SOCIAL
PSYCHOLOGY

Sixth Canadian Edition

Mc Graw Hill Education | McGraw-Hill Ryerson

MYERS • SPENCER • JORDAN

Social Psychology
Sixth Canadian Edition

ISBN-13: 978-125902465-8
ISBN-10: 1-25-902465-2

2 3 4 5 6 7 8 9 10 CTPS 1 9 8 7 6 5

Printed and bound in China.

Director of Product Management: *Rhondda McNabb*
Product Manager: *Jason Chih*
Senior Marketing Manager: *Margaret Greenfield*
Product Developer: *Katherine Goodes*
Senior Product Team Associate: *Marina Seguin*
Supervising Editor: *Stephanie Gay*
Photo/Permissions Editor: *Marnie Lamb*
Copy Editor: *Michael Kelly*
Plant Production Coordinator: *Scott Morrison*
Manufacturing Production Coordinator: *Emily Hickey*
Cover and Interior Design: *Michelle Losier*
Cover Image: *Robert Daly/Royalty Free Getty Images*
Page Layout: *Laserwords Private Limited*
Printer: *China Translation & Printing Services Limited*

Library and Archives Canada Cataloguing in Publication

Myers, David G., author
    Social psychology / Myers, Spencer, Jordan.—Sixth Canadian edition.

Includes bibliographical references and index.
ISBN 978-125902465-8-(bound)

    1. Social psychology—Textbooks. I. Spencer, Steven J., author   II. Jordan, Christian H. (Christian Hywel), 1974-, author   III. Title.
HM1033.M947 2015   302   C2014-905559-5

About the Authors

David G. Myers, since receiving his Ph.D. from the University of Iowa, has spent his career at Michigan's Hope College where he is a professor of psychology and has taught dozens of social psychology sections. Hope College students have invited him to be their commencement speaker and named him "outstanding professor."

He also communicates psychology science to the general public. His writings have appeared in four dozen magazines, from *Today's Education* to *Scientific American*. His 17 books include *The Pursuit of Happiness* and *Intuition: Its Powers and Perils*.

Myers' research and writings have been recognized for the Gordon Allport Prize, for an "honored scientist" award from the Federation of Associations in the Brain and Behavioral Sciences, and for the Award for Distinguished Service on Behalf of Personality-Social Psychology.

Steven J. Spencer is a professor and chair of the social psychology division at the University of Waterloo. He teaches popular classes in introductory psychology, social psychology, and social cognition. He is known for his lively lectures and engaging classroom demonstrations.

Dr. Spencer also maintains an active research program that investigates self-image maintenance processes, motivated social perception, stereotyping, and social norms. In particular, he has examined how threats to the self-concept can lead people to stereotype others and how being stereotyped by others can threaten people and undermine their performance on academic tasks. His work has been published in the *Psychological Bulletin, Psychological Science, Journal of Personality and Social Psychology, Personality and Social Psychology Bulletin*, and *Journal of Experimental Social Psychology*. He has served his discipline as a consulting editor to the *Journal of Personality and Social Psychology* and as an associate editor to the *Journal of Experimental Social Psychology*.

In his spare time, he enjoys running half marathons and spending time with his family. He has a daughter and a son.

Christian H. Jordan is an associate professor and graduate officer for the psychology department at Wilfrid Laurier University. He teaches lecture courses and seminars in social psychology and research methods at both the undergraduate and graduate levels.

Dr. Jordan is also an active researcher, studying self-esteem, narcissism, and self-enhancement processes. His work has been published in a number of scholarly handbooks and journals, including the *Journal of Personality and Social Psychology, Journal of Experimental Psychology, Journal of Experimental Social Psychology, Personality and Social Psychology Bulletin, Self and Identity,* and *Journal of Social and Clinical Psychology.* He has also written popular instructional pieces on how to effectively read journal articles and how to conduct and report persuasive psychology experiments.

In his spare time, he spends time with his family and friends, reads, listens to music, and exercises outdoors or at the gym. Christian and Lynne Jordan have two sons, Grayson and Hayden, and a daughter, Reilly, whom they lost to leukemia.

Brief Contents

Preface xi

CHAPTER 1   Introducing Social Psychology   3

Part One   Social Thinking   33

CHAPTER 2   The Self in a Social World   35
CHAPTER 3   Social Beliefs and Judgments   77
CHAPTER 4   Behaviour and Attitudes   121

Part Two   Social Influence   155

CHAPTER 5   Persuasion   157
CHAPTER 6   Conformity   195
CHAPTER 7   Group Influence   231

Part Three   Social Relations   271

CHAPTER 8   Altruism: Helping Others   273
CHAPTER 9   Aggression: Hurting Others   309
CHAPTER 10   Attraction and Intimacy: Liking
             and Loving Others   351
CHAPTER 11   Sources of Prejudice   397
CHAPTER 12   Consequences of Prejudice   427

Modules: Social Psychology Applied   451

MODULE A   Social Psychology in Conflict and Peacemaking   452
MODULE B   Social Psychology in the Clinic   470
MODULE C   Social Psychology in Court   496
MODULE D   Social Psychology and the Sustainable Future   514

Glossary GL-1
References. RE-1
Acknowledgements AK-1
Name Index NI-1
Subject Index SI-1

Table of Contents

Preface   xi

CHAPTER 1
Introducing Social Psychology   3

WHAT IS SOCIAL PSYCHOLOGY?   4

WHAT ARE THE MAJOR THEMES
IN SOCIAL PSYCHOLOGY?   6

We Construct Our Social Reality   6
Our Social Intuitions Are Often
    Powerful but Sometimes Perilous   6
Social Influences Shape Our Behaviour   8
Personal Attitudes and Dispositions
    Also Shape Behaviour   8
Social Behaviour Is Biologically Rooted   9
Relating to Others Is a Basic Need   9
Social Psychology's Principles Are
    Applicable in Everyday Life   10

HOW DO VALUES AFFECT SOCIAL
PSYCHOLOGY?   10

Obvious Ways in Which Values Enter Social
    Psychology   11
Not-So-Obvious Ways in Which Values
    Enter Social Psychology   11

IS SOCIAL PSYCHOLOGY MERELY
COMMON SENSE?   13

RESEARCH METHODS: HOW DO
WE DO SOCIAL PSYCHOLOGY?   16

Forming and Testing Hypotheses   16
Correlational Research: Detecting Natural Associations   18
Experimental Research: Searching for Cause and Effect   24
Generalizing from Laboratory to Life   29

PART ONE
Social Thinking   33

CHAPTER 2
The Self in a Social World   35

SELF-CONCEPT: WHO AM I?   37

Your Sense of Self   37
Possible Selves   38
Social Identity   38
Self and Culture   41
Self-Knowledge   47

WHAT IS THE NATURE AND
MOTIVATING POWER OF SELF-ESTEEM?   51

Self-Esteem Motivation   52
The "Dark Side" of Self-Esteem   53

WHAT DOES IT MEAN TO HAVE
PERCEIVED SELF-CONTROL?   56

Self-Control   56
Learned Helplessness versus Self-Determination   57

WHAT IS SELF-SERVING BIAS?   60

Explaining Positive and Negative Events   60
Can We All Be Better Than Average?   61
Unrealistic Optimism   63
False Consensus and Uniqueness   65
Temporal Comparison   66
Explaining Self-Serving Bias   68
Reflections on Self-Esteem and Self-Serving Bias   68

HOW DO PEOPLE MANAGE
THEIR SELF-PRESENTATION?   70

Self-Handicapping   71
Impression Management   71

CHAPTER 3
Social Beliefs and Judgments   77

HOW DO WE PERCEIVE OUR
SOCIAL WORLDS?   78

Priming   79
Perceiving and Interpreting Events   80
Belief Perseverance   83
Constructing Memories of Ourselves
    and Our Worlds   84

HOW DO WE JUDGE OUR
SOCIAL WORLDS?   87

Intuitive Judgments   87
Overconfidence   90

Heuristics: Mental Shortcuts 94
Counterfactual Thinking 96
Illusory Thinking 97
Mood and Judgment 99

HOW DO WE EXPLAIN OUR SOCIAL WORLDS? 101

Attributing Causality: To the Person or the Situation? 101
The Fundamental Attribution Error 104
Why We Make the Attribution Error 107
Cultural Differences 109
Why We Study Attribution Errors 110

HOW DO OUR EXPECTATIONS OF OUR SOCIAL WORLDS MATTER? 111

Teacher Expectations and Student Performance 111
Getting from Others What We Expect 113

WHAT CAN WE CONCLUDE FROM RESEARCH ON SOCIAL BELIEFS AND JUDGMENTS? 115

CHAPTER 4
Behaviour and Attitudes 121

HOW WELL DO OUR ATTITUDES PREDICT OUR BEHAVIOURS? 122

Are We All Hypocrites? 123
When Attitudes Predict Behaviour 124

WHEN DOES OUR BEHAVIOUR AFFECT OUR ATTITUDES? 129

Role-Playing 129
When Saying Becomes Believing 132
The Foot-in-the-Door Phenomenon 133
Evil and Moral Acts 135
Social Movements 138

WHY DOES OUR BEHAVIOUR AFFECT OUR ATTITUDES? 139

Self-Presentation: Impression Management 139
Self-Justification: Cognitive Dissonance 140
Culture and Cognitive Dissonance 144
Self-Perception 145
Comparing the Theories 150

PART TWO
Social Influence 155

CHAPTER 5
Persuasion 157

WHAT PATHS LEAD TO PERSUASION? 159

The Central Route 160
The Peripheral Route 160
Different Routes for Different Purposes 161

WHAT ARE THE ELEMENTS OF PERSUASION? 162

Who Says? The Communicator 162
What Is Said? The Message Content 166
How Is It Said? The Channel of Communication 174
To Whom Is It Said? The Audience 178

EXTREME PERSUASION: HOW DO CULTS INDOCTRINATE? 181

Attitudes Follow Behaviour 183
Persuasive Elements 183
Group Effects 185

HOW CAN PERSUASION BE RESISTED? 187

Strengthening Personal Commitment 187
Inoculation Programs 188
Implications of Attitude Inoculation 191

CHAPTER 6
Conformity 195

WHAT IS CONFORMITY? 196

WHAT ARE THE CLASSIC CONFORMITY AND OBEDIENCE STUDIES? 197

Sherif's Studies of Norm Formation 197
Asch's Studies of Group Pressure 200
Milgram's Obedience Studies 203
What Breeds Obedience? 206
Reflections on the Classic Studies 209

WHAT PREDICTS CONFORMITY? 214

Group Size 214
Unanimity 215
Cohesion 216

Status 217
Public Response 217
No Prior Commitment 217

WHY CONFORM? 219

WHO CONFORMS? 221
Personality 222
Culture 223
Social Roles 224

DO WE EVER WANT TO BE DIFFERENT? 225
Reactance 225
Asserting Uniqueness 226

CHAPTER 7
Group Influence 231

WHAT IS A GROUP? 233

SOCIAL FACILITATION: HOW ARE WE AFFECTED BY THE PRESENCE OF OTHERS? 233
The Mere Presence of Others 233
Crowding: The Presence of Many Others 236
Why Are We Aroused in the Presence of Others? 237

SOCIAL LOAFING: DO INDIVIDUALS EXERT LESS EFFORT IN A GROUP? 238
Many Hands Make Light Work 238
Social Loafing in Everyday Life 240

DEINDIVIDUATION: WHEN DO PEOPLE LOSE THEIR SENSE OF SELF IN GROUPS? 243
Doing Together What We Would Not Do Alone 243
Diminished Self-Awareness 247

GROUP POLARIZATION: DO GROUPS INTENSIFY OUR OPINIONS? 247
The Case of the "Risky Shift" 248
Impact of Group Discussion on Individuals' Opinions 249
Explaining Polarization 252

GROUPTHINK: DO GROUPS HINDER OR ASSIST GOOD DECISIONS? 255
Symptoms of Groupthink 256
Critiquing Groupthink 259
Preventing Groupthink 260

Group Problem-Solving 261

LEADERSHIP: HOW DO LEADERS SHAPE THE GROUP'S ACTIONS? 264
Task Leadership and Social Leadership 264
Transactional Leadership 265
Transformational Leadership 265

THE INFLUENCE OF THE MINORITY: HOW DO INDIVIDUALS INFLUENCE THE GROUP? 266
Consistency 267
Self-Confidence 268
Defections from the Majority 268

PART THREE
Social Relations 271

CHAPTER 8
Altruism: Helping Others 273

WHY DO WE HELP? 274
Social Exchange 274
Social Norms 280
Evolutionary Psychology 282
Comparing and Evaluating Theories of Altruism 285

WHEN WILL WE HELP? 290
Number of Bystanders 290
Helping When Someone Else Does 297
Time Pressures 297
Similarity to the Victim 298

WHO HELPS? 298
Personality Traits 299
Gender 300

HOW CAN WE INCREASE HELPING? 300
Reduce Ambiguity, Increase Responsibility 300
Guilt and Concern for Self-Image 302
Socializing Prosocial Behaviour 303

CHAPTER 9
Aggression: Hurting Others 309

WHAT IS AGGRESSION? 310

WHAT ARE SOME THEORIES OF AGGRESSION? — 311

Aggression as a Biological Phenomenon — 311
Aggression as a Response to Frustration — 316
Aggression as Learned Social Behaviour — 319

WHAT ARE SOME INFLUENCES ON AGGRESSION? — 322

Aversive Incidents — 322
Arousal — 324
Aggression Cues — 325
Media Influences: Pornography and Sexual Violence — 327
Media Influences: Television — 331
Media Influences: Video Games — 337
Group Influences — 342

HOW CAN AGGRESSION BE REDUCED? — 344

Catharsis? — 344
A Social Learning Approach — 346
Culture Change and World Violence — 348

CHAPTER 10

Attraction and Intimacy: Liking and Loving Others — 351

WHAT LEADS TO FRIENDSHIP AND ATTRACTION? — 355

Proximity — 355
Physical Attractiveness — 359
Similarity versus Complementarity — 368
Liking Those Who Like Us — 371
Relationship Rewards — 375

WHAT IS LOVE? — 376

Passionate Love — 377
Companionate Love — 380

WHAT ENABLES CLOSE RELATIONSHIPS? — 382

Attachment — 382
Equity — 385
Self-Disclosure — 387

HOW DO RELATIONSHIPS END? — 389

Divorce — 391
The Detachment Process — 392

CHAPTER 11

Sources of Prejudice — 397

WHAT IS PREJUDICE? — 398

Defining Prejudice — 398
Prejudice: Overt, Subtle, and Automatic — 400

WHAT ARE THE SOCIAL SOURCES OF PREJUDICE? — 401

Social Inequalities: Justifying the Status Quo — 401
Socialization — 403
Institutional Supports — 406

WHAT ARE THE MOTIVATIONAL SOURCES OF PREJUDICE? — 407

Frustration and Aggression: The Scapegoat Theory — 407
Social Identity Theory: Feeling Superior to Others — 408
Motivation to See the World as Just — 414
Motivation to Avoid Prejudice — 416

WHAT ARE THE COGNITIVE SOURCES OF PREJUDICE? — 417

Categorization: Classifying People into Groups — 417
Distinctiveness: Perceiving People Who Stand Out — 420
Attributions: Discounting Important Situational Forces — 423

CHAPTER 12

Consequences of Prejudice — 427

WHAT ARE THE CONSEQUENCES OF RACIAL AND GENDER-BASED PREJUDICE? — 428

Prejudice Based on Race — 428
Prejudice Based on Gender — 433

CAN PREJUDICE CREATE ITS OWN REALITY? — 436

Self-Perpetuating Prejudgments — 436
Impact of Discrimination: The Self-Fulfilling Prophecy — 438
Stereotype Threat — 440
Stereotypes and Personal Judgment — 442

HOW DO PEOPLE REACT TO FACING PREJUDICE AND STEREOTYPING? — 446

Perception of Discrimination — 447

MODULES:
Social Psychology Applied   451

MODULE A
Social Psychology in Conflict and Peacemaking   452

WHAT CREATES CONFLICT?   453

Social Dilemmas   453
Perceived Injustice   460
Misperception   460

HOW CAN PEACE BE ACHIEVED?   462

Bargaining   462
Mediation   463
Arbitration   466
Conciliation   467

MODULE B
Social Psychology in the Clinic   470

WHAT INFLUENCES THE ACCURACY OF CLINICAL JUDGMENTS?   471

Illusory Correlations   472
Hindsight and Overconfidence   473
Self-Confirming Diagnoses   473
Implications for Better Clinical Practice   475

WHAT COGNITIVE PROCESSES ACCOMPANY BEHAVIOUR PROBLEMS?   475

Depression   475
Anxiety and Shyness   480

WHAT IS HEALTH PSYCHOLOGY AND THE PSYCHOLOGY OF ILLNESS?   482

Reactions to Illness   482
Emotions and Illness   483

HOW DO SOCIAL RELATIONSHIPS SUPPORT HEALTH AND WELL-BEING?   487

Close Relationships and Health   487
Close Relationships and Happiness   491

MODULE C
Social Psychology in Court   496

HOW RELIABLE IS EYEWITNESS TESTIMONY?   497

How Persuasive Is Eyewitness Testimony?   498
When Eyes Deceive   498
The Misinformation Effect   500
Retelling   502
Reducing Error   503

WHAT INFLUENCES A JURY?   506

Physical Attractiveness of the Defendant   506
The Judge's Instructions   506
The Story of the Trial   507
Statistical Information   507
Increasing Jurors' Understanding   508
Group Influences in Juries   508
From Lab to Life: Simulated and Real Juries   510

MODULE D
Social Psychology and the Sustainable Future   514

HOW CAN HUMANITY CREATE A SUSTAINABLE FUTURE?   515

Psychology and Climate Change   516
New Technologies   518
Reducing Consumption   519

DOES MONEY BUY HAPPINESS?   521

Increased Materialism   521
Wealth and Well-Being   521
Materialism Fails to Satisfy   522
Toward Sustainability and Survival   525

Glossary   GL-1
References   RE-1
Acknowledgements   AK-1
Name Index   NI-1
Subject Index   SI-1

Preface

Welcome to the sixth Canadian edition of *Social Psychology*. When I was asked to write this book, I was excited, but I also knew it would be a challenge. I was thrilled to be working with David Myers. He is known for his wonderful textbooks, which are solidly scientific and warmly human, factually rigorous, and intellectually provocative. His texts are simply the best. In addition, David is a fantastic friend, generous colleague, and one of my favourite undergraduate instructors—he was one of the readers on my honours thesis and has shaped my career from its very beginning. I knew him well and thought we could work well together. I expected that David would be a terrific mentor, and he has more than exceeded my expectations.

I also had the privilege of working with Christian Jordan. Christian is a fabulous writer, fantastic scholar, and a generous colleague. I first met Christian when he was an undergraduate, and it was my great fortune to work with him while he was a graduate student. As Christian's career developed, I hoped to bring him on as an author on this textbook, and I could not be more pleased with his tremendous job on this book the past couple of editions.

Christian and I continue to meet the challenge of creating a comprehensive Canadian social psychology text. How does one select the material for inclusion in a "reasonably comprehensive" introduction to one's discipline—a text long enough to allow rich narrative (to weave a story) but crisp enough not to overwhelm? Further, what Canadian content will most capture the imaginations of Canadian students? We have sought to present theories and findings that are not too esoteric but that capture the fundamental concepts of the field in a scientifically rigorous manner. In doing so, we have sought to balance classic findings with significant current Canadian research. We think you will find that as the book emphasizes the Canadian context, it also has a strong research focus presented in an understandable and engaging style.

ORGANIZATION

The book opens with a single chapter that includes our methods of inquiry. The chapter also warns students about how findings can seem obvious—once you know them—and how social psychologists' own values permeate the discipline. The intent is to give students just enough background to prepare them for what follows.

The book then unfolds around its definition of social psychology: the scientific study of how people *think about* (Part One), *influence* (Part Two), and *relate to* (Part Three) one another.

Part One on *social thinking* examines how we view ourselves and others. It assesses the accuracy of our impressions, intuitions, and explanations; and it examines the relation of our behaviour and our attitudes.

Part Two explores *social influence*. In this edition, we begin by discussing how social influence can shape attitudes—that is, how persuasion occurs. This structure allows instructors to focus on attitude formation and change in a unit that covers Chapters 4 and 5. We continue to examine social influence by examining the nature of conformity, and group influence.

Part Three considers the attitudinal and behavioural manifestations of both negative and positive *social relations*. It flows from altruism to aggression and attraction to prejudice. Notably in this edition, we have split the material on prejudice into two chapters, focusing on the causes of prejudice in Chapter 11 and the consequences of prejudice in Chapter 12. Research in prejudice has grown considerably in the last decade, and there is simply too much research at this point to cover in a single chapter.

Applications of social psychology are both interwoven throughout every chapter and highlighted in the four concluding modules: **"Social Psychology in Conflict and Peacemaking," "Social Psychology in the Clinic," "Social Psychology in Court,"** and **"Social Psychology and the Sustainable Future."** These modules are not meant to be comprehensive treatments of these issues, but focus on interesting and engaging issues. They are meant to be included as supplements to the other chapters in the book when instructors want to emphasize these issues.

This book also has a multicultural emphasis that we seek to stress in every chapter in the book. All authors are creatures of their cultures, and we are no exceptions. Yet by reading the world's social psychology literature, by corresponding with researchers worldwide, and by examining Canada's extensive research on the many cultures represented in this country, we have sought to present a multicultural text to a Canadian audience. The book's focus remains the *fundamental principles of social thinking, social influence, and social relations as revealed by careful empirical research*. However, hoping to broaden our awareness of the human family, we aim to illustrate these principles multiculturally.

To assist readers, we have organized chapters into three or four readable-length sections. Each begins with a preview and ends with a summary that highlights the organization and key concepts.

In agreement with Thoreau's beliefs that "anything living is easily and naturally expressed in popular language," we have sought, paragraph by paragraph, to craft the most engaging and effective book possible. A bright, four-colour design complements the text revision and enhances the impact of the photos and figures. The definitions of key terms appear both in the margins and in the end-of-book Glossary.

HIGHLIGHTS OF THE SIXTH CANADIAN EDITION

- **Current research.** The text's extensive references, more than 2700 in total, have been thoroughly updated to include the most cutting-edge research in social psychology. The latest findings on automatic processing, evolutionary psychology, video games and aggression, perceptions of media bias, counter-arguments and attitude inoculation, culture and helping strangers, motivational sources of prejudice, and misperceptions of outgroups are just some of the examples of updated research in this new edition.

- **Additional coverage of culture.** Coverage of culture is integrated in every relevant chapter throughout the text. As this literature has grown and formed an important subfield in social psychology, it seemed that comprehensive coverage of this topic required more than just a single chapter.

- **Additional coverage of gender.** Research on gender continues to evolve. Gender is examined by a number of different researchers in a number of different contexts. As such, it seems that gender is less a subfield of social psychology and more a very important variable that is studied in many contexts. Given this evolution, gender is covered throughout the book in many subsections.

- **Additional coverage of social cognitive neuroscience.** New developments in brain imaging and recording have provided a number of new insights in the field. These findings make a substantial contribution to a number of chapters.

- **Strong pedagogy.** Readers benefit from features designed to engage interest while encouraging understanding of core concepts. Pedagogical elements include section previews; numerous photos, figures, and tables; a running glossary; Focus On boxes highlighting applied concepts; The Inside Story vignettes written by leading researchers; a summary of each major section within the text; the Summing Up sections moved to the end of each chapter, to become a source for students reviewing for exams; and an index printed on the inside covers highlighting coverage of concepts such as culture, ethics, gender, law and justice, and sexuality.

- **Relevant examples.** Drawn from the arts, business, sports, and currents events, the text's examples appeal to students from a variety of majors and academic backgrounds.

WHAT'S NEW IN THE SIXTH CANADIAN EDITION

Highlights of new and updated material in the sixth Canadian edition include the following.

CHAPTER 1: INTRODUCING SOCIAL PSYCHOLOGY

- Extended coverage of the ethics of research
- Updated and recent research incorporated throughout the chapter

CHAPTER 2: THE SELF IN A SOCIAL WORLD

- Updated and recent research incorporated throughout the chapter
- Revised coverage of ego depletion to reflect recent research about the psychological mechanisms underlying ego depletion effects
- Extended coverage of narcissism—including research on rising rates of narcissism among young people—and revised coverage of both the benefits and "dark side" of self-esteem
- New coverage of research on the costs of excess choice

CHAPTER 3: SOCIAL BELIEFS AND JUDGMENTS

- Added new examples of behavioural priming
- Added new key term—*embodied cognition*—with research examples
- Updated and incorporated recent research throughout the chapter

CHAPTER 4: BEHAVIOUR AND ATTITUDES

- Added coverage of implicit attitude research
- Updated coverage of cognitive dissonance
- New explanations and current examples for expressions and attitude
- Two new "The Inside Story" boxes

CHAPTER 5: PERSUASION

- Added new chapter opener on the powers of persuasion
- Updated coverage of the effects of arousing fear and persuasion
- Incorporated an introduction of *gain-framed* and *loss-framed messages* in persuasion
- New explanations and current examples for elements of persuasion

CHAPTER 6: CONFORMITY

- Added coverage on the neuroscience of compliance and acceptance, including a discussion of how Asch's procedure became the standard for hundreds of later experiments
- New material on Milgram and the power of the situation, on cohesion as a factor in predicting conformity, and on conformity in relation to cultural differences
- Inclusion of new functional magnetic resonance imaging studies identifying neural activity associated with normative influence

CHAPTER 7: GROUP INFLUENCE

- Expanded coverage of physical anonymity
- New discussion on group polarization on the Internet and in terrorist organizations
- Expanded coverage of the normative influence of group polarization
- Updated and recent research incorporated throughout the chapter

CHAPTER 8: ALTRUISM: HELPING OTHERS

- Updated and recent research incorporated throughout the chapter
- New research covering the reciprocity norm
- Expanded coverage of genuine altruism with new examples
- Updated coverage of modelling prosocial behaviour

CHAPTER 9: AGGRESSION: HURTING OTHERS

- Updated and recent research incorporated throughout the chapter
- New discussion on bullying

- Expanded coverage of instinct theory with new examples
- Newly treated and enhanced coverage of biochemical influences on aggression
- New section on poor diet as an influence on aggression
- Added section on the culture of violence
- Expanded section on media influences related to pornography and sexual violence
- New section on Stephen Pinker's evidence for a decrease in world violence
- Enhanced coverage of the Internet and aggression
- Discussion of desensitization and TV's cognitive effects expanded
- First-time coverage of TV as a time drain
- Expanded coverage on whether playing video games causes aggression

CHAPTER 10: ATTRACTION AND INTIMACY: LIKING AND LOVING OTHERS

- Updated and recent research incorporated throughout the chapter, including ostracism as pain, attractiveness, liking begetting liking, attachment styles, theory of love, evolution and attraction, and how relationships end
- New "Focus On" box describing research that speaks to whether the Internet fosters greater intimacy or isolation
- Updated chapter opener with more discussion of ostracism
- Treatment of avoidant attachment for the first time in this text

CHAPTER 11: SOURCES OF PREJUDICE

- Expanded coverage of the authoritarian personality as it relates to socialization
- New examples throughout the chapter
- Expanded coverage of in-group bias
- New research related to motivation to avoid prejudice

CHAPTER 12: CONSEQUENCES OF PREJUDICE

- Updated and recent research incorporated throughout the chapter
- Expanded coverage of stereotype threat

MODULE A: SOCIAL PSYCHOLOGY IN CONFLICT AND PEACEMAKING

- New definition for *conflict*
- Updated figures in discussion of the prisoner's dilemma
- Updated and recent research incorporated throughout the chapter

MODULE B: SOCIAL PSYCHOLOGY IN THE CLINIC

- Expanded discussion of clinicians' clinical versus statistical prediction
- New coverage of loneliness
- New treatment of stress and illness

MODULE C: SOCIAL PSYCHOLOGY IN COURT

- New coverage examining the confidence of witnesses
- New research into misinformation-induced false memories
- Revised coverage of training for police interviewers
- Revised coverage of minimizing false lineup identifications
- New section examining the physical attractiveness of the defendant and the judge's instructions during a trial

MODULE D: SOCIAL PSYCHOLOGY AND THE SUSTAINABLE FUTURE

- Fully updated to include the newest research on creating a sustainable future

FEATURES

In addition to the authors' renowned engaging and personal writing style, which reflects their enthusiasm for the subject, *Social Psychology*, Sixth Canadian Edition, also offers pedagogical elements designed to help students get the most out of the text.

SECTION PREVIEWS

These previews introduce each major section within a chapter, bringing forward the concepts and issues to be discussed in the ensuing pages.

> ### ● HOW WELL DO OUR ATTITUDES PREDICT OUR BEHAVIOURS?
>
> *To what extent, and under what conditions, do attitudes drive our outward actions? Why were social psychologists at first surprised by a seemingly small connection between attitudes and actions?*

KEY TERMS

Every key concept is defined and placed in the margin to correspond to the term's use in the text. In addition, key terms are collected in the Glossary at the back of the text.

> **Implicit Association Test (IAT)**
> a computer-driven assessment of implicit attitudes that uses reaction times to measure people's automatic associations between attitude objects and evaluative words, where easier pairings

A newer and widely used attitude measure, the Implicit Association Test (IAT), uses reaction times to measure how quickly people associate concepts (Greenwald et al., 2002; Greenwald, Nosek, & Banaji, 2003). One can, for example, measure implicit racial attitudes by assessing whether White people take longer to associate positive words with Black than with White faces. Implicit attitude researchers have offered various IAT assessments online (projectimplicit.net). The some 5 million completed tests since 1998 have, they report, shown the following:

- *Implicit biases are pervasive.* For example, 80 percent of people show more implicit negativity toward the elderly compared with the young.

QUOTATIONS

Found throughout the text in the margins, quotations from philosophers, writers, and scientists highlight how social psychological concepts relate to many aspects of everyday society.

students felt that the Holocaust occurred in the more distant past when they read about German atrocities committed at that time (Peetz, Gunn, & Wilson, 2010). Our glory days may often feel like yesterday, while our defeats and transgressions feel like ancient history.

To sum up, these tendencies toward self-serving attributions, self-congratulatory comparisons, illusory optimism, and false consensus for our failings are major sources of self-serving bias (Figure 2–9).

> *"The past is to be respected and acknowledged, but not to be worshipped. It is our future in which we will find our greatness."*
> PIERRE ELLIOT TRUDEAU, *CANADIAN MUSEUM OF CIVILIZATION LIBRARY*

THE INSIDE STORY

In their own words, prominent social psychologists explain the motives and methods behind the studies conducted in their areas of expertise. These vignettes give students a first-hand account of studies cited in the text.

THE >>> INSIDE STORY

I vividly remember the afternoon I began to appreciate the far-reaching implications of physical attractiveness. Graduate student Karen Dion (now a professor at the University of Toronto) learned that some researchers at our Institute of Child Development had collected popularity ratings from nursery school children and taken a photo of each child. Although teachers and caregivers of children had persuaded us that "all children are beautiful" and no physical-attractiveness discriminations could be made, Dion suggested we instruct some people to rate each child's looks and correlate these with popularity. After doing so, we realized our long shot had hit home: Attractive children were popular children. Indeed, the effect was far

more potent than we and others had assumed, with a host of implications that investigators are still tracing.

Ellen Berscheid, *University of Minnesota*

FOCUS ON BOXES

In these boxes, a point–counterpoint approach to issues encourages students to apply the concepts of social psychology to their real-world experience.

FOCUS ON › Money, Happiness, and Helping •

Imagine that you won a million dollars in the lottery. How would you spend it? Do you think that spending the money would make you happy? If you are like most people, you probably thought about buying some nice things for yourself with the money. Recent research by University of British Columbia researcher Elizabeth Dunn and her colleagues (Dunn, Aknin, & Norton, 2008), however, suggests one of the common ways that we mispredict our future emotional reactions is that we think that spending money on ourselves will make us happy, when it usually does not. In contrast, we think that spending money on other people will bring us little joy when, in fact, spending money on others usually makes us quite happy.

To test the impact of spending money on oneself versus others, Dunn and her colleagues gave students an envelope with a fresh new bill (either a 5 or a 20) and told them either to spend the money on a gift for themselves or to spend the money on a gift for someone else or a charitable donation. Later that evening, they called the students and asked them how happy they were. Students who spent the money on themselves (regardless of the amount they spent) were less happy than those who spent money on others. These experimental findings mirror what is seen in correlational data as well. When people make more money, on average this only has a small effect on their happiness; but if they spend money on others—regardless of how much they make—they tend to be a lot happier.

This line of research is a dramatic example of how the internal rewards for helping others can have a larger impact on happiness than even a powerful external reward like money.

SUMMING UP

Found at the end of each major section within a chapter, this feature summarizes key concepts and draws connections between important issues.

▶ SUMMING UP

HOW WELL DO OUR ATTITUDES PREDICT OUR BEHAVIOURS?

- Attitudes do not predict behaviour as well as most people believe.
- Attitudes are better predictors of behaviour; however, when social influences are minimal, attitudes are specific to behaviours, and attitudes are potent (strong and on one's mind).

WHEN DOES OUR BEHAVIOUR AFFECT OUR ATTITUDES?

- When taking on a role, our actions in that role often shape our attitudes.
- When we state a belief (even if we do not initially believe it), our words often shape our attitudes.
- When we engage in small actions inconsistent with our attitudes, these small actions can lead to larger actions that can dramatically shape our attitudes and behaviour.
- When we engage in moral or evil acts, these actions can powerfully shape our attitudes.
- When we participate in social movements, our actions can profoundly shape our attitudes.

CONNECT

McGraw-Hill Connect™ is a web-based assignment and assessment platform that gives students the means to better connect with their coursework, with their instructors, and with the important concepts that they will need to know for success now and in the future.

With Connect, instructors can deliver assignments, quizzes, and tests online. Instructors can edit existing questions and author entirely new problems, track individual student performance—by question, by assignment, or in relation to the class overall—with detailed grade reports, integrate grade reports easily with Learning Management Systems (LMS), and much more.

By choosing Connect, instructors are providing their students with a powerful tool for improving academic performance and truly mastering course material. Connect allows students to practise important skills at their own pace and on their own schedule. Importantly, students' assessment results and instructors' feedback are all saved online, so students can continually review their progress and plot their course to success.

Connect also provides 24/7 online access to an eBook—an online edition of the text to aid them in successfully completing their work, wherever and whenever they choose.

KEY FEATURES

Simple Assignment Management

With Connect, creating assignments is easier than ever, so you can spend more time teaching and less time managing.

- Create and deliver assignments easily and test bank material to assign online.
- Streamline lesson planning, student progress reporting, and assignment grading to make classroom management more efficient than ever.
- Go paperless with the eBook and online submission and grading of student assignments.

Smart Grading

When it comes to studying, time is precious. Connect helps students learn more efficiently by providing feedback and practice material when they need it, where they need it.

- Automatically score assignments, giving students immediate feedback on their work and side-by-side comparisons with correct answers.
- Access and review each response; manually change grades or leave comments for students to review.
- Reinforce classroom concepts with practice tests and instant quizzes.

Instructor Library

The Connect Instructor Library is your course creation hub. It provides all the critical resources you'll need to build your course, just how you want to teach it.

- Assign eBook readings and draw from a rich collection of textbook-specific assignments.
- Access instructor resources, including ready-made PowerPoint presentations and media to use in your lectures.

- View assignments and resources created for past sections.
- Post your own resources for students to use.

eBook

Connect reinvents the textbook learning experience for the modern student. Every Connect subject area is seamlessly integrated with Connect eBooks, which are designed to keep students focused on the concepts key to their success.

- Provide students with a Connect eBook, allowing for anytime, anywhere access to the textbook.
- Merge media, animation, and assessments with the text's narrative to engage students and improve learning and retention.
- Pinpoint and connect key concepts in a snap using the powerful eBook search engine.
- Manage notes, highlights, and bookmarks in one place for simple, comprehensive review.

LearnSmart

LEARNSMART

No two students are alike. Why should their learning paths be? LearnSmart uses revolutionary adaptive technology to build a learning experience unique to each student's individual needs. It starts by identifying the topics a student knows and does not know. As the student progresses, LearnSmart adapts and adjusts the content based on his or her individual strengths, weaknesses, and confidence, ensuring that every minute spent studying with LearnSmart is the most efficient and productive study time possible.

SmartBook

SMARTBOOK

As the first and only adaptive reading experience, SmartBook is changing the way students read and learn. SmartBook creates a personalized reading experience by highlighting the most important concepts a student needs to learn at that moment. As students engage with Smart-Book, the reading experience continuously adapts by highlighting content based on what each student knows and doesn't know. This ensures that students are focused on the content needed to close specific knowledge gaps, while it simultaneously promotes long-term learning.

Instructor Supplements

Connect is a one-stop shop for instructor resources, including the following:

- **Instructor's Manual** (by Steven Smith, Saint Mary's University): Each chapter in the Instructor's Manual contains key learning points, lecture ideas, class discussion topics, and more.
- **Computerized Test Bank** (by Barbara Bond, Trent University and Sir Sandford Fleming College): The Test Bank provides a variety of questions, including multiple choice, true/false, and short answer. The multiple-choice and true/false questions include the answer as well as the page number in the main text where the material appears.
- **Microsoft® PowerPoint® Presentations** (by Barbara Bond, Trent University and Sir Sandford Fleming College): These visual presentations, crafted for each chapter, include useful outlines, summaries, and visuals.

STUDENT SUPPLEMENTS

Connect for Students

By choosing Connect, instructors are providing their students with a powerful tool for improving academic performance and truly mastering course material. Connect allows students to study and practise important skills at their own pace and on their own schedule with pre- and post-tests, additional quizzing material, social psychology videos, and an eBook for easy reference. Pre- and post-practice tests are tied to learning objectives and allow students to continually review their progress and plot their course to success. Online access to Connect with eBook is included with all Connect printed textbooks—no extra charge to the student.

Superior Learning Solutions and Support

The McGraw-Hill Ryerson team is ready to help you assess and integrate any of our products, technology, and services into your course for optimal teaching and learning performance. Whether it's helping your students improve their grades, or putting your entire course online, the McGraw-Hill Ryerson team is here to help you do it. Contact your Learning Solutions Consultant today to learn how to maximize all of McGraw-Hill Ryerson's resources!

For more information on the latest technology and Learning Solutions offered by McGraw-Hill Ryerson and its partners, please visit us online at **www.mcgrawhill.ca/he/solutions.**

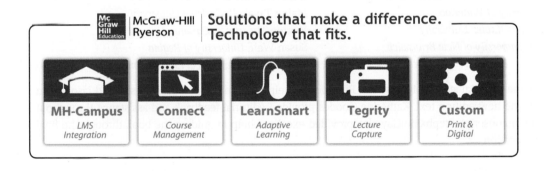

IN APPRECIATION

We would like to thank the many people, past and present, who helped us in writing and revising this book. The following Canadian scholars provided thoughtful and thorough reviews, and their suggestions have greatly improved each edition:

Craig Blatz, *Grant MacEwan University*

Susan Boon, *University of Calgary*

Rena Borovilo, *Humber College*

David Bourgeois, *Saint Mary's University*

Delbert A. Brodie, *St. Thomas University*

Irene Cheung, *University of Western Ontario*

Greg Chung-Yan, *University of Windsor*

Ken Cramer, *University of Windsor*

Jill Esmonde, *Georgian College*

Deborah Flynn, *Nipissing University*

Ken Fowler, *Memorial University of Newfoundland*

James Gibson, *University of Victoria*

Gerald Goldberg, *York University*

Stephanie Hancock, *University of Lethbridge*

Gabriella Ilie, *University of Toronto Scarborough*

Linda Jessup, *University of Waterloo*

Erika Koch, *St. Francis Xavier University*

Diane Lachapelle, *University of New Brunswick*

Stephen Livingstone, *University of Toronto*

Christine Lomore, *St. Francis Xavier University*

Tara MacDonald, *Queen's University*

Stacey L. MacKinnon, *University of Prince Edward Island*

Christopher Motz, *Carleton University*

Tom Murphy, *University of Western Ontario*

Jennifer Ostovich, *McMaster University*

Stephen B. Perrott, *Mount Saint Vincent University*

Jason Plaks, *University of Toronto St. George*

Kelley Robinson, *University of Manitoba*

Stanley Sadava, *Brock University*

Saba Safdar, *University of Guelph*

Rodney Schmaltz, *University of Alberta*

Kelly Schwartz, *University of Calgary*

Monika Stelzl, *St. Thomas University*

Mahin Tavakoli, *Carleton University*

Warren Thorngate, *Carleton University*

Susan Weir, *University of Regina*

Anne E. Wilson, *Wilfrid Laurier University*

We also want to thank the editorial staff at McGraw-Hill Ryerson for their excellent work. Kim Brewster and Jason Chih followed the vision for the new edition text. Katherine Goodes provided editorial feedback and assistance throughout the development of the manuscript. Stephanie Gay also provided excellent help in guiding the book through the final changes needed for publication.

Steven J. Spencer
University of Waterloo
Waterloo, ON N2L 3G4
Email: sspencer@watarts.uwaterloo.ca

Christian Jordan
Wilfrid Laurier University
Waterloo, ON N2L 3C5
Email: cjordan@wlu.ca

CHAPTER ONE
Introducing Social Psychology

▶CHAPTER OUTLINE

● WHAT IS SOCIAL PSYCHOLOGY?

● WHAT ARE THE MAJOR THEMES OF SOCIAL PSYCHOLOGY?

● HOW DO VALUES AFFECT SOCIAL PSYCHOLOGY?

● IS SOCIAL PSYCHOLOGY MERELY COMMON SENSE?

● RESEARCH METHODS: HOW DO WE DO SOCIAL PSYCHOLOGY?

There once was a man whose second wife was a vain and selfish woman. This woman had two daughters who were similarly vain and selfish. The man's own daughter, however, was sweet and kind. This sweet, kind daughter, whom we all know as Cinderella, learned early on that she had best do as she was told, accept insults, and not upstage her vain stepsisters.

But then, thanks to her fairy godmother, Cinderella was able to escape her situation and go to a grand ball, where she attracted a handsome prince. When the lovestruck prince later encountered a homelier Cinderella back in her degrading home, he at first failed to recognize her.

Implausible? The folk tale demands that we accept the power of the situation. In the presence of her oppressive stepmother, Cinderella was humble and unattractive. At the ball, Cinderella felt more beautiful—and walked and talked and smiled as if she were. In one situation, she cowered. In the other, she charmed.

The French philosopher–novelist Jean-Paul Sartre (1946) would have had no problem accepting the Cinderella premise. We humans are "first of all beings in a situation," he believed. "We cannot be distinguished from our situations, for they form us and decide our possibilities" (pp. 59–60, paraphrased).

WHAT IS SOCIAL PSYCHOLOGY?

What are the parameters of social psychology?

social psychology
the scientific study of how people think about, influence, and relate to one another

Social psychology is a science that studies the influences of our situations, with special attention to how we view and affect one another. Said more precisely, it is the scientific study of how people think about, influence, and relate to one another (Figure 1–1).

Social psychology lies at psychology's boundaries with sociology. Compared with sociology (the study of people in groups and societies), social psychology focuses more on individuals with methods that more often use experimentation. Compared with personality psychology,

FIGURE 1–1

SOCIAL
PSYCHOLOGY IS . . .

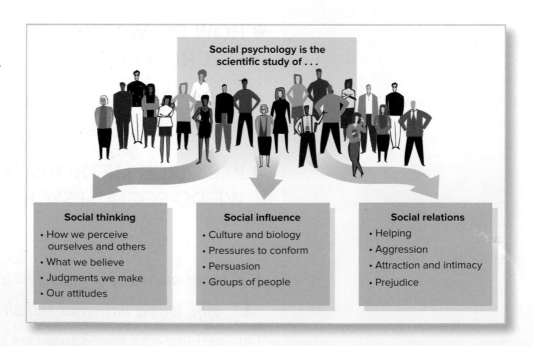

Social psychology is the scientific study of . . .

Social thinking
- How we perceive ourselves and others
- What we believe
- Judgments we make
- Our attitudes

Social influence
- Culture and biology
- Pressures to conform
- Persuasion
- Groups of people

Social relations
- Helping
- Aggression
- Attraction and intimacy
- Prejudice

social psychology focuses less on differences among individuals, and more on how individuals, in general, view and affect one another.

Social psychology is still a young science. The first social psychology experiments were barely more than a century ago (1898), and the first social psychology texts did not appear until just before and after 1900, in France, Italy, and Germany (Smith, 2005). Not until the 1930s did social psychology assume its current form. And not until the Second World War did it begin to emerge as the vibrant field it is today.

Social psychology studies our thinking, influence, and relationships by asking questions that have intrigued us all. Here are some examples:

How much of our social world is just in our heads?

As we will see in later chapters, our social behaviour varies not just with the objective situation, but with how we construe it. Social beliefs can be self-fulfilling. For example, happily married people will attribute their spouse's acid "Can't you ever put that where it belongs?" to something external ("He must have had a frustrating day."). Unhappily married people will attribute the same remark to a mean disposition ("Is he ever hostile!") and may, therefore, respond with a counterattack. Moreover, expecting hostility from their spouse, they may behave resentfully, thereby eliciting the hostility they expect.

A memorial to Robert Dziekanski who died at the Vancouver International Airport after he was tasered by authorities. He became confused and agitated after a long flight and could not understand authorities as they tried to deal with his behaviour. They followed protocol and shot him with a taser. Tragically, he died. Social psychologists ask, Could such an incident have been averted if rules allowed more-flexible responses to altercations with authorities?

Would you be cruel if ordered?

How did Nazi Germany implement the inconceivable slaughter of 6 million Jews? These evil acts occurred because thousands of people followed orders. They put the prisoners on trains, herded them into crowded showers, and poisoned them with gas. How could people engage in such horrific actions? Were these folks normal human beings? Stanley Milgram (1974) wondered. So he set up a situation where people were ordered to administer increasing levels of electric shock to someone who was having difficulty learning a series of words. As we will see in Chapter 6, the experimental results were quite disturbing: Nearly two-thirds of the participants fully complied.

To help others? Or to help yourself?

As bags of cash tumbled from an armoured truck on a fall day in 1987, $2 million was scattered along a Toronto, Ontario, street. Some motorists who stopped to help returned $100 000. Judging from what disappeared, many more stopped to help themselves. When similar incidents occurred in San Francisco, California, and Columbus, Ohio, the results were the same: Passersby grabbed most of the money (Bowen, 1988). A more recent example occurred during the August 2011 riots in London, England: A YouTube video showed young people approaching a man who had been injured; one young man seemed to help him, while another took the opportunity to rob him.

Throughout this book, sources for information are cited parenthetically, and then fully provided in the References section at the end of this book.

What situations trigger people to be helpful or greedy? Do some cultural contexts—perhaps villages and small towns—breed greater helpfulness?

A common thread runs through these questions: They all deal with how people view and affect one another. And that is what social psychology is all about. Social psychologists study attitudes and beliefs, conformity and independence, love and hate.

● WHAT ARE THE MAJOR THEMES IN SOCIAL PSYCHOLOGY?

What are social psychology's big lessons—its overarching themes?

In many academic fields, the results of tens of thousands of studies, the conclusions of thousands of investigators, and the insights of hundreds of theorists can be boiled down to a few central ideas. Biology offers us principles such as natural selection and adaptation. Sociology builds on concepts such as social structure and organization. Music harnesses our ideas of rhythm, melody, and harmony.

What concepts are on social psychology's list of central ideas? What themes, or fundamental principles, will be worth remembering long after you have forgotten most of the details? At a broad level, the fundamental principles of social psychology can be captured by a classic statement by one of its founders, Kurt Lewin, who said, "behaviour is a function of the person and the situation" (1952). From this general principle, we have developed a short list of "great ideas we ought never to forget," each of which we will unpack in chapters to come (Figure 1–2).

WE CONSTRUCT OUR SOCIAL REALITY

We humans have an irresistible urge to explain behaviour, to attribute it to some cause, and therefore, to make it seem orderly, predictable, and controllable. You and I may react differently to similar situations because we think differently. As mentioned earlier, how we react to a spouse's insult depends on whether we attribute it to hostility or to a bad day.

In a way, we are all intuitive scientists. We explain people's behaviour, usually with enough speed and accuracy to suit our daily needs. When someone's behaviour is consistent and distinctive, we attribute their behaviour to their personality. For example, if we observe someone who makes repeated snide comments, we may infer that that person has a nasty disposition, and then we might try to avoid the person.

Our beliefs about ourselves also matter. Do we have an optimistic outlook? Do we see ourselves as in control of things? Do we view ourselves as relatively superior or inferior? Our answers influence our emotions and actions. How we construe the world, and ourselves, matters.

OUR SOCIAL INTUITIONS ARE OFTEN POWERFUL BUT SOMETIMES PERILOUS

Our intuitions shape our fears (Is flying dangerous?), impressions (Can I trust him?), and relationships (Does she like me?). Intuitions influence leaders in times of crisis, gamblers at the table, jurors in their assessments of guilt, and personnel directors when eyeing applicants. Such intuitions are commonplace.

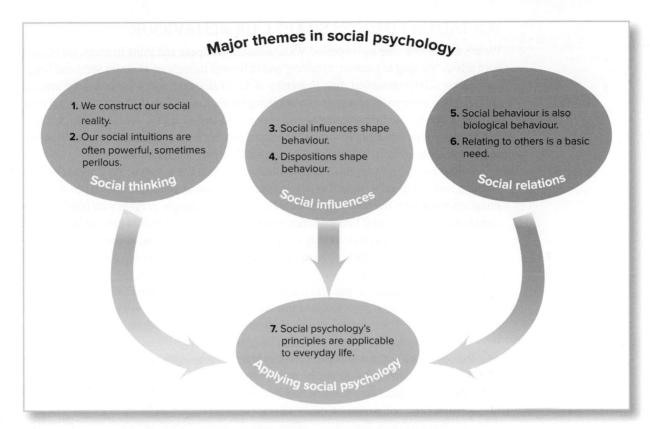

Major themes in social psychology

1. We construct our social reality.

2. Our social intuitions are often powerful, sometimes perilous.

Social thinking

3. Social influences shape behaviour.

4. Dispositions shape behaviour.

Social influences

5. Social behaviour is also biological behaviour.

6. Relating to others is a basic need.

Social relations

7. Social psychology's principles are applicable to everyday life.

Applying social psychology

FIGURE 1–2

MAJOR THEMES IN SOCIAL PSYCHOLOGY.

Indeed, psychological science reveals a fascinating unconscious mind—an intuitive back-stage mind—that Freud never told us about. More than we realized a decade or more ago, thinking occurs not onstage, in full view of others, but offstage, out of sight. As we will see, studies of automatic processing, implicit memory, heuristics, spontaneous trait inference, instant emotions, and nonverbal communication unveil our intuitive capacities. Thinking, memory, and attitudes all operate on two levels—one conscious and deliberate, the other unconscious and automatic. "Dual processing," today's researchers call it. We know more than we know we know.

Intuitions are powerful, but they are also perilous. Thinking occurs offstage, with the results occasionally displayed onstage. We misperceive others, and we often fail to appreciate how our expectations shape our evaluations. Even our intuitions about ourselves often err. We intuitively trust our memories more than we should. We misread our own minds; in experiments, subjects have denied being affected by things that did influence them. We mispredict our own feelings—how bad we'll feel a year from now if we lose our job or our romance breaks up, and how good we'll feel a year from now if we win our province's lottery. And we often mispredict our own future—when buying clothes, people approaching middle age will still buy snug, claiming, "I anticipate shedding a bit of weight"; rarely does anyone say, more realistically, "I'd better buy a relatively loose fit; people my age tend to put on weight."

Our social intuitions, then, are noteworthy for both their power and their perils. By reminding us of intuition's gifts and alerting us to its pitfalls, social psychologists aim to fortify our thinking. In most situations, "fast and frugal" snap judgments serve us well enough. But in others, where accuracy matters—as when needing to fear the right things and spend our resources accordingly—we had best restrain our impulsive intuitions with critical thinking.

SOCIAL INFLUENCES SHAPE OUR BEHAVIOUR

We are, as Aristotle long ago observed, social animals. We speak and think in words we learned from others. We long to connect, to belong, and to be well thought of. Matthias Mehl and James Pennebaker (2003) quantified their University of Texas students' social behaviour by inviting them to wear microcassette recorders and microphones. Once every 12 minutes during their waking hours, the computer-operated recorder would imperceptibly record for 30 seconds. Although the observation period covered only weekdays (including class time), almost 30 percent of their time was spent talking. Relationships are a large part of being human.

As social creatures, we respond to our immediate contexts. Sometimes, the power of a social situation leads us to act in ways that depart from our espoused attitudes. Indeed, powerful evil situations sometimes overwhelm good intentions, inducing people to agree with falsehoods or comply with cruelty: Under Nazi influence, many otherwise decent people became instruments of the Holocaust. Other situations may elicit great generosity and compassion: After the earthquake and tsunami that struck Japan in 2011, for example, people throughout the world gave generously to provide relief.

The power of the situation was also dramatically evident in varying attitudes toward the 2003 war against Iraq. Opinion polls revealed that Americans and Israelis overwhelmingly favoured this waging of war. Their distant cousins elsewhere in the world overwhelmingly opposed it. Tell a social psychologist where you live and he or she will make a reasonable guess as to what your attitudes were as the war began. (Tell that social psychologist your educational level and what media you watch and read, and he or she will make an even more confident guess of how you construed the war.) Regardless of how history judges the war, this much is evident: Your situation matters.

Your culture helps define your situation; your standards regarding promptness, frankness, and clothing vary with your culture. Here are some examples:

- Whether you prefer a slim or voluptuous body depends on when and where in the world you live.

- Whether you define social justice as equality (all receive the same) or as equity (those who earn more receive more) depends on whether your ideology has been shaped more by socialism or by capitalism.

- Whether you tend to be expressive or reserved, casual or formal, hinges partly on your culture and your ethnicity.

- Whether you focus primarily on yourself—your personal needs, desires, and morality—or on your family, clan, and communal groups depends on how much you are a product of modern Western individualism.

Social psychologist Hazel Markus (2005) summed it up: "People are, above all, malleable." Said differently, we adapt to our social context. Our behaviour is shaped by external forces.

PERSONAL ATTITUDES AND DISPOSITIONS ALSO SHAPE BEHAVIOUR

Internal forces also matter. We are not passive tumbleweeds, merely blown this way and that by the social winds. Our inner attitudes affect our behaviour. Our political attitudes influence our voting behaviour. Our attitudes toward smoking influence our susceptibility to peer pressures to smoke. Our attitudes toward poor people influence our willingness to support them. (As we will see, attitudes also follow behaviour, which leads us to believe strongly in those things for which we have committed ourselves or suffered.)

Personality dispositions also affect behaviour. Facing the same situation, different people may react differently. Emerging from years of political imprisonment, one person exudes bitterness and seeks revenge. Another, such as South Africa's Nelson Mandela, seeks reconciliation and unity with one-time enemies.

SOCIAL BEHAVIOUR IS BIOLOGICALLY ROOTED

Twenty-first-century social psychology is providing us with ever-growing insights into our behaviour's biological foundations. Many of our social behaviours reflect a deep biological wisdom.

Everyone who has taken introductory psychology knows that nature and nurture together form who we are. As the area of a field is determined by both its length and its width, so do biology and experience together create us. As evolutionary psychologists remind us, our inherited human nature predisposes us to behave in ways that helped our ancestors survive and reproduce. We carry the genes of those whose traits enabled them and their children to survive and reproduce. Thus, evolutionary psychologists ask how natural selection might predispose our actions and reactions when dating and mating, hating and hurting, caring and sharing. Nature also endows us with an enormous capacity to learn and to adapt to varied environments. We are sensitive and responsive to our social context.

If every psychological event (every thought, every emotion, every behaviour) is simultaneously a biological event, then we can also examine the neurobiology that underlies social behaviour. What brain areas enable our experiences of love and contempt, helping and aggression, perception and belief? How do mind and behaviour function together as one coordinated system? What does the timing of brain events reveal about how we process information? Such questions are asked by those in **social neuroscience** (Cacioppo et al., 2010; Klein et al., 2010).

Social neuroscientists do not reduce complex social behaviours, such as helping and hurting, to simple neural or molecular mechanisms. Their point is this: To understand social behaviour, we must consider both under-the-skin (biological) and between-skins (social) influences. Mind and body are one grand system. Stress hormones affect how we feel and act. Social ostracism elevates blood pressure. Social support strengthens the disease-fighting immune system.

We are bio-psycho-social organisms. We reflect the interplay of our biological, psychological, and social influences. And that is why today's psychologists study behaviour from these different levels of analysis.

social neuroscience an integration of biological and social perspectives that explores the neural and psychological bases of social and emotional behaviours

RELATING TO OTHERS IS A BASIC NEED

We want to fit in with others, and our relationship with others can be an important source of stress and pain as well as joy and comfort. Kip Williams and his colleagues (Williams, 2002; Williams, Cheung, & Choi, 2000; Williams & Zadro, 2001) have shown that feeling left out can have dramatic effects on how people feel about themselves. They had university students play a simple computer game in which each player was represented by a cartoon figure on the screen and the figures passed a ball to one another. When confederates of the experimenter passed the ball to one another and left the real participants out of the action, the participants felt miserable and reported steep drops in their self-esteem. Apparently, even university students can feel the pain that many schoolchildren experience when they are not included. Acts of aggression and prejudice inflict this sort of pain.

Of course, relating to others is not all pain. When others help, when we form romantic relationships, and when we promote harmony between groups, interpersonal relations can be an important source of joy and comfort. In fact, according to Mark Leary and Roy Baumeister, our relationships with others form the basis of our self-esteem (Leary & Baumeister, 2000). In fact, they argue that our self-esteem is nothing more than a reading of how accepted we feel by others. In this view, relating to others is a basic need that shapes all our social actions.

> "You can never foretell what any man [person] will do, but you can say with precision what an average number will be up to. Individuals may vary, but percentages remain constant."
>
> SHERLOCK HOLMES, IN SIR ARTHUR CONAN DOYLE'S *A STUDY IN SCARLET*, 1887

SOCIAL PSYCHOLOGY'S PRINCIPLES ARE APPLICABLE IN EVERYDAY LIFE

Social psychology has the potential to illuminate your life, to make visible the subtle forces that guide your thinking and acting. It also offers many ideas about how to know ourselves better, how to win friends and influence people, how to transform closed fists into open arms.

Scholars are also applying social psychological insights to other disciplines. Principles of social thinking, social influence, and social relations have implications for human health and well-being, for judicial procedures and juror decisions in courtrooms, and for the encouragement of behaviours that will enable an environmentally sustainable human future.

As but one perspective on human existence, psychological science does not seek to engage life's ultimate questions: What is the meaning of human life? What should be our purpose? What is our ultimate destiny? But social psychology does give us a method for asking and answering some exceedingly interesting and important questions. Social psychology is all about life—your life: your beliefs, your attitudes, your relationships.

● HOW DO VALUES AFFECT SOCIAL PSYCHOLOGY?

Social psychologists' values penetrate their work in ways both obvious and subtle. What are these ways?

Social psychology is less a collection of findings than a set of strategies for answering questions. In science, as in courts of law, personal opinions are inadmissible. When ideas are put on trial, evidence determines the verdict. But are social psychologists really this objective? Because they are human beings, don't their values—their personal convictions about what is desirable and how people ought to behave—seep into their work? And if so, can social psychology really be scientific?

There are two general ways that values enter psychology: the obvious and the subtle.

OBVIOUS WAYS IN WHICH VALUES ENTER SOCIAL PSYCHOLOGY

Values enter the picture with our choice of research topics. These choices typically reflect social history (Kagan, 2009). It was no accident that the study of prejudice flourished during the 1940s as fascism raged in Europe; that the 1950s, a time of look-alike fashions and rows of identical suburban homes, gave us studies of conformity; that the 1960s saw interest in aggression increase with riots and rising crime rates; that the 1970s feminist movement helped stimulate a wave of research on gender and sexism; that the 1980s offered a resurgence of attention to psychological aspects of the arms race; and that the 1990s were marked by heightened interest in how people respond to cultural diversity. These trends reflect the social concerns of their time. Social psychology reflects social history (Kagan, 2009).

Values differ not only across time but also across cultures. In Europe, people take pride in their nationalities. The Scots are self-consciously distinct from the English, and the Austrians from the Germans. Consequently, Europe has given us a major theory of "social identity," whereas North American social psychologists have focused more on individuals—how one person thinks about others, is influenced by them, and relates to them (Fiske, 2004; Tajfel, 1981; Turner, 1984). Australian social psychologists have drawn theories and methods from both Europe and North America (Feather, 2005).

Values also influence the types of people attracted to various disciplines (Campbell, 1975a; Moynihan, 1979). At your school, too, do the students attracted to the humanities, the natural sciences, and the social sciences noticeably differ? Do psychology and sociology attract people who are eager to challenge tradition, people who would rather shape the future than preserve the past?

Finally, values obviously enter the picture as the object of social-psychological analysis. Social psychologists investigate how values form, why they change, and how they influence attitudes and actions. None of this, however, tells us which values are "right."

NOT-SO-OBVIOUS WAYS IN WHICH VALUES ENTER SOCIAL PSYCHOLOGY

We less often recognize the subtler ways in which value commitments masquerade as objective truth. Consider these not-so-obvious ways in which values enter social psychology and related areas.

The subjective aspects of science

Scientists and philosophers now agree: Science is not purely objective. Scientists do not simply read the book of nature. Rather, they interpret nature, using their own mental categories. In our daily lives, too, we view the world through the lens of our preconceptions.

While reading these words, you have been unaware that you are also looking at your nose. Your mind blocks from awareness something that is there, if only you were predisposed to perceive it. This tendency to prejudge reality based on our expectations is a basic fact about the human mind.

Because scholars at work in any given area often share a common viewpoint or come from the same **culture**, their assumptions may go unchallenged. What we take

culture
the enduring behaviours, ideas, attitudes, traditions, products, and institutions shared by a large group of people and transmitted from one generation to the next

social representations socially shared beliefs; widely held ideas and values, including our assumptions and cultural ideologies. Our social representations help us make sense of our world

for granted—the shared beliefs that European social psychologists call our **social representations** (Augoustinos & Innes, 1990; Moscovici, 1988, 2001)—are our most important but often most unexamined convictions. Sometimes, however, someone from outside the camp will also call attention to these assumptions. During the 1980s, feminists and Marxists exposed some of social psychology's unexamined assumptions. Feminist critics called attention to subtle biases—for example, the political conservatism of many scientists who favour a biological interpretation of gender differences in social behaviour (Unger, 1985). Marxist critics called attention to competitive, individualist biases—for example, the assumptions that conformity is bad and that individual rewards are good. Marxists and feminists, of course, make their own assumptions, as critics of academic "political correctness" are fond of noting. Social psychologist Lee Jussim (2005), for example, argues that progressive social psychologists sometimes feel compelled to deny group differences and to assume that stereotypes of group difference are never rooted in reality but always in racism.

> *"Science does not simply describe and explain nature; it is part of the interplay between nature and ourselves; it describes nature as exposed to our method of questioning."*
> WERNER HEISENBERG, *PHYSICS AND PHILOSOPHY*, 1958

In Chapter 3, we will see more ways in which our preconceptions guide our interpretations. What's crucial for our behaviour is less the situation-as-it-is than the situation-as-we-construe-it.

The hidden values in psychological concepts

Implicit in our understanding that psychology is not objective is the realization that psychologists' own values play an important part in the theories and judgments they support. Psychologists refer to people as mature or immature, as well-adjusted or poorly adjusted, as mentally healthy or mentally ill. They talk as if they were stating facts, when really they are value judgments. Here are some examples:

- *Forming concepts.* Hidden values even seep into psychology's research-based concepts. Pretend you have taken a personality test and the psychologist, after scoring your answers, announces, "You scored high in self-esteem. You are low in anxiety. And you have exceptional ego-strength." "Ah," you think, "I suspected as much, but it feels good to know that." Now another psychologist gives you a similar test. For some peculiar reason, this test asks some of the same questions. Afterwards, the psychologist informs you that you seem defensive, for you scored high in "repressiveness." "How could this be?" you wonder. "The other psychologist said such nice things about me." It could be because all these labels describe the same set of responses (a tendency to say nice things about oneself and not to acknowledge problems). Shall we call it high self-esteem or defensiveness? The label reflects a value judgment.

- *Labelling.* Value judgments are often hidden within our social-psychological language—but that is also true of everyday language. Here are some examples:
  - Whether we label someone engaged in guerrilla warfare a "terrorist" or a "freedom fighter" depends on our view of the cause.
  - Whether we view wartime civilian deaths as "the loss of innocent lives" or as "collateral damage" affects our acceptance of the deaths.
  - Whether we call public assistance "welfare" or "aid to the needy" reflects our political views.

- When "they" exalt their country and people, it's nationalism; when "we" do it, it's patriotism.

- Whether someone involved in an extramarital affair is practising "open marriage" or "adultery" depends on our personal values.

- "Brainwashing" is social influence we do not approve of.

- *Naturalistic fallacy.* A seductive error for those who work in the social sciences is sliding from a description of *what is* into a prescription of *what ought to be.* Philosophers call this the naturalistic fallacy. The gulf between "is" and "ought to be," between scientific description and ethical prescription, remains as wide today as when philosopher David Hume pointed it out 200 years ago. No survey of human behaviour—say, of sexual practices—logically dictates what is "right" behaviour. If most people don't do something, that does not make it wrong. If most people do it, that does not make it right. We inject our values whenever we move from objective statements of fact to prescriptive statements of what ought to be.

Hidden (and not-so-hidden) values seep into psychological advice. They permeate popular psychology books that offer guidance on living and loving.

As these examples indicate, values lie hidden within our cultural definitions of mental health, our psychological advice for living, our concepts, and our psychological labels. Throughout this book, we will call your attention to additional examples of hidden values. The point is never that the implicit values are necessarily bad. The point is that scientific interpretation, even at the level of labelling a phenomenon, is a human activity. It is, therefore, natural and inevitable that prior beliefs and values will influence what social psychologists think and write.

Should we dismiss science because it has its subjective side? Quite the contrary: The realization that human thinking always involves interpretation is precisely why we need researchers with varying biases to undertake scientific analysis. By constantly checking our beliefs against the facts, as best we know them, we check and retrain our biases. Systematic observation and experimentation help us clean the lens through which we see reality.

naturalistic fallacy
the error of defining what is good in terms of what is observable: for example, what's typical is normal; what's normal is good

● IS SOCIAL PSYCHOLOGY MERELY COMMON SENSE?

Is social psychology simply common sense? Do social psychology's theories provide new insight into the human condition? Or do they only describe the obvious?

Many of the conclusions presented in this book will probably have already occurred to you, for social psychology is all around you. We constantly observe people thinking about, influencing, and relating to one another. Much of our thinking aims to discern and explain relationships among social events. It pays to discern what that facial expression predicts, how to get someone to do something, or whether to regard another person as friend or foe. For centuries, philosophers, novelists, and poets have observed and commented on social behaviour, often with keen insight.

Does this mean that social psychology is only common sense in fancy words? We wouldn't have written this book if we thought so. Nevertheless, it must be acknowledged that social psychology faces two contradictory criticisms: first, that it is trivial because it documents the obvious; second, that it is dangerous because its findings could be used to manipulate people.

We will explore the second criticism in Chapter 5. For the moment, let's examine the first objection.

Do social psychology and the other social sciences simply formalize what any amateur already knows intuitively? Writer Cullen Murphy (1990) thought so: "Day after day social scientists go out into the world. Day after day they discover that people's behaviour is pretty much what you'd expect." Nearly a half-century earlier, historian Arthur Schlesinger, Jr. (1949) reacted with similar scorn to social scientists' studies of Second World War soldiers.

What were the findings? Another reviewer, Paul Lazarsfeld (1949), offered a sample with interpretive comments, four of which we paraphrase:

1. Better-educated soldiers suffered more adjustment problems than did less-educated soldiers. (Intellectuals were less prepared for battle stresses than street-smart people.)

2. Soldiers from southern climates coped better with the hot South Sea Island weather than did northern soldiers. (People from southern climates are more accustomed to hot weather.)

3. Soldiers from rural backgrounds were usually in better spirits during their army life than soldiers from city backgrounds. (After all, they are more accustomed to hardships.)

4. Soldiers were more eager to return home during the fighting than they were after the German surrender. (You cannot blame people for not wanting to be killed.)

> *"A first-rate theory predicts; a second-rate theory forbids; and a third-rate theory explains after the event."*
> ALEKSANDER ISAAKOVICH KITAIGORODSKII

As you read those findings, did you agree that they were basically common sense? If so, you might be surprised to learn that Lazarsfeld went on to say, "Every one of these statements is the direct opposite of what was actually found." In reality, it was found that less-educated soldiers adapted more poorly. People from southern climates were not more likely than people from northern climates to adjust to tropical weather. Soldiers from city backgrounds were usually in better spirits than soldiers from rural backgrounds. And soldiers were actually more eager to come home after the fighting ended than while it was still ongoing. "If we had mentioned the actual results of the investigation first [as Schlesinger experienced], the reader would have labelled these 'obvious' also."

One problem with common sense, however, is that we invoke it after we know the facts. Events are far more "obvious" and predictable in hindsight than beforehand. Experiments reveal that when people learn the outcome of an experiment, that outcome suddenly seems unsurprising—certainly less surprising than it is to people who are simply told about the experimental procedure and the possible outcomes (Slovic & Fischhoff, 1977).

Likewise, in everyday life, we often do not expect something to happen until it does. We *then* suddenly see clearly the forces that brought it about and feel unsurprised. After the Quebec sovereignty vote of 1995, commentators—forgetting they had predicted a large win for the federalists—found the close vote unsurprising. It seems we often think we knew what we actually did not. As the philosopher–theologian Søren Kierkegaard put it, "Life is lived forwards, but understood backwards."

If this **hindsight bias** (also called the I-knew-it-all-along phenomenon) is pervasive, you may now be feeling that you already knew about it. Indeed, almost any conceivable result of a psychological experiment can seem like common sense—*after* you know the result.

You can demonstrate the phenomenon yourself. Take a group of people and tell half of them one psychological finding and the other half the opposite result. For example, tell half as follows:

> Social psychologists have found that, whether choosing friends or falling in love, we are most attracted to people whose traits are different from our own. There seems to be wisdom in the old saying, "Opposites attract."

Tell the other half:

> Social psychologists have found that, whether choosing friends or falling in love, we are most attracted to people whose traits are similar to our own. There seems to be wisdom in the old saying, "Birds of a feather flock together."

Ask the people to explain the result. Then ask them to say whether it is "surprising" or "not surprising." Virtually all will find whichever result they were given "not surprising."

Indeed, we can draw upon our stockpile of proverbs to make almost any result seem to make sense. If a social psychologist reports that separation intensifies romantic attraction, Joe Public responds, "You get paid for this? Everybody knows that 'absence makes the heart grow fonder.'" Should it turn out that separation weakens attraction, Judy Public may say, "My grandmother could have told you, 'Out of sight, out of mind.'"

Karl Teigen (1986) must have had a few chuckles when he asked University of Leicester (England) students to evaluate actual proverbs and their opposites. When given the proverb "Fear is stronger than love," most rated it as true. But so did students who were given its reversed form, "Love is stronger than fear." Likewise, a genuine proverb, "He that is fallen cannot help him who is down," was rated highly; but so, too, was "He that is fallen can help him who is down." Our favourites, however, were the two highly rated proverbs: "Wise men make proverbs and fools repeat them" (authentic) and its made-up counterpart, "Fools make proverbs and wise men repeat them."

The hindsight bias creates a problem for many psychology students. Sometimes, results are genuinely surprising (for example, that Olympic *bronze* medallists take more joy in their achievement than do *silver* medallists). More often, when you read the results of experiments in your textbooks, the material seems easy, even obvious. When you later take a multiple-choice test during which you must choose among several plausible conclusions, the task may become surprisingly difficult. "I don't know what happened," the befuddled student later moans. "I thought I knew the material." (A word to the wise: Beware of this phenomenon when studying for exams, lest you fool yourself into thinking that you know the material better than you do.)

hindsight bias
the tendency to exaggerate, after learning an outcome, one's ability to have foreseen how something turned out; also known as the *I-knew-it-all-along phenomenon*

In hindsight, events seem obvious and predictable.
ScienceCartoonsPlus.com

"It is easy to be wise after the event."
SHERLOCK HOLMES, IN ARTHUR
CONAN DOYLE'S "THE PROBLEM OF
THOR BRIDGE," 1922

So what do we conclude—that common sense is usually wrong? Sometimes it is. Until science dethroned the common-sense view, centuries of daily experience assured people that the sun revolved around the earth. Medical experience assured doctors that bleeding was an effective treatment for typhoid fever, until someone in the middle of the last century bothered to experiment—to divide patients into two groups, one bled, the other given mere bed rest.

Other times, conventional wisdom is right—or it falls on both sides of an issue: Does happiness come from knowing the truth or preserving illusions? From being with others or living in peaceful solitude? Opinions are a dime a dozen; no matter what we find, there will be someone who foresaw it. (Mark Twain jested that Adam was the only person who, when saying a good thing, knew that nobody had said it before.) But which of the many competing ideas best fit reality?

The point is not that common sense is predictably wrong. Rather, common sense usually is right *after the fact.* We, therefore, easily deceive ourselves into thinking that we know and knew more than we do and did. And this is precisely why we need science—to help us sift reality from illusion and genuine predictions from easy hindsight.

● RESEARCH METHODS: HOW DO WE DO SOCIAL PSYCHOLOGY?

How does social psychology try to accomplish its goals?

We have considered some of the intriguing questions social psychology seeks to answer. We have also seen the ways in which subjective, often unconscious processes influence the work that social psychologists do. Now let's consider the scientific methods that make social psychology a science.

"Nothing has such power to broaden the mind as the ability to investigate systematically and truly all that comes under thy observation in life."
MARCUS AURELIUS, *MEDITATIONS*

In their quest for insight, social psychologists propose theories that organize their observations and imply testable hypotheses and practical predictions. To test a hypothesis, social psychologists may do research that predicts behaviour using correlational studies, often conducted in natural settings. Or they may seek to explain behaviour by conducting experiments that manipulate one or more factors under controlled conditions. Once they have conducted a research study, they explore ways to apply their findings to improve people's lives.

We are all amateur social psychologists. People-watching is a universal hobby in parks, on the street, at school. As we observe people, we form ideas about how humans think about, influence, and relate to one another. Professional social psychologists do the same, only more systematically (by forming theories) and painstakingly (often with experiments that create miniature social dramas to pin down cause and effect).

FORMING AND TESTING HYPOTHESES

theory
an integrated set of principles that explain and predict observed events

We social psychologists have a hard time thinking of anything more fascinating than human existence. As we wrestle with human nature to pin down its secrets, we organize our ideas and findings into theories. A **theory** is an integrated set of principles that explain and predict observed events. Theories are a scientific shorthand.

In everyday conversation, "theory" often means "less than fact"—a middle rung on a confidence ladder from guess to theory to fact. Thus, people may, for example, dismiss Charles Darwin's theory of evolution as "just a theory." Indeed, noted Alan Leshner (2005), "Evolution *is* only a theory, but so is gravity." People often respond that gravity is a fact—but the fact is that your keys fall to the ground when dropped. Gravity is the theoretical explanation that accounts for such observed facts.

To a scientist, facts and theories are apples and oranges. Facts are agreed-upon statements that we observe. Theories are ideas that summarize and explain facts. "Science is built up with facts, as a house is with stones," wrote French scientist Jules Henri Poincaré (1905), "but a collection of facts is no more a science than a heap of stones is a house."

Theories not only summarize; they also imply testable predictions, called **hypotheses**. Hypotheses serve several purposes. First, they allow us to test the theory on which they are based. By making specific predictions, a theory puts its money where its mouth is. Second, predictions give direction to research. Any scientific field will mature more rapidly if its researchers have a sense of direction. Theoretical predictions suggest new areas for research; they send investigators looking for things they might never have thought of. Third, the predictive feature of good theories can also make them practical. What, for example, would be of greater practical value today than a theory of aggression that would predict when to expect aggression and how to control it?

When testing our theories with specific hypotheses, however, we must always translate variables that are described at the theoretical level into the specific variables that we are going to observe. This process called *operationalization* is often as much an art as a science.

Consider how this works. Say we observe that people who loot, taunt, or attack others (i.e., exhibit extreme violence) often do so in crowds. We might, therefore, theorize that the presence of others in a crowd leads to extreme violence. Let's play with this idea for a moment. In order to test this hypothesis, we need to translate our theoretical variable "crowd" into a meaningful example of it that we will observe. In this case, maybe we would operationalize this variable as 20 strangers together in a relatively small room, even though this definition of "crowd" would probably be different from the crowds we originally observed. The crucial question for this study would be this: Does our operational variable of "crowd" represent what we mean theoretically by a crowd? The answer to that question determines whether our operational variable is a *valid* measure of our theoretical variable. If we can accept it as valid, then we can go on to test our hypothesis. If we can't accept it as valid, then the proposed research will not tell us much about our theory and we should develop a new operationalization. What do you think of this operationalization of "crowd"? Could you do better? Good social psychology requires both following the principles of science and developing tests of theories that creatively capture the essence of the theory being tested.

If we are going to test our hypothesis, however, we would also need to operationalize extreme violence. What if we asked individuals in "crowds" to administer punishing shocks to a hapless victim without knowing which one of the group was actually shocking the victim? Would these individuals administer stronger shocks than individuals acting alone, as our theory predicts? In this example, administering punishing shocks would be the operational variable of our concept of extreme violence. To be a good operationalization, we would need to believe that it is a valid measure of violence; we would also need to believe that by using this measure, differences in violence could emerge and we would get basically the same results if we did the study over again. That is, we would need to believe that it is a *reliable* measure. If this measure of violence sometimes showed violence and other times didn't, we might very well miss our effect.

hypotheses
testable propositions that describe relationships that may exist between events

When we test our theories, we necessarily must make observations; and when we make observations, we have to decide what we are going to observe. This process of deciding on our observations, called operationalization, is how science puts its theories to test. A good operationalization captures the essence of the theoretical concept—that is, it is valid—and it does so sensitively and consistently—that is, reliably—so that tests of the theory can be observed.

You will note throughout the text, however, that quite regularly more than one theory can explain what we know about a given phenomenon. Not only must we test our own theory, but science often proceeds by testing between two theories. How do we conclude that one theory is better than another? A good theory accomplishes the following:

- It effectively summarizes many observations.
- It makes clear predictions that we can use to do the following:
  - Confirm or modify the theory.
  - Generate new exploration.
  - Suggest practical applications.

When we discard theories, usually it's not because they have been proved false. Rather, like old cars, they get replaced by newer, better models.

CORRELATIONAL RESEARCH: DETECTING NATURAL ASSOCIATIONS

Let's go backstage now and take a brief look at how social psychology is done. This glimpse behind the scenes will be just enough, we trust, for you to appreciate findings discussed later and to think critically about everyday social events.

field research
research done in natural, real-life settings outside the laboratory

Social-psychological research varies by location. It can take place in the laboratory (a controlled situation) or it can be **field research** (everyday situations). And it varies by method—being **correlational research** (asking whether two or more factors are naturally associated) or **experimental research** (manipulating some factor to see its effect on another). If you want to be a critical reader of psychological research reported in newspapers and magazines, it will pay to understand the difference between correlational and experimental research.

correlational research
the study of the naturally occurring relationships among variables

Using some real examples, let's first consider the advantages of correlational research (often involving important variables in natural settings) and the disadvantages (ambiguous interpretation of cause and effect). As we will see in Module B, today's psychologists are relating personal and social factors to human health. Among the researchers are Douglas Carroll at Glasgow Caledonian University and his colleagues, George Davey Smith and Paul Bennett (1994). In search of possible links between socio-economic status and health, the researchers ventured into Glasgow's old graveyards. As a measure of health, they noted from grave markers the lifespans of 843 individuals. As an indication of status, they measured the height of the pillars over the graves, reasoning that height reflected cost and, therefore, affluence. As Figure 1–3 shows, higher markers were also related to longer lives, for both men and women.

experimental research
studies that seek clues to cause–effect relationships by manipulating one or more factors (independent variables) while controlling others (holding them constant)

Carroll and his colleagues explain how other researchers, using contemporary data, have confirmed the status–longevity correlation. Scottish postal-code regions having the least overcrowding and unemployment also have the greatest longevity. In contemporary Britain, occupational status correlates with longevity. One study followed 17 350 British civil service workers over 10 years. Compared to top-grade administrators, those at the professional-executive grade were 1.6 times more likely to die. Clerical workers were 2.2 times and labourers 2.7 times more likely to have died (Adler et al., 1993, 1994). Across times and places, the status–longevity correlation seems reliable.

Correlation versus causation

The status–longevity question illustrates the most irresistible thinking error made by both amateur and professional social psychologists: When two factors like status and health go together, it is terribly tempting to

Commemorative markers in the Glasgow Cathedral graveyard.

conclude that one is causing the other. Status, we might presume, somehow protects a person from health risks. Or might it be the other way around? Maybe health promotes vigour and success. Perhaps people who live longer accumulate more wealth (enabling them to have more expensive grave markers). Correlational research allows us to predict, but it cannot tell us whether changing one variable (such as social status) will cause changes in another (such as health).

The correlation–causation confusion is behind much muddled thinking in popular psychology. Consider another very real correlation—between self-esteem and academic achievement. Children with high self-esteem tend also to have high academic achievement. (As with any

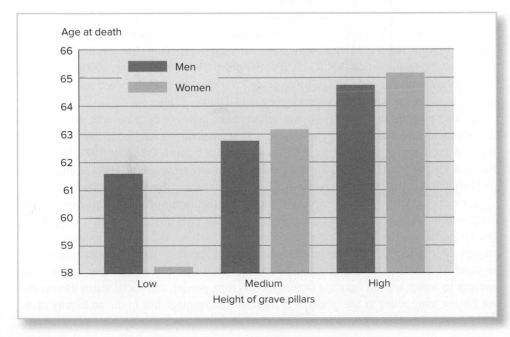

Age at death

Height of grave pillars

FIGURE 1–3

STATUS AND LONGEVITY.

Tall grave pillars commemorated people who also tended to live longer.

FIGURE 1–4

CORRELATION
AND CAUSATION.

When two variables
correlate, any
combination of
three explanations is
possible.

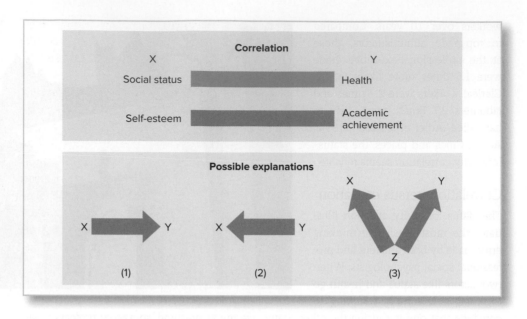

correlation, we can also state this the other way around: High achievers tend to have high self-esteem.) Why do you suppose this is? (See Figure 1–4 for a representation of three possible scenarios.)

Some people believe a "healthy self-concept" contributes to achievement. Thus, boosting a child's self-image may also boost school achievement. But others, including psychologists William Damon (1995), Robyn Dawes (1994), Mark Leary (1998), and Martin Seligman (1994), doubted that self-esteem is really "the armor that protects kids" from underachievement (or drug abuse and delinquency). Perhaps it's the other way around: Perhaps problems and failures cause low self-esteem. Perhaps self-esteem often reflects the reality of how things are going for us. Perhaps self-esteem grows from hard-won achievements. Do well, and you will feel good about yourself; goof off and fail, and you will feel like a dolt. A study of 635 Norwegian schoolchildren suggests that a string of gold stars beside one's name on the spelling chart and constant praise from an admiring teacher can boost a child's self-esteem (Skaalvik & Hagtvet, 1990). Or perhaps, as in a recent study of nearly 6000 German grade 7 students, the traffic between self-esteem and academic achievement runs both ways (Trautwein & Lüdtke, 2006).

It's also possible that self-esteem and achievement correlate because both are linked to underlying intelligence and family social status. That possibility was raised in two studies—one study of 1600 young men, another of 715 teenagers (Bachman & O'Malley, 1977; Maruyama, Rubin, & Kingbury, 1981). When the researchers statistically removed the effect of intelligence and family status, the correlation between self-esteem and achievement evaporated.

Correlations quantify, with a coefficient known as r, the degree of relationship between two factors—from -1.0 (as one factor score goes up, the other goes down), through 0, to $+1.0$ (the two factors' scores rise and fall together). Scores on self-esteem and depression tests correlate negatively (r is about -0.6). The intelligence scores of identical twins correlate positively (r is about $+0.08$). The strength of correlational research is that it tends to occur in real-world settings in which we can examine factors such as race, gender, and social status (factors that we cannot manipulate in the laboratory). Its great disadvantage lies in the ambiguity of the results. The point is so important that even if it fails to impress people the first 25 times they hear it, it is worth repeating a 26th time: Knowing that two variables change together (correlate) enables us to predict one when we know the other, but correlation does not specify cause and effect.

When correlational research is extended over time, it is called longitudinal research. Longitudinal research can begin to sort out cause and effect because we know that some things happen before others. Causes always happen before effects, so if we know that children almost always have a healthy positive self-image before they start to show more achievement than their peers, then we can rule out that it is achievement that causes a healthy positive self-image. Advanced correlational techniques can suggest cause–effect relations. *Time-lagged* correlations reveal the sequence of events (for example, by indicating whether changed achievement more often precedes or follows changed self-esteem). Researchers can also use statistical techniques that extract the influence of "confounded" variables, as when the correlation between self-esteem and achievement evaporated after extracting intelligence and family status. Recall our earlier mention of a third variable, such as diet. Thus, the Scottish research team wondered whether the status–longevity relationship would survive their removing the effect of cigarette smoking, which is now much less common among those of higher status. It did, which suggested that some other factors, such as increased stress and decreased feelings of control, may also account for poorer people's earlier mortality.

Survey research

How do we measure such variables as status and health? One way is by surveying representative samples of people. Survey researchers obtain a representative group by taking a **random sample**—one in which every person in the population being studied has an equal chance of inclusion. With this procedure, any subgroup of people—red-haired people, for example—will tend to be represented in the survey to the extent that they are represented in the total population.

> **random sample**
> survey procedure in which every person in the population being studied has an equal chance of inclusion

It is an amazing fact that whether we survey people in a city or in a whole country, 1200 randomly selected participants will enable us to be 95 percent confident of describing the entire population with an error margin of 3 percentage points or less. Imagine a huge jar filled with beans, 50 percent red and 50 percent white. Randomly sample 1200 of these, and you will be 95 percent certain to draw out between 47 percent and 53 percent red beans—regardless of whether the jar contains 10 000 beans or 100 million beans. If we think of the red beans as supporters of one political party and the white beans as supporters of the other party, we can understand why polls taken just before national elections have diverged from election results by an average of less than 2 percent. As a few drops of blood can speak for the whole body, so can a random sample speak for a population.

Bear in mind that polls do not literally *predict* voting; they only *describe* public opinion as of the moment they are taken. Public opinion can shift. For example, in the 2011 federal election, surveys just two days before the election (LISPOP, 2011) suggested that the Liberal Party would get as many seats as the New Democratic Party (NDP); but clearly the NDP was gaining momentum and ended up capturing many more seats than the Liberals.

To evaluate surveys, we must also bear in mind four potentially biasing influences: unrepresentative samples, the order of the questions, the response options, and the wording of the questions.

Unrepresentative samples

How closely the sample represents the population under study matters greatly. In 1984, columnist Ann Landers accepted a letter writer's challenge to poll her readers on the question of whether women find affection more important than sex. Her question: "Would you be content to be held close and treated tenderly and forget about 'the act'?" Of the more than 100 000 women who replied, 72 percent said yes. An avalanche of worldwide publicity followed. In response to critics, Landers (1985, p. 45) granted that "the sampling may not be representative of all American women. But it does provide honest—valuable—insights from a cross-section of the public. This is because my column is read by people from every walk of life, approximately 70 million of them." Still, one wonders, are the 70 million readers representative of the entire population? And are the 1 in 700 readers who participated representative of the 699 in 700 who did not?

The importance of representativeness was effectively demonstrated in the 1936 U.S. presidential election, when a weekly news magazine, *Literary Digest,* mailed a postcard election poll to more than 10 million people. Among the more than 2 million returns, Alf Landon won by a landslide over Franklin D. Roosevelt. When the actual votes were counted a few days later, the results were the opposite: Roosevelt won in a landslide over Landon. The magazine had sent the poll only to people whose names it had obtained from telephone books and automobile registrations—thus omitting all those who could afford neither (Cleghorn, 1980).

Order of the questions

Given a representative sample, we must also contend with other sources of bias, such as the order in which we ask questions. Asked whether "the Japanese government should be allowed to set limits on how much American industry can sell in Japan," most Americans answered no. Simultaneously, two-thirds of an equivalent sample were answering yes to the same question because they were first asked whether "the American government should be allowed to set limits on how much Japanese industry can sell in the United States." Most of these people said the United States has the right to limit imports. To appear consistent, they then said that Japan should have the same right (Schuman & Ludwig, 1983).

Response bias and social desirability

Consider, too, the dramatic effects of the response options. When Joop van der Plight and his co-workers (1987) asked English voters what percentage of Britain's energy they wished came from nuclear power, the average preference was 41 percent. They asked others what percentage they wished came from (1) nuclear, (2) coal, and (3) other sources. Their average preference for nuclear power was 21 percent.

It is not just the response options, however, that can bias people's responses. Sometimes people don't want to admit their true actions and beliefs either to the experimenter or sometimes even to themselves. Questions about prejudice often show very low levels of reported prejudice by the respondents. Yet systematic experiments demonstrate that prejudice is all too common. Why the difference in findings? People may not want to admit on a survey or even to themselves that they harbour some feelings of prejudice. This tendency for people to say what they want others to hear or what they want to believe about themselves is called *social desirability*. Recently, social psychologists have developed new methods of measuring people's beliefs without them knowing that their beliefs are being measured. These *implicit measures* are often used when concerns about social desirability arise.

Wording of the questions

Given a representative sample, we must also contend with other sources of bias, such as the wording of questions. For example, one poll found that people favoured cutting "foreign aid" yet opposed cutting funding "to help hungry people in other nations" (Simon, 1996). Even subtle changes in the tone of a question can have large effects (Schuman & Kalton, 1985). Thus it is not surprising that politicians in Ottawa and Quebec have fought bitterly about the wording of referendum questions about Quebec sovereignty. Federalists have long charged that the Parti Québécois purposely has devised questions that are unclear and designed to elicit a "yes" vote in favour of sovereignty. In the 1995 election, Quebecers voted on the question, "Do you agree that Quebec should become sovereign, after having made a formal offer to Canada for a new economic and political partnership, within the scope of the Bill respecting the future of Quebec and the agreement signed on June 12, 1995?" Did this question affect the outcome of the election? It certainly might have because even when people say they feel strongly about an issue, a question's form and wording may affect their answer (Krosnick & Schuman, 1988). Survey researchers must be sensitive to subtle—and not so subtle—biases.

Knowledge of the issues, however, can sometimes interact with the wording of the question to influence responses. Consider a study conducted by Darin Lehman of the University of British Columbia and his colleagues (Lehman et al., 1992). They had students read a number of newspaper clippings preceding a provincial election. The clippings were a mixed bag, some siding with the New Democratic Party (NDP), others siding with the Social Credit Party (SCP)—the two main rivals in the election. After the students had read the articles, Lehman and his colleagues asked the students in one condition to respond to a series of questions about how fair the articles were to the NDP. The students in the other condition were asked to respond to nearly the same questions, except that they rated how fair the articles were to the SCP. The questions tended to lead students to see bias against one party over the other. Did the wording of the question affect all students equally? No. It primarily affected students

DOONESBURY © 1990 G.B. Trudeau. Reprinted with permission of Universal Press Syndicate. All rights reserved.

who were less knowledgeable about the issues in the election. These students saw more bias against the NDP when the questions were about the NDP and more bias against the SCP when the questions were about the SCP. More knowledgeable students, on the other hand, were unaffected by the wording of the question.

EXPERIMENTAL RESEARCH: SEARCHING FOR CAUSE AND EFFECT

The difficulty of discerning cause and effect among naturally correlated events prompts most social psychologists to create laboratory simulations of everyday processes whenever this is feasible and ethical. These simulations are roughly similar to how aeronautical engineers work. They don't begin by observing how flying objects perform in a wide variety of natural environments. The variations in both atmospheric conditions and flying objects are so complex that they would surely find it difficult to organize and use such data to design better aircraft. Instead, they construct a simulated reality that is under their control—a wind tunnel. Then they can manipulate wind conditions and observe the precise effect of particular wind conditions on particular wing structures.

Control: Manipulating variables

independent variables
experimental factors that a researcher manipulates

Like aeronautical engineers, social psychologists experiment by constructing social situations that simulate important features of our daily lives. By varying just one or two factors at a time—called **independent variables**—the experimenter pinpoints how changes in these one or two things affect us. Just as the wind tunnel helps the aeronautical engineer discover principles of aerodynamics, so the experiment enables the social psychologist to discover principles of social thinking, social influence, and social relations. The ultimate aim of wind tunnel simulations is to understand and predict the flying characteristics of complex aircraft. Social psychologists experiment to understand and predict human behaviour.

Historically, social psychologists have used the experimental method in about three-fourths of their research studies (Higbee, Millard, & Folkman, 1982), and in two out of three studies, the setting has been a research laboratory (Adair, Dushenko, & Lindsay, 1985). To illustrate the laboratory experiment, consider two experiments that typify research from upcoming chapters on prejudice and aggression. Each suggests possible cause–effect explanations of correlational findings.

① *Correlational and experimental studies of prejudice against the obese*

The first experiment concerns prejudice against people who are obese. People often perceive the obese as slow, lazy, and sloppy (Ryckman et al., 1989). Do such attitudes spawn discrimination? In hopes of finding out, Steven Gortmaker and his colleagues (1993) studied 370 obese 16- to 24-year-olds. When they restudied them seven years later, two-thirds of the women were still obese, and these women were less likely to be married and earning high salaries than a comparison group of some 5000 other women. Even after correcting for any differences in aptitude test scores, race, and parental income, the obese women's incomes were $7000 a year below average. *Note:* Obesity correlated with marital status and income.

Correcting for certain other factors makes it look like discrimination might explain the correlation between obesity and lower status, but we can't be sure. (Can you think of other possibilities?) Enter social psychologists Mark Snyder and Julie Haugen (1994, 1995). They asked 76 University of Minnesota men students to have a getting-acquainted phone conversation with one of 76 women students. Each man was shown a photo *said* to picture his conversational partner. Half were shown an obese woman (not the actual partner); the other half were shown a normal-weight woman. Whom the men were shown—a normal or an overweight woman—was the independent variable.

In one part of the experiment, the men were asked to form an impression of the women's traits. Later analysis of just the women's side of the conversation revealed that when women were being evaluated, the men spoke less warmly and happily if the women were presumed obese. Clearly, the men's beliefs induced the men to behave in a way that led their supposedly obese partners to confirm the idea that such women are undesirable. Prejudice and discrimination were having an effect. Recalling the effect of the stepmother's attitudes, perhaps we should call this "the Cinderella effect."

② *Correlational and experimental studies of TV violence viewing*

As a second example of how an experiment can clarify causation, consider the correlation between television viewing and children's behaviour. Children who watch many violent television programs tend to be more aggressive than those who watch few. This suggests that children might be learning from what they see on the screen. But, as we hope you now recognize, this is a correlational finding. There are at least two other cause–effect interpretations that do not implicate television as the cause of the children's aggression. (What are they?)

Social psychologists have, therefore, brought television viewing into the laboratory, where they control the amount of violence the children see. By exposing children to violent and non-violent programs, researchers can observe how the amount of violence affects behaviour. Chris Boyatzis and his colleagues (1995) showed some elementary schoolchildren, but not others, an episode of the 1990s' most popular—and violent—children's television program, *Power Rangers*. Immediately after viewing the episode, the viewers committed seven times as many aggressive acts per two-minute interval as the non-viewers. We call the observed aggressive acts the **dependent variable**. Such experiments indicate that television can be one cause of children's aggressive behaviour.

So far we have seen that the logic of experimentation is simple: By creating and controlling a miniature reality, we can vary one factor and then another and discover how these factors, separately or in combination, affect people. Now let's go a little deeper and see how an experiment is done.

Every social-psychological experiment has two essential ingredients. We have just considered one—*control*. We manipulate one or two independent variables while trying to hold everything else constant. The other ingredient is *random assignment*.

dependent variable
the variable being measured, so called because it may *depend* on manipulations of the independent variable

Does viewing violence on TV or in other media lead to imitation? Experiments suggest that it does, especially among children.

TABLE 1–1   RECOGNIZING CORRELATIONS AND EXPERIMENTAL RESEARCH

	Can participants be randomly assigned to condition?	Independent variable	Dependent variable
Are early maturing children more confident?	No → Correlational		
Do students learn more in online or classroom courses?	Yes → Experimental	Take class online or in classroom	Learning
Do school grades predict vocational success?	No → Correlational		
Does playing violent video games increase aggressiveness?	Yes → Experimental	Play violent or non-violent game	Aggressiveness
Do people find comedy funnier when alone or with others?	(you answer)		
Do higher-income people have higher self-esteem?	(you answer)		

Random assignment: The great equalizer

Recall that we were reluctant, on the basis of a correlation, to assume that obesity *caused* lower status (via discrimination) or that viewing violence *caused* aggressiveness (see Table 1–1 for more examples). A survey researcher might measure and statistically extract other possibly pertinent factors and see if the correlations survive. But researchers can never control for all the factors that might distinguish obese from non-obese, and violence viewers from non-viewers. Maybe violence viewers differ in education, culture, intelligence, or in dozens of ways the researcher hasn't considered.

    In one fell swoop, **random assignment** eliminates all such extraneous factors. With random assignment, each person has an equal chance of viewing the violence or the non-violence. Thus the people in both groups would, in every conceivable way—family status, intelligence, education, initial aggressiveness—average about the same. Highly intelligent people, for example, are equally likely to appear in both groups. Because random assignment creates equivalent groups, any later aggression difference between the two groups must have something to do with the only way they differ—whether or not they viewed violence (Figure 1–5).

random assignment
the process of assigning participants to the conditions of an experiment such that all persons have the same chance of being in a given condition

FIGURE 1–5

RANDOM ASSIGNMENT.

Experiments randomly assigning people either to a condition that receives the experimental treatment or to a control condition that does not. This gives the researcher confidence that any later difference is somehow caused by the treatment.

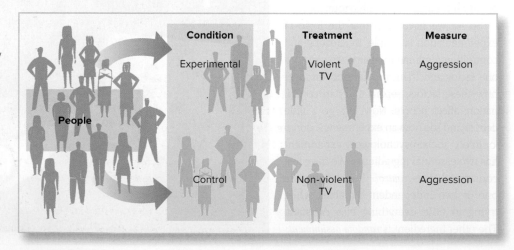

Note the distinction between random *assignment* in experiments and random *sampling* in surveys. Random assignment helps us infer cause and effect. Random sampling helps us generalize to a population.

The ethics of experimentation

Our television example illustrates why some experiments are ethically sensitive. Social psychologists would not, over long time periods, expose one group of children to brutal violence. Rather, they briefly alter people's social experience and note the effects. Sometimes, the experimental treatment is a harmless, perhaps even enjoyable, experience to which people give their knowing consent. Sometimes, however, researchers find themselves operating in a grey area between the harmless and the risky.

Social psychologists often venture into that ethical grey area when they design experiments that engage intense thoughts and emotions. Experiments need not have what Elliot Aronson, Marilynn Brewer, and Merrill Carlsmith (1985) called **mundane realism**. That is, laboratory behaviour (for example, delivering electric shocks as part of an experiment on aggression) need not be literally the same as everyday behaviour. For many researchers, that sort of realism is, indeed, mundane—not important. But the experiment *should* have **experimental realism**—it should absorb and involve the participants. Experimenters do not want their people consciously play-acting; they want to engage real psychological processes. Forcing people to choose whether to give intense or mild electric shock to someone else can, for example, be a realistic measure of aggression. It functionally simulates real aggression.

Achieving experimental realism sometimes requires deceiving people with a plausible cover story. If the person in the next room actually is not receiving the shocks, the experimenter does not want the participants to know this. That would destroy the experimental realism. Thus, about one-third of social-psychological studies (though a decreasing number) have required deception (Korn & Nicks, 1993; Vitelli, 1988).

Experimenters also seek to hide their predictions lest the participants, in their eagerness to be "good subjects," merely do what's expected or, in an ornery mood, do the opposite. In subtle ways, the experimenter's words, tone of voice, and gestures may call forth desired responses. To minimize such **demand characteristics**—cues that seem to "demand" certain behaviour—experimenters typically standardize their instructions or even use a computer to present them.

Researchers often walk a tightrope in designing experiments that will be involving yet ethical. To believe that you are hurting someone, or to be subjected to strong social pressure to see if it will change your opinion or behaviour, may be temporarily uncomfortable. Such experiments raise the age-old question of whether ends justify means. Do the insights gained justify deceiving and sometimes distressing people?

mundane realism
degree to which an experiment is superficially similar to everyday situations

experimental realism
degree to which an experiment absorbs and involves its participants

demand characteristics
cues in an experiment that tell the participant what behaviour is expected

What influences occasionally trigger post-game violence among European soccer fans—and Canadian hockey fans? Social psychologists have proposed hypotheses that have been tested with groups behaving under controlled conditions.

University ethics committees now review social-psychological research to ensure that it will treat people humanely. Ethical principles developed by major psychological organizations and government organizations, such as Canada's Tri-Council, which funds natural science, social science, humanities, and health research, urge investigators to follow these practices:

informed consent
an ethical principle requiring that research participants be told enough to enable them to choose whether they wish to participate

- Tell potential participants enough about the experiment to enable their **informed consent**.

- Be truthful. Use deception only if essential and justified by a significant purpose and if there is no alternative.

- Protect people from harm and significant discomfort.

- Treat information about the individual participants confidentially.

- Debrief participants. Fully explain the experiment afterward, including any deception. The only exception to this rule is when the feedback would be distressing, such as by making participants realize they have been stupid or cruel.

The experimenter should be sufficiently informative and considerate to leave subjects feeling at least as good about themselves as when they came in. Better yet, the participants should be repaid by having learned something (Sharpe & Faye, 2009). When treated respectfully, few participants mind being deceived (Epley & Huff, 1998; Kimmel, 1998). Indeed, say social psychology's defenders, professors provoke far greater anxiety and distress by giving and returning course exams than researchers now do in their experiments.

Increasingly, social psychologists have recognized that research ethics go beyond how participants in their studies are treated. Part of this realization occurred when three established social psychologists were exposed for making up all or part of their data in several experiments (Funder et al., 2013).

The shock from these cases of fraud caused most social psychologists to do a lot of soul searching about how this could happen in the field. How could someone work in the field for 20 years, make up the data from all or most of their papers, and by all appearances be successful? Why didn't colleagues, editors, reviewers, and students notice? The answers to these questions have not been simple and have caused social psychologists to rethink the standards for conducting, reporting, and reviewing research (John, Loewenstein, & Prelec, 2012).

Researchers now have become more vigilant not only about trying to detect and eliminate fraud, which is obviously wrong, but also in conducting and reviewing research to eliminate subtle biases, such as the tendency to confirm hypotheses, as much as possible. Among the practices that are gaining wider adoption are making the data from one's experiments publicly available, providing fuller reports of the methods used in experiments, and carefully describing the statistical tests used to test hypotheses. It remains to be seen whether these practices will make fraud more difficult, but they do reflect a trend among researchers to hold one another to a higher standard and to reduce bias in the conducting of research.

GENERALIZING FROM LABORATORY TO LIFE

As the research on children, television, and violence illustrates, social psychology mixes everyday experience and laboratory analysis. Throughout this book, we will do the same by drawing our data mostly from the laboratory and our illustrations mostly from life. Social psychology displays a healthy interplay between laboratory research and everyday life. Hunches gained from everyday experience often inspire laboratory research, which deepens our understanding of our experience.

This interplay appears in the children's television experiment. What people saw in everyday life suggested experimental research. Network and government policymakers, those with the power to make changes, are now aware of the results. This consistency of findings on television's effects—in the lab and in the field—is true of research in many other areas, including studies of helping, leadership style, depression, and achievement. The effects found in the lab have been mirrored by effects in the field. "The psychology laboratory has generally produced psychological truths rather than trivialities," noted Craig Anderson and his colleagues (1999).

We need to be cautious, however, in generalizing from the laboratory to life. Although the laboratory uncovers basic dynamics of human existence, it is still a simplified, controlled reality. It tells us what effect to expect of variable X, all other things being equal—which in real life they never are. Moreover, as you will see, the participants in many experiments are university students. Although this may help you identify with them, university students are hardly a random sample of all humanity. Would we get similar results with people of different ages, educational levels, and cultures? This is always an open question.

FIGURE 1–6

TWO METHODS OF DOING RESEARCH: CORRELATIONAL AND EXPERIMENTAL.

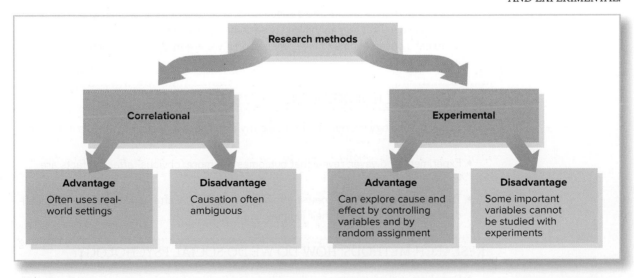

⋯▸ SUMMING UP

WHAT IS SOCIAL PSYCHOLOGY?

- *Social psychology* is the scientific study of how people think about, influence, and relate to one another. Its central themes are listed below.

WHAT ARE THE MAJOR THEMES OF SOCIAL PSYCHOLOGY?

- We construct our social reality.
- Our social intuitions are often powerful but sometimes perilous.
- Social influences shape our behaviour.
- Personal attitudes and dispositions also shape behaviour.
- Social behaviour is biologically rooted.
- Relating to others is a basic need.
- Social psychology's principles are applicable in everyday life.

HOW DO VALUES AFFECT SOCIAL PSYCHOLOGY?

- Social psychologists' values penetrate their work in obvious ways, such as their choice of research topics and the types of people who are attracted to various fields of study.
- They also do this in subtler ways, such as their hidden assumptions when forming concepts, choosing labels, and giving advice.
- This penetration of values into science is not a reason to fault social psychology or any other science. That human thinking is seldom dispassionate is precisely why we need systematic observation and experimentation if we are to check our cherished ideas against reality.

IS SOCIAL PSYCHOLOGY MERELY COMMON SENSE?

- Social psychology is criticized for being trivial because it documents things that seem obvious.
- Experiments, however, reveal that outcomes are more "obvious" *after* the facts are known.
- This *hindsight bias* (the *I-knew-it-all-along phenomenon*) often makes people overconfident about the validity of their judgments and predictions.

RESEARCH METHODS: HOW DO WE DO SOCIAL PSYCHOLOGY?

- Social psychologists organize their ideas and findings into *theories*. A good theory will distill an array of facts into a much shorter list of predictive principles. We can use those predictions to confirm or modify the theory, to generate new research, and to suggest practical application.

- Most social-psychological research is either *correlational* or *experimental*. Correlational studies, sometimes conducted with systematic survey methods, discern the relationship between variables, such as between amount of education and amount of income. Knowing two things are naturally related is valuable information, but it is not a reliable indicator of what is causing what—or whether a third variable is involved.

- When possible, social psychologists prefer to conduct experiments that explore cause and effect. By constructing a miniature reality that is under their control, experimenters can vary one thing and then another and discover how those things, separately or in combination, affect behaviour. We *randomly assign* participants to an experimental condition, which receives the experimental treatment, or to a control condition, which does not. We can then attribute any resulting difference between the two conditions to the *independent variable* (Figure 1–6).

- In creating experiments, social psychologists sometimes stage situations that engage people's emotions. In doing so, they are obliged to follow professional ethical guidelines, such as obtaining people's *informed consent,* protecting them from harm, and fully disclosing afterward any temporary deceptions. Laboratory experiments enable social psychologists to test ideas gleaned from life experience and then to apply the principles and findings to the real world.

1

SOCIAL THINKING

This book unfolds around its definition of social psychology: the scientific study of how we *think about* (Part One), *influence* (Part Two), and *relate to* (Part Three) one another.

Part One examines the scientific study of how we think about one another (also called social cognition). Each chapter confronts some overriding questions: How reasonable are our social attitudes, explanations, and beliefs? Are our impressions of ourselves and others generally accurate? How does our social thinking form? How is it prone to bias and error, and how might we bring it closer to reality?

Chapter 2 explores the interplay between our sense of self and our social worlds. How do our social surroundings shape our self-identities? How does self-interest colour our social judgments and motivate our social behaviour?

Chapter 3 looks at the amazing and sometimes rather amusing ways we form beliefs about our social worlds. It also alerts us to some pitfalls of social thinking and suggests how to avoid them and think smarter.

Chapter 4 explores the links between our thinking and our actions, between our attitudes and behaviours: Do our attitudes determine our behaviours, or vice versa? Or does it work both ways?

CHAPTER TWO
The Self in a
Social World

CHAPTER OUTLINE

● SELF-CONCEPT: WHO AM I?

● WHAT IS THE NATURE
AND MOTIVATING POWER
OF SELF-ESTEEM?

● WHAT DOES IT MEAN TO HAVE
PERCEIVED SELF-CONTROL?

● WHAT IS SELF-SERVING BIAS?

● HOW DO PEOPLE MANAGE THEIR
SELF-PRESENTATION?

*A*t the centre of our worlds, more pivotal
for us than anything else, is ourselves.
As we navigate our daily lives, our sense of
self continually engages the world.

Put yourself in the shoes of students showing up for a simple experiment by Jacquie Vorauer from the University of Manitoba and Dale Miller from Princeton University (1997). The experimenter explains to you and one other participant that the study explores students' experiences at the university. By a coin toss, the other participant is sent off to complete a questionnaire while you collect your thoughts before being interviewed. Fifteen minutes later, the experimenter gives you a peek at the other student's glum report:

> I guess I don't really feel like I have had very many positive academic experiences. . . . I've found a lot of the material very difficult. . . . The worst moment I can think of was my French final; I went completely blank at the start. . . . I haven't made many new friends since I got to Princeton. Mostly, I have to rely on the people that I knew before.

"There are three things extremely hard: steel, a diamond, and to know one's self."
BENJAMIN FRANKLIN

Now, it's your turn. Will you describe your personal experiences more negatively than if you had just read (as other subjects did) a report of someone who wrote "doing well in my courses. . . . I have had some wonderful friendships and roommates. . . . I feel more socially accepted than I used to"? So it happened with the actual student subjects. The positivity of their self-presentations echoed those of the other student. Yet, remarkably, they did not recognize this social influence on their self-presentation. They were blind to the interplay between their social surroundings and their self-presentation.

This is but one of many examples of the subtle connections between what happens in the world around us and what goes on in our heads. Here are some more examples:

- *Social surroundings affect our self-awareness.* When we are the only members of our race, gender, or nationality in a group, we notice how we differ and how others are reacting to our difference. The only woman in an executive meeting or math class is likely to be acutely aware of her gender. One of the authors has noticed that he is quite aware of his gender when volunteering at his children's school, where almost all the teachers and volunteers are women.

- *Self-interest colours our social judgment.* When problems arise in a close relationship such as marriage, we usually attribute more responsibility to our partners than to ourselves. When things go well at home or work or play, we see ourselves as more responsible. After Canadians Frederick Banting and John Macleod received a 1923 Nobel Prize for discovering insulin, they both thought the discovery was primarily their own. Banting claimed that Macleod, who headed the laboratory, had been more a hindrance than a help. Macleod omitted Banting's name in speeches about the discovery (Ross, 1981).

- *Self-concern motivates our social behaviour.* In hopes of making a positive impression, we agonize about our appearance. Like savvy politicians, we also monitor others' behaviour and expectations and adjust our behaviour accordingly.

- *Social relationships help define the self.* In our varied relationships, we have varying selves (Andersen & Chen, 2002). We may be one self with Mom, another with friends, another with teachers. How we think of ourselves is linked to the person we're with at the moment. And when relationships change, our self-concepts can change as well. College students who recently broke up with a romantic partner shifted their self-perceptions and felt less certain about who they were—one reason breakups can be so emotionally distressing (Slotter, Gardner, & Finkel, 2010).

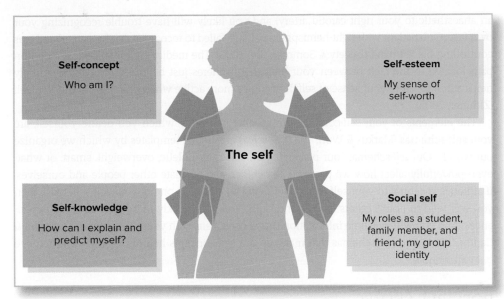

FIGURE 2–1
THE SELF.

Self-concept
Who am I?

Self-esteem
My sense of
self-worth

The self

Self-knowledge
How can I explain and
predict myself?

Social self
My roles as a student,
family member, and
friend; my group
identity

As these examples suggest, the traffic between self and society runs both ways. Our ideas and feelings about ourselves affect how we respond to others. And others help shape our sense of self.

No topic in psychology is more researched today than the self. In 2013, the word "self" appeared in 20 734 book and article summaries in *PsycINFO* (the online archive of psychological research)—more than 20 times the number that appeared in 1970. Our sense of self organizes our thoughts, feelings, and actions (Figure 2–1). Our sense of self enables us to remember our past, assess our present, and project our future—and thus to behave adaptively.

In later chapters, we will see that much of our behaviour is not consciously controlled but, rather, automatic and un-self-conscious. However, the self does enable long-term planning, goal setting, and restraint. It imagines alternatives, compares itself with others, and manages its reputation and relationships. Moreover, as Mark Leary (2004a) has noted, the self can sometimes be an impediment to a satisfying life. Its egocentric preoccupations are what religious meditation practices seek to prune, by quieting the self, reducing its attachments to material pleasures, and redirecting it. "Mysticism," adds psychologist Jonathan Haidt (2006), "everywhere and always, is about losing the self, transcending the self, and merging with something larger than the self."

In the remainder of this chapter, we will take a look at self-concept (how we come to know ourselves) and at the self in action (how our sense of self drives our attitudes and actions).

● SELF-CONCEPT: WHO AM I?

How and how accurately do we know ourselves? What determines our self-concept?

YOUR SENSE OF SELF

The most important aspect of yourself is your self. To discover where this sense of self arises, neuroscientists are exploring the brain activity that underlies your constant sense of being yourself. Some studies suggest an important role for the right hemisphere. Put yours to sleep (with

self-concept
how a person answers the question, "Who am I?" provides a glimpse of his or her self-concept

an anaesthetic to your right carotid artery) and you likely will have trouble recognizing your own face. One patient with right-hemisphere damage failed to recognize that he owned and was controlling his left hand (Decety & Sommerville, 2003). The medial prefrontal cortex, a neuron path located in the cleft between your brain hemispheres just behind your eyes, seemingly helps stitch together your sense of self. It becomes more active when you think about yourself (Zimmer, 2005).

self-schemas
beliefs about self that organize and guide the processing of self-relevant information

The elements of your self-concept, the specific beliefs by which you define yourself, are your **self-schemas** (Markus & Wurf, 1987). *Schemas* are mental templates by which we organize our worlds. Our *self*-schemas—our perceiving ourselves as athletic, overweight, smart, or whatever—powerfully affect how we perceive, remember, and evaluate other people and ourselves. If athletics is central to your self-concept (if being an athlete is one of your self-schemas), then you will tend to notice others' bodies and skills. You will quickly recall sports-related experiences. And you will welcome information that is consistent with your self-schema (Kihlstrom & Cantor, 1984). The self-schemas that make up our self-concepts help us organize and retrieve our experiences.

POSSIBLE SELVES

possible selves
images of what we dream of or dread becoming in the future

Our self-concepts include not only our self-schemas about who we currently are but also who we might become—our **possible selves**. Hazel Markus and her colleagues (Inglehart, Markus, & Brown, 1989; Markus & Nurius, 1986) noted that our possible selves include our visions of the self we dream of becoming—the rich self, the thin self, the passionately loved and loving self. They also include the self we fear becoming—the underemployed self, the unloved self, the academically failed self. Such possible selves motivate us with a vision of the life we long for—or to avoid the one we dread.

Development of the social self

The self-concept has become a major social-psychological focus because it helps organize our thinking and guide our social behaviour. But what determines our self-concept? Studies of twins point to genetic influences on personality and self-concept, but social experience also plays a part. Among these influences are the following:

- The social identities we form
- The comparisons we make with others
- Our successes and failures
- How other people judge us
- The surrounding culture

social identity
the "we" aspect of our self-concept; the part of our answer to "Who am I?" that comes from our group memberships (examples: "I am Australian." "I am Catholic.")

SOCIAL IDENTITY

Our self-concept—our sense of who we are—contains not just our personal identity (our sense of our personal attributes) but also our **social identity**. The social definition of who you are—your race, religion, sex, academic major, and so forth—implies, too, a definition of who you are not.

When we're part of a small group surrounded by a larger group, we are often conscious of our social identity; when our social group is the majority, we think less about it. As a solo female in a group of men, or as an Asian student on a mostly White campus, we are conscious of our uniqueness. In Canada, most people identify themselves as "Canadian," except in Quebec, where francophones are more likely to identify themselves as "Québécois" (Kalin & Berry, 1995).

Social comparisons

How do we decide if we are rich, smart, or short? One way is through **social comparison** (Festinger, 1954). Others around us help to define the standard by which we define ourselves as rich or poor, smart or dumb, tall or short: We compare ourselves with those around us and become conscious of how we differ. We then use others as a benchmark by which we can evaluate our performance and our beliefs.

social comparison evaluating your abilities and opinions by comparing yourself to others

Consider a study conducted by Penelope Lockwood of the University of Toronto and Ziva Kunda of the University of Waterloo (Lockwood & Kunda, 1997). They exposed first-year or fourth-year accounting students to an article about a star accounting student who had won numerous awards, attained a very high grade average, and landed a spectacular job. For first-year students, this role model represented an achievement they could hope to attain. If all went well, they too could have such a fantastic future. For fourth-year students, however, this role model did not present such hope. They knew all too well that at this point in their studies they would never measure up to such a superstar. As you can see in Figure 2–2, such comparisons had strong effects on these students' self-evaluations. When first- and fourth-year students did not compare to the superstar, they had similar self-evaluations. But when they were exposed to the superstar, first-year students seemed inspired; their self-evaluations rose dramatically. Fourth-year students, on the other hand, seemed dejected; their self-evaluations dropped. This research demonstrates the fundamental principle that our comparisons to others are a strong determinant of our self-views.

Social comparison explains why students tend to have a higher academic self-evaluation if they attend a school with mostly average students (Marsh, Kong, & Hau, 2000), and how that self-evaluation can be threatened after graduation when a student who excelled in an average high school goes on to an academically selective university. The "big fish" is no longer in a small pond.

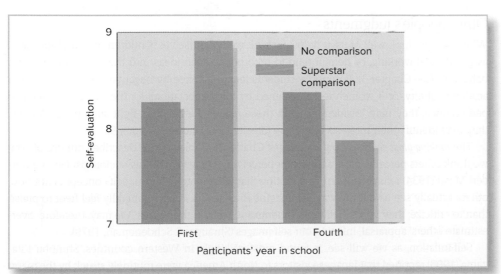

FIGURE 2–2

SOCIAL COMPARISON AND SELF-EVALUATION.

People are inspired by a role model if they can attain similar success, but they are demoralized if they cannot. (Data from Lockwood & Kunda, 1997)

Much of life revolves around social comparisons. We feel handsome when others seem homely, smart when others seem dull, caring when others seem callous. When we witness a peer's performance, we cannot resist implicitly comparing ourselves (Gilbert, Giesler, & Morris, 1995). We may, therefore, privately take some pleasure in a peer's failure, especially when it happens to someone we envy and when we don't feel vulnerable to such misfortune ourselves (Lockwood, 2002; Smith et al., 1996).

Social comparisons can also diminish our satisfaction. When we experience an increase in affluence, status, or achievement, we "compare upward"—we raise the standards by which we evaluate our attainments. When climbing the ladder of success, we tend to look up, not down; we compare ourselves with others doing even better (Gruder, 1977; Suls & Tesch, 1978; Wheeler, Koestner, & Driver, 1982). When facing competition, we often protect our shaky self-concept by perceiving the competitor as advantaged. For example, college swimmers believed that their competitors had better coaching and more practice time (Shepperd & Taylor, 1999).

> *"Make no comparisons!"*
> –KING CHARLES I, 1600–49

Success and failure

Self-concept is also fed by our daily experiences. To undertake challenging yet realistic tasks and to succeed is to feel more competent. After experiencing academic success, students believe they are better at school, which often stimulates them to work harder and achieve more (Felson, 1984; Marsh & Young, 1997).

This success-feeds-self-esteem principle has led several research psychologists to question efforts to boost achievement by raising self-esteem with positive messages ("You are somebody! You're special!"). Self-esteem comes not only from telling children how wonderful they are, but also—and perhaps more importantly—from hard-earned achievements. Feelings follow reality. When they don't, it can cause problems. Joanne Wood of the University of Waterloo and her colleagues recently found that repeating positive self-statements, like "I am a lovable person," can actually backfire. Doing so made people with high self-esteem feel a bit better about themselves, but made people with low self-esteem—those who needed a boost the most—feel worse (Wood, Perunovic, & Lee, 2009).

Other people's judgments

When people think well of us, it helps us think well of ourselves. Children whom others label as gifted, hard-working, or helpful tend to incorporate such ideas into their self-concepts and behaviour (see Chapter 3). If minority students feel threatened by negative stereotypes of their academic ability, or if women feel threatened by low expectations for their math and science performance, they may "disidentify" with those realms. Rather than fight such prejudgments, they may identify their interests elsewhere (Steele, 1997; and see Chapter 9).

The *looking-glass self* was how sociologist Charles H. Cooley (1902) described our use of how we think others perceive us as a mirror for perceiving ourselves. Fellow sociologist George Herbert Mead (1934) refined this concept, noting that what matters for our self-concept is not how others actually see us but the way we imagine they see us. People generally feel freer to praise than to criticize; they voice their compliments and restrain their gibes. We may, therefore, over-estimate others' appraisal, inflating our self-images (Shrauger & Schoeneman, 1979).

Self-inflation, as we will see, is found most strikingly in Western countries. Shinobu Kitayama (1996) reported that Japanese visitors to North America were routinely struck by the many words of praise that friends offer one another. When he and his colleagues asked people how many days ago they last complimented someone, the most common American response was one day. In Japan, where people are socialized less to feel pride in personal achievement and more to feel shame in failing others, the most common response was four days.

Our ancestors' fate depended on what others thought of them. Their survival was enhanced when protected by their group. When perceiving their group's disapproval, there was biological wisdom to their feeling shame and low self-esteem. As their heirs, having a similar deep-seated need to belong, we feel the pain of low self-esteem when we face social exclusion, noted Mark Leary (1998, 2004b). Self-esteem, he argued, is a psychological gauge by which we monitor and react to how others appraise us.

Our self-esteem tracks how we see ourselves on traits that we believe are valued by others. People believe that social acceptance often depends on easily observable traits, such as physical appearance and social skills. Though people say they value communal traits—traits that denote a concern and connection to other people, such as kindness and understanding—they recognize that appearance is often what attracts others. And self-esteem corresponds more closely to such superficial traits than to communal qualities (Anthony, Holmes, & Wood, 2007).

Self-esteem is, however, predicted by communal qualities for people whose roles make these qualities attractive to others. Our society values kindness and caring in women (more so than in men) and in people in romantic relationships. For these individuals, self-esteem tracks communal qualities. Self-esteem thus depends on whether or not we believe we have traits that make us attractive to others, and not necessarily on the traits that we say we value most.

SELF AND CULTURE

How would you complete this statement: "I am ___"? Would you give information about your personal traits, such as "I am honest," "I am tall," or "I am outgoing"? Or would you also describe your social identity, such as "I am a Pisces," "I am a MacDonald," or "I am a Muslim"?

For some people, especially those in industrialized Western cultures, **individualism** prevails. Identity is self-contained. Adolescence is a time of separating from parents, becoming self-reliant, and defining one's personal, **independent self**. One's identity—as a unique individual with particular abilities, traits, values, and dreams—remains fairly constant.

The psychology of Western cultures assumes that your life will be enriched by believing in your power of personal control. Western literature, from *The Iliad* to *Anne of Green Gables*, celebrates the self-reliant individual more than the person who fulfills others' expectations. Movie plots feature rugged heroes who buck the establishment. Songs proclaim "I Did It My Way" and "I Gotta Be Me," and declare that "The Greatest Love of All" is loving oneself (Schoeneman, 1994). Individualism flourishes when people experience affluence, mobility, urbanism, and mass media (Freeman, 1997; Marshall, 1997; Triandis, 1994).

Most cultures native to Asia, Africa, and Central and South America place a greater value on **collectivism**. They nurture what Shinobu Kitayama and Hazel Markus (1995) call the **interdependent self**. In these cultures, people are more self-critical and have less need for positive self-regard (Heine et al., 1999). Malaysians, Indians, Japanese, and traditional Kenyans such as the Maasai, for example, are much more likely than Australians, Canadians, Americans, and the British to complete the "I am" statement with their group identities (Kanagawa, Cross, & Markus, 2001; Ma & Schoeneman, 1997). When speaking, people using the languages of

individualism
the concept of giving priority to one's own goals over group goals and defining one's identity in terms of personal attributes rather than group identifications

independent self
construing one's identity as a unique individual with particular abilities, traits, values, and dreams

collectivism
giving priority to the goals of one's groups (often, one's extended family or work group) and defining one's identity accordingly

interdependent self
construing one's identity in relation to others

collectivist countries say "I" less often (Kashima & Kashima, 1998, 2003). A person might say, "Went to the movie," rather than "I went to the movie." Compared with U.S. church websites, Korean church websites place more emphasis on social connections and participation and less on personal spiritual growth and self-betterment (Sasaki & Kim, 2011).

Pigeonholing cultures as solely individualist or collectivist oversimplifies: Within any culture, individualism varies from person to person (Oyserman, Coon, & Kemmelmeier, 2002a; Oyserman, Kemmelmeier, & Coon, 2002b). There are individualist Chinese and collectivist Americans, and most of us sometimes behave communally, sometimes individualistically (Bandura, 2004). Individualism–collectivism also varies across a country's regions and political views. Conservatives tend to be economic individualists ("don't tax or regulate me") and moral collectivists ("legislate against immorality"). Liberals tend to be economic collectivists (supporting universal health care) and moral individualists ("let people choose for themselves"). Despite individual and subcultural variations, however, researchers continue to regard individualism and collectivism as genuine cultural variables (Schimmack, Oishi, & Diener, 2005).

Culture and cognition

In his book *The Geography of Thought* (2003), social psychologist Richard Nisbett contends that collectivism also results in different ways of thinking. Consider: Which two, of a panda, a monkey, and a banana, go together? Perhaps a monkey and a panda, because they both fit the category "animal"? Asians more often than Americans see relationships: monkey eats banana. When shown an animated underwater scene (Figure 2–3), Japanese respondents spontaneously recalled 60 percent more background features than did Americans, and they spoke of more relationships (the frog beside the plant). Americans look more at the focal object, such as a single big fish, and less at the surroundings (Chua, Boland, & Nisbett, 2005; Nisbett, 2003), a result duplicated in studies examining activation in different areas of the brain (Goh et al., 2007; Lewis, Goto, & Kong, 2008). When shown drawings of groups of children, Japanese students took the facial expressions of all of the children into account when rating the happiness or anger of an individual child, whereas Americans focused on only the child they were asked to rate (Masuda et al., 2008). Nisbett and Takahido Masuda (2003) concluded from

FIGURE 2–3

ASIAN AND WESTERN THINKING.

When shown an underwater scene such as this one, Asians often describe the environment and the relationships among the fish. Americans attend more to a single big fish (Nisbett, 2003).

such studies that East Asians think more holistically—perceiving and thinking about objects and people in relationship to one another and to their environment.

If you grew up in a Western culture, you were probably told to "express yourself"—through writing, through the choices you make, through the products you buy, and perhaps through your tattoos or piercings. When asked about the purpose of language, American students were more likely to explain that it allows self-expression, whereas Korean students focused on how language allows communication with others. American students were also more likely to see their choices as expressions of themselves and to evaluate their choices more favourably (Kim & Sherman, 2007). The individualized latté—"decaf, single shot, skinny, extra hot"—that seems just right at a North American espresso shop would seem strange in Seoul, noted Heejun Kim and Hazel Markus (1999). In Korea, people place less value on expressing their uniqueness and more on tradition and shared practices (Choi & Choi, 2002; and Figure 2–4). Korean advertisements tend to feature people together; they seldom highlight personal choice or freedom (Markus, 2001; Morling & Lamoreaux, 2008).

With an interdependent self, people have a greater sense of belonging. If they were uprooted and cut off from family, colleagues, and loyal friends, interdependent people would lose the social connections that define who they are. When Chinese participants were asked to think about their mothers, a brain region associated with the self became activated—an area that became more active for Western participants only when they thought about themselves (Zhu et al., 2007). Interdependent selves have not one self but many selves: self-with-parents, self-at-work, self-with-friends (Cross, Liao, & Josephs, 1992). As Figure 2–5 and Table 2–1 suggest, the interdependent self is embedded in social memberships. Conversation is less direct and more polite (Holtgraves, 1997), and people focus more on gaining social approval (Lalwani, Shavitt, & Johnson, 2006). The goal of social life is to harmonize with and support one's communities, not—as it is in more individualistic societies—to enhance one's individual self.

Even within one culture, personal history can influence self-views. People who have moved from place to place are happier when people understand their constant, personal selves; people who have always lived in the same town are more pleased when someone recognizes their collective identity (Oishi, Lun, & Sherman, 2007). Our self-concepts seem to adjust to our situation: If

The Self in a Social World
© Jack Ziegler/The New Yorker Collection/www.cartoonbank.com

FIGURE 2–4 WHICH PEN WOULD YOU CHOOSE?

When Heejun Kim and Hazel Markus (1999) invited people to choose one of these pens, 77 percent of Americans but only 31 percent of Asians chose the uncommon colour (regardless of whether it was orange, as here, or green). This result illustrates differing cultural preferences for uniqueness and conformity, noted Kim and Markus.

FIGURE 2–5

SELF-CONSTRUAL AS INDEPENDENT OR INTERDEPENDENT.

The independent self acknowledges relationships with others; the interdependent self is more deeply embedded in others (Markus & Kitayama, 1991).

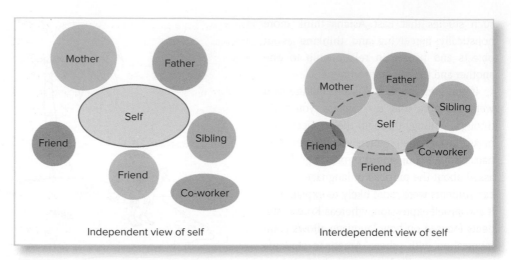

you interact with the same people all your life, they are more important to your identity than if you are uprooted every few years and must make new friends. Your self becomes your constant companion ("Wherever you go, there you are.").

Culture and self-esteem

Self-esteem in collectivist cultures correlates closely with "what others think of me and my group." Self-concept in these cultures is malleable (context-specific) rather than stable (enduring across situations). In one study, four in five Canadian students but only one in three Chinese and Japanese students agreed that "the beliefs that you hold about who you are (your inner self) remain the same across different activity domains" (Tafarodi et al., 2004).

For those in individualistic cultures, self-esteem is more personal and less relational. Threaten our *personal* identity and we'll feel angrier and gloomier than when someone threatens our collective identity (Gaertner, Sedikides, & Graetz, 1999). Unlike Japanese subjects who persist more on tasks when they are failing (wanting not to fall short of others' expectations), people in individualistic countries persist more when succeeding, because for them, success elevates self-esteem (Heine et al., 2001). Western individualists like to make comparisons with

TABLE 2-1   SELF-CONCEPT: INDEPENDENT OR INTERDEPENDENT.

	Independent	Interdependent
Identity is	Personal, defined by individual traits and goals	Social, defined by connections with others
What matters	Me—personal achievement and fulfillment; my rights and liberties	We—group goals and solidarity; our social responsibilities and relationships
Disapproves of	Conformity	Egotism
Illustrative motto	"To thine own self be true"	"No one is an island"
Cultures that support	Individualistic Western	Collectivistic Asian and developing world

others that boost their self-esteem. Asian collectivists make comparisons (often upward, with those doing better) in ways that facilitate self-improvement (White & Lehman, 2005).

So when, do you suppose, are university students in collectivist Japan and individualist United States most likely to report positive emotions such as happiness and elation? For Japanese students, happiness comes with positive social engagement—with feeling close, friendly, and respectful. For American students, it more often comes with disengaged emotions—with feeling effective, superior, and proud (Kitayama & Markus, 2000). Conflict in collectivist cultures often takes place between groups; individualist cultures breed more conflict (and crime and divorce) between individuals (Triandis, 2000).

When Kitayama (1999), after 10 years of teaching and researching in America, visited his Japanese alma mater, Kyoto University, graduate students were "astounded" when he explained the Western idea of the independent self. "I persisted in explaining this Western notion of self-concept—one that my American students understood intuitively—and finally began to persuade them that, indeed, many Americans do have such a disconnected notion of self. Still, one of them, sighing deeply, said at the end, 'Could this really be true?'"

When East meets West—as happens, for example, thanks to Western influences in urban Japan and to Japanese exchange students visiting Western countries—does the self-concept become more individualized? Are the Japanese influenced when exposed to Western promotions based on individual achievement, with admonitions to "believe in one's own possibilities," and with movies in which the heroic individual police officer catches the crook *despite* others' interference? They seem to be, report Steven Heine and his co-researchers (1999). Personal self-esteem increased among Japanese exchange students after spending seven months at the University of British Columbia. Individual self-esteem is also higher among long-term Asian immigrants to Canada than among more recent immigrants (and than it is among those living in Asia).

Collectivism in action: Following the 2010 earthquake in Haiti, people acted together to help one another.

THE >>> INSIDE STORY

We began our collaboration by wondering out loud. Shinobu wondered why American life was so weird. Hazel countered with anecdotes about the strangeness of Japan. Cultural psychology is about making the strange familiar and the familiar strange. Our shared cultural encounters astonished us and convinced us that when it comes to psychological functioning, place matters.

After weeks of lecturing in Japan to students with a good command of English, Hazel wondered why the students did not say anything—no questions, no comments. She assured students she was interested in ideas that were different from hers, so why was there no response? Where were the arguments, debates, and signs of critical thinking? Even if she asked a straightforward question—for example, "Where is the best noodle shop?"—the answer was invariably an audible intake of air followed by "It depends." Didn't Japanese students have preferences, ideas, opinions, and attitudes? What is inside a head if it isn't these things? How could you know someone if she didn't tell you what she was thinking?

On the other hand, Shinobu was curious about why students shouldn't just listen to a lecture and why American students felt the need to be constantly interrupting each other and talking over each other and the professor. Why did the comments and questions reveal strong emotions and have a competitive edge? What was the point of this arguing? Why did intelligence seem to be associated with getting the best of another person, even within a class where people knew each other well?

Shinobu expressed his amazement at American hosts who bombard their guests with choices. Do you want wine or beer, or soft drinks or juice, or coffee or tea? Why burden the guest with trivial decisions? Surely the host knew what would be good refreshment on this occasion and could simply provide something appropriate.

Offering a guest with a choice of beverage may be greeted with surprise by people from some cultures.

Choice as a burden? Hazel wondered if this could be the key to one particularly humiliating experience in Japan. A group of eight was in a French restaurant, and everyone was following the universal restaurant script and was studying the menu. The waiter approached and stood nearby. Hazel announced her choice of appetizer and entrée. Next was a tense conversation among the Japanese host and the Japanese guests. When the meal was served, it was not what she had ordered. Everyone at the table was served the same meal. This was deeply disturbing. If you can't choose your own dinner, how could it be enjoyable? What was the point of the menu if everybody is served the same meal? Could a sense of sameness be a good or a desirable feeling in Japan?

When Hazel walked around the grounds of a temple in Kyoto, there was a fork in the path and a sign that read, "ORDINARY PATH." Who would want to take the ordinary path? Where was the special, less travelled path? Choosing the non-ordinary path may be an obvious course for Americans, but in this case, it led to the temple dump outside the temple grounds. The ordinary path did not denote the dull and unchallenging way; it meant the good and appropriate way.

(continued)

(continued)

These exchanges inspired our experimental studies and reminded us that there are ways of life beyond the ones that each of us knows best. So far, most of psychology has been produced by psychologists in middle-class White American settings studying middle-class White American respondents. In other socio-cultural contexts, there can be different ideas and practices about how to be a person and how to live a meaningful life, and these differences have an influence on psychological functioning. It is this realization that fuels our continuing interest in collaboration and in cultural psychology.

Hazel Rose Markus, *Stanford University*
Shinobu Kitayama, *University of Michigan*

SELF-KNOWLEDGE

Why did you choose your university? Why did you lash out at your roommate? Why did you fall in love with that special person? Sometimes we know. Sometimes we don't. Asked why we have felt or acted as we have, we produce plausible answers. Yet, when causes are subtle, our self-explanations are often wrong. We may dismiss factors that matter and inflate others that don't. People may misattribute their rainy-day gloom to life's emptiness (Schwarz & Clore, 1983). And people routinely deny being influenced by the media, which, they readily acknowledge, affects others.

Also thought-provoking are studies in which people recorded their moods every day for two or three months (Stone et al., 1985; Weiss & Brown, 1976; Wilson, Laser, & Stone, 1982). They also recorded factors that might affect their moods: the day of the week, the weather, the amount they slept, and so forth. At the end of each study, the people judged how much each factor had affected their moods. Remarkably (given that their attention was being drawn to their daily moods), there was little relationship between their perceptions of how well a factor predicted their mood and how well it actually did so. These findings raise a disconcerting question: How much insight do we really have into what makes us happy or unhappy? As Dan Gilbert notes (2007, 2011), not much: We are remarkably bad predictors of what will make us happy. "We seem to know less about the worlds inside our heads than about the world our heads are inside."

> *"You don't know your own mind."*
> JONATHAN SWIFT, *POLITE CONVERSATION*, 1738

Predicting behaviour

People also err when predicting their behaviour. Dating couples tend to predict the longevity of their relationships through rose-coloured glasses. Their friends and family often know better, reported Tara MacDonald and Michael Ross (1997). Among University of Waterloo students, their roommates were better predictors of whether their romances would survive than they were. Medical residents weren't very good at predicting whether they would do well on a surgical skills exam, but their peers in the program predicted each other's performance with startling accuracy (Lutsky, Risucci, & Tortolani, 1993). So if you're in love and want to know whether it will last, don't listen to your heart–ask your roommate. And if you want to predict your routine daily behaviours–how much time you will spend laughing, on the phone, or watching TV, for example–your close friends' estimates will likely prove at least as accurate as your own (Vazire & Mehl, 2008).

planning fallacy
the tendency to underestimate how long it will take to complete a task

One of the most common errors in behaviour prediction is underestimating how long it will take to complete a task (called the **planning fallacy**). The Sydney Opera House was supposed to be completed in six years; it took sixteen years. In 1969, Montreal Mayor Jean Drapeau proudly announced that a stadium with a retractable roof would be built for the 1976 Olympics; the roof was completed in 1989. In one study, Wilfrid Laurier University students writing an honours thesis were asked to predict when they would complete the project. On average, students finished three weeks later than their "most realistic" estimate–and a week later than their "worst-case scenario" estimate (Buehler, Griffin, & Ross, 2002)! However, friends and teachers were able to predict just how late these papers would be. Just as you should ask your friends how long your relationship is likely to survive, if you want to know when you will finish your term paper, ask your roommate or your mom. You could also do what Microsoft does: Managers automatically add 30 percent onto a software developer's estimate of completion–and 50 percent if the project involves a new operating system (Dunning, 2006).

Are people equally bad at predicting how much money they will spend? Johanna Peetz of Carleton University and Roger Buehler of Wilfrid Laurier University (2009) found that the answer was yes. Undergraduates predicted that they would spend $94 over the next week but actually spent $122. Considering they had spent $126 in the week before the study, their guess should have been more accurate. When they came back a week later, they still predicted they would spend only $85 in the coming week. Students who said they wanted to save money were more likely to predict they would spend less–but ended up spending the same amount as everyone else. So just as we think we will complete tasks quickly, we think we will save our money. The difficulty lies in actually doing so. If Lao-tzu was right–"He who knows others is learned. He who knows himself is enlightened."–then most people, it would seem, are more learned than enlightened.

Predicting feelings

Many of life's big decisions involve predicting our future feelings. Would marrying this person lead to lifelong contentment? Would entering this profession make for satisfying work? Would going on this vacation produce a happy experience? Or would the likelier results be divorce, job burnout, and holiday disappointment?

"When a feeling was there, they felt as if it would never go; when it was gone, they felt as if it had never been; when it returned, they felt as if it had never gone."
GEORGE MACDONALD, *WHAT'S MINE'S MINE,* 1886

Sometimes we know how we will feel–if we fail that exam, win that big game, or take that half-hour jog. We know what exhilarates us, and what makes us anxious or bored. Other times we may mispredict our responses. Asked how they would feel if asked sexually harassing questions on a job interview, most women studied by Julie Woodzicka and Marianne LaFrance (2001) said they would feel angry. When actually asked such questions, however, women more often experienced fear.

Studies of "affective forecasting" reveal that people have the greatest difficulty predicting the intensity and the duration of their future emotions (Wilson & Gilbert, 2003). People have mispredicted how they would feel some time after a romantic breakup, receiving a gift, losing an election, winning a game, and being insulted (Gilbert & Ebert, 2002; Loewenstein & Schkade, 1999). Some examples follow:

- When young men are sexually aroused by erotic photographs and then exposed to a passionate date scenario in which their date asks them to "stop," they admit that they might not stop. If not shown sexually arousing pictures first, they more often deny the possibility of being sexually aggressive. When not aroused, one easily mispredicts how one will feel and act when aroused—a phenomenon that leads to professions of love during lust, to unintended pregnancies, and to repeat offences among sex abusers who have sincerely vowed "never again."

- Hungry shoppers do more impulse buying ("Those doughnuts would be delicious!") than when shopping after eating a mega-sized blueberry muffin (Gilbert & Wilson, 2000). When hungry, we mispredict how gross those deep-fried doughnuts will seem when sated. When stuffed, we underestimate how yummy a doughnut might be with a late-night glass of milk.

- How much will you like the guy you're about to speed-date? Ask the woman who went before you. Female university students predicted their enjoyment of a date better when another woman who had speed-dated him clued them in than when relying on facts such as a picture and a profile. Yet at the end of the experiment, most women still said that relying on the profile would be a better predictor of their feelings than the subjective opinion of another speed-dater (Gilbert et al., 2009).

- When natural disasters like hurricanes occur, people predict that their sadness will be greater if more people are killed. But after Hurricane Katrina struck in 2005, students' sadness was similar when they believed 50 people had been killed or 1000 had been killed (Dunn & Ashton-James, 2008). What did influence how sad people felt? Seeing pictures of victims. Poignant images on TV have a great deal of influence on us after disasters.

- People overestimate how much their well-being would be affected by both bad events (a romantic breakup, failing to reach an athletic goal [Eastwick et al., 2007a; van Dijk, Finkenauer, & Pollmann, 2008]) and good events (warmer winters, losing weight, more television channels, or more free time). Even extreme events, such as winning a provincial lottery or suffering a paralyzing accident, affect long-term happiness less than most people suppose.

Our intuitive theory seems to be: We want. We get. We are happy. If that were true, this chapter would have fewer words. In reality, noted Daniel Gilbert and Timothy Wilson (2000), we often "miswant." People who imagine an idyllic desert island holiday with sun, surf, and sand may be disappointed when they discover "how much they require daily structure, intellectual stimulation, or regular infusions of Pop Tarts." We think that if our candidate or team wins we will be delighted for a long while. But study after study reveals our vulnerability to **impact bias**—overestimating the enduring impact of emotion-causing events. Faster than we expect, the emotional traces of such good tidings evaporate.

impact bias
overestimating the enduring impact of emotion-causing events

Moreover, we are especially prone to impact bias after negative events. When Gilbert and his colleagues (1998) asked assistant professors to predict their happiness a few years after achieving tenure or not, most believed that achieving tenure was important for their future happiness. "Losing my job would crush my life's ambitions. It would be terrible." Yet when surveyed several years after the event, those denied tenure were about as happy as those who received it. Impact bias is important, said Wilson and Gilbert (2005), because people's "affective forecasts"—their predictions of their future emotions—influence their decisions. If people overestimate the intensity and duration of the pleasure they will gain from purchasing a new car or undergoing cosmetic

Predicting behaviour, even one's own, is no easy matter, which may be why this visitor goes to a tarot card reader in hope of help.

surgery, then they may make ill-advised investments in that new Mercedes or extreme makeover.

Let's make this personal. Gilbert and Wilson invite us to imagine how we might feel a year after losing our non-dominant hands. Compared with today, how happy would you be?

Thinking about that, you perhaps focused on what the calamity would mean: no clapping, no shoe tying, no competitive basketball, no speedy keyboarding. Although you likely would forever regret the loss, your general happiness some time after the event would be influenced by "two things: (a) the event, and (b) everything else" (Gilbert & Wilson, 2000). In focusing on the negative event, we discount the importance of everything else that contributes to happiness and so overpredicted our enduring misery. "Nothing that you focus on will make as much difference as you think," concurred researchers David Schkade and Daniel Kahneman (1998).

Moreover, said Wilson and Gilbert (2003), people neglect the speed and power of their *psychological immune system,* which includes their strategies for rationalizing, discounting, forgiving, and limiting emotional trauma. Being largely ignorant of our psychological immune system (a phenomenon Gilbert and Wilson called **immune neglect**), we adapt to disabilities, romantic breakups, exam failures, tenure denials, and personal and team defeats more readily than we would expect. Ironically, Gilbert and his colleagues report (2004), major negative events (which activate our psychological defences) can be less enduringly distressing than minor irritations (which don't activate our defences). In other words, under most circumstances, we are remarkably resilient.

immune neglect
the human tendency to underestimate the speed and the strength of the "psychological immune system," which enables emotional recovery and resilience after bad things happen

The wisdom and illusions of self-analysis

To a striking extent, then, our intuitions are often dead wrong about what has influenced us and what we will feel and do. But let's not overstate the case. When the causes of our behaviour are conspicuous and the correct explanation fits our intuition, our self-perceptions will be accurate (Gavanski & Hoffman, 1987). When the causes of behaviour are obvious to an observer, they are usually obvious to us as well.

As Chapter 3 will explore further, we are unaware of much that goes on in our minds. Studies of perception and memory show that we are more aware of the results of our thinking than its process. We experience the results of our mind's unconscious workings when we set a mental clock to record the passage of time and to awaken us at an appointed hour, or when we somehow achieve a spontaneous creative insight after a problem has unconsciously "incubated." Similarly, creative scientists and artists, for example, often cannot report the thought processes that produced their insights, although they have superb knowledge of the results.

Timothy Wilson (1985, 2002) offers a bold idea: The mental processes that *control* our social behaviour are distinct from the mental processes through which we *explain* our behaviour. Our rational explanations may, therefore, omit the unconscious attitudes that actually guide our behaviour. In nine experiments, Wilson and his colleagues (1989, 2008) found that the attitudes people consciously expressed toward things or people usually predicted their subsequent behaviour reasonably well. Their attitude reports became useless, however, if the participants were first asked to analyze their feelings. For example, dating couples' current happiness with their relationship accurately predicted whether they would still be dating several months later. But participants who first listed all the reasons they could think of why their relationship was good or bad before rating their happiness were misled—their happiness ratings were useless in predicting the future of the relationship! Apparently, the process of dissecting the relationship drew attention to easily verbalized factors that actually were less important than aspects of the relationship that were harder to verbalize. We are often "strangers to ourselves," Wilson concluded (2002).

Such findings illustrate that we have **dual attitudes**, said Wilson and his colleagues (Wilson, Lindsey, & Schooler, 2000). Our automatic *implicit* attitudes regarding someone or something often differ from our consciously controlled, *explicit* attitudes (Gawronski & Bodenhausen, 2006; Nosek, 2007). From childhood, for example, we may retain a habitual, automatic fear or dislike of people for whom we now verbalize respect and appreciation. Although explicit attitudes may change with relative ease, noted Wilson, "implicit attitudes, like old habits, change more slowly." With repeated practice, acting on the new attitude, new habitual attitudes can, however, replace old ones.

This research on the limits of our self-knowledge has two practical implications. The first is for psychological inquiry. Self-reports are often untrustworthy. Errors in self-understanding limit the scientific usefulness of subjective personal reports.

The second implication is for our everyday lives. The sincerity with which people report and interpret their experiences is no guarantee of the validity of those reports. Personal testimonies are powerfully persuasive (as we will see in Module C, "Social Psychology in Court"). But they may also be wrong. Keeping this potential for error in mind can help us feel less intimidated by others and be less gullible.

dual attitudes
differing implicit (automatic) and explicit (consciously controlled) attitudes toward the same object. Verbalized explicit attitudes may change with education and persuasion; implicit attitudes change slowly, with practice that forms new habits.

> "Self-contemplation is a curse that makes an old confusion worse."
> THEODORE ROETHKE, *THE COLLECTED POEMS OF THEODORE ROETHKE*, 1975

WHAT IS THE NATURE AND MOTIVATING POWER OF SELF-ESTEEM?

People desire self-esteem, which they are motivated to enhance. But how can self-esteem also be problematic?

Is **self-esteem**—our overall self-evaluation—the sum of all our self-schemas and possible selves? If we see ourselves as attractive, athletic, smart, and destined to be rich and loved, will we have high self-esteem? Yes, said Jennifer Crocker and Connie Wolfe (2001), when we feel good about the domains (looks, smarts, or whatever) important to our self-esteem. "One person may have self-esteem that is highly contingent on doing well in school and being physically attractive, whereas another may have self-esteem that is contingent on being loved by God and adhering to moral standards." Thus, the first person will feel high self-esteem when made to feel smart and good-looking, the second person when made to feel moral.

But Jonathon Brown and Keith Dutton (1994) argued that this "bottom-up" view of self-esteem is not the whole story. The causal arrow, they believed, also goes the other way. People

self-esteem
a person's overall self-evaluation or sense of self-worth

who value themselves in a general way—those with high self-esteem—are more likely to value their looks, abilities, and so forth. They are like new parents who, loving their infant, delight in the baby's fingers, toes, and hair: The parents do not first evaluate their infant's fingers or toes and then decide how much to value the whole baby.

Specific self-perceptions do have some influence, however. If you think you're good at math, you will be more likely to do well at math. Although general self-esteem does not predict academic performance very well, academic self-concept—whether you think you are good in school—does predict performance (Marsh & O'Mara, 2008). Of course, each causes the other: Doing well at math makes you think you are good at math, which then motivates you to do even better. So if you want to encourage someone (or yourself!), it's better if your praise is specific ("You're good at math.") instead of general ("You're great."), and it's better if your kind words reflect true ability and performance ("You really improved on your last test.") rather than unrealistic optimism ("You can do anything."). Feedback is best when it is true and specific (Swann, Chang-Schneider, & Angulo, 2007).

Imagine you're getting your grade back for the first test in a psychology class. When you see your grade, you groan—you're hovering somewhere between a D and an F. But then you get an encouraging e-mail with some review questions for the class and this message: "Students who have high self-esteem not only get better grades, but they remain self-confident and assured. . . . Bottom line: Hold your head—and your self-esteem—high." Another group of students instead get a message about taking personal control of their performance, or receive review questions only. So how would each group do on the final exam? To the surprise of the researchers in one study, the students whose self-esteem was boosted did by far the worst on the final; in fact, they flunked it (Forsyth et al., 2007). Struggling students told to feel good about themselves, the researchers suggested, may have thought, "I'm already great—why study?"

SELF-ESTEEM MOTIVATION

Most people are extremely motivated to maintain their self-esteem. In fact, a study found that university students preferred a boost to their self-esteem to eating their favourite food, engaging in their favourite sexual activity, seeing a best friend, drinking alcohol, or receiving a paycheque (Bushman, Moeller, & Crocker, 2011). So, somewhat incredibly, self-esteem was more important than sex, pizza, and beer! WEIRD

What happens when your self-esteem is threatened—for example, by a failure or an unflattering comparison with someone else? When brothers have markedly different ability levels—for example, one is a great athlete and the other is not—they report not getting along well (Tesser, 1988).

Self-esteem threats occur among friends, whose success can be more threatening than that of strangers (Zuckerman & Jost, 2001). In contrast, researchers at the University of Toronto have found that people often react more positively to upward than downward comparisons to romantic partners (Pinkus et al., 2008). When a partner outperforms us in a domain important to both our identities, we may reduce the threat by affirming our relationship, saying, "My capable partner, with whom I'm very close, is part of who I am" (Lockwood et al., 2004).

What underlies the motive to maintain or enhance self-esteem? Mark Leary (1998, 2004b, 2007) believed that our self-esteem feelings are like a fuel gauge. Relationships enable surviving and thriving. Thus, the self-esteem gauge alerts us to threatened social rejection, motivating us to act with greater sensitivity to others' expectations. Studies confirmed that social

Among sibling relationships, the threat to self-esteem is greatest for an older child with a highly capable younger brother or sister.

rejection lowers our self-esteem and makes us more eager for approval. Spurned or jilted, we feel unattractive or inadequate. Like a blinking dashboard light, this pain can motivate action—self-improvement and a search for acceptance and inclusion elsewhere.

Jeff Greenberg (2008) offered another perspective, called "terror management theory," which argues that humans must find ways to manage their overwhelming fear of death. If self-esteem were only about acceptance, he counters, why do "people strive to be great rather than to just be accepted"? The reality of our own death, he argued, motivates us to gain recognition from our work and values. There's a worm in the apple, however: Not everyone can achieve such recognition, which is exactly why it is valuable, and why self-esteem can never be wholly unconditional. ("You're special just for being you" is an example of self-esteem being granted unconditionally.) To feel our lives are not in vain, Greenberg maintained, we must continually pursue self-esteem by meeting the standards of our societies.

THE "DARK SIDE" OF SELF-ESTEEM

People with low self-esteem often have problems in their lives—they make less money, abuse drugs, and are more likely to be depressed (Salmela-Aro & Nurmi, 2007; Trzesniewski et al., 2006). As you learned in Chapter 1, though, a correlation between two variables is sometimes caused by a third factor. Maybe people low in self-esteem also faced poverty as children, experienced sexual abuse, or had parents who used drugs—all possible causes of later struggling. Sure enough, a study that controlled for these factors found that the link between self-esteem and negative outcomes disappeared (Boden, Fergusson, & Horwood, 2008). In other words, low self-esteem was not the cause of these young adults' problems—the seeming cause, instead, was that many could not escape their tough childhoods.

High self-esteem does have some benefits: It fosters initiative, resilience, and pleasant feelings (Baumeister et al., 2003). Yet teen males who engage in sexual activity at an "inappropriately young age" tend to have higher than average self-esteem. So do teen gang leaders, extreme ethnocentrists, terrorists, and men in prison for committing violent crimes (Bushman & Baumeister, 1998; Dawes, 1994, 1998).

Narcissism: Self-esteem's conceited sister

High self-esteem becomes especially problematic if it crosses over into narcissism or having an inflated sense of self. Most people with high self-esteem value both individual achievement and relationships with others. Narcissists usually have high self-esteem, but they are missing the piece about caring for others (Campbell, Rudich, & Sedikides, 2002). Although narcissists are often outgoing and charming early on, their self-centredness often leads to relationship problems in the long run (Campbell, 2005). The link between narcissism and problematic social relations led Delroy Paulhus and Kevin Williams (2002) of the University of British Columbia to include narcissism in the "Dark Triad" of negative traits, along with Machiavellianism (manipulativeness) and antisocial psychopathy.

In a series of experiments conducted by Brad Bushman and Roy Baumeister (1998), undergraduate volunteers wrote essays and received rigged feedback that said, "This is one of the worst essays I've read!" Those who scored high on narcissism were much more likely to retaliate, blasting painful noise into the headphones of the student they believed had criticized them. Narcissists weren't aggressive toward someone who praised them ("Great essay!"); it was the insult that set them off. But what about self-esteem? Maybe only the "insecure" narcissists—those low in self-esteem—would lash out. But that's not how it turned out; instead, the students high in both self-esteem and narcissism were the most aggressive. The same was true in a classroom setting: Those who were high in narcissism were most likely to retaliate against a classmate's criticism by giving him or her a bad grade (Bushman et al., 2009; Figure 2–6). Narcissists can be charming and entertaining, but as one wit has said, "God help you if you cross them."

It's also possible to have too much narcissistic pride in your group, not just yourself. Polish undergraduates who displayed a "collective narcissism," believing their country was superior to

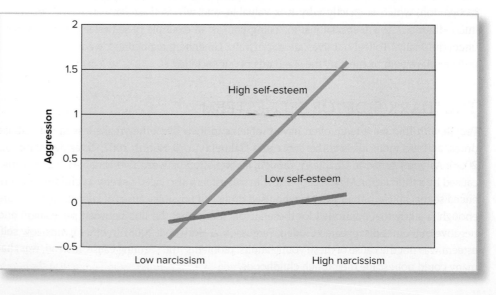

FIGURE 2–6

NARCISSISM, SELF-ESTEEM, AND AGGRESSION.

Narcissism and self-esteem interact to influence aggression. In an experiment by Brad Bushman and colleagues (2009), the recipe for retaliation against a critical classmate required both narcissism and high self-esteem.

others, were more prejudiced against Jewish people. Mexican undergraduates high in collective narcissism were more likely to view the construction of a U.S.–Mexico border wall as an insult and to endorse a boycott of U.S. products in retaliation (Golec de Zavala et al., 2009). So whether someone has excessive pride in themselves or their group, others may end up suffering.

Some studies have found small correlations between low self-esteem and antisocial behaviour, even when IQ and family income were taken into account (Donnellan, Larsen-Rife, & Conger, 2005; Trzesniewski et al., 2006). However, another study found that the link between low self-esteem and antisocial behaviour disappeared when sexual abuse and earlier behavioural problems were considered (Boden, Fergusson, & Horwood, 2007). Kids aren't acting aggressively because they have low self-esteem, it seems, but because they were hurt in the past. "The enthusiastic claims of the self-esteem movement mostly range from fantasy to hogwash," says Baumeister (1996), who suspects he has "probably published more studies on self-esteem than anybody else. . . . The effects of self-esteem are small, limited, and not all good." Folks with high self-esteem, he reports, are more likely to be obnoxious, to interrupt, and to talk at people rather than with them (in contrast to the more shy, modest, folks with low self-esteem). "My conclusion is that self-control is worth 10 times as much as self-esteem."

What about the idea that an overinflated ego is just a cover for deep-seated insecurity? Do narcissistic people actually dislike themselves "deep down inside"? Many researchers have tried to find low self-esteem beneath such an outer crust. But studies of bullies, gang members, genocidal dictators, and obnoxious narcissists have turned up no sign of it. "Hitler had very high self-esteem," noted Baumeister and his co-authors (2003).

Narcissism on the rise

After tracking self-importance across the past several decades, psychologist Jean Twenge (2006; Twenge et al., 2008) reports that today's young generation—*Generation Me*, she calls it—expresses more narcissism (by agreeing with statements such as "If I ruled the world, it would be a better place" or "I think I am a special person"). Narcissism scores rose over time on university campuses (Stewart & Bernhardt, 2010; Twenge & Foster, 2008, 2010). Narcissism correlates with materialism, the desire to be famous, inflated expectations, fewer committed relationships and more "hooking up," more gambling, and more cheating, all of which have also risen as narcissism has increased. Narcissism is also linked to a lack of empathy—the ability to take someone else's perspective and be concerned about their problems—and empathy has dropped precipitously among university students (Konrath, O'Brien, & Hsing, 2011). The researchers speculate that today's generation may be so wrapped up in online interaction that their in-person interaction skills have atrophied. Or, they say, empathy might have declined because young people today are "feeling too busy on their paths to success," single-mindedly concentrating on their own achievement because the world is now so competitive. Yet ironically, those high in narcissism and low in empathy are less—not more—successful in the long run, making lower grades in university and performing poorly at work (Judge, LePine, & Rich, 2006; Robins & Beer, 2001).

Fragile versus secure self-esteem

The findings linking highly positive self-views with negative behaviour—what Baumeister and his colleagues called "the dark side of high self-esteem"—exist in tension with findings that people expressing low self-esteem are more vulnerable to assorted clinical problems, including anxiety, loneliness, and eating disorders. When feeling bad or threatened, low-self-esteem people tend to take a negative view of everything. They notice and remember others' worst behaviours and think their partners don't love them (Murray et al., 1998, 2002a; Ybarra, 1999).

Christian Jordan from Wilfrid Laurier University and his colleagues (2003, 2005) suggested that this tension may be more apparent than real. They suggested that not all high-self-esteem people are alike. New research indicates that self-esteem, like attitudes, comes in two forms— *explicit* (consciously controlled) and *implicit* (automatic or intuitive). Jordan and his colleagues argue that when people have conscious views of themselves that are positive, but have low implicit self-esteem, they are likely to have fragile self-views. In several studies, they found that people with such fragile high self-esteem are more defensive: They rationalize their decisions more, and discriminate more against Aboriginal Canadians than other people do. Ian McGregor and his colleagues (McGregor & Marigold, 2003; McGregor et al., 2005) similarly found that York University students with fragile high self-esteem responded defensively to uncertainty by compensating with increased convictions in their political and social opinions and by perceiving greater popularity for their views.

Unlike a fragile self-esteem, a secure self-esteem—one rooted more in feeling good about who one is than on grades, looks, money, or others' approval—is conducive to long-term well-being (Kernis, 2003; Schimel et al., 2001). Jennifer Crocker and her colleagues (2002, 2003, 2004, 2005) confirmed this in studies with University of Michigan students. Those whose self-worth was most fragile—most contingent on external sources—experienced more stress, anger, relationship problems, drug and alcohol use, and eating disorders than did those whose worth was rooted more on internal sources, such as personal virtues. Ironically, noted Crocker and Lora Park (2004), those who pursue self-esteem, perhaps by seeking to become beautiful, rich, or popular, may lose sight of what really makes for quality of life. Moreover, if feeling good about ourselves is our goal, then we may become less open to criticism, more likely to blame than empathize with others, and more pressured to succeed at activities rather than enjoy them. Over time, such pursuit of self-esteem can fail to satisfy our deep needs for competence, relationship, and autonomy, noted Crocker and Park. To focus less on one's self-image, and more on developing one's talents and relationships, eventually leads to greater well-being. Kristin Neff (2011) suggests we label this approach self-compassion—leaving behind comparisons with others and instead treating ourselves with kindness. As an Indian proverb puts it, "There is nothing noble in being superior to some other person. The true nobility is in being superior to your previous self."

● WHAT DOES IT MEAN TO HAVE PERCEIVED SELF-CONTROL?

Several lines of research point to the significance of our perceived self-control and how we manage the self in action. What concepts emerge from this research?

We have considered what our self-concept is, how it develops, and how well (or poorly) we know ourselves. Now let's see why our self-concept matters, by viewing the self in action.

SELF-CONTROL

The self's capacity for action has limits, note Roy Baumeister and his colleagues (1998, 2000; Muraven, Tice, & Baumeister, 1998). Consider the following:

- People who exert self-control—by forcing themselves to eat radishes rather than chocolates, or by suppressing forbidden thoughts—subsequently quit faster when given unsolvable puzzles.
- People who have tried to control their emotional responses to an upsetting movie exhibit decreased physical stamina.
- People who have spent their willpower on tasks such as controlling their emotions during an upsetting film later become more aggressive and more likely to fight with their partners (DeWall et al., 2007; Finkel & Campbell, 2001). They also become less restrained in their sexual thoughts and behaviours. When asked to express intimacy with their partner, those with depleted willpower were more likely to passionately kiss their partner and even remove some clothing right in the lab (Gailliot & Baumeister, 2007).

Effortful self-control depletes our limited willpower reserves. Our brain's "central executive" consumes available blood sugar when engaged in self-control (Gailliot, 2008). Self-control, therefore, operates similarly to muscular strength, concluded Baumeister and Julia Exline (2000): Both are weaker after exertion, replenished with rest, and strengthened by exercise. Self-control depletion may, however, also reflect a motivational failure. After an initial act of self-control, people may "feel justified in slacking off" or indulging themselves (Inzlicht & Schmeichel, 2012). Consistent with this view, incentives to exert self-control in secondary tasks stop self-control depletion from occurring (Muraven & Slessareva, 2003). In addition, personal beliefs about self-control affect its depletion: People who believe that self-control is unlimited show no self-control depletion after earlier exertions (Job, Dweck, & Walton, 2010).

Our self-concepts do influence our behaviour (Graziano, Jensen-Campbell, & Finch, 1997). Given challenging tasks, people who imagine themselves as hard-working and successful outperform those who imagine themselves as failures (Ruvolo & Markus, 1992). Envision your positive possibilities and you become more likely to plan and enact a successful strategy.

LEARNED HELPLESSNESS VERSUS SELF-DETERMINATION

The benefits of feelings of control also appear in animal research. In research done before today's greater concern for animal welfare, dogs taught that they cannot escape shocks while confined will learn a sense of helplessness. Later, these dogs cower passively in other situations when they *could* escape punishment. Dogs that learn personal control (by successfully escaping their first shocks) adapt easily to a new situation. Researcher Martin Seligman (1975, 1991) noted similarities to this **learned helplessness** in human situations. Depressed or oppressed people, for example, become passive because they believe their efforts have no effect. Helpless dogs and depressed people both suffer paralysis of the will, passive resignation, even motionless apathy (Figure 2–7).

On the other hand, people benefit by training their self-control "muscles." University students who practised self-control by sticking with an exercise program or reducing their impulse buying also ate less junk food, cut down on alcohol, and studied more (Oaten & Cheng, 2006a, 2006b). So if you learn how to exert willpower in one area of your life, resisting temptation in other areas becomes easier too.

Ellen Langer and Judith Rodin (1976) tested the importance of personal control by treating elderly patients in a highly rated nursing home in one of two ways. With one group, the

learned helplessness
the hopelessness and resignation learned when a human or animal perceives no control over repeated bad events

FIGURE 2–7

LEARNED HELPLESSNESS.

When animals and people experience uncontrollable bad events, they learn to feel helpless and resigned.

benevolent caregivers stressed "our responsibility to make this a home you can be proud of and happy in." They gave the passive patients their normal well-intentioned, sympathetic care, and they allowed them to assume a passive care-receiving role. Three weeks later, most were rated by themselves, by interviewers, and by nurses as further debilitated. Langer and Rodin's other treatment promoted personal control. It emphasized opportunities for choice, the possibilities for influencing nursing-home policy, and the person's responsibility "to make of your life whatever you want." These patients were given small decisions to make and responsibilities to fulfill. Over the ensuing three weeks, 93 percent of this group showed improved alertness, activity, and happiness.

Studies have confirmed that systems of governing or managing people that promote self-efficacy—a belief in your own competence—will, indeed, promote health and happiness (Deci & Ryan, 1987). Here are some additional examples:

- University students who develop a sense of control over school gain a greater sense of control over their lives (Guay, Mageau, & Vallerand, 2003).

- Prisoners given some control over their environments—by being able to move chairs, control TV sets, and switch the lights—experience less stress, exhibit fewer health problems, and commit less vandalism (Ruback, Carr, & Hoper, 1986; Wener, Frazier, & Farbstein, 1987).

- Workers given leeway in carrying out tasks and making decisions experience improved morale (Miller & Monge, 1986). So do telecommuting workers who have more flexibility in balancing their work and personal life (Valcour, 2007).

- In all countries studied, including Canada, people who perceive themselves as having free choice experience greater satisfaction with their lives. And countries where people experience more freedom have more satisfied citizens (Inglehart & Welzel, 2005).

The costs of excess choice

Can there ever be too much of a good thing such as freedom and self-determination? Barry Schwartz (2000, 2004) contends that individualistic modern cultures indeed have "an excess of freedom," causing decreased life satisfaction and increased rates of clinical depression. Too many choices can lead to paralysis, or what Schwartz calls "the tyranny of freedom." After choosing from among 30 kinds of jams or chocolates, people express less satisfaction with their choices than those choosing from among 6 options (Iyengar & Lepper, 2000). Making choices is also tiring. Students who read the catalogue and chose which classes they would take during the upcoming semester—versus those who simply read it but made no choices—were later less likely to study for an important test and more likely to procrastinate by playing video games and reading magazines. In another study, students who chose among an array of consumer products were later less able to consume an unsavoury but healthy drink (Vohs et al., 2008). So after choosing among the 19 000 possible beverage combinations at Starbucks or the 40 000 items at the average grocery store, you might be less satisfied with your choices and more likely to go home and eat the ice cream straight from the container.

Christopher Hsee and Reid Hastie (2006) illustrate how choice may enhance regret. Give employees a free trip to either Paris or Hawaii and they will be happy. But give them a choice between the two and they may be less happy. People who choose Paris may regret that it lacks the warmth and the ocean. Those who choose Hawaii may regret the lack of great museums.

"This gives my confidence a real boost."

Confidence and feelings of self-efficacy grow from successes.

© Edward Koren/The New Yorker Collection/www.cartoonbank.com

In other experiments, people have expressed greater satisfaction with irrevocable choices (such as those made in an "all purchases final" sale) than with reversible choices (as when allowing refunds or exchanges). Ironically, people like and will pay for the freedom to reverse their choices. Yet, note Daniel Gilbert and Jane Ebert (2002), that same freedom "can inhibit the psychological processes that manufacture satisfaction."

That principle may help explain a curious social phenomenon (Myers, 2000): National surveys show that people expressed more satisfaction with their marriages several decades ago when marriage was more irrevocable ("all purchases final"). Today, despite greater freedom to escape bad marriages and try new ones, people tend to express somewhat less satisfaction with the marriage that they have.

Research on self-control gives us greater confidence in traditional virtues such as perseverance and hope. Bandura (2004) acknowledges that self-efficacy is fed by social persuasion ("You have what it takes to succeed.") and by self-persuasion ("I think I can, I think I can."). Modelling—seeing similar others succeed with effort—helps, too. But the biggest source of self-efficacy, he says, is *mastery experiences.* "Successes build a robust belief in one's efficacy." If your initial efforts to lose weight, stop smoking, or improve your grades succeed, your self-efficacy increases.

"Argue for your limitations, and sure enough they're yours."
RICHARD BACH, ILLUSIONS: *ADVENTURES OF A RELUCTANT MESSIAH*, 1977

A team of researchers led by Roy Baumeister (Baumeister et al., 2003) concurs with Bandura's conclusion about mastery experiences. "Praising all the children just for being themselves," they contend, "simply devalues praise." Better to praise and bolster self-esteem "in recognition of good performance. . . . As the person performs or behaves better, self-esteem is encouraged to rise, and the net effect will be to reinforce both good behavior and improvement. Those outcomes are conducive to both the happiness of the individual and the betterment of society."

● WHAT IS SELF-SERVING BIAS?

As we process self-relevant information, a potent bias intrudes. We readily excuse our failures, accept credit for our successes, and in many ways see ourselves as better than average. Such self-enhancing perceptions enable many people to enjoy the benefits of high self-esteem, while occasionally suffering the perils of pride.

Most of us have a good reputation with ourselves. In studies of self-esteem, even low-scoring people respond in the mid-range of possible scores. (A low-self-esteem person responds to such statements as "I have good ideas" with a qualifying modifier, such as "somewhat" or "sometimes.") In a study of self-esteem across 53 nations, including Canada, the average self-esteem score was above the midpoint in every single country (Schmitt & Allik, 2005). One of social psychology's most provocative yet firmly established conclusions concerns the potency of **self-serving bias**.

self-serving bias
the tendency to perceive yourself favourably

self-serving attributions
a form of self-serving bias; the tendency to attribute positive outcomes to yourself and negative outcomes to other factors

The self-serving bias.
© Jean Sorensen.

EXPLAINING POSITIVE AND NEGATIVE EVENTS

Many dozens of experiments have found that people accept credit when told they have succeeded. They attribute the success to their ability and effort, but they attribute failure to such external factors as bad luck or the problem's inherent "impossibility" (Campbell & Sedikides, 1999). Similarly, in explaining their victories, athletes commonly credit themselves, but they attribute losses to something else: bad breaks, bad referee calls, or the other team's super effort or dirty play (Grove, Hanrahan, & McInman, 1991; Lalonde, 1992; Mullen & Riordan, 1988). And how much responsibility do you suppose car drivers tend to accept for their accidents? On insurance forms, drivers have described their accidents in words such as these: "An invisible car came out of nowhere, struck my car and vanished," "As I reached an intersection, a hedge sprang up, obscuring my vision, and I did not see the other car," and "A pedestrian hit me and went under my car" (*Toronto News*, 1977).

Situations that combine skill and chance (games, exams, job applications) are especially prone to the phenomenon: Winners can easily attribute their successes to their skill, while losers can attribute their losses to chance. When you win at Scrabble, it's because of your verbal dexterity; when you lose, it's "Who could get anywhere with a Q but no U?" Politicians similarly tend to attribute their wins to themselves (hard work, constituent service, reputation, and strategy) and their losses to factors beyond their control (their district's party makeup, their opponent's name, and political trends) (Kingdon, 1967). This phenomenon of **self-serving attributions** (attributing positive outcomes to oneself and negative outcomes to something else) is one of the most potent of human biases. That might be for a good reason: Making self-serving attributions activates brain areas associated with reward and pleasure (Seidel et al., 2010).

Self-serving attributions contribute to marital discord, worker dissatisfaction, and bargaining impasses (Kruger & Gilovich, 1999). Small wonder that divorced people usually blame their partner for the breakup (Gray & Silver, 1990), or that managers usually blame poor performance on workers' lack of ability or effort (Imai, 1994; Rice, 1985). (Workers, on the other hand, are more likely to blame something external—inadequate supplies, excessive workload, difficult co-workers, or ambiguous assignments.) Small wonder, too, that people evaluate reward distributions such as pay raises as fairer when they receive a bigger raise than most of their co-workers (Diekmann et al., 1997).

Ironically, we are even biased against seeing our own bias. People claim they avoid self-serving bias themselves, but readily acknowledge that others commit this bias (Pronin, Lin, & Ross, 2002). This "bias blind spot" can have serious consequences during conflicts. If you're negotiating with your roommate over who does household chores and you believe your roommate has a biased view of the situation, you're much more likely to become angry (Pronin & Ross, 2006). Apparently we see ourselves as objective and everyone else as biased. No wonder we fight: We're each convinced we're "right" and free from bias. As the T-shirt slogan says, "Everyone is entitled to my opinion."

Is the self-serving bias universal, or are people in collectivistic cultures immune? People in collectivistic cultures associate themselves with positive words and valued traits (Gaertner, Sedikides, & Chang, 2008; Yamaguchi et al., 2007). However, in some studies, collectivists are less likely to self-enhance by believing they are better than others (Heine & Hamamura, 2007), particularly in individualistic domains (Sedikides, Gaertner, & Toguchi, 2003).

CAN WE ALL BE BETTER THAN AVERAGE?

Self-serving bias also appears when people compare themselves with others. If Chinese philosopher Lao-tzu was right that "at no time in the world will a man who is sane overreach himself, overspend himself, overrate himself," then most of us are a little insane. For on *subjective, socially desirable,* and *common* dimensions, most people see themselves as better than the average person. Compared with people in general, most people see themselves as more ethical, more competent at their job, friendlier, more intelligent, better looking, less prejudiced, healthier, and even more insightful and less biased in their self-assessments (see "Focus on: Self-Serving Bias— How Do I Love Me? Let Me Count the Ways," on page 63).

Every community, it seems, is like Garrison Keillor's fictional Lake Wobegon, where "all the women are strong, all the men are good-looking, and all the children are above average." Many people believe that they will become even more above average in the future—"If I'm good now, I will be even better soon," they seem to think (Kanten & Teigen, 2008). One of Freud's favourite jokes was the husband who told his wife, "If one of us should die, I think I would go live in Paris."

Michael Ross and Fiore Sicoly (1979) observed that the self-serving bias is also common in marriages. They found that young married Canadians usually felt they did more of the work of cleaning the house and caring for the children than their spouses believed they did. In a 2008 survey, 49 percent of married men said they did half to most of the child care. But only 31 percent of wives said their husbands did this much. In the same survey, 70 percent of women said they do most of the cooking, but 56 percent of the men said *they* do most of the cooking (Galinsky, Aumann, & Bond, 2009). The general rule: Group members' estimates of how much they contribute to a joint task typically sum to more than 100 percent (Savitsky et al., 2005).

Within commonly considered domains, *subjective behaviour dimensions* (such as "disciplined") trigger greater self-serving bias than *objective behaviour dimensions* (such as "punctual"). Subjective qualities give us leeway in constructing our own definitions of success (Dunning,

Meyerowitz, & Holzberg, 1989; Dunning, Perie, & Story, 1991). Rating my "athletic ability," I ponder my basketball play, not the agonizing weeks I spent as a Little League baseball player hiding in right field. Assessing my "leadership ability," I conjure up an image of a great leader whose style is similar to mine. By defining ambiguous criteria in our own terms, each of us can see ourselves as relatively successful. In one University Entrance Examination Board survey of 829 000 high school seniors, *none* rated themselves below average in "ability to get along with others" (a subjective, desirable trait), 60 percent rated themselves in the top 10 percent, and 25 percent saw themselves among the top 1 percent! In 2011, 77 percent of incoming university students described themselves as above average in their "drive to achieve," another subjective and desirable trait (Pryor et al., 2010).

Researchers have wondered: Do people really believe their above-average self-estimates? Is their self-serving bias partly a function of how the questions are phrased (Krizan & Suls, 2008)? When Elanor Williams and Thomas Gilovich (2008) had people bet real money when estimating their relative performance on tests, they found that, yes, "people truly believe their self-enhancing self-assessments."

THE >>> INSIDE STORY

Suppose that you have collaborated on a project with another student and that the two of you evaluated each other's contributions to the final product. You may be disappointed to discover that your partner is less impressed with the quality and extent of your contribution than you are. In the history of science, there are many examples of such disagreements; erstwhile friends and colleagues become bitter enemies as they contest each other's contributions to important discoveries.

[Fiore] Sicoly and I suggested that individuals generally tend to accept more responsibility for a joint product than other contributors attribute to them. In many everyday activities, participants are unaware of their divergent views because they don't share their opinions with each other. After cleaning the kitchen, for example, spouses don't usually discuss how much each contributed to the cleanup.

When such opinions are voiced, people are likely to be upset because they believe that the other person is not giving them sufficient credit. If the consequences are high (e.g., academic grades, job promotions, or Nobel Prizes at stake), they may well assume that their partner is deliberately downgrading their contributions to enhance his or her own achievements.

In our research, Sicoly and I showed that differences in assessments of responsibility are common in many everyday contests, and that contrasting judgments may reflect normal cognitive processes rather than deliberate deceit. Differences in judgment can result from honest evaluations of information that is differentially available to the two participants.

Michael Ross *University of Waterloo*

UNREALISTIC OPTIMISM

Optimism predisposes a positive approach to life. "The optimist," noted H. Jackson Brown (1990, p. 79), "goes to the window every morning and says, 'Good morning, God.' The pessimist goes to the window and says, 'Good god, morning.'" Studies of more than 90 000 people across 22 cultures reveal that most humans are more disposed to optimism than pessimism (Fischer & Chalmers, 2008). Indeed, many of us have what researcher Neil Weinstein (1980, 1982) termed "an unrealistic optimism about future life events." Partly because of their relative pessimism about others' fates (Hoorens, Smits, & Shepperd, 2008; Shepperd, 2003), students perceive themselves as far more likely than their classmates to get a good job, draw a good salary, and own a home. They also see themselves as far less likely to experience negative events, such as developing a drinking problem, having a heart attack before age 40, or being fired. Adult women are much more likely

> *"Views of the future are so rosy that they would make Pollyanna blush."*
> SHELLEY E. TAYLOR, *POSITIVE ILLUSIONS*, 1989

FOCUS ON ⟩ Self-Serving Bias—How Do I Love Me? Let Me Count the Ways

"The one thing that unites all human beings, regardless of age, gender, religion, economic status or ethnic background," noted Dave Barry (1998), "is that deep down inside, we all believe that we are above-average drivers." We also believe we are above average on most any other subjective and desirable trait. Among the many faces of self-serving bias are these:

- *Ethics.* Most businesspeople see themselves as more ethical than the average businessperson (Baumhart, 1968; Brenner & Molander, 1977). One national survey asked, "How would you rate your own morals and values on a scale from 1 to 100 (100 being perfect)?" Fifty percent of people rated themselves 90 or above; only 11 percent said 74 or less (Lovett, 1997).

- *Professional competence.* Ninety percent of business managers rated their performance as superior to their average peer (French, 1968). In Australia, 86 percent of people rated their job performance as above average, 1 percent as below average (Headey & Wearing, 1987). Most surgeons believed their patients' mortality rate to be lower than average (Gawande, 2002).

- *Virtues.* In the Netherlands, most high school students rated themselves as more honest, persistent, original, friendly, and reliable than the average high school student (Hoorens, 1993, 1995).

- *Intelligence.* Most people perceive themselves as more intelligent, better looking, and much less prejudiced than their average peer (Public Opinion, 1984; Wylie, 1979). When someone outperforms them, people tend to think of the other as a genius (Lassiter & Munhall, 2001).

- *Parental support.* Most adults believe they support their aging parents more than do their siblings (Lerner et al., 1991).

- *Health.* Los Angeles residents view themselves as healthier than most of their neighbours, and most university students believe they will outlive their actuarially predicted age of death by about 10 years (Larwood, 1978; C. R. Snyder, 1978).

- *Insight.* Others' words and deeds reveal their natures, we presume. Our private thoughts do the same. Thus, most of us believe we know and understand others better than they know and understand us. We also believe we know ourselves better than others know themselves (Pronin et al., 2001). Few university students see themselves as more naïve or more gullible than others; many more think they're less naïve and gullible (Levine, 2003).

- *Driving.* Most drivers—even most drivers who have been hospitalized for accidents—believe themselves to be safer and more skilled than the average driver (Guerin, 1994; McKenna & Myers, 1997; Svenson, 1981). Dave Barry got it right!

to be unduly optimistic than pessimistic about their relative risk of breast cancer (Waters et al., 2011). Football fans believe their favourite team has a 77 percent chance of winning their first game. Even after four months when (on average) their team won only half the time, they still hold out hope and predict a 70 percent chance of their team winning (Massey, Simmons, & Armor, 2011).

Parents extend their unrealistic optimism to their children, assuming their child is less likely to drop out of college, become depressed, or get lung cancer than the average child, but more likely to complete university, remain healthy, and stay happy (Lench, Quas, & Edelstein, 2006).

Illusory optimism increases our vulnerability. Believing ourselves immune to misfortune, we do not take sensible precautions. Sexually active undergraduate women who don't consistently use contraceptives perceive themselves, compared to other women at their university, as much *less* vulnerable to unwanted pregnancy (Burger & Burns, 1988). Elderly drivers who rated themselves as "above average" were four times more likely than more modest drivers to flunk a driving test and be rated "unsafe" (Freund et al., 2005). Students who enter university with inflated assessments of their academic ability often suffer deflating self-esteem and well-being and are more likely to drop out (Robins & Beer, 2001).

Those who cheerfully deny the effects of smoking or stumble into ill-fated relationships remind us that blind optimism, like pride, may go before a fall. When gambling, optimists persist longer than pessimists, even when piling up losses (Gibson & Sanbonmatsu, 2004). If those who deal in the stock market or in real estate perceive their business intuition to be superior to that of their competitors, they, too, may be in for severe disappointment. Even the seventeenth-century economist Adam Smith, a defender of human economic rationality, foresaw that people would overestimate their chances of gain. This "absurd presumption in their own good fortune," he said, arises from "the overweening conceit which the greater part of men have of their own abilities" (Spiegel, 1971, p. 243).

Unrealistic optimism appears to be on the rise. In the 1970s, half of American high school seniors predicted that they would be "very good" workers as adults—the highest rating available in the study, and thus the equivalent of giving themselves five stars out of five. By 2006, two-thirds of teens believed they would achieve this stellar outcome (Twenge & Campbell, 2008). Even more striking, half of high school seniors in 2000 believed that they would earn a graduate degree—even though only 9 percent were likely to actually do so (Reynolds et al., 2006).

Although aiming high has benefits for success, those who aim too high may struggle with depression as they learn to adjust their goals to more realistic heights (Wrosch & Miller, 2009).

Optimism definitely beats pessimism in promoting self-efficacy, health, and well-being (Armor & Taylor, 1996). If our optimistic ancestors were more likely than their pessimistic neighbours to surmount challenges and survive, then small wonder that we are disposed to optimism (Haselton & Nettle, 2006). Yet a dash of realism can save us from the perils of unrealistic optimism. Students who exhibit excess optimism (as many students destined for low grades do) can benefit from having some self-doubt, which motivates study (Prohaska, 1994; Sparrell & Shrauger, 1984). Students who are overconfident tend to underprepare, whereas their equally able but less confident peers study harder and get higher grades (Goodhart, 1986; Norem & Cantor, 1986; Showers & Ruben, 1987). The moral: Success in school and beyond requires enough optimism to sustain hope and enough pessimism to motivate concern.

FALSE CONSENSUS AND UNIQUENESS

We have a curious tendency to further enhance our self-images by overestimating or underestimating the extent to which others think and act as we do. On matters of *opinion*, we find support for our positions by overestimating the extent to which others agree—a phenomenon called the **false consensus effect** (Krueger & Clement, 1994; Marks & Miller, 1987; Mullen & Goethals, 1990). Sharad Goel, Winter Mason, and Duncan Watts (2010) found that Facebook users were 90 percent accurate in guessing when they agreed with their friends on political and other issues, but they were only 41 percent accurate in guessing disagreement. In other words, most of the time they thought their friends agreed with them when they didn't. Business students asked to make decisions about ethical dilemmas overestimated how many other students made the same choice (Flynn & Wiltermuth, 2010). White Australians prejudiced against Aborigines were more likely to believe that other Whites were also prejudiced (Watt & Larkin, 2010). The sense we make of the world seems like common sense.

> **false consensus effect** the tendency to overestimate the commonality of one's opinions and one's undesirable or unsuccessful behaviours

When we behave badly or fail in a task, we reassure ourselves by thinking that such lapses also are common. After one person lies to another, the liar begins to perceive the *other* person as dishonest (Sagarin, Rhoads, & Cialdini, 1998). They guess that others think and act as they do: "I lie, but doesn't everyone?" If we smoke or cheat on our income taxes, we are likely to overestimate the number of other people who do likewise. If we feel sexual desire toward someone, we may overestimate that person's reciprocal desire. "We don't see things as they are," says a proverb. "We see things as we are."

> *"I think few people have conventional family relationships."*
> MADONNA, 2000

False consensus may occur because we generalize from a limited sample, which prominently includes ourselves (Dawes, 1990). Lacking other information, why not "project" ourselves; why not impute our own knowledge to others and use our responses as a clue to their likely responses? Also, we're more likely to associate with people who share our attitudes and behaviours and then to judge the world from the people we know. Small wonder that Germans tend to think that the typical European looks rather German, whereas the Portuguese see Europeans as looking more Portuguese (Imhoff et al., 2011).

On matters of ability or when we behave well or successfully, however, a **false uniqueness effect** more often occurs (Goethals, Messick, & Allison, 1991). We serve our self-image by seeing our talents and moral behaviours as relatively unusual. Dutch college students preferred being

> **false uniqueness effect** the tendency to underestimate the commonality of one's abilities and one's desirable or successful behaviours

part of a larger group in matters of opinion such as politics (false consensus) but wanted to be part of a smaller group in matters of taste such as musical preferences (false uniqueness; Spears, Ellemers, & Doosje, 2009). After all, a band isn't cool anymore if too many people like it. Female college students who protect themselves while drinking by, for example, designating a driver or drinking only with a meal underestimate how many other women do the same (Benton et al., 2008). Thus we may see our failings as relatively normal and our virtues as relatively exceptional.

temporal comparisons
comparisons between how the self is viewed now and how the self was viewed in the past or how the self is expected to be viewed in the future

TEMPORAL COMPARISON

Comparisons with others can contribute to the self-serving bias, and so can comparisons to the person we used to be. **Temporal comparisons** with our own past selves typically cast the current self in a positive light.

Anne Wilson of Wilfrid Laurier University and Mike Ross of the University of Waterloo (Wilson & Ross, 2001; Ross & Wilson, 2002) have studied temporal comparisons extensively. They found that people maintain a positive view of themselves by disparaging their distant past selves and complimenting their recent past selves. In one experiment, for example, Wilson and Ross had university students and their parents rate the students on a number of traits, both as they currently were and as they were when they were 16. As can be seen in Figure 2–8, both students and their parents believed that they had improved significantly with time. This evidence suggests that people may disparage their past selves, but it could simply indicate a developmental trend—maybe people just get better with time. However, Wilson and Ross (2001) also had students rate themselves at the beginning of term and then retrospectively rate their beginning-of-term self again at the end of term. The students remembered themselves as being much worse at the beginning of term than they actually rated themselves at the time—their sense of improvement was thus more illusion than reality.

> *"Everybody says I'm plastic from head to toe. Can't stand next to a radiator or I'll melt. I had (breast) implants, but so has every single person in L.A."*
> ACTRESS PAMELA ANDERSON (QUOTED BY TALBERT, 1997)

Ross and Wilson (2002) also found that we perceive positive past selves as closer in time and negative past selves as more distant. In one study, they had students rate their social success in high school and later rate how psychologically distant high school seemed. For those who were popular in high school, it felt more recent than for those who were less popular. Drawing positive past selves closer and pushing negative past selves away is one way to self-enhance. This tendency even extends to our social groups: German but not Canadian

Illusory optimism: Most couples marry feeling confident of long-term love. Actually, in individualistic cultures, new marriages often fail.

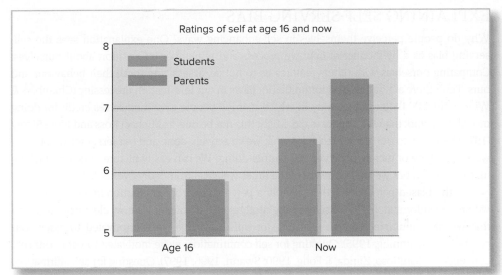

FIGURE 2–8

BETTER WITH TIME?
Both university students and their parents believe they have improved with time (Data from Wilson & Ross, 2001).

students felt that the Holocaust occurred in the more distant past when they read about German atrocities committed at that time (Peetz, Gunn, & Wilson, 2010). Our glory days may often feel like yesterday, while our defeats and transgressions feel like ancient history.

To sum up, these tendencies toward self-serving attributions, self-congratulatory comparisons, illusory optimism, and false consensus for our failings are major sources of self-serving bias (Figure 2–9).

"The past is to be respected and acknowledged, but not to be worshipped. It is our future in which we will find our greatness."
PIERRE ELLIOT TRUDEAU, *CANADIAN MUSEUM OF CIVILIZATION LIBRARY*

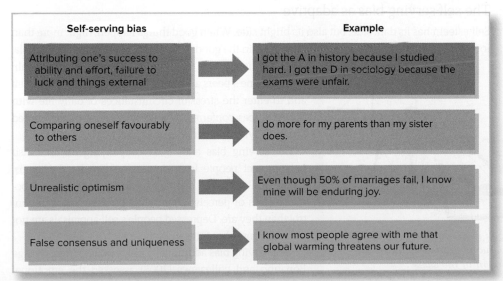

FIGURE 2–9

HOW SELF-SERVING BIAS WORKS.

EXPLAINING SELF-SERVING BIAS

Why do people perceive themselves in self-enhancing ways? One explanation sees the self-serving bias as a by-product of how we process and remember information about ourselves. Comparing ourselves with others requires us to notice, assess, and recall their behaviour and ours. Thus, there are multiple opportunities for flaws in our information processing (Chambers & Windschitl, 2004). Recall the study in which married people gave themselves credit for doing more housework than their spouses did. Might this not be due, as Michael Ross and Fiore Sicoly (1979) believed, to our greater recall for what we've actively done and our lesser recall for what we've not done or merely observed our partner doing? We can easily picture ourselves picking up the laundry, but we are less aware of the times we absentmindedly overlook it.

Are the biased perceptions, then, simply a perceptual error, an emotion-free glitch in how we process information? Or are self-serving motives also involved? It's now clear from research that we have multiple motives. Questing for self-knowledge, we're motivated to assess our competence (Dunning, 1995). Questing for self-confirmation, we're motivated to verify our self-conceptions (Sanitioso, Zunda, & Fong, 1990; Swann, 1996, 1997). Questing for self-affirmation, we're especially motivated to enhance our self-image (Sedikides, 1993). Self-esteem motivation helps power self-serving bias. As social psychologist Daniel Batson (2006) surmised, "The head is an extension of the heart."

REFLECTIONS ON SELF-ESTEEM AND SELF-SERVING BIAS

If you are like some readers, by now you are finding the self-serving bias either depressing or contrary to your own occasional feelings of inadequacy. Even the people who exhibit the self-serving bias may feel inferior to specific individuals, especially those who are a step or two higher on the ladder of success, attractiveness, or skill. Moreover, not everyone operates with a self-serving bias. Some people do suffer from low self-esteem. Positive self-esteem does have some benefits.

The self-serving bias as adaptive

Self-esteem has its dark side, but also its bright side. When good things happen, high- more than low-self-esteem people tend to savour and sustain the good feelings (Wood, Heimpel, & Michela, 2003). "Believing one has more talents and positive qualities than one's peers allows one to feel good about oneself and to enter the stressful circumstances of daily life with the resources conferred by a positive sense of self," noted Shelley Taylor and her co-researchers (2003).

Self-serving bias and its accompanying excuses also help protect people from depression (Snyder & Higgins, 1988). Non-depressed people excuse their failures on laboratory tasks or perceive themselves as being more in control than they are. Depressed people's self-appraisals are not inflated (more about this in Module B).

Self-serving bias additionally helps buffer stress. George Bonanno and colleagues (2005) assessed the emotional

"I admit it does look very impressive. But you see nowadays everyone graduates in the top ten percent of his class".

resiliency of workers who escaped the World Trade Center or its environs on September 11, 2001. They found that those who displayed self-enhancing tendencies were the most resilient.

In their "terror management theory," Jeff Greenberg, Sheldon Solomon, and Tom Pyszczynski (1997) proposed another reason why positive self-esteem is adaptive: It buffers anxiety, including anxiety related to our certain death. In childhood, the theory posits, we learn that when we meet the standards taught to us by our parents, we are loved and protected; when we don't, love and protection may be withdrawn. We, therefore, come to associate viewing ourselves as good with feeling secure. Greenberg and colleagues argued that positive self-esteem—viewing ourselves as good and secure—even protects us from feeling terror over our eventual death. Their research shows that reminding people of their mortality (say, by writing a short essay on dying) motivates them to affirm their self-worth. Moreover, when facing threats, increased self-esteem leads to decreased anxiety.

"Then we're in agreement. There's nothing rotten in Denmark. Something is rotten everywhere else."

© Dana Fradon/The New Yorker Collection/ www.cartoonbank.com

As research on depression and anxiety suggests, there may be some practical wisdom in self-serving perceptions. It may be strategic to believe we are smarter, stronger, and more socially successful than we are. Cheaters may give a more convincing display of honesty if they believe themselves honourable. Belief in our superiority can also motivate us to achieve—creating a self-fulfilling prophecy—and can sustain a sense of hope through difficult times (Willard & Gramzow, 2009).

The self-serving bias as maladaptive

Although self-serving pride may help protect us from depression, it can at times be maladaptive. People who blame others for their social difficulties are often unhappier than people who can acknowledge their mistakes (C. A. Anderson, Horowitz, & French, 1983; Newman & Langer, 1981; Peterson, Schwartz, & Seligman, 1981).

Research by Barry Schlenker (1976; Schlenker & Miller, 1977a, 1977b) has also shown how self-serving perceptions can poison a group. As a rock band guitarist during his college days, Schlenker noted that "rock band members typically overestimated their contributions to a group's success and underestimated their contributions to failure. I saw many good bands disintegrate from the problems caused by these self-glorifying tendencies." In his later life as a University of Florida social psychologist, Schlenker explored group members' self-serving perceptions. In nine experiments, he had people work together on some task. He then falsely informed them that their group had done either well or poorly. In every one of these studies, the members of successful groups claimed more responsibility for their group's performance than did members of groups that supposedly failed at the task.

"Victory finds a hundred fathers but defeat is an orphan."
COUNT GALEAZZO CIANO, *THE CIANO DIARIES*, 1938

If most group members believe they are underpaid and underappreciated relative to their better-than-average contributions, disharmony and envy are likely. University presidents and academic deans will readily recognize the phenomenon. Ninety percent or more of university faculty members rate themselves as superior to their average colleague (Blackburn et al., 1980; Cross, 1977). It is, therefore, inevitable that when merit salary raises are announced and half receive an average raise or less, many will feel themselves victims of injustice.

Self-serving biases also inflate people's judgments of their groups, a phenomenon called **group-serving bias**. When groups are comparable, most people consider their own group superior (Codol, 1976; Jourden & Heath, 1996; Taylor & Doria, 1981). Consider the following:

group-serving bias explaining away out-group members' positive behaviours; also attributing negative behaviours to their dispositions (while excusing such behaviour by one's own group)

- Most university sorority members perceive those in their sorority as far less likely to be conceited and snobby than those in other sororities (Biernat, Vescio, & Green, 1996).

- Fifty-three percent of Dutch adults rate their marriage or partnership as better than that of most others; only 1 percent rate it as worse than most (Buunk & van der Eijnden, 1997).

- Most corporation presidents and production managers overpredict their own firms' productivity and growth (Kidd & Morgan, 1969; Larwood & Whittaker, 1977).

That people see themselves and their groups with a favourable bias is hardly new. The tragic flaw portrayed in ancient Greek drama was *hubris,* or pride. Like the subjects of our experiments, the Greek tragic figures were not self-consciously evil; they merely thought too highly of themselves. In literature, the pitfalls of pride are portrayed again and again. In theology, pride has long been first among the "seven deadly sins."

If pride is akin to the self-serving bias, then what is humility? Is it self-contempt? Humility is not handsome people trying to believe they are ugly and clever people trying to believe they are slow-witted. False modesty can actually be a cover for pride in one's better-than-average humility. (James Friedrich [1996] reports that most students congratulate themselves on being better than average at not thinking themselves better than average!) True humility is more like self-forgetfulness than false modesty. It leaves people free to rejoice in their special talents and, with the same honesty, to recognize the talents of others.

After just one brief conversation with a prospective employee, interviewers are prone to overconfidence in their intuitive judgments.

- Such perceptions arise partly from a motive to maintain and enhance self-esteem, a motive that protects people from depression but contributes to misjudgment and group conflict.

- Self-serving bias can be adaptive in that it allows us to savour the good things that happen in our lives. When bad things happen, however, self-serving bias can have the maladaptive effect of causing us to blame others or feel cheated out of something we "deserved."

....

● HOW DO PEOPLE MANAGE THEIR SELF-PRESENTATION?

....

Humans seem motivated not only to perceive themselves in self-enhancing ways but also to present themselves favourably to others. How might people's tactics of "impression management" lead to false modesty or to self-defeating behaviour?

So far we have seen that the self is at the centre of our social worlds, that self-esteem and self-efficacy pay dividends, and that self-serving bias influences self-evaluations. But are self-enhancing expressions always sincere? Do people have the same feelings privately as they express publicly? Or are they just putting on a positive face even while living with self-doubt?

SELF-HANDICAPPING

Sometimes, people sabotage their chances for success by creating impediments that make success less likely. Far from being deliberately self-destructive, such behaviours typically have a self-protective aim (Arkin, Lake, & Baumgardner, 1986; Baumeister & Scher, 1988; Rhodewalt, 1987): "I'm really not a failure—I would have done well except for this problem."

Why would people handicap themselves with self-defeating behaviour? Recall that we eagerly protect our self-images by attributing failures to external factors. Can you see why, fearing failure, people might handicap themselves by partying half the night before a job interview or playing video games instead of studying before a big exam? When self-image is tied up with performance, it can be more self-deflating to try hard and fail than to procrastinate and have a ready excuse. If we fail while working under a handicap, we can cling to a sense of competence; if we succeed under such conditions, it can only boost our self-image. Handicaps protect both self-esteem and public image by allowing us to attribute failures to something temporary or external ("I was feeling sick." or "I was out too late the night before.") rather than to lack of talent or ability.

> *"With no attempt there can be no failure; with no failure no humiliation."*
> WILLIAM JAMES, *PRINCIPLES OF PSYCHOLOGY*, 1890

Steve Berglas and Edward Jones (1978) confirmed this analysis of **self-handicapping**. One experiment was announced as concerning "drugs and intellectual performance." Imagine yourself in the position of their participants. You guess answers to some difficult aptitude questions and then are told, "Yours was one of the best scores seen to date!" Feeling incredibly lucky, you are then offered a choice between two drugs before answering more of these items. One drug will aid intellectual performance and the other will inhibit it. Which drug do you want? Most students wanted the drug that would supposedly disrupt their thinking and thus provide a handy excuse for anticipated poorer performance.

self-handicapping protecting one's self-image with behaviours that create a handy excuse for later failure

Researchers have documented other ways in which people self-handicap. Fearing failure, people will do the following:

- Reduce their preparation for important individual athletic events (Rhodewalt, Saltzman, & Wittmer, 1984).
- Give their opponent an advantage (Shepperd & Arkin, 1991).
- Perform poorly at the beginning of a task in order not to create unreachable expectations (Baumgardner & Brownlee, 1987).
- Not try as hard as they could during a tough, ego-involving task (Hormuth, 1986; Pyszczynski & Greenberg, 1987; Riggs, 1992; Turner & Pratkanis, 1993).

IMPRESSION MANAGEMENT

Self-serving bias, false modesty, and self-handicapping reveal the depth of our concern for self-image. To varying degrees, we are continually managing the impressions we create. Whether we wish to impress, to intimidate, or to seem helpless, we are social animals, playing to an audience. So great is the human desire for social acceptance that it can lead people to risk harming themselves through smoking, binge eating, premature sex, or drug and alcohol abuse (Rawn & Vohs, 2011).

self-presentation
the act of expressing yourself and behaving in ways designed to create a favourable impression or an impression that corresponds to your ideals

Self-presentation refers to our wanting to present a desired image both to an external audience (other people) and to an internal audience (ourselves). We work at managing the impressions we create. We excuse, justify, or apologize as necessary to shore up our self-esteem and verify our self-image (Schlenker & Weigold, 1992). Just as we preserve our self-esteem, we also must make sure not to brag too much and risk the disapproval of others (Anderson et al., 2006). Social interaction is a careful balance of looking good while not looking *too* good.

In familiar situations, self-presentation happens without conscious effort. In unfamiliar situations, perhaps at a party with people we would like to impress or in conversation with someone we have romantic interest in, we are acutely self-conscious of the impressions we are creating and we are, therefore, less modest than when among friends who know us well (Leary et al., 1994; Tice et al., 1995). Preparing to present ourselves in a photograph, we may even try out different faces in a mirror. We do so even though active self-presentation depletes energy, which often leads to diminished effectiveness—for example, to less persistence on a tedious experimental task or more difficulty stifling emotional expressions (Vohs, Baumeister, & Ciarocco, 2005). The upside is that self-presentation can unexpectedly improve mood. People feel significantly better than they thought they would after doing their best to "put their best face forward" and concentrate on making a positive impression on their boyfriend or girlfriend. Elizabeth Dunn of the University of British Columbia and her colleagues (2008) concluded that "date nights" for long-term couples work because they encourage active self-presentation, which improves mood.

> *"Public opinion is always more tyrannical towards those who obviously fear it than towards those who feel indifferent to it."*
> BERTRAND RUSSELL, *THE CONQUEST OF HAPPINESS*, 1930

Social networking sites such as Facebook provide a new and sometimes intense venue for self-presentation. They are, according to communications professor Joseph Walther, "like impression management on steroids" (Rosenbloom, 2008). Users make careful decisions about which pictures, activities, and interests to highlight in their profiles. Some even think about how their friends will affect the impression they make on others; one study found that those with more attractive friends were perceived as more attractive themselves (Walther et al., 2008). Given the concern with status and attractiveness on social networking sites, it is not surprising that people high in narcissistic traits thrive on Facebook, tallying up more friends and choosing more attractive pictures of themselves to display (Buffardi & Campbell, 2008).

Given our concern for self-presentation, it's no wonder, say self-presentation researchers, that people will self-handicap when failure might make them look bad. It's no wonder that people take health risks—tanning their skin with wrinkle- and cancer-causing radiation; having piercings or tattoos done without proper hygiene; becoming anorexic; or yielding to peer pressures to smoke, get drunk, and do drugs (Leary et al., 1994). It's no wonder that people express more modesty when their self-flattery is vulnerable to being debunked, perhaps by experts who will be scrutinizing their self-evaluations (Arkin, Appleman, & Burger, 1980; Riess et al., 1981; Weary et al., 1982). Professor Smith will express less confidence in the significance of her work, for example, when presenting it to professional colleagues than when presenting it to students.

> *"It is not, therefore, necessary for a prince to have all the desirable qualities . . . but it is very necessary to seem to have them."*
> NICCOLO MACHIAVELLI, 1469-1527

For some people, conscious self-presentation is a way of life. They continually monitor their own behaviour and note how others react, then adjust their social performance to gain a desired effect. Those who score high on a scale of **self-monitoring** (who, for example, agree that "I tend to be what people expect me to be") act like social chameleons—they adjust their behaviour in response to external situations (Gangestad & Snyder, 2000; Snyder, 1987). Having attuned their behaviour to the situation, they are more likely to espouse attitudes they don't really hold (Zanna & Olson, 1982). Being conscious of others, they are less likely to act on their own attitudes. As Mark Leary (2004b) observed, the self they know often differs from the self they show. As social chameleons, those who score high in self-monitoring are also less committed to their relationships and more likely to be dissatisfied in their marriages (Leone & Hawkins, 2006).

self-monitoring
being attuned to the way you present yourself in social situations and adjusting your performance to create the desired impression

Those who score low in self-monitoring care less about what others think. They are more internally guided and thus more likely to talk and act as they feel and believe (McCann & Hancock, 1983). For example, if asked to list their thoughts about gay couples, they simply express what they think, regardless of the attitudes of their anticipated audience (Klein, Snyder, & Livingston, 2004). As you might imagine, someone who is extremely low in self-monitoring could come across as an insensitive boor, whereas extremely high self-monitoring could result in dishonest behaviour worthy of a con artist. Most of us fall somewhere between those two extremes.

Presenting oneself in ways that create a desired impression is a delicate balancing act. People want to be seen as able, but also as modest and honest (Carlston & Shovar, 1983). In most situations, modesty creates a good impression, unsolicited boasting a bad one (Forsyth, Berger, & Mitchell, 1981; Holtgraves & Srull, 1989; Schlenker & Leary, 1982). Hence the false modesty phenomenon: We often display lower self-esteem than we privately feel (Miller & Schlenker, 1985). But when we have obviously done extremely well, the insincerity of a disclaimer ("I did well, but it's no big deal.") may be evident. To make good impressions—as modest yet competent—requires social skill.

Group identity: In Asian countries, self-presentation is restrained. Children learn to identify themselves with their groups.

Self-presented modesty is greatest in cultures that value self-restraint, such as those of China and Japan (Heine & Lehman, 1995, 1997; Lee & Seligman, 1997; Markus & Kitayama, 1991; Wu & Tseng, 1985). In China and Japan, people exhibit less self-serving bias. Unlike Westerners, who (as we have seen in this chapter) tend to take credit for successes and attribute failures to the situation, Japanese children learn to share credit for success and to accept responsibility for failures. "When I fail, it's my fault, not my group's" is a typical Japanese attitude (Anderson, 1999).

▶ SUMMING UP

SELF-CONCEPT: WHO AM I?

- Our sense of self helps organize our thoughts and actions. Self-concept consists of two elements: the self-schemas that guide our processing of self-relevant information, and the possible selves that we dream of or dread.

- Cultures shape the self, too. Many people in individualistic Western cultures assume an independent self. Others, often in collectivistic cultures, assume a more interdependent self. These contrasting ideas contribute to cultural differences in social behaviour.

- Our self-knowledge is curiously flawed. We often do not know why we behave the way we do. When influences upon our behaviour are not conspicuous enough for any observer to see, we, too, can miss them. The unconscious, implicit processes that control our behaviour may differ from our conscious, explicit explanations of it.

- We also tend to mispredict our emotions. We underestimate the power of our psychological immune systems and thus tend to overestimate the durability of our emotional reactions to significant events.

WHAT IS THE NATURE AND MOTIVATING POWER OF SELF-ESTEEM?

- Self-esteem is the overall sense of self-worth we use to appraise our traits and abilities. Our self-concepts are determined by multiple influences, including the roles we play, the comparisons we make, our social identities, how we perceive others appraising us, and our experiences of success and failure.

- Self-esteem motivation influences our cognitive processes: Facing failure, high-self-esteem people sustain their self-worth by perceiving other people as failing, too, and by exaggerating their superiority over others.

- Although high self-esteem is generally more beneficial than low, researchers have found that people high in both self-esteem and narcissism are the most aggressive. Someone with a big ego who is threatened or deflated by social rejection is potentially aggressive.

WHAT DOES IT MEAN TO HAVE PERCEIVED SELF-CONTROL?

- Our sense of self helps organize our thoughts and actions.

- Our ability to effortfully regulate our behaviour, or willpower, works similarly to muscular strength. It can be exhausted by use in the short term, but can also be strengthened by regular exercise.

- Learned helplessness often occurs when attempts to improve a situation have proven fruitless; self-determination, in contrast, is bolstered by experiences of successfully exercising control and improving one's situation.
- People who believe in their own competence and effectiveness cope better and achieve more than those who have learned a helpless, pessimistic outlook.

WHAT IS SELF-SERVING BIAS?

- Contrary to the presumption that most people suffer from feelings of inferiority, researchers consistently find that most people exhibit a self-serving bias. In experiments and everyday life, we often take credit for successes while blaming failures on the situation.
- Most people rate themselves as better than average on subjective, desirable traits and abilities. We exhibit unrealistic optimism about our futures. And we overestimate the commonality of our opinions and foibles (false consensus) while underestimating the commonality of our abilities and virtues (false uniqueness). We also remember ourselves in the past in ways that flatter the current self.

HOW DO PEOPLE MANAGE THEIR SELF-PRESENTATION?

- As social animals, we adjust our words and actions to suit our audiences. To varying degrees, we self-monitor; we note our performance and adjust it to create the impressions we desire.
- Such impression management tactics explain examples of false modesty, in which people put themselves down, extol future competitors, or publicly credit others when privately they credit themselves.
- Sometimes, people will even self-handicap with self-defeating behaviours that protect self-esteem by providing excuses for failure.
- Self-presentation refers to our wanting to present a favourable image both to an external audience (other people) and to an internal audience (ourselves). With regard to an external audience, those who score high on a scale of self-monitoring adjust their behaviour to each situation, whereas those low in self-monitoring may do so little social adjusting that they seem insensitive.

CHAPTER THREE
Social Beliefs and Judgments

CHAPTER OUTLINE

● HOW DO WE PERCEIVE OUR SOCIAL WORLDS?

● HOW DO WE JUDGE OUR SOCIAL WORLDS?

● HOW DO WE EXPLAIN OUR SOCIAL WORLDS?

● HOW DO OUR EXPECTATIONS OF OUR SOCIAL WORLDS MATTER?

● WHAT CAN WE CONCLUDE FROM RESEARCH ON SOCIAL BELIEFS AND JUDGMENTS?

*I*n June 2010, Canada hosted a G20 summit of world financial leaders. To prepare for the summit, being held at the Metro Toronto Convention Centre, an Integrated Security Unit was formed of police officers and Canadian military personnel. Large segments of downtown Toronto were cordoned off to secure the summit and protect delegates from harm. Then, just prior to the summit, a bank in Ottawa was firebombed by a group of anarchists who threatened to be in Toronto to violently oppose the meeting.

As the summit began, many activist groups gathered in downtown Toronto to protest issues such as poverty, indigenous rights, and capitalism and globalization. A few downtown streets were closed off to accommodate the growing number of protestors. Most of the protests were peaceful. Some individuals, however, began using "black bloc" tactics: They dressed entirely in black, concealed their faces, and vandalized local businesses, broke windows, and set police cruisers on fire.

In response, over the course of the weekend, the Toronto police (as part of the Integrated Security Unit) arrested over 900 people. Many were detained for hours without any charges, including hundreds of citizens who, without warning, were corralled and held in the pouring rain at the corner of Spadina Avenue and Queen Street. Cold, wet, and hungry, without access to bathrooms, most were ultimately released without questioning.

To what should we attribute the police's actions? Should protestors and onlookers have expected such treatment by getting so close to the summit with tensions running high? Were the police simply reacting as best they could to control a complex and perilous situation? Or did they unjustifiably abuse their power, ignoring citizens' rights and treating everyone like "black bloc" hooligans?

These differing reactions illustrate the extent to which we construct social perceptions and beliefs:

- We perceive and recall events through the filters of our own assumptions.
- We judge events, informed by our intuition, by implicit rules that guide our snap judgments, and by our moods.
- We explain events by sometimes attributing them to the situation, sometimes to the person.
- We expect certain events, and our expectation sometimes helps bring them about.

This chapter explores how we perceive, judge, and explain our social worlds, and how—and to what extent—our expectations matter.

● HOW DO WE PERCEIVE OUR SOCIAL WORLDS?

Striking research reveals the extent to which our assumptions and prejudgments can bias our perceptions, interpretations, and recall.

Chapter 1 noted a significant fact about the human mind: that our preconceptions guide how we perceive and interpret information. We construe the world through belief-tinted glasses. "Sure, preconceptions matter," people will agree; yet, they fail to realize how great the effect is.

Let's consider some provocative experiments. The first group of experiments examines how *pre*dispositions and *pre*judgments affect how we perceive and interpret information. The second group plants a judgment in people's minds after they have been given information to study how after-the-fact ideas bias recall. The overarching point: We respond not to reality as it is but to reality as we construe it.

PRIMING

Unattended stimuli can subtly influence how we interpret and recall events. Imagine yourself, during an experiment, wearing earphones and concentrating on ambiguous spoken sentences such as "We stood by the bank." When a pertinent word (*river* or *money*) is simultaneously sent to your other ear, you don't consciously hear it. Yet the word "primes" your interpretation of the sentence (Baars & McGovern, 1994).

Our memory system is a web of associations, and **priming** is the awakening or activating of certain associations. Priming experiments reveal how one thought, even without awareness, can influence another thought, or even an action. John Bargh and his colleagues (1996) asked people to complete sentences containing words such as "old," "wise," and "retired." Shortly after, they observed these people walking more slowly to the elevator than did those not primed with aging-related words. Moreover, the slow walkers had no awareness of their walking speed or of having just viewed words that primed aging. Similarly, fast food can prime impatience (DeVoe, House, & Zhong, 2013; Zhong & DeVoe, 2010). Participants surveyed in front of a fast-food restaurant preferred to receive a smaller amount of money immediately rather than wait for a larger sum, compared to people surveyed at another spot along the same street.

Often, our thinking and acting are primed by events of which we are unaware. In another experiment, Rob Holland and his colleagues (2005) observed that Dutch students exposed to the scent of an all-purpose cleaner were quicker to identify cleaning-related words. In follow-up experiments, other students exposed to a cleaning scent recalled more cleaning-related activities when describing their day's activities and even kept their desks cleaner while eating a crumbly cookie. Moreover, all these effects occurred without the participants' conscious awareness of the scent and its influence.

Priming experiments have their counterparts in everyday life:

* Watching a scary movie alone at home can prime our thinking, by activating emotions that, without our realizing it, cause us to interpret furnace noises as a possible intruder.

* Depressed moods, as this chapter explains later, prime negative associations. But put people in a *good* mood and suddenly their past seems more wonderful, their future brighter.

* For many psychology students, reading about psychological disorders primes how they interpret their own anxieties and gloomy moods. Reading about disease symptoms similarly primes medical students to worry about their congestion, fever, or headache.

In a host of studies, priming effects surface even when the stimuli are presented subliminally—too briefly to be perceived consciously. What's out of sight may not be completely out of mind. An electric shock that is too slight to be felt may increase the perceived intensity of a later shock. An imperceptibly flashed word, "bread," may prime people to detect a related word such as "butter" more quickly than an unrelated word such as "bottle" or "bubble." A subliminal colour name facilitates speedier identification when the colour appears on the computer screen, whereas an unseen wrong name delays colour identification (Epley, Savitsky, & Kachelski, 1999;

priming
activating particular associations in memory

Merikle, Smilek, & Eastwood, 2001). In each case, an invisible image or word primes a response to a later task.

Studies of how implanted ideas and images can prime our interpretations and recall illustrate one of this book's take-home lessons from twenty-first-century social psychology: Much of our social information processing is automatic. It is unintentional, out of sight, and happens without our conscious awareness.

embodied cognition
the mutual influence of bodily sensations on cognitive preferences and social judgments

Even physical sensations, thanks to our **embodied cognition**, prime our social judgments and vice versa. After holding a warm drink, people become more likely to rate someone more warmly and behave more generously (Ijzerman & Semin, 2009; Williams & Bargh, 2008). After receiving a cold shoulder treatment, people judge the experimental room as colder than do those treated warmly (Zhong & Leonardelli, 2008). Physical warmth accentuates social warmth, and social exclusion literally feels cold.

PERCEIVING AND INTERPRETING EVENTS

Despite some startling and oft-confirmed biases and logical flaws in how we perceive and understand one another, we're mostly accurate (Jussim, 2005). Our first impressions of one another are more often right than wrong. Moreover, the better we know people, the more accurately we can read their minds and feelings.

But on occasion, our prejudgments err. The effects of prejudgments and expectations are standard fare for psychology's introductory course. Consider this phrase:

A

BIRD

IN THE

THE HAND

"As I am, so I see."
RALPH WALDO EMERSON, *ESSAYS*

Did you notice anything wrong with it? There is more to perception than meets the eye. The same is true of social perception. Because social perceptions are very much in the eye of the beholder, even a simple stimulus may strike two people quite differently. Saying that Stephen Harper is "an okay prime minister" may sound like a put-down to those who ardently admire him but like praise to those who regard him with contempt. When social information is subject to multiple interpretations, preconceptions matter (Hilton & von Hippel, 1990).

"Once you have a belief, it influences how you perceive all other relevant information. Once you see a country as hostile, you are likely to interpret ambiguous actions on their part as signifying their hostility."
POLITICAL SCIENTIST ROBERT JERVIS (1985)

An experiment by Robert Vallone, Lee Ross, and Mark Lepper (1985) reveals just how powerful preconceptions can be. The researchers showed pro-Israeli and pro-Arab students six network news segments describing the 1982 killing of civilian refugees at two camps in Lebanon. As Figure 3–1 illustrates, each group perceived the networks as hostile to its side.

The phenomenon is commonplace: Sports fans perceive referees as partial to the other side. Presidential candidates and their supporters nearly always view the media as unsympathetic to their cause.

It's not just fans and politicians. People everywhere perceive media and mediators as biased against their position. "There is no subject about which people are less objective than objectivity," noted one media commentator (Poniewozik, 2003). Indeed, people's perceptions of bias

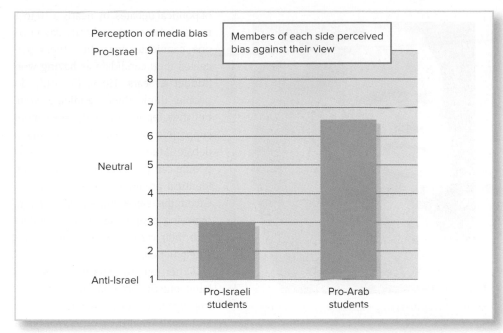

Perception of media bias

Members of each side perceived bias against their view

Pro-Israel 9

8

7

6

Neutral 5

4

3

2

Anti-Israel 1

Pro-Israeli students

Pro-Arab students

FIGURE 3–1

PERCEPTION OF BIAS.

Pro-Israeli and pro-Arab students who viewed network news descriptions of the "Beirut massacre" believed the coverage was biased against their point of view. (Data from Vallone, Ross, & Lepper, 1985)

Supporters of a particular cause or candidate tend to see the media as favouring the other side.

can be used to assess their attitudes (Saucier & Miller, 2003). Tell someone where you see bias, and you will reveal your attitudes.

Our assumptions about the world can even make contradictory evidence seem supportive. For example, Ross and Lepper assisted Charles Lord (1979) in asking students to evaluate the results of two supposedly new research studies. Half the students favoured capital punishment and half opposed it. Of the studies they evaluated, one confirmed and the other disconfirmed the students' beliefs about the deterrent effect of the death penalty. The results: Both proponents and opponents of capital punishment readily accepted evidence that confirmed their belief but were sharply critical of disconfirming evidence. Showing the two sides an identical body of mixed evidence had, therefore, not lessened their disagreement but increased it. Likewise, when Anthony Bastardi and co-researchers (2011) showed people mixed evidence about the effects of daycare on children, those planning to use daycare found the evidence more supportive of their plans.

Is that why, in politics, religion, and science, ambiguous information often fuels conflict? When political debates have no clear-cut winner, they mostly reinforce pre-debate opinions. In one study of three different series

FIGURE 3–2

CRUEL OR KIND?

Judge for yourself: Is this person's expression cruel or kind? If told he was a Nazi, would your reading of his face differ?

of political debates, by nearly a 10-to-1 margin, those who already favoured one candidate over the others perceived their candidate as having won (Kinder & Sears, 1985). Not only do people think their candidate won, but they report becoming even more supportive of them after viewing a debate (Munro et al., 1997). It seems people can perceive and interpret the identical arguments quite differently. Given the same mixed information, opposing people can each assimilate it to their views and find their views strengthened.

Other experiments have manipulated preconceptions with astonishing effects on how people interpret and recall what they observe. Myron Rothbart and Pamela Birrell (1977) had students assess the facial expression of a man (Figure 3–2). Those told he was a Gestapo leader responsible for barbaric medical experiments on concentration camp inmates during the Second World War intuitively judged his expression as cruel. (Can you see that barely suppressed sneer?) Those told he was a leader in the anti-Nazi underground movement whose courage saved thousands of Jewish lives judged his facial expression as warm and kind. (Just look at those caring eyes and that almost smiling mouth.)

Filmmakers control people's perceptions of emotion by manipulating the setting in which they see a face. They call this the "Kulechov effect," after a Russian film director who would skillfully guide viewers' inferences by manipulating their assumptions. Kulechov demonstrated the phenomenon by creating three short films that presented identical footage of the face of an actor with a neutral expression after viewers had first been shown one of three scenes: a dead woman, a dish of soup, or a girl playing. As a result, in the first film, the actor seemed sad, in the second thoughtful, and in the third happy.

Construal processes also colour others' perceptions of us. When we say something good or bad about someone else, people will tend to associate that trait with us, reported Lynda Mae, Donal Carlston, and John Skowronski (1999; Carlston & Skowronski, 2005)—a phenomenon they called *spontaneous trait transference*. If we go around talking about others being gossipy, people may then unconsciously associate "gossip" with us. Call someone a jerk and folks may later construe *you* as one. Describe someone as sensitive, loving, and compassionate, and you may seem more so. There is, it appears, intuitive wisdom in the childhood taunt, "I'm rubber, you're glue; what you say bounces off me and sticks to you."

"The error of our eye directs our mind: What error leads must err."
SHAKESPEARE, *TROILUS AND CRESSIDA*, 1601–1602

The bottom line: We view our social worlds through the spectacles of our beliefs, attitudes, and values. This is one reason our beliefs and schemas are so important; they shape our interpretation of everything else.

BELIEF PERSEVERANCE

Imagine a babysitter who decides, during an evening with a crying infant, that bottle-feeding produces colicky babies: "Come to think of it, cow's milk obviously better suits calves than babies." If the infant turns out to be suffering a high fever, will the sitter nevertheless persist in believing that bottle-feeding causes colic (Ross & Anderson, 1982)?

To find out, Craig Anderson, Lee Ross, and their colleagues (1980) planted a falsehood in people's minds and then tried to discredit it. Their experiments reveal that it is surprisingly difficult to demolish a falsehood, once the person conjures up a rationale for it. Each experiment first implanted a belief, either by proclaiming that it was true or by showing the participants some anecdotal evidence. Then the participants were asked to explain *why* it is true. Finally, the researchers totally discredited the initial information by telling the person the truth: The information was manufactured for the experiment, and half the people in the experiment had received opposite information. Nevertheless, the new belief survived about 75 percent intact, presumably because the participants still retained their invented explanations for the belief. This phenomenon, named **belief perseverance**, shows that beliefs can take on a life of their own and survive the discrediting of the evidence that inspired them.

An example: Anderson, Lepper, and Ross (1980) asked people to decide whether people who take risks make good or bad firefighters. One group considered a risk-prone person who was a successful firefighter and a cautious person who was an unsuccessful one. The other group considered cases suggesting the opposite conclusion. After forming their theory that risk-prone people make better or worse firefighters, the individuals wrote explanations for it—for example, that risk-prone people are brave or that cautious people are careful. Once formed, each explanation could exist independently of the information that initially created the belief. When that information was discredited, the people still held their self-generated explanations and, therefore, continued to believe that risk-prone people really *do* make better or worse firefighters.

These experiments also show that the more we examine our theories and explain how they *might* be true, the more closed we become to information that challenges our belief. Once we consider why an accused person might be guilty, why someone of whom we have a negative first impression acts that way, or why a favoured stock might rise in value, our explanations may survive challenges (Davies, 1997; Jelalian & Miller, 1984).

The evidence is compelling: Our beliefs and expectations powerfully affect how we mentally construct events. Usually, we benefit from our preconceptions, just as scientists benefit from creating theories that guide them in noticing and interpreting events. But the benefits sometimes entail a

> *"We hear and apprehend only what we already half know."*
> HENRY DAVID THOREAU, 1817–1862

belief perseverance persistence of your initial conceptions, as when the basis for your belief is discredited but an explanation of why the belief might be true survives

Do people who take risks make the best firefighters? Or the worst?

> "No one denies that new evidence can change people's beliefs. Children do eventually renounce their belief in Santa Claus. Our contention is simply that such changes generally occur slowly, and that more compelling evidence is often required to alter a belief than to create it."
>
> LEE ROSS & MARK LEPPER (1980)

cost: We become prisoners of our own thought patterns. Thus, the "canals" that were so often seen on Mars turned out to be the product of intelligent life—an intelligence on earth's side of the telescope.

Is there a remedy for belief perseverance? There is: Explain the opposite. Charles Lord, Mark Lepper, and Elizabeth Preston (1984) repeated the capital punishment study described earlier and added two variations. First, they asked some of their subjects when evaluating the evidence to be "as *objective* and *unbiased* as possible." It was to no avail; whether for or against capital punishment, those who received this plea made evaluations as biased as those who had not.

The researchers asked a third group of subjects to consider the opposite—to ask themselves "whether you would have made the same high or low evaluations had exactly the same study produced results on the *other* side of the issue." After imagining an opposite finding, these people were much less biased in their evaluations of the evidence for and against their views. In his experiments, Craig Anderson (1982; Anderson & Sechler, 1986) consistently found that explaining why an opposite theory might be true—why a cautious rather than a risk-taking person might be a better firefighter—reduces or eliminates belief perseverance. Indeed, explaining *any* alternative outcome, not just the opposite, drives people to ponder various possibilities (Hirt & Markman, 1995).

CONSTRUCTING MEMORIES OF OURSELVES AND OUR WORLDS

Do you agree or disagree with this statement?

Memory can be likened to a storage chest in the brain into which we deposit material and from which we can withdraw it later if needed. Occasionally, something is lost from the "chest," and then we say we have forgotten.

About 85 percent of university students surveyed agreed (Lamal, 1979). As one magazine ad put it, "Science has proven the accumulated experience of a lifetime is preserved perfectly in your mind."

Actually, psychological research has proved the opposite. Many memories are not copies of experiences that remain on deposit in a memory bank. Rather, we construct memories at the time of withdrawal. Like a paleontologist inferring the appearance of a dinosaur from bone fragments, we reconstruct our distant past by using our current feelings and expectations to combine fragments of information (Hirt, 1990; Ross & Buehler, 1994). Thus, we can easily (though unconsciously) revise our memories to suit our current knowledge. When one of the authors' sons complained, "The June issue of *Cricket* never came," and was then shown where it was, he delightedly responded, "Oh good, I knew I'd gotten it."

> "Memory isn't like reading a book: it's more like writing a book from fragmentary notes."
>
> JOHN F. KIHLSTROM, 1994

When an experimenter or a therapist manipulates people's presumptions about their past, a sizable fraction will construct false memories. Asked to vividly imagine a childhood time when they ran, tripped, fell, and stuck their hand through a window, or a time when they knocked over a punch bowl at a wedding, about one-fourth will later recall the fictitious event as something that actually happened (Loftus & Bernstein, 2005). In its search for truth, the mind sometimes constructs a falsehood.

In experiments involving more than 20 000 people, Elizabeth Loftus (2003, 2007) and her collaborators explored our mind's tendency to construct memories. In the typical experiment, people witnessed an event, received misleading information about it (or not), and then took a memory test. The repeated finding was the **misinformation effect**. People incorporate the misinformation into their memories: They recall a yield sign as a stop sign, hammers as screwdrivers, *Vogue* magazine as *Mademoiselle*, Dr. Henderson as "Dr. Davidson," breakfast cereal as eggs, and a clean-shaven man as a fellow with a moustache. Suggested misinformation may even produce false memories of supposed child sexual abuse, argued Loftus.

This process affects our recall of social as well as physical events. Jack Croxton and his colleagues (1984) had students spend 15 minutes talking with someone. Those later informed that this person reported liking them recalled the person's behaviour as relaxed, comfortable, and happy. Those informed that the person disliked them recalled the person as nervous, uncomfortable, and not so happy.

Reconstructing past attitudes

Five years ago, how did you feel about nuclear power? About Canada's prime minister? About your parents? If your attitudes have changed, what do you think is the extent of the change?

Experimenters have tried to answer such questions, and the results have been unnerving. People whose attitudes have changed often insist that they have always felt much as they now feel. Daryl Bem and Keith McConnell (1970) conducted a survey to test these ideas among students at their university. Buried in it was a question concerning student control over the university curriculum. A week later, the students agreed to write an essay opposing student control. After doing so, their attitudes shifted toward greater opposition to student control. When asked to recall how they had answered the question before writing the essay, they "remembered" holding the opinion that they *now* held and denied that the experiment had affected them.

After observing students similarly denying their former attitudes, researchers D. R. Wixon and James Laird (1976) commented, "The speed, magnitude, and certainty" with which the students revised their own histories "was striking." As George Vaillant (1977, p. 197) noted after following adults through time, "It is all too common for caterpillars to become butterflies and then to maintain that in their youth they had been little butterflies. Maturation makes liars of us all."

The construction of positive memories does brighten our recollections. Terence Mitchell, Leigh Thompson, and their colleagues (1994, 1997) reported that people often exhibit *rosy retrospection*—they recall mildly pleasant events more favourably than they experienced them. University students on a three-week bike trip, older adults on a guided tour of Austria, and undergraduates on vacation all reported enjoying their experiences as they have them. But they later recalled such experiences even more fondly, minimizing the unpleasant or boring aspects and remembering the high points. Thus, the pleasant times during which one of the authors has sojourned in Scotland he now (back in his office facing deadlines and interruptions) romanticizes as pure bliss. With any positive experience, some of the pleasure resides in the anticipation, some in the actual experience, and some in the rosy retrospection.

misinformation effect incorporating "misinformation" into one's memory of the event, after witnessing an event and then receiving misleading information about it

"A man should never be ashamed to own that he has been in the wrong, which is but saying, in other words, that he is wiser today than he was yesterday."
JONATHAN SWIFT, *THOUGHTS ON VARIOUS SUBJECTS*, 1711

"Travel is glamorous only in retrospect."
PAUL THEROUX, IN *THE OBSERVER*

Cathy McFarland and Michael Ross (1985) found that we also revise our recollections of other people as our relationships with them change. They had university students rate their steady dating partners. Two months later, they rated them again. Students who were more in love than ever had a tendency to recall love at first sight. Those who had broken up were more likely to recall having recognized the partner as somewhat selfish and bad-tempered.

Diane Holmberg and John Holmes (1994) discovered the same phenomenon among 373 newlywed couples, most of whom reported being very happy. When resurveyed two years later, those whose marriages had soured recalled that things had always been bad. The results are "frightening," said Holmberg and Holmes: "Such biases can lead to a dangerous downward spiral. The worse your current view of your partner is, the worse your memories are, which only further confirms your negative attitudes."

> "Vanity plays lurid tricks with our memory."
> NOVELIST JOSEPH CONRAD, 1857–1924

It's not that we are totally unaware of how we used to feel, just that when memories are hazy, current feelings guide our recall. Parents of every generation bemoan the values of the next generation, partly because they misrecall their youthful values as being closer to their current values.

Unlike photos, memories get reconstructed when withdrawn from the memory bank.

Reconstructing past behaviour

Memory construction enables us to revise our own histories. Michael Ross, Cathy McFarland, and Garth Fletcher (1981) exposed some students to a message convincing them of the desirability of toothbrushing. Later, in a supposedly different experiment, these students recalled brushing their teeth more often during the preceding two weeks than did students who had not heard the message. Likewise, projecting from surveys, people reported smoking many fewer cigarettes than were actually sold (Hall, 1985). And they recalled casting more votes than were actually recorded (Census Bureau, 1993).

Social psychologist Anthony Greenwald (1980) noted the similarity of such findings to happenings in George Orwell's novel *1984*, in which it was "necessary to remember that events happened in the desired manner." Indeed, argued Greenwald, we all have "totalitarian egos" that revise the past to suit our present views. Thus, we under-report bad behaviour and over-report good behaviour.

Sometimes, our present view is that we've improved—in which case we may misrecall our past as more unlike the present than it actually was. This tendency resolves a puzzling pair of consistent findings: Those who participate in psychotherapy and self-improvement programs for weight control, anti-smoking, and exercise show only modest improvement on average. Yet they often claim considerable benefit (Myers, 2010). Michael Conway and Michael Ross (1985, 1986) explained why: Having expended so much time, effort, and money on self-improvement, people may think, "I may not be perfect now, but I was worse before; this did me a lot of good."

● HOW DO WE JUDGE OUR SOCIAL WORLDS?

As we have already noted, our cognitive mechanisms are efficient and adaptive, yet occasionally error-prone. Usually they serve us well, but sometimes clinicians misjudge patients, employers misjudge employees, people of one race misjudge people of another, and spouses misjudge their mates. The results are misdiagnoses, labour strife, prejudices, and divorces. So, how—and how well—do we make intuitive social judgments?

When historians describe social psychology's first century, they will surely record the last 30 years as the era of social cognition. By drawing upon advances in cognitive psychology—in how people perceive, represent, and remember events—social psychologists have shed welcome light on how we form impressions. Let's look at what this research reveals of the marvels and mistakes of our social judgments.

When historians describe social psychology's first century, they will surely record 1980 to 2010 as the era of social cognition. By drawing on advances in cognitive psychology—in how people perceive, represent, and remember events—social psychologists have shed welcome light on how we form judgments. Let's look at what the research reveals about the marvels and mistakes of our social intuition.

① INTUITIVE JUDGMENTS

What are our powers of intuition—of immediately knowing something without reasoning or analysis? Advocates of "intuitive management" believe we should tune into our hunches. When judging others, they say, we should plug into the nonlogical smarts of our "right brain." When hiring, firing, and investing, we should listen to our premonitions. In making judgments, we should trust the force within.

Are the intuitionists correct that important information is immediately available apart from our conscious analysis? Or are the skeptics right in saying that intuition is "our knowing we are right, whether we are or not"?

Priming research suggests that the unconscious indeed controls much of our behaviour. As John Bargh and Tanya Chartrand (1999) explained, "Most of a person's everyday life is determined not by their conscious intentions and deliberate choices but by mental processes that are put into motion by features of the environment and that operate outside of conscious awareness and guidance." When the light turns red, we react and hit the brake before consciously deciding to do so. Indeed, reflected Neil Macrae and Lucy Johnston (1998), "to be able to do just about anything at all (e.g., driving, dating, dancing), action initiation needs to be decoupled from the inefficient (i.e., slow, serial, resource consuming) workings of the conscious mind, otherwise inaction inevitably would prevail."

The powers of intuition

"The heart has its reasons which reason does not know," observed seventeenth-century philosopher–mathematician Blaise Pascal. Three centuries later, scientists have proved Pascal correct. We know more than we know we know. Studies of our unconscious information processing confirm our limited access to what's going on in our minds (Bargh, 1997; Greenwald & Banaji, 1995; Strack & Deutsch, 2004). Our thinking is partly **controlled processing** (reflective,

controlled processing explicit thinking that is deliberate, reflective, and conscious

deliberate, and conscious) and—more than psychologists once supposed—partly **automatic processing** (impulsive, effortless, and without our awareness). Automatic, intuitive thinking occurs not "on-stage" but "off-stage," out of sight, where reason does not go. Consider these examples of automatic thinking:

- *Schemas*—mental templates—intuitively guide our perceptions and interpretations of our experience. Whether we hear someone speaking of religious *sects* or *sex* depends not only on the word spoken but also on how we automatically interpret the sound.

- *Emotional reactions* are often nearly instantaneous, before there is time for deliberate thinking. One neural shortcut takes information from the eye or ear to the brain's sensory switchboard (the thalamus) and out to its emotional control centre (the amygdala) before the thinking cortex has had any chance to intervene (LeDoux, 1994, 1996). Our ancestors who intuitively feared a sound in the bushes were usually fearing nothing, but they were more likely to survive to pass their genes down to us than their more deliberative cousins.

- Given sufficient *expertise,* people may intuitively know the answer to a problem. Master chess players intuitively recognize meaningful patterns that novices miss and often make their next move with only a glance at the board, as the situation cues information stored in their memory. Similarly, without knowing quite how, we recognize a friend's voice after the first spoken word of a phone conversation.

- Faced with a decision but lacking the expertise to make an informed snap judgment, our unconscious thinking may guide us toward a satisfying choice. That's what University of Amsterdam psychologist Ap Dijksterhuis and his collaborators (2006a, 2006b) discovered after showing people, for example, a dozen pieces of information about each of four potential apartments. Compared to people who made instant decisions or were given time to analyze the information, the most satisfying decisions were made by those who were distracted and unable to focus consciously on the problem. Although these findings are controversial (Gonzalez-Vallejo et al., 2008; Newell et al., 2008), this much seems true: When facing a tough decision, it often pays to take our time—even to sleep on it—and await the intuitive result of our out-of-sight information processing.

Some things—facts, names, and past experiences—we remember explicitly (consciously). But other things—skills and conditioned dispositions—we remember *implicitly,* without consciously knowing or declaring that we know. It's true of us all, but most strikingly evident in people with brain damage who cannot form new explicit memories. One such person never could learn to recognize her physician, who would need to reintroduce himself with a handshake each day. One day, the physician affixed a tack to his hand, causing the patient to jump with pain. When the physician next returned, he was still unrecognized (explicitly). But the patient, retaining an implicit memory, would not shake his hand.

Equally dramatic are the cases of *blindsight.* Having lost a portion of the visual cortex to surgery or stroke, people may be functionally blind in part of their field of vision. Shown a series of sticks in the blind field, they reported seeing nothing. When asked to guess whether the sticks were vertical or horizontal, the patients, remarkably, got them all right. Like the patient who "remembered" the painful handshake, these people knew more than they know they know.

Subliminal stimuli, as we have already noted, can have intriguing effects. Consider the following study: Mark Baldwin of McGill University and his colleagues (1989) had Catholic women read a sexually explicit passage and then subliminally flashed either a picture of the Pope frowning, a picture

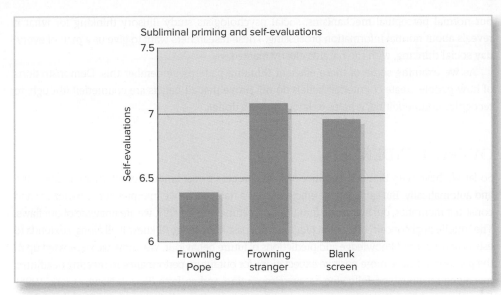

Subliminal priming and self-evaluations

FIGURE 3-3

SUBLIMINAL PRIMING AND SELF-EVALUATIONS.

Catholic students primed with a subliminal picture of the Pope frowning rated themselves lower on a number of traits. (Data from Baldwin, Carrell, & Lopez, 1989)

of a stranger frowning, or a blank screen. As you can see in Figure 3-3, the women subsequently reported lower self-esteem if they were exposed to the frowning Pope. This effect was particularly pronounced for women who reported being more devout Catholics. Even outside awareness, the image of a disapproving Pope made these women feel worse after reading a steamy passage.

So, many routine cognitive functions occur automatically, unintentionally, without awareness. We might remember how automatic processing helps us get through life by picturing our minds as functioning like big corporations. Our CEO—our controlled consciousness—attends to many of the most important, complex, and novel issues, while subordinates deal with routine affairs and matters requiring instant action. This delegation of resources enables us to react to many situations quickly and efficiently. The bottom line: Our brain knows much more than it tells us.

The limits of intuition

We have seen how automatic, intuitive thinking can "make us smart" (Gigerenzer, 2007). Elizabeth Loftus and Mark Klinger (1992), nevertheless, spoke for other cognitive scientists in having doubts about the brilliance of intuition. They reported "a general consensus that the unconscious may not be as smart as previously believed." For example, although subliminal stimuli can trigger a weak, fleeting response—enough to evoke a feeling if not conscious awareness—there is no evidence that commercial subliminal tapes can "reprogram your unconscious mind" for success. In fact, a significant body of evidence indicates that they can't (Greenwald, 1992).

Social psychologists have explored not only our error-prone hindsight judgments but also our capacity for illusion—for perceptual misinterpretations, fantasies, and constructed beliefs. Michael Gazzaniga (1992, 1998, 2008) reported that patients whose brain hemispheres have been surgically separated will instantly fabricate—and believe—explanations of their own puzzling behaviours. If the patient gets up and takes a few steps after the experimenter flashes the instruction "walk" to the patient's nonverbal right hemisphere, the verbal left hemisphere will instantly provide the patient with a plausible explanation ("I felt like getting a drink").

Illusory thinking also appears in the vast new literature on how we take in, store, and retrieve social information. As perception researchers study visual illusions for what they reveal about

ILLUSORY THINKING

our normal perceptual mechanisms, social psychologists study illusory thinking for what it reveals about normal information processing. These researchers want to give us a map of everyday social thinking, with the hazards clearly marked.

As we examine some of these efficient thinking patterns, remember this: Demonstrations of how people create counterfeit beliefs do not prove that all beliefs are counterfeit (though, to recognize counterfeiting, it helps to know how it's done).

OVERCONFIDENCE

So far we have seen that our cognitive systems process a vast amount of information efficiently and automatically. But our adaptive efficiency has a trade-off; as we interpret our experiences and construct memories, our automatic intuitions sometimes err. Usually, we are unaware of our flaws. The "intellectual conceit" evident in judgments of past knowledge ("I knew it all along") extends to estimates of current knowledge and predictions of future behaviour. We know we've messed up in the past. But we have more positive expectations for our future performance in meeting deadlines, managing relationships, following an exercise routine, and so forth (Ross & Newby-Clark, 1998). Even thinking of realistic obstacles to exercising did not dissuade University of Guelph students from predicting that they would exercise more in the coming month (Newby-Clark, 2005).

overconfidence phenomenon
the tendency to be more confident than correct—to overestimate the accuracy of one's beliefs

To explore this **overconfidence phenomenon**, Daniel Kahneman and Amos Tversky (1979) gave people factual questions and asked them to fill in the blanks, as in the following: "I feel 98 percent certain that the air distance between New Delhi and Beijing is more than ____ miles but less than ____ miles." Most subjects were overconfident: About 30 percent of the time, the correct answer lay outside the range they felt 98 percent confident about.

To find out whether overconfidence extends to social judgments, David Dunning and his associates (1990) created a little game show. They asked students to guess a stranger's answers to a series of questions, such as "Would you prepare for a difficult exam alone or with others?" and "Would you rate your lecture notes as neat or messy?" Knowing the type but not the actual questions, the subjects first interviewed their target person about background, hobbies, academic interests, aspirations, astrological sign—anything they thought might be helpful. Then, while the targets privately answered 20 of the two-choice questions, the interviewers predicted their target's answers and rated their own confidence in the predictions.

The interviewers guessed right 63 percent of the time, beating chance by 13 percent. But, on average, they *felt* 75 percent sure of their predictions. When guessing their own roommates' responses, they were 68 percent correct and 78 percent confident. Moreover, the most confident people were most likely to be *over*confident. People are also markedly overconfident when judging whether someone is telling the truth, or when estimating such things as the sexual history of their dating partner or the activity preferences of their roommates (DePaulo et al., 1997; Swann & Gill, 1997).

Ironically, incompetence feeds overconfidence. It takes competence to recognize what competence is, noted Justin Kruger and David Dunning (1999). Students who score at the bottom on tests of grammar, humour, and logic are most prone to overestimating their gifts at such. Those who don't know what good logic or grammar is are often unaware that they lack it. If you make a list of all the words you can form out of the letters in "psychology," you may feel brilliant—but then stupid when a friend starts naming the ones you missed. Deanna Caputo and Dunning (2005) recreated this phenomenon in experiments, confirming that our ignorance of our

DOONESBURY © 2000
G. B. Trudeau. Reprinted
with permission of
Universal Press Syndicate.
All rights reserved.

ignorance sustains our self-confidence. Follow-up studies indicate that this "ignorance of one's incompetence" occurs mostly on relatively easy-seeming tasks, such as forming words out of "psychology." On really hard tasks, poor performers more often appreciate their lack of skill (Burson et al., 2006).

Ignorance of one's own incompetence helps explain Dunning's (2005) startling conclusion from employee assessment studies that "what others see in us. . . tends to be more highly correlated with objective outcomes than what we see in ourselves." In one study, participants watched someone walk into a room, sit, read a weather report, and walk out (Borkenau & Liebler, 1993). Based on nothing more than that, their estimate of the person's intelligence correlated with the person's intelligence score (.30) about as well as did the person's own self-estimate (.32)! If ignorance can beget false confidence, then—yikes!—where, we may ask, are you and I unknowingly deficient?

In Chapter 2, we noted how poorly people overestimate their long-term emotional responses to good and bad happenings. Are people better at predicting their own *behaviour?* To find out, Robert Vallone and his colleagues (1990) had university students predict in September whether they would drop a course, declare a major, elect to live off campus next year, and so forth. Although the students felt, on average, 84 percent sure of these self-predictions, they were wrong nearly twice as often as they expected to be. Even when feeling 100 percent sure of their predictions, they erred 15 percent of the time.

Part of the problem is that people may often give too much weight to their current intentions when predicting their future behaviour (Koehler & Poon, 2006; Koehler, White, & John, 2011). When University of Waterloo students predicted whether they would donate blood, they relied heavily on their intentions to do so. But their intentions did not predict their actual donations well. The students failed to appreciate how much their busy schedules, looming deadlines, or simple forgetfulness would get in the way of donating.

THE >>> INSIDE STORY

As a graduate student, I noticed something peculiar about my work-related predictions. Most evenings, I would stuff my briefcase with work to complete at home and then return the following day with much of it untouched. Yet each time I packed that briefcase, I was sure my plans were realistic. In my Ph.D. dissertation and subsequent research (conducted with Dale Griffin and Michael Ross), I have addressed two related questions: Why do people often underestimate how long it will take to finish tasks? Why don't people learn from past experience and adjust their estimates accordingly? The findings suggest that people's unwarranted optimism stems in part from a desire to finish projects promptly and in part from the thought processes that they naturally engage in to generate predictions. People tend to focus narrowly on their plans for completing the task at hand and consequently dismiss other valuable sources of information, such as how long similar tasks have taken in the past. These research

insights have, unfortunately, had little impact on my own predictions, and I'm still lugging around an overweight briefcase.

Roger Buehler *Wilfrid Laurier University*

In estimating their chances for success on a task, such as a major exam, people's confidence runs highest when removed in time from "the moment of truth." By exam day, the possibility of failure looms larger and confidence typically drops (Gilovich, Kerr, & Medvec, 1993). Roger Buehler and his colleagues (1994, 2010) reported that most students also confidently underestimated how long it would take them to complete papers and other major assignments and overestimated how much money they would save in coming weeks (Peetz & Buehler, 2009). They are not alone:

- Planners routinely underestimate the time and expense of projects. In 1969, Montreal Mayor Jean Drapeau proudly announced that a $120-million stadium with a retractable roof would be built for the 1976 Olympics. The roof was completed in 1989 and cost $120 million by itself.

- Investment experts market their services with the confident presumption that they can beat the stock market average, forgetting that for every stockbroker or buyer saying "Sell!" at a given price there is another saying "Buy!" A stock's price is the balance point between these mutually confident judgments. Thus, incredible as it may seem, economist Burton Malkiel (1985, 1995) reported that mutual fund portfolios selected by investment analysts had not outperformed randomly selected stocks.

- Overconfident decision-makers can wreak havoc. It was a confident Adolf Hitler who from 1939 to 1945 waged war against the rest of Europe. In 1812, it was a confident James Madison who led the newly formed United States into a war to take over Upper Canada.

What produces overconfidence? Why does experience not lead us to a more real-istic self-appraisal? For one thing, people tend to recall their mistaken judgments as times when they were *almost* right. Phillip Tetlock (1998, 1999, 2005) observed this after inviting various academic and government experts to project—from their view-point in the late 1980s—the future governance of the Soviet Union, South Africa, and Canada. Five years later, communism had collapsed, South Africa had become a multiracial democracy, and Quebec had not seceded from Canada. Experts who had felt more than 80 percent confident were right in predicting these turns of events less than 40 percent of the time. Yet, reflecting on their judgments, those who erred believed they were still basically right. I was "almost right," said many. "The hardliners almost succeeded in their coup attempt against Gorbachev." "The Québécois separatists almost won the secessionist referendum." "But for the coincidence of de Klerk and Mandela, there would have been a lot bloodier transition to black majority rule in South Africa." Among politi-cal experts—and stock market forecasters, mental health workers, and sports prognosticators—overconfidence is hard to dislodge.

> *"When you know a thing, to hold that you know it; and when you do not know a thing, to allow that you do not know it; this is knowledge."*
> CONFUCIUS, *ANALECTS*

Confirmation bias

People also tend not to seek information that might disprove what they believe. P. C. Wason (1960) demonstrated this, as you can, by giving people a sequence of three numbers—2, 4, 6 —that conformed to a rule he had in mind (the rule was simply *any three ascending numbers*). To enable the people to discover the rule, Wason invited each person to generate sets of three num-bers. Each time, Wason told the person whether or not the set conformed to his rule. When they were sure they had discovered the rule, the people were to stop and announce it.

The result? Seldom right but never in doubt: 23 of the 29 people convinced themselves of a wrong rule. They typically formed some erroneous belief about the rule (for example, counting by twos) and then searched for *confirming* evidence (for example, by testing 8, 10, 12) rather than attempting to *disconfirm* their hunches. We are eager to verify our beliefs but less inclined to seek evidence that might disprove them. We call this phenomenon the **confirmation bias**.

confirmation bias
a tendency to search for information that confirms one's preconceptions

Confirmation helps explain why our self-images are so remarkably stable. In several experi-ments, William Swann and Stephen Read (1981; Swann et al., 1992a, 1992b, 2007) discovered that students seek, elicit, and recall feedback that confirms their beliefs about themselves. People seek as friends and spouses those who bolster their own self-views—even if they think poorly of themselves (Swann et al., 1991, 2003).

Swann and Read liken this *self-verification* to how someone with a domineering self-image might behave at a party. Upon arriving, the person seeks those guests whom she knows acknowledge her dominance. In conversation, she then presents her views in ways that elicit the respect she expects. After the party, she has trouble recalling conversations in which her influence was minimal and more easily recalls her persuasiveness in the conversations that she dominated. Thus her experience at the party confirms her self-image.

Remedies for overconfidence

What lessons can we draw from research on overconfidence? One lesson is to be careful about other people's dogmatic statements. Even when people seem sure they are right, they may be wrong. Confidence and competence need not coincide.

Three techniques have successfully reduced the overconfidence bias. One is prompt feedback (Lichtenstein & Fischhoff, 1980). In everyday life, weather forecasters and those who set the odds in horse racing both receive clear, daily feedback. Experts in both groups, therefore, do quite well at estimating their probable accuracy (Fischhoff, 1982).

To reduce "planning fallacy" overconfidence, people can be asked to "unpack" a task—to break it into its subcomponents—and estimate the time required for each. Justin Kruger and Matt Evans (2004) reported that doing so led to more realistic estimates of completion time.

When people think about why an idea might be true, it begins to seem true (Koehler, 1991). Thus, a third way to reduce overconfidence is to get people to think of one good reason why their judgments might be wrong: Force them to consider disconfirming information (Koriat, Lichtenstein, & Fischhoff, 1980). Managers might foster more realistic judgments by insisting that all proposals and recommendations include reasons why they might not work.

Still, we should be careful not to undermine people's self-confidence to a point where they spend too much time in self-analysis or where self-doubts begin to cripple decisiveness. In times when their wisdom is needed, those lacking self-confidence may shrink from speaking up or making tough decisions. Overconfidence can cost us, but realistic self-confidence is adaptive.

HEURISTICS: MENTAL SHORTCUTS

heuristics
a thinking strategy that enables quick, efficient judgments

With precious little time to process so much information, our cognitive system specializes in mental shortcuts. With remarkable ease, we form impressions, make judgments, and invent explanations. We do so by using **heuristics**—simple, efficient thinking strategies. In many situations, our snap generalizations—"That's dangerous!"—are adaptive. Their speed promotes our survival. The biological purpose of thinking is less to make us right than to keep us alive. In some situations, however, haste makes error.

Representativeness heuristic

Suppose a panel of psychologists interviewed a sample of 30 engineers and 70 lawyers and summarized their impressions in thumbnail descriptions. The following description, they were told, was drawn at random from the sample of 30 engineers and 70 lawyers:

> Twice divorced, Frank spends most of his free time hanging around the country club. His clubhouse bar conversations often centre on his regrets at having tried to follow his esteemed father's footsteps. The long hours he had spent at academic drudgery would have been better invested in learning how to be less quarrelsome in his relations with other people. *Question:* What is the probability that Frank is a lawyer rather than an engineer?

representativeness heuristic
the tendency to presume, sometimes despite contrary odds, that someone or something belongs to a particular group if resembling (representing) a typical member

Asked to guess Frank's occupation, more than 80 percent of students surmised he was one of the lawyers (Fischhoff & Bar-Hillel, 1984). Fair enough. But how do you suppose their estimates changed when the sample description was changed to say that 70 percent were engineers? Not in the slightest. The students took no account of the base rate of engineers and lawyers; in their minds, Frank was more *representative* of lawyers, and that was all that seemed to matter.

To judge something by intuitively comparing it to our mental representation of a category is to use the **representativeness heuristic**. Heuristics are implicit rules of thumb. Like most heuristics, representativeness usually is a reasonable guide to reality. But not always. Consider Linda, who is 31, single, outspoken, and very bright. She majored in philosophy in university. As a student, she was deeply concerned with discrimination and other social issues, and she participated in anti-nuclear demonstrations. Based on this description, which would you say it is more likely?

a. Linda is a bank teller.

b. Linda is a bank teller and active in the feminist movement.

Most people think *b* is more likely, partly because Linda better *represents* their image of feminists. Consider: Is there a better chance that Linda is *both* a bank teller *and* a feminist than that she's a bank teller (whether feminist or not)? As Amos Tversky and Daniel Kahneman (1983) remind us, the conjunction of two events can't be more likely than either event alone.

Availability heuristic

Consider: Do more people live in Iraq or in Tanzania?

You probably answered in terms of how readily Iraqis and Tanzanians come to mind. If examples are readily *available* in our memory—as Iraqis may tend to be—then we presume that the event is commonplace. Usually it is, so we are often well served by this cognitive rule, called the **availability heuristic**. Said simply, the more easily we can recall something, the more likely it seems.

But sometimes the rule deludes us. If people hear a list of famous people of one sex (Oprah Winfrey, Lady Gaga, Margaret Atwood) intermixed with an equal size list of unfamous people of the other sex (Donald Scarr, William Wood, Mel Jasper), the famous names will later be more cognitively available. Most people will, therefore, recall having heard more (in this instance) women's names (McKelvie, 1995, 1997; Tversky & Kahneman, 1973). Likewise, media attention to gay–lesbian issues makes gays and lesbians cognitively available. Thus, the average person in one survey estimated that 25 percent of people are gay or lesbian (Morales, 2011)—some seven times the number who, in surveys, actually self-identify as gay, lesbian, or bisexual (Gates, 2011).

Even fictional happenings in novels, television, and movies leave images that later penetrate our judgments (Gerrig & Prentice, 1991; Green, Strange, & Brock, 2002). The more absorbed and "transported" the reader ("I could easily picture the events"), the more the story affects the reader's later beliefs (Diekman, McDonald, & Gardner, 2000). Readers who are captivated by romance novels, for example, may gain readily available sexual scripts that influence their own sexual attitudes and behaviours.

In one clever experiment that demonstrates the availability heuristic, Norbert Schwarz and his colleagues (1991) had students list either 12 times they had been assertive or 6 times they had been assertive. For most students, it was easy to come up with 6 times they were assertive, but hard to come up with 12 times they were assertive. The students then rated how assertive they were. Those who listed 6 times they were assertive reported being more assertive than those who listed 12 times they were assertive. It seems that easily thinking about being assertive had more influence on the students than the number of instances that they thought about.

Our use of the availability heuristic highlights a basic principle of social thinking: People are slow to deduce particular instances from a general truth, but they are remarkably quick to infer general truth from a vivid instance. No wonder that after hearing and reading stories of rapes,

availability heuristic
a cognitive rule that judges the likelihood of things in terms of their availability in memory. If instances of something come readily to mind, we presume it to be commonplace.

robberies, and beatings, 9 out of 10 Canadians overestimate—usually by a considerable margin—the percentage of crimes that involve violence (Doob & Roberts, 1988).

The availability heuristic explains why powerful anecdotes are often more compelling than statistical information. We fret over extremely rare child abduction, even if we don't buckle our children in the backseat. We dread terrorism but are indifferent to global climate change—"Armageddon in slow motion." Especially after the 2011 Japanese tsunami and nuclear power catastrophe, we fear nuclear power, with little concern for the many more deaths related to coal mining and burning (von Hippel, 2011). In short, we worry about remote possibilities while ignoring higher probabilities, a phenomenon that Cass Sunstein (2007) called our "probability neglect."

Because news footage of airplane crashes is a readily available memory for most of us, we often suppose we are more at risk travelling in commercial airplanes than in cars. Actually, from 2003 to 2005, U.S. travellers were 230 times more likely to die in a car crash than on a commercial flight covering the same distance (National Safety Council, 2008). For most air travellers, the most dangerous part of the journey is the drive to the airport.

By now it is clear that our naive statistical intuitions, and our resulting fears, are driven not by calculation and reason but by emotions attuned to the availability heuristic. After this book is published, there likely will be another dramatic natural or terrorist event, which will again propel our fears, vigilance, and resources in a new direction. Terrorists, aided by the media, may again achieve their objective of capturing our attention, draining our resources, and distracting us from the mundane, undramatic, insidious risks that, over time, devastate lives, such as the rotavirus that each day claims the equivalent of four 747s filled with children (Parashar et al., 2006). But then again, dramatic events can also serve to awaken us to real risks. That, say some scientists, is what happened when the extreme floods, droughts, snows, and tornadoes of 2011 raised concern that global climate change, by raising sea levels and spawning extreme weather, is destined to become nature's own weapon of mass destruction. For Australians and Americans, a temporary hot day can prime people to believe more in global warming (Li et al., 2011). Even feeling hot in an *indoor* room increases people's belief in global warming (Risen & Critcher, 2011).

Answer to question on page 95: Tanzania's 44 million people greatly outnumber Iraq's 30 million. Most people, having more vivid images of Iraqis, guess wrong.

COUNTERFACTUAL THINKING

Easily imagined (cognitively available) events also influence our experiences of guilt, regret, frustration, and relief. If our team loses (or wins) a big game by one point, we can easily imagine how the game might have gone the other way, and thus we feel greater regret (or relief). Imagining worse alternatives helps us feel better. Imagining better alternatives, and pondering what we might do differently next time, helps us prepare to do better in the future (Epstude & Roese, 2008).

In Olympics competition, athletes' emotions after an event reflect mostly how they did relative to expectations; but they also reflect the athletes' **counterfactual thinking**—their mental simulation of what might have been (McGraw, Mellers, & Tetlock, 2005; Medvec, Madey, & Gilovich, 1995). Bronze medallists (who could easily imagine finishing without a medal) exhibited more joy than silver medallists (who could more easily imagine having won the gold). On the medal stand, it has been said, happiness is as simple as 1-3-2. Similarly, the higher a

counterfactual thinking
imagining alternative scenarios and outcomes that might have happened, but didn't

student's score within a grade category (such as B+), the *worse* they feel (Medvec & Savitsky, 1997). The B+ student who misses an A− by a point feels worse than the B+ student who actually did worse and just made a B+ by a point.

Counterfactual thinking occurs when we can easily picture an alternative outcome (Kahneman & Miller, 1986; Markman & McMullen, 2003; Petrocelli et al., 2011): If we barely miss a plane or bus, we imagine making it *if only* we had left at our usual time, taken our usual route, not paused to talk. If we change an exam answer, then get it wrong, we inevitably think, "If only . . ." and will vow next time to trust our immediate intuition—although, contrary to student lore, answer changes are more often from incorrect to correct (Kruger et al., 2005).

Counterfactual thinking underlies our feelings of luck. When we have barely escaped a bad event—avoiding defeat with a last-minute goal or standing nearest a falling icicle—we easily imagine a negative counterfactual (losing, being hit) and, therefore, feel "good luck" (Teigen et al., 1999). "Bad luck," on the other hand, refers to bad events that did happen but might not have.

The more significant the event, the more intense the counterfactual thinking. Bereaved people who have lost a spouse or child in a vehicle accident, or a child to sudden infant death syndrome, commonly report replaying and undoing the event (Davis et al., 1995, 1996). One individual, having lost his wife, daughter, and mother in a head-on collision with a drunk driver, reported that "For months I turned the events of that day over and over in my mind. I kept reliving the day, changing the order of events so that the accident wouldn't occur" (Sittser, 1994).

Across both Asian and Western cultures, most people, however, live with less regret over things done than over things they failed to do, such as, "I wish I had been more serious in college" or "I should have told my father I loved him before he died" (Gilovich & Medvec, 1994; Gilovich et al., 2003; Savitsky, Medvec, & Gilovich, 1997). In one survey of adults, the most common regret was not taking their education more seriously (Kinnier & Metha, 1989). Would we live with less regret if we dared more often to reach beyond our comfort zone—to venture out, risking failure, but at least having tried?

ILLUSORY THINKING

Another influence on everyday thinking is our search for order in random events, a tendency that can lead us down all sorts of wrong paths.

Illusory correlation

It's easy to see a correlation where none exists. When we expect significant relationships, we easily associate random events, perceiving an **illusory correlation**. William Ward and Herbert Jenkins (1965) showed people the results of a hypothetical 50-day cloud-seeding experiment. They told their subjects which of the 50 days the clouds had been seeded and which days it had rained. This information was nothing more than a random mix of results: Sometimes it rained after seeding; sometimes it didn't. People nevertheless became convinced—in conformity with their ideas about the effects of cloud seeding—that they really had observed a relationship between cloud seeding and rain.

Other experiments confirmed that people easily misperceive random events as confirming their beliefs (Crocker, 1981; Jennings, Amabile, & Ross, 1982; Trolier & Hamilton, 1986). If we believe a correlation exists, we are more likely to notice and recall confirming instances. If we believe that premonitions correlate with events, we

illusory correlation perception of a relationship where none exists, or perception of a stronger relationship than actually exists

"I see men ordinarily more eager to discover a reason for things than to find out whether the things are so."
FRENCH ESSAYIST MONTAIGNE, 1533–1592

notice and remember the joint occurrence of the premonition and the event's later occurrence. We seldom notice or remember all the times unusual events do not coincide. If, after we think about a friend, the friend calls us, we notice and remember this coincidence. We don't notice all the times we think of a friend without any ensuing call, or receive a call from a friend about whom we've not been thinking.

Illusion of control

illusion of control
perception of uncontrollable events as subject to one's control or as more controllable than they are

Our tendency to perceive random events as related feeds an **illusion of control**—the idea that chance events are subject to our influence. This is what keeps gamblers going and what makes the rest of us do all sorts of unlikely things.

Gambling

Ellen Langer (1977) demonstrated the illusion of control with experiments on gambling. Compared to those given an assigned lottery number, people who chose their own number demanded four times as much money when asked about selling their ticket. When playing a game of chance against an awkward and nervous person, they bet significantly more than when playing against a dapper, confident opponent. Michael Wohl of Carleton University and Michael Enzle of the University of Alberta have found that being the person who throws the dice or spins the wheel increases people's confidence (Wohl & Enzle, 2002). In these and other ways, more than 50 experiments have consistently found people acting as if they can predict or control chance events (Presson & Benassi, 1996).

Observations of real-life gamblers confirm these experimental findings. Dice players may throw softly for low numbers and hard for high numbers (Henslin, 1967). The gambling industry thrives on gamblers' illusions. Gamblers attribute wins to their skill and foresight. Losses become "near misses" or "flukes"—perhaps (for the sports gambler) a bad call by the referee or a freakish bounce of the ball (Gilovich & Douglas, 1986).

Regression toward the average

regression toward the average
the statistical tendency for extreme scores or extreme behaviour to return toward the person's average

Tversky and Kahneman (1974) noted another way by which an illusion of control may arise: We fail to recognize the statistical phenomenon of **regression toward the average**. Because exam scores fluctuate partly by chance, most students who get extremely high scores on an exam will get lower scores on the next exam. If their first score is at the ceiling, their second score is more likely to fall back ("regress") toward their own average than to push the ceiling even higher. Conversely, the lowest-scoring students on the first exam are likely to improve. If those who scored lowest go for tutoring after the first exam, the tutors are likely to feel effective when the student improves, even if the tutoring had no effect.

Indeed, when things reach a low point, we will try anything, and whatever we try—going to a psychotherapist, starting a new diet–exercise plan, reading a self-help book—is more likely to be followed by improvement than by further deterioration. Sometimes we recognize that events are not likely to continue at an unusually good or bad extreme. Experience has taught us that when everything is going great, something will go wrong, and that when life is dealing us terrible blows, we can usually look forward to things getting better. Often, though, we fail to recognize this regression effect. We puzzle at why baseball's rookie-of-the-year often has a more ordinary second year—did he become overconfident? Self-conscious? We forget that exceptional performance tends to regress toward normality.

Regression toward the average: When we are at an extremely low point, anything we try, like meditation or yoga, will usually seem effective as we return to our more usual state.

By simulating the consequences of using praise and punishment, Paul Schaffner (1985) showed how the illusion of control might infiltrate human relations. He invited students to train an imaginary fourth-grade boy, "Harold," to come to school by 8:30 each morning. For each school day of a three-week period, a computer displayed Harold's arrival time, which was always between 8:20 and 8:40. The subjects would then select a response to Harold, ranging from strong praise to strong reprimand. As you might expect, they usually praised Harold when he arrived before 8:30 and reprimanded him when he arrived after 8:30. Because Schaffner had programmed the computer to display a random sequence of arrival times, Harold's arrival time tended to improve (to regress toward 8:30) after being reprimanded. For example, if Harold arrived at 8:39, he was almost sure to be reprimanded, and his randomly selected next-day arrival time was likely to be earlier than 8:39. Thus, even though their reprimands were having no effect, most subjects ended the experiment believing that their reprimands had been effective.

This experiment demonstrates Tversky and Kahneman's provocative conclusion: Nature operates in such a way that we often feel punished for rewarding others and rewarded for punishing them. In actuality, as every student of psychology knows, positive reinforcement for doing things right is usually more effective and has fewer negative side effects.

MOOD AND JUDGMENT

Social judgment involves efficient, though fallible, information processing. It also involves our feelings: Our moods infuse our judgments. We are not cool computing machines; we are emotional creatures. Some studies compare happy and sad individuals (Myers, 1993, 2000). Unhappy people—especially those bereaved or depressed—tend to be more self-focused and brooding. A depressed mood motivates intense thinking—a search for information that makes one's environment more understandable and controllable (Weary & Edwards, 1994).

Happy people, by contrast, are more trusting, more loving, more responsive. If people are made temporarily happy by receiving a small gift while shopping, they will report, a few moments later on an unrelated survey, that their cars and TV sets are working beautifully—better, if you took their word for it, than those belonging to folks who replied after not receiving gifts.

Moods pervade our thinking. To Germans enjoying their team's World Cup soccer victory (Schwarz et al., 1987) and to Australians emerging from a heartwarming movie (Forgas & Moylan, 1987), people seem good-hearted, life seems wonderful. After (but not before) a 1990 football game between rivals Alabama and Auburn, victorious Alabama fans deemed war less likely and potentially devastating than did the gloomier Auburn fans (Schweitzer et al., 1992). When we are in a happy mood, the world seems friendlier, decisions are easier, good news more readily comes to mind (DeSteno et al., 2000; Isen & Means, 1983; Stone & Glass, 1986).

Let a mood turn gloomy, however, and thoughts switch onto a different track. Off come the rose-coloured glasses; on go the dark glasses. Now the bad mood primes our recollections of negative events (Bower, 1987; Johnson & Magaro, 1987). Our relationships seem to sour. Our self-image takes a dive. Our hopes for the future dim. Other people's behaviour seems more sinister (Brown & Taylor, 1986; Esses, 1989; Mayer & Salovey, 1987).

University of New South Wales social psychologist Joseph Forgas (1999) had often been struck by how moody people's "memories and judgments change with the color of their mood." To understand this "mood infusion," he began to experiment. Imagine yourself in one such study. Using hypnosis, Forgas and his colleagues (1984) put you in a good or bad mood and then have you watch a videotape (made the day before) of yourself talking with someone. If made to feel happy, you feel pleased with what you see, and you are able to detect many instances of your poise, interest, and social skill. If you've been put in a bad mood, viewing the same tape seems to reveal a quite different you—one who is stiff, nervous, and inarticulate (Figure 3–4). Given how your mood colours your judgments, you feel relieved at how things brighten when the experimenter switches you to a happy mood before leaving the experiment. Curiously, noted Michael Ross and Garth Fletcher (1985), we don't attribute our changing perceptions to our mood shifts. Rather, the world really seems different.

Our moods colour how we see our worlds partly by bringing to mind past experiences associated with the mood. In a bad mood, we have more depressing thoughts. Mood-related thoughts may distract us from complex thinking about something else. Thus, when emotionally aroused—when angry or even in a very good mood—we become more likely to make snap judgments and evaluate others based on stereotypes (Bodenhausen, Sheppard, & Kramer, 1994;

FIGURE 3–4

MOOD AND PERCEPTION.

A temporary good or bad mood strongly influenced people's ratings of their videotaped behaviour. Those in a bad mood detected far fewer positive behaviours. (Forgas, Bower, & Krantz, 1984)

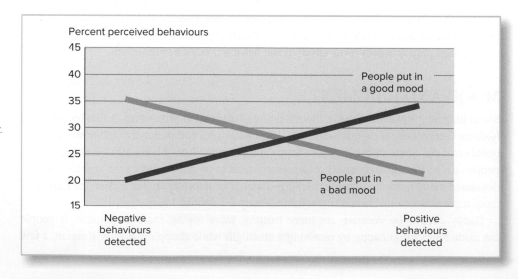

Percent perceived behaviours

People put in a good mood

People put in a bad mood

Negative behaviours detected

Positive behaviours detected

We all know moody people, and I have often been struck by how their feelings seem to invade their thinking. It almost appears that their memories and judgments change with the colour of their mood. For some years now, I have been trying to understand how and why this mood infusion occurs.

One day while sitting in a restaurant, I noticed an odd couple at the next table—a beautiful young woman with an unattractive elderly man. As I found myself repeatedly wondering about this relationship, it occurred to me that the more I thought about them, the more opportunity there might be for my mood to infuse my thoughts. Testing this idea in the laboratory, we found that, indeed, mood had a greater effect on complex judgments of odd couples than on snap judgments of well-matched couples. Such findings have helped us to develop a theory that predicts when moodiness will infuse judgments.

Joseph Forgas *University of New South Wales, Sydney, Australia*

Paulhus & Lim, 1994). But if our attention is drawn to our moods, we may "correct" our judgments. People in a foul mood had less flattering views of another person than did people in a happy mood, unless they first attended to their moods. In that case, mood had little impact on impressions of the other person (McFarland, White, & Newth, 2006). It seems that if we acknowledge our moods, we can keep them from biasing our judgments.

HOW DO WE EXPLAIN OUR SOCIAL WORLDS?

People make it their business to explain other people, and social psychologists make it their business to explain people's explanations.

Our judgments of people depend on how we explain their behaviour. Depending on our explanation, we may judge killing as murder, manslaughter, self-defence, or heroism. Depending on our explanation, we may view a homeless person as lacking initiative or as victimized by job and social assistance cutbacks. Depending on our explanation, we may attribute someone's friendly behaviour as genuine warmth or as ingratiation. Attribution theory helps us make sense of how this explanation works.

ATTRIBUTING CAUSALITY: TO THE PERSON OR THE SITUATION?

We endlessly analyze and discuss why things happen as they do, especially when we experience something negative or unexpected (Weiner, 1985, 2008, 2010). If worker productivity declines, do we assume the workers are getting lazier? Or has their workplace become less effi-cient? Does a young boy who hits his classmates have a hostile personality? Or is he respond-ing to relentless teasing? Researchers found that married people often analyze their partners' behaviours, especially their negative behaviours. Cold hostility is more likely than a warm hug to leave the partner wondering "why?" (Holtzworth-Munroe & Jacobson, 1985; Holtzworth & Jacobson, 1988).

Spouses' answers correlate with their marriage satisfaction. Unhappy couples usually offer distress-maintaining explanations for negative acts ("She was late because she doesn't care about me"). Happy couples more often externalize ("She was late because of heavy traffic"). With positive partner behaviour, their explanations similarly work either to maintain distress ("He brought me flowers because he wants sex") or to enhance the relationship ("He brought me flowers to show he loves me") (Hewstone & Fincham, 1996; McNulty, O'Mara, & Karney, 2008; Weiner, 1995).

Antonia Abbey (1987, 1991) and her colleagues repeatedly found that men are more likely than women to attribute a woman's friendliness to mild sexual interest. Men's misreading of women's warmth as a sexual come-on—an example of **misattribution**—can lead to behaviour that women regard as sexual harassment or even to rape (Farris et al., 2008; Kolivas & Gross, 2007; Pryor et al., 1997). Many believe women are flattered by repeated requests for dates, which women more often view as harassment (Rotundo, Nguyen, & Sackett, 2001).

Misattribution is especially likely when men are in positions of power. A male manager may misinterpret a subordinate woman's submissive or friendly behaviour and, full of himself, may see women only in sexual terms (Bargh & Raymond, 1995). Men may greatly overestimate the sexual significance of a woman's courtesy smile (Levesque, Nave, & Lowe, 2006; Nelson & LeBoeuf, 2002).

Such misattributions help explain the greater sexual assertiveness exhibited by men across the world and the greater tendency of men in various cultures, from Boston to Bombay, to justify rape by arguing that the victim consented or implied consent (Kanekar & Nazareth, 1988; Muehlenhard, 1988; Shotland, 1989). Women more often judge the same behaviour as merit-ing conviction and a stiff sentence (Schutte & Hosch, 1997). Misattributions also help explain why the 23 percent of American women who say they have been forced into unwanted sex-ual behaviour is eight times the 3 percent of American men who say they have ever forced a woman into a sexual act (Laumann et al., 1994).

Attribution theory analyzes how we explain people's behaviour. The variations of attribu-tion theory share some common assumptions. As Daniel Gilbert and Patrick Malone (1995) explained, each "construes the human skin as a special boundary that separates one set of 'causal forces' from another. On the sunny side of the epidermis are the external or situational forces that press inward upon the person, and on the meaty side are the internal or personal forces that exert pressure outward. Sometimes these forces press in conjunction, sometimes in opposition, and their dynamic interplay manifests itself as observable behavior."

Attribution theory pioneer Fritz Heider (1958) and others after him analyzed the "common-sense psychology" by which people explain everyday events. They concluded that when we observe someone acting intentionally, we sometimes attribute that person's behaviour to *inter-nal* causes (for example, the person's disposition) or *external* causes (for example, something about the person's situation). A teacher may wonder whether a child's underachievement is due to lack of motivation and ability (a **dispositional attribution**) or to physical and social

misattribution
mistakenly attributing a behaviour to the wrong cause

attribution theory
the theory of how people explain the behaviour of others—for example, by attributing it either to internal dispositions (enduring traits, motives, and attitudes) or to external situations

dispositional attribution
attributing behaviour to the person's disposition and traits

To what should we attribute this student's sleepiness? Lack of sleep? Boredom? Whether we make internal or external attributions depends on whether we notice her consistently sleeping in this and other classes, and whether other students react as she does to this particular class.

circumstances (a **situational attribution**). Some people are more inclined to attribute behaviour to stable personality; others tend more to attribute behaviour to situations (Bastian & Haslam, 2006; Robins et al., 2004).

situational attribution
attributing behaviour to the environment

Inferring traits

Edward Jones and Keith Davis (1965) noted that we often infer that other people's actions are indicative of their intentions and dispositions. If I observe Rick making a sarcastic comment to Linda, I infer that Rick is a hostile person. Jones and Davis's "theory of correspondent inferences" specifies the conditions under which such attributions are most likely. For example, normal or expected behaviour tells us less about the person than does unusual behaviour. If Samantha is sarcastic in a job interview, where a person would normally be pleasant, this tells us more about Samantha than if she is sarcastic with her siblings.

The ease with which we infer traits—a phenomenon called **spontaneous trait inference**—is remarkable. In one set of experiments, James Uleman (1989) gave students statements to remember, like "The librarian carries the old woman's groceries across the street." The students would instantly, unintentionally, and unconsciously infer a trait. When later they were helped to recall the sentence, the most valuable clue word was not "books" (to cue librarian) or "bags" (to cue groceries) but "helpful"—the inferred trait that we suspect you, too, spontaneously attributed to the librarian. Given even 1/10th of a second exposure to someone's face, people will spontaneously infer some personality traits (Willis & Todorov, 2006).

spontaneous trait inference
an effortless, automatic inference of a trait after exposure to someone's behaviour

Common-sense attributions

As the theory of correspondent inference suggests, attributions often are rational. In testimony to the reasonable ways in which we explain behaviour, attribution theorist Harold Kelley (1973) described how we use information about "consistency," "distinctiveness," and "consensus"

FIGURE 3–5

HAROLD KELLEY'S
THEORY OF
ATTRIBUTIONS.

Consistency: How
consistent is the
person's behaviour in
this situation?
Distinctiveness: How
specific is the person's
behaviour to this
particular situation?
Consensus: To what
extent do others in
this situation behave
similarly?

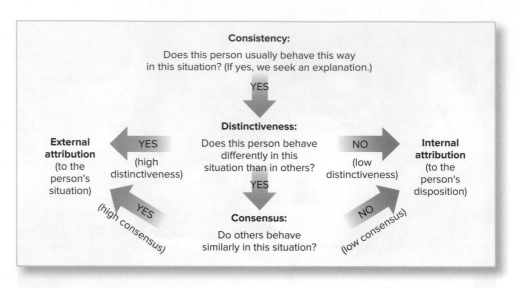

(Figure 3–5). When explaining why Edgar is having trouble with his computer, most people use information concerning *consistency* (Is Edgar usually unable to get his computer to work?), *distinctiveness* (Does Edgar have trouble with other computers, or only this one?), and *consensus* (Do other people have similar problems with this make of computer?). If we learn that Edgar alone consistently has trouble with this and other computers, we likely will attribute the troubles to Edgar, not to defects in this computer.

So our common-sense psychology often explains behaviour logically. But Kelley also found that people often discount a contributing cause of behaviour if other plausible causes are already known. If we can specify one or two reasons why a student might have done poorly on an exam, we may ignore or discount other possibilities (McClure, 1998). When given information about people's university grade average and asked to judge their suitability for graduate school, people discount the school's grading leniency (Moore et al., 2010).

THE FUNDAMENTAL ATTRIBUTION ERROR

Social psychology's most important lesson concerns the influence of our social environment. At any moment, our internal state, and, therefore, what we say and do, depends on the situation, as well as on what we bring to the situation. In experiments, a slight difference between two situations sometimes greatly affects how people respond. As professors, we have seen this when teaching classes at both 8:30 A.M. and 7:00 P.M. Silent stares greet us at 8:30; at 7:00, one of the authors had to break up a party. In each situation, some individuals were more talkative than others, but the difference between the two situations exceeded the individual differences.

Attribution researchers have found that we often fail to appreciate this important lesson. When explaining someone's behaviour, we underestimate the impact of the situation and overestimate the extent to which it reflects the individual's traits and attitudes. Thus, even knowing the effect of the time of day on classroom conversation, we have found it terribly tempting to assume that the people in the 7:00 P.M. class are more extroverted than the "silent types" who come at 8:30 A.M. Likewise, we may infer that people fall because they're clumsy rather than because they were tripped, that people smile because they're happy rather than faking friendliness, and that people speed past us on the highway because they're aggressive rather than late for an important meeting. This discounting of the situation, dubbed by Lee Ross (1977) as the **fundamental attribution error**, appears in many experiments. In the first such study, Edward Jones and Victor Harris (1967) had students read debaters' speeches supporting or attacking Cuba's leader, Fidel Castro. When the position taken was said to have been chosen by the debater, the students logically enough assumed it reflected the person's own attitude. But what happened when the students were told that the debate coach had assigned the position? People who were merely feigning a position wrote stronger statements than you'd expect (Allison et al., 1993; Miller, Ashton, & Mishal, 1990). Thus, even knowing that the debater had been told to take a pro-Castro position did not prevent students from inferring that the debater, in fact, had some pro-Castro leanings (Figure 3–6). People seemed to think, "Yeah, I know he was assigned that position, but to some extent I think he really believes it."

Even when people know they are *causing* someone else's behaviour, they still underestimate external influences. If subjects dictate an opinion that someone else must then express, they still tend to see the person as actually holding that opinion (Gilbert & Jones, 1986). If subjects are asked to be either self-enhancing or self-deprecating during an interview, they are very aware of why they are acting so. But they are *un*aware of their effect on another person. If Juan acts modestly, his naive partner Bob is likely to exhibit modesty as well. Juan will easily understand his own behaviour, but he will think that poor Bob suffers low self-esteem (Baumeister et al., 1988). In short, we tend to presume that others *are* the way they act. Observing Cinderella cowering

> **fundamental attribution error**
> the tendency for observers to underestimate situational influences and overestimate dispositional influences on others' behaviour; also called *correspondence bias*, because we so often see behaviour as corresponding to a disposition

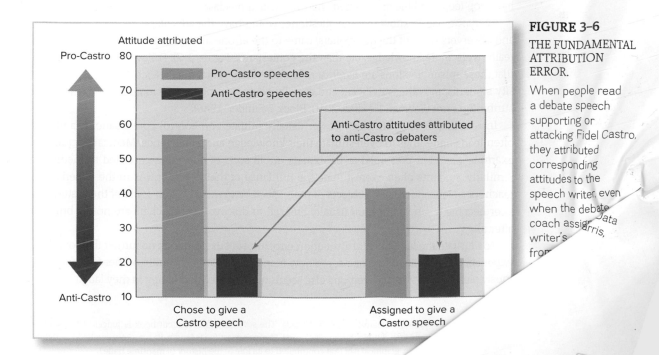

FIGURE 3–6

THE FUNDAMENTAL ATTRIBUTION ERROR.

When people read a debate speech supporting or attacking Fidel Castro, they attributed corresponding attitudes to the speech writer, even when the debate coach assigned the writer's from

People often attribute keen intelligence to those, such as teachers and quiz show hosts, who test others' knowledge.

in her oppressive home, people infer she is meek; dancing with her at the ball, the prince sees a suave and glamorous person.

The discounting of social constraints was further evident in a thought-provoking experiment by Lee Ross and his collaborators (1977). The experiment recreated Ross's first-hand experience of moving from graduate student to professor. His doctoral oral exam had proved a humbling experience as his apparently brilliant professors quizzed him on topics they specialized in. Six months later, *Dr.* Ross was himself an examiner, now able to ask penetrating questions on *his* favourite topics. Ross's hapless student later confessed to feeling exactly as Ross had a half-year before—dissatisfied with his ignorance and impressed with the apparent brilliance of the examiners.

In the experiment, with Teresa Amabile and Julia Steinmetz, Ross (1977) set up a simulated quiz game. He randomly assigned some students to play the role of questioner, some to play the role of contestant, and others to observe. The researchers invited the questioners to make up difficult questions that would demonstrate their wealth of knowledge. Any one of us can imagine such questions using our own domain of competence: "Where are the clearest waters for scuba diving in Canada?" "What is the seventh book in the Old Testament?" "Which has the longer coastline, Europe or Africa?" If even these few questions have you feeling a little uninformed, then you will appreciate the results of this experiment.*

Everyone had to know that the questioner would have the advantage. Yet both contestants and observers (but not the questioners) came to the erroneous conclusion that the questioners really were more knowledgeable than the contestants (Figure 3–7). Follow-up research shows that these misimpressions are hardly a reflection of low social intelligence. If anything, university students and other intelligent and socially competent people are more likely to make the attribution error (Bauman & Skitka, 2010; Block & Funder, 1986).

In real life, those with social power usually initiate and control conversations, and this often leads underlings to overestimate their knowledge and intelligence. Medical doctors, for example, are often presumed to be experts on all sorts of questions unrelated to medicine. Similarly, students often overestimate the brilliance of their teachers. (As in the experiment, teachers are questioners on subjects of their special expertise.) When some of these students later become teachers, they are usually amazed to discover that teachers are not so brilliant after all.

To illustrate the fundamental attribution error, most of us need look no further than our own experience. Determined to make some new friends, Bev plasters a smile on her face and anxiously plunges into a party. Everyone else seems quite relaxed and happy as they laugh and talk

*Tobermory, Ontario, has the clearest waters in Canada. The seventh Old Testament book is Judges. Although the _can continent is more than double the area of Europe, Europe's coastline is longer. (It is more convoluted, with lots ours and inlets, a geographical fact that contributed to its role in the history of maritime trade.)

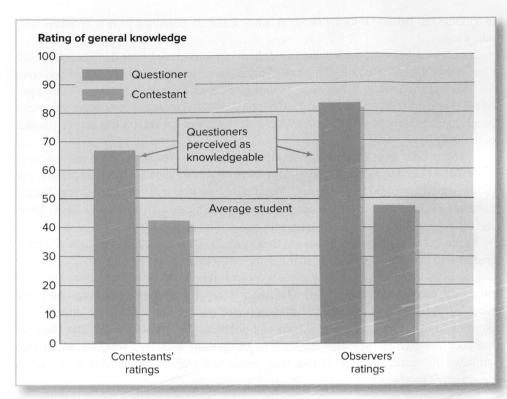

FIGURE 3–7

MISPERCEPTIONS AND THE FUNDAMENTAL ATTRIBUTION ERROR.

Both contestants and observers of a simulated quiz game assumed that a person who had been randomly assigned the role of questioner was far more knowledgeable than the contestant. Actually, the assigned roles of questioner and contestant simply made the questioner seem more knowledgeable. The failure to appreciate this illustrates the fundamental attribution error. (Data from Ross, Amabile, & Steinmetz, 1977)

with one another. Bev wonders to herself, "Why is everyone always so at ease in groups like this while I'm feeling shy and tense?" Actually, everyone else is feeling nervous, too, and making the same attribution error in assuming that Bev and the others are as they appear—confidently convivial.

WHY WE MAKE THE ATTRIBUTION ERROR

So far, we have seen a bias in the way we explain other people's behaviour: We often ignore powerful situational determinants. Why do we tend to underestimate the situational determinants of others' behaviour but not of our own?

Perspective and situational awareness

An actor–observer difference

Attribution theorists point out that we observe others from a different perspective than we observe ourselves (Jones & Nisbett, 1971; Jones, 1976). When we act, the *environment* commands our attention. When we watch another person act, that *person* occupies the centre of our attention and the situation becomes relatively invisible. If I'm mad, it's the situation that's making me angry. But someone observing us may spontaneously infer a trait.

From his analysis of 173 studies, Bertram Malle (2006) concluded that the actor–ob difference is often minimal. When our action feels intentional and admirable, we att our own good reasons, not the situation. It's only when we behave badly that we to attribute our behaviour to the situation, while someone observing us may spontaneously infer a trait.

In some experiments, people viewed a videotape of a suspect confessing during a police interview. If they viewed the confession through a camera focused on the suspect, they perceived the confession as genuine. If they viewed it through a camera focused on the detective, they perceived it as more coerced (Lassiter et al., 1986, 2005, 2007). The camera perspective influenced people's guilt judgments even when the judge instructed them not to allow it to happen (Lassiter et al., 2002).

In courtrooms, most confession videotapes focus on the confessor. As we might expect, noted Daniel Lassiter and Kimberly Dudley (1991), such tapes yield a nearly 100 percent conviction rate when played by prosecutors. Aware of this research, reported Lassiter, New Zealand has made it a national policy that police interrogations are filmed with equal focus on the officer and the suspect, such as by filming them with side profiles of both.

As the once-visible person recedes in their memory, observers often give more and more credit to the situation. Immediately after hearing someone argue an assigned position, people assume that's how the person really felt. A week later, they are much more likely to credit the situational constraints (Burger, 1991). The day after a major election, Jerry Burger and Julie Pavelich (1994) asked voters why the election turned out the way it did. Most attributed the outcome to the candidates' personal traits and positions (the winner was likeable; the loser had poor ideas). When they asked the same voters the same question a year later, only a third attributed the verdict to the candidates. More people now credited the circumstances, such as the country's good mood and the robustness of the economy.

Let's make this personal: Are you generally quiet or talkative, or does it depend on the situation? "Depends on the situation" is a common answer. Likewise, when asked to predict their feelings two weeks after receiving grades or learning the outcome of their country's national election, people expect the situation to rule their emotions; they underestimate the importance of their own sunny or dour dispositions (Quoidbach & Dunn, 2010). But when asked to describe a friend—or to describe what they were like five years ago—people more often ascribed definite trait descriptions. When recalling our past, we become like observers of someone else, noted researchers Emily Pronin and Lee Ross (2006). For most of us, the "old you" is someone other than today's "real you." We regard our distant past selves (and our distant future selves) almost as if they were other people occupying our body.

All these experiments point to a reason for the attribution error: We find causes where we look for them. To see this in your own experience, consider: Would you say your social psychology instructor is a quiet or a talkative person?

Our guess is you inferred that he or she is fairly outgoing. But consider the situation further: Your attention focuses on your instructor while he or she behaves in a public context that demands speaking. The instructor, on the other hand, observes his or her own behaviour in many different situations—in the classroom, in meetings, at home. "Me talkative?" your instructor might say. "Well, it all depends on the situation. When I'm in class or with good friends, I'm rather outgoing. But at conventions and in unfamiliar situations, I feel and act rather shy." Because we are acutely aware of how our behaviour varies with the situation, we see ourselves as more variable than other people (Baxter & Goldberg, 1987; Kammer, 1982; Sande, Goethals, & Radloff, 1988). "Nigel is uptight, Fiona is relaxed. With ⁀e, it varies."

CULTURAL DIFFERENCES

Cultures also influence attribution errors (Ickes, 1980; Watson, 1982). A Western worldview predisposes people to assume that people, not situations, cause events. Internal explanations are more socially approved (Jellison & Green, 1981). "You can do it!" we are assured by the pop psychology of positive-thinking Western culture. You get what you deserve and deserve what you get.

As children grow up in Western culture, they learn to explain behaviour in terms of others' personal characteristics (Rholes, Newman, & Ruble, 1990; Rose, 1981). As a first-grader, one of the authors' sons

The fundamental attribution error: People are biased to assume that people's behaviour corresponds to their inner dispositions. Such assumptions are sometimes, but not always, correct. Some weekend bikers are weekday professionals.

brought home an example. He unscrambled the words "gate the sleeve caught Tom on his" into "The gate caught Tom on his sleeve." His teacher, applying the Western cultural assumptions of the curriculum materials, marked that wrong. The "right" answer located the cause within Tom: "Tom caught his sleeve on the gate."

The fundamental attribution error occurs across varied cultures (Krull et al., 1999). Yet people in Eastern Asian cultures are somewhat more sensitive to the importance of situations. Thus, when aware of the social context, they are less inclined to assume that others' behaviour corresponds to their traits (Choi, Nisbett, & Norenzayan, 1999; Farwell & Weiner, 2000; Masuda & Kitayama, 2004). Past situations and actions may also provide context for understanding present events, and the Chinese are more sensitive to the relevance of past information than are Canadians (Ji et al., 2009).

Some languages promote external attributions. Instead of "I was late," Spanish idiom allows one to say, "The clock caused me to be late." In collectivist cultures, people less often perceive others in terms of personal dispositions (Lee, Hallahan, & Herzog, 1996; Zebrowitz-McArthur, 1988). They are less likely to spontaneously interpret a behaviour as reflecting an inner trait (Newman, 1993). When told of someone's actions, Hindus in India are less likely than Americans to offer dispositional explanations ("She is kind") and more likely to offer situational explanations ("Her friends were with her") (Miller, 1984).

The fundamental attribution error is, however, fundamental because it colours our explanations in basic and important ways. Researchers in Britain, India, Australia, and the United States have found, for example, that people's attributions predict their attitudes toward the poor and unemployed (Feather, 1983; Furnham, 1982; Pandey et al., 1982; Wagstaff, 1983; Weiner, Osborne, & Rudoph, 2011). Those who attribute poverty and unemployment to personal dispositions ("They're just lazy and undeserving") tend to adopt political positions unsympathetic to such people (Figure 3–8). This *dispositional attribution* ascribes behaviour to the person's dispositions and traits. Those who make *situational attributions* ("If you or I were to live with the same overcrowding, poor education, and discrimination, would we be any better off?") tend to adopt political positions that offer more direct support to the poor.

"Most poor people are no[t] lazy. . . . They catch [the] early bus. . . . Th[ey . . .] other people[. . .]S. No, They cle[. . .] —JACKSON, no, th[. . .] DEMOCRATIC TH[. . .]TION, JULY 1988

FIGURE 3–8

ATTRIBUTIONS
AND REACTIONS.

How we explain
someone's negative
behaviour determines
how we feel about it.

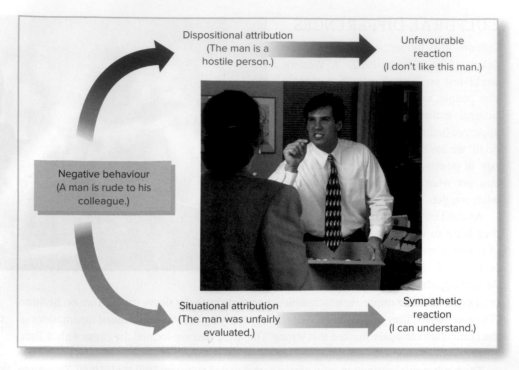

WHY WE STUDY ATTRIBUTION ERRORS

This chapter, like the one before, explains some foibles and fallacies in our social thinking. Reading these may make it seem, as one of our students put it, that "social psychologists get their kicks out of playing tricks on people." Actually, the experiments are not designed to demonstrate "what fools these mortals be" (although some of the experiments *are* amusing); their purpose is to reveal how we think about ourselves and others.

If our capacity for illusion and self-deception is shocking, remember that our modes of thought are generally adaptive. Illusory thinking is often a by-product of our mind's strategies for simplifying complex information. It parallels our perceptual mechanisms, which generally give us a useful image of the world, but sometimes lead us astray.

A second reason for focusing on biases such as the fundamental attribution error is humanitarian. One of social psychology's "great humanizing messages," noted Thomas Gilovich and Richard Eibach (2001), is that people should not always be blamed for their problems. "Failure, disability, and misfortune are more often than people are willing to acknowledge the product of real environmental causes."

A third reason for focusing on the biases is that we are mostly unaware of them and can benefit from greater awareness. As with other biases, such as the self-serving bias (Chapter 2), people see themselves as less susceptible than others to attribution errors (Pronin, Gilovich, & Ross, 2004). Our hunch is that you will find more surprises, more challenges, and more benefit in an analysis of errors and biases than you would in a string of testimonies to the human capacity for logic and intellectual achievement. That is also why world literature so often portrays pride and other human failings. Social psychology aims to expose us to fallacies in our thinking in the hope that we will become more rational, more in touch with reality.

HOW DO OUR EXPECTATIONS OF OUR SOCIAL WORLDS MATTER?

Having considered how we explain and judge others—efficiently, adaptively, but sometimes erroneously—we conclude by pondering the effects of our social judgments. Do our beliefs about social reality matter? Do they change reality?

Our social beliefs and judgments do matter. They influence how we feel and act, and by so doing may generate their own reality. When our ideas lead us to act in ways that produce their apparent confirmation, they have become what sociologist Robert Merton (1948) termed **self-fulfilling prophecies**—false beliefs that lead to their own fulfillment. If, led to believe that their bank is about to crash, the bank's customers race to withdraw their money, their false perceptions may create reality, noted Merton. If people are led to believe that stocks are about to soar, they will indeed.

self-fulfilling prophecies
beliefs that lead to their own fulfillment

In his well-known studies of "experimenter bias," Robert Rosenthal (1985, 2006) found that research participants sometimes live up to what is expected of them. In one study, experimenters asked individuals to judge the success of people in various photographs. The experimenters read the same instructions to all their participants and showed them the same photos. Nevertheless, experimenters led to expect high ratings obtained higher ratings than did those who expected their participants to see the photographed people as failures. Even more startling—and controversial—are reports that teachers' beliefs about their students similarly serve as self-fulfilling prophecies. If a teacher believes a student is good at math, will the student do well in the class? Let's examine this.

TEACHER EXPECTATIONS AND STUDENT PERFORMANCE

Teachers do have higher expectations for some students than for others. Perhaps you have detected this yourself after having a brother or sister precede you in school, after receiving a label such as "gifted" or "learning disabled," or after being tracked with "high-ability" or "average-ability" students. Or perhaps your new teacher scrutinized your school file or discovered your family's social status. Do such teacher expectations affect student performance? It's clear that teachers' evaluations *correlate* with student achievement: Teachers think well of students who do well. That's mostly because teachers accurately perceive their students' abilities and achievements. "About 75 percent of the correlation between teacher expectations and student future achievement reflects accuracy," report Lee Jussim, Stacy Robustelli, and Thomas Cain (2009).

But are teachers' evaluations ever a *cause* as well as a consequence of student performance? One correlational study of 4300 British schoolchildren by William Crano and Phyllis Mellon (1978) suggested yes. Not only is high performance followed by higher teacher evaluations, but the reverse is true as well.

CANT ASSUME CAUSATION

Could we test this "teacher-expectations effect" experimentally? Pretend we gave a teacher the impression that Dana, Marisa, Todd, and Jamal—four randomly selected students—are unusually capable. Will the teacher give special treatment to these four and elicit superior performance from them? In a now famous experiment, Rosenthal and Lenore Jacobson (1968) reported precisely that. Randomly selected children in an elementary school who were said (on the basis of a fictitious test) to be on the verge of a dramatic intellectual spurt did then spurt ahead in IQ sco

That dramatic result seemed to suggest that the school problems of "disadvantaged" children might reflect their teachers' low expectations. The findings were soon publicized in the media as well as in many university textbooks in psychology and education. However, further analysis—which was not as highly publicized—revealed the teacher-expectations effect to be not so powerful and reliable as this initial study had led many people to believe (Jussim et al., 2009; Spitz, 1999). By Rosenthal's own count, in only about 4 in 10 of the 448 published experiments did expectations significantly affect performance (Rosenthal, 1991, 2002). Low expectations do not doom a capable child, nor do high expectations magically transform a slow learner into a valedictorian. Human nature is not so pliable.

High expectations do, however, seem to boost low achievers, for whom a teacher's positive attitude may be a hope-giving breath of fresh air (Madon, Jussim, & Eccles, 1997). How are such expectations transmitted? Rosenthal and other investigators reported that teachers look, smile, and nod more at "high-potential students." Teachers also may teach more to their "gifted" students, set higher goals for them, call on them more, and give them more time to answer (Cooper, 1983; Harris & Rosenthal, 1985, 1986; Jussim, 1986).

In one study, Elisha Babad, Frank Bernieri, and Rosenthal (1991) videotaped teachers talking to, or about, unseen students for whom they held high or low expectations. A random 10-second clip of either the teacher's voice or face was enough to tell viewers—both children and adults—whether this was a good or poor student and how much the teacher liked the student. (You read that right: 10 seconds.) Although teachers may think they can conceal their feelings, students are acutely sensitive to teachers' facial expressions and body movements (Figure 3–9).

Reading the experiments on teacher expectations makes us wonder about the effect of *students'* expectations on their teachers. You no doubt begin many of your courses having heard "Professor Smith is interesting" and "Professor Jones is a bore." Robert Feldman and Thomas Prohaska (1979; Feldman & Theiss, 1982) found that such expectations can affect both student and teacher. Students in a learning experiment who expected to be taught by a competent teacher perceived their teacher (who was unaware of their expectations) as more competent and interesting than did students with low expectations. Furthermore, the students actually learned more. In a later experiment, women who were led to expect their male instructor to be sexist

FIGURE 3–9

SELF-FULFILLING PROPHECIES. Teacher expectations can become self-fulfilling prophecies. _____ m & Harber,

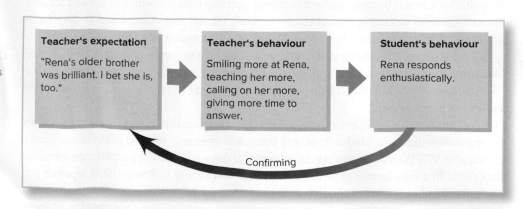

Teacher's expectation	Teacher's behaviour	Student's behaviour
"Rena's older brother was brilliant. I bet she is, too."	Smiling more at Rena, teaching her more, calling on her more, giving more time to answer.	Rena responds enthusiastically.

Confirming

had a less positive experience with him, performed worse, and rated him as less competent than did women not given the sexist expectation (Adams et al., 2006).

Were these results due entirely to the students' perceptions or also to a self-fulfilling prophecy that affected the teacher? In a follow-up experiment, Feldman and Prohaska videotaped teachers and had observers rate their performances. Teachers were judged most capable when assigned a student who nonverbally conveyed positive expectations.

To see whether such effects might also occur in actual classrooms, a research team led by David Jamieson (Jamieson et al., 1987) experimented with four Ontario high school classes taught by a newly transferred teacher. During individual interviews, researchers told students in two of the classes that both other students and the research team rated the teacher very highly. Compared to the control classes, whose expectations they did not raise, the students given positive expectations paid better attention during class. At the end of the teaching unit, they also got better grades and rated the teacher as clearer in her teaching. The attitudes that a class has toward its teacher are as important, it seems, as the teacher's attitude toward the students.

GETTING FROM OTHERS WHAT WE EXPECT

So the expectations of experimenters and teachers, though usually reasonably accurate assessments, occasionally act as self-fulfilling prophecies. How widespread are self-fulfilling prophecies? Do we get from others what we expect of them? Studies show that our perceptions of others are more accurate than biased (Jussim, 2012). Self-fulfilling prophecies have "less than extraordinary power." Yet sometimes, self-fulfilling prophecies do operate in work settings (with managers who have high or low expectations), in courtrooms (as judges instruct juries), and in simulated police contexts (as interrogators with guilty or innocent expectations interrogate and pressure suspects) (Kassin, Goldstein, & Savitsky, 2003; Rosenthal, 2003).

Do self-fulfilling prophecies colour our personal relationships? There are times when negative expectations of someone lead us to be extra nice to that person, which induces them to be nice in return—thus *dis*confirming our expectations. But a more common finding in studies of social interaction is that, yes, we do to some extent get what we expect (Olson, Roese, & Zanna, 1996).

What we believe about someone can lead us to treat the person in ways that create a self-fulfilling prophecy. Consider this in the context of Internet dating and e-mail exchange with strangers.

In laboratory games, hostility nearly always begets hostility: People who perceive their opponents as non-cooperative will readily induce them to be non-cooperative (Kelley & Stahelski, 1970). Each party's perception of the other as aggressive, resentful, and vindictive induces the other to display these behaviours in self-defence, thus creating a vicious self-perpetuating circle. In another experiment, people anticipated interacting with another person of a different race. When led to expect that the person disliked interacting with someone of their race, they felt more anger and displayed more hostility toward the person (Butz & Plant, 2006). Likewise, whether a husband expects his wife to be in a bad mood or in a warm, loving mood may affect how he relates to her, thereby inducing her to confirm his belief.

So do intimate relationships prosper when partners idealize each other? Are positive illusions of the other's virtues self-fulfilling? Or are they more often self-defeating, by creating expectations that can't be met? Among University of Waterloo dating couples followed by Sandra Murray and associates (1996a, 2000), positive ideals of one's partner were good omens. Idealization helped buffer conflict, bolster satisfaction, and turn self-perceived frogs into princes or princesses. When someone loves and admires us, it helps us become more the person he or she imagines us to be.

When dating couples deal with conflicts, hopeful optimists and their partners tend to perceive each other as engaging constructively. Compared to those with more pessimistic expectations, they then feel more supported and more satisfied with the outcome (Srivastava et al., 2006). Among married couples, too, those who worry that their partner doesn't love and accept them interpret slight hurts as rejections, which motivate them to devalue the partner and distance themselves. Those who presume their partner's love and acceptance respond less defensively and even may be closer to their partner (Murray et al., 2003). Love helps create its presumed reality.

Several experiments conducted by Mark Snyder (1984) show how, once formed, erroneous beliefs about the social world can induce others to confirm those beliefs, a phenomenon called **behavioural confirmation**. In a classic study, Snyder, Elizabeth Tanke, and Ellen Berscheid (1977) had male students talk on the telephone with women they thought (from having been shown a picture) were either attractive or unattractive. Analysis of just the women's comments during the conversations revealed that the supposedly attractive women spoke more warmly than the supposedly unattractive women. The men's erroneous beliefs had become a self-fulfilling prophecy by leading them to act in a way that influenced the women to fulfill their stereotype that beautiful people are desirable people.

behavioural confirmation
a type of self-fulfilling prophecy whereby people's social expectations lead them to act in ways that cause others to confirm their expectations

Behavioural confirmation also occurs as people interact with partners holding mistaken beliefs. People who are believed lonely behave less sociably (Rotenberg, Gruman, & Ariganello, 2002). Men who are believed sexist behave less favourably toward women (Pinel, 2002). Job interviewees who are believed to be warm behave more warmly.

Imagine yourself as one of the 60 young men or 60 young women in an experiment by Robert Ridge and Jeffrey Reber (2002). Each man is to interview one of the women to assess her suitability for a teaching assistant position. Before doing so, he is told either that she feels attracted to him (based on his answers to a biographical questionnaire) or not attracted. (Imagine being told that someone you were about to meet reported considerable interest in getting to know you and in dating you.) The result was behavioural confirmation: Applicants believed to feel an attraction exhibited more flirtatiousness (and without being aware of doing so). This process may be one of the roots of sexual harassment, Ridge and Reber suggested. If a woman's behaviour seems to confirm a man's beliefs, he may then escalate his overtures until they become sufficiently overt for the woman to recognize and interpret them as inappropriate or harassing.

Expectations influence children's behaviour, too. After observing the amount of litter in three classrooms, Richard Miller and his colleagues (1975) had the teacher and others repeatedly tell one class that they should be neat and tidy. This persuasion increased the amount of litter placed in wastebaskets from 15 to 45 percent, but only temporarily. Another class, which also had been placing only 15 percent of its litter in wastebaskets, was repeatedly congratulated for being so neat and tidy. After eight days of hearing this, and still two weeks later, these children were fulfilling the expectation by putting more than 80 percent of their litter in wastebaskets. Repeatedly tell children they are hard-working and kind (rather than lazy and mean), and they may live up to their label.

These experiments help us understand how social beliefs, such as stereotypes about people with disabilities or about people of a particular race or sex, may be self-confirming. We help construct our own social realities. How others treat us reflects how we and others have treated them.

WHAT CAN WE CONCLUDE FROM RESEARCH ON SOCIAL BELIEFS AND JUDGMENTS?

Social cognition studies reveal that our information-processing powers are impressive for their efficiency and adaptiveness (We are "in apprehension how like a god!" as Shakespeare's Hamlet exclaimed), yet vulnerable to predictable errors and misjudgments (The brain is a "headpiece filled with straw," according to T. S. Eliot). What practical lessons, and what insights into human nature, can we take home from all of this research?

We have reviewed reasons why people sometimes form false beliefs. We cannot easily dismiss these experiments: Most of their participants were intelligent people, mostly students at leading universities. Moreover, people's intelligence scores are uncorrelated with their vulnerability to many different thinking biases (Stanovich & West, 2008). One can be very smart and exhibit seriously bad judgment.

Trying hard doesn't eliminate biased thinking. These predictable distortions and biases occurred even when payment for right answers motivated people to think optimally. As one researcher concluded, the illusions "have a persistent quality not unlike that of perceptual illusions" (Slovic, 1972).

Research in cognitive social psychology thus mirrors the mixed review given humanity in literature, philosophy, and religion. Many research psychologists have spent lifetimes exploring the awesome capacities of the human mind. We are smart enough to have cracked our own genetic code, to have invented talking computers, to have sent people to the moon. Three cheers for human reason.

Well, two cheers—because the mind's premium on efficient judgment makes our intuition more vulnerable to misjudgment than we suspect. With remarkable ease, we form and sustain false beliefs. Led by our preconceptions, overconfident, persuaded by vivid anecdotes, perceiving correlations and control even where none may exist, we construct our social beliefs and then influence others to confirm them. "The naked intellect," observed novelist Madeleine L'Engle, "is an extraordinarily inaccurate instrument."

But have these experiments just been intellectual tricks played on hapless participants, thus making them look worse than they are? Richard Nisbett and Lee Ross (1980) contended that, if anything, laboratory procedures overestimate our intuitive powers.

The experiments usually present people with clear evidence and warn them that their reasoning ability is being tested. Seldom does life say to us, "Here is some evidence. Now put on your intellectual Sunday best and answer these questions."

Often, our everyday failings are inconsequential, but not always. False impressions, interpretations, and beliefs can produce serious consequences. Even small biases can have profound social effects when we are making important social judgments: Why are so many people homeless? Unhappy? Homicidal? Does my friend love me or my money? Cognitive biases even creep into sophisticated scientific thinking. Apparently, human nature has not changed in the 3000 years since the Psalmist noted that "no one can see his own errors."

Is this too cynical? Leonard Martin and Ralph Erber (2005) invited us to imagine that an intelligent being swooped down just for a moment and begged for information that would help it understand the human species. When you hand it this social psychology text, the alien says, "Thank you," and zooms back off into space. After (we'd like to presume) resolving your remorse over giving up this book, how would you feel about having offered social psychology's analysis? Joachim Krueger and David Funder (2003a, 2003b) wouldn't feel too good. Social psychology's preoccupation with human foibles needs balancing with "a more positive view of human nature," they argued.

Fellow social psychologist Lee Jussim (2005) agreed, adding, "Despite the oft-demonstrated existence of a slew of logical flaws and systematic biases in lay judgment and social perception, such as the fundamental attribution error, false consensus, over-reliance on imperfect heuristics, self-serving biases, etc., people's perceptions of one another are surprisingly (though rarely perfectly) accurate." The elegant analyses of the imperfections of our thinking are themselves a tribute to human wisdom. Were one to argue that all human thought is illusory, the assertion would be self-refuting, for it, too, would be but an illusion. It would be logically equivalent to contending, "All generalizations are false, including this one."

As medical science assumes that any given body organ serves a function, so behavioural scientists find it useful to assume that our modes of thought and behaviour are adaptive (Funder, 1987; Kruglanski & Ajzen, 1983; Swann, 1984). The rules of thought that produce false beliefs and striking deficiencies in our statistical intuition usually serve us well. Frequently, the errors are a by-product of our mental shortcuts that simplify the complex information we receive.

Nobel laureate psychologist Herbert Simon (1957) was among the modern researchers who first described the bounds of human reason. Simon contended that to cope with reality, we simplify it. Consider the complexity of a chess game: The number of possible games is greater than the number of particles in the universe. How do we cope? We adopt some simplifying rules of thumb—heuristics. These heuristics sometimes lead us to defeat. But they do enable us to make efficient snap judgments.

Illusory thinking can likewise spring from useful heuristics that aid our survival. In many ways, as mentioned earlier in the chapter, heuristics "make us smart" (Gigerenzer & Gaissmaier, 2011). The belief in our power to control events helps maintain hope and effort. If things are sometimes subject to control and sometimes not, we maximize our outcomes by positive thinking. Optimism pays dividends. We might even say that our beliefs are like scientific theories—sometimes in error yet useful as generalizations. As Susan Fiske (1992) said, "Thinking is for doing."

Might we reduce errors in our social thinking? In school, math teachers teach, teach, teach, until the mind is finally trained to process numerical information accurately and automatically. We assume that such ability does not come naturally; otherwise, why bother with the years of training? Research psychologist Robyn Dawes (1980b)—who was dismayed that "study after study has shown [that] people have very limited abilities to process information on a conscious level, particularly social information"—suggested that we should also teach, teach, teach how to process social information.

Richard Nisbett and Lee Ross (1980) believed that education could, indeed, reduce our vulnerability to certain types of error. They offered the following recommendations:

- Train people to recognize likely sources of error in their own social intuition.

- Set up statistics courses geared to everyday problems of logic and social judgment. Given such training, people do, in fact, reason better about everyday events (Lehman, Lempert, & Nisbett, 1988; Nisbett et al., 1987).

- Make such teaching more effective by richly illustrating it with concrete, vivid anecdotes and examples from everyday life.

- Teach memorable and useful slogans, such as these: "It's an empirical question." "Which hat did you draw that sample out of?" "You can lie with statistics, but a well-chosen example does the job better."

▶ SUMMING UP

HOW DO WE PERCEIVE OUR SOCIAL WORLDS?

- Our schemas and preconceptions strongly influence how we interpret and remember events. In a phenomenon called priming, people's prejudgments have striking effects on how they perceive and interpret information.

- Other experiments have planted judgments or false ideas in people's minds *after* they have been given information. These experiments reveal that as before-the-fact judgments bias our perceptions and interpretations, so after-the-fact judgments bias our recall.

- *Belief perseverance* is the phenomenon in which people cling to their initial beliefs and the reasons why a belief might be true, even when the basis for the belief is discredited.

- Far from being a repository for facts about the past, our memories are actually formed when we retrieve them; they are subject to strong influence by the attitudes and feelings we hold at the time of retrieval.

HOW DO WE JUDGE OUR SOCIAL WORLDS?

- We have an enormous capacity for automatic, efficient, intuitive thinking. Our cognitive efficiency, though generally adaptive, comes at the price of occasional error. Since we are generally unaware of those errors entering our thinking, it is useful to identify ways in which we form and sustain false beliefs.

- First, we often overestimate our judgments. This overconfidence phenomenon stems partly from the much greater ease with which we can imagine why we might be right than why we might be wrong. Moreover, people are much more likely to search for information that can confirm their beliefs than information that can disconfirm them.

- Second, when given compelling anecdotes or even useless information, we often ignore useful base-rate information. This is partly due to the later ease of recall of vivid information (the availability heuristic).

- Third, our emotional experiences are powerfully influenced by our imagination of how things might have happened differently. Counterfactual thinking shapes our feelings of guilt, regret, frustration, or relief.

- Fourth, we are often swayed by illusions of correlation and personal control. It is tempting to perceive correlations where none exist (illusory correlation) and to think we can predict or control chance events (the illusion of control).

- Finally, moods infuse judgments. Good and bad moods trigger memories of experiences associated with those moods. Moods colour our interpretation of current experiences. And by distracting us, moods can also influence how deeply or superficially we think when making judgments.

HOW DO WE EXPLAIN OUR SOCIAL WORLDS?

- Attribution theory involves how we explain people's behaviour. When will we attribute someone's behaviour to a person's disposition and when to the situation?

- By and large, we make reasonable attributions. When explaining other people's behaviour, however, we often commit the fundamental attribution error (also called correspondence bias). We attribute their behaviour so much to their inner traits and attitudes that we discount situational constraints, even when those are obvious.

- We make this attribution error partly because when we watch someone act, that person is the focus of our attention and the situation is relatively invisible.

- When we act, our attention is usually on what we are reacting to—the situation is more visible.

HOW DO OUR EXPECTATIONS OF OUR SOCIAL WORLDS MATTER?

- Our beliefs sometimes take on a life of their own. Usually, our beliefs about others have a basis in reality. But studies of experimenter bias and teacher expectations show that an erroneous belief that certain people are unusually capable (or incapable) can lead teachers and researchers to give those people special treatment. This may elicit superior (or inferior) performance and, therefore, seem to confirm an assumption that is actually false.

- Similarly, in everyday life, we often get behavioural confirmation of what we expect. Told that someone we are about to meet is intelligent and attractive, we may come away impressed with just how intelligent and attractive he or she is.

WHAT CAN WE CONCLUDE FROM RESEARCH ON SOCIAL BELIEFS AND JUDGMENTS?

- Research on social beliefs and judgments reveals how we form and sustain beliefs that usually serve us well, but sometimes lead us astray. A balanced social psychology will appreciate both the powers and perils of social thinking.

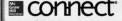 

CHAPTER FOUR
Behaviour and Attitudes

CHAPTER OUTLINE

● HOW WELL DO OUR ATTITUDES PREDICT OUR BEHAVIOURS?

● WHEN DOES OUR BEHAVIOUR AFFECT OUR ATTITUDES?

● WHY DOES OUR BEHAVIOUR AFFECT OUR ATTITUDES?

Rebecca is active and health conscious. She enjoys rock climbing, cycling, and ultimate Frisbee, and she recently ran a half marathon. She eats well and takes good care of her body with one exception: She smokes. Rebecca started smoking when she was 14

Attitudes and actions: Many sports events, which glorify health and physical prowess, are sponsored by manufacturers of products like cigarettes and alcohol, which are dangerous to health.

attitude
a favourable or unfavourable evaluative reaction toward something or someone, exhibited in one's beliefs, feelings, or intended behaviour

and has tried to quit several times. One time she quit for almost two years, but returned to smoking when hanging out with a group of friends who smoked. How are we to understand Rebecca's behaviour (i.e., smoking) and her attitudes (i.e., being health conscious)? What is the relationship between what we *are* (on the inside) and what we *do* (on the outside)? Philosophers, theologians, and educators have long speculated about the connections between attitude and action, character and conduct, private word and public deed. Underlying most teaching, counselling, and child-rearing is an assumption: Our private beliefs and feelings determine our public behaviour, so if we wish to change behaviour we must first change hearts and minds.

In the beginning, social psychologists agreed: To know people's attitudes is to predict their actions. As demonstrated by genocidal killers and suicide bombers, extreme attitudes can produce extreme behaviour. Countries whose people detest another country's leaders are more likely to produce terrorist acts against them (Krueger & Malečková, 2009). Hateful attitudes spawn violent behaviour.

But in 1957, Leon Festinger concluded that the evidence showed that *changing* people's attitudes hardly affects their behaviour. Festinger believed the attitude–behaviour relation works the other way around. As Robert Abelson (1972) put it, we are "very well trained and very good at finding reasons for what we do, but not very good at doing what we find reasons for." This chapter explores the interplay between attitudes and behaviour.

When social psychologists talk about someone's attitude, they refer to beliefs and feelings related to a person or an event and the resulting behaviour tendency. Taken together, favourable or unfavourable evaluative reactions toward something—often rooted in beliefs and exhibited in feelings and inclinations to act—define a person's **attitude** (Olson & Zanna, 1993). Thus, a person may have a negative attitude toward coffee, a neutral attitude toward the French, and a positive attitude toward the next-door neighbour. Attitudes efficiently size up the world. When we have to respond quickly to something, how we feel about it can guide how we react (Bassili & Roy, 1998; Breckler & Wiggins, 1989; Sanbonmatsu & Fazio, 1990). For example, a person who believes a particular ethnic group is lazy and aggressive may feel dislike for such people and, therefore, tend to act in a discriminatory manner. You can remember these three dimensions as the ABCs of attitudes: *a*ffect (feelings), *b*ehaviour tendency, and *c*ognition (thoughts).

● HOW WELL DO OUR ATTITUDES PREDICT OUR BEHAVIOURS?

To what extent, and under what conditions, do attitudes drive our outward actions? Why were social psychologists at first surprised by a seemingly small connection between attitudes and actions?

ARE WE ALL HYPOCRITES?

A blow to the supposed power of attitudes came when social psychologist Allan Wicker (1969) reviewed several dozen research studies covering a wide variety of people, attitudes, and behaviours, and offered a shocking conclusion: People's expressed attitudes hardly predicted their varying behaviours.

> *"The ancestor of every action is a thought."*
> RALPH WALDO EMERSON, *ESSAYS, FIRST SERIES*, 1841

- Student attitudes toward cheating bore little relation to the likelihood of their actually cheating.
- Attitudes toward the church were only modestly linked with church attendance on any given Sunday.
- Self-described racial attitudes provided little clue to behaviours in actual situations. Many people *say* they express being upset with someone making racist remarks; yet, when they hear racism (such as someone using the N-word) respond indifferently (Kawakami et al., 2009).

An example of the disjuncture between attitudes and actions is what Daniel Batson and his colleagues (1997, 2001, 2002; Valdesolo & DeSteno, 2007, 2008) called "moral hypocrisy" (appearing moral without being so). Their studies presented people with an appealing task (where the participant could earn raffle tickets toward a $30 prize) and a dull task with no rewards. The participants had to assign themselves to one of the tasks and a supposed second participant to the other. Only 1 in 20 believed that assigning the positive task to themselves was the most moral thing to do, yet 80 percent did so. In follow-up experiments on moral hypocrisy, participants could toss a coin to assign roles—privately, if they wished. Even if they chose to use a coin toss, 90 percent assigned themselves to the positive task! Was this because they could specify the consequences of heads and tails after the coin toss? In yet another experiment, Batson put a sticker on each side of the coin, indicating what the flip outcome would signify. Still, 24 of 28 people who made the toss assigned themselves to the positive task. When morality and greed were put on a collision course, greed won.

If people don't walk the same line that they talk, it's little wonder that attempts to change behaviour by changing attitudes often fail. Warnings about the dangers of smoking only minimally affect those who already smoke. Increasing public awareness of the desensitizing and brutalizing effects of a prolonged diet of television violence has stimulated many people to voice a desire for less violent programming—yet they still watch media murder as much as ever. Sex education programs have often influenced attitudes toward abstinence and condom use without affecting long-term abstinence and condom-use behaviours. We are, it seems, at base all hypocrites.

All in all, the developing picture of what controls behaviour emphasized external social influences, such as others' behaviour and expectations, and played down internal factors, such as attitudes and personality. The original thesis that attitudes determine actions was countered during the 1960s by the antithesis that attitudes determine virtually nothing.

> *"It may be desirable to abandon the attitude concept."*
> ALLAN WICKER, 1971

Thesis. Antithesis. Is there a synthesis? The surprising finding that what people say often differs from what they do sent social psychologists scurrying to find out why. Surely, we reasoned, convictions and feelings sometimes make a difference.

Indeed. In fact, what we are about to explain now seems so obvious that we wonder why most social psychologists (ourselves included) were not thinking this way before the early 1970s. We must remind ourselves that truth never seems obvious until it is known.

WHEN ATTITUDES PREDICT BEHAVIOUR

The reason—now obvious—why our behaviour and our expressed attitudes differ is that both are subject to other influences. One social psychologist counted 40 separate factors that complicate their relationship (Triandis, 1982; see also Kraus, 1995). Our attitudes do predict our behaviour when these other influences on what we say and do are minimal, when the attitude is specific to the behaviour, and when the attitude is potent (that is, strong and on our mind).

When social influences on what we say are minimal

Unlike a physician measuring heart rate, social psychologists never get a direct reading on attitudes. Rather, we measure expressed attitudes. Like other behaviours, expressions are subject to outside influences. This was vividly demonstrated when politicians once overwhelmingly passed a salary increase for themselves in an off-the-record vote, then moments later overwhelmingly defeated the same bill on a roll-call vote. Fear of criticism had distorted the true sentiment on the roll-call vote. We sometimes say what we think others want to hear.

Today's social psychologists have some clever means at their disposal for minimizing social influences on people's attitude reports. Some of these complement traditional self-report measures of *explicit* (conscious) attitudes with measures of *implicit* (unconscious) attitudes. One such test measures facial muscle responses to various statements (Cacioppo & Petty, 1981). Those measurements, the researchers hope, can reveal enough of a microsmile or a microfrown to indicate the participant's attitude about a given statement.

Implicit Association Test (IAT)
a computer-driven assessment of implicit attitudes that uses reaction times to measure people's automatic associations between attitude objects and evaluative words, where easier pairings (and faster responses) are taken to indicate stronger unconscious associations

A newer and widely used attitude measure, the **Implicit Association Test (IAT)**, uses reaction times to measure how quickly people associate concepts (Greenwald et al., 2002; Greenwald, Nosek, & Banaji, 2003). One can, for example, measure implicit racial attitudes by assessing whether White people take longer to associate positive words with Black than with White faces. Implicit attitude researchers have offered various IAT assessments online (projectimplicit.net). The some 5 million completed tests since 1998 have, they report, shown the following:

- *Implicit biases are pervasive.* For example, 80 percent of people show more implicit negativity toward the elderly compared with the young.
- *People differ in implicit bias.* Depending on their group memberships, their conscious attitudes, and the bias in their immediate environment, some people exhibit more implicit bias than others.
- *People are often unaware of their implicit biases.* Despite thinking themselves unprejudiced, even the researchers exhibit some implicit biases (negative associations with various social groups).

Do implicit biases predict behaviour? A review of the available research (now over 200 investigations) reveals that both explicit (self-report) and implicit attitudes help predict people's behaviours and judgments (Greenwald et al., 2008; Nosek, Hawkins, & Frazier, 2011). Thus, explicit and implicit attitudes may together predict behaviour better than either alone (Spence & Townsend,

2007). The behaviour predictions range from dental flossing to the fate of romantic relationships to suicide attempts (Lee, Rogge, & Reis, 2010; Millar, 2011; Nock et al., 2010). In one study, hiring managers received job applications that were matched on credential strength, but with one, the applicants' photos were digitally altered to make them appear obese. Several months later, when 153 of the managers completed an IAT, their automatic anti-obesity bias score predicted which applicants they had invited for interviews (Agerström & Rooth, 2011).

For attitudes formed early in life—such as racial and gender attitudes— implicit and explicit attitudes frequently diverge, with implicit attitudes often being the better predictor of behaviour.

THE >>> INSIDE STORY

Graduating from high school in India at age 15, I had but a single goal—to leave my well-adjusted and secure family to live the patently more daring and exciting life of a secretarial assistant. Proficient at typing scores of words a minute, I looked forward to a life of independence that involved living a block away from my parents. My mother, despite not having attended college, persuaded me to try college—but only for a semester, we agreed, after which I would be free to choose my path.

The end of my first semester at Nizam College came and went. Mother didn't ask about my plans. I didn't have to swallow and tell. Just before one holiday trip home, I bought the five volumes of the 1968 *Handbook of Social Psychology* for the equivalent of a dollar apiece (it seemed like a lot of book for the money). By the end of a 24-hour train ride home, I had polished off one volume and knew with blunt clarity that this science, which studied social processes experimentally, was something I had to do.

Doctoral and postdoctoral fellowships enabled me to work with three remarkable people early in my career: Tony Greenwald at Ohio State, and Claude Steele and Elizabeth Loftus at the University of Washington. At Yale, while still interested in human memory researchers, I discovered that memories come in both explicit (conscious) and implicit (unconscious) forms. Might this also be true of attitudes, beliefs, and values? Hesitantly, I wrote the words "Implicit Attitudes" as the title of a grant proposal, not knowing

it would become such a central part of what my students and I would study for the next two decades.

With Tony Greenwald and Brian Nosek, I have enjoyed an extended collaboration on implicit social cognition that few scientists are blessed with. From the hundreds of studies that have used the Implicit Association Test (projectimplicit.net) and the millions of tests taken, we now know that people carry knowledge (stereotypes) and feelings (attitudes) of which they are unaware, and which often contrast with their conscious expressions. We know that subcortical brain activity can be an independent marker of implicit attitudes, that people differ in their implicit attitudes, and that such attitudes and stereotypes predict real-life behaviour. Most optimistically, we know that implicit attitudes, even old ones, can be modified by experience.

Mahzarin R. Banaji *Harvard University*

For example, implicit racial attitudes have successfully predicted interracial roommate relationships (Towles-Schwen & Fazio, 2006). For other attitudes, such as those related to consumer behaviour and support for political candidates, explicit self-reports are the better predictor. (See the nearby "The Inside Story" box from Mahzarin R. Banaji.)

Recent neuroscience studies have identified brain centres that produce our automatic, implicit reactions (Stanley, Phelps, & Banaji, 2008). One area deep in the brain (the amygdala, a centre for threat perception) is active as we automatically evaluate social stimuli. For example, White people who show strong unconscious racial bias on the IAT also exhibit high amygdala activation when viewing unfamiliar Black faces. Other frontal lobe areas are involved in detecting and regulating implicit attitudes.

A word of caution: Despite much excitement over these recent studies of implicit attitudes hiding in the mind's basement, the Implicit Association Test has detractors (Arkes & Tetlock, 2004; Blanton et al., 2006, 2007). They note that, unlike an aptitude test, the IAT is not reliable enough for use in assessing and comparing individuals. Moreover, a score that suggests some relative bias doesn't distinguish a positive bias for one group (or greater familiarity with one group) from a negative bias against another. The critics also wonder whether compassion and guilt rather than latent hostility might slow one's speed in associating Blacks with positive words. Regardless, the existence of distinct explicit and implicit attitudes confirms one of twenty-first-century psychology's biggest lessons: our "dual processing" capacity for both *controlled* (deliberate, conscious, explicit) and *automatic* (effortless, habitual, implicit) thinking.

When other influences on behaviour are minimal

On any occasion, it's not only our inner attitudes that guide us but also the situation we face. As Chapters 5 to 8 will illustrate again and again, social influences can be enormous—enormous enough to induce people to violate their deepest convictions. Government aides may go along with actions they know are wrong. Prisoners of war may lie to placate their captors.

So, would averaging many occasions enable us to detect more clearly the impact of our attitudes? Predicting people's behaviour is like predicting a baseball or cricket player's hitting. The outcome of any particular time at bat is nearly impossible to predict, because it is affected not only by the batter but also by what the pitcher throws and by chance factors. When we aggregate many times at bat, we neutralize these complicating factors. Knowing the players, we can predict their approximate batting averages.

> *"Do I contradict myself? Very well then I contradict myself. (I am large, I contain multitudes.)"*
> WALT WHITMAN, *SONG OF MYSELF*, 1855

To use a research example, people's general attitude toward religion poorly predicts whether they will go to worship next weekend (because the weather, the preacher, how they are feeling, and so forth also influence attendance). But religious attitudes predict quite well the total quantity of religious behaviours over time (Fishbein & Ajzen, 1974; Kahle & Berman, 1979). The findings define a *principle of aggregation:* The effects of an attitude on behaviour become more apparent when we look at a person's aggregate or average behaviour rather than at isolated acts.

When attitudes specific to behaviour are examined

Other conditions further improve the predictive accuracy of attitudes. As Icek Ajzen and Martin Fishbein (1977; Ajzen, 1982) point out, when the measured attitude is a general one—say, an attitude toward Asians—and the behaviour is very specific—say, a decision whether to help a particular Asian couple—we should not expect a close correspondence between words and actions. Indeed, reported Fishbein and Ajzen, in 26 out of 27 such research studies, attitudes did not predict behaviour. But attitudes *did* predict behaviour in all 26 studies they could find in which the measured attitude was directly pertinent to the situation. Thus, attitudes toward the general concept of "health fitness" poorly predict specific exercise and dietary practices, but an individual's attitudes about the costs and benefits of jogging are a fairly strong predictor of whether he or she jogs regularly.

Better yet for predicting behaviour, said Ajzen in his and Fishbein's "theory of planned behaviour," is knowing people's *intended* behaviours, and their perceived self-efficacy and control (Figure 4-1). Moreover, four dozen experimental tests confirmed that inducing new intentions induces new behaviour (Webb & Sheeran, 2006). Even simply asking people about their intentions to engage in a behaviour increases its likelihood (Levav & Fitzsimons, 2006). Ask people if they intend to floss their teeth in the next two weeks or to vote in an upcoming election, and they will become more likely to do so.

Further studies—more than 700 studies with 276 000 participants—confirmed that specific, relevant attitudes do predict intended and actual behaviour (Armitage & Conner, 2001; Bassili, 1995; Six & Eckes, 1996; Wallace et al., 2005). For example, attitudes toward condoms strongly predict condom use (Albarracin et al., 2001). And attitudes toward recycling (but not general attitudes toward environmental issues) predict participation in recycling (Oskamp, 1991). To change habits through persuasion, we had best alter people's attitudes toward *specific* practices.

So far we have seen two conditions under which attitudes will predict behaviour: (1) when we minimize other influences on our attitude statements and our behaviour, and (2) when the attitude is specifically relevant to the observed behaviour. There is a third condition: An attitude predicts behaviour better when it is potent (strong and on one's mind).

When attitudes are potent

Much of our behaviour is automatic. We act out familiar scripts, without reflecting on what we're doing. We respond to people we meet in the hall with an automatic "Hi." We answer the restaurant cashier's question, "How was your meal?" by saying, "Fine," even if we found it tasteless.

FIGURE 4-1

THE THEORY OF PLANNED BEHAVIOUR.

Icek Ajzen, working with Martin Fishbein, has shown that one's (a) attitudes, (b) perceived social norms, and (c) feelings of control together determine one's intentions, which guide behaviour.

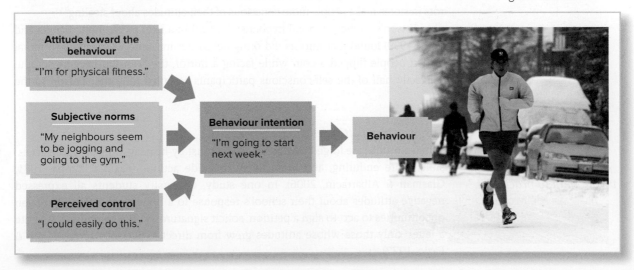

Such mindless reaction is adaptive. It frees our minds to work on other things. For habitual behaviours—seat belt use, coffee consumption, class attendance—conscious intentions are hardly activated (Ouellette & Wood, 1998). As the philosopher Alfred North Whitehead argued, "Civilization advances by extending the number of operations which we can perform without thinking about them."

Bringing attitudes to mind

If we were prompted to think about our attitudes before acting, would we be truer to ourselves? Mark Snyder and William Swann (1976) wanted to find out. So two weeks after 120 of their students indicated their attitudes toward affirmative-action employment policies, Snyder and Swann invited them to act as jurors in a sex-discrimination court case. Only if they first induced the students to remember their attitudes—by giving them "a few minutes to organize your thoughts and views on the affirmative-action issue"—did attitudes predict verdicts. Similarly, people who take a few moments to review their past behaviour express attitudes that better predict their future behaviour (Zanna, Olson, & Fazio, 1981). Our attitudes become potent *if* we think about them.

> "Thinking is easy, acting difficult, and to put one's thoughts into action, the most difficult thing in the world."
> GERMAN POET JOHANN WOLFGANG VON GOETHE, 1749–1832

Self-conscious people usually are in touch with their attitudes (Miller & Grush, 1986). This suggests another way to induce people to focus on their inner convictions: Make them self-conscious, perhaps by having them act in front of a mirror (Carver & Scheier, 1981). Maybe you can recall suddenly being acutely aware of yourself upon entering a room with a large mirror. Making people self-aware in this way promotes consistency between words and deeds (Froming, Walker, & Lopyan, 1982; Gibbons, 1978).

> "Without doubt it is a delightful harmony when doing and saying go together."
> MONTAIGNE, *ESSAYS*, 1588

Edward Diener and Mark Wallbom (1976) noted that nearly all university students say that cheating is morally wrong. But will they follow the advice of Shakespeare's Polonius, "To thine own self be true"? Diener and Wallbom set students to work on an anagram-solving task (said to predict IQ) and told them to stop when a bell in the room sounded. Left alone, 71 percent cheated by working past the bell. Among students made self-aware—by working in front of a mirror while hearing their tape-recorded voices—only 7 percent cheated. It makes one wonder: Would eye-level mirrors in stores make people more conscious of their attitudes about stealing?

Remember Batson's studies of moral hypocrisy (p. 123) In a later experiment, Batson and his colleagues (1999) found that mirrors did bring behaviour into line with espoused moral attitudes. When people flipped a coin while facing a mirror, the coin flip became scrupulously fair. Exactly half of the self-conscious participants assigned the other person to the positive task.

Forging strong attitudes through experience

> "It is easier to preach virtue than to practise it."
> LA ROCHEFOUCAULD, *MAXIMS*, 1665

When attitudes are forged by experience, not just by hearsay, they are more accessible, more enduring, and more likely to guide actions (Fazio & Zanna, 1981; Glasman & Albarracin, 2006). In one study, university students all expressed negative attitudes about their school's response to a housing shortage. But given opportunities to act—to sign a petition, solicit signatures, join a committee, or write a letter—only those whose attitudes grew from direct experience acted (Regan & Fazio, 1977).

WHEN DOES OUR BEHAVIOUR AFFECT OUR ATTITUDES?

If social psychology has taught us anything during the last 25 years, it is that we are likely not only to think ourselves into a way of acting but also to act ourselves into a way of thinking. What lines of evidence support this assertion?

Now we turn to a more startling idea: behaviour determines attitudes. It's true that we sometimes stand up for what we believe. But it's also true that we come to believe in what we stand up for. Social-psychological theories inspired much of the research that underlies this conclusion. Instead of beginning with these theories, however, let's first see what there is to explain. As we engage evidence that behaviour affects attitudes, speculate *why* this is and then compare your ideas with social psychologists' explanations.

> *"Thought is the child of Action."*
>
> BENJAMIN DISRAELI, *VIVIAN GREY*, 1826

Consider the following incidents, each based on actual happenings:

- Sarah is hypnotized and told to take off her shoes when a book drops on the floor. Fifteen minutes later, a book drops, and Sarah quietly slips out of her loafers. "Sarah," asks the hypnotist, "why did you take off your shoes?" "Well . . . my feet are hot and tired," Sarah replies. "It has been a long day." The act produces the idea.

- George has electrodes temporarily implanted in the brain region that controls his head movements. When neurosurgeon José Delgado (1973) stimulates the electrode by remote control, George always turns his head. Unaware of the remote stimulation, he offers a reasonable explanation for it: "I'm looking for my slipper." "I heard a noise." "I'm restless." "I was looking under the bed."

- Carol's severe seizures were relieved by surgically separating her two brain hemispheres. Now, in an experiment, psychologist Michael Gazzaniga (1985) flashes a picture of a nude woman to the left half of Carol's field of vision and thus to her nonverbal right hemisphere. A sheepish smile spreads over her face, and she begins chuckling. Asked why, she invents— and apparently believes—a plausible explanation: "Oh—that funny machine." Frank, another split-brain patient, has the word "smile" flashed to his nonverbal right hemisphere. He obliges and forces a smile. Asked why, he explains, "This experiment is very funny."

The mental after-effects of our behaviour also appear in many social-psychological examples of self-persuasion. As we will see over and over, attitudes follow behaviour.

ROLE-PLAYING

The word **role** is borrowed from the theatre and, as in the theatre, refers to actions expected of those who occupy a particular social position. Each social position is defined by a set of prescribed **norms** for behaviour. When stepping into a new social role, we must perform its actions, even if we feel phony. But our unease seldom lasts.

Think of a time when you stepped into some new role—perhaps your first days on a job, at university, or in a sorority or fraternity. That first week on campus, for example, you may have been supersensitive to your new social situation and tried valiantly to act appropriately and root out your high school behaviour. At such times, we feel self-conscious. We observe our new speech and actions because they aren't natural to us. Then one day, an amazing thing happens:

role
a set of norms that define how people in a given social position ought to behave

norms
rules for accepted and expected behaviour, that prescribe "proper" behaviour

Guards and prisoners in a prison simulation quickly absorbed the roles they played.

We notice that our sorority enthusiasm or our pseudo-intellectual talk no longer feels forced. The role has begun to fit as comfortably as our old jeans and T-shirt.

In one study, university men volunteered to spend time in a simulated prison constructed in the psychology department by Philip Zimbardo (1971). Zimbardo, like so many others, wondered whether prison brutality is a product of evil prisoners and malicious guards or whether the institutional roles of guard and prisoner would embitter and harden even compassionate people. Do the people make the place violent, or does the place make the people violent?

By a flip of a coin, he designated some students as guards. He gave them uniforms, billy clubs, and whistles, and instructed them to enforce the rules. The other half, the prisoners, were locked in cells and made to wear humiliating outfits. After a jovial first day of "playing" their roles, the guards and prisoners, and even the experimenters, got caught up in the situation. The guards began to disparage the prisoners, and some devised cruel and degrading routines. The prisoners broke down, rebelled, or became apathetic. There developed, reported Zimbardo (1972), a "growing confusion between reality and illusion, between role-playing and self-identity. . . . This prison which we had created . . . was absorbing us as creatures of its own reality." Observing the emerging social pathology, Zimbardo was forced to call off the planned two-week simulation after only six days.

U.S. soldiers acting as prison guards engaged in brutal and demeaning treatment of their Iraqi prisoners. Most soldiers sat by and watched the atrocities occur without raising a warning or trying to stop them. This reaction, too, resembled the Stanford prison experiment. The role of prison guard brought out hostility in some, but an even more common result of the role seems to be that it prevents intervening even to help those who are clearly in need.

The deeper lesson of role-playing studies concerns how what is unreal (an artificial role) can evolve into what is real. In a new career, as teacher, soldier, or businessperson, we act a role that shapes our attitudes.

Take the case of Stephen Reid. In the 1970s, Reid was part of the notorious group of bank robbers called the "Stop Watch Gang." They robbed over 100 banks, stealing more than $15 million. Reid was eventually arrested. While in prison, he wrote the highly regarded novel, *Jackrabbit Parole*. Award-winning Canadian poet Susan Musgrave edited the book and then asked Reid to marry her. They were married; when he was released, they raised two children. By all accounts, Reid was a happy and devoted husband and father. He was fond of saying, "My criminal career ended the day I began writing."

Sadly his criminal career had not ended. In 1998, Reid began using drugs and became addicted. On June 9, 1999, he robbed a Victoria bank, shot at a police officer, and held an elderly couple hostage.

If Reid had been a bank robber all along and only pretended to be a good family man, people could have more easily understood his actions. What they could not

> *"No man, for any considerable period, can wear one face to himself and another to the multitude without finally getting bewildered as to which may be true."*
> NATHANIEL HAWTHORNE, 1850

After the degradation of Iraqi prisoners by some U.S. military personnel, Philip Zimbardo (2004a, 2004b) noted "direct and sad parallels between similar behaviour of the 'guards' in the Stanford Prison Experiment." Such behaviour, he contended, is attributable to a toxic situation that can make good people into perpetrators of evil. "It's not that we put bad apples in a good barrel. We put good apples in a bad barrel. The barrel corrupts anything that it touches."

understand was that he could really be a bank robber, then really a devoted husband and father, and then really a bank robber again.

Could such a thing happen to you or me? Yes and no. Our actions depend not only on the social situation but also on our dispositions. Reid may have had a predisposition to drug abuse, which probably played a role in his criminal activities. You might well have responded differently.

Nevertheless, some social situations can move most "normal" people to behave in "abnormal" ways. This is clear from experiments that put well-intentioned people in a bad situation to see whether good or evil prevails. To a dismaying extent, evil wins. Nice guys often don't finish nice.

Stephen Reid, serving his sentence for bank robbery (left), and with his wife, poet and author Susan Musgrave (right).

Gender roles

One prominent role given to us by our society is our gender. Early on, we are socialized into gender roles. Gender socialization, it has been said, gives girls "roots" and boys "wings." In Caldecott Award–winning children's books over the last half-century, girls have four times more often than

boys been shown using household objects (such as a broom, sewing needle, or pots and pans), and boys have five times more often than girls been shown using production objects (such as a pitchfork, plough, or gun) (Crabb & Bielawski, 1994). The adult result: "Everywhere," reported the United Nations (1991), women do most household work. And "everywhere, cooking and dishwashing are the least shared household chores." Such behaviour expectations for males and females define **gender roles**.

gender roles
behaviour expectations (norms) for males and females

In an experiment with undergraduate women, Mark Zanna and Susan Pack (1975) showed the impact of gender role expectations. The women answered a questionnaire on which they described themselves to a man they expected to meet, a man they were told was tall, unattached, and a fourth-year student. Those led to believe the man's ideal woman was home-oriented and deferential to her husband presented themselves as more traditionally feminine than did women expecting to meet a man who liked strong, ambitious women. Moreover, given a problem-solving test, those expecting to meet the non-sexist man behaved more intelligently: They solved 18 percent more problems than those expecting to meet the man with the traditional views. This adapting of themselves to fit the man's image was much less pronounced if the man was less desirable—a short, already attached first-year student. In a companion experiment by Dean Morier and Cara Seroy (1994), men similarly adapted their self-presentations to meet desirable women's gender role expectations. Clearly our gender roles can shape our actions.

Do you ever present oneself to members of your own sex and a different self to members of the other sex?

WHEN SAYING BECOMES BELIEVING

People often adapt what they say to please their listeners. They are quicker to tell people good news than bad, and they adjust their message toward the listener's position (Manis, Cornell, & Moore, 1974; Tesser, Rosen, & Conlee, 1972; Tetlock, 1983). When induced to give spoken or written support to something they doubt, people will often feel bad about the deceit. Nevertheless, they begin to believe what they are saying—provided they weren't bribed or coerced into doing so. When there is no compelling external explanation for one's words, saying becomes believing (Klaas, 1978).

© J. B. Handelsman/The New Yorker Collection/www.cartoonbank.com.

Tory Higgins and his colleagues (Higgins & McCann, 1984; Higgins & Rholes, 1978) illustrated how saying becomes believing. They had university students read a personality description of someone and then summarize it for someone else who was believed either to like or to dislike this person. The students wrote a more positive description when the recipient liked the person, and, having said positive things, then liked

"That was a fine report, Barbara. But since the sexes speak different languages, I probably didn't understand a word of it."

the person more themselves. Asked to recall what they had read, they remembered the description as being more positive than it was. In short, it seems that we are prone to adjust our messages to our listeners and, having done so, to believe the altered message.

THE FOOT-IN-THE-DOOR PHENOMENON

Most of us can recall times when, after agreeing to help out with a project or an organization, we ended up more involved than we ever intended, vowing that in the future we would say no to such requests. How does this happen?

In keeping with the "attitude follows behaviour" principle, experiments suggest that if you want people to do a big favour for you, one technique is to get them to do a small favour first. In the best-known demonstration of this **foot-in-the-door phenomenon**, researchers posing as safety-drive volunteers asked people to permit the installation of a huge, poorly lettered "Drive Carefully" sign in their front yards. Only 17 percent consented. Others were first approached with a small request: Would they display a 7.5 cm "Be a safe driver" window sign? Nearly all readily agreed. When approached two weeks later to allow the large, ugly sign in their front yards, 76 percent consented (Freedman & Fraser, 1966). One project helper who went from house to house later recalled that, not knowing who had been previously visited, "I was simply stunned at how easy it was to convince some people and how impossible to convince others" (Ornstein, 1991).

Other researchers have confirmed the foot-in-the-door phenomenon with altruistic behaviours.

- Patricia Pliner and her collaborators (1974) found 46 percent of Toronto suburbanites willing to give to the Cancer Society when approached directly. Others, asked a day ahead to wear a lapel pin publicizing the drive (which all agreed to do), were nearly twice as likely to donate.

- Angela Lipsitz and others (1989) reported that ending blood-drive reminder calls with "We'll count on seeing you then, OK? [pause for response]" increased the show-up rate from 62 to 81 percent.

- In Internet chat rooms, Paul Markey and his colleagues (2002) requested help ("I can't get my e-mail to work. Is there any way I can get you to send me an e-mail?"). Help increased—from 2 to 16 percent—by including a smaller prior request ("I am new to this whole computer thing. Is there any way you can tell me how to look at someone's profile?").

- Nicolas Gueguen and Celine Jacob (2001) tripled the rate of French Internet users contributing to a child land-mine victims organization (from 1.6 to 4.9 percent) by first inviting them to sign a petition against land mines.

Note that in these experiments, as in many of the 1001 other foot-in-the-door experiments, the initial compliance—signing a petition, wearing a lapel pin, stating one's intention—was voluntary (Burger & Guadagno, 2003). We will see again and again that when people commit themselves to public behaviours and perceive these acts to be their own doing, they come to believe more strongly in what they have done.

Social psychologist Robert Cialdini is a self-described "patsy." "For as long as I can recall, I've been an easy mark for the pitches of peddlers, fundraisers, and operators of

foot-in-the-door phenomenon the tendency for people who have first agreed to a small request to comply later with a larger request

"You will easily find folk to do favours if you cultivate those who have done them."
PUBLILIUS SYRUS, 42 B.C.

THE >>> INSIDE STORY

When I began my career at Princeton in 1970, the first group of female undergraduates had just enrolled at this formerly all-male bastion. These pioneers were incredibly bright and very ambitious. Indeed, the majority intended to become doctors, lawyers, or professors! It was Susan Pack's intuition that, despite the great capabilities and high achievement motivation of her female peers, they still "acted dumb" when confronted with the typical attractive, though chauvinistic, Princeton male.

Susan's undergraduate honours thesis, designed to test this notion, demonstrated that Princeton females "acted dumb" or "acted smart" depending, in part, on whether they believed an attractive Princeton male held chauvinistic or liberated attitudes about women. I wonder: Would these results hold today at Princeton? At other colleges? Would males, too, act to fulfill the gender stereotypes of attractive females?

Mark Zanna *University of Waterloo*

one sort or another." To better understand why one person says yes to another, he spent three years as a trainee in various sales, fundraising, and advertising organizations, discovering how they exploit "the weapons of influence." He also put those weapons to the test in simple experiments. In one, Cialdini and his collaborators (1978) explored a variation of the foot-in-the-door phenomenon by experimenting with the **low-ball technique**. After the customer agrees to buy a new car because of its bargain price and begins completing the sales forms, the salesperson removes the price advantage by charging for options the customer thought were included or by checking with a boss who disallows the deal because "we'd be losing money." Folklore has it that more customers stick with the higher-priced purchase than would have agreed to it at the outset.

low-ball technique
a tactic for getting people to agree to something. People who agree to an initial request will often still comply when the requester ups the ante. People who receive only the costly request are less likely to comply with it.

Cialdini and his collaborators found that this technique indeed works. When they invited introductory psychology students to participate in an experiment at 7:00 a.m., only 24 percent showed up. But if the students first agreed to participate without knowing the time and only then were asked to participate at 7:00 a.m., 53 percent came.

Marketing researchers and salespeople have found that the principle works even when we are aware of a profit motive (Cialdini, 1988). A harmless initial commitment—returning a card for more information and a gift, agreeing to listen to an investment possibility—often moves us toward a larger commitment. Salespeople may exploit the power of small commitments when trying to bind people to purchase agreements. Many places now have laws that allow customers of door-to-door salespeople a few days to think over their purchases and cancel. (For example, the Ontario *Consumer Protection Act* of 2002 allows a 10-day "cooling-off period" during which you may cancel a contract.) To combat the effect of these laws, many companies use what the sales-training program of one encyclopedia company calls "a very important psychological aid in preventing customers from backing out of their contracts" (Cialdini, 1988, p. 78). They simply have the customer, rather than the salesperson, fill out the agreement. Having written it themselves, people usually live up to their commitment.

The foot-in-the-door phenomenon is well worth learning about. Someone trying to seduce us—financially, politically, or sexually—usually will try to create a momentum of compliance. Before agreeing to a small request, think about what may follow.

EVIL AND MORAL ACTS

The attitudes-follow-behaviour principle works with more immoral acts as well. Evil sometimes results from gradually escalating commitments. A trifling evil act can make a worse act easier. Evil acts gnaw at the actor's moral sensitivity. To paraphrase La Rochefoucauld's *Maxims* (1665), it is not as difficult to find a person who has never succumbed to a given temptation as to find a person who has succumbed only once. After telling a "white lie" and thinking, "Well, that wasn't so bad," the person may go on to tell a bigger lie.

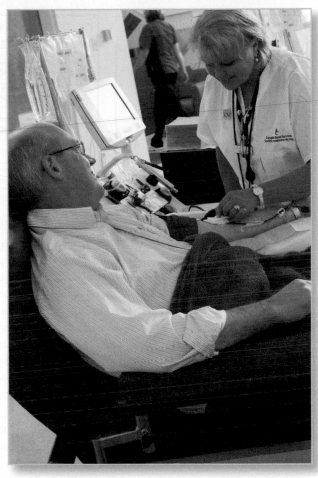

A foot in the door. To get people to donate blood or money, it often helps to first elicit a smaller commitment to the same cause.

Another way in which evil acts influence attitudes is the paradoxical fact that we tend not only to hurt those we dislike but also to dislike those we hurt. Several studies (Berscheid, Boye, & Walster, 1968; Davis & Jones, 1960; Glass, 1964) found that harming an innocent victim—by uttering hurtful comments or delivering electric shocks—typically leads aggressors to disparage their victims, thus helping them justify their cruel behaviour. This is especially so when we are coaxed into it, not coerced. When we voluntarily agree to do a deed, we take more responsibility for it.

The phenomenon appears in wartime. Prisoner-of-war camp guards would sometimes display good manners to captives in their first days on the job, but those behaviours didn't last. Soldiers ordered to kill may initially react with revulsion to the point of sickness over their act, but not for long (Waller, 2002). Often they will denigrate their enemies with dehumanizing nicknames.

Attitudes also follow behaviour in peacetime. A group that holds another in slavery will likely come to perceive the slaves as having traits that justify their oppression. For example, prison staff who participate in executions experience "moral disengagement" by coming to believe (more strongly than do other prison staff) that their

"Our self-definitions are not constructed in our heads; they are forged by our deeds."
ROBERT MCAFEE BROWN,
CREATIVE DISLOCATION—THE MOVEMENT OF GRACE, 1980

The low-ball technique.

The Born Loser © Newspaper Enterprise Association.

victims deserve their fate (Osofsky, Bandura, & Zimbardo, 2005). Actions and attitudes feed each other, sometimes to the point of moral numbness. The more one harms another and adjusts one's attitudes, the easier harm-doing becomes. Conscience is corroded.

To simulate the "killing begets killing" process, Andy Martens and his collaborators (2007) asked University of Arizona students to kill some bugs. They wondered: Would killing initial bugs in a "practice" trial increase students' willingness to kill more bugs later? To find out, they asked some students to look at one small bug in a container, then to dump it into a coffee grinder and press the "on" button for three seconds. (No bugs were actually killed. An unseen stopper at the base of the insert tube prevented the bug from actually entering the opaque killing machine, which had torn bits of paper to simulate the sound of a killing.) Others, who initially killed five bugs (or so they thought), went on to "kill" significantly more bugs during an ensuing 20-second period.

Harmful acts shape the self, but, thankfully, so do moral acts. Character, it is said, is reflected in what we do when we think no one is looking. Researchers have tested character by giving children temptations when it seems no one is watching. Consider what happens when children resist the temptation. They internalize the conscientious act if the deterrent is strong enough to elicit the desired behaviour yet mild enough to leave them with a sense of choice. In a dramatic experiment, Jonathan Freedman (1965) introduced elementary school children to an enticing battery-controlled robot, instructing them not to play with it while he was out of the room. Freedman used a severe threat with half the children and a mild threat with the others. Both were sufficient to deter the children.

Several weeks later, a different researcher, with no apparent relation to the earlier events, left each child to play in the same room with the same toys. Of the 18 children who had been given the severe threat, 14 now freely played with the robot, but two-thirds of those who had been given the mild deterrent still resisted playing with it. Having earlier made a conscious choice not to play with the toy, the mildly deterred children apparently internalized their decision. This new attitude controlled their subsequent action. Thus, moral action, especially when chosen rather than coerced, affects moral thinking.

If moral action feeds moral attitudes, can laws and rules that require moral conduct lead to genuine moral beliefs? Elliot Aronson (1992) argued that such change is possible. His argument went like this: If we wait for the heart to change—through preaching and teaching—we will wait a long time. But if we legislate moral action, we can, under the right conditions, indirectly affect heartfelt attitudes.

Mourners walked with the hearse carrying murder victim David Rosenzweig following his funeral service at Toronto in July 2002. Rosenzweig was the victim of an alleged hate crime. Acts like this can compound fear or even breed more prejudice.

The idea runs counter to the presumption that "you can't legislate morality." Yet attitude change has, in fact, followed changes in the laws. Consider some of the following:

- In the 1980s and 1990s, many governments began requiring the use of seat belts by all people riding in automobiles. Initially, these laws were seen as burdensome and were opposed by many. But over time, seat belt use has risen dramatically. Now, most people in these jurisdictions favour mandatory seat belt laws.

- In 1954, the Supreme Court of the United States ruled that schools segregated by race were inherently unfair and that such schools were required to desegregate. Since that decision, the percentage of Whites in the U.S. favouring integrated schools has more than doubled and now includes nearly everyone.

- In the 1970s, many National Hockey League players did not wear helmets. Older players saw this as a measure of toughness. But in the 1980s, almost all bantam and junior hockey leagues required players to wear helmets. Now, all players in the NHL wear helmets and see them as an important safety measure. Having grown up with helmets, they now believe they are useful.

Do laws always lead to the adoption of consistent attitudes? Almost certainly not. There are times when it is true that "you can't legislate morality." But research in social psychology confirms that, under the right conditions, people's attitudes follow their behaviours even when these behaviours are required.

Experiments demonstrate that positive behaviour toward someone fosters liking for that person. Doing a favour for an experimenter or another subject, or tutoring a student, usually increases liking of the person helped (Blanchard & Cook, 1976). It is a lesson worth remembering: If you wish to love someone more, act as if you do.

"We do not love people so much for the good they have done us, as for the good we have done them."
LEO TOLSTOY, *WAR AND PEACE*, 1867–1869

SOCIAL MOVEMENTS

We have now seen that a society's laws, and therefore its behaviour, can have a strong influence on people's behaviour. But a danger lies in the possibility of employing the same idea for political socialization on a mass scale. For many Germans during the 1930s, participation in Nazi rallies, wearing uniforms, demonstrating, and especially the public greeting "Heil Hitler" established a profound inconsistency between behaviour and belief. Historian Richard Grunberger (1971) reported that for those who had their doubts about Hitler, "The 'German greeting' was a powerful conditioning device. Having once decided to intone it as an outward token of conformity, many experienced schizophrenic discomfort at the contradiction between their words and their feelings. Prevented from saying what they believed, they tried to establish their psychic equilibrium by consciously making themselves believe what they said" (p. 27).

"One does what one is; one becomes what one does."
ROBERT MUSIL, *KLEINE PROSA*, 1930

The practice is not limited to totalitarian regimes. Political rituals, such as singing the national anthem, use public conformity to build a private belief in patriotism. One of the authors was amazed at the strong sense of being a Canadian that his son developed in junior kindergarten. Before school, his son had virtually no identity as a Canadian; but after three weeks of singing *O Canada* on Mondays, he was Canadian through and through. Observers noted how the civil rights marches of the 1960s strengthened the demonstrators' commitments. Their actions expressed an idea whose time had come and drove that idea more deeply into their hearts. The 1980s' move toward gender-inclusive language similarly strengthened inclusive attitudes.

Many people assume that most social indoctrination comes through *brainwashing,* a term coined to describe what happened to prisoners of war (POWs) during the Korean War in the 1950s. Actually, this Chinese "thought-control" program, developed to re-educate the Chinese populace into communism and used during the Korean War, was not nearly as irresistible as this term suggests. But the results still were disconcerting. Hundreds of prisoners cooperated with their captors. Twenty-one chose to remain after being granted permission to return to their home countries. And many of those who returned to the United States arrived believing that "although communism won't work in America, I think it's a good thing for Asia" (Segal, 1954).

Edgar Schein (1956) interviewed many of the POWs during their journey home and reported that the captors' methods included a gradual escalation of demands. The Chinese always started with trivial requests and gradually worked up to more significant ones. "Thus after a prisoner had once been 'trained' to speak or write out trivia, statements on more important issues were demanded." Moreover, they

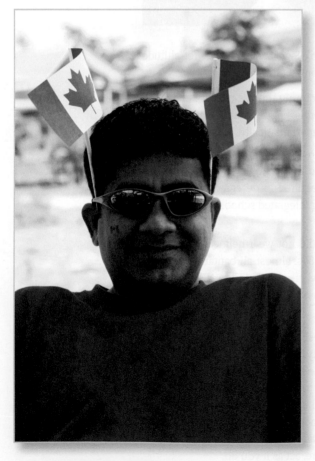

Celebrating Canada Day:
Patriotic actions strengthen patriotic attitudes.

always expected active participation, be it just copying something or participating in group discussions, writing self-criticism, or uttering public confessions. Once a prisoner had spoken or written a statement, he felt an inner need to make his beliefs consistent with his acts. This often drove prisoners to persuade themselves of the good of what they had done. The "start-small-and-build" tactic was an effective application of the foot-in-the-door technique, as it continues to be today in the socialization of terrorists and torturers (Chapter 6).

Now let me ask you, before reading further, to play theorist. Ask yourself: Why in these studies and real-life examples did attitudes follow behaviour? Why might playing a role or making a speech influence your attitude?

> *"You can use small commitments to manipulate a person's self-image; you can use them to turn citizens into 'public servants,' prospects into 'customers,' prisoners into 'collaborators.'"*
> ROBERT CIALDINI, *INFLUENCE*, 1988

● WHY DOES OUR BEHAVIOUR AFFECT OUR ATTITUDES?

What theories help explain the attitudes-follow-behaviour phenomenon? How do the tests between these competing ideas illustrate the process of scientific explanation?

We have seen that several streams of evidence merge to form a river: the effect of actions on attitudes. Do these observations contain any clues to why action affects attitude? Social psychology's detectives suspect three possible sources. Self-presentation theory assumes that for strategic reasons, we express attitudes that make us appear consistent. Cognitive dissonance theory assumes that to reduce discomfort, we justify our actions to ourselves. Self-perception theory assumes that our actions are self-revealing (when uncertain about our feelings or beliefs, we look to our behaviour, much as anyone else would). Let's examine each explanation.

SELF-PRESENTATION: IMPRESSION MANAGEMENT

The first explanation began as a simple idea, which you may recall from Chapter 2. Who among us does not care what people think? We spend countless dollars on clothes, diets, cosmetics, even plastic surgery—all because we worry about what others think of us. We see making a good impression as a way to gain social and material rewards, to feel better about ourselves, even to become more secure in our social identities (Leary, 1994, 2001, 2004b, 2007, 2010).

No one wants to look foolishly inconsistent. To avoid seeming so, we express attitudes that match our actions. To appear consistent, we may pretend those attitudes. Even if that means displaying a little insincerity or hypocrisy, it can pay off in managing the impression we are making. Or so self-presentation theory suggests.

Does our feigning consistency explain why expressed attitudes shift toward consistency with behaviour? To some extent, yes. People exhibit a much smaller attitude change when a bogus pipeline—a technique in which researchers lead participants to believe that any false statements will be detected—inhibits trying to make a good impression (Paulhus, 1982; Tedeschi, Nesler, & Taylor, 1987).

But there is more to the attitude changes we have reviewed than self-presentation, for people express their changed attitudes even to someone who doesn't know how they have behaved.

Two other theories explain why people sometimes internalize their self-presentations as genuine attitude changes.

SELF-JUSTIFICATION: COGNITIVE DISSONANCE

One theory is that our attitudes change because we are motivated to maintain consistency among our cognitions. This is the implication of Leon Festinger's (1957) **cognitive dissonance theory**. The theory is simple, but its range of application is enormous. It assumes we feel tension ("dissonance") when two simultaneously accessible thoughts or beliefs ("cognitions") are psychologically inconsistent—as when we decide to say or do something we have mixed feelings about. Festinger argued that to reduce this unpleasant arousal, we often adjust our thinking. This simple idea and some surprising predictions derived from it have spawned more than 2000 studies (Cooper, 1999).

One way people minimize dissonance, Festinger believed, is through selective exposure to agreeable information. Studies have asked people about their views on various topics, and then invited them to choose whether they wanted to view information supporting or opposing their viewpoint. By about a two-to-one ratio, people (less secure and open-minded people, especially) preferred supporting rather than challenging information (Fischer & Greitemeyer, 2010; Hart et al., 2009; Sweeny et al., 2010). People are especially keen on reading information that supports their political, religious, and ethical views—a phenomenon that most of us can illustrate from our own favourite news and blog sources. On more practical and less values-relevant topics, "accuracy motives" are more likely to drive us. Thus, we welcome a home inspection before buying or a second opinion before surgery.

Dissonance theory pertains mostly to discrepancies between behaviour and attitudes. We are aware of both. Thus, if we sense some inconsistency, perhaps some hypocrisy, we feel pressure for change. That helps explain why, in a British survey, half of cigarette smokers disagreed with the near-consensus among non-smokers that smoking is "really as dangerous as people say" (Eiser, Sutton, & Wober, 1979; Saad, 2002) and why the perception of risk among those who have quit declines after relapsing (Gibbons, Eggleston, & Benthin, 1997).

Cognitive dissonance theory offers several surprising predictions. See if you can anticipate them.

① Insufficient justification

Imagine you are a participant in a famous experiment staged by the creative Festinger and his student, J. Merrill Carlsmith (1959). For an hour, you are required to perform dull tasks, such as turning wooden knobs again and again. After you finish, the experimenter (Carlsmith) explains that the study concerns how expectations affect performance. The next subject, waiting outside, must be led to expect an interesting experiment. The seemingly distraught experimenter, whom Festinger had spent hours coaching until he became extremely convincing, explains that the assistant who usually creates this expectation couldn't make this session. Wringing his hands, he pleads, "Could you fill in and do this?"

It's for science and you are being paid, so you agree to tell the next subject (who is actually the experimenter's real assistant) what a delightful experience you have just had. "Really?" responds the supposed subject. "A friend of mine was in this experiment a week ago, and she said it was boring." "Oh, no," you respond, "it's really very

cognitive dissonance theory
tension that arises when we are simultaneously aware of two inconsistent cognitions. For example, dissonance may occur when we realize that we have, with little justification, acted contrary to our attitudes or made a decision favouring one alternative despite reasons favouring another.

"A foolish consistency is the hobgoblin of little minds."
RALPH WALDO EMERSON, "SELF-RELIANCE," 1841

interesting. You get good exercise while turning some knobs. I'm sure you'll enjoy it." Finally, someone else who is studying how people react to experiments has you complete a questionnaire that asks how much you actually enjoyed your knob-turning experience.

Now for the prediction: Under which condition are you most likely to believe your little lie and say the experiment was, indeed, interesting? When paid $1 for doing so, as some of the subjects were? Or when paid a then-generous $20, as others were? Contrary to the common notion that big rewards produce big effects, Festinger and Carlsmith made an outrageous prediction: Those paid just $1 (hardly sufficient justification for a lie) would be most likely to adjust their attitudes to their actions. Having **insufficient justification** for their action, they would experience more discomfort (dissonance) and thus be more motivated to believe in what they had done. Those paid $20 had sufficient justification for what they did and hence should have experienced less dissonance. As Figure 4–2 shows, the results fit this intriguing prediction.*

In dozens of later experiments, the attitudes-follow-behaviour effect was strongest when people felt some choice and when their actions had foreseeable consequences. One experiment had people read disparaging lawyer jokes into a recorder (for example, "How can you tell when a lawyer is lying? His lips are moving."). The reading produced more negative attitudes toward lawyers when it was a chosen rather than coerced activity (Hobden & Olson, 1994). Other experiments have engaged people to write an essay for a measly $1.50 or so. When the essay argues something they don't believe in—say, a tuition increase—the underpaid writers begin to feel somewhat greater sympathy with the policy. Advocating a policy favourable to another race may improve your attitudes not only toward the policy but toward the race. This is especially so if something makes you face the inconsistency or if you think important people will actually

> **insufficient justification**
> reduction of dissonance by internally justifying one's behaviour when external justification is "insufficient"

THE >>> INSIDE STORY

Following a 1934 earthquake in India, there were rumours outside the disaster zone of worse disasters to follow. It occurred to me that these rumours might be "anxiety-justifying"—cognitions that would justify their lingering fears. From that germ of an idea, I developed my theory of dissonance reduction—making your view of the world fit with how you feel or what you've done.

Leon Festinger (1920–1989)

---

*There is a seldom-reported final aspect of this 1950s experiment. Imagine yourself finally back with the experimenter, who is truthfully explaining the whole study. Not only do you learn that you've been duped, but the experimenter asks for the $20 back. Do you comply? Festinger and Carlsmith noted that all their student subjects willingly reached into their pockets and gave back the money. This is a foretaste of some quite amazing observations on compliance and conformity discussed in Chapter 6. As we will see, when the social situation makes clear demands, people usually respond accordingly.

FIGURE 4-2

INSUFFICIENT JUSTIFICATION.

Dissonance theory predicts that when our actions are not fully explained by external rewards or coercion, we will experience dissonance, which we can reduce by believing in what we have done. (Data from Festinger & Carlsmith, 1959)

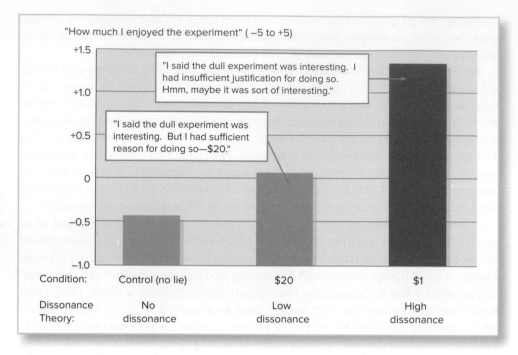

read an essay with your name on it (Leippe & Eisenstadt, 1994; Leippe & Elkin, 1987). Feeling responsible for statements you have made, you will now believe them more strongly. Pretence becomes reality.

Earlier, we noted how the insufficient justification principle works with punishments. Children were more likely to internalize a request not to play with an attractive toy if given a mild threat that insufficiently justified their compliance. When a parent says, "Clean up your room, Johnny, or I'll knock your block off," Johnny won't need to internally justify cleaning his room. The severe threat is justification enough.

Note that cognitive dissonance theory focuses on what induces a desired action, rather than the relative effectiveness of rewards and punishments administered after the act. It aims to have Johnny say, "I am cleaning up my room because I want a clean room," rather than, "I am cleaning up my room because my parents will kill me if I don't." Students who perceive their required community service as something they would have chosen to do are more likely to anticipate future volunteering than those who feel coerced (Stukas, Snyder, & Clary, 1999). The principle: Attitudes follow behaviours for which we feel some responsibility.

Authoritarian management will be effective, the theory predicts, only when the authority is present—because people are unlikely to internalize forced behaviour. Bree, a formerly enslaved talking horse in C. S. Lewis's *The Horse and His Boy* (1974), observes that "One of the worst results of being a slave and being forced to do things is that when there is no one to force you any more you find you have almost lost the power of forcing yourself" (p. 193). Dissonance theory insists that encouragement and inducement should be enough to elicit the desired action. But it suggests that managers, teachers, and parents should use only enough incentive to elicit the desired behaviour.

② Dissonance after decisions

The emphasis on perceived choice and responsibility implies that decisions produce dissonance. When faced with an important decision—what university to attend, whom to date, which job to accept—we are sometimes torn between two equally attractive alternatives. Perhaps you can recall a time when, having committed yourself, you became painfully aware of dissonant cognitions—the desirable features of what you rejected and the undesirable features of what you chose. If you decided to live on campus, you may have realized you were forgoing the spaciousness and freedom of an apartment in favour of cramped, noisy dorm quarters. If you elected to live off campus, you may have realized that your decision meant physical separation from campus and friends and having to cook for yourself.

After making important decisions, we usually reduce dissonance by upgrading the chosen alternative and downgrading the unchosen option. In the first published dissonance experiment (1956), Jack Brehm had women rate eight products, such as a toaster, a radio, and a hair dryer. Brehm then showed the women two objects they had rated closely and told them they could have whichever they chose. Later, when re-rating the eight objects, the women increased their evaluations of the item they had chosen and decreased their evaluations of the rejected item. It seems that after we have made our choice, the grass does *not* then grow greener on the other side of the fence. (Afterwards, Brehm confessed he couldn't afford to let them keep what they chose.)

Dissonance theory suggests that parents should aim to elicit desired behaviour non-coercively, thus motivating children to internalize the appropriate attitudes.

With simple decisions, this deciding-becomes-believing effect can breed overconfidence (Blanton et al., 2001): "What I have decided must be right." The effect can occur very quickly. Robert Knox and James Inkster (1968) found that bettors at a Vancouver racetrack who had just put down their money on a horse felt more optimistic about their bet than did those who were about to bet. In the few moments that intervened between standing in line and walking away from the betting window, nothing had changed—except the decisive action and the person's feelings about it. Contestants in carnival games of chance feel more confident of winning right after agreeing to play than right before. And voters indicate more esteem and confidence in a candidate just after voting than just before (Younger, Walker, & Arrowood, 1977).

Our preferences influence our decisions, which then sharpen our preferences. This choices-influence-preferences effect occurs even after people press a button to choose what they think was a subliminally presented vacation alternative (nothing was actually shown them). They later tended to prefer the holiday that they believed they had chosen (Sharot, Velasquez, & Dolan, 2010).

> *"Every time you make a choice you are turning the central part of you, the part of you that chooses, into something a little different from what it was before."*
>
> C. S. LEWIS, *MERE CHRISTIANITY*, 1943

And it's not just grown-ups who do this. A Yale University team led by Louisa Egan (2007) invited 4-year-olds to rate different stickers on a scale of smiley faces. With each child, the researchers then picked three stickers which that child had rated equally, and randomly identified two (let's call them Sticker A and Sticker B) from which the children could choose one to take home. Next they let the child choose one more—either the unchosen sticker or the third one, Sticker C. The result (which put a smiley on our faces): The children apparently reduced dissonance by downplaying the appeal of the unchosen first sticker, thus moving them to favour Sticker C 63 percent of the time (rather than half the time, as we might have expected). They repeated the experiment with capuchin monkeys using alternative sweets instead of stickers. As with the children, so with the monkeys: They, too, revised their attitudes after making an initial decision.

CULTURE AND COGNITIVE DISSONANCE

Do cultural differences lead to differences in the experience of cognitive dissonance? Recall from Chapter 2 that people from Eastern cultures tend to have a more collectivist self-concept, whereas people from Western cultures tend to have a more individualistic self-concept. Note that all the early studies on dissonance after decision took place in Western cultures. Does the tendency in these studies for people to justify their decisions arise out of a Western cultural desire to individualistically claim that they made good choices?

Steve Heine and Darrin Lehman (1997a) from the University of British Columbia thought so. They had Canadian students from U.B.C. and Japanese exchange students complete a typical dissonance experiment. All the students were asked to rate a number of compact discs (CDs), and then were given a choice between two of the CDs as a reward for being in the experiment. Previous studies conducted in individualistic cultures have shown that when people are given such a choice and then rate the CDs again, their ratings of the CD they chose become more positive and their ratings of the CD they did not choose become more negative. Heine and Lehman found this exact pattern among their Canadian participants. Apparently, Canadians protected their individualistic self-concepts by seeing their choices as good choices.

But what about the Japanese participants? Did they protect themselves by justifying their choices? No. Showing no evidence of the typical pattern, they rated the CDs the same regardless of what choice they had made.

Does this mean that people who have a collectivistic self-concept do not experience cognitive dissonance? Etsuko Hoshino-Browne and her colleagues (Hoshino-Browne et al., 2005) thought they would experience dissonance if their collectivist self-concepts were threatened. They tested this idea by modifying the typical dissonance experiment. They had University of Waterloo students born in Canada or Kyoto University students from Japan make a choice for themselves or for a close friend. They reasoned that when Canadian students made a choice for themselves, their individualistic self-concept would be threatened, but when Japanese students made a choice for a friend, their collectivistic self-concept would be threatened. Consistent with this reasoning, they found that Canadian students justified the choices they made for themselves, but not the choices they made for their friends; Japanese students, on the other hand, justified the choices they made for their friends, but not the choices they made for themselves.

These studies suggest that culture can shape the experience of cognitive dissonance. Having an individualistic versus a collectivistic self-concept will affect when and how people experience cognitive dissonance. They also suggest, however, that the experience of feeling cognitive dissonance may be shared across many cultures.

SELF-PERCEPTION

Although dissonance theory has inspired much research, an even simpler theory explains its phenomena. Consider how we make inferences about other people's attitudes. We see how a person acts in a particular situation, and then we attribute the behaviour either to the person's traits and attitudes or to environmental forces. If we see parents coercing their little Susie into saying, "I'm sorry," we attribute Susie's reluctant behaviour to the situation, not to her personal regret. If we see Susie apologizing with no apparent inducement, we attribute the apology to Susie herself.

Self-perception theory (proposed by Daryl Bem, 1972) assumes that we make similar inferences when we observe our own behaviour. When our attitudes are weak or ambiguous, we are in the position of someone observing us from the outside. Hearing myself talk informs me of my attitudes; seeing my actions provides clues to how strong my beliefs are. This is especially so when you can't easily attribute your behaviour to external constraints. The acts we freely commit are self-revealing (Figure 4–3).

The pioneering psychologist William James proposed a similar explanation for emotion a century ago. We infer our emotions, he suggested, by observing our bodies and our behaviours. A stimulus such as a growling bear confronts a woman in the forest. She tenses, her heartbeat increases, adrenalin flows, and she runs away. Observing all this, she then experiences fear. Before big lectures, one of the authors often wakes before dawn and is unable to get back to sleep. Noting his wakefulness, he concludes that he must be anxious.

self-perception theory
the theory that when unsure of our attitudes, we infer them much as would someone observing us—by looking at our behaviour and the circumstances under which it occurs

FIGURE 4–3
ATTITUDES FOLLOW BEHAVIOUR.
Why do actions affect attitudes?

Do people who observe themselves agreeing to a small request come to perceive themselves as the helpful sort of person who responds positively to requests for help? Is that why, in the foot-in-the-door experiments, people will then later agree to larger requests? Indeed, yes, reported Jerry Burger and David Caldwell (2003). Behaviour can modify self-concept.

Expressions and attitude

You may be skeptical of the self-perception effect. We were when we first heard it. Experiments on the effects of facial expressions, however, suggest a way for you to experience it.

> *"Self-knowledge is best learned, not by contemplation, but action."*
> GOETHE, 1749–1832

When James Laird (1974, 1984; Duclos et al., 1989) induced university students to frown while attaching electrodes to their faces—"contract these muscles," "pull your brows together"—the students reported feeling angry. It's more fun to try out Laird's other finding: Those induced to make a smiling face felt happier and found cartoons more humorous. Those induced to repeatedly practise happy (versus sad or angry) expressions may recall more happy memories and find the happy mood lingering (Schnall & Laird, 2003). A Japanese research team created similar expressions—and emotions—by taping rubber bands to the sides of the face and then running them over either the top of the head (raising the cheeks into a smile) or under the chin (Mori & Mori, 2009).

Clever follow-up studies have found more examples of this facial (and body) feedback effect:

- Botox smoothes emotional wrinkles. If it's hard for us to know what the frozen-faced Botoxed are feeling, it's also hard for them to know themselves. Paralyzing the frowning muscles with Botox slows activity in people's emotion-related brain circuits and slows their reading of sadness- or anger-related sentences (Havas et al., 2010; Hennenlotter et al., 2008). Moreover, being unable to mimic others' expressions, it's harder for them to understand others' emotions (Neal & Chartrand, 2011).

- When people are instructed to sit straight and push out their chest, they feel more confidence in their written ideas than when sitting slouched forward and with eyes downcast (Briñol, Petty, & Wagner, 2009).

- People who assume high-power rather than low-power poses (think hands on hips rather than a contracted posture) experience increased testosterone, feelings of power, and risk tolerance (Carney, Cuddy, & Yap, 2010).

We have all experienced this phenomenon. We're feeling crabby, but then the phone rings or someone comes to the door and elicits from us warm, polite behaviour. "How's everything?"

According to German psychologist Fritz Strack and his colleagues (1988), people found cartoons funnier while holding a pen with their teeth (using a smiling muscle) than while holding it with their lips (using muscles incompatible with smiling).

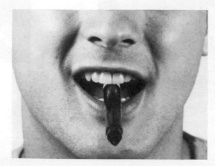
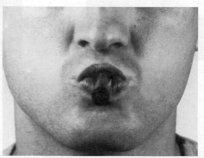

Natural mimicry and emotional contagion. People in sync, like these children working out math problems, feel more rapport with each other.

"Just fine, thanks. How are things with you?" "Oh, not bad. . . ." If our feelings are not intense, this warm behaviour may change our whole attitude. It's tough to smile and feel grouchy. When Miss Universe parades her smile, she may, after all, be helping herself feel happy. As Rodgers and Hammerstein reminded us, when we are afraid, it may help to "whistle a happy tune." Going through the motions can trigger the emotions. It is also true, however, that extending the middle finger makes others' ambiguous expressions seem more hostile (Chandler & Schwarz, 2009).

Even your gait can affect how you feel. When you get up from reading this chapter, walk for a minute taking short, shuffling steps, with eyes downcast. It's a great way to feel depressed. "Sit all day in a moping posture, sigh, and reply to everything with a dismal voice, and your melancholy lingers," noted William James (1890, p. 463). Want to feel better? Walk for a minute taking long strides with your arms swinging and your eyes straight ahead.

If our expressions influence our feelings, then would imitating others' expressions help us know what they are feeling? An experiment by Katherine Burns Vaughan and John Lanzetta (1981) suggested it would. They asked students to observe someone receiving electric shock. They told some of the observers to make a pained expression whenever the shock came on. If, as Freud and others supposed, expressing an emotion allows us to discharge it, then the pained expression should be inwardly calming (Cacioppo et al., 1991). Actually, compared to other students who did not act out the expressions, these grimacing students perspired more and had a faster heart rate whenever they saw the person shocked. Acting out the person's emotion apparently enabled the observers to feel more empathy. The implication: To sense how other people are feeling, let your own face mirror their expressions.

Actually, you hardly need try. Observing others' faces, postures, and voices, we naturally and unconsciously mimic their moment-to-moment reactions (Hatfield, Cacioppo,

"I can watch myself and my actions, just like an outsider."
ANNE FRANK, *THE DIARY OF A YOUNG GIRL*, 1947

"The free expression by outward signs of emotion intensifies it. On the other hand, the repression as far as possible, of all outward signs softens our emotions."
CHARLES DARWIN, *THE EXPRESSION OF THE EMOTIONS IN MAN AND ANIMALS*, 1897

& Rapson, 1992; Ireland & Pennebaker, 2010). We synchronize our movements, postures, and tones of voice with theirs. Doing so helps us tune in to what they're feeling. It also makes for "emotional contagion," helping explain why it's fun to be around happy people and depressing to be around depressed people (see Module B).

Our facial expressions also influence our attitudes. In a clever experiment, Gary Wells and Richard Petty (1980) had University of Alberta students "test headphone sets" by making either vertical or horizontal head movements while listening to a radio editorial. Who most agreed with the editorial? Those who had been nodding their heads up and down. Why? Wells and Petty surmised that positive thoughts are compatible with vertical nodding and incompatible with horizontal motion. Try it yourself when listening to someone: Do you feel more agreeable when nodding rather than shaking your head?

At the University of Cologne, Thomas Mussweiler (2006) likewise discovered that stereotyped actions feed stereotyped thinking. In one clever experiment, he induced some people to move about in the portly manner of an obese person—by having them wear a life vest and putting weights on their wrists and ankles—and then give their impression of someone described on paper. Those whose movements simulated obesity, more than those in a control condition, perceived the person (described on paper) as exhibiting traits (friendliness, sluggishness, unhealthiness) that people often perceive in obese people. In follow-up experiments, people induced to move slowly, as an elderly person might, ascribed more elderly stereotypic traits to a target person. Doing influenced thinking.

Postures also affect performance. After noting that people associate an arms-folded posture with determination and persistence, Ron Friedman and Andrew Elliot (2008) had students attempt to solve impossible anagrams. Those instructed to work with their arms folded persevered for an average 55 seconds, nearly double the 30 seconds of those with their hands on their thighs.

Overjustification and intrinsic motivations

Recall the insufficient justification effect—the smallest incentive that will get people to do something is usually the most effective in getting them to like the activity and keep on doing it. Cognitive dissonance theory offers one explanation for this: When external inducements are insufficient to justify our behaviour, we reduce dissonance by internally justifying the behaviour.

Self-perception theory offers another explanation: People explain their behaviour by noting the conditions under which it occurs. Imagine hearing someone proclaim the wisdom of a tuition increase after being paid $20 to do so. Surely the statement would seem less sincere than if you thought the person was expressing those opinions for no pay. Perhaps we make similar inferences when observing ourselves. We observe our uncoerced action and infer our attitude.

Self-perception theory goes even a step further. Contrary to the notion that rewards always increase motivation, it suggests that unnecessary rewards sometimes have a hidden cost. Rewarding people for doing what they already enjoy may lead them to attribute their doing it to the reward, thus undermining their self-perception that they do it because they like it. Experiments by Edward Deci and Richard Ryan (1991, 1997), by Mark Lepper and David Greene (1979), and by Ann Boggiano and her colleagues (1985, 1987) confirmed this **overjustification effect**. Pay people for playing with puzzles, and they will later play with the puzzles less than those who play without being paid; promise children a reward for doing what they intrinsically enjoy (for example, playing with magic markers) and you will turn their play into work (Figure 4–4).

overjustification effect
the result of bribing people to do what they already like doing; they may then see their action as externally controlled rather than intrinsically appealing

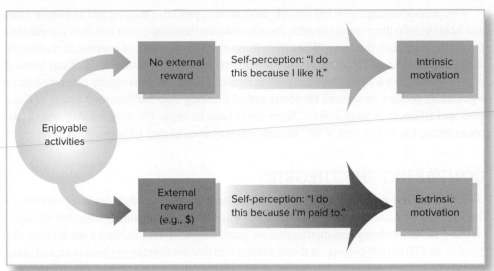

FIGURE 4–4

INTRINSIC AND EXTRINSIC MOTIVATION.

When people do something they enjoy, without reward or coercion, they attribute their behaviour to their love of the activity. External rewards undermine intrinsic motivation by leading people to attribute their behaviour to the incentive.

A folk tale illustrates the overjustification effect. An old man lived alone on a street where boys played noisily every afternoon. The din annoyed him, so one day he called the boys to his door. He told them he loved the cheerful sound of children's voices and promised them each 50 cents if they would return the next day. Next afternoon, the youngsters raced back and played more lustily than ever. The old man paid them and promised another reward the next day. Again they returned, whooping it up, and the man again paid them; this time 25 cents. The following day they got only 15 cents, and the man explained that his meagre resources were being exhausted. "Please, though, would you come to play for 10 cents tomorrow?" The disappointed boys told the man they would not be back. It wasn't worth the effort, they said, to play all afternoon at his house for only 10 cents.

As self-perception theory implies, an unanticipated reward does not diminish intrinsic interest, because people can still attribute their action to their own motivation (Bradley & Mannell, 1984; Tang & Hall, 1995). (It's like the heroine who, having fallen in love with the woodcutter, now learns that he's really a prince.) And if compliments for a good job make us feel more competent and successful, this can actually increase our intrinsic motivation. When rightly administered, rewards may also boost creativity (Eisenberger & Armeli, 2001; Eisenberger & Cameron, 1999; Eisenberger & Rhoades, 2001; Eisenberger, Rhoades, & Cameron, 1999; Eisenberger & Shanock, 2003).

The overjustification effect occurs when someone offers an unnecessary reward beforehand in an obvious effort to control behaviour. What matters is what a reward implies: Rewards and praise that inform people of their achievements (that make them feel, "I'm very good at this") boost intrinsic motivation. Rewards that seek to control people and lead them to believe it was the reward that caused their effort ("I did it for the money") diminish the intrinsic appeal of an enjoyable task (Freedman, Cunningham, & Krismer, 1992; Rosenfeld, Folger, & Adelman, 1980; Sansone, 1986).

How then can we cultivate people's enjoyment of tasks that are not intrinsically appealing? Young Maria may find her first piano lessons frustrating. Toshi may not have an intrinsic love of fifth-grade science. Sandra may not look forward to making those first sales calls. In such cases, the parent, teacher, or manager should probably use some incentives to coax the desired behaviour (Boggiano & Ruble, 1985; Cooke et al., 2011; Workman & Williams, 1980). After the person complies, suggest an intrinsic reason for doing so: "I'm not surprised that sales call went well, because you are so good at making a first impression."

If we provide students with just enough justification to perform a learning task and use rewards and labels to help them feel competent, we may enhance their enjoyment and their eagerness to pursue the subject on their own. When there is too much justification—as happens in classrooms where teachers dictate behaviour and use rewards to control the children—child-driven learning may diminish (Deci & Ryan, 1985, 1991, 2008). One of the authors' sons eagerly consumed six or eight library books a week—until his library started a reading club that promised a party to those who read 10 books in three months. Three weeks later, he began checking out only one or two books during his weekly visit. Why? "Because you only need to read 10 books, you know."

COMPARING THE THEORIES

We have seen one explanation of why our actions seem to affect our attitudes (self-presentation theory). And we have seen two explanations of why our actions genuinely affect our attitudes: (1) the dissonance-theory assumption that we justify our behaviour to reduce our internal discomfort, and (2) the self-perception theory assumption that we observe our behaviour and make reasonable inferences about our attitudes, as we observe other people and infer their attitudes.

The last two explanations seem to contradict one another. Which is right? It's difficult to find a definitive test. In most instances, they make the same predictions, and we can bend each theory to accommodate most of the findings we have considered (Greenwald, 1975). Daryl Bem (1972), the self-perception theorist, even suggested it boils down to a matter of loyalties and aesthetics. This illustrates the subjectivity of scientific theorizing (see Chapter 1). Neither dissonance theory nor self-perception theory has been handed to us by nature. Both are products of human imagination—creative attempts to simplify and explain what we've observed.

It is not unusual in science to find that a principle, such as "attitudes follow behaviour," is predictable from more than one theory. Physicist Richard Feynman (1967) marvelled that "one of the amazing characteristics of nature" is the "wide range of beautiful ways" in which we can describe it: "I do not understand the reason why it is that the correct laws of physics seem to be expressible in such a tremendous variety of ways" (pp. 53–55). Like different roads leading to the same place, different sets of assumptions can lead to the same principle. If anything, this *strengthens* our confidence in the principle. It becomes credible not only because of the data supporting it but also because it rests on more than one theoretical pillar.

Dissonance as arousal

Can we say that one of our theories is better? On one key point, strong support has emerged for dissonance theory. Recall that dissonance is, by definition, an aroused state of uncomfortable tension. To reduce this tension, we supposedly change our attitudes. Self-perception theory says nothing about tension being aroused when our actions and attitudes are not in harmony. It assumes merely that when our attitudes are weak to begin with, we will use our behaviour and its circumstances as a clue to those attitudes (like the person who said, "How do I know how I feel until I hear what I say?" [Forster, 1976]).

Are conditions that supposedly produce dissonance (for example, making decisions or acting contrary to one's attitudes) actually uncomfortably arousing? Clearly yes, considering the classic study by the University of Waterloo's Mark Zanna and Princeton University's Joel Cooper (1974). They had students write an essay banning all speakers on campus, a view with which all the students disagreed. Half the students were told that they had no choice but to write the essay, while the other half were given the illusion that they chose to write the essay. Thus far, the study

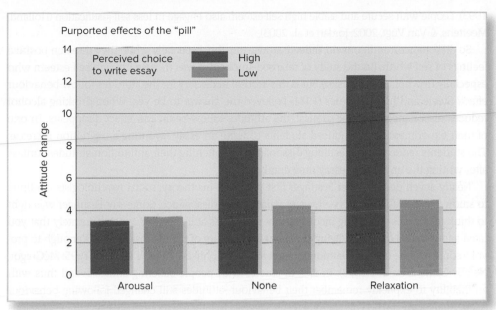

FIGURE 4–5

DISSONANCE AND THE PILL.

When people attributed their arousal to a pill they had taken, they did not change their attitudes, demonstrating the role of dissonance in attitude change. (Data from Zanna & Cooper, 1974)

is just a replication of many previous dissonance studies, but Zanna and Cooper added a simple manipulation that helped establish arousal as central to the experience of dissonance. They had all the students take a pill (actually filled with powdered milk) at the beginning of the experiment. One-third of the students were told that the pill would make them feel aroused, one-third were told that it would make them feel relaxed, and one-third were given no information about the effects of the pill. Zanna and Cooper reasoned that if students thought the pill would make them feel aroused, when they experienced the arousal from the cognitive dissonance they were feeling, they would blame the arousal on the pill and would not change their attitude.

As you can see in Figure 4–5, the results of the experiment supported this reasoning. When students thought the pill would be arousing, students who had high and low choice to write the essay did not differ in their attitudes. When they were given no information about the pill, students showed the typical dissonance pattern of attitude change—students who were given the illusion of choice to write the essay changed their attitudes more than students who were given no choice to write it. Finally, the students who were told the pill would be relaxing showed an especially large amount of attitude change. These results demonstrate that feeling aroused is a central part of the experience of cognitive dissonance and that people must attribute this arousal to their own actions before they engage in self-justifying attitude change.

Why is "volunteering" to say or do undesirable things so arousing? Because, suggests Claude Steele's (1988) **self-affirmation theory**, such acts are embarrassing. They make us feel foolish. They threaten our sense of personal competence and goodness. Justifying our actions and decisions is, therefore, self-affirming; it maintains our sense of integrity and self-worth. And when people engage in dissonance-generating actions—uncoerced counter-attitudinal actions—their thinking left frontal lobes buzz with extra arousal (Harmon-Jones, Gerdjikov, & Harmon-Jones, 2008). This is the grinding gears of belief change at work.

What do you suppose happens if, after committing a self-contradictory act, we offer people some other way to reaffirm their sense of self-worth, such as by doing a good deed? In several experiments, Steele found that, with their self-concepts secure, people (especially those who came to the experiments with strong self-concepts) feel much less need to justify their acts (Steele, Spencer, & Lynch,

self-affirmation theory
a theory that people often experience self-image threat after engaging in an undesirable behaviour, and they compensate for this threat by affirming another aspect of the self. Threaten people's self-concept in one domain, and they will compensate either by refocusing or by doing good deeds in some other domain.

1993). People with secure and stable high self-esteem also engage in less self-justification (Holland, Meertens, & Van Vugt, 2002; Jordan et al., 2003).

So dissonance conditions do, indeed, arouse tension, especially when they threaten positive feelings of self-worth. (In the study of relapsed smokers, it was those with high self-esteem who especially downplayed the risks.) But is this arousal necessary for the attitudes-follow-behaviour effect? Steele and his colleagues (1981) believed the answer to be yes. When drinking alcohol reduces dissonance-produced arousal, the attitudes-follow-behaviour effect disappears. In one of their experiments, they induced students to write an essay favouring a big tuition increase. The students reduced their resulting dissonance by softening their anti-tuition attitudes—unless after writing the unpleasant essay they drank alcohol.

Nearly seven decades after Festinger first proposed his theory, social psychologists continue to study and debate alternative views of what causes dissonance. Some say Festinger was right to think that merely behaving inconsistently with one's attitudes—say, writing privately that you liked a foul-tasting drink and being simultaneously aware of the inconsistency—is enough to provoke some attitude change (Harmon-Jones et al., 1996; Johnson, Kelly, & LeBlanc, 1995; McGregor, Newby-Clark, & Zanna, 1998). In fact, in studies with people suffering amnesia—and thus with an inability to explicitly remember their behaviour—attitudes still changed following behaviour (Lieberman et al., 2001). (This startling result suggests that there's more to the effect than conscious self-justification. Unconscious processing also seems to be at work.) Others argue that the crucial inconsistency is between one's behaviour and one's self-concept (Prislin & Pool, 1996; Stone et al., 1999). Although the dust has not settled, this much is clear, said Richard Petty, Duane Wegener, and Leandre Fabrigar (1997): "Dissonance theory has captivated the imagination of social psychologists as virtually no other, and it has continued to generate interesting new research."

Self-perceiving when not self-contradicting

Dissonance procedures are uncomfortably arousing, which leads to self-persuasion after acting contrary to one's attitudes. But dissonance theory cannot explain all the findings. When people argue a position that is in line with their opinion, although a step or two beyond it, procedures that usually eliminate arousal do not eliminate attitude change (Fazio, Zanna, & Cooper, 1977, 1979). Dissonance theory also does not explain the overjustification effect, since being paid to do what you like to do should not arouse great tension. And what about situations where the action does not contradict any attitude—when, for example, people are induced to smile or grimace? Here, too, there should be no dissonance. For these cases, self-perception theory has a ready explanation.

In short, it appears that dissonance theory successfully explains what happens when we act contrary to clearly defined attitudes: We feel tension, so we adjust our attitudes to reduce it. Dissonance theory, then, explains attitude change. In situations where our attitudes are not well formed, self-perception theory explains attitude formation. As we act and reflect, we develop a more readily accessible attitude to guide our future behaviour (Fazio, 1987; Roese & Olson, 1994).

People rarely internalize coerced behaviour.

© Charles Barsotti/The New Yorker Collection/www. cartoonbank.com.

"No, Hoskins, you're not going to do it just because I'm telling you to do it. You're going to do it because you believe in it."

⋯▶ SUMMING UP

HOW WELL DO OUR ATTITUDES PREDICT OUR BEHAVIOURS?

- Attitudes do not predict behaviour as well as most people believe.
- Attitudes are better predictors of behaviour; however, when social influences are minimal, attitudes are specific to behaviours, and attitudes are potent (strong and on one's mind).

WHEN DOES OUR BEHAVIOUR AFFECT OUR ATTITUDES?

- When taking on a role, our actions in that role often shape our attitudes.
- When we state a belief (even if we do not initially believe it), our words often shape our attitudes.
- When we engage in small actions inconsistent with our attitudes, these small actions can lead to larger actions that can dramatically shape our attitudes and behaviour.
- When we engage in moral or evil acts, these actions can powerfully shape our attitudes.
- When we participate in social movements, our actions can profoundly shape our attitudes.

WHY DOES OUR BEHAVIOUR AFFECT OUR ATTITUDES?

- One reason our behaviours affect our attitudes is that we want to present ourselves to others and ourselves as consistently rational people.
- Our behaviours also affect our attitudes because holding beliefs that are inconsistent with our actions is arousing and uncomfortable. Because it is often easier to change our beliefs than our actions, we change our beliefs to match our actions and reduce the discomfort.
- Cultures vary in what beliefs and actions arouse feelings of discomfort, but when discrepancies between beliefs and action cause discomfort, similar processes of reducing this discomfort seem to occur across cultures.
- We also change our beliefs to match our actions because in observing our actions we have powerful clues about our beliefs.
- Several theories have been proposed to explain how our behaviour shapes our attitudes (i.e., self-presentation theory, cognitive dissonance theory, and self-perception theory). All three theories account for important phenomena, but cognitive dissonance theory is best at explaining what happens when the discrepancy between attitudes and behaviour is large, and self-perception theory is best at explaining what happens when the discrepancy between attitudes and behaviour is small.

For more information on the resources available from McGraw-Hill Ryerson, go to **www.mheducation.ca/he/solutions**

Mc Graw Hill Education **connect** · Mc Graw Hill Education **SMARTBOOK** · Mc Graw Hill Education **LEARNSMART**

2

SOCIAL INFLUENCE

So far in this book we have considered mostly "within-the-skin" phenomena—how we think about one another. Now we consider "between-skins" happenings—how we influence and relate to one another. Therefore, in Chapters 5 through 7, we probe social psychology's central concern: the powers of social influence.

What are these unseen social forces that push and pull us? How powerful are they? Research on social influence helps illuminate the invisible strings by which our social worlds move us about. This part reveals these subtle powers, especially the principles of persuasion (Chapter 5), the forces of social conformity (Chapter 6), the consequences of participation in groups (Chapter 7), and how all these influences operate together in everyday situations.

Seeing these influences, we may better understand why people feel and act as they do. And we may ourselves become less vulnerable to unwanted manipulation and more adept at pulling our own strings.

CHAPTER FIVE
Persuasion

▶ CHAPTER OUTLINE

● WHAT PATHS LEAD TO
  PERSUASION?

● WHAT ARE THE ELEMENTS
  OF PERSUASION?

● EXTREME PERSUASION: HOW DO
  CULTS INDOCTRINATE?

● HOW CAN PERSUASION BE
  RESISTED?

Many of life's powers can either harm or help us. Nuclear power enables us to light up homes or wipe out cities. Sexual power helps us to express committed love

Persuasion is everywhere. When we approve of it, we may call it "education."

persuasion
the process by which a message induces change in beliefs, attitudes, or behaviours

or to seek selfish gratification. Similarly, **persuasion**'s power enables us to promote health or to sell addiction, to advance peace or stir up hate, to enlighten or deceive. And such powers are great. Consider the following:

- *The spread of weird beliefs:* About one American in five thinks the sun revolves around the earth (Dean, 2005). Others deny that the moon landing and the Holocaust happened.

- *Climate change skepticism:* The scientific community, represented by various national academies of science and the Intergovernmental Panel on Climate Change, is in a virtual consensus about three facts of life: (1) Atmospheric greenhouse gases are accumulating; (2) diminishing sea ice and rising land, sea, and atmospheric temperatures all confirm the world's warming; and (3) this climate change will almost certainly produce rising sea levels and more extreme weather, including record floods, tornadoes, droughts, and high temperatures. Nevertheless, as the past decade was ending, popular climate *skepticism* was growing. The number of people who believed global warming has been happening declined from 84 to 74 percent between 2007 and 2010 in the U.S., as concern diminished (Krosnick, 2010). In Britain, the proportion who believed climate change was not only happening but also "now established as largely manmade" dropped from 41 percent in 2009 to 26 percent in 2010. And the number of Germans fearing global warming dropped to 42 percent, from 62 percent four years earlier (Rosenthal, 2010). Researchers wondered: Why is the scientific consensus failing to persuade and to motivate action? And what might be done?

"To swallow and follow, whether old doctrine or new propaganda, is a weakness still dominating the human mind."
CHARLOTTE PERKINS GILMAN, *HUMAN WORK,* 1904

- *Promoting healthier living:* Due partly to health-promotion campaigns, the Canadian Tobacco Use Monitoring Survey reveals that the Canadian smoking rate has plunged to 18 percent, less than half the rate of 30 years ago. And the rate of lifetime abstainers from alcohol use among Canadian university students had increased to 9.9 percent in 2004, based on reports from the Canadian Centre on Substance Abuse.

"Speech has power. Words do not fade. What starts out as a sound ends in a deed."
RABBI ABRAHAM HESCHEL, 1961

As these examples show, efforts to persuade are sometimes diabolical, sometimes controversial, and sometimes beneficial. Persuasion is neither inherently good nor inherently bad. It is usually the content of the message that elicits judgments of good or bad. The bad we call "propaganda"; the good we call "education." Education is more factually based and less coercive than propaganda. Yet generally we call it "education" when we believe it, "propaganda" when we don't (Lumsden, Zanna, & Darley, 1980).

Persuasion—whether it be education or propaganda—is inevitable. Indeed, persuasion is everywhere—at the heart of politics, marketing, courtship, parenting, negotiation, evangelism, and courtroom decision-making. Social psychologists, therefore, seek to understand what leads to effective, long-lasting attitude change. What factors affect persuasion? And how, as persuaders, can we most effectively "educate" others?

Imagine that you are a marketing or advertising executive. Or imagine that you are a preacher, trying to increase love and charity among your parishioners. Or imagine that you want to promote energy conservation, to encourage breast-feeding, or to campaign for a political candidate. What could you do to make yourself and your message persuasive? And if you are wary of being influenced, to what tactics should you be alert?

To answer such questions, social psychologists usually study persuasion the way some geologists study erosion—by observing the effects of various factors in brief, controlled experiments. The effects are small and are most potent on weak attitudes that don't touch on our values. Yet they enable us to understand how, given enough time, such factors could produce big effects.

> "A fanatic is one who can't change his mind and won't change the subject."
> WINSTON CHURCHILL, 1954

> "Remember that to change thy mind and to follow him that sets thee right, is to be none the less a free agent."
> MARCUS AURELIUS ANTONINUS, *MEDITATIONS*, VIII. 16, 121–1804

WHAT PATHS LEAD TO PERSUASION?

What two paths lead to influence? What type of cognitive processing does each involve—and with what effects?

When people try to persuade others, they can try to use good arguments; they can convince people that if they really think through the issues, they will become persuaded to change their minds. At the opposite extreme, they can try to change people's minds without having them think about the issue at all.

Perhaps the best way to convince people that something is good is just to associate it with something positive. Think of your favourite television ad. Most people like TV ads because they are funny or contain captivating images. Such ads can be effective ways to sell products, even if they have few—if any—convincing arguments.

In the 1940s and 1950s, Carl Hovland and his colleagues (Hovland, Lumsdaine, & Sheffield, 1949) at Yale University studied the barriers that can prevent a message from being persuasive. They approached their task carefully, manipulating factors related to the communicator, the content of the message, the channel of communication, and the audience.

Researchers at Ohio State University then focused on people's thoughts in response to persuasive messages. If a message is clear but unconvincing, then you will easily counter-argue the message and won't be persuaded. If the message offers convincing arguments, then your thoughts will be more favourable and you will most likely be persuaded. People's "cognitive response" matter. As shown in Figure 5-1, persuasion entails clearing several hurdles. Any factors that help people clear the persuasion increase persuasion. For example, if an attractive source increases your attention to a message, then the message should have a better chance of persuading you.

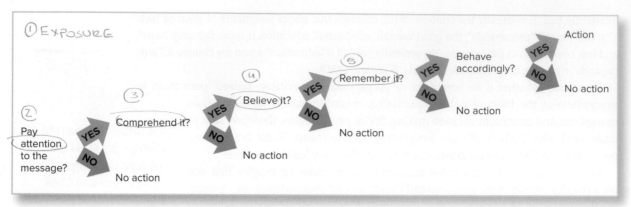

FIGURE 5-1

THE PROCESS OF PERSUASION.

To elicit action, a persuasive message must clear several hurdles. What is crucial is not so much remembering the message itself as remembering one's own thoughts in response. (Adapted from W. J. McGuire. "An Information-Processing Model of Advertising Effectiveness," in *Behavioral and Management Science in Marketing*, H. L. Davis and A. J. Silk, eds. Copyright © 1978. Reprinted by permission of John Wiley & Sons.)

central route to persuasion
occurs when interested people focus on the arguments and respond with favourable thoughts

peripheral route to persuasion
occurs when people are influenced by incidental cues, such as a speaker's attractiveness

THE CENTRAL ROUTE

Richard Petty and John Cacioppo (1986; Petty & Wegener, 1999) and Alice Eagly and Shelly Chaiken (1993, 1998) took this one step further. They theorized that persuasion is likely to occur via one of two routes (Figure 5-2). When people are motivated and able to think systematically about an issue, they are likely to take the central route to persuasion—focusing on the arguments. If those arguments are strong and compelling, persuasion is likely. If the message only contains weak arguments, thoughtful people will notice that the arguments aren't very compelling and will counter-argue.

THE PERIPHERAL ROUTE

But sometimes the strength of the arguments doesn't matter. Sometimes we're not motivated enough or able to think carefully. If we're distracted, uninvolved, or just plain busy, we may not take the time to reflect on the message's content. Rather than noticing whether the arguments are particularly compelling, we might follow the peripheral route to persuasion—focusing on cues that trigger acceptance without much thinking. In these situations, easily understood familiar statements are more persuasive than novel statements with the same meaning. Thus, for uninvolved or distracted people, "Don't put all your eggs in one basket" has more impact than "Don't risk everything on a single venture" (Howard, 1997).

Smart advertisers adapt ads to their consumers' thinking. They do so for good reason. Much of consumers' behaviour—such as one's spontaneous decision, while shopping, to pick up some ice cream of a particular brand—is made unthinkingly (Dijksterhuis et al., 2005). Billboards and television commercials—media that consumers are able to take in only for brief amounts of time—typically use visual images as peripheral cues. Our opinions regarding products such as food, drink, and clothing are often based more on feelings than on logic. Ads for such products often use visual peripheral cues. Instead of providing arguments in favour of consuming alcohol, beer ads associate the product with images of beauty and pleasure. Tim Hortons ads promote its coffee and donuts as being quintessentially Canadian. On the other hand, computer ads, which interested, logical consumers may pore over for some time, seldom feature Hollywood stars or great athletes; instead, they offer customers information on competitive features and prices.

These two routes to persuasion—one explicit and reflective, the other more implicit and automatic—were forerunners to today's "dual processing" models of the human mind. Central

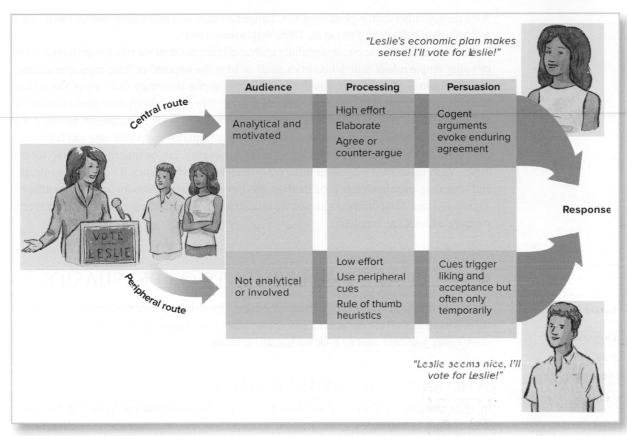

FIGURE 5–2
THE CENTRAL AND PERIPHERAL ROUTES TO PERSUASION.
Computer ads typically take the central route, by assuming their audience wants to systematically compare features and prices. Soft-drink ads usually take the peripheral route, by merely associating their product with glamour, pleasure, and good moods. Central route processing more often produces enduring attitude change.

route processing often swiftly changes explicit attitudes. Peripheral route processing more slowly builds implicit attitudes, through repeated associations between an attitude object and an emotion (Jones, Fazio, & Olson, 2009; Petty & Brinol, 2008; Walther, Weil, & Düsing, 2011).

DIFFERENT ROUTES FOR DIFFERENT PURPOSES

The ultimate goal of the advertiser, the preacher, and even the teacher is not just to have people pay attention to the message and move on. Typically, the goal is behaviour change (buying a product, quitting smoking, or studying more effectively). Are both routes to persuasion equally likely to fulfill that goal? Petty and his colleagues (Petty, Haugtvedt, & Smith, 1995) noted how central route processing can lead to more enduring change than does the peripheral route. When people are thinking carefully and mentally elaborating on issues, they rely not just on the strength of persuasive appeals but on their own thoughts in response as well. It's not so much the arguments that are persuasive as the way they get people thinking. And when people

> *"All effective propaganda must be limited to a very few points and must harp on these in slogans until the last member of the public understands."*
> ADOLF HITLER, *MEIN KAMPF*

> *"Attitude changes are stronger the more they are based on issue-relevant thinking."*
> RICHARD PETTY AND DUANE WEGENER (1998)

think deeply rather than superficially, any changed attitude will more likely persist, resist attack, and influence behaviour (Petty et al., 1995; Verplanken, 1991).

None of us has the time to thoughtfully analyze all issues. Often we take the peripheral route, by using simple rule-of-thumb heuristics, such as "trust the experts" or "long messages are credible" (Chaiken & Maheswaran, 1994). The professors at the university that one of the authors works at recently voted to hire a new dean of science. The author didn't have time to review all of the candidates' files or attend their interviews (he had this book to write). But he noted that several people he liked and respected on the hiring committee supported one candidate over the others. So he used a simple heuristic—friends and experts can be trusted—and voted accordingly. We all make snap judgments using other rule-of-thumb heuristics: If a speaker is articulate and appealing, has apparently good motives, and has several arguments (or better, if the different arguments come from different sources), we usually take the easy peripheral route and accept the message without much thought.

● WHAT ARE THE ELEMENTS OF PERSUASION?

Among the primary ingredients of persuasion explored by social psychologists are these four: (1) the communicator, (2) the message, (3) how the message is communicated, and (4) the audience. In other words, who says what by what method, and to whom?

WHO SAYS? THE COMMUNICATOR

Imagine the following scene: I. M. Wright, a hockey fan who was the "goon" on his junior hockey team, is watching a sports program. One sportswriter complains about a vicious hit she saw recently and says, "This guy meant to hurt the other player, and he never got suspended. It's awful. This kind of thing should be stopped. . . ." Angered, Mr. Wright mutters to his wife, "I'm sick of these people who know nothing about hockey trying to ruin it. Good hits are just part of the game." Now switch the scene. Imagine Mr. Wright hearing these same statements from Don Cherry on *Coach's Corner* describing a vicious hit by a Swedish player on a Canadian star. Do you think Mr. Wright would react differently?

Social psychologists have found that who is saying something affects how an audience receives it. In one experiment, when the Socialist and Liberal leaders in the Dutch parliament argued identical positions using the same words, each was most effective with members of his own party (Wiegman, 1985). It's not just the central message that matters, but also who says it. What, then, makes one communicator more persuasive than another?

Credibility

Any of us would find a statement about the benefits of exercise more believable if it came from a scientific journal rather than from a tabloid newspaper. But the effects of source **credibility** (perceived expertise and trustworthiness) diminish after a month or so. If a credible person's message is persuasive, its impact may fade as its source is forgotten or dissociated from the message. And the impact of a non-credible person may correspondingly increase over time if people remember the message better than the reason for discounting it (Cook & Flay, 1978; Gruder et al., 1978; Pratkanis et al., 1988). This delayed persuasion, after people forget the source or its connection with the message, is called the **sleeper effect**.

---

credibility
believability. A credible communicator is perceived as both expert and trustworthy.

sleeper effect
a delayed impact of a message; occurs when we remember the message but forget a reason for discounting it

"If I seem excited, Mr. Bolling, it's only because I know that I can make you a very rich man."

Skilled persuaders know how to convey a message effectively.

© Charles Barsotti/The New Yorker Collection/ www.cartoonbank.com.

Perceived expertise

How does one become an authoritative "expert"? One way is to begin by saying things the audience agrees with, which makes one seem smart. One reason the scientific consensus about climate change fails to persuade is that people count as "expert" someone whose conclusions support their own pre-existing values and views. Researchers have observed this "congenial views seem more expert" phenomenon on topics ranging from climate change to nuclear waste to gun laws (Kahan, Jenkins-Smith, & Braman, 2010).

It also helps to be seen as *knowledgeable* on the topic. A message about tooth brushing from "Dr. James Rundle of the Canadian Dental Association" is much more convincing than the same message from "Jim Rundle, a local high school student who did a project with some of his classmates on dental hygiene" (Olson & Cal, 1984). After more than a decade studying high-school marijuana use, researchers concluded that scare messages from unreliable sources did not affect marijuana use during the 1960s and 1970s. However, from a credible source, scientific reports of the biological and psychological results of long-term marijuana use "can play an important role in reducing . . . drug use" (Bachman et al., 1988).

Another way to appear credible is to speak confidently. Whether pitching a business plan or giving advice, a charismatic, energetic, confident-seeming person often is convincing (Moore & Swift, 2011; Pentland, 2010). Bonnie Erickson and her collaborators (1978) had students evaluate courtroom testimony given in the straightforward manner or in a more hesitant manner. Here is an example:

"Believe an expert."
VIRGIL, *AENEID*

QUESTION: Approximately how long did you stay there before the ambulance arrived?
ANSWER A: [*Straightforward*] Twenty minutes. Long enough to help get Mrs. David straightened out.
ANSWER B: [*Hesitating*] Oh, it seems like it was about, uh, 20 minutes. Just long enough to help my friend Mrs. David, you know, get straightened out.

The students found the straightforward witnesses much more competent and credible.

Perceived trustworthiness

Speech style also affects a speaker's apparent trustworthiness. Gordon Hemsley and Anthony Doob (1978) found that if, while testifying, videotaped witnesses looked their questioner straight in the eye instead of gazing downward, they impressed people as more believable.

Trustworthiness is also higher if the audience believes the communicator is not trying to persuade them. In an experimental version of what later became the "hidden-camera" method of television advertising, Elaine Hatfield and Leon Festinger (Walster & Festinger, 1962) had some undergraduates eavesdrop on graduate students' conversations. (What they actually heard was a tape recording.) When the conversational topic was relevant to the eavesdroppers (having to do with campus regulations), the speakers had more influence if the listeners presumed the speakers were unaware of the eavesdropping. After all, if people don't know someone's listening, why would they be less than fully honest?

We also perceive as sincere those who argue against their own self-interest. Alice Eagly, Wendy Wood, and Shelly Chaiken (1978) presented students with a speech attacking a company's pollution of a river. When they said the speech was given by a political candidate with a business background or to an audience of company supporters, it seemed unbiased and was persuasive. When a supposedly pro-environment politician gave the same anti-business speech to environmentalists, listeners could attribute the politician's arguments to personal bias or to the audience. Being willing to suffer for one's beliefs—which Gandhi, Nelson Mandela, Martin Luther King, Jr., and other great leaders have done—also helps convince people of one's sincerity (Knight & Weiss, 1980).

Norman Miller and his colleagues (1976) found that trustworthiness and credibility increase when people talk fast. People who listened to tape-recorded messages rated fast speakers (about 190 words per minute) as more objective, intelligent, and knowledgeable than slow speakers (about 110 words per minute). They also found the more rapid speakers more persuasive.

Some television ads are obviously constructed to make the communicator appear both expert and trustworthy. A drug company may promote its pain relievers using a speaker in a white lab coat, who declares confidently that most doctors recommend their ingredient (which is merely aspirin). Given such peripheral cues, people who don't care enough to analyze the evidence may reflexively infer that the product is special. Other ads seem not to use the credibility principle. It's not primarily for his expertise about sports apparel that Nike paid Tiger Woods $100 million to appear in its ads.

Thus, communicators gain credibility if they seem expert and trustworthy (Pornpitakpan, 2004). When we know in advance that a source is credible, we think more favourable thoughts in response to the message. If we learn the source after a message generates favourable thoughts, high credibility strengthens our confidence in our thinking, which strengthens the persuasive impact of the message (Briñol, Petty, & Tormala, 2004; Briñol, Tormala, & Petty, 2002; Tormala, Briñol, & Petty, 2006).

Attractiveness and liking

Most of us deny that endorsements by star athletes and entertainers affect us. We know that stars are seldom knowledgeable about the products they endorse. Besides, we know the intent is to persuade us: We don't just casually get to observe Ryan Reynolds's morning routine, getting dressed and spraying himself with a specific brand of cologne. Such ads are based on another characteristic of an effective communicator: **attractiveness**.

attractiveness
having qualities that appeal to an audience. An appealing communicator (often someone similar to the audience) is most persuasive on matters of subjective preference.

We may think we are not influenced by attractiveness or likeability, but researchers have found otherwise. We're more likely to respond to those we like, a phenomenon well-known to those organizing charitable solicitations and candy sales. Even a fleeting conversation with someone is enough to increase our liking for that person and our responsiveness to his or her influence (Burger et al., 2001). Our liking may open us up to the communicator's arguments (central route persuasion), or it may trigger positive associations when we see the product later (peripheral route persuasion). As with credibility, the liking-begets-persuasion principle suggests applications (see Table 5–1).

? COMPLIANCE.

TABLE 5–1 SIX PERSUASION PRINCIPLES

In his book *Influence: Science and Practice,* persuasion researcher Robert Cialdini (2000) illustrates six principles that underlie human relationships and human influence.

Principle	Application
Authority: People defer to credible experts.	Establish your expertise; identify problems you have solved and people you have served.
Liking: People respond more affirmatively to those they like.	Win friends and influence people. Create bonds based on similar interests; praise freely.
Social proof: People allow the example of others to validate how to think, feel, and act.	Use "peer power"—have respected others lead the way.
Reciprocity: People feel obliged to repay in kind what they've received.	Be generous with your time and resources. What goes around, comes around.
Consistency: People tend to honour their public commitments.	Have others write or voice their intentions. Don't say "Please do this by. . . ." Instead, elicit a "yes" by asking.
Scarcity: People prize what's scarce.	Highlight genuinely exclusive information or opportunities.

Attractiveness exists in several forms. Physical attractiveness is one. Arguments, especially emotional ones, are often more influential when they come from people we consider beautiful (Chaiken, 1979; Dion & Stein, 1978; Pallak, Murroni, & Koch, 1983). Most people understand that attractiveness matters most when people are making superficial judgments. In experiments, people exploit opportunities to use attractive communicators with less analytical recipients (Vogel et al., 2010).

Similarity is another. As Chapter 10 will emphasize, we tend to like people who are like us. We also are influenced by them, a fact that has been harnessed by a successful anti-smoking campaign that features youth appealing to other youth through ads that challenge the tobacco industry about its destructiveness and its marketing practices (Krisberg, 2004). People who act as we do, subtly mimicking our postures, are likewise more influential (Bailenson & Yee, 2005). Thus, salespeople are sometimes taught to "mimic and mirror": If the customer's arms or legs are crossed, cross yours; if she smiles, smile back.

Another example: Theodore Dembroski, Thomas Lasater, and Albert Ramirez (1978) gave Black junior high school students a taped appeal for proper dental care. When a dentist assessed the cleanliness of their teeth the next day, those who heard the appeal from a Black dentist had cleaner teeth. As a general rule, people respond better to a message that comes from someone in their group (Van Knippenberg & Wilke, 1992; Wilder, 1990).

Is similarity more important than credibility? Sometimes yes, sometimes no. Timothy Brock (1965) found that paint store customers were more influenced by the testimony of an ordinary person who had recently bought the same amount of paint they planned to buy than by an expert who had recently purchased 20 times as much. But recall that when discussing dental hygiene, a leading dentist (a dissimilar but expert source) was more persuasive than a student (a similar but inexpert source).

Such seemingly contradictory findings bring out the detective in us. They suggest that an undiscovered factor is at work—that similarity is more important given the presence of factor X, and credibility is more important given the absence of factor X. Factor X, as George Goethals and Erick Nelson (1973) discovered, is whether the topic is one of subjective preference or objective reality. When the choice concerns matters of personal value, taste, or way of life, similar communicators have the most influence. But on judgments of fact—Does Sydney have less rainfall than London?—confirmation of belief by a dissimilar person does more to boost confidence. A dissimilar person provides a more independent judgment.

WHAT IS SAID? THE MESSAGE CONTENT

It matters not only who says something, but also what that person says. If you were to help organize an appeal to get people to vote for an increase in school taxes, or to stop smoking, or to give money to world hunger relief, you might wonder how to concoct a recipe for central route persuasion. Common sense could lead you to either side of these questions:

- Is a logical message more persuasive—or one that arouses emotion?
- Will you get more opinion change by advocating a position that is only slightly different from the listeners' existing opinions or by advocating an extreme point of view?
- Should the message express your side only, or should it acknowledge and refute the opposing views?
- If people are to present both sides—say, in successive talks at a community meeting or in a political debate—is there an advantage to going first or last?

Let's take these questions one at a time.

Reason versus emotion

Suppose you were campaigning in support of world hunger relief. Would it be best to itemize your arguments and cite an array of impressive statistics? Or would you be more effective presenting an emotional approach—say, the compelling story of one starving child? Of course, an argument can be both reasonable and emotional. You can marry passion and logic. Still, which is more influential—reason or emotion? Was Shakespeare's Lysander right: "The will of man is by his reason sway'd"? Or was Lord Chesterfield's advice wiser: "Address yourself generally to the senses, to the heart, and to the weaknesses of mankind, but rarely to their reason"?

Attractive communicators, such as Rihanna endorsing her perfume, often trigger peripheral route persuasion. We associate their message or product with our good feelings toward the communicator, and we approve and believe.

The answer: It depends on the audience. Well-educated or analytical people are responsive to rational appeals (Cacioppo et al., 1996; Cacioppo, Petty, & Morris, 1983; Hovland et al., 1949). Thoughtful, involved audiences travel the central route; they are most responsive to reasoned arguments. Disinterested audiences travel the peripheral route; they are more affected by how much they like the communicator (Chaiken, 1980; Petty, Cacioppo, & Goldman, 1981).

It also depends on how people's attitudes were formed. When people's initial attitudes are formed primarily through emotion, they are more persuaded by later emotional appeals; when their initial attitudes are formed primarily through reason, they are more persuaded by later intellectual arguments (Edwards, 1990; Fabrigar & Petty, 1999). New emotions may sway an emotion-based attitude. But to change an information-based attitude, more information may be needed.

The effect of good feelings

Messages also become more persuasive through association with good feelings. Irving Janis and his colleagues (1965; Dabbs & Janis, 1965) found that students were more convinced by persuasive messages if they were allowed to enjoy peanuts and Pepsi while reading them (Figure 5–3). Similarly, Mark Galizio and Clyde Hendrick (1972) found that students were more persuaded by folk-song lyrics accompanied by pleasant guitar music than by unaccompanied lyrics. There is, it seems, something to be gained from conducting business over sumptuous lunches with pleasant background music.

Good feelings often enhance persuasion, partly by enhancing positive thinking and partly by linking good feelings with the message (Petty et al., 1993). As noted in Chapter 3, in a good mood, people view the world through rose-coloured glasses. But they also make faster, more impulsive decisions; they rely more on peripheral cues (Bodenhausen, 1993; Moons & Mackie, 2007). Unhappy people ruminate more before reacting, so they are less easily swayed by weak arguments. (They also produce more cogent persuasive messages [Forgas, 2007].) Thus, if you can't make a strong case, it's a smart idea to put your audience in a good mood and hope they'll feel good about your message without thinking too much about it.

Knowing that humour can put people in a good mood, a Dutch research team led by Madelijn Strick (Strick et al., 2009) invited people to view ads in the vicinity of either funny cartoons (Figure 5–4) or the same cartoons altered to be unfunny.

> *"The truth is always the strongest argument."*
> SOPHOCLES, *PHAEDRA*

> *"Opinion is ultimately determined by the feelings and not by the intellect."*
> HERBERT SPENCER, *SOCIAL STATICS*, 1851

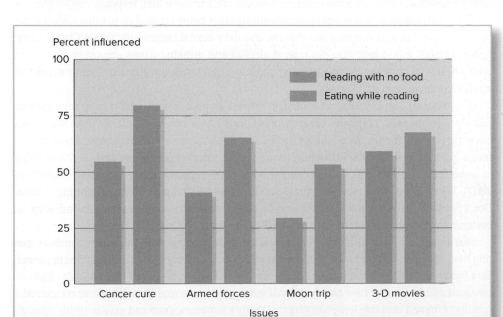

FIGURE 5–3

PERSUASION AND GOOD FEELINGS.

People who snacked as they read were more persuaded than those who read without snacking. (Data from Janis, Kaye, & Kirschner, 1965)

"If the jury had been sequestered in a nicer hotel, this would probably never have happened. "

Good feelings help create positive attitudes.

© Frank Cotham/The New Yorker Collection/www.cartoonbank.com.

Their finding: Products associated with humour were better liked, as measured by an implicit attitude test, and were more often chosen.

The effect of arousing fear

Messages also can be effective by evoking negative emotions. When trying to convince people to cut down on smoking, brush their teeth more often, get a tetanus shot, or drive carefully, a fear-arousing message can be potent (de Hoog, Stroebe, & de Wit, 2007; Muller & Johnson, 1990). By requiring cigarette makers to include graphic warning labels depicting the hazards of smoking on each pack of cigarettes, the Canadian government assumed—correctly, it turns out—that showing cigarette smokers the horrible things that can happen to smokers adds to persuasiveness (O'Hegarty et al., 2007; Peters et al., 2007; Stark et al., 2008).

But how much fear should you arouse? Should you evoke just a little fear, lest people become so frightened that they tune out your painful message? Or should you try to scare the daylights out of them? Experiments by Howard Leventhal (1970) and his collaborators, by Ronald Rogers and his collaborators (Robberson & Rogers, 1988), and by Natascha de Hoog and her colleagues (2007) show that, often, the more frightened people are, the more they respond.

The effectiveness of fear-arousing communications is being applied in ads discouraging not only smoking, but also drinking and driving, and risky sexual behaviours. When Claude Levy-Leboyer (1988) found that attitudes toward alcohol and drinking habits among French youth were effectively changed by fear-arousing pictures, the French government incorporated this kind of information in its TV spots.

One effective anti-smoking ad campaign offered graphic "truth" ads. In one, vans pull up outside an unnamed corporate tobacco office. Teens pile out and unload 1200 body bags covering two city blocks. As a curious corporate suit peers out a window above, a teen shouts into a loudspeaker: "Do you know how many people tobacco kills every day? . . . We're going to leave these here for you, so you can see what 1200 people actually look like" (Nicholson, 2007). While teens who viewed a simultaneous cerebral Philip Morris ad (lecturing, "Think. Don't Smoke") were not less likely to smoke, those viewing the more dramatic and edgy ad became significantly less inclined to smoke (Farrelly et al., 2002, 2008).

Fear-arousing communications are increasing people's detection behaviours, such as getting mammograms, doing breast or testicular self-exams, and checking for signs of skin cancer. Sara Banks, Peter Salovey, and their colleagues (1995) had women aged 40 to 66 who had not obtained mammograms view an educational video on mammography. Of those who received a positively framed message (emphasizing that getting a mammogram can save your life through early detection), only half got a mammogram within 12 months. Of those who received a

FIGURE 5–4

In experiments at Radboud University Nijmegen, humour enhanced people's liking for products such as these.

fear-framed message (emphasizing that not getting a mammogram can cost you your life), two-thirds got a mammogram within 12 months.

Playing on fear works best if a message leads people not only to fear the severity and likelihood of a threatened event but also to perceive a solution and feel capable of implementing it (Devos-Comby & Salovey, 2002; Maddux & Rogers, 1983). Many ads aimed at reducing sexual risks aim both to arouse fear—"AIDS kills"—and to offer a protective strategy: Abstain, or wear a condom, or save sex for a committed relationship. Also, "gain-framed" messages are often equally effective as "loss-framed" messages (O'Keefe & Jensen, 2011). Gain-framed messages focus on the advantages of healthy behaviour (for example, "If you wear sunscreen, you'll have attractive skin" rather than "If you don't wear sunscreen, you'll have unattractive skin"). Thus, a global climate change article that ends by describing future catastrophic consequences is less persuasive to many skeptics than one that concludes by discussing possible solutions (Feinberg & Willer, 2010).

Vivid propaganda often exploits fears. The Nazi newspaper *Der Stürmer* aroused fear with hundreds upon hundreds of unsubstantiated anecdotes about Jews who were said to have ground rats to make hash, seduced non-Jewish women, and cheated families out of their life savings. These appeals, like most Nazi propaganda, were emotional, not logical. The appeals also gave clear, specific instructions on how to combat "the danger": They listed Jewish businesses so readers would avoid them, encouraged readers to submit for publication the names of Germans who patronized Jewish shops and professionals, and directed readers to compile lists of Jews in their area (Bytwerk & Brooks, 1980).

Vivid stories can also, however, be used for good, especially when what's most memorable conveys the central message rather than distracting from it (Guadagno, Rhoads, & Sagarin, 2011). After the genocidal conflict between Rwanda's Hutus and Tutsi, a year-long field experiment explored the impact of a radio soap opera that featured stories of prejudice, conflict, communication, reconciliation, and even love across group lines in two fictional communities. Compared with a control group exposed to a health-related radio soap opera, listeners became more accepting of empathy, cooperation, trauma healing, and even intermarriage (Paluck, 2009). Fiction fostered forbearance.

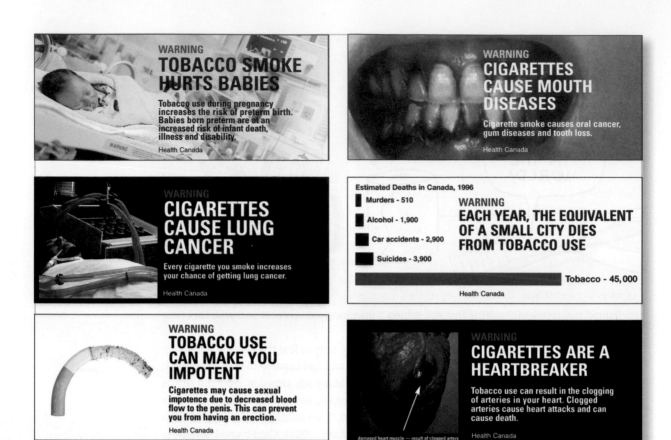

Canadian cigarette
warnings, sampled here,
use fear arousal.

Discrepancy

Picture the following scene: Nicole arrives home on spring vacation and hopes to convert her portly, middle-aged father to her new "health-fitness lifestyle." She runs eight kilometres a day. Her father says his idea of exercise is "channel surfing." Nicole thinks, "Would I be more likely to get Dad off his duff by urging him to try a modest exercise program, say a daily walk, or by trying to get him involved in something strenuous, like a program of calisthenics and running? Maybe if I asked him to take up a rigorous exercise program, he would compromise and at least do something worthwhile. But then again, maybe he'd write me off and do nothing."

Like Nicole, social psychologists can reason either way. Disagreement produces discomfort, and discomfort prompts people to change their opinions. (Recall from Chapter 4 the effects of dissonance.) So perhaps greater disagreement will produce more change. Then again, a communicator who proclaims an uncomfortable message may be discredited. People who disagree with conclusions drawn by a newscaster rate the newscaster as more biased, inaccurate, and untrustworthy. People are more open to conclusions within their range of acceptability (Liberman & Chaiken, 1992; Zanna, 1993). So perhaps greater disagreement will produce less change.

Elliot Aronson, Judith Turner, and Merrill Carlsmith (1963) reasoned that a credible source— one hard to discount—would elicit considerable opinion change when advocating a position greatly discrepant from the recipient's. Sure enough, when credible T. S. Eliot was said to have highly praised a disliked poem, people changed their opinion more than when he gave it faint praise. But when the less credible "Agnes Stearns," a teacher's college student, evaluated a disliked poem, high praise was no more persuasive than faint praise. Thus, as Figure 5-5 shows, discrepancy and credibility interact: The effect of a large versus small discrepancy depends on whether the communicator is credible.

So the answer to Nicole's question "Should I argue an extreme position?" is "It depends." Is Nicole in her adoring father's eyes a highly prestigious, authoritative source? If so, she should push for a complete fitness program. If not, she would be wise to make a more modest appeal.

The answer also depends on how involved her father is in the issue. Deeply involved people tend to accept only a narrow range of views. To them, a moderately discrepant message may seem foolishly radical, especially if the message argues an opposing view rather than being a more extreme version of their own view (Maio, Bell, & Esses, 1996; Pallak et al., 1972; Petty & Cacioppo, 1979; Rhine & Severance, 1970). Thus, social psychologists Arie Kruglanski, Michele Gelfand, and Rohan Gunaratna (2010) advise how to construct messages that may help deradicalize committed terrorists: Build such messages upon elements of their pre-existing beliefs.

On the other hand, if Nicole's father has not yet thought or cared much about exercise, she can probably take a more extreme position. So, if you are a credible authority and your audience isn't much concerned with your issue, go for it: Advocate a discrepant view.

One-sided versus two-sided appeals

Persuaders face another practical issue: how to deal with opposing arguments. Once again, common sense offers no clear answer. Acknowledging the opposing arguments might confuse the audience and weaken the case. On the other hand, a message might seem fairer and be more disarming if it recognizes the opposition's arguments.

Carol Werner and her colleagues (2002) showed the disarming power of a simple two-sided message in experimental messages that promoted aluminum can recycling. Signs added to wastebaskets in a university classroom said, for example, "No Aluminum Cans Please!!!!! Use the Recycler Located on the First Floor, Near the Entrance." When a final persuasive message

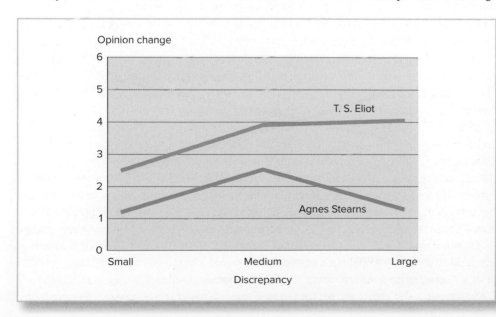

FIGURE 5–5

DISCREPANCY INTERACTS WITH COMMUNICATOR CREDIBILITY.

Only a highly credible communicator maintains effectiveness when arguing an extreme position. (Data from Aronson, Turner, & Carlsmith, 1963)

acknowledged and responded to the main counter-argument—"It May Be Inconvenient. But It Is Important!!!!!!!!!!"—recycling reached 80 percent (double the rate before any message, and more than in other message conditions).

After Germany's defeat in the Second World War, the Allies did not want soldiers to relax and think that the still ongoing war with Japan would become easy. So Carl Hovland and his colleagues (1949) designed two radio broadcasts arguing that the war in the Pacific would last at least two more years. One broadcast was one-sided; it did not acknowledge the existence of contradictory arguments, such as the advantage of fighting only one enemy instead of two. The other broadcast was two-sided; it mentioned and responded to the opposing arguments. As Figure 5–6 illustrates, the effectiveness of the message depended on the listener. A one-sided appeal was most effective with those who already agreed. An appeal that acknowledged opposing arguments worked better with those who disagreed.

Experiments also revealed that a two-sided presentation is more persuasive and enduring if people are (or will be) aware of opposing arguments (Jones & Brehm, 1970; Lumsdaine & Janis, 1953). In simulated trials, a defence case becomes more credible when the defence brings up damaging evidence before the prosecution does (Williams, Bourgeois, & Croyle, 1993). Thus, a political candidate speaking to a politically informed group would, indeed, be wise to respond to the opposition. So if your audience will be exposed to opposing views, offer a two-sided appeal.

> *"Opponents fancy they refute us when they repeat their own opinion and pay no attention to ours."*
> GOETHE (1749–1832), *MAXIMS AND REFLECTIONS*

This interaction effect typifies persuasion research. For optimists, positive persuasion works best ("The new plan reduces tuition in exchange for part-time university service."). For pessimists, negative persuasion is more effective ("All students will have to work part-time for the university, lest they pay exorbitant tuition fees.") (Geers, Handley, & McLarney, 2003). We might wish that persuasion variables had simple effects. (It would make this an easier chapter to study.) Alas, most variables, noted Richard Petty and Duane Wegener (1998), "have complex effects—increasing persuasion in some situations and decreasing it in others."

FIGURE 5–6

THE INTERACTION OF INITIAL OPINION WITH ONE- VERSUS TWO-SIDEDNESS.

After Germany's defeat in the Second World War, Allied soldiers skeptical of a message suggesting Japan's strength were more persuaded by a two-sided communication. Soldiers initially agreeing with the message were strengthened more by a one-sided message. (Data from Hovland, Lumsdaine, & Sheffield, 1949)

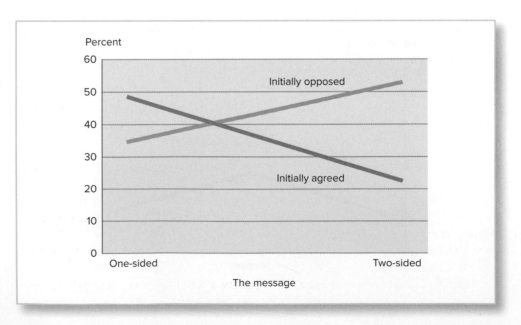

As students and scientists, we cherish "Occam's razor"—seeking the simplest possible principles. But if human reality is complex, our principles will need to have some complexity—to acknowledge interaction effects—as well.

Primacy versus recency

Imagine that you are a consultant to a prominent politician who must soon debate another politician regarding a proposed arms limitation treaty. Three weeks before the vote, each politician is to appear on the nightly news and present a prepared statement. By the flip of a coin, your side receives the choice of whether to speak first or last. Knowing that you are a former social psychology student, everyone looks to you for advice.

You mentally scan your old books and lecture notes. Would first be best? People's preconceptions control their interpretations. Moreover, a belief, once formed, is difficult to discredit. So going first could give people ideas that would favourably bias how they would perceive and interpret the second speech. Besides, people may pay most attention to what comes first. But then again, people remember recent things best. Might it really be more effective to speak last?

Your first line of reasoning predicts what is most common, **primacy effect:** Information presented early is most persuasive. First impressions *are* important. For example, can you sense a difference between these two descriptions?

- John is intelligent, industrious, impulsive, critical, stubborn, and envious.
- John is envious, stubborn, critical, impulsive, industrious, and intelligent.

When Solomon Asch (1946) gave these sentences to university students, those who read the adjectives in the intelligent-to-envious order rated the person more positively than did those given the envious-to-intelligent order. The earlier information seemed to colour their interpretation of the later information, producing the primacy effect. Some other primacy effect examples:

- In some experiments, people have succeeded on a guessing task 50 percent of the time. Those whose successes come early seem more able than those whose successes come after early failures (Jones et al., 1968; Langer & Roth, 1975; McAndrew, 1981).
- In political polls and in election voting, candidates benefit from being listed first on the ballot (Moore, 2004).
- Norman Miller and Donald Campbell (1959) gave university students a condensed transcript from an actual civil trial. They placed the plaintiff's testimony and arguments in one block, and those for the defence in another. The students read both blocks. When they returned a week later to declare their opinions, most sided with the information they had read first.

What about the opposite possibility? Would our better memory for the most recent information we've received ever create a **recency effect?** We have all experienced what the book of Proverbs observed: "The one who first states a case seems right, until the other comes and cross-examines." We know from our experience (as well as from memory experiments) that today's events can temporarily outweigh significant past events. As we noted in Chapter 3, today's blizzard makes long-term global warming seem less a threat, just as today's sweltering heat makes it seem more a threat.

To test for a possible recency effect, Miller and Campbell (1959) gave another group of students one block of testimony to read. A week later, the researchers had them read the second

primacy effect
other things being equal, information presented first usually has the most influence

recency effect
information presented last sometimes has the most influence. Recency effects are less common than primacy effects.

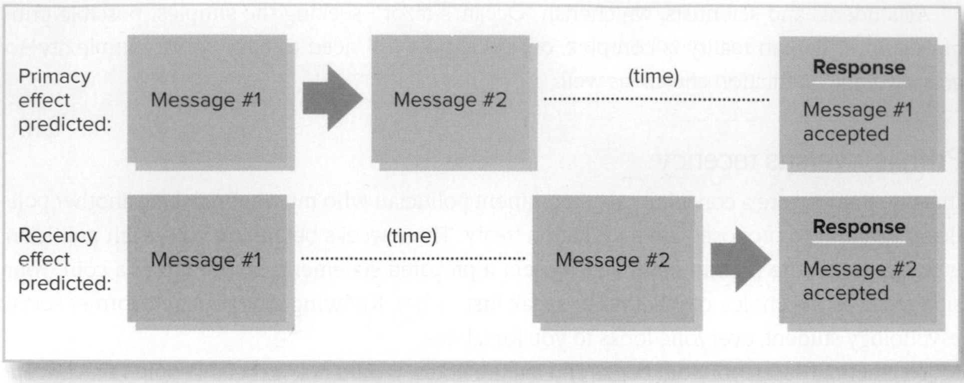

FIGURE 5–7

PRIMACY EFFECT VERSUS RECENCY EFFECT.

When two persuasive messages are back to back and the audience then responds at some later time, the first message has the advantage (primacy effect). When the two messages are separated in time and the audience responds soon after the second message, the second message has the advantage (recency effect).

block and then immediately state their opinions. Now the results were just the reverse—a recency effect. Apparently, the first block of arguments, being a week old, had largely faded from memory.

Forgetting creates the recency effect (1) when enough time separates the two messages, and (2) when the audience commits itself soon after the second message. When the two messages are back to back, followed by a time gap, a primacy effect usually occurs (Figure 5–7). This is especially so when the first message stimulates thinking (Haugtvedt & Wegener, 1994). So what advice would you now give to the political debater?

HOW IS IT SAID? THE CHANNEL OF COMMUNICATION

For persuasion to occur, there must be communication. And for communication to occur, there must be a **channel of communication:** a face-to-face appeal, a written sign or document, a media advertisement, or some other method.

channel of communication
the way the message is delivered—whether face to face, in writing, on film, or in some other way

Common-sense psychology places faith in the power of written words. How do we try to get people out to a campus event? We post notices. How do we get drivers to slow down and keep their eyes on the road? We put "Drive Carefully" messages on billboards. How do we discourage students from dropping garbage on campus? We post anti-litter messages on campus bulletin boards.

Active experience or passive reception?

Are spoken appeals more persuasive? Not necessarily. Those of us who do public speaking can become so easily enamoured of our spoken words that we are tempted to overestimate their power. Ask university students what aspect of their school experience has been most valuable or what they remember from their first year, and few, we are sad to say, recall the brilliant lectures that we faculty remember giving.

Thomas Crawford (1974) and his associates tested the impact of the spoken word by going to the homes of people from 12 churches shortly before and after they heard sermons opposing racial bigotry and injustice. When asked during the second interview whether they had heard or read anything about racial prejudice or discrimination since the previous interview, only 10 percent recalled the sermons spontaneously. When the remaining 90 percent were asked directly whether their priest had "talked about prejudice or discrimination in the last couple of weeks," more than 30 percent denied hearing such a sermon. The end result: The sermons left racial attitudes unaffected.

"The medium is the message."
MARSHALL MCLUHAN

When you stop to think about it, an effective preacher has many hurdles to surmount. As Figure 5–1 (page 160) showed, a persuasive speaker must deliver a message that not only gets attention but also is understandable, convincing, memorable, and compelling. A carefully thought-out appeal must consider each of those steps in the persuasion process.

Consider another well-intentioned effort. At one university, a week-long anti-litter campaign urged students with slogans such as "Let's clean up our garbage." Such slogans were placed in students' mailboxes each morning and displayed on prominent posters. The day before the campaign began, social psychologist Raymond Paloutzian (1979) placed litter near a garbage can along a well-travelled sidewalk. Then he stepped back to record the behaviour of 180 passersby. No one picked up anything. On the last day of the campaign, he repeated the test with 180 more passersby. Did the pedestrians now race one another in their zeal to comply with the appeals? Hardly. Only two of the 180 picked up the trash.

Passively received appeals, however, are not always futile. A drugstore that one of the authors shops at sells two brands of aspirin, one heavily advertised and one unadvertised. Apart from slight differences in how fast each tablet crumbles in your mouth, any pharmacist will tell you the two brands are identical. Aspirin is aspirin. Our bodies cannot tell the difference. But our pocketbooks can. The advertised brand sells for three times the price of the unadvertised brand.

With such power, can the media help a wealthy political candidate buy an election? In politics, those who spend the most usually get the most votes (Grush, 1980; Open Secrets, 2005). Advertising exposure helps make an unfamiliar candidate into a familiar one. As we will see in Chapter 10, mere exposure to unfamiliar stimuli breeds liking. Moreover, mere repetition can make things believable (Dechêne et al., 2010; Moons, Mackie, & Garcia-Marques, 2009). Researcher Hal Arkes (1990) calls such findings "scary." As political manipulators know, believable lies can displace hard truths. Repeated clichés can cover complex realities. Even repeatedly saying that a consumer claim ("Shark cartilage is good for arthritis.") is false can, when the discounting is presented amid other true and false claims, lead older adults to later misremember it as true (Skurnik et al., 2005). As they forget the discounting, their lingering familiarity with the claim can make it seem believable.

> *"In study after study, most people agree that mass media influence attitudes—other people's attitudes, but not their own."*
> DUCK, HOGG, & TERRY, 1995

Mere repetition of a statement also serves to increase its fluency—the ease with which it spills off our tongue—which increases believability (McGlone & Tofighbakhsh, 2000). Other factors, such as rhyming, also increase fluency—and believability. "Haste makes waste" may say essentially the same thing as "rushing causes mistakes," but it seems more true. Whatever makes for fluency (familiarity, rhyming) also makes for credibility.

Because passively received appeals are sometimes effective and sometimes not, can we specify in advance the topics on which a persuasive appeal will be successful? There is a simple rule: Persuasion decreases as the significance of the issue increases. On minor issues, such as which brand of aspirin to buy, it's easy to demonstrate the media's power. On more important issues, such as whether the federal government is doing enough to reduce greenhouse gas emissions, persuading people is like trying to push a piano uphill. It is not impossible, but one shove won't do it.

As we saw in Chapter 4, active experience also strengthens attitudes. When we act, we amplify the idea behind what we've done, especially when we feel responsible. What is more, attitudes more often endure and influence our behaviour when rooted in our own experience. Compared with attitudes formed passively, experience-based attitudes are more confident, more stable, and less vulnerable to attack. These principles are evident in many studies that show that the most effective HIV-prevention interventions not only give people information but also give them behavioural training, such as practising assertiveness in refusing sex and using protection (Albarracin et al., 2005).

Personal versus media influence

Persuasion studies demonstrate that the major influence on us is not the media but our contact with people. Modern selling strategies seek to harness the power of word-of-mouth personal influence through "viral marketing," "creating a buzz," and "seeding" sales (Walker, 2004). The *Harry Potter* series was not expected to be a bestseller (*Harry Potter and the Philosopher's Stone* had a first printing of 500 copies), but kids talking to other kids made it so.

Two classic field experiments illustrate the strength of personal influence. Some years ago, Samuel Eldersveld and Richard Dodge (1954) studied political persuasion in a local election. They divided citizens intending not to vote for a revision of the city charter into three groups. Among those exposed only to what they saw and heard in the mass media, 19 percent changed their minds and voted in favour of the revision on election day. Of a second group, who received four mailings in support of the revision, 45 percent voted for it. Among people in a third group, who were visited personally and given the appeal face-to-face, 75 percent cast their votes for the revision.

> *"You do realize, you will never make a fortune out of writing children's books?"*
>
> J. K. ROWLING'S LITERARY AGENT BEFORE THE RELEASE OF *HARRY POTTER AND THE PHILOSOPHER'S STONE*

In another field experiment, a research team led by John Farquhar and Nathan Maccoby (Farquhar et al., 1977; Maccoby, 1980; Maccoby & Alexander, 1980) tried to reduce the frequency of heart disease among middle-aged adults in three small California cities. To check the relative effectiveness of personal and media influence, they interviewed and medically examined some 1200 people before the project began and at the end of each of the following three years. Residents of Tracy, California, received no persuasive appeals other than those occurring in their regular media. In Gilroy, California, a two-year multimedia campaign used TV, radio, newspapers, and direct mail to teach people about coronary risk and what they could do to reduce it. In Watsonville, California, this media campaign was supplemented by personal contacts with two-thirds of those whose blood pressure, weight, and age put them in a high-risk group. Using behaviour-modification principles, the researchers helped people set specific goals and reinforced their successes.

As Figure 5–8 shows, after one, two, and three years, the high-risk people in Tracy (the control town) were about as much at risk as before. High-risk people in Gilroy, which was deluged with media appeals, improved their health habits and were now somewhat less at risk. Those in Watsonville, who also received the personal contacts, changed most.

Media influence: The two-step flow

Although face-to-face influence is usually greater than media influence, we should not underestimate the media's power. Those who personally influence our opinions must get their ideas from somewhere, and often their sources are the media. Elihu Katz (1957) observed that much of the media's effects operate in a **two-step flow of communication:** from media to opinion leaders to the rank and file. In any large group, it is these opinion leaders and trendsetters—"the influentials"—that marketers and politicians seek to woo (Keller & Berry, 2003). Opinion leaders are individuals perceived as experts. They may include talk show hosts and editorial columnists; doctors, teachers, and scientists; and people in all walks of life who have made it their business to absorb information and to inform their friends and family. If a father wants to evaluate computer equipment, he may defer to the opinions of his daughter, who gets many of her ideas from the printed page. Sell the daughter, and you sell the father too.

two-step flow of communication
the process by which media influence often occurs through opinion leaders, who in turn influence others

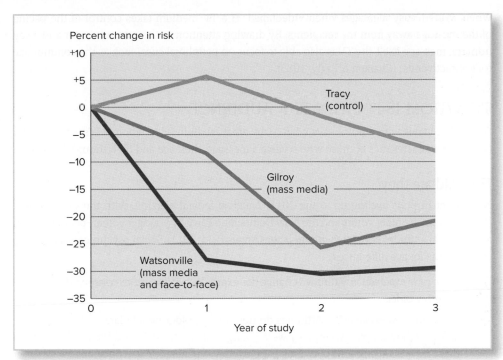

Percent change in risk

Tracy (control)

Gilroy (mass media)

Watsonville (mass media and face-to-face)

Year of study

FIGURE 5–8

IMPACT OF HEALTH EDUCATION.

Percentage change from baseline (0) in coronary risk after one, two, or three years of health education. (Data from Maccoby, 1980)

The two-step flow of information may influence the drugs your physician prescribes (Nair, Manchanda, & Bhatia, 2008). Physicians look to opinion leaders within their social network–often, a university hospital–based specialist–when deciding what drugs to favour. For more than nine in ten physicians, this influence comes through personal contact. The largest drug companies know that opinion leaders drive sales, and, therefore, they target about one-third of their marketing dollars on these influential people.

The two-step flow model reminds us that media influences penetrate the culture in subtle ways. Even if the media had little direct effect on people's attitudes, they could still have a big indirect effect. Those rare children who grow up without watching television do not grow up beyond television's influence. Unless they live as hermits, they will join in TV-imitative play on the school playground. They will ask their parents for the TV-related toys their friends have. They will beg or demand to watch their friend's favourite programs. Parents can say no, but they cannot switch off television's influence.

Comparing media

Lumping together all media, from mass mailings to television to social networking, oversimplifies. Studies comparing different media find that the more lifelike the medium, the more persuasive its message. Thus, the order of persuasiveness seems to be this: live (face-to-face), videotaped, audiotaped, and written.

To add to the complexity, messages are best comprehended and recalled when written. Comprehension is one of the first steps in the persuasion process. So Shelly Chaiken and Alice Eagly (1976) reasoned that if a message is difficult to comprehend, persuasion should be greatest when the message is written, because readers will be able to work through the message at their own pace. The researchers gave students easy or difficult messages in writing, on audiotape, or on videotape. Figure 5–9 displays their results: Difficult messages were, indeed, most persuasive when written, easy messages when videotaped. The TV medium takes control of the pacing of the message away from the recipients. By drawing attention to the communicator and away from the message itself, the TV is also able to focus on peripheral cues, such as the communicator's attractiveness (Chaiken & Eagly, 1983).

TO WHOM IS IT SAID? THE AUDIENCE

Persuasion varies with who . . . says what . . . by what medium . . . to whom. Let's also consider two other characteristics of those who receive a message: their age and their thoughtfulness.

How old are they?

As evident in polls leading up to the 2011 Canadian federal election—with the Conservative Party favoured by older voters and the New Democratic Party by younger voters—people's social and political attitudes correlate with their age (Angus Reid, 2011). Social psychologists offer two explanations for age differences:

1. • *A life cycle explanation:* Attitudes change (for example, become more conservative) as people grow older.

2. • *A generational explanation:* Attitudes do not change; older people largely hold onto the attitudes they adopted when they were young. Because these attitudes are different from those now being adopted by young people today, a generation gap develops.

The evidence mostly supports the generational explanation. In surveying and resurveying groups of younger and older people over several years, the attitudes of older people usually change less than those of younger people. As David Sears (1979, 1986) put it, researchers have "almost invariably found generational rather than life cycle effects."

The teens and early twenties are important formative years (Koenig, McGue, & Iacono, 2008; Krosnick & Alwin, 1989). Attitudes are changeable during that time, and the attitudes formed then tend to stabilize through middle adulthood. Gallup interviews of more than 120 000 people suggested that political attitudes formed at age 18 tend to last (Silver, 2009). Young people might, therefore, be advised to choose their social influences—the groups they join, the media they imbibe, the roles they adopt—carefully.

A striking example: During the late 1930s and early 1940s, students at one small prestigious school—women from privileged, conservative families—encountered a free-spirited environment led by a left-leaning young faculty. One member of the faculty, social psychologist Theodore Newcomb, later denied the faculty was trying to make "good little liberals" out of its students. Nevertheless, they succeeded. The students became much more liberal than was typical of those from their social backgrounds. Moreover, attitudes formed at the school

MORE EVIDENCE →

Although currently banned, cigarette advertising was once common. This photo shows models practising the "correct" pucker and blow technique for a 1950s TV ad.

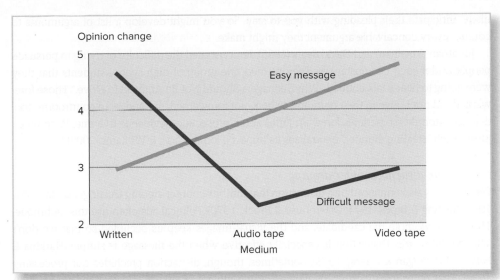

FIGURE 5–9

WRITTEN VS. TAPED MESSAGES.

Easy-to-understand messages are most persuasive when videotaped. Difficult messages are most persuasive when written. Thus, the difficulty of the message interacts with the medium to determine persuasiveness (Data from Chaiken & Eagly, 1976)

endured. A half-century later, the women, now in their seventies, voted for liberal candidates by a 3 to 1 margin in the 1984 U.S. national election, while other university-educated women in their seventies were voting for conservative candidates by a 3 to 1 margin (Alwin, Cohen, & Newcomb, 1991). The views embraced at an impressionable time had survived a lifetime of wider experience.

Adolescent and early-adulthood experiences are formative partly because they make deep and lasting impressions. When Howard Schuman and Jacqueline Scott (1989) asked people to name the one or two most important world events of the previous half-century, most recalled events from their teens or early twenties. For those who experienced the Great Depression or the Second World War as 16- to 24-year-olds, those events overshadowed more recent events that were imprinted on the minds of those who experienced them as 16- to 24-year olds. We may, therefore, expect that today's young adults will include events such as 9/11 and Canada's military presence in Afghanistan or the ensuing economic recession as memorable turning points.

That is not to say that older adults are inflexible. Studies conducted by Norval Glenn (1980) found that most people in their fifties and sixties had more liberal sexual and racial attitudes than they had in their thirties and forties. Given the "sexual revolution" that began in the 1960s and became mainstream in the 1970s, these middle-aged people had apparently changed with the times. Few of us are utterly uninfluenced by changing cultural norms. Moreover, near the end of their lives, older adults may again become more susceptible to attitude change, perhaps because of the decline in the strength of their attitudes (Visser & Krosnick, 1998).

What are they thinking?

The crucial aspect of central route persuasion is not the message but the responses it evokes in a person's mind. Our minds are not sponges that soak up whatever pours over them. If the message summons favourable thoughts, it persuades us. If it provokes us to think of contrary arguments, we remain unpersuaded.

Forewarned is forearmed—if you care enough to counter-argue

What circumstances breed counter-arguing? One is a warning that someone is going to try to persuade you. If you had to tell your family that you wanted to drop out of school, you would likely anticipate their pleading with you to stay. So you might develop a list of arguments to counter every conceivable argument they might make.

Jonathan Freedman and David Sears (1965) demonstrated the difficulty of trying to persuade people under such circumstances. They warned one group of high school students that they were going to hear a talk entitled "Why Teenagers Should Not Be Allowed to Drive." Those forewarned did not budge in their opinions. Others, not forewarned, did budge. In courtrooms, too, defence attorneys sometimes forewarn juries about prosecution evidence to come. With mock juries, such "stealing thunder" neutralizes its impact (Dolnik, Case, & Williams, 2003).

Distraction disarms counter-arguing

Persuasion is also enhanced by a distraction that inhibits counter-arguing (Festinger & Maccoby, 1964; Keating & Brock, 1974; Osterhouse & Brock, 1970). Political ads often use this technique. The words promote the candidate, and the visual images keep us occupied so that we don't analyze the words. Distraction is especially effective when the message is simple (Harkins & Petty, 1981; Regan & Cheng, 1973). Sometimes, though, distraction precludes our processing an ad. That helps explain why ads viewed during violent or sexual TV programs are so often unremembered and ineffective (Bushman, 2005, 2007).

Uninvolved audiences use peripheral cues

Recall the two routes to persuasion—the central route of systematic thinking and the peripheral route of heuristic cues. Like the road through town, the central route has starts and stops as the mind analyzes arguments and formulates responses. Like the highway around town, the peripheral route zips people to their destination. Analytical people—those with a high **need for cognition**—enjoy thinking carefully and prefer central routes (Cacioppo et al., 1996). People who like to conserve their mental resources—those with a low need for cognition—are quicker to respond to such peripheral cues as the communicator's attractiveness and the pleasantness of the surroundings.

But the issue matters, too. All of us struggle actively with issues that involve us while making snap judgments about things that matter little (Johnson & Eagly, 1990; Maio & Olson, 1990). The more we think about an issue, the more we take the central route. Consider the following study conducted by Queen's University's Leandre Fabrigar and his colleagues (1998). They made some students think a lot about their attitudes toward vegetarianism by asking them a lot of questions about it; others were asked about their views only once. As you can see in Figure 5–10, those who had thought a lot about their views were persuaded by strong arguments about vegetarianism but were uninfluenced by weak arguments. But for people who had not thought much about the topic, the strength of the arguments did not matter.

This simple theory—that what we think in response to a message is crucial, especially if we are motivated and able to think about it—has generated many predictions, most of which have been confirmed by Petty, Cacioppo, and others (Axsom, Yates, & Chaiken, 1987; Haddock et al., 2008; Harkins & Petty, 1987). Many experiments have explored different ways to stimulate people's thinking:

- By using rhetorical questions
- By presenting multiple speakers (for example, having three speakers each give one argument instead of one speaker giving three)

need for cognition the motivation to think and analyze; assessed by agreement with items such as "the notion of thinking abstractly is appealing to me" and disagreement with items such as "I only think as hard as I have to"

"To be forewarned and therefore forearmed ... is eminently rational if our belief is true; but if our belief is a delusion, this same forewarning and forearming would obviously be the method whereby the delusion rendered itself incurable."
C. S. LEWIS, *SCREWTAPE PROPOSES A TOAST*, 1965

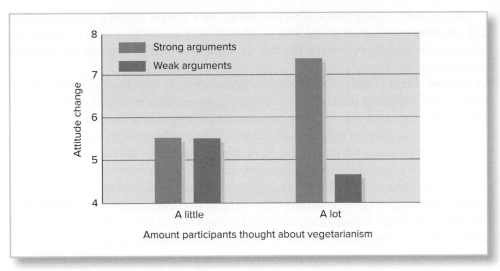

FIGURE 5–10
ATTITUDE
ACCESSIBILITY AND
PERSUASION.
When people's
attitudes are
accessible—that is,
when their attitudes
come easily to
mind—they process
information through
the central route; but
when their attitudes
are less accessible,
they process
information through
the peripheral route.
(Based on Fabrigar
et al., 1998)

- By making people feel responsible for evaluating or passing along the message
- By repeating the message
- By getting people's undistracted attention

The consistent finding with each of these techniques: Stimulating thinking makes strong messages more persuasive and (because of counter-arguing) weak messages less persuasive.

The theory also has practical implications. Effective communicators care not only about their images and their messages but also about how their audience is likely to react. The best instructors tend to get students to think actively. They ask rhetorical questions, provide intriguing examples, and challenge students with difficult problems. Such techniques foster the central route to persuasion. In classes where the instruction is less engaging, you can provide your own central processing. If you think about the material and elaborate on the arguments, you are likely to do better in the course.

EXTREME PERSUASION: HOW DO CULTS INDOCTRINATE?

What persuasion and group influence principles are harnessed by new religious movements ("cults")?

On March 22, 1997, Marshall Herff Applewhite and 37 of his disciples decided the time had come to shed their bodies—mere "containers"—and be whisked up to a UFO trailing Hale-Bopp Comet, en route to heaven's gate. So they put themselves to sleep by mixing phenobarbital into pudding or applesauce, washing it down with vodka, and then fixing plastic bags over their heads so they would suffocate in their slumber. On that same day, a cottage in the French-Canadian village of St. Casimir exploded in an inferno, consuming five people—the latest of 74 members of the Order of the Solar Temple to have committed suicide in Canada, Switzerland, and France. All were hoping to be transported to the star Sirius, nine light-years away.

The question on many minds: What persuades people to leave behind their former beliefs and join these mental chain gangs? Shall we attribute their strange behaviours to strange personalities? Or do their experiences illustrate the common dynamics of social influence and persuasion?

Bear two things in mind: First, this is hindsight analysis. It uses persuasion principles as categories for explaining, after the fact, a troubling social phenomenon. Second, explaining why people believe something says nothing about the truth of their beliefs. That is a logically separate issue. A psychology of religion might tell us why a theist believes in God and an atheist disbelieves, but it cannot tell us who is right. Explaining either belief does not change its validity. If someone tries to discount your beliefs by saying, "You just believe that because . . . ," you might recall Archbishop William Temple's reply to a questioner who challenged, "Well, of course, Archbishop, the point is that you believe what you believe because of the way you were brought up." To which the archbishop replied, "That is as it may be. But the fact remains that you believe I believe what I believe because of the way I was brought up, because of the way you were brought up."

cults
groups typically characterized by (1) the distinctive ritual of its devotion to a god or a person, (2) isolation from the surrounding "evil" culture, and (3) a charismatic leader; also called *new religious movements*. (A sect, by contrast, is a spinoff from a major religion.)

In recent decades, several **cults**—which some social scientists prefer to call new religious movements—have gained much publicity: Sun Myung Moon's Unification Church, Jim Jones's People's Temple, David Koresh's Branch Davidians, and Marshall Applewhite's Heaven's Gate. Sun Myung Moon's mixture of Christianity, anticommunism, and glorification of Moon himself as a new messiah attracted a worldwide following. In response to Moon's declaration, "What I wish must be your wish," many committed themselves and their incomes to the Unification Church.

In 1978 in Guyana, 914 followers of the Reverend Jim Jones, who had followed him there from San Francisco, shocked the world when they died by following his order to down a strawberry drink laced with tranquilizers, painkillers, and a lethal dose of cyanide.

In 1993, high-school dropout David Koresh used his talent for memorizing scripture and mesmerizing people to seize control of a faction of a sect called the Branch Davidians. Over time, members were gradually relieved of their bank accounts and possessions. Koresh also persuaded the men to be celibate while he slept with their wives and daughters, and he convinced his 19 "wives" that they should bear his children. Under siege after a shootout that killed six members and four U.S. federal agents, Koresh told his followers they would soon die and go with him straight to heaven. Federal agents rammed the compound with tanks, hoping to inject tear gas. By the end of the assault, 86 people were consumed in a fire.

Marshall Applewhite was not similarly tempted to command sexual favours. Having been fired from two music teaching jobs for affairs with students, he sought sexless devotion by castration, as had 7 of the other 17 Heaven's Gate men who died with him (Chua-Eoan, 1997; Gardner, 1997). While in a psychiatric hospital in 1971, Applewhite had linked up with nurse and astrology dabbler Bonnie Lu Nettles, who gave the intense and charismatic Applewhite a cosmological vision of a route to "the next level." Preaching with passion, he persuaded his followers to renounce families, sex, drugs, and personal money with promises of a spaceship voyage to salvation.

How could these things happen? What persuaded these people to give such total allegiance to these leaders? Shall we make dispositional explanations—by blaming the victims? Shall we dismiss them as gullible or unbalanced? Or can familiar principles of conformity, compliance, dissonance, persuasion, and group influence explain their behaviour—putting them on common ground with the rest of us who in our own ways are shaped by such forces?

ATTITUDES FOLLOW BEHAVIOUR

As Chapter 4 showed over and over again, people usually internalize commitments made voluntarily, publicly, and repeatedly. Cult leaders seem to know this.

Compliance breeds acceptance

New converts soon learn that membership is no trivial matter. They are quickly made active members of the team. Behavioural rituals, public recruitment, and fund-raising strengthen the initiates' identities as members. As those in social-psychological experiments come to believe in what they bear witness to (Aronson & Mills, 1959; Gerard & Mathewson, 1966), cult initiates become committed advocates. The greater the personal commitment, the more the need to justify it.

The foot-in-the-door phenomenon

How are people induced to make such a drastic life change? Seldom by an abrupt, conscious decision. One does not just decide, "I'm through with mainstream religion. I'm gonna find a cult." Nor do cult recruiters approach people on the street saying, "Hi. I'm a Moonie. Care to join us?" Rather, the recruitment strategy exploits the foot-in-the-door principle. Unification Church recruiters, for example, would invite people to a dinner and then to a weekend of warm fellowship and discussions of philosophies of life. At the weekend retreat, they encouraged the attenders to join them in songs, activities, and discussion. Potential converts were then urged to sign up for longer training retreats. Eventually, the activities became more arduous, culminating in having recruits solicit contributions and attempt to convert others.

Once into the cult, converts find that monetary offerings are at first voluntary, then mandatory. Jim Jones inaugurated a required 10-percent-of-income contribution, which soon increased to 25 percent. Finally, he ordered members to turn over to him everything they owned. Workloads also became progressively more demanding. Former cult member Grace Stoen recalls the gradual progress:

> Nothing was ever done drastically. That's how Jim Jones got away with so much. You slowly gave up things and slowly had to put up with more, but it was always done very gradually. It was amazing, because you would sit up sometimes and say, wow, I really have given up a lot. I really am putting up with a lot. But he did it so slowly that you figured, I've made it this far, what the hell is the difference? (Conway & Siegelman, 1979, p. 236)

PERSUASIVE ELEMENTS

We can also analyze cult persuasion using the factors discussed in this chapter (and summarized in Figure 5-11): *Who* (the communicator) said *what* (the message) *how* (the channel) to *whom* (the audience)?

The communicator

Successful cults typically have a charismatic leader—someone who attracts and directs the members. As in experiments on persuasion, a credible communicator is someone the audience perceives as expert and trustworthy—for example, as "Father" Moon.

Jim Jones used "psychic readings" to establish his credibility. Newcomers were asked to identify themselves as they entered the church before services. Then one of his aides would call the person's home and say, "Hi. We're doing a survey, and we'd like to ask you some questions." During the service, one ex-member recalled, Jones would call out the person's name and say things like this:

> Have you ever seen me before? Well, you live in such and such a place, your phone number is such and such, and in your living room you've got this, that, and the other, and on your sofa you've got such and such a pillow. . . . Now do you remember me ever being in your house? (Conway & Siegelman, 1979, p. 234)

Trust is another aspect of credibility. Cult researcher Margaret Singer (1979) noted that middle-class youths are more vulnerable because they are more trusting. They lack the "street smarts" of lower-class youths (who know how to resist a hustle) and the wariness of upper-class youths (who have been warned of kidnappers since childhood). Many cult members have been recruited by friends or relatives, people they trust (Stark & Bainbridge, 1980). Hundreds of thousands of people in recent years have been recruited by members of some 2500 religious cults, but seldom through an abrupt decision.

The message

The vivid, emotional messages and the warmth and acceptance with which the group showers them can be strikingly appealing: Trust the master, join the family; we have the answer, the "one way." The message echoes through channels as varied as lectures, small-group discussions, and direct social pressure.

The audience

FIGURE 5–11

VARIABLES KNOWN TO AFFECT THE IMPACT OF PERSUASIVE COMMUNICATIONS.

In real life, these variables may interact; the effect of one may depend on the level of another.

Recruits are often young people under 25, still at that comparatively open age before attitudes and values stabilize. Some, such as the followers of Jim Jones, are less-educated people who like the simplicity of the message and find it difficult to counter-argue. But most are educated, middle-class people who, taken by the ideals, overlook the contradictions in those who profess selflessness and practise greed, who pretend concern and behave callously.

Potential converts often are at a turning point in their lives, facing a personal crisis, or vacationing or living away from home. They have needs; the cult offers them an answer (Lofland & Stark, 1965; Singer, 1979). Gail Maeder joined Heaven's Gate after her T-shirt shop had failed. David Moore joined when he was 19, just out of high school and searching for direction. Times of social and economic upheaval are especially conducive to someone who can make apparent

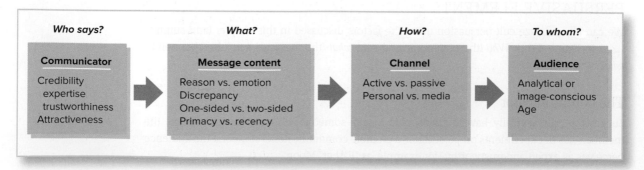

simple sense out of the confusion (O'Dea, 1968; Sales, 1972).

Most of those who have carried out suicide bombings in the Middle East (and other places such as Bali, Madrid, and London) were, likewise, young men at the transition between adolescence and maturity. Like cult recruits, they come under the influence of authoritative, religiously oriented communicators who indoctrinate them into seeing themselves as "living martyrs" whose fleeting moment of self-destruction will be their portal into bliss and heroism. To overcome the will to survive, each candidate makes public commitments—creating a will, writing goodbye letters, making a farewell video—that create a psychological point of no return (Kruglanski & Golec de Zavala, 2005). All of this typically transpires in the relative isolation of small cells, with group influences that fan hatred for the enemy.

"You go on home without me, Irene. I'm going to join this man's cult."

GROUP EFFECTS

Cults also illustrate the theme of upcoming Chapter 7: the power of a group to shape members' views and behaviour. The cult typically separates members from their previous social support systems and isolates them with other cult members. There may then occur what Rodney Stark and William Bainbridge (1980) called a "social implosion": External ties weaken until the group collapses inward socially, each person engaging only with other group members. Cut off from families and former friends, they lose access to counter-arguments. The group now offers identity and defines reality. Because the cult frowns on or punishes disagreements, the apparent consensus helps eliminate any lingering doubts. Moreover, stress and emotional arousal narrow attention, making people "more susceptible to poorly supported arguments, social pressure, and the temptation to derogate non-group members" (Baron, 2000).

Marshall Applewhite and Bonnie Nettles at first formed their own group of two, reinforcing each other's aberrant thinking—a phenomenon that psychiatrists call *folie à deux* (French for "insanity of two"). As others joined them, the group's social isolation facilitated more peculiar thinking. Internet conspiracy groups can likewise foster paranoia. Heaven's Gate was skilled in Internet recruiting.

These techniques—increasing behavioural commitments, persuasion, and group isolation—do not, however, have unlimited power. The Unification Church has successfully recruited fewer than one in ten people who attend its workshops (Ennis & Verrilli, 1989). Most who joined Heaven's Gate had left before that fateful day. David Koresh ruled with a mix of persuasion, intimidation, and violence. As Jim Jones made his demands more extreme, he, too, increasingly had to control people with intimidation. He used threats of harm to those who fled the

Military training creates cohesion and commitment through some of the same tactics used by leaders of new religious movements, fraternities, and therapeutic communities.

community, beatings for non-compliance, and drugs to neutralize disagreeable members. By the end, he was as much an arm-twister as a mind-bender.

Some of these cult influence techniques bear similarities to techniques used by more-benign, widely accepted groups. Buddhist and Catholic monasteries, for example, have cloistered adherents with kindred spirits. Fraternity and sorority members have reported that the initial "love bombing" of potential cult recruits is not unlike their own "rush" period. Members lavish prospective pledges with attention and make them feel special. During the pledge period, new members are somewhat isolated, cut off from old friends who did not pledge. They spend time studying the history and rules of their new group. They suffer and commit time on its behalf. They are expected to comply with all of its demands. The result is usually a committed new member.

Much the same is true of some therapeutic communities for recovering drug and alcohol abusers. Zealous self-help groups form a cohesive "social cocoon," have intense beliefs, and exert a profound influence on members' behaviour (Galanter, 1989, 1990).

Another constructive use of persuasion is in counselling and psychotherapy, which social-counselling psychologist Stanley Strong viewed "as a branch of applied social psychology" (1978, p. 101). Like Strong, psychiatrist Jerome Frank (1974, 1982) recognized years ago that it takes persuasion to change self-defeating attitudes and behaviours. Frank noted that the psychotherapy setting, like cults and zealous self-help groups, provides (1) a supportive, confiding social relationship; (2) an offer of expertise and hope; (3) a special rationale that explains one's difficulties and offers a new perspective; and (4) a set of rituals and learning experiences that promises a new sense of peace and happiness.

We chose the examples of fraternities, sororities, self-help groups, and psychotherapy not to disparage them but to illustrate two concluding observations. First, if we attribute new religious movements to the leader's mystical force or to the followers' peculiar weaknesses, we may delude ourselves into thinking we are immune to social control techniques. In truth, our own groups—and countless political leaders, educators, and other persuaders—successfully use many of these tactics on us. Between education and indoctrination, enlightenment and propaganda, conversion and coercion, therapy and mind control, there is but a blurry line.

Second, the fact that Jim Jones and other cult leaders abused the power of persuasion does not mean persuasion is intrinsically bad. Knowing that persuasive power, like nuclear power, can be harnessed for evil purposes should alert us, as scientists and citizens, to guard against its immoral use. But the power itself is neither inherently evil nor inherently good; it is how we use it that determines whether its effect is destructive or constructive. Condemning persuasion because of deceit is like condemning eating because of gluttony.

HOW CAN PERSUASION BE RESISTED?

What are some tactics for resisting influence? How might we prepare people to resist unwanted persuasion?

Martial arts trainers devote as much time to teaching defensive blocks, deflections, and parries as they do to teaching attack. "On the social influence battlefield," noted Brad Sagarin and his colleagues (2002), researchers have focused more on persuasive attack than on defence. Being persuaded comes naturally, Daniel Gilbert and his colleagues (Gilbert, Krull, & Malone, 1990; Gilbert, Tafarodi, & Malone, 1993) reported. It is easier to accept persuasive messages than to doubt them. To understand an assertion (say, that lead pencils are a health hazard) is to believe it—at least temporarily, until one actively undoes the initial, automatic acceptance. If a distracting event prevents the undoing, the acceptance lingers.

Still, blessed with logic, information, and motivation, we do resist falsehoods. If the credible-seeming repair person's uniform and the doctor's title have intimidated us into unquestioning agreement, we can rethink our habitual responses to authority. We can seek more information before committing time or money. We can question what we don't understand.

STRENGTHENING PERSONAL COMMITMENT

Before encountering others' judgments, you can resist persuasion by making a public commitment to your position. Having stood up for your convictions, you will become less susceptible (or should we say less "open") to what others have to say. In mock civil trials, straw polls of jurors can foster a hardening of expressed positions, leading to more deadlocks (Davis et al., 1993).

Challenging beliefs

How might we stimulate people to commit themselves? Charles Kiesler (1971) offered one possible way: Mildly attack their position. Kiesler found that when committed people were attacked strongly enough to cause them to react, but not so strongly as to overwhelm them, they became even more committed. Kiesler explained: "When you attack committed people and your attack is of inadequate strength, you drive them to even more extreme behaviours in defense of their previous commitment" (p. 88). Perhaps you can recall a time when this happened in an argument, as those involved escalated their rhetoric, committing themselves to increasingly extreme positions.

A "poison parasite" ad.

Developing counter-arguments

There is a second reason a mild attack might build resistance. Like inoculations against disease, even weak arguments will prompt counter-arguments, which are then available for a stronger attack. William McGuire (1964) documented this in a series of experiments. McGuire wondered if we could inoculate people against persuasion much as we inoculate them against a virus? Is there such a thing as **attitude inoculation?** Could we take people raised in a "germ-free ideological environment"—people who hold some unquestioned belief—and stimulate their mental defences? And would subjecting them to a small dose of belief-threatening material inoculate them against later persuasion?

attitude inoculation
exposing people to
weak attacks on their
attitudes so that when
stronger attacks come,
they will have refutations
available

That is what McGuire did. First, he found some cultural truisms, such as, "It's a good idea to brush your teeth after every meal if at all possible." He then showed that people were vulnerable to a massive, credible assault on these truisms (for example, prestigious authorities were said to have discovered that too much tooth brushing can damage your gums). If, however, before having their belief attacked, they were "immunized" by first receiving a small challenge to their belief, and if they read or wrote an essay in refutation of this mild attack, then they were better able to resist the powerful attack.

Robert Cialdini and his colleagues (2003) agree that appropriate counter-arguments are a great way to resist persuasion, but they wondered how to bring them to mind in response to an opponent's ads. The answer, they suggest, is a "poison parasite" defence—one that combines a poison (strong counter-arguments) with a parasite (retrieval cues that bring those arguments to mind when seeing the opponent's ads). In their studies, participants who viewed a familiar political ad were least persuaded by it when they had earlier seen counter-arguments overlaid on a replica of the ad. Seeing the ad again thus also brought to mind the puncturing counter-arguments. Anti-smoking ads have effectively done this, for example, by re-creating a "Marlboro Man" commercial set in the rugged outdoors but now showing a coughing, decrepit cowboy.

INOCULATION PROGRAMS

Could attitude inoculation indeed prepare people to resist unwanted persuasion? Applied research on smoking prevention and consumer education offers encouraging answers.

Inoculating children against peer pressure to smoke

Consider how laboratory research findings can lead to practical applications. One research team had high school students "inoculate" students in grade 7 against peer pressures to smoke (McAlister et al., 1980). The grade 7 students were taught to respond to advertisements implying that liberated women smoke by saying, "She's not really liberated if she is hooked on tobacco." They also acted in role plays; after being called "chicken" for not taking a cigarette, they answered with statements like "I'd be a real chicken if I smoked just to impress you." After several of these sessions during grades 7 and 8, the inoculated students were half as likely to begin smoking as uninoculated students at another junior high school that had an identical parental smoking rate (Figure 5–12).

Other research teams have confirmed that such inoculation procedures, sometimes supplemented by other life skills training, reduce teen smoking (Botvin, Epstein, & Griffin, 2008; Botvin, Schinke, & Orlandi, 1995; Evans, Smith, & Raines, 1984; Flay et al., 1985). Most newer efforts emphasize strategies for resisting social pressure. One study exposed students in grades 6 to 8 to anti-smoking films or to information about smoking, together with role plays of student-generated ways of refusing a cigarette (Hirschman & Leventhal, 1989). A year and a half later, 31 percent of those who watched the anti-smoking films had taken up smoking. Among those who role-played refusing, only 19 percent had begun smoking.

Anti-smoking and drug education programs apply other persuasion principles, too. They use attractive peers to communicate information. They trigger the students' own cognitive processing ("Here's something you might want to think about."). They get the students to make a public commitment (by making a rational decision about smoking and then announcing it, along with their reasoning, to their classmates). Some of these smoking-prevention programs require only two to six hours of class, using prepared printed materials or videotapes. Today, any school district or teacher wishing to use the social-psychological approach to smoking prevention can do so easily, inexpensively, and with the hope of significant reductions in future smoking rates and associated health costs.

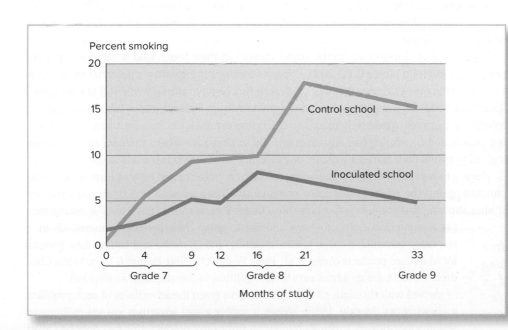

FIGURE 5–12

IMPACT OF "INOCULATION" AGAINST SMOKING.

The percentage of cigarette smokers at an "inoculated" junior high school was much less than at a matched control school using a more typical smoking education program. (Data from McAlister et al., 1980; Telch et al., 1981)

I confess to having felt like Mr. Clean when doing this immunization work because I was studying how to help people resist being manipulated. Then, after our research was published, an advertising executive called and said, "Very interesting, Professor; I was delighted to read about it." Somewhat righteously, I replied, "Very nice of you to say that, Mr. Executive, but I'm really on the other side. You're trying to persuade people, and I'm trying to make them more resistant." "Oh, don't underrate yourself, Professor," he said. "We can use what you're doing to diminish the effect of our competitor's ads." And sure enough, it has become almost standard for advertisers to mention other brands and deflate their claims.

William McGuire (1925–2007),
Yale University

Inoculating children against the influence of advertising

Belgium, Denmark, Greece, Ireland, Italy, and Sweden all restrict advertising that targets children (McGuire, 2002). Advertising to children is prohibited by law in Quebec and regulated in other provinces. Nevertheless, in North America, noted Robert Levine in *The Power of Persuasion: How We're Bought and Sold,* the average child sees over 10 000 commercials a year. "Two decades ago," he noted, "children drank twice as much milk as soda. Thanks to advertising the ratio is now reversed" (2003, p. 16).

Smokers often develop an "initial brand choice" in their teens, said a 1981 report from researchers at Philip Morris (FTC, 2003). "Today's teenager is tomorrow's potential regular customer, and the overwhelming majority of smokers first begin to smoke while still in their teens" (Lichtblau, 2003). That explains why some cigarette and smokeless tobacco (snuff and chewing tobacco) companies aggressively market to U.S. university students, by advertising, by sponsoring parties, and by offering free cigarettes (usually in situations where students are also drinking), all as part of their marketing of nicotine to "entry level" smokers (Farrell, 2005).

Hoping to restrain advertisers' influence, researchers have studied how to immunize young children against the effects of television commercials. Their research was prompted partly by studies showing that children, especially those under 8 years old, (1) have trouble distinguishing commercials from programs and fail to grasp their persuasive intent, (2) trust television advertising rather indiscriminately, and (3) desire and badger their parents for advertised products (Adler et al., 1980; Feshbach, 1980; Palmer & Dorr, 1980). Children, it seems, are an advertiser's dream: gullible, vulnerable, and an easy sell.

"In general, my children refuse to eat anything that hasn't danced on television."
ERMA BOMBECK

Armed with this data, citizens' groups have given the advertisers of such products a chewing out (Moody, 1980): "When a sophisticated advertiser spends millions to sell unsophisticated, trusting children an unhealthy product, this can only be called exploitation." In "Watch Out for Children: A Mothers' Statement to Advertisers" (Motherhood Project, 2001), a broad coalition of women echoed this outrage:

> For us, our children are priceless gifts. For you, our children are customers, and childhood is a "market segment" to be exploited.... The line between meeting and creating consumer needs and desire is increasingly being crossed, as your battery of highly trained and creative experts study, analyze, persuade, and manipulate our children. . . . The driving messages are "You deserve a break today," "Have it your way," "Follow your instincts. Obey your thirst," "Just Do It," "No Boundaries," "Got the Urge?" These [exemplify] the dominant message of advertising and marketing: that life is about selfishness, instant gratification, and materialism.

Children are the advertiser's dream. Researchers have, therefore, studied ways to inoculate children against the 20 000 or so ads they see each year, many as they are glued to a TV set.

On the other side are the commercial interests. They claim that ads allow parents to teach their children consumer skills and, more important, finance children's television programs. Government agencies that oversee the media are often stuck in the middle, pushed by research findings and political pressures while trying to decide whether to place new constraints on TV ads aimed at underage youth.

Meanwhile, researchers have found that inner-city grade 7 students who are able to think critically about ads—who have "media resistance skills"—also better resist peer pressure as grade 8s, and are less likely to drink alcohol as grade 9s (Epstein & Botvin, 2008). Researchers have also wondered whether children can be taught to resist deceptive ads. In one such effort, a team of investigators led by Norma Feshbach (1980; Cohen, 1980) gave small groups of elementary schoolchildren three half-hour lessons in analyzing commercials. The children were inoculated by viewing ads and discussing them. For example, after viewing a toy ad, they were immediately given the toy and challenged to make it do what they had just seen in the commercial. Such experiences helped breed a more realistic understanding of commercials.

Consumer advocates worry that inoculation may be insufficient. Better to clean the air than to wear a gas mask. It is no surprise, then, that parents resent it when advertisers market products to children and then place them on lower store shelves where kids will see them, pick them up, and nag and whine until they sometimes wear the parent down. For that reason, urges the "Mothers' Code for Advertisers," there should be no advertising in schools, no targeting of children under 8 years of age, no product placement in movies and programs targeting children and adolescents, and no ads directed at children and adolescents "that promote an ethic of selfishness and a focus on instant gratification" (Motherhood Project, 2001).

IMPLICATIONS OF ATTITUDE INOCULATION

The best way to build resistance to brainwashing probably is not just stronger indoctrination into one's current beliefs. If parents are worried that their children could become members of a cult, they might better teach their children about the various cults and prepare them to counter persuasive appeals.

For the same reason, religious educators should be wary of creating a "germ-free ideological environment" in their churches and schools. People who live amid diverse views become more discerning and more likely to modify their views only in response to credible arguments (Levitan & Visser, 2008). Also, a challenge to one's views, if refuted, is more likely to solidify one's position than to undermine it, particularly if the threatening material can be examined with like-minded others (Visser & Mirabile, 2004). Cults apply this principle by forewarning members of how families and friends will attack the cult's beliefs. When the expected challenge comes, the member is armed with counter-arguments.

Another implication is that, for the persuader, an ineffective appeal can be worse than none. Can you see why? Those who reject an appeal are inoculated against further appeals. Consider an experiment in which Susan Darley and Joel Cooper (1972) invited students to write essays advocating a strict dress code. Because that was against the students' own positions and the essays were to be published, all chose not to write the essay—even those offered money to do so. After turning down the money, they became even more extreme and confident in their anti–dress-code opinions. Those who have rejected initial appeals to quit smoking may likewise become immune to further appeals. Ineffective persuasion, by stimulating the listener's defences, may be counterproductive. It may "harden the heart" against later appeals.

⋯▶ SUMMING UP

WHAT PATHS LEAD TO PERSUASION?

- Sometimes persuasion occurs as people focus on arguments and respond with favourable thoughts. Such systematic, or "central route," persuasion occurs when people are naturally analytical or involved in the issue.
- When issues don't engage systematic thinking, persuasion may occur through a faster "peripheral route" as people use heuristics or incidental cues to make snap judgments.
- Central route persuasion, being more thoughtful and less superficial, is more durable and more likely to influence behaviour.

WHAT ARE THE ELEMENTS OF PERSUASION?

- What makes persuasion effective? Researchers have explored four factors: the communicator (who says it), the message (what is said), the channel (how it is said), and the audience (to whom it is said).
- Credible communicators have the best success in persuading. People who speak unhesitatingly, who talk fast, and who look listeners straight in the eye seem more credible. So do people who argue against their own self-interest. An attractive communicator is effective on matters of taste and personal values.
- The message itself persuades; associating it with good feelings makes it more convincing. People often make quicker, less reflective judgments while in good moods. Fear-arousing messages can also be effective, especially if recipients can take protective action.

- How discrepant a message should be from an audience's existing opinions depends on the communicator's credibility. And whether a one- or a two-sided message is most persuasive depends on whether the audience already agrees with the message, is unaware of opposing arguments, and is unlikely later to consider the opposition.

- When two sides of an issue are included, the primacy effect often makes the first message more persuasive. If a time gap separates the presentations, the more likely result will be a recency effect in which the second message prevails.

- Another important consideration is how the message is communicated. Usually face-to-face appeals work best. Print media can be effective for complex messages; the mass media can be effective when the issue is minor or unfamiliar, and when the media reach opinion leaders.

- The age of the audience makes a difference; young people's attitudes are more subject to change. What does the audience think while receiving a message? Do they think favourable thoughts? Do they counter-argue? Were they forewarned?

EXTREME PERSUASION: HOW DO CULTS INDOCTRINATE?

- The successes of religious cults provide an opportunity to see powerful persuasion processes at work.

- It appears that the success of cults has resulted from three general techniques: eliciting behavioural commitments (as described in Chapter 4); applying principles of effective persuasion (this chapter); and isolating members in like-minded groups (to be discussed in Chapter 7).

HOW CAN PERSUASION BE RESISTED?

- How do people resist persuasion? A prior public commitment to one's own position, stimulated perhaps by a mild attack on the position, breeds resistance to later persuasion.

- A mild attack can also serve as an inoculation, stimulating one to develop counter-arguments that will then be available if and when a strong attack comes.

- This implies, paradoxically, that one way to strengthen existing attitudes is to challenge them, though the challenge must not be so strong as to overwhelm them.

 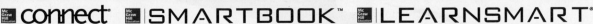

CHAPTER SIX
Conformity

CHAPTER OUTLINE

- WHAT IS CONFORMITY?

- WHAT ARE THE CLASSIC CONFORMITY AND OBEDIENCE STUDIES?

- WHAT PREDICTS CONFORMITY?

- WHY CONFORM?

- WHO CONFORMS?

- DO WE EVER WANT TO BE DIFFERENT?

*Y*ou have surely experienced the phenomenon: As a controversial speaker
or music concert finishes, the admiring fans

near the front leap to their feet, applauding. The approving folks just behind them follow their example and join the standing ovation. Now the wave of people standing reaches people who, unprompted, would merely be giving polite applause from their comfortable seats. Seated among them, part of you wants to stay seated ("This speaker doesn't represent my views at all."). But as the wave of standing people sweeps by, will you alone stay seated? It's not easy, being a minority of one.

Unless you heartily dislike what you've heard, you will probably rise to your feet, at least briefly. Such scenes of conformity raise this chapter's questions:

- Why, given our diversity, do we so often behave as social clones?
- Under what circumstances are we most likely to conform?
- Are certain people more likely than others to conform?
- Who resists the pressure to conform?
- Is conformity as bad as our image of a docile "herd" implies? Should we instead be describing their "group solidarity" and "social sensitivity"?

● WHAT IS CONFORMITY?

Let us take the last question first. Is conformity good or bad? That question has no scientific answer. Assuming the values most of us share, conformity is at times bad (when it leads someone to drink and drive or to join in racist behaviour), at times good (when it inhibits people from cutting in front of us in a theatre line), and at times inconsequential (when it disposes tennis players to wear white).

"The social pressures community brings to bear are a mainstay of our moral values."
AMITAI ETZIONI, *THE SPIRIT OF COMMUNITY*, 1993

"The race of men, while sheep in credulity, are wolves for conformity."
CARL VAN DOREN, *WHY I AM AN UNBELIEVER*

In Western individualistic cultures, where submitting to peer pressure is not admired, the word "conformity" tends to carry a negative connotation. How would you feel if you overheard someone describing you as a "real conformist"? I suspect you would feel hurt. North American and European social psychologists, reflecting their individualistic cultures, give conformity negative labels (submission, compliance) rather than positive ones (communal sensitivity, responsiveness, cooperative team play).

In Japan, going along with others is a sign not of weakness but of tolerance, self-control, and maturity (Markus & Kitayama, 1994). "Everywhere in Japan," observed Lance Morrow (1983), "one senses an intricate serenity that comes to a people who know exactly what to expect from each other." Such is also true of self-organized U2 fans whom Marie Helweg-Larsen and Barbara LoMonaco (2008) observed queuing overnight for unreserved concert places at or near the front rail. A U2 fan code of honour mandates first come, first served, with disdain for line-cutters.

The moral: We choose labels to suit our values and judgments. Labels both describe and evaluate, and they are inescapable. We cannot discuss the topics of this chapter without labels. So let us be clear on the meanings of the following labels: conformity, obedience, compliance, and acceptance.

Conformity is not just acting as other people act; it is also being affected by how they act. It is acting or thinking differently from the way you would act and think if you were alone. Thus **conformity** is a change in behaviour or belief to accord with others. When, as part of a crowd, you rise to cheer a game-winning goal, are you conforming? When, along with millions

conformity
a change in behaviour or belief to accord with others

of others, you drink milk or coffee, are you conforming? When you and everyone else agree that women look better with longer hair than with crewcuts, are you conforming? Maybe, maybe not. The key is whether your behaviour and beliefs would be the same apart from the group. Would you rise to cheer the goal if you were the only fan in the stands?

There are several varieties of conformity (Nail, MacDonald, & Levy, 2000). Consider three: compliance, obedience, and acceptance. Sometimes we conform to an expectation or request without really believing in what we are doing. We put on the necktie or dress, though we dislike doing so. This insincere, outward conformity is **compliance**. We comply primarily to reap a reward or avoid a punishment. If our compliance is to an explicit command, we call it **obedience**.

Sometimes we genuinely believe in what the group has persuaded us to do. We may join millions of others in exercising because we have all been told that exercise is healthy and we accept that as true. This sincere, inward conformity is called **acceptance**. There is even a neuroscience of compliance and acceptance: The shorter-lived memories that underlie public compliance have a different neural basis than the memories that underlie longer-term private acceptance (Edelson et al., 2011; Zaki, Schirmer, & Mitchell, 2011).

Acceptance sometimes follows compliance; we may come to inwardly believe something we initially questioned. As Chapter 4 emphasized, attitudes follow behaviour. Unless we feel no responsibility for our behaviour, we usually become sympathetic to what we have stood up for.

> *"Whatever crushes individuality is despotism, by whatever name it may be called."*
> JOHN STUART MILL, *ON LIBERTY*, 1859

compliance
conformity that involves publicly acting in accord with social pressure while privately disagreeing

obedience
acting in accord with a direct order

acceptance
conformity that involves both acting and believing in accord with social pressure

....

WHAT ARE THE CLASSIC CONFORMITY AND OBEDIENCE STUDIES?

....

How have social psychologists studied conformity in the laboratory? What do their results reveal about the potency of social forces and the nature of evil?

Researchers who study conformity construct miniature social worlds—laboratory microcultures that simplify and simulate important features of everyday social influence. Some of these studies revealed such startling findings that they have been widely replicated and widely reported by other researchers, earning them the name of "classic" experiments. We will consider three, each of which provides a method for studying conformity—and plenty of food for thought.

© Alex Gregory/The New Yorker Collection/www.cartoonbank.com.

SHERIF'S STUDIES OF NORM FORMATION

The first of the three classics bridges between culture's power to create and perpetuate arbitrary norms and processes of conformity. Muzafer Sherif (1935, 1937) wondered whether it was possible to observe the emergence of a social norm in the laboratory. Like biologists seeking to isolate

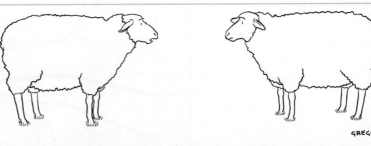

"*Sure, I follow the herd—not out of brainless obedience, mind you, but out of a deep and abiding respect for the concept of community.*"

a virus so they can then experiment with it, Sherif wanted to isolate and then experiment with the social phenomenon of norm formation.

Imagine yourself a participant in one of Sherif's experiments. You find yourself seated in a dark room. Five metres in front of you a pinpoint of light appears. At first, nothing happens. Then for a few seconds it moves erratically and finally disappears. Now you must guess how far it moved. The dark room gives you no way to judge distance, so you offer an uncertain "15 centimetres." The experimenter repeats the procedure. This time you say "25 centimetres." With further repetitions, your estimates continue to average about 20 centimetres.

The next day you return, joined by two other participants who had the same experience the day before. When the light goes off for the first time, the other two people offer their best guesses from the day before. "Five centimetres," says one. "Two centimetres," says the other. A bit taken aback, you nevertheless say, "15 centimetres." With successive repetitions of this group experience, both on this day and for the next two days, will your responses change? The participants whom Sherif tested changed their estimates markedly. As Figure 6–1 illustrates, a group norm typically emerged. (The norm was false. Why? The light never moved! Sherif had taken advantage of an optical illusion called the **autokinetic phenomenon**.)

Sherif and others have used this technique to answer questions about people's suggestibility. When people were retested alone a year later, would their estimates again diverge or would they continue to follow the group norm? Remarkably, they continued to support the group norm (Rohrer et al., 1954). (Does this suggest compliance or acceptance?)

Struck by culture's seeming power to perpetuate false beliefs, Robert Jacobs and Donald Campbell (1961) studied the transmission of false beliefs. Using the autokinetic phenomenon, they had a **confederate** give an inflated estimate of how far the light moved. The confederate

autokinetic phenomenon
self (*auto*) motion (*kinetic*). The apparent movement of a stationary point of light in the dark. Perhaps you have experienced this when thinking you have spotted a moving satellite in the sky, only to realize later that it was merely an isolated star.

confederate
an accomplice of the experimenter

FIGURE 6–1

A SAMPLE GROUP FROM SHERIF'S STUDY OF NORM FORMATION.

Three individuals converge as they give repeated estimates of the apparent movement of a point of light. (Data from Sherif & Sherif, 1969, p. 209)

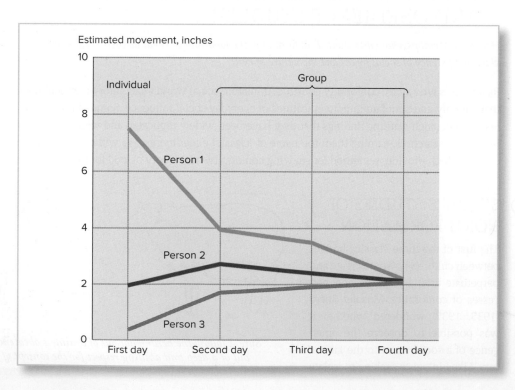

then left the experiment and was replaced by another real subject who was in turn replaced by a still newer member. The inflated illusion persisted (although diminishing) for five generations of participants. These people had become "unwitting conspirators in perpetuating a cultural fraud." The lesson of these experiments: Our views of reality are not ours alone.

In everyday life, the results of suggestibility are sometimes amusing. One person coughs, laughs, or yawns, and others are soon doing the same. Comedy show laugh tracks capitalize on our suggestibility. Laugh tracks work especially well when we presume that the laughing audience is like us—other students at the same university, for participants in one study by Michael Platow and colleagues (2005)—rather than a group that's unlike us. Just being around happy people can help us feel happier, a phenomenon that Peter Totterdell and his colleagues (1998) called "mood linkage." In their studies of British nurses and accountants, people within the same work groups tended to share up and down moods. People within a social network also move toward sharing similar obesity, sleep loss, loneliness, happiness, and drug use (Christakis & Fowler, 2009). Friends function as a social system.

Another form of social contagion is what Tanya Chartrand and John Bargh (1999) called "the chameleon effect." Picture yourself in one of their experiments, working alongside a confederate who occasionally either rubbed her face or shook her foot. Would you—like their participants—be more likely to rub your face when with a face-rubbing person and shake your foot when with a foot-shaking person? If so, it would quite likely be an automatic behaviour, done without any conscious intention to conform. Behaviour synchronizing includes speaking; people tend to mirror grammar that they read and hear (Ireland & Pennebaker, 2010). And because our behaviour influences our attitudes and emotions, our natural tendency to mimic inclines us to feel what the other feels (Neumann & Strack, 2000).

An experiment in the Netherlands by Rick van Baaren and his colleagues (2004) indicates that your mimicry would also incline the other person to like you and be helpful to you and to others. People become more likely to help pick up dropped pens for someone whose behaviour has mimicked their own. Being mimicked seems to enhance social bonds, which can even lead to donating more money to a charity. In a follow-up experiment, Chartrand, van Baaren, and their colleagues had an interviewer invite students to try a new sports drink, while sometimes mirroring the students' postures and movements, with just enough delay to make it not noticeable (Tanner et al., 2008). By the experiment's end, the copied students became more likely to consume the new drink and say they would buy it.

Suggestibility can also occur on a large scale. In late March 1954, one city's newspapers reported damage to car windshields in an area 125 kilometres to the north. On the morning of April 14, similar windshield damage was reported 105 kilometres away and later that day only 70 kilometres away. By nightfall, whatever was causing the windshield-pitting had reached the city itself. Before the end of April 15, the police department had received complaints of damage to more than 3000 windshields (Medalia & Larsen, 1958). That evening, the mayor called on the federal government for help.

David Myers was an 11-year-old at the time. He recalls searching the family car's windshield, frightened by the

"I don't know why. I just suddenly felt like calling."

> *"Why doth one man's yawning make another yawn?"*
> ROBERT BURTON, *ANATOMY OF MELANCHOLY*, 1621

explanation that an H-bomb test was raining fallout on his city. On April 16, however, the newspapers hinted that the real culprit might be mass suggestibility. After April 17, there were no more complaints. Later analysis of the pitted windshields concluded that the cause was ordinary road damage. Why did people notice this only after April 14? Given the suggestion, they had looked carefully at their windshields instead of through them.

Suggestibility is not always so amusing. Hijackings, UFO sightings, and even suicides tend to come in waves. Shortly after the 1774 publication of *The Sorrows of Young Werther*, Johann Wolfgang von Goethe's first novel, young European men started dressing in yellow trousers and blue jackets, as had Goethe's protagonist, a young man named Werther. Although the fashion epidemic triggered by the book was amusing, another apparent effect was less amusing and led to the book's banning in several areas. In the novel, Werther commits suicide with a pistol after being rejected by the woman whose heart he failed to win; after the book's publication, reports began accumulating of young men imitating Werther's desperate act.

Two centuries later, sociologist David Phillips confirmed such imitative suicidal behaviour and described it as "the Werther effect." Phillips and his colleagues (1985, 1989) discovered that suicides, as well as fatal auto accidents and private airplane crashes (which sometimes disguise suicides), increase after well-publicized suicides. For example, following Marilyn Monroe's August 6, 1962, suicide, there were 200 more August suicides than normal. Moreover, the increase happened only in areas where the suicide story is publicized. The more publicity, the greater the increase in later fatalities.

Although not all studies have found the copycat suicide phenomenon, it has surfaced in Germany; in a London psychiatric unit that experienced 14 patient suicides in one year; and in one high school that, within 18 days after one student committed suicide, suffered 2 suicides, 7 suicide attempts, and 23 students reporting suicidal thoughts (Joiner, 1999; Jonas, 1992). In both Germany and the United States, suicide rates rise slightly following fictional suicides on soap operas, and, ironically, even after serious dramas that focus on the suicide problem (Gould & Shaffer, 1986). Phillips reports that teenagers are most susceptible, a finding that would help explain the occasional clusters of teen copycat suicides. In the days following Saddam Hussein's widely publicized hanging, boys in at least five countries slipped nooses around their own heads and hanged themselves, apparently accidentally (AP, 2007).

② ASCH'S STUDIES OF GROUP PRESSURE

Participants in Sherif's darkened-room autokinetic experiments faced an ambiguous reality. Consider a less ambiguous perceptual problem faced by a young boy named Solomon Asch (1907–1996). While attending the traditional Jewish seder at Passover, Asch recalled:

> I asked my uncle, who was sitting next to me, why the door was being opened. He replied, "The prophet Elijah visits this evening every Jewish home and takes a sip of wine from the cup reserved for him."
>
> I was amazed at this news and repeated, "Does he really come? Does he really take a sip?"

My uncle said, "If you watch very closely, when the door is opened you will see—you watch the cup—you will see that the wine will go down a little."

And that's what happened. My eyes were riveted upon the cup of wine. I was determined to see whether there would be a change. And to me it seemed—it was tantalizing, and of course, it was hard to be absolutely sure—that indeed something was happening at the rim of the cup, and the wine did go down a little. (quoted by Aron & Aron, 1989, p. 27)

Years later, social psychologist Asch recreated his boyhood experience in his laboratory. Imagine yourself as one of Asch's volunteer subjects. You are seated sixth in a row of seven people. After explaining that you will be taking part in a study of perceptual judgments, the experimenter asks you to say which of the three lines in Figure 6-2 matches the standard line. You can easily see that it's line 2. So it's no surprise when the five people responding before you all say, "Line 2."

The next comparison proves as easy, and you settle in for what seems to be a simple test. But the third trial startles you. Although the correct answer seems just as clear-cut, the first person gives a wrong answer. When the second person gives the same wrong answer, you sit up in your chair and stare at the cards. The third person agrees with the first two. Your jaw drops; you start to perspire. "What is this?" you ask yourself. "Are they blind? Or am I?" The fourth and fifth people agree with the others. Then the experimenter looks at you. Now you are experiencing an epistemological dilemma: "How am I to know what is true? Is it what my peers tell me or what my eyes tell me?"

Dozens of university students experienced this conflict during Asch's experiments. Those in a control condition who answered alone were correct more than 99 percent of the time. Asch wondered: If several others (confederates coached by the experimenter) gave identical wrong answers, would people declare what they would otherwise have denied? Although some people never conformed, three-quarters did so at least once. All told, 37 percent of the responses were conforming (or should we say "trusting of others").

Of course, that means 63 percent of the time people did not conform. The experiments show that most people "tell the truth even when others do not," noted Bert Hodges and Ann Geyer (2006). Despite the independence shown by many of his subjects, Asch's (1955) feelings about the conformity were as clear as the correct answers to his questions: "That reasonably intelligent and well-meaning young people are willing to call white black is a matter of concern. It raises questions about our ways of education and about the values that guide our conduct."

Asch's procedure became the standard for hundreds of later experiments. These experiments lack what Chapter 1 called the "mundane realism" of everyday conformity, but they do have "experimental realism." People became emotionally involved in the experience. The Sherif and Asch results are startling because they involve no obvious pressure to conform—there are no rewards for "team play," no punishments for individuality. Other experiments have explored conformity in everyday situations, such as these:

> *"He who sees the truth, let him proclaim it, without asking who is for it or who is against it."*
> HENRY GEORGE, *THE IRISH LAND QUESTION*, 1881

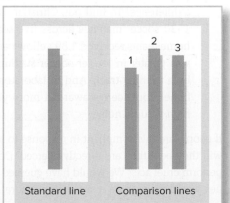

FIGURE 6–2

SAMPLE COMPARISON FROM SOLOMON ASCH'S CONFORMITY PROCEDURE.

The participants judged which of three comparison lines matched the standard.

In one of Asch's conformity experiments, subject number six experienced uneasiness and conflict after hearing five people before him give a wrong answer.

- *Dental flossing.* Sarah Schmiege and her colleagues (2010) told students either that "Our studies show that [fellow students] your age floss approximately [X] times per week," where X was either the participant's own flossing rate, as reported in prior questioning, or five greater than that number. Those given the inflated estimate not only expressed increased intent to floss, but also flossed more over the ensuing three months.

- *Cancer screening.* Monika Sieverding and her colleagues (2010) approached middle-aged German men on the street and invited them to sign up to receive information about cancer screening. If led to believe few ("only 18 percent!") of other men in Germany had undergone the screening, a similar 18 percent signed up. But 39 percent signed up after being told that most other men ("indeed 65 percent!") had been screened. Health education campaigns had best not publicize low participation rates, surmised the researchers.

- *Soccer referee decisions.* In many sports, from figure skating to soccer, referees make instantaneous decisions amid crowd noise. When rating a skating performance or deciding whether a soccer player collision merits a yellow card, does the crowd noise—which increases when an opposing player commits a seeming infraction—make a difference? To find out, Christian Unkelbach and Daniel Memmert (2010) examined 1530 soccer matches across five seasons in Germany's premier league. On average, home teams received 1.89 yellow cards and away teams 2.35. Moreover, the difference was greater in louder soccer stadiums where fans were not separated from the field by a running track. And in laboratory experiments, professional referees who judged filmed foul scenes awarded more yellow cards when a scene was accompanied by high-volume noise.

If people are this compliant in response to such minimal pressure, how much more compliant will they be if they are directly coerced? Could someone force an average North American to perform cruel acts? We would have guessed not: Their humane, democratic, individualistic values would make them resist such pressure. Besides, the easy verbal pronouncements of these experiments are a giant step away from actually harming someone; we would never yield to coercion to hurt another. Or would we? Social psychologist Stanley Milgram wondered.

③ MILGRAM'S OBEDIENCE STUDIES

Milgram's (1965, 1974) controversial studies—"the most famous, or infamous, stud[ies] in the annals of scientific psychology" (Benjamin & Simpson, 2009)—tested what happens when the demands of authority clash with the demands of conscience. "Perhaps more than any other empirical contributions in the history of social science," noted Lee Ross (1988), "they have become part of our society's shared intellectual legacy—that small body of historical incidents, biblical parables, and classic literature that serious thinkers feel free to draw on when they debate about human nature or contemplate human history." Although you may, therefore, recall a mention of this research in a prior course, let's go backstage and examine the studies in depth.

Here is the scene staged by Milgram, a creative artist who wrote stories and stage plays: Two men come to the psychology laboratory to participate in a study of learning and memory. A stern experimenter in a grey technician's coat explains that this is a pioneering study of the effect of punishment on learning. The experiment requires one of them to teach a list of word pairs to the other and to punish errors by delivering shocks of increasing intensity. To assign the roles, they draw slips out of a hat. One of the men (a mild-mannered, 47-year-old accountant who is the experimenter's confederate) says that his slip says "learner," and he is ushered into an adjacent room. The other man (a volunteer who has come in response to a newspaper ad) is assigned to the role of "teacher." He takes a mild sample shock and then looks on as the experimenter straps the learner into a chair and attaches an electrode to his wrist.

"It is too easy to go over to the majority."
SENECA, *EPISTULAE AD LUCILIUM*

Teacher and experimenter then return to the main room (Figure 6–3) where the teacher takes his place before a "shock generator" with switches ranging from 15 to 450 volts in 15-volt increments. The switches are labelled "Slight Shock," "Very Strong Shock," "Danger: Severe Shock,"

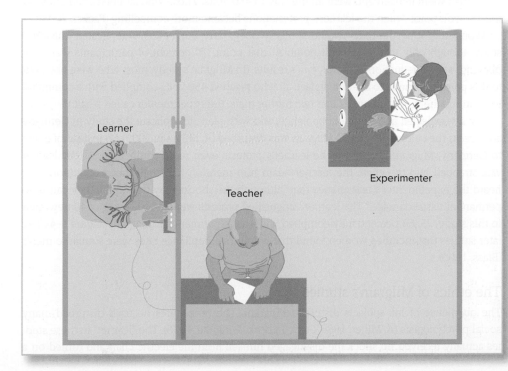

FIGURE 6–3

SETUP FOR MILGRAM'S OBEDIENCE EXPERIMENT.

Source: Milgram, 1974.

and so forth. Under the 435- and 450-volt switches appears "XXX." The experimenter tells the teacher to "move one level higher on the shock generator" each time the learner gives a wrong answer. With each flick of a switch, lights flash, relay switches click, and an electric buzzer sounds.

If the participant complies with the experimenter's requests, he hears the learner grunt at 75, 90, and 105 volts. At 120 volts, the learner shouts that the shocks are painful; at 150 volts, he cries out, "Experimenter, get me out of here! I won't be in the experiment anymore! I refuse to go on!" By 270 volts, his protests have become screams of agony, and his pleas to be let out continue. At 300 and 315 volts, he screams his refusal to answer. After 330 volts, he falls silent. In answer to the teacher's inquiries and pleas to end the experiment, the experimenter states that the non-responses should be treated as wrong answers. To keep the participant going, he uses four verbal prods:

> Prod 1: Please continue (*or* Please go on).
>
> Prod 2: The experiment requires that you continue.
>
> Prod 3: It is absolutely essential that you continue.
>
> Prod 4: You have no other choice; you *must* go on.

How far would you go? Milgram described the study to 110 psychiatrists, university students, and middle-class adults. People in all three groups guessed that they would disobey by about 135 volts, which perhaps isn't surprising. But they also said that they thought other people would disobey by 200 volts and virtually no one expected anyone to proceed to XXX on the shock panel. (The psychiatrists guessed about one in a thousand.)

But when Milgram conducted the study with 40 men—a vocational mix of 20- to 50-year-olds—26 of them (65 percent) went all the way to 450 volts. Those who stopped often did so at the 150-volt point, when the learner's protestations became more compelling (Packer, 2008).

Wondering if people today would similarly obey, Jerry Burger (2009) replicated Milgram's study—though only to the 150-volt point. At that point, 70 percent of participants were still obeying, a slight reduction from Milgram's results. (In Milgram's study, most who were obedient to this point continued to the end. In fact, all who reached 450 volts complied with a command to continue the procedure until, after two further trials, the experimenter called a halt.)

Having expected a low rate of obedience, and with plans to replicate the study in Germany and assess the culture difference, Milgram was disturbed (A. Milgram, 2000). So instead of going to Germany, Milgram next made the learner's protests even more compelling. As the learner was strapped into the chair, the teacher heard him mention his "slight heart condition" and heard the experimenter's reassurance that "although the shocks may be painful, they cause no permanent tissue damage." The learner's anguished protests were to little avail; of 40 new men in this study, 25 (63 percent) fully complied with the experimenter's demands (Figure 6–4). Ten later studies that included women found that women's compliance rates were similar to men's (Blass, 1999).

The ethics of Milgram's studies

The obedience of his subjects disturbed Milgram. The procedures he used disturbed many social psychologists (A. Miller, 1986; Stam, Lubeck, & Radtke, 1998). The "learner" in these studies actually received no shock (he disengaged himself from the electric chair and turned on a

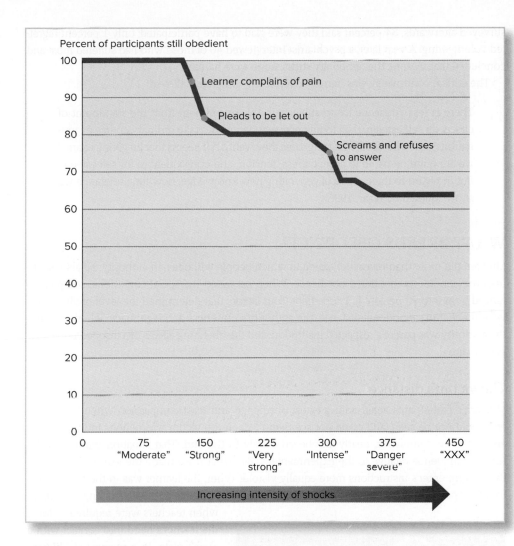

FIGURE 6–4

RESULTS FOR
THE MILGRAM
OBEDIENCE STUDY.

This graph shows
the percentage of
subjects complying
despite the learner's
cries of protest and
failure to respond.
(Milgram, 1965)

tape recorder that delivered the protests). Nevertheless, some critics said that Milgram did to his participants what they did to their victims: He stressed them against their will. Indeed, many of the "teachers" did experience agony. They sweated, trembled, stuttered, bit their lips, groaned, or even broke into uncontrollable nervous laughter. A *New York Times* reviewer complained that the cruelty inflicted by the studies "upon their unwitting subjects is surpassed only by the cruelty that they elicit from them" (Marcus, 1974).

Critics also argued that the participants' self-concepts may have been altered. One participant's wife told him, "You can call yourself Eichmann" (referring to Nazi death camp administrator Adolf Eichmann). CBS television depicted the results and controversy in a two-hour dramatization starring William Shatner as Milgram. "A world of evil so terrifying no one dares penetrate its secret. Until now!" declared a *TV Guide* ad for the program (Elms, 1995).

In his own defence, Milgram pointed to the lessons taught by his nearly two dozen studies with a diverse sample of more than 1000 participants. He also reminded critics of the support he received from the participants after the deception was revealed and the study explained. When surveyed afterwards, 84 percent said they were glad to have participated; only 1 percent regretted volunteering. A year later, a psychiatrist interviewed 40 of those who had suffered most and concluded that, despite the temporary stress, none were harmed.

The ethical controversy was "terribly overblown," Milgram believed:

> There is less consequence to subjects in this experiment from the standpoint of effects on self-esteem, than to university students who take ordinary course examinations, and who do not get the grades they want.... It seems that [in giving exams] we are quite prepared to accept stress, tension, and consequences for self-esteem. But in regard to the process of generating new knowledge, how little tolerance we show. (quoted by Blass, 1996)

WHAT BREEDS OBEDIENCE?

Milgram did more than reveal the extent to which people will obey an authority; he also examined the conditions that breed obedience. When he varied the social conditions, compliance ranged from 0 to 93 percent fully obedient. Four factors that determined the level of obedience were the victim's emotional distance, the authority's closeness and legitimacy, whether or not the authority was part of a respected institution, and the liberating effects of a disobedient fellow participant.

The victim's distance

Milgram's participants acted with greatest obedience and least compassion when the "learners" could not be seen (and could not see them). When the victim was remote and the "teachers" heard no complaints, nearly all obeyed calmly to the end. That situation minimized the learner's influence relative to the experimenter's. But what if we made the learner's pleas and the experimenter's instructions more equally visible? When the learner was in the same room, "only" 40 percent obeyed to 450 volts. Full compliance dropped to a still-astonishing 30 percent when teachers were required to force the learner's hand into contact with a shock plate. In a re-enacted Milgram experiment—with videotaped actors who were either hidden or seen on a computer screen and known to be feigning hurt—participants were, again, much less obedient when the victim was visible (Dambrun & Vatiné, 2010).

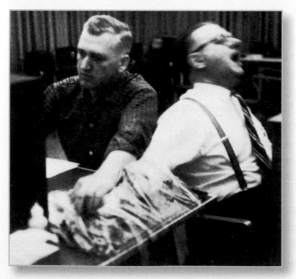

An obedient subject in Milgram's "touch" condition forces the victim's hand onto the shock plate. Usually, however, those in the teacher role were more merciful to victims who were this close to them.

In everyday life, too, it is easiest to abuse someone who is distant or depersonalized. People who might never be cruel to someone in person may be downright nasty when posting comments aimed at anonymous people on Internet discussion boards. Throughout history, executioners have often depersonalized those being executed by placing hoods over their heads. The ethics of war allow a soldier to bomb a helpless village from 13 000 metres but not to shoot an equally helpless villager. In combat with an enemy they can see, many soldiers either do not fire or do not aim. Such disobedience is rare among those given orders to kill with the more distant artillery or aircraft weapons (Padgett, 1989).

As the Holocaust began, some Germans, under orders, used machine guns or rifles to kill men, women, and children standing before them. But others could not bring themselves to do so, and some who did were left shaken by the experience of face-to-face killing. That led Heinrich Himmler, the Nazi "architect of genocide," to devise a "more humane" killing, one that would visually separate the killers and their victims. The solution was the construction of concrete gas chambers, where the killers would not see or hear the human consequences of their horror (Russell & Gregory, 2005).

On the positive side, people act most compassionately toward those who are personalized. This is why appeals for the unborn or the hungry are nearly always personalized with a compelling photograph or description. Perhaps even more compelling is an ultrasound picture of one's own developing fetus. When queried by John Lydon and Christine Dunkel-Schetter (1994), expectant women expressed more commitment to their pregnancy if they had earlier seen an ultrasound picture of their fetus that clearly displayed body parts.

Closeness and legitimacy of the authority

The physical presence of the experimenter also affected obedience. When Milgram gave the commands by telephone, full obedience dropped to 21 percent (although many lied and said they were obeying). Other studies confirmed that when the one making the request is physically close, compliance increases. Given a light touch on the arm, people were more likely to comply by lending a dime, signing a petition, or sampling a new pizza (Kleinke, 1977; Smith, Gier, & Willis, 1982; Willis & Hamm, 1980).

The authority, however, must be perceived as legitimate. In another twist on the basic study, the experimenter received a rigged telephone call that required him to leave the laboratory. He said that since the equipment recorded data automatically, the "teacher" should just go ahead. After the experimenter left, another person who had been assigned a clerical role (actually a second confederate) assumed command. The clerk "decided" that the shock should be increased one level for each wrong answer and instructed the teacher accordingly. Now 80 percent of the teachers refused to comply fully. The confederate, feigning disgust at this defiance, sat down in front of the shock generator and tried to take over the teacher's role. At this point, most of the defiant participants protested. Some tried to unplug the generator. One large man lifted the zealous confederate from his chair and threw him across the room. This rebellion against an illegitimate authority contrasted sharply with the deferential politeness usually shown the experimenter.

It also contrasts with the behaviour of hospital nurses who in one study were called by an unknown physician and ordered to administer an obvious overdose of a drug (Hofling et al., 1966). The researchers told one group of nurses and nursing students about the experiment and asked how they would react. Nearly all said they would not have given the medication as ordered. One explained that she would have replied, "I'm sorry, sir, but I am not authorized to give any medication without a written order, especially one so large over the usual dose and one that I'm unfamiliar with. If it were possible, I would be glad to do it, but this is against hospital policy and my own ethical standards." Nevertheless, when 22 other nurses were actually given the phoned-in overdose order, all but one obeyed without delay (until being intercepted on their way to the patient). Although not all nurses are so compliant (Krackow & Blass, 1995; Rank & Jacobson, 1977), these nurses were following a familiar script: Doctor (a legitimate authority) orders; nurse obeys.

Compliance with legitimate authority was also apparent in the strange case of the "rectal earache" (Cohen & Davis, 1981). A doctor ordered ear drops given to a patient suffering infection in the right ear. On the prescription, the doctor abbreviated "place in right ear" as "place in *R ear.*" Reading the order, the compliant nurse put the required drops in the compliant patient's rectum.

The compliant nurse might empathize with the reported 70 fast-food restaurant managers who, between 1995 and 2006, were caught in this scam: They complied with orders from a self-described authority, usually posing as a police officer over the phone (ABC News, 2004; Snopes, 2008; Wikipedia, 2008). This supposed officer described a generic employee or customer. Once the manager had identified someone fitting the description, the authoritative-sounding caller gave an order to strip-search the person to see if he or she had stolen property. One male Taco Bell manager pulled aside a 17-year-old female customer who fit the description and, with the caller giving orders, carried out a search that included body cavities. After forcing a 19-year-old female employee to strip against her will, a restaurant manager explained, "I never wanted to do it. . . . I was just doing what he told me to do." The manager feared that disobedience might mean losing his job or going to jail, explained his defence lawyer.

In another incident, a McDonald's manager received a call from an "Officer Scott" who described an employee he said was suspected of purse stealing. The female manager brought an 18-year-old woman who fit the description into the office and followed a series of orders to have her empty her pockets and successive pieces of clothing. Over 3½ hours of humiliating detention, the requests became progressively more bizarre, including sexual contact with a male. The traumatized teen sued McDonald's, claiming they had not adequately forewarned staff of the scam, and was awarded $6.1 million (CNN, 2007).

Institutional authority

If the prestige of the authority is important, then perhaps the institutional prestige of Yale University, where the Milgram studies were conducted, legitimized the commands. In post-study interviews, many participants volunteered that had it not been for Yale's reputation, they would not have obeyed. To see whether this was true, Milgram moved the study to Bridgeport, Connecticut. He set himself up in a modest commercial building as the "Research Associates of Bridgeport." When the "learner-has-a-heart-condition" study was run with the same personnel, what percentage of the men do you suppose fully obeyed? Although the obedience rate (48 percent) was still remarkably high, it was significantly lower than the 65 percent rate at Yale.

The liberating effects of group influence

These classic experiments give us a negative view of conformity. But conformity can also be constructive. The heroic figures who rushed into the flaming World Trade Center towers were "incredibly brave," noted Susan Fiske and her colleagues (2004), but they were also "partly obeying their superiors, partly conforming to extraordinary group loyalty." Consider, too, the occasional liberating effect of conformity. Perhaps you can recall a time you felt justifiably angry

Given orders, most soldiers will torch people's homes or kill people—behaviours that in other contexts they would consider immoral.

at an unfair teacher, or with someone's offensive behaviour, but you hesitated to object. Then one or two others objected, and you followed their example. Milgram captured this liberating effect of conformity by placing the teacher with two confederates who were to help conduct the procedure. During the study, both defied the experimenter, who then ordered the real subject to continue alone. Did he? No. Ninety percent liberated themselves by conforming to the defiant confederates.

REFLECTIONS ON THE CLASSIC STUDIES

The common response to Milgram's results is to note their counterparts in recent history: the "I was only following orders" defences of Adolf Eichmann in Nazi Germany; of Lieutenant William Calley, who in 1968 directed the unprovoked slaughter of hundreds of Vietnamese in the village of My Lai; and of the "ethnic cleansing" occurring more recently in Iraq, Rwanda, Bosnia, and Kosovo.

Soldiers are trained to obey superiors. Thus, one participant in the My Lai massacre recalled:

> [Lieutenant Calley] told me to start shooting. So I started shooting, I poured about four clips into the group. . . . They were begging and saying, "No, no." And the mothers were hugging their children and. . . . Well, we kept right on firing. They were waving their arms and begging (Wallace, 1969).

The "safe" scientific contexts of the obedience studies differ from the wartime contexts. Moreover, much of the mockery and brutality of war and genocide goes beyond obedience (L. Miller, 2004). Some of those who implemented the Holocaust were "willing executioners" who hardly needed to be commanded to kill (Goldhagen, 1996).

The obedience studies also differ from the other conformity studies in the strength of the social pressure: Obedience is explicitly commanded. Without the coercion, people did not act cruelly. Yet both the Asch and Milgram studies share certain

"If the commander-in-chief tells this lieutenant colonel to go stand in the corner and sit on his head, I will do so."
OLIVER NORTH, 1987

commonalities. They show how compliance can take precedence over moral sense. They succeeded in pressuring people to go against their own conscience. They did more than teach us an academic lesson; they sensitized us to moral conflicts in our own lives. And they illustrated and affirmed some familiar social psychological principles: the link between behaviour and attitudes and the power of the situation.

Behaviour and attitudes

Chapter 4 noted a situation in which attitudes fail to determine behaviour: when external influences override inner convictions. These experiments vividly illustrated that principle. When responding alone, Asch's subjects nearly always gave the correct answer. It was another matter when they stood alone against a group.

In the obedience studies, a powerful social pressure (the experimenter's commands) overcame a weaker one (the remote victim's pleas). Torn between the pleas of the victim and the orders of the experimenter, between the desire to avoid doing harm and the desire to be a good participant, a surprising number chose to obey.

Why were the participants unable to disengage themselves? How had they become trapped? Imagine yourself as the teacher in yet another version of Milgram's study, one he never conducted. Assume that when the learner gives the first wrong answer, the experimenter asks you to zap him with 330 volts. After flicking the switch, you hear the learner scream, complain of a heart disturbance, and plead for mercy. Do you continue?

We doubt it. Recall the step-by-step entrapment of the foot-in-the-door phenomenon (Chapter 4) as we compare this hypothetical experiment to what Milgram's participants experienced. Their first commitment was mild—15 volts—and it elicited no protest. You, too, would agree to do that much. By the time they delivered 75 volts and heard the learner's first groan, they had already complied five times, and the next request was to deliver only slightly more. By the time they delivered 330 volts, the participants had complied 22 times and reduced some of their dissonance. They were, therefore, in a different psychological state from that of someone beginning the experiment at that point. The same thing occurred with the fast-food restaurant managers in the strip search scam, after they had complied with initially reasonable-seeming orders from a supposed authority. As we saw in Chapter 4, external behaviour and internal disposition can feed one another, sometimes in an escalating spiral. Thus, reported Milgram (1974, p. 10):

Maybe I was too patriotic." So said ex-torturer Jeffrey Benzien, shown here demonstrating the "wet bag" technique to South Africa's Truth and Reconciliation Commission. He would place a cloth over victims' heads, bringing them to the terrifying brink of asphyxiation over and over again. Such terror by the former security police, who routinely denied such acts, was used to get an accused person to disclose, for example, where guns were hidden. "I did terrible things," Benzien admitted with apologies to his victims, though he claimed only to be following orders.

Many subjects harshly devalue the victim as a consequence of acting against him. Such comments as "He was so stupid and stubborn he deserved to get shocked" were common. Once having acted against the victim, these subjects found it necessary to view him as an unworthy individual, whose punishment was made inevitable by his own deficiencies of intellect and character.

While working for Solomon E. Asch, I wondered whether his conformity experiments could be made more humanly significant. First, I imagined an experiment similar to Asch's except that the group induced the person to deliver shocks to a protesting victim. But a control was needed to see how much shock a person would give in the absence of group pressure. Someone, presumably the experimenter, would have to instruct the subject to give the shocks. But now a new question arose: Just how far would a person go when ordered to administer such shocks? In my mind, the issue had shifted to the willingness of people to comply with destructive orders. It was an exciting moment for me. I realized that this simple question was both humanly important and capable of being precisely answered.

The laboratory procedure gave scientific expression to a more general concern about authority, a concern forced upon members of my generation, in particular upon Jews such as myself, by the atrocities of the Second World War. The impact of the Holocaust on my own psyche energized my interest in obedience and shaped the particular form in which it was examined.

Stanley Milgram (1933–1984)

Abridged from the original for this book and from Milgram, 1977, with permission of Alexandra Milgram.

During the early 1970s, Greece's military junta used this "blame-the-victim" process to train torturers (Haritos-Fatouros, 1988; Staub, 1989, 2003). There, as in the training of SS officers in Nazi Germany, the military selected candidates based on their respect for and submission to authority. But such tendencies alone do not a torturer make. Thus they would first assign the trainee to guard prisoners, then to participate in arrest squads, then to hit prisoners, then to observe torture, and only then to practise it. Step by step, an obedient but otherwise decent person evolved into an agent of cruelty. Compliance bred acceptance. If we focus on the end point—450 volts of torture administered—we are aghast at the evil conduct. If we consider how one gets there—in tiny steps—we understand.

As a Holocaust survivor, social psychologist Ervin Staub knows too well the forces that can transform citizens into agents of death. From his study of human genocide across the world, Staub (2003) showed where this process can lead. Too often, criticism produces contempt, which licenses cruelty, which, when justified, leads to brutality, then killing, then systematic killing. Evolving attitudes both follow and justify actions. Staub's disturbing conclusion: "Human beings have the capacity to come to experience killing other people as nothing extraordinary" (1989, p. 13).

But humans also have a capacity for heroism. During the Holocaust, the French village of Le Chambon sheltered 5000 Jews and other refugees destined for deportation to Germany. These people were mostly Protestants, whose own authorities, their pastors, had taught them to "resist whenever our adversaries will demand of us obedience contrary to the orders of the Gospel" (Rochat, 1993; Rochat & Modigliani, 1995). Ordered to expose the sheltered Jews, the head pastor modelled disobedience: "I don't

"Men's actions are too strong for them. Show me a man who has acted and who has not been the victim and slave of his action."

RALPH WALDO EMERSON, *REPRESENTATIVE MAN*, 1850

know of Jews, I only know of human beings." Without knowing how terrible the war would be or how much they would suffer, the resisters made an initial commitment and then—supported by their beliefs, by their own authorities, and by one another—remained defiant to the war's end. Here and elsewhere, the ultimate response to Nazi occupation came early. Initial helping heightened commitment, leading to more helping.

The power of the situation

This chapter's most important lesson—that immediate situational forces are powerful—reveals the strength of the social context. To feel this for yourself, imagine violating some minor norms: standing up in the middle of a class, singing out loud in a restaurant, greeting some distinguished senior professors by their first names, playing golf in a suit. In trying to break with social constraints, we suddenly realize how strong they are.

The students in one recent experiment found it surprisingly difficult to violate the norm of being "nice" rather than confrontational. Participants imagined themselves discussing with three others whom to select for survival on a desert island. They were asked to imagine one of the others, a man, injecting three sexist comments, such as "I think we need more women on the island to keep the men satisfied." How would they react to such sexist remarks? Only 5 percent predicted they would ignore each of the comments or wait to see how others reacted. But when Janet Swim and Lauri Hyers (1998) engaged other students in discussions where such comments were actually made by a male confederate, 55 percent (not 5 percent) said nothing. Likewise, although people predicted they would be upset by witnessing a person making a racial slur—and would avoid picking the racist person as a partner in an experiment—Kerry Kawakami of York University and her colleagues (2009) found that people actually experiencing such an event typically exhibited indifference. These experiments demonstrated the power of normative pressures and showed how hard it is to predict behaviour, even our own behaviour.

This lesson is further illustrated by a painful episode in Canadian history. In 1994, two soldiers in the Canadian Airborne Regiment tortured and killed Shidane Arone, a Somali teenager who was caught stealing from their camp in Somalia. An inquiry into Arone's death suggested that 16 people passed through the area where he was tortured and that his screams could be heard throughout the camp, yet no one intervened. The Canadian public was outraged: They had prided their military as peacekeepers and did not believe that such atrocity could happen on Canada's watch. They likely believed that they would have stepped in to stop torture. But the lessons of history, of bystander response (see Chapter 8), and of these experiments remind us that *saying* what we would do in a hypothetical situation is often easier than *doing* it in a real situation.

Milgram's studies also offer a lesson about evil. According to what we see in horror movies and suspense novels, evil results from a few bad apples, a few depraved killers. In real life, we similarly think of Hitler's extermination of Jews or of Osama bin Laden's terrorist plots. But evil also results from social forces—from the heat, humidity, and disease that help make a whole barrel of apples go bad. The U.S. military police, whose abuse of Iraqi prisoners at Abu Ghraib prison horrified the world, were under stress, taunted by many of those they had come to save, angered by comrades' deaths, overdue to return home, and under lax supervision—an evil situation that produced evil behaviour (Fiske et al., 2004). Similar conditions prevailed in Somalia when Canadian soldiers turned a blind eye to Shidane Arone's murder. Situations can induce ordinary people to capitulate to cruelty.

This is especially true when, as happens often in complex societies, the most terrible evil evolves from a sequence of small evils. German civil servants surprised Nazi leaders with their willingness to handle the paperwork of the Holocaust. They were not killing Jews, of course; they were merely pushing paper (Silver & Geller, 1978). When fragmented, evil becomes easier. Milgram studied this compartmentalization of evil by involving yet another 40 men more indirectly. Rather than trigger the shock, they had only to administer the learning test. Under those conditions, 37 of the 40 fully complied.

So it is in our everyday lives: The drift toward evil usually comes in small increments, without any conscious intent to do evil. Procrastination involves a similar unintended drift, toward self-harm (Sabini & Silver, 1982). A student knows the deadline for a term paper weeks ahead. Each diversion from work on the paper—a video game here, a TV program there—seems harmless enough. Yet gradually, the student veers toward not doing the paper without ever consciously deciding not to do it.

It is tempting to assume that Eichmann and the Auschwitz death camp commanders were uncivilized monsters. Indeed, their evil was fuelled by virulent anti-Semitism. And the social situation alone does not explain why, in the same death camp, some personalities displayed vicious cruelty and others heroic kindness. Still, the commanders would not have stood out to us as monsters. After a hard day's work, they would relax by listening to Beethoven and Schubert. Like most other Nazis, Eichmann himself was outwardly indistinguishable from common people with ordinary jobs (Arendt, 1963). Or consider the German police battalion responsible for shooting nearly 40 000 Jews in Poland, many of them women, children, and elderly people who were gruesomely shot in the back of the head. Christopher Browning (1992) portrayed the "normality" of these men. Like the many, many others who ravaged Europe's Jewish ghettos, operated the deportation trains, and administered the death camps (Goldhagen, 1996), they were not Nazis, SS members, or racial fanatics. They were labourers, salesmen, clerks, and artisans—family men who were too old for military service, but who, when directly ordered to kill, were unable to refuse.

As Milgram noted (1974, p. 6), "The most fundamental lesson of our study is that ordinary people, simply doing their jobs, and without any particular hostility on their part, can become agents in a terrible destructive process." Under the sway of evil forces, even nice people are sometimes corrupted as they construct moral rationalizations for immoral behaviour (Tsang, 2002). So it is that ordinary soldiers will follow orders to shoot defenceless civilians, ordinary employees will follow instructions to produce and distribute degrading products, and ordinary group members will heed commands to brutally haze initiates.

So, does a situational analysis of harm-doing exonerate harm-doers? Does it absolve them of responsibility? In laypeople's minds, the answer is to some extent yes, noted Arthur Miller (2006). But the psychologists who study the roots of evil insist otherwise. To explain is not to excuse. To understand is not to forgive. You can forgive someone whose behaviour you don't understand, and you can understand someone whom you do not forgive. Moreover, added James Waller (2002), "When we understand the ordinariness of extraordinary evil, we will be less surprised by evil, less likely to be unwitting contributors to evil, and perhaps better equipped to forestall evil."

Finally, a comment on the experimental method used in conformity research (see synopsis, Table 6-1): Conformity situations in the laboratory differ from those in

"Eichmann did not hate Jews, and that made it worse, to have no feelings. To make Eichmann appear a monster renders him less dangerous than he was. If you kill a monster you can go to bed and sleep, for there aren't many of them. But if Eichmann was normality, then this is a far more dangerous situation."

HANNAH ARENDT, *EICHMANN IN JERUSALEM*, 1963

TABLE 6–1   SUMMARY OF CLASSIC OBEDIENCE STUDIES

Topic	Researcher	Method	Real-Life Example
Norm formation	Sherif	Assessing suggestibility regarding seeming movement of light	Interpreting events differently after hearing from others; appreciating a tasty food that others love
Conformity	Asch	Agreement with others' obviously wrong perceptual judgments	Doing as others do; fads such as tattoos
Obedience	Milgram	Complying with commands to shock another	Soldiers or employees following questionable orders

everyday life. How often are we asked to judge line lengths or administer shock? But as combustion is similar for a burning match and a forest fire, so we assume that psychological processes in the laboratory and in everyday life are similar (Milgram, 1974). We must be careful in generalizing from the simplicity of a burning match to the complexity of a forest fire. Yet controlled experiments on burning matches can give us insights into combustion that we cannot gain by observing forest fires. So, too, the social-psychological experiment offers insights into behaviour not readily revealed in everyday life. The experimental situation is unique, but so is every social situation. By testing with a variety of unique tasks, and by repeating experiments in different times and places, researchers probe for the common principles that lie beneath the surface diversity.

The classic conformity studies answered some questions but raised others: Sometimes people conform; sometimes they do not. (1) When do they conform? (2) Why do people conform? Why don't they ignore the group and "to their own selves be true?" (3) Is there a type of person who is likely to conform? In the next section, we will address these questions one at a time.

WHAT PREDICTS CONFORMITY?

Some situations trigger much conformity, others little conformity. If you want to produce maximum conformity, what conditions would you choose?

Social psychologists wondered: If even Asch's non-coercive, unambiguous situation could elicit a 37 percent conformity rate, would other settings produce even more? Researchers soon discovered that conformity did grow if the judgments were difficult or if the subjects felt incompetent. The more insecure we are about our judgments, the more influenced we are by others.

Group attributes also matter. Conformity is highest when the group has three or more people and is cohesive, unanimous, and high in status. Conformity is also highest when the response is public and made without prior commitment. Let's look at each of these conditions.

GROUP SIZE

In laboratory experiments, a group need not be large to have a large effect. Asch and other researchers found that three to five people will elicit much more conformity than just one or two. Increasing the number of people beyond five yields diminishing returns (Gerard, Wilhelmy,

& Conolley, 1968; Rosenberg, 1961). In a field experiment, Milgram and his colleagues (1969) had 1, 2, 3, 5, 10, or 15 people pause on a busy sidewalk and look up. As Figure 6–5 shows, the percentage of people passing by who also looked up increased as the number looking up increased from one to five persons.

The way the group is "packaged" also makes a difference. Researcher David Wilder (1977) gave students a jury case. Before giving their own judgments, the students watched videotapes of four confederates giving their judgments. When the confederates were presented as two independent groups of two people, the participants conformed more than when the four confederates presented their judgments as a single group. Similarly, two groups of three people elicited more conformity than one group of six, and three groups of two people elicited even more. The agreement of several small groups makes a position more credible.

UNANIMITY

Imagine yourself in a conformity experiment in which all but one of the people responding before you give the same wrong answer. Would the example of this one nonconforming confederate be as liberating as it was for the subjects in Milgram's obedience experiment? Several experiments reveal that someone who punctures a group's unanimity deflates its social power (Allen & Levine, 1969; Asch, 1955; Morris & Miller, 1975). As Figure 6–6 illustrates, people will nearly always voice their convictions if just one other person has also differed from the majority. The participants in such experiments often later say they felt warm toward and close to their nonconforming ally. Yet they deny that the ally influenced them: "I would have answered just the same if he weren't there."

It's difficult to be a minority of one; few juries are hung because of one dissenting juror. Conformity experiments teach the practical lesson that it is easier to stand up for something if you can find someone else to stand up with you. Many religious groups recognize this. Following the example of Jesus, who sent his disciples out in pairs, Jehovah's Witnesses send two

FIGURE 6–5

GROUP SIZE AND CONFORMITY.

The percentage of passersby who imitated a group looking upward increased as group size increased to five persons. (Data from Milgram, Bickman, & Berkowitz, 1969)

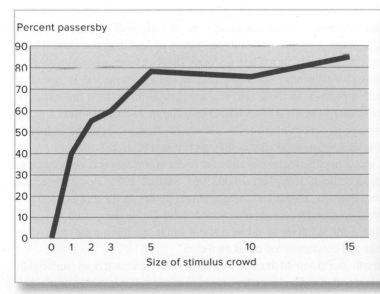

Percent passersby

Size of stimulus crowd

FIGURE 6–6

THE EFFECT OF UNANIMITY ON CONFORMITY.

When someone giving correct answers punctures the group's unanimity, individuals conform only one-fourth as often. (Data from Asch, 1955)

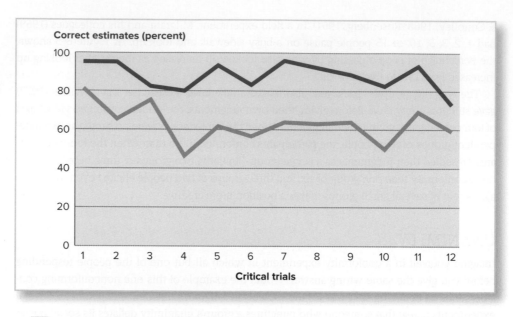

> "My opinion, my conviction, gains infinitely in strength and success, the moment a second mind has adopted it."
>
> NOVALIS, *FRAGMENT*

missionaries into a neighbourhood together. The support of the one comrade greatly increases a person's social courage.

Observing someone else's dissent–even when it is wrong–can increase our own independence. Charlan Nemeth and Cynthia Chiles (1988) discovered this after having people observe a lone individual in a group of four misjudge blue stimuli as green. Although the dissenter was wrong, observing him enabled the observers to exhibit their own form of independence: 76 percent of the time they correctly labelled red slides "red" even when everyone else was calling them "orange." Participants who had no opportunity to observe the "green" dissenter conformed 70 percent of the time.

COHESION

A minority opinion from someone outside the groups we identify with–from someone at another university or of a different religion, for example–sways us less than the same minority opinion from someone within our group (Clark & Maass, 1988). A heterosexual arguing for gay rights would sway heterosexuals more effectively than would a homosexual. People even comply more readily with requests from those said to share their birthday, their first name, or features of their fingerprint (Burger et al., 2004; Silvia, 2005). The more **cohesiveness** a group exhibits, the more power it gains over its members. In university sororities, for example, friends tend to share binge-eating tendencies, especially as they grow closer (Crandall, 1988).

In experiments, too, group members who feel attracted to the group are more responsive to its influence (Berkowitz, 1954; Boldt, 1976; Lott & Lott, 1961; Sakurai, 1975). Fearing rejection by group members whom they like, they allow them a certain power. In his *Essay Concerning Human Understanding,* the seventeenth-century philosopher John Locke recognized the cohesiveness factor: "Nor is there one in ten thousand who is stiff and insensible enough to bear up under the constant dislike and condemnation of his own club."

Our inclination to go with our group–to think what it thinks and do what it does–surfaced in one experiment as people reported greater liking for a piece of music that was said to be liked by

cohesiveness
a "we feeling"—the extent to which members of a group are bonded together, such as by attraction for one another

people akin to themselves (but disliked the music more when it was liked by someone unlike themselves [Hilmert, Kulik, & Christenfeld, 2006]). Likewise, when university students compare themselves with drinkers who are dissimilar from themselves, they become *less* likely to drink (Lane et al., 2011). And after observing cheating by someone wearing a T-shirt from their own university, participants in another experiment became more likely to cheat. But if the cheater wore a T-shirt from a competing university, it had the opposite effect: the participants became more honest (Gino, Ayal, & Ariely, 2009). Cohesion-fed conformity also appears in university dorms, where students' attitudes over time become more similar to those living near them (Cullum & Harton, 2007).

STATUS

As you might suspect, higher-status people tend to have more impact (Driskell & Mullen, 1990). Junior group members—even junior social psychologists—acknowledge more conformity to their group than do senior group members (Jetten, Hornsey, & Adarves-Yorno, 2006). Or consider this: U.S. studies of jaywalking behaviour, conducted with the unwitting aid of nearly 24 000 pedestrians, revealed that the baseline jaywalking rate of 25 percent decreases to 17 percent in the presence of a non-jaywalking confederate and increases to 44 percent in the presence of another jaywalker (Mullen, Copper, & Driskell, 1990). The non-jaywalker best discourages jaywalking when well dressed. Even chimps are more likely to imitate the behaviours of high-ranking group members (Horner et al., 2010). Among both humans and other primates, prestige begets influence. Milgram (1974) reported that in his obedience studies, people of lower status accepted the experimenter's commands more readily than people of higher status. After delivering 450 volts, one participant, a 37-year-old welder, turned to the experimenter and deferentially asked, "Where do we go from here, Professor?" (p. 46). Another participant, a divinity school professor who disobeyed at 150 volts, said, "I don't understand why the experiment is placed above this person's life," and plied the experimenter with questions about "the ethics of this thing" (p. 48).

PUBLIC RESPONSE

One of conformity researchers' first questions was this: Would people conform more in their public responses than in their private opinions? Or would they wobble more in their private opinions but be unwilling to conform publicly, lest they appear wishy-washy?

The answer is now clear: As shown in experiments, people conform more when they must respond in front of others rather than writing their answer privately. Asch's participants, after hearing others respond, were less influenced by group pressure if they could write an answer that only the experimenter would see. Likewise, when university instructors ask controversial questions, students express more diverse opinions when answering anonymously, with clickers, than when raising hands (Stowell, Oldham, & Bennett, 2010). It is much easier to stand up for what we believe in the privacy of the voting booth than before a group.

NO PRIOR COMMITMENT

In 1980, Genuine Risk became the second filly ever to win the Kentucky Derby. In her next race, the Preakness, she came off the last turn gaining on the leader, Codex, a colt.

> *"If you worry about missing the boat— remember the Titanic."*
> ANONYMOUS

Did Codex brush against Genuine Risk? Once race referees publicly announced their decision, no amount of evidence could budge them.

"Those who never retract their opinions love themselves more than they love truth."
JOUBERT, *PENSÉES*

As they came out of the turn neck and neck, Codex moved sideways toward Genuine Risk, causing her to hesitate and giving him a narrow victory. Had Codex brushed Genuine Risk? Had his jockey even whipped Genuine Risk in the face? The race referees huddled. After a brief deliberation, they judged that no foul had occurred and confirmed Codex as the winner. The decision caused an uproar. Televised instant replays showed that Codex had, indeed, brushed Genuine Risk, the sentimental favourite. A protest was filed. The officials reconsidered their decision, but they did not change it.

Did their declared judgment immediately after the race affect officials' openness toward reaching a different decision later? We will never know for sure. We can, however, put people through a laboratory version of this event—with and without the immediate commitment—and observe whether the commitment makes a difference. Again, imagine yourself in an Asch-type experiment. The experimenter displays the lines and asks you to respond first. After you have given your judgment and then heard everyone else disagree, the experimenter offers you an opportunity to reconsider. In the face of group pressure, do you now back down?

People almost never do (Deutsch & Gerard, 1955). Once having made a public commitment, they stick to it. At most, they will change their judgments in later situations (Saltzstein & Sandberg, 1979). We may, therefore, expect that judges of diving or gymnastics competitions, for example, will seldom change their ratings after seeing the other judges' ratings, although they might adjust their later performance ratings.

Prior commitment: Once they commit themselves to a position, people seldom yield to social pressure. Real umpires and referees rarely reverse their initial judgments.
© Robert Mankoff/The New Yorker Collection/www.cartoonbank.com

"All right! Have it your own way. It was a ball."

Prior commitments restrain persuasion, too. When simulated juries make decisions, hung verdicts are more likely in cases when jurors are polled by a show of hands rather than by secret ballot (Kerr & MacCoun, 1985). Making a public commitment makes people hesitant to back down.

Smart persuaders know this. Salespeople ask questions that prompt us to make statements for, rather than against, what they are marketing. Environmentalists ask people to commit themselves to recycling, energy conservation, or bus riding. That's because behaviour then changes more than when environmental appeals are heard without inviting a commitment (Katzev & Wang, 1994).

WHY CONFORM?

What two forms of social influence explain why people will conform to others?

"Do you see yonder cloud that's almost in the shape of a camel?" asks Shakespeare's Hamlet of Polonius. "Tis like a camel indeed," replies Polonius. "Methinks it is a weasel," says Hamlet a moment later. "It is backed like a weasel," acknowledges Polonius. "Or like a whale?" wonders Hamlet. "Very like a whale," agrees Polonius. Question: Why does Polonius so readily agree with Hamlet every time he changes his mind?

Or consider this nonfictional situation: One of the authors was attending his first lecture during an extended visit at a German university. As the lecturer finished, the author lifted his hands to join in the clapping. But rather than clap, the other people began rapping the tables with their knuckles. What did this mean? Did they disapprove of the speech? Surely, not everyone would be so openly rude. Nor did their faces express displeasure. No, the author decided, this must be a German ovation. Whereupon, he added his knuckles to the chorus.

What causes such conformity? There are two possibilities: A person may bow to the group (a) to be accepted and avoid rejection or (b) to obtain important information. Morton Deutsch and Harold Gerard (1955) named these two possibilities **normative influence** and **informational influence**. The first springs from our desire to be liked, and the second from our desire to be right.

Normative influence is "going along with the crowd" to avoid rejection, to stay in people's good graces, or to gain their approval. In the laboratory and in everyday life, groups often reject those who consistently deviate (Miller & Anderson, 1979; Schachter, 1951). That's a lesson learned by a media studies professor who became an outcast while playing the online game "City of Heroes" (Vargas, 2009). The professor, with whom we empathize, played by the rules but did not conform to the customs. Much as drivers who go 70 in a 100 km/h zone are disliked for violating norms but not rules, the professor was derided with instant messages: "I hope your mother gets cancer." "EVERYONE HATES YOU." "If you kill me one more time I will come and kill you for real and I am not kidding."

As most of us know, social rejection is painful; when we deviate from group norms, we often pay an emotional price. Brain scans show that group judgments differing from one's own activate a brain area that also is active when one feels the pain of bad betting decisions (Klucharev et al., 2009). Gerard (1999) recalled that in one of his conformity experiments, an initially friendly participant became upset, asked to leave the room, and returned looking

normative influence
conformity based on a person's desire to fulfill others' expectations, often to gain acceptance

informational influence
conformity that results from accepting evidence about reality provided by other people

sick and visibly shaken. I became worried and suggested that we discontinue the session. He absolutely refused to stop and continued through all 36 trials, not yielding to the others on a single trial. After the experiment was over and I explained the subterfuge to him, his entire body relaxed and he sighed with relief. Colour returned to his face. I asked him why he had left the room. "To vomit," he said. He did not yield, but at what a price! He wanted so much to be accepted and liked by the others and was afraid he would not be because he had stood his ground against them. There you have normative pressure operating with a vengeance.

Sometimes, the high price of deviation compels people to support what they do not believe in or at least to suppress their disagreement.

Informational influence, on the other hand, leads people to privately accept others' influence. When reality is ambiguous, as it was for subjects in the autokinetic situation, other people can be a valuable source of information. The participant may reason, "I can't tell how far the light is moving. But this guy seems to know."

Our friends have extra influence on us for informational as well as normative reasons (Denrell, 2008; Denrell & Le Mens, 2007). If our friend buys a particular car and takes us to a particular restaurant, we will gain information that may lead us to like what our friend likes—even if we don't care what our friend likes. Our friends influence the experiences that inform our attitudes.

To discover what the brain is doing when people experience an Asch-type conformity experiment, a neuroscience team put participants in a functional magnetic resonance imaging (fMRI) brain scanner while having them answer perceptual questions after hearing others' responses (Berns et al., 2005). (The task involved mentally rotating a figure to find its match among several possibilities.) When the participants conformed to a wrong answer, the brain regions dedicated to perception became active. And when they went *against* the group, brain regions associated with emotion became active. These results suggest that when people conform, their perceptions may be genuinely influenced. Follow-up fMRI studies have identified neural activity associated with normative influence (in a brain area that is active when people are anxious about social rejection) and with informational influence (in areas involved with one's judgments of a stimulus) (Zaki et al., 2011).

So, concern for social image produces normative influence, and the desire to be correct produces informational influence. In day-to-day life, normative and informational influence often occur together. Dale Griffin of the University of British Columbia and Roger Buehler of Wilfrid Laurier University even found that normative influence can cause informational influence as people construct reasons to justify their conformity (Griffin & Buehler, 1993). They found that participants who conformed to a group standard subsequently interpreted information in ways that upheld their decision to conform. Participants read about "Robert" who needed to decide whether to take a chance and pursue his dream of studying music or play it safe and accept an offer to attend medical school. Some participants were told that "most people" thought Robert should make the risky choice and pursue his dream. Others were told "most people" thought he should play it safe. As Figure 6–7 demonstrates, participants who conformed changed their perceptions of acceptable risk for Robert. Those who conformed to the recommendation that Robert attend medical school subsequently believed he should consider studying music only if he was quite certain of success; those who conformed to the recommendation that Robert study music thought

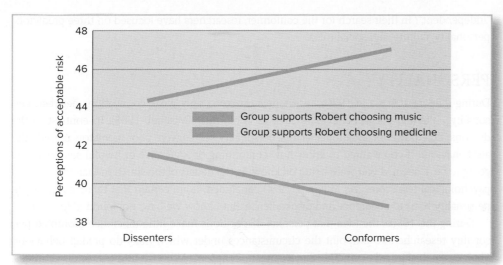

FIGURE 6–7

CHANGING OUR
BELIEFS AFTER WE
CONFORM.

Sometimes we
change what we say
if the basis of our
beliefs is a result
of our conformity.
(Data from Buehler &
Griffin, 1993)

he should do so even if success was only a remote possibility. Participants also changed their construal of the situation in ways that justified their decision to conform or dissent. Those who conformed to the recommendation that Robert go to the music conservatory, for example, thought "success" meant "international fame," rather than a career with a "local symphony orchestra." Thus, the act of dissenting or conforming—driven by normative influence—led participants to interpret the situation differently.

Normative influence: Newly elected politicians often dream of changing the system. Then, seeking to climb within the system, normative influences compel them to comply with its social rules.

Conformity experiments have sometimes isolated either normative or informational influence. Conformity is greater when people respond before a group; this surely reflects normative influence (because subjects receive the same information whether they respond publicly or privately). On the other hand, conformity is greater when participants feel incompetent, when the task is difficult, and when the subjects care about being right—all signs of informational influence.

> *"Do as most do and men will speak well of thee."*
> THOMAS FULLER, *GNOMOLOGIA*

WHO CONFORMS?

Conformity varies not only with situations but also with personality differences. How much so? And in what social contexts do personality traits shine through?

Are some people generally more susceptible (or, should we say, more open) to social influence? Among your friends, can you identify some who are "conformists" and others who are "independent"? In their search for the conformer, researchers have focused on three predictors: personality, culture, and social roles.

PERSONALITY

During the late 1960s and 1970s, researchers observed only weak connections between personality traits and social behaviours such as conformity (Mischel, 1968). In contrast to the demonstrable power of situational factors, personality scores were poor predictors of individuals' behaviour. If you wanted to know how conforming or aggressive or helpful someone was going to be, it seemed you were better off knowing the details of the situation than the person's psychological test scores. As Milgram (1974) concluded, "I am certain that there is a complex personality basis to obedience and disobedience. But I know we have not found it" (p. 205).

During the 1980s, the idea that personal dispositions make little difference prompted personality researchers to pinpoint the circumstances under which traits do predict behaviour. Their research affirmed a principle that we met in Chapter 4: Although internal factors (attitudes, traits) seldom precisely predict a specific action, they better predict a person's average behaviour across many situations (Epstein, 1980; Rushton, Brainerd, & Pressley, 1983). An analogy may help: Just as your response to a single test item is hard to predict, so is your behaviour in a single situation. And just as your total score across the many items of a test is more predictable, so is your total conformity (or outgoingness or aggressiveness) across many situations.

Personality also predicts behaviour better when social influences are weak. Milgram's obedience studies created "strong" situations; their clear-cut demands made it difficult for personality differences to operate. Even so, Milgram's participants differed widely in how obedient they were, and there is good reason to suspect that sometimes his participants' hostility, respect for

Personality effects loom larger when we note people's differing reactions to the same situation, as when one person reacts with delight and another with terror to a roller coaster ride.

authority, and concern for meeting expectations affected their obedience (Blass, 1990, 1991). In "weaker" situations—as when two strangers sit in a waiting room with no cues to guide their behaviour—individual personalities are even freer to shine (Ickes et al., 1982; Monson, Hesley, & Chernick, 1982).

> *"I don't want to get adjusted to this world."*
> WOODY GUTHRIE

The pendulum of professional opinion swings. Without discounting the undeniable power of social forces, the pendulum is now swinging back toward an appreciation of individual personality and its genetic predispositions. Like the attitude researchers we considered earlier, personality researchers are clarifying and reaffirming the connection between who we are and what we do. Thanks to their efforts, today's social psychologists now agree with pioneering theorist Kurt Lewin's (1936) dictum: "Every psychological event depends upon the state of the person and at the same time on the environment, although their relative importance is different in different cases" (p. 12).

CULTURE

Does cultural background help predict how conforming people will be? Indeed it does. James Whittaker and Robert Meade (1967) repeated Asch's conformity experiment in several countries and found similar conformity rates in most—31 percent in Lebanon, 32 percent in Hong Kong, 34 percent in Brazil—but 51 percent among the Bantu of Zimbabwe, a tribe with strong sanctions for nonconformity. When Milgram (1961) used a different conformity procedure to compare Norwegian and French students, he consistently found the French students to be less conforming. An analysis by Roy Bond and Peter Smith (1996) of 133 studies in 17 countries showed how cultural values influence conformity. Compared with people in individualistic countries, those in collectivist countries (where social harmony is prized) are more responsive to others' influence. In collectivist Japan, Western observers were struck by the absence of looting and lawlessness following the 2011 earthquake and tsunami; respect for social norms prevailed (Cafferty, 2011). In individualist countries, university students see themselves as more nonconforming than others in their consumer purchases and political views—as individuals amid the sheep (Pronin, Berger, & Molouki, 2007).

Why do people in some countries conform more than others? Conformity may reflect an evolutionary response to survival threats, such as disease-bearing pathogens. Norms for food preparation and personal hygiene protect people from pathogens, and conformity to these norms reduces the spread of disease. Damian Murray and his collaborators (2011) at the University of British Columbia found that cultures that display greater conformity in experiments had historically greater prevalence of pathogens such as malaria, dengue, and tuberculosis. Cultural norms promoting greater conformity may have emerged in these areas to protect people from these dangerous diseases. Cultural differences also exist within any country. For example, in five studies, Nicole Stephens and her co-researchers (2007) found that working-class people tend to prefer similarity to others while middle-class people more strongly preferred to see themselves as unique individuals. In one experiment, people chose a pen from among five green and orange pens (with three or four of one colour). Of university students from working-class backgrounds, 72 percent picked one from the majority colour, as did only 44 percent of those from middle-class backgrounds (with a university-graduate parent). Those from working-class backgrounds also came to like their chosen pen more after seeing someone else make the same choice. They responded more positively to a friend's knowingly buying the same car they had just bought. And they were also more likely to prefer visual images that they knew others had chosen.

In addition, cultures may change over time. Replication of Asch's experiment with university students in Canada, Britain, and the United States sometimes triggers less conformity than Asch observed two or three decades earlier (Lalancette & Standing, 1990; Larsen, 1974, 1990; Nicholson, Cole, & Rocklin, 1985; Perrin & Spencer, 1981). So conformity and obedience are universal phenomena, yet they vary across cultures and eras.

SOCIAL ROLES

All the world's a stage,
And all the men and women merely players:
They have their exits and their entrances;
And one man in his time plays many parts.
—William Shakespeare

Role theorists assume, as did William Shakespeare's character Jaques in *As You Like It,* that social life is like acting on a theatrical stage, with all its scenes, masks, and scripts. And those roles have much to do with conformity. Social roles allow some freedom of interpretation to those who act them out, but some aspects of any role *must* be performed. A student must at least show up for exams, turn in papers, and maintain some minimum grade point average.

When only a few norms are associated with a social category (for example, riders on an escalator should stand to the right and walk to the left), we do not regard the position as a social role. It takes a whole cluster of norms to define a role. The authors could readily generate a long list of norms prescribing our activities as professors or as fathers. Although we may acquire our particular images by violating the least important norms (e.g., rarely arriving early for anything), violating our role's most important norms (failing to meet classes, abusing our children) could lead to being fired or having our children removed from our care.

Roles have powerful effects. In Chapter 4, we noted that we tend to absorb our roles. On a first date or on a new job, we may act the role self-consciously. As we internalize the role, self-consciousness subsides. What felt awkward now feels genuine.

That is the experience of many immigrants and international students and executives. After arriving in a new country, it takes time to learn how to talk and act appropriately in the new context—to conform, as the author did with the Germans who rapped their knuckles on their desks. And the almost universal experience of those who repatriate back to their home country is re-entry distress (Sussman, 2000). In ways they may not have been aware of, their behaviour, values, and identity will have shifted to accommodate a different place. They must "re-conform" to their former roles before being back in sync.

"Nowhere is social psychology further apart from public consciousness," noted Philip Brickman (1978), "than in its understanding of how things become real for people." Our actions depend not only on the social situation but also on our personalities. Not everyone responds in the same way to the pressure to conform.

So far in this chapter, we have discussed classic studies of conformity and obedience, identified the factors that predict conformity, and considered who conforms and why. Remember that our primary quest in social psychology is not to catalogue differences but to identify universal principles of behaviour. Social roles will always vary with culture, but the processes by which those roles influence behaviour vary much less. People in Nigeria and Japan define teen roles differently from people in Europe and North America, for example; but in all cultures, role expectations guide the conformity found in social relations.

DO WE EVER WANT TO BE DIFFERENT?

Will people ever actively resist social pressure? When compelled to do A, will they instead do Z? What would motivate such anticonformity?

This chapter emphasizes the power of social forces. It is, therefore, fitting that we conclude by again reminding ourselves of the power of the person. We are not just billiard balls moving where pushed. We may and can act according to our own values, independently of the forces that push on us. Knowing that someone is trying to coerce us may even prompt us to react in the opposite direction.

> *"To do just the opposite is also a form of imitation."*
> LICHTENBERG, *APHORISMEN*, 1764–1799

REACTANCE

Individuals value their sense of freedom and self-efficacy. When blatant social pressure threatens their sense of freedom, they often rebel. Think of Romeo and Juliet, whose love was intensified by their families' opposition. Or think of children asserting their freedom and independence by doing the opposite of what their parents ask. Savvy parents, therefore, offer their children choices instead of commands: "It's time to clean up: Do you want a bath or a shower?"

The theory of psychological **reactance**—that people act to protect their sense of freedom—was supported by experiments showing that attempts to restrict a person's freedom often produce an anti-conformity "boomerang effect" (Brehm & Brehm, 1981; Nail et al., 2000). In one field experiment, many non-"nerdy" students stopped wearing a "Livestrong" wristband when nearby "nerdy" academic students started wearing the band (Berger & Heath, 2008). Likewise, rich Brits dissociated themselves from a dissimilar group when they stopped wearing Burberry caps after they caught on among soccer hooligans (Clevstrom & Passariello, 2006).

Reactance may contribute to underage drinking. A survey of 18- to 24-year-olds by the Canadian Centre on Substance Abuse (1997) revealed that 69 percent of those over the legal drinking age had been drunk in the last year, as had 77 percent of those who were underage. Likewise, 21.5 percent of underage drinkers, but only 17 percent of legal drinkers, reported that their drinking had caused personal problems in their life. Researchers suspected that this reflects a reactance against the restriction.

reactance
a motive to protect or restore one's sense of freedom. Reactance arises when someone threatens our freedom of action.

NON SEQUITUR © 1997 / Wiley Miller. Reprinted with permission of Universal Press Syndicate. All Rights Reserved.

ASSERTING UNIQUENESS

Imagine a world of complete conformity, where there were no differences among people. Would such a world be a happy place? If nonconformity can create discomfort, can sameness create comfort?

"When I'm in America, I have no doubt I'm a Jew, but I have strong doubts about whether I'm really an American. And when I get to Israel, I know I'm an American, but I have strong doubts about whether I'm a Jew."
LESLIE FIEDLER, *FIEDLER ON THE ROOF*, 1991

People feel uncomfortable when they appear too different from others. But, at least in Western cultures, they also feel uncomfortable when they appear exactly like everyone else. As experiments by C. R. Snyder and Howard Fromkin (1980) have shown, people feel better when they see themselves as moderately unique. Moreover, they act in ways that will assert their individuality. In one experiment, Snyder (1980) led university students to believe that their "10 most important attitudes" were either distinct from or nearly identical to the attitudes of 10 000 other students. When they then participated in a conformity experiment, those deprived of their feeling of uniqueness were most likely to assert their individuality by nonconformity. Moreover, individuals who have the highest "need for uniqueness" tend to be the least responsive to majority influence (Imhoff & Erb, 2009).

Seeing oneself as unique also appears in people's "spontaneous self-concepts." William McGuire and his colleagues (McGuire & Padawer-Singer, 1978; McGuire, McGuire, & Winton, 1979) reported that when children are invited to "tell us about yourself," they are

Reactance at work? Underage students have been found to be less often abstinent and more often drinking to excess than students over the legal drinking age.

most likely to mention their distinctive attributes. Foreign-born children are more likely than others to mention their birthplace. Redheads are more likely than black- and brown-haired children to volunteer their hair colour. Light and heavy children are the most likely to refer to their body weight. Minority children are the most likely to mention their race.

Likewise, we become more keenly aware of our gender when we are with people of the other gender (Cota & Dion, 1986). When one of the authors attended a Psychological Association meeting with 10 others—all women, as it happened—he immediately was aware of his gender. As the group took a break at the end of the second day, he joked that the line would be short at his bathroom, triggering the woman sitting next to him to notice what hadn't crossed her mind—the group's gender makeup.

The principle, says McGuire, is that "one is conscious of oneself insofar as, and in the ways that, one is different." Thus, "If I am a Black woman in a group of White women, I tend to think of myself as a Black; if I move to a group of Black men, my blackness loses salience and I become more conscious of being a woman" (McGuire et al., 1978). This insight helps us understand why White people who grow up amid non-White people tend to have a strong White identity, and why any minority group tends to be conscious of its distinctiveness and how the surrounding culture relates to it (Knowles & Peng, 2005). The majority group, being less conscious of race, may see the minority group as hypersensitive.

When the people of two cultures are nearly identical, they still will notice their differences, however small. Even trivial distinctions may provoke scorn and conflict. Jonathan Swift satirized the phenomenon in *Gulliver's Travels* with the Little-Endians' war against the Big-Endians. Their difference: The Little-Endians preferred to break their eggs on the small end, the Big-Endians on the large end. On a world scale, the differences may not seem great between Scots and English, Hutus and Tutsis, Serbs and Croatians, or Catholic and Protestant Northern Irish. But small differences can mean big conflicts (Rothbart & Taylor, 1992). Rivalry is often most intense when the other group closely resembles your own.

So, although we do not like being greatly deviant, we are, ironically, all alike in wanting to feel distinctive and in noticing how we are distinctive. But as research on self-serving bias (Chapter 2) has made clear, it is not just any kind of distinctiveness we seek but distinctiveness in the right direction. Our quest is not merely to be different from the average, but to be better than average.

> *"There are no exceptions to the rule that everybody likes to be an exception to the rule."*
> MALCOLM FORBES, *FORBES MAGAZINE*

Asserting our uniqueness. While not wishing to be greatly deviant, most of us express our distinctiveness through our personal styles and dress.

⋮⋯▶ SUMMING UP

WHAT IS CONFORMITY?

- *Conformity*—changing one's behaviour or belief as a result of group pressure—comes in two forms. *Compliance* is outwardly going along with the group while inwardly disagreeing; a subset of compliance is *obedience*, compliance with a direct command. *Acceptance* is believing as well as acting in accord with social pressure.

WHAT ARE THE CLASSIC CONFORMITY AND OBEDIENCE STUDIES?

Three classic sets of experiments illustrate how researchers have studied conformity:

- Muzafer Sherif observed that others' judgments influenced people's estimates of the movement of a point of light that actually did not move. Norms for "proper" answers emerged and survived both over long periods of time and through succeeding generations of research participants.

- Solomon Asch had people listen to others' judgments of which of three comparison lines was equal to a standard line and then make the same judgment themselves. When the others unanimously gave a wrong answer, the subjects conformed 37 percent of the time.

- Stanley Milgram's obedience studies elicited an extreme form of compliance. Under optimum conditions—a legitimate, close-at-hand commander, a remote victim, and no one else to exemplify disobedience—65 percent of his adult male subjects fully obeyed instructions to deliver what were supposedly traumatizing electric shocks to a screaming innocent victim in an adjacent room.

- These classic studies expose the potency of several phenomena. Behaviour and attitudes are mutually reinforcing, enabling a small act of evil to foster the attitude that leads to a larger evil act. The power of the situation is seen when good people, faced with dire circumstances, commit reprehensible acts (although dire situations may produce heroism in others).

WHAT PREDICTS CONFORMITY?

- Using conformity testing procedures, experimenters have explored the circumstances that produce conformity. Certain situations appear to be especially powerful. For example, conformity is affected by the characteristics of the group: People conform most when faced with the unanimous reports of three or more people, or groups, who model the behaviour or belief.

- Conformity is reduced if the model behaviour or belief is not unanimous.

- Conformity is enhanced by group cohesion.

- The higher the status of those modelling the behaviour or belief, the greater likelihood of conformity.

- People also conform most when their responses are public (in the presence of the group).

- A prior commitment to a certain behaviour or belief increases the likelihood that a person will stick with that commitment rather than conform.

WHY CONFORM?

Experiments reveal two reasons people conform:

- Normative influence results from a person's desire for acceptance: We want to be liked. The tendency to conform more when responding publicly reflects normative influence.

- Informational influence results from others' providing evidence about reality. The tendency to conform more on difficult decision-making tasks reflects informational influence: We want to be right.

WHO CONFORMS?

- The question "Who conforms?" has produced few definitive answers. Personality scores are poor predictors of specific acts of conformity but better predictors of average conformity. Trait effects sometimes seem strongest in "weak" situations where social forces do not overwhelm individual differences.

- Although conformity and obedience are universal, culture socializes people to be more or less socially responsive.

- Social roles involve a certain degree of conformity, and conforming to expectations is an important task when stepping into a new social role.

DO WE EVER WANT TO BE DIFFERENT?

- Social psychology's emphasis on the power of social pressure must be joined by a complementary emphasis on the power of the person. We are not puppets. When social coercion becomes blatant, people often experience reactance—a motivation to defy the coercion in order to maintain a sense of freedom.

- We are not comfortable being too different from a group, but neither do we want to appear the same as everyone else. Thus, we act in ways that preserve our sense of uniqueness and individuality. In a group, we are most conscious of how we differ from the others.

CHAPTER SEVEN
Group Influence

▶ CHAPTER OUTLINE

● WHAT IS A GROUP?

● SOCIAL FACILITATION: HOW ARE WE AFFECTED BY THE PRESENCE OF OTHERS?

● SOCIAL LOAFING: DO INDIVIDUALS EXERT LESS EFFORT IN A GROUP?

● DEINDIVIDUATION: WHEN DO PEOPLE LOSE THEIR SENSE OF SELF IN GROUPS?

● GROUP POLARIZATION: DO GROUPS INTENSIFY OUR OPINIONS?

● GROUPTHINK: DO GROUPS HINDER OR ASSIST GOOD DECISIONS?

● LEADERSHIP: HOW DO LEADERS SHAPE THE GROUP'S ACTIONS?

● THE INFLUENCE OF THE MINORITY: HOW DO INDIVIDUALS INFLUENCE THE GROUP?

Tawna is nearing the end of her daily run. Her mind prods her to keep going; her body begs her to just walk home. She compromises and slowly jogs home. The next day, conditions are identical, except that two friends run with her. Tawna runs her route two minutes faster. She wonders, "Did I run better merely because Gail and Rachel went along? Would I always run better in a group?"

At almost every turn, we are involved in groups. Our world contains not only more than 7 billion individuals but also 193 nation-states, 4 million local communities, 20 million economic organizations, and hundreds of millions of other formal and informal groups—couples having dinner, housemates hanging out, clubs planning activities. How do these groups influence individuals?

Group interactions often have more dramatic effects. Intellectual university students hang out with other intellectuals, accentuating one another's intellectual interests. Deviant youth hang out with other deviant youth, amplifying one another's antisocial tendencies. But how do groups affect attitudes? And what influences lead groups to smart and foolish decisions?

Individuals influence their groups. As the 1957 movie *Twelve Angry Men* opens, 12 wary murder trial jurors file into the jury room. It is a hot day. The tired jurors are close to agreement and eager for a quick verdict convicting a teenage boy of knifing his father. But one maverick, played by Henry Fonda, refuses to vote guilty. As the heated deliberation proceeds, the jurors one by one change their verdict until consensus is reached: "Not guilty." In real trials, a lone individual seldom sways the entire group. Yet, minorities that sway majorities make history. What helps make a minority—or an effective leader—persuasive?

We will examine these intriguing phenomena of group influence one at a time. But first things first: What is a group and why do groups exist?

● WHAT IS A GROUP?

The answer to this question seems self-evident—until several people compare their definitions. Are jogging partners a group? Are airplane passengers a group? Is a group a set of people who identify with one another, who sense they belong together? Is a group those who share common goals and rely on one another? Does a group form when individuals become organized? When their relationships with one another continue over time? These are among the social psychological definitions of a group (McGrath, 1984).

Group dynamics expert Marvin Shaw (1981) argued that all groups have one thing in common: Their members interact. He, therefore, defined a **group** as two or more people who interact and influence one another. Moreover, suggested Australian National University social psychologist John Turner (1987), groups perceive themselves as "us" in contrast to "them." A pair of jogging companions, then, would indeed constitute a group. Different groups help us meet different human needs—to affiliate (to belong to and connect with others), to achieve, and to gain a social identity (Johnson et al., 2006).

By Shaw's definition, students working individually in a computer room would not be a group. Although physically together, they are more a collection of individuals than an interacting group (though each may be part of a group with dispersed others in an online chat room). The distinction between collections of unrelated individuals in a computer lab and the more influential group behaviour among interacting individuals sometimes blurs. People who are merely in one another's presence do sometimes influence one another. At a hockey game, they may perceive themselves as "us" fans in contrast with "them" who root for the other team.

In this chapter, we consider three examples of such collective influence: social facilitation, social loafing, and deindividuation. These three phenomena can occur with minimal interaction (in what we call "minimal group situations"), but they also influence people's behaviour while interacting. Then we will consider four examples of social influence in interacting groups: group polarization, groupthink, leadership, and minority influence.

group
two or more people who, for longer than a few moments, interact with and influence one another and perceive one another as "us"

● SOCIAL FACILITATION: HOW ARE WE AFFECTED BY THE PRESENCE OF OTHERS?

Let's explore one of social psychology's most elementary questions: Are we affected by the mere presence of another person? "Mere presence" means that the people are not competing, do not reward or punish, and in fact do nothing except be present as a passive audience or as co-actors*. Would the mere presence of others affect a person's jogging, eating, ice skating, or exam performance? The search for the answer is a scientific mystery story.*

co-actors
a group of people working simultaneously and individually on a non-competitive task

THE MERE PRESENCE OF OTHERS

More than a century ago, Norman Triplett (1898), a psychologist interested in bicycle racing, noticed that cyclists' times were faster when racing together than when racing alone against the

social facilitation
(1) original meaning: the tendency of people to perform simple or well-learned tasks better when others are present; (2) current meaning: the strengthening of dominant (prevalent, likely) responses owing to the presence of others

clock. Before he peddled his hunch (that the presence of others boosts performance), Triplett conducted one of social psychology's early laboratory experiments. Children told to wind string on a fishing reel as rapidly as possible wound faster when they worked with co-actors than when they worked alone. "The bodily presence of another contestant . . . serves to liberate latent energy," concluded Triplett.

A modern reanalysis of Triplett's data revealed that the difference did not reach statistical significance (Stroebe, 2012; Strube, 2005). But ensuing experiments found that the presence of others improves the speed with which people do simple multiplication problems and cross out designated letters. It also improves the accuracy with which people perform simple motor tasks, such as keeping a metal stick in contact with a dime-sized disk on a moving turntable (F. W. Allport, 1920; Dashiell, 1930; Travis, 1925). This **social facilitation** effect also occurs with animals. In the presence of others of their species, ants excavate more sand, chickens eat more grain, and sexually active rat pairs mate more often (Bayer, 1929; Chen, 1937; Larsson, 1956).

Social facilitation: The motivating presence of a co-actor or audience strengthens well-learned responses.

But wait: Other studies revealed that on some tasks the presence of others hinders performance. In the presence of others, cockroaches, parakeets, and green finches learn mazes more slowly (Allee & Masure, 1936; Gates & Allee, 1933; Klopfer, 1958). This disruptive effect also occurs with people. The presence of others diminishes efficiency at learning nonsense syllables, completing a maze, and performing complex multiplication problems (Dashiell, 1930; Pessin, 1933; Pessin & Husband, 1933).

Saying that the presence of others sometimes facilitates performance and sometimes hinders it is about as satisfying as a weather forecast predicting that it might be sunny but then again it might rain. By 1940, research activity in this area had ground to a halt. It lay dormant for 25 years until awakened by the touch of a new idea.

Social psychologist Robert Zajonc (pronounced *Zyence;* rhymes with *science*) wondered whether these seemingly contradictory findings could be reconciled. As often happens at creative moments in science, Zajonc (1965) used one field of research to illuminate another. The illumination came from a well-established principle in experimental psychology: Arousal enhances whatever response tendency is dominant. Increased arousal enhances performance on easy tasks for which the most likely—"dominant"—response is correct. People solve easy anagrams, such as *akec,* fastest when they are anxious. On complex tasks, for which the correct answer is not dominant, increased arousal promotes incorrect responding. On harder anagrams, such as *theloacco,* people do worse when anxious.

Could this principle solve the mystery of social facilitation? It seemed reasonable to assume that others' presence will arouse or energize people (Mullen, Bryant, & Driskell, 1997); most of us can recall feeling more tense or excited before an audience. If social arousal

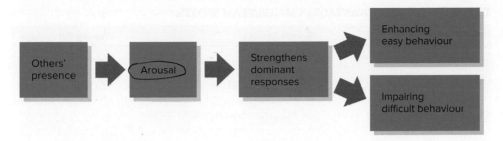

facilitates dominant responses, it should boost performance on easy tasks and hurt performance on difficult tasks.

With that explanation, confusing results made sense. Winding fishing reels, doing simple multiplication problems, and eating were all easy tasks for which the responses were well-learned or naturally dominant. Sure enough, having others around boosted performance. Learning new material, doing a maze, and solving complex math problems were more difficult tasks for which the correct responses were initially less probable. In these cases, the presence of others increased the number of incorrect responses on these tasks. The same general rule—arousal facilitates dominant responses—worked in both cases (see Figure 7-1). Suddenly, what had looked like contradictory results no longer seemed contradictory.

Zajonc's solution, so simple and elegant, left other social psychologists thinking what Thomas H. Huxley thought after first reading Darwin's *Origin of the Species:* "How extremely stupid not to have thought of that!" It seemed obvious—once Zajonc had pointed it out. Perhaps, however, the pieces appeared to merge so neatly only because we viewed them through the spectacles of hindsight. Would the solution survive direct experimental tests?

After almost 300 studies, conducted with the help of more than 25 000 volunteers, the solution has survived (Bond & Titus, 1983; Guerin, 1993, 1999). Social arousal facilitates dominant responses, whether right or wrong. For example, Peter Hunt and Joseph Hillery (1973) found that in the presence of others, students took less time to learn a simple maze and more time to learn a complex one (just as the cockroaches do!). And James Michaels and his collaborators (1982) found that good pool players (who had made 71 percent of their shots while being unobtrusively observed) did even better (80 percent) when four observers came up to watch them play. Poor shooters (who had previously averaged 36 percent) did even worse (25 percent) when closely observed. Likewise, novice drivers more often fail driving tests when tested with another to-be-tested person in the car rather than alone (Rosenbloom et al., 2007).

Athletes, actors, and musicians perform well-practiced skills, which helps explain why they often perform best when energized by the responses of a supportive audience. Studies of more than 80 000 university and professional athletic events in Canada, the United States, and Great Britain revealed that home teams win about six in ten games (somewhat fewer for baseball and football, somewhat more for basketball and soccer; see Table 7-1). The home advantage may, however, also stem from the players' familiarity with their home environment, less travel fatigue, feelings of dominance derived from territorial control, or increased team identity when cheered by fans (Zillmann & Paulus, 1993).

FIGURE 7–1

THE EFFECTS OF SOCIAL AROUSAL.

Robert Zajonc reconciled apparently conflicting findings by proposing that arousal from others' presence strengthens dominant responses (the correct responses only on easy or well-learned tasks).

"Mere social contact begets . . . a stimulation of the animal spirits that heightens the efficiency of each individual workman."
KARL MARX, *DAS KAPITAL*, 1867

"Discovery consists of seeing what everybody has seen and thinking what nobody has thought."
ALBERT AXENT-GYORGYI, *THE SCIENTIST SPECULATES*

TABLE 7-1   HOME ADVANTAGE IN MAJOR TEAM SPORTS.

Sport	Games Studied	Winning Percentage
Baseball	135 665	54.3%
Football	2592	57.3
Hockey	4322	61.1
Basketball	13 596	64.4
Soccer	37 202	69.0

Data from Courneya & Carron (1992), except for Major League Baseball, 1900 to 1992, from Schlenker et al. (1995).

A good house is a full house, as James Maas's Cornell University introductory psychology students experienced in this 2000-seat auditorium. If the class had 100 students meeting in this large space, it would feel much less energized.

CROWDING: THE PRESENCE OF MANY OTHERS

So people do respond to the mere presence of others. But does the presence of observers always arouse people? In times of stress, a comrade can be comforting. Nevertheless, with others present, people perspire more, breathe faster, tense their muscles more, and have higher blood pressure and a faster heart rate (Geen & Gange, 1983; Moore & Baron, 1983). Even a supportive audience may elicit poorer performance on challenging tasks (Butler & Baumeister, 1998). Having your family at your first piano recital likely won't boost your performance.

The effect of others' presence increases with their number (Jackson & Latané, 1981; Knowles, 1983). Sometimes, the arousal and self-conscious attention created by a large audience interferes even with well-learned, automatic behaviours, such as speaking. Given extreme pressure, we're vulnerable to "choking." Stutterers tend to stutter more in front of larger audiences than when speaking to just one or two people (Mullen, 1986b).

Being in a crowd also intensifies positive or negative reactions. When they sit close together, friendly people are liked even more, and unfriendly people are disliked even more (Schiffenbauer & Schiavo, 1976; Storms & Thomas, 1977). In experiments with Columbia University students and with Ontario Science Centre visitors, Jonathan Freedman and his co-workers (1979, 1980) had an accomplice listen to a humorous tape or watch a movie with other participants. When they all sat close together, the accomplice could more readily induce them to laugh and clap. As theatre directors and sports fans know, and as researchers have confirmed, a "good house" is a full house (Agnew & Carron, 1994; Aiello, Thompson, & Brodzinsky, 1983; Worchel & Brown, 1984).

Perhaps you've noticed that a class of 35 students feels warmer and livelier in a room that seats just 35 than when spread around a room that seats 100. When others are close by, we are more likely to notice and join in their laughter or clapping. But crowding also enhances arousal, as Gary Evans (1979) found. He tested 10-person groups, either in a room 7 by 10 metres or in one 3 by 4 metres. Compared to those in the large room, those densely packed had higher pulse rates and blood pressure (indicating arousal). On difficult tasks, they made more errors, an effect of crowding replicated by Dinesh Nagar and Janak Pandey (1987) with university students in India. Crowding, then, has a similar effect to being observed by a crowd: It enhances arousal, which facilitates dominant responses.

> "*Heightened arousal in crowded homes also tends to increase stress. Crowding produces less distress in homes divided into many spaces, however, enabling people to withdraw in privacy.*"
> EVANS, LEPORE, & SCHROEDER, 1996

WHY ARE WE AROUSED IN THE PRESENCE OF OTHERS?

What you do well, you will be energized to do best in front of others (unless you become hyper-aroused and self-conscious). What you find difficult may seem impossible in the same circumstances. What is it about other people that creates arousal? There is evidence to support three possible factors (Aiello & Douthitt, 2001): evaluation apprehension, distraction, and mere presence.

① Evaluation apprehension

Nickolas Cottrell surmised that observers make us apprehensive because we wonder how they are evaluating us. To test whether **evaluation apprehension** exists, Cottrell and his associates (1968) examined social facilitation for the pronunciation of nonsense syllables and well-learned easy-to-pronounce syllables. In this "mere presence" condition, they blindfolded observers, supposedly in preparation for a perception experiment. In contrast to the effect of the watching audience, the mere presence of these blindfolded people did not boost well-practiced responses.

evaluation apprehension concern for how others are evaluating us

Other experiments confirmed Cottrell's conclusion: The enhancement of dominant responses is strongest when people think they are being evaluated. In one experiment, joggers on a jogging path sped up as they came upon a woman seated on the grass—if she was facing them rather than sitting with her back turned (Worringham & Messick, 1983).

The self-consciousness we feel when being evaluated can also interfere with behaviours that we perform best automatically (Mullen & Baumeister, 1987). If self-conscious basketball players analyze their body movements while shooting critical free throws, they are more likely to miss.

② Driven by distraction

Glenn Sanders, Robert Baron, and Danny Moore (1978; Baron, 1986) carried evaluation apprehension a step further. They theorized that when people wonder how co-actors are doing or how an audience is reacting, they get distracted. This *conflict* between paying attention to others and paying attention to the task overloads our cognitive system, causing arousal. We are "driven by distraction." This arousal comes not just from the presence of another person but even from a non-human distraction, such as bursts of light (Sanders, 1981a, 1981b).

③ Mere presence

Zajonc, however, believed that the mere presence of others produces some arousal even without evaluation apprehension or arousing distraction. Recall that facilitation effects also occur with non-human creatures such as cockroaches. This finding hints at an innate social arousal mechanism common to much of the zoological world. (Animals probably are not consciously worrying about how other animals are evaluating them.) At the human level, most runners are energized when running with someone else, even one who neither competes nor evaluates. And university rowing team members, perhaps aided by an endorphin boost from the communal activity, tolerate twice as much pain after rowing together rather than solo (Cohen et al., 2009).

This is a good time to remind ourselves that a good theory is scientific shorthand: It simplifies and summarizes a variety of observations. Social facilitation theory does this well. It is a simple summary of many research findings. A good theory also offers clear predictions that (1) help confirm or modify the theory, (2) guide new exploration, and (3) suggest practical application. Social facilitation theory has definitely generated the first two types of prediction: (1) The basics of the theory (that the presence of others is arousing and that this social arousal enhances dominant responses) have been confirmed, and (2) the theory has brought new life to a long-dormant field of research.

Are there (3) some practical applications? We can make some educated guesses. Many new office buildings have replaced private offices with large, open areas divided by low partitions. Might the resulting awareness of others' presence help boost the performance of well-learned tasks, but disrupt creative thinking on complex tasks? Can you think of other possible applications?

● SOCIAL LOAFING: DO INDIVIDUALS EXERT LESS EFFORT IN A GROUP?

In a team tug-of-war, will eight people on a side exert as much force as the sum of their best efforts in individual tugs of war? If not, why not? What level of individual effort can we expect from members of work groups?

Social facilitation usually occurs when people work toward individual goals and when their efforts, whether winding fishing reels or solving math problems, can be individually evaluated. These situations parallel some everyday work situations—not those where people cooperatively pool their efforts toward a common goal but those where individuals are not accountable for their efforts. A team tug-of-war provides one such example. Organizational fund-raising—pooling candy-sale proceeds to pay for the class trip—provides another. So does a class project where all get the same grade. On such "additive tasks"—tasks where the group's achievement depends on the sum of the individual efforts—will team spirit boost productivity? Will bricklayers lay bricks faster when working as a team than when working alone? One way to attack such questions is with laboratory simulations.

MANY HANDS MAKE LIGHT WORK

Nearly a century ago, French engineer Max Ringelmann (reported by Kravitz & Martin, 1986) found that the collective effort of tug-of-war teams was but half the sum of the individual efforts. Contrary to the common notion that "in unity there is strength," this suggested that group members may actually be less motivated when performing additive tasks. Maybe, though, poor performance stemmed from poor coordination—people pulling a rope in slightly different directions at slightly different times. A group of researchers led by Alan Ingham (1974) cleverly eliminated this problem by making individuals think others were pulling with them, when in fact they were pulling alone. Blindfolded participants who were assigned the first position in the apparatus shown in Figure 7–2 and told to "pull as hard as you can" pulled 18 percent harder when they knew they were pulling alone than when they believed that behind them two to five people were also pulling.

Researchers Bibb Latané, Kipling Williams, and Stephen Harkins (1979; Harkins, Latané, & Williams, 1980) kept their ears open for other ways to investigate this phenomenon, which they labelled **social loafing**. They observed that the noise produced by six people shouting or clapping "as loud as you can" was less than three times that produced by one person alone. Like the tug-of-war task, however, noisemaking is vulnerable to group inefficiency. So Latané and his associates followed Ingham's example by leading their participants to believe others were shouting or clapping with them, when in fact they were doing so alone.

Their method was to blindfold six people, seat them in a semicircle, and have them put on headphones, over which they were blasted with the sound of people shouting or clapping. People could not hear their own shouting or clapping, much less that of others. On various trials, they were instructed to shout or clap either alone or along with the group. People who were told about this experiment guessed the participants would shout louder when with others, because they would be less inhibited (Harkins, 1981). The actual result? Social loafing. When the participants believed five others were also either shouting or clapping, they produced one-third less noise than when they thought themselves alone. Social loafing occurred even when the participants were high school cheerleaders who believed themselves to be cheering together rather than alone (Hardy & Latané, 1986).

Curiously, those who clapped both alone and in groups did not view themselves as loafing; they perceived themselves as clapping equally in both situations. This parallels what happens

social loafing
the tendency for people to exert less effort when they pool their efforts toward a common goal than when they are individually accountable

FIGURE 7–2

THE ROPE-PULLING APPARATUS.

People in the first position pulled less hard when they thought people behind them were also pulling. (Data from Ingham, Levinger, Graves, & Peckham, 1974; photo by Alan G. Ingham)

when students work on group projects for a shared grade. Williams reports that all agree that loafing occurs—but no one admits to doing the loafing.

John Sweeney (1973), a political scientist interested in the policy implications of social loafing, obtained similar results. Students pumped exercise bicycles more energetically (as measured by electrical output) when they knew they were being individually monitored than when they thought their output was being pooled with that of other riders. In the group condition, people were tempted to **free-ride** on the group effort.

In this and some 160 other studies (Karau & Williams, 1993; Figure 7–3), we see a twist on one of the psychological forces that makes for social facilitation: evaluation apprehension. In the social loafing experiments, individuals believe they are evaluated only when they act alone. The group situation (rope pulling, shouting, and so forth) decreases evaluation apprehension. When people are not accountable and cannot evaluate their own efforts, responsibility is diffused across all group members (Harkins & Jackson, 1985; Kerr & Bruun, 1981). By contrast, the social facilitation experiments increased exposure to evaluation. When made the centre of attention, people self-consciously monitor their behaviour (Mullen & Baumeister, 1987). So, when being observed increases evaluation concerns, social facilitation occurs; when being lost in a crowd decreases evaluation concerns, social loafing occurs (Figure 7–4).

To motivate group members, one strategy is to make individual performance identifiable. Some football coaches do this by filming and evaluating each player individually. Whether in a group or not, people exert more effort when their outputs are individually identifiable: University swim team members swim faster in intrasquad relay races when someone monitors and announces their individual times (Williams et al., 1989).

SOCIAL LOAFING IN EVERYDAY LIFE

How widespread is social loafing? In the laboratory, the phenomenon occurs not only among people who are pulling ropes, cycling, shouting, and clapping but also among those who are

free-ride
benefiting from the group, but giving little in return

↓ EVALUATION
 APPREHENSION
DIFFUSION OF
RESPONSIBILITY

FIGURE 7–3

EFFORT DECREASES AS GROUP SIZE INCREASES.

A statistical digest of 49 studies, involving more than 4000 participants, revealed that effort decreases (loafing increases) as the size of the group increases. Each dot represents the aggregate data from one of these studies. (From K. D. Williams, J. M. Jackson, & S. J. Karau, in *Social Dilemmas: Perspectives on Individuals and Groups,* edited by D. A. Schroeder. Copyright © 1992 by Praeger Publishers. Reprinted with permission of Greenwood Publishing Group, Inc., Westport, CT.)

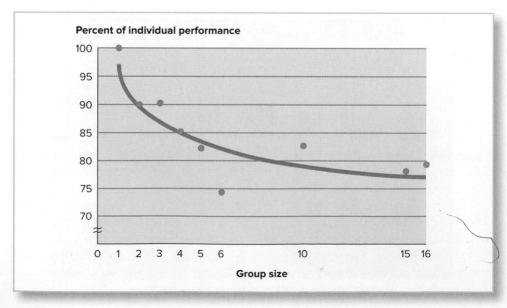

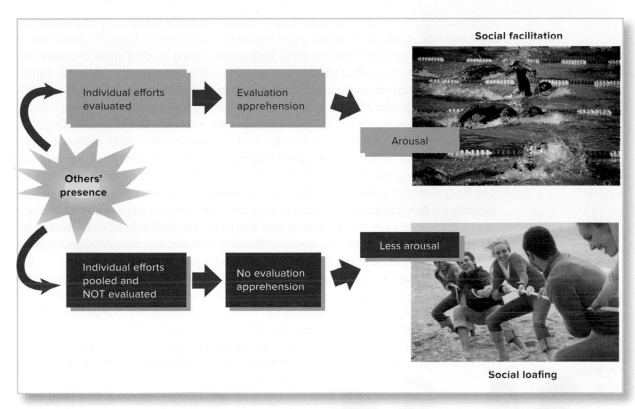

Social facilitation

Others' presence → Individual efforts evaluated → Evaluation apprehension → Arousal

Others' presence → Individual efforts pooled and NOT evaluated → No evaluation apprehension → Less arousal

Social loafing

FIGURE 7–4

SOCIAL FACILITATION OR SOCIAL LOAFING?

When individuals cannot be evaluated or held accountable, loafing becomes more likely. An individual swimmer is evaluated on his or her ability to win the race. In tug of war, no single person on the team is held accountable, so any one member might relax or loaf.

pumping water or air, evaluating poems or editorials, producing ideas, typing, and detecting signals. Do these results generalize to everyday worker productivity?

In one small experiment, assembly-line workers produced 16 percent more product when their individual output was identified, even though they knew their pay would not be affected (Faulkner & Williams, 1996). And consider: A key job in a pickle factory is picking the right-size dill-pickle halves off the conveyor belt and stuffing them in jars. Unfortunately, workers are tempted to stuff any size pickle in, because their output is not identifiable (the jars go into a common hopper before reaching the quality-control section). Williams, Harkins, and Latané (1981) noted that research on social loafing suggests "making individual production identifiable, and raises the question: 'How many pickles could a pickle packer pack if pickle packers were only paid for properly packed pickles?'"

Researchers have also found evidence of social loafing in varied cultures, particularly by assessing agricultural output in formerly communist countries. On their collective farms under communism, Russian peasants worked one field one day, another field the next, with little direct responsibility for any given plot. For their own use, they were given small private plots. One analysis found that the private plots occupied 1 percent of the agricultural land, yet produced 27 percent of the Soviet farm output (H. Smith, 1976). In communist Hungary, private plots accounted for 13 percent of the farmland but produced one-third of the output (Spivak, 1979). When China began allowing farmers to sell food grown in excess of that owed to the state, food production jumped 8 percent per year—2.5 times the annual increase in the preceding 26 years (Church, 1986). In an effort to tie rewards to productive effort, today's Russia is "decollectivizing" many of its farms (Kramer, 2008).

What about collectivist cultures under non-communist regimes? Latané and his co-researchers (Gabrenya et al., 1985) repeated their sound-production experiments in Japan, Thailand, Taiwan, India, and Malaysia. Their findings? Social loafing was evident in all of those countries, too. Seventeen later studies in Asia revealed that people in collectivist cultures do, however, exhibit less social loafing than do people in individualist cultures (Karau & Williams, 1993; Kugihara, 1999). As we noted in Chapter 2, loyalty to family and work groups runs strong in collectivist cultures. Likewise, women tend to be less individualistic than men—and to exhibit less social loafing.

In North America, workers who do not pay dues or volunteer time to their unions or professional associations nevertheless are usually happy to accept the benefits those organizations provide. So, too, are public television viewers who don't respond to their station's fund drives. This hints at another possible explanation of social loafing. When rewards are divided equally, regardless of how much one contributes to the group, any individual gets more reward per unit of effort by free-riding on the group. So people may be motivated to slack off when their efforts are not individually monitored and rewarded. Situations that welcome free riders can, therefore, be, in the words of one commune member, a "paradise for parasites."

But surely collective effort does not always lead to slacking off. Sometimes, the goal is so compelling and maximum output from everyone is so essential that team spirit maintains or intensifies effort. In an Olympic crew race, will the individual rowers in a four-person crew pull their oars with less effort than those in a one- or two-person crew?

People usually give reduced effort when working in a group; but when group members are highly committed to one another and the success of the group—like these rowers for the Canadian national team—such social loafing may not occur.

The evidence assures us they will not. People in groups loaf less when the task is challenging, appealing, or involving (Karau & Williams, 1993). On challenging tasks, people may perceive their efforts as indispensable (Harkins & Petty, 1982; Kerr, 1983; Kerr & Bruun, 1983). When people see others in their group as unreliable or as unable to contribute much, they work harder (Plaks & Higgins, 2000; Williams & Karau, 1991). But in many situations, so do less capable individuals as they strive to keep up with others' greater productivity (Weber & Hertel, 2007). Adding incentives or challenging a group to strive for certain standards also promotes collective effort (Harkins & Szymanski, 1989; Shepperd & Wright, 1989). Group members will work hard when convinced that high effort will bring rewards (Shepperd & Taylor, 1999).

Groups also loaf less when their members are friends or are identified with or indispensable to their group (Davis & Greenlees, 1992; Gockel et al., 2008; Karau & Williams, 1997; Worchel, Jenner, & Hebl, 1998). Even just expecting to interact with someone again serves to increase efforts on team projects (Groenenboom, Wilke, & Wit, 2001). Collaborate on a class project with others whom you will be seeing often, and you will probably feel more motivated than you would if you never expect to see them again. Cohesiveness intensifies effort.

These findings parallel those from studies of everyday work groups. When groups are given challenging objectives, when they are rewarded for group success, and when there is a spirit of commitment to the "team," group members work hard (Hackman, 1986). Keeping work groups small can also help members believe their contributions are indispensable (Comer, 1995). Social loafing is common when group members work without individual accountability; so it would seem that many hands need not always make light work.

DEINDIVIDUATION: WHEN DO PEOPLE LOSE THEIR SENSE OF SELF IN GROUPS?

Group situations may cause people to lose self-awareness, with resulting loss of individuality and self-restraint. What circumstances trigger such "deindividuation"?

In the spring of 1993, soldiers from the Canadian Airborne Regiment were stationed in the remote town of Belet Huen, Somalia. On March 4, a group of soldiers shot two young Somalis for stealing supplies and killed one of the young men with a point-blank shot to the head. A few days later, the group captured, tortured, and killed a 16-year-old Somali named Shidane Arone. Pictures of the torture eventually made their way back to Canada, shocking the nation into a prolonged discussion of the state of the military and group violence. People wondered: Where was the soldiers' humanity? What had happened to standards of military conduct? What could cause such behaviour?

DOING TOGETHER WHAT WE WOULD NOT DO ALONE

Social facilitation experiments show that groups can arouse people, and social loafing experiments show that groups can diffuse responsibility. When arousal and diffused responsibility combine and normal inhibitions diminish, the results may be startling. Acts may range from a mild lessening of restraint (throwing food in the dining hall, snarling at a referee, screaming during a rock concert) to impulsive self-gratification (group vandalism, orgies, thefts) to destructive social explosions (police brutality, riots, mass suicide).

These unrestrained behaviours have something in common: They are somehow provoked by the power of a group. Groups can generate a sense of excitement, of being caught up in something bigger than one's self. It is hard to imagine a single rock fan screaming deliriously at a private rock concert, or a single fan setting multiple cars on fire after a championship win. In certain kinds of group situations, people are more likely to abandon normal restraints, to lose their sense of individual responsibility, a state that Leon Festinger, Albert Pepitone, and Theodore Newcomb (1952) labelled as **deindividuation**. What circumstances elicit this psychological state?

Circumstances for deindividuation.

(1) ## Group size

A group has the power not only to arouse its members but also to render them unidentifiable. The snarling crowd hides the snarling hockey fan. A mob enables its members to believe they will not be prosecuted; they perceive the action as the group's. Rioters, made faceless by the mob, are freed to loot. Interestingly, this seems to occur even when people are identifiable and will be prosecuted. In the riots that ensued after the Vancouver Canucks lost the Stanley Cup in 2011, people acted as if they would not be identified and prosecuted even though several people were. In an analysis of 21 instances in which crowds were present as someone

deindividuation loss of self-awareness and evaluation apprehension; occurs in group situations that foster anonymity and draw attention away from the individual

Prompted by group influence, an anarchist vandalized a police cruiser on Bay Street in Toronto before setting it on fire, Saturday, June 26, 2010.

threatened to jump from a building or bridge, Leon Mann (1981) found that when the crowd was small and exposed by daylight, people usually did not try to bait the person. But when a large crowd or the cover of night gave people anonymity, the crowd usually baited and jeered.

From sports crowds to rioters, evaluation apprehension plummets. And because "everyone is doing it," all can attribute their behaviour to the situation rather than to their own choices.

Physical anonymity

"A mob is a society of bodies voluntarily bereaving themselves of reason."

RALPH WALDO EMERSON, "COMPENSATION," *ESSAYS, FIRST SERIES*, 1841

How can we be sure that the effect of crowds means greater anonymity? We can't. But we can experiment with anonymity to see if it actually lessens inhibitions. Philip Zimbardo (1970, 2002) got the idea for such an experiment from his undergraduate students, who questioned how good boys in William Golding's *Lord of the Flies* could so suddenly become monsters after painting their faces. To experiment with such anonymity, he dressed women in identical white coats and hoods, rather like Ku Klux Klan members (Figure 7–5). Asked to deliver electric shocks to a woman, they pressed the shock button twice as long as did women who were visible and wearing large name tags.

The Internet offers similar anonymity. The anonymity offered by chat rooms, newsgroups, and listservs also has been observed to foster higher levels of hostile, uninhibited "flaming" behaviour than observed in face-to-face conversations (Douglas & McGarty, 2001). Internet bullies who would never to someone's face say, "Get a life, you phony," will hide behind their anonymity. Facebook, to its credit, requires people to use their real names, which constrains the bullying, hate-filled, and inflammatory comments.

On several occasions, anonymous online bystanders have egged on people threatening suicide, sometimes with live video feeding the scene to scores of people. Online communities "are like the crowd outside the building with the guy on the ledge," noted one analyst of technology's social effects (quoted by Stelter, 2008). Sometimes, a caring person tried to talk the person down, while others, in effect, chanted, "Jump, jump." "The anonymous nature of these communities only emboldens the meanness or callousness of the people on these sites."

FIGURE 7–5

EFFECT OF PHYSICAL ANONYMITY.

Anonymous women delivered longer electric shocks to helpless victims than did identifiable women.

Testing deindividuation on the streets, Patricia Ellison, John Govern, and their colleagues (1995) had a confederate driver stop at a red light and wait for 12 seconds whenever she was followed by a convertible or 4x4 vehicle. While enduring the wait, she recorded any horn-honking (a mild aggressive act) by the car behind. Compared to drivers of convertibles and 4x4s with the top down, those with the top up, who were relatively anonymous, honked one-third sooner, twice as often, and for nearly twice as long.

A research team led by Ed Diener (1976) cleverly demonstrated the effect both of being in a group and of being physically anonymous. At Halloween, they observed 1352 children trick-or-treating. As the children, either alone or in groups, approached 1 of 27 homes scattered throughout the city, an experimenter greeted them warmly, invited them to "take *one* of the candies," and then left the room. Hidden observers noted that, compared to solo children, those in groups were more than twice as likely to take extra candy. Also, compared to children who had been asked their names and where they lived, those left anonymous were also more than twice as likely to transgress. As Figure 7–6 shows, the transgression rate thus varied dramatically with the situation. When deindividuated by group immersion combined with anonymity, most children stole extra candy.

These experiments make us wonder about the effect of wearing uniforms. Preparing for battle, warriors in some tribal cultures (like rabid fans of some sports teams) depersonalize themselves with body and face paints or special masks. After the battle, some cultures kill, torture, or mutilate any remaining enemies; other cultures take prisoners alive. Robert Watson (1973) scrutinized anthropological files and discovered that the cultures with depersonalized warriors were also the cultures that brutalized the enemy. The uniformed Canadian soldiers who tortured and killed Shidane Arone were angered and aroused by their frustrating mission and the brutal desert heat; enjoying one another's camaraderie, they were unaware that outsiders would view their actions. Thus, forgetting their normal standards, they were swept away by the situation. During the 2010 G20 summit in Toronto, many of the police officers violated explicit

"The use of self-control is like the use of brakes on a train. It is useful when you find yourself going in the wrong direction, but merely harmful when the direction is right."
BERTRAND RUSSELL, *MARRIAGE AND MORALS*

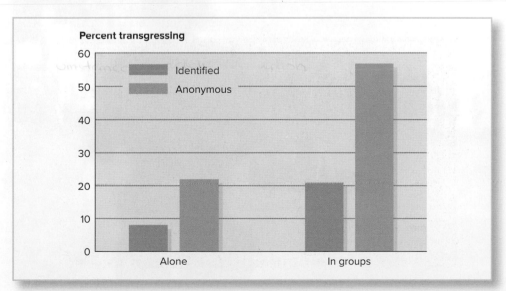

FIGURE 7–6
EFFECT OF GROUP IMMERSION AND ANONYMITY.

Children were more likely to transgress by taking extra Halloween candy when in a group, when anonymous, and, especially, when deindividuated by the combination of group immersion and anonymity. (Data from Diener et al., 1976)

regulations and did not wear their name tags or other identification. Did this anonymity contribute to some instances of violence enacted by the police?

Does becoming physically anonymous always unleash our worst impulses? Fortunately, no. For one thing, the situations in which some of these experiments took place had clear antisocial cues. Robert Johnson and Leslie Downing (1979) pointed out that the Klan-like outfits worn by Zimbardo's subjects may have encouraged hostility. In an experiment, they had women put on nurses' uniforms before deciding how much shock someone should receive. When those wearing the nurses' uniforms were made anonymous, they became *less* aggressive in administering shocks than when their names and personal identities were stressed. From their analysis of 60 deindividuation studies, Tom Postmes and Russell Spears (1998; Reicher, Spears, & Postmes, 1995) concluded that being anonymous makes one less self-conscious, and more responsive to cues present in the situation, whether negative (Klan uniforms) or positive (nurses' uniforms). In the 2011 riots after the Vancouver Stanley Cup defeat, one couple engaged in an extended kiss that was captured by a photographer. It seems that anonymity can lead to affection as well as violence (Gergen, Gergen, & Barton, 1973).

Arousing and distracting activities

Aggressive outbursts by large crowds are often preceded by minor actions that arouse and divert people's attention. Group shouting, chanting, clapping, or dancing serve both to hype people up and to reduce self-consciousness.

Ed Diener's experiments (1976, 1979) showed that such activities as throwing rocks and group singing can set the stage for more uninhibited behaviour. There is a self-reinforcing pleasure in doing an impulsive act while observing others doing it also. When we see others act as we are acting, we think they feel as we do, which reinforces our own feelings (Orive, 1984). Moreover, impulsive group action absorbs our attention. When we yell at the referee, we are not thinking about our values; we are reacting to the immediate situation. Later, when we stop

Deindividuation, such as is seen in a riot, can lead to expressions of affection as well as violence.

to think about what we have done or said, we sometimes feel chagrined. Sometimes. At other times, we seek deindividuating group experiences—dances, worship experiences, group encounters—where we can enjoy intense positive feelings and feel close to others.

DIMINISHED SELF-AWARENESS

Group experiences that diminish self-consciousness tend to disconnect behaviour from attitudes. Experiments by Ed Diener (1980) and Steven Prentice-Dunn and Ronald Rogers (1980, 1989) revealed that un-self-conscious, deindividuated people are less restrained, less self-regulated, more likely to act without thinking about their own values, and more responsive to the situation. These findings complement and reinforce the experiments on self-awareness considered in Chapter 3.

Self-awareness is the opposite of deindividuation. Those made self-aware—say, by acting in front of a mirror or TV camera—exhibit increased self-control; their actions more clearly reflect their attitudes. In front of a mirror, people taste-testing cream cheese varieties eat less of the high-fat alternative (Sentyrz & Bushman, 1997).

People made self-aware are also less likely to cheat (Beaman et al., 1979; Diener & Wallbom, 1976). So are those who generally have a strong sense of themselves as distinct and independent (Nadler, Goldberg, & Jaffe, 1982). In Japan, where (mirror or no mirror) people more often imagine how they might look to others, people are no more likely to cheat when not in front of a mirror (Heine et al., 2008). The principle: People who are self-aware, or who are temporarily made so, exhibit greater consistency between their words outside a situation and their deeds in it.

We can apply those findings to many situations in everyday life. Circumstances that decrease self-awareness, as alcohol consumption does, increase deindividuation (Hull & Young, 1983). And deindividuation decreases in circumstances that increase self-awareness: mirrors and cameras, small towns, bright lights, large name tags, undistracted quiet, individual clothes and houses (Ickes, Layden, & Barnes, 1978). When a teenager leaves for a party, a parent's parting advice should perhaps be this: "Have fun, and remember who you are." In other words, enjoy being with the group, but be self-aware; maintain your personal identity; and be wary of being deindividuated.

> *"Attending a service in the Gothic cathedral, we have the sensation of being enclosed and steeped in an integral universe, and of losing a prickly sense of self in the community of worshippers."*
> YI-FU TUAN, 1982

● GROUP POLARIZATION: DO GROUPS INTENSIFY OUR OPINIONS?

Many conflicts grow as people on both sides talk mostly with like-minded others. Does such interaction amplify pre-existing attitudes? If so, why?

Which effects—good or bad—does group interaction more often have? Police brutality and mob violence demonstrate its destructive potential. Yet support-group leaders, management consultants, and educational theorists proclaim its benefits; and social and religious movements urge their members to strengthen their identities by fellowship with like-minded others.

Studies of people in small groups have produced a principle that helps explain both bad and good outcomes: Group discussion often strengthens members' initial inclinations. The unfolding of this research on group polarization illustrates the process of inquiry—how an interesting discovery often leads researchers to hasty and erroneous conclusions, which ultimately are replaced with more accurate conclusions. This is a scientific mystery we can discuss firsthand, having been one of the detectives.

THE CASE OF THE "RISKY SHIFT"

More than 300 studies of risk-taking behaviour was a study by James Stoner (1961), a study that led to a surprising result. For his master's thesis in industrial management, Stoner compared risk-taking by individuals and groups. To test the commonly held belief that groups are more cautious than individuals, Stoner posed decision dilemmas faced by fictional characters. The participant's task was to advise the imagined character how much risk to take. Put yourself in the participant's shoes: What advice would you give the character in this situation?

> Helen is a writer who is said to have considerable creative talent but who so far has been earning a comfortable living by writing cheap westerns. Recently she has come up with an idea for a potentially significant novel. If it could be written and accepted, it might have considerable literary impact and be a big boost to her career. On the other hand, if she cannot work out her idea or if the novel is a flop, she will have expended considerable time and energy without remuneration.
>
> Imagine that you are advising Helen. Please check the *lowest* probability that you would consider acceptable for Helen to attempt to write the novel.
>
> Helen should attempt to write the novel if the chances that the novel will be a success are at least
>
> _____ 1 in 10
> _____ 2 in 10
> _____ 3 in 10
> _____ 4 in 10
> _____ 5 in 10
> _____ 6 in 10
> _____ 7 in 10
> _____ 8 in 10
> _____ 9 in 10
> _____ 10 in 10 (Place a check here if you think Helen should attempt the novel only if it is certain that the novel will be a success.)

After making your decision, guess what this book's average reader would advise.

Having marked their advice on a dozen such items, five or so individuals would then discuss and reach agreement on each item. How do you think the group decisions compared to the average decision before the discussions? Would the groups be likely to take greater risks? Be more cautious? Stay the same?

To everyone's amazement, the group decisions were usually riskier. Dubbed the "risky shift phenomenon," this finding set off a wave of investigation into group risk-taking. The studies revealed that this effect occurs not only when a group decides by consensus; after a brief discussion, individuals, too, will alter their decisions. What is more, researchers successfully repeated Stoner's finding with people of varying ages and occupations in a dozen different nations.

During discussion, opinions converged. Curiously, however, the point toward which they converged was usually a lower (riskier) number than their initial average. Here was a delightful puzzle. The small risky shift effect was reliable, unexpected, and without any immediately obvious explanation. What group influences produce such an effect? And how widespread is it? Do discussions in juries, business committees, and military organizations also promote risk-taking? Does this explain why teenage reckless driving, as measured by death rates, nearly doubles when a 16- or 17-year-old driver has two teenage passengers rather than none (Chen et al., 2000)? Does it explain stock bubbles, as people discuss why stocks are rising, thus creating an informational cascade that drives stocks even higher (Sunstein, 2009)?

After several years of study and speculation about group risk-taking, we became aware that the risky shift was not universal. We could write decision dilemmas on which people became more cautious after discussion. One of these featured "Roger," a young married man with two school-age children and a secure but low-paying job. Roger can afford life's necessities but few of its luxuries. He hears that the stock of a relatively unknown company may soon triple in value if its new product is favourably received or the stock may decline considerably if the product does not sell. Roger has no savings. To invest in the company, he is considering selling his life insurance policy.

Can you see a general principle that predicts both the tendency to give riskier advice after discussing Helen's situation and more cautious advice after discussing Roger's? If you are like most people, you would advise Helen to take greater risk than Roger, even before talking with others. It turns out that there is a strong tendency for discussion to accentuate these initial leanings; groups discussing the "Roger" dilemma became more risk-averse than they were before discussion.

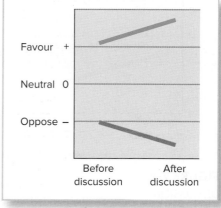

FIGURE 7-7
GROUP POLARIZATION.

The group-polarization hypothesis predicts that discussion will strengthen an attitude shared by group members. If people initially tend to favour something (say, risk on a life dilemma question), they tend to favour it even more after discussion, and vice versa.

IMPACT OF GROUP DISCUSSION ON INDIVIDUALS' OPINIONS

This group phenomenon was not a consistent shift to risk, but rather a tendency for group discussion to enhance the individuals' initial leanings. This idea led investigators to propose what Serge Moscovici and Marisa Zavalloni (1969) called a **group polarization** phenomenon: Discussion typically strengthens the average inclination of group members.

Group polarization experiments

This new view of the changes induced by group discussion prompted experimenters to have people discuss statements that most of them favoured or most of them opposed. Would talking in groups enhance their initial inclinations as it did with the decision dilemmas? That's what the group polarization hypothesis predicts (Figure 7–7).

Dozens of studies confirm group polarization. Moscovici and Zavalloni (1969) observed that discussion enhanced French students' initially positive attitude toward their premier and negative attitude toward Americans. Mititoshi Isozaki (1984) found that Japanese university students gave more pronounced "guilty" judgments after discussing a traffic case. Markus Brauer and

group polarization group-produced enhancement of members' pre-existing tendencies; a strengthening of the members' *average* tendency, not a split within the group

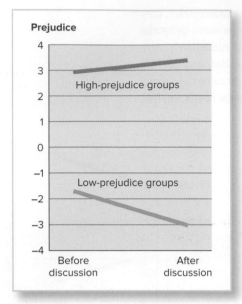

FIGURE 7–8

DISCUSSION
AND GROUP
POLARIZATION.

Discussion increased
polarization between
homogeneous groups
of high- and low-
prejudice high-school
students. Talking
over racial issues
increased prejudice in
a high-prejudice group
and decreased it in a
low-prejudice group.
(Data from Myers &
Bishop, 1970)

his co-workers (2001) found that French students' dislike for certain other people was exacerbated after discussing their shared negative impressions. And Glen Whyte (1993) reported that groups exacerbate the "too much invested to quit" phenomenon that has cost many businesses huge sums of money. Canadian business students imagined themselves having to decide whether to invest more money in the hope of preventing losses in various failing projects (for example, whether to make a high-risk loan to protect an earlier investment). They exhibited the typical effect: 72 percent reinvested money they would seldom have invested if they were considering it as a new investment on its own merits. When making the same decision in groups, 94 percent opted for reinvestment.

Another research strategy has been to pick issues on which opinions are divided and then isolate people who hold the same view. Does discussion with like-minded people strengthen shared views? Does it magnify the attitude gap that separates the two sides? George Bishop and David Myers wondered. So they set up groups of relatively prejudiced and unprejudiced high-school students and asked them to respond—before and after discussion—to issues involving racial attitudes, such as property rights versus open housing (Myers & Bishop, 1970). They found that the discussions among like-minded students did, indeed, increase the initial gap between the two groups (Figure 7–8).

Group polarization in everyday life

In everyday life, people associate mostly with others whose attitudes are similar to their own (Chapter 10—or just look at your own circle of friends). Does everyday group interaction with like-minded friends intensify shared attitudes?

Group polarization in schools

One real-life parallel to the laboratory phenomenon is what education researchers have called the "accentuation phenomenon": Over time, initial differences among groups of university students become accentuated. If the students at university X are initially more intellectual than the students at university Y, that gap is likely to grow during university. Likewise, compared to fraternity and sorority members, independents tend to have more liberal political attitudes, a difference that grows with time in university (Pascarella & Terenzini, 1991). Researchers believe this results partly from group members reinforcing shared inclinations.

Group polarization in communities

Polarization also occurs in communities. During community conflicts, like-minded people associate increasingly with one another, amplifying their shared tendencies. Gang hostility emerges from a process of mutual reinforcement within neighbourhood gangs, whose members share attributes and hostilities (Cartwright, 1975). If, on your block, "a second out-of-control 15-year-old moves in," surmised David Lykken (1997), "the mischief they get into as a team is likely to be more than merely double what the first would do on his own. . . . A gang is more dangerous than the sum of its individual parts." Indeed, "unsupervised peer groups" are "the strongest predictor" of a neighbourhood's crime victimization rate, reported Bonita Veysey and Steven

Messner (1999). Moreover, experimental interventions that group young offenders with other young offenders actually—no surprise to any group polarization researcher—increase the rate of problem behaviour (Dishion, McCord, & Poulin, 1999).

Group polarization on the Internet

E-mail, blogs, and electronic chat rooms offer a potential new medium for group interaction. At websites like myspace.com, for example, there are hundreds of thousands of groups of kindred spirits discussing music, cars, politics, religion, hobbies—you name it. The Internet's countless virtual groups enable peacemakers and neo-Nazis, geeks and goths, conspiracy theorists and cancer survivors to isolate themselves with one another and find support for their shared concerns, interests, and suspicions (Gerstenfeld, Grant, & Chiang, 2003; McKenna & Bargh, 1998, 2000; Sunstein, 2001, 2009). Indeed, most of us read blogs that reinforce rather than challenge our views, and those blogs link mostly to like-minded blogs—connecting liberals with liberals, conservatives with conservatives—like having conversations with the bathroom mirror (Lazer et al., 2009). Will such discussions produce group polarization? Will socially networked birds of a feather find support for their shared beliefs, values, and suspicions? Will peacemakers become more pacifistic and militia members more terror prone? E-mail, Google, and chat rooms "make it much easier for small groups to rally like-minded people, crystallize diffuse hatreds, and mobilize lethal force," observes Robert Wright (2003). As broadband spreads, Internet-spawned polarization will increase, he speculates. According to one University of Haifa analysis, terrorist websites—which grew from a dozen in 1997 to some 4700 at the end of 2005—increased more than four times faster than the total number of websites (Ariza, 2006).

Group polarization in terrorist organizations

From their analysis of terrorist organizations throughout the world, Clark McCauley and Mary Segal (1987; McCauley, 2002) note that terrorism does not erupt suddenly. Rather, it arises among people whose shared grievances bring them together and fan their fire. As they interact in isolation from moderating influences, they become progressively more extreme. The social amplifier brings the signal in more strongly. The result is violent acts that the individuals, apart from the group, would never have committed.

According to one analysis of terrorists who were members of the Salafi Jihad, 70 percent joined while living as expatriates. After moving to foreign places in search of jobs or education, they became keenly mindful of their Muslim identity and often gravitated to mosques and moved in with other expatriate Muslims, who sometimes recruited them into cell groups that provided "mutual emotional and social support" and "development of a common identity" (Sageman, 2004).

Massacres, similarly, have been found to be group phenomena. The violence is enabled and escalated by the killers egging one another on, noted Robert Zajonc (2000), who knew violence as a survivor of a World War II Warsaw air raid that killed both his parents (Burnstein, 2009). It is difficult to influence someone once "in the pressure cooker of the terrorist group," notes Jerrold Post (2005) after interviewing many accused terrorists. "In the long run, the most effective antiterrorist policy is one that inhibits potential recruits from joining in the first place."

EXPLAINING POLARIZATION

In two trials, South African courts reduced sentences after learning how social-psychological phenomena, including deindividuation and group polarization, led crowd members to commit murderous acts (Colman, 1991). Would you agree that courts should consider social-psychological phenomena as possible extenuating circumstances?

Why do groups adopt stances that are more exaggerated than the average opinions of their individual members? Researchers hoped that solving the mystery of group polarization might provide some insights. Solving small puzzles sometimes provides clues for solving larger ones.

Among several proposed theories of group polarization, two have survived scientific scrutiny. One deals with the arguments presented during a discussion, the other with how members of a group view themselves vis-à-vis the other members. The first idea is an example of what Chapter 6 called informational influence (influence that results from accepting evidence about reality). The second is an example of normative influence (influence based on a person's desire to be accepted or admired by others).

Polarization is caused by:

① Informational influence and group polarization

According to the best-supported explanation, group discussion elicits a pooling of ideas, most of which favour the dominant viewpoint. Ideas that were common knowledge to group members will often be brought up in discussion or, even if unmentioned, will jointly influence their discussion (Gigone & Hastie, 1993; Larson, Foster-Fishman, & Keys, 1994; Stasser, 1991). Other ideas mentioned in discussion may include persuasive arguments that some group members had not previously considered. When discussing Helen the writer, someone may say, "Helen should go for it, because she has little to lose. If her novel flops, she can always go back to writing cheap westerns." Such statements often entangle information about the person's arguments with cues concerning the person's position on the issue. But when people hear relevant arguments without learning the specific stands other people assume, they still shift their positions (Burnstein & Vinokur, 1977; Hinsz, Tindale, & Vollrath, 1997). Arguments, in and of themselves, matter.

But there's more to attitude change than merely hearing someone else's arguments. Active participation in discussion produces more attitude change than does passive listening. Participants and observers hear the same ideas; but when participants put them into their own words, the verbal commitment magnifies the impact. The more group members repeat one another's ideas, the more they rehearse and validate them (Brauer, Judd, & Gliner, 1995).

This illustrates a point made in Chapter 5: People's minds are not just blank tablets for persuaders to write on. In central route persuasion, what people think in response to a message is crucial; in fact, just thinking about an issue for a couple of minutes can strengthen opinions (Tesser, Martin, & Mendolia, 1995). (Perhaps you can recall your feelings becoming polarized as you merely ruminated about someone you disliked, or liked.) Even expecting to discuss an issue with an equally expert person holding an opposing view can motivate people to marshal their arguments and thus to adopt a more extreme position (Fitzpatrick & Eagly, 1981).

② Normative influence and group polarization

A second explanation of polarization involves comparison with others. As Leon Festinger (1954) argued in his influential theory of social comparison, and as already discussed in Chapter 2, it is human nature to want to evaluate our abilities and opinions, something we can do by comparing our views with those of others. We are most persuaded by people in our "reference groups"—groups

Animal gangs: The pack is more than the sum of the wolves in it.

we identify with (Abrams et al., 1990; Hogg, Turner, & Davidson, 1990). Moreover, wanting people to like us, we may express stronger opinions after discovering that others share our views.

When we ask people (as we asked you earlier) to predict how others would respond to items such as the "Helen" dilemma, they typically exhibit **pluralistic ignorance**: They don't realize how strongly others support the socially preferred tendency (in this case, writing the novel). A typical person will advise writing the novel even if its chance of success is only 4 in 10 but will estimate that most other people would require 5 or 6 in 10. (This finding is reminiscent of the self-serving bias: People tend to view themselves as better-than-average embodiments of socially desirable traits and attitudes.) When the discussion begins, most people discover they are not outshining the others as they had supposed. In fact, some others are ahead of them, having taken an even stronger position in favour of writing the novel. No longer restrained by a misperceived group norm, they are liberated to voice their preferences more strongly.

Perhaps you have been in the situation where you have wanted to go out with someone, but you were afraid to make the first move. You wait and watch, but the other person doesn't seem to be expressing any interest in you, so you think that he or she would probably reject you. Have you ever stopped to think that the other person might be doing the same thing you are? University of Manitoba researchers Jacquie Vorauer and Rebecca Ratner (1996) have shown that such reactions make it difficult for people to start up relationships.

Dale Miller and Cathy McFarland (1987) created a similar phenomenon in a laboratory experiment. They asked people to read an article and to seek help if they ran into "any really serious problems in understanding the paper." Although the article was incomprehensible, none of the subjects sought help; but they presumed other subjects would not be similarly restrained by fear of embarrassment. They wrongly inferred that people who didn't seek help didn't need any. To overcome such pluralistic ignorance, someone must break the ice and enable others to reveal and reinforce their shared reactions.

Social comparison theory prompted experiments that exposed people to others' positions but not to their arguments. This is roughly the experience we have when reading the results of an opinion poll. When people learn others' positions—without discussion—will they adjust

pluralistic ignorance
a false impression of how other people are thinking, feeling, or responding

FIGURE 7–9

RISK OR CAUTION?

On "risky" dilemma items (such as the case of "Helen"), mere exposure to others' judgments enhanced individuals' risk-prone tendencies. On "cautious" dilemma items (such as the case of "Roger"), exposure to others' judgments enhanced their cautiousness. (Data from Myers, 1978)

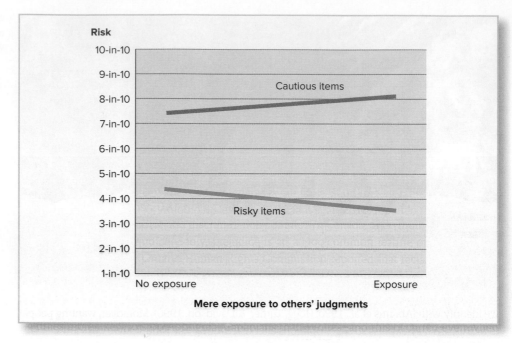

their responses to maintain a socially favourable position? When people have made no prior commitment to a particular response, seeing others' responses does stimulate a small polarization (Goethals & Zanna, 1979; Sanders & Baron, 1977). (See Figure 7–9 for an example.) This polarization from mere social comparison is usually less than that produced by a lively discussion. Still, it's surprising that, instead of simply conforming to the group average, people often go it one better.

Merely learning others' choices also contributes to the bandwagon effect that creates blockbuster songs, books, and movies. Sociologist Matthew Salganik and colleagues (2006) experimented with the phenomenon by engaging 14 341 Internet participants in listening to and, if they wished, downloading previously unknown songs. The researchers randomly assigned some participants to a condition that disclosed previous participants' download choices. Among those given that information, popular songs became more popular and unpopular songs became less popular. This finding is reminiscent of the self-serving bias (Chapter 2): People tend to view themselves as better-than-average embodiments of socially desirable traits and attitudes.

Group polarization research illustrates the complexity of social-psychological inquiry. As much as we like our explanations of a phenomenon to be simple, one explanation seldom accounts for all the data. Because people are complex, more than one factor frequently influences an outcome. In group discussions, persuasive arguments predominate on issues that have a factual element ("Is she guilty of the crime?"). Social comparison sways responses on value-laden judgments ("How long a sentence should she serve?") (Kaplan, 1989). On the many issues that have both factual and value-laden aspects, the two factors work together. Discovering that others share one's feelings (social comparison) unleashes arguments (informational influence) supporting what everyone secretly favours.

FACTS =
Persuasive
Arguments
Judgements =
Social
Comparison

● GROUPTHINK: DO GROUPS HINDER OR ASSIST GOOD DECISIONS?

When do group influences hinder smart decisions? When do groups promote good decisions, and how can we lead groups to make optimal decisions?

Do the social-psychological phenomena we have been considering in these first seven chapters occur in sophisticated groups like corporate boards where people are professionals and know each other well? Is there likely to be self-justification? Self-serving bias? A cohesive "we feeling" provoking conformity and rejection of dissent? Public commitment producing resistance to change? Group polarization? Social psychologist Irving Janis (1971, 1982) wondered whether such phenomena might help explain good and bad decisions made by a number of leaders and their advisers. In particular, he analyzed the decision-making procedures that led to several major fiascos. Although Janis did not analyze it, the sinking of the *Titanic*—the worst seafaring accident in history—provides a compelling example of the type of disasters Janis analyzed.

We will try to give an accurate account of this tragedy, but the particulars of the disaster will probably always be a bit of a mystery. Most of you have probably seen the movie *Titanic* written and directed by Canadian James Cameron, as it was the most widely seen movie of all time; but there are many accounts, and it is often hard to sort out the truth. Playwright George Bernard Shaw and mystery writer Sir Arthur Conan Doyle, creator of the Sherlock Holmes character, fought bitterly back and forth about many of the details in the years after the shipwreck. Sherlock himself might not have been able to solve all the mysteries of this disaster. Nevertheless, here are some of the basic facts that are not in dispute.

On April 10, 1912, the *Titanic* left Southampton, England, on her maiden voyage across the Atlantic Ocean. At the time, the *Titanic* was the largest and most fabulous ship in the world.

Groupthink on a titanic scale. Despite four messages of possible icebergs ahead and the lookout person's unheeded plea for binoculars, Captain Edward Smith—a directive and respected leader—kept his ship sailing at full speed into the night. There was an illusion of invulnerability ("God Himself could not sink this ship," a crew member had said). There was conformity pressure (crew mates chided the lookout for not being able to use his naked eye, and they dismissed his misgivings). And there was mindguarding (a *Titanic* telegraph operator failed to pass the last and most complete iceberg warning to Captain Smith).

It was as tall as an 11-storey building, as long as eight football fields, and it weighed 1000 tonnes more than any other ship. It had a double hull system that made many believe the ship was unsinkable. It was the pride of the White Star line of ships. The ship was cruising briskly across the Atlantic when on Sunday, April 12, the ship received several messages that a group of icebergs was ahead. At least four of these messages reached the captain; at least one of them reached the president of the cruise line, who was aboard the ship. Despite these warnings, the ship did not slow down. At about 11:40 p.m., one of the lookouts saw an iceberg straight ahead and sounded the warning. The first officer, who was at the helm, swung the ship to the port but only fast enough to avoid hitting the iceberg head-on. The ice tore a huge gash in the side of the ship. It didn't take the crew a great deal of time to know the extent of the damage—by 12:15 A.M., they knew the ship was going to sink. The *Titanic* had only 20 lifeboats, which was not even enough for half of the passengers. These lifeboats were lowered and filled—or only partially filled—with passengers, and distress calls were sent out to other ships. The ship finally went under at 2:20 A.M. Only 705 people survived the shipwreck; at least twice that many died. The exact number is one of the facts that is in dispute. The estimates range from 1490 to 1635.

Janis believed that such tragedies could be traced to the tendency of decision-making groups to suppress dissent in the interests of group harmony, a phenomenon he called **groupthink**. In work groups, camaraderie boosts productivity (Mullen & Copper, 1994). Moreover, team spirit is good for morale. But when making decisions, close-knit groups may pay a price. Janis believed that the soil from which groupthink sprouts includes an amiable, cohesive group, relative isolation of the group from dissenting viewpoints, and a directive leader who signals what decision he or she favours. When deciding what to do with the threat of the icebergs ahead, there is little doubt that Captain Edward J. Smith, the senior captain of the cruise line, who had served for 38 years, was a strong and directive leader. He and his crew enjoyed a strong *esprit de corps*. As one source (Lord, 1955) put it, Smith was "worshipped by crew and passenger alike. . . . They loved everything about him." It is also clear that in the middle of the Atlantic they were isolated from other points of view. It is quite possible that groupthink may have influenced their decision-making. Let's see if they displayed the symptoms of groupthink.

groupthink
"The mode of thinking that persons engage in when concurrence-seeking becomes so dominant in a cohesive in-group that it tends to override realistic appraisal of alternative courses of action."— Irving Janis (1971)

SYMPTOMS OF GROUPTHINK

From historical records and the memoirs of participants and observers, Janis identified eight groupthink symptoms. These symptoms are a collective form of dissonance reduction that surfaces as group members try to maintain the positive group feeling when facing a threat (Turner et al., 1992, 1994).

The first two groupthink symptoms lead group members to <u>overestimate their group's might and right</u>:

- **An illusion of invulnerability:** There is little question that Captain Smith and his crew had developed an illusion that nothing bad could happen to them or their ship. Five years before the crash, it was clear that Smith believed a disaster with loss of life could not happen to one of his ships. He was quoted saying, "I cannot conceive of any vital disaster happening . . . Modern shipbuilding has gone beyond that" (Marshall, 1912). As the ship departed from Southampton, one of the crew members expressed a view that seemed to be widespread. When asked if the *Titanic* was really unsinkable, he replied, "God Himself could not sink this ship" (Lord, 1955).

- **Unquestioned belief in the group's morality:** Group members assume the inherent morality of their group and ignore ethical and moral issues. Looking back on the tragedy of the *Titanic*, it is clear that there should have been more lifeboats aboard the vessel, and sadly, this would not have been difficult. But the builders of the ship and especially the president of the cruise line decided they were not needed.

Group members also become closed-minded:

- **Rationalization:** The group discounts challenges by collectively justifying their decisions. The officers on the *Titanic* knew they were in the vicinity of icebergs, but went on at full speed. In one critical conversation at 9:00 P.M., the second officer and Captain Smith discussed how they should handle the ship. Both knew that they were in the vicinity of icebergs, but Smith remarked that it was an exceptionally clear night and, therefore, they did not need to slow down (Davie, 1986).

- **Stereotyped view of opponent:** One of the most controversial stories surrounding the *Titanic* is whether the ship was trying to break a speed record in crossing the Atlantic. You may recall that the movie *Titanic* portrayed the president of the cruise line as pressuring the captain to do so. This story has been suggested several times and many believe it—even though the president of the cruise line, who survived, vehemently denied it. One reason the story is believable to some is that the shipping business was intensely competitive in the early 1900s; cruise lines had very derogatory views of other cruise lines. These stereotyped views of their opponents might well have led Smith and his crew to ignore the warnings from other ships.

Finally, the group suffers from pressures toward uniformity:

- **Conformity pressure:** Group members rebuff those who raise doubts about the group's assumptions and plans, at times not by argument but by ridicule. When Fredrick Fleet—the lookout who eventually saw the iceberg—complained that the crew did not have binoculars, he was chided by his colleagues for not being able to use his naked eye.

- **Self-censorship:** Since disagreements are often uncomfortable and the groups seem in consensus, members often withhold or discount their misgivings. Despite Fleet's belief that he needed a pair of binoculars for his task as a lookout, he did not suggest that they pick up a new pair at the next port. He was at a loss to describe his failure to do so. He maintained until his dying day that if he had had a pair of binoculars, he would have seen the iceberg soon enough to avoid hitting it.

Self-censorship contributes to an illusion of unanimity.

© Henry Martin/The New Yorker Collection/www.cartoonbank.com

- **Illusion of unanimity:** Self-censorship and pressure not to puncture the consensus create an illusion of unanimity. What is more, the apparent consensus confirms the group's decision. Did none of the experienced crew on the *Titanic* think they should slow down? It seems likely that the apparent unanimity about the decision to go full speed ahead was merely an illusion. This sort of illusion has been

> People "are never so likely to settle a question rightly as when they discuss it freely."
>
> JOHN STUART MILL, *ON LIBERTY*, 1859

seen in other groups as well. Albert Speer (1971), an adviser to Hitler, described the atmosphere around Hitler as one where pressure to conform suppressed all deviance. The absence of dissent created the illusion of unanimity:

In normal circumstances people who turn their backs on reality are soon set straight by the mockery and criticism of those around them, which makes them aware that they have lost credibility. In the Third Reich there were no such correctives, especially for those who belonged to the upper stratum. On the contrary, every self-deception was multiplied as in a hall of distorting mirrors, becoming a repeatedly confirmed picture of a fantastical dream world which no longer bore any relationship to the grim outside world. In those mirrors I could see nothing but my own face reproduced many times over. No external factors disturbed the uniformity of hundreds of unchanging faces, all mine. (p. 379)

Protect group from info that indicates they were wrong

• **Mindguards:** Some members protect the group from information that would call into question the effectiveness or the morality of its decisions. The telegraph operator on the *Titanic* provided a compelling example of this symptom. After receiving several warning messages about icebergs, he failed to take down the final and most complete message about the iceberg that was struck and he failed to pass this message to the captain. Thus the operator deprived Captain Smith of the latest information that would challenge Smith's decision to go full steam ahead.

The contaminated water tragedy in Walkerton, Ontario, demonstrated the negative aspects of groupthink in action.

Groupthink symptoms can produce a failure to seek and discuss contrary information and alternative possibilities. When a leader promotes an idea and when a group insulates itself from dissenting views, groupthink may produce defective decisions (McCauley, 1989).

The management of the Walkerton, Ontario, water crisis in May 2000 by Stan Koebel, who ran the water treatment plant, shows many of the symptoms of groupthink. Koebel and his employees certainly showed an illusion of invulnerability. They believed that the water in Walkerton had always been safe and that little needed to be done to ensure its safety. They viewed the new chlorinator that they never installed as unnecessary. Koebel even continued to drink tap water long after people began getting sick and he knew the water tested positive for E. coli. The men at the water plant also engaged in massive rationalization. Even though they knew the water tested positive for contaminants, they continued to believe for days that the water was not what was making people sick. Self-censorship was also an important part of the group's response. Frank Koebel (Stan's brother) testified in the inquiry into the crisis that he knew the failure to chlorinate the water and to take proper samples could lead to problems, but he never raised his objections to his brother. Finally, the group clearly employed mindguards by failing to report the results of the tainted water to the Ministry of Environment and the Officer of Health.

CRITIQUING GROUPTHINK

Although Janis's ideas and observations have received enormous attention, some researchers are skeptical (Fuller & Aldag, 1998; t'Hart, 1998). The evidence being retrospective, Janis could pick supporting cases.

Some follow-up experiments have supported aspects of Janis's theory:

- Directive leadership is indeed associated with poorer decisions, because subordinates sometimes feel too weak or insecure to speak up (Granstrom & Stiwne, 1998; McCauley, 1998).

- Groups that make smart decisions have widely distributed conversation, with socially attuned members who take turns speaking (Woolley et al., 2010).

- Groups do prefer supporting over challenging information (Schulz-Hardt et al., 2000).

- When members look to a group for acceptance, approval, and social identity, they may suppress disagreeable thoughts (Hogg & Hains, 1998; Turner & Pratkanis, 1997).

- Groups with diverse perspectives outperform groups of like-minded experts (Nemeth & Ormiston, 2007; Page, 2007). Engaging people who think differently from you can make you feel uncomfortable; but compared with comfortably homogeneous groups, diverse groups tend to produce more ideas and greater creativity.

- In discussion, information that is shared by group members does tend to dominate and crowd out unshared information, meaning that groups often do not benefit from all that their members know (Sunstein & Hastie, 2008).

Yet, friendships need not breed groupthink (Esser, 1998; Mullen et al., 1994). In a secure, highly cohesive group (say, a family), committed members will often care enough to voice disagreement (Packer, 2009). The norms of a cohesive group can favour either consensus, which can lead to groupthink, or critical analysis, which prevents it (Postmes, Spears, & Cihangir, 2001). When academic colleagues in a close-knit department share their draft manuscripts with one another, they want critique: "Do what you can to save me from my own mistakes." In a free-spirited atmosphere, cohesion can enhance effective teamwork.

When Philip Tetlock and his colleagues (1992) looked at a broader sample of historical episodes, it became clear that even good group procedures sometimes yield ill-fated decisions. As Jimmy Carter and his advisers plotted their humiliating attempt to rescue hostages in Iran in 1980, they welcomed different views and realistically considered the perils. Except for a helicopter problem, the rescue might have succeeded. (Carter later reflected that had he sent in one more helicopter he believed they would have succeeded.) To reword Mister Rogers, sometimes good groups do bad things.

Reflecting on the critiques of groupthink, Paul Paulus (1998) reminds us of Leon Festinger's (1987) observation that only an untestable theory is unchanging. "If a theory is at all testable, it will not remain unchanged. It has to change. All theories are wrong." Thus, said Festinger, we shouldn't ask whether a theory is right or wrong, but rather "how much of the empirical realm can it handle and how must it be modified." Irving Janis, having tested and modified his own theory before his death in 1990, would surely have welcomed others continuing to reshape it; in science, that is how we grope our way toward truth, by testing our ideas against reality, revising them, and then testing them some more.

PREVENTING GROUPTHINK

Flawed group dynamics help explain many failed decisions; sometimes too many cooks spoil the broth. But given open leadership, a cohesive team spirit can improve decisions. Sometimes two (or more) heads are better than one.

In search of conditions that breed good decisions, Janis also analyzed two seemingly successful ventures: the formulation of the Marshall Plan for getting Europe back on its feet after the Second World War and the handling of the former U.S.S.R.'s attempts to install missile bases in Cuba in 1962. Janis's (1982) recommendations for preventing groupthink incorporate many of the effective group procedures used in both cases:

STRATEGIES FOR PREVENTING GROUPTHINK

- Be impartial—do not endorse any position. Don't start group discussions by having people state their positions; doing so suppresses information sharing and degrades the quality of decisions (Mojzisch & Schulz-Hardt, 2010).

- Encourage critical evaluation; assign a "devil's advocate." Better yet, welcome the input of a genuine critic, which does even more to stimulate original thinking and to open a group to opposing views, report Charlan Nemeth and her colleagues (2001a, 2001b).

- Occasionally subdivide the group, and then reunite to air differences.

- Welcome critiques from outside experts and associates.

- Before implementing, call a "second-chance" meeting to air any lingering doubts.

Some of these practical principles for improved group dynamics are now being taught to airline flight crews. Training programs called crew resource management developed from the realization that flight crew mistakes contribute to more than two-thirds of plane accidents. Having two or three people in the cockpit should increase the odds that someone will notice a problem or see its solution—if the information is shared. Sometimes, however, groupthink pressures lead to conformity or self-censorship.

On the night of September 2, 1998, Swiss Air flight 111 crashed just off of Peggy's Cove, Nova Scotia, killing all 229 people on board. The crash appears to have occurred because faulty wiring led to a fire in the cockpit. Several stories in the media reported that the two pilots were at odds in how to respond to the fire. These reports suggested that the co-pilot wanted to forget about procedure and land the plane immediately. The pilot, on the other hand, was allegedly firm in his insistence that they follow the standard procedure, and was so busy with a checklist that he was not able to discuss a plan of action with the co-pilot. Could these faulty group dynamics have played a role in the crash? We do not even know if the media reports are accurate, but faulty group dynamics have been linked to other crashes (Helmrich, 1997).

But not always. In 1989, a three-person crew facing a similar problem responded as a model team to imminent disaster. The crew, which had been trained in crew resource management, faced the disintegration of the centre engine, severing lines to the rudder and ailerons needed to manoeuvre the plane. In the 34 minutes before crash-landing just short of the airport runway, the crew had to devise a strategy for bringing the plane under control, assessing damage, choosing a landing site, and preparing the crew and passengers for the crash. Minute-by-minute analysis of the cockpit conversation revealed intense interaction—31 communications per minute (one per second at its peak). In these minutes, the crew members recruited a fourth pilot who was flying as a passenger, prioritized their work, and kept one another aware of unfolding events and decisions. Junior crew members freely suggested alternatives, and the captain responded with

Effective group dynamics enabled the crew of a disabled Denver-to-Chicago United flight to devise a technique for steering by adjusting relative power from its two remaining engines, enabling the survival of most passengers. Recognizing the importance of cockpit group dynamics, airlines now provide crew management training and seek pilots who are capable of functioning as team members.

appropriate commands. Bursts of social conversation provided emotional support, enabling the crew to cope with the extreme stress and to save the lives of 185 of the 296 people on board.

GROUP PROBLEM-SOLVING

Not every group decision is flawed by groupthink. Under some conditions, two or more heads *are* better than one. Patrick Laughlin and his colleagues (Laughlin & Adamopoulos, 1980; Laughlin, 1996; Laughlin et al., 2003) have shown this with various intellectual tasks. Consider one of their analogy problems:

Assertion is to *disproved* as *action* is to

a. *hindered*

b. *opposed*

c. *illegal*

d. *precipitate*

e. *thwarted*

Most university students miss this question when answering alone, but choose the correct answer (*thwarted*) after discussion. Moreover, Laughlin finds that if two members of a six-person group are initially correct, two-thirds of the time they convince all the others. (If only one person is correct, on the other hand, this "minority of one" almost three-fourths of the time fails to convince the group.) And when given tricky logic problems, three, four, or five heads are better than two (Laughlin et al., 2006).

Dell Warnick and Glenn Sanders (1980) and Verlin Hinsz (1990) confirmed that several heads can be better than one when they studied the accuracy of eyewitness reports of a videotaped crime or job interview. Groups of eyewitnesses gave accounts that were much more accurate than those provided by the average isolated individual. Several heads critiquing each other can also allow the group to avoid some forms of cognitive bias and produce some higher-quality ideas (McGlynn, Tubbs, & Holzhausen, 1995; Wright, Lüüs, & Christie, 1990). In science, the benefits of diverse

THE >>>
INSIDE
STORY

In the spring of 1969, Amos Tversky, my younger colleague at the Hebrew University of Jerusalem, and I met over lunch and shared our own recurrent errors of judgment. From there were born our studies of human intuition.

I had enjoyed collaboration before, but this was magical. Amos was very smart, and also very funny. We could spend hours of solid work in continuous mirth. His work was always characterized by confidence and by a crisp elegance, and it was a joy to find those characteristics now attached to my ideas as well. As we were writing our first paper, I was conscious of how much better it was than the more hesitant piece I would have written by myself.

All our ideas were jointly owned. We did almost all the work on our joint projects while physically together, including the drafting of questionnaires and papers. Our principle was to discuss every disagreement until it had been resolved to our mutual satisfaction.

Some of the greatest joys of our collaboration—and probably much of its success—came from our ability to elaborate on each other's nascent thoughts: If I expressed a half-formed idea, I knew that Amos would be there to understand it, probably more clearly than I did, and that if it had merit, he would see it.

Amos and I shared the wonder of together owning a goose that could lay golden eggs—a joint mind that was better than our separate minds. We were a team, and we remained in that mode for well over a decade. The Nobel Prize was awarded for work that we produced during that period of intense collaboration.

Daniel Kahneman *Princeton University*
Nobel Laureate, 2002

minds collaborating has led to more and more "team science"—to an increasing proportion of scientific publication, especially highly cited publication, by multi-author teams (Cacioppo, 2007).

But contrary to the popular idea that face-to-face brainstorming generates more creative ideas than do the same people working alone, researchers agree it isn't so (Paulus, Dzindolet, & Kohn, 2011; Paulus, Larey, & Ortega, 1995; Paulus, & Yang, 2000; Stroebe & Diehl, 1994). And contrary to the popular idea that brainstorming is most productive when the brainstormers are admonished "not to criticize," encouraging people to debate ideas appears to stimulate ideas and to extend creative thinking beyond the brainstorming session (Nemeth et al., 2004).

People feel more productive when generating ideas in groups (partly because people disproportionately credit themselves for the ideas that come out). But time and again, researchers have found that people working alone usually will generate more good ideas than will the same people in a group (Nijstad, Stroebe, & Lodewijkx, 2006; Rietzschel, Nijstad, & Stroebe, 2006). Large brainstorming groups are especially inefficient. In accord with social loafing theory, large groups cause some individuals to free-ride on others' efforts. In accord with normative influence theory, they cause others to feel apprehensive about voicing oddball ideas. And they cause "production blocking"—losing one's ideas while awaiting a turn to speak (Nijstad & Stroebe, 2006). As James Watson and Francis Crick demonstrated in discovering DNA, challenging two-person conversations can more effectively engage creative thinking. Watson later recalled that he and Crick benefited from *not* being the most brilliant people seeking to crack the genetic code. The most brilliant researcher "was so intelligent that she rarely sought advice" (quoted by Cialdini,

2005). If you are (and regard yourself as) the most gifted person, why seek others' input? Like Watson and Crick, psychologists Daniel Kahneman and the late Amos Tversky similarly collaborated in their exploration of intuition and its influence on economic decision making. (See "The Inside Story" shown above.)

However, Vincent Brown and Paul Paulus (2002) have identified three ways to enhance group brainstorming:

- **Combine group and solitary brainstorming.** Their data suggest using group brainstorming followed by solo brainstorming rather than the reverse order or either alone. With new categories primed by the group brainstorming, individuals' ideas can continue flowing without being impeded by the group context that only allows one person to speak at a time. Creative work teams also tend to be small and to alternate working alone, working in pairs, and meeting as a circle (Paulus & Coskun, 2012).

[handwritten margin note: GROUP 1st ALONE 2nd.]

- **Have group members interact by writing.** Another way to take advantage of group priming, without being impeded by the one-at-a-time rule, is to have group members write and read, rather than speak and listen. Brown and Paulus described this process of passing notes and adding ideas, which has everyone active at once, as "brainwriting" (see also Heslin, 2009; Kohn, Paulus, & Choi, 2011). Moreover, when leaders urge people to generate lots of ideas (rather than just good ideas), they generate both more ideas *and* more good ideas (Paulus et al., 2011). So whatever comes to mind, put it down.

- **Incorporate electronic brainstorming.** There is a potentially more efficient way to avoid the verbal traffic jams of traditional group brainstorming in larger groups: Let individuals produce and read ideas on networked computers.

So, when group members freely combine their creative ideas and varied insights, the frequent result is not groupthink but group problem-solving.

The wisdom of groups is evident in everyday life as well as in the laboratory:

- **Weather forecasting.** "Two forecasters will come up with a forecast that is more accurate than either would have come up with working alone," reported Joel Myers (1997), president of the largest private forecasting service.

- **Google.** Google has become a dominant search engine by harnessing what James Surowiecki (2004) called "the wisdom of crowds." Google interprets a link to Page X as a vote for Page X, and weights most heavily links from pages that are themselves highly ranked. Harnessing the democratic character of the web, Google often takes less than one-tenth of a second to lead you right to what you want.

- **Game shows.** For a befuddled contestant on *Who Wants to Be a Millionaire?*, a valuable lifeline was to "ask the audience," which usually offered wisdom superior to the contestant's intuition. This is because the average judgment from a crowd of people typically errs less than does the average judgment by an individual.

- **The "crowd within."** Likewise, the average of different guesses from the same person tends to surpass the person's individual guesses (Herzog & Hertwig, 2009). Edward Vul and Harold Pashler (2008) discovered this when asking people to guess the correct answers to factual questions such as "What percentage of the world's airports are in the United States?" Then the researchers asked their participants to make a second guess, either immediately or three weeks later. The result? "You can gain about 1/10th as much from asking yourself the same question twice as you can from getting a second opinion from someone else, but if you wait three weeks, the benefit of re-asking yourself the same question rises to 1/3 the value of a second opinion."

- **Prediction markets.** In U.S. presidential elections since 1988, the final public opinion polls have provided a good gauge to the election result. An even better predictor, however, has been the Iowa Election Market. Taking everything (including polls) into account, people buy and sell shares in candidates. Other prediction markets have harnessed collective wisdom in gauging the likelihood of other events, such as an avian flu epidemic (Arrow et al., 2008; Stix, 2008).

Thus, we can conclude that when information from many diverse people is combined, all of us together can become smarter than almost any of us alone. We're in some ways like a flock of geese, no one of which has a perfect navigational sense. Nevertheless, by staying close to one another, a group of geese can navigate accurately. The flock is smarter than the bird.

● LEADERSHIP: HOW DO LEADERS SHAPE THE GROUP'S ACTIONS?

What is leadership, and what roles do effective leaders perform in groups?

In 1910, the Norwegians and the English engaged in an epic race to the South Pole. The Norwegians, effectively led by Roald Amundsen, made it. The English, ineptly led by Robert Falcon Scott, did not; Scott and three team members died. Some coaches move from team to team, transforming losers into winners each time; for example, Scotty Bowman has led three different teams to Stanley Cup championships.

TASK LEADERSHIP AND SOCIAL LEADERSHIP

leadership
the process by which certain group members motivate and guide the group

Some leaders are formally appointed or elected; others emerge informally as the group interacts. What makes for good **leadership** often depends on the situation—the best person to lead an engineering team may not make the best leader of a sales force. Some people excel at *task leadership*—at organizing work, setting standards, and focusing on goal attainment. Others excel at *social leadership*—at building teamwork, mediating conflicts, and being supportive.

Task leaders often have a directive style—one that can work well if the leader is bright enough to give good orders (Fiedler, 1987). Being goal oriented, such leaders also keep the group's attention and effort focused on its mission. Experiments show that the combination of specific, challenging goals and periodic progress reports helps motivate high achievement (Locke & Latham, 1990). Task leaders also can effectively keep poorly functioning groups under control. Thus, task leaders seem to get the most out of very high-achieving and very low-achieving groups.

Social leaders often have a democratic style—one that delegates authority, welcomes input from team members, and, as we have seen, helps prevent groupthink. Many experiments reveal that such leadership is good for morale. Group members usually feel more satisfied when they participate in making decisions (Spector, 1986; Vanderslice, Rice, & Julian, 1987). Given control over their tasks, workers also become more motivated to achieve (Burger, 1987). People who value good group feeling and take pride in achievement, therefore, thrive under democratic leadership (Lortie-Lussier, Lemieux, & Godbout, 1989).

M/C?

Democratic leadership can be seen in the move by many businesses toward participative management, a management style common in Sweden and Japan (Naylor, 1990; Sundstrom, De Meuse, & Futrell, 1990). Ironically, a major influence on this "Japanese-style" management was social psychologist Kurt Lewin. In laboratory and factory experiments, Lewin and his students demonstrated the benefits of inviting workers to participate in decision-making. Shortly before the Second World War, Lewin visited Japan and explained his findings to industrial and academic leaders (Nisbett & Ross, 1991). Japan's collectivist culture provided a receptive audience for Lewin's ideas about teamwork. Eventually, his influence circled back to North America.

> *Women more often than men have a democratic leadership style.*
> EAGLY & JOHNSON, 1990

TRANSACTIONAL LEADERSHIP →Both task & social leadership

The once-popular "great person" theory of leadership—that all great leaders share certain traits—has fallen into disrepute. Effective leadership styles, we now know, vary with the situation. People who know what they are doing may resent task leadership, while those who don't may welcome it. Recently, however, social psychologists have again wondered if there might be qualities that mark a good leader in many situations (Hogan, Curphy, & Hogan, 1994). British social psychologists Peter Smith and Monir Tayeb (1989) reported that studies done in India, Taiwan, and Iran found that the most effective supervisors in coal mines, banks, and government offices score high on tests of both task and social leadership. They are actively concerned with how work is progressing and sensitive to the needs of their subordinates.

These transactional leaders (Hollander, 1958) focus on getting to know their subordinates and listening carefully. They seek to fulfill the subordinates' needs but maintain high expectation for how subordinates will perform. Such leaders, who allow people to express their opinions, both learn from others and receive strong support from their followers (Tyler, Rasinski, & Spodick, 1985).

TRANSFORMATIONAL LEADERSHIP = ↑ minority views

Studies also reveal that many effective leaders of laboratory groups, work teams, and large corporations exhibit behaviours that help make a minority view persuasive. Such leaders engender trust by consistently sticking to their goals. And they often exude a self-confident charisma that kindles the allegiance of their followers (Bennis, 1984; House & Singh, 1987). Charismatic leaders typically have a compelling vision of some desired state of affairs, an ability to communicate this to others in clear and simple language, and enough optimism and faith in their group to inspire others to follow.

trust + consistent + confident

In one analysis of 50 Dutch companies, the highest morale was at firms with chief executives who most inspired their colleagues "to transcend their own self-interests for the sake of the collective" (de Hoogh et al., 2004). Leadership of this kind—transformational leadership—motivates others to identify with and commit themselves to the group's mission. Transformational leaders—many of whom are charismatic, energetic, self-confident extroverts—articulate high standards, inspire people to share their vision, and offer personal attention (Bono & Judge, 2004). The frequent result of such leadership in organizations is a more engaged, trusting, and effective workforce (Turner et al., 2002).

To be sure, groups also influence their leaders. Sometimes, those at the front of the herd have simply sensed where it is already heading. Political candidates know how to read the opinion

Participative management, illustrated in this "quality circle," requires democratic rather than autocratic leaders.

polls. A leader who deviates too radically from the group's standards may be rejected. Smart leaders usually remain with the majority and spend their influence prudently. Nevertheless, effective individual leaders can sometimes exhibit a type of minority influence by mobilizing and guiding their group's energy.

In rare circumstances, the right traits matched with the right situation yield history-making change, noted Dean Keith Simonton (1994). To have a Winston Churchill or a Margaret Thatcher, a Pierre Trudeau or a Karl Marx, a Napoleon or an Adolf Hitler, a Wilfrid Laurier or a Martin Luther King, Jr., takes a certain person in a certain place at a certain time. When an apt combination of intelligence, skill, determination, self-confidence, and social charisma meets a rare opportunity, the result is sometimes a new government, a Nobel Prize, or a social revolution.

● THE INFLUENCE OF THE MINORITY: HOW DO INDIVIDUALS INFLUENCE THE GROUP?

Groups influence individuals, but when—and how—do individuals influence their groups?

Each chapter in this social influence unit concludes with a reminder of our power as individuals. We have seen these phenomena:

- Cultural situations mould us, but we also help create and choose these situations.
- Pressures to conform sometimes overwhelm our better judgment, but blatant pressure can motivate us to assert our individuality and freedom.
- Persuasive forces are powerful, but we can resist persuasion by making public commitments and by anticipating persuasive appeals.

This chapter has emphasized group influences on the individual, so we conclude by seeing how individuals and minorities can influence their groups. (Note that in this context, "minority influence" refers to minority opinions, not to ethnic minorities.)

At the beginning of most social movements, a small minority will sometimes sway, and then even become, the majority. "All history," wrote Ralph Waldo Emerson, "is a record of the power of minorities, and of minorities of one." For good or bad, minorities of one often have a huge impact. Think of Copernicus, Hitler, Galileo, and Pol Pot. In Canadian history, the Meech Lake Accord might well have been ratified as part of the Constitution if not for the efforts of Elijah Harper, a member of the Manitoba legislature. Innovative minorities also make technological history. As Robert Fulton developed his steamboat—"Fulton's Folly"—he endured constant derision: "Never did a single encouraging remark, a bright hope, a warm wish, cross my path" (Cantril & Bumstead, 1960).

What makes a minority persuasive? What might the crew of the *Titanic* have done to convince Captain Smith that the ship needed to slow down? Experiments initiated by Serge Moscovici in Paris have identified several determinants of minority influence: consistency, self-confidence, and defection.

CONSISTENCY

More influential than a minority that wavers is a minority that sticks to its position. Moscovici and his associates (Moscovici, 1985; Moscovici, S., Lage, S., & Naffrechoux, 1969) found that if a minority consistently judges blue slides as green, members of the majority will occasionally agree. But if the minority wavers, saying "blue" to one-third of the blue slides and "green" to the rest, virtually no one in the majority will ever agree with "green."

Experiments show—and experience confirms—that nonconformity, especially persistent nonconformity, is often painful (Levine, 1989; Lücken & Simon, 2005). That helps explain a *minority slowness effect*—a tendency for people with minority views to express them less quickly than people in the majority (Bassili, 2003). If you set out to be Emerson's minority of one, prepare yourself for ridicule—especially when you argue an issue that's personally relevant to the majority and when the group wants to settle an issue by reaching consensus (Kameda & Sugimori, 1993; Kruglanski & Webster, 1991; Trost, Maass, & Kenrick, 1992). Even when people in the majority know that the disagreeing person is factually or morally right, they may still, unless they change their position, dislike the person (Chan, Louis, & Jetten, 2010).

> *"If the single man plant himself indomitably on his instincts, and there abide, the huge world will come round to him."*
> RALPH WALDO EMERSON, *NATURE, ADDRESS, AND LECTURES: THE AMERICAN SCHOLAR,* 1849

People may attribute your dissent to psychological peculiarities (Papastamou & Mugny, 1990). When Charlan Nemeth (1979, 2011) planted a minority of two within a simulated jury and had them oppose the majority's opinions, the two were inevitably disliked. Nevertheless, the majority acknowledged that the persistence of the two did more than anything else to make them rethink their positions. Compared to majority influence that often triggers unthinking agreement, minority influence stimulates a deeper processing of arguments, often with increased creativity (Kenworthy et al., 2008; Martin, Hewstone, & Martin, 2007; Martin et al., 2008).

On the other hand, a minority may stimulate creative thinking (Martin, 1996; Mucchi-Faina, Maass, & Volpato, 1991; Peterson & Nemeth, 1996). With dissent from within one's own group, people take in more information, think about the issue in new ways, and often make better decisions (Page, 2007). Believing that one need not win friends to influence people, Nemeth quotes Oscar Wilde: "We dislike arguments of any kind; they are always vulgar, and often convincing."

A persistent minority is influential, even if not popular, partly because it soon becomes the focus of debate (Schachter, 1951). Being the centre of conversation allows one to contribute a disproportionate number of arguments. And Nemeth reported that in experiments on minority influence, as in the studies dealing with group polarization, the position supported by the most arguments usually wins. Talkative group members are usually influential (Mullen, Salas, & Driskell, 1989).

② SELF-CONFIDENCE

Consistency and persistence convey self-confidence. Furthermore, Nemeth and Joel Wachtler (1974) reported that any behaviour by a minority that conveys self-confidence–for example, taking the head seat at the table–tends to raise self-doubts among the majority. By being firm and forceful, the minority's apparent self-assurance may prompt the majority to reconsider its position. This is especially so on matters of opinion rather than fact. In research at Italy's University of Padova, Anne Maass and her colleagues (1996) reported that minorities are less persuasive regarding fact ("from which country does Italy import most of its raw oil?") than regarding attitude ("from which country should Italy import most of its raw oil?").

③ DEFECTIONS FROM THE MAJORITY

↓ Illusion of unanimity

A persistent minority punctures any illusion of unanimity. When a minority consistently doubts the majority wisdom, majority members become freer to express their own doubts and may even switch to the minority position. John Levine (1989) found that a minority person who had defected from the majority was more persuasive than a consistent minority voice. In her jury-simulation experiments, Nemeth found that once defections begin, others often soon follow, initiating a snowball effect.

Are these factors that strengthen minority influence unique to minorities? Sharon Wolf and Bibb Latané (1985; Wolf, 1987) and Russell Clark (1995) believed not. They argued that the same social forces work for both majorities and minorities. Informational and normative influence fuels both group polarization and minority influence. And if consistency, self-confidence, and defections from the other side strengthen the minority, such variables also strengthen a majority. The social impact of any position depends on the strength, immediacy, and number of those who support it. Minorities have less influence than majorities simply because they are smaller.

Anne Maass and Russell Clark (1984, 1986) agreed with Moscovici, however, that minorities are more likely to convert people to accepting their views. And from their analyses of how groups evolve over time, John Levine and Richard Moreland (1985) concluded that new recruits to a group exert a different type of minority influence than do longtime members. Newcomers exert influence through the attention they receive and the group awareness they trigger in the old-timers. Established members feel freer to dissent and to exert leadership.

There is a delightful irony in this new emphasis on how individuals can influence the group. Until recently, the idea that the minority could sway the majority was itself a minority view in social psychology. Nevertheless, by arguing consistently and forcefully, Moscovici, Nemeth, Maass, Clark, and others have convinced the majority of group influence researchers that minority influence is a phenomenon worthy of study.

And the way that several of these minority influence researchers came by their interests should, perhaps, not surprise us. Anne Maass (1998) became interested in how minorities could effect social change after growing up in post-war Germany and hearing her grandmother's personal accounts of fascism. Charlan Nemeth (1999) developed her interest while she was a visiting professor in Europe "working with Henri Tajfel and Serge Moscovici. The three of us were 'outsiders'–I am an American Roman Catholic female in Europe, they having survived World War II as Eastern European Jews. Sensitivity to the value and the struggles of the minority perspective came to dominate our work."

▶ SUMMING UP

WHAT IS A GROUP?

- A group exists when two or more people interact for more than a few moments, affect one another in some way, and think of themselves as "us."

SOCIAL FACILITATION: HOW ARE WE AFFECTED BY THE PRESENCE OF OTHERS?

- The presence of others is arousing and helps our performance on easy tasks better, but hurts our performance on difficult tasks.

- Being in a crowd, or in crowded conditions, is similarly arousing and has the same types of effects on performance.

- But why are we aroused by others' presence? Partly because we worry about how we are evaluated by others. Others presence is also distracting and that accounts for some of the affects as well. Still, the mere presence of others seems to be arousing through the animal kingdom and may be a part of our evolutionary heritage.

SOCIAL LOAFING: DO INDIVIDUALS EXERT LESS EFFORT IN A GROUP?

- When people's efforts are pooled and individual effort is not evaluated, people generally exert less effort in groups than individually.

- Such social loafing is common in everyday life, but when the task is challenging, the group is cohesive, and people are committed to the group, social loafing is less evident.

DEINDIVIDUATION: WHEN DO PEOPLE LOSE THEIR SENSE OF SELF IN GROUPS?

- When people are in a large group, are physically anonymous, and are aroused and distracted.

- The resulting diminished self-awareness and self-restraint tend to increase people's responsiveness to the immediate situation, be it negative or positive.

GROUP POLARIZATION: DO GROUPS INTENSIFY OUR OPINIONS?

- When researchers originally studied the way groups make decisions differently from individuals, they found that groups make riskier decisions; but as they examined more types of decisions, they found that groups make more polarized decisions. If individuals would tend to be risky, then groups would make riskier decisions, but if individuals would tend to play it safe, then groups would make less risky decisions.

- Groups intensify decisions through group discussions.

- Group discussions intensify decisions by exposing us to new arguments and through our comparisons with others in the group.

GROUPTHINK: DO GROUPS HINDER OR ASSIST GOOD DECISIONS?

- Analysis of several international fiascos indicates that group cohesion can override realistic appraisal of a situation, leading to bad decisions. This is especially true when group members strongly desire unity, when they are isolated from opposing ideas, and when the leader signals what he or she wants from the group.
- Symptomatic of this overriding concern for harmony, labelled groupthink, are (1) an illusion of invulnerability, (2) rationalization, (3) unquestioned belief in the group's morality, (4) stereotyped views of the opposition, (5) pressure to conform, (6) self-censorship of misgivings, (7) an illusion of unanimity, and (8) "mindguards" who protect the group from unpleasant information.
- Critics have noted that some aspects of Janis's groupthink model (such as directive leadership) seem more implicated in flawed decisions than others (such as cohesiveness).
- Both in experiments and in actual history, groups sometimes decide wisely. These cases suggest ways to prevent groupthink: upholding impartiality, encouraging "devil's advocate" positions, subdividing and then reuniting to discuss a decision, seeking outside input, and having a "second-chance" meeting before implementing a decision.
- Research on group problem-solving suggests that groups can be more accurate than individuals; groups also generate more and better ideas if the group is small or if, in a large group, individual brainstorming follows the group session.

LEADERSHIP: HOW DO LEADERS SHAPE THE GROUP'S ACTIONS?

- Some leaders focus more on tasks and other leaders focus more on the social functioning of the group. Leaders who focus on tasks are often most effective for very high- and very low-functioning groups.
- Some leaders, however, combine social and task leadership by listening to followers and seeking to meet their needs, but at the same time holding them to high standards for performance. These transactional leaders are often very effective.
- Other leaders gain a following through their charisma and by offering personal attention. These transformational leaders inspire people to make self-sacrifices for the sake of the group and can lead others to be committed and engaged in the task at hand.

THE INFLUENCE OF THE MINORITY: HOW DO INDIVIDUALS INFLUENCE THE GROUP?

- When minority group members are consistent, they are more likely to influence the group.
- When minority group members have self-confidence, they are more likely to influence the group.
- When minority group members are consistent and self-confident, they create an atmosphere in which majority members can join their cause.

3

SOCIAL RELATIONS

Social psychology is the scientific study of how people think about, influence, and relate to one another. Having explored how we think about (Part One) and influence (Part Two) one another, we now consider social psychology's third facet—how we relate to one another. Our feelings and actions toward people are sometimes negative, sometimes positive. Chapter 8, "Altruism," and Chapter 9, "Aggression," examine why and when we help and hurt one another. Then in Chapter 10, "Attraction and Intimacy," Chapter 11, "Causes of Prejudice," and Chapter 12, "Effects of Prejudice," we explore why and when we love and hate one another.

CHAPTER EIGHT
Altruism: Helping Others

► **CHAPTER OUTLINE**

● WHY DO WE HELP?

● WHEN WILL WE HELP?

● WHO HELPS?

● HOW CAN WE INCREASE HELPING?

*H*elping comes in many forms, most strikingly in heroic, caring acts.

On November 12, 1999, Rohan Wilson saw smoke and flames spewing out of an Edmonton, Alberta, apartment building. He quickly called 911 and then climbed up the outside of the building to a balcony where three children were stranded. He brought them down to safety and then climbed to another balcony and saved a pregnant woman. When asked if he was a hero, he said, "Someone needed help, I hope someone would do the same for me if I was in that position" (CBC 4 Kids, 1999).

On a hillside in Jerusalem, 800 trees form a simple line, the Avenue of the Righteous. Beneath each tree is a plaque with the name of a European Christian who gave refuge to one or more Jews during the Nazi Holocaust. These "righteous Gentiles" knew that if the refugees were discovered, Nazi policy dictated that both host and refugee would suffer a common fate. Many did (Hellman, 1980; Wiesel, 1985).

Less dramatic acts of comforting, caring, and helping abound: Without asking anything in return, people offer directions, donate money, give blood, volunteer time.

- Why, and when, will people help?
- Who will help?
- What can be done to lessen indifference and increase helping?

Those are this chapter's primary questions.

Altruism is selfishness in reverse. An altruistic person is concerned and helpful even when no benefits are offered or expected in return. In the parable of the Good Samaritan, Jesus provided the classic illustration:

> A man was going down from Jerusalem to Jericho, and fell into the hands of robbers, who stripped him, beat him, and went away, leaving him half dead. Now by chance a priest was going down that road; and when he saw him, he passed by on the other side. So likewise a Levite, when he came to the place and saw him, passed by on the other side. But a Samaritan while travelling came near him; and when he saw him, he was moved with pity. He went to him and bandaged his wounds, having poured oil and wine on them. Then he put him on his own animal, brought him to an inn, and took care of him. The next day he took out two denarii, gave them to the innkeeper, and said, "Take care of him; and when I come back, I will repay you whatever more you spend." (Luke 10:30–35)

The Samaritan illustrates pure altruism. Filled with compassion, he gives a total stranger time, energy, and money while expecting neither repayment nor appreciation.

altruism
a motive to increase another's welfare without conscious regard for one's self-interests

● WHY DO WE HELP?

To study altruistic acts, social psychologists identify circumstances in which people perform such deeds. Before looking at what the experiments reveal, let's consider what motivates helping.

SOCIAL EXCHANGE

Several theories of helping agree that, in the long run, helping benefits the giver as well as the receiver. One explanation assumes that human interactions are guided by a "social economics." We exchange not only material goods and money but also social goods—love, services, information, status (Foa & Foa, 1975). In doing so, we use a "minimax" strategy—minimize costs, maximize rewards. **Social-exchange theory** does not contend that we consciously monitor costs and rewards, only that such considerations predict our behaviour.

Suppose your campus is having a blood drive and someone asks you to participate. Might you not implicitly weigh the costs of donating (needle prick, time, fatigue) against those of not donating (guilt, disapproval)? Might you not also weigh the benefits of donating (feeling good about helping someone, free refreshments) against those of not donating (saving the time, discomfort, and anxiety)? According to social-exchange theory—supported by studies of Wisconsin blood donors by Jane Allyn Piliavin and her research team (Piliavin, 2003; Piliavin, Evans, & Callero, 2003)—such subtle calculations precede decisions to help or not.

social-exchange theory
the theory that human interactions are transactions that aim to maximize one's rewards and minimize one's costs

Rewards

Rewards that motivate helping may be external or internal. When businesses donate money to improve their corporate images or when someone offers someone else a ride hoping to receive appreciation or friendship, the reward is external. We give to get. Thus we are most eager to help someone attractive to us, someone whose approval we desire (Krebs, 1970; Unger, 1979). In experiments, and in everyday life, public generosity boosts one's status, while selfish behaviour can lead to punishment (Hardy & Van Vugt, 2006; Henrich et al., 2006).

Rewards may also be internal. Nearly all blood donors in Jane Piliavin's research agreed that giving blood "makes you feel good about yourself" and "gives you a feeling of self-satisfaction." This helps explain why people far from home will leave tips for waiters and do kindnesses for strangers whom they will never see again.

Helping's boost to self-worth explains why so many people feel good after doing good. One month-long study of 85 couples found that giving emotional support to one's partner was positive for the giver; giving support boosted the giver's mood (Gleason et al., 2003). Piliavin (2003) and Susan Andersen (1998) reviewed studies that showed that youth who engaged in community service projects, school-based "service learning," or tutoring children develop social skills and positive social values. Such youth are at markedly less risk for delinquency, pregnancy, and school dropout and are more likely to become engaged citizens. Volunteering likewise benefits morale and health, especially when self-initiated rather than pressured (Weinstein & Ryan, 2010). Bereaved spouses recover from their depressed feelings faster when they are engaged in helping others (S. L. Brown et al., 2008, 2009). Those who do good tend to do well.

"Men do not value a good deed unless it brings a reward."
OVID, *EPISTULAE EX PONTO*

Ditto for giving money. Making donations activates brain areas linked with reward (Harbaugh, Mayr, & Burghart, 2007). Generous people are happier than those whose spending is self-focused. In one experiment, people received an envelope with cash that some were instructed to spend on themselves, while others were directed to spend it on other people. At the day's end, the happiest people were those assigned to the spend-it-on-others condition (Dunn et al., 2008). Other research confirms that giving increases happiness (Anik et al., 2010).

This cost-benefit analysis can seem demeaning. In defence of the theory, however, is it not a credit to humanity that much of our behaviour is not antisocial but "prosocial," and that we can find fulfillment in the giving of love? How much worse if we gained pleasure only by serving ourselves.

"True," some readers may reply. "Still, doesn't social-exchange theory imply that a helpful act is never truly altruistic—that we merely call it 'altruistic' when its rewards are inconspicuous? If we help the screaming woman so we can gain social approval, relieve our distress, or boost our self-image, is it really altruistic?" This is reminiscent of B. F. Skinner's (1971) analysis of altruism. We credit people for their good deeds, said Skinner, only when we can't explain them. We attribute their behaviour to their inner dispositions only when we lack external explanations. When the external causes are obvious, we credit the causes, not the person.

There is, however, a weakness in social-exchange theory: It easily degenerates into explaining-by-naming. If someone volunteers for the Big Sister tutor program, it is tempting to "explain" her compassionate action by the satisfaction it brings her. But such after-the-fact naming of rewards creates a circular explanation: "Why did she volunteer?" "Because of the inner rewards." "How do you know there are inner rewards?" "Why else would she have volunteered?" Because of this circular reasoning, egoism—the idea that self-interest motivates all behaviour—has fallen into disrepute.

To escape the circularity, we must define the rewards and costs independently of the helping behaviour. If social approval motivates helping, then in experiments we should find that when approval follows helping, helping increases. And it does (Staub, 1978).

egoism
a motive (supposedly underlying all behaviour) to increase your own welfare; the opposite of *altruism*, which aims to increase someone else's welfare.

Internal rewards

So far, we have considered external rewards for helping. We also need to consider internal factors, such as the helper's emotional state or personal traits.

The benefits of helping include internal self-rewards. Near someone in distress, we may feel distress. A woman's scream outside your window arouses and distresses you. If you cannot reduce your arousal by interpreting the scream as a playful shriek, then you may investigate or give aid, thereby reducing your distress (Piliavin & Piliavin, 1973). Altruism researcher Dennis Krebs (1975) found that university men whose physiological responses and self-reports revealed the most arousal in response to another's distress also gave the most help to the person.

Guilt

Distress is not the only negative emotion we act to reduce. Throughout recorded history, guilt has been a painful emotion that people avoid and seek to relieve. As Everett Sanderson remarked after heroically saving a child who had fallen onto subway tracks in front of an approaching train, "If I hadn't tried to save that little girl, if I had just stood there like the others, I would have died inside. I would have been no good to myself from then on."

Cultures have institutionalized ways to relieve guilt: animal and human sacrifices, offerings of grain and money, penitent behaviour, confession, denial. In ancient Israel, the sins of the people were periodically laid on a "scapegoat" animal that was then led into the wilderness to carry away the people's guilt.

To examine the consequences of guilt, social psychologists have induced people to transgress: to lie, to deliver shock, to knock over a table loaded with alphabetized cards, to break a machine, to cheat. Afterwards, the guilt-laden participants may be offered a way to relieve their guilt: by confessing, by disparaging the one harmed, or by doing a good deed to offset the bad one. The results are remarkably consistent: People will do whatever can be done to expunge the guilt and restore their self-image.

Picture yourself as a participant in one such experiment conducted with university students by David McMillen and James Austin (1971). You and another student, each seeking to earn credit toward a course requirement, arrive for the experiment. Soon after, a confederate enters, portraying himself as a previous subject looking for a lost book. He strikes up a conversation in which he mentions that the experiment involves taking a multiple-choice test, for which most of the correct answers are "B." After the accomplice departs, the experimenter arrives, explains the experiment, and then asks, "Has either of you been in this experiment before or heard anything about it?"

Would you lie? The behaviour of those who have gone before you in this experiment—100 percent of whom told the little lie—suggests that you would. After you have taken the test (without receiving any feedback on it), the experimenter says: "You are free to leave. However, if you have some spare time, I could use your help in scoring some questionnaires." Assuming you have told the lie, do you think you would now be more willing to volunteer some time? Judging from the results, the answer again is yes. On average, those who had not been induced to lie volunteered only two minutes of time. Those who had lied were apparently eager to redeem their self-image; on average, they offered a whopping 63 minutes. One moral of this experiment was well expressed by a 7-year-old girl, who, in one of our own experiments, wrote this: "Don't Lie or you! Live with gilt" (and you will feel a need to relieve it).

Our eagerness to do good after doing bad reflects both our need to reduce private guilt and to restore our shaken self-image and our desire to reclaim a positive public image. We are more likely to redeem ourselves with helpful behaviour when other people know about our misdeeds (Carlsmith & Gross, 1969).

All in all, guilt leads to much good. By motivating people to confess, apologize, help, and avoid repeated harm, it boosts sensitivity and sustains close relationships.

Among adults, the inner rewards of prosocial behaviour—feeling good about oneself after donating blood or helping pick up someone's dropped materials—can offset other negative moods as well (Cialdini, Kenrick, & Baumann, 1981; Williamson & Clark, 1989). Thus, when an adult is in a guilty, sad, or otherwise negative mood, a helpful deed (or any other mood-improving experience) helps neutralize the bad feelings.

> *"Open confession is good for the soul."*
> OLD SCOTTISH PROVERB

Exceptions to the feel bad–do good scenario

Among well-socialized adults, should we always expect to find the "feel bad–do good" phenomenon? No. One negative mood, anger, produces anything but compassion (as we will see in Chapter 9). Another exception is depression, which is characterized by brooding self-concern (Carlson & Miller, 1987; Wood, Saltzberg, & Goldsamt, 1990a). Yet another exception is profound grief. People who suffer the loss of a spouse or a child, whether through death or separation, often undergo a period of intense self-preoccupation, a state that makes it difficult to be giving (Aderman & Berkowitz, 1983; Gibbons & Wicklund, 1982).

In a powerfully involving laboratory simulation of self-focused grief, William Thompson, Claudia Cowan, and David Rosenhan (1980) had Stanford University students privately listen to a taped description of a person (whom they were to imagine was their best friend of the other sex) dying of cancer. (The examples below are for a female subject.) The experiment focused some subjects' attention on their own worry and grief:

> He could die and you would lose him, never be able to talk to him again. Or worse, he could die slowly. You would know every minute could be your last time together. For months, you would have to be cheerful for him while you were sad.

You would have to watch him die in pieces, until the last piece finally went, and you would be alone.

For others, it focused their attention on the friend:

He spends his time lying in bed, waiting those interminable hours, just waiting and hoping for something to happen. Anything. He tells you that it's not knowing that is the hardest.

The researchers reported that regardless of which tape the participants heard, they were profoundly moved and sobered by the experience, yet not at all regretful of participating (although some participants who listened to a boring control condition tape were regretful). Did their mood affect their helpfulness? When immediately thereafter they were given a chance to anonymously help a graduate student with her research, 25 percent of those whose attention had been self-focused helped. Of those whose attention was other-focused, 83 percent helped. The two groups were equally touched. But only the other-focused participants found helping someone especially rewarding. In short, the feel bad–do good effect occurs with people whose attention is on others, people for whom prosocial behaviour is, therefore, rewarding (Barnett et al., 1980; McMillen, Sanders, & Solomon, 1977). If not self-preoccupied by depression or grief, sad people are sensitive, helpful people.

Feel good–do good

Are happy people unhelpful? Quite the contrary. There are few more consistent findings in the entire literature of psychology: Happy people are helpful people. This effect occurs with both children and adults, regardless of whether the good mood comes from a success, from thinking happy thoughts, or from any of several other positive experiences (Salovey, Mayer, & Rosenhan, 1991). One woman recalled her experience after falling in love:

At the office, I could hardly keep from shouting out how deliriously happy I felt. The work was easy; things that had annoyed me on previous occasions were taken in stride. And I had strong impulses to help others; I wanted to share my joy. When Mary's typewriter broke down, I virtually sprang to my feet to assist. Mary! My for-mer "enemy"! (Tennov, 1979, p. 22)

In experiments on happiness and helpfulness, the person who is helped may be someone seeking a donation, an experimenter seeking help with paperwork, or a woman who drops papers. Here are three other examples:

- Joseph Forgas and his colleagues (2008) had a confederate offer either a mood-boosting compliment to a Target department store salesperson or a neutral or mood-deflating comment. Moments later, a second confederate, who was "blind" to the mood-induction condition, sought the employee's help in locating a non-existent item. Among less-experienced staff (who lacked a practised routine for answering such requests), those receiving the mood boost made the greatest effort to help.

- Dariusz Dolinski and Richard Nawrat (1998) found that a positive mood of relief can dramatically boost helping. Imagine yourself as one of their unwitting subjects. After illegally parking your car for a few moments, you return to discover what looks like a ticket under your windshield wiper (where parking tickets are placed). Groaning inwardly, you pick up the apparent ticket, and then are much relieved to discover it is only an ad (or a blood drive appeal). Moments later, a university student approaches you and asks you to spend 15 minutes answering questions—to "help me complete my M.A. thesis." Would your positive, relieved mood make you more likely to help? Indeed, 62 percent of people whose fear had just turned to relief agreed willingly. That was nearly double the number who did so when no ticket-like paper was left or when it was left on the car door (not a place for a ticket).

- Alice Isen, Margaret Clark, and Mark Schwartz (1976) had a confederate call people who had received a free sample of stationery 0 to 20 minutes earlier. The confederate said she had used her last dime to dial this (supposedly wrong) number and asked each person to relay a message by phone. As Figure 8–1 shows, the individuals' willingness to relay the phone message rose during the five minutes afterward. Then, as the good mood wore off, helpfulness dropped.

If sad people are sometimes extra helpful, how can it be that happy people are also helpful? Experiments reveal that several factors are at work (Carlson, Charlin, & Miller, 1988; Schaller & Cialdini, 1990). Helping softens a bad mood and sustains a good mood. (Perhaps you can recall feeling good after giving someone directions.) A positive mood is, in turn, conducive to positive thoughts and positive self-esteem, which predispose us to positive behaviour (Berkowitz, 1987; Cunningham et al., 1990; Isen et al., 1978). In a good mood—after being given a gift or while feeling the warm glow of success—people are more likely to have positive thoughts and to have positive associations with being helpful. Positive thinkers are likely to be positive actors.

"It's curious how, when you're in love, you yearn to go about doing acts of kindness to everybody."
P. G. WODEHOUSE, *THE MATING SEASON*, 1949

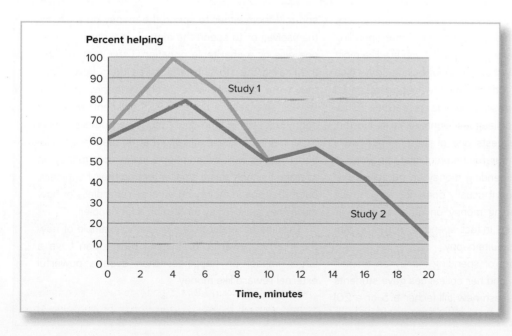

FIGURE 8–1

MOOD AND HELPFULNESS.

This graph shows the percentage of subjects willing to relay a phone message 0 to 20 minutes after receiving a free sample. Of control subjects who did not receive a gift, only 10 percent helped. (Data from Isen et al., 1976)

SOCIAL NORMS

Often, we help others not because we have consciously calculated that such behaviour is in our self-interest but simply because something tells us we ought to. We ought to help a new neighbour move in. We ought to return the wallet we found. We ought to protect our combat buddies from harm. Norms, the *oughts* of our lives, are social expectations. They prescribe proper behaviour. Researchers studying helping behaviour have identified two social norms that motivate prosocial behaviour: the reciprocity norm and the social-responsibility norm.

The reciprocity norm

reciprocity norm
an expectation that people will help, not hurt, those who have helped them

One universal moral code is a **reciprocity norm**: *To those who help us, we should return help, not harm* (Gouldner, 1960). This norm is as universal as the incest taboo. We "invest" in others and expect dividends. Politicians know that the one who gives a favour can later expect a favour. Mail surveys and solicitations sometimes include a little gift of money or personalized address labels, assuming some people will reciprocate the favour. Even 21-month-old infants display reciprocity, by being more willing to help those who have tried to give them a toy (Dunfield & Kuhlmeier, 2010). The reciprocity norm even applies in marriage. At times, one may give more than one receives, but in the long run, the exchange should balance out. In all such interactions, to receive without giving in return violates the reciprocity norm.

FOCUS ON > Money, Happiness, and Helping

Imagine that you won a million dollars in the lottery. How would you spend it? Do you think that spending the money would make you happy? If you are like most people, you probably thought about buying some nice things for yourself with the money. Recent research by University of British Columbia researcher Elizabeth Dunn and her colleagues (Dunn, Aknin, & Norton, 2008), however, suggests one of the common ways that we mispredict our future emotional reactions is that we think that spending money on ourselves will make us happy, when it usually does not. In contrast, we think that spending money on other people will bring us little joy when, in fact, spending money on others usually makes us quite happy.

To test the impact of spending money on oneself versus others, Dunn and her colleagues gave students an envelope with a fresh new bill (either a 5 or a 20)

and told them either to spend the money on a gift for themselves or to spend the money on a gift for someone else or a charitable donation. Later that evening, they called the students and asked them how happy they were. Students who spent the money on themselves (regardless of the amount they spent) were less happy than those who spent money on others. These experimental findings mirror what is seen in correlational data as well. When people make more money, on average this only has a small effect on their happiness; but if they spend money on others—regardless of how much they make—they tend to be a lot happier.

This line of research is a dramatic example of how the internal rewards for helping others can have a larger impact on happiness than even a powerful external reward like money.

Reciprocity within social networks helps define the "social capital"—the supportive connections, information flow, trust, and cooperative actions—that keeps a community healthy. Neighbours keeping an eye on each other's homes is social capital in action.

The norm operates most effectively as people respond publicly to deeds earlier done to them. In laboratory games as in everyday life, fleeting one-shot encounters produce greater selfishness than sustained relationships. But even when people respond anonymously, they sometimes do the right thing and repay the good done to them. In one experiment, Mark Whatley and his colleagues (1999) found that more university students willingly made a pledge to the charity of someone who had previously bought them some candy (Figure 8–2).

When people cannot reciprocate, they may feel threatened and demeaned by accepting aid. Thus, proud, high self-esteem people are often reluctant to seek help (Nadler & Fisher, 1986). Receiving unsolicited help can take one's self-esteem down a notch (Schneider et al., 1996; Shell & Eisenberg, 1992). Studies show this can happen to beneficiaries of affirmative action, especially when affirmative action fails to affirm the person's competence and chances for future success (Pratkanis & Turner, 1996). Asians, for whom social ties and the reciprocity norm are stronger than for North Americans, are therefore more likely to refuse a gift from a casual acquaintance to avoid the felt need to reciprocate (Shen, Wan, & Wyer, 2011).

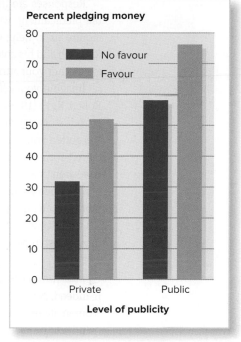

Percent pledging money

No favour
Favour

Private / Public

Level of publicity

FIGURE 8–2

PRIVATE AND PUBLIC RECIPROCATION OF A FAVOUR.

People were more willing to pledge to an experimental confederate's charity if the confederate had done a small favour for them earlier, especially when their reciprocation was made known to the confederate. (Whatley et al., 1999)

social-responsibility norm
an expectation that people will help those dependent upon them

The social-responsibility norm

The reciprocity norm reminds us to balance giving and receiving in social relations. If the only norm was reciprocity, however, the Samaritan would not have been the Good Samaritan. In the parable, Jesus obviously had something more humanitarian in mind, something explicit in another of his teachings: "I say to you, Love your enemies . . . If you love those who love you [the reciprocity norm], what right have you to claim any credit?" (Matthew 5:44, 46).

With people who clearly are dependent and unable to reciprocate, such as children, the severely impoverished, and those with disabilities, another social norm motivates our helping. The **social-responsibility norm** is the belief that people should help those who need help, without regard to future exchanges (Berkowitz, 1975; Schwartz, 1975). If a person on crutches drops a book, you honour the social-responsibility norm as you pick it up. In India, a relatively collectivist culture, people support the social-responsibility norm more strongly than in the individualist West (Baron & Miller, 2000). They voice an obligation to help even when the need is not life-threatening or the needy person—perhaps a stranger needing a bone marrow transplant—is outside their family circle.

Even when helpers in Western countries remain anonymous and have no expectation of any reward, they often help needy people (Harrel, 1994; Shotland & Stebbins, 1983). However, they usually apply the social-responsibility norm selectively to those whose need appears not to be due to their own negligence. Especially among political conservatives (Skitka & Tetlock, 1993), the norm seems to be this: Give people what they deserve. If they are victims of circumstance, such as a natural disaster, then by all means be compassionate (Goetz, Keltner, & Simon-Thomas, 2010; Zagefka et al., 2011). If they seem to have created their own problems (by laziness, immorality, or lack of foresight, for example), then the norm suggests they don't deserve help.

Responses are thus closely tied to attributions. If we attribute the need to an uncontrolla-ble predicament, we help. If we attribute the need to the person's choices, fairness does not require us to help; we say it's the person's own fault (Weiner, 1980). The key, suggested Udo Rudolph and his colleagues (2004) from their review of more than three dozen pertinent studies, is whether your attributions evoke sympathy, which in turn motivates helping.

Imagine yourself as one of the students in a study by Richard Barnes, William Ickes, and Robert Kidd (1979). You receive a call from a "Tony Freeman" who explains that he is in your introductory psychology class. He says that he needs help for the upcoming exam and that he has gotten your name from the class roster. "I don't know. I just don't seem to take good notes in there," Tony explains. "I know I can, but sometimes I just don't feel like it, so most of the notes I have aren't very good to study with." How sympathetic would you feel toward Tony? How much of a sacrifice would you make to lend him your notes? If you are like the students in this experi-ment, you would probably be much less inclined to help than if Tony had just explained that his troubles were beyond his control. Thus, the social-responsibility norm compels us to help those most in need and those most deserving.

Gender and receiving help

If, indeed, perception of someone else's need strongly determines your willingness to help, will women, if perceived as less competent and more dependent, receive more help than men? That is indeed the case. Alice Eagly and Maureen Crowley (1986) located 35 studies that compared help received by male or female victims. (Virtually all the studies involved short-term encoun-ters with strangers in need—the very situations in which people expect males to be chivalrous, noted Eagly and Crowley.)

Women offered help equally to males and females, whereas men offered more help when the strangers in need were females. Several experiments in the 1970s found that women with disabled cars (for example, with a flat tire) got many more offers of help than did men (Penner, Dertke, & Achenbach, 1973; Pomazal & Clore, 1973; West, Whitney, & Schnedler, 1975). Similarly, solo female hitchhikers received far more offers of help than solo males or couples (Pomazal & Clore, 1973; Snyder, Grether, & Keller, 1974). Of course, men's chivalry toward lone women may have been motivated by something other than altruism. Mating motives increase men's spend-ing on conspicuous luxuries, and they also motivate displays of heroism (Griskevicius et al., 2007). Not surprisingly, men more frequently helped attractive than unattractive women (Mims, Hartnett, & Nay, 1975; Stroufe et al., 1977; West & Brown, 1975).

Women receive more offers of help in certain situations; they also seek more help (Addis & Mahalik, 2003). They are twice as likely to seek medical and psychiatric help. They are the majority of callers to radio counselling programs and clients of college and university counselling centres. They more often welcome help from friends. Arie Nadler (1991), a Tel Aviv University expert on help-seeking, attributed this to gender differences in independence versus interdependence.

EVOLUTIONARY PSYCHOLOGY

Another explanation of helping comes from evolutionary theory. Evolutionary psychology con-tends that the essence of life is gene survival. Our genes drive us in ways that have maximized their chance of survival. When our ancestors died, their genes lived on, predisposing us to behave in ways that will spread them into the future.

As suggested by the title of Richard Dawkins' (1976) book *The Selfish Gene,* evolutionary psychology offers a humbling human image—one that psychologist Donald Campbell (1975b) called a biological reaffirmation of a deep, self-serving "original sin." Genes that predispose individuals to self-sacrifice in the interests of strangers' welfare would not survive in the evolutionary competition. Evolutionary success does, however, come from cooperation. And humans, say Martin Nowak and Roger Highfield (2011), are the animal kingdom's super-cooperators because we exhibit multiple mechanisms for overcoming selfishness, including the following:

- *Kin selection:* If you carry my genes, I'll favour you.
- *Direct reciprocity:* We scratch each other's backs.
- *Indirect reciprocity:* I'll scratch your back, you scratch someone's, and someone will scratch mine.
- *Group selection:* Back-scratching groups survive.

> *"Fallen heroes do not have children. If self-sacrifice results in fewer descendants, the genes that allow heroes to be created can be expected to disappear gradually from the population."*
> E. O. WILSON, *ON HUMAN NATURE,* 1978

Kin selection

Our genes dispose us to care for relatives. Thus, one form of self-sacrifice that would increase gene survival is devotion to one's children. Compared with neglectful parents, parents who put their children's welfare ahead of their own are more likely to pass their genes on. As evolutionary psychologist David Barash (1979, p. 153) wrote, "Genes help themselves by being nice to themselves, even if they are enclosed in different bodies." Genetic egoism (at the biological level) fosters parental altruism (at the psychological level). Although evolution favours self-sacrifice for one's children, children have less at stake in the survival of their parents' genes. Thus, according to the theory, parents will generally be more devoted to their children than their children are to them.

Other relatives share genes in proportion to their biological closeness. You share one-half of your genes with your brothers and sisters, one-eighth with your cousins. **Kin selection**—favouritism toward those who share our genes—led the evolutionary biologist J. B. S. Haldane to joke that while he would not give up his life for his brother, he would sacrifice himself for three brothers—or for nine cousins. Haldane would not have been surprised that, compared to fraternal twins, genetically identical twins are noticeably more mutually supportive (Segal, 1984; Stewart-Williams, 2007). In one laboratory game experiment, identical twins were half again as likely to cooperate with their twin for a shared gain when playing for money (Segal & Hershberger, 1999).

kin selection
the idea that evolution has selected altruism toward one's close relatives to enhance the survival of mutually shared genes

The point is not that we calculate genetic relatedness before helping but that nature (as well as culture) programs us to care about close relatives. The Carnegie medal for heroism is seldom awarded for saving an immediate family member. When Carlos Rogers of the Toronto Raptors NBA basketball team volunteered to end his career and donate a kidney to his sister (who died before she received it), people applauded his self-sacrificial love. But such acts for close kin are not totally unexpected. What we do not expect (and, therefore, honour) is the altruism of those who, like our apartment fire hero Rohan Wilson, risk themselves to save a stranger. We share common genes with many besides our relatives. Blue-eyed people share particular genes with other blue-eyed people. How do we detect the people in which copies of our genes occur most abundantly? As the blue-eyes example suggests, one clue lies in physical similarities.

Physical similarities & proximity

> "Morality governs our actions toward others in much the same way that gravity governs the motions of the planets: its strength is in inverse proportion to the square of the distance between them."
>
> JAMES Q. WILSON, "THE UNIVERSAL ASPIRATION," 1993

Also, in evolutionary history, genes were shared more with neighbours than with foreigners. Are we, therefore, biologically biased to be more helpful to those who look similar to us and those who live near us? In the aftermath of natural disasters and other life-and-death situations, the order of who gets helped would not surprise an evolutionary psychologist: the children before the old, family members before friends, neighbours before strangers (Burnstein, Crandall, & Kitayama, 1994; Form & Nosow, 1958). We feel more empathy for a distressed or tortured person in our in-group, and even *Schadenfreude* (secret pleasure at their misfortune) for rival or out-group members (Batson, Chao, & Givens, 2009; Cikara, Bruneau, & Saxe, 2011; Tarrant, Dazeley, & Cottom, 2009). Helping stays close to home.

Some evolutionary psychologists note that kin selection predisposes ethnic in-group favouritism—the root of countless historical and contemporary conflicts (Rushton, 1991). E. O. Wilson (1978) noted that kin selection is "the enemy of civilization. If human beings are to a large extent guided . . . to favour their own relatives and tribe, only a limited amount of global harmony is possible" (p. 167).

Reciprocity

Genetic self-interest also predicts reciprocity. One organism helps another, biologist Robert Trivers argued, because it expects help in return (Binham, 1980). The giver expects later to be the getter, whereas failure to reciprocate is punished: The cheat, the turncoat, and the traitor are universally despised.

Reciprocity works best in small, isolated groups, groups in which one will often see the people for whom one does favours. Sociable female baboons—those who groom and stay in close contact with their peers—gain a reproductive advantage: Their infants more often live to see a first birthday (Silk, Alberts, & Altmann, 2003). If a vampire bat has gone a day or two without food—it can't go much more than 60 hours without starving to death—it asks a well-fed nestmate to regurgitate food for a meal (Wilkinson, 1990). The donor bat does so willingly, losing fewer hours till starvation than the recipient gains. But such favours occur only among familiar nestmates who share in the give-and-take. Those who always take and never give, and those who have no relationship with the donor bat, go hungry. It pays to have friends.

For similar reasons, reciprocity is stronger in the remote Cook Islands of the South Pacific than in New York City (Barash, 1979, p. 160). Small schools, towns, churches, work teams, and dorms are all conducive to a community spirit in which people care for each other. Compared to people in small-town or rural environments, those in big cities are less willing to relay a phone message, less likely to mail "lost" letters, less cooperative with survey interviewers, less helpful to a lost child, and less willing to do small favours (Hedge & Yousif, 1992; Steblay, 1987).

Group selection

If individual self-interest inevitably wins in genetic competition, then why will we help strangers? Why will we help those whose limited resources or abilities preclude their reciprocating? What caused Mother Teresa to act as she did? What causes soldiers to throw themselves on grenades? One answer, initially favoured by Darwin (then discounted by selfish gene theorists, but now back again) is group selection: When groups are in competition, groups of mutually supportive altruists outlast groups of non-altruists (Krebs, 1998; Sober & Wilson, 1998; Wilson & Wilson, 2008). This is most dramatically evident with the social insects, who function like cells in a body. Bees and ants will labour sacrificially for their colony's survival.

To a much lesser extent, humans exhibit in-group loyalty, by sometimes sacrificing to support "us" against "them." Natural selection is, therefore, "multi-level," according to some researchers (Mirsky, 2009): It operates at both individual and group levels.

Donald Campbell (1975a, 1975b) offered another basis for unreciprocated altruism: Human societies evolved ethical and religious rules that serve as brakes on the biological bias toward self-interest. Commandments such as "Love your neighbour" admonish us to balance self-concern with concern for the group, and so contribute to the survival of the group. Richard Dawkins (1976) offered a similar conclusion: "Let us try to teach generosity and altruism, because we are born selfish. Let us understand what our selfish genes are up to, because we may then at least have the chance to upset their designs, something no other species has ever aspired to" (p. 3).

COMPARING AND EVALUATING THEORIES OF ALTRUISM

By now, you have perhaps noticed similarities among the social-exchange, social norm, and evolutionary views of altruism. As Table 8–1 shows, each proposes two types of prosocial behaviour: a tit-for-tat reciprocal exchange and a more unconditional helpfulness. They do so at three complementary levels of explanation. If the evolutionary view is correct, then our genetic predispositions should manifest themselves in psychological and sociological phenomena.

Each theory appeals to logic. Yet each is vulnerable to charges of being speculative and after the fact. When we start with a known effect (the give-and-take of everyday life) and explain it by conjecturing a social-exchange process, a "reciprocity norm," or an evolutionary origin, we might be merely explaining-by-naming. The argument that a behaviour occurs because of its survival function is hard to disprove. With hindsight, it's easy to think it had to be that way. If we can explain any conceivable behaviour after the fact as the result of a social exchange, a norm, or natural selection, then we cannot disprove the theories. Each theory's task is, therefore, to generate predictions that enable us to test it.

An effective theory also provides a coherent scheme for summarizing a variety of observations. On this criterion, the three altruism theories get higher marks. Each offers us a broad perspective from which we can understand both enduring commitments and spontaneous help.

TABLE 8–1 COMPARING THEORIES OF ALTRUISM.

		How Is Altruism Explained?	
Theory	**Level of Explanation**	**Mutual Altruism**	**Intrinsic Altruism**
Social norms	Sociological	Reciprocity norm	Social-responsibility norm
Social exchange	Psychological	External rewards for helping	Distress $\rightarrow$ inner rewards for helping
Evolutionary	Biological	Reciprocity	Kin selection

THE >>> INSIDE STORY

The reasons why people do things aren't always what they seem. For instance, the things I'll tell you shortly may imply that my motive for going to graduate school was to study interesting questions about helping behaviour. It's more likely, though, that I went to graduate school because I didn't fancy having to find a job in the real world. Before going to graduate school, I heard about research suggesting that the emotional experience of empathy leads to a truly altruistic motive to help others. I didn't buy it. Neither did Bob Cialdini, and so I chose to go work with him.

We conducted several studies supporting the hypothesis that the alleged altruistic motive to help is actually a mood-management motive in disguise. So even when people feel empathic toward someone else, they may help that person for selfish, not selfless, motives. Of course, these motives may not account fully for the effects of empathy on helping behaviour. Recently, I've been thinking that some of the effects on helping may be so automated that they may not be driven by motives and goals at all, even though they appear to be. After all, the reasons why people do things aren't always what they seem.

Mark Schaller, *University of British Columbia*

Genuine altruism

Are life-saving heroes, everyday blood donors, and relief workers *ever* motivated by an ultimate goal of selfless concern for others? Or is their ultimate goal always some form of self-benefit, such as relief from distress or avoidance of guilt?

Philosophers have debated this question for centuries. Consider the case of Rohan Wilson, which was described at the beginning of the chapter. He risked his life to save three young children and a pregnant woman. But do we really know that this was a selfless act of concern? Perhaps he only helped because he would not have been able to live with himself if he had not. Or maybe he helped because he expected the praise and accolades he received. The skeptic can always see a hidden motive of self-interest in even the most heroic acts. We can all be skeptical of some acts of helping. Take as an example corporate donations to charity. John Cleghorn (2000), the chairman and CEO of Royal Bank, noted that in 1999 his bank gave over $25 million to charity. Yet even he had to admit that "In some cases the line between marketing and philanthropic activities has become increasingly blurred." So, do people help just so they won't feel bad, and do companies give to charities only to increase their bottom lines? Until recently, psychologists have generally argued that self-interest is behind most instances of helping.

Helpfulness so reliably makes helpers feel better that Daniel Batson (2011) has devoted much of his career to discerning whether helpfulness also contains a streak of genuine altruism. Batson theorizes that our willingness to help is influenced by both self-serving and selfless considerations (Figure 8–3). Distress over someone's suffering motivates us to relieve

"Are you all right, Mister? Is there anything I can do?"

"Young man, you're the only one who bothered to stop! I'm a millionaire and I'm going to give you five thousand dollars!"

our upset feelings, either by escaping the distressing situation (like the priest and Levite) or by helping (like the Samaritan). But especially when we feel attached to someone, reported Batson and a team of attachment researchers led by Mario Mikulincer (2005), we also feel **empathy**. Loving parents suffer when their children suffer and rejoice over their children's joys—an empathy lacking in child abusers and other perpetrators of cruelty (Miller & Eisenberg, 1988).

We also feel empathy for those we identify with. In September 1997, millions of people who never came within 80 kilometres of Princess Diana (but who felt as if they knew her after hundreds of tabloid stories and 44 *People* magazine cover articles) wept for her and her motherless sons—but shed no tears for the nearly 1 million faceless Rwandans murdered or dying in squalid refugee camps since 1994. We feel more empathy for a real person than a suffering aggregate, more sadness over the death of a Diana than over a mass "statistic." This "collapse of compassion"—decreasing concern as the number of suffering people increases—also occurs as people regulate their painful emotional responses to large tragedies (Cameron & Payne, 2011).

When we feel empathy, we focus not so much on our own distress as on the sufferer. Genuine sympathy and compassion motivate us to help others for their own sakes. When we value another's welfare, perceive the person as in need, and take the person's perspective, we feel empathic concern (Batson et al., 2007).

To increase empathy, it helps to get a small dose of what another feels. A specific torture technique becomes less acceptable when people experience even a small dose of it. For example,

We never know what benefits may come from helping someone in distress.

© Barney Tobey/The New Yorker Collection/www.cartoonbank.com.

empathy
the vicarious experience of someone else's feeling; putting yourself in someone else's shoes

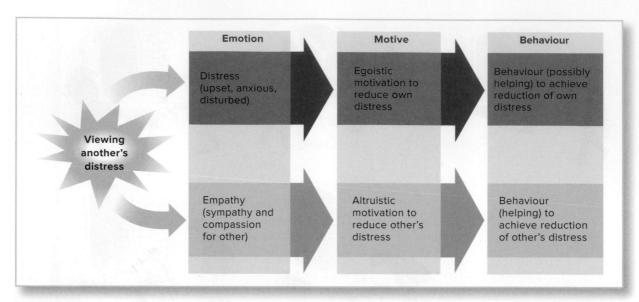

Emotion	Motive	Behaviour
Distress (upset, anxious, disturbed)	Egoistic motivation to reduce own distress	Behaviour (possibly helping) to achieve reduction of own distress
Empathy (sympathy and compassion for other)	Altruistic motivation to reduce other's distress	Behaviour (helping) to achieve reduction of other's distress

Viewing another's distress

FIGURE 8–3

EGOISTIC AND ALTRUISTIC ROUTES TO HELPING.

Viewing someone else's distress can evoke a mixture of self-focused distress and other-focused empathy. Researchers agree that distress triggers egoistic motives. But they debate whether empathy can trigger a pure altruistic motive. (Adapted from Batson, Fultz, & Schoenrade, 1987)

when moderately sleep-deprived, people become more likely to say that, yes, extreme sleep deprivation is torture (Nordgren, Banas, & MacDonald, 2011).

In humans, empathy comes naturally. Even day-old infants cry more when they hear another infant cry (Hoffman, 1981). In hospital nurseries, one baby's crying sometimes evokes a chorus of crying. Most 18-month-old infants, after observing an unfamiliar adult accidentally drop a marker or clothespin and have trouble reaching it, will readily help (Tomasello, 2009). To some, this suggests that humans are hard-wired for empathy. Primates and even mice also display empathy, indicating that the building blocks of prosocial behaviour predate humanity (de Waal, 2005; de Waal, Leimgruber, & Greenberg, 2008; Langford et al., 2006; Wynne & de Waal, 2006). In one classic experiment, most rhesus monkeys refused to operate a device that gained them food if it would cause another monkey to receive an electric shock (Masserman, Wechkin, & Terris, 1964). Chimpanzees will choose a token that gives both themselves and another chimp a food treat over a token that gratifies only themselves (Horner et al., 2010).

Often, distress and empathy together motivate responses to a crisis (Gordon & Mentzel, 1990). In 1983, people watched on television as an Australian bushfire wiped out hundreds of homes near Melbourne. Afterwards, Paul Amato (1986) studied donations of money and goods. He found that those who felt angry or indifferent gave less than those who felt either distressed (shocked and sickened) or empathic (sympathetic and worried for the victims).

To separate egoistic distress reduction from altruistic empathy, Batson's research group conducted studies that aroused feelings of empathy. Then the researchers noted whether the aroused people would reduce their own distress by escaping the situation or whether they would go out of their way to aid the person. The results were consistent: Their empathy aroused, they usually helped.

In one of these experiments, Batson and his associates (1981) had women observe a young woman suffering while she supposedly received electric shocks. During a pause in the experiment, the obviously upset victim explained to the experimenter that a childhood fall against an electric fence left her acutely sensitive to shocks. In sympathy, the experimenter suggested that perhaps the observer (the actual subject in this experiment) might trade places and take the remaining shocks for her. Previously, half of these actual subjects had been led to believe that the suffering person was a kindred spirit on matters of values and interests (thus arousing their empathy). Some also were led to believe that their part in the experiment was completed, so that in any case they were done observing the woman's suffering. Nevertheless, their empathy aroused, virtually all these student observers willingly offered to substitute for the victim. Might genuine altruism motivate an international health educator working with children in Uganda? Daniel Batson suggested it might.

Is this genuine altruism? Mark Schaller and Robert Cialdini (1988) doubted it. Feeling empathy for a sufferer makes one sad, they noted. In one of their experiments, they led people to believe that their sadness was going to be relieved by a different sort of mood-boosting experience—listening to a comedy tape. Under such conditions, people who felt empathy were not especially helpful. Schaller and Cialdini concluded that if we feel empathy but know that something else will make us feel better, we aren't so likely to help.

Might genuine empathy motivate humanitarian aid workers to travel across the world? This Red Cross worker believes yes.

Everyone agrees that some helpful acts are either obviously egoistic (done to gain rewards or avoid punishment) or subtly egoistic (done to relieve inner distress). Is there a third type of helpfulness—an altruism that aims simply to increase another's welfare (producing happiness for oneself merely as a by-product)? Is empathy-based helping a source of such altruism? Cialdini (1991) and his colleagues Mark Schaller and Jim Fultz thought not. They noted that no experiment rules out all possible egoistic explanations for helpfulness.

However, after some 25 experiments testing egoism versus empathy, Batson (2001) and others (Dovidio, 1991; Staub, 1991) believed that sometimes people do focus on the welfare of others, not on their own. Batson, a former philosophy and theology student, had begun his research feeling "excited to think that if we could ascertain whether people's concerned reactions were genuine, and not simply a subtle form of selfishness, then we could shed new light on a basic issue regarding human nature" (1999a). Two decades later, Batson believed he had his answer. Genuine "empathy-induced altruism is part of human nature" (1999b). And that, said Batson, raises the hope—confirmed by research—that inducing empathy might improve attitudes toward stigmatized people—people with AIDS, the homeless, the imprisoned, and other minorities.

> "*How selfish soever man may be supposed, there are evidently some principles in his nature, which interest him in the fortune of others, and render their happiness necessary to him, though he derives nothing from it except the pleasure of seeing it.*"
> ADAM SMITH, *THE THEORY OF MORAL SENTIMENTS,* 1759

● WHEN WILL WE HELP?

What circumstances prompt people to help, or not to help? How is helping influenced by the number and behaviour of other bystanders, and why?

On March 13, 1964, bar manager Kitty Genovese was set upon by a knife-wielding rapist as she returned to her apartment house at 3:00 A.M. Her screams of terror and pleas for help—"Oh my God, he stabbed me! Please help me! Please help me!"—aroused 38 of her neighbours. Many came to their windows and saw her plight while she struggled for 35 minutes to escape her attacker. Not until her attacker departed did anyone so much as call the police. Soon after, she died.

A later analysis disputed the initial report that there were actually 38 witnesses who observed the murder yet remained inactive (Manning, Levine, & Collins, 2007). Nevertheless, the story helped inspire research on bystander inaction, which was illustrated in other incidents:

- Seventeen-year-old Andrew Mormille was knifed in the stomach as he rode the subway home. After his attackers left the car, 11 other riders watched the young man bleed to death.

- Eleanor Bradley tripped and broke her leg while shopping. Dazed and in pain, she pleaded for help. For 40 minutes, the stream of pedestrians simply parted and flowed around her. Finally, a cab driver helped her to a doctor (Darley & Latané, 1968).

- As more than a million locals and tourists mingled in the warm sun during and after a June 2000 parade alongside New York's Central Park, a pack of alcohol-fuelled young men became sexually aggressive—groping, and in some cases stripping, 60 women. In the days that followed, media attention focused on the mob psychology behind this sexual aggression and on police inaction (at least two victims had approached nearby police, who failed to respond). But what about the thousands of people milling around? Why did they tolerate this? Among the many bystanders with cellphones, why did not one person call 911 (*Dateline*, 2000)?

What is shocking is not that in these cases some people failed to help; what is really shocking is that in each of these groups, almost 100 percent of those involved failed to respond. Why? In the same or similar situations, would you or I react as they did?

Social psychologists were curious and concerned about bystanders' lack of involvement. So they undertook experiments to identify when people will help in an emergency, and when they will not.

NUMBER OF BYSTANDERS

Bystander passivity during emergencies has prompted social commentators to lament people's "alienation," "apathy," "indifference," and "unconscious sadistic impulses." By attributing the non-intervention to the bystanders' dispositions, we can reassure ourselves that as caring people, *we* would have helped. But were the bystanders such inhumane characters?

Social psychologists Bibb Latané and John Darley (1970) were unconvinced. So they staged ingenious emergencies and found that a single situational factor—the presence of other bystanders—greatly decreased intervention. By 1980, some four dozen experiments had compared help given by bystanders who perceived themselves to be either alone or with others. Given unrestricted communication among the bystanders, a person was at least as likely to be helped by a lone bystander as when observed by several bystanders (Latané & Nida, 1981; Stalder, 2008). In Internet communication, people are more likely to respond helpfully to a request for help (such as from someone seeking the link to the campus library) if they believe they alone (and not several others as well) have received the request (Blair, Thompson, & Wuensch, 2005).

Sometimes, the victim was actually less likely to get help when many people were around. When Latané, James Dabbs (1975), and 145 collaborators "accidentally" dropped coins or pencils during 1497 elevator rides, they were helped 40 percent of the time when one other person was on the elevator and less than 20 percent of the time when there were six passengers.

Why does the presence of other bystanders sometimes inhibit helping? Latané and Darley surmised that as the number of bystanders increases, any given bystander is less likely to notice the incident, less likely to interpret the incident as a problem or emergency, and less likely to assume responsibility for taking action (Figure 8–4).

Noticing

Twenty minutes after Eleanor Bradley has fallen and broken her leg on a crowded city sidewalk, you come along. Your eyes are on the backs of the pedestrians in front of you (it is bad manners to stare at those you pass), and your private thoughts are on the day's events. Would you, therefore, be less likely to notice the injured woman than if the sidewalk were virtually deserted?

To find out, Latané and Darley (1968) had men fill out a questionnaire in a room, either by themselves or with two strangers. While they were working (and being observed through a one-way mirror), there was a staged emergency: Smoke poured into the room through a wall vent. Solitary students, who often glanced idly about the room while working, noticed the smoke almost immediately—usually in less than five seconds. Those in groups kept their eyes on their work. It typically took them about 20 seconds to notice the smoke.

Interpreting

Once we notice an ambiguous event, we must interpret it. Put yourself in the room filling with smoke. Though worried, you don't want to embarrass yourself by getting flustered. You glance at

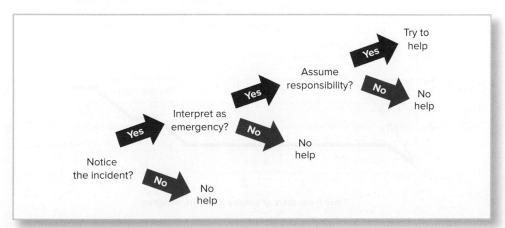

FIGURE 8–4

LATANÉ AND DARLEY'S DECISION TREE.

Only one path up the tree leads to helping. At each fork of the path, the presence of other bystanders may divert a person down a branch toward not helping. (Adapted from Darley & Latané, 1968)

the others. They look calm, indifferent. Assuming everything must be okay, you shrug it off and go back to work. Then one of the others notices the smoke and, noting your apparent unconcern, reacts similarly. This is an example of informational influence. Each person uses others' behaviour as clues to reality. Such misinterpretations can contribute to a delayed response to actual fires in offices, restaurants, and other multiple-occupancy settings (Canter, Breaux, & Sime, 1980).

The misinterpretations are fed by what Thomas Gilovich, Kenneth Savitsky, and Victoria Husted Medvec (1998) called an *illusion of transparency*—a tendency to overestimate others' ability to "read" our internal states. More than we usually suppose, our disgust, our deceit, and our alarm are opaque. Keenly aware of our emotions, we presume that others see right through us. Sometimes others do. But often we appear quite effectively to keep our cool. The result is what Chapter 7 called pluralistic *ignorance*—the assumption that others are thinking and feeling what we are. Thus, in emergencies, each person may think "I'm very concerned," but perceive others as not looking alarmed—"so maybe it's not an emergency."

So it happened in the actual experiment. When those working alone noticed the smoke, they usually hesitated a moment, then got up, walked over to the vent, felt, sniffed, and waved at the smoke, hesitated again, and then went to report it. In dramatic contrast, those in groups of three did not move. Among the 24 men in eight groups, only one person reported the smoke within the first four minutes (Figure 8–5). By the end of the six-minute experiment, the smoke was so thick it was obscuring the men's vision and they were rubbing their eyes and coughing. Still, in only three of the eight groups did even a single person leave to report the problem.

Equally interesting, the group's passivity affected its members' interpretations. What caused the smoke? "A leak in the air conditioning." "Chemistry labs in the building." "Steam pipes." "Truth gas." They offered many explanations. Not one said, "Fire." The group members, by serving as non-responsive models, influenced each other's interpretation of the situation.

That experimental dilemma parallels dilemmas each of us faces. Are the shrieks outside merely playful antics or the desperate screams of someone being assaulted? Is the boys' scuffling

FIGURE 8–5

THE SMOKE-FILLED ROOM EXPERIMENT.

Smoke pouring into the testing room was much more likely to be reported by individuals working alone than by three-person groups. (Data from Darley & Latané, 1968)

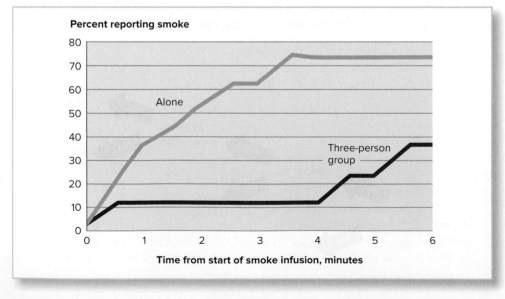

a friendly tussle or a vicious fight? Is the person slumped in the doorway sleeping, high on drugs, or seriously ill, perhaps in a diabetic coma? That surely was the question confronting those who passed by Sidney Brookins (Goleman, 1993; AP, 1993). Brookins, who had suffered a concussion when beaten, died after lying near the door to his apartment house for two days. That may also have been the question for those who in 2003 watched Brandon Vedas overdose and die online. As his life ebbed, his audience, which was left to wonder whether he was putting on an act, failed to decipher available clues to his whereabouts and to contact police (Nichols, 2003).

Unlike the smoke-filled-room experiment, however, each of these everyday situations involves someone in desperate need. To see if the same **bystander effect** occurs in such situations, Latané and Judith Rodin (1969) staged an experiment around a woman in distress. A female researcher set men to work on a questionnaire and then left through a curtained doorway to work in an adjacent office. Four minutes later, she could be heard (from a tape recorder) climbing on a chair to reach some papers. This was followed by a scream and a loud crash as the chair collapsed and she fell to the floor. "Oh, my God, my foot . . . I . . . I . . . can't move it," she sobbed. "Oh . . . my ankle . . . I . . . can't get this . . . thing . . . off me." Only after two minutes of moaning did she manage to make it out her office door.

Seventy percent of those alone when they overheard the "accident" came into the room or called out to offer help. Among pairs of strangers confronting the emergency, only 40 percent of the time did either person offer help. Those who did nothing apparently interpreted the situation as a non-emergency. "A mild sprain," said some. "I didn't want to embarrass her," explained others. This again demonstrates the bystander effect: As the number of people known to be aware of an emergency increases, any given person becomes less likely to help. For the victim, there is, therefore, no safety in numbers.

People's interpretations also affect their reactions to street crimes. In staging physical fights between a man and a woman, Lance Shotland and Margaret Straw (1976) found that bystanders intervened 65 percent of the time when the woman shouted, "Get away from me; I don't know you," but only 19 percent of the time when she shouted, "Get away from me; I don't know why I ever married you." People seemed to think it wasn't their business when the woman was married to the attacker. Spousal abuse, it seems, just doesn't trigger as much concern as stranger abuse. In such dangerous situations with a perpetrator present and intervention requiring physical risk, the bystander effect is less (Fischer et al., 2011).

Assuming responsibility

Failing to notice and misinterpretation is not the only cause of the bystander effect. Even when a shabby 14-year-old was the "burglar," when someone simultaneously broke into two adjacent cars, or when onlookers saw a different person breaking into the car than had just gotten out of it, Takooshian and Bodinger (1982) reported that there still was virtually no intervention. And what about those times when an emergency is obvious? Those who saw and heard Kitty Genovese's pleas for help correctly interpreted what was happening. But the lights and silhouetted figures in neighbouring windows told them that others were also watching. This diffused the responsibility for action.

bystander effect
the finding that a person is less likely to provide help when there are other bystanders

Interpretations matter: Is this man locked out of his car or is he a burglar? Our answer affects how we respond.

Few of us have observed a murder. But all of us have at times been slower to react to a need when others were present. Passing a stranded motorist on a highway, we are less likely to offer help than on a country road. To explore bystander inaction in clear emergencies, Darley and Latané (1968) simulated the Genovese drama. They placed people in separate rooms from which the participants would hear a victim crying for help. To create this situation, Darley and Latané asked some students to discuss their problems with university life over a laboratory intercom. They told the students that to guarantee their anonymity, no one would be visible, nor would the experimenter eavesdrop. During the ensuing discussion, the participants heard one person, when the experimenter turned his microphone on, lapse into an epileptic seizure. With increasing intensity and speech difficulty, he pleaded for someone to help.

Of those led to believe they were the only listener, 85 percent left their room to seek help. Of those who believed four others also overheard the victim, only 31 percent went for help. Were those who didn't respond apathetic and indifferent? When the experimenter came in to end the experiment, she did not find this response. Most immediately expressed concern. Many had trembling hands and sweating palms. They believed an emergency had occurred but were undecided whether to act.

After the smoke-filled room, the woman-in-distress, and the seizure experiments, Latané and Darley asked the participants whether the presence of others had influenced them. We know the others had a dramatic effect. Yet the participants almost invariably denied the influence. The typical reply? "I was aware of the others, but I would have reacted just the same if they weren't there." This response reinforces a familiar point: We often do not know why we do what we do. That is why experiments such as these are revealing. A survey of uninvolved bystanders following a real emergency would have left the bystander effect hidden.

Responsibility diffusion: The nine paparazzi photographers on the scene immediately after Princess Diana's car accident all had cellphones. With one exception, no one called for help. Their almost unanimous explanation was that they assumed "someone else" had already called (Sancton, 1997).

Further experiments revealed situations in which the presence of others sometimes did not inhibit people from offering help. Irving Piliavin and his colleagues (1969) staged an emergency in a laboratory on wheels, the unwitting subjects being 4450 riders of the subway. On each of 103 occasions, a confederate entered a subway car and stood in the centre next to a pole. After the train pulled out of the station, he staggered, then collapsed. When the victim carried a cane, one or more bystanders almost always promptly offered help. Even when the victim carried a bottle and smelled of liquor, he was often promptly offered aid—aid that was especially prompt when several male bystanders were close by. Why? Did the presence of other passengers provide a sense of security to those who helped? Was it because the situation was unambiguous? (The passengers couldn't help noticing and realizing what was happening.)

To test this latter possibility, Linda Solomon, Henry Solomon, and Ronald Stone (1978) conducted experiments in which people either saw and heard someone's distress, as in the subway experiment, or only heard it, as in the woman-in-distress experiment (leaving the situation more open to interpretation). When the emergencies were very clear, those in groups were only slightly less likely to help than were those alone. When the emergencies were somewhat ambiguous, however, the subjects in groups were far less likely to help than were solitary bystanders.

Most people who live in large cities are seldom alone in public places, which helps account for why city people often are less helpful than country people. *Compassion fatigue* and *sensory overload* from encountering so many people in need further restrain helping in large cities across the world (Yousif & Korte, 1995). This explains what happened when Robert Levine and colleagues (1994) approached several thousand people in 36 cities, dropping an unnoticed pen, asking for change, simulating a blind person needing help at a corner, and so forth. The bigger and more densely populated the city, the less likely people were to help. In large cities, bystanders are also more often strangers—whose increasing numbers depress helping. When bystanders are friends or people who share a group identity, increased numbers may, instead, increase helping (M. Levine & Crowther, 2008).

Compassion fatigue helps explain why those seeking help receive fewer responses from city people than from country people.

Levine and his collaborators (R. V. Levine, 2001; R. V. Levine, 2003; R. V. Levine, Norenzayan, & Philbrick, 2001) found that willingness to help strangers also varies around the world (Figure 8-6). People in economically advanced countries tended to offer less help to strangers, and those in cultures marked by amiable and agreeable "simpatia" (in Spanish) or "simpatico" (in Portuguese) were more helpful.

Nations, too, have often been bystanders to catastrophes, even to genocide. As 750 000 people were murdered in Rwanda, we all stood by. "With many potential actors, each feels less responsible," noted Ervin Staub (1997a). "It's not our responsibility," say the leaders of unaffected nations. Psychologist Peter Suedfeld (2000)—like Staub, a Holocaust survivor—notes that the diffusion of responsibility also helps explain "why the vast majority of European citizens stood idly by during the persecution, removal, and killing of their Jewish compatriots."

Revisiting research ethics

These experiments raise an ethical issue. Is it right to force unwitting people to overhear someone's apparent collapse? Were the researchers in the seizure experiment ethical when they forced people to decide whether to interrupt their discussion to report the problem? Would you object to being in such a study? Note that it would have been impossible to get your "informed consent"; doing so would have destroyed the experiment's cover.

The researchers were always careful to debrief the laboratory participants. After explaining the seizure experiment, probably the most stressful, the experimenter gave the participants a questionnaire. One hundred percent said the deception was justified and that they would be willing to take part in similar experiments in the future. None reported feeling angry at the experimenter. Other researchers have confirmed that the overwhelming majority of participants in such experiments say that their participation was both instructive and ethically justified (Schwartz & Gottlieb, 1981). In field experiments, an accomplice assisted the victim if no one else did, thus reassuring bystanders that the problem was being dealt with.

Remember that the social psychologist has a twofold ethical obligation: to protect the participants and to enhance human welfare by discovering influences upon human behaviour. Such discoveries can alert us to unwanted influences and show us how we might exert positive

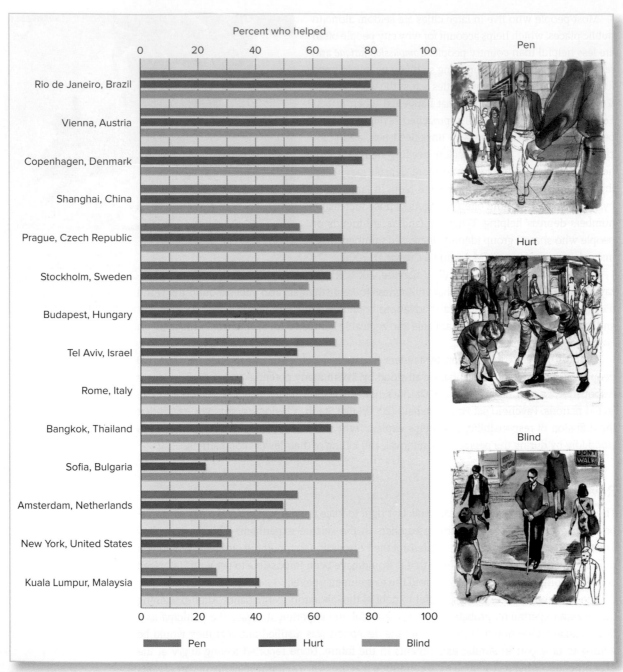

FIGURE 8–6

A WORLD OF DIFFERENCE IN HELPING STRANGERS.

To compare helping in different cities and cultures, Robert Levine and his collaborators would "accidentally" drop a pen, drop magazines while limping with an apparently injured leg, or feign blindness when approaching an intersection as the light turned green. Those dropping a pen in Rio were, for example, four times more likely to be helped than those doing so in New York City or Kuala Lumpur. (This is a sample of data from 14 countries.) (Adapted from R. V. Levine. [2003]. The kindness of strangers. *American Scientist, 91,* 226–233.)

influences. The ethical principle seems to be this: After protecting participants' welfare, social psychologists fulfill their responsibility to society by giving us insight into our behaviour.

HELPING WHEN SOMEONE ELSE DOES

Imagine hearing a crash followed by sobs and moans. If another bystander said, "Uh oh. This is an emergency! We've got to do something," would this stimulate others to help?

The evidence is clear: Prosocial models do promote prosoical behaviour. Here are some examples:

- In one field study, James Bryan and Mary Ann Test (1967) found that drivers were more likely to offer help to a female driver with a flat tire if a quarter-mile (0.4 km) earlier they witnessed someone helping another woman change a tire.

- In another experiment, Bryan and Test observed that Christmas shoppers were more likely to drop money in a Salvation Army kettle if they had just seen someone else do the same.

- Philippe Rushton and Anne Campbell (1977) found British adults more willing to donate blood if they were approached after observing a confederate consent to donating.

- A glimpse of extraordinary human kindness and charity—such as we gave you in the examples of heroic altruism at this chapter's outset—often triggers what Jonathan Haidt (2003) called *elevation,* "a distinctive feeling in the chest of warmth and expansion" that may provoke chills, tears, and throat-clenching and that often inspires people to become more self-giving.

> *"We are, in truth, more than half what we are by imitation. The great point is, to choose good models and to study them with care."*
> LORD *CHESTERFIELD, LETTERS, JANUARY* 18, 1750

One of these findings is especially meaningful for parents: Models sometimes contradict in practice what they preach. Parents may tell their children, "Do as I say, not as I do." Experiments show that children learn moral judgments from both what they hear preached and what they see practised (Rice & Grusec, 1975; Rushton, 1975). When exposed to hypocrites, they imitate: They say what the model says and do what the model does.

TIME PRESSURES

Darley and Batson (1973) discerned another determinant of helping in the Good Samaritan parable. The priest and the Levite were both busy, important people, probably hurrying to their duties. The lowly Samaritan was perhaps less pressed for time. To see whether people in a hurry would behave as the priest and Levite did, Darley and Batson cleverly staged the situation described in the parable.

After collecting their thoughts prior to recording a brief extemporaneous talk (which, for half the participants, was on the Good Samaritan parable), theological seminary students were directed to a recording studio in an adjacent building. En route, they passed a man sitting slumped in a doorway, head down, coughing and groaning. Some of the students had been sent off nonchalantly:

"It will be a few minutes before they're ready for you, but you might as well head on over." Of these, almost two-thirds stopped to offer help. Others were told, "Oh, you're late. They were expecting you a few minutes ago . . . so you'd better hurry." Of these, only 10 percent offered help.

Reflecting on these findings, Darley and Batson remarked:

> A person not in a hurry may stop and offer help to a person in distress. A person in a hurry is likely to keep going. Ironically, he is likely to keep going even if he is hurrying to speak on the parable of the Good Samaritan, thus inadvertently confirming the point of the parable. (Indeed, on several occasions, a seminary student going to give his talk on the parable of the Good Samaritan literally stepped over the victim as he hurried on his way!) (p. 107)

Are we being unfair to the seminary students, who were, after all, hurrying to help the experimenter? Perhaps they keenly felt the social-responsibility norm but found it pulling them two ways—toward the experimenter and toward the victim. In another enactment of the Good Samaritan situation, Batson and his associates (1978) directed 40 university students to an experiment in another building. Half were told they were late; half knew they had plenty of time. Half thought their participation was vitally important to the experimenter; half thought it was not essential. The results: Those on their way to an unimportant appointment usually stopped to help. But people seldom stopped to help if, like the White Rabbit in *Alice's Adventures in Wonderland,* they were late for a very important date.

Can we conclude that those who were rushed were callous? Did the seminarians notice the victim's distress and then consciously choose to ignore it? No. In their hurry, they never fully grasped the situation. Harried, preoccupied, rushing to meet a deadline, they simply did not take time to tune in to the person in need. As social psychologists have so often observed, their behaviour was influenced more by context than by conviction.

SIMILARITY TO THE VICTIM

Because similarity is conducive to liking, and liking is conducive to helping, we are more empathic and helpful toward those similar to us (Miller, Kozu, & Davis, 2001). This similarity bias applies to both dress and beliefs. Tim Emswiller and his fellow researchers (1971) had confederates, dressed either conservatively or in counter-culture garb, approach "conservative" or "hip" students seeking money for a phone call. Fewer than half the students did the favour for those dressed differently than themselves. Two-thirds did so for those dressed similarly. Likewise, Scottish shoppers in a more anti-gay era were less willing to make change for someone if the person wore a T-shirt with a pro-gay slogan (Gray, Russell, & Blockley, 1991).

No face is more familiar than one's own. That explains why, when Lisa DeBruine (2002) had McMaster University students play an interactive game with a supposed other player, they were more trusting and generous when the other person's pictured face had some features of their own morphed into it (Figure 8–7). In me I trust. Even just sharing a birthday, a first name, or a fingerprint pattern leads people to respond more to a request for help (Burger et al., 2004).

● WHO HELPS?

Surely some characteristics must distinguish the Mother Teresa types. Faced with identical situations, some people will respond helpfully, and others won't bother. Who are the likely helpers?

We have considered internal influences on the decision to help (such as guilt and mood) and external influences as well (such as social norms, number of bystanders, time pressure, and similarity to the victim). We also need to consider the helper's personality and gender.

PERSONALITY TRAITS

Surely some traits must distinguish the Mother Teresa types from others. Faced with identical situations, some people will respond helpfully, while others won't bother. Who are the likely helpers?

For many years, social psychologists were unable to discover a single personality trait that predicted altruistic behaviour with anything close to the predictive power of the situation, guilt, and mood factors. Modest relationships were found between helping and certain personality variables, such as need for social approval. But by and large, the personality tests were unable to identify the helpers. Studies of rescuers of Jews in Nazi Europe reveal a similar conclusion: Although the social context clearly influenced willingness to help, there was no definable set of altruistic personality traits (Darley, 1995).

If that has a familiar ring, it could be from a similar conclusion by conformity researchers (Chapter 6): Conformity, too, seemed more influenced by the situation than by measurable personality traits. Perhaps, though, you recall from Chapter 2 that who we are does affect what we do. Attitude and trait measures seldom predict a specific act, which is what most experiments on prosocial behaviour measure, in contrast to the lifelong altruism of someone like Mother Teresa. But they better predict average behaviour across many situations more accurately.

Personality researchers have responded to the challenge. First, they have found individual differences in helpfulness, and they have shown that these differences persist over time and are noticed by a person's peers (Hampson, 1984; Rushton, Chrisjohn, & Fekken, 1981). Some people are reliably more helpful.

Second, they are gathering clues to the network of traits that predispose a person to helpfulness. Those high in emotionality, empathy, and self-efficacy are most likely to be concerned and helpful (Eisenberg et al., 1991; Krueger, Hicks, & McGue, 2001; Walker & Frimer, 2007).

Third, personality influences how particular people react to particular situations (Carlo et al., 1991; Romer, Gruder, & Lizzadro, 1986; Wilson & Petruska, 1984). Those high in self-monitoring

> *"There are . . . reasons why personality should be rather unimportant in determining people's reactions to the emergency. For one thing, the situational forces affecting a person's decision are so strong."*
> BIBB LATANÉ AND JOHN DARLEY (1970, P. 115)

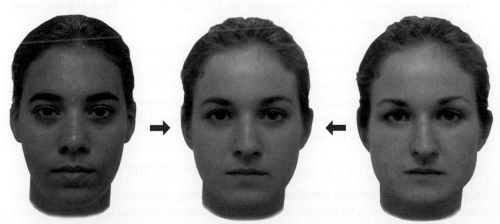

FIGURE 8–7

SIMILARITY BREEDS COOPERATION.

Lisa DeBruine (2002) morphed participants' faces (left) with strangers' faces (right) to make the composite faces (centre)—toward whom the participants were more generous than toward the stranger.

are attuned to the expectations of others and are especially helpful if they think helpfulness will be socially rewarded (White & Gerstein, 1987). Others' opinions matter less to internally guided, low self-monitoring people.

GENDER

This interaction of person and situation also appears in the 172 studies that have compared the helpfulness of nearly 50 000 male and female subjects. After analyzing these results, Alice Eagly and Maureen Crowley (1986) reported that when faced with potentially dangerous situations in which strangers need help (such as with a flat tire or a fall in a subway), men more often help. Eagly (2009) also reported that among 6767 individuals who have received the Carnegie medal for heroism in saving human life, 90 percent have been men.

Would gender norms—"women and children first"—more likely come into play in situations when people have time to reflect on social norms (as opposed to acting instinctively, on impulse)? To explore this possibility, some fiendish experimenter might wish to assign passengers to fast- or slow-sinking ships and observe behaviour. Actually, note Zurich researcher Bruno Frey and his colleagues (2010), the course of human events has conducted this experiment. In 1915, a German U-boat sank the passenger liner, the *Lusitania*, in a panicked 18 minutes, with women on board being 1 percent less likely to survive than men. In 1912, the *Titanic*, carrying a similar mix of passengers, hit an iceberg and took nearly three hours to sink—and women were 53 percent more likely to survive than men. In this natural experiment, time enabled prosocial behaviour and the activation of gender norms.

In safer situations, such as volunteering to help with an experiment or spend time with children with developmental disabilities, women are slightly more likely to help. In one survey of 272 036 university students, 63 percent of men and 75 percent of women rated "helping others in difficulty" as "very important" or "essential" (Pryor et al., 2007). Women also have been as likely as, or more likely than, men to risk death as Holocaust rescuers, to donate a kidney, and to volunteer with the Peace Corps and Doctors of the World (Becker & Eagly, 2004). Faced with a friend's problems, women respond with greater empathy and spend more time helping (George et al., 1998). Thus, the gender difference interacts with (depends on) the situation.

● HOW CAN WE INCREASE HELPING?

To increase helping, we can reverse the factors that inhibit helping, or we can teach altruistic norms and socialize people to see themselves as helpful.

As social scientists, our goal is to understand human behaviour, thus also suggesting ways to improve it. So, how might we apply research-based understanding to increase helping? One way to promote prosocial behaviour is to reverse those factors that inhibit it. Given that hurried, preoccupied people are less likely to help, can we think of ways to encourage them to slow down and turn their attention outward? If the presence of others diminishes each bystander's sense of responsibility, how can we enhance responsibility?

REDUCE AMBIGUITY, INCREASE RESPONSIBILITY

If Latané and Darley's decision tree (Figure 8–4) describes the dilemmas bystanders face, then assisting people to interpret an incident correctly and to assume responsibility should increase their involvement. Leonard Bickman and his colleagues (1975, 1979; Bickman & Green, 1977) tested this presumption in a series of experiments on crime reporting. In each, supermarket or bookstore shoppers witnessed a shoplifting. Some witnesses had seen signs that attempted to sensitize them to shoplifting and to inform them how to report it. But the signs had little effect. Other witnesses heard a bystander interpret the incident: "Say, look at her. She's shoplifting. She put that into her purse." (The bystander then left to look for a lost child.) Still others heard this person add, "We saw it. We should report it. It's our responsibility." Both face-to-face comments substantially boosted reporting of the crime.

The potency of personal influence is no longer in doubt. Robert Foss (1978) surveyed several hundred blood donors and found that neophyte donors, unlike veterans, were usually there at someone's personal invitation. Leonard Jason and his collaborators (1984) confirmed that personal appeals for blood donation are much more effective than posters and media announcements—if the personal appeals come from friends.

Personal appeal

Personalized nonverbal appeals can also be effective. Mark Snyder and his co-workers (1974; Omoto & Snyder, 2002) found that hitchhikers doubled the number of ride offers by looking drivers straight in the eye, and that most AIDS volunteers got involved through someone's personal influence. A personal approach makes people feel less anonymous, more responsible.

Henry Solomon and Linda Solomon (1978; Solomon et al., 1981) explored ways to reduce anonymity. They found that bystanders who had identified themselves to one another—by name, age, and so forth—were more likely to offer aid to a sick person than were anonymous bystanders. Similarly, when a female experimenter caught the eye of another shopper and gave her a warm smile prior to stepping on an elevator, that shopper was far more likely than other shoppers to offer help when the experimenter later said, "Damn. I've left my glasses. Can anyone tell me what floor the umbrellas are on?" Even a trivial momentary conversation with someone ("Excuse me, aren't you Suzie Spear's sister?" "No, I'm not") dramatically increased the person's later helpfulness.

Helpfulness also increases when one expects to meet the victim and other witnesses again. Using a laboratory intercom system, Jody Gottlieb and Charles Carver (1980) led students to believe they were discussing problems of university living with other students. (Actually, the other discussants were tape-recorded.) When one of the supposed fellow discussants had a choking fit and cried out for help, she was helped most quickly by subjects who believed they would soon be meeting the discussants face-to-face. In short, anything that personalizes bystanders—a personal request, eye contact, stating one's name, anticipation of interaction—increases willingness to help. In experiments, restaurant patrons have tipped more when their servers introduced themselves by name, touched guests on the arm or shoulder, sat or squatted at the table during the service encounter, and wrote friendly messages on checks before they gave them to customers (Leodoro & Lynn, 2007; Schirmer et al., 2011).

Personal treatment makes bystanders more self-aware and, therefore, more attuned to their own altruistic ideals. Recall from earlier chapters that people made self-aware by acting in front of a mirror or TV camera exhibited increased consistency between attitudes and actions. By contrast, *deindividuated* people were less responsible. Thus, circumstances that promote self-awareness—name tags, being watched and evaluated, undistracted quiet—should also increase helping.

Shelley Duval, Virginia Duval, and Robert Neely (1979) confirmed this. They showed some women their own image on a TV screen or had them complete a biographical questionnaire just before giving them a chance to contribute time and money to people in need. Those made self-aware contributed more. Similarly, pedestrians who have just had their picture taken by someone became more likely to help another pedestrian pick up dropped envelopes (Hoover, Wood, & Knowles, 1983). And among those who had just seen themselves in a mirror, 70 percent of Italian pedestrians helped a stranger by mailing a postcard, as did 13 percent of others approached (Abbate et al., 2006). Self-aware people more often put their ideals into practice.

GUILT AND CONCERN FOR SELF-IMAGE

Previously, we noted that people who feel guilty will act to reduce guilt and restore their self-worth. Can awakening people's guilt therefore increase their desire to help? Have university students think about their past transgressions and they become more likely to agree to volunteer to help with a school project.

A research team led by Richard Katzev (1978) experimented with guilt-induced helping in everyday contexts. When visitors to an art museum disobeyed a "Please do not touch" sign, experimenters reprimanded some of them: "Please don't touch the objects. If everyone touches them, they will deteriorate." Likewise, when visitors to a zoo fed unauthorized food to the bears, some of them were admonished with, "Hey, don't feed unauthorized food to the animals. Don't you know it could hurt them?" In both cases, 58 percent of the now guilt-laden subjects shortly thereafter offered help to another experimenter who had "accidentally" dropped something. Of those not reprimanded, only one-third helped. Guilt-laden people are helpful people.

People also care about their public image. When Robert Cialdini and his colleagues (1975) asked some of their university students to chaperone delinquent children on a zoo trip, only 32 percent agreed to do so. With other students, the questioner first made a very large request—that the students commit two years as volunteer counsellors to delinquent children. After getting the *door-in-the-face* in response to this request (all refused), the questioner then counter-offered with the chaperoning request, saying, in effect, "Okay, if you won't do that, would you do just this much?" With this **door-in-the-face technique**, nearly twice as many—56 percent—agreed to help.

Cialdini and David Schroeder (1976) offered another practical way to trigger concern for self-image: Ask for a contribution so small that it's hard to say no without feeling like a Scrooge. Cialdini (1995) discovered this when a United Way canvasser came to his door. As she solicited his contribution, he was mentally preparing his refusal—until she said magic words that demolished his financial excuse: "Even a penny will help." "I had been neatly finessed into compliance," recalled Cialdini. "And there was another interesting feature of our exchange as well. When I stopped coughing (I really had choked on my attempted rejection), I gave her not the penny she had mentioned but the amount I usually allot to legitimate charity solicitors. At that, she thanked me, smiled innocently, and moved on."

door-in-the-face technique
a strategy for gaining a concession. After someone first turns down a large request (the door-in-the-face), the same requester counter-offers with a more reasonable request.

Door-in-the-face technique.

HI & LOIS © King Features Syndicate.

Was Cialdini's response atypical? To find out, he and Schroeder had a solicitor approach suburbanites. When the solicitor said he or she was collecting money for the Cancer Society, 29 percent contributed an average of $1.44 each. When the solicitor added, "Even a penny will help," 50 percent contributed an average of $1.54 each. When James Weyant (1984) repeated this experiment, he found similar results: The "even a penny will help" boosted the number contributing from 39 to 57 percent. And when 6000 people were solicited by mail for the Cancer Society, those asked for small amounts were more likely to give—and gave no less on aver-age—than those asked for larger amounts (Weyant & Smith, 1987). When approaching previous donors, bigger requests (within reason) do elicit bigger donations (Doob & McLaughlin, 1989). But with door-to-door solicitation, there is more success with requests for small contributions, which are difficult to turn down and still allow the person to maintain an altruistic self-image.

Labelling people as helpful can also strengthen a helpful self-image. After they had made a charitable contribution, Robert Kraut (1973) told women, "You are a generous person." Two weeks later, these women were more willing than those not labelled this way to contribute to a different charity.

SOCIALIZING PROSOCIAL BEHAVIOUR

If we can learn prosocial behaviour, then how might we teach it? Here are five ways.

Teaching moral inclusion

Rescuers of Jews in Nazi Europe, relief workers in foreign countries, and volunteers at homeless shelters share at least one thing in common: **moral inclusion**. They include people who differ from themselves within the human circle to which their moral values and rules of justice apply. These people are morally inclusive, as illustrated by one rescuer who faked a pregnancy on behalf of a pregnant hidden Jew—thus including the soon-to-be-born child within the circle of her own children's identities (Fogelman, 1994).

moral inclusion
regarding others as within your circle of moral concern

Moral exclusion—omitting certain people from one's circle of moral concern—has the oppo-site effect. It justifies all sorts of harm, from discrimination to genocide (Opotow, 1990; Staub, 1990; Tyler & Lind, 1990). Exploitation or cruelty becomes acceptable, even appropriate, toward those we regard as undeserving or as non-persons. The Nazis excluded Jews from their moral community; so does anyone who participates in enslavement, death squads, or torture. To a lesser extent, moral exclusion describes any of us who concentrate our concerns, favours, and financial inheritance on "our people" (for example, our children) to the exclusion of others.

moral exclusion
the perception of certain individuals or groups as outside the boundary within which you apply moral values and rules of fairness

We easily become numbed by impersonal big numbers of out-group fatalities, note Paul Slovic (2007) and Elizabeth Dunn and Claire Ashton-James (2008). People presume that they would be more upset about a hurricane that killed 5000 rather than 50 people. But whether Dunn and Ashton-James told people that Hurricane Katrina claimed 50, 500, 1000, or 5000 lives, their sadness was unaffected by the number. Ditto for the scale of other tragedies, includ-ing a forest fire in Spain and the war in Iraq. "If I look at the mass I will never act," said Mother Teresa. "If I look at the one, I will." Shown a single victim, a 7-year-old girl named Rokia, people responded with more money for a hunger charity than when told the organization was working to save millions (Slovic & Västfjäll, 2010).

A first step toward socializing prosocial behaviour is, therefore, to counter the natural in-group bias favouring kin and tribe by broadening the range of people whose well-being concerns us. Daniel Batson (1983) noted how religious teachings do this. They extend the reach of kin-linked prosocial behaviour by urging "brotherly and sisterly" love toward all "children of

God" in the whole human "family." If everyone is part of our family, then everyone has a moral claim on us. The boundaries between "us" and "them" fade. Inviting advantaged people to put themselves in others' shoes, to imagine how less advantaged people feel, also helps (Batson et al., 2003). To "do unto others as you would have them do unto you," one must take the others' perspective (see Figure 8–8).

Modelling prosocial behaviour

Previously, we noted that seeing unresponsive bystanders makes us less likely to help. People reared by extremely punitive parents, as were many delinquents and chronic criminals, also show much less of the empathy and principled caring that typify altruists.

If we see or read about someone helping, we are more likely to offer assistance. It's better, found Robert Cialdini (2003), not to publicize rampant tax cheating, littering, and teen drinking, and instead to emphasize—to define a norm of—people's widespread honesty, cleanliness, and abstinence. In one experiment, researchers asked visitors not to remove petrified wood from along the paths of the U.S. Petrified Forest National Park. Some subjects were also told that "past visitors have removed the petrified wood." Those subjects who were told that "past visitors have left the petrified wood" in order to preserve the park were much less likely to pick up samples placed along a path.

Modelling effects were also apparent in the families of European Christians who risked their lives to rescue Jews in the 1930s and 1940s and in the civil rights activists of the late 1950s. In both cases, these exceptional altruists had warm and close relationships with at least one parent who was, similarly, a strong "moralist" or committed to humanitarian causes (London, 1970; Oliner & Oliner, 1988; Rosenhan, 1970). Their family—and often their friends and church—had taught them the norm of helping and caring for others. This *prosocial value orientation* led them to include people from other groups in their circle of moral concern and to feel responsible for others' welfare (Staub, 1989, 1991, 1992).

Do television's positive models promote helping, much as its aggressive portrayals promote aggression? Prosocial TV models have actually had even greater effects than antisocial models. Susan Hearold (1986) statistically combined 108 comparisons of prosocial programs with neutral programs or no program. She found that, on average, "If the viewer watched prosocial programs instead of neutral programs, he would [at least temporarily] be elevated from the 50th to the 74th percentile in prosocial behaviour—typically altruism."

FIGURE 8–8
PRACTICAL WAYS
TO INCREASE
HELPING.

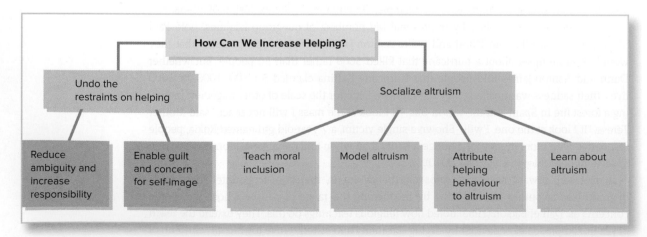

In one such study, researchers Lynette Friedrich and Aletha Stein (1973; Stein & Friedrich, 1972) showed preschool children *Mister Rogers' Neighborhood* episodes each day for four weeks as part of their nursery school program. (*Mister Rogers* aimed to enhance young children's social and emotional development.) During this viewing period, children from less educated homes became more cooperative, helpful, and likely to state their feelings. In a follow-up study, kindergartners who viewed four *Mister Rogers* programs were able to state its prosocial content, both on a test and in puppet play (Friedrich & Stein, 1975; also Coates, Pusser, & Goodman, 1976).

Other media also effectively model prosocial behaviour. Recent studies show positive effects on attitudes or behaviour from playing prosocial video games and listening to prosocial music lyrics (Gentile et al., 2009; Greitemeyer, 2009; Greitemeyer, Osswald, & Brauer, 2010). For example, playing *Lemmings,* where the goal is to help others, increases later real-life empathy and helping in response to another's misfortune (Greitemeyer & Osswald, 2010; Greitemeyer et al., 2010). Listening to prosocial songs, such as Michael Jackson's "Heal the World," made listeners more likely to help someone pick up dropped pencils and less likely to say harsh things about a job candidate or give someone a large dose of disliked chili sauce (Greitemeyer, 2009, 2011).

Warren Buffett earned the admiration of millions by pledging to give away 99 percent of his fortune to philanthropic causes.

Learning by doing

Ervin Staub (2005) has shown that just as immoral behaviour fuels immoral attitudes, so helping increases future helping. Children and adults learn by doing. In a series of studies with children near age 12, Staub and his students found that after children were induced to make toys for hospitalized children or for an art teacher, they became more helpful. So were children after teaching younger children to make puzzles or use first aid.

When children act helpfully, they develop helping-related values, beliefs, and skills, noted Staub. Helping also contributes to satisfying their needs for a positive self-concept. On a larger scale, community service and volunteer programs woven into a school curriculum have been shown to increase later citizen involvement, social responsibility, cooperation, and leadership (Andersen, 1998; Putnam, 2000). Attitudes follow behaviour. Helpful actions, therefore, promote the self-perception that one is caring and helpful, which in turn promotes further helping.

Attributing helpful behaviour to altruistic motives

Another clue to socializing prosocial behaviour comes from research on the overjustification effect (see also Chapter 4): When the justification for an act is more than sufficient, the person may attribute the act to the extrinsic justification rather than to an inner motive. Rewarding people for doing what they would do anyway undermines intrinsic motivation. We can state the principle positively: By providing people with just enough justification to prompt a good deed (weaning them from bribes and threats when possible), we may increase their pleasure in doing such deeds on their own.

Daniel Batson and his associates (1978, 1979) put the overjustification phenomenon to work. In several experiments, they found that University of Kansas students felt most altruistic after they agreed to help someone without payment or implied social pressure. When pay had been offered or social pressures were present, people felt less altruistic after helping.

In another experiment, the researchers led students to attribute a helpful act to compliance ("I guess we really don't have a choice") or to compassion ("The guy really needs help"). Later, when the students were asked to volunteer their time to a local service agency, 25 percent of those who had been led to perceive their previous helpfulness as mere compliance now volunteered; of those led to see themselves as compassionate, 60 percent volunteered. The moral? When people wonder, "Why am I helping?" it's best if the circumstances enable them to answer, "Because help was needed, and I am a caring, giving, helpful person."

As you may recall from Chapter 4, rewards undermine intrinsic motivation when they function as controlling bribes. An unanticipated compliment, however, can make people feel competent and worthy. When Joe is coerced with "If you quit being chicken and give blood, we'll win the fraternity prize for most donations," he isn't likely to attribute his donation to altruism. When Jocelyn is rewarded with "That's terrific that you'd choose to take an hour out of such a busy week to give blood," she's more likely to walk away with an altruistic self-image—and thus to contribute again (Piliavin et al., 1982; Thomas & Batson, 1981; Thomas, Batson, & Coke, 1981).

To predispose more people to help in situations where most don't, it can also pay to induce a tentative positive commitment, from which people may infer their own helpfulness. Delia Cioffi and Randy Garner (1998) observed that only about 5 percent of students responded to a campus blood drive after receiving an e-mail announcement a week ahead. They asked other students to reply to the announcement with a "yes," "if you think you probably will donate." Of these, 29 percent replied and the actual donation rate was 8 percent. They asked a third group to reply with a "no" if they did not anticipate donating. Now 71 percent implied they might give (by not replying). Imagine yourself in this third group. Might you have decided not to say no because, after all, you are a caring person so there's a chance you might give. And might that thought have opened you to persuasion as you encountered campus posters and flyers during the ensuing week? That apparently is what happened, because 12 percent of these students—more than twice the normal rate—showed up to offer their blood.

Inferring that one is a helpful person seems also to have happened when Dariusz Dolinski (2000) stopped pedestrians on the streets of Wroclaw, Poland, and asked them for directions to a non-existent "Zubrzyckiego Street" or to an illegible address. Everyone tried unsuccessfully to help. After doing so, about two-thirds (twice the number of those not given the opportunity to try to help) agreed when asked by someone 100 metres farther down the road to watch their heavy bag or bicycle for five minutes.

Learning about prosocial behaviour

Researchers have found another way to boost prosocial behaviour, one that provides a happy conclusion to this chapter. Some social psychologists worry that as people become more aware of social psychology's findings, their behaviour may change, thus invalidating the findings (Gergen, 1982). Will learning about the factors that inhibit helping reduce their influence? Sometimes, such "enlightenment" is not our problem but one of our goals.

Experiments by Arthur Beaman and his colleagues (1978) revealed that once people understand why the presence of bystanders inhibits helping, they become more likely to help in group situations. The researchers used a lecture to inform some students how bystander inaction can affect the interpretation of an emergency and feelings of responsibility. Other students heard either a different lecture or no lecture at all. Two weeks later, as part of a different experiment in a different location, the participants found themselves walking (with an unresponsive confederate) past someone slumped over or past a person sprawled beneath a bicycle. Of those who had not heard the helping lecture, a fourth paused to offer help; twice as many of those who had been "enlightened" did so.

Having read this chapter, you, too, have perhaps changed. As you come to understand what influences people's responses, will your attitudes and your behaviour be the same?

⋯▶ SUMMING UP

WHY DO WE HELP?

- Because of social exchange: We help those who have helped us.
- Because social norms dictate helping in some situations.
- To aid our survival—helping kin and those who may help us make it more likely for us to pass on our genes.

WHEN WILL WE HELP?

- When there are few bystanders.
- When we observe someone else helping.
- When we are not in a hurry.
- When the person needing help is similar to us.

WHO HELPS?

- People high in emotionality, empathy, and self-efficacy.
- Men in risky situations, but women in less risky situations. Overall, men and women do not differ in helpfulness.

HOW CAN WE INCREASE HELPING?

- By reducing ambiguity and increasing responsibility.
- By evoking feelings of guilt.
- By socializing prosocial behaviour.

CHAPTER NINE
Aggression: Hurting Others

CHAPTER OUTLINE

- WHAT IS AGGRESSION?

- WHAT ARE SOME THEORIES OF AGGRESSION?

- WHAT ARE SOME INFLUENCES ON AGGRESSION?

- HOW CAN AGGRESSION BE REDUCED?

*D*uring the last century, 250 wars killed 110 million people, enough to populate a "nation of the dead" with more than the combined population of France, Belgium, the

> *"Every gun that is made, every warship launched, every rocket fired signifies, in the final sense, a theft from those who hunger and are not fed, those who are cold and are not clothed."*
> PRESIDENT DWIGHT EISENHOWER, SPEECH TO THE AMERICAN SOCIETY OF NEWSPAPER EDITORS, 1953

Netherlands, Denmark, Finland, Norway, and Sweden (Sivard, 1996). The tolls came not only from the world wars, but also from genocides, including the 1915 to 1923 genocide of 1 million Armenians by the Ottoman Empire, the 1971 Pakistani genocide of 3 million Bangladeshis, and the 1.5 million Cambodians murdered in a reign of terror starting in 1975 (Dutton, Boyanowsky, & Bond, 2005; Sternberg, 2003). As Hitler's genocide of millions of Jews, Stalin's genocide of millions of Russians, Mao's genocide of millions of Chinese, and the genocide of millions of Aboriginal Americans from the time of Columbus through the nineteenth century make plain, the human potential for extraordinary cruelty crosses cultures and races.

Less severe, but still harmful, aggression is even more common. In a survey of children across 35 countries, more than 1 out of 10 reported being bullied at school (Craig & Harel, 2004). Among a sample of Canadian middle school and high school students, half said they had been bullied online in the previous three months. Their experiences included being called names, having rumours spread about them, or having their private pictures distributed without their consent (Mishna et al., 2010).

> *"Is there any way of delivering mankind from the menace of war?"*
> ALBERT EINSTEIN, LETTER TO SIGMUND FREUD, 1932

Are we like the mythical Minotaur, half human, half beast? What explains that midsummer day in 1941 when the non-Jewish half of the Polish town of Jebwabne murdered the other half in a macabre frenzy of violence, leaving only a dozen or so survivors among the 1600 Jews (Gross, 2001)? Why would a university student broadcast his gay roommate's sexual encounter, driving him to suicide, as happened at Rutgers University in 2010? Why, in 2011, would a gunman in peaceful Norway bomb government buildings and then shoot and kill 69 people, mostly teenagers? What explains such monstrous behaviour? In this chapter, we ask the following:

- Is aggression biologically predisposed, or do we learn it?
- What circumstances prompt hostile outbursts?
- Do the media influence aggression?
- How might we reduce aggression?

First, however, we need to clarify the term *aggression*.

● WHAT IS AGGRESSION?

Should all harm be considered aggression? Are there different kinds of aggression that serve different goals?"

[different from assertiveness.]

The original Thugs, members of a criminal fraternity in northern India, were aggressing when between 1550 and 1850 they strangled more than 2 million people, and claimed to do so in the service of the goddess Kali. But people also use "aggressive" to describe a dynamic salesperson. Social psychologists distinguish such self-assured, energetic, go-getting behaviour from behaviour that hurts, harms, or destroys. The former is assertiveness, the latter aggression.

aggression
physical or verbal behaviour intended to hurt someone

To a social psychologist, **aggression** is physical or verbal behaviour intended to cause harm. This definition excludes unintentional harm, such as auto accidents or sidewalk collisions; it also excludes actions that may involve pain as an unavoidable side effect of helping someone, such as dental treatments or—in the extreme—assisted suicide. It includes kicks and slaps, threats and insults, even gossipy or snide "digs." It includes decisions during experiments about how much to hurt someone, such as how much electric shock to impose. It also includes destroying property, lying, and other behaviour whose goal is to hurt.

This definition covers two distinct types of aggression. Animals exhibit *social* aggression, characterized by displays of rage, and *silent* aggression, as when a predator stalks its prey. Social and silent aggressions involve separate brain regions. In humans, psychologists label the two types *hostile* and *instrumental* aggression. Hostile aggression springs from anger; its goal is to injure. Instrumental aggression aims to injure too—but only as a means to some other end.

Most terrorism is instrumental aggression. "What nearly all suicide terrorist campaigns have in common is a specific secular and strategic goal," concluded Robert Pape (2003) after studying all suicide bombings from 1980 to 2001. That goal is "to compel liberal democracies to withdraw military forces from territory that the terrorists consider to be their homeland." Terrorism is rarely committed by someone with a psychological pathology, noted Arie Kruglanski and Shira Fishman (2006); rather, it is a strategic tool used during conflict.

Most wars are instrumental aggression. In 2003, U.S. and British leaders justified attacking Iraq not as a hostile effort to kill Iraqis but as an instrumental act of liberation and of self-defence against presumed weapons of mass destruction. Adolescents who bully others—either verbally or physically—are also engaged in instrumental aggression, because they often seek to demonstrate their dominance and high status. In the strange hierarchy of adolescence, being mean and disliked can sometimes make you popular and revered (Salmivalli, 2009). Most murders, however, are hostile aggression. Approximately half erupt from arguments, while others result from romantic triangles, or from brawls while under the influence of alcohol or drugs (Ash, 1999). Such murders are impulsive, emotional outbursts—which helps explain why data from 110 nations show that enforcing the death penalty has not resulted in fewer homicides (Costanzo, 1998; Wilkes, 1987). Some murders and many other violent acts of retribution and sexual coercion, however, are instrumental (Felson, 2000). Most of Chicago's more than 1000 murders carried out by organized crime during the prohibition era and the years following were cool and calculated.

hostile aggression
aggression driven by anger and performed as an end in itself

instrumental aggression
aggression that is a means to some other end

● WHAT ARE SOME THEORIES OF AGGRESSION?

In analyzing causes of hostile and instrumental aggression, social psychologists have focused on three big ideas: biological influences, frustration, and learned behaviour.

AGGRESSION AS A BIOLOGICAL PHENOMENON

Philosophers have debated whether our human nature is fundamentally that of a benign, contented "noble savage" or that of a brute. The first view, argued by the eighteenth-century French philosopher Jean-Jacques Rousseau (1712–1778), blames society, not human nature, for social evils. The second, associated with the English philosopher Thomas Hobbes (1588–1679), sees society's laws as necessary to restrain and control the human brute. In the twentieth century, the "brutish" view—that aggressive drive is inborn and thus inevitable—was argued by Sigmund Freud in Vienna and Konrad Lorenz, an animal behaviour expert, in Germany.

"Our behaviour toward each other is the strangest, most unpredictable, and most unaccountable of all the phenomena with which we are obliged to live. In all of nature, there is nothing so threatening to humanity as humanity itself."
LEWIS THOMAS (1981)

BIOLOGICAL

① ## Instinct theory and evolutionary psychology

Freud speculated that human aggression springs from a self-destructive impulse. It redirects toward others the energy of a primitive death urge (the *death instinct*). Lorenz saw aggression as adaptive rather than self-destructive. Both agreed that aggression is instinctive behaviour (unlearned and universal). If not discharged, it supposedly builds up until it explodes or until an appropriate stimulus "releases" it, like a mouse releasing a mousetrap.

instinctive behaviour
an innate, unlearned behaviour pattern exhibited by all members of a species

The idea that aggression is an instinct collapsed as the list of supposed human instincts grew to include nearly every conceivable human behaviour. Nearly 6000 supposed instincts were enumerated in one 1924 survey of social science books (Barash, 1979). What the social scientists had tried to do was explain social behaviour by naming it. It's tempting to play this explaining-by-naming game: "Why do sheep stay together?" "Because of their herd instinct." "How do you know they have a herd instinct?" "Just look at them: They're always together!"

Instinct theory also fails to account for the variation in aggressiveness, from person to person and culture to culture. How would a shared human instinct for aggression explain the difference between the peaceful Iroquois before White invaders came and the hostile Iroquois after the invasion (Hornstein, 1976)? Although aggression is biologically influenced, the human propensity to aggress does not qualify as instinctive behaviour.

Throughout much of human history, men especially have found aggression adaptive, note evolutionary psychologists such as John Archer (2006) and Francis McAndrew (2009). Purposeful aggression improved the odds of survival and reproduction. The losers, notes McAndrew, "ran the risk of genetic annihilation." Aggression often occurs when males are competing with other males, or when a man's social status is challenged. "Violence committed against the right people at the right time was a ticket to social success," McAndrew observes.

Consider professional basketball player Charles Barkley, who was drinking in a bar in 1997 when a man threw a glass of water at him. Barkley promptly hurled the man through a plate-glass window—even though Barkley was not hurt by the water, even though the man might have retaliated, and even though Barkley was arrested within minutes of the assault. Nevertheless, witnesses praised Barkley in news reports, seemingly impressed by his aggression. When Barkley was asked if he regretted throwing the man through the window, he replied, "I regret we weren't on a higher floor" (Griskevicius et al., 2009).

Apparently, Barkley was not an isolated example. Across three experiments, college men motivated to increase their status were more aggressive toward others in face-to-face confrontations (Griskevicius et al., 2009). Status-based aggression also helps explain why aggression is highest during adolescence and early adulthood, when the competition for status and mates is the most intense. Although violence is less rewarded than it once was, young men scuffling for status and mates are still very much in evidence at many bars and campuses around the world.

② ## Neural influences

Because aggression is a complex behaviour, no one spot in the brain controls it. But researchers have found neural systems in both animals and humans that facilitate aggression. When the scientists activate these areas in the brain, hostility increases; when they deactivate them, hostility decreases. Docile animals can thus be provoked into rage, and raging animals into submission.

In one experiment, researchers placed an electrode in an aggression-inhibiting area of a domineering monkey's brain. A smaller monkey, given a button that activated the electrode, learned to push it every time the tyrant monkey became intimidating. Brain activation works with humans, too. After receiving painless electrical stimulation in her amygdala (a part of the brain core), one woman became enraged and smashed her guitar against the wall, barely missing her psychiatrist's head (Moyer, 1976, 1983).

Does this mean that violent people's brains are in some way abnormal? To find out, Adrian Raine and his colleagues (1998, 2000, 2005, 2008) used brain scans to measure brain activity in murderers and to measure the amount of grey matter in men with antisocial conduct disorder. They found that the prefrontal cortex, which acts like an emergency brake on deeper brain areas involved in aggressive behaviour, was 14 percent less active than normal in murderers (excluding those who had been abused by their parents) and 15 percent smaller in the antisocial men. As other studies of murderers and death-row inmates confirm, abnormal brains can contribute to abnormally aggressive behaviour (Davidson, Putnam, & Larson, 2000; Lewis, 1998; Pincus, 2001).

③ Genetic influences

Heredity influences the neural system's sensitivity to aggressive cues. It has long been known that animals of many species can be bred for aggressiveness. Sometimes, this is done for practical purposes (the breeding of guard dogs). Sometimes, breeding is done for research. Finnish psychologist Kirsti Lagerspetz (1979) took normal albino mice and bred the most aggressive ones together and the least aggressive ones together. After repeating the procedure for 26 generations, she had one set of fierce mice and one set of placid mice.

Aggressiveness similarly varies among individuals (Asher, 1987; Bettencourt et al., 2006; Denson, Pedersen, & Miller, 2006; Olweus, 1979). Our temperaments—how intense and reactive we are—are partly brought with us into the world, influenced by our sympathetic nervous system's reactivity (Kagan, 1989; Wilkowski & Robinson, 2008). A person's temperament, observed in infancy, usually endures (Larsen & Diener, 1987; Wilson & Matheny, 1986). A 3-year-old who exhibits little conscientiousness and self-control is more vulnerable to substance abuse and arrest by age 32 (Moffitt et al., 2011). A child who is non-aggressive at age 8 will very likely still be non-aggressive at age 48 (Huesmann et al., 2003). Identical twins, when asked separately, are more likely than fraternal twins to agree on whether they have "a violent temper" or have gotten in fights (Rushton et al., 1986; Rowe, Almeida, & Jacobson, 1999). Of convicted criminals who are twins, fully half of their identical twins (but only one in five fraternal twins) also have criminal records (Raine, 1993, 2008).

Genes predispose the pit bull's aggressiveness.

In a study examining 12.5 million residents of Sweden, those with a genetic sibling convicted of a violent crime were four times as likely to be convicted themselves. Rates were much lower for adopted siblings, suggesting a strong genetic component and a more modest environmental influence (Frisell, Lichtenstein, & Långström, 2011). Long-term studies following several hundred New Zealand children reveal that the recipe for aggressive behaviour combines a gene that alters neurotransmitter balance with childhood maltreatment (Caspi et al., 2002; Moffitt et al., 2003). Neither "bad" genes nor a "bad" environment alone predispose later aggressiveness and antisocial behaviour; rather, genes predispose some children to be more sensitive and responsive to maltreatment. Nature and nurture interact.

④ Biochemical influences

Blood chemistry also influences neural sensitivity to aggressive stimulation.

Alcohol

Both laboratory experiments and police data indicate that alcohol unleashes aggression when people are provoked (Bushman, 1993; Bushman & Cooper, 1990; Taylor & Chermack, 1993). Consider the following:

- When asked, in experiments, to think back on relationship conflicts, intoxicated people administered stronger shocks and felt angrier than did sober people (MacDonald, Zanna, & Holmes, 2000).

- In 65 percent of homicides and 55 percent of in-home fights and assaults, the assailant and/or the victim had been drinking (American Psychological Association, 1993). Four in ten prisoners convicted of a violent crime were drinking when they committed murder, assault, robbery, or sexual assault (Karberg & James, 2005).

- Heavy men who drank alcohol were significantly more aggressive after drinking alcohol, but alcohol had little effect on women's or smaller men's aggression. Alcohol, note the researchers, seemed to encourage "heavy men to 'throw their weight around' and intimidate others by behaving aggressively" (DeWall et al., 2010a). Apparently, people really are wise to avoid the "big, drunk guy" in the bar.

"Ordinary men who drank too much" was the *New York Times* description of the mob that openly assaulted some 50 women attending a June 2000 parade. "Stoked with booze, they worked up from hooting at women, to grabbing them, to drenching them with water and pulling off their tops and pants" (Staples, 2000).

Alcohol enhances aggressiveness by reducing people's self-awareness, by focusing their attention on a provocation, and by people's mentally associating alcohol with aggression (Bartholow & Heinz, 2006; Giancola & Corman, 2007; Ito, Miller, & Pollock, 1996). Alcohol also predisposes people to interpret ambiguous acts (such as a bump in a crowd) as provocations (Begue et al., 2010). Alcohol deindividuates, and it disinhibits.

Testosterone

Hormonal influences appear much stronger in lower animals than in humans. But human aggressiveness does correlate with the male sex hormone, testosterone. Consider the following:

- Drugs that diminish testosterone levels in violent human males will subdue their aggressive tendencies.

- After people reach age 25, their testosterone and rates of violent crime decrease together.

- Testosterone levels tend to be higher among prisoners convicted of planned and unprovoked violent crimes than among prisoners convicted of non-violent crimes (Dabbs, 1992; Dabbs et al., 1995; Dabbs, Riad, & Chance, 2001; Dabbs, Strong, & Milun, 1997).

- Among the normal range of teen boys and adult men, those with high testosterone levels are more prone to delinquency, hard drug use, and aggressive responses to provocation (Archer, 1991; Dabbs & Morris, 1990; Olweus et al., 1988).

Young, male, and restless. In the 2011 riots that swept English cities, those arrested overwhelmingly shared one genetic characteristic—a Y chromosome—and were testosterone-fuelled teens or people in their early 20s (*Guardian*, 2011).

- After handling a gun, people's testosterone levels rise, and the more their testosterone rises, the more they seek to inflict pain on someone else (Kleinsmith, Kasser, & McAndrew, 2006).

- In men, testosterone increases the facial width-to-height ratio. And sure enough, in the laboratory, men with relatively wider faces display more aggression. Ditto in the hockey rink, where varsity and professional hockey players with relatively wide faces spend more time in the penalty box (Carré & McCormick, 2008; Stirrat & Perrett, 2010).

Testosterone, said James Dabbs (2000), "is a small molecule with large effects." Injecting a man with testosterone won't automatically make him aggressive, yet men with low testosterone are somewhat less likely to react aggressively when provoked (Geen, 1998). Testosterone is roughly like battery power. Only if the battery levels are very low will things noticeably slow down.

Poor diet

When British researcher Bernard Gesch first tried to study the effect of diet on aggression, he stood in front of hundreds of inmates at an English prison—but no matter how loudly he talked, none of them would listen. Finally, he talked privately to the "daddy"—the inmates' "tough guy" leader—and 231 inmates signed on to receive nutritional supplements or a placebo. Prisoners who got the extra nutrition were involved in 35 percent fewer violent incidents (Gesch et al., 2002). Such programs may eventually help people outside of prison as well, because many people have diets deficient in important nutrients, such as omega-3 fatty acids (found in fish and important for brain function) and calcium (which guards against impulsivity).

Biology and behaviour interact

The traffic between biology and behaviour flows both ways. Testosterone, for example, may facilitate dominance and aggressiveness, but dominating or defeating behaviour

Some violent sex offenders, wishing to free themselves of persistent, damaging impulses and to reduce their prison terms, have requested castration. Should their requests be granted? If so, and if they are deemed no longer at risk of sexual violence, should their prison terms be reduced or eliminated?

"Of course, we'll never actually use it against a potential enemy, but it will allow us to negotiate from a position of strength."

Humanity has armed its capacity for destruction without comparably arming its capacity for the inhibition of aggression.

© John Ruge. Reprinted with permission of General Media Magazines.

also boosts testosterone levels (Mazur & Booth, 1998). After a World Cup soccer match or a big basketball game between arch-rivals, testosterone levels rise in the winning fans and fall in the losing fans (Bernhardt et al., 1998). The phenomenon also occurs in the laboratory, where socially anxious men exhibit a pronounced drop in their testosterone level after losing a rigged face-to-face competition (Maner et al., 2008). The interaction between testosterone surges and celebration-related drinking probably explains the finding of Cardiff University researchers that fans of *winning* rather than losing soccer and rugby teams commit more post-game assaults (Sivarajasingam, Moore, & Shepherd, 2005).

So neural, genetic, and biochemical influences predispose some people to react aggressively to conflict and provocation. But is aggression so much a part of human nature that it makes peace unattainable? The International Council of Psychologists has joined other organizations in unanimously endorsing a statement on violence developed by scientists from a dozen nations (Adams, 1991): "It is scientifically incorrect [to say that] war or any other violent behaviour is genetically programmed into our human nature [or that] war is caused by 'instinct' or any single motivation." Thus there are, as we will see, ways to reduce human aggression.

AGGRESSION AS A RESPONSE TO FRUSTRATION

It is a warm evening. Tired and thirsty after two hours of studying, you borrow some change from a friend and head for the nearest soft-drink machine. As the machine devours the change, you can almost taste the cold, refreshing cola. But when you push the button, nothing happens. You push it again. Then you flip the coin return button. Still nothing. Again, you hit the buttons. You slam the machine. Alas, no money and no drink. You stomp back to your studies, empty-handed and short-changed. Should your roommate beware? Are you now more likely to say or do something hurtful?

frustration-aggression theory
the theory that frustration triggers a readiness to aggress

frustration
the blocking of goal-directed behaviour

One of the first psychological theories of aggression, the popular **frustration-aggression theory**, answers yes. "Frustration always leads to some form of aggression," said John Dollard and his colleagues (1939, p. 1). **Frustration** is anything (such as the malfunctioning vending machine) that blocks our attainment of a goal. Frustration grows when our motivation to achieve a goal is very strong, when we expected gratification, and when the blocking is complete. When Rupert Brown and his colleagues (2001) surveyed British ferry passengers heading to France, they found much higher aggressive attitudes on a day when French fishing boats blockaded the port, preventing their travel. Blocked from obtaining their goal, the passengers became more likely (in responding to various vignettes) to agree with an insult toward a French person who had spilled coffee.

displacement
the redirection of aggression to a target other than the source of the frustration. Generally, the new target is a safer or more socially [ac]ceptable target.

The aggressive energy need not explode directly against its source. Most people learn to inhibit direct retaliation, especially when others might disapprove or punish; instead, we displace our hostilities to safer targets. **Displacement** occurs in the old anecdote about a man who, humiliated by his boss, berates his wife, who yells at their son, who kicks the dog, which bites the mail carrier (who goes home and berates his wife . . .). In experiments and in real life, displaced aggression is most likely when the target shares some similarity to the instigator

317

and does some minor irritating act that unleashes the displaced aggression (Marcus-Newhall et al., 2000; Pedersen, Gonzales, & Miller, 2000). When a person is harbouring anger, even a trivial offence—one that would normally produce no response—may elicit an explosive overreaction.

In one experiment, Eduardo Vasquez and his co-researchers (2005) provoked some university students (but not others) by having an experimenter insult their performance on an anagram-solving test. Shortly after-ward, the students had to decide how long another supposed student should be required to immerse his or her hand in painful cold water while completing a task. When the supposed student committed a trivial

offence—by giving a mild insult—the previously provoked participants responded punitively, by recommending a longer cold-water treatment than did the unprovoked participants. This phe-nomenon of displaced aggression helps us understand, noted Vasquez, why a previously pro-voked and still-angry person might respond to mild highway offences with road rage, or react to spousal criticism with spouse abuse. It also helps explain why frustrated major league baseball pitchers, in one analysis of nearly 5 million at-bats from 74 197 games since 1960, were most likely to hit batters after the batter hit a home run the last time at bat, or after the previous batter did so (Timmerman, 2007).

Frustration-triggered aggression sometimes appears as road rage. Road rage is fed by perceptions of hostile intentions from other drivers, as when someone is cut off in traffic (Britt & Garrity, 2006).

Frustration-aggression theory revised

Laboratory tests of the frustration-aggression theory produced mixed results: Sometimes frustration increased aggressiveness, sometimes not. For example, if the frustration was understandable—if, as in one experiment, a confederate disrupted a group's problem-solv-ing because his hearing aid malfunctioned (rather than just because he paid no attention)—then frustration led to irritation, but not aggression (Burnstein & Worchel, 1962). Similarly, if someone frustrates us, we are less likely to respond aggressively if that person apolo-gizes, accepts responsibility, or otherwise tries to make amends (Eaton & Struthers, 2006).

Leonard Berkowitz (1978, 1989) realized that the original theory overstated the frustration-aggression connection, so he revised it. Berkowitz theorized that frustration produces anger, an emotional readiness to aggress. Anger arises when someone who frustrates us could have chosen to act otherwise (Averill, 1983; Weiner, 1981). A frustrated person is especially likely to lash out when aggressive cues pull the cork, releasing bottled-up anger (Figure 9–1). Sometimes the cork will blow without such cues. But, as we will see, cues associated with aggression amplify aggression (Carlson, Marcus-Newhall, & Miller, 1990).

> *"The war on terrorism will not be won until we have come to grips with the problem of poverty, and thus the sources of discontent."*
> JAMES WOLFENSOHN, FORMER WORLD BANK PRESIDENT

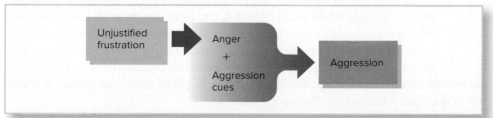

FIGURE 9–1

SIMPLIFIED FRUSTRATION-AGGRESSION THEORY.

A simplified synopsis of Leonard Berkowitz's revised frustration-aggression theory.

Relative deprivation

Frustration is not only caused by complete deprivation; more often, *frustration arises from the gap between expectations and attainments.* The most economically frustrated people are probably not the impoverished residents of African shantytowns, who might know no other way of life, but middle-class North Americans who aspire to be rich—or at least upper-middle class. When your expectations are fulfilled by your attainments, and when your desires are reachable at your income, you feel satisfied rather than frustrated (Solberg et al., 2002).

> *"Evils which are patiently endured when they seem inevitable become intolerable when once the idea of escape from them is suggested."*
> ALEXIS DE TOCQUEVILLE, 1856

Frustration is often compounded when we compare ourselves with others. Workers' feelings of well-being depend on whether their compensation compares favourably with that of others in their line of work (Yuchtman, 1976). A raise in salary for a city's police officers, while temporarily lifting their morale, may deflate that of the firefighters. It seems that frustration is in the eye of the beholder. Objective reality may have little to do with people's experience of frustration, but even irrational frustration can lead to devastating violence.

> *"A house may be large or small; as long as the surrounding houses are equally small, it satisfies all social demands for a dwelling. But let a palace arise beside the little house, and it shrinks from a little house into a hut."*
> KARL MARX

Marc Lepine wanted to be an engineer from the time he was a boy, but he was unable to get into a program to study engineering. He blamed his frustration on women, and on feminists in particular, who he felt were denying him his lifelong dream. On December 6, 1989, his frustration broke out into horrifying aggression. He took a semi-automatic rifle and went to the École Polytechnique de Montréal, the engineering school he had always wanted to attend. He entered one classroom and ordered the women to line up on one side. He opened fire, shooting them all at close range. He entered another classroom and did the same. He prowled the hallways killing any women he could find. In the end, he killed 14 women before turning the gun on himself. A full understanding of Lepine's actions may never be possible, but it seems clear that his attainments in life fell far short of his expectations. And it seems plausible that this gap between his achievements and his aspirations may have fuelled his frustration and contributed to this tragedy.

relative deprivation
the perception that one is less well off than others to whom one compares oneself

Such feelings, called **relative deprivation**, explain why happiness tends to be lower and crime rates higher in communities and nations with large income inequality (Hagerty, 2000; Kawachi, Kennedy, & Wilkinson, 1999). They predict reactions to perceived inequities by minority groups (K. L. Dion, 1985; Kawakami & Dion, 1993, 1995). They also explain why women who make less than men working in the same occupations feel underpaid only if they compare themselves with male rather than female colleagues (Bylsma & Major, 1994; Zanna, Crosby, & Loewenstein, 1987). And it explains why the former East Germans revolted against their communist regime: They had a higher standard of living than some Western European countries, but a frustratingly lower one than their West German neighbours (Baron, Kerr, & Miller, 1992).

> *"Women's discontent increases in exact proportion to her development."*
> ELIZABETH CADY STANTON, 1815–1902, AMERICAN SUFFRAGETTE

The term *relative deprivation* was coined by researchers studying the satisfaction felt by soldiers in World War II (Merton & Kitt, 1950; Stouffer et al., 1949). Ironically, those in the air corps felt more frustrated about their own rate of promotion than those in the military police, for whom promotions were actually slower. The air corps' promotion rate was rapid, and most air corps personnel probably perceived themselves as better than the average air corps member (the self-serving bias). Thus, their aspirations soared higher than their achievements. The result? Frustration.

One possible source of such frustration today is the affluence depicted in television programs and commercials. In cultures where television is a universal appliance, it helps turn absolute deprivation (lacking what others have) into relative deprivation (feeling deprived). Karen Hennigan and her co-workers (1982) analyzed crime rates in several cities around the time television was introduced. In 34 cities where television ownership became widespread in 1951, the 1951 larceny theft rate (for crimes such as shoplifting and bicycle stealing) took an observable jump. In 34 other cities, where a government freeze had delayed the introduction of television until 1955, a similar jump in the theft rate occurred—in 1955.

AGGRESSION AS LEARNED SOCIAL BEHAVIOUR

Theories of aggression based on instinct and frustration assume that hostile urges erupt from inner emotions, which naturally "push" aggression from within. Social psychologists contend that learning also "pulls" aggression out of us.

The rewards of aggression

By experience and by observing others, we learn that aggression often pays. Experiments have transformed animals from docile creatures into ferocious fighters. Severe defeats, on the other hand, create submissiveness (Ginsburg & Allee, 1942; Kahn, 1951; Scott & Marston, 1953).

People, too, can learn the rewards of aggression. A child whose aggressive acts successfully intimidate other children will likely become increasingly aggressive (Patterson, Littman, &

Bricker, 1967). Aggressive hockey players—the ones sent most often to the penalty box for rough play—score more goals than non-aggressive players (McCarthy & Kelly, 1978a, 1978b). Canadian teenage hockey players whose fathers applaud physically aggressive play show the most aggressive attitudes and style of play (Ennis & Zanna, 1991). In the waters off Somalia, paying ransom to hijackers of ships—a reported $150 million in 2008 (BBC, 2008)—rewarded the pirates, thus fuelling further hijackings. In these cases, aggression is instrumental in achieving certain rewards.

The same is true of terrorist acts, which enable powerless people to garner widespread attention. "The primary targets of suicide-bombing attacks are not those who are injured but those who are made to witness it through media coverage," noted Paul Marsden and Sharon Attia (2005). Terrorism's purpose is, with the help of media amplification, to terrorize. "Kill one, frighten ten thousand," asserts an ancient Chinese proverb. Deprived of what Margaret Thatcher called "the oxygen of publicity," terrorism would surely diminish, concluded Jeffrey Rubin (1986). It's like the 1970s incidents of naked spectators "streaking" onto football fields for a few seconds of television exposure. Once the networks decided to ignore the incidents, the phenomenon ended.

Observational learning

social learning theory
the theory that we learn social behaviour by observing and imitating and by being rewarded and punished

Albert Bandura (1997) proposed a **social learning theory** of aggression. He believed that we learn aggression not only by experiencing its payoffs but also by observing others. As with most social behaviours, we acquire aggression by watching others act and noting the consequences.

Picture this scene from one of Bandura's experiments (Bandura, Ross, & Ross, 1961). A preschool child is put to work on an interesting art activity. An adult is in another part of the room, where there are Tinker Toys, a mallet, and a big, inflated "Bobo" doll. After a minute of working with the Tinker Toys, the adult gets up and for almost 10 minutes attacks the inflated doll. She pounds it with the mallet, kicks it, and throws it, all the while yelling, "Sock him in the nose. . . . Knock him down. . . . Kick him."

After observing this outburst, the child goes to a different room with many very attractive toys. But after two minutes, the experimenter interrupts, saying these are her best toys and she must "save them for the other children." The frustrated child now goes into another room with various toys for aggressive and non-aggressive play, two of which are a Bobo doll and a mallet.

Seldom did children not exposed to the aggressive adult model display any aggressive play or talk. Although frustrated, they nevertheless played calmly. Those who had observed the aggressive adult were many times more likely to pick up the mallet and lash out at the doll. Watching the adult's aggressive behaviour lowered their inhibitions. Moreover, the children often reproduced the model's acts and said her words. Observing aggressive behaviour had both lowered their inhibitions and taught them ways to aggress.

Bandura (1979) believed that everyday life exposes us to aggressive models in the family, in one's subculture, and, as we will see, in the mass media.

The family

Physically aggressive children tend to have physically punitive parents; their parents modelled aggression by disciplining them with screaming, slapping, and beating (Patterson, Chamberlain, & Reid, 1982). These parents often had parents who were themselves physically punitive (Bandura & Walters, 1959; Straus & Gelles, 1980). A study of 975 Canadian children 6 years of age

Monkey see, monkey do: In Bandura's famous experiment, children exposed to an adult's aggression against a Bobo doll were likely to reproduce the observed aggression.

or younger found that those with more hostile parents were more aggressive (Benzies, Keown, & Magill-Evans, 2009). Such punitive behaviour may escalate into abuse, and although most abused children do not become criminals or abusive parents, 30 percent do later abuse their own children—four times the general population rate (Kaufman & Zigler, 1987; Widom, 1989). Even more mild physical punishment, such as spanking, is linked to later aggression (Gershoff, 2002). Violence often begets violence.

The culture

The social environment outside the home also provides models. In communities where "macho" images are admired, aggression is readily transmitted to new generations (Cartwright, 1975; Short, 1969). The violent subculture of teenage gangs, for instance, provides its junior members with aggressive models. Among adolescents who are otherwise equally at risk for violence, those who have observed gun violence were twice as likely to be (Bingenheimer, Brennan, & Earls, 2005).

The broader culture also matters. Show social psychologists a man from a non-democratic culture that is economically underdeveloped, that has great economic inequality, that prepares men to be warriors, and that has engaged in war, and they will show you someone who is predisposed to aggressive behaviour (Bond, 2004).

Richard Nisbett and Dov Cohen (Cohen, 1998; Cohen & Nisbett, 1997; Cohen et al., 1996) have explored the effects of culture on attitudes toward violence.. They report that the U.S. South, settled by Scots-Irish herders ever wary of threats to their flocks, has a "culture of honour," which maintains that insults deserve retaliation. After squeezing by another man in a hallway and hearing him mutter an insult, White Southern men expressed more aggressive thoughts and experienced a surge in testosterone. White Northern men were more likely to find the encounter funny (Cohen et al., 1996). To the present day, U.S. cities populated by southerners have higher-than-average White homicide rates (Vandello, Cohen, & Ransom, 2008). More students in "culture of honour" states bring weapons to school, and these states have had three times as many school shootings as others (R. P. Brown, Osterman, & Barnes, 2009).

People learn aggressive responses both by experience and by observing aggressive models. But when will aggressive responses actually occur? Bandura (1979) contended that aggressive acts are motivated by a variety of aversive experiences—frustration, pain, insults (Figure 9–2). Such experiences arouse us emotionally. But whether we act aggressively depends on the

FIGURE 9–2

THE SOCIAL LEARNING VIEW OF AGGRESSION.

The emotional arousal from an aversive experience motivates aggression. Whether aggression or some other response actually occurs depends on what consequences we have learned to expect. (Based on Bandura, 1979, 1997)

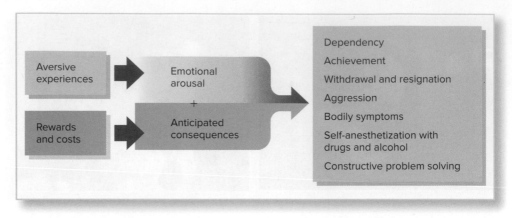

consequences we anticipate. Aggression occurs most likely when we are aroused *and* when it seems safe and rewarding to aggress.

WHAT ARE SOME INFLUENCES ON AGGRESSION?

Under what conditions do we aggress?

In the previous section, we examined some theories of aggression. Now we dig deeper and examine some specific influences: aversive incidents, arousal, aggression cues, the media, and the group context.

① AVERSIVE INCIDENTS

Recipes for aggression often include some type of aversive experience. These include pain, uncomfortable heat, or an attack.

Pain

Researcher Nathan Azrin (1967) was doing experiments with laboratory rats in a cage wired to deliver shocks to the animals' feet. Azrin wanted to know if switching off the foot shocks would reinforce two rats' positive interactions with each other. Azrin planned to turn on the shock and then, once the rats approached each other, cut off the pain. To his great surprise, the experiment proved impossible. As soon as the rats felt pain, they attacked each other, before the experimenter could switch off the shock. The greater the shock (and pain), the more violent the attack. The same effect occurred across a long list of species, including cats, turtles, and snakes. The animals were not selective about their targets. They would attack animals of their own species and those of a different species, or stuffed dolls, or even tennis balls.

Today's ethical guidelines restrict researchers' use of painful stimuli.

The researchers also varied the source of pain. They found that shocks weren't the only stimuli that induced attack; intense heat and "psychological pain"—for example, suddenly not rewarding hungry pigeons that had been trained to expect a grain reward after pecking at a disk—brought the same reaction as shocks. This "psychological pain" is, of course, frustration.

Pain heightens aggressiveness in humans, also. Many of us can recall such a reaction after stubbing a toe or suffering a headache. Leonard Berkowitz and his associates demonstrated this by having students hold one hand in lukewarm water or painfully cold water. Those whose hands were submerged in the cold water reported feeling more irritable and more annoyed, and they were more willing to blast another person with unpleasant noise. In view of such results, Berkowitz (1983, 1989) proposed that aversive stimulation rather than frustration is the basic trigger of hostile aggression. Frustration is certainly one important type of unpleasantness. But any aversive event, whether a dashed expectation, a personal insult, or physical pain, can incite an emotional outburst. Even the torment of a depressed state increases the likelihood of hostile aggressive behaviour.

Heat

People have theorized for centuries about the effect of climate on human action. Hippocrates (ca. 460–377 B.C.) compared the civilized Greece of his day to the savagery in the region further north (what is now Germany and Switzer-

Pain attack. Frustrated after losing the first two rounds of his 1997 heavyweight championship fight with Evander Holyfield, and feeling pain from an accidental head butt, Mike Tyson reacted by biting off part of Holyfield's ear.

land), and decided that northern Europe's harsh climate was to blame. Later, the English attributed their "superior" culture to England's ideal climate. French thinkers proclaimed the same for France. Because climate remains relatively steady while cultural traits change over time, the climate theory of culture obviously has limited validity.

Temporary climate variations can, however, affect behaviour. Offensive odours, cigarette smoke, and air pollution have all been linked with aggressive behaviour (Rotton & Frey, 1985). But the most-studied environmental irritant is heat. William Griffitt (1970; Griffitt & Veitch, 1971) found that compared to students who answered questionnaires in a room with a normal temperature, those who did so in an uncomfortably hot room (over 32°C/90°F) reported feeling more tired and aggressive and expressed more hostility toward a stranger. Follow-up experiments revealed that heat also triggers retaliative actions (Bell, 1980; Rule, Taylor, & Dobbs, 1987).

Does uncomfortable heat increase aggression in the real world as well as in the laboratory? Consider the following:

- In hot weather, drivers without air-conditioning are more likely to honk at a stalled car (Kenrick & MacFarlane, 1986).

- In an analysis of 57 293 Major League Baseball games since 1952, batters were more likely to be hit by a pitch during hot weather—nearly 50 percent more likely when the temperature was 32°C or above (versus 27°C or below) and when three of the pitcher's teammates had previously been hit (Larrick et al., 2011). Pitchers weren't wilder on hot days—they had no more walks or wild pitches. They just clobbered more batters.

- Studies in six cities have found that when the weather is hot, violent crimes are more likely (Anderson & Anderson, 1984; Cohn, 1993; Cotton, 1981, 1986; Harries & Stadler, 1988; Rotton & Frey, 1985).

- Across the northern hemisphere, it is not only hotter days that have more violent crimes, but also hotter seasons of the year, hotter summers, hotter years, hotter cities, and hotter regions (Anderson & Anderson, 1998; Anderson et al., 2000). Anderson and his colleagues projected that if a 4-degree-Fahrenheit (about 2°C) global warming occurs, the United States alone will see at least 50 000 more serious assaults annually.

> *"I pray thee, good Mercutio, let's retire; The day is hot, the Capulets abroad, And, if we meet, we shall not 'scape a brawl, For now, these hot days, is the mad blood stirring."*
> SHAKESPEARE, *ROMEO AND JULIET*

Do these findings show that heat discomfort directly fuels aggressiveness? Although the conclusion appears plausible, these correlations between temperature and aggression don't prove it. People certainly could be more irritable in hot, sticky weather. And in the laboratory, hot temperatures do increase arousal and hostile thoughts and feelings (Anderson et al., 1999). There may be other contributing factors, however. Maybe hot summer evenings drive people into the streets. There, other group influence factors may well take over. Then again (researchers have debated this), maybe there comes a point where stifling heat suppresses violence (Bell, 2005; Bushman, Wang, & Anderson, 2005a, 2005b; Cohn & Rotton, 2005).

Attacks

Being attacked or insulted by someone is especially conducive to aggression. Several experiments, including one at Osaka University by Kennichi Ohbuchi and Toshihiro Kambara (1985), have confirmed that intentional attacks breed retaliatory attacks. In most of these experiments, one person competed with another in a reaction-time contest. After each test trial, the winner chose how much shock to give the loser. Actually, each subject was playing a programmed opponent, who steadily escalated the amount of shock. Did the real subjects respond more charitably? Hardly. Extracting "an eye for an eye" was the more likely response.

(z) AROUSAL

So far we have seen that various aversive stimulations can arouse anger and aggression. Do other types of arousal, such as those that accompany exercise or sexual excitement, have a similar effect? Imagine that Tawna, having just finished a stimulating short run, comes home to discover that her date for the evening has called and left word that he has made other plans. Will Tawna more likely explode in fury after her run than if she discovered the same message after awakening from a nap? Or, having just exercised, will her aggressive tendencies be exorcised? To discover an answer, let's examine some intriguing research on how we interpret and label our bodily states.

In a famous experiment, Stanley Schachter and Jerome Singer (1962) found that we can experience an aroused bodily state in different ways. They aroused men by injecting adrenalin. The drug produced body flushing, heart palpitation, and more rapid breathing. When forewarned that the drug would produce these effects, the men felt little emotion, even when waiting with either a hostile or a euphoric person. Of course, they could readily attribute their bodily sensations to the drug. Schachter and Singer led another group of men to believe the drug produced no such side effects. Then they, too, were placed in the company of a hostile or euphoric person. How did they feel and act? They were angered when with the hostile person, amused when with the person who was euphoric. The principle seemed to be this: A given state of bodily arousal feeds one emotion or another, depending on how the person interprets and labels the arousal.

Other experiments indicate that arousal is not as emotionally undifferentiated as Schachter believed. Yet being physically stirred up does intensify just about any emotion (Reisenzein, 1983). For example, Paul Biner (1991) reported that subjects found radio static unpleasant, especially when they were aroused by bright lighting. And Dolf Zillmann (1988), Jennings Bryant, and their collaborators (Zillmann, 1989b) found that people who had just pumped an exercise bike or watched a film of a Beatles rock concert found it easy to misattribute their arousal to a provocation. They then retaliated with heightened aggression. Although common sense might lead us to assume that Tawna's run would have drained her aggressive tensions, enabling her to accept bad news calmly, these studies showed that arousal feeds emotions.

Sexual arousal and other forms of arousal, such as anger, can, therefore, amplify one another (Zillmann, 1989a). Love is never so passionate as after a fight or a fright. In the laboratory, erotic stimuli are more arousing to people who have just been frightened. Similarly, the arousal of a roller-coaster ride or a horror movie may spill over into romantic feelings for one's partner.

Some people, called sensation seekers, crave being in a heightened state of arousal—they love to take risks and need the rush of constant stimulation. Consistent with the idea that aggression increases arousal and vice versa, sensation seekers are also more likely to be aggressive (Wilson & Scarpa, 2011).

A frustrating, hot, or insulting situation heightens arousal. When it does, the arousal, combined with hostile thoughts and feelings, may form a recipe for aggressive behaviour (Figure 9–3).

③ AGGRESSION CUES

As we noted when considering the frustration-aggression hypothesis, violence is more likely when aggressive cues release pent-up anger. Leonard Berkowitz (1968, 1981, 1995) and others have found that the sight of a weapon is such a cue. In one experiment, children who had just played with toy guns became more willing to knock down another child's blocks. In another, angered University of Wisconsin men gave more electric shocks to their tormenter when a rifle and a revolver (supposedly

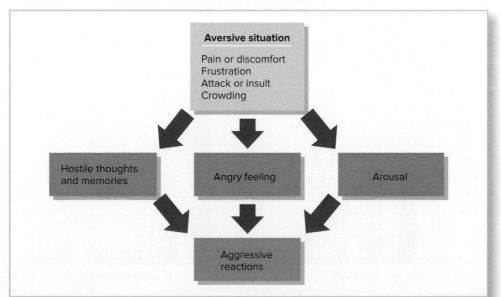

FIGURE 9–3

ELEMENTS OF HOSTILE AGGRESSION.

An aversive situation can trigger aggression by provoking hostile cognitions, hostile feelings, and arousal. These reactions make us more likely to perceive harmful intent and to react aggressively. (Simplified from Anderson, Deuser, & DeNeve, 1995)

The NHL's Steve Moore collapsed on the ice with three broken vertebrae and a concussion after being viciously sucker-punched by Todd Bertuzzi in March 2004. Bertuzzi's captain had taken a hard hit earlier in the season, and it appears the attack on Moore was retaliatory.

left over from a previous experiment) were nearby than when badminton racquets had been left behind (Berkowitz & LePage, 1967). Guns prime hostile thoughts and punitive judgments (Anderson, Benjamin, & Bartholow, 1998; Dienstbier et al., 1998). What's within sight is within mind. This is especially so when a weapon is perceived as an instrument of violence rather than a recreational item. For hunters, for example, seeing a hunting rifle does not prime aggressive thoughts, though it does for non-hunters (Bartholow et al., 2004).

Berkowitz was not surprised that in the United States, a country with some 200 million privately owned guns, half of all murders are committed with handguns, or that handguns in homes are far more likely to kill household members than intruders. "Guns not only permit violence," he reported, "they can stimulate it as well. The finger pulls the trigger, but the trigger may also be pulling the finger."

Berkowitz was also not surprised that countries that ban handguns have lower murder rates. Compared to the United States, Britain has one-fourth as many people and one-sixteenth as many murders. The United States has 10 000 handgun homicides a year; Australia has about a dozen, Britain two dozen, and Canada 100. Vancouver, British Columbia, and Seattle, Washington, have similar populations, climates, economies, and rates of criminal activity and assault—except that Vancouver, which carefully restricts handgun ownership, had one-fifth as many handgun murders as Seattle and thus a 40 percent lower overall murder rate (Sloan et al., 1988). Not only does Canada have a much lower murder rate than the U.S., but the difference in the percentage of murders that occur by the use of a gun is also striking. As you can see in Figure 9–4, Americans are more than twice as likely as Canadians to use guns when they commit murder.

FIGURE 9–4

CANADA VS. U.S.: WEAPONS USED.

(Adapted from Statistics Canada, Canadian Crime Statistics, 1996, Catalogue no. 85-002-XPE, Vol. 17, no. 8; and U.S. Federal Bureau of Investigation Uniform Crime Report. This does not constitute an endorsement by Statistics Canada of this product.)

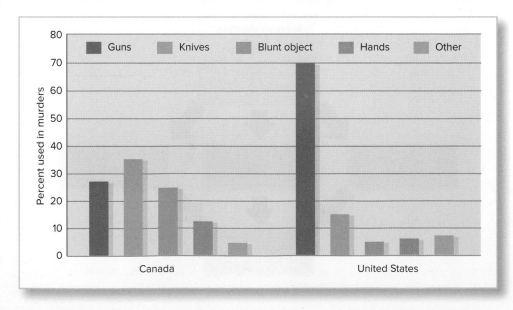

Changes in gun laws do seem to affect murder rates. For example, when Washington, D.C., adopted a law restricting handgun possession, the number of gun-related murders dropped about 25 percent. No changes occurred in other methods of murder, nor did adjacent areas outside the reach of this law experience any such declines (Loftin et al., 1991).

Researchers also have examined risks of violence in homes with and without guns. This is controversial research because such homes may differ in many ways. One study compared gun owners and non-owners of the same sex, race, age, and neighbourhood. The ironic and tragic result was that those who kept a gun in the home (often for protection) were 2.7 times more likely to be murdered—nearly always by a family member or close acquaintance (Kellermann, 1997; Kellermann et al., 1993). Another study found that the risk of suicide in homes with guns was five times as high as in homes without them (Taubes, 1992). A newer study found a slightly weaker, but still significant, link between guns and homicide or suicide. Compared with others of the same gender, age, and race, people with guns at home were 41 percent more likely to be homicide victims and 3.4 times as likely to die of suicide (Wiebe, 2003). A gun in the home has often meant the difference between a fight and a funeral, or between suffering and suicide.

Is violent crime rising? Perceptions of increased crime can trigger gun purchases, but these guns are more likely to be used against a household member than as originally intended—against an intruder or attacker. Countries with fewer guns have lower murder rates.

Guns serve as aggression cues, and they also put psychological distance between aggressor and victim. As Milgram's obedience studies taught us, remoteness from the victim facilitates cruelty. A knife can kill someone, but a knife attack is more difficult than pulling a trigger from a distance.

(4) MEDIA INFLUENCES: PORNOGRAPHY AND SEXUAL VIOLENCE

Pornography is now a bigger business in the North America than professional football, basketball, and baseball combined, thanks to some $13 billion a year spent on the industry's cable and satellite networks, theatres and pay-per-view movies, in-room hotel movies, phone sex, sex magazines, and Internet sites (D'Orlando, 2011; Richtel, 2007). The easy availability of pornography on the Internet has accelerated its popularity. In a recent survey of 18- to 26-year-old men, 87 percent said they viewed pornography at least once a month, and nearly half used it at least once a week (Carroll et al., 2008). However, only 31 percent of women reported viewing pornography at all. Social-psychological research on pornography has focused mostly on depictions of sexual violence, which is commonplace in popular recent adult videos (Sun et al., 2008). A typical sexually violent episode finds a man forcing himself on a woman.

Repeated exposure to erotic films featuring quick, uncommitted sex also tends to

- *decrease attraction for one's partner*
- *increase acceptance of extramarital sex and of women's sexual submission to men*
- *increase men's perceiving women in sexual terms*

N. MYERS (2000)

She at first resists and tries to fight off her attacker. Gradually she becomes sexually aroused, and her resistance melts. By the end, she is in ecstasy, pleading for more. We have all viewed or read non-pornographic versions of this sequence: She resists, he persists. Dashing man grabs and forcibly kisses protesting woman. Within moments, the arms that were pushing him away are clutching him tight, her resistance overwhelmed by her unleashed passion. The problem, of course, is that women do not actually respond this way to rape. Social psychologists report that viewing such fictional scenes of a man overpowering and arousing a woman can (a) distort one's perceptions of how women actually respond to sexual coercion and (b) increase men's aggression against women.

Distorted perceptions of sexual reality

Does viewing sexual violence reinforce the "rape myth"—that some women would welcome sexual assault and that "no doesn't really mean no"? Researchers have observed a correlation between the amount of TV viewing and rape myth acceptance (Kahlor & Morrison, 2007). To explore the relationship experimentally, Neil Malamuth and James Check (1981) showed University of Manitoba men either two non-sexual movies or two movies depicting a man sexually overcoming a woman. A week later, when surveyed by a different experimenter, those who saw the films with mild sexual violence were more accepting of violence against women.

"Pornography that portrays sexual aggression as pleasurable for the victim increases the acceptance of the use of coercion in sexual relations."
SOCIAL SCIENCE CONSENSUS AT SURGEON GENERAL'S WORKSHOP ON PORNOGRAPHY AND PUBLIC HEALTH (KOOP, 1987)

Other studies have confirmed that exposure to pornography increases acceptance of the rape myth (Oddone-Paolucci, Genuis, M., & Violato, 2000). For example, while spending three evenings watching sexually violent movies, male viewers in an experiment by Charles Mullin and Daniel Linz (1995) became progressively less bothered by the raping and slashing. Compared with others not exposed to the films, three days later they expressed less sympathy for domestic violence victims, and they rated the victims' injuries as less severe. In fact, said researchers Edward Donnerstein, Daniel Linz, and Steven Penrod (1987), what better way for an evil character to get people to react calmly to the torture and mutilation of women than to show a gradually escalating series of such films?

Note that the sexual message (that many women enjoy being "taken") was subtle and unlikely to elicit counter-arguing. Given frequent media images of women's resistance melting in the arms of a forceful man, we shouldn't be surprised that even women often believe that some *other* woman might enjoy being sexually overpowered—though virtually none think it of themselves (Malamuth et al., 1980).

Aggression against women

Evidence also suggests that pornography contributes to men's actual aggression toward women (Kingston et al., 2009). Nathaniel Lambert and his colleagues (2012) asked male and female college and university students, "Approximately how many times in the past 30 days have you viewed a pornographic website?" Even after taking gender into account, those who had viewed porn more frequently were also more likely to physically assault friends and romantic partners over the next three weeks, and were more aggressive toward another student in a lab experiment. When given the chance to stick pins into a doll representing their relationship partner, those who viewed more Internet porn symbolically stabbed their partner with more pins.

Pornography also affects the children who see it. Among 1000 10- to 15-year-old boys and girls, those who saw movies, magazines, or websites with violent sexual content were six times more likely to be sexually aggressive toward others (defined as "kissed, touched, or done anything sexual with another person when that person did not want you to do so"), even after adjusting for factors such as gender, aggressive traits, and family background (Ybarra et al., 2011).

Canadian and American sexual offenders commonly acknowledge pornography use. Among 155 men arrested for Internet-based child pornography, 85 percent admitted they had molested a child at least once, and the average offender had 13 victims (Bourke & Hernandez, 2009). The reverse is also true: rapists, serial killers, and child molesters report using pornography at unusually high rates (Bennett, 1991; Ressler, Burgess, & Douglas, 1988). Among university men, high pornography consumption has predicted sexual aggressiveness even after controlling for other predictors of antisocial behaviour, such as general hostility (Vega & Malamuth, 2007).

Was Paul Bernardo's use of pornography (in whose house police found pornographic tapes) merely a symptom of his derangement or was it a cause? Could the viewing of pornography actually have pushed him over the edge and led him to begin raping and murdering young girls? Notorious serial killer Ted Bundy saw such a role for pornography in his own life. On the eve of his execution, he argued, "The most damaging kinds of pornography [involve] sexual violence. Like an addiction, you keep craving something that is harder, harder, something which, which gives you a greater sense of excitement. Until you reach a point where the pornography only goes so far, you reach that jumping off point where you begin to wonder if maybe actually doing it would give you that which is beyond just reading it or looking at it."

But perhaps pornography doesn't actually cause violence, but instead, violent men like violent pornography. To rule out this explanation, it is necessary to perform an experiment—for example, to randomly assign some people to watch pornography. In one such study, 120 men watched a neutral, an erotic, or an aggressive-erotic (rape) film. Then the men, supposedly as part of another experiment, "taught" a male or female confederate some nonsense syllables by choosing how much shock to administer for incorrect answers. The men who had watched the rape film administered markedly stronger shocks (Figure 9–5), especially when angered and with a female confederate. A consensus statement by 21 leading social scientists summed up the results of experiments in this area: "Exposure to violent pornography increases punitive behavior toward women" (Koop, 1987).

If the ethics of conducting such experiments trouble you, rest assured that these researchers appreciate the controversial and powerful experience they are giving participants. Only after giving their knowing consent do people participate. Moreover, after the experiment, researchers debunk any myths the film communicated (Check & Malamuth, 1984). Another experiment avoided the ethical dilemma by asking college and university students who usually consumed pornography to abstain from consumption for a month. Compared with those who instead gave up

> *"What we're trying to do is raise the level of awareness of violence against women and pornography to at least the level of racist and Ku Klux Klan literature."*
> GLORIA STEINEM (1988)

FIGURE 9–5

PORNOGRAPHY
AND PUNITIVE
BEHAVIOUR.

After viewing an
aggressive-erotic
film, university and
college men delivered
stronger shocks than
before, especially to
a woman. (Data from
Donnerstein, 1980)

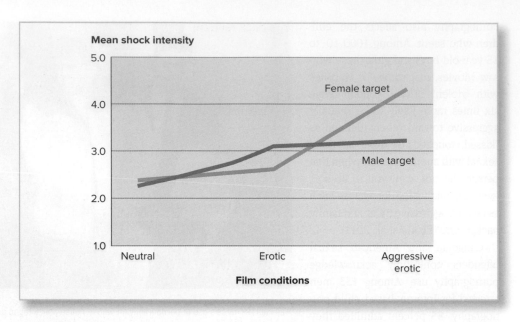

a favourite food, those who had dialled back on their porn consumption were less aggressive (Lambert et al., 2012).

Justification for this experimentation is not only scientific but also humanitarian. In a sample of 9684 North Americans, 11 percent of women reported experiencing forced sex at some point in their lives (Basile et al., 2007; CDC, 2008). Surveys in many industrialized countries produced similar results (Table 9–1). Three in four stranger rapes and nearly all acquaintance rapes went unreported to police. Thus, the official rape rate *greatly* underestimates the actual rape rate.

Women are most at risk when encountering men who exhibit the promiscuous behaviour and hostile attitudes pornography cultivates (Figure 9–6).

Media awareness education

As most Germans quietly tolerated the degrading anti-Semitic images that fed the Holocaust, so most people today tolerate media images of women that feed sexual harassment,

TABLE 9–1   REPORTED RAPE EXPERIENCES IN FIVE COUNTRIES.

Country	Sample of Women	Completed and Attempted Rape
Canada	Student national sample at 95 colleges and universities	23% rape or sexual assault
Berlin, Germany	Late adolescents	17% criminal sexual violence
New Zealand	Sample of psychology students	25%
United Kingdom	Student sample at 22 universities	19%
United States	Representative sample at 32 colleges and universities	28%
Seoul, Korea	Adult women	22%

Source: Studies reported by Koss, Heise, and Russo (1994), and Krahé (1998).

abuse, and rape. Should such portrayals, which demean and violate women, be restrained by law?

In the contest between individual and collective rights, people in most Western nations side with individual rights. As an alternative to censorship, many psychologists favour "media awareness training." You will recall that pornography researchers have successfully resensitized and educated participants to women's actual responses to sexual violence. Could educators similarly promote critical-viewing skills? By sensitizing people to the view of women that predominates in pornography and to issues of sexual harassment and violence, it should be possible to counter the myth that women enjoy being coerced. "Our utopian and perhaps naive hope," said Edward Donnerstein, Daniel Linz, and Steven Penrod (1987, p. 196), "is that in the end the truth revealed through good science will prevail and the public will be convinced that these images demean not only those portrayed but also those who view them."

Is such a hope naive? Consider: Without a ban on cigarettes, the number of Canadian smokers dropped from 48 percent in 1972 to 16 percent in 2012 (Health Canada, 2012). Without censorship of racism, once-common media images of Blacks as childlike, superstitious buffoons have nearly disappeared. As public consciousness changed, scriptwriters, producers, and media executives shunned exploitative images of minorities. Will we one day look back with embarrassment on the time when movies entertained people with scenes of exploitation, mutilation, and sexual coercion?

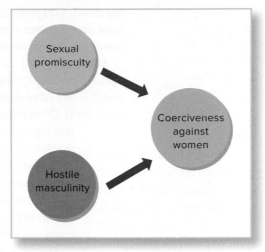

FIGURE 9–6

SEXUALLY AGGRESSIVE MEN.

Men who sexually coerce women often combine a history of impersonal sex with hostile masculinity. (Malamuth, 1996, 2003; Jacques-Tiura et al., 2007)

⑤ MEDIA INFLUENCES: TELEVISION

We have seen that watching an aggressive model attack a Bobo doll can unleash children's aggressive urges and teach them new ways to aggress. And we have seen that after viewing movies depicting sexual violence, many angry men will act more violently toward women. Does everyday television viewing have any similar effects?

Although very recent data are scarce (funding for media monitoring waned after the early 1990s), these facts about television watching remain: Today, in much of the industrialized world, 98 percent of households have a TV set, more than have telephones (Trewin, 2001). Most homes have more than one set, which helps explain why parents and children often give differing reports of what the children are watching (Donnerstein, 1998).

In the average home, the set is on seven hours a day, with individual teens averaging four hours and adults three hours. Thanks to digital video recorders (DVRs) that allow people to "time-shift" their TV watching, people in 2008 watched more TV than ever before (Nielsen, 2008a, 2008b). During all those hours, what social behaviours are modelled? From 1994 to 1997, bleary-eyed employees of the National Television Violence Study (1997) analyzed some 10 000 programs from the major networks and cable channels. Their findings? Six in ten programs contain violence ("physically compelling action that threatens to hurt or kill, or actual hurting or killing"). During fistfights, people who went down usually shook it off and came back stronger—unlike most real fistfights that last one punch (often resulting in a broken jaw or hand). In 73 percent of violent scenes, the aggressors went unpunished. In 58 percent, the victim was not shown to experience pain. In children's programs, only 5 percent of violence was shown to have any long-term consequences; two-thirds depicted violence as funny. To adults, violence seems less violent when humorous (Kirsh, 2006).

What does it add up to? All told, television beams its electromagnetic waves into children's eyeballs for more growing-up hours than they spend in school. More hours, in fact than they spend in any other waking activity. By the end of elementary school, the average child views some 8000 TV murders and 100 000 other violent acts (Huston et al., 1992). According to one content analysis, prime-time violence increased 75 percent between 1998 and the 2005–2006 season, which averaged 4.41 violent events per hour (PTC, 2007). Reflecting on his 22 years of cruelty counting, media researcher George Gerbner (1994) lamented, "Humankind has had more bloodthirsty eras but none as filled with *images* of violence as the present. We are awash in a tide of violent representations the world has never seen . . . drenching every home with graphic scenes of expertly choreographed brutality."

> *"One of television's great contributions is that it brought murder back into the home where it belongs. Seeing a murder on television can be good therapy. It can help work off one's antagonisms."*
> ALFRED HITCHCOCK

Studies of television viewing and aggression aim to identify effects more subtle and pervasive than the occasional "copy-cat" murders that capture public attention. They ask this question: How does television affect viewers' behaviour and viewers' thinking?

Television's effects on behaviour

Do viewers imitate violent models? Examples abound of people re-enacting television crimes. In one survey of 208 prison convicts, nine out of ten admitted that they learned new criminal tricks by watching crime programs. Four out of ten said they had attempted specific crimes seen on television (*TV Guide,* 1977).

Correlating TV viewing and behaviour

Stories of TV-inspired crime are not scientific evidence. Researchers, therefore, use correlational and experimental studies to examine the effects of viewing violence. One technique, commonly used with schoolchildren, correlates their TV watching with their aggressiveness. The frequent result: The more violent the content of the child's TV viewing, the more aggressive the child (Eron, 1987; Kuntsche et al., 2006; Turner, Hesse, & Peterson-Lewis, 1986). The relationship is modest but consistently found in North America, Europe, and Australia. British girls who most often view programs that model gossiping, backbiting, and social exclusion also more often display such behaviour (Coyne & Archer, 2005).

Can we conclude that a diet of violent TV fuels aggression? Perhaps you are already thinking that because this is a correlational study, the cause–effect relation could also work in the opposite direction. Maybe aggressive children prefer aggressive programs. Or maybe some underlying third factor, such as lower intelligence, predisposes some children both to prefer aggressive programs and to exhibit aggressive behaviour.

Researchers have developed two ways to test these alternative explanations. They test the "hidden third factor" explanation by statistically pulling out the influence of some of these possible factors. For example, British researcher William Belson (1978; Muson, 1978) studied 1565 London boys. Compared to those who watched little violence, those who watched a great deal (especially realistic rather than cartoon violence) admitted to 50 percent more violent acts during the preceding six months (for example, vandalizing a public telephone). Belson also examined 22 likely third factors, such as family size. The heavy and light viewers still differed after equating them with respect to potential third factors. So Belson surmised that the heavy viewers were, indeed, more violent *because* of their TV exposure.

Similarly, Leonard Eron and Rowell Huesmann (1980, 1985) found that violence viewing among 875 eight-year-olds correlated with aggressiveness even after statistically pulling out several obvious possible third factors. Moreover, when they restudied these individuals as 19-year-olds, they discovered that viewing violence at age 8 modestly predicted aggressiveness at age 19, but that aggressiveness at age 8 did not predict viewing violence at age 19. Aggression followed viewing, not the reverse. Moreover, by age 30, those who had watched the most violence in childhood were more likely to have been convicted of a serious crime (Figure 9–7).

Follow-up studies have confirmed these findings in various ways, including the following:

- Correlating 8-year-olds' violence viewing with their later likelihood of adult spousal abuse (Huesmann et al., 1984, 2003)

- Correlating adolescents' violence viewing with their later likelihood of assault, robbery, and threats of injury (Johnson et al., 2002)

- Correlating elementary schoolchildren's violent media exposure with how often they got into fights when restudied two to six months later (Gentile et al., 2004)

In all these studies, the investigators were careful to adjust for likely "third factors," such as pre-existing lower intelligence or hostility.

Another fact to ponder: Where television goes, increased violence follows. Even murder rates increase when and where television comes. In Canada, the homicide rate doubled between

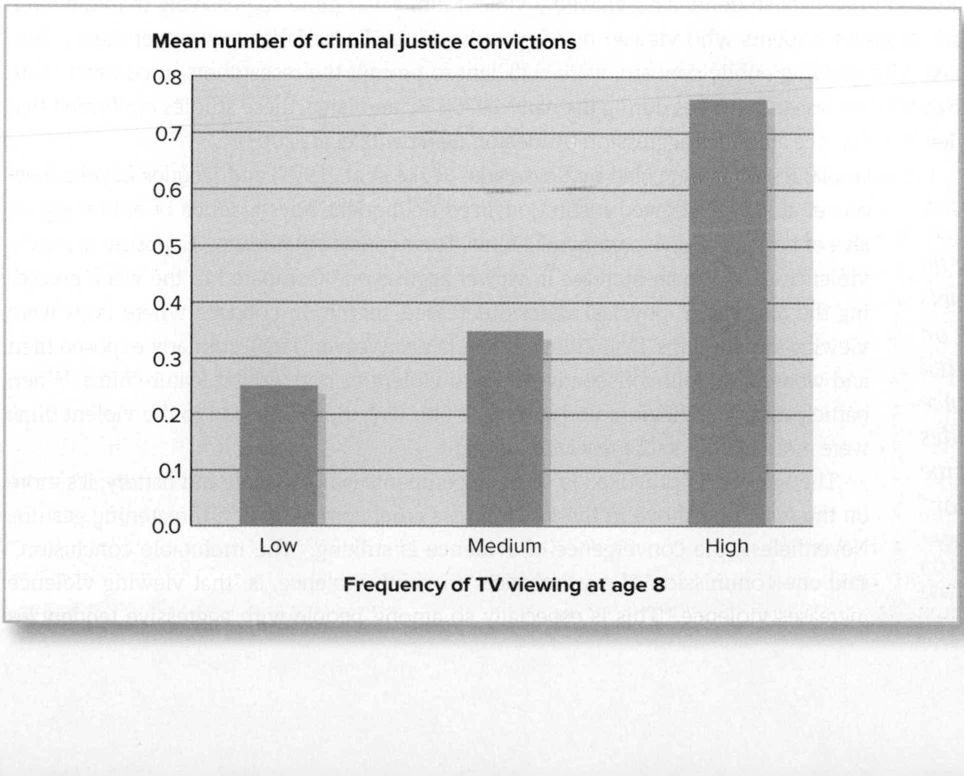

> *"I rarely turn down an invitation to speak to a PTA meeting or other civic groups in order to warn parents and other caretakers that they must control their children's viewing habits."*
> LEONARD ERON (1985)

Mean number of criminal justice convictions

Frequency of TV viewing at age 8

(Bar chart showing values approximately: Low ≈ 0.25, Medium ≈ 0.35, High ≈ 0.75, on a vertical axis from 0.0 to 0.8)

FIGURE 9–7

CHILDREN'S TELEVISION VIEWING AND LATER CRIMINAL ACTIVITY.

Violence viewing at age 8 was a predictor of a serious criminal offence by age 30. (Data from Eron and Huesmann, 1984)

1957 and 1974 as violent television spread. In census regions where television came later, the homicide rate jumped later, too. In South Africa, where television was not introduced until 1975, a similar near doubling of the homicide rate did not begin until after 1975 (Centerwall, 1989). And in a closely studied rural Canadian town where television came late, playground aggression doubled soon after (Williams, 1986).

Many people now spend more screen time in front of their computers than in front of the television. In many ways, the Internet allows an even greater variety of options for viewing violence than television does, including violent videos, violent pictures, and hate-group websites (Donnerstein, 2011). It also allows people to create and distribute violent media themselves, and to bully others through e-mail, instant messaging, or social networking websites (Donnerstein, 2011). In a survey of European adolescents, one-third reported seeing violent or hateful content online (Livingstone & Haddon, 2009). Among U.S. youth, those who frequently visited violent websites were five times more likely to report engaging in violent behaviour (Ybarra et al., 2008).

Notice that these studies illustrate how researchers are now using correlational findings to suggest cause and effect. Yet an infinite number of possible third factors could be creating a merely coincidental relation between viewing violence and aggression. Fortunately, however, the experimental method can control these extraneous factors. If we randomly assign some children to watch a violent film and others a non-violent film, any later aggression difference between the two groups will be due to the only factor that distinguishes them: what they watched.

> "Then shall we simply allow our children to listen to any story anyone happens to make up, and so receive into their minds ideas often the very opposite of those we shall think they ought to have when they are grown up?"
> PLATO, *REPUBLIC*

TV viewing experiments

The pioneering experiments by Albert Bandura and Richard Walters (1963) sometimes had young children view the adult pounding the inflated doll on film instead of observing it live—with much the same effect. Then Leonard Berkowitz and Russell Geen (1966) found that angered university students who viewed a violent film acted more aggressively than did similarly angered students who viewed non-aggressive films. These laboratory experiments, coupled with growing public concern, were sufficient to prompt the researchers to conduct more than 50 new research studies during the early 1970s. By and large, these studies confirmed that viewing violence amplifies aggression (Anderson, Berkowitz et al., 2003).

For example, research teams led by Ross Parke (Parke et al., 1977) and Jacques Leyens (Leyens et al., 1975) showed institutionalized delinquent boys a series of either aggressive or non-aggressive commercial films. Their consistent finding: "Exposure to movie violence . . . led to an increase in viewer aggression." Compared to the week preceding the film series, physical attacks increased sharply in cottages where boys were viewing violent films. Dolf Zillmann and James Weaver (1999) similarly exposed men and women, on four consecutive days, to violent or non-violent feature films. When participating in a different project on the fifth day, those exposed to the violent films were more hostile to the research assistant.

> "There is absolutely no doubt that higher levels of viewing violence on television are correlated with increased acceptance of aggressive attitudes and increased aggressive behavior."
> AMERICAN PSYCHOLOGICAL ASSOCIATION COMMISSION ON VIOLENCE AND YOUTH, 1993

The aggression provoked in these experiments is not assault and battery; it's more on the scale of a shove in the lunch line, a cruel comment, or a threatening gesture. Nevertheless, the convergence of evidence is striking. "The irrefutable conclusion," said one commission of psychologists on youth violence, is "that viewing violence increases violence." This is especially so among people with aggressive tendencies and when, in the violent depiction, an attractive person commits justified, realistic violence that goes unpunished and that shows no pain or harm (Comstock, 2008; Gentile, Saleem, & Anderson, 2007; Zillmann & Weaver, 2007).

All in all, concluded researchers Brad Bushman and Craig Anderson (2001), the evidence for media effects on aggression is now "overwhelming." The research base is large, the methods diverse, and the overall findings consistent, echoed a task force of leading media violence researchers (C. A. Anderson et al., 2003). "Our in-depth review . . . reveals unequivocal evidence that exposure to media violence can increase the likelihood of aggressive and violent behaviour in both immediate and long-term contexts."

Why does TV viewing affect behaviour?

Given the convergence of correlational and experimental evidence, researchers have explored why viewing violence has this effect. Consider three possibilities (Geen & Thomas, 1986). One is the arousal it produces (Mueller, Donnerstein, E., & Hallam, 1983; Zillmann, 1989a). As we noted earlier, arousal tends to spill over: One type of arousal energizes other behaviours.

Other research shows that viewing violence disinhibits; that is, it lowers inhibitions. In Bandura's experiment, the adult's punching of the Bobo doll seemed to legitimize such outbursts and to lower the children's inhibitions. Viewing violence primes the viewer for aggressive behaviour by activating violence-related thoughts (Berkowitz, 1984; Bushman & Geen, 1990; Josephson, 1987). Listening to music with sexually violent lyrics seems to have a similar effect (Barongan & Hall, 1995; J. D. Johnson, Jackson, & Gatto, 1995; Pritchard, 1998).

Media portrayals also evoke imitation. The children in Bandura's experiments re-enacted the specific behaviours they had witnessed. The commercial television industry is hard-pressed to dispute that television leads viewers to imitate what they have seen: Its advertisers model consumption. Are media executives right, however, to argue that TV merely holds a mirror to a violent society? That art imitates life? That the "reel" world, therefore, shows us the real world? Actually, on TV programs, acts of assault outnumber affectionate acts 4 to 1. In other ways as well, television models an unreal world.

But there is good news here, too. If the ways of relating and problem-solving modelled on television do trigger imitation, especially among young viewers, then modelling **prosocial behaviour** should be socially beneficial. Chapter 8 explored how television's subtle influence can, indeed, teach children positive lessons in behaviour.

prosocial behaviour
positive, constructive, helpful social behaviour; the opposite of antisocial behaviour

Television's effects on thinking

We have focused on television's effect on behaviour, but researchers have also examined the cognitive effects of viewing violence: Does prolonged viewing desensitize us to cruelty? Does it give us mental scripts for how to act? Does it distort perceptions of reality? Does it prime aggressive thoughts?

Desensitization

Repeat an emotion-arousing stimulus, such as an obscene word, over and over. What happens? From introductory psychology, you may recall that the emotional response will "extinguish." After witnessing thousands of acts of cruelty, there is good reason to expect a similar emotional numbing. The most common response might well become, "Doesn't bother me at all." Such a response is precisely what Barbara Krahe and her colleagues (2010) observed when they

> *"All television is educational. The question is, what is it teaching?"*
>
> NICHOLAS JOHNSON, FORMER COMMISSIONER, FEDERAL COMMUNICATIONS COMMISSION, 1978

measured the physiological arousal of 303 university students who watched a clip from a violent movie. Regular viewers of violence on TV and movies showed a lessened response, compared to infrequent viewers, reacting to violence with a shrug rather than concern.

In a clever experiment, Brad Bushman and Craig Anderson (2009) had a young woman with a taped-up ankle drop her crutches while outside a movie theatre and then struggle to retrieve them. Moviegoers who had just seen a violent film (*The Ruins*) took longer to help than those who had just seen a non-violent film (*Nim's Island*). When the woman dropped her crutches before the movie, however, there was no difference in helping—suggesting it was the violent film itself, and not the type of people who watch violent films, that desensitized moviegoers to her dilemma.

As television and movies have become more sexually explicit—the number of prime-time American TV scenes involving sexual talk or behaviour nearly doubled between 1998 and 2005 (Kaiser Family Foundation, 2005)—teen concern about media sex depictions has similarly declined. Today's teens "appear to have become considerably more desensitized to graphic depictions of violence and sex than their parents were at their age," concludes Gallup researcher Josephine Mazzuca (2002). Media portrayals desensitize.

Social scripts

social scripts
culturally provided mental instructions for how to act in various situations

When we find ourselves in new situations, uncertain how to act, we often rely on social scripts—culturally provided mental instructions for how to act. After so many action films, youngsters may acquire a script that is played when they face real-life conflicts. Challenged, they may "act like a man" by intimidating or eliminating the threat. Likewise, after viewing multiple sexual innuendoes and acts on TV and in music lyrics—mostly involving impulsive or short-term relationships—youths may acquire sexual scripts they later enact in real-life relationships (Escobar-Chaves & Anderson, 2008; Fischer & Greitemeyer, 2006; Kunkel, 2001). Thus, the more sexual content that adolescents view (even when controlling for other predictors of early sexual activity), the more likely they are to perceive their peers as sexually active, to develop sexually permissive attitudes, and to experience early intercourse (Escobar-Chaves et al., 2005; Martino et al., 2005). Media portrayals implant social scripts.

Altered perceptions

> *"The more fully that any given generation was exposed to television in its formative years, the lower its civic engagement [its rate of voting, joining, meeting, giving, and volunteering]."*
>
> ROBERT PUTNAM, *BOWLING ALONE* (2000)

Does television's fictional world also mould our conceptions of the real world? George Gerbner and his associates (1979, 1994) suspect this is television's most potent effect. Their surveys of both adolescents and adults showed that heavy viewers (four hours a day or more) are more likely than light viewers (two hours or fewer) to exaggerate the frequency of violence in the world around them and to fear being personally assaulted. Similar feelings of vulnerability have been expressed by South African women after viewing violence against women (Reid & Finchilescu, 1995). One survey of 7- to 11-year-old children found that heavy viewers were more likely than light viewers to admit fears "that somebody bad might get into your house" or that "when you go outside, somebody might hurt you" (Peterson & Zill, 1981). For those who watch a lot of television, the world becomes a scary place. Media portrayals shape perceptions of reality.

Cognitive priming

Evidence also reveals that watching violent videos primes aggressive-related ideas (Bushman, 1998). After viewing violence, people offer more hostile explanations for others' behaviour (was the shove intentional?). They interpret spoken homonyms with the more aggressive meaning (interpreting "punch" as a hit rather than a drink). And they recognize aggressive words more quickly. Media portrayals prime thinking.

Time drain

Perhaps television's biggest effect relates not to its quality but to its quantity. Compared with more active recreation, TV watching sucks people's energy and dampens their moods (Kubey & Csikszentmihaly, 2002). Moreover, TV annually replaces in people's lives a thousand or more hours of other activities. If, like most others, you have spent a thousand-plus hours per year watching TV, think how you might have used that time if there were no television. What difference would that have made in who you are today? In seeking to explain the post-1960 decline in civic activities and organizational memberships, Robert Putnam (2000) reported that every added hour a day spent watching TV competes with civic participation. Television steals time from club meetings, volunteering, congregational activity, and political engagement.

(Dan Perkins/THIS MODERN WORLD)

People who watch many hours of television see the world as a dangerous place.

© 2009 Tom Tomorrow. Reprinted with permission of Dan Perkins.

⑥ MEDIA INFLUENCES: VIDEO GAMES

"The scientific debate over the effects of media violence is basically over," contended Douglas Gentile and Craig Anderson (2003). Researchers are now shifting their attention to video games, which are extremely popular among teens and can be extremely violent. Educational research shows that "video games are excellent teaching tools," noted Gentile and Anderson. "If health video games can successfully teach health behaviours, and flight simulator video games can teach people how to fly, then what should we expect violent murder-simulating games to teach?"

The games kids play

In 2012, the video game industry celebrated its 40th birthday. Since the first video game in 1972, we have moved from electronic Ping-Pong to splatter games (Anderson, Gentile, & Buckley, 2007). In a 2008 poll, 97 percent of 12- to 17-year-olds said they play video games. Half had played a video game the day before. Many of these games were violent—half of the teens said they played first-person shooter games, such as Halo or Counter-Strike, and two out of three played action games that often involve violence, such as Grand Theft Auto (Pew Research Center, 2008). Younger children are also playing violent games: In one survey of grade 4 students, 59 percent of girls and 73 percent of boys reported their favourite games as violent ones (Anderson, 2003, 2004). Games rated "M" (mature) are supposedly intended for sale only to those 17 and older but often get marketed to those younger. The U.S. Federal Trade Commission found that in four out of five attempts, underage children could easily purchase them (Pereira, 2003).

> *"We had an internal rule that we wouldn't allow violence against people."*
> NOLAN BUSHNELL, ATARI FOUNDER

In the popular video game "Grand Theft Auto: San Andreas," youth are invited to play psychopath, noted Gentile (2004). "You can run down pedestrians with the car, you can do carjackings, you can do drive-by shootings, you can run down to the red-light district, pick up a prostitute, have sex with her in your car, and then kill her to get your money back." In effective 3D graphics, you can knock people over, stomp on them until they cough up blood, and watch them die.

Effects of the games kids play

Concerns about violent video games heightened after teen assassins enacted in school shootings the horrific violence they had so often played on-screen; concerns emerged again after the 2011 slaughter of Norwegians by an avid World of Warcraft gamer. People wondered: What do youth learn from endless hours of role-play attacking and dismembering people? And was anything accomplished when some Norwegian stores responded to the killings by pulling violent games from their shelves (Anderson, 2011)?

Most smokers don't die of lung cancer. Most abused children don't become abusive. And most people who spend hundreds of hours rehearsing human slaughter live gentle lives. This enables video game defenders, like tobacco and TV interests, to say their products are harmless. "There is absolutely no evidence, none, that playing a violent game leads to aggressive behavior," contended Doug Lowenstein (2000), president of the Interactive Digital Software Association.

Gentile and Anderson offer some reasons why violent game-playing might have a more toxic effect than watching violent television. With game-playing, players do the following:

- Identify with, and play the role of, a violent character.
- Actively rehearse violence; they don't just passively watch it.
- Engage in the whole sequence of enacting violence—selecting victims, acquiring weapons and ammunition, stalking the victim, aiming the weapon, pulling the trigger.
- Are engaged with continual violence and threats of attack.
- Repeat violent behaviours over and over.
- Are rewarded for violent acts.

For such reasons, military organizations often prepare soldiers to fire in combat (which many in the Second World War reportedly were hesitant to do) by engaging them with attack simulation games.

But do people who play violent video games go on to behave aggressively outside the game? "I play violent video games," some may protest, "and I'm not aggressive." As columnist Roger Simon (2011) wrote about research showing that media violence leads to real-life aggression, "Such claims bewilder me. I grew up playing with toy guns and have never shot anybody (though I know plenty who deserve it)." The problem with this common argument is that one isolated example proves nothing—it's not a scientific study. A better approach is to examine large samples of people to find out if, on average, violent video games increase aggression.

A large body of research shows that playing violent video games does, on average, increase aggressive behaviour, thoughts, and feelings. Combining data from 381 studies with 130 296 participants, Craig Anderson and his colleagues (2010) found a clear effect: Violent video game-playing increased aggression—for children, adolescents, and young adults; in North America, Japan, and Western Europe; and across three research designs (correlational, experimental, and longitudinal). That means violent video games caused aggression even when participants were randomly assigned to play them (vs. a non-violent game), which rules out the possibility that, for example, aggressive people like to play aggressive games. Longitudinal studies, which follow people over time, produce similar results: Among German adolescents, today's violent game-playing predicted later aggression, but today's aggression did not predict future violent game-playing (Moller & Krahe, 2008).

Playing violent video games has an array of effects, including the following:

- **Increases in aggressive behaviours.** After violent game play, children and youth play more aggressively with their peers, get into more arguments with their teachers, and participate in more fights. The effect occurs inside and outside of the laboratory; across self-reports, teacher reports, and parent reports; and for reasons illustrated in Figure 9–8. Even among young adolescents who scored low in hostility, 10 times more of the heavy violent gamers got into fights compared with their non-gaming counterparts. And after they started playing the violent games, previously non-hostile kids became more likely to have fights (Gentile et al., 2004). In Japan, too, playing violent games early in a school year predicted physical aggressiveness later in the year, even after controlling for gender and prior aggressiveness (Anderson et al., 2008).

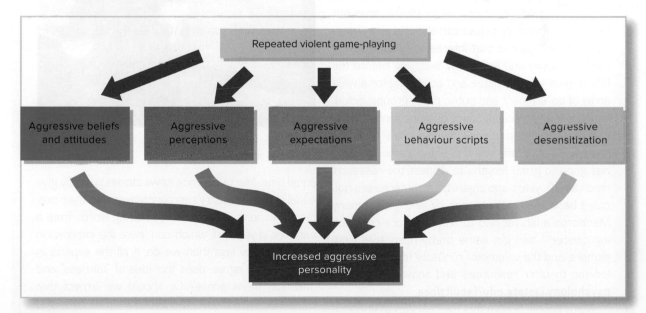

FIGURE 9–8

VIOLENT VIDEO GAME INFLUENCES ON AGGRESSIVE TENDENCIES.

(Adapted from Craig A. Anderson & Brad J. Bushman, 2001)

- **Increases in aggressive thoughts.** After playing a violent game, students became more likely to guess that a man whose car was just rear-ended would respond aggressively, by using abusive language, kicking out a window, or starting a fight (Bushman & Anderson, 2002).

- **Increases in aggressive feelings.** Including hostility, anger, or revenge.

- **Decreases in helping others and in empathy for others.** Students randomly assigned to play a violent or non-violent video game later overheard a loud fight that ended with one person writhing on the floor in pain from a sprained ankle. Students who had just played a violent game took more than one minute on average to come to the person's aid, almost four times as long as those who had played a non-violent game (Bushman & Anderson, 2009).

After violent video game-playing, people became more likely to exploit rather than to trust and cooperate with a partner (Sheese & Graziano, 2005). They also became desensitized to violence, as revealed by decreased brain activity associated with emotion (Bartholow, Bushman, & Sestir, 2006; Carnagey, Anderson, & Bushman, 2007). Tobias Greitemeyer and Neil McLatchie (2011) explored a specific kind of desensitization: Seeing other people as less human. Among British university students, those randomly assigned to play a violent game were more likely to describe in non-human terms someone who had insulted them. And the less human they saw the person, the more aggressive they were.

THE >>> INSIDE STORY

Understanding the clearly harmful effects being documented by TV/film researchers, I was disturbed as I noticed the increasing violence in video games. With one of my graduate students, Karen Dill, I therefore began correlational and experimental investigations that intersected with growing public concern and led to my testifying before the U.S. Senate subcommittee and consulting for a wide array of government and public policy groups, including parent and child advocacy organizations.

Although it is gratifying to see one's research have a positive impact, the video game industry has gone to great lengths to dismiss the research, much as 30 years ago cigarette manufacturers ridiculed basic medical research by asking how many Marlboros a lab rat had to smoke before contracting cancer. I also got some pretty nasty mail from gamers, and the volume of requests for information led me to offer resources and answers at **www.psychology.iastate.edu/faculty/caa**.

Many people believe that the best way to enhance understanding of a complicated topic is to find people who will give opposite views and give each "side"

Is violent video game-playing cathartic? Toxic? Or neutral? Experiments offer some answers.

equal time. Media violence news stories typically give equal time to industry representatives and their preferred "experts" along with reassuring words from a carefree 4-year-old, which can leave the impression that we know less than we do. If all the experts in a given area agree, does this idea of "fairness" and "balance" make sense? Or should we expect that legitimate experts will have published peer-reviewed original research articles on the issue at hand?

Craig A. Anderson *Iowa State University*

Moreover, the more violent the games played, the bigger the effects. The bloodier the game (for example, the higher the blood level setting in one experiment with Mortal Kombat players), the greater the gamer's after-game hostility and arousal (Barlett, Harris, & Bruey, 2008). More-realistic games—showing violence more likely to happen in real life—also produced more aggressive feelings than less-realistic games (Barlett & Rodeheffer, 2009). Video games have become more violent, which helps explain why newer studies find the biggest effects. Although much remains to be learned, these studies challenge the **catharsis** hypothesis—the idea that violent games allow people to safely express their aggressive tendencies and "get their anger out" (Kutner & Olson, 2008). Practising violence breeds rather than releases violence, say catharsis critics. Yet the idea that games might relieve angry feelings is one of the main draws of violent video games for angry people (Bushman & Whitaker, 2010). Unfortunately, say critics, this strategy is likely to backfire, leading to more anger and aggression.

In 2005, California State Senator Leland Yee proposed a law banning the sale of violent video games to those under 18. The bill was signed into law, but video game manufacturers immediately sued, and it never went into effect. The U.S. Supreme Court heard the case in 2010, and more than 100 social scientists signed a statement in support of the law, writing that "Overall, the research data conclude that exposure to violent video games causes an increase in the likelihood of aggressive behavior." In 2011, the Supreme Court struck down the law, primarily citing the First Amendment to the U.S. Constitution's guarantee of free speech but also expressing doubts that the research showed "a direct causal link between playing violent video games and actual harm to minors" (Scalia, 2011).

Similarly, academic researchers are not unanimous in the view that violent video games have meaningful effects on real-world behaviour. Christopher Ferguson and John Kilburn (2010), for example, signed a statement to the U.S. Supreme Court criticizing the California law. They point out that from 1996 to 2006, when violent video game sales were increasing, real-life youth violence was decreasing. Ferguson and Kilburn also argue that the effects of violent video games on aggression are small—only some people who play violent video games will act aggressively in real life. Their skepticism helped persuade the Australian Attorney General's department (2010) that research on violent video game effects "is contested and inconclusive." Brad Bushman and his colleagues (2010) argue that the violent gaming effect is larger than the toxic effects of asbestos or the effect of second-hand smoke on lung cancer. Not everyone exposed to asbestos or second-hand smoke will develop cancer, they point out, but they are still considered public health dangers.

Of course, video games are not all bad—not all of them are violent, and even the violent games improve hand-eye coordination and reaction time (Dye, Green, & Bavelier, 2009). Moreover, game-playing is focused fun that helps satisfy basic needs for a sense of competence, control, and social connection (Przybylski, Rigby, & Ryan, 2010). No wonder an experiment that randomly assigned 6- to 9-year-old boys to receive a game system found them spending an average of 40 minutes a day on it over the next few months. The downside: They spent less time on schoolwork, resulting in lower reading and writing scores than the control group that did not get a game system (Weis & Cerankosky, 2010).

What about playing prosocial games in which people help each other—the conceptual opposite of violent games? In three studies with children and adults in Singapore, Japan, and the United States, those who played prosocial video games helped others, shared, and cooperated more in real-life situations (Gentile et al., 2009). As Douglas Gentile and Craig Anderson (2011)

catharsis
emotional release. The catharsis view of aggression is that aggressive drive is reduced when one "releases" aggressive energy, either by acting aggressively or by fantasizing aggression.

conclude, "Video games are excellent teachers." Educational games teach children reading and math, prosocial games teach prosocial behaviour, and violent games teach violence, they note. We do what we're taught to do, whether that's to help or to hurt.

As a concerned scientist, Craig Anderson (2003, 2004; see "The Inside Story," above) therefore encourages parents to discover what their kids are ingesting and to ensure that their media diet, at least in their own home, is healthy. Parents may not be able to control what their child watches, plays, and eats in someone else's home. Nor can they control the media's effect on their children's peer culture. (That is why advising parents to "just say no" is naive.) But parents can oversee consumption in their own home and provide increased time for alternative activities. Networking with other parents can build a kid-friendly neighbourhood. And schools can help by providing media awareness education.

GROUP INFLUENCES

We have considered what provokes individuals to aggress. If frustrations, insults, and aggressive models heighten the aggressive tendencies of isolated people, then such factors are likely to prompt the same reaction in groups. As a riot begins, aggressive acts often spread rapidly after the "trigger" example of one antagonistic person. Seeing looters freely helping themselves to TV sets, normally law-abiding bystanders may drop their moral inhibitions and imitate.

Groups can amplify aggressive reactions partly by diffusing responsibility. Decisions to attack in war typically are made by strategists remote from the front lines. They give orders, but others carry them out. Does such distancing make it easier to recommend aggression?

Jacquelin Gaebelein and Anthony Mander (1978) simulated this situation in the laboratory. They asked their university student participants either to shock someone or to advise someone how much shock to administer. When the recipient was innocent of any provocation, as are most victims of mass aggression, the advisers recommended more shock than given by the front-line participants, who felt more directly responsible for any hurt.

Diffusion of responsibility increases not only with distance but with numbers. (Recall from Chapter 7 the phenomenon of deindividuation.) When Brian Mullen (1986a) analyzed information from 60 lynchings that occurred between 1899 and 1946, he made an interesting discovery: The greater the number of people in a lynch mob, the more vicious the murder and mutilation.

Through social "contagion," groups magnify aggressive tendencies, much as they polarize other tendencies. Examples include youth gangs, soccer fans, rapacious soldiers, urban rioters, and what Scandinavians call "mobbing"—schoolchildren in groups repeatedly harassing or attacking an insecure, weak schoolmate (Lagerspetz et al., 1982). Mobbing is a group activity.

Youths sharing antisocial tendencies and lacking close family bonds and expectations of academic success may find social identity in a gang. As group identity develops, conformity pressures and deindividuation increase (Staub, 1996). Self-identity diminishes as members give themselves over to the group, often feeling a satisfying oneness with the others. The frequent result is social contagion—group-fed arousal, disinhibition, and polarization. As gang expert Arnold Goldstein

Social contagion: When 17 juvenile, orphaned male bull elephants were relocated during the mid-1990s to a South African park, they became an out-of-control adolescent gang and killed 40 white rhinoceros. When, in 1998, concerned park officials relocated six older, stronger bull elephants into their midst, the rampaging soon quieted down (Slotow et al., 2000). One of these dominant bulls, at left, faces down several of the juveniles.

(1994) observed, until gang members marry out, age out, get a job, go to prison, or die, they hang out. They define their turf, display their colours, challenge rivals, and sometimes commit delinquent acts and fight over drugs, territory, honour, women, or insults.

The twentieth-century massacres that have claimed more than 150 million lives were "not the sums of individual actions," noted Robert Zajonc (2000). "Genocide is not the plural of homicide." Massacres are social phenomena fed by "moral imperatives"—a collective mentality (including images, rhetoric, and ideology) that mobilizes a group or a culture for extraordinary actions. The massacres of Rwanda's Tutsis, of Europe's Jews, and of North America's Aboriginal population were collective phenomena requiring widespread support, organization, and participation. Before launching the genocidal initiative, Rwanda's Hutu government and business leaders bought and distributed 2 million Chinese machetes. Over three months, the Hutu attackers reportedly would get up, eat a hearty breakfast, gather together, and then go hunt their former neighbours, who had fled. They would hack to death anyone they found, then return home, wash, and socialize over a few beers (Dalrymple, 2007; Hatzfeld, 2007).

Experiments in Israel (Jaffe & Yinon, 1983) confirmed that groups can amplify aggressive tendencies. In one such experiment, university men angered by a supposed fellow participant retaliated with decisions to give much stronger shocks when in groups than when alone. In another experiment (Jaffe, Shapir, & Yinon, 1981), people decided, either alone or in groups, how much punishing shock to give someone for incorrect answers on a task. As Figure 9–9 shows, individuals gave progressively more of the assumed shock as the experiment proceeded, and group decision-making magnified this individual tendency. When circumstances provoke an individual's aggressive reaction, the addition of group interaction will often amplify it.

Perhaps you can remember a time in school when you or someone you knew were bullied—either verbally or physically. Often, other students watch bullying as it happens. These bystanders can play an active role in the aggressive act of bullying—for example, by contributing to the humiliation by laughing or cheering (Salmivalli et al., 1999). Or they may defend the victim. An effective anti bullying program in Finland found that when bystanders stop rewarding bullies with positive feedback and status, bullying declined (Karna et al., 2011).

Aggression studies provide an apt opportunity to ask how well social psychology's laboratory findings generalize to everyday life. Do the circumstances that trigger someone to deliver electric shock or other aversive stimuli really tell us anything about the circumstances that trigger verbal abuse or a punch in the face? Craig Anderson and Brad Bushman (1997; Bushman & Anderson, 1998) noted that social psychologists have studied aggression in both the laboratory and the everyday world, and the findings are strikingly consistent. In both contexts, increased aggression is predicted by the following:

- Male actors
- Aggressive or anger-prone personalities
- Alcohol use
- Violence viewing
- Anonymity
- Provocation
- The presence of weapons
- Group interaction

"Genocide is not the plural of homicide."
ROBERT ZAJONC, "MASSACRES: MASS MURDERS IN THE NAME OF MORAL IMPERATIVES," 2000

FIGURE 9–9

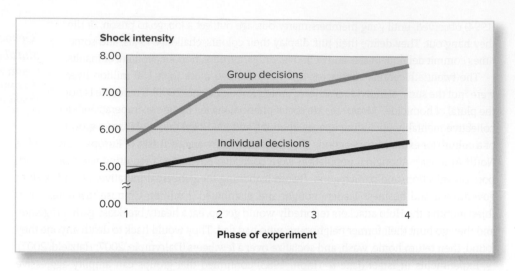

FIGURE 9–9

GROUP-ENHANCED AGGRESSION.

When individuals chose how much shock to administer as punishment for wrong answers, they escalated the shock level as the experiment proceeded. Group decision-making further polarized this tendency.
(Data from Jaffe et al., 1981)

The laboratory allows us to test and revise theories under controlled conditions. Real-world events inspire ideas and provide the venue for applying our theories. Aggression research illustrates that an interplay between studies in the controlled lab and the complex real world advances psychology's contribution to human welfare. Hunches gained from everyday experience inspire theories, which stimulate laboratory research, which then deepens our understanding and our ability to apply psychology to real problems.

● HOW CAN AGGRESSION BE REDUCED?

Can we reduce aggression? Here we look at how theory and research suggest ways to control it.

CATHARSIS?

"Youngsters should be taught to vent their anger." So commented advice columnist Ann Landers (1969). If a person "bottles up his rage, we have to find an outlet. We have to give him an opportunity of letting off steam." So asserted the once-prominent psychiatrist Fritz Perls (1973). Both statements assume the "hydraulic model," which implies accumulated aggressive energy, like dammed-up water, needs a release.

The concept of catharsis is usually credited to Aristotle. Although Aristotle actually said nothing about aggression, he did argue that we can purge emotions by experiencing them and that viewing the classic tragedies, therefore, enabled a catharsis (purging) of pity and fear. To have an emotion excited, he believed, is to have that emotion released (Butcher, 1951). The catharsis hypothesis has been extended to include the emotional release supposedly obtained not only by observing drama but also through recalling and reliving past events, through expressing emotions, and through our actions.

Assuming that aggressive action or fantasy drains pent-up aggression, some therapists and group leaders encourage people to ventilate suppressed aggression by acting it out—by whopping one another with foam bats or beating a bed with a tennis racquet while screaming. If led to believe that catharsis effectively vents emotions, people will react more aggressively to an insult as a way to improve their mood (Bushman, Baumeister, & Phillips, 2001). Some psychologists, believing that catharsis is therapeutic, advise parents to encourage children's release of emotional tension through aggressive play.

Many laypeople have also bought the catharsis idea, as reflected in their nearly two-to-one agreement with the statement, "Sexual materials provide an outlet for bottled up impulses" (Niemi, Mueller, & Smith, 1989). But other surveys reveal that most people also agree that "Sexual materials lead people to commit rape." So is the catharsis approach valid or not?

Consider: If viewing erotica provides an outlet for sexual impulses, people should experience diminished sexual desire afterward, and men should be less likely to view and treat women as sexual objects. But studies show the opposite (Kelley, Dawson, & Musialowski, 1989; McKenzie-Mohr & Zanna, 1990). Sexually explicit videos are an aphrodisiac; they feed sexual fantasies that fuel a variety of sexual behaviours.

Researcher Brad Bushman (2002) noted, "Venting to reduce anger is like using gasoline to put out a fire." For example, Robert Arms and his associates reported that Canadian and American spectators of football, wrestling, and hockey matches exhibited more hostility after viewing the event than before (Arms, Russell, & Sandilands, 1979; Goldstein & Arms, 1971; Russell, 1983).

In laboratory tests of the catharsis hypothesis, Brad Bushman (2002) invited angered participants to hit a punching bag while either ruminating about the person who angered them or thinking about becoming physically fit. A third group did not hit the punching bag. Then, when given a chance to administer loud blasts of noise to the person who angered them, people in the "punching bag plus rumination" condition felt angrier and were most aggressive. Moreover, doing nothing at all more effectively reduced aggression than did "blowing off steam" by hitting the bag.

In some real-life experiments, too, aggressing has led to heightened aggression. Ebbe Ebbesen and his co-researchers (1975) interviewed 100 engineers and technicians shortly after they were angered by layoff notices. Some were asked questions that gave them an opportunity to express hostility against their employer or supervisors—for example, "What instances can you think of where the company has not been fair with you?" Afterward, they answered a questionnaire assessing attitudes toward the company and the supervisors. Did the opportunity to express their hostility reduce it? To the contrary, their hostility increased. Expressing hostility bred more hostility.

Sound familiar? Recall from Chapter 4 that cruel acts beget cruel attitudes. Furthermore, as we noted in analyzing Stanley Milgram's obedience studies, small aggressive acts can breed their own justification. People derogate their victims, rationalizing further aggression.

Retaliation may, in the short run, reduce tension and even provide pleasure (Ramirez, Bonniot-Cabanac, & Cabanac, 2005). But in the long run, it fuels more negative feelings. When people who have been provoked hit a punching bag, even when they believe it will be cathartic, the effect is the opposite—leading them to exhibit more cruelty, reported Bushman and his colleagues (Bushman, Baumeister, & Stack, 1999; Bushman, Baumeister, & Phillips, 2000). "It's like the old joke," reflected Bushman (1999). "'How do you get

"The worst barbarity of war is that it forces men collectively to commit acts against which individually they would revolt with their whole being."
ELLEN KEY, *WAR, PEACE, AND THE FUTURE*, 1916

"He who gives way to violent gestures will increase his rage."
CHARLES DARWIN, *THE EXPRESSION OF EMOTION IN MAN AND ANIMALS*, 1872

to Carnegie Hall? Practice, practice, practice.' How do you become a very angry person? The answer is the same. Practice, practice, practice."

Should we, therefore, bottle up anger and aggressive urges? Silent sulking is hardly more effective, because it allows us to continue reciting our grievances as we conduct conversations in our head. Brad Bushman and his colleagues (2005) experimented with the toxic effect of such rumination. First, an obnoxious experimenter provoked subjects with insults such as "Can't you follow directions? Speak louder!" Then half were given a distraction (by being asked to write an essay about their campus landscape), and half were induced to ruminate (by writing an essay about their experiences as a research participant). Next they were mildly insulted by a supposed fellow participant (actually a confederate), to whom they responded by prescribing a hot sauce dose this person would have to consume. The distracted participants, their anger now abated, prescribed only a mild dose; the still-seething ruminators displaced their aggressive urge and prescribed twice as much.

Fortunately, there are non-aggressive ways to express our feelings and to tell others how their behaviour affects us. Across cultures, those who reframe accusatory "you" messages as "I" messages—"I feel angry about what you said" or "I get irritated when you leave dirty dishes"— communicate their feelings in a way that better enables the other person to make a positive response (Kubany et al., 1995). We can be assertive without being aggressive.

A SOCIAL LEARNING APPROACH

If aggressive behaviour is learned, then there is hope for its control. Let us briefly review factors that influence aggression and speculate how to counteract them.

Aversive experiences such as frustrated expectations and personal attacks predispose hostile aggression. So it is wise to refrain from planting false, unreachable expectations in people's minds. Anticipated rewards and costs influence instrumental aggression. This suggests that we should reward cooperative, non-aggressive behaviour.

In experiments, children become less aggressive when caregivers ignore their aggressive behaviour and reinforce their non-aggressive behaviour (Hamblin et al., 1969). Punishing the aggressor is less consistently effective. Threatened punishment deters aggression only under ideal conditions: when the punishment is strong, prompt, and sure; when it is combined with reward for the desired behaviour; and when the recipient is not angry (Baron, 1977).

Moreover, there are limits to punishment's effectiveness. Most homicide is impulsive, hot aggression—the result of an argument, an insult, or an attack. If mortal aggression were cool and instrumental, we could hope that waiting until it happens and severely punishing the criminal afterwards would deter such acts. In that world, countries that impose the death penalty might have a lower murder rate than countries without the death penalty. But in our world of hot homicide, that is not so (Costanzo, 1998). As John Darley and Adam Alter (2009) noted, "A remarkable amount of crime is committed by impulsive individuals, frequently young males, who are frequently drunk or high on drugs, and who often are in packs of similar and similarly mindless young men." No wonder, they say, that trying to reduce crime by increasing sentences has proven so fruitless, while on-the-street policing that produces more arrests has produced encouraging results, such as a 50 percent drop in gun-related crimes in some cities.

Thus, we must prevent aggression before it happens. We must teach non-aggressive conflict-resolution strategies. When psychologists Sandra Jo Wilson and Mark Lipsey (2005) assembled data from 249 studies of school violence-prevention programs, they found encouraging results, especially for programs focused on selected "problem" students. After being taught problem-solving skills, emotion-control strategies, and conflict-resolution techniques, the typical 20 percent of students engaging in some violent or disruptive behaviour in a typical school year was reduced to 13 percent.

Physical punishment can also have negative side effects. Punishment is aversive stimulation; it models the behaviour it seeks to prevent. And it is coercive (recall that we seldom internalize actions coerced with strong external justifications). These are reasons violent teenagers and child-abusing parents so often come from homes where discipline took the form of harsh physical punishment.

To foster a gentler world, we could model and reward sensitivity and cooperation from an early age, perhaps by training parents how to discipline without violence. Training programs encourage parents to reinforce desirable behaviours and to frame statements positively ("When you finish cleaning your room, you can go play," rather than "If you don't clean your room, you're grounded.") One "aggression-replacement program" has reduced re-arrest rates of juvenile offenders and gang members by teaching the youths and their parents communication skills, training them to control anger, and raising their level of moral reasoning (Goldstein & Glick, 1994).

If observing aggressive models lowers inhibitions and elicits imitation, then we might also reduce brutal, dehumanizing portrayals in films and on television—steps comparable to those already taken to reduce racist and sexist portrayals. We can also inoculate children against the effects of media violence. Wondering if the TV networks would ever "face the facts and change their programming," Eron and Huesmann (1984) taught 170 children that television portrays the world unrealistically, that aggression is less common and effective than TV suggests, and that aggressive behaviour is undesirable. (Drawing upon attitude research, Eron and Huesmann encouraged children to draw these inferences themselves and to attribute their expressed criticisms of television to their own convictions.) When restudied two years later, these children were less influenced by TV violence than were untrained children. In a more recent study, Stanford University used 18 classroom lessons to persuade children to simply reduce their TV watching and video game-playing (Robinson et al., 2001). They reduced their TV viewing by a third—and their aggressive behaviour at school dropped 25 percent compared to children in a control school. Even music can help reduce aggression when it models the right attitude: German students who were randomly assigned to hear prosocial music like "We Are the World" and "Help" behaved less aggressively than those who heard neutral music (Greitemeyer, 2011).

Suggestions such as these can help us minimize aggression. But given the complexity of aggression's causes and the difficulty of controlling them, it is difficult to feel the optimism expressed by Andrew Carnegie's forecast that in the twentieth century, "To kill a man will be considered as disgusting as we in this day consider it disgusting to eat one." Since Carnegie uttered those words in 1900, some 200 million human beings have been killed. It is a sad irony that, although today we understand human aggression better than ever before, humanity's inhumanity endures.

CULTURE CHANGE AND WORLD VIOLENCE

Nevertheless, cultures can change. "The Vikings slaughtered and plundered," noted science writer Natalie Angier. "Their descendants in Sweden haven't fought a war in nearly 200 years." Indeed, as psychologist Steven Pinker (2011) documents, across centuries, humans have become more civilized and all forms of violence—including wars, genocide, and murders—have declined. We've graduated from plundering neighbouring tribes to economic interdependence, from a world in which Western European countries initiated two new wars per year over 600 years to, for the past seven decades, zero wars. Surprisingly, to those of us who love modern British murder mysteries, "a contemporary Englishman has about a 50-fold less chance of being murdered than his compatriot in the Middle Ages," notes Pinker. In all but one Western democracy, the death penalty has been abolished. And the sole exception—the United States—no longer practises it for witchcraft, counterfeiting, and horse theft, and has seen declines in, or the disappearance of, lynching, hate crimes, rapes, corporal punishment, and anti-gay attitudes and intimidation. We can, Pinker concludes, be grateful "for the institutions of civilization and enlightenment [economic trade, education, government policing, and justice] that have made it possible."

┅▶ SUMMING UP

WHAT IS AGGRESSION?

- Aggression is defined as verbal or physical behaviour intended to cause harm.
- Aggression manifests itself in two forms: hostile aggression, which springs from emotions such as anger and intends to injure, and instrumental aggression, which is a means to some other end.

WHAT ARE SOME THEORIES OF AGGRESSION?

There are three broad theories of aggression:

- The instinct view, most commonly associated with Sigmund Freud and Konrad Lorenz, contended that aggressive energy will accumulate from within, like water accumulating behind a dam. Although the available evidence offers little support for this view, aggression is biologically influenced by heredity, blood chemistry, and the brain.
- According to the second view, frustration causes anger and hostility. Given aggressive cues, this anger may provoke aggression. Frustration stems not from deprivation itself but from the gap between expectations and achievements.
- The social learning view presents aggression as learned behaviour. By experience and by observing others' success, we sometimes learn that aggression pays. Social learning enables family and subculture influences on aggression, as well as media influences.

WHAT ARE SOME INFLUENCES ON AGGRESSION?

- Many factors exert influence on aggression. One factor is aversive experiences, which include not only frustrations but also discomfort, pain, and personal attacks, both physical and verbal.

- Arousal from almost any source, even physical exercise or sexual stimulation, can be transformed into anger.

- Aggressive cues, such as the presence of a gun, increase the likelihood of aggressive behaviour.

- Viewing violence (1) breeds a modest increase in aggressive behaviour, especially in people who are provoked; (2) desensitizes viewers to aggression; and (3) alters viewers' perceptions of reality. These findings parallel the results of research on the effects of viewing violent pornography, which can increase men's aggression against women and distort their perceptions of women's responses to sexual coercion.

- Television permeates the daily life of millions of people and portrays considerable violence. Correlational and experimental studies converge on the conclusion that heavy exposure to televised violence correlates with aggressive behaviour.

- Repeatedly playing violent video games may increase aggressive thinking, feelings, and behaviour even more than television or movies do, as the experience involves much more active participation than the other media.

- Circumstances that provoke individuals may also provoke groups by diffusing responsibility and polarizing actions; group situations amplify aggressive reactions.

HOW CAN AGGRESSION BE REDUCED?

- How can we minimize aggression? Contrary to the catharsis hypothesis, expressing aggression by catharsis tends to breed further aggression, not reduce it.

- The social learning approach suggests controlling aggression by counteracting the factors that provoke it: by reducing aversive stimulation, by rewarding and modelling non-aggression, and by eliciting reactions incompatible with aggression.

CHAPTER TEN

Attraction and Intimacy: Liking and Loving Others

▶ **CHAPTER OUTLINE**

● WHAT LEADS TO FRIENDSHIP AND ATTRACTION?

● WHAT IS LOVE?

● WHAT ENABLES CLOSE RELATIONSHIPS?

● HOW DO RELATIONSHIPS END?

Our lifelong dependence on one another puts relationships at the core of our existence. In your beginning, there very likely was an attraction—the attraction between a particular man and a particular woman. Aristotle called humans "the social animal."

need to belong
a motivation to
bond with others in
relationships that
provide ongoing, positive
interactions

Indeed, we have what today's social psychologists call a **need to belong**—to connect with others in enduring, close relationships.

Social psychologists Roy Baumeister and Mark Leary (1995) illustrated the power of social attachments:

- For our ancestors, mutual attachments enabled group survival. When hunting game or erecting shelter, ten hands were better than two.

- For heterosexual women and men, the bonds of love can lead to children, whose survival chances are boosted by the nurturing of two bonded parents who support each other.

- For children and their caregivers, social attachments enhance survival. Unexplainably separated from one another, parent and toddler may both panic, until reunited in a tight embrace. Reared under extreme neglect or in institutions without belonging to anybody, children become pathetic, anxious creatures.

- For university students, relationships consume much of life. How much of your waking life is spent talking with people? One sampling of 10 000 tape recordings of half-minute slices of students' waking hours (using belt-worn recorders) found them talking to someone 28 percent of the time—and that doesn't count the time they spent listening to someone (Mehl & Pennebaker, 2003).

- When not face-to-face, the world's 7 billion people connect by voice and texting through their more than 5 billion cellphone subscriptions (International Telecommunication Union, 2010) or through social networks such as Facebook. Half of all connected teens send 50 or more texts daily (Lenhart, 2010). Our need to belong motivates our investment in being continuously connected.

- For people everywhere (no matter their sexual orientation), actual and hoped-for close relationships can dominate thinking and emotions. Finding a supportive soulmate in whom we can confide, we feel accepted and prized. Falling in love, we feel irrepressible joy. When relationships with partners, family, and friends are healthy, self-esteem—a barometer of our relationships—rides high (Denissen et al., 2008). Longing for acceptance and love, we spend billions on cosmetics, clothes, and diets. Even people who seem unconcerned with pleasing others relish being accepted (Carvallo & Gabriel, 2006).

- Exiled, imprisoned, or in solitary confinement, people ache for their own people and places. Rejected, we are at risk for depression (Nolan, Flynn, & Garber, 2003). Time goes slower and life seems less meaningful (Twenge, Catanese, & Baumeister, 2003). When queried three months after arriving on a large university campus, many international students, like some homesick domestic students, reported declining feelings of well-being (Cemalcilar & Falbo, 2008).

- For the jilted, the widowed, and the sojourner in a strange place, the loss of social bonds triggers pain, loneliness, or withdrawal. Losing a close relationship, adults feel jealous, lonely, distraught, or bereaved, as well as more mindful of death and the fragility of life (Strachman & Schimel, 2006). After relocating, people—especially those with the strongest need to belong—typically feel homesick (Watt & Badger, 2009).

- Reminders of death in turn heighten our need to belong, to be with others, and to hold close those we love (Mikulincer, Florian, & Hirschberger, 2003; Wisman & Koole, 2003). The shocking death of a classmate, co-worker, or family member brings people together, their differences no longer mattering.

A recipe for violence: an unstable disposition plus ostracism. Mark Leary and colleagues (2003) report that in all but 2 of 15 school shootings from 1995 to 2001, such as by Eric Harris and Dylan Klebold at Columbine High School, the assailants had experienced ostracism.

We are indeed social animals. We need to belong. As with other motivations, thwarting the need to belong intensifies it; satisfying the need reduces the motivation (DeWall et al., 2009; DeWall & Bushman, 2011). And as Module A confirms, when we do belong—when we feel supported by close, intimate relationships—we tend to be healthier and happier. Satisfy the need to belong in balance with two other human needs—to feel *autonomy* and *competence*—and the typical result is a deep sense of well-being (Deci & Ryan, 2002; Milyavskaya et al., 2009; Sheldon & Niemiec, 2006). Happiness is feeling connected, free, and capable.

Social psychologist Kipling Williams (2002, 2007) has explored what happens when our need to belong is thwarted by ostracism (acts of excluding or ignoring). Humans in all cultures, whether in schools, workplaces, or homes, use ostracism to regulate social behaviour. Some of us know what it is like to be shunned—to be avoided, met with averted eyes, or given the silent treatment. Even just being among people speaking a language one doesn't know can leave one feeling excluded (Dotan-Eliaz, Sommer, & Rubin, 2009).

People (women especially) respond to ostracism with depressed mood, anxiety, hurt feelings, efforts to restore relationship, and eventual withdrawal (Baumeister, DeWall, & Vohs, 2009; Blackhart et al., 2009; Gerber & Wheeler, 2009a, 2009b). The silent treatment is "emotional abuse" and "a terrible, terrible weapon to use," say those who have experienced it from a family member or co-worker. In experiments, people who are left out of a simple game of ball tossing feel deflated and stressed. Ostracism hurts, and the social pain is keenly felt—more than those who are not ostracized ever know (Nordgren, Banas, & MacDonald, 2011). If only we better empathized with those rejected, there might be less tolerance of emotional bullying.

Sometimes deflation turns nasty. In several studies, Jean Twenge and her collaborators (2001, 2002, 2007; DeWall, Maner, & Rouby, 2009; Leary, Twenge, & Quinlivan, 2006) gave some people an experience of being socially included while others experienced temporary exclusion: They were either told that (based on a personality test) they "were likely to end up alone later in life" or that others whom they'd met didn't want them in their group. Those led to feel excluded became not only more likely to engage in self-defeating behaviours, such as underperforming on an aptitude test, but also less able to regulate their behaviour (they drank less of a healthy but bad-tasting drink and ate more unhealthy but good-tasting cookies). They also became more likely to disparage or deliver a blast of noise to someone who had insulted them. If a small laboratory experience could produce such aggression, noted the researchers, what aggressive tendencies "might arise from a series of important rejections or chronic exclusion"?

Williams and Steve Nida (2011) were surprised to discover that even "cyberostracism," by faceless people whom one will never meet, takes a toll. (Perhaps you have experienced this when feeling ignored in a chat room or when your e-mail is not answered.) The researchers have had more than 5000 participants from dozens of countries play a web-based game of throwing a flying disc with two others (actually, computer-generated fellow players). Those ostracized by the other players experienced poorer moods and became more likely to conform to others' wrong judgments on a subsequent perceptual task. Exclusion hurts longest for anxious people, and hurts even when it's by a disliked out-group—Australian KKK members, in one experiment (Gonsalkorale & Williams, 2006; Zadro, Boland, & Richardson, 2006).

Williams and his colleagues (Williams, Cheung, & Choi, 2000) even found ostracism stressful when each of them was ignored for an agreed-upon day by the unresponsive four others. Contrary to their expectations that this would be a laughter-filled role-playing game, the simulated ostracism disrupted work, interfered with pleasant social functioning, and "caused temporary concern, anxiety, paranoia, and general fragility of spirit." To thwart our deep need to belong is to unsettle our life.

Evidence collected by Geoff MacDonald of the University of Toronto and his colleagues suggests a convergence between social and physical pain (MacDonald & Leary, 2005). Ostracized people exhibit heightened activity in a brain cortex area that also is activated in response to physical pain (Figure 10–1). Ostracism's social pain, much like physical pain, increases aggression (Riva, Wirth, & Williams, 2011). Hurt feelings are also embodied in a depressed heart rate (Moor, Crone, & van der Molen, 2010). Heartbreak makes for heart brake.

Indeed, the pain of social rejection is so real that a pain-relieving Tylenol can reduce hurt feelings (DeWall et al., 2010b; DeWall & Bushman, 2011). Ostracism's opposite—feeling love—activates brain reward systems. When looking at their beloved's picture, deeply in love university students feel markedly less thermal pain (Younger et al., 2010). Ostracism is a real pain. And love is a natural painkiller.

Asked to recall a time when they were socially excluded—perhaps left alone in the dorm when others went out—University of Toronto students in one experiment even perceived the

FIGURE 10–1

THE PAIN OF REJECTION.

Naomi Eisenberger, Matthew Lieberman, and Kipling Williams (2003) reported that social ostracism evokes a brain response similar to that triggered by physical pain, activating the anterior cingulate (A) and the right ventral prefrontal cortex (B).

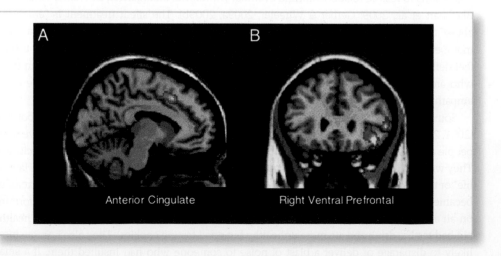

room temperature as five degrees colder than did those asked to recall a social acceptance experience (Zhong & Leonardelli, 2008). Such recollections come easily: People remember and relive past social pain more easily than past physical pain (Chen et al., 2008). Roy Baumeister (2005) found a silver lining in the rejection research. When recently excluded people experience a safe opportunity to make a new friend, they "seem willing and even eager to take it." They become more attentive to smiling, accepting faces (DeWall, Maner, & Rouby, 2009). An exclusion experience also triggers increased mimicry of others' behaviour as a non-conscious effort to build rapport (Lakin, Chartrand, & Arkin, 2008). And at a societal level, noted Baumeister, meeting the need to belong should pay dividends:

> My colleagues in sociology have pointed out that minority groups who feel excluded show many of the same patterns that our laboratory manipulations elicit: high rates of aggression and antisocial behaviour, decreased willingness to cooperate and obey rules, poorer intellectual performance, more self-destructive acts, short-term focus, and the like. Possibly, if we can promote a more inclusive society in which more people feel themselves to be accepted as valued members, some of these tragic patterns could be reduced.

WHAT LEADS TO FRIENDSHIP AND ATTRACTION?

What factors nurture liking and loving? Let's start with those that help initiate attraction: proximity, physical attractiveness, similarity, and feeling liked.

What predisposes one person to like, or to love, another? Few questions about human nature arouse greater interest. The ways affections flourish and fade form the stuff and fluff of soap operas, popular music, novels, and much of our everyday conversation.

So much has been written about liking and loving that almost every conceivable explanation—and its opposite—has already been proposed. For most people—and for you—what factors nurture liking and loving? Does absence make the heart grow fonder, or is someone who is out of sight also out of mind? Is it similarities that attract, or opposites? How much do good looks matter? What has fostered your close relationships? Let's start with those factors that help a friendship begin and then consider those that sustain and deepen a relationship, thus satisfying our need to belong.

"I cannot tell how my ankles bend, nor whence the cause of my faintest wish, nor the cause of the friendship I emit, nor the cause of the friendship I take again."
WALT WHITMAN, "SONG OF MYSELF," 1855

PROXIMITY

One powerful predictor of whether any two people are friends is sheer **proximity**. Proximity can also breed hostility; most assaults and murders involve people living close together. But far more often, proximity kindles liking. Mitja Back and his colleagues (2008) confirmed this by randomly assigning students to seats at their first class meeting, and then having each make a brief self-introduction to the whole class. One year after this one-time seating assignment, students reported greater friendship with those who just happened, during that first class, to be seated next to or near them.

proximity
geographical nearness. Proximity (more precisely, "functional distance") powerfully predicts liking.

> *"I don't believe that friends are necessarily the people you like best, they are merely the people who got there first."*
>
> SIR PETER USTINOV, *DEAR ME*, 1979

Though it may seem trivial to those pondering the mysterious origins of romantic love, sociologists long ago found that most people marry someone who lives in the same neighbourhood, or works at the same company or job, or sits in the same class (Bossard, 1932; Burr, 1973; Clarke, 1952; Katz & Hill, 1958). In a survey of people married or in long-term relationships, 38 percent met at work or at school; some of the rest met when their paths crossed in their neighbourhood, church, or gym, or while growing up (Pew Research Center, 2006). Look around. If you marry, it will likely be to someone who has lived or worked or studied within walking distance.

Interaction

Even more significant than geographical distance is "functional distance"—how often people's paths cross. We frequently become friends with those who use the same entrances, parking lots, and recreation areas. Randomly assigned university roommates, who can hardly avoid frequent interaction, are far more likely to become good friends than enemies (Newcomb, 1961). At the university where one of us teaches, the men and women once lived on opposite sides of the campus. They understandably bemoaned the lack of cross-sex friendships. Now that they occupy different areas of the same dormitories and share common sidewalks, lounges, and laundry facilities, cross-sex friendships are far more frequent. Interaction enables people to explore their similarities, to sense one another's liking, and to perceive themselves as a social unit (Arkin & Burger, 1980).

> *"When I'm not near the one I love, I love the one I'm near."*
>
> E. Y. HARBURG, *FINIAN'S RAINBOW*, LONDON: CHAPPELL MUSIC, 1947

So if you're new in town and want to make friends, try to get an apartment near the mailboxes, an office desk near the coffee pot, a parking spot near the main buildings. Such is the architecture of friendship.

The chance nature of such contacts helps explain a surprising finding. Consider this: If you had an identical twin who became engaged to someone, wouldn't you (being in so many ways similar to your twin) expect to share your twin's attraction to this person? But no, reported researchers David Lykken and Auke Tellegen (1993); only half of identical twins recalled really liking their twin's selection, and only 5 percent said, "I could have fallen for my twin's fiancée." Romantic love is often rather like ducklings' imprinting, in which ducklings bond to whoever is near, surmised Lykken and Tellegen. With repeated exposure to someone, our infatuation may fix on almost anyone who has roughly similar characteristics and who reciprocates our affection. Why does proximity breed liking? One factor is availability; obviously there are fewer opportunities to get to know someone who attends a different school or lives in another town. But there is more to it than that. Most people like their roommates, or those one door away, better than

"Sometimes I think you only married me because I lived next door!"

those two doors away. Those just a few doors away, or even a floor below, hardly live at an inconvenient distance. Moreover, those close by are potential enemies as well as friends. So why does proximity encourage affection more often than animosity?

Anticipation of interaction

Proximity enables people to discover commonalities and exchange rewards, but merely anticipating interaction also boosts liking. John Darley and Ellen Berscheid (1967) discovered this when they gave women ambiguous information about two other women, one of whom they expected to talk with intimately. Asked how much they liked each one, the women preferred the person they expected to meet. Expecting to date someone similarly boosts liking (Berscheid et al., 1976).

The phenomenon is adaptive. Anticipatory liking–expecting that someone will be pleasant and compatible–increases the chance of a rewarding relationship (Klein & Kunda, 1992; Knight & Vallacher, 1981; Miller & Marks, 1982). It's a good thing that we are biased to like those we often see, for our lives are filled with relationships with people whom we may not have chosen but with whom we need to have continuing interactions–roommates, siblings, grandparents, teachers, classmates, co-workers. Liking such people is surely conducive to better relationships with them, which in turn makes for happier, more productive living.

Mere exposure

Proximity leads to liking not only because it enables interaction and anticipatory liking but also for another reason: More than 200 experiments revealed that, contrary to an old proverb, familiarity does not breed contempt. Rather, it fosters fondness (Bornstein, 1989, 1999). The **mere-exposure effect** refers to the tendency for all sorts of novel stimuli–nonsense syllables, Chinese calligraphy characters, musical selections, faces–boosts people's ratings of them. Do the supposed Turkish words *nansoma, saricik,* and *afworbu* mean something better or something worse than the words *iktitaf, biwojni,* and *kudirga?* Students tested by Robert Zajonc (1968, 1970)

mere-exposure effect the tendency for novel stimuli to be liked more or rated more positively after the rater has been repeatedly exposed to them

Feeling close to those close by: People often become attached to, and sometimes fall in love with, familiar co-workers.

preferred whichever of these words they had seen most frequently. The more times they had seen a meaningless word or a Chinese ideograph, the more likely they were to say it meant something good. This can make for a good class demonstration. Periodically flash certain non-sense words on a screen. By the end of the semester, students will rate those "words" more positively than other nonsense words they have never before seen.

Or consider: What are your favourite letters of the alphabet? People of differing nationalities, languages, and ages prefer the letters appearing in their own names and those that frequently appear in their own languages (Hoorens et al., 1990, 1993; Kitayama & Karasawa, 1997; Nuttin, 1987). French students rate capital *W*, the least frequent letter in French, as their least favourite letter. Japanese students prefer not only letters from their names but also numbers corresponding to their birth dates.

The mere-exposure effect violates the common-sense prediction of boredom—decreased interest—regarding repeatedly heard music or frequently tasted foods (Kahneman & Snell, 1992). Unless the repetitions are incessant ("Even the best song becomes tiresome if heard too often," says a Korean proverb), familiarity usually doesn't breed contempt; rather, it increases liking. When completed in 1889, the Eiffel Tower in Paris was mocked as grotesque (Harrison, 1977). Today, it is the beloved symbol of Paris.

So, do visitors to the Louvre in Paris really adore the *Mona Lisa* for the artistry it displays, or are they simply delighted to find a familiar face? It might be both: To know her is to like her. Eddie Harmon-Jones and John Allen (2001) explored this phenomenon experimentally. When they showed people a woman's face, their cheek (smiling) muscle typically became more active with repeated viewings. Mere exposure breeds pleasant feelings.

Zajonc and his co-workers, William Kunst-Wilson and Richard Moreland, reported that even exposure without awareness leads to liking (Kunst-Wilson & Zajonc, 1980; Moreland & Zajonc, 1977; Wilson, 1979). In fact, mere exposure has an even stronger effect when people perceive stimuli without awareness (Bornstein & D'Agostino, 1992). In one experiment, women students using headphones listened in one ear to a prose passage. They also repeated the words out loud and compared them to a written version to check for errors. Meanwhile, brief, novel melodies played in the other ear. This procedure focused attention on the verbal material and away from the tunes. Later, when the women heard the tunes interspersed among similar ones not previously played, they did not recognize them. Nevertheless, they liked best the tunes they had previously heard.

Note that conscious judgments about the stimuli in these experiments provided fewer clues to what people had heard or seen than did their instant feelings. You can probably recall immediately liking or disliking something or someone without consciously knowing why. Zajonc (1980) argued that emotions are often more instantaneous than thinking.

The mere-exposure effect has "enormous adaptive significance," noted Zajonc (1998). It is a "hard-wired" phenomenon that predisposes our attractions and attachments, and that helped our ancestors categorize things and people as either familiar and safe, or unfamiliar and possibly dangerous. The more two strangers interact, the more attractive they tend to find each other (Reis et al., 2011). The mere-exposure effect colours our evaluations of others: We like familiar people (Swap, 1977). It works the other way around too: People we like (for example, smiling rather than unsmiling strangers) seem more familiar (Garcia-Marques et al., 2004).

The phenomenon's negative side, as we will note in Chapter 11, is our wariness of the unfamiliar—which may explain the automatic, unconscious prejudice people often feel when confronting those who are different from themselves. Fearful or prejudicial feelings are not always expressions of stereotyped beliefs; sometimes, the beliefs arise later as justifications for intuitive feelings. Infants as young as three months exhibit an own-race preference: If they are typically surrounded by others of the same race in their environments, then they prefer to gaze at faces of their own familiar race (Bar-Haim et al., 2006; Kelly et al., 2005, 2007).

We even like ourselves better when we are the way we're used to seeing ourselves. In a delightful experiment, Theodore Mita, Marshall Dermer, and Jeffrey Knight (1977) photographed women students and later showed each one her actual picture along with a mirror image of it. Asked which picture they liked better, most preferred the mirror image—the image they were used to seeing. (No wonder our photographs never look quite right.) When close friends of the subjects were shown the same two pictures, they preferred the true picture—the image *they* were used to seeing.

Advertisers and politicians exploit this phenomenon. When people have no strong feelings about a product or a candidate, repetition alone can increase sales or votes (McCullough & Ostrom, 1974; Winter, 1973). After endless repetition of a commercial, shoppers often have an unthinking, automatic, favourable response to the product. If candidates are relatively unknown, those with the most media exposure usually win (Patterson, 1980; Schaffner, Wandersman, & Stang, 1981). Political strategists who understand the mere-exposure effect have replaced reasoned argument with brief ads that hammer home a candidate's name and a sound-bite message.

PHYSICAL ATTRACTIVENESS

What do (or did) you look for in a potential date? Sincerity? Character? Humour? Good looks? Sophisticated, intelligent people are unconcerned with such superficial qualities as good looks; they know "beauty is only skin deep" and "you can't judge a book by its cover." At least they know that's how they ought to feel. As Cicero counselled, "Resist appearance."

The belief that looks are unimportant may be another instance of how we deny real influences on us, for there is now a filing cabinet full of research studies showing that appearance does matter. The consistency and pervasiveness of this effect is astonishing. Good looks are a great asset.

> *"We should look to the mind, and not to the outward appearances."*
> AESOP, *FABLES*

> *"Personal beauty is a greater recommendation than any letter of introduction."*
> ARISTOTLE, *DIOGENES LAERTIUS*

Attractiveness and dating

Like it or not, a young woman's physical attractiveness is a moderately good predictor of how frequently she dates, and a young man's attractiveness is a modestly good predictor of how frequently he dates (Berscheid et al., 1971; Krebs & Adinolfi, 1975; Reis et al., 1982; Reis, Nezlek, & Wheeler, 1980; Walster et al., 1966). Women more than men say they would prefer a mate who's homely and warm over one who's attractive and cold (Fletcher et al., 2004). In a worldwide BBC Internet survey of nearly 220 000 people, men more than women ranked attractiveness as important in a mate, while women more than men assigned importance to honesty, humour, kindness, and dependability (Lippa, 2007).

Do such self-reports imply, as many have surmised, that women are better at following Cicero's advice? Or that nothing has changed since 1930, when the English philosopher Bertrand Russell wrote, "On the whole women tend to love men for their character while men tend to love women for their appearance." Or does it merely reflect the fact that men more often do the

Attractiveness and dating: For Internet dating customers, looks are part of what is offered and sought.

inviting? If women were to indicate their preferences among various men, would looks be as important to them as men?

To see whether men are, indeed, more influenced by looks, researchers have provided male and female students with various pieces of information about someone of the other sex, including the person's picture. Or they have briefly introduced a man and a woman and later asked each about their interest in dating the other. In such experiments, men do put somewhat more value on opposite-sex physical attractiveness (Feingold, 1990, 1991; Sprecher et al., 1994). Perhaps sensing this, women worry more about their appearance and constitute nearly 90 percent of cosmetic surgery patients (Crowley, 1996; Dion, Dion, & Keelan, 1990). Women also better recall others' appearance, as when asked to recall someone's clothing or hair (Mast & Hall, 2006).

Do women respond to men's looks? In one ambitious study, Elaine Hatfield and her co-workers (1966) matched 752 first-year students for a "Welcome Week" computer dance. The researchers gave each student personality and aptitude tests but then matched the couples randomly. On the night of the dance, the couples danced and talked for two-and-a-half hours and then took a brief intermission to evaluate their dates. How well did the personality and aptitude tests predict attraction? Did people like someone better who was high in self-esteem, or low in anxiety, or different from themselves in outgoingness? The research-ers examined a long list of possibilities. But as far as they could determine, only one thing mattered: how physically attractive the person was (as previously rated by the researchers). The more attractive a woman was, the more he liked her and wanted to date her again. And the more attractive the man was, the more she liked him and wanted to date him again.

More recent studies have gathered data from speed-dating evenings, during which people interact with a succession of potential dates for only a few minutes each and later indicate which ones they would like to see again (mutual "yeses" are given contact information). The procedure is rooted in research showing that we can form durable impressions of others based on seconds-long "thin slices" of their social behaviour (Ambady, Bernieri, & Richeson, 2000). In speed-dating research by Paul Eastwick and Eli Finkel (2008), men more than women presumed the importance of a potential date's physical attractiveness; but in reality, a prospect's attractive-ness was similarly important to both men and women.

Looks even influence voting, or so it seems from a study by Alexander Todorov and col-leagues (2005). They showed university students photographs of two major candidates in 695 political elections. Based on looks alone, the students preferred competent-looking over more baby-faced candidates; in doing so, they correctly guessed the winners of 67 percent of the elections. In a follow-up study by Joan Chiao and her co-researchers (2008) confirmed the find-ing that voters prefer competent-looking candidates. But gender also mattered: Men were more likely to vote for physically attractive female candidates, and women were more likely to vote for approachable-looking male candidates. Likewise, heterosexual people display a positive bias toward attractive job candidates and university applicants—*if* they are of the other sex (Agthe, Spörrle, & Maner, 2011).

The matching phenomenon

Not everyone can end up paired with someone stunningly attractive. So how do people pair off? Judging from research by Bernard Murstein (1986) and others, they get real. They pair off with people who are about as attractive as they are. Several studies have found a strong correspondence between the attractiveness of husbands and wives, of dating partners, and even of those within particular fraternities (Feingold, 1988; Montoya, 2008). People tend to select as friends and especially to marry those who are a "good match" not only to their level of intelligence but also to their level of attractiveness (Taylor et al., 2011).

Experiments confirm this **matching phenomenon**. When choosing whom to approach, knowing the other is free to say yes or no, people usually approach someone whose attractiveness roughly matches (or exceeds but only slightly) their own (Berscheid et al., 1971; Huston, 1973; Van Straaten et al., 2009). Good physical matches may also be conducive to good relationships, as Gregory White (1980) found in a study of dating couples. Those who were most similar in physical attractiveness were most likely, nine months later, to have fallen more deeply in love.

Perhaps this research prompts you to think of happy couples who differ in perceived "hotness." In such cases, the less attractive person often has compensating qualities. Each partner brings assets to the social marketplace, and the value of the respective assets creates an equitable match. Personal advertisements exhibit this exchange of assets (Cicerello & Sheehan, 1995; Hitsch, Hortacsu, & Ariely, 2006; Koestner & Wheeler, 1988; Rajecki, Bledsoe, & Rasmussen, 1991). Men typically offer wealth or status and seek youth and attractiveness; women more often do the reverse: "Attractive, bright woman, 26, slender, seeks warm, professional male." Moreover, men who advertise their income and education, and women who advertise their youth and looks, receive more responses to their ads (Baize & Schroeder, 1995). The asset-matching process helps explain why beautiful young women often marry older men of higher social status (Elder, 1969).

> *"If you would marry wisely, marry your equal."*
> OVID, 43 B.C.–A.D. 17

matching phenomenon
the tendency for men and women to choose as partners those who are a "good match" in attractiveness and other traits

Asset matching: High-status Rolling Stones guitarist Keith Richards has been married to supermodel Patti Hansen, 19 years his junior, since 1983.

The physical-attractiveness stereotype

Does the attractiveness effect spring entirely from sexual attractiveness? Clearly not, as Vicky Houston and Ray Bull (1994) discovered when they used a makeup artist to give an accomplice an apparently scarred, bruised, or birthmarked face. When riding on a Glasgow commuter rail line, people of both sexes avoided sitting next to the accomplice when she appeared facially disfigured. Moreover, much as adults are biased toward attractive adults, young children are biased toward attractive children (Dion, 1973; Dion & Berscheid, 1974; Langlois et al., 2000). To judge from how long they gaze at someone, even three-month-old infants prefer attractive faces (Langlois et al., 1987).

Adults show a similar bias when judging children. Margaret Clifford and Elaine Hatfield (Clifford & Walster, 1973) gave grade 5 teachers identical information about a boy or girl, but with the photograph of an attractive or unattractive child attached. The teachers perceived the attractive child as more intelligent and successful in school. Think of yourself as a playground supervisor having to discipline an unruly child. Might you, like the women studied by Karen Dion (1972), show less warmth and tact to an unattractive child? The sad truth is that most of us assume that homely children are less able and socially competent than their beautiful peers.

What is more, we assume that beautiful people possess certain desirable traits. Other things being equal, we guess beautiful people are happier, sexually warmer, and more outgoing, intelligent, and successful—though not more honest or concerned for others (Eagly et al., 1991; Feingold, 1992; Jackson, Hunter, & Hodge, 1995). We are more eager to bond with attractive people, which motivates our projecting desirable attributes such as kindness and reciprocal interest onto them (Lemay, Clark, & Greenberg, 2010).

physical-attractiveness stereotype
the presumption that physically attractive people possess other socially desirable traits as well: What is beautiful is good.

Added together, the findings define a **physical-attractiveness stereotype**: What is beautiful is good. Children learn the stereotype quite early—and one of the ways they learn it is through stories told to them by adults. "Disney movies promote the stereotype that what is beautiful is good," report Doris Bazzini and colleagues (2010) from an analysis of human characters in 21 animated films. Snow White and Cinderella are beautiful—and kind. The witch and the stepsisters are ugly—and wicked. "If you want to be loved by somebody who isn't already in your family, it doesn't hurt to be beautiful," surmised one 8-year-old girl. Or as one kindergarten girl put it when asked what it means to be pretty, "It's like to be a princess. Everybody loves you" (Dion, 1979).

If physical attractiveness is that important, then permanently changing people's attractiveness should change the way others react to them. But is it ethical to alter someone's looks? Such manipulations are performed millions of times a year by plastic surgeons and orthodontists. With teeth and nose straightened, hair replaced and dyed, face lifted, fat liposuctioned, and breasts enlarged, lifted, or reduced, most self-dissatisfied people do express satisfaction with the results of their procedures, though some unhappy patients seek out repeat procedures (Honigman, Phillips, & Castle, 2004).

To examine the effect of such alterations, Michael Kalick (1977) had students rate their impressions of eight women based on profile photographs taken before or after cosmetic surgery. They judged the women not only as more physically attractive after the surgery but also as kinder, more sensitive, more sexually warm and responsive, more likeable, and so on.

First impressions

To say that attractiveness is important, other things being equal, is not to say that physical appearance always outranks other qualities. Some people more than others judge people by their looks (Livingston, 2001). Moreover, attractiveness probably most affects first impressions. But first impressions are important—and are becoming more so as societies become increasingly mobile and urbanized and as contacts with people become more fleeting (Berscheid, 1981). Your Facebook self-presentation starts with . . . your face. In speed-dating experiments, the attractiveness effect is strongest when people's choices are superficially made—when meeting lots of people quickly (Lenton & Francesconi, 2010). That helps explain why attractiveness better predicts happiness and social connections for those in urban rather than rural settings (Plaut, Adams, G., & Anderson, 2009).

Though interviewers may deny it, attractiveness and grooming affect first impressions in job interviews—especially when the evaluator is of the other sex (Agthe et al., 2011; Cash & Janda, 1984; Mack & Rainey, 1990; Marvelle & Green, 1980). People rate new products more favourably when they are associated with attractive inventors (Baron, Markman, & Bollinger, 2006). Such impressions help explain why attractive people and tall people have more prestigious jobs and make more money (Engemann & Owyang, 2003; Persico, Postelwaite, & Silverman, 2004).

Patricia Roszell and her colleagues (1990) looked at the incomes of a national sample of Canadians whom interviewers had rated on a 1 (homely) to 5 (strikingly attractive) scale. They found that for each additional scale unit of rated attractiveness, people earned, on average, an additional $1988 annually. Irene Hanson Frieze and her associates (1991) did the same analysis with 737 MBA graduates after rating them on a similar 1-to-5 scale using student yearbook photos. For each additional scale unit of rated attractiveness, men earned an added $2600 and women earned an additional $2150. In *Beauty Pays*, economist Daniel Hamermesh (2011) argues that, for a man, good looks have the earnings effect of another year-and-a-half of schooling.

The speed with which first impressions form, and their influence on thinking, helps explain why good-looking people prosper. Even an exposure as brief as 0.013 second—too brief to actually discern a face—is enough to enable people to guess a face's attractiveness (Olson & Marchuetz, 2005). Moreover, when categorizing subsequent words as either good or bad, an attractive face predisposes people to categorize good words faster. Attractiveness is perceived promptly and primes positive processing.

Is the "beautiful is good" stereotype accurate?

Do beautiful people, indeed, have desirable traits? Or was Leo Tolstoy correct when he wrote that it's "a strange illusion . . . to suppose that beauty is goodness"? There is some truth to the stereotype. Attractive children and young adults are somewhat more relaxed, outgoing, and socially polished (Feingold, 1992; Langlois et al., 2000). William Goldman and Philip Lewis (1977) demonstrated this by having 60 men call and talk for five minutes with each of three women students. Afterwards, the men and women rated the most attractive of their unseen telephone partners as somewhat more socially skillful and likeable. Physically attractive individuals tend also to be more popular, more outgoing, and more gender-typed—more traditionally masculine, if male; more traditionally feminine, if female (Langlois et al., 1996).

These small average differences between attractive and unattractive people probably result from self-fulfilling prophecies. Attractive people are valued and favoured, and so may develop more social self-confidence. (Recall from Chapter 3 an experiment in which men evoked a warm

response from unseen women they *thought* were attractive.) By that analysis, what's crucial to your social skill is not how you look but how people treat you and how you feel about yourself—whether you accept yourself, like yourself, feel comfortable with yourself.

Who is attractive?

We have described attractiveness as if it were an objective quality like height, which some people have more of, some less. Strictly speaking, attractiveness is whatever the people of any given place and time find attractive. This, of course, varies. The beauty standards by which Miss Universe is judged hardly apply to the whole planet. People in various places and times have pierced noses, lengthened necks, dyed hair, bound feet, or painted skin; they have gorged themselves to become voluptuous and starved themselves to become thin; they have bound themselves with leather garments to make their breasts seem small and used silicone and padded bras to make them seem big. For cultures with scarce resources and for poor or hungry people, plumpness seems attractive; for cultures and individuals with abundant resources, beauty more often equals slimness (Nelson & Morrison, 2005). Moreover, attractiveness influences life outcomes less in cultures where relationships are based more on kinship or social arrangement than on personal choice (S. L. Anderson, Adams, & Plaut, 2008).

Despite such variations, there remains "strong agreement both within and across cultures about who is and who is not attractive," noted Judith Langlois and her colleagues (2000). To be really attractive is, ironically, to be perfectly average (Rhodes, 2006). Research teams led by Judith Langlois and Lorri Roggman (1990; Langlois, Roggman, & Musselman, 1994) at the University of Texas, and Anthony Little and David Perrett (2002) working with Ian Penton-Voak at the University of St. Andrews, have digitized multiple faces and averaged them using a computer. Inevitably, people find the composite faces more appealing than almost all of the actual faces (Figure 10–2). Across 27 nations, even an average leg-length-to-body ratio looks more attractive than very short or long legs (Sorokowski et al., 2011). With both humans and animals, averaged looks best embody prototypes (for your typical man, woman, dog, or whatever), and

FIGURE 10–2

WHO'S THE FAIREST OF THEM ALL?

Each year's selection of Miss Germany provides one country's answer. A University of Regensburg student research team, working with a German television channel, offered an alternative. Christof Braun and his compatriots (Gruendl, 2005) photographed the twenty-two 2002 "Queen of Beauty" finalists, without makeup and with hair tied back, and then created a "Virtual Miss Germany" that was the blended composite of them all (right). When adults in a local shopping mall were shown the finalists and the Virtual Miss Germany, they easily rated Virtual Miss Germany as the most attractive of them all. Although the winning real Miss Germany (left) may have been disappointed by the news that everyone preferred her virtual competitor to herself, she can reassure herself that she will never meet her virtual competitor.

thus are easy for the brain to process and categorize, noted Jamin Halberstadt (2006). Perfectly average is easy on the eyes (and brain).

Computer-averaged faces tend also to be perfectly symmetrical—another characteristic of strikingly attractive (and reproductively successful) people (W. M. Brown et al., 2008; Gangestad & Thornhill, 1997). A University of Western Australia research team led by Gillian Rhodes (2006; Rhodes, Sumich, & Byatt, 1999) and research by Ian Penton-Voak (Penton-Voak, Perrett, & Peirce, 2001) have shown that if you could merge either half of your face with its mirror image—thus forming a perfectly symmetrical new face—you would boost your looks. Averaging a number of such attractive, symmetrical faces produces an even better-looking face.

Evolution and attraction

Psychologists working from the evolutionary perspective explain the human preference for attractive partners in terms of reproductive strategy. They assume that beauty signals biologically important information: health, youth, and fertility. And so it does, report Gordon Gallup and colleagues (2008). Men with attractive faces have higher-quality sperm. Women with hourglass figures have more regular menstrual cycles and are more fertile. Over time, men who preferred fertile-looking women out-reproduced those who were as happy to mate with post-menopausal females. That, David Buss (1989) believed, explains why the males he studied in 37 cultures—from Australia to Zambia—did, indeed, prefer youthful female characteristics that signify reproductive capacity.

Evolutionary psychologists also assume that evolution predisposes women to favour male traits that signify an ability to provide and protect resources. No wonder physically attractive females tend to marry high-status males, and men compete with such determination to display status by achieving fame and fortune. In screening potential mates, reported Norman Li and his follow researchers (2002), men require a modicum of physical attractiveness, women require status and resources, and both welcome kindness and intelligence.

Evolutionary psychologists have also explored men's and women's responses to other cues to reproductive success. Judging from glamour models and beauty pageant winners, men everywhere have felt most attracted to women whose waists are 30 percent narrower than their hips—a shape associated with peak sexual fertility (Singh, 1993, 1995; Singh & Randall, 2007; Streeter & McBurney, 2003). Circumstances that reduce a woman's fertility—malnutrition, pregnancy, menopause—also change her shape.

When judging males as potential marriage partners, women, too, prefer a male waist-to-hip ratio suggesting health and vigour. They rate muscular men as sexier, and muscular men do feel sexier and report more lifetime sex partners (Frederick & Haselton, 2007). This makes evolutionary sense, noted Jared Diamond (1996): A muscular hunk was more likely than a scrawny fellow to gather food, build houses, and defeat rivals. But today's women prefer men with high incomes even more (Singh, 1995).

During ovulation, women show heightened preference for men with masculinized faces, voices, and bodies (Gallup & Frederick, 2010; Gangestad et al., 2004; Macrae et al., 2002). They show increased accuracy in judging male sexual orientation, finds Nicholas Rule of the University of Toronto and his colleagues (2011). And they show increased wariness of out-group men (McDonald et al., 2011). One study found that, when ovulating, young women tend to wear and prefer more revealing outfits than when infertile. In another study, ovulating lap dancers averaged $70 in tips per hour—double the $35 of those who were menstruating (G. Miller, Tybur, & Jordan, 2007).

We are, evolutionary psychologists suggest, driven by primal attractions. Like eating and breathing, attraction and mating are too important to leave to the whims of culture.

Social comparison

Although our mating psychology has wisdom, attraction is not all hard-wired. What's attractive to you also depends on your comparison standards.

Douglas Kenrick and Sara Gutierres (1980) had male confederates interrupt men in their dormitory rooms and explain, "We have a friend coming to town this week and we want to fix him up with a date, but we can't decide whether to fix him up with her or not, so we decided to conduct a survey … We want you to give us your vote on how attractive you think she is … on a scale of 1 to 7." Shown a picture of an average young woman, those who had just been watching *Charlie's Angels* (a television show featuring three beautiful women) rated her as less attractive than those who hadn't.

Laboratory experiments confirm this "contrast effect." To men who have recently been gazing at centrefolds, average women or even their own wives seem less attractive (Kenrick, Gutierres,

Maxine!Comix © Marian Henley. Reprinted by permission of the artist.

& Goldberg, 1989). Viewing pornographic films simulating passionate sex similarly decreases satisfaction with the viewer's own partner (Zillmann, 1989b). Being sexually aroused may temporarily make a person of the other sex seem more attractive. But the lingering effect of exposure to perfect "10s," or of unrealistic sexual depictions, is to make a person's own partner seem less appealing—more like a "6" than an "8."

It works the same way with our self-perceptions. After viewing a super attractive person of the same sex, people rate themselves as being less attractive than after viewing a homely person (J.D. Brown et al., 1992; Thornton & Maurice, 1997). Men's self-rated desirability is also deflated by exposure to more dominant, successful men. Thanks to modern media, we may see in an hour "dozens of individuals who are more attractive and more successful than any of our ancestors would have seen in a year, or even a lifetime," noted Sara Gutierres and her co-researchers (1999). Such extraordinary comparison standards trick us into devaluing our potential mates and ourselves and spending billions and billions of dollars on cosmetics, diet aids, and plastic surgery. But even after another 12 million annual cosmetic procedures, there may be no net gain in human satisfaction. If others get their teeth straightened, capped, and whitened, and you don't, the social comparison may leave you more dissatisfied with your normal, natural teeth than you would have been if you were surrounded by peers whose teeth were also natural.

"Love is only a dirty trick played on us to achieve a continuation of the species."
NOVELIST W. SOMERSET MAUGHAM, 1874–1965

The attractiveness of those we love

Let's conclude our discussion of attractiveness on an upbeat note. First, a 17-year old girl's facial attractiveness is a surprisingly weak predictor of her attractiveness at ages 30 and 50. Sometimes, an average-looking adolescent becomes a quite attractive middle-aged adult (Zebrowitz, Collins, & Dutta, 1998; Zebrowitz, Olson, & Hoffman, 1993).

Second, not only do we perceive attractive people as likeable, we also perceive likeable people as attractive. Perhaps you can recall individuals who, as you grew to like them, became more attractive. Their physical imperfections were no longer so noticeable. Alan Gross and Christine Crofton (1977) had students view someone's photograph after reading a favourable or unfavourable description of the person's personality. Those portrayed as warm, helpful, and considerate also looked more attractive. It may be true, then, that "handsome is as

"Do I love you because you are beautiful, or are you beautiful because I love you?"
PRINCE CHARMING, IN RODGERS & HAMMERSTEIN'S *CINDERELLA*

Standards of beauty differ from culture to culture. Yet some people are considered attractive throughout most of the world.

handsome does." Discovering someone's similarities to us also makes the person seem more attractive (Beaman & Klentz, 1983; Klentz et al., 1987).

Moreover, love sees loveliness: The more in love a woman is with a man, the more physically attractive she finds him (Price et al., 1974). And the more in love people are, the less attractive they find all others of the opposite sex (Johnson & Rusbult, 1989; Simpson, Gangestad, & Lerma, 1990). Research by John Lydon of McGill University and his colleagues (1999) suggests this is especially true for people in more committed relationships. They had people in relationships of varying commitment rate an attractive, "single and not currently involved" member of the opposite sex who was apparently also a participant in the study. This attractive person was supposedly matched with them randomly (a moderate threat to their relationship) or because he or she thought the participant was attractive (a more serious threat). As you can see in Figure 10–3, when people were threatened at the same level as they were committed, they saw the competition as less attractive. It seems that people modulate how attractive they find others in a way that maintains their close relationships. Beauty really is, to some extent, in the eye of the beholder.

> *"Can two walk together except they be agreed?"*
>
> AMOS 3:3

(3) SIMILARITY VERSUS COMPLEMENTARITY

From our discussion so far, one might surmise Leo Tolstoy was entirely correct: "Love depends . . . on frequent meetings, and on the style in which the hair is done up, and on the colour and cut of the dress." As people get to know one another, however, other factors influence whether acquaintance develops into friendship.

Do birds of a feather flock together?

Of this much we may be sure: Birds that flock together are of a feather. Friends, engaged couples, and spouses are far more likely than people randomly paired to share common attitudes, beliefs,

FIGURE 10–3

RELATED ATTRACTIVENESS AND RELATIONSHIP COMMITMENT.

When an attractive member of the opposite sex threatens people's relationships, they rate this person as less attractive if the threat posed by the person matches their level of commitment. (Based on Lydon et al., 1999)

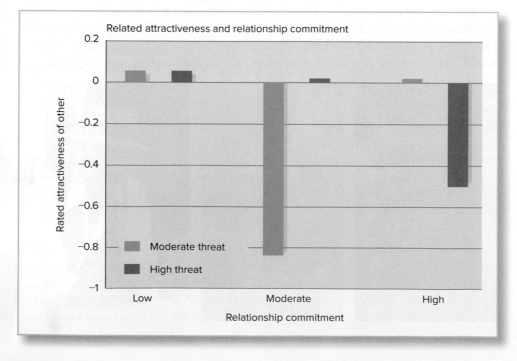

and values. Furthermore, the greater the similarity between husband and wife, the happier they are and the less likely they are to divorce (Byrne, 1971; Caspi & Herbener, 1990). Such correlational findings are intriguing. But cause and effect remain an enigma. Does similarity lead to liking? Or does liking lead to similarity?

Likeness begets liking

To discern cause and effect, we experiment. Imagine that at a campus party Lakesha gets involved in a long discussion of politics, religion, and personal likes and dislikes with Les and Lon. She and Les discover they agree on almost everything, she and Lon on few things. Afterwards, she reflects, "Les is really intelligent . . . and so likeable. I hope we meet again." In experiments, Donn Byrne (1971) and his colleagues captured the essence of Lakesha's experience. Over and over again, they found that the more similar someone's attitudes are to your own, the more likeable you will find the person. Likeness produces liking not only for college and university students but also for children and the elderly, for people of various occupations, and for those in various cultures.

The likeness-leads-to-liking effect has been tested in real-life situations:

Henry James's description of novelist George Eliot (the pen name of Mary Ann Evans): "She is magnificently ugly—deliciously hideous. She has a low forehead, a dull grey eye, a vast pendulous nose, a huge mouth, full of uneven teeth, and a chin and jaw-bone *qui n'en finissent pas.* . . Now in this vast ugliness resides a most powerful beauty which, in a very few minutes, steals forth and charms the mind, so that you end as I ended, in falling in love with her."

- At the University of Michigan, Theodore Newcomb (1961) studied two groups of 17 unacquainted male transfer students. After 13 weeks of boardinghouse life, those whose agreement was initially highest were most likely to have formed close friendships. One group of friends was composed of five liberal arts students, each a political liberal with strong intellectual interests. Another was made up of three conservative veterans who were all enrolled in the engineering college.

- At two of Hong Kong's universities, Royce Lee and Michael Bond (1996) found that roommate friendships flourished over a six-month period when roommates shared values and personality traits, but more so when they perceived their roommates as similar. As so often happens, reality matters, but perception matters more.

- In various settings, researchers at Wilfrid Laurier University found that people entering a room of strangers sit closer to those like themselves (Mackinnon, Jordan, & Wilson, 2011). People with glasses sit closer to others with glasses. Long-haired people sit closer to people with long hair. Dark-haired people sit closer to people with dark hair (even after controlling for race and sex).

- People like not only those who think as they do, but also those who act as they do. Subtle mimicry fosters fondness. Have you noticed that when someone nods their head as you do and echoes your thoughts, you feel a certain rapport and liking? That's a common experience, reported Rick van Baaren and his colleagues (2003a, 2003b), and one result is higher tips for Dutch restaurant servers who mimic their customers by merely repeating their order. Natural mimicry increases rapport, noted Jessica Lakin and Tanya Chartrand (2003), and desire for rapport increases mimicry.

- Whether in China or the Western world, similar attitudes, traits, and values help bring couples together and predict their satisfaction (Chen et al., 2009; Gaunt, 2006; Gonzaga, Campos, & Bradbury, 2007). Speed-daters are drawn to those who share their speaking style (Ireland et al., 2011). Even morning and evening types tend to find one another (Randler & Kretz, 2011). One psychologist-founded Internet dating site claims to match singles using the similarities that mark happy couples (Carter & Snow, 2004; Warren, 2005).

So similarity breeds content. Birds of a feather *do* flock together. Surely you have noticed this upon discovering a special someone who shares your ideas, values, and desires—a soulmate who likes the same music, the same activities, even the same foods you do. (When liking the same music as another, people infer similar values as well [Boer et al., 2011].)

Dissimilarity breeds dislike

We have a bias—the false consensus bias—toward assuming that others share our attitudes. Getting to know someone—and discovering that the person is actually dissimilar—tends to decrease liking (Norton, Frost, & Ariely, 2007). If those dissimilar attitudes pertain to our strong moral convictions, we dislike and distance ourselves from them all the more (Skitka, Bauman, & Mullen, 2004). People in one political party often are not so much fond of fellow party members as they are disdainful of the opposition (Hoyle, 1993; Rosenbaum, 1986). Straight men often disdain gay men, who are doubly dissimilar to themselves—in perceived gender traits and sexuality (Lehavot & Lambert, 2007).

In general, dissimilar attitudes depress liking more than similar attitudes enhance it (Singh & Ho, 2000; Singh & Teoh, 1999). Within their own groups, where they expect similarity, people find it especially hard to like someone with dissimilar views (Chen & Kenrick, 2002). That perhaps explains why dating partners and roommates become more similar over time in their emotional responses to events and in their attitudes (C. Anderson, Keltner, & John, 2003; Davis & Rusbult, 2001). "Attitude alignment" helps promote and sustain close relationships, a phenomenon that can lead partners to overestimate their attitude similarities (Kenny & Acitelli, 2001; Murray et al., 2002b).

Whether people perceive those of another race as similar or dissimilar influences their racial attitudes. Wherever one group of people regards another as "other"—as creatures who speak differently, live differently, and think differently—the potential for conflict is high. In fact, except for intimate relationships such as dating, the perception of like minds seems more important for attraction than like skins. Most Whites have expressed more liking for, and willingness to work with, a like-minded Black than a dissimilarly minded White (Insko, Nacoste, & Moe, 1983; Rokeach, 1968). The more that Whites presume that Blacks support their values, the more positive their racial attitudes (Biernat, Vescio, & Theno, 1996). Likewise, the more Montreal residents perceived a Canadian ethnic group as similar to themselves, the more willing they were to associate with its members (Osbeck, Moghaddam, & Perreault, 1996).

"Cultural racism" persists, argued social psychologist James Jones (1988, 2003, 2004), because cultural differences are a fact of life. Black culture tends to be present-oriented, spontaneously expressive, spiritual, and emotionally driven. White culture tends to be more future-oriented, materialistic, and achievement-driven. Rather than trying to eliminate such differences,

The most appealing people are those most like us.

© Warren Miller/The New Yorker Collection/www.cartoonbank.com

"Actually, Lou, I think it was more than just my being in the right place at the right time. I think it was my being the right race, the right religion, the right sex, the right socioeconomic group, having the right accent, the right clothes, going to the right schools . . ."

suggested Jones, we might better appreciate what they "contribute to the cultural fabric of a multicultural society." There are situations in which expressiveness is advantageous and situations in which future orientation is advantageous. Each culture has much to learn from the other. In countries such as Canada, Britain, and the United States, where migration and different birthrates make for growing diversity, educating people to respect and enjoy those who differ is a major challenge. Given increasing cultural diversity and given our natural wariness of differences, this may, in fact, be the major social challenge of our time.

Do opposites attract?

Are we not also attracted to people who in some ways differ from ourselves? We are attracted to people whose scent suggests dissimilar enough genes to prevent inbreeding (Garver-Apgar et al., 2006). But what about attitudes and behavioural traits? Researchers have explored this question by comparing not only friends' and spouses' attitudes and beliefs but also their age, religion, race, smoking behaviour, economic level, education, height, intelligence, and appearance. In all these ways and more, similarity still prevails (Buss, 1985; Kandel, 1978). Smart birds flock together. So do rich birds, Protestant birds, tall birds, pretty birds.

Still we resist: Are we not attracted to people whose needs and personalities complement our own? Would a sadist and a masochist find true love? Even the *Reader's Digest* has told us that "opposites attract. . . . Socializers pair with loners, novelty-lovers with those who dislike change, free spenders with scrimpers, risk-takers with the very cautious" (Jacoby, 1986). Sociologist Robert Winch (1958) reasoned that the needs of someone who is outgoing and domineering would naturally complement those of someone who is shy and submissive. The logic seems compelling, and most of us can think of couples who view their differences as complementary. "My husband and I are perfect for each other. I'm Aquarius—a decisive person. He's Libra—can't make decisions. But he's always happy to go along with arrangements I make."

Given the idea's persuasiveness, the inability of researchers to confirm it is astonishing. For example, most people feel attracted to expressive, outgoing people (Friedman, Riggio, & Casella, 1988). Would this be especially so when one is down in the dumps? Do depressed people seek those whose gaiety will cheer them up? To the contrary, it is non-depressed people who most prefer the company of happy people (Locke & Horowitz, 1990; Rosenblatt & Greenberg, 1988, 1991; Wenzlaff & Prohaska, 1989). When you're feeling blue, someone else's bubbly personality can be aggravating. The contrast effect that makes average people feel homely in the company of beautiful people also makes sad people more conscious of their misery in the company of cheerful people.

Some **complementarity** may evolve as a relationship progresses (even a relationship between identical twins). Yet people seem slightly more prone to like and to marry those whose needs and personalities are similar (Botwin, Buss, & Shackelford, 1997; Buss, 1984; Fishbein & Thelen, 1981a, 1981b; Nias, 1979). Perhaps we shall yet discover some ways (other than heterosexuality) in which differences commonly breed liking. Dominance/submissiveness may be one such way (Dryer & Horowitz, 1997). And we tend not to feel attracted to those who show our own worst traits (Schimel et al., 2000). But as a general rule, opposites do not attract.

complementarity
the popularly supposed tendency, in a relationship between two people, for each to complete what is missing in the other

(4) LIKING THOSE WHO LIKE US

Liking is usually mutual. Proximity and attractiveness influence our initial attraction to someone, and similarity influences longer-term attraction as well. If we have a deep need to belong

"Well—and I'm not just saying this because you're my husband—it stinks."

© Robert Mankoff/The New Yorker Collection/www.cartoonbank.com

and to feel liked and accepted, would we not also take a liking to those who like us? Are the best friendships mutual admiration societies? Indeed, one person's liking for another does predict the other's liking in return (Kenny & Nasby, 1980; Montoya & Insko, 2008).

But does one person's liking another cause the other to return the appreciation? People's reports of how they fell in love suggest yes (Aron et al., 1989). Discovering that an appealing someone really likes you seems to awaken romantic feelings. Experiments confirm it: Those told that certain others like or admire them usually feel a reciprocal affection (Berscheid & Walster, 1978). And all the better, one speed-dating experiment suggested, when someone likes you especially, more than others (Eastwick et al., 2007b). A dash of uncertainty can also fuel desire. Thinking that someone probably likes you—but you aren't sure—tends to increase your thinking about, and feeling attracted to, another (Whitechurch, Wilson, & Gilbert, 2011).

And consider this finding by Ellen Berscheid and her colleagues (1969): Student subjects liked better another student who said eight positive things about them than one who said seven positive things and one negative thing. We are sensitive to the slightest hint of criticism. Writer Larry L. King spoke for many in noting, "I have discovered over the years that good reviews strangely fail to make the author feel as good as bad reviews make him feel bad."

> *"The average man is more interested in a woman who is interested in him than he is in a woman with beautiful legs."*
> ACTRESS MARLENE DIETRICH
> (1901–1992)

Whether we are judging ourselves or others, negative information carries more weight because, being less usual, it grabs more attention (Yzerbyt & Leyens, 1991). People's votes are more influenced by their impressions of candidates' weaknesses than by their impressions of strengths (Klein, 1991), a phenomenon that has not been lost on those who design negative campaigns. It's a general rule of life, noted Roy Baumeister and his colleagues (2001): Bad is stronger than good.

Our liking for those we perceive as liking us was recognized long ago. Observers from the ancient philosopher Hecato ("If you wish to be loved, love") to Ralph Waldo Emerson ("The only way to have a friend is to be one") to Dale Carnegie ("Dole out praise lavishly") anticipated the findings. What they did not anticipate was the precise conditions under which the principle works.

Attribution

As we've seen, flattery will get you somewhere—but not everywhere. If praise clearly violates what we know is true—if someone says, "Your hair looks great," when we haven't washed it in days—we may lose respect for the flatterer and wonder whether the compliment springs from ulterior motives (Shrauger, 1975). Thus we often perceive criticism to be more sincere than praise (Coleman, Jussim, & Abraham, 1987).

ingratiation
the use of strategies, such as flattery, by which people seek to gain another's favour

Laboratory experiments reveal something we've noted in previous chapters: Our reactions depend on our attributions. Do we attribute the flattery to ingratiation—to a self-serving strategy? Is the person trying to get us to buy something, to acquiesce sexually, to do a favour? If so, both the flatterer and the praise lose appeal (Gordon, 1996; Jones, 1964). But if there is no apparent ulterior motive, then we warmly receive both flattery and flatterer.

Some people embrace compliments more readily than do others, however. Denise Marigold of Renison University College and her colleagues found that people with low self-esteem focus narrowly on the literal meaning of compliments—to them, "You have a nice smile," means just that (Marigold, Holmes, & Ross, 2007). People with high self-esteem, in contrast, attribute more abstract significance to compliments—that their partner is attentive, values and cares for them—and they feel more secure in their relationships. It's not that low self-esteem people can't derive the same benefit from compliments; they do if they are directed to consider what compliments mean for their relationship. Everyone feels more secure and valued if they attribute compliments to caring and affection, but people with low self-esteem need more encouragement to do so.

Self-esteem and attraction

Elaine Hatfield (Walster, 1965) wondered if another's approval is especially rewarding after we have been deprived of approval, much as eating is most powerfully rewarding after fasting. To test this idea, she gave some women either very favourable or very unfavourable analyses of their personalities, affirming some and wounding others. Then she asked them to evaluate several people, including an attractive male confederate who just before the experiment had struck up a warm conversation with each woman and had asked each for a date. (Not one turned him down.) Which women do you suppose most liked the man? It was those whose self-esteem had been temporarily shattered and who were presumably hungry for social approval.

This helps explain why people sometimes fall passionately in love on the rebound, after an ego-bruising rejection. Indeed, after a breakup, the prospect of someone new helps people (particularly those who are characteristically anxious about relationships) get over their ex-partners (Spielman, MacDonald, & Wilson, 2009). Unfortunately, low self-esteem individuals tend to underestimate how much potential partners will accept them. Jessica Cameron of the University of Manitoba, Danu Stinson of the University of Victoria, and their collaborators (2010) found that, even when partners behave in an equally friendly way, low self-esteem individuals believe they will be less accepted than high self-esteem individuals. These lower expectations of acceptance lead low self-esteem individuals to behave in a less warm and friendly manner, which ultimately leads them to really be less accepted by others (Stinson et al., 2009).

Even in established relationships, low self-esteem people underestimate how much their romantic partners value them. They also have less generous views of their partner and are, therefore, less happy with the relationship (Murray et al., 2000). If you feel down about yourself, you will likely feel pessimistic about your relationships. Feel good about yourself and you're more likely to feel confident of your dating partner's or spouse's regard. Accordingly, when low self-esteem people are focused on their own strengths, they feel more secure in their relationships (Murray et al., 2005).

Gaining another's esteem

If approval that comes after disapproval is powerfully rewarding, then would we most like someone who liked us after initially disliking us? Or would we most like someone who liked us from the start (and, therefore, gave us more total approval)? Ray is in a small discussion class with his roommate's cousin, Sophia. After the first week of classes, Ray learns via his "pipeline" that Sophia thinks him rather shallow. As the semester progresses, however, he learns that Sophia's opinion of him is steadily rising; gradually, she comes to view him as bright, thoughtful, and charming. Would Ray like Sophia more if she had thought well of him from the beginning? If Ray is simply counting the number of approving comments he receives, then the answer will be yes: He would like Sophia better had she consistently praised him. But if after her initial disapproval, Sophia's rewards become more potent, Ray then might like her better than if she had been consistently affirming.

To see which is more often true, Elliot Aronson and Darwyn Linder (1965) captured the essence of Ray's experience in a clever experiment. They "allowed" 80 women to overhear a sequence of evaluations of themselves by another woman. Some women heard consistently positive things about themselves, some consistently negative. Others heard evaluations that changed either from negative to positive (like Sophia's evaluations of Ray) or from positive to negative. In this and other experiments, the target person was well-liked when the subject experienced a gain in the other's esteem, especially when the gain occurred gradually and reversed the earlier criticism (Aronson & Mettee, 1974; Clore, Wiggins, & Itkin, 1975). Perhaps Sophia's nice words have more credibility coming after her not-so-nice words. Or perhaps after being withheld, they are especially gratifying.

Aronson speculated that constant approval can lose value. When a husband says for the 500th time, "Gee, honey, you look great," the words carry far less impact than were he now to say, "Gee, honey, you look awful in that dress." A loved one you've doted upon is hard to reward but easy to hurt. This suggests that an open, honest relationship—one where people enjoy one another's esteem and acceptance yet are honest—is more likely to offer continuing rewards than one dulled by the suppression of unpleasant emotions, one in which people try only, as Dale Carnegie advised, to "lavish praise." Aronson (1988) put it this way:

> As a relationship ripens toward greater intimacy, what becomes increasingly important is authenticity—our ability to give up trying to make a good impression and begin to reveal things about ourselves that are honest even if unsavory. . . . If two people are genuinely fond of each other, they will have a more satisfying and exciting relationship over a longer period of time if they are able to express both positive and negative feelings than if they are completely "nice" to each other at all times. (p. 323)

In most social interactions, we self-censor our negative feelings. Thus, noted William Swann and his colleagues (1991), some people receive no corrective feedback. Living in a world of pleasant illusion, they continue to act in ways that alienate their would-be friends. A true friend is one who can let us in on bad news.

Someone who really loves us will be honest with us but will also tend to see us through rose-coloured glasses. When Sandra Murray and her colleagues (Murray & Holmes, 1997; Murray, Holmes, & Griffin, 1996a, 1996b) studied dating and married couples from the University of Waterloo, they found that the happiest (and those who became happier) were those who idealized one another, who even saw their partners more positively than their partners saw themselves.

When we're in love, we're inclined to find those we love not only physically attractive, but socially attractive as well (Boyes & Fletcher, 2007). Moreover, the most satisfied married couples tend to have idealized one another as newlyweds and to approach problems without immediately criticizing their partners and finding fault (P. J. E. Miller, Niehuis, & Huston, 2006). Honesty has its place in a good relationship, but so does a presumption of the other person's basic goodness.

> "Hatred which is entirely conquered by love passes into love, and love on that account is greater than if it had not been preceded by hatred."
> BENEDICT SPINOZA, *ETHICS*

> "It takes your enemy and your friend, working together, to hurt you to the heart; the enemy to slander you and the friend to get the news to you."
> MARK TWAIN, *PUDD'NHEAD WILSON'S NEW CALENDAR*, 1897

⑤ RELATIONSHIP REWARDS

Asked why they are friends with someone or why they were attracted to their partner, most people can readily answer. "I like Carol because she's warm, witty, and well-read." What such explanations leave out—and what social psychologists believe is most important—is ourselves. Attraction involves the one who is attracted as well as the attractor. Thus a more psychologically accurate answer might be, "I like Carol because of how I feel when I'm with her." We are attracted to those we find it satisfying and gratifying to be with. Attraction is in the eye (and brain) of the beholder.

The point can be expressed as a simple **reward theory of attraction:** Those who reward us, or whom we associate with rewards, we like. If a relationship gives us more rewards than costs, we will like it and will wish it to continue. This will be especially true if the relationship is more profitable than alternative relationships (Rusbult, 1980). Mutual attraction flourishes when each meets the other's unmet needs (Byers & Wang, 2004).

We not only like people who are rewarding to be with, but also, according to the second version of the reward principle, we like those we associate with good feelings. Conditioning creates positive feelings toward things and people linked with rewarding events (Byrne & Clore, 1970; De Houwer, Thomas, & Baeyens, 2001; Lott & Lott, 1974). When, after a strenuous week, we relax in front of a fire, enjoying good food, drink, and music, we will likely feel a special warmth toward those around us. We are less likely to take a liking to someone we meet while suffering a splitting headache.

Pawel Lewicki (1985) tested this liking-by-association principle. In one experiment, University of Warsaw students were virtually 50–50 in choosing which of two pictured women (A or B in Figure 10-4) looked friendlier. Other students, having interacted with a warm, friendly experimenter who resembled woman A, chose woman A, by a 6-to-1 margin. In a follow-up study, the experimenter acted *unfriendly* toward half the subjects. When these subjects later had to turn in their data to one of two women, they nearly always avoided the one who resembled the experimenter. (Perhaps you can recall a time when you reacted positively or negatively to someone who reminded you of someone else.)

reward theory of attraction
the theory that we like those whose behaviour is rewarding to us or whom we associate with rewarding events

"No one is perfect until you fall in love with them."
ANDY ROONEY

FIGURE 10–4

LIKING BY ASSOCIATION.

After interacting with a friendly experimenter, people preferred someone who looked like her (Person A) to one who didn't (Person B). After interacting with an unfriendly experimenter, people avoided the woman who resembled her (Lewicki, 1985).

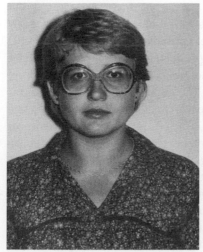

Experimenter   Person A   Person B

> *"Friendship is a scheme for the mutual exchange of personal advantages and favours whereby self-esteem may profit."*
>
> LA ROCHEFOUCAULD, *MAXIMS*, 1665

Other experiments confirm this phenomenon of liking—and disliking—by association. Elaine Hatfield and William Walster (1978) found a practical tip in these research studies: "Romantic dinners, trips to the theatre, evenings at home together, and vacations never stop being important. . . . If your relationship is to survive, it's important that you both continue to associate your relationship with good things."

This simple theory of attraction—we like those who reward us and those whom we associate with rewards—helps us understand why people everywhere feel attracted to those who are warm, trustworthy, and responsive (Fletcher et al., 1999; Regan, 1998; Wojciszke, Bazinska, & Jaworski, 1998). The reward theory also helps explain some of the influences on attraction:

- Proximity is rewarding. It costs less time and effort to receive friendship's benefits with someone who lives or works close by.

- We like attractive people because we perceive that they offer other desirable traits and because we benefit by associating with them.

- If others have similar opinions, we feel rewarded because we presume that they like us in return. Moreover, those who share our views help validate those views. We especially like people if we have successfully converted them to our way of thinking (Lombardo, Weiss, & Buchanan, 1972; Riordan, 1980; Sigall, 1970).

- We like to be liked and love to be loved. Thus, liking is usually mutual. We like those who like us.

Researchers report that sustained eye contact, nodding, and smiling are indicators of passionate love.

● WHAT IS LOVE?

What are the varieties and components of love?

Loving is more complex than liking and thus more difficult to measure, more perplexing to study. People yearn for it, live for it, die for it.

Most attraction researchers have studied what is most easily studied—responses during brief encounters between strangers. The influences on our initial liking of another—proximity, attractiveness, similarity, being liked, and other rewarding traits—also influence our long-term, close relationships. The impressions that dating couples quickly form of each other provide a clue to their long-term future (Berg, 1984; Berg & McQuinn, 1986). If North American romances flourished randomly, though, without regard to proximity and similarity, then most Catholics (being a minority) would marry Protestants, most Blacks would marry Whites, and college graduates would be as apt to marry high-school dropouts as fellow graduates.

So first impressions are important. Nevertheless, long-term loving is not merely an intensification of initial liking. Social psychologists have, therefore, shifted their attention from the mild attraction experienced during first encounters to the study of enduring, close relationships.

2 'KINDS' OF LOVE

① PASSIONATE LOVE

The first step in scientifically studying romantic love, as in studying any variable, is to decide how to define and measure it. We have ways to measure aggression, altruism, prejudice, and liking—but how do we measure love?

"How do I love thee? Let me count the ways," wrote Elizabeth Barrett Browning. Social scientists have counted various ways. Psychologist Robert Sternberg (1998) viewed love as a triangle consisting of three components: passion, intimacy, and commitment (Figure 10–5). Some elements are common to all loving relationships: mutual understanding, giving and receiving support, enjoying the loved one's company. On the other hand, some elements of passionate love are distinctive. If we experience passionate love, we express it physically, we expect the relationship to be exclusive, and we are intensely fascinated with our partner. You can see it in our eyes.

Zick Rubin confirmed this (Rubin, 1973). He administered a love scale to hundreds of dating couples. Later, from behind a one-way mirror in a laboratory waiting room, he clocked eye contact among "weak-love" and "strong-love" couples. Other research indicates that mutual gaze conveys liking and averted eye gaze conveys ostracism (Wirth et al., 2010). So Rubin's result will not surprise you: The strong-love couples gave themselves away by gazing for a long time into one another's eyes. When talking, they also nod their head, smile naturally, and lean forward (Gonzaga et al., 2001). When observing speed-daters, it takes but a few seconds to make a reasonably accurate guess as to whether one person is interested in another (Place et al., 2009).

Passionate love is emotional, exciting, intense. Elaine Hatfield (1988) defined it as "a state of intense longing for union with another" (p. 193). If reciprocated, a person feels fulfilled and joyous; if not, he or she feels empty or despairing. Like other forms of emotional excitement, passionate love involves a mix of elation and gloom, tingling exhilaration and dejected misery.

Passionate love is what you feel not only when you love someone but also when you are "in love" with him or her. As Sarah Meyers and Ellen Berscheid (1997) note, we understand that someone who says, "I love you, but I'm not in love with you," means to say, "I like you. I care about you. I think you're marvellous. But I don't feel sexually attracted to you." That person feels friendship but not passion.

passionate love
a state of intense longing for union with another. Passionate lovers are absorbed in one another; they feel ecstatic at attaining their partner's love, and they are disconsolate on losing it.

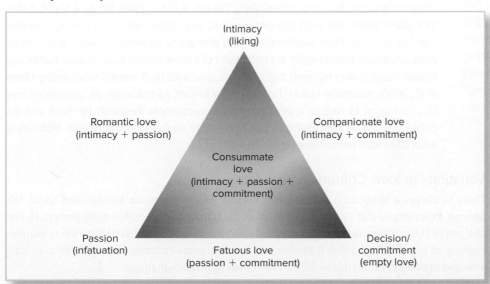

FIGURE 10–5

KINDS OF LOVE.

Robert Sternberg's (1998) conception of kinds of loving as combinations of three basic components of love.

Intimacy
(liking)

Romantic love
(intimacy + passion)

Companionate love
(intimacy + commitment)

Consummate
love
(intimacy + passion +
commitment)

Passion
(infatuation)

Fatuous love
(passion + commitment)

Decision/
commitment
(empty love)

A theory of passionate love

To explain passionate love, Hatfield noted that a given state of arousal can be steered into any of several emotions, depending on how we attribute the arousal. An emotion involves both body and mind—both arousal and how we interpret and label that arousal. Imagine yourself with pounding heart and trembling hands: Are you experiencing fear, anxiety, joy? Physiologically, one emotion is quite similar to another. You may, therefore, experience the arousal as joy if you are in a euphoric situation, as anger if your environment is hostile, or as passionate love if the situation is romantic. In this view, passionate love is the psychological experience of being biologically aroused by someone we find attractive.

If, indeed, passion is a revved-up state that's labelled "love," then whatever revs one up should intensify feelings of love. In several experiments, university men aroused sexually by reading or viewing erotic materials had a heightened response to a woman—for example, by scoring much higher on a love scale when describing their girlfriends (Carducci, Cosby, & Ward, 1978; Dermer & Pyszczynski, 1978; Stephan, Berscheid, & Walster, 1971). Proponents of the **two-factor theory of emotion**, developed by Stanley Schachter and Jerome Singer (1962) argue that when the revved-up men responded to a woman, they easily misattributed some of their arousal to her.

two-factor theory of emotion
arousal × its label = emotion

According to this theory, being aroused by any source should intensify passionate feelings—providing the mind is free to attribute some of the arousal to a romantic stimulus. In a dramatic illustration of this phenomenon, Donald Dutton and Arthur Aron (1974, 1989) had an attractive young woman approach individual young men as they crossed a narrow, wobbly, 150-metre-long suspension walkway hanging 75 metres above British Columbia's rocky Capilano River. The woman asked each man to help her fill out a class questionnaire. When he had finished, she scribbled her name and phone number and invited him to call if he wanted to hear more about the project. Most accepted the phone number, and half who did so called. By contrast, men approached by the woman on a low, solid bridge, and men approached on the high bridge by a male interviewer, rarely called. Once again, physical arousal accentuated romantic responses.

> *"The 'adrenaline' associated with a wide variety of highs can spill over and make passion more passionate. (Sort of a 'Better loving through chemistry' phenomenon.)"*
> ELAINE HATFIELD AND RICHARD RAPSON (1987)

Scary movies, roller-coaster rides, and physical exercise have the same effect, especially to those we find attractive (Cohen, Waugh, & Place, 1989; White & Kight, 1984). The effect holds true with married couples, too. Those who do exciting activities together report the best relationships. And after doing an arousing rather than a mundane laboratory task (roughly the equivalent of a three-legged race on their hands and knees), couples also reported higher satisfaction with their overall relationship (Aron et al., 2000). Adrenalin makes the heart grow fonder. As this suggests, passionate love is a biological as well as a psychological phenomenon. Research by Aron and his colleagues (2005) indicated that passionate love engages dopamine-rich brain areas associated with reward (see Figure 10-6).

Variations in love: Culture and gender

There is always a temptation to assume that most others share our feelings and ideas. We assume, for example, that love is a precondition for marriage. Most cultures—89 percent in one analysis of 166 cultures—do have a concept of romantic love, as reflected in flirtation or couples running off together (Jankowiak & Fischer, 1992). But in some cultures, notably those practising arranged marriages, love tends to follow rather than to precede marriage.

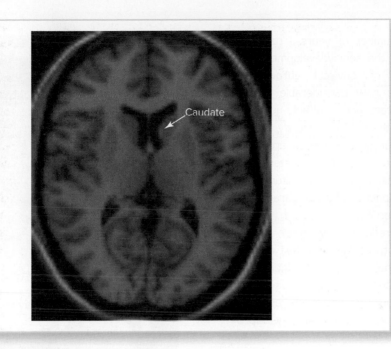

FIGURE 10–6

LOVE IS IN THE BRAIN.

MRI scans from young adults intensely in love revealed areas, such as the caudate nucleus, which became more active when gazing at the loved one's photo (but not when gazing at the photo of another acquaintance). (Aron et al., 2005)

Do males and females differ in how they experience passionate love? Studies of men and women falling in and out of love reveal some surprises. Most people, including the writer of the following letter to a newspaper advice columnist, suppose that women fall in love more readily:

Dear Dr. Brothers:

Do you think it's effeminate for a 19-year-old guy to fall in love so hard it's like the whole world's turned around? I think I'm really crazy because this has happened several times now and love just seems to hit me on the head from nowhere. . . . My father says this is the way girls fall in love and that it doesn't happen this way with guys—at least it's not supposed to. I can't change how I am in this way but it kind of worries me.—P.T. (quoted by Dion & Dion, 1985)

P.T. would be reassured by the repeated finding that it is actually men who tend to fall in love more readily (Ackerman, Griskevicius, & Li, 2011; Dion & Dion, 1985; Peplau & Gordon, 1985). Men also seem to fall out of love more slowly and are less likely than women to break up a premarital romance. Surprisingly to most people, in heterosexual relationships, it's men, not women, who most often are first to say "I love you" (Ackerman et al., 2011).

Once in love, however, women are typically as emotionally involved as their partners, or more so. They are more likely to report feeling euphoric and "giddy and carefree," as if they were "floating on a cloud." Women are also somewhat more likely than men to focus on the intimacy of the friendship and on their concern for their partner. Men are more likely than women to think about the playful and physical aspects of the relationship (Hendrick & Hendrick, 1995).

THE >>> INSIDE STORY

For a number of years, I have been studying the social/developmental psychology of physical attractiveness. There is now considerable evidence that attractiveness affects judgments and evaluations of others. More recently, I've been interested in whether cultural values are related to the occurrence and/or strength of stereotyping based on attractiveness. Are there culture-related differences in the impact of physical attractiveness on evaluations of others?

This question reflects my more general research interest in the cultural context of attraction and interpersonal relationships. Increasingly, the importance of cultural perspectives is being acknowledged by social psychologists, as well as researchers in other areas of psychology—a promising trend within the field.

Karen Dion, *University of Toronto*

(z) COMPANIONATE LOVE

Although passionate love burns hot, it inevitably simmers down. The longer a relationship endures, the fewer its emotional ups and downs (Berscheid, Snyder, & Omoto, 1989). The high of romance may be sustained for a few months, even a couple of years. But no high lasts forever. "When you're in love, it's the most glorious two-and-a-half days of your life," jested comedian Richard Lewis. The novelty, the intense absorption in the other, the thrill of the romance, the giddy "floating on a cloud" feeling, fades. After two years of marriage, spouses express affection about half as often as when they were newlyweds (Huston & Chorost, 1994). About four years after marriage, the divorce rate peaks in cultures worldwide (H. Fisher, 1994). If a close relationship is to endure, it will settle to a steadier but still warm afterglow that Hatfield calls **companionate love**. The passion-facilitating hormones (testosterone, dopamine, adrenaline) subside, while the hormone oxytocin supports feelings of attachment and trust (Taylor, Saphire-Bernstein, & Seeman, 2010).

companionate love
the affection we feel for those with whom our lives are deeply intertwined

Unlike the wild emotions of passionate love, companionate love is lower key; it's a deep, affectionate attachment. It activates different parts of the brain (Aron et al., 2005). And it is just as real. Nisa, a !Kung San woman of the African Kalahari Desert, explained it this way: "When two people are first together, their hearts are on fire and their passion is very great. After a while, the fire cools and that's how it stays. They continue to love each other, but it's in a different way—warm and dependable" (Shostak, 1981).

"Don't it always seem to go that you don't know what you've got 'til it's gone."
JONI MITCHELL, "BIG YELLOW TAXI," 1970

The flow and ebb of romantic love follows the pattern of addictions to coffee, alcohol, and other drugs. At first, a drug gives a big kick, perhaps a high. With repetition, opponent emotions gain strength and tolerance develops. An amount that once was highly stimulating no longer gives a thrill. Stopping the substance, however, does not

Unlike passionate love, companionate love can last a lifetime.

return you to where you started. Rather, it triggers withdrawal symptoms—malaise, depression, the blahs. The same often happens in love. The passionate high is fated to become lukewarm. The no-longer-romantic relationship becomes taken for granted—until it ends. Then the jilted lover, the widower, and the divorcee are surprised at how empty life now seems without the person they long ago stopped feeling passionately attached to. Having focused on what was not working, they stopped noticing what was (Carlson & Hatfield, 1992).

The cooling of passionate love over time and the growing importance of other factors, such as shared values, can be seen in the feelings of those who enter arranged versus love-based marriages in India. Usha Gupta and Pushpa Singh (1982) asked 50 couples in Jaipur, India, to complete a love scale. They found that those who married for love reported diminishing feelings of love after a five-year newlywed period. By contrast, those in arranged marriages reported more love if their marriage was five or more years old (Figure 10–7).

The cooling of intense romantic love often triggers a period of disillusion, especially among those who believe that passionate love is essential both for a marriage and for its continuation. Compared to North Americans, Asians tend to focus less on personal feelings and more on the practical aspects of social attachments (Dion & Dion, 1988; Sprecher et al., 1994). Thus, they are less vulnerable to disillusionment. Asians are also less prone to the self-focused individualism that in the long run can undermine a relationship and lead to divorce (Dion & Dion, 1991, 1996; Triandis et al., 1988).

"Grow old along with me! The best is yet to be."
ROBERT BROWNING

The decline in intense mutual fascination may be natural and adaptive for species survival. The result of passionate love frequently is children, whose survival is aided by the parents' waning obsession with one another (Kenrick & Trost, 1987). Nevertheless, for those married more than 20 years, some of the lost romantic feeling is often renewed as the family nest empties and the parents are once again free to focus their attention on each other (Hatfield & Sprecher, 1986). "No man or woman really knows what love is until they have been

FIGURE 10–7

ROMANTIC LOVE
BETWEEN PARTNERS
IN ARRANGED OR
LOVE MARRIAGES
IN JAIPUR, INDIA.

(Data from Gupta &
Singh, 1982)

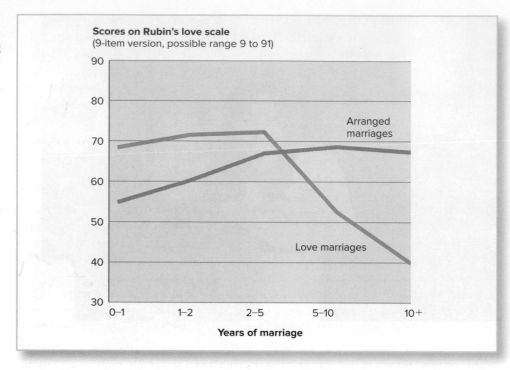

married a quarter of a century," said Mark Twain. If the relationship has been intimate, mutually rewarding, and rooted in a shared life history, companionate love deepens.

WHAT ENABLES CLOSE RELATIONSHIPS?

What factors influence the ups and downs of our close relationships? Let's consider three factors: attachment styles, equity, and self-disclosure.

ATTACHMENT

Love is a biological imperative. We are, in our roots, social creatures, destined to bond with others. Our need to belong is adaptive. Cooperation promotes survival. In solo combat, our ancestors were not the toughest predators. But as hunter-gatherers, and in fending off predators, they gained strength from numbers. Because group dwellers survived and reproduced, we today carry genes that predispose us to form such bonds.

Researchers have found that different forms of a particular gene predict mammalian pair bonding. In the mouse-like prairie vole, and in humans, injections of hormones such as oxytocin (which is released in females during nursing and during mating) and vasopressin produce good feelings that trigger male–female bonding (Donaldson & Young, 2008; Young, 2009). In humans, genes associated with vasopressin activity predict marital stability (Walum et al., 2008). Such is the biology of enduring love.

Our infant dependency strengthens our human bonds. Soon after birth, we exhibit various social responses—love, fear, anger. But the first and greatest of these is love. As babies, we almost immediately prefer familiar faces and voices. We coo and smile when our parents give us attention. By eight months, we crawl after mother or father and typically let out a wail when separated from them. Reunited, we cling. By keeping infants close to their caregivers, social attachment serves as a powerful survival impulse.

Deprived of familiar attachments, sometimes under conditions of extreme neglect, children may become withdrawn, frightened, silent. After studying the mental health of homeless children for the World Health Organization, psychiatrist John Bowlby (1980, p. 442) reflected, "Intimate attachments to other human beings are the hub around which a person's life revolves . . . From these intimate attachments a person draws his strength and enjoyment of life."

Researchers have compared the nature of attachment and love in various close relationships—between parents and children, same-sex friends, and spouses or lovers (K. E. Davis, 1985; Maxwell, 1985; Sternberg & Grajek, 1984). Some elements are common to all loving attachments: mutual understanding, giving and receiving support, valuing and enjoying being with the loved one. Passionate love is, however, spiced with some added features: physical affection, an expectation of exclusiveness, and an intense fascination with the loved one.

Passionate love is not just for lovers. The intense love of parent and infant for each other qualifies as a form of passionate love, even to the point of engaging brain areas akin to those enabling passionate romantic love. Phillip Shaver and Mario Mikulincer (2011) noted that year-old infants, much like young adult lovers, welcome physical affection, feel distress when separated, express intense affection when reunited, and take great pleasure in the significant other's attention and approval. Infants vary in their styles of relating to caregivers. Likewise, adults display varying attachment styles in their relationships. These two facts made Shaver and Cindy Hazan (1993, 1994) wonder whether infant attachment styles might carry over to adult relationships.

Attachment styles

About 7 in 10 infants, and nearly that many adults, exhibit **secure attachment** (Baldwin et al., 1996; Jones & Cunningham, 1996; Mickelson, Kessler, & Shaver, 1997). When placed as infants in a strange situation (usually a laboratory playroom), they play comfortably in their mother's presence, happily exploring this strange environment. If she leaves, they get distressed; when she returns, they run to her, hold her, then relax and return to exploring and playing (Ainsworth, 1973, 1979). This trusting attachment style, many researchers believe, forms a working model of intimacy—a blueprint for one's adult intimate relationships, in which underlying trust sustains relationships through times of conflict (P. J. E. Miller & Rempel, 2004). Secure adults find it easy to get close to others and don't fret about getting too dependent or being abandoned. As lovers, they enjoy sexuality within the context of a continuing relationship. And their relationships tend to be satisfying and enduring (Feeney, 1996; Feeney & Noller, 1990; Keelan, Dion & Dion, 1998; Simpson, Rholes, & Nelligan, 1992).

Approximately 2 in 10 infants and adults exhibit **avoidant attachment**. Although internally aroused, avoidant infants reveal little distress during separation, or clinging upon reunion. Avoiding closeness, avoidant adults tend to be less invested in relationships and more likely to leave them. They also are more likely to engage in one-night stands of sex without love. Kim Bartholomew of Simon Fraser University and Leonard Horowitz of Stanford University (1991) note that avoidant individuals may be either *fearful* ("I am uncomfortable getting close to others.") or *dismissing* ("It is very important to me to feel independent and self-sufficient.").

secure attachment
attachments rooted in trust and marked by intimacy

avoidant attachment
attachments are marked by discomfort over, or resistance to, being close to others

THE >>> INSIDE STORY

My interest in adult attachment stems from an obvious, but perplexing, observation. On the one hand, people are highly motivated to form satisfying intimate relationships. And yet, despite this motivation, the goal of finding and maintaining the perfect (or at least good enough) intimate relationship all too often proves elusive. I have looked to attachment theory as a theoretical framework for understanding the range of difficulties people experience in their intimate relationships. My research has focused on how adult attachment orientations, as assessed through semi-structured interviews, may affect functioning in close relationships. During the course of a longitudinal study of attachment processes in young established couples, I became acutely aware of the high levels of abuse in some relationships and the surprisingly high stability of most of these relationships. Through this work and through an association with Donald Dutton, a family-violence researcher at U.B.C., my students and I became interested in violent relationships. Working with both clinical and community samples, we have applied an attachment perspective to understanding the dynamics of abusive relationships and the difficulty many individuals experience leaving

abusive relationships. We have observed that individuals who lack confidence in the acceptance and responsiveness of their partners are prone to experience high levels of attachment anxiety, leading them (in some cases) to act in aggressive, seemingly counterproductive, ways in an attempt to gain proximity to their partners. In our most recent line of research, we are investigating attachment, childhood socialization, and partner abuse in gay men.

Kim Bartholomew, *Simon Fraser University*

---

insecure attachment
attachments are
marked by anxiety or
ambivalence

Approximately 1 in 10 infants and adults exhibit the anxiousness and ambivalence that mark **insecure attachment** (also described as *preoccupied*). In the strange situation, infants are more likely to cling tightly to their mother. If she leaves, they cry; when she returns, they may be indifferent or hostile. As adults, anxious-ambivalent individuals are less trusting, and more possessive and jealous. They may break up repeatedly with the same person. When discussing conflicts, they get emotional and often angry (Cassidy, 2000; Simpson, Rholes, & Phillips, 1996).

Some researchers attribute these varying attachment styles, which have been observed across 62 cultures (Schmitt et al., 2004), to parental responsiveness. Cindy Hazan (2004) summed up the idea: "Early attachment experiences form the basis for *internal working models* or characteristic ways of thinking about relationships." Thus, sensitive, responsive mothers—mothers who engender a sense of basic trust in the world's reliability—typically have securely attached infants, observed Mary Ainsworth (1979) and Erik Erikson (1963). In fact, one study of 100 Israeli grandmother–daughter–granddaughter threesomes found intergenerational

Attachment, especially to caretakers, is a powerful survival impulse.

consistency of attachment styles (Besser & Priel, 2005). And youths who have experienced nurturing and involved parenting teams tend later to have warm and supportive relationships with their romantic partners (Conger et al., 2000).

Other researchers believe attachment styles may reflect inherited temperament (Gillath et al., 2008; Harris, 1998). A gene that predisposes prairie voles to cuddle and mate for life (and has the same effect on laboratory mice genetically engineered to have the gene) has varying human forms. One is more commonly found in faithful, married men; another in those who are unmarried or unfaithful (Caldwell et al., 2008; Walum et al., 2008). Moreover, teens who are prone to anger and anxiety tend to have, as young adults, more fragile relationships (Donnellan et al., 2005). For better or for worse, early attachment styles do seem to lay a foundation for future relationships.

EQUITY

If each partner in a relationship pursues his or her personal desires willy-nilly, the relationship will die. Therefore, our society teaches us to exchange rewards by what Elaine Hatfield, William Walster, and Ellen Berscheid (1978) have called an **equity** principle of attraction: What you and your partner get out of a relationship should be proportional to what you each put into it. If two people receive equal outcomes, they should contribute equally; otherwise, one or the other will feel it is unfair. If both feel their outcomes correspond to the assets and efforts each contributes, then both perceive equity.

Strangers and casual acquaintances maintain equity by exchanging benefits: You lend me your class notes; later, I'll lend you mine. I invite you to my party; you invite me to yours. Those in an enduring relationship, including roommates and those in love, do not feel bound to trade similar benefits—notes for notes, parties for parties (Berg, 1984). They feel freer to maintain

equity
a condition in which the outcomes people receive from a relationship are proportional to what they contribute to it. *Note:* Equitable outcomes needn't always be equal outcomes.

equity by exchanging a variety of benefits ("When you drop by to lend me your notes, why don't you stay for dinner?") and eventually to stop keeping track of who owes whom.

Long-term equity

Is it crass to suppose that friendship and love are rooted in an equitable exchange of rewards? Don't we sometimes give in response to a loved one's need, without expecting any sort of return? Indeed, those involved in an equitable, long-term relationship are unconcerned with short-term equity. Margaret Clark and Judson Mills (1979, 1993; Clark, 1984, 1986) argued that people even take pains to avoid calculating any exchange benefits. When we help a good friend, we do not want instant repayment. If someone invites us for dinner, we wait before reciprocating, lest the person attribute the motive for our return invitation to be merely paying off a social debt. True friends tune in to one another's needs even when reciprocation is impossible (Clark, Mills, & Corcoran, 1989; Clark, Mills, & Powell, 1986). Similarly, happily married people tend not to keep score of how much they are giving and getting (Buunk & Van Yperen, 1991). As people observe their partners being self-giving, their sense of trust grows (Wieselquist et al., 1999).

"Love is the most subtle kind of self-interest."
HOLBROOK JOHNSON

In a series of experiments, Clark and Mills confirmed that *not* being calculating is a mark of friendship. Tit-for-tat exchanges boosted people's liking when the relationship was relatively formal but diminished liking when the two sought friendship. Clark and Mills surmised that marriage contracts in which each partner specifies what is expected from the other are more likely to undermine than enhance love. Only when the other's positive behaviour is voluntary can we attribute it to love.

Previously, we noted an equity principle at work in the matching phenomenon: People usually bring equal assets to romantic relationships. Often, they are matched for attractiveness, status, and so forth. If they are mismatched in one area, such as attractiveness, they tend to be mismatched in some other area, such as status. But in total assets, they are an equitable match. No one says, and few even think, "I'll trade you my good looks for your big income." But especially in relationships that last, equity is the rule.

Perceived equity and satisfaction

In one large-scale survey, "sharing household chores" ranked third (after "faithfulness" and a "happy sexual relationship") among nine things that people saw as marks of successful marriages (Pew Research Center, 2007). Indeed, those in an equitable relationship are more content (Fletcher et al., 1987; Hatfield et al., 1985; Van Yperen & Buunk, 1990). Those who perceive their relationship as inequitable feel discomfort: The one who has the better deal may feel guilty, and the one who senses a raw deal may feel strong irritation. (Given the self-serving bias—most husbands perceive themselves as contributing more housework than their wives credit them for—the person who is "overbenefited" is less sensitive to the inequity.)

Robert Schafer and Patricia Keith (1980) surveyed several hundred married couples of all ages, noting those who felt their marriages were somewhat unfair because one spouse contributed too little to the cooking, housekeeping, parenting, or providing. Inequity took its toll: Those who perceived inequity also felt more distressed and depressed. During the child-rearing years, when wives often feel underbenefited and husbands overbenefited, marital satisfaction tends to dip. During the honeymoon and empty-nest stages, spouses are more likely to perceive equity and to feel satisfaction with their marriages (Feeney, Peterson, & Noller, 1994). When both partners freely give and receive, and make decisions together, the odds of sustained, satisfying love are good.

Perceived inequity triggers marital distress, agreed Nancy Grote and Margaret Clark (2001) from their tracking of married couples over time. But they also reported that the traffic between inequity and distress runs both ways: Marital distress exacerbates the perception of unfairness (Figure 10–8).

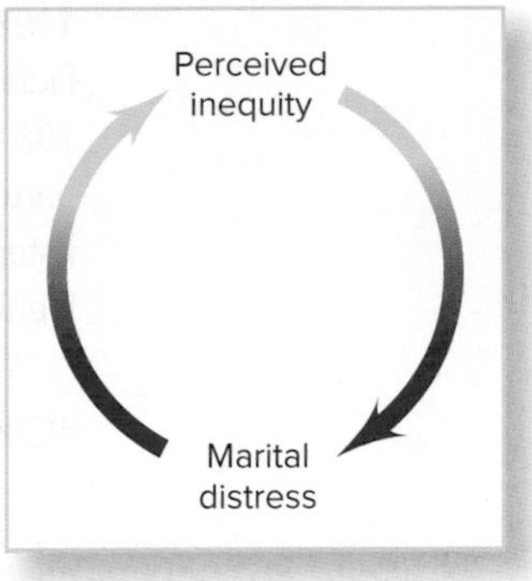

③ SELF-DISCLOSURE

Deep, companionate relationships are intimate. They enable us to be known as we truly are and feel accepted. We discover this exquisite experience in a good marriage or a close friendship—a relationship where trust displaces anxiety and where we are free to open ourselves without fear of losing the other's affection (Holmes & Rempel, 1989). Such relationships are characterized by what the late Sidney Jourard called **self-disclosure** (Derlega et al., 1993). As a relationship grows, self-disclosing partners reveal more and more of themselves to one another; their knowledge of one another penetrates to deeper and deeper levels. In relationships that flourish, much of this self-disclosure shares successes, triumphs, and mutual delight over good happenings (Gable, Gonzaga, & Strachman, 2006). When a friend rejoices with us over good news, it not only increases our joy about the happy event but also helps us feel better about the friendship (Reis et al., 2010).

Research studies find that most of us enjoy such intimacy. We feel pleased when a normally reserved person says that something about us "made me feel like opening up," when that person shares confidential information (Archer & Cook, 1986; D. Taylor, Gould, & Brounstein, 1981). It's gratifying to be singled out for another's disclosure. Not only do we like those who disclose, but we also disclose to those whom we like. And after disclosing to them, we like them more (Collins & Miller, 1994). Lacking opportunities for intimacy, we experience the pain of loneliness (Berg & Peplau, 1982; Solano, Batten, & Parish, 1982).

Experiments have probed both the causes and the effects of self-disclosure. When are people most willing to disclose intimate information concerning "what you like and don't like about yourself" or "what you're most ashamed and most proud of"? And what effects do such revelations have on those who reveal and receive them?

The most reliable finding is the **disclosure reciprocity** effect: Disclosure begets disclosure (Berg, 1987; L. C. Miller, 1990; Reis & Shaver, 1988). We reveal more to those who have been open with us. But intimacy is seldom instant. (If it is, the person may seem indiscreet and unstable.) Appropriate intimacy progresses like a dance: I reveal a little, you reveal a little—but not too much. You then reveal more, and I reciprocate.

For those in love, deepening intimacy is exciting. "Rising intimacy will create a strong sense of passion," noted Roy Baumeister and Ellen Bratslavsky (1999). This helps explain why those who remarry after the loss of a spouse tend to begin the new marriage with an increased frequency of sex, and why passion often rides highest when intimacy is restored following severe conflict.

Some people—most of them women—are especially skilled "openers"; they easily elicit intimate disclosures from others, even from those who normally don't reveal very much of themselves (L. C. Miller, Berg, & Archer, 1983; Pegalis et al., 1994; Shaffer, Pegalis, & Bazzini,

FIGURE 10–8

INEQUITY AND MARITAL DISTRESS.

Perceived inequities trigger marital distress, which fosters the perception of inequities. (Adapted from Grote & Clark, 2001)

self-disclosure
revealing intimate aspects of oneself to others.

disclosure reciprocity
the tendency for one person's intimacy of self-disclosure to match that of a conversational partner

1996). Such people tend to be good listeners. During conversation, they maintain attentive facial expressions and appear to be comfortably enjoying themselves (Purvis, Dabbs, & Hopper, 1984). They may also express interest by uttering supportive phrases while their conversational partner is speaking. They are what psychologist Carl Rogers (1980) called "growth-promoting" listeners—people who are genuine in revealing their own feelings, who are accepting of others' feelings, and who are empathic, sensitive, reflective listeners.

What are the effects of such self-disclosure? Humanistic psychologist Sidney Jourard (1964) argued that dropping our masks, letting ourselves be known as we are, nurtures love. He presumed that it is gratifying to open up to another and then to receive the trust another implies by being open with us. People feel better on days when they have disclosed something significant about themselves, such as their being lesbian or gay, and feel worse when concealing their identity (Beals, Peplau, & Gable, 2009). Those whose days include more deep or substantive discussions, rather than just small talk, tend to be happier. That's what Mathias Mehl and co-researchers (2010) found after equipping 70 undergraduates with recording devices that snatched 30-second conversational snippets five times each hour over four days.

> "A friend is a person with whom you dare to be yourself."
>
> FRANK CRANE, "A DEFINITION OF FRIENDSHIP"

Having an intimate friend with whom we can discuss threats to our self-image seems to help us survive such stresses (Swann & Predmore, 1985). A true friendship is a special relationship that helps us cope with our other relationships. "When I am with my friend," reflected the Roman playwright Seneca, "methinks I am alone, and as much at liberty to speak anything as to think it." At its best, marriage is such a friendship, sealed by commitment.

Intimate self-disclosure is also one of companionate love's delights. The most self-revealing dating and married couples tend to enjoy the most satisfying and enduring relationships (Berg & McQuinn, 1986; Hendrick, Hendrick, & Adler, 1988; Sprecher, 1987). In a study of newlywed couples who were all equally in love, those who most deeply and accurately knew each other were most likely to enjoy enduring love (Neff & Karney, 2005). Married partners who most strongly agree that "I try to share my most intimate thoughts and feelings with my partner" tend to have the most satisfying marriages (Sanderson & Cantor, 2001). For very reticent people, marriage may not be as satisfying as it is for those more willing to share their feelings (Baker & McNulty, 2010).

Researchers have also found that women are often more willing to disclose their fears and weaknesses than are men (Cunningham, 1981). As feminist writer Kate Millett (1975) put it, "Women express, men repress." Nevertheless, men today, particularly men with egalitarian gender-role attitudes, seem increasingly willing to reveal intimate feelings and to enjoy the satisfactions that accompany a relationship of mutual trust and self-disclosure. And that, say Arthur Aron and Elaine Aron (1994), is the essence of love—two selves connecting, disclosing, and identifying with one another; two selves, each retaining their individuality, yet sharing activities, delighting in similarities, and mutually supporting. The result for many romantic partners is "self-other integration": intertwined self-concepts (Slotter & Gardner, 2009; Figure 10–9). More satisfied couples are more likely even to display merged self-concepts symbolically by including relationship partners in their Facebook profile pictures (Saslow et al., 2013).

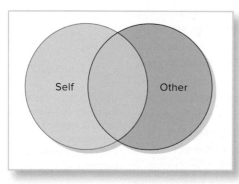

FIGURE 10–9

LOVE: AN OVERLAPPING OF SELVES—YOU BECOME PART OF ME, I PART OF YOU.

From A. L. Weber and J. Harvey, *Perspective on Close Relationships.* Published by Allyn & Bacon, Boston, MA. Copyright © 1994 by Pearson Education. Reprinted by permission of the publishers.

That being so, might we cultivate closeness by experiences that mirror the escalating closeness of budding friendships? The Arons and their collaborators (1997) wondered. They paired volunteer students who were strangers to each other. The students talked for 45 minutes. For the first 15 minutes, they shared thoughts on a list of personal but low-intimacy topics, such as "When did you last sing to yourself?" The next 15 minutes were spent on more intimate topics, such as "What is your most treasured memory?" The last 15 minutes invited even more self-disclosure, with questions such as this: "Complete this sentence: 'I wish I had someone with whom I could share . . .'" and "When did you last cry in front of another person? By yourself?"

Compared to control participants who spent the 45 minutes in small talk ("What was your high school like?" "What is your favourite holiday?"), those who experienced the escalating self-disclosure ended the hour feeling remarkably close to their conversation partners; in fact, "closer than the closest relationship in the lives of 30 percent of similar students," reported the researchers. These relationships surely were not yet marked by the loyalty and commitment of true friendship. Nevertheless, the experiment provided a striking demonstration of how readily a sense of closeness to others can grow, given open self-disclosure.

To promote self-disclosure in ongoing dating relationships, Richard Slatcher and James Pennebaker (2006) invited one member of 86 couples to spend 20 minutes on each of three days writing their deepest thoughts and feelings about the relationship (or, in a control condition, writing merely about their daily activities). Those who pondered and wrote about their feelings expressed more emotion to their partners in the days following. Three months later, 77 percent were still dating (compared with 52 percent in the control group).

● HOW DO RELATIONSHIPS END?

Often love dies. What factors predict marital dissolution? How do couples typically detach or renew their relationships?

In 1971, a man wrote a love poem to his bride, slipped it into a bottle, and dropped it into the Pacific Ocean. A decade later, a jogger found it on a Guam beach:

> If, by the time this letter reaches you, I am old and grey, I know that our love will be as fresh as it is today. It may take a week or it may take years for this note to find you. . . . If this should never reach you, it will still be written in my heart that I will go to extreme means to prove my love for you. Your husband, Bob.

The woman to whom the love note was addressed was reached by phone. When the note was read to her, she burst out laughing. And the more she heard, the harder she laughed. "We're divorced," she finally said, and slammed down the phone.

So it often goes. Comparing their unsatisfying relationship with the support and affection they imagine is available elsewhere, many relationships end. Each year, Canada and the United States record one divorce for every two marriages. As economic and social barriers to divorce weakened during the 1960s and 1970s, thanks partly to women's increasing employment, divorce rates rose. "We are living longer, but loving more briefly," quipped Os Guiness (1993, p. 309).

Britain's royal House of Windsor knows well the hazards of modern marriage. The fairy-tale marriages of Princess Margaret, Princess Anne, Prince Charles, and Prince Andrew all crumbled,

FOCUS ON Does the Internet Create Intimacy or Isolation?

As a reader of this university text, you are almost surely one of the world's 2.3 billion (as of 2012) Internet users. It took the telephone seven decades to go from 1 percent to 75 percent penetration of North American households. Internet access reached 75 percent penetration in approximately 7 years (Putnam, 2000). You enjoy social networking, web surfing, texting, and perhaps participating in listservs, news groups, or chat rooms (Internetworldstats.com).

What do you think: Is computer-mediated communication within virtual communities a poor substitute for in-person relationships? Or is it a wonderful way to widen our social circles? Does the Internet do more to connect people or to drain time from face-to-face relationships? Consider the emerging debate.

Point: The Internet, like the printing press and the telephone, expands communication, and communication enables relationships. Printing reduced face-to-face storytelling and the telephone reduced face-to-face chats, but both enable us to reach and be reached by people without limitations of time and distance. Social relations involve networking, and the Net is the ultimate network. It enables efficient networking with family, friends, and kindred spirits—including people we otherwise never would have found, be they fellow MS patients, St. Nicholas collectors, or Harry Potter fans.

Counterpoint: True, but computer communication is impoverished. It lacks the nuances of eye-to-eye contact punctuated with nonverbal cues and physical touches. Except for simple emoticons—such as a :-) for an unnuanced smile—electronic messages are devoid of gestures, facial expressions, and tones of voice. No wonder it's so easy to misread them. The absence of expressive e-motion makes for ambiguous emotion.

For example, vocal nuances can signal whether a statement is serious, kidding, or sarcastic. Research by Justin Kruger and colleagues (2006) shows that communicators often think their "just kidding" intent is equally clear, whether e-mailed or spoken. Actually, when e-mailed, the intent often isn't clear. Thanks also to one's anonymity in virtual discussions, the result is sometimes a hostile "flame war."

A Stanford University survey found that 25 percent of more than 4000 adults surveyed reported that their time online had reduced time spent in person and on the phone with family and friends (Nie & Erbring, 2000). The Internet, like television, diverts time from real relationships. Internet romances are not the developmental equivalent of real dating. Cybersex is artificial intimacy. Individualized web-based entertainment displaces getting together for bridge. Such artificiality and isolation is regrettable because our ancestral history predisposes our needing real-time relationships, replete with smirks and smiles.

Point: But most folks don't perceive the Internet to be isolating. Another national survey found that "Internet users in general—and women online in particular—believe that their use of e-mail has strengthened their relationships and increased their contact with relatives and friends" (Pew Research Center, 2000). Internet use may displace in-person intimacy, but it also displaces television watching. If one-click cyber-shopping is bad for your local bookstore, it frees time for relationships. Telecommuting does the same, enabling people to work from home and thereby spend more time with their families.

smiles replaced with stony stares. Shortly after her 1986 marriage to Prince Andrew, Sarah Ferguson gushed, "I love his wit, his charm, his looks. I worship him." Andrew reciprocated her euphoria: "She is the best thing in my life." Six years later, Andrew, having decided her friends were "philistines," and Sarah, having derided Andrew's boorish behaviour as "terribly gauche," called it quits (*Time*, 1992).

And why say that computer-formed relationships are unreal? On the Internet, your looks and location cease to matter. Your appearance, age, and race don't deter people from relating to you based on what's more genuinely important—your shared interests and values. In workplace and professional networks, computer-mediated discussions are less influenced by status and are therefore more candid and equally participatory. Computer-mediated communication fosters more spontaneous self-disclosure than face-to-face conversation (Joinson, 2001).

Most Internet flirtations go nowhere. "Everyone I know who has tried online dating . . . agrees that we loathe spending (wasting?) hours gabbing to someone and then meeting him and realizing that he is a creep," observed one Toronto woman (Dicum, 2003). This experience would not surprise Eli Finkel and his fellow social psychologists (2012). Nearly a century of research on romantic compatibility leads them to conclude that the formulas of online matchmaking sites are unlikely to do what they claim. The best predictors of relationship success, such as communication patterns and other indications of compatibility, emerge only *after* people meet and get to know one another. Nevertheless, friendships and romantic relationships that form on the Internet are more likely than in-person relationships to last for at least two years, report Katelyn McKenna and John Bargh and their colleagues (Bargh & McKenna, 2004; Bargh, McKenna, & Fitzsimons, 2002; McKenna & Bargh, 1998, 2000; McKenna, Green, & Gleason, 2002). In one experiment, they found that people disclosed more, with greater honesty and less posturing, when they met people online. They also felt more liking for people with whom they conversed online for 20 minutes than for those met for the same time face-to-face. This was true even when they unknowingly met the very same person in both contexts. People surveyed similarly feel that Internet friendships are as real, important, and close as offline relationships.

Counterpoint: The Internet allows people to be who they really are, but also to feign who they really aren't, sometimes in the interests of sexual exploitation. Internet sexual media, like other forms of pornography, likely serve to distort people's perceptions of sexual reality, decrease the attractiveness of their real-life partner, prime men to perceive women in sexual terms, make sexual coercion seem more trivial, provide mental scripts for how to act in sexual situations, increase arousal, and lead to disinhibition and imitation of loveless sexual behaviours.

Finally, suggests Robert Putnam (2000), the social benefits of computer-mediated communication are constrained by "cyberbalkanization." The Internet enables those of us with hearing loss to network, but it also enables White supremacists to find one another and thus contributes to social and political polarization.

As the debate over the Internet's social consequences continues, "the most important question," says Putnam (p. 180), will be "not what the Internet will do to us, but what we will do with it? . . . How can we harness this promising technology for thickening community ties? How can we develop the technology to enhance social presence, social feedback, and social cues? How can we use the prospect of fast, cheap communication to enhance the now fraying fabric of our real communities?"

DIVORCE

To predict a culture's divorce rates, it helps to know its values (Triandis, 1994). Individualistic cultures (where love is a feeling and people ask, "What does my heart say?") have more divorce than do communal cultures (where love entails obligation and people ask, "What will other

"Passionate love is in many ways an altered state of consciousness. . . . In many states today, there are laws that a person must not be in an intoxicated condition when marrying. . . . But passionate love is a kind of intoxication."

ROY BAUMEISTER, *MEANINGS OF LIFE*, 1991

people say?"). Individualists marry "for as long as we both shall love," collectivists more often for life. Individualists expect more passion and personal fulfillment in a marriage, which puts greater pressure on the relationship (Dion & Dion, 1993). "Keeping romance alive" was rated as important to a good marriage by 78 percent of American women surveyed and 29 percent of Japanese women (*American Enterprise*, 1992).

Even in Western society, however, those who enter relationships with a long-term orientation and an intention to persist do experience healthier, less turbulent, and more durable partnerships (Arriaga, 2001; Arriaga & Agnew, 2001). Enduring relationships are rooted in enduring love and satisfaction, but also in fear of the termination cost, a sense of moral obligation, and inattention to possible alternative partners (Adams & Jones, 1997; Maner et al., 2009; R. S. Miller, 1997). Those who especially fear being single, who dread the thought of growing old alone, are likely to persist in unsatisfying relationships (Spielmann et al., 2013a).

Those whose commitment to a union outlasts the desires that gave birth to it will endure times of conflict and unhappiness. One national survey found that 86 percent of those who were unhappily married but who stayed with the marriage were, when reinterviewed five years later, now mostly "very" or "quite" happy with their marriages (Popenoe, 2002). By contrast, "narcissists"—those more focused on their own desires and image—enter relationships with less commitment and less likelihood of long-term relational success (Campbell & Foster, 2002).

Risk of divorce also depends on who marries whom (Fergusson et al., 1984; Myers, 2000; Tzeng, 1992). People in the following situations usually stay married:

- Married after age 20
- Both grew up in stable, two-parent homes
- Dated for a long while before marriage
- Are well and similarly educated
- Enjoy a stable income from a good job
- Live in a small town or on a farm
- Did not cohabit or become pregnant before marriage
- Are religiously committed
- Are of similar age, faith, and education

None of these predictors, by itself, is essential to a stable marriage. But if none of these things is true for someone, marital breakdown is an almost sure bet. If all are true, they are very likely to stay together until death. The English perhaps had it right, several centuries ago, when presuming that the temporary intoxication of passionate love was a foolish basis for permanent marital decisions. Better, they felt, to choose a mate based on stable friendship and compatible backgrounds, interests, habits, and values (Stone, 1977).

THE DETACHMENT PROCESS

Our close relationships help define the social identity that shapes our self-concept (Slotter, Gardner, & Finkel, 2010). Thus, much as we experience life's best moments when relationships begin—when having a baby, making a friend, falling in love—so we experience life's worst moments when relationships end, with death or a broken bond (Jaremka, Gabriel, & Carvallo, 2011). Severing bonds produces a predictable sequence of agitated preoccupation with the lost partner, followed by deep sadness and, eventually, the beginnings of emotional detachment and a return to normal living (Hazan & Shaver, 1994; Lewandowski & Bizzoco, 2007; Spielmann, MacDonald, & Wilson, 2009). Even newly separated couples who have long ago ceased feeling affection are often surprised at their desire to be near the former partner. Deep and long-standing attachments seldom break quickly; detaching is a process, not an event. And people may have difficulty reaping the rewards of new relationships if they have not yet gotten over ex-partners (Spielmann et al., 2013b).

"Don't you understand? I love you! I need you! I want to spend the rest of my vacation with you!"

© Mike Twohy/The New Yorker Collection/ www.cartoonbank.com

Among dating couples, the closer and longer the relationship and the fewer the available alternatives, the more painful the breakup (Simpson, 1987). Surprisingly, Roy Baumeister and Sara Wotman (1992) reported that, months or years later, people recall more pain over spurning someone's love than over having been spurned. Their distress arises from guilt over hurting someone, from upset over the heartbroken lover's persistence, or from uncertainty over how to respond. Among married couples, breakup has additional costs: shocked parents and friends, guilt over broken vows, anguish over reduced household income, and possibly restricted parental rights. Still, each year millions of couples are willing to pay those costs to extricate themselves from what they perceive as the greater price of continuing a painful, unrewarding relationship. That price included, in one study of 328 married couples, a tenfold increase in depression symptoms when a marriage is marked by discord rather than satisfaction (O'Leary, Christian, & Mendell, 1994).

When relationships suffer, those without better alternatives or who feel invested in a relationship (through time, energy, mutual friendships, possessions, and perhaps children) will seek alternatives to exiting the relationship. Caryl Rusbult and her colleagues (1986, 1987) have explored three ways of coping with a failing relationship. Some people exhibit loyalty—by waiting for conditions to improve. The problems are too painful to speak of and the risks of separation are too great, so the loyal partner perseveres, hoping the good old days will return. Others (especially men) exhibit neglect; they ignore the partner and allow the relationship to deteriorate. With painful dissatisfactions ignored, an insidious emotional uncoupling ensues as the partners talk less and begin redefining their lives without each other. Still others will voice their concerns and take active steps to improve the relationship by discussing problems, seeking advice, and attempting to change. Study after study—in fact, 115 studies of 45 000 couples— reveal that unhappy couples disagree, command, criticize, and put down. Happy couples more often agree, approve, assent, and laugh (Karney & Bradbury, 1995; Noller & Fitzpatrick, 1990). After observing 2000 couples, John Gottman (1994) noted that healthy marriages were not necessarily devoid of conflict. Rather, they were marked by an ability to reconcile differences and to overbalance criticism with affection. In successful marriages, positive interactions (smiling, touching, complimenting, laughing) outnumbered negative interactions (sarcasm, disapproval, insults) by at least a 5-to-1 ratio.

Successful couples have learned, sometimes aided by communication training, to restrain the poisonous putdowns and gut-level reactions and to think and behave more positively

(McNulty, 2010). They fight fairly (by stating feelings without insulting). They depersonalize conflict with comments like "I know it's not your fault" (Markman et al., 1988; Notarius & Markman, 1993; Yovetich & Rusbult, 1994).

Would unhappy relationships get better if the partners agreed to act more as happy couples do—by complaining and criticizing less? By affirming and agreeing more? By setting time aside to voice their concerns? By having fun together daily? As attitudes trail behaviours, do affections trail actions? Joan Kellerman, James Lewis, and James Laird (1989) wondered. They knew that among couples passionately in love, eye gazing is typically prolonged and mutual (Rubin, 1973). Would intimate eye gazing similarly stir feelings between those not in love (much as 45 minutes of escalating self-disclosure evoked feelings of closeness among those unacquainted students)? To find out, they asked unacquainted male–female pairs to gaze intently for two minutes either at one another's hands or in one another's eyes. When they separated, the eye gazers reported a tingle of attraction and affection toward each other. Simulating love had begun to stir it.

By enacting and expressing love, researcher Robert Sternberg (1988) believed the passion of initial romance can evolve into enduring love:

> "Living happily ever after" need not be a myth, but if it is to be a reality, the happiness must be based upon different configurations of mutual feelings at various times in a relationship. Couples who expect their passion to last forever, or their intimacy to remain unchallenged, are in for disappointment. . . . We must constantly work at understanding, building, and rebuilding our loving relationships. Relationships are constructions, and they decay over time if they are not maintained and improved. We cannot expect a relationship simply to take care of itself, any more than we can expect that of a building. Rather, we must take responsibility for making our relationships the best they can be.

▶ SUMMING UP

WHAT LEADS TO FRIENDSHIP AND ATTRACTION?

- The best predictor of whether any two people are friends is their sheer proximity to one another. Proximity is conducive to repeated exposure and interaction, which enables us to discover similarities and to feel one another's liking.

- A second determinant of initial attraction is physical attractiveness. Both in laboratory studies and in field experiments involving blind dates, university students tend to prefer attractive people. In everyday life, however, people tend actually to choose and marry someone whose attractiveness roughly matches their own (or someone who, if less attractive, has other compensating qualities).

- Liking is greatly aided by similarity of attitudes, beliefs, and values. Likeness leads to liking; opposites rarely attract.
- We are also likely to develop friendships with people who like us.
- According to the reward theory of attraction, we like people whose behaviour we find rewarding or whom we have associated with rewarding events.

WHAT IS LOVE?

- Researchers have characterized love as having components of intimacy, passion, and commitment. Passionate love is experienced as a bewildering confusion of ecstasy and anxiety, elation and pain. The two-factor theory of emotion suggests that in a romantic context, arousal from any source, even painful experiences, can be steered into passion.
- In the best of relationships, the initial romantic high settles to a steadier, more affectionate relationship called companionate love.

WHAT ENABLES CLOSE RELATIONSHIPS?

- From infancy to old age, attachments are central to human life. Secure attachments, as in an enduring marriage, mark happy lives.
- Companionate love is most likely to endure when both partners feel the partnership is equitable, with both perceiving themselves receiving from the relationship in proportion to what they contribute to it.
- One reward of companionate love is the opportunity for intimate self-disclosure, a state achieved gradually as each partner reciprocates the other's increasing openness.

HOW DO RELATIONSHIPS END?

- Often love does not endure. As divorce rates rose in the twentieth century, researchers discerned predictors of marital dissolution. One predictor is an individualistic culture that values feelings over commitment; other factors include the couple's age, education, values, and similarity.
- Researchers are also identifying the process through which couples either detach or rebuild their relationships, and they are identifying the positive and non-defensive communication styles that mark healthy, stable marriages.

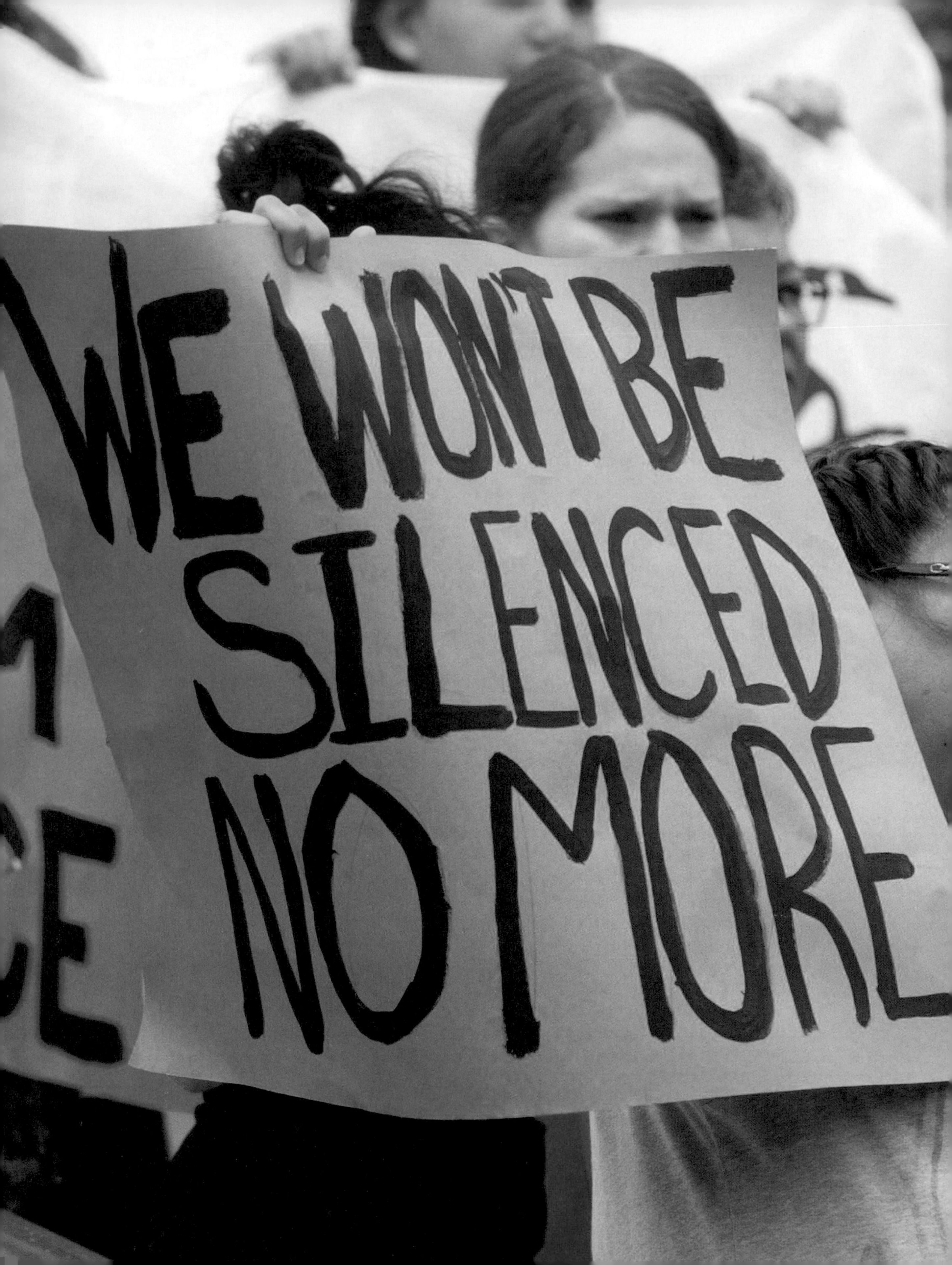
WE WON'T BE
SILENCED
NO MORE

CHAPTER ELEVEN
Sources of Prejudice

▶ CHAPTER OUTLINE

● WHAT IS PREJUDICE?

● WHAT ARE THE SOCIAL SOURCES OF PREJUDICE?

● WHAT ARE THE MOTIVATIONAL SOURCES OF PREJUDICE?

● WHAT ARE THE COGNITIVE SOURCES OF PREJUDICE?

In the summer of 2007, Shayne Berwick, Ray Lam, and a group of their friends went fishing near the Mossington Bridge on Lake Simcoe in central Ontario. They had fished often in this spot, but this night was different. A group of local young men including Trevor Middleton came and, by one account, threw one of the men from Toronto into the lake. A scuffle ensued.

Shayne and his friends got into their Honda Civic and fled the scene. Trevor jumped into his truck, chased them down, and ran them off the road. In the accident, Shayne was thrown from the car and suffered a brain injury that has left him with severe brain damage. What makes this incident different from many other fights between groups of young men? Shayne's friends are Asian-Canadian, and Trevor and his friends are European-Canadian; the Ontario Human Rights Commission has ruled that this specific case was racially motivated—a case of, what is called in the area, "nipper-tipping." In that one summer, there were at least three other cases of Asian-Canadians being thrown into Lake Simcoe, a disturbing pattern of racially motivated attacks (Doolittle, 2007; Edwards, 2010).

Are such acts of prejudice and discrimination common in Canada, or do multicultural values blunt the impact of prejudice? Sadly, prejudice is an all-too-common feature of the Canadian landscape. In 2003, the Ontario Human Rights Commission reported that racial profiling was a commonly occurring practice in Ontario. Blacks, Latinos, Aboriginal Canadians, and Middle Easterners commonly receive greater scrutiny from law enforcement and customs officers. In one study in Kingston, Ontario, police officers were 3.7 times more likely to stop Blacks and 1.4 times more likely to stop Aboriginal Canadians than Whites—and this occurred even when the officers knew their stops would be evaluated for evidence of racial profiling (CBC, 2005).

● WHAT IS PREJUDICE?

How is "prejudice" distinct from "stereotyping," "discrimination," "racism," and "sexism"? Are stereotypes necessarily false or malicious? What forms does prejudice assume today?

DEFINING PREJUDICE

Prejudice, stereotyping, discrimination, racism, sexism—the terms often overlap. Let's clarify them. Each of the situations just described involved a negative evaluation of some group. And that is the essence of **prejudice**: a negative prejudgment of a group and its individual members. (Some prejudice definitions include positive prejudgments as well, but nearly all uses of "prejudice" refer to negative tendencies—or what Gordon Allport termed in his classic, *The Nature of Prejudice*, "an antipathy based upon a faulty and inflexible generalization" [1954, p. 9].)

Prejudice is an attitude. As we noted in Chapter 4, an attitude is a distinct combination of feelings, inclinations to act, and beliefs. This combination is the ABC of attitudes: affect (feelings), behaviour tendency (inclination to act), and cognition (beliefs). A prejudiced person might dislike people who are different from self and behave in a discriminatory manner, believing them ignorant and dangerous. Like many attitudes, prejudice is complex; for example, it may include a component of patronizing affection that serves to keep the target disadvantaged.

The negative evaluations that mark prejudice often are supported by negative beliefs, called **stereotypes**. To stereotype is to generalize. To simplify the world, we generalize: The British are reserved; Italians are outgoing; professors are absent-minded. Here are some widely shared stereotypes:

prejudice
a negative prejudgment of a group and its individual members

stereotypes
beliefs about the personal attributes of a group of people. Stereotypes can be overgeneralized, inaccurate, and resistant to new information.

- During the 1980s, women who assumed the title of "Ms." were seen as more assertive and ambitious than those who called themselves "Miss" or "Mrs." (Dion, 1987; Dion & Cota, 1991; Dion & Schuller, 1991). Now that "Ms." is the standard female title, the stereotype has shifted. Now, married women who keep their own surname are seen as assertive and ambitious (Crawford, Stark, & Renner, 1998; Etaugh et al., 1999).

- Public opinion surveys reveal that Europeans have definite ideas about other Europeans. They see Germans as relatively hard-working, the French as pleasure-loving, the British as cool and unexcitable, Italians as amorous, and the Dutch as reliable. (Coming from Willem Koomen and Michiel Bähler, 1996, at the University of Amsterdam, these findings one expects to be reliable.)

- Europeans also view southern Europeans as more emotional and less efficient than northern Europeans (Linssen & Hagendoorn, 1994). The stereotype of the southerner as more expressive even holds within countries: James Pennebaker and his colleagues (1996) reported that across 20 Northern Hemisphere countries (but not in six Southern Hemisphere countries), southerners within a country are perceived as more expressive than northerners.

Stereotypes sometimes reflect reality. People with sub-Saharan African ancestry comprise 12 percent of the world's people; and in 2000, they held the top 15 world running records, ranging from the 100 metres to the marathon (DiPietro, 2000). Even when describing reality with more or less accuracy, however, stereotypes do not explain causation.

Such generalizations can be more or less true (and are not always negative). Old people are more frail. Southern countries in the northern hemisphere do have higher rates of violence. People living in the south in these countries do report being more expressive than those in the northern regions of their country. "Stereotypes," noted Lee Jussim, Clark McCauley, and Yueh-Ting Lee (1995), "may be positive or negative, accurate or inaccurate." An accurate stereotype may even be desirable. We call it "sensitivity to diversity" or "cultural awareness in a multicultural world." To stereotype the British as more concerned about punctuality than are Mexicans is to understand what to expect and how to get along in each culture.

The problem with stereotypes arises when they are overgeneralized or just plain wrong. To presume that most Aboriginal Canadians need treatment for alcoholism is to overgeneralize, because it just isn't so. Another problem arises when people attribute negatively evaluated differences to biology, ignoring toxic social forces. People may see that women are less likely than men to become engineers or chief executive officers, but they often do not see the underlying causes that prevent women from succeeding. People are quick to judge that women do not have the math or leadership ability to succeed in these fields, but the evidence suggests otherwise (Eagly, Karau, & Makhijani, 1995; Hyde, Fennema, & Lamon, 1990; Kimball, 1989; Walton & Spencer, 2009). The barriers that actually prevent women's success, such as unfair evaluations and self-fulfilling prophecies, are much harder for people to recognize.

Familiar stereotypes: "Heaven is a place with an American house, Chinese food, British police, a German car, and French art. Hell is a place with a Japanese house, Chinese police, British food, German art, and a French car."
ANONYMOUS, AS REPORTED BY YUEH-TING LEE (1996)

discrimination
unjustifiable negative behaviour toward a group or its members

Prejudice is a negative attitude; discrimination is negative behaviour. Discriminatory behaviour often, but not always, has its source in prejudicial attitudes (Dovidio et al., 1996; Wagner, Christ, & Pettigrew, 2008). As Chapter 4 emphasized, however, attitudes and behaviour are often loosely linked, partly because our behaviour reflects more than our inner convictions. Prejudiced attitudes need not breed hostile acts, nor does all oppression spring from prejudice. Racism and sexism are institutional practices that discriminate, even when there is no prejudicial intent. If word-of-mouth hiring practices in an all-White business have the effect of excluding potential non-White employees, the practice could be called racist. And if word-of-mouth hiring practices in an all-male business have the effect of excluding potential female employees, the practice could be called sexist. Both situations are discriminatory, even if an employer intended no discrimination. When job ads for male-dominated vocations feature words associated with male stereotypes ("We are a dominant engineering firm seeking individuals who can perform in a competitive environment"), and job ads for female-dominated vocations feature the opposite ("We seek people who will be sensitive to clients' needs and can develop warm client relationships"), the result may be institutional sexism. Without intending any prejudice, the gendered wording helps sustain gender inequality (Gaucher, Friesen, & Kay, 2011). We will examine discrimination more fully in Chapter 12.

racism
(1) an individual's prejudicial attitudes and discriminatory behaviour toward people of a given race, or (2) institutional practices (even if not motivated by prejudice) that subordinate people of a given race

sexism
(1) an individual's prejudicial attitudes and discriminatory behaviour toward people of a given sex, or (2) institutional practices (even if not motivated by prejudice) that subordinate people of a given sex

PREJUDICE: OVERT, SUBTLE, AND AUTOMATIC

The attitude of prejudice, like other attitudes, can be measured by asking people a number of straightforward questions, such as "Is it true that Blacks have gotten more economically than they deserve?" (McConahay, 1986) or "Is it true that the government and news media have been showing more concern about the treatment of women than is warranted by women's actual experiences?" (Swim et al., 1995). Such measures of people's prejudice have been collected for more than 75 years, and an interesting pattern has emerged. For most social groups, overt expressions of prejudice have decreased. For example, national surveys suggest that outright prejudice is less common than it was 30 years ago. Kalin and Barry (1995) noted that despite some remaining prejudice toward members of ethnic groups, Canadians are genuinely motivated to develop a truly multicultural society.

Does that mean that prejudice is no longer a serious social problem? Unfortunately, after many experiments, it has become clear that such an optimistic view is not warranted. Although overt expression of prejudice has decreased, subtle forms of prejudice are still widespread.

Although prejudice dies last in socially intimate contacts, interracial marriage has increased in most countries.

Subtle forms of prejudice

When White students indicate racial attitudes and men indicate their sympathy for women's rights while hooked up to a supposed lie detector, they admit to prejudice, but they hide such prejudice when not hooked up to a lie detector (Roese & Jamieson, 1993). Indeed, prejudiced attitudes seem to surface when they can hide behind the screen of some other motive. In France, Britain, Germany, Australia, and the Netherlands, subtle prejudice—exaggerating ethnic differences, feeling less admiration and affection for immigrant minorities, rejecting them for supposedly non-racial reasons—is replacing blatant prejudice (Pedersen & Walker, 1997; Pettigrew, 1998). Some researchers call such subtle prejudice "modern racism" or "cultural racism." Modern prejudice often appears subtly, in our preferences for what is familiar, similar, and comfortable (Dovidio et al., 1992; Esses, Haddock, & Zanna, 1993a).

Automatic prejudice

Prejudice provides one of the best examples of our dual attitude system (Chapter 4). We can have differing explicit (conscious) and implicit (automatic) attitudes toward the same target, as shown by 500 studies using the Implicit Association Test (Carpenter, 2008). The test, which Chapter 4 introduced and which has been taken online by some 6 million people, assesses "implicit cognition"—what you know without knowing that you know (Greenwald et al., 2008). It does so by measuring people's speed of associations. Much as we more quickly associate a hammer with a nail than with a pail, so the test can measure how speedily we associate "White" with "good" versus "Black" with "good." Thus, we may retain from childhood a habitual, automatic fear or dislike of people for whom we now express respect and admiration. Although explicit attitudes may change dramatically with education, implicit attitudes may linger, changing only as we form new habits through practice (Kawakami et al., 2000).

> *"Many [people] have confessed to me . . . that even though in their minds they no longer feel prejudice towards Blacks, they still feel squeamish when they shake hands with a Black. These feelings are left over from what they learned in their families as children."*
> THOMAS PETTIGREW (1987)

A raft of experiments (Banaji, 2004; Bargh & Chartrand, 1999; Devine & Sharp, 2008; Fazio, 2007; Fazio et al., 1995; Greenwald et al., 2000; Nosek et al., 2007; Wittenbrink, 2007; Wittenbrink, Judd, & Park, 1997) have confirmed that prejudice can occur outside of people's awareness. Some of these studies briefly flash words or faces that prime (automatically activate) stereotypes of some racial, gender, or age group. Without their awareness, the participants' activated stereotypes may then bias their behaviour. Having been primed with images associated with Blacks, for example, they may then react with more hostility to an experimenter's (intentionally) annoying request. In clever experiments by Anthony Greenwald and his colleagues (1998, 2000), nine in ten White people took longer to identify pleasant words (such as *peace* and *paradise*) as "good" when associated with Black rather than White faces. The participants typically expressed little or no prejudice, only an unconscious, unintended response.

WHAT ARE THE SOCIAL SOURCES OF PREJUDICE?

As we have emphasized throughout this book, the social situations we encounter are powerful forces that shape our attitudes and behaviours. The formation of prejudice is no exception to this general rule. Unequal status and conflict between groups, the desire to see our own groups positively, conformity pressures, and fears and hostilities can all fuel the formation of prejudice.

SOCIAL INEQUALITIES: JUSTIFYING THE STATUS QUO

A principle to remember: Unequal status breeds prejudice. Masters viewed slaves as lazy, irresponsible, lacking ambition—as having just those traits that justified the slavery. Historians debate the forces that create unequal status. But once these inequalities exist, prejudice helps justify the economic and social superiority of those who have wealth and power. Tell us the economic relationship between two groups, and we'll predict the intergroup attitudes. Upper-class individuals are more likely than those in poverty to see people's fortunes as the outcomes they have earned, thanks to skill and effort, and not as the result of having connections, money, and good luck (Kraus, Piff, & Keltner, 2011).

> *"Prejudice is never easy unless it can pass itself off for reason."*
> WILLIAM HAZLITT, 1778–1830, "ON PREJUDICE"

Examples abound. Until recently, prejudice everywhere in the world was greatest in regions where slavery was practised. Nineteenth-century European politicians and writers justified imperial expansion by describing exploited colonized people as "inferior," "requiring protection," and a "burden" to be borne (G. W. Allport, 1958, pp. 204–205). Six decades ago, sociologist Helen Mayer Hacker (1951) noted how stereotypes of Blacks and women helped rationalize the inferior status of each: Many people thought both groups were mentally slow, emotional, primitive, and "contented" with their subordinate role. Blacks were "inferior"; women were "weak." Blacks were all right in their place; women's place was in the home.

Theresa Vescio and her colleagues (2005) tested that reasoning. They found that powerful men who stereotype their female subordinates give them plenty of praise but fewer resources, thus undermining their performance. This sort of patronizing behaviour allows the men to maintain their positions of power. In the laboratory, too, patronizing benevolent sexism (statements implying that women, as the weaker sex, need support) has undermined women's cognitive performance by planting intrusive thoughts—self-doubts, preoccupations, and decreased self-esteem (Dardenne, Dumont, & Bollier, 2007).

> *"It is human nature to hate those whom we have injured."*
> TACITUS, *AGRICOLA*

Peter Glick and Susan Fiske's distinction between "hostile" and "benevolent" sexism extends to other prejudices (2001). We see other groups as competent or as likeable, but usually not as both. These two culturally universal dimensions of social perception—likeability (warmth) and competence—were illustrated by one European's comment that "Germans love Italians, but don't admire them. Italians admire Germans, but don't love them" (Cuddy & others, 2009). We typically *respect* the competence of those high in status and *like* those who agreeably accept a lower status. In the United States, reported Fiske and her colleagues (1999), Asians, Jews, Germans, non-traditional women, and assertive Blacks and gay men tend to be respected but not liked so well. Traditionally subordinate Blacks, traditional women, feminine gay men, and people with disabilities tend to be seen as less competent but liked for their emotional, spiritual, artistic, or athletic qualities.

Racial prejudice often begins during times of conflict, as during the Second World War when Japanese Canadians were sent to internment camps.

Aaron Kay, John Jost, and their colleagues (Jost & Kay, 2005; Kay, Jost, & Young, 2005; Kay et al., 2007) argued that the motive to see the system as just, fair, and benevolent lies behind these complimentary stereotypes. They argued that by seeing strengths and weaknesses in all group differences and positive and negative outcomes for all groups, that differences in power and opportunities are glossed over and allow people to see the social system in a positive light.

Some people, more than others, notice and justify status differences. Those high in **social dominance orientation** tend to view people in terms of hierarchies. They like their social groups to be high status; that is, they like to be on the top of the hierarchy. Being in a dominant high-status position also tends to promote this orientation (Guimond et al., 2003). Jim Sidanius, Felicia Pratto, and their colleagues (Levin et al., 2011; Pratto et al., 1994; Sidanius et al., 2004) suggested that this desire to be on top leads people high in social dominance to embrace prejudice and to support political positions that justify prejudice. Indeed, people high in social dominance orientation often support policies that maintain hierarchies, such as tax cuts for the well-off, and oppose policies that undermine the hierarchy, such as affirmative action. People high in social dominance orientation also prefer professions, such as politics and business, which increase their status and maintain hierarchies. And they express more negative attitudes toward minority persons who exhibit strong racial identities (Kaiser & Pratt-Hyatt, 2009). They avoid jobs, such as social work, that undermine hierarchies. Status may breed prejudice, but some people seek to maintain status.

Social inequalities breed not only prejudice but also mistrust. Experiments confirm that correlation: Groups receiving more unequal distributions exhibit less trust and cooperation (Cozzolino, 2011). Societies with the greatest income disparity tend also to exhibit less communal health and more anxiety, obesity, homicides, teen births, drug use, prisons, and police (Pickett & Wilkinson, 2011).

> **social dominance orientation**
> a motivation to have your own group be dominant over other social groups

② SOCIALIZATION

Prejudice springs from unequal status, and from other social sources, including our acquired values and attitudes. The influence of family socialization appears in children's prejudices, which often mirror those perceived in their mothers (Castelli et al., 2007). Children's automatic racial attitudes reflect their parents' explicit prejudice (Sinclair, Dunn, & Lowery, 2004). Our families and cultures pass on all kinds of information—how to find mates, how to drive cars, how to divide the household chores, and whom to distrust and dislike.

The authoritarian personality

In the 1940s, University of California at Berkeley researchers—two of whom had fled Nazi Germany—set out on an urgent research mission: to uncover the psychological roots of an anti-Semitism so poisonous that it caused the slaughter of millions of Jews and turned many millions of Europeans into indifferent spectators. In studies of American adults, Theodor Adorno and his colleagues (1950) discovered that hostility toward Jews often coexisted with hostility toward other minorities. Prejudice appeared to be less an attitude specific to one group than a way of thinking about those who are different. Moreover, these judgmental, **ethnocentric** people shared authoritarian tendencies—intolerance for weakness, a punitive attitude, and a submissive respect for their in-group's authorities, as reflected in their agreement with such statements as this: "Obedience and respect for authority are the most important virtues children should learn."

More recent inquiry into authoritarian people's early lives has revealed that, as children, they often face harsh discipline. Militant extremism, on both the political left and right, shares some common themes, such as catastrophizing, desiring vengeance, and dehumanizing the enemy

> **ethnocentric**
> believing in the superiority of your own ethnic and cultural group, and having a corresponding disdain for all other groups

(Saucier et al., 2009). This extremism supposedly leads the individuals affected to repress their hostilities and impulses, which they project onto out-groups. Research into authoritarianism also suggests that the insecurity of authoritarian individuals predisposes them toward an excessive concern with power and status and an inflexible right-wrong way of thinking that makes ambiguity difficult to tolerate. Such people therefore tend to be submissive to those with power over them and aggressive or punitive toward those whom they consider lower in status than themselves. In other words, "My way or the highway."

Scholars criticized the research for focusing on right-wing authoritarianism and overlooking the dogmatic authoritarianism of the left. Still, contemporary studies of right-wing authoritarians by University of Manitoba psychologist Bob Altemeyer (1988, 1992) confirmed that there are individuals whose fears and hostilities surface as prejudice. Their feelings of moral superiority may go hand in hand with brutality toward perceived inferiors. Altemeyer also concludes that right-wing authoritarians tend to be "equal opportunity bigots." Different forms of prejudice—toward Blacks, gays and lesbians, women, Muslims, immigrants, the homeless—*do* tend to coexist in the same individuals (Zick, Pettigrew, & Wagner, 2008). Moreover, authoritarian tendencies, sometimes reflected in ethnic tensions, surge during threatening times of economic recession and social upheaval (Cohrs & Ibler, 2009; Doty, Peterson, & Winter, 1991; Sales, 1973).

Particularly striking are people high in social dominance orientation and authoritarian personality. Altemeyer (2004) reported that these "Double Highs" are, not surprisingly, "among the most prejudiced persons in our society." What is perhaps most surprising and more troubling is that they seem to display the worst qualities of each type of personality, striving for status often in manipulative ways while being dogmatic and ethnocentric. Altemeyer argued that although these people are relatively rare, they are predisposed to be leaders of hate groups.

Although authoritarianism and social dominance can coexist, it appears they have different ideological bases and different functions. Authoritarianism appears more related to concern with security and control, whereas social dominance orientation appears more related to a person's group status (Cohrs et al., 2005). They can function together to form a toxic environment in groups, however. Leanne Son Hing from the University of Guelph and her colleagues (Son Hing et al., 2007) examined combinations of authoritarian and high social dominance leaders and followers. They found that high social dominance orientation leaders who had high authoritarian followers were more likely than any other combination to throw ethics out the window in the blind pursuit of profit.

Religion and prejudice

Those who benefit from social inequalities while avowing that "all are created equal" need to justify keeping things the way they are. What could be a more powerful justification than to believe God has ordained the existing social order? For all sorts of cruel deeds, noted William James, "Piety is the mask" (1902, p. 264).

In almost every country, leaders invoke religion to sanctify the present order. The use of religion to support injustice helps explain a consistent pair of findings concerning Christianity, North America's dominant religion: (1) Church members express more racial prejudice than non-members, and (2) those professing traditional or fundamentalist Christian beliefs express more prejudice than those professing more progressive beliefs (Altemeyer & Hunsberger, 1992; Hall, Matz, & Wood, 2010; Johnson et al., 2011).

Knowing the correlation between two variables—religion and prejudice—tells us nothing about their causal connection. There might be no connection at all. Perhaps people with less education are both more fundamentalist and more prejudiced. Perhaps prejudice causes religion, by leading people to create religious ideas to support their prejudices. Or perhaps religion causes prejudice, by leading people to believe that because all individuals possess free will, impoverished minorities have themselves to blame for their status.

If, indeed, it is religion that causes prejudice, then more religious church members should also be more prejudiced. But three other findings consistently indicate otherwise:

> *"We have just enough religion to make us hate, but not enough to make us love one another."*
> JONATHAN SWIFT, "THOUGHTS ON VARIOUS SUBJECTS," 1706

- Among church members, faithful church attenders were, in 24 out of 26 comparisons, less prejudiced than occasional attenders (Batson & Ventis, 1982).

- Those for whom religion is an end in itself (those who agree, for example, with the statement, "My religious beliefs are what really lie behind my whole approach to life") express less prejudice than those for whom religion is more a means to other ends (who agree that "A primary reason for my interest in religion is that my church is a congenial social activity") (Allport & Ross, 1967). And those who score highest on Gallup's "spiritual commitment" index are more welcoming of a person of another race moving in next door (Gallup & Jones, 1992).

- Protestant ministers and Roman Catholic priests give more support to human rights than do laypeople (Fichter, 1968; Hadden, 1969). In Germany, 45 percent of clergy in 1934 had aligned themselves with the Confessing Church, which was organized to oppose the Nazi regime (Reed, 1989).

What, then, is the relationship between religion and prejudice? The answer we get depends on how we ask the question. If we define religiousness as church membership or willingness to agree at least superficially with traditional beliefs, then the more religious people are the more racially prejudiced. Bigots often rationalize bigotry with religion. If we assess depth of religious commitment in any of several other ways, however, then the very devout are less prejudiced—hence the religious roots of the modern civil rights movement, among whose leaders were many ministers and priests. It was Thomas Clarkson and William Wilberforce's faith-inspired values ("Love your neighbor as yourself") that, two centuries ago, motivated their successful campaign to end the British Empire's slave trade and the practice of slavery. As Gordon Allport concluded, "The role of religion is paradoxical. It makes prejudice and it unmakes prejudice" (1958, p. 413).

Conformity

Once established, prejudice is maintained largely by inertia. If prejudice is socially accepted, many people will follow the path of least resistance and conform to the fashion. They will act not so much out of a need to hate as out of a need to be liked and accepted. Thus, people become more likely to favour (or oppose) discrimination after hearing someone else do so, and they are less supportive of women after hearing sexist humour (Ford et al., 2008; Zitek & Hebl, 2007).

Thomas Pettigrew's (1958) studies of Whites in South Africa and the American South revealed that, during the 1950s, those who conformed most to other social norms were also most prejudiced; those who were less conforming mirrored less of the surrounding prejudice.

Conformity also maintains gender prejudice. "If we have come to think that the nursery and the kitchen are the natural sphere of a woman," wrote George Bernard Shaw in an 1891 essay, "we have done so exactly as English children come to think that a cage is the natural sphere of a parrot—because they have never seen one anywhere else." Children who have seen women elsewhere—children of employed women—have less stereotyped views of men and women (Hoffman, 1977).

In all these findings, there is a message of hope. If prejudice is not deeply ingrained in personality, then as fashions change and new norms evolve, prejudice can diminish. And so it has.

③ INSTITUTIONAL SUPPORTS

Social institutions (schools, government, the media) reinforce dominant cultural attitudes. One analysis of stories in 134 children's readers written before 1970 found that male characters outnumbered female characters three to one (Women on Words and Images, 1972). Who was portrayed as showing initiative, bravery, and competence? Note the answer in this excerpt from the classic *Dick and Jane* children's reader: Jane, sprawled out on the sidewalk, her roller skates beside her, listens as Mark explains to his mother:

> "She cannot skate," said Mark.
> "I can help her.
> "I want to help her.
> "Look at her, Mother.
> "Just look at her.
> "She's just like a girl.
> "She gives up."

Institutional supports for prejudice, like that reader, are often unintended and unnoticed. Not until the 1970s, when changing ideas about males and females brought new perceptions of such portrayals, was this blatant (to us now) stereotyping widely noticed and dealt with.

What contemporary examples of institutionalized biases still go unnoticed? Here is one that most of us failed to notice, although it was right before our eyes: By examining 1750 photographs of people in magazines and newspapers, Dane Archer and his associates (1983) discovered that about two-thirds of the average male photo, but less than half of the average female

photo, was devoted to the face. As Archer widened his search, he discovered that such "face-ism" is common. He found it in the periodicals of 11 other countries, in 920 portraits gathered from the artwork of six centuries, and in the amateur drawings of students. Georgia Nigro and her colleagues (1988) confirmed the face-ism phenomenon in more magazines, including *Ms.*

The researchers suspect that the visual prominence given the faces of men and, relatively speaking, the bodies of women both reflects and perpetuates gender bias. In research in Germany, Norbert Schwarz and Eva Kurz (1989) confirmed that people whose faces are prominent in photos seem more intelligent and ambitious.

● WHAT ARE THE MOTIVATIONAL SOURCES OF PREJUDICE?

Prejudice may be bred by social situations, but motivation underlies both the hostilities of prejudice and the desire to be unbiased. Frustration can feed prejudice, as can the desire to see your own group as superior, and the desire to see the world as just. But at times, people are also motivated to avoid prejudice.

FRUSTRATION AND AGGRESSION: THE SCAPEGOAT THEORY

As we discussed in Chapter 9, pain and frustration (the blocking of a goal) often evoke hostility. When the cause of our frustration is intimidating or vague, we often redirect our hostility. This phenomenon of "displaced aggression" may have contributed to the lynchings of Blacks in the southern United States after the Civil War. Between 1882 and 1930, there were more lynchings in years when cotton prices were low and economic frustration was, therefore, presumably high (Hepworth & West, 1988; Hovland & Sears, 1940). When living standards are rising, societies tend to be more open to diversity and to the passage and enforcement of antidiscrimination laws (Frank, 1999). Ethnic peace is easier to maintain during prosperous times.

Targets for this displaced aggression vary. Following their defeat in the First World War and their country's subsequent economic chaos, many Germans saw Jews as villains. Long before Hitler came to power, one German leader explained it this way: "The Jew is just convenient. . . . If there were no Jews, the anti-Semites would have to invent them" (quoted by G. W. Allport, 1958, p. 325). In earlier centuries, people vented their fear and hostility on witches, whom they sometimes burned or drowned in public. Passions provoke prejudice.

Competition is an important source of frustration that can fuel prejudice. When two groups compete for jobs, housing, or social prestige, one group's goal fulfillment can become the other group's frustration. Thus, the **realistic group conflict theory** suggests that prejudice arises when groups compete for scarce resources (Esses, Jackson, & Armstrong, 1998; Maddux, Mullen, & Galinsky, 2008; Pereira, Vala, & Costa-Lopes, 2010; Sassenberg et al., 2007). A corresponding ecological principle, Gause's law, states that maximum competition will exist between species with identical needs.

realistic group conflict theory
the theory that prejudice arises from competition between groups for scarce resources

In Canada, opposition to immigration since 1975 has gone up and down with the unemployment rate (Palmer, 1996). In Western Europe, some people agree, "Over the last five years, people like yourself have been economically worse off than most [name of country's minority group]."

These frustrated people express relatively high levels of blatant prejudice (Pettigrew & Meertens, 1995; Pettigrew et al., 2008a). And in South Africa, dozens of African immigrants were killed by mobs, and 35 000 people were hounded from squatter camps by poor South Africans who resented the economic competition. "These foreigners have no IDs, no papers, and yet they get the jobs," said one unemployed South African, noting that "They are willing to work for 15 rand [about $2] a day" (Bearak, 2010). When interests clash, prejudice may be the result.

SOCIAL IDENTITY THEORY: FEELING SUPERIOR TO OTHERS

Humans are a group-bound species. Our ancestral history prepares us to feed and protect ourselves—to live—in groups. Humans cheer for their groups, kill for their groups, die for their groups. Evolution prepares us, when encountering strangers, to make a quick judgment: friend or foe? Those from our group, those who look like us, even those who *sound* like us—with accents like our own—we instantly tend to like (Gluszek & Dovidio, 2010; Kinzler et al., 2009).

Not surprisingly, we also define ourselves by our groups, noted Australian social psychologists John Turner (1981, 2000), Michael Hogg (1992, 2006, 2008, 2010), and their colleagues. Self-concept—our sense of who we are—contains not just a personal identity (our sense of our personal attributes and attitudes) but also a social identity (Chapter 2) (Chen, Boucher, & Tapias, 2006). Fiona identifies herself as a woman, an Aussie, a supporter of the Labour Party, a University of New South Wales student, a member of the MacDonald family. We carry such social identities like playing cards, playing them when appropriate.

Working with the late British social psychologist Henri Tajfel, Turner proposed social identity theory. Turner and Tajfel observed the following:

- **We categorize:** We find it useful to put people, ourselves included, into categories. To label someone as a Hindu, a Scot, or a bus driver is a shorthand way of saying some other things about the person.

- **We identify:** We associate ourselves with certain groups (our **in-groups**), and gain self-esteem by doing so.

- **We compare:** We contrast our groups with other groups (**out-groups**), with a favourable bias toward our own groups.

in-groups
"us"—groups of people who share a sense of belonging, a feeling of common identity

out-groups
"them"—groups that people perceive as distinctively different from or apart from their in-group

We humans naturally divide others into those inside and those outside our group. We also evaluate ourselves partly by our group memberships. Having a sense of "we-ness" strengthens our self-concept. It feels good. We seek not only respect for ourselves but also pride in our groups (Smith & Tyler, 1997). Moreover, seeing our groups as superior helps us feel even better. It's as if we all think, "I am an X [name your group]. X is good. Therefore, I am good."

Lacking a positive personal identity, people often seek self-esteem by identifying with a group. Thus, many youths find pride, power, and identity in gang affiliations. When people's personal and social identities become fused—when the boundary between self and group blurs—they become more willing to fight or die for their group (Gómez et al., 2011; Swann et al., 2009). Many super-patriots define themselves by their national identities (Staub, 1997b, 2005). And many people at loose ends find identity in their associations with new religious movements, self-help groups, or fraternal clubs (Figure 11-1).

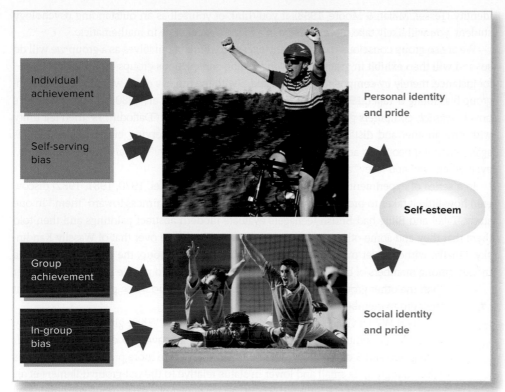

FIGURE 11–1

IDENTITY AND SELF-ESTEEM.

Personal identity and social identity together feed self-esteem.

In-group bias

The group definition of who you are—your race, religion, gender, academic major—implies a definition of who you are not. The circle that includes "us" (the in-group) excludes "them" (the out-group). The more that ethnic Turks in the Netherlands see themselves as Turks or as Muslims, the less they see themselves as Dutch (Verkuyten & Yildiz, 2007).

The mere experience of being formed into groups may promote **in-group bias.** Ask children, "Which are better, the children in your school or the children at [another school nearby]?" Virtually all will say their own school has the better children. For adults, too, the closer to home, the better things seem. More than 80 percent of both Whites and Blacks say race relations are generally good in their neighbourhoods, but fewer than 60 percent see relations as generally good in the country as a whole (Sack & Elder, 2000). Merely sharing a birthday with someone creates enough of a bond to evoke heightened cooperation in a laboratory experiment (D. T. Miller, Downs, & Prentice, 1998).

In-group bias is one more example of the human quest for a positive self-concept (Chapter 2). Most people have a positive self-image, which they project to their in-groups more than to out-groups (DiDonato, Ullrich, & Krueger, 2011). Their in-group bias expresses their positive self-concept, but it also supports their self-concept. When our group has been successful, we can make ourselves feel better by identifying more strongly with it. College and university students whose team has just been victorious frequently report, "*We* won." After their team's defeat, students are more likely to say, "*They* lost." Basking in the reflected glory of a successful in-group is strongest among those who have just experienced an ego blow, such as learning they did poorly on a "creativity test" (Cialdini et al., 1976). We can also bask in the reflected glory of a friend's achievement—except when the friend outperforms us on something pertinent to our

in-group bias
the tendency to favour your own group

identity (Tesser, Millar, & Moore, 1988). If you think of yourself as an outstanding psychology student, you will likely take more pleasure in a friend's excellence in mathematics.

We are so group conscious that given any excuse to think of ourselves as a group we will do so—and will then exhibit in-group bias. Even forming conspicuous groups on no logical basis—for instance, merely by composing groups X and Y with the flip of a coin—will produce some in-group bias (Billig & Tajfel, 1973; Brewer & Silver, 1978; Locksley et al., 1980). In Kurt Vonnegut's novel *Slapstick*, computers gave everyone a new middle name; all "Daffodil-11s" then felt unity with one another and distance from "Raspberry-13s." The self-serving bias (Chapter 2) rides again, enabling people to achieve a more positive social identity: "We" are better than "they," even when "we" and "they" are defined randomly!

In a series of experiments, Tajfel and Michael Billig (1974; Tajfel, 1970, 1981, 1982) discovered how little it takes to provoke favouritism toward "us" and unfairness toward "them." In one study, Tajfel and Billig had British teenagers evaluate modern abstract paintings and then told them that they and some others had favoured the art of Paul Klee over that of Wassily Kandinsky. Finally, without ever meeting the other members of their group, the teens divided some money among members of both groups. They gave more money to people in their group rather than the other group, even though they had no idea who these people were or what their group membership meant.

David Wilder (1981) summarized the typical result: "When given the opportunity to divide 15 points [worth money], subjects generally award 9 or 10 points to their own group and 5 or 6 points to the other group." We are more prone to in-group bias when our group is small and lower in status relative to the out-group (Ellemers et al., 1997; Mullen, Brown, & Smith, 1992). When we're part of a small group surrounded by a larger group, we are conscious of our group membership; when our in-group is the majority, we think less about it. To be a foreign student, to be gay or lesbian, or to be

In-group bias is behind the animosity between Palestine and Israel.

of a minority race or gender at some social gathering is to feel your own social identity more keenly and to react accordingly.

Does in-group bias reflect liking for the in-group, dislike for the out-group, or both? Does ethnic pride cause prejudice? Does a strong feminist identity lead feminists to dislike non-feminists? Does loyalty to a particular fraternity or sorority lead its members to deprecate independents and members of other fraternities and sororities? Or do people merely favour their own group without any animosity toward others?

Experiments have suggested that in-group favouritism reflects both a liking for our own group and a dislike for the other group. Out-group stereotypes prosper when people feel keenly their in-group identity, such as when they are with other in-group members (Wilder & Shapiro, 1991). At a club meeting, we sense most strongly our differences from those in another club.

Basking in reflected glory: After Jamaican-Canadian sprinter Ben Johnson won the Olympic 100-metre race in 1988, Canadian media described this victory by a "Canadian." After Johnson's gold medal was taken away due to steroid use, Canadian media then emphasized his "Jamaican" identity (Stelzl, Janes, & Seligman, 2008).

We also ascribe uniquely human emotions (love, hope, contempt, resentment) to in-group members and are more reluctant to see such human emotions in out-group members (Demoulin, Saroglou, & Van Pachterbeke, 2008; Leyens et al., 2003, 2007). There is a long history of denying human attributes to out-groups—a process called "infrahumanization." European explorers pictured many of the peoples they encountered as savages ruled by animal instinct. "Africans have been likened to apes, Jews to vermin, and immigrants to parasites," noted Australian social psychologists Stephen Loughman and Nick Haslam (2007).

Yet in-group bias results as much or more from perceiving that your own group is good (Brewer, 1979) as from a sense that other groups are bad (Rosenbaum & Holtz, 1985). Even when there is no "them" (imagine yourself bonding with a handful of fellow survivors on a deserted island), one can come to love "us" (Gaertner et al., 2006). So it seems that positive

"Uh-oh! They seem to have loved it!"

Something favoured by an out-group may be cast in a negative light.

© Ed Fisher/The New Yorker Collection/www.cartoonbank.com.

> *"Father, Mother, and Me,*
> *Sister and Auntie say*
> *All the people like us are*
> *We, And every one else is*
> *They. And They live over*
> *the sea, While We live*
> *over the way. But would*
> *you believe it? They look*
> *upon We As only a sort of*
> *They!"*
>
> RUDYARD KIPLING, 1926 (QUOTED
> BY MULLEN, 1991)

feelings for our own groups need not be mirrored by equally strong negative feelings for out-groups.

Need for status, self-regard, and belonging

Status is relative: To perceive ourselves as having status, we need people below us. Thus one psychological benefit of prejudice, or of any status system, is a feeling of superiority. Most of us can recall a time when we took secret satisfaction in someone else's failure—perhaps seeing a brother or sister punished or a classmate failing a test. In Europe and North America, prejudice is often greater among those low or slipping on the socio-economic ladder and among those whose positive self-image is being threatened (Lemyre & Smith, 1985; Pettigrew et al., 2008b; Thompson & Crocker, 1985). In one study, members of lower-status sororities were more disparaging of other sororities than were members of higher-status sororities (Crocker et al., 1987). If our status is secure, we have less need to feel superior.

In study after study, thinking about your own mortality—by writing a short essay on dying and the emotions aroused by thinking about death—also provokes enough insecurity to intensify in-group favouritism and out-group prejudice (Greenberg et al., 1990, 1994; Harmon-Jones et al., 1996; Schimel et al., 1999; Solomon, Greenberg, & Pyszczynski, 2000). Among Whites, thinking about death can even promote liking for racists who argue for their group's superiority

---

THE >>> INSIDE STORY

I grew up in Toronto and watched it evolve from a very homogeneous city to one of the most ethnically diverse cities in the world. This planted the seed for my later interest in studying intergroup attitudes. I began to study intergroup attitudes as a postdoctoral fellow at the University of Waterloo in the late 1980s, conducting research on the effects of mood on the expression of ethnic stereotypes, and the role of values, stereotypes, and emotions in determining intergroup attitudes. Since then, my interest in this topic has moved in several different directions. One important direction is the investigation of attitudes toward immigrants and immigration, which again came out of my experiences in Toronto. It struck me that immigrants seemed to be the target of considerable prejudice and discrimination, even among people who were themselves immigrants only a generation or two ago. In addition, it seemed that people justified their negative attitudes and behaviour toward immigrants on the basis of

competition for resources, such as jobs. This led to my research on the role of group competition in determining prejudice and discrimination toward immigrants. I feel fortunate to be able to work in an area in which I can apply theory and research in social psychology to important social issues.

Victoria Esses
University of Western Ontario

(Greenberg et al., 2008). With death on their minds, people exhibit "terror management" by derogating those who further arouse their anxiety by challenging their world views. When people are already feeling vulnerable about their mortality, prejudice helps bolster a threatened belief system. The news is not all bad, however. Thinking about death can also lead people to pursue communal feelings such as togetherness and altruism (McGregor et al., 2001; Sani, Herrera, & Bowe, 2009).

All this suggests that a man who doubts his own strength and independence might, by proclaiming women to be pitifully weak and dependent, boost his masculine image. Indeed, when Joel Grube, Randy Kleinhesselink, and Kathleen Kearney (1982) had Washington State University men view young women's videotaped job interviews, men with low self-acceptance disliked strong, non-traditional women. Men with high self-acceptance preferred them. Similarly, James Meindl and Melvin Lerner (1984) found that a humiliating experience—accidentally knocking over a stack of someone's important computer cards—provoked English-speaking Canadian students to express increased hostility toward French-speaking Canadians. Experiments confirm the connection between self-image and prejudice: Affirm people and they will evaluate an out-group more positively; threaten their self-esteem and they will restore it by denigrating an out-group (Fein & Spencer, 1997; Spencer et al., 1998).

Despised out-groups can also serve the need to strengthen the in-group. As we will note in Module A, the perception of a common enemy unites a group. School spirit is seldom so strong as when the game is with the archrival. The sense of comradeship among workers is often highest when they all feel a common antagonism toward management. To solidify the Nazi hold over Germany, Hitler used the "Jewish menace." Despised out-groups can strengthen the in-group. But when the need to belong is met, people become more accepting of outgroups, report Mario Mikulincer and Phillip Shaver (2001). They subliminally primed some Israeli students

> *"By exciting emulation and comparisons of superiority, you lay the foundation of lasting mischief; you make brothers and sisters hate each other."*
> SAMUEL JOHNSON, QUOTED IN JAMES BOSWELL'S *LIFE OF SAMUEL JOHNSON*, 1791

The curse of cliques? Did the tendency of high school students to form in-groups and disparage out-groups—jocks, preppies, goths, geeks contribute to a tribal atmosphere that helped form the context for school massacres, here at Colorado's Columbine High School, or elsewhere?

"It's not enough that we succeed. Cats must also fail."

Something favoured by an out-group may be cast in a negative light.

© Leo Cullum/The New Yorker Collection/www.cartoonbank.com.

just-world phenomenon the tendency of people to believe that the world is just, and that, therefore, people get what they deserve and deserve what they get

with words that fostered a sense of belonging (*love, support, hug*) and others with neutral words. The students then read an essay that was supposedly written by a fellow Jewish student and another by an Arab student. When primed with neutral words, the Israeli students evaluated the supposed Israeli student's essay as superior to the supposed Arab student's essay. When the participants were primed with a sense of belonging, that bias disappeared.

MOTIVATION TO SEE THE WORLD AS JUST

In a series of experiments conducted at the Universities of Waterloo and Kentucky, Melvin Lerner and his colleagues (Lerner & Miller, 1978; Lerner, 1980) discovered that merely observing another innocent person being victimized is enough to make the victim seem less worthy. Lerner noted that such disparaging of hapless victims results from the human need to believe that "I am a just person living in a just world, a world where people get what they deserve." From early childhood, he argued, we are taught that good is rewarded and evil punished. Hard work and virtue pay dividends; laziness and immorality do not. From this, it is but a short leap to assuming that those who flourish must be good and those who suffer must deserve their fate.

Numerous studies have confirmed this **just-world phenomenon** (Hafer & Bègue, 2005). Imagine that you, along with some others, are participating in one of Lerner's studies—supposedly on the perception of emotional cues (Lerner & Simmons, 1966). One of the participants, a confederate, is selected by lottery to perform a memory task. This person receives painful shocks whenever she gives a wrong answer. You and the others note her emotional responses.

After watching the victim receive these apparently painful shocks, the experimenter asks you to evaluate her. How would you respond? With compassionate sympathy? We might expect so. As Ralph Waldo Emerson wrote, "The martyr cannot be dishonoured." On the contrary, the experiments revealed that martyrs can be dishonoured. When observers were powerless to alter the victim's fate, they often rejected and devalued the victim. Juvenal, the Roman satirist, anticipated these results: "The Roman mob follows after Fortune . . . and hates those who have been condemned." And the more ongoing the suffering, as with Jews even after the Holocaust, the greater the dislike of the victims (Imhoff & Banse, 2009).

Linda Carli and her colleagues (Carli, 1999; Carli & Leonard, 1989) reported that this just-world phenomenon colours our impressions of rape victims. Carli had people read detailed descriptions of interactions between a man and a woman. For example, a woman and her boss meet for dinner, go to his home, and each have a glass of wine. Some read a scenario that has a happy ending: "Then he led me to the couch. He held my hand and asked me to marry him." In hindsight, people find the ending unsurprising and admire the man's and woman's character traits. Others read the same scenario with a different ending: "But then he became very rough and pushed me onto the couch. He held me down on the couch and raped me." Given this ending, people see it as inevitable and blame the woman for behaviour that seems faultless in the first scenario.

Recently, Carolyn Hafer from Brock University and her colleagues (Hafer, 2000; Hafer & Bègue, 2005; Hafer & Olson, 2003) have provided compelling evidence that an innocent

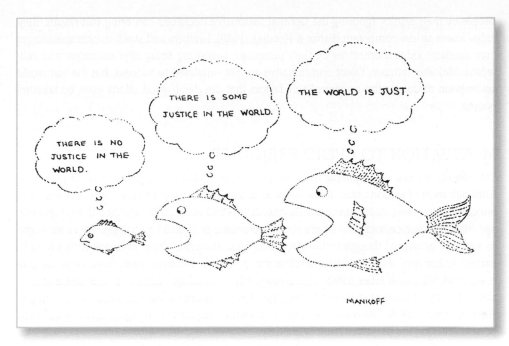

victim threatens people's sense of justice. In one study, for example, students watched a boy describe how he had been beaten and robbed while he was travelling in South America; other students did not experience this story. Those who watched the innocent victim describe his assault were especially slow at reading words related to justice, in much the same way that spider phobics are slow to read words about spiders. People seemed afraid to think about justice when confronted with an innocent victim. In a later study, they demonstrated that watching the same video led students to distance themselves from the victim—they said they weren't like him. And the more they distanced themselves from him, the more they derogated him.

Research on the motive to see the world as just suggests that this motive is so strong that it can lead people to ignore gross injustice and instead see no injustice at all. Those who assume a just world believe that rape victims must have behaved seductively (Borgida & Brekke, 1985), that battered spouses must have provoked their beatings (Summers & Feldman, 1984), that poor people don't deserve better (Furnham & Gunter, 1984), and that sick people are responsible for their illnesses (Gruman & Sloan, 1983). When researchers activate the concept of choice by having people record others' choices, participants display less empathy for disadvantaged individuals, engage in more victim-blaming, and show reduced support for social policies such as affirmative action (Savani, Stephens, & Markus, 2011).

Such beliefs enable rich and successful people to reassure themselves that they, too, deserve what they have. The wealthy and healthy can see their own good fortune, and others' misfortune, as justly deserved. Linking good fortune with virtue and misfortune with moral failure enables the fortunate to feel pride and to avoid responsibility for the unfortunate.

People loathe a loser even when the loser's misfortune quite obviously stems from mere bad luck. People know that gambling outcomes are just good or bad luck and should not affect their evaluations of the gambler. Still, they can't resist playing Monday-morning quarterback—judging people by their results. Ignoring the fact that reasonable decisions can bring bad results, they judge losers as less competent (Baron & Hershey, 1988). Lawyers and stock market speculators may similarly judge themselves by their outcomes, becoming smug after successes and self-reproachful after failures. Talent and initiative are not unrelated to success, but the just-world assumption discounts the uncontrollable factors that can derail good efforts even by talented people.

MOTIVATION TO AVOID PREJUDICE

Motivations not only lead people to be prejudiced; they also lead people to avoid prejudice. Although most of us don't want to be prejudiced, a prejudice habit lingers. Patricia Devine and her colleagues (1989, 2005; Amodio & Devine, 2010; Plant et al., 2010) reported that people low and high in prejudice sometimes have similar automatic prejudicial responses. Try as we might to suppress unwanted thoughts—thoughts about food, thoughts about romance with a friend's partner, judgmental thoughts about another group—they sometimes refuse to go away (Macrae et al., 1994; Wegner & Erber, 1992). This is especially so for older adults, who lose some of their ability to inhibit unwanted thoughts and, therefore, to suppress old stereotypes (von Hippel, Silver, & Lynch, 2000). The result for all of us: Unwanted (dissonant) thoughts and feelings often persist. Breaking the prejudice habit is not easy.

In real life, encountering a minority person may trigger a similar knee-jerk stereotype. Those with accepting attitudes and those with disapproving attitudes toward homosexuals may both feel uncomfortable sitting with a gay male on a bus seat (Monteith, 1993). Encountering an unfamiliar Black male, White people—even those who pride themselves on not being prejudiced—may respond warily. Seeking not to appear prejudiced, they may divert their attention away from the person (Richeson & Trawalter, 2008).

In one experiment by E. J. Vanman and colleagues (1990), White people viewed slides of White and Black people, imagined themselves interacting with them, and rated their probable liking of each person pictured. Although the participants saw themselves liking the Black people more than the White people, their facial muscles told a different story. Instruments revealed that when a Black face appeared, there tended to be more activity in frowning than smiling muscles. An emotion-processing centre in the brain also becomes more active as a person views an unfamiliar person of another race (Hart et al., 2000).

Researchers who study stereotyping contend, however, that prejudicial reactions are not inevitable (Crandall, Eshleman, & O'Brien, 2002; Kunda & Spencer, 2003). The motivation to avoid prejudice can lead people to modify their thoughts and actions. Aware of the gap between how they should feel and how they do feel, self-conscious people will feel guilt and try to inhibit their prejudicial response (Bodenhausen & Macrae, 1998; Dasgupta & Rivera, 2006; Zuwerink et al., 1996). Even automatic prejudices subside, noted Devine and her colleagues (2005), when people's motivation to avoid prejudice is internal (because prejudice is wrong) rather than external (because they don't want others to think badly of them).

The moral: Overcoming what Devine called "the prejudice habit" isn't easy. But it can be done, as Devine and her colleagues (2012) discovered, after raising the awareness and concern of willing volunteers and training them to replace biased with unbiased knee-jerk responses. Throughout the two-year study follow-up period, participants in the experimental intervention condition displayed reduced implicit prejudice. If you find yourself reacting with knee-jerk presumptions or feelings, don't despair; that's not unusual. It's what you do with that awareness that matters. Do you let those feelings hijack your behaviour? Or do you compensate by monitoring and correcting your behaviour in future situations?

WHAT ARE THE COGNITIVE SOURCES OF PREJUDICE?

To understand stereotyping and prejudice, it also helps to remember how our minds work. How do the ways in which we think about the world, and simplify it, influence our stereotypes? And how do our stereotypes affect our judgments?

CATEGORIZATION: CLASSIFYING PEOPLE INTO GROUPS

Prejudice arises not only from social and motivational influences but also at times from cool calculation. The same processes that allow people to simplify and make sense of the world, also at times lead people to make prejudicial evaluations of others. One way we simplify our environment is to "categorize"—to organize the world by clustering objects into groups (Macrae & Bodenhausen, 2000, 2001). A biologist classifies plants and animals. Most of us classify people. Having done so, we can think about them more easily. If people in a group are similar, knowing their group can provide useful information with minimal effort (Macrae, Stangor, & Milne, 1994). Stereotypes sometimes offer "a beneficial ratio of information gained to effort expended" (Sherman et al., 1998). Stereotypes represent cognitive efficiency. They are energy-saving schemes for making speedy judgments and predicting how others will think and act. Thus, stereotypes and out-group bias may, as Carlos David Navarrete and others (2010) have noted, "serve ultimate, evolutionary functions," by enabling our ancestors to cope and survive.

Spontaneous categorization

We find it especially easy and efficient to rely on stereotypes under the following conditions:

- When pressed for time (Kaplan, Wanshula, & Zanna, 1993)
- When preoccupied (Gilbert & Hixon, 1991)
- When tired (Bodenhausen, 1990)
- When emotionally aroused (Esses, Haddock, & Zanna, 1993b; Stroessner & Mackie, 1993)
- When too young to appreciate diversity (Biernat, 1991)

Ethnicity and sex are, in our current world, powerful ways of categorizing people. Imagine Tom, a 45-year-old Black real estate agent in New Brunswick. We suspect that your image of "Black male" predominates over the categories "middle-aged," "businessperson," and "easterner."

Experiments expose our spontaneous categorization of people by race. Much as we organize what is actually a colour continuum into what we perceive as distinct colours, so we cannot resist categorizing people into groups. We label people of widely varying ancestry as simply "Black" or "White," as if such categories were black and white. When subjects view different people making statements, they often forget who said what, yet remember the race of the person who made each statement (Hewstone, Hantzi, & Johnston, 1991; Stroessner, Hamilton, & Lepore,

FIGURE 11–2

RACIAL CATEGORIZATION.

Quickly: What race is this person? Less prejudiced people respond more quickly, with less apparent concern with possibly misclassifying someone (as if thinking, who cares?).

out-group homogeneity effect perception of out-group members as more similar to one another than are in-group members. Thus, "they are alike; we are diverse."

1990; Taylor, Sheatsley, & Greeley, 1978). By itself, such categorization is not prejudice, but it does provide a foundation for prejudice.

In fact, it's necessary for prejudice. Social identity theory implies that those who feel their social identity keenly will concern themselves with correctly categorizing people as us or them. To test this prediction, Jim Blascovich, Natalie Wyer, Laura Swart, and Jeffrey Kibler (1997) compared racially prejudiced people (who feel their racial identity keenly) with non-prejudiced people. Both groups proved equally speedy at classifying white, black, and grey ovals. But how much time did each group take to categorize *people* by race? Especially when shown faces whose race was somewhat ambiguous (Figure 11–2), prejudiced people took longer, with more apparent concern for classifying people as us (their own race) or them (another race).

Perceived similarities and differences

Picture the following objects: apples, chairs, pencils.

There is a strong tendency to see objects within a group as being more uniform than they really are. Were your apples all red? Your chairs all straight-backed? Your pencils all yellow? Once we classify two days in the same month, they seem more alike, temperature-wise, than the same interval across months. People guess the eight-day average temperature difference between, say, November 15 and 23, to be less than the eight-day difference between November 30 and December 8 (Krueger & Clement, 1994).

It's the same with people. Once we assign people to groups—athletes, drama majors, psychology professors—we are likely to exaggerate the similarities within groups and the differences between them (S. E. Taylor, 1981; Wilder, 1978). Just dividing into groups can create an **out-group homogeneity effect**—a sense that they are "all alike" and different from us and our group (Ostrom & Sedikides, 1992). Because we generally like people we think are similar to us and dislike those we perceive as different, the natural result is in-group bias (Byrne & Wong, 1962; Rokeach & Mezei, 1966; Stein, Hardyck, & Smith, 1965).

The mere fact of a group decision can also lead outsiders to overestimate a group's unanimity. If the Conservative Party wins a national election by a slim majority, observers infer "the people have turned Conservative." If the Liberal Party wins by a similarly slim margin, voter attitudes would hardly have differed, but observers would now attribute a "Liberal mood" to the country. Whether a decision is made by majority rule or by a designated group executive, people usually presume that it reflects the entire group's attitudes, observed Scott Allison and his co-workers (Allison & Messick, 1985; Allison, Mackie, & Messick, 1996). When the Onex Corporation tried to take over Air Canada, Buzz Hargrove, then-president of the Canadian Auto Workers (CAW), sided with Onex. The media reported that the CAW was behind Onex, even though it was clear that many union members felt otherwise.

When the group is our own, we are more likely to see diversity:

- Many non-Europeans see the Swiss as a fairly homogeneous people. But to the people of Switzerland, the Swiss are diverse, encompassing French-, German-, and Italian-speaking groups.

- Those in a minority tend to feel more shared identity than those in the majority (Haslam & Oakes, 1995; Ryan, 1996). Nevertheless, those in the minority are especially likely to see important differences between their own subgroup and other subgroups, while those in the majority tend to lump all minority group members together (Huddy & Virtanen, 1995).

- Sorority sisters perceive the members of any other sorority as less diverse than the mix in their own (Park & Rothbart, 1982); and business majors and engineering majors overestimate the uniformity of the other group's traits and attitudes (Judd, Ryan, & Park, 1991).

> *"Women are more like each other than men [are]."*
> LORD (NOT LADY) CHESTERFIELD

In general, the greater our familiarity with a social group, the more we see its diversity (Brown & Wootton-Millward, 1993; Linville, Gischer, & Salovey, 1989). The less our familiarity, the more we stereotype. Also, the smaller and less powerful the group, the more we stereotype (Fiske, 1993; Hancock & Rhodes, 2008; Mullen & Hu, 1989). To those in power, we pay attention.

Perhaps you have noticed: They—the members of any racial group other than your own—even look alike. Many of us can recall embarrassing ourselves by confusing two people of another racial group, prompting the person we've misnamed to say, "You think we all look alike." Experiments by John Brigham, June Chance, Alvin Goldstein, and Roy Malpass in the United States and by Hayden Ellis in Scotland revealed that people of other races do, in fact, seem to look more alike than do people of your own race (Brigham & Williamson, 1979; Chance & Goldstein, 1981; Ellis, 1981; Meissner & Brigham, 2001; Sporer & Horry, 2011). When White students are shown faces of a few White and a few Black individuals and then asked to pick these individuals out of a photographic lineup, they show an **own-race bias.** They more accurately recognize the White faces than the Black, and they often falsely recognize Black faces never before seen.

As Figure 11–3 illustrates, Blacks more easily recognize another Black than they do a White (Bothwell, Brigham, & Malpass, 1989). Likewise, British South Asians are quicker than White Brits to recognize South Asian faces (Walker & Hewstone, 2008). And 10- to 15-year-old Turkish children are quicker than Austrian children to recognize Turkish faces (Sporer, Trinkl, & Guberova, 2007). Even infants as young as 9 months display better own-race recognition of faces (Kelly et al., 2005, 2007).

own-race bias
the tendency for people to more accurately recognize faces of their own race

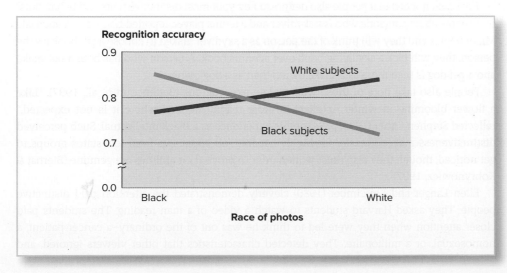

FIGURE 11–3

THE OWN-RACE BIAS.

White subjects more accurately recognize the faces of Whites than of Blacks; Black subjects more accurately recognize the faces of Blacks than of Whites. (From P. G. Devine and R. S. Malpass, 1985)

The term "own-race bias" is a misnomer in the case of Anglo and Hispanic identifications. Most Hispanic people are classified as Caucasians.

It's true outside the laboratory as well, as Daniel Wright and his colleagues (2001) found after either a Black or a White researcher approached Black and White people in South African and English shopping malls. When later asked to identify the researcher from lineups, people recognized better those of their own race. It's not that we cannot perceive differences among faces of another race. Rather, when looking at a face from another racial group, we often pay attention, first, to race ("that man is Black") rather than to individual features. When viewing someone of our own race, we are less attentive to the race category and more attentive to individual details (Bernstein, Young, & Hugenberg, 2007; Hugenberg et al., 2010; Shriver et al., 2008; Young, Bernstein, & Hugenberg, 2010).

Our attending to someone's being in a different social category may also be contributing to a parallel own-age bias—the tendency for both children and older adults to more accurately identify faces from their own age groups (Anastasi & Rhodes, 2005, 2006; He, Ebner, & Johnson, 2011; Wright & Stroud, 2002). (Perhaps you have noticed that senior citizens look more alike than do your fellow students?)

② DISTINCTIVENESS: PERCEIVING PEOPLE WHO STAND OUT

Other ways we perceive our worlds also breed stereotypes. Distinctive people and vivid or extreme occurrences often capture attention and distort judgments.

Distinctive people

Have you ever found yourself in a situation where you were the only person of your sex, race, or nationality present? If so, your difference from the others probably made you more noticeable and the object of more attention. A Black in an otherwise White group, a man in an otherwise female group, and a woman in an otherwise male group seem more prominent and influential; they appear to have exaggerated good and bad qualities (Crocker & McGraw, 1984; S. E. Taylor et al., 1979). When someone in a group is made conspicuous, we tend to see that person as causing whatever happens (S. E. Taylor & Fiske, 1978). If we are positioned to look at Joe, even if Joe is an average group member, Joe will seem to have a greater-than-average influence on the group.

Have you noticed that people also define you by your most distinctive traits and behaviours? Tell people about someone who is a skydiver and a tennis player, reported Lori Nelson and Dale Miller (1995), and they will think of the person as a skydiver. Asked to choose a gift book for the person, they will pick a skydiving book over a tennis book. A person who has both a pet snake and a pet dog is seen more as a snake owner than as a dog owner.

People also take note of those who violate expectations (Bettencourt et al., 1997). "Like a flower blooming in winter, intellect is more readily noticed where it is not expected," reflected Stephen Carter (1993, p. 54) on his experience as a Black intellectual. Such perceived distinctiveness makes it easier for highly capable job applicants from low-status groups to get noticed, though they also must work harder to prove their abilities are genuine (Biernat & Kobrynowicz, 1997).

Ellen Langer and Lois Imber (1980) cleverly demonstrated the attention paid distinctive people. They asked Harvard students to watch a video of a man reading. The students paid closer attention when they were led to think he was out of the ordinary—a cancer patient, a homosexual, or a millionaire. They detected characteristics that other viewers ignored, and their evaluation of him was more extreme. Those who thought the man a cancer patient noticed distinctive facial characteristics and bodily movements and thus perceived him as much more "different from most people" than did the other viewers. The extra attention we pay to distinctive people creates an illusion that they differ more from others than they really do. If people thought you had the IQ of a genius, they would probably notice things about you that otherwise would pass unnoticed.

Distinctive cases

Our minds also use distinctive cases as a shortcut to judging groups. Are Blacks good athletes? "Well, there's Lennox Lewis and Marion Jones and Jarome Iginla. Yeah, I'd say so." Note the thought processes at work here: Given lim-

Distinctive people, such as the Houston Rockets' 7'6" player Yao Ming, now retired, draw attention.

ited experience with a particular social group, we recall examples of it and generalize from those (Sherman, 1996). Moreover, encountering exemplars of negative stereotypes (a hostile Black person in one recent experiment) can prime such stereotypes, leading people to minimize contact with the group (Hendersen-King & Nisbett, 1996).

Such generalizing from single cases can cause problems. Vivid instances, though more available in memory, are seldom representative of the larger group. Exceptional athletes, though distinctive and memorable, are not the best basis for judging the distribution of athletic talent in an entire group.

Those in a numerical minority, being more distinctive, also may be numerically overestimated by the majority. What proportion of your country's population would you say is Muslim? People in non-Muslim countries often overestimate this proportion. (In Canada, for example, less than 2 percent declared themselves as Muslim in the 2001 Census.) Or consider a U.S. poll that found the average American thinking 21 percent of men were gay and 22 percent of women were lesbian (Robinson, 2002). Repeated surveys suggest that actually about 3 or 4 percent of men and 1 or 2 percent of women have a same-sex orientation (National Center for Health Statistics, 1991; T. W. Smith, 1998; Tarmann, 2002).

Myron Rothbart and his colleagues (1978) showed how distinctive cases also fuel stereotypes. They had University of Oregon students view 50 slides, each of which stated the man's height. For one group of students, 10 of the men were slightly over 6 feet (up to 6 feet, 4 inches). For other students, these 10 men were well over 6 feet (up to 6 feet, 11 inches). When asked later how many of the men were over 6 feet, those given the moderately tall examples recalled

5 percent too many. Those given the extremely tall examples recalled 50 percent too many. In a follow-up experiment, students read descriptions of the actions of 50 men, 10 of whom had committed either non-violent crimes, such as forgery, or violent crimes, such as rape. Of those shown the list with the violent crimes, most overestimated the number of criminal acts.

Distinctive events

Stereotypes assume a correlation between group membership and individuals' characteristics ("Italians are emotional," "Jews are shrewd," "Accountants are perfectionists"). Even under the best of conditions, our attentiveness to unusual occurrences can create illusory correlations (Chapter 3). Because we are sensitive to distinctive events, the co-occurrence of two such events is especially noticeable—more noticeable than each of the times the unusual events do not occur together.

David Hamilton and Robert Gifford (1976) demonstrated illusory correlation in a clever experiment. They showed students slides on which various people, members of "Group A" or "Group B," were said to have done something desirable or undesirable; for example, "John, a member of Group A, visited a sick friend in the hospital." Twice as many statements described members of Group A as Group B, but both groups did nine desirable acts for every four undesirable behaviours. Since both Group B and the undesirable acts were less frequent, their co-occurrence—for example, "Allen, a member of Group B, dented the fender of a parked car and didn't leave his name"—was an unusual combination that caught people's attention. The students then overestimated the frequency with which the "minority" group (B) acted undesirably and judged Group B more harshly.

Remember, Group B members actually committed undesirable acts in the same proportion as Group A members. Moreover, the students had no pre-existing biases for or against Group B, and they received the information more systematically than daily experience ever offers it. Although researchers debate why it happens, they agree that illusory correlation occurs and provides yet another source for the formation of racial stereotypes (Berndsen et al., 2002). Thus, the features that most distinguish a minority from a majority are those that become associated with it (Sherman et al., 2009). Your ethnic or social group may be like other groups in most ways, but people will notice how it differs.

In experiments, even single co-occurrences of an unusual act by someone in an atypical group—"Ben, a Jehovah's Witness, owns a pet sloth"—can embed illusory correlations in people's minds (Risen, Gilovich, & Dunning, 2007). This enables the mass media to feed illusory correlations. When a self-described gay man murders someone, his sexual orientation often gets mentioned. When a straight man murders someone, his sexual orientation is seldom mentioned. Likewise, when ex–mental patients Mark Chapman and John Hinckley, Jr., shot John Lennon and U.S. President Ronald Reagan, respectively, the assailants' mental histories commanded attention. Assassins and mental hospitalization are both relatively infrequent, making the combination especially newsworthy. Such reporting adds to the illusion of a large correlation between (1) violent tendencies and (2) homosexuality or mental hospitalization.

Unlike the students who judged Groups A and B, we often have pre-existing biases. David Hamilton's further research with Terrence Rose (1980) revealed that our pre-existing stereotypes can lead us to "see" correlations that aren't there. The researchers had University of California Santa Barbara students read sentences in which various adjectives described the members of different occupational groups ("Doug, an accountant, is timid and thoughtful"). In actuality, each occupation was described equally often by each adjective; accountants, doctors, and salespeople were equally often timid, wealthy, and talkative. The students, however, thought they had more often read descriptions of timid accountants, wealthy doctors, and talkative salespeople. Their stereotyping led them to perceive correlations that weren't there, thus helping to perpetuate the stereotypes.

Likewise, guess what happened when Vaughn Becker and his colleagues (2010) invited university students to view a White and a Black face—one angry, one not—for one-tenth of a second. Then, as a brief distraction, they added two numbers that accompanied the faces. The participants' subsequent recollections of what they had viewed revealed racial bias. "White anger flowed to neutral Black faces (34 percent likelihood) more readily than Black anger flowed to neutral White faces (19 percent likelihood)."

③ ATTRIBUTIONS: DISCOUNTING IMPORTANT SITUATIONAL FORCES

In explaining others' actions, we frequently commit the fundamental attribution error (Chapter 3). We attribute others' behaviour so much to their inner dispositions that we discount important situational forces. The error occurs partly because our attention focuses on the person, not on the situation. A person's race or sex is vivid and gets attention; the situational forces working on that person are usually less visible. Slavery was often overlooked as an explanation for slave behaviour; the behaviour was instead attributed to the slaves' own nature. Until recently, the same was true of how we explained the perceived differences between women and men. Because gender-role constraints were hard to see, we attributed men's and women's behaviour solely to their innate dispositions. The more people assume that human traits are fixed dispositions, the stronger are their stereotypes (Levy, Stroessner, & Dweck, 1998; Williams & Eberhardt, 2008).

Group-serving bias

Thomas Pettigrew (1979, 1980) argued that attribution errors can bias people's explanations of group members' behaviours. We grant members of our own group the benefit of the doubt: "She donated because she has a good heart; he refused because he had to under the circumstances." When explaining acts by members of other groups, we more often assume the worst: "He donated to gain favour; she refused because she's selfish." Hence, as we noted earlier in this chapter, the shove that Whites perceive as mere "horsing around" when done by another White becomes a "violent gesture" when done by a Black (Duncan, 1976).

This group-serving bias (Chapter 2) also means that positive behaviour by out-group members is more often dismissed. It may be seen as a "special case" ("He is certainly bright and hard-working—not at all like other Aboriginals"), as owing to luck or some special advantage ("She probably got admitted just because her med school had to fill its quota for women applicants"), as demanded by the situation ("Under the circumstances, what could the cheap Scot do but pay the whole cheque?"), or as attributable to extra effort ("Jewish students get better grades because they're so compulsive"). Disadvantaged groups exhibit less of the group-serving bias (Fletcher & Ward, 1989; Heine & Lehman, 1997; Jackson, Sullivan, & Hodge, 1993).

The group-serving bias can subtly colour our language. A team of University of Padova (Italy) researchers led by Anne Maass (1995, 1999) found that positive behaviours by another in-group

TABLE 11-1   HOW SELF-ENHANCING SOCIAL IDENTITIES SUPPORT STEREOTYPES

	In-group	Out-group
Attitude	Favouritism	Denigration
Perceptions	Heterogeneity (we differ)	Homogeneity (they're all alike)
Attributions for negative behaviour	To situations	To dispositions

member are often described as general dispositions (for example, "Lucy is helpful"). When performed by an out-group member, the same behaviour is often described as a specific, isolated act ("Maria opened the door for the man with the cane"). With negative behaviour, the specificity reverses: "Joe shoved her" vs. "Juan was aggressive." Maass called this group-serving bias the *linguistic intergroup bias*.

Earlier we noted that blaming the victim can justify the blamer's own superior status (Table 11-1). Blaming occurs as people attribute an out-group's failures to its members' flawed dispositions, noted Miles Hewstone (1990): "They fail because they're stupid; we fail because we didn't try." If women, Blacks, or Jews have been abused, they must somehow have brought it on themselves. When the British made a group of German civilians walk through the Bergen-Belsen concentration camp at the close of the Second World War, one German responded, "What terrible criminals these prisoners must have been to receive such treatment."

▶ SUMMING UP

WHAT IS PREJUDICE?

- Prejudice is a preconceived negative attitude. Stereotypes are beliefs about another group—beliefs which may be accurate, inaccurate, or overgeneralized but which are based on a kernel of truth. Discrimination is unjustified negative behaviour. Racism and sexism may refer to individuals' prejudicial attitudes or discriminatory behaviour, or to oppressive institutional practices (even if not intentionally prejudicial).

- Prejudice exists in subtle and unconscious guises as well as overt, conscious forms. Researchers have devised subtle survey questions and indirect methods for assessing people's attitudes and behaviour to detect unconscious prejudice.

WHAT ARE THE SOCIAL SOURCES OF PREJUDICE?

- A group that enjoys social and economic superiority will often use prejudicial beliefs to justify its privileged position.

- Children are also brought up in ways that foster or reduce prejudice. The family, religious communities, and the broader society can sustain or reduce prejudices.

- Social institutions (government, schools, the media) also support prejudice, sometimes through overt policies and sometimes through unintentional inertia.

WHAT ARE THE MOTIVATIONAL SOURCES OF PREJUDICE?

- Frustration breeds hostility, which people sometimes vent on scapegoats and sometimes express more directly against competing groups.

- People are motivated to view themselves and their groups as superior to other groups. Even trivial group memberships lead people to favour their own group over others. A threat to self-image heightens such in-group favouritism, as does the need to belong.

- The motive to see the world as just can also powerfully shape people's views of others.

- On a more positive note, if people are motivated to avoid prejudice, they can break the prejudice habit.

WHAT ARE THE COGNITIVE SOURCES OF PREJUDICE?

- Clustering people into categories exaggerates the uniformity within a group and the differences between groups.

- A distinctive individual, such as a lone minority person, has a compelling quality that makes us aware of differences that would otherwise go unnoticed. The occurrence of two distinctive events (for example, a minority person committing an unusual crime) helps create an illusory correlation between people and behaviour.

- Attributing others' behaviour to their dispositions can lead to the group-serving bias: assigning out-group members' negative behaviour to their natural character while explaining away their positive behaviours.

CHAPTER TWELVE
Consequences of Prejudice

▶ **CHAPTER OUTLINE**

● WHAT ARE THE CONSEQUENCES OF RACIAL AND GENDER-BASED PREJUDICE?

● CAN PREJUDICE CREATE ITS OWN REALITY?

● HOW DO PEOPLE REACT TO FACING PREJUDICE AND STEREOTYPING?

It was 30 degrees below zero in Saskatoon, January 28, 2000. Darrell Night recalls being picked up by the police outside a friend's apartment after midnight. He admits that he was intoxicated that night, but he tells a chilling story: Police took him to an isolated area on the outskirts of town, opened the car door, and said, "Get the f—out of here, you f—ing Indian." Many were disinclined to believe Night's story, but its credibility was enhanced when the frozen bodies of two other Aboriginal men were found in the same isolated location (*Toronto Sun,* February 20, 2000).

As this example illustrates, prejudicial attitudes can lead to discriminatory behaviours. Although attitudes do not always lead to behaviours, they often do (Chapter 4). Given this relation between attitudes and behaviour, it should come as no surprise that one of the important consequences of prejudice is discrimination. In this chapter, we will review two common and widely studied forms of discrimination—racial discrimination and gender-based discrimination—and their consequences. Then we will look at the many and varied results of stereotyping.

● WHAT ARE THE CONSEQUENCES OF RACIAL AND GENDER-BASED PREJUDICE?

Discrimination is the primary consequence of prejudice, but it can take on many forms, affecting career availability, income levels, and the likelihood of suspicion of criminal activity.

PREJUDICE BASED ON RACE

In the context of the world, every race is a minority. People of European descent, for example, are only one-fifth of the world's population and will be one-eighth within another half-century. Thanks to mobility and migration over the past two centuries, the world's races now intermingle, in relations that are sometimes hostile, sometimes amiable.

To a molecular biologist, skin colour is a trivial human characteristic, one controlled by a minuscule genetic difference. Moreover, nature doesn't cluster races in neatly defined categories. It is people, not nature, who label Barack Obama, the son of a White woman, as "Black."

Africville: A symbol of African identity in Nova Scotia and the fight against racism.

Is racial prejudice disappearing?

Explicit prejudicial attitudes can change very quickly. In 1942, most Americans agreed that "There should be separate sections for Negroes on streetcars and buses" (Hyman & Sheatsley, 1956). Today, the question would seem bizarre, because such blatant prejudice has nearly disappeared. In 1942, fewer than a third of all American Whites (only 1 in 50 in the South) supported school integration; by 1980, support for it was 90 percent. Considering what a thin slice of history is covered by the years since 1942 or even since slavery was practised, the changes are dramatic. In Britain, overt racial prejudice, as expressed in opposition to interracial marriage or having an ethnic minority boss, has similarly plummeted, especially among younger adults (Ford, 2008).

Africville was a small town on the north end of Halifax, Nova Scotia. It was founded in the early 1800s by freed slaves from the U.S. and free Canadians of African descent. In the 1950s and 1960s, Halifax "reclaimed" this land from Africville residents and relocated them in slum housing, transporting their belongings in garbage trucks. Meagre or no compensation was offered. In the twenty-first century, such blatant discrimination is a major embarrassment, and the Halifax Regional Municipality has apologized for its actions (CBC, 2002).

> *Psychologists usually capitalize Black and White to emphasize that these are socially applied race labels, not literal colour labels for persons of African and European ancestry.*

Shall we conclude, then, that racial prejudice is extinct in countries such as the United States, Britain, and Canada? Not if we consider the 7772 perpetrators of reported hate crimes during 2006 in the U.S. or the 762 racially motivated hate crimes reported in Canada in 2009 (Federal Bureau of Investigation [FBI], 2008; Statistics Canada, 2009). Note that the incidence of these crimes in Canada and the U.S. is about proportional—10 times as many people in the U.S. as in Canada and 10 times as many hate crimes.

So, how great is the progress toward racial equality? Majority group members tend to compare the present with the oppressive past and to perceive swift and radical progress. Minority group members tend to compare the present with their ideal world, which has not yet been realized, and to perceive somewhat less progress (Eibach & Ehrlinger, 2006).

Subtle forms of prejudice

The subtle influence of prejudice on discrimination appears to be widespread. A number of experiments have assessed people's behaviour toward Blacks and Whites. As we saw in Chapter 11, Whites are equally helpful to any person in need—except when the person in need is remote (say, a wrong-number caller with an apparent Black accent who needs a message relayed). Likewise, when asked to use electric shocks to "teach" a task, White people have given no more (if anything, less) shock to a Black than to a White person—except when they were angered or when the recipient couldn't retaliate or know who did it (Crosby, Bromley, & Saxe, 1980; Rogers & Prentice-Dunn, 1981).

> *"I cannot totally grasp all that I am. . . . For that darkness is lamentable in which the possibilities in me are hidden from myself."*
> ST. AUGUSTINE, *CONFESSIONS*, A.D. 398

We can also detect bias in behaviour in the results of these studies:

- To test for possible labour market discrimination, M.I.T. researchers sent 5000 resumés out in response to 1300 varied employment ads (Bertrand & Mullainathan, 2003). Applicants randomly assigned White names (Emily, Greg) received one callback for every 10 resumés sent. Those given Black names (Lakisha, Jamal) received one callback for every 15 resumés sent.

- In one analysis of traffic stops, African-Americans and Latinos were four times more likely than Whites to be searched, twice as likely to be arrested, and three times more likely to be handcuffed and to have excessive force used against them (Lichtblau, 2005).

- In 2002, the *Toronto Star* analyzed single possession drug arrests of Black and White Toronto residents, in an article called "Police target black drivers." Over 76 percent of Whites were released at the scene in such arrests, but only 61.8 percent of Blacks; and Blacks were twice as likely to be held for bail.

- In 2005, according to the Ontario Human Rights Commission, racial profiling was common in Ontario. For example, analysis of traffic stops in Kingston, Ontario, in 2005 found that police were 3.7 times as likely to stop a Black driver and 1.4 times as likely to stop Aboriginal-Canadian drivers as White drivers (CBC, 2005).

Another subtle form of prejudice appears as race sensitivity that leads to exaggerated reactions to isolated minority persons—overpraising their accomplishments, overcriticizing their mistakes, and failing to warn Black students, as they would White students, about potential academic difficulty (Crosby & Monin, 2007; Fiske, 1989; Hart & Morry, 1997; Hass et al., 1991). It also appears as patronization; for example, Kent Harber (1998) gave White students at Stanford University a poorly written essay to evaluate. When the students thought the writer was Black, they gave it a higher grade than when they were led to think the author was White; and they rarely offered harsh criticisms to the supposedly Black student. The evaluators, perhaps wanting to avoid the appearance of bias, patronized the Black essayists with lower standards. Such "inflated praise and insufficient criticism" may hinder minority student achievement, Harber noted. In follow-up research, Harber and his colleagues (2010) found that Whites concerned about appearing biased not only rate and comment more favourably on weak essays attributed to Black students, they also recommend less time for skill development. To protect their own self-image as unprejudiced, they bend over backward to give positive and unchallenging feedback.

Discrimination without awareness

In the incidences describe above, discrimination may be subtle, but presumably people have some awareness that they may be treating people of different races differently. The existence of automatic prejudice described in Chapter 11, however, suggests that discrimination that results from prejudice about which people are unaware may lead to discrimination about which they are unaware. People may genuinely believe they are acting in an egalitarian fashion, but their behaviour might well be discriminatory. Let's look at some examples:

- In a Swedish study, a measure of implicit biases against Arab-Muslims predicted the likelihood of 193 corporate employers not interviewing applicants with Muslim names (Rooth, 2007).

- In a medical study of 287 physicians, those exhibiting the most implicit racial bias were the least likely to recommend clot-busting drugs for a Black patient described as complaining of chest pain (Green et al., 2007).

- In a study of 44 Australian drug and alcohol nurses, those displaying the most implicit bias against drug users were also the most likely, when facing job stress, to want a different job (von Hippel, Brener, & von Hippel, 2008).

- Kurt Hugenberg and Galen Bodenhausen (2003) showed university students a movie of faces morphing from angry to happy. Those who had scored as most prejudiced (on an implicit racial attitudes test) perceived anger lingering more in ambiguous Black than White faces (Figure 12–1).

In some situations, automatic, implicit prejudice can have life or death consequences. In separate experiments, Joshua Correll and his co-workers (2002, 2006, 2007) and Anthony Greenwald

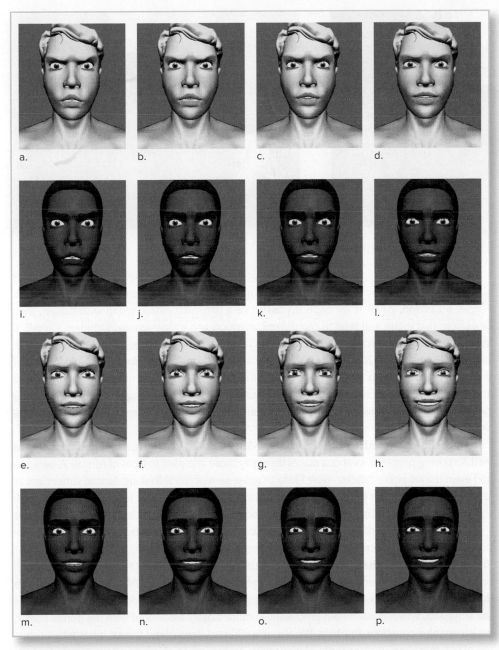

a.   b.   c.   d.

i.   j.   k.   l.

e.   f.   g.   h.

m.   n.   o.   p.

FIGURE 12–1

FACING PREJUDICE.

University students watched a movie of faces morphing from angry to happy. Those who had scored as most prejudiced (on an implicit racial attitudes test) perceived anger lingering longer in ambiguous Black than White faces. (Hugenberg & Bodenhausen, 2003)

and his co-workers (2003) invited people to press buttons quickly to "shoot" or "not shoot" men who suddenly appeared on-screen holding either a gun or a harmless object such as a flashlight or a bottle. The participants (both Blacks and Whites, in one of the studies) more often mistakenly shot harmless targets who were Black. (Follow-up computerized simulations revealed that it's Black *male* suspects—not females, whether Black or White—that are more likely to be associated with threat and to be shot [Plant, Goplen, & Kunstman, 2011].)

Automatic prejudice: When Joshua Correll and his colleagues invited people to react quickly to individuals holding either a gun or a harmless object, race influenced perceptions and reactions.

In the aftermath of London police shooting dead a man who *looked* Muslim, researchers also found Australians more ready to shoot someone wearing Muslim headgear (Unkelbach, Forgas, & Denson, 2008). If we implicitly associate a particular ethnic group with danger, then faces from that group will tend to capture our attention and trigger arousal (Donders, Correll, & Wittenbrink, 2008; Dotsch & Wigboldus, 2008; Trawalter et al., 2008). In a related series of studies, Keith Payne (2001, 2006) and Charles Judd and colleagues (2004) found that when primed with a Black rather than a White face, people think guns: They more quickly recognize a gun and they more often mistake a tool, such as a wrench, for a gun. Even when race does not bias perception, it may bias reaction—as people require more or less evidence before firing (Klauer & Voss, 2008).

Jennifer Eberhardt and her colleagues (2004) demonstrated that the reverse effect can occur as well. Exposing people to weapons makes them pay more attention to faces of African-Americans and even makes police officers more likely to judge stereotypical-looking African-Americans as criminals. These studies help explain why Amadou Diallo, a Guinean immigrant in New York City, was shot 41 times by police officers for removing his wallet from his pocket (Cooper, 1999).

It also appears that different brain regions are involved in automatic and consciously controlled stereotyping (Correll et al., 2006; Cunningham, Raye, & Johnson, 2004; Eberhardt, 2005). Pictures of out-groups that elicit the most disgust (such as drug addicts and the homeless) elicit brain activity in areas associated with disgust and avoidance (Harris & Fiske, 2006). This suggests that automatic prejudices involve primitive regions of the brain associated with fear, such as the amygdala, whereas controlled processing is more closely associated with the frontal cortex, which enables conscious thinking. We also use different parts of our frontal lobes when thinking about ourselves or groups we identify with, versus when thinking about people that we perceive as dissimilar to us (Jenkins, Macrae, & Mitchell, 2008; Mitchell, McCrae, & Banaji, 2006).

Even the social scientists who study prejudice seem vulnerable to automatic prejudice, noted Anthony Greenwald and Eric Schuh (1994). They analyzed biases in authors' citations of social science articles by people with selected non-Jewish names (Erickson, McBride, etc.) and Jewish names (Goldstein, Siegel, etc.). Their analysis of nearly 30 000 citations, including 17 000 citations of prejudice research, found something remarkable: Compared with Jewish authors, non-Jewish authors had 40 percent higher odds of citing non-Jewish names. (Greenwald and

Schuh could not determine whether Jewish authors were overciting their Jewish colleagues or whether non-Jewish authors were overciting their non-Jewish colleagues, or both.)

PREJUDICE BASED ON GENDER

How pervasive is prejudice against women? In Chapter 4, we examined gender-role norms—people's ideas about how women and men ought to behave. Here we consider gender stereotypes—people's beliefs about how women and men do behave. Norms are prescriptive; stereotypes are descriptive.

Gender stereotypes

Culture, as we noted earlier, is what's shared by a large group and transmitted across generations—ideas, attitudes, behaviours, and traditions. We can see the shaping power of culture in ideas about how men and women should behave—and in the scorn that they endure when violating expectations (Kite, 2001). In countries everywhere, girls spend more time helping with housework and child care, while boys spend more time in unsupervised play (Edwards, 1991). Even in contemporary, dual-career, North American marriages, men do most of the household repairs and women arrange the child care (Bianchi et al., 2000; Biernat & Wortman, 1991).

As we noted in Chapter 4, gender socialization, it has been said, gives girls "roots" and boys "wings." A study of children's books showed that even in Caldecott Award–winning books, girls were pictured using household objects (such as broom, sewing needle, or pots and pans) four times more often than boys, and boys were pictured five times more often than girls using production objects (such as pitchfork, plough, or gun) (Crabb & Bielawski, 1994). The adult result: According to a United Nations report (1991), "Everywhere," women do most household work. And "everywhere, cooking and dishwashing are the least shared household chores."

In the last half-century—a thin slice of our long history—gender roles have begun to change. In 1938, one in five approved "of a married woman earning money in business or industry if she has a husband capable of supporting her." By 1980, the percentage of women in the full-time workforce had steadily increased to 32 percent, and by 1997, to 39 percent (Statistics Canada, 1997). A similar influx of women in the workforce has occurred in Australia, Great Britain, and the U.S. Since 1975, increasing numbers of women have been training to become lawyers, doctors, and engineers—though gains in engineering have been modest.

On paper-and-pencil questionnaires, however, Janet Swim and her co-researchers (1995, 1997) have found a subtle ("modern") sexism that parallels subtle ("modern") racism. Both forms appear in denials of discrimination and in antagonism toward efforts to promote equality (as in agreeing with a statement such as "Women are getting too demanding in their push for equal rights").

We can also detect gender-based discrimination in other ways. One research team led by Ian Ayres (1991) visited 90 Chicago-area car dealers, using a uniform strategy to negotiate the lowest price on a new car that cost the dealer about $11 000. White males were given a final price that averaged $11 362, White females were given an average price of $11 504, the average price for Black males was $11 783, and for Black females, it was $12 237—almost 8 percent higher than the average for White males.

> *Canadian husbands do 67 percent of the maintenance and repairs around the home, but only 27 percent of the meal preparation and cleanup, and only 23 percent of the housecleaning.*
> STATISTICS CANADA, 1998

Do you ever present one self to members of your own sex and a different self to members of the other sex?

From research on stereotypes, two conclusions are indisputable: Strong gender stereotypes exist; and, as often happens, members of the stereotyped group accept the stereotypes (W. Wood et al., 2005). Men and women agree that you *can* judge the book by its sexual cover. In one survey, Mary Jackman and Mary Senter (1981) found that gender stereotypes were much stronger than racial stereotypes. For example, only 22 percent of men thought the two sexes equally "emotional." Of the remaining 78 percent, those who believed females were more emotional outnumbered those who thought males were by 15 to 1. And what did the women believe? To within 1 percentage point, their responses were identical.

Remember that stereotypes are generalizations about a group of people, and may be true, false, or overgeneralized from a kernel of truth (Chapter 11). The average man and woman do differ somewhat in social connectedness, empathy, social power, aggressiveness, and sexual initiative (though not in intelligence). Do we then conclude that gender stereotypes are accurate? Sometimes, stereotypes exaggerate differences. But not always, observed Janet Swim (1994). She found that Pennsylvania State University students' stereotypes of men's and women's restlessness, nonverbal sensitivity, aggressiveness, and so forth were reasonable approximations of actual gender differences. Moreover, such stereotypes have persisted across time and culture. Averaging data from 27 countries, John Williams and his colleagues (Williams, Satterwhite, & Best, 1999, 2000) found that folks everywhere perceive women as more agreeable, men as more outgoing. The persistence and omnipresence of gender stereotypes leads some evolutionary psychologists to believe they reflect innate, stable reality (Lueptow, Garovich, & Lueptow, 1995).

"All the pursuits of men are the pursuits of women also, and in all of them a woman is only a lesser man."
PLATO, *REPUBLIC*, 360 B.C.

Stereotypes (which are beliefs) are not prejudices (which are attitudes). Stereotypes may support prejudice, but they don't necessarily do so. One might believe, without prejudice, that men and women are "different yet equal." Let us, therefore, see how researchers probe for gender prejudice.

Gender-based discrimination: Benevolent and hostile

Judging from what people tell survey researchers, attitudes toward women have changed as rapidly as racial attitudes. Alice Eagly and her associates (1991) and Geoffrey Haddock and Mark Zanna (1994) also report that people don't respond to women with gut-level negative emotions as they do to certain other groups; in fact, most people like women more than men. They perceive women as more understanding, kind, and helpful. A *favourable* stereotype, which Eagly (1994) dubs the *women-are-wonderful effect,* results in a favourable attitude.

But gender attitudes often are ambivalent, report Peter Glick, Susan Fiske, and their colleagues (1996, 2007) from their surveys of 15 000 people in 19 nations. They frequently mix a *benevolent sexism* ("Women have a superior moral sensibility") with a *hostile sexism* ("Once a man commits, she puts him on a tight leash").

Stereotypes about men also come in contrasting pairs. Glick and his colleagues (Glick & Fiske, 2007; Glick et al., 2004) report ambivalent sexism toward men—with *benevolent* attitudes of men as powerful and *hostile* attitudes that characterized men as immoral. People who endorse benevolent sexism toward women also tend to endorse benevolent sexism toward men. These complementary ambivalent sexist views of men and women may serve to justify the status quo in gender relations (Jost & Kay, 2005; Lau, Kay, & Spencer, 2008).

Gender-based discrimination: Good news?

Being male isn't all roses. Compared to women, men are three times more likely to commit suicide and be murdered. They are nearly all the battlefield and death row casualties. They die five years sooner. And males represent the majority with mental retardation or autism, as well as students in special education programs (Baumeister, 2007; S. Pinker, 2008).

One heavily publicized finding of discrimination against women came from a 1968 study in which Philip Goldberg gave women several short articles and asked them to judge the value of each. Sometimes, a given article was attributed to a male author (for example, John T. McKay), and sometimes to a female author (for example, Joan T. McKay). In general, the articles received lower ratings when attributed to a female. The historic mark of oppression—self-deprecation—surfaced clearly: Women were discriminating against women.

But there is good news for those who are upset by such findings. Eager to demonstrate the subtle reality of gender discrimination, David Myers obtained Goldberg's materials in 1980 and repeated the experiment with his own students. They (women and men) showed no such tendency to deprecate women's work. So Janet Swim, Eugene Borgida, Geoffrey Maruyama, and David Myers (1989) searched the literature and corresponded with investigators to learn all they could about studies of gender bias in the evaluation of men's and women's work. To their surprise, the biases that occasionally surfaced were as often against men as against women. But the most common result across 104 studies involving almost 20 000 people was *no difference*. On most comparisons, judgments of someone's work were unaffected by whether the work was attributed to a female or a male. Summarizing other studies of people's evaluations of women and men as leaders, professors, and so forth, Alice Eagly (1994) concluded, "Experiments have *not* demonstrated any *overall* tendency to devalue women's work."

Is gender bias fast becoming extinct in Western countries? Has the women's movement nearly completed its work? (See Figure 12–2.) As with racial prejudice, blatant

Question: *"Misogyny" is the hatred of women. What is the corresponding word for the hatred of men?* **Answer:** *In most dictionaries, no such word exists.*

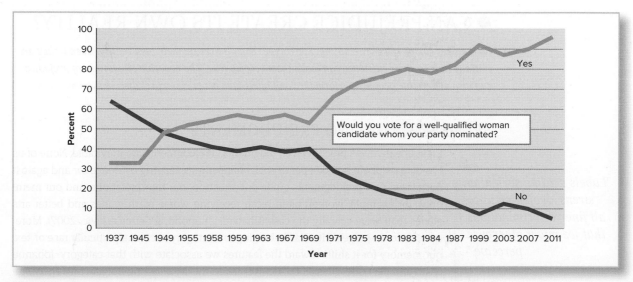

FIGURE 12–2 CHANGING GENDER ATTITUDES FROM 1937 TO 2011.

Data from Gallup Polls (www.gallup.com/poll/4729/presidency.aspx)

gender prejudice is dying, but subtle bias lives. Violate gender stereotypes, and people may react. People take notice of a cigar-smoking woman and a tearful man, and denigrate them (Phelan & Rudman, 2010).

In the world beyond democratic Western countries, gender discrimination looms even larger.

- Two-thirds of the world's un-schooled children are girls (United Nations, 1991).

- In some countries, discrimination extends to violence, even to being prosecuted for adultery after being raped or to being doused with kerosene and set ablaze by dissatisfied husbands (UN, 2006).

- In Saudi Arabia, women are forbidden to drive (Beyer, 1990).

- Around the world, people tend to prefer having baby boys. In the United States in 1941, 38 percent of expectant parents said they preferred a boy if they could have only one child, 24 percent preferred a girl, and 23 percent said they didn't care. In 2003, the answers were virtually unchanged with 38 percent still preferring a boy (Lyons, 2003; Simmons, 2000). With the widespread use of ultrasound to determine the sex of a fetus and the growing availability of abortion, these preferences are affecting the number of boys and girls. The 2000 China census revealed 119 newborn boys for every 100 girls (Walfish, 2001). The 2001 India census reported that Punjab province had 126 newborn boys for every 100 girls (Dugger, 2001). The net result is tens of millions of "missing women."

To conclude, overt prejudice against people of colour and against women is far less common today than it was in the mid-twentieth century. Nevertheless, techniques that are sensitive to subtle prejudice still detect widespread bias. And in parts of the world, gender prejudice makes for misery.

● CAN PREJUDICE CREATE ITS OWN REALITY?

Stereotypes can be self-perpetuating. Stereotypes can also create their own reality. Even if they are initially untrue, their existence can make them become true. The negative allegations of prejudice can also undermine people's performance and affect how people interpret discrimination.

SELF-PERPETUATING PREJUDGMENTS

"Labels act like shrieking sirens, deafening us to all finer discriminations that we might otherwise perceive."
GORDON ALLPORT, *THE NATURE OF PREJUDICE,* 1954

Prejudice involves preconceived judgments.. Prejudgments are inevitable: None of us is a dispassionate bookkeeper of social happenings, tallying evidence for and against our biases. Our prejudgments guide our attention, our interpretations, and our memories; for example, women often recall receiving worse math grades and better arts grades than were actually the case (Chatard, Guimond, & Selimbegovic, 2007). Moreover, once we judge an item as belonging to a category such as a particular race or sex, our memory for it shifts toward the features we associate with that category. Johanne Huart and her colleagues (2005) demonstrated this by showing Belgian university students a computer-generated face that was a blend of 70 percent of the features of the typical male and 30 percent female (or vice versa). Later, those shown the 70 percent of the features of a typical male recalled seeing a male (as you might expect), but also misrecalled the face as being more typically male than it actually was.

Prejudgments are self-perpetuating. Whenever a member of a group behaves as expected, we duly note the fact; our prior belief is confirmed. When a member of a group behaves inconsistently with our expectation, we may explain away the behaviour as due to special circumstances (Crocker, Hannah, & Weber, 1983). The contrast to a stereotype can also make someone seem exceptional. Telling someone that "Maria played hockey" and others that "Mark played hockey" may make Maria seem more athletic than Mark (Biernat, 2003). Stereotypes can, therefore, influence how we construe someone's behaviour (Kunda & Sherman-Williams, 1993; Sanbonmatsu, Akimoto, & Gibson, 1994; Stangor & McMillan, 1992). Prime White folks with negative

When people violate our stereotypes, we salvage the stereotype by splitting off a new subgroup stereotype, such as "senior athletes."

media images of Black folks, and the activated stereotype may be poisonous. In one experiment, such images produced reduced empathy for other Black people in need (Johnson, Bushman, & Dovidio, 2008).

Perhaps you, too, can recall a time when, try as you might, you could not overcome someone's opinion of you, a time when no matter what you did you were misinterpreted. Misinterpretations are likely when someone expects an unpleasant encounter with you (Wilder & Shapiro, 1989). William Ickes and his colleagues (1982) demonstrated this in an experiment with pairs of university-age men. Upon arrival, the experimenters falsely forewarned one member of each pair that the other subject was "one of the unfriendliest people I've talked to lately." The two were then introduced and left alone together for five minutes. Students in another condition were led to think the other subject was exceptionally friendly.

Those in both conditions were friendly to the new acquaintance. In fact, those who expected him to be unfriendly went out of their way to be friendly, and their smiles and other friendly behaviours elicited a warm response. But unlike the positively biased students, those expecting an unfriendly person attributed this reciprocal friendliness to their own "kid-gloves" treatment of him. Afterwards, they expressed more mistrust and dislike for the person and rated his behaviour as less friendly. Despite their partner's actual friendliness, the negative bias induced these students to "see" hostility lurking beneath his "forced smiles." They would never have seen it if they hadn't first believed it.

We do notice information that is strikingly inconsistent with a stereotype, but even this information has less impact than might be expected. When we focus on an atypical example, we can salvage the stereotype by splitting off a new category (Brewer, 1988; Hewstone, 1994; Kunda & Oleson, 1995, 1997). For instance, the positive image that British schoolchildren formed of their friendly school police officers (whom they perceived as a special category) didn't improve their image of police officers in general (Hewstone, Hopkins, & Routh, 1992). This **subtyping**—putting people who deviate into a different class of people—helps maintain the stereotype that police officers are unfriendly and dangerous (Figure 12–3). A different way to accommodate the inconsistent information is to recognize that the stereotype does not apply for everyone in the category. White homeowners, who may have harboured prejudices related to Blacks but

subtyping
accommodating groups of individuals who deviate from one's stereotype by thinking of them as a special category of people with different properties

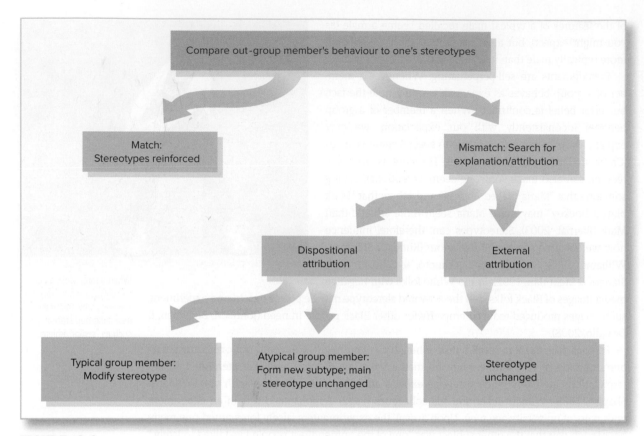

FIGURE 12–3

ATTRIBUTION AND STEREOTYPE CHANGE.

When someone's behaviour doesn't fit our stereotype, we can change the stereotype, split off a subtype, or attribute the behaviour to the peculiar situation. (Based on Wilder, Simon, & Faith, 1996)

subgrouping
accommodating groups of individuals who deviate from one's stereotype by forming a new stereotype about this subset of the group

who now enjoy their Black neighbours, can form a new and different stereotype of "professional, middle-class Blacks." This subgrouping—forming a subgroup stereotype—tends to lead to modest change in the stereotype as the stereotype becomes more differentiated (Richards & Hewstone, 2001). Subtypes are exceptions to the group; subgroups are acknowledged as a part of the overall group.

IMPACT OF DISCRIMINATION: THE SELF-FULFILLING PROPHECY

Attitudes may coincide with the social hierarchy not only as a rationalization for it but also because discrimination affects its victims. "One's reputation," wrote Gordon Allport, "cannot be hammered, hammered, hammered into one's head without doing something to one's character" (1958, p. 139). If we could snap our fingers and end all discrimination, it would be naive then to say, "The tough times are all over, folks! You can now put on suits or dresses and be attaché-carrying executives and professionals." When the oppression ends, its effects linger, like a societal hangover.

In *The Nature of Prejudice*, Allport catalogued 15 possible effects of victimization. Allport believed these reactions were reducible to two basic types—those that involve blaming yourself (withdrawal, self-hate, aggression against your own group) and those that involve blaming external causes (fighting back, suspiciousness, increased group pride). If the net results are negative—say, higher rates of crime—people can use them to justify the discrimination that helps maintain them: "If we let those people in our nice neighbourhood, property values will plummet."

Does discrimination affect its victims in this way? We must be careful not to overstate the point. The soul and style of Black culture is for many a proud heritage, not just a response to victimization (J. M. Jones, 1983). Thus, while White youth are learning to de-emphasize ethnic differences and avoid stereotypes, Black youth "are increasingly taking pride in their ethnicity and positively valuing ethnic differences," reported Charles Judd and his co-researchers (1995).

Nevertheless, social beliefs can be self-confirming, as demonstrated in a clever pair of experiments by Carl Word, Mark Zanna, and Joel Cooper (1974). In the first experiment, Princeton University White men interviewed White and Black research assistants posing as job applicants. When the applicant was Black, the interviewers sat farther away, ended the interview 25 percent sooner, and made 50 percent more speech errors than when the applicant was White. Imagine being interviewed by someone who sat at a distance, stammered, and ended the interview rather quickly. Would it affect your performance or your feelings about the interviewer?

To find out, the researchers conducted a second experiment in which trained interviewers treated students in the same way as the interviewers in the first experiment had treated either the White or Black applicants. When videotapes of the interviews were later rated, those who were treated like the Blacks in the first experiment seemed more nervous and less effective. Moreover, the interviewees could themselves sense a difference; those treated as were the Blacks judged their interviewers to be less adequate and less friendly. The experimenters concluded that part of "the 'problem' of black performance resides . . . within the interaction setting itself." As with other self-fulfilling prophecies (recall Chapter 3), prejudice affects its targets.

> *"It is understandable that the suppressed people should develop an intense hostility towards a culture whose existence they make possible by their work, but in whose wealth they have too small a share."*
> SIGMUND FREUD, *THE FUTURE OF AN ILLUSION*, 1927

Distinctiveness and self-consciousness

One such effect of prejudice is that feeling distinctive leads people to feel self-conscious. When surrounded by Whites, Blacks sometimes detect people reacting to their distinctiveness. Many report being stared or glared at, being subject to insensitive comments, and receiving bad service (Swim, Cohen, & Hyers, 1998). Sometimes, we misperceive others as reacting to our distinctiveness. At Dartmouth College, researchers Robert Kleck and Angelo Strenta (1980) discovered this when they led college women to feel disfigured. The women thought the purpose of the experiment was to assess how someone would react to a facial scar created with theatrical makeup; the scar was on the right cheek, running from the ear to the mouth. Actually, the purpose was to see how the women themselves, when made to feel deviant, would perceive others' behaviour toward them. After applying the makeup, the experimenter gave each woman a small hand mirror so that she could see the authentic-looking scar. When she put the mirror down, the experimenter then applied some "moisturizer" to "keep the makeup from cracking." What the "moisturizer" really did was remove the scar.

The scene that followed was poignant. A young woman, feeling terribly self-conscious about her supposedly disfigured face, talked with another woman who saw no such disfigurement and knew nothing of what had gone on before. If you have ever felt similarly self-conscious—perhaps about a physical handicap, acne, even just a bad hair day—then perhaps you can empathize with the self-conscious woman. Compared with women who were led to believe their conversational partners merely thought they had an allergy, the "disfigured" women became acutely sensitive to how their partners were looking at them. They rated their partners as more tense, distant, and patronizing. In fact, observers who later analyzed videotapes of how the partners treated "disfigured" persons could find no such differences in treatment. Self-conscious about being different, the "disfigured" women misinterpreted mannerisms and comments they would otherwise not have noticed.

Self-conscious interactions between a majority and a minority person can, therefore, feel tense even when both are well-intentioned (Devine, Evett, & Vasquez-Suson, 1996). Tom, who is known to be gay, meets Bill, who is straight. Tolerant Bill wants to respond without prejudice. But feeling unsure of himself, he holds back a bit. Tom, expecting negative attitudes from most people, misreads Bill's hesitancy as hostility and responds with a seeming chip on his shoulder.

> "If we foresee evil in our fellow man, we tend to provoke it; if good, we elicit it."
>
> GORDON ALLPORT, *THE NATURE OF PREJUDICE*, 1958

Anyone can experience this phenomenon. Majority group members (Manitoba White people in one study) often have beliefs—"meta-stereotypes"—about how minorities stereotype them (Vorauer, Main, & O'Connell, 1998). Even relatively unprejudiced Canadian Whites, Israeli Jews, or American Christians may sense that out-group minorities stereotype them as prejudiced, arrogant, or patronizing. If George worries that Gamal perceives him as "your typical educated racist," he may be on guard when talking with Gamal.

Stigma consciousness

People vary in *stigma consciousness*—in how likely they are to expect that others will stereotype them. Gays and lesbians, for example, differ in how much they suppose others "interpret all my behaviours" in terms of their sexual orientation (Pinel, 1999). Seeing oneself as a victim of pervasive prejudice has its ups and downs (Branscombe, Schmitt, & Harvey, 1999; Dion, 1998). The downside is that those who perceive themselves as frequent victims live with the stress of stereotype threats and presumed antagonism and, therefore, experience lower well-being. While living in Europe, stigma-conscious Americans—people who perceive Europeans as resenting Americans—live more fretfully than those who feel accepted.

The upside is that perceptions of prejudice buffer individual self-esteem. If someone is nasty, "Well, it's not directed at me personally." Moreover, perceived prejudice and discrimination enhance our feelings of social identity and prepare us to work together to overcome discrimination.

STEREOTYPE THREAT

Feeling self-conscious about being stereotyped can siphon off our mental energy and attention; the result can be diminished mental and physical stamina (Inzlicht, McKay, & Aronson, 2006). For example, one of the authors is a short man in his late 50s. When he joins a pick-up basketball game with bigger, younger players, he often suspects that they expect him to be a detriment to their team and that tends to undermine his confidence and performance. Claude Steele and his colleagues called this phenomenon **stereotype threat**—a self-confirming apprehension that one will be evaluated based on a negative stereotype (Steele, 2010; Steele, Spencer, & Aronson, 2002). Unlike self-fulfilling prophecies that gradually hammer one's reputation into one's self-concept, stereotype threat situations have immediate effects even if they aren't incorporated into the self-concept.

In several experiments, Steven Spencer, Claude Steele, and Diane Quinn (1999) gave a very difficult math test to men and women students who had similar math backgrounds. When told

stereotype threat
a disruptive concern, when facing a negative stereotype, that one will be evaluated based on a negative stereotype

that there were *no* gender differences on the test and no evaluation of any group stereotype, the women's performance consistently equalled the men's. Told that there *was* a gender difference, the women dramatically confirmed the stereotype (Figure 12–4). Frustrated by the extremely difficult items, they apparently felt added apprehension, which undermined their performances. For female engineering students, interacting with a sexist man likewise undermines test performance (Logel et al., 2009a). Even before exams, stereotype threat can also hamper women's learning math rules and operations (Rydell, Rydell, & Boucher, 2010).

The media can provoke stereotype threat. Paul Davies and his colleagues (2002) had women and men watch a series of commercials expecting that they would be tested for their memory of details. For half the participants, the commercials contained only neutral stimuli; for the other half, some of the commercials contained images of "air-headed" women. After seeing the stereotypic images, women not only performed worse than men on a math test, they also reported less interest in obtaining a math or science major or entering a math or science career.

> *"Math class is tough!"*
> "TEEN TALK" BARBIE (LATER REMOVED FROM THE MARKET)

Might racial stereotypes be similarly self-fulfilling? Claude Steele and Joshua Aronson (1995) confirmed that they are when giving difficult verbal abilities tests to Whites and Blacks. Blacks underperformed Whites only when taking the tests under conditions high in stereotype threat. Jeff Stone and his colleagues (1999) reported that stereotype threat affects athletic performance, too. Blacks did worse than usual when a golf task was framed as a test of "sports intelligence," and Whites did worse when it was a test of "natural athletic ability." "When people are reminded of a negative stereotype about themselves—'White men can't jump' or 'Black men can't think'—it can adversely affect performance," Stone (2000) surmised.

If you tell students they are at risk of failure (as is often suggested by minority support programs in the U.S.), the stereotype may erode their performance, suggested Steele (1997); it may cause them to "disidentify" with school and seek self-esteem elsewhere (Figure 12–5). Indeed, studies have shown that, as Black students move from grade 8 to grade 10, there is a weakening connection between their school performance and self-esteem (Osborne, 1995). Moreover, students led to think they have benefited from gender- or race-based preferences in

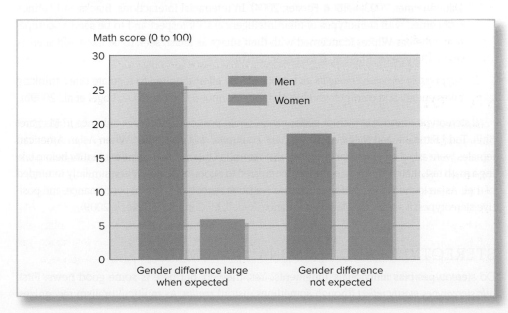

FIGURE 12–4

STEREOTYPE THREAT AND WOMEN'S MATH PERFORMANCE.

Experiments confirmed the effects of stereotype threat on women's math scores (Spencer, Steele, & Quinn, 1999).

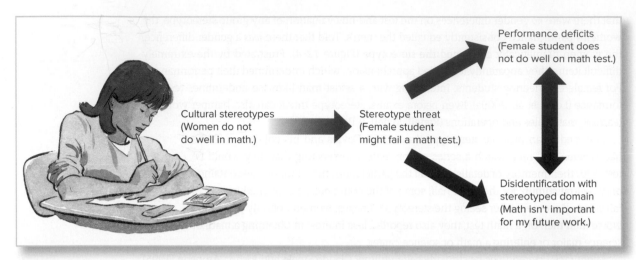

FIGURE 12–5

EFFECTS OF
STEREOTYPE
THREAT.

Threat from facing a
negative stereotype
can produce
performance deficits
and disidentification.

gaining admission to a college or an academic group tend to underperform those who are led to feel competent (R. P. Brown et al., 2000). Better, therefore, to challenge students to believe in their potential, observed Steele. In another of his research team's experiments, Black students responded well to criticism of their writing when also told, "I wouldn't go to the trouble of giving you this feedback if I didn't think, based on what I've read in your letter, that you are capable of meeting the higher standard that I mentioned" (Cohen, Steele, & Ross, 1999).

How does stereotype threat undermine performance? It does so in three ways, contend Toni Schmader, Michael Johns, and Chad Forbes (2008):

1. *Stress.* fMRI brain scans suggest that the stress of stereotype threat impairs brain activity associated with mathematical processing and increases activity in areas associated with emotion processing (Derks, Inzlicht, & Kang, 2008; Krendl et al., 2008; Wraga et al., 2007).

2. *Self-monitoring.* Worrying about making mistakes disrupts focused attention (Keller & Dauenheimer, 2003; Seibt & Forster, 2004). In interracial interactions, Blacks and Latinos (concerned with stereotypes of their intelligence) seek respect and to be seen as competent, whereas Whites (concerned with their image as racist) seek to be liked and seen as moral (Bergsieker, Shelton, & Richeson, 2010).

3. *Suppressing unwanted thoughts and emotions.* The effort required to regulate one's thinking takes energy and disrupts working memory (Bonnot & Croizet, 2007; Logel et al., 2009b).

If stereotype threats can disrupt performance, could positive stereotypes enhance it? Margaret Shih, Todd Pittinsky, and Nalini Ambady (1999) confirmed this possibility. When Asian-American females were asked biographical questions that reminded them of their gender identity before taking a math test, their performance plunged (compared to a control group). When similarly reminded of their Asian identity, their performance rose. Negative stereotypes disrupt performance, and positive stereotypes, it seems, facilitate performance (Rydell, McConnell, & Beilock, 2009).

STEREOTYPES AND PERSONAL JUDGMENT

Do stereotypes bias individuals' judgments? Yes, they do; but here is some good news: First, *our stereotypes mostly reflect* (though sometimes distort) *reality.* As multiculturalism recognizes, people differ—and can perceive and appreciate those differences. "Stereotype accuracy is one of the largest effects in all of social psychology," argues Lee Jussim (2012). Second, *people often evaluate individuals more positively than the groups they compose* (Miller & Felicio, 1990). Anne Locksley, Eugene Borgida, and Nancy Brekke have found that once someone knows a person, "Stereotypes may have minimal, if any, impact on judgments about that person" (Borgida, Locksley, & Brekke, 1981; Locksley et al., 1980; Locksley, Hepburn, & Ortiz, 1982). They discovered this by giving university students anecdotal information about recent incidents in the life of "Nancy." In a supposed transcript of a telephone conversation, Nancy told a friend how she responded to three different situations (for example, being harassed by a seedy character while shopping). Some of the students read transcripts portraying Nancy responding assertively (telling the seedy character to leave); others read a report of passive responses (simply ignoring the character until he finally drifts away). Still other students received the same information, except that the person was named "Paul" instead of Nancy. A day later, the students predicted how Nancy (or Paul) would respond to other situations.

Did knowing the person's sex have any effect on these predictions? None at all. Expectations of the person's assertiveness were influenced solely by what the students had learned about that individual the day before. Even their judgments of masculinity and femininity were unaffected by knowing the person's sex. Gender stereotypes had been left on the shelf; the students evaluated Nancy and Paul as individuals.

An important principle discussed in Chapter 3 explains that finding. Given (1) general (base-rate) information about a group and (2) trivial but vivid information about a particular group

---

During a committee meeting on campus diversity at the University of Michigan in the late 1980s, I noticed an interesting fact: At every level of entering SAT score, minority students were getting lower college grades than their non-minority counterparts. Soon, Steven Spencer, Joshua Aronson, and I found that this was a national phenomenon; it happened at most colleges and it happened to other groups whose abilities were negatively stereotyped, such as women in advanced math classes. This underperformance wasn't caused by group differences in preparation. It happened at all levels of preparation (as measured by SATs).

Eventually, we produced this underperformance in the laboratory by simply having motivated people perform a difficult task in a domain where their group was negatively stereotyped. We also found that we could eliminate this underperformance by making the same task irrelevant to the stereotype, by removing the "stereotype threat," as we had come

to call it. This latter finding spawned more research: figuring out how to reduce stereotype threat and its ill effects. Through this work, we have gained an appreciation for two big things: first, the importance of life context in shaping psychological functioning, and second, the importance of social identities like age, race, and gender in shaping that context.

Claude Steele, *Stanford University*

member, the vivid information usually overwhelms the effect of the general information. This is especially so when the person doesn't fit our image of the typical group member (Fein & Hilton, 1992; Lord et al., 1991). For example, imagine yourself being told how most people in an experiment actually behaved and then viewing a brief interview with one of the supposed subjects. Would you react like the typical viewer—by guessing the person's behaviour from the interview, ignoring the base-rate information on how most people actually behaved?

People often believe such stereotypes, yet ignore them when given vivid, anecdotal information. Thus, many people believe "politicians are crooks" but "our MP Mr. Jones has integrity." (No wonder people have such a low opinion of politicians yet usually re-elect their own representatives.) These findings resolve a puzzling set of findings considered early in this chapter. We know that gender stereotypes (1) are strong, yet (2) have little effect on people's judgments of work attributed to a man or a woman. Now we see why. People may have strong gender stereotypes yet ignore them when judging a particular individual.

Impact of strong stereotypes

However, stereotypes, when *strong*, do colour our judgments of individuals (Krueger & Rothbart, 1988). When Thomas Nelson, Monica Biernat, and Melvin Manis (1990) had students estimate the heights of individually pictured men and women, they judged the individual men as taller—even when their heights were equal, even when they were told that in this sample sex didn't predict height, and even when they were offered cash rewards for accuracy.

In a follow-up study, Nelson, Michele Acker, and Manis (1996) showed university students photos of other students from the university's engineering and nursing schools, along with descriptions of each student's interests. Even when informed that the sample contained an equal number of males and females from each school, a description was judged more likely to come from a nursing student when attached to a female face. Thus, even when a strong gender stereotype is known to be irrelevant, it has an irresistible force.

Bias in interpretations and memories

Stereotypes also colour how we interpret events, noted David Dunning and David Sherman (1997). If told, "some felt the politician's statements were untrue," people will infer the politician was lying. If told, "some felt the physicist's statements were untrue," they infer only that the physicist was mistaken. When told two people had an altercation, people perceive it as a fist fight if told it involved two lumberjacks, but as a verbal spat if told it involved two marriage counsellors. A person concerned about her physical condition seems vain if she is a model but health-conscious if a triathlete. Indeed, subjects will often later "recognize" false descriptions of an event that fit their stereotype-influenced interpretations. Just as a prison guides and constrains its inmates, concluded Dunning and Sherman, the "cognitive prison" of our stereotypes guides and constrains our impressions.

Sometimes we make judgments, or begin interacting with someone, with little to go on but our stereotype. In such cases, stereotypes can strongly bias our interpretations and memories of that person. For example, Charles Bond and his colleagues (1988) found that, after getting to know their patients, White psychiatric nurses equally often put Black and White patients in physical restraints. But they restrained incoming Black patients more often than their White counterparts. With little else to go on, stereotypes mattered.

Such bias can also operate more subtly. In an experiment by John Darley and Paget Gross (1983), students viewed a videotape of a grade 4 girl, Hannah. The tape depicted her either in a depressed urban neighbourhood, supposedly the child of lower-class parents, or in an affluent suburban setting, the child of professional parents. Asked to guess Hannah's ability level in various subjects, both groups of viewers refused to use Hannah's class background to prejudge her ability level; each group rated her ability level at her grade level.

Other students also viewed a second videotape, showing Hannah taking an oral achievement test in which she got some questions right and some wrong. Those who had previously been introduced to upper-class Hannah judged her answers as showing high ability and later recalled her getting most questions right; those who had met lower-class Hannah judged her ability as below grade level and recalled her missing almost half the questions. But remember: The second videotape was identical for both groups. So we see that when stereotypes are strong and the information about someone is ambiguous (unlike the cases of Nancy and Paul), stereotypes can subtly bias our judgments of individuals.

Finally, we evaluate people more extremely when their behaviour violates our stereotypes (Bettencourt & Dorr, 1997). A woman who rebukes someone cutting in front of her in a movie line ("Shouldn't you go to the end of the line?") may seem more assertive than a man who reacts similarly (Manis, Nelson, & Shedler, 1988). Do such processes affect your ratings of your professors? A series of studies by University of Winnipeg professor Lisa Sinclair and University of Waterloo professor Ziva Kunda suggests that they might very well be. They analyzed students' evaluations of their professors and found that when students get good grades they tend to like their professors; this is true whether their professors are men or women. When students get bad grades, however, they are especially harsh on female professors. (Kunda & Sinclair, 1999; Sinclair & Kunda, 1999, 2000)

Kunda and Sinclair have found similar findings in a series of laboratory studies. After completing a test of leadership ability while being watched by a "manager" in an adjacent room, for example, participants were praised or criticized on their performance by the manager. When

THE >>> INSIDE STORY

Ziva Kunda had long been interested in how people's motives and desires coloured their judgment. Her earlier work suggested that people attempted to be rational, and drew their desired conclusions only if they could justify them. However, they often did not realize that their justifications could be biased by their motives—when constructing justifications, people search selectively for those beliefs that lend support to their desired conclusion. If they could successfully recruit such beliefs, they could draw their desired conclusion, not realizing that they may also possess other beliefs that argue against it. It occurred to Kunda and Lisa Sinclair that a negative group stereotype may sometimes provide a handy justification for disparaging a group member whom one is otherwise motivated to discredit. People may be motivated to discredit anyone who has criticized them, but may be better able to justify disparaging a woman or a member of a visible minority than disparaging a White man. As a result, people may view a woman or a Black man who criticizes them more negatively than they view a White man who delivers the same criticism.

Ziva Kunda, *University of Waterloo*

FIGURE 12–6

HARSHER EVALUATION OF A STEREOTYPED TARGET.

When University of Waterloo students received positive feedback from a "manager," his race did not matter; but when they received negative feedback, they saw a Black manager as less competent than a White manager. (Data from Kunda & Sinclair, 1999)

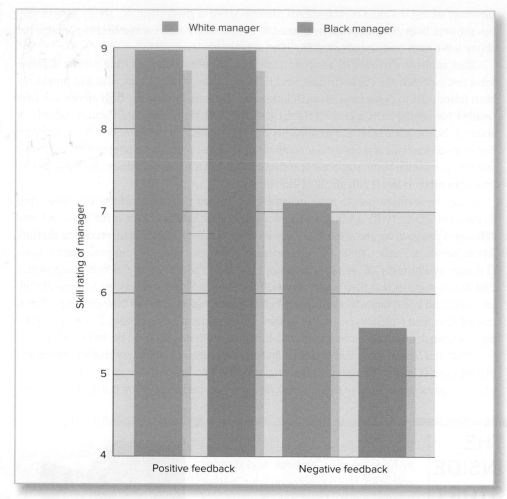

they were praised, the participants liked both the male and the female manager; but when they were criticized, they evaluated the female manager much more negatively. In another study, they found similar results with White and Black male managers (see Figure 12–6).

● HOW DO PEOPLE REACT TO FACING PREJUDICE AND STEREOTYPING?

Over the last 15 years, numerous studies have begun to investigate "the other side of prejudice"— that is, how people cope with prejudiced evaluation by others. Prejudice has consequences. People who experience discrimination know these consequences all too well, but they do not always acknowledge them.

Despite the fact that people are reluctant to acknowledge experiencing personal discrimination, they understand that there are times when they are being discriminated against; this understanding has costs and benefits. On the one hand, if people come to believe that others will be prejudiced against them, they can lose a sense of control over their environment. In general, the more that people believe they experience discrimination, the more anxious and depressed they are (Branscombe et al., 1999). Believing that you experience pervasive prejudice has a negative impact on the individual.

On the other hand, believing that you experience discrimination can also protect your self-esteem. Crocker and Major (1989) first noted this in reviewing the level of self-esteem of a number of groups in society. You will recall from Chapter 2 that we often form our views of ourselves from how we are viewed by others. Applying this theory to groups that experience prejudice, it seems that these groups would have lower self-esteem; but, in general, they do not. Negatively valued ethnic groups, the physically handicapped, and the facially disfigured all have self-esteem as high as or higher than those who do not face these challenges. What would account for these robust feelings of self-esteem? Crocker and Major argued that one way such groups protect their self-esteem is by attributing the negative evaluations they face in specific situations to prejudice.

The first studies to test these ideas were conducted by Ken Dion and his colleagues at the University of Toronto (Dion, 1975; Dion & Earn, 1975). In one study (Dion, 1975), Dion had women receive either a few or a lot of tickets from confederates who were either male or female. When women received only a few tickets from the male confederates, they attributed the males' actions to prejudice, but they did not do so when the confederates were female. These ground-breaking studies demonstrate that people who face prejudice are vigilant to the possibility that others may discriminate against them.

But do such attributions protect self-esteem? A number of studies by Crocker, Major, and their colleagues suggest that they do (Major, Quinton, & McCoy, 2002). In one study (Crocker et al., 1991), the researchers gave Blacks and Whites positive or negative feedback from a fellow student who either listened to their performance in an adjacent room (and could not see them because blinds separating the rooms were drawn) or listened to and watched their performance with the blinds open. When Blacks were negatively evaluated with the blinds closed, their self-esteem suffered; but when the blinds were open, they appeared to be protected from the negative feedback and their self-esteem was unaffected.

So, do perceptions help or hurt? The answer seems to be that it depends on whether these perceptions are chronic or in response to a specific situation. Those who perceive chronic prejudice in their lives suffer; in response to a specific negative event, however, believing that the event was due to prejudice can protect one's self-esteem.

PERCEPTION OF DISCRIMINATION

Most women know that gender bias exists. They believe that sex discrimination affects most working women, as shown by the lower salaries for women and especially for jobs, such as child care, that are filled mostly by women. Garbage haulers (mostly men) make more than preschool teachers (mostly women). Curiously, however, Faye Crosby and her colleagues (1989) have repeatedly found that most women deny feeling personally discriminated against. Discrimination, they believe, is something *other* women face. Their employers are not villainous. They are doing better than the average woman. Conversely, hearing no complaints, managers—even in discriminatory organizations—can persuade themselves that justice prevails.

Similar denials of personal disadvantage, while perceiving discrimination against one's group, occur among unemployed people, out-of-the-closet lesbians, and Canadian minorities (Dion & Kawakami, 1996; D. M. Taylor et al., 1990). This *personal/group discrimination discrepancy*, as Donald Taylor and his colleagues (1990) labelled the phenomenon, enables individuals to maintain a perception of control over their performance and relationships (see Figure 12–7). (Curiously however, personal/group discrepancy extends to non-discriminatory events. People also see others as more likely than themselves to be affected by, say, an economic recession, rising health costs, and better physical fitness facilities [Moghaddam & Studer, 1997].)

It is not only the concerns of those who have traditionally faced prejudice but also the concerns of those who have not that make social interactions difficult. Jacquie Vorauer from the University of Manitoba and her colleagues (Vorauer et al., 1998, 2000) have examined the concerns that members of dominant groups have about the stereotypes that others have of them—meta-stereotypes (stereotypes about stereotypes). They found that at the University of Manitoba, White students have very clear ideas about the stereotypes that Aboriginal Canadians may have about them. They are concerned that First Nations people may view them as prejudiced, unfair, selfish, arrogant, phony, etc.

In a series of studies, they led White students to believe that they would be interacting with Aboriginal Canadians. The more that students expected to be perceived in terms of the meta-stereotype, the more they anticipated experiencing negative emotions in the interaction. Interestingly, highly prejudiced White students expected to be perceived in terms of the meta-stereotype more than less prejudiced students. These meta-stereotypes were more important in predicting their reaction to the situation than the students' level of prejudice itself.

Vorauer along with Nicole Shelton and Jennifer Richeson (Shelton, Richeson, & Vorauer, 2006) have described how these processes affect inter-ethnic interactions. They found that concerns about being seen in a stereotypic way lead to awkward interactions (Shelton & Richeson, 2006) and decreased executive functioning among White students (Trawalter & Richeson, 2006). Overcoming these obstacles seems to be an essential step in promoting better relationships across groups.

FIGURE 12–7

THE PERSONAL/ GROUP DISCRIMINATION DISCREPANCY.

People report experiencing very little discrimination personally, but they do perceive discrimination against their group. (Based on Taylor et al., 1990)

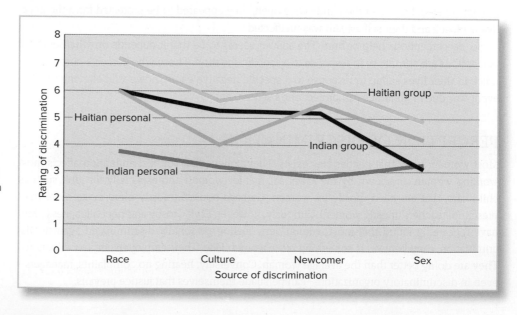

THE >>> INSIDE STORY

We were on a mission to get mainstream social psychology to broaden its individualistic emphasis and recognize intergroup relations as a central topic. Systemic discrimination was a key preoccupation for us and being the "white male" I would often ask female and visible minority students to describe their experiences with discrimination. I began to notice a theme to their responses, which took the form—"Well, I personally have never faced discrimination, but my group is unfairly treated in the following ways."

We were embarking on a large field study involving visible minority immigrants to Canada from all walks of life, and wanted to gauge the extent to which they felt discriminated against. We decided to ask participants to rate, in two separate questions, the extent to which their group, and they personally as a member of their group, had been discriminated against.

The personal/group discrimination discrepancy was born. Respondents consistently rated discrimination directed at their group to be higher than discrimination directed at themselves personally, as a member of that group.

The methodological implications were immediate and obvious. Any attempt to gauge societal prejudice and discrimination would produce very different conclusions depending on the focus of the question, personal or group. A group-based question would portray society as relatively prejudiced, whereas a question about personal discrimination would give the impression that society was relatively free from bigotry.

The bigger challenge, of course, is to explain the personal/group discrimination discrepancy. Perhaps one of you will take it up.

Don Taylor, *McGill University*

▶ SUMMING UP

WHAT ARE THE CONSEQUENCES OF RACIAL AND GENDER-BASED PREJUDICE?

- Racial discrimination was common in the U.S., Britain, and Canada until the 1960s; since that time, overt discrimination has become far less prevalent, but subtle and automatic discrimination is still evident.
- Similarly, discrimination against women has lessened in recent decades. Nevertheless, strong gender stereotypes and a fair amount of gender discrimination are still found in Canada and, to a greater degree, around the world.

CAN PREJUDICE CREATE ITS OWN REALITY?

- Prejudice and stereotyping have important consequences for those who face them, especially when strongly held and when judging unknown individuals.
- Once formed, stereotypes tend to perpetuate themselves and resist change. They also create their own realities through self-fulfilling prophecies.
- Prejudice can also undermine people's performance through stereotype threat, by making people apprehensive that others will view them stereotypically.
- Stereotypes, especially when strong, can predispose how we perceive people and interpret events.

HOW DO PEOPLE REACT TO FACING PREJUDICE AND STEREOTYPING?

- Reactions to experiencing prejudice and discrimination are varied.
- Blaming poor performance on prejudice can be a way to protect self-esteem.
- People are reluctant to acknowledge that they individually experience prejudice. Targets of prejudice are often vigilant to the possibility of being discriminated against but also are motivated to deny that such discrimination actually occurs.

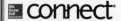 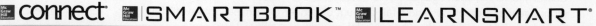 

SOCIAL PSYCHOLOGY APPLIED

Throughout this book, we have aimed to link laboratory to life by relating social psychology's principles and findings to everyday happenings. We now conclude by recollecting a number of these big ideas and applying them in four practical contexts. Module A, "Social Psychology in Conflict and Peacemaking," considers how social conflicts develop and how they can be justly and amicably resolved. Module B, "Social Psychology in the Clinic," applies social psychology to evaluating and promoting mental and physical health. Module C, "Social Psychology in Court," explores social thinking and social influences on witnesses and juries. Module D, "Social Psychology and the Sustainable Future," asks what social psychological principles might contribute to help avert an ecological holocaust triggered by increasing population, consumption, and global warming.

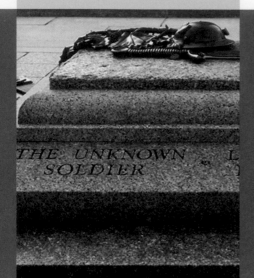

MODULE A
Social Psychology in Conflict and Peacemaking

CHAPTER OUTLINE

- WHAT CREATES CONFLICT?

- HOW CAN PEACE BE ACHIEVED?

There is a speech that has been spoken in many languages by the leaders of many countries. It goes like this: "The intentions of our country are entirely peaceful. Yet, we are also aware that other nations, with their new weapons, threaten us. Thus we must defend ourselves against attack. By so doing, we shall protect our way of life and preserve the peace" (Richardson, 1960). Almost every nation claims concern only for peace but, mistrusting other nations, arms itself in self-defence. The result is a world that has been spending $5 billion per day on arms and armies while hundreds of millions die of malnutrition and untreated disease (SIPRI, 2011).

The elements of **conflict** are similar at many levels, whether we examine conflict between nations in an arms race, religious factions disputing points of doctrine, corporate executives and workers disputing salaries, or a bickering married couple. Whether their perceptions are accurate or inaccurate, people in conflict sense that one side's gain is the other's loss.

> **conflict**
> a perceived incompatibility of actions or goals

"We want more pay."

"We can't afford to give it to you."

"I'd like the music off."

"I'd like it on."

Sometimes, the result is that everybody loses, as when a salary cap impasse between owners and players caused the 2005 National Hockey League season to be cancelled.

A relationship or an organization without conflict is probably apathetic. Conflict signifies involvement, commitment, and caring. If understood, if recognized, it can stimulate renewed and improved human relations. Harmony occurs when justice and mutual respect prevail but also when "everyone knows their place" in an unjust world (Dixon et al., 2010). Without conflict, people seldom face and resolve their problems.

Genuine peace is more than the suppression of open conflict, more than a fragile superficial calm. Peace is the outcome of a creatively managed conflict. Peace is the parties reconciling their perceived differences to reach genuine accord. "We got our increased pay. You got your increased profit. Now we're helping each other achieve our aspirations." Peace, said peace researcher Royce Anderson (2004), "is a condition in which individuals, families, groups, communities, and/or nations experience low levels of violence and engage in mutually harmonious relationships."

● WHAT CREATES CONFLICT?

Social-psychological studies have identified several ingredients that create conflict. What is striking (and what simplifies our task) is that these ingredients are common to all levels of social conflict, whether interpersonal, intergroup, or international.

SOCIAL DILEMMAS

Several of the problems that most threaten our human future—nuclear arms, global warming, overpopulation, natural resource depletion—arise as various parties pursue their self-interest, to their collective detriment. Any individual can think, "It would cost me lots to buy expensive pollution controls. Besides, by itself my pollution is trivial." Many others reason similarly, and the result is unclean air and water.

In some societies, individuals benefit by having many children who, they assume, can assist with the family tasks and provide security in the parents' old age. But when most families have many children, the result is the collective devastation of overpopulation. A choice that is individually rewarding becomes collectively punishing. We, therefore, have an urgent dilemma: How can we reconcile individuals' well-being, including their right to pursue their personal interests, with communal well-being?

Although workers and management often cooperate, they also can experience conflict, which is most evident during a strike.

To isolate and illustrate this dilemma, social psychologists have used laboratory games that expose the heart of many real social conflicts. By showing us how well-meaning people become trapped in mutually destructive behaviour, they illuminate some fascinating, yet troubling, paradoxes of human existence.

Let's consider two laboratory games that are each an example of a **social trap**: the Prisoners' Dilemma and the Tragedy of the Commons.

social trap
a situation in which the conflicting parties, by rationally pursuing their own self-interest, become caught in mutually destructive behaviour

The Prisoners' Dilemma

This dilemma derives from an anecdote concerning two suspects questioned separately by the Crown attorney (Rapoport, 1960). They are jointly guilty; however, the Crown has only enough evidence to convict them of a lesser offence. So the Crown creates an incentive for each to confess privately:

If Prisoner A confesses and Prisoner B doesn't, the Crown will grant the confessor immunity to A, and will use the confession to convict B of a maximum offence (and vice versa if B confesses and A doesn't).

If both confess, each will receive a moderate sentence.

If neither confesses, each will be convicted of a lesser crime and receive a light sentence.

The matrix of Figure A–1 summarizes the choices. If you were a prisoner faced with such a dilemma, with no chance to talk to the other prisoner, would you confess?

Many people say they would confess to be granted immunity, even though mutual non-confession elicits lighter sentences than mutual confession. Perhaps this is because (as shown in the matrix of Figure A–1) no matter what the other prisoner decides, each is better off confessing

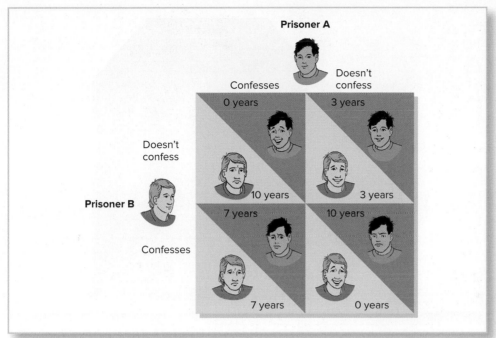

FIGURE A–1

THE PRISONERS' DILEMMA.

In each box, the number above the diagonal is prisoner A's outcome. Thus, if both prisoners confess, both get seven years. If neither confesses, each gets three years. If one confesses, that prisoner is set free in exchange for evidence used to convict the other of a crime bringing a 10-year sentence. If you were one of the prisoners, would you confess?

than being convicted individually. If the other also confesses, the sentence is moderate rather than severe. If the other does not confess, one goes free.

In some 2000 studies (Dawes, 1991), university students have faced variations of the Prisoners' Dilemma with the choices being to defect or cooperate, and the outcome not being prison terms but chips, money, or course points. As Figure A–2 illustrates, on any given decision, a person is better off defecting (because such behaviour exploits the other's cooperation or protects against the other's exploitation). However—and here's the rub—by not cooperating, both parties end up far worse off than if they had trusted each other and thus had gained a joint profit. This dilemma often traps each one in a maddening predicament in which both realize they *could* mutually profit. But, unable to communicate and mistrusting one another, they become "locked in" to not cooperating.

"When multiplied by 2, a national policy of Peace Through Strength leads inevitably to an arms race."
GEORGE LEVINGER (1987)

The Tragedy of the Commons

Many social dilemmas involve more than two parties. Global warming stems from widespread deforestation and from the carbon dioxide emitted by the world's cars, furnaces, and coal-fired power plants. Each gas-guzzling SUV contributes infinitesimally to the problem, and the harm each does is diffused over many people. To model such social predicaments, researchers have developed laboratory dilemmas that involve multiple people.

A metaphor for the insidious nature of social dilemmas is what ecologist Garrett Hardin (1968) called the "tragedy of the commons." He derived the name from the centrally located pasture area in old English towns.

In today's world, the "commons" can be air, water, whales, cookies, or any shared and limited resource. If all use the resource in moderation, it may replenish itself as rapidly as it's harvested. The grass will grow, the whales will reproduce, and the cookie jar will get restocked. If not, there

FIGURE A–2

LABORATORY VERSION OF THE PRISONERS' DILEMMA.

The numbers represent some reward, such as money. In each box, the number above the diagonal lines is the outcome for person A. Unlike the Prisoners' Dilemma (a one-shot decision), most laboratory versions involve repeated plays.

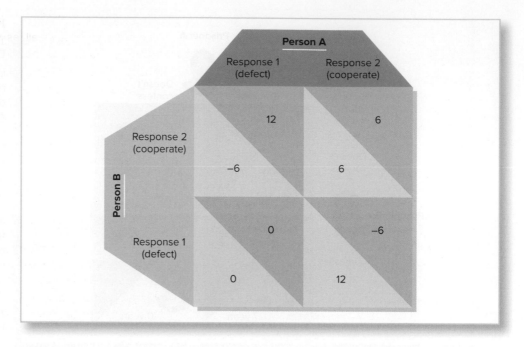

occurs a tragedy of the commons. Imagine 100 farmers surrounding a commons capable of sustaining 100 cows. When each grazes one cow, the common feeding ground is optimally used. But then someone reasons, "If I put a second cow in the pasture, I'll double my output, minus the mere 1 percent overgrazing." So this farmer adds a second cow. So do each of the other farmers. The inevitable result? The tragedy of the commons—a grassless mud field.

Many real predicaments parallel this story. Internet congestion occurs as unregulated individuals, seeking to maximize their own gain, surf the web, filling its pipelines with graphical information (Huberman & Lukose, 1997). Likewise, environmental pollution is the sum of many minor pollutions, each of which benefits the individual polluters much more than they could benefit themselves (and the environment) if they stopped polluting. We litter public places—parks, zoos, residence lounges—while keeping our personal spaces clean. And we deplete our natural resources because the immediate personal benefits of, say, taking a long, hot shower outweigh the seemingly inconsequential costs. Whalers knew that others would exploit the whales if they didn't and that taking a few whales would hardly diminish the species. Therein lay the tragedy. Everybody's business—conservation—becomes nobody's business.

Is such individualism unique to Western societies? Kaori Sato (1987) gave students in a more collective culture, Japan, opportunities to harvest—for actual money—trees from a simulated forest. When the students shared equally the costs of planting the forest, the result was like those in Western cultures. More than half the trees were harvested before they had grown to the most profitable size.

Sato's forest reminds us of the cookie jars in our homes. What we *should* do is conserve cookies during the interval between weekly restockings, so that each day we can each munch two or three. Lacking regulation and fearing that other family members will soon deplete the resource, what we actually do is maximize our individual cookie consumption by downing one after the other. The result: Within 24 hours, the cookie glut will often end, the jar sitting empty for the rest of the week.

I am brash enough to believe that laboratory studies of conflict can illumine our understanding of the dynamics of war, peace, and social justice. From small groups to nations, the social processes appear similar. Thus, social psychologists who study conflict are in much the same position as the astronomers. We cannot conduct true experiments with large-scale social events. But we can identify the conceptual similarities between the large scale and the small, as the astronomers have between the planets and Newton's apple. By experimenting with small-scale social situations, we may thus be able to understand, predict, and influence large-scale social processes. That is why the games people play as subjects in our laboratory may advance our understanding of war, peace, and social justice.

Morton Deutsch, *Columbia University*

When resources are not partitioned, people often consume more than they realize (Herlocker et al., 1997). As a bowl of mashed potatoes is passed around a table of 10, it is likely that more people will scoop out a disproportionate share than when a platter of 10 chicken drumsticks is passed.

The Prisoners' Dilemma and the Tragedy of the Commons games have several similar features. First, both tempt people to explain their own behaviour situationally ("I had to protect myself against exploitation by my opponent") and to explain their partners' behaviour dispositionally ("She was greedy," "He was untrustworthy"). Most never realize that their counterparts are viewing them with the same fundamental attribution error (Hine & Gifford, 1996). People with self-inflating, self-focused narcissistic tendencies are especially unlikely to display empathy for others' perspectives (Campbell et al., 2005).

Second, motives often change. At first, people are eager to make some easy money, then to minimize their losses, and finally to save face and avoid defeat (Brockner et al., 1982; Teger, 1980). These shifting motives can make it harder to negotiate a solution. Early on, mediators can focus on proposing resolutions that maximize the benefits to both sides. As time progresses, however, solutions must increasingly address the substantive issues, and they must also let all parties enter an agreement with the sense that they have prevented important losses and avoided defeat.

Third, most real-life conflicts, like the Prisoners' Dilemma and the Tragedy of the Commons, are **non-zero-sum games**. The two sides' profits and losses need not add up to zero. Both can win; both can lose. Each game pits the immediate interests of individuals against the well-being of the group. Each is a diabolical social trap that shows how, even when individuals behave "rationally," harm can result. No malicious person planned for Los Angeles to be smothered in smog, for the horrendous destruction of the Bosnian conflict, or for the earth's atmosphere to be warmed by a blanket of carbon dioxide.

non-zero-sum games games in which outcomes need not sum to zero. With cooperation, both can win; with competition, both can lose. (Also called *mixed-motive situations.*)

Not all self-serving behaviour leads to collective doom. In a plentiful commons—as in the world of the eighteenth-century capitalist economist Adam Smith (1976, p. 18)—individuals who seek to maximize their own profit may also give the community what it needs: "It is not from the benevolence of the butcher, the brewer, or the baker, that we expect our dinner," he observed, "but from their regard to their own interest."

Resolving social dilemmas

Faced with social traps, how can we induce people to cooperate for their mutual betterment? Research with the laboratory dilemmas reveals several ways (Gifford & Hine, 1997).

Regulation

If taxes were entirely voluntary, how many would pay their full share? Surely, many would not, which is why modern societies do not depend on charity to pay for social and military security. We also develop rules to safeguard our common good. Fishing and hunting have long been regulated by local seasons and limits; at the global level, an International Whaling Commission sets an agreed-upon "harvest" that enables whales to regenerate. Likewise, where fishing industries, such as the Alaskan halibut fishery, have implemented "catch shares"—guaranteeing each fisher a percentage of each year's allowable catch—competition and overfishing have been greatly reduced (Costello, Gaines, & Lynham, 2008).

In everyday life, however, regulation has costs—the cost of administering and enforcing the regulations, for example, and the cost of diminished personal freedom. A volatile political question thus arises: At what point does a regulation's cost exceed its benefits?

Small is beautiful

There is another way to resolve social dilemmas: Make the group small. In small commons, each person feels more responsible and effective (Kerr, 1989). As a group grows larger, people more often think "I couldn't have made a difference anyway"—a common excuse for non-cooperation (Kerr & Kaufman-Gilliland, 1997). In small groups, people also feel more identified with a group's success. Anything else that enhances group identity will also increase cooperation. Even just a few minutes of discussion, or just believing that one shares similarities with others in the group, can increase "we feeling" and cooperation (Brewer, 1987; Orbell, van de Kragt, & Dawes, 1988).

In small rather than large groups, individuals are also less likely to take more than their equal share of available resources (Allison, McQueen, & Schaerfl, 1992). On the Puget Sound island where one of the authors grew up, the small neighbourhood shared a communal water supply. On hot summer days when the reservoir ran low, a light came on, signalling the community's 15 families to conserve. Recognizing their responsibility to one another, and feeling as if conservation really mattered, each family conserved. Never did the reservoir run dry.

> "For that which is common to the greatest number has the least care bestowed upon it."
> ARISTOTLE

In a much larger commons—say, a city—voluntary conservation is less successful. Because the harm one does diffuses across many others, each individual can rationalize away personal accountability; therefore, some political theorists and social psychologists argue that, where feasible, the commons should be divided into smaller territories (Edney, 1980). In his *Mutual Aid* (1902), the Russian revolutionary Pyotr Kropotkin set down a vision of small communities rather than central government making consensus decisions for the benefit of all (Gould, 1988).

Evolutionary psychologist Robin Dunbar (1992, 2010) notes that hunter-gatherer societies often travel together as groups of 30 to 35 people, that tribal villages and clans often have averaged about 150 people—enough to afford mutual support and protection but not more people than one can monitor. He suspects it's not a coincidence that the average number of Facebook friends—about 125—echoes the size of our ancestral tribal villages, which reflect the number of people with whom we can have meaningful, supportive relationships. This seemingly natural group size is also, he believes, the optimum size for business organizations, religious congregations, and military fighting units.

Appeals to altruistic norms

In Chapter 8, we described how increasing people's feelings of responsibility for others boosts altruism. Can we, therefore, assume that appeals to altruistic motives will prompt people to act for the common good?

The evidence is mixed. On the one hand, it seems that just knowing the dire consequences of non-cooperation has little effect. In laboratory games, people realize that their self-serving choices are mutually destructive, yet they continue to make them. Outside the laboratory, warnings of doom and appeals to conserve have brought little response. Pleas to carpool, conserve water, and refrain from littering, often go unheeded. In the summer of 2003, the town of Guelph, Ontario, which is near the home of one of the authors, had a ban on lawn sprinkling, yet about 80 percent of the lawns in town remained green. Knowing the good does not necessarily lead to doing the good.

Still, most people do adhere to norms of social responsibility, reciprocity, equity, and keeping one's commitments (Kerr, 1992). The problem is how to tap such feelings. One such way is by defining situations in ways that imply cooperative norms. Lee Ross and Andrew Ward (1996) invited Stanford dormitory advisers to nominate male students they thought would be especially likely to cooperate and others they thought would be likely to defect while playing a prisoners' dilemma game. In reality, the two groups of students were equally likely to cooperate. What dramatically affected cooperation was whether the researchers labelled the simulation the "Wall Street Game" (in which case one-third of the participants cooperated) or the "Community Game" (in which case two-thirds cooperated).

To change behaviour, many cities have changed the payoff matrix. Fast carpool-only lanes increase the benefits of carpooling and increase the costs of driving alone.

Communication can also tap altruistic norms. When permitted to communicate, participants in laboratory games frequently appeal to the social-responsibility norm: "If you defect on the rest of us, you're going to have to live with it for the rest of your life" (Dawes, McTavish, & Shaklee, 1977). Noting this, researcher Robyn Dawes (1980a) and his associates gave people a short sermon about group benefits, exploitation, and ethics. Then the people played a dilemma game. The appeal worked: People were convinced to forgo immediate personal gain for the common good.

Could such appeals work in large-scale dilemmas? Jeffery Scott Mio and his colleagues (1993) found that after reading about the commons dilemma (as you have), theatre patrons littered less than patrons who read about voting. Moreover, when cooperation obviously serves the public good, one can usefully appeal to the social-responsibility norm (Lynn & Oldenquist, 1986). When, for example, people believe public transportation can save time, they will be more likely to use it if they also believe it reduces pollution (Van Vugt, Van Lange, & Meertens, 1996). In the struggle for civil rights, many marchers willingly agreed, for the sake of the larger group, to suffer harassment, beatings, and jail. In wartime, people make great personal sacrifices for the good of their group. As Winston Churchill said of the Battle of Britain, the actions of the Royal Air Force pilots were genuinely altruistic: A great many people owed a great deal to those who flew into battle knowing there was a high probability they would not return (Levinson, 1950).

To summarize, we can minimize destructive entrapment in social dilemmas by establishing rules that regulate self-serving behaviour, by keeping groups small, and by invoking altruistic norms.

"Never in the field of human conflict was so much owed by so many to so few."
SIR WINSTON CHURCHILL, HOUSE OF COMMONS, AUGUST 20, 1940

PERCEIVED INJUSTICE

"That's unfair!" "What a rip-off!" "We deserve better!" Such comments typify conflicts bred by perceived injustice. But what is "justice"? According to some social-psychological theorists, people perceive justice as equity—the distribution of rewards in proportion to individuals' contributions (Walster, Walster, & Berscheid, 1978). If you and I have a relationship (employer–employee, teacher–student, husband–wife, colleague–colleague), it is equitable if

$$\frac{\text{My outcomes}}{\text{My outputs}} = \frac{\text{Your outcome}}{\text{Your output}}$$

If you contribute more and benefit less than I do, you will feel exploited and irritated; I may feel exploitative and guilty. Chances are, though, that you more than I will be sensitive to the inequity (Greenberg, 1986; Messick & Sentis, 1979).

We may agree with the equity principle's definition of justice yet disagree on whether our relationship is equitable. If two people are colleagues, what will each consider a relevant input? The one who is older may favour basing pay on seniority; the other may favour basing pay on current productivity. Given such a disagreement, whose definition is likely to prevail? More often than not, those with social power convince themselves and others that they deserve what they're getting (Mikula, 1984). This has been called a "golden" rule: Whoever has the gold makes the rules.

> *"Do unto others 20% better than you would expect them to do unto you, to correct for subjective error."*
> LINUS PAULING (1962)

Knowing that one's group has overbenefited can trigger collective guilt, much as individuals can feel guilt when receiving what's undeserved. To restore a sense of justice, such collective guilt can motivate an apology or an offer of compensation (Mallet & Swim, 2003). However, the exploiter can also relieve guilt by devaluing others' inputs. As we described in Chapter 11, those who inflict harm may blame the victim and thus maintain their belief in a just world.

> *"From each according to his abilities, to each according to his needs."*
> KARL MARX

Critics argue that equity is not the only conceivable definition of justice. (Pause a moment: Can you imagine any other?) Edward Sampson (1975) pointed out that equity theorists wrongly assume that the economic principles that guide Western, capitalist nations are universal. Some non-capitalist cultures define justice not as equity but as either **equality** or **need-based distribution**. When rewards are distributed to those within one's group, people socialized under the influence of collectivist cultures, such as China and India, likewise favour need or equality more than do individualistic Westerners (Hui, Triandis, & Yee, 1991; Leung & Bond, 1984; Murphy-Berman et al., 1984).

equality
the equal distribution of rewards to all individuals

need-based distribution
the distribution of rewards based on need for those rewards

On what basis *should* rewards be distributed? Need? Equality? Merit? Some combination of these? Political philosopher John Rawls (1971) invited us to consider a future in which our own place on the economic ladder was unknown. Which standard of justice would we prefer? Gregory Mitchell and his colleagues (1993) reported that university students wanted enough priority placed on equality to meet their own needs, should they find themselves at the bottom.

MISPERCEPTION

Recall that conflict is a *perceived* incompatibility of actions or goals. Many conflicts contain but a small core of truly incompatible goals; the bigger problem is the misperceptions of the other's motives and goals (Figure A–3).

In earlier chapters, we considered the seeds of such misperception. The self-serving bias leads individuals and groups to accept credit for their good deeds and shuck responsibility for bad deeds, without according others the same benefit of the doubt. A tendency to self-justify further inclines people to deny the wrong of the evil acts that they cannot really justify. Because of the fundamental attribution error, each side sees the other's hostility as reflecting an evil disposition. People then filter the information and interpret it to fit their preconceptions. Groups frequently polarize these self-serving, self-justifying, biasing tendencies. Groupthink causes people to perceive their own group as moral and strong, the opposition as evil and weak. Terrorist acts that are despicable brutality to most people are "holy war" to others. Indeed, the mere fact of being in a group triggers an in-group bias. And negative stereotypes, once formed, are often resistant to contradictory evidence.

So it should not surprise us, though it should sober us, to discover that people in conflict form distorted images of one another. Ervin Staub and Daniel Bar-Tal (2003) argued that groups in intractable conflict almost always do the following:

- They see their own goals as supremely important.
- They take pride in their own group and devalue the out-group.
- They believe themselves victimized.
- They elevate patriotism, solidarity, and loyalty to the group's needs.
- They celebrate self sacrifice and suppress criticism.

Although one side to a conflict may, indeed, be acting with greater moral virtue, the point is that ways of thinking about the enemy are fairly predictable.

> *"Solutions to the distribution problem are nontrivial. Children fight, colleagues complain, group members resign, tempers flare, and nations battle over issues of fairness. As parents, employers, teachers, and presidents know, the most frequent response to an allocation decision is 'not fair.'"*
>
> ARNOLD KAHN & WILLIAM GAEDDERT (1985)

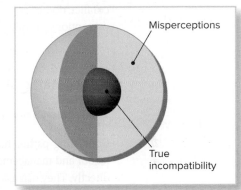

FIGURE A–3

INCOMPATIBLE GOALS VS. MISPERCEPTIONS

Many conflicts contain a core of truly incompatible goals surrounded by a larger exterior of misperceptions.

Simplistic thinking

When tension rises—as happens during an international crisis—rational thinking becomes more difficult (Janis, 1989). Views of the enemy become more simplistic and stereotyped, and seat-of-the-pants judgments become more likely. Experiments by Peter Carnevale and Tahira Probst (1998) showed that even the mere expectation of conflict can serve to freeze thinking and impede creative problem-solving.

Researchers have also analyzed political rhetoric preceding the outset of major wars, surprise military attacks, regional conflicts, and revolutions (Conway, Suedfeld, & Tetlock, 2001). In nearly every case, attacking leaders displayed increasingly simplistic we-are-good/they-are-bad thinking immediately prior to their aggressive actions; but shifts *away* from simplistic rhetoric typically preceded major peace agreements.

Shifting perceptions

If misperceptions accompany conflict, then they should appear and disappear as conflicts wax and wane. And they do, with startling ease. The same processes that create the enemy's image can reverse that image when the enemy becomes an ally. Thus, the "bloodthirsty, cruel, treacherous Japs" of the Second World War (who were deemed so dangerous that Canadian citizens of Japanese descent were sent to internment camps) soon became our "intelligent, hard-working, self-disciplined, resourceful allies." Our Second World War allies, the Russians, then became the "warlike, treacherous" ones.

The Germans, who after two world wars were hated, then admired, and then again hated, were once again admired—apparently no longer plagued by what earlier was presumed to be cruelty in their national character. So long as Iraq was attacking Iran, even while using chemical weapons and massacring its own Kurds, many nations supported it. Our enemy's enemy is our friend. When Iraq ended its war with Iran and invaded oil-rich Kuwait, Iraq's behaviour suddenly became "barbaric." Clearly, images of our enemies not only justify our actions but also change with amazing ease.

The extent of misperceptions during conflict provides a chilling reminder that people need not be insane or abnormally evil to form these distorted images of their antagonists. When in conflict with another nation, another group, or a roommate or parent, we readily develop misperceptions that allow us to perceive our own motives and actions as wholly good and the other's as totally evil. Our antagonists usually form a mirror-image perception of us.

So, with antagonists trapped in a social dilemma, competing for scarce resources, or perceiving injustice, the conflict continues until something enables both parties to peel away their misperceptions and work at reconciling their actual differences. Good advice, then: When in conflict, do not assume that the other fails to share your values and morality; instead, compare perceptions, assuming that the other is likely perceiving the situation differently.

● HOW CAN PEACE BE ACHIEVED?

What strategies can be used to alleviate or end conflicts?

Conflicting parties have other ways to resolve their differences. When husband and wife, or labour and management, or nation X and nation Y disagree, they can bargain with one another directly. They can ask a third party to mediate by making suggestions and facilitating their negotiations. Or they can arbitrate by submitting their disagreement to someone who will study the issues and impose a settlement.

BARGAINING

bargaining
seeking an agreement
through direct
negotiation between
parties to a conflict

If we want to buy or sell a new car, are we better off adopting a tough **bargaining** stance—opening with an extreme offer so that splitting the difference will yield a favourable result? Or are we better off beginning with a sincere "good-faith" offer?

Experiments suggest no simple answer. On the one hand, those who demand more will often get more. Robert Cialdini, Leonard Bickman, and John Cacioppo (1979) provided a typical result: In a control condition, they approached various Chevrolet dealers and asked the price of a new Monte Carlo sports coupe with designated options. In an experimental condition, they approached other dealers and first struck a tougher bargaining stance, asking for and rejecting a price on a different car ("I need a lower price than that. That's a lot"). When they then asked the price of the Monte Carlo, exactly as in the control condition, they received offers that averaged some $200 lower.

Tough bargaining may lower the other party's expectations, making the other side willing to settle for less (Yukl, 1974). But toughness can sometimes backfire. Many a conflict is not over a pie of fixed size but over a pie that shrinks if the conflict continues. A time delay is often a lose-lose scenario. When a strike is prolonged, both labour and management lose. Being tough is another potential lose–lose scenario. If the other party responds with an equally tough stance, both may be locked into positions from which neither can back down without losing face. The nurses' strike in Quebec in the summer of 1999 had some of these features. Premier Lucien Bouchard had announced before the strike that he would not give a raise greater than 5 percent over three years, and the nurses announced they would not accept such a deal. After such statements, it is difficult for either side to compromise and reach an agreement.

MEDIATION

A third-party mediator may offer suggestions that enable conflicting parties to make concessions and still save face (Pruitt, 1998). If my concession can be attributed to **mediation**, which also is gaining an equal concession from my antagonist, then neither of us will be viewed as caving in to the other's demands.

mediation
an attempt by a neutral third party to resolve a conflict by facilitating communication and offering suggestions

Turning win–lose into win–win

Mediators also help resolve conflicts by facilitating constructive communication. Their first task is to help the parties rethink the conflict and gain information about the other's interests (Thompson, 1998). Typically, people on both sides have a competitive "win–lose" orientation: They think that they are successful if their opponent is unhappy with the result, and unsuccessful if their opponent is pleased (Thompson, Valley, & Kramer, 1995). The mediator aims to replace this win–lose orientation with a cooperative "win–win" orientation, by prodding them to set aside their conflicting demands and instead to think about each other's underlying needs, interests, and goals. In experiments, Leigh Thompson (1990) found that, with experience, negotiators become better able to make mutually beneficial trade-offs and thus to achieve win–win resolutions.

A classic story of such a resolution concerns the two sisters who quarrelled over an orange (Follett, 1940). Finally they compromised and split the orange in half, whereupon one sister squeezed her half for juice while the other used the peel to make a cake. In a series of compelling experiments, Dean Pruitt and his associates induced bargainers to search for **integrative agreements**. If the sisters had agreed to split the orange, giving one sister all the juice and the other all the peel, they would have hit on such an agreement, one that integrates both parties' interests (Kimmel et al., 1980; Pruitt & Lewis, 1975, 1977). Compared to compromises, in which each party sacrifices something important, integrative agreements are more enduring. Because they are mutually rewarding, they also lead to better ongoing relationships (Pruitt, 1986).

integrative agreements
win–win agreements that reconcile both parties' interests to their mutual benefit

Unravelling misperceptions with controlled communications

Communication often helps reduce self-fulfilling misperceptions. Perhaps you can recall experiences similar to that of this university student:

> Often, after a prolonged period of little communication, I perceive Martha's silence as a sign of her dislike for me. She, in turn, thinks that my quietness is a result of my being mad at her. My silence induces her silence, which makes me even more silent . . . until this snowballing effect is broken by some occurrence that makes it

necessary for us to interact. And the communication then unravels all the misinterpretations we had made about one another.

The outcome of such conflicts often depends on how people communicate their feelings to one another. Roger Knudson and his colleagues (1980) invited married couples to come to the psychology laboratory and relive, through role-playing, one of their past conflicts. Before, during, and after their conversation (which often generated as much emotion as the actual previous conflict), the couples were closely observed and questioned. Couples who evaded the issue—by failing to make their positions clear or failing to acknowledge their spouse's position—left with the illusion that they were more in harmony and agreement than they really were. Often, they came to believe they now agreed more when actually they agreed less. In contrast, those who engaged the issue—by making their positions clear and by taking one another's views into account—achieved more actual agreement and gained more accurate information about one another's perceptions. That helps explain why couples who communicate their concerns directly and openly are usually happily married (Grush & Glidden, 1987).

Such findings have triggered new programs that teach couples and children how to manage conflicts constructively (Horowitz & Boardman, 1994). If managed constructively, conflict provides opportunities for reconciliation and more genuine harmony. Psychologists Ian Gotlib and Catherine Colby (1988) offered advice on how to avoid destructive quarrels and how to have good quarrels (see Table A–1). Children, for example, learn that conflict is normal, that people can learn to get along with those who are different, that most disputes can be resolved with two winners, and that non-violent communication strategies are an alternative to a world of bullies and victims. This "violence prevention curriculum . . . is not about passivity," noted Deborah Prothrow-Stith (1991, p. 183). "It is about using anger not to hurt oneself or one's peers, but to change the world."

David Johnson and Roger Johnson (1995, 2000, 2003) put children from grades one to nine through about a dozen hours of conflict resolution training in six schools, with very heartening results. Before the training, most students were involved in daily conflicts—put-downs and

TABLE A–1   HOW TO FIGHT CONSTRUCTIVELY.

Do Not	**Do**
• apologize prematurely.	• fight privately away from children.
• evade the argument, give the silent treatment, or walk out.	• clearly define the issue and repeat the other's arguments in your own words.
• use your intimate knowledge of the other person to hit below the belt and humiliate.	• divulge your positive and negative feelings.
• bring in unrelated issues.	• welcome feedback about your behaviour.
• feign agreement while harbouring resentment.	• clarify where you agree and disagree and what matters most to each of you.
• tell the other party how she or he is feeling.	• ask questions that help the other find words to express the concern.
• attack indirectly by criticizing someone or something the other person values.	• wait for spontaneous explosions to subside, without retaliating.
• undermine the other by intensifying their insecurity or threatening disaster.	• offer positive suggestions for mutual improvement.

teasing, playground turn-taking conflicts, conflicts over possessions—conflicts that nearly always resulted in a winner and a loser. After training, the children more often found win–win solutions, better mediated friends' conflicts, and retained and applied their new skills in and out of school throughout the school year. When implemented with a whole student body, the result is a more peaceful student community and increased academic achievement.

Conflict researchers report that a key factor is trust (Noor et al., 2008; Ross & Ward, 1995). If you believe the other person is well-intentioned, you are then more likely to divulge your needs and concerns. Lacking such trust, you may fear that being open will give the other party information that might be used against you. Even simple behaviours can enhance trust. In experiments, negotiators who were instructed to mimic the others' mannerisms, as naturally empathic people in close relationships often do, elicited more trust and greater discovery of compatible interests and mutually satisfying deals (Maddux et al., 2008).

> *"[There is] a psychological barrier between us, a barrier of suspicion, a barrier of rejection; a barrier of fear, of deception, a barrier of hallucination. . . ."*
> PRESIDENT ANWAR AL-SADAT, TO THE ISRAELI KNESSET, 1977

When the two parties mistrust each other and communicate unproductively, a third-party mediator—a marriage counsellor, a labour mediator, a diplomat—sometimes helps. Often, the mediator is someone trusted by both sides. In the 1980s, it took an Algerian Muslim to mediate the conflict between Iran and Iraq, and the Pope to resolve a geographical dispute between Argentina and Chile (Carnevale & Choi, 2000).

After coaxing the conflicting parties to rethink their perceived win–lose conflict, the mediator often has each party identify and rank its goals. When goals are compatible, the ranking procedure makes it easier for each to concede on less important goals so that both achieve their chief goals (Erickson et al., 1974; Schulz & Pruitt, 1978). South Africa achieved internal peace when White and Black South Africans granted each other's top priorities—replacing apartheid with majority rule and safeguarding the security, welfare, and rights of Whites (Kelman, 1998).

When labour and management both believe that management's goal of higher productivity and profit is compatible with labour's goal of better wages and working conditions, they can begin to work for an integrative win–win solution. If workers will forgo benefits that are moderately beneficial to them but very costly to management (perhaps company-provided dental care), and if management will forgo moderately valuable arrangements that workers very much resent (perhaps inflexibility of working hours), then both sides may gain (Ross & Ward, 1995). Rather than seeing itself as making a concession, each side can see the negotiation as an effort to exchange bargaining chips for things more valued.

When the parties convene to communicate directly, the mediator does not usually leave them on their own, eyeball to eyeball. In the midst of a threatening, stressful conflict, emotions often disrupt the ability to understand the other party's point of view. Communication may become most difficult just when it is most needed (Tetlock, 1985).

The mediator will, therefore, often structure the encounter to help each party understand and feel understood by the other. The mediator may ask the conflicting parties to restrict their arguments to statements of fact, including statements of how they feel and how they respond when the other acts in a given way ("I" statements): "I enjoy having music on. When you play it loud, I find it hard to concentrate. That makes me crabby." Also, the mediator may ask people to reverse roles and argue the other's position. (Experiments show that inducing empathy decreases stereotyping and increases cooperation [Batson & Moran, 1999; Galinsky & Muskowitz, 2000].) The mediator may have them restate one another's positions before replying with their own: "It annoys you when I play my music and you're trying to study."

Communication facilitators work to break down barriers, as in this diversity training exercise for teenagers.

Neutral third parties may also suggest mutually agreeable proposals that would be dismissed—*reactively devalued*—if offered by either side. The very same proposal that is seen as a cheap trick when presented by the opposition is often seen as an interesting suggestion when presented by the mediator. Even good proposals are greeted with suspicion when presented by the opposition. Likewise, people will often reactively devalue a concession offered by an adversary ("they must not value it"); the same concession may seem less like a token gesture when suggested by a third party.

These peacemaking principles, based partly on laboratory experiments, partly on practical experience, have helped mediate both international and industrial conflicts (Blake & Mouton, 1962, 1979; R. J. Fisher, 1994; Wehr, 1979). Social psychologists have conducted workshops that promote healing and reconciliation, bringing together influential Arabs and Israelis, Pakistanis and Indians, and Tutsi and Hutu in Rwanda (Kelman, 1997; Staub & Pearlman, 2005a, 2005b). Using methods such as those we've considered, these psychologists countered misperceptions and had participants creatively seek solutions for their common good. The participants were free to speak directly to their adversaries without fear of their constituents' second-guessing what they were saying. The result? Those from both sides typically came to understand the other side's perspective, and they understood how the other side responded to their own group's actions.

ARBITRATION

Some conflicts are so intractable, the underlying interests so divergent, that a mutually satisfactory resolution is unattainable. Bosnian Serbs and Muslims could not both have jurisdiction over the same homelands. In a divorce dispute over custody of a child, both parents cannot enjoy full custody. In these and many other cases (disputes over tenants' repair bills, athletes' wages, and national territories), a third-party mediator may—or may not—help resolve the conflict.

If not, the parties may turn to **arbitration** by having the mediator or another third party impose a settlement. Disputants usually prefer to settle their differences without arbitration, so they retain control over the outcome. Neil McGillicuddy and others (1987) observed this preference in an experiment involving disputants coming to one arbitration centre. When people knew they would face an arbitrated settlement if mediation failed, they tried harder to resolve the problem, exhibited less hostility, and thus were more likely to reach agreement.

In cases where differences seem large and irreconcilable, however, the prospect of arbitration may have the opposite effect (Pruitt, 1986). The disputants may freeze their positions, hoping to gain an advantage when the arbitrator chooses a compromise. To combat this tendency, some disputes, such as those involving salaries of individual baseball players, are settled with "final-offer arbitration" in which the third party chooses one of the two final offers. Final-offer arbitration motivates each party to make a reasonable proposal.

Typically, however, the final offer is not as reasonable as it would be if each party, free of self-serving bias, saw its own proposal through others' eyes. Negotiation researchers report that most disputants are made stubborn by "optimistic overconfidence" (Kahneman & Tversky, 1995). Successful mediation is hindered when, as often happens, both parties believe they have a two-thirds chance of winning a final-offer arbitration (Bazerman, 1986, 1990).

> **arbitration**
> resolution of a conflict by a neutral third party who studies both sides and imposes a settlement

> *"In the research on the effects of mediation one finding stands out: The worse the state of the parties' relationship is with one another, the dimmer the prospects that mediation will be successful."*
> KENNETH KRESSEL
> & DEAN PRUITT (1985)

CONCILIATION

Sometimes, tension and suspicion run so high that communication, much less resolution, becomes all but impossible. Each party may threaten, coerce, or retaliate against the other. Unfortunately, such acts tend to be reciprocated, thus escalating the conflict. So would a strategy of appeasing the other party by being unconditionally cooperative produce a satisfying result? Often not. In laboratory games, those who are 100 percent cooperative often get exploited. Politically, a one-sided pacifism is out of the question.

Social psychologist Charles Osgood (1962, 1980) advocated a third alternative—one that is conciliatory, rather than retaliatory, yet strong enough to discourage exploitation. Osgood called it "graduated and reciprocated initiatives in tension reduction," nicknamed **GRIT**.

GRIT requires one side to initiate a few small de-escalatory actions, after announcing a conciliatory intent. The initiator states a desire to reduce tension, declares each conciliatory act prior to making it, and invites the adversary to reciprocate. Such announcements create a framework that helps the adversary correctly interpret what otherwise might be seen as weak or tricky actions. They also bring public pressure on the adversary to follow the reciprocity norm.

> **GRIT**
> acronym for "graduated and reciprocated initiatives in tension reduction"—a strategy designed to de-escalate international tensions

Next, the initiator establishes credibility and genuineness by carrying out, exactly as announced, several verifiable conciliatory acts. This intensifies the pressure to reciprocate. Making conciliatory acts diverse—perhaps offering medical information, closing a military base, and lifting a trade ban—keeps the initiator from making a significant sacrifice in any one area and leaves the adversary freer to choose its own means of reciprocation. If the adversary reciprocates voluntarily, this conciliatory behaviour may soften its attitudes.

GRIT *is* conciliatory. But it is not "surrender on the installment plan." The remaining aspects of the plan protect each side's self-interest by maintaining retaliatory capability. The initial conciliatory steps entail some small risk but do not jeopardize either one's security; rather, they are

> *"I am not suggesting that principles of individual behavior can be applied to the behavior of nations in any direct, simpleminded fashion. What I am trying to suggest is that such principles may provide us with hunches about internation behavior that can be tested against experience in the larger arena."*
>
> CHARLES E. OSGOOD (1966)

calculated to begin edging both sides down the tension ladder. If one side takes an aggressive action, the other side reciprocates in kind, making it clear it will not tolerate exploitation. Yet the reciprocal act is not an over-response that would re-escalate the conflict. If the adversary offers its own conciliatory acts, these, too, are matched or even slightly exceeded.

Does GRIT really work? In laboratory dilemma games, a successful strategy has proved to be simple "tit-for-tat," which begins with a cooperative opening play and thereafter matches the other party's last response (Axelrod & Dion, 1988; Parks & Rumble, 2001; Van Lange & Visser, 1999). Although initially friendly, tit-for-tat immediately punishes non-cooperation but also immediately forgives wayward opponents who again cooperate. In a lengthy series of experiments, Svenn Lindskold and his associates (1976 to 1988) tested other aspects of the GRIT strategy. Lindskold (1978) reported that his own and others' studies provide "strong support for the various steps in the GRIT proposal." In laboratory games, announcing cooperative intent *does* boost cooperation. Repeated conciliatory acts *do* breed greater trust (although self-serving biases often make one's own acts seem more conciliatory and less hostile than those of the adversary). Maintaining an equality of power *does* protect against exploitation.

Applications in the real world

Peace-creating strategies have been tried outside the laboratory, with promising results. One of the best examples of such a strategy was Lester B. Pearson's handling of the Suez Canal crisis. In the summer of 1956, Egyptian president Gamal Abdal Nasser declared that the Egyptian government was taking control of the Suez Canal. He hoped to raise money from tolls charged to ships going through the canal to finance the Aswan High Dam on the Nile River. A company controlled by British and French interests had previously controlled the canal. England and France were taken aback by the announcement and were worried that Egyptian control of the canal might eventually restrict the flow of goods (particularly oil) to Western Europe. In October 1956, these worries led England, France, and their ally Israel to invade the canal zone. They gained control of the area but were roundly criticized in international circles, precipitating a major international crisis. Would the Soviet Union come to Egypt's aid? Would the world powers stumble into another war? International outrage forced Britain, France, and Israel to withdraw from the canal zone, and Anthony Eden, the British foreign minister, had to resign.

Into this pressure cooker of a situation stepped Lester B. Pearson, then the foreign minister of Canada. He formulated a plan where concessions were made to both Egypt and Britain, as well as France and Israel. In exchange, United Nations peacekeeping troops were sent into the canal zone to ensure that the plan would be implemented. Egypt was allowed to collect tolls on ships going through the canal to finance the building of the Aswan High Dam. Britain and France were assured that the canal would remain open and that trade would not be restricted to Western Europe. Israel was given shipping rights that they had not previously enjoyed.

Lester B. Pearson received international acclaim (and the Nobel Peace Prize in 1957) for his role in handling the crisis; and, of course, he went on to become prime minister of Canada.

Might conciliatory efforts also help reduce tension between individuals? There is every reason to expect so. When a relationship is strained and communication non-existent, it sometimes takes only a conciliatory gesture—a soft answer, a warm smile, a gentle touch—for both parties to begin easing down the tension ladder, to a rung where contact, cooperation, and communication again become possible.

⋯▸ SUMMING UP

WHAT CREATES CONFLICT?

- Whenever two people, two groups, or two nations interact, their perceived needs and goals may conflict.

- Many social problems arise as people pursue individual self-interest, to their collective detriment. Two laboratory games, the Prisoners' Dilemma and the Tragedy of the Commons, capture this clash of individual versus communal well-being.

- In real life, as in laboratory experiments, we can avoid such traps by establishing rules that regulate self-serving behaviour, by keeping social groups small so people feel responsibility for one another, and by invoking altruistic norms.

- Conflicts also arise when people feel unjustly treated. According to equity theory, people define justice as the distribution of rewards in proportion to one's contributions. Conflicts occur when people disagree on the extent of their contributions and thus on the equity of their outcomes.

- Conflicts frequently contain a small core of truly incompatible goals, surrounded by a thick layer of misperceptions of the adversary's motives and goals.

HOW CAN PEACE BE ACHIEVED?

- Although conflicts are readily kindled and fuelled by social dilemmas and misperceptions, some equally powerful forces, such as bargaining, mediation, arbitration, and conciliation, can transform hostility into harmony.

- Conflicting parties can seek to resolve their differences by bargaining either directly or through a third-party mediator.

- Third-party mediators can help by prodding the antagonists to replace their competitive win–lose view of the conflict with a more cooperative win–win orientation. Mediators can structure communications that will peel away misperceptions and increase mutual understanding and trust.

- When a negotiated settlement is not reached, the conflicting parties may defer the outcome to an arbitrator, who either dictates a settlement or selects one of the two final offers.

- When tensions run so high that genuine communication is impossible, small conciliatory gestures by one party may elicit reciprocal conciliatory acts by the other party. One such conciliatory strategy, GRIT (graduated and reciprocated initiatives in tension reduction), aims to alleviate tense international situations.

- Those who mediate tense labour-management and international conflicts sometimes use another peacemaking strategy. They instruct the participants, as this chapter instructed you, in the dynamics of conflict and peacemaking in the hope that understanding can help them establish and enjoy peaceful, rewarding relationships.

MODULE B
Social Psychology in the Clinic

CHAPTER OUTLINE

● WHAT INFLUENCES THE ACCURACY OF CLINICAL JUDGMENTS?

● WHAT COGNITIVE PROCESSES ACCOMPANY BEHAVIOUR PROBLEMS?

● WHAT IS HEALTH PSYCHOLOGY AND THE PSYCHOLOGY OF ILLNESS?

● HOW DO SOCIAL RELATIONSHIPS SUPPORT HEALTH AND WELL-BEING?

If you are a typical university student, you may occasionally feel mildly depressed. Perhaps you have felt dissatisfied with life, discouraged about the future, sad, lacking appetite and energy, unable to concentrate, perhaps even wondering if life is worth living. Maybe disappointing grades have seemed to jeopardize your career goals. Perhaps the breakup of a relationship has left you in despair. At such times, you may fall into self-focused brooding that only worsens your feelings. In one large-scale survey of university students, 31 percent reported that during the last school year they had at some point felt "so depressed it was difficult to function" (ACHA, 2009). For 13 percent of men and 22 percent of women, life's down times are not just temporary blue moods in response to bad events; rather, they define a major depressive episode that lasts for weeks without any obvious cause—and thus, at some point, a diagnosis of depression (Pelham, 2009).

Among the many thriving areas of applied social psychology is one that relates social psychology's concepts to depression; to other problems such as loneliness, anxiety, and physical illness; and to happiness and well-being. This bridge-building research between social psychology and **clinical psychology** seeks answers to four important questions:

- As laypeople or as professional psychologists, how can we improve our judgments and predictions about others?

- How do the ways in which we think about self and others fuel problems such as depression, loneliness, anxiety, and ill health?

- How might people reverse these maladaptive thought patterns?

- What part do close, supportive relationships play in health and happiness?

clinical psychology
the study, assessment, and treatment of people with psychological difficulties

WHAT INFLUENCES THE ACCURACY OF CLINICAL JUDGMENTS?

Do the influences on our social judgment (discussed in Chapters 2 through 4) also affect clinicians' judgments of clients? If so, what biases should clinicians and their clients be wary of?

A parole board talks with a convicted rapist and ponders whether to release him. A clinical psychologist ponders whether her patient is seriously suicidal. A physician notes a patient's symptoms and decides whether to recommend an invasive test. A school social worker ponders whether a child's overheard threat was a macho joke, a one-time outburst, or a signal indicating a potential school assassin.

All these professionals must decide whether to make their judgments subjectively or objectively. Should they listen to their gut instincts, their hunches, their inner wisdom? Or should they rely on the wisdom embedded in formulas, statistical analyses, and computerized predictions?

Clinical judgments are also social judgments, noted social-clinical psychologist James Maddux (2008). The social construction of mental illness works like this, he explained: Someone observes a pattern of atypical or unwanted thinking and acting. A powerful group sees the desirability or profitability of diagnosing and treating this problem, and thus gives it a name. News about the disease spreads, and people begin seeing it in themselves or in family members. And thus is born Body Dysmorphic Disorder (for those preoccupied with an appearance defect), Oppositional Defiance Disorder (for toddlers throwing tantrums), Hypoactive Sexual Desire Disorder (for those not wanting sex often enough), or Orgasmic Disorder (for those having orgasms too late or too soon). "The science of medicine is not diminished by acknowledging that the notions of *health* and *illness* are socially constructed," noted Maddux, "nor is the science of economics diminished by acknowledging that the notions of *poverty* and *wealth* are socially constructed."

As social phenomena, clinical judgments are thus vulnerable to illusory correlations, overconfidence bred by hindsight, and self-confirming diagnoses (Garb, 2005; Maddux, 1993). Let's see why alerting mental health workers to how people form impressions (and misimpressions) might help avert serious misjudgments.

ILLUSORY CORRELATIONS

As we noted in Chapter 3, it is tempting to see correlations where none exist. If we expect two things to be associated—if, for example, we believe that premonitions predict events—it's easy to perceive illusory correlations. Even when shown random data, we may notice and remember instances when premonitions and events are coincidentally related, and soon forget all the instances when premonitions aren't borne out and when events happen without a prior premonition.

> "To free a man of error is to give, not to take away. Knowledge that a thing is false is a truth."
> ARTHUR SCHOPENHAUER, 1788-1860

Clinicians, like all of us, may perceive illusory correlations. If they are expecting particular responses to Rorschach inkblots to be more common among people with paranoid delusions, they may, in reflecting on their experience, believe they have witnessed such associations. To discover when such a perception is an illusory correlation, psychological science offers a simple method: Have one clinician administer and interpret the test. Have another clinician assess the same person's symptoms. Repeat this process with many people. The proof of the pudding is in the eating: Are test outcomes, in fact, correlated with reported symptoms? Some tests are, indeed, predictive. Others, such as the Rorschach inkblots and the Draw-a-Person test, have far weaker correlations than their users suppose (Lilienfeld et al., 2000, 2005).

Why, then, do clinicians continue to express confidence in uninformative or ambiguous tests? Pioneering experiments by Loren Chapman and Jean Chapman (1969, 1971) help us see why. They invited both university students and professional clinicians to study some test performances and diagnoses. If the students or clinicians expected a particular association, they generally perceived it, regardless of whether the data were supportive. For example, clinicians who believed that suspicious people draw peculiar eyes on the Draw-a-Person test did, in fact, perceive such a relationship—even when shown cases in which suspicious people drew peculiar eyes *less* often than non-suspicious people. If they believed in a connection, they were more likely to notice confirming instances.

> "No one can see his own errors."
> PSALMS 19:12

In fairness to clinicians, illusory thinking also occurs among political analysts, historians, sportscasters, personnel directors, stockbrokers, and many other professionals, including research psychologists. As researchers, we have often been blind to the shortcomings of our theoretical analyses. We so eagerly presume that our idea of truth is *the* truth that, no matter how hard we try, we cannot see our own errors. This is evident in the editorial review process that precedes any research publication. Over the years, we have read dozens of reviews of our own manuscripts and have been reviewers for dozens of others. Our experience is that it is far easier to spot someone else's sloppy thinking than to perceive our own.

HINDSIGHT AND OVERCONFIDENCE

If someone we know commits suicide, how do we react? One common reaction is to think that we, or those close to the person, should have been able to predict and to prevent the suicide: "We should have known!" In hindsight, we can see the suicidal signs and the pleas for help. One experiment gave people a description of a depressed person. Some participants were told that the person subsequently committed suicide. Compared to those not informed of the suicide, those who were informed became more likely to say they "would have expected" it (Goggin & Range, 1985). Moreover, those told of the suicide viewed the victim's family more negatively. After a tragedy, an I-should-have-known-it-all-along phenomenon can leave family, friends, and therapists feeling guilty.

David Rosenhan (1973) and seven associates provided a striking example of potential error in after-the-fact explanations. To test mental health workers' clinical insights, they each made an appointment with a different mental hospital admissions office and complained of "hearing voices." Apart from giving false names and vocations, they reported their life histories and emotional states honestly and exhibited no further symptoms. Most were diagnosed as schizophrenic and remained hospitalized for two to three weeks. Hospital clinicians then searched for early incidents in the pseudo-patients' life histories and hospital behaviour that "confirmed" and "explained" the diagnosis.

Rosenhan told of one pseudo-patient who truthfully explained to the interviewer that he had a close relationship with his mother but was rather remote from his father during his early childhood. During adolescence and beyond, however, his father became a close friend, while his relationship with his mother cooled. His present relationship with his wife was characteristically close and warm. Apart from occasional angry exchanges, friction was minimal. The children had rarely been spanked.

The interviewer, "knowing" the person suffered from schizophrenia, explained the problem this way:

> This white 39-year-old male . . . manifests a long history of considerable ambivalence in close relationships, which begins in early childhood. A warm relationship with his mother cools during his adolescence. A distant relationship to his father is described as becoming very intense. Affective stability is absent. His attempts to control emotionality with his wife and children are punctuated by angry outbursts and, in the case of the children, spankings. And while he says that he has several good friends, one senses considerable ambivalence embedded in those relationships also.

Rosenhan later told some staff members (who had heard about his controversial experiment but doubted such mistakes could occur in their hospital) that during the next three months one or more pseudo-patients would seek admission to their hospital. After the three months, he asked the staff to guess which of the 193 patients admitted during that time were really pseudo-patients. Of the 193 new patients, 41 were accused by at least one staff member of being pseudo-patients. Actually, there were none.

SELF-CONFIRMING DIAGNOSES

So far we've seen that mental health workers sometimes perceive illusory correlations and that hindsight explanations are often questionable. A third problem with clinical judgment is that people may also supply information that fulfills clinicians' expectations. To get a feel for how this phenomenon might be tested experimentally, imagine yourself on a blind date with someone who has been told that you are an uninhibited, outgoing person. To see whether this is true, your date slips questions into the conversation, such as "Have you ever done anything crazy in front of other people?" As you answer such questions, will you reveal a different "you" than if your date had been told you were shy and retiring?

In a clever series of experiments, Mark Snyder (1984), in collaboration with William Swann and others, gave interviewers some hypotheses to test concerning individuals' traits. Snyder and Swann found that people often test for a trait by looking for information that confirms it. As in the above blind-date example, if people are trying to find out if someone is an extrovert, they often solicit instances of extroversion ("What would you do if you wanted to liven things up at a party?"). Testing for introversion, they are more likely to ask, "What factors make it hard for you to really open up to people?" In response, those probed for extroversion seem more sociable, and those probed for introversion seem more shy. Our assumptions and expectations about the other person help create the kind of person we see.

Russell Fazio and his colleagues (Fazio, Effrein, & Falender, 1981) reproduced this finding and also discovered that those asked the "extroverted questions" later perceived themselves as actually more outgoing than those asked the introverted questions. Moreover, they really became noticeably more outgoing. An accomplice of the experimenter later met each participant in a waiting room and 70 percent of the time correctly guessed from the person's behaviour which condition the person had come from.

Confirmation bias also occurs when people evaluate themselves. Consider for a moment: Are you happy with your social life? Ziva Kunda and colleagues (Kunda, Fong et al., 1993) put this question to students at the University of Waterloo and elsewhere. The students searched their memories for confirming instances and thus ended up feeling happier than students asked, "Are you unhappy with your social life?" Seek and you shall find.

In other experiments, Snyder and his colleagues (1982) tried to get people to search for behaviours that would disconfirm the trait they were testing. In one experiment, they told the interviewers, "It is relevant and informative to find out ways in which the person . . . may not be like the stereotype." In another experiment, Snyder (1981) offered "$25 to the person who develops the set of questions that tell the most about . . . the interviewee." Still, confirmation bias persisted: People resisted choosing "introverted" questions when testing for extroversion.

"As is your sort of mind, So is your sort of search: You'll find What you desire."
ROBERT BROWNING, 1812–1889

Given such experiments, can you see why the behaviours of people undergoing psychotherapy come to fit their therapists' theories (Whitman, Kramer, & Baldridge, 1963)? When Harold Renaud and Floyd Estess (1961) conducted life-history interviews of 100 healthy, successful adult men, they were startled to discover that their subjects' childhood experiences were loaded with "traumatic events," tense relations with certain people, and bad decisions by their parents—the very factors usually used to explain psychiatric problems. When Freudian therapists go fishing for traumas in early childhood experiences, they often find their hunches confirmed. Thus, Snyder (1981) surmised:

> The psychiatrist who believes (erroneously) that adult gay males had bad childhood relationships with their mothers may meticulously probe for recalled (or fabricated) signs of tension between their gay clients and their mothers, but neglect to so carefully interrogate their heterosexual clients about their

maternal relationships. No doubt, any individual could recall some friction with his or her mother, however minor or isolated the incidents.

IMPLICATIONS FOR BETTER CLINICAL PRACTICE

Professional clinicians are human; they are "vulnerable to insidious errors and biases," concluded James Maddux (1993). As we have seen, they are as follows:

- Frequently the victims of illusory correlation
- Too readily convinced of their own after-the-fact analyses
- Unaware that erroneous diagnoses can be self-confirming
- Likely to overestimate their clinical intuition

The implications for mental health workers are easily stated:

- Be mindful that clients' verbal agreement with what you say does not prove its validity.
- Beware of the tendency to see relationships that you expect to see or that are supported by striking examples readily available in your memory.
- Rely on your notes more than on your memory.
- Recognize that hindsight is seductive: It can lead you to feel overconfident and sometimes to judge yourself too harshly for not having foreseen outcomes.
- Guard against the tendency to ask questions that assume your preconceptions are correct; consider opposing ideas and test them, too (Garb, 1994).

> *"One thing I have learned in a long life: that all our science, measured against reality, is primitive and childlike—and yet it is the most precious thing we have."*
> ALBERT EINSTEIN, IN B. HOFFMAN & H. DUKES, *ALBERT EINSTEIN: CREATOR AND REBEL,* 1973

● WHAT COGNITIVE PROCESSES ACCOMPANY BEHAVIOUR PROBLEMS?

Let's next consider how people's thinking affects their feelings. What are the memories, attributions, and expectations of depressed, lonely, shy, or illness-prone people?

DEPRESSION

People who feel depressed tend to think in negative terms. They view life through dark-coloured glasses. With seriously depressed people—those who are feeling worthless, lethargic, indifferent toward friends and family, and unable to sleep or eat normally—the negative thinking is self-defeating. Their intensely pessimistic outlook leads them to magnify every bad experience and minimize every good one. As one depressed young woman reported, "The real me is worthless and inadequate. I can't move forward with my work because I become frozen with doubt" (Burns, 1980, p. 29).

> *"Life is the art of being well deceived."*
> WILLIAM HAZLITT, 1778–1830

Distortion or realism?

Are all depressed people unrealistically negative? To find out, Lauren Alloy and Lyn Abramson (1979) studied university students who were either mildly depressed or not depressed. They had the students press a button, and observe that the button controlled a light coming on. Surprisingly, the depressed students were quite accurate in estimating their degree of control. It was the non-depressives whose judgments were distorted; they exaggerated the extent of their control. Despite their self-preoccupation, mildly depressed people also are more attuned to others' feelings (Harkness et al., 2005).

depressive realism the tendency of mildly depressed people to make accurate rather than self-serving judgments, attributions, and predictions

This surprising phenomenon of **depressive realism,** nicknamed the "sadder-but-wiser effect," shows up in various judgments of a person's control or skill (Ackermann & DeRubeis, 1991; Alloy et al., 1990). Shelley Taylor (1989, p. 214) explained:

> Normal people exaggerate how competent and well liked they are. Depressed people do not. Normal people remember their past behaviour with a rosy glow. Depressed people [unless severely depressed] are more evenhanded in recalling their successes and failures. Normal people describe themselves primarily positively. Depressed people describe both their positive and negative qualities. Normal people take credit for successful outcomes and tend to deny responsibility for failure. Depressed people accept responsibility for both success and failure. Normal people exaggerate the control they have over what goes on around them. Depressed people are less vulnerable to the illusion of control. Normal people believe to an unrealistic degree that the future holds a bounty of good things and few bad things. Depressed people are more realistic in their perceptions of the future. In fact, on virtually every point on which normal people show enhanced self-regard, illusions of control, and unrealistic visions of the future, depressed people fail to show the same biases. "Sadder but wiser" does indeed appear to apply to depression.

Underlying the thinking of depressed people are their attributions of responsibility. Consider: If you fail an exam and blame yourself, you may conclude that you are stupid or lazy; consequently, you may feel depressed. If you attribute the failure to an unfair exam or to other circumstances beyond your control, you may feel angry. In over 100 studies involving 15 000 subjects, depressed people have been more likely than non-depressed people to exhibit a negative **explanatory style** (Peterson & Steen, 2002; Sweeney, Anderson, & Bailey, 1986). As shown in Figure B–1, this explanatory style attributes failure and setbacks to causes that are stable ("It's going to last forever"), global ("It's going to affect everything I do"), and internal ("It's all my fault"). The result of this pessimistic, overgeneralized, self-blaming thinking, said Abramson and her colleagues (1989), is a depressing sense of hopelessness.

explanatory style a person's habitual way of explaining life events. A negative, pessimistic, and depressive explanatory style attributes failures to stable, global, and internal causes.

Is negative thinking a cause or a result of depression?

The cognitive accompaniments of depression raise a chicken-and-egg question: Do depressed moods cause negative thinking, or does negative thinking cause depression?

Depressed moods cause negative thinking

As we noted in Chapter 3, our moods definitely colour our thinking. When we feel happy, we think happy. We see and recall a good world. But let our mood turn gloomy and our thoughts switch onto a different track. Off come the rose-coloured glasses; on go the dark glasses. Now the bad mood primes our recollections of negative events (Bower, 1987; Johnson & Magaro, 1987). Our relationships seem to sour, our self-images tarnish, our hopes for the future dim, people's behaviour seems more sinister (Brown & Taylor, 1986; Mayer & Salovey, 1987). As

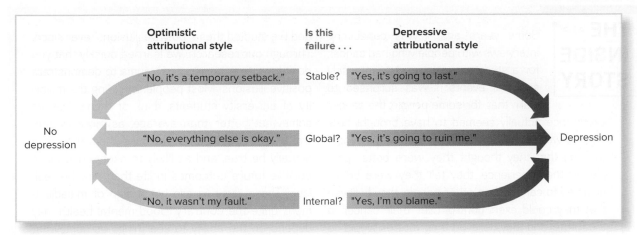

FIGURE B–1

DEPRESSIVE EXPLANATORY STYLE.

Depression is linked with a negative, pessimistic way of explaining and interpreting failures.

depression deepens, memories and expectations plummet; when depression lifts, thinking brightens (Barnett & Gotlib, 1988; Kuiper & Higgins, 1985). As an example, currently depressed people recall their parents as having been rejecting and punitive. But formerly depressed people recall their parents in the same positive terms as do never-depressed people (Lewinsohn & Rosenbaum, 1987). Thus, when you hear depressed people trashing their parents, remember: Moods modify memory.

By studying basketball fans, Edward Hirt and his colleagues (1992) demonstrated that even a temporary bad mood can darken our thinking. After the fans were either depressed by watching their team lose or elated by a victory, the researchers asked them to predict the team's future performance, and their own. After a loss, people offered bleaker assessments not only of the team's future but also of their own likely performance at throwing darts, solving anagrams, and getting a date. When things aren't going our way, it may seem as though they never will.

A depressed mood also affects behaviour. When depressed, we tend to be withdrawn, glum, and quick to complain. Stephen Strack and James Coyne (1983) found that depressed people were realistic in thinking that others didn't appreciate their behaviour; their pessimism and bad moods can even trigger social rejection (Carver, Kus, & Scheier, 1994). Depressed behaviour can also trigger reciprocal depression in others. College and university students who have depressed roommates tend to become a little depressed themselves (Burchill & Stiles, 1988; Joiner, 1994; Sanislow, Perkins, & Balogh, 1989). In dating couples, too, depression is often contagious (Katz, Beach, & Joiner, 1999). (Better news comes from a study that followed nearly 5000 residents of one Massachusetts city for 20 years. Happiness is also contagious. When surrounded by happy people, people become more likely to be happy in the future [Fowler & Christakis, 2008].)

We can see, then, that being depressed has cognitive and behavioural effects. Does it also work the other way? Does depression have cognitive origins?

Negative thinking causes depressed moods

Depression is natural when experiencing severe stress—losing a job, getting divorced or rejected, or suffering any experience that disrupts our sense of who we are and why we are worthy human beings. The brooding that comes with this short-term depression can be adaptive. Much as nausea and pain protect the body from toxins, so depression protects us, by slowing us down, causing us to reassess, and then redirecting our energy in new ways (Watkins, 2008).

THE >>>
INSIDE
STORY

Some years ago, I was conducting interviews with people who had cancer, for a study on adjustment to intensely stressful events. I was surprised to learn that, for some people, the cancer experience actually seemed to have brought benefits, as well as the expected liabilities. Many people told me that they thought they were better people for the experience, they felt they were better adjusted to cancer than other people, they believed that they could exert control over their cancer in the future, and they believed their futures would be cancer-free, even when we knew from their medical histories that their cancers were likely to recur.

As a result, I became fascinated by how people can construe even the worst of situations as good,

and I've studied these "positive illusions" ever since. Through our research, we learned quickly that you don't have to experience a trauma to demonstrate positive illusions. Most people, including the majority of university students, think of themselves as somewhat better than average, as more in control of the circumstances around them than may actually be true, and as likely to experience more positive future outcomes in life than may be realistic. These illusions are not a sign of maladjustment; quite the contrary. Good mental health may depend on the ability to see things as somewhat better than they are and to find benefits even when things seem most bleak.

Shelley Taylor, *UCLA*

Insights gained during times of depressed inactivity may later result in better strategies for interacting with the world. But depression-prone people respond to bad events with self-focused rumination and self-blame (Mor & Winquist, 2002; Pyszczynski et al., 1991; Wood et al., 1990a, 1990b). Their self-esteem fluctuates more rapidly, up with boosts and down with threats (Butler, Hokanson, & Flynn, 1994).

Why are some people so affected by even minor stresses? Evidence suggests that when stress-induced rumination is filtered through a negative explanatory style, the frequent outcome is depression (Robinson & Alloy, 2003). Colin Sacks and Daphne Bugental (1987) asked some young women to get acquainted with a stranger who sometimes acted cold and unfriendly, creating an awkward social situation. Unlike optimistic women, those with a pessimistic explanatory style—who characteristically offer stable, global, and internal attributions for bad events—reacted to the social failure by feeling depressed. Moreover, they then behaved more antagonistically toward the next people they met. Their negative thinking led to a negative mood, which then led to negative behaviour.

Such depressive rumination is more common among women, reported Susan Nolen-Hoeksema (2003). When trouble strikes, men tend to act, women tend to think—and often to "overthink," she reported. And that helps explain why, beginning in adolescence, women have, compared with men, a doubled risk of depression (Hyde, Mezulis, & Abramson, 2008).

Outside the laboratory, studies of children, teenagers, and adults confirm that those with the pessimistic explanatory style are more likely to become depressed when bad things happen. One study monitored university students every six weeks for two-and-a-half years (Alloy et al., 1999). Only 1 percent of those who began college with optimistic thinking styles had a first depressive episode, but 17 percent of those with pessimistic thinking styles did. "A recipe for severe depression is pre-existing pessimism encountering failure," noted Martin Seligman (1991, p. 78). Researcher Peter Lewinsohn and his colleagues (1985) assembled these findings into a coherent psychological understanding of depression. The negative self-image, attributions, and expectations of a depressed person are, they reported, an essential link in a vicious cycle that is triggered by negative experience—perhaps academic or vocational failure, or family conflict, or social rejection (Figure B–2). Such ruminations create a depressed mood that drastically alters the way a person thinks and acts, which then fuels further negative experiences, self-blame, and depressed mood. In experiments, mildly depressed people's moods brighten when a task diverts their attention to something external (Nix et al., 1995). Depression is, therefore, both a cause and a consequence of negative cognitions.

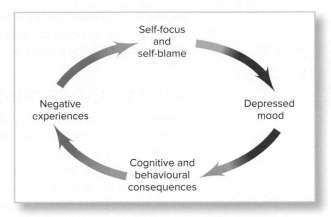

FIGURE B–2
THE VICIOUS CYCLE OF DEPRESSION.

Martin Seligman (1991, 1998, 2002) believes that self-focus and self-blame help explain the near-epidemic levels of depression in the Western world today. In North America, for example, young adults today are three times as likely as their grandparents to have suffered depression—despite their grandparents' experiencing a lower standard of living and greater hardship (Cross-National Collaborative Group, 1992; Swindle et al., 2000). Seligman believes that the decline of religion and family, plus the growth of individualism, breeds hopelessness and self-blame when things don't go well. Failed courses, careers, and marriages produce despair when we stand alone, with nothing and no one to fall back on. If, as a macho *Fortune* ad declared, you can "make it on your own," on "your own drive, your own guts, your own energy, your own ambition," then whose fault is it if you don't make it?

In non-Western cultures, where close-knit relationships and cooperation are the norm, major depression is less common and less tied to guilt and self-blame over perceived failure. In Japan, for example, depressed people instead tend to report feeling shame over letting down their family or co-workers (Draguns, 1990).

These insights into the thinking style linked with depression have prompted social psychologists to study thinking patterns associated with other problems. How do those who are

THE >>> INSIDE STORY

My dual background in social and personality psychology often leads me to topics at the intersection of the two fields; for example, how do personality impressions develop in social contexts? Several speculations about the topic arose from the inclusion of discussion groups in some of my undergraduate courses. When students met several times to work on a task, one thing became clear: First impressions don't always rule. For certain personality types, the first impression they make on other group members does not necessarily match the group's final impression of them. So my graduate students and I designed a series of studies to follow one type of individual whose bad first impression improves over time, namely, the shy person. We also studied another type of individual whose good shiny first impression gradually darkens, namely the narcissist. The moral of this scientific story: Social perceptions are a constantly shifting product of the context, the time frame, and the target's actual personality.

Del Paulhus, *University of British Columbia*

plagued with excessive anxiety, shyness, or substance abuse view themselves? How well do they recall their successes and their failures? To what do they attribute their ups and downs? Where is their attention focused—on themselves or on others?

ANXIETY AND SHYNESS

Shyness is a form of social anxiety characterized by self-consciousness and worry about what others think (Anderson & Harvey, 1988; Asendorpf, 1987; Carver & Scheier, 1986). Being interviewed for a much-wanted job, dating someone for the first time, stepping into a roomful of strangers, performing before an important audience, or giving a speech (one of the most common phobias) can make almost anyone feel anxious. But some people feel anxious in almost any situation in which they might be evaluated, such as having a casual lunch with a co-worker. For these people, anxiety is more a trait than a temporary state.

Doubting our ability in social situations

What causes us to feel anxious in social situations? Why are some people shackled in the prison of their own social anxiety? Barry Schlenker and Mark Leary (1982, 1985; Leary & Kowalski, 1995) answered those questions by applying self-presentation theory. As you may recall from Chapters 2 and 4, self-presentation theory assumes that we are eager to present ourselves in ways that make a good impression. The implications for anxiety in social situations are straightforward: We feel anxious when we are motivated to impress others but have self-doubts. This simple principle helps explain a variety of research findings, each of which may ring true in your own experience. We feel most anxious when we are in the following situations:

- With powerful, high-status people—people whose impressions of us matter
- In an evaluative context, as when making a first impression on the parents of your fiancé
- Self-conscious (as shy people often are), and our attention is focused on ourselves and how we are coming across
- Focused on something central to our self-image, as when a university professor presents ideas before peers at a professional convention
- In novel or unstructured situations, such as a first school dance or first formal dinner, where we are unsure of the social rules

For most people, the natural tendency in all such situations is to be cautiously self-protective: to talk less; to avoid topics that reveal ignorance; to be guarded about yourself; to be unassertive, agreeable, and smiling. Ironically, such anxious concern with making a good impression often makes a bad impression (Broome & Wegner, 1994; Meleshko & Alden, 1993).

With time, however, shy people often become well liked. Consider a series of interesting studies conducted by Del Paulhus (Paulhus, 1998; Paulhus & Morgan, 1997) at the University of British Columbia. He examined how people perceive each other over time. In the short run, self-enhancing people were evaluated positively, and shy people were evaluated negatively. After seven meetings, however, this pattern reversed—the egotistical self-enhancers got on people's nerves, but the modesty, sensitivity, and discretion of shy people eventually led people to like them.

Overpersonalizing situations

Compared with unshy people, shy, self-conscious people (whose numbers include many adolescents) see incidental events as somehow related to themselves (Fenigstein, 1984; Fenigstein & Vanable, 1992). Shy, anxious people overpersonalize situations, a tendency that breeds anxious concern and, in extreme cases, paranoia. They also overestimate the extent to which other people are watching and evaluating them. If they are having a bad hair day, or they have a facial blemish, they assume everyone else notices and judges them accordingly. Shy people may even be conscious of their self-consciousness. They wish they could stop worrying about blushing, about what others are thinking, or about what to say next.

To reduce anxiety in social situations, some people turn to alcohol. Alcohol lowers anxiety as it reduces self-consciousness (Hull & Young, 1983). Thus, chronically self-conscious people are especially likely to drink following a failure. If recovering from alcoholism, they are more likely than those low in self-consciousness to relapse when they again experience stress or failure.

Alcohol can also reduce social anxiety by restricting people's ability to think about their internal states. Claude Steele and Robert Josephs (1990) have called this effect "alcohol myopia." In their research, Steele and Josephs showed that when people are intoxicated they can focus on only the most salient cues in their environment. If drinking at a rowdy party, anxious people are likely to focus on the party and not on their anxiety. On the other hand, if they drink alone in a quiet room, they are more likely to focus on their anxiety (as there is little else to focus on) and become more anxious. This may be one reason why people drink mainly in social situations.

Alcohol myopia can have serious consequences, as Queen's University professor Tara MacDonald and University of Waterloo professors Mark Zanna and Geoff Fong (1995) have shown. They had students at a campus bar answer a survey about drinking and driving either when they arrived at the bar (i.e., when they were sober) or at the end of the night after they'd been drinking. They either asked people their attitudes about "drinking and driving" or about "drinking and driving only a short distance." They found that the way they asked the question made no difference to sober students, but the students who were intoxicated were more accepting of drinking and driving "only a short distance" (see Figure B–3). It seems that alcohol myopia

FIGURE B–3

ALCOHOL MYOPIA AND ATTITUDES TOWARD DRUNK DRIVING.

When people are intoxicated, they can only focus on a very limited amount of information, an effect called alcohol myopia. If people focus on cues that lower their inhibition, such as the short distance home, then they may be more likely to drink and drive. (Adapted from MacDonald, Zanna, & Fong, 1995)

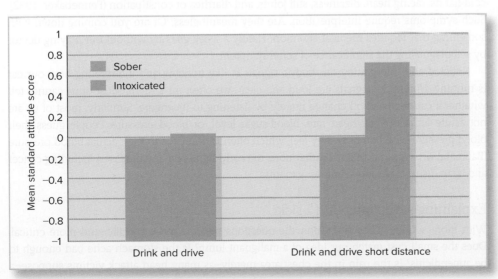

made these students focus on the encouraging cue that it was just a short distance, and not their more general belief that drinking and driving is dangerous. This same effect of alcohol—a narrowing of attention—can contribute to potentially costly decisions to have unprotected casual sex (MacDonald et al., 2000).

● WHAT IS HEALTH PSYCHOLOGY AND THE PSYCHOLOGY OF ILLNESS?

Health psychology examines how psychological processes influence our physical health. Our thoughts and emotions affect how we interpret symptoms, whether we seek treatment, and how we respond to treatment when we do seek it.

In the industrialized world, at least half of all deaths are linked with behaviour—with consuming cigarettes, alcohol, drugs, and harmful foods; with reactions to stress; with lack of exercise; and with not following a doctor's advice. A new interdisciplinary field called **behavioural medicine** studies these behavioural contributions to illness. Psychology's contribution to this interdisciplinary science is its subfield, **health psychology**. Health psychologists study how people respond to illness symptoms and how emotions and explanations influence health.

behavioural medicine
an interdisciplinary field that integrates and applies behavioural and medical knowledge about health and disease

health psychology
the study of the psychological roots of health and illness. It provides psychology's contribution to behavioural medicine.

REACTIONS TO ILLNESS

How do people decide whether they are ill? How do they explain their symptoms? What influences their willingness to seek and follow treatment?

Noticing symptoms

Chances are you have recently experienced at least one of these physical complaints: headache, stomach ache, nasal congestion, sore muscles, ringing in the ears, excess perspiration, cold hands, racing heart, dizziness, stiff joints, and diarrhea or constipation (Pennebaker, 1982). Such symptoms require interpretation. Are they meaningless? Or are you coming down with something that requires medical attention? Hardly a week goes by without our playing doctor by self-diagnosing the significance of some symptom.

Noticing and interpreting our body's signals is like noticing and interpreting how our car is running. Unless the signals are loud and clear, we often miss them. Most of us cannot tell whether a car needs an oil change merely by listening to its engine. Similarly, most of us are not astute judges of our heart rate, blood-sugar level, or blood pressure. People guess their blood pressure based on how they feel, which often is unrelated to their actual blood pressure (Baumann & Leventhal, 1985). Furthermore, the early signs of many illnesses, including cancer and heart disease, are subtle and easy to miss.

Explaining symptoms: Am I sick?

With more serious aches and pains, the questions become more specific—and more critical. Does the small cyst match our idea of a malignant lump? Is the stomach ache bad enough to be appendicitis? Is the pain in the chest area merely—as many heart attack victims suppose—a muscle spasm? Indeed, half or more of heart attack victims die without having sought medical help (Friedman & DiMatteo, 1989). What factors influence how we explain symptoms?

Once we notice symptoms, we tend to interpret them according to familiar disease schemas (Bishop, 1991). In medical schools, this can have amusing results. As part of their training, medical students learn the symptoms associated with various diseases. Because they also experience various symptoms, they sometimes attribute their symptoms to recently learned disease schemas. ("Maybe this wheeze is the beginning of pneumonia.") As you may have discovered, psychology students are prone to this same effect as they read about psychological disorders.

Do I need treatment?

When people notice a symptom and interpret it as possibly serious, several factors influence their decision to seek medical care. People more often seek treatment if they believe their symptoms have a physical rather than a psychological cause (Bishop, 1987). They may delay seeking help, however, if they feel embarrassed, if they think the likely benefits of medical attention won't justify the cost and inconvenience, or if they want to avoid a possibly devastating diagnosis.

Numerous studies have found a gender difference in decisions to seek medical treatment: Compared to men, women report more symptoms, use more prescription and non-prescription drugs, and visit physicians 40 percent more often for preventative care. Women also visit psychotherapists 50 percent more often than men (Olfson & Pincus, 1994).

So are women more often sick? Apparently not. In fact, men may be more disease-prone. Among other problems, men have higher rates of hypertension, ulcers, and cancer, as well as shorter life expectancies. So why are women more likely to see a doctor? Perhaps women are more attentive to their internal states. Perhaps they are less reluctant to admit "weakness" and seek help (Bishop, 1984).

Patients are more willing to follow treatment instructions when they have a warm relationship with their doctor, when they help plan their treatment, and when options are framed attractively. People are more likely to elect an operation when given "a 40-percent chance of surviving" than when given "a 60-percent chance of not surviving" (Rothman & Salovey, 1997; Wilson, Kaplan, & Schneiderman, 1987). Such "gain-framed" messages also persuade more people to use sunscreen, eschew cigarettes, and get HIV tests (Detweiler et al., 1999; Salovey, Schneider, & Apanovitch, 2002; Schneider et al., 2000). Better to tell people that "sunscreen maintains healthy, young-looking skin" than to tell them that "not using sunscreen decreases your chances of healthy, young-looking skin." Framing a desired exercise program as minutes per day, rather than hours per week, similarly increases people's willingness to commit to it (Peetz, Buehler, & Britten, 2011).

EMOTIONS AND ILLNESS

Do our emotions predict our susceptibility to heart disease, stroke, cancer, and other ailments (Figure B–4)?

Heart disease has been linked with a competitive, impatient, and—the aspect that matters most—anger-prone personality (Chida & Steptoe, 2009; Kupper & Denollet, 2007). When under stress, reactive, anger-prone, "Type A" people secrete more of the stress hormones believed to accelerate the buildup of plaque on the walls of the heart's arteries.

FIGURE B–4

STRESS AND
ILLNESS.

Stress-caused
negative emotions
may have various
effects on health. This
is especially so for
depressed or anger-
prone people.

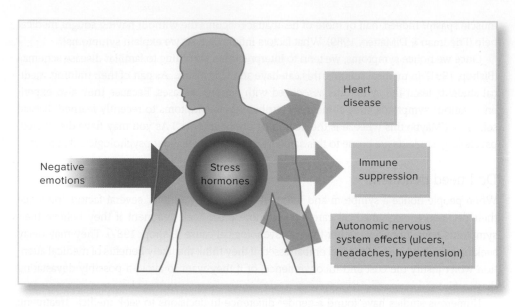

Depression also increases the risk of various ailments. Mildly depressed people are more vulnerable to heart disease, even after controlling for differences in smoking and other disease-related factors (Anda et al., 1993; Boehm et al., 2011). The year after a heart attack, depressed people have a doubled risk of further heart problems (Frasure-Smith et al., 1995, 1999, 2005). The toxicity of negative emotions contributes to the high rate of depression and anxiety among chronically ill people (Cohen & Rodriguez, 1995). The association between depression and heart disease may result from stress-related inflammation of the arteries (Matthews, 2005; Miller & Blackwell, 2006). Stress hormones enhance protein production that contributes to inflammation, which helps fight infections. But inflammation can also exacerbate asthma, clogged arteries, and depression.

George Vaillant (1997) witnessed the effect of distress when he followed a group of male university graduates from mid-life into old age. Of those whom, at age 52, he classified as "squares" (having never abused alcohol, used tranquilizers, or seen a psychiatrist), only 5 percent had died by age 75. Of those classified as "distressed" (who had abused alcohol and either used tranquilizers or seen a psychiatrist), 38 percent had died.

Optimism and health

Stories abound of people who took a sudden turn for the worse when something makes them lose hope, or who suddenly improved when hope is renewed. As cancer attacked the liver of 9-year-old Jeff, his doctors feared the worst. But Jeff remains optimistic. He is determined to grow up to be a cancer research scientist. One day, Jeff is elated. A specialist who has taken a long-distance interest in his case was planning to stop off while on a cross-country trip. There is so much Jeff wants to tell the doctor and to show him from the diary he has kept since he got sick. On the anticipated day, fog blankets his city. The doctor's plane was diverted to another city, from which the doctor flew on to his final destination. Hearing the news, Jeff cries quietly. The next morning, pneumonia and fever have developed, and Jeff lies listless. By evening, he is in a coma. The next afternoon, he dies (Visintainer & Seligman, 1983).

Understanding the links between attitudes and disease requires more than dramatic true stories. If hopelessness coincides with cancer, we are left to wonder: Does cancer breed hopelessness, or does hopelessness also hinder resistance to cancer? To resolve this chicken-and-egg riddle, researchers have (1) experimentally created hopelessness by subjecting organisms to uncontrollable stresses and (2) correlated the hopeless explanatory style with future illnesses.

Stress and illness

The clearest indication of the effects of hopelessness—what Chapter 2 labels learned helplessness—comes from experiments that subject animals to mild but uncontrollable electric shocks, loud noises, or crowding. Such experiences do not cause diseases such as cancer, but they do lower the body's resistance. Rats injected with live cancer cells more often develop and die of tumours if they also receive inescapable shocks than if they receive either escapable shocks or no shocks. Moreover, compared to juvenile rats given controllable shocks, those given uncontrollable shocks are twice as likely in adulthood to develop tumours if given cancer cells and another round of shocks (Visintainer & Seligman, 1985). Animals that have learned helplessness react more passively, and blood tests reveal a weakened immune response.

It's a big leap from rats to humans. But a growing body of evidence reveals that people who undergo highly stressful experiences become more vulnerable to disease (Segerstrom & Miller, 2004). Stress doesn't make us sick, but it does divert energy from our disease-fighting immune system, leaving us more vulnerable to infections and malignancy (S. Cohen, 2002, 2004). The death of a spouse, the stress of a space flight landing, even the strain of an exam week have all been associated with depressed immune defences (Jemmott & Locke, 1984).

Consider the following:

- Stress magnifies the severity of respiratory infections and of symptoms experienced by volunteers who are knowingly infected with a cold virus (S. Cohen et al., 2003, 2006; Pedersen, Zachariae, & Bovbjerg, 2010).

- Newlywed couples who became angry while discussing problems suffered more immune system suppression the next day (Kiecolt-Glaser et al., 1993). When people are stressed by marital conflict, laboratory puncture wounds take a day or two longer to heal (Kiecolt-Glaser et al., 2005). Studies in 11 countries following 6.5 million lives through time reveal that, among men and younger adults, divorce increases the ensuing risk of early death (Sbarra, Law, & Portley, 2011).

- Work stress can literally be disheartening. In one study that followed 17 415 middle-aged women, researchers found that significant work stress predicted an 88 percent increased risk of heart attacks (Slopen et al., 2010). In Denmark, a study of 12 116 female nurses found that those reporting "much too high" work pressures had a 40 percent increased risk of heart disease (Allesøe et al., 2010).

- Stress increases the production of inflammation-producing proteins. Those who experience social stress, including children reared in abusive families, are therefore more prone to inflammation responses (Dickerson et al., 2009; Miller, Chen, & Parker, 2011). Inflammation fights infections, but persistent inflammation contributes to asthma, clogged arteries, and depression. Researchers have even discovered molecular, "epigenetic" mechanisms by which stress, in some people, activates genes that control inflammation (Cole et al., 2010).

Explanatory style and illness

If uncontrollable stress affects health, depresses immune functioning, and generates a passive, hopeless resignation, then will people who exhibit such pessimism be more vulnerable to illness? Several studies have confirmed that a pessimistic style of explaining bad events (saying, "It's going to last, it's going to undermine everything, and it's my fault") makes illness more likely (Carver, Scheier, & Segerstrom, 2010). Christopher Peterson and Martin Seligman (1987) studied the press quotations of 94 members of baseball's Hall of Fame and gauged how often they offered pessimistic (stable, global, internal) explanations for bad events, such as losing big games. Those who routinely did so tended to die at somewhat younger ages. Optimists—who offered stable, global, and internal explanations for good events—usually outlived the pessimists.

Other studies have followed lives through time:

- Harvard graduates who expressed the most optimism in 1946 were the healthiest when restudied 34 years later (Peterson, Seligman, & Vaillant, 1988).

- One Dutch research team followed 941 older adults for nearly a decade (Giltay et al., 2004, 2007). Among those in the upper optimism quartile, only 30 percent died, compared with 57 percent of those in the lower optimism quartile.

- Catholic nuns who expressed the most positive feelings at an average age of 22 outlived their more dour counterparts by an average of seven years over the ensuing half-century and more (Danner, Snowdon, & Friesen, 2001).

It is important to note, however, that healthy behaviours—exercise, good nutrition, not drinking to excess—are essential contributors to the longevity of many optimists (Peterson & Bossio, 2000; Whooley et al., 2008).

From their own studies, researchers Howard Tennen and Glenn Affleck (1987) agree that a positive, hopeful explanatory style is generally good medicine. But they also remind us that every silver lining has a cloud. Optimists may see themselves as invulnerable and thus fail to

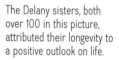

The Delany sisters, both over 100 in this picture, attributed their longevity to a positive outlook on life.

take sensible precautions; for example, those who smoke cigarettes optimistically underestimate the risks involved (Segerstrom et al., 1993). And when things go wrong in a big way—when the optimist encounters a devastating illness—adversity can be shattering. Optimism is good for health, but even optimists have a mortality rate of 100 percent.

● HOW DO SOCIAL RELATIONSHIPS SUPPORT HEALTH AND WELL-BEING?

There is one other major topic in the social psychology of mental and physical well-being. Supportive close relationships—feeling liked, affirmed, and encouraged by intimate friends and family—predict both health and happiness.

Our relationships are fraught with stress. "Hell is others," wrote Jean-Paul Sartre. When Peter Warr and Roy Payne (1982) asked a representative sample of British adults what, if anything, had emotionally strained them the day before, "family" was their most frequent answer. And stress, as we have seen, aggravates health problems such as coronary heart disease, hypertension, and suppression of our disease-fighting immune system.

Still, on balance, close relationships contribute less to illness than to health and happiness. Asked what prompted yesterday's times of pleasure, the same British sample, by an even larger margin, again answered, "Family." Close relationships provide our greatest heartaches, but also our greatest joys.

CLOSE RELATIONSHIPS AND HEALTH

Eight extensive investigations, each interviewing thousands of people across several years, have reached a common conclusion: Close relationships predict health (Berkman, 1995; Ryff & Singer, 2000). Health risks are greater among lonely people, who often experience more stress, sleep less well, and commit suicide more often (Cacioppo & Patrick, 2008). Compared with those with few social ties, those who have close relationships with friends, family, or other members of close-knit religious or community organizations are less likely to die prematurely. Outgoing, affectionate, relationship-oriented people have more friends, and they are also less susceptible to cold viruses (see Figure B–5; S. Cohen et al., 1997, 2003).

Married couples also tend to live healthier, longer lives than their unmarried counterparts. One major study found that people, regardless of age, sex, race, and income, tend to be healthier if married (NCHS, 2008). Married folks experience less pain from headaches and backaches, suffer less stress, and drink and smoke less. One experiment subjected married women to the threat of electric ankle shocks as they lay in an fMRI brain scanning machine (Coan, Schaefer, & Davidson, 2006). Meanwhile, some of the women held their husband's hand, some held an anonymous person's hand, and some held no hand at all. While awaiting the shocks, the threat-responsive areas of the women's brains were less active if they held their husband's hand. Consistent with the finding that it's happy, supportive marriages that are conducive to health (De Vogli, Chandola, & Marmot, 2007), the soothing hand-holding benefit was greatest for those reporting the happiest marriages.

Giving social support also matters. In one five-year study of 423 elderly married couples, those who gave the most social support (from rides and errands for friends and neighbours to

FIGURE B–5

RATE OF COLDS BY SOCIABILITY.

After a cold virus injection, highly sociable people were less vulnerable to catching colds. (From S. Cohen et al., 2003)

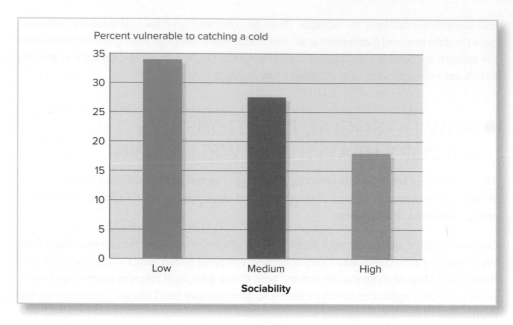

emotional support of their spouse) enjoyed greater longevity, even after controlling for age, sex, initial health, and economic status (S. L. Brown et al., 2003). Especially among women, suggests a Finnish study that tracked more than 700 people's illnesses, it is better to give social support than to only receive it (Väänänen et al., 2005).

Moreover, losing social ties heightens the risk of disease:

- A Finnish study of 96 000 widowed people found their risk of death doubled in the week following their partner's death (Kaprio, Koskenvuo, & Rita, 1987).

- An American National Academy of Sciences study revealed that those who are recently widowed become more vulnerable to disease and death (Dohrenwend et al., 1982).

- A study of 30 000 men revealed that when a marriage ends, men drink and smoke more and eat fewer vegetables and more fried foods (Eng et al., 2001).

Confiding and health

So there is a link between social support and health. Why? Perhaps those who enjoy close relationships eat better, exercise more, and smoke and drink less. Perhaps a supportive network helps us evaluate and overcome stressful events (S. E. Taylor, Repetti, & Seeman, 1997). In more than 80 studies, social support has been linked with better-functioning cardiovascular and immune systems (Uchino, Cacioppo, & Kiecolt-Glaser, 1996). Thus, when we are wounded by someone's dislike or by the loss of a job, the advice, help, and reassurance of a friend may be good medicine (Cutrona, 1986; Rook, 1987). Even when the problem isn't mentioned, friends provide us with distraction and a sense that, come what may, we're accepted, liked, and respected.

With someone we consider a close friend, we may confide painful feelings. In one study, James Pennebaker and Robin O'Heeron (1984) contacted the surviving spouses of suicide or car accident victims. Those who bore their grief alone had more health problems than those who expressed it openly. When Pennebaker (1990) surveyed more than 700 university women, he found one in twelve reported a traumatic sexual experience in childhood. Compared with women who had experienced non-sexual traumas, such as parental death or divorce, the sexually abused women reported more headaches, stomach ailments, and other health problems—especially if they had kept their history of abuse secret.

To isolate the confiding, confessional side of close relationships, Pennebaker asked the bereaved spouses to share what upsetting events had been weighing on their minds. Those they first asked to describe a trivial event were physically tense. They stayed tense until they confided their troubles. Then they relaxed. Writing about personal traumas in a diary also seems to help. When volunteers in another experiment did so, they had fewer health problems during the next six months. One participant explained, "Although I have not talked with anyone about what I wrote, I was finally able to deal with it, work through the pain instead of trying to block it out. Now it doesn't hurt to think about it." Even if it's only "talking to my diary," and even if the writing is about your future dreams and life goals, it helps to be able to confide (Burton & King, 2006; King, 2001; Lyubomirksy, Sousa, & Dickerhoof, 2006).

Other experiments confirm the benefits of engaging rather than suppressing stressful experiences. In one, Stephen Lepore and his colleagues (2000) had students view a stressful slide show and video on the Holocaust and either talk about it immediately afterwards or not. Two days later, those who talked were experiencing less stress and fewer intrusive thoughts.

Poverty, inequality, and health

We have seen connections between health and the feelings of control that accompany a positive explanatory style, and we have seen connections between health and social support. Feelings of control and support together with health care and nutrition help explain why economic status correlates with longevity. Recall from Chapter 1 the study of old grave markers in Glasgow, Scotland: Those with the costliest, highest pillars (indicating affluence) tended to have lived the longest (Carroll et al., 1994). Still today, in Scotland, Canada, and the United States, poorer people are at greater risk for premature death. Poverty predicts perishing. Being wealthy predicts being healthy.

The correlation between poverty and ill health could run either way. Bad health isn't good for a person's income. But most evidence indicates that the causal arrow runs from poverty toward ill health (Sapolsky, 2005). So how does poverty "get under the skin"? The answers include (a) reduced access to quality health care, (b) unhealthier lifestyles (smoking is much more common among less educated and lower-income people), and, to a striking extent, (c) increased stress. To be poor is to be at risk for increased stress, negative emotions, and a toxic environment (Adler & Snibbe, 2003; Chen, 2004; Gallo & Matthews, 2003). To be poor is to more often be sleep-deprived after working a second job, earning paycheques that don't cover the bills, commuting on crowded public transit, living in a high-pollution area, and doing hard labour that's controlled by someone else. Even among lower-order primates, those with the least control—at the bottom of the social pecking order—are most vulnerable when exposed to a cold-like virus (S. Cohen et al., 1997).

Poverty also helps explain a curious but oft-reported correlation between intelligence and health. Ian Deary (2005) and his colleagues observed this correlation after stumbling across data from an intelligence test administered on June 1, 1932, to virtually all Scots born in 1921. When they searched Scotland's death records, they found, as have researchers in other countries since,

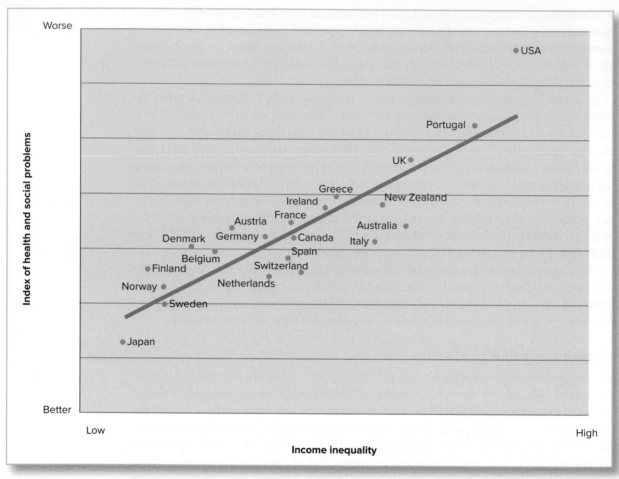

FIGURE B–6

SOCIAL AND PHYSICAL HEALTH PROBLEMS ARE GREATER IN COUNTRIES WITH HIGH INCOME INEQUALITY.

This health problems index is a composite of lower life expectancy, infant mortality, obesity, teen births, mental illness, imprisonment, and lower levels of literacy, social trust, and social mobility. (Richard Wilkinson and Kate Pickett, *The Spirit Level: Why Greater Equality Makes Societies Stronger* [Penguin, 2009])

that "whether you live to collect your old-age pension depends in part on your IQ at age 11. You just can't keep a good predictor down." Partly, the low-intelligence risk factor–which is roughly equivalent to that of obesity or high blood pressure, Deary reported–is due to the low-IQ persons having been less likely to cease smoking after its risks became known, and therefore more likely to die of lung cancer. Poverty-related stresses and lack of control also contribute, he notes.

People also die younger in regions with great income inequality (Kawachi et al., 1999; Lynch et al., 1998; see Figure B–6). People in Britain and Canada have larger income disparities and lower life expectancies than people in Japan and Sweden. Where inequality has grown over the last decade, as in Eastern Europe and Russia, life expectancy has been at the falling end of the teeter-totter.

Is inequality merely an indicator of poverty? The mixed evidence indicates that poverty matters but that inequality matters, too. John Lynch and his colleagues (1998, 2000) reported that people at every income level are at greater risk of early death if they live in a community with great income inequality. It's not just being poor, it's also *feeling* poor, relative to your surroundings that proves toxic. And that, Robert Sapolsky (2005) suggested, helps explain why the United States, which has the greatest income inequality of Westernized nations, simultaneously ranks number 1 in the world on health care expenditures and number 29 on life expectancy.

Inequality may also lead to a more inefficient health care system. Not only does the U.S. rank low on life expectancy; when you look at any number of specific outcomes, it is clear that the U.S. mix of private and public funding is much less efficient than the Canadian system of publicly funded health care (Woolhandler, Campbell, & Himmelstein, 1991). Canada spends far less on health care than the U.S., but the care received by and the subsequent health of Canadians is noticeably better than the typical person in the U.S. This health care advantage is especially large for those with the lowest incomes, but it extends to all income levels.

CLOSE RELATIONSHIPS AND HAPPINESS

Confiding painful feelings is good not only for the body but also for the soul. That's the conclusion of studies showing that people are happier when supported by a network of friends and family.

Some studies, summarized in Chapter 2, compared people in a competitive, individualistic culture, such as that of Canada, Australia, or the United States, with those in collectivist cultures, such as Japan and many developing countries. Individualistic cultures offer independence, privacy, and pride in personal achievements. The tighter social bonds of collectivist cultures offer protection from loneliness, alienation, divorce, and stress-related diseases.

> *"Woe to him who is alone when he falls and has not another to lift him up."*
> ECCLESIASTES 4:10B

Friendships and happiness

Other studies compare individuals with few or many close relationships. Being attached to friends with whom we can share intimate thoughts has two effects, observed the seventeenth-century philosopher Francis Bacon. "It redoubleth joys, and cutteth griefs in half." So it seems from answers to a question asked in one large-scale survey (Burt, 1986): "Looking over the last six months, who are the people with whom you discussed matters important to you?" Compared to those who could name five or six such intimates, those who could name no such person were twice as likely to report being "not very happy."

Other findings confirm the importance of having a network of friends. Across the lifespan, friendships foster self-esteem and well-being (Hartup & Stevens, 1997). For example:

- The happiest university students are those who feel satisfied with their love life (Emmons et al., 1983).

- Those who enjoy close relationships cope better with various stresses, including bereavement, rape, job loss, and illness (Abbey & Andrews, 1985; Perlman & Rook, 1987).

- Among 800 alumni who are of one university surveyed by Wesley Perkins, those who preferred having very close friends and a close marriage to having a high income and occupational success were twice as likely as their former classmates to describe themselves as "fairly" or "very" happy (Perkins, 1991). When asked, "What is necessary for your happiness?" or "What is it that makes your life meaningful?" most people mention—before anything else—satisfying close relationships with family, friends, or romantic partners (Berscheid, 1985; Berscheid & Peplau, 1983). Happiness hits close to home.

> *"The sun looks down on nothing half so good as a household laughing together over a meal."*
> C. S. LEWIS, "MEMBERSHIP," 1949

Marital attachment and happiness

For more than nine in ten people worldwide, one eventual example of a close relationship is marriage. Does marriage correlate positively with happiness? Or is there more happiness in the pleasure-seeking single life than in the "bondage," "chains," and "yoke" of marriage?

A mountain of data reveal that most people are happier attached than unattached. Survey after survey of many tens of thousands of Europeans and North Americans has produced a consistent result: Compared to those who are single or widowed, and especially compared to those who are divorced or separated, married people report being happier and more satisfied with life (Gove, Style, & Hughes, 1990; Inglehart, 1990). In Canada, married people are more satisfied with their lives than people who have never been married, who are more satisfied than people who have been widowed or divorced (Tepperman & Curtis, 1995). This marriage–happiness link occurs across ethnic groups (Parker, Ortega, & VanLaningham, 1995). Lesbian couples, too, report greater well-being than those who are alone (Peplau & Fingerhut, 2007). This is but one illustration of what social psychologist Bella DePaulo (2006) documented: There are multiple ways to satisfy the human need to belong. Nevertheless, there are few stronger predictors of happiness than a close, nurturing, equitable, intimate, lifelong companionship with one's best friend.

Is marriage, as is so often supposed, more strongly associated with men's happiness than women's? Given women's greater contribution to household work and to supportive nurturing, we might expect so. The married versus never-married happiness gap, however, is only slightly greater among men than women. In European surveys, and in a statistical digest of 93 other studies, this happiness gap is virtually identical for men and women (Inglehart, 1990; Wood, Rhodes, & Whelan, 1989). Although a bad marriage is often more depressing to a woman than to a man, the myth that single women are happier than married women can be laid to rest. Throughout the Western world, married people of both sexes report more happiness than those never married, divorced, or separated (Figure B–7).

FIGURE B–7
MARITAL STATUS AND DEPRESSION.

The Canadian Community Health Survey, a large-scale study, found depression rates were significantly higher among single and especially separated or divorced adults than among those who were married. (Based on Akhtar-Danesh & Landeen, 2007)

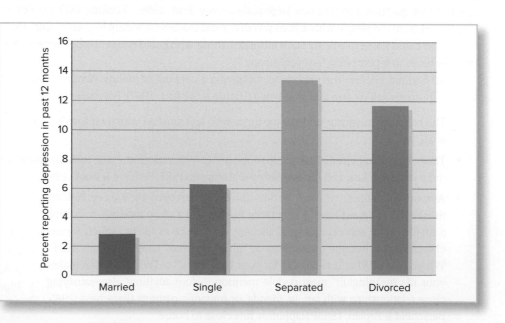

More important than being married, however, is the marriage's quality. People who say their marriage is satisfying—who find themselves still in love with their partner—rarely report being unhappy, discontented with life, or depressed. Fortunately, most married people do declare their marriages happy ones. In one large survey, almost two-thirds say their marriages are "very happy." Three out of four say their spouses are their best friends. Four out of five people say they would marry the same people again. As a consequence, most such people feel quite happy with life as a whole.

Why are married people generally happier? Does marriage promote happiness? Or is it the other way around—does happiness promote marriage? Are happy people more appealing as marriage partners? Do grouchy or depressed people more often stay single or suffer divorce? Certainly, happy people are more fun to be with. They are also more outgoing, trusting, compassionate, and focused on others (Myers, 1993). Unhappy people, as we have noted, are more often socially rejected. Depression often triggers marital stress, which deepens the depression (Davila et al., 1997). So, positive, happy people more readily form happy relationships.

But "the prevailing opinion of researchers," reported University of Oslo sociologist Arne Mastekaasa (1995), is that the marriage–happiness connection is "mainly due" to the beneficial effects of marriage. Think about this: If the happiest people marry sooner and more often, then as people age (and progressively less happy people move into marriage), the average happiness of both married and never-married people should decline. (The older, less happy newlyweds would pull down the average happiness of married people, and the unmarried group would be more and more left with the unhappy people.) But the data do not support this prediction. This suggests that marital intimacy does—for most people—pay emotional dividends. One team that followed 1380 adults over 15 years concurred (Horwitz, White, & Howell-White, 1997). The tendency for married people to be less depressed occurs even after controlling for premarital happiness.

Marriage enhances happiness for at least two reasons. First, married people are more likely to enjoy an enduring, supportive, intimate relationship, and are less likely to suffer loneliness. No wonder male medical students in a study by Robert Coombs survived medical school with less stress and anxiety if married (Coombs, 1991). A good marriage gives each partner a dependable companion, lover, and friend.

There is a second, more prosaic, reason why marriage promotes happiness, or at least buffers us from misery. Marriage offers the roles of spouse and parent, which can provide additional sources of self-esteem (Crosby, 1987). True, multiple roles can multiply stress. Our circuits can and do overload. Yet each also provides rewards, status, avenues to enrichment, and escape from stress faced in other parts of life. A self with many identities is like a mansion with many rooms. When fire struck one wing of Windsor Castle, most of the castle still remained for royals and tourists to enjoy. When our personal identity stands on several legs, it, too, holds up under the loss of any one of them. If we mess up at work, well, we can tell ourselves we're still good husbands and fathers; and in the final analysis, these parts of us are what matter most.

⋯▶ SUMMING UP

WHAT INFLUENCES THE ACCURACY OF CLINICAL JUDGMENTS?

- As psychiatrists and clinical psychologists diagnose and treat their clients, they may perceive illusory correlations.
- Hindsight explanations of people's difficulties are sometimes too easy. Indeed, after-the-fact explaining can breed overconfidence in clinical judgment.
- When interacting with clients, erroneous diagnoses are sometimes self-confirming, because interviewers tend to seek and recall information that verifies what they are looking for.
- Research on the errors that so easily creep into intuitive judgments illustrates the need for rigorous testing of intuitive conclusions.

WHAT COGNITIVE PROCESSES ACCOMPANY BEHAVIOUR PROBLEMS?

- Social psychologists are actively exploring the attributions and expectations of depressed and socially anxious people.
- Depressed people have a negative explanatory style, interpreting negative events as being stable, global, and internally caused.
- Despite their more negative judgments, mildly depressed people in laboratory tests tend to be surprisingly realistic.
- Depression can be a vicious circle in which negative thoughts elicit self-defeating behaviours and vice versa.
- Most people experience anxiety in situations where they are being evaluated; but shy individuals are extremely prone to anxiety even in friendly, casual situations. This can be another vicious circle in which anxious feelings elicit awkward, off-putting behaviour.

WHAT IS HEALTH PSYCHOLOGY AND THE PSYCHOLOGY OF ILLNESS?

- Social psychologists are also exploring the attributions and expectations of physically ill people.
- Researchers in the mushrooming field of health psychology are exploring how people decide they are ill, how they explain their symptoms, and when they seek and follow treatment.
- Psychologists are also exploring the effects of negative emotions and the links among illness, stress, and a pessimistic explanatory style.

HOW DO SOCIAL RELATIONSHIPS SUPPORT HEALTH AND WELL-BEING?

- Health and happiness are influenced not only by social cognition but also by social relations. People who enjoy close, supportive relationships are at less risk for illness and premature death. Such relationships assist people's coping with stress, especially when they enable people to confide their intimate emotions.

- Close relationships foster happiness. People who have intimate, long-term attachments with friends and family members cope better with loss and report greater happiness.
- Compared to unmarried adults, those who are married are much more likely to report being very happy, and are less at risk for depression. This appears due both to the greater social success of happy people and to the well-being engendered by a supportive life companion.

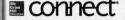 

MODULE C
Social Psychology in Court

► CHAPTER OUTLINE

● HOW RELIABLE IS EYEWITNESS TESTIMONY?

● WHAT INFLUENCES A JURY?

On January 31, 1969, Gail Miller set out in –42 degree Celsius weather for her job as a nursing assistant at the Saskatoon City Hospital. She never made it. She was found later that day lying face down in a snow bank, lifeless. She had been brutally beaten, raped, and stabbed. A trail of evidence (blood, a knife handle, a boot, and a wallet) led to a building not far away. There, visiting an acquaintance with two of his travelling companions, was a 16-year-old drifter named David Milgaard.

Milgaard was questioned; he denied any involvement in the murder. His companions, when questioned, backed his alibi; but after extensive questioning (and deprivation from the drugs they were addicted to), they changed their story. One companion said he could not account for Milgaard's whereabouts, and the other said that she saw Milgaard commit the murder. The police felt they had their man. Milgaard was tried, convicted, and sentenced to life in prison.

Larry Fisher was living in the building where David Milgaard had stayed that fateful night. In 1970, Fisher confessed to a series of rapes in Saskatoon that winter; DNA testing later demonstrated that he was the man who had killed Gail Miller.

David Milgaard spent 23 years in prison for a crime he did not commit. How could the criminal justice system fail him in such a fundamental way? The case raised other questions as well, all examined in social psychological experiments:

- There were no true eyewitnesses to this crime. How influential was the eyewitness testimony? What makes a credible witness?

- Milgaard was a drifter, and people saw him as a hippie. Can jurors ignore, as they should, their prejudices and the defendant's appearance and social status?

- How well do jurors comprehend important information, such as the statistical probabilities involved in DNA blood tests? Has the number of forensic dramas on television created unrealistic expectations in jurors—a "*CSI* effect"?

Such questions fascinate lawyers, judges, and defendants. And they are questions to which social psychology can suggest answers, as most law schools have recognized when they hire professors of "law and social science."

We can think of a courtroom as a miniature social world, one that magnifies everyday social processes with major consequences for those involved. In criminal cases, psychological factors may influence decisions involving arrest, interrogation, prosecution, plea bargaining, sentencing, and parole. Of criminal cases disposed of in Canadian courts, three in four never come to trial (Statistics Canada, 1997). Much of the trial lawyer's work, therefore, "is not persuasion in the courtroom but bargaining in the conference room" (Saks & Hastie, 1978, pp. 119–120). Even in the conference room, decisions are made based on speculation about what a jury or judge might do.

So, whether a case reaches a jury verdict or not, the social dynamics of the courtroom matter. Let's consider two sets of factors that have been heavily researched: (1) features of the courtroom drama that can influence jurors' judgments of a defendant and (2) characteristics of both the jurors and their deliberations.

● HOW RELIABLE IS EYEWITNESS TESTIMONY?

As the courtroom drama unfolds, jurors hear testimony, form impressions of the defendant, listen to instructions from the judge, and render a verdict. Let's discuss these steps one at a time, starting with eyewitness testimony.

HOW PERSUASIVE IS EYEWITNESS TESTIMONY?

In Chapter 3, we noted that anecdotes and personal testimonies, being vivid and concrete, can be powerfully persuasive, often more so than information that is logically compelling but abstract. There's no better way to end an argument than to say, "I saw it with my own eyes!"

Elizabeth Loftus (1974, 1979, 2011) found that those who had "seen" were, indeed, believed, even when their testimony was shown to be useless. When students were presented with a hypothetical robbery–murder case with circumstantial evidence but no eyewitness testimony, only 18 percent voted for conviction. Other students received the same information but with the addition of a single eyewitness. Now, knowing that someone had declared, "That's the one!" 72 percent voted for conviction. For a third group, the defence attorney discredited this testimony (the witness had 20/400 vision and was not wearing glasses). Did this discrediting reduce the effect of the testimony? In this case, not much; 68 percent still voted for conviction.

Later experiments revealed that discrediting may reduce somewhat the number of guilty votes (Whitley, 1987). But unless contradicted by another eyewitness (Leippe, 1985), a vivid eyewitness account is difficult to erase from jurors' minds. That helps explain why, compared to criminal cases lacking eyewitness testimony, those that have eyewitness testimony are more likely to produce convictions (Visher, 1987).

Can't jurors spot erroneous testimony? To find out, Gary Wells, R. C. L. Lindsay, and their colleagues staged hundreds of eyewitnessed thefts of a University of Alberta calculator. Afterwards, they asked each eyewitness to identify the culprit from a photo lineup. Other people, acting as jurors, observed the eyewitnesses being questioned and then evaluated their testimony. Are incorrect eyewitnesses believed less often than those who are accurate? As it happened, both correct and incorrect eyewitnesses were believed 80 percent of the time (Wells et al., 1979). This led the researchers to speculate that "human observers have absolutely no ability to discern eyewitnesses who have mistakenly identified an innocent person" (Wells et al., 1980).

Eyewitness recall of detail is sometimes impressive. When John Yuille and Judith Cutshall (1986) studied accounts of a mid-afternoon murder on a busy Burnaby, British Columbia, street, they found that eyewitnesses' recall for detail was 80 percent accurate.

In a follow-up experiment, Lindsay, Wells, and Carolyn Rumpel (1981) staged the theft under conditions that sometimes allowed witnesses a good, long look at the thief and sometimes didn't. The jurors believed the witnesses more when conditions were good. But even when conditions were so poor that two-thirds of the witnesses had actually misidentified an innocent person, 62 percent of the jurors still believed the witnesses.

Wells and Michael Leippe (1981) also found that jurors are more skeptical of eyewitnesses whose memory for trivial details is poor—though these tend to be the most accurate witnesses. Jurors think a witness who can remember that there were three pictures hanging in the room must have "really been paying attention" (Bell & Loftus, 1988, 1989). Actually, those who pay attention to details are less likely to pay attention to the culprit's face.

WHEN EYES DECEIVE

David Milgaard is not the only person who has been falsely accused of a crime. Stories abound of innocent people who have wasted years in prison because of the testimony of eyewitnesses who were sincerely wrong (Brandon & Davies, 1973). Yet there are tens of thousands of cases each year that depend on eyewitness testimony, so even dozens of such cases would not prove that eyewitness accounts are unreliable. To assess the accuracy of eyewitness recollections, we need to learn their overall rates of "hits" and "misses." One way to gather such information is to stage crimes comparable to those in everyday life and then solicit eyewitness reports.

This has now been done many times, sometimes with disconcerting results (Sporer, 2008). In one study, 141 students witnessed an "assault" on a professor. Seven weeks later, when Robert Buckhout (1974) asked them to identify the assailant from a group of six photographs, 60 percent chose an innocent person. No wonder eyewitnesses to actual crimes sometimes disagree about what they saw. Later studies have confirmed that eyewitnesses often are more confident than correct. For example, Brian Bornstein and Douglas Zickafoose (1999) found that students felt, on average, 74 percent sure of their later recollections of a classroom visitor, but they were only 55 percent correct.

Of course, some witnesses are more confident than others. Wells and colleagues (2002, 2006) report that it's the confident witnesses whom jurors find most believable. Unless their credibility is punctured by an obvious error, confident witnesses seem more credible (Tenney et al., 2007). Confident witnesses are somewhat more accurate, especially when making quick and confident identifications soon after the event (Sauer et al., 2010; Sauerland & Sporer, 2009). In 57 percent of DNA exoneration cases that included eyewitness testimony, the eyewitnesses initially were uncertain (Garrett, 2011). Still, the overconfidence phenomenon (Chapter 3) affects witnesses, too. Under many conditions, report Neil Brewer and Gary Wells (2011), witnesses that feel 90 to 100 percent confident tend to be approximately 75 to 90 percent accurate. Moreover, some people—whether right or wrong—chronically express themselves more assertively. And that, says Michael Leippe (1994), explains why mistaken eyewitnesses are so often persuasive.

The situation can also affect confidence without affecting accuracy. For example, Rod Lindsay and his colleagues (2008) found that people were quite poor at estimating the distance they were from a crime they had observed, but distance did not affect their accuracy in making an identification of the perpetrator. It did, however, affect their confidence. This finding would surely come as a surprise to many judges. In most cases, the law is such that judges are supposed to take a witness's certainty of his or her testimony into account. One panel of judges declared that among the factors to be considered in determining accuracy is "the level of certainty demonstrated by the witness" (Wells & Murray, 1983). If judges and juries take this to heart, they will often be swayed by certain but wrong testimony.

> *"Certitude is not the test of certainty."*
> OLIVER WENDELL HOLMES, *COLLECTED LEGAL PAPERS*

Errors sneak into our perceptions and our memories because our minds are not videotape machines. People are quite good at recognizing a pictured face when later shown the same picture alongside a new face. But University of Stirling face researcher Vicki Bruce (1998) was surprised to discover that subtle differences in views, expression, or lighting "are hard for human vision to deal with." We construct our memories, based partly on what we perceived at the time and partly on our expectations, beliefs, and current knowledge.

The strong emotions that accompany witnessed crimes and traumas may further corrupt eyewitness memories. In one experiment, visitors wore heart rate monitors while in the London Dungeon's Horror Labyrinth. Those exhibiting the most emotion later made the most mistakes in identifying someone they had encountered (Valentine & Mesout, 2009).

Charles Morgan and his colleagues (2004) documented the effects of stress on memory with more than 500 soldiers at survival schools—mock prisoner-of-war camps that were training the soldiers to withstand deprivation of food and sleep, combined with intense, confrontational interrogation. A day after release from the camp, when the soldiers were asked to identify their intimidating interrogators from a 15-person lineup, only 30 percent could do so, although 62 percent could recall a low-stress interrogator. Thus, conclude the researchers, "contrary to popular conception that most people would never forget the face of a clearly seen individual who had physically confronted them and threatened them for more than 30 minutes, [many] were unable to correctly identify the perpetrator." We are most at risk for false recollections made with high confidence with faces of another race (Brigham et al., 2006; Meissner, Brigham, & Butz, 2005).

THE MISINFORMATION EFFECT

Elizabeth Loftus and her associates (1978) provided a dramatic demonstration of memory construction. They showed students 30 slides depicting successive stages of an automobile–pedestrian accident. One critical slide showed a red Datsun stopped at either a stop sign or a yield sign. Afterwards, the researchers asked half the students, among other questions, "Did another car pass the red Datsun while it was stopped at the stop sign?" They asked the other half the same question but with the words "stop sign" replaced by "yield sign." Later, all viewed both slides in Figure C–1 and recalled which one they had previously seen. Those earlier asked the question consistent with what they had seen were 75 percent correct. Those previously asked the misleading question were only 41 percent correct; more often than not, they *denied* seeing what they had actually seen and instead "remembered" the picture they had never seen!

In other studies of this misinformation effect (Chapter 3), Loftus (1979a, 1979b, 2001) found that after suggestive questions, witnesses may believe that a red light was actually green or that a robber had a moustache when he didn't. When questioning eyewitnesses, police and attorneys commonly ask questions framed by their own understanding of what happened. So it is troubling to discover how easily witnesses incorporate misleading information into their memories,

FIGURE C–1

THE MISINFORMATION EFFECT.

When shown this picture and the picture on page 501 and then asked a question suggesting the sign from the other photo, most people later "remembered" seeing the sign they had not actually seen.

especially when they believe the questioner is well-informed and when suggestive questions are repeated (Smith & Ellsworth, 1987; Zaragoza & Mitchell, 1996).

It is also troubling to realize that false memories feel and look like real memories. Thus, they can be as persuasive as real memories—convincingly sincere, yet sincerely wrong. This is true of young children (who are especially susceptible to misinformation) as well as adults. Stephen Ceci and Maggie Bruck (1993a, 1993b) demonstrated children's suggestibility by asking children, once a week for 10 weeks, to "Think real hard, and tell me if this ever happened to you." For example, "Can you remember going to the hospital with the mousetrap on your finger?" Remarkably, when then interviewed by a new adult who asked the same question, 58 percent of preschoolers produced false and often detailed stories about the fictitious event. One boy explained that his brother had pushed him into a basement woodpile, where his finger got stuck in the trap. "And then we went to the hospital, and my mommy, daddy, and Colin drove me there, to the hospital in our van, because it was far away. And the doctor put a bandage on this finger."

Given such vivid stories, professional psychologists were often fooled. They could not reliably separate real from false memories—nor could the children. Told the incident never actually happened, some protested. "But it really did happen. I remember it!" For Bruck and Ceci (1999, 2004), such findings raise the possibility of false accusations, as in alleged child sex abuse cases where children's memories may have been contaminated by repeated suggestive questioning and where there is no corroborating evidence. Given suggestive interview questions, Bruck and Ceci reported, most preschoolers and many older children will produce false reports, such as seeing a thief steal food in their daycare centre.

Even among university students, imagining childhood events, such as breaking a window with their hand or having a nurse remove a skin sample, led one fourth to recall that the imagined event actually happened (Garry et al., 1996; Mazzoni & Memom, 2003). This "imagination

FIGURE C–1

THE MISINFORMATION EFFECT.

When shown this picture and the picture on page 500 and then asked a question suggesting the sign from the other photo, most people later "remembered" seeing the sign they had not actually seen.

inflation" happens partly because visualizing something activates similar areas in the brain as does actually experiencing it (Gonsalves et al., 2004).

Misinformation-induced false memories provide one explanation for a peculiar phenomenon: *false confessions* (Kassin et al., 2010; Lassiter, 2010; Loftus, 2011). Among 250 closely studied cases in which DNA evidence cleared wrongfully convicted people, 40 involved false confessions (Garrett, 2011). Many of these were *compliant confessions*—people who confessed when worn down and often sleep-deprived ("If you will just tell us you accidentally rather than deliberately set the fire, you can go home."). Others were *internalized confessions*—ones apparently believed after people were fed misinformation.

RETELLING

Retelling events commits people to their recollections, accurate or not. An accurate retelling helps them later resist misleading suggestions (Bregman & McAllister, 1982). Other times, the more we retell a story, the more we convince ourselves of a falsehood. Wells, Ferguson, and Lindsay (1981) demonstrated this by having eyewitnesses to a staged theft rehearse their answers to questions before taking the witness stand. Doing so increased the confidence of those who were wrong, and thus made jurors who heard their false testimony more likely to convict the innocent person.

In Chapter 4, we noted that we often adjust what we say to please our listeners and, having done so, come to believe the altered message ourselves. Imagine witnessing an argument that erupts into a fight in which one person injures the other. Afterwards, the injured party sues. Before the trial, a smooth lawyer for one of the two parties interviews you. Might you slightly adjust your testimony, giving a version of the fight that supports this lawyer's client? If you did so, might your later recollections in court be similarly slanted?

Blair Sheppard and Neil Vidmar (1980) reported that the answer to both questions is yes. At the University of Western Ontario, they had some students serve as witnesses to a fight and others as lawyers and judges. When interviewed by lawyers for the defendant, the witnesses later gave the judge testimony that was more favourable to the defendant. In a follow-up experiment, Vidmar and Nancy Laird (1983) noted that witnesses did not omit important facts from their testimony; they just changed their tone of voice and choice of words depending on

THE INSIDE STORY

The legal system has always struck me as relying heavily on doctrine and precedent in making assumptions. What attracted me to social psychology was the possibility of scientifically testing many of these assumptions. Consider the assumption that eyewitnesses to crimes can report reliably on events they have observed. Using staged crimes, I have shown that eyewitnesses can be highly inaccurate and yet sincerely confident. This research reveals that people's confidence in the accuracy of their memories reflects social and personality factors rather than the quality of their memories. One exciting development from this research is that I have been able to devise ways to improve eyewitness accuracy. This shows that social psychologists can do more than identify problems; we can also develop solutions.

Gary L. Wells, *Iowa State University*

whether they thought they were a witness for the defendant or for the plaintiff. Even this was enough to bias the impressions of those who heard the testimony. So it's not only suggestive questions that can distort eyewitness recollections but also their own retellings, which may be subtly adjusted to suit their audience.

REDUCING ERROR

Given these error-prone tendencies, what constructive steps can be taken to increase the accuracy of eyewitnesses and jurors? Experts have several ideas.

Training for police interviewers

When Ronald Fisher and his co-workers (1987, 1989) examined tape-recorded interviews of eyewitnesses conducted by experienced Florida police detectives, they found a typical pattern. Following an open-ended beginning ("Tell me what you recall"), the detectives would occasionally interrupt with follow-up questions, including questions eliciting terse answers ("How tall was he?").

Fisher and Edward Geiselman (1992) said interviews should begin by allowing eyewitnesses to offer their own unprompted recollections. The recollections will be most complete if the interviewer jogs the memory by first guiding people to reconstruct the setting. Have them visualize the scene and what they were thinking and feeling at the time. Even showing pictures of the setting—of, say, the store checkout lane with a clerk standing where she was robbed—can promote accurate recall (Cutler & Penrod, 1988). After giving witnesses ample, uninterrupted time to report everything that comes to mind, the interviewer then jogs their memory with evocative questions ("Was there anything unusual about the voice? Was there anything unusual about the person's appearance or clothing?").

When Fisher and colleagues (Fisher, Geiselman, & Amador, 1989; Fisher, McCauley, & Geiselman, 1994; P. Fischer et al., 2011) trained detectives to question in this way, the eyewitnesses' information increased 25 to 50 percent without increasing the false memory rate. A later statistical summary of 46 published studies confirmed that this "cognitive interview" substantially increases details recalled, with no loss in accuracy (Memon, Meissner, & Fraser, 2011). In response to such results, most police agencies in North America and Britain have adopted the cognitive interview procedure (Dando & others, 2009). (The procedure also shows promise for enhancing information gathered in oral histories and medical surveys.)

> *"While the rules of evidence and other safeguards provide protection in the courtroom, they are absent in the backroom of the precinct station."*
> ERNEST HILGARD & ELIZABETH LOFTUS (1979)

Accurate identifications tend to be automatic and effortless (Sauer et al., 2010). The right face just pops out. In studies by David Dunning and Scott Perretta (2002), eyewitnesses who make their identifications in less than 10 to 12 seconds were nearly 90 percent accurate; those taking longer were only about 50 percent accurate. Although other studies challenge a neat 10- to 12-second rule, they confirm that quicker identifications are generally more accurate (Weber et al., 2004). For example, when Tim Valentine and co-workers (2003) analyzed 640 eyewitness viewings of London police lineups, they, too, found that nearly nine in ten "fast" identifications were of the actual suspect, as were fewer than four in ten slower identifications. Younger eyewitnesses, and those who had viewed the culprit for more than one minute, were also more accurate than older eyewitnesses and those who had less than one minute's exposure.

Minimizing false lineup identifications

The case of Ron Shatford illustrates how the composition of a police lineup can promote misidentification (Doob & Kirshenbaum, 1973). After a suburban Toronto department store robbery, the cashier involved could only recall that the culprit was not wearing a tie and was "very neatly dressed and rather good-looking." When police put the good-looking Shatford in a lineup with 11 unattractive men, all of whom wore ties, the cashier readily identified him as the culprit. Only after he had served 15 months of a long sentence did another person confess, allowing Shatford to be retried and found not guilty.

If a suspect has a distinguishing feature—a tie, a tattoo, or an eye patch—false identifications are reduced by putting a similar feature on other lineup "foils" (Zarkadi & others, 2009). Gary Wells (1984, 1993, 2005, 2008) reports that another way to reduce misidentifications is to remind witnesses that the person they saw may or may not be in the lineup. Alternatively, give eyewitnesses a "blank" lineup that contains no suspects and screen out those who make false identifications. Those who do not make such errors turn out to be more accurate when they later face the actual lineup.

Dozens of studies in Europe, North America, Australia, and South Africa show that mistakes also subside when witnesses simply make individual yes or no judgments in response to a *sequence* of people (Lindsay & Wells, 1985; Meissner et al., 2005; Steblay et al., 2001). A simultaneous lineup tempts people to pick the person who, among the lineup members, most resembles the perpetrator. Witnesses viewing just one suspect at a time are less likely to make false identifications.

If witnesses view several photos or people simultaneously, they are more likely to choose whoever most resembles the culprit. (When not given a same-race lineup, witnesses may pick someone of the culprit's race, especially when it's a different race from their own [Wells & Olson, 2003].) With a "sequential lineup," eyewitnesses compare each person with their memory of the culprit and make an absolute decision—match or no-match (Goodsell, Gronlund, & Carlson, 2010; Gronlund, 2004a, 2004b). In one large study based on cases from several cities, the sequential lineup reduced the misidentification of foils from 18 to 12 percent, with no reduction in accurate identifications (Wells et al., 2011).

These no-cost procedures make police lineups more like good experiments. They contain a control group—a no-suspect lineup or a lineup in which witnesses try to guess the suspect based merely on a general description. They have an experimenter who is blind to the hypotheses—an officer who doesn't know which person is the suspect. Questions are scripted and neutral, so they don't subtly demand a particular response (the procedure doesn't imply the culprit is in the lineup). And confidence-inflating post-lineup comments ("you got him") are prohibited prior to trial testimony. Such procedures greatly reduce the natural human confirmation bias (having an idea and seeking confirming evidence). Lineups can also now be effectively administered by computers (MacLin, Zimmerman, & Malpass, 2005).

Although procedures such as double-blind testing are common in psychological science, they are still uncommon in criminal procedures (Wells & Olson, 2003). But their time may be coming. Police could use a new procedure developed by Queen's University researchers Sean Pryke, Rod Lindsay, and their colleagues (2004). They invited students to identify a prior class visitor from multiple lineups that separately presented face, body, and voice samples. Their findings: An eyewitness who consistently identified the same suspect—by face, by body, and by voice—was nearly always an accurate eyewitness.

Education for jurors

Do jurors evaluate eyewitness testimony rationally? Do they intuitively understand how the circumstances of a lineup determine its reliability? Do they know whether to take an eyewitness's self-confidence into account? Do they realize how memory can be influenced by earlier misleading questions, by stress at the time of the incident, by the interval between the event and the questioning, by whether the suspect is of their race or of a different race, by whether recall of other details is sharp or hazy? Studies in Canada, Great Britain, and the United States reveal that jurors discount most of these factors, all of which are known to influence eyewitness testimony (Cutler, Penrod, & Stuve, 1988; Devenport et al., 2002; Noon & Hollin, 1987; Wells & Turtle, 1987; Yarmey, 2003a, 2003b).

To educate jurors, experts are now frequently asked (usually by defence attorneys) to testify about eyewitness testimony. Their aim is to offer jurors the sort of information you have been reading, to help them evaluate the testimony of both prosecution and defence witnesses. Table C–1, drawn from a survey of 64 experts on eyewitness testimony, lists the most agreed-upon phenomena.

Taught the conditions under which eyewitness accounts *are* trustworthy, jurors become more likely to trust such testimony (Cutler, Penrod, & Dexter, 1989; Wells, 1986). Moreover, attorneys and judges are recognizing the importance of some of these factors when deciding when to ask for or permit suppression of lineup evidence (Stinson et al., 1996, 1997). Efforts at educating the public about such issues have gradually begun to affect potential jurors (Desmarais & Read, 2011; Read & Desmarais, 2009). On many questions on topics such as lineup instructions and confidence malleability, at least 70 percent of potential jurors are able to identify the correct

TABLE C–1 INFLUENCES ON EYEWITNESS TESTIMONY.

Phenomenon	Eyewitness Experts Agreeing*
Question wording. An eyewitness's testimony about an event can be affected by how the questions put to that eyewitness are worded.	98%
Lineup instructions. Police instructions can affect an eyewitness's willingness to make an identification.	98%
Confidence malleability. An eyewitness's confidence can be influenced by factors that are unrelated to identification accuracy.	95%
Mug-shot-induced bias. Exposure to mug shots of a suspect increases the likelihood that the witness will later choose that suspect in a lineup.	95%
Post-event information. Eyewitnesses' testimony about an event often reflects not only what they actually saw but information they obtained later on.	94%
Attitudes and expectations. An eyewitness's perception and memory of an event may be affected by his or her attitudes and expectations.	92%
Cross-race bias. Eyewitnesses are more accurate when identifying members of their own race than when identifying members of other races.	90%
Accuracy versus confidence. An eyewitness's confidence is not a good predictor of his or her identification accuracy.	87%

*"This phenomenon is reliable enough for psychologists to present it in courtroom testimony."

Source: Adapted from S. M. Kassin, V. A. Tubb, H. M. Hosch, & A. Memon, "On the 'general acceptance' of eyewitness testimony research: A new survey of the experts," *American Psychologist, 56*(5), 405–416. Copyright © 2001 by the American Psychological Association. Adapted with permission.

response, and this knowledge has increased with time. Despite this progress, however, there are still a number of questions on which potential jurors have little knowledge, such as the cross-race bias and accuracy versus confidence.

WHAT INFLUENCES A JURY?

Verdicts depend on what happens in the courtroom—the eyewitness testimonies, the defendant's characteristics, the judge's instructions. But verdicts also depend on how the individual jurors process information and on how the members of the jury influence one another.

PHYSICAL ATTRACTIVENESS OF THE DEFENDANT

In Chapter 9, we noted a physical attractiveness stereotype: Beautiful people seem like good people. Michael Efran (1974) wondered whether that stereotype would bias students' judgments of someone accused of cheating. He asked some of his University of Toronto students whether attractiveness should affect presumption of guilt. They answered, "No, it shouldn't." But did it? Yes. When Efran gave other students a description of the case with a photograph of either an attractive or an unattractive defendant, they judged the more attractive as less guilty and recommended that person for lesser punishment.

Other experimenters have confirmed that when the evidence is meagre or ambiguous, justice is not blind to a defendant's looks (Mazzella & Feingold, 1994). Diane Berry and Leslie Zebrowitz-McArthur (1988) discovered this when they asked people to judge the guilt of baby-faced and mature-faced defendants. Baby-faced adults (people with large, round eyes and small chins) seemed more naive and were found guilty more often of crimes of mere negligence but less often of intentional criminal acts. If found guilty, unattractive people also strike people as more dangerous, especially if they are sexual offenders (Esses & Webster, 1988).

In a mammoth experiment conducted with BBC Television, Richard Wiseman (1998) showed viewers evidence about a burglary, with just one variation. Some viewers saw the defendant played by an actor who fit what a panel of 100 people judged as the stereotypical criminal—unattractive, crooked nose, small eyes. Among 64 000 people phoning in their verdict, 41 percent judged him guilty. British viewers elsewhere saw an attractive, baby-faced defendant with large blue eyes. Only 31 percent found him guilty.

To see if these findings extend to the real world, Chris Downs and Phillip Lyons (1991) asked police escorts to rate the physical attractiveness of 1742 defendants appearing before 40 Texas judges in misdemeanour cases that were serious (such as forgery), moderate (such as harassment), or minor (such as public intoxication). In each type of case, the judges set higher bails and fines for less attractive defendants. What explains this dramatic effect? Are unattractive people also lower in status? Are they more likely to flee or to commit another crime, as the judges perhaps suppose? Or do judges simply ignore the Roman statesman Cicero's advice: "The final good and the supreme duty of the wise man is to resist appearance."

THE JUDGE'S INSTRUCTIONS

All of us can recall courtroom dramas in which an attorney exclaimed, "Your honour, I object!" whereupon the judge sustains the objection and instructs the jury to ignore the other attorney's suggestive question or the witness's remark. How effective are such instructions?

Several experimenters report that jurors show concern for due process (Fleming, Wegener, & Petty, 1999) but that they find it difficult to ignore inadmissible evidence, such as the defendant's previous convictions. In one study, Stanley Sue, Ronald Smith, and Cathy Caldwell (1973) gave students a description of a grocery store robbery–murder and a summary of the prosecution's case and the defence's case. When the prosecution's case was weak, no one judged the defendant guilty. When a tape recording of an incriminating phone call made by the defendant was added to the weak case, approximately one-third judged the person guilty. The judge's instructions that the tape was not legal evidence and should be ignored did nothing to erase the effect of the damaging testimony.

Indeed, a judge's order to ignore testimony—"It must play no role in your consideration of the case. You have no choice but to disregard it."—can even boomerang, adding to the testimony's impact (Wolf & Montgomery, 1977). Perhaps such statements create reactance in the jurors. Or perhaps they sensitize jurors to the inadmissible testimony, as when I warn you not to notice your nose as you finish this sentence. Judges can more easily strike inadmissible testimony from the court records than from the jurors' minds. As trial lawyers sometimes say, "You can't unring a bell."

This is especially so with emotional information (Edwards & Bryan, 1997). When jurors are told vividly about a defendant's record ("hacking up a woman"), a judge's instructions to ignore are more likely to boomerang than when the inadmissible information is less emotional ("assault with a deadly weapon"). Even if jurors later claim to have ignored the inadmissible information, it may alter how they construe other information.

THE STORY OF THE TRIAL

To gain insight into how jurors process information, Nancy Pennington and Reid Hastie (1993) studied the thought processes of mock jurors, sampled from courthouse jury pools, while viewing re-enactments of actual trials.

In making their decisions, jurors first construct a story that made sense of all the evidence. After observing one murder trial, some jurors concluded that a quarrel made the defendant angry, triggering him to get a knife, search for the decedent, and stab him to death. Others surmised that the frightened defendant picked up a knife that he used to defend himself when he later encountered the decedent.

When jurors begin deliberating, they are often surprised to discover that others have constructed different stories. This implies—and research confirms—that jurors are persuaded when attorneys present evidence as a narrative (a story). In felony cases—where the conviction rate can be as high as 80 percent—the Crown case follows a story structure more often than the defence case.

STATISTICAL INFORMATION

People also have a hard time comprehending statistics and scientific information when it is presented as evidence. When Larry Fisher was finally tried for Gail Miller's murder in 1999, the jury was presented with evidence that there was only one chance in 950 trillion that the DNA from the sperm found on Gail Miller's clothes belonged to anyone other than Larry Fisher. This evidence by all rational accounts should have ruled David Milgaard out as a suspect in the case. These sorts of statistics, however, are difficult to comprehend, and jurors often have trouble figuring out exactly what they mean. Perhaps aware of jurors' fragile understanding of such statistical principles, Fisher's lawyer tried to argue that despite the DNA evidence there was still a good chance that David Milgaard was the person who really raped and murdered Gail Miller. In this instance, the jury was able to see through the lawyer's erroneous argument. Unfortunately, juries are not always able to do so. The more typical finding is that juries do not pay enough attention to statistical evidence.

Gary Wells (1992) reported that even when people (including experienced trial judges) understand naked statistical probabilities, they may be unpersuaded. The numbers, it seems, must be supported by a convincing story. Thus, reported Wells, one Toronto mother lost a paternity suit seeking child support from her child's alleged father despite a blood test showing a 99.8 percent probability that the man was her child's father. She lost after the man took the stand and persuasively denied the allegation.

INCREASING JURORS' UNDERSTANDING

Understanding how jurors misconstrue judicial instructions and statistical information is a first step toward better decisions. A next step might be giving jurors access to transcripts rather than forcing them to rely on their memories in processing complex information (Bourgeois, Horowitz, & Lee, 1993). A further step would be devising and testing clearer, more effective ways to present information—a task on which several social psychologists have worked. For example, when a judge quantifies the required standard of proof (as, say, 51, 71, or 91 percent certainty), jurors understand and respond appropriately (Kagehiro, 1990).

And surely there must be a simpler way to tell jurors, as required by the Illinois Death Penalty Act, not to impose the death sentence in murder cases when there are justifying circumstances: "If you do not unanimously find from your consideration of all the evidence that there are no mitigating factors sufficient to preclude imposition of a death sentence, then you should sign the verdict requiring the court to impose a sentence other than death" (Diamond, 1993). When jurors are given instructions rewritten into simple language, they are less susceptible to the judge's biases (Halverson et al., 1997; Smith & Haney, 2011).

Phoebe Ellsworth and Robert Mauro (1998) sum up the dismal conclusions of jury researchers: "Legal instructions are typically delivered in a manner likely to frustrate the most conscientious attempts at understanding . . . The language is technical and . . . no attempt is made either to assess jurors' mistaken preconceptions about the law or to provide any kind of useful education."

GROUP INFLUENCES IN JURIES

Imagine a jury that, having finished a trial, has entered the jury room to begin its deliberations. Researchers Harry Kalven and Hans Zeisel (1966) reported that chances are about two in three that the jurors will initially *not* agree on a verdict. Yet, after discussion, 95 percent emerge with a consensus. Obviously, group influence has occurred.

Thousands of times a year small groups sampled from the people called for jury duty convene to seek a group decision (Kagehiro, 1990). Are they subject to the social influences that mould other decision groups—to patterns of majority and minority influence, to group polarization, to groupthink (Chapter 7)? Let's start with a simple question: If we knew the jurors' initial leanings, could we predict their verdict?

The law prohibits observation of actual juries. So researchers simulate the jury process by presenting a case to mock juries and having them deliberate as a real jury would. In a series of such studies, James Davis, Robert Holt, Norbert Kerr, and Garold Stasser tested various mathematical schemes for predicting group decisions, including decisions by mock juries (Davis et al., 1975, 1977, 1989; Kerr et al., 1976). Will some mathematical combination of initial decisions predict the final group decision? Davis and his colleagues found that the scheme that predicts best varies according to the nature of the case. But in several experiments, a "two-thirds-majority" scheme fared best: The group verdict was usually the alternative favoured by at least two-thirds of the jurors at the outset. Without such a majority, a hung jury was likely.

Likewise, in Kalven and Zeisel's survey of juries, nine in ten reached the verdict favoured by the majority on the first ballot. Although you might fantasize about someday being the courageous lone juror who sways the majority, as Henry Fonda's character did in the famous play and movie *Twelve Angry Men*, the fact is that it seldom happens.

Minority influence

Sometimes, however, what was initially a minority prevails. A typical 12-person jury is like a typical small university class: The three quietest people rarely talk and the three most vocal people contribute more than half the talking (Hastie, Penrod, & Pennington, 1983). If jurors who favoured a particular verdict are vocal and persist in their views, they are more likely to eventually prevail. From the research on minority influence, we know that jurors in the minority will be most persuasive when they are consistent, persistent, and self-confident. This is especially so if they can begin to trigger some defections from the majority (Gordijn, De Vries, & De Dreu, 2002; Kerr, 1981).

Group polarization

Jury deliberation shifts people's opinions in other intriguing ways as well. In experiments, deliberation often magnifies initial sentiments. For example, Robert Bray and Audrey Noble (1978) had University of Kentucky students listen to a 30-minute tape of a murder trial. Then, assuming the defendant was found guilty, they recommended a prison sentence. Groups of high authoritarians initially recommended strong punishments (56 years) and after deliberation were even more punitive (68 years). The low-authoritarian groups were initially relatively lenient (38 years) and after deliberation became even more so (29 years).

Confirmation that group polarization can occur in juries comes from an ambitious study in which Reid Hastie, Steven Penrod, and Nancy Pennington (1983) put together 69 twelve-person juries from Massachusetts citizens on jury duty. Each jury was shown a re-enactment of an actual murder case, with roles played by an experienced judge and actual attorneys. Then they were given unlimited time to deliberate the case in a jury room. As Figure C–2 shows, the evidence was incriminating: Four out of five jurors voted guilty before deliberation, but felt unsure enough that a weak verdict of manslaughter was their most popular preference. After deliberation, nearly all agreed that the accused was guilty, and most now preferred a stronger verdict—second-degree murder. Through deliberation, their initial leanings had grown stronger.

FIGURE C–2

GROUP POLARIZATION IN JURIES.

In highly realistic simulations of a murder trial, 828 Massachusetts jurors stated their initial verdict preferences, and then deliberated the case for periods ranging from three hours to five days. Deliberation strengthened initial tendencies, which favoured the prosecution. (From Hastie et al., 1983)

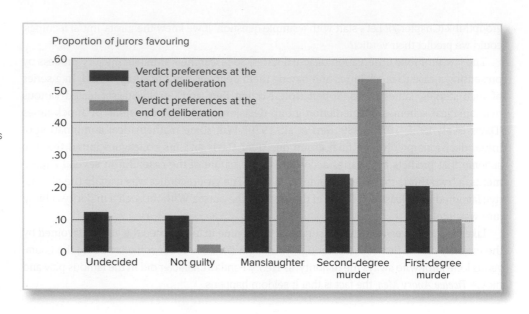

Proportion of jurors favouring

Verdict preferences at the start of deliberation

Verdict preferences at the end of deliberation

Undecided   Not guilty   Manslaughter   Second-degree murder   First-degree murder

Leniency

In many experiments, one other curious effect of deliberation has surfaced: Especially when the evidence is not highly incriminating, as it was in the experiment just described, deliberating jurors often become more lenient (MacCoun & Kerr, 1988). This qualifies the "two-thirds-majority-rules" finding, for if even a bare majority initially favours acquittal, it usually will prevail (Stasser, Kerr, & Bray, 1981). Moreover, a minority that favours acquittal stands a better chance of prevailing than one that favours conviction (Tindale et al., 1990).

Once again, a survey of actual juries confirms the laboratory results. Kalven and Zeisel (1966) reported that in those cases where the majority does not prevail, it usually shifts to acquittal. When a judge disagrees with the jury's decision, it is usually because the jury acquits someone the judge would have convicted.

Might "informational influence" (stemming from others' persuasive arguments) account for the increased leniency? The "innocent-unless-proved-guilty" and "proof-beyond-a-reasonable-doubt" rules put the burden of proof on those who favour conviction. Perhaps this makes evidence of the defendant's innocence more persuasive. Or perhaps "normative influence" creates the leniency effect, as jurors who view themselves as fair-minded confront other jurors who are even more concerned with protecting a possibly innocent defendant.

> *"It is better that ten guilty persons escape than one innocent suffer."*
> WILLIAM BLACKSTONE, 1769

FROM LAB TO LIFE: SIMULATED AND REAL JURIES

Perhaps while reading this chapter, you have wondered what some critics (Tapp, 1980; Vidmar, 1979) have wondered: Isn't there an enormous gulf between college and university students discussing a hypothetical case and real jurors deliberating a real person's fate?

Indeed there is. It is one thing to ponder a pretend decision given minimal information and quite another to agonize over the complexities and profound consequences of an actual case. So Reid Hastie, Martin Kaplan, James Davis, Eugene Borgida, and others have asked their participants, who sometimes are drawn from actual juror pools, to view enactments of actual trials. The enactments are so realistic that sometimes participants forget the trial they are watching on television is staged (Thompson et al., 1981).

Researchers also defend the laboratory simulations, by noting that the laboratory offers a practical, inexpensive method for studying important issues under controlled conditions (Bornstein & Greene, 2011; Bray & Kerr, 1982; Dillehay & Nietzel, 1980). What is more, as researchers have begun testing them in more realistic situations, findings from the laboratory studies have often held up quite well. No one contends that the simplified world of the jury experiment mirrors the complex world of the real courtroom; rather, the experiments help us formulate theories with which we interpret what goes on in the courtroom.

Are these jury simulations any different from social psychology's other experiments, all of which create simplified versions of complex realities? By varying just one or two factors at a time in this simulated reality, the experimenter pinpoints how changes in one or two aspects can affect us. And that is the essence of social psychology's experimental method.

▶ SUMMING UP

HOW RELIABLE IS EYEWITNESS TESTIMONY?

- In hundreds of experiments, social psychologists have found that the accuracy of eyewitness testimony can be impaired by a host of factors.
- Some eyewitnesses express themselves more assertively than others. The assertive witness is more likely to be believed, although assertiveness is actually a trait of the witness and not of the certainty of the information.
- The human eye is not a video camera; it is vulnerable to variations in light, angle, and other changes that impair recognition of a face.
- As the sequence of events in a crime is told repeatedly, errors may creep in and become embraced by the witness as part of the true account.
- To reduce such errors, interviewers are advised to let the witness tell what he or she remembers without interruption, and to encourage the witness to visualize the scene of the incident and the emotional state he or she was in when the incident occurred.
- Educating jurors about the pitfalls of eyewitness testimony can improve the way testimony is received and, ultimately, the accuracy of the verdict.

WHAT INFLUENCES A JURY?

- Jurors view attractive defendants more leniently than unattractive defendants.
- Jurors have difficulty in following a judge's instructions to ignore evidence.
- Jurors construct a story when presented with evidence in a trial, and this story has a major impact on how they see evidence and come to a verdict.
- One major concern is jurors' ability to comprehend evidence, especially when it involves statistics indicating the probability that a given person committed the crime.

- Understanding jurors' limitations in understanding instructions can be a first step in developing better instructions for juries.

- Juries are groups, and they are swayed by the same influences that bear upon other types of groups, including that opposing views may become more entrenched and polarized.

- Deliberation may make jurors more lenient than they originally were, especially when evidence is not highly incriminating.

- Simulated juries are not real juries, so we must be cautious in generalizing research findings to actual courtrooms. Yet, like all experiments in social psychology, laboratory jury experiments help us formulate theories and principles that we can use to interpret the more complex world of the courtroom.

MODULE D
Social Psychology and the Sustainable Future[1]

CHAPTER OUTLINE

- HOW CAN HUMANITY CREATE A SUSTAINABLE FUTURE?

- DOES MONEY BUY HAPPINESS?

*L*ife is good. Today, the average North American enjoys luxuries unknown even to royalty in centuries past: hot showers, flush toilets, central air-conditioning, microwave ovens, jet travel, wintertime fresh fruit, big-screen digital television, e-mail, and Post-it notes. But on the horizon, beyond the

[1] Parts of this module are adapted from David G. Myers's book, *The American Paradox: Spiritual Hunger in an Age of Plenty* (Yale University Press, 2000), where further information about materialism and about wealth, inequality, and well-being may be found.

sunny skies of comfort and convenience, dark clouds of an environmental disaster are gathering. In scientific gatherings hosted by the United Nations, Britain's Royal Society, and the U.S. National Academy of Sciences, a consensus has emerged: Increasing population and increasing consumption have combined to overshoot the Earth's ecological carrying capacity (Figure D–1).

HOW CAN HUMANITY CREATE A SUSTAINABLE FUTURE?

Although these are, materially, the best of times for many people on Earth, humanity is creating a climate change that may, if human behaviour does not change, become a weapon of mass destruction. Although increasing population and consumption have overshot the world's carrying capacity, new technologies together with reduced consumption may enable sustainable living.

In 1960, the Earth carried 3 billion people and 127 million motor vehicles. Today, it has more than 7 billion people and nearly 1 billion motor vehicles (Davis, Diegel, & Boundy, 2011). The greenhouse gases emitted by motor vehicles, along with the burning of coal and oil to generate electricity and heat homes and buildings, are changing the Earth's climate. To ascertain how much and how fast climate change is occurring, several thousand scientists worldwide have collaborated to create and review the evidence via the Intergovernmental Panel on Climate Change (IPCC). The past chair of its scientific assessment committee, John Houghton (2011), reports that their conclusions— supported by the national academies of science of the world's 11 most developed countries—are undergirded by the most "thoroughly researched and reviewed" scientific effort in human history.

As the IPCC reports illustrate, converging evidence verifies climate change:

- **A warming greenhouse gas blanket is growing.** About half the carbon dioxide emitted by human activity since the Industrial Revolution (since 1750) remains in the atmosphere (Royal Society, 2010).

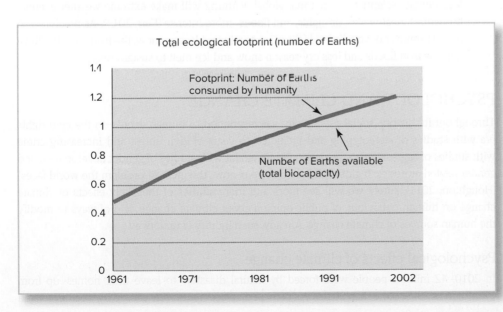

FIGURE D–1

THE ECOLOGICAL OVERSHOOT.

The human demand for things such as land, timber, fish, and fuels is increasingly exceeding the Earth's regenerative capacity. (Data from Global Footprint Network, 2006, www .footprintnetwork.org)

- **Reported emissions levels are increasing.** There is now 39 percent more atmospheric carbon dioxide and 158 percent more atmospheric methane than before industrial times—and the increase has recently accelerated (World Meteorological Organization, 2011). As the permafrost thaws, methane gas release threatens to compound the problem (Gillis, 2011).

- **Sea and air temperatures are rising.** The numbers—the facts—have no political leanings. Every decade since the 1970s has been warmer than the one preceding it, with nine of the ten warmest years on record since 2001 (Royal Society, 2010). If the world were not warming, random weather variations should produce equal numbers of record-breaking high and low temperatures. In reality, record highs have been greatly outnumbering record lows—by about 2 to 1 in the United States, for example (Meehl et al., 2009). After amassing 1.6 billion temperature reports from more than 39 000 weather stations, one-time climate change skeptic Richard Muller (2011) became convinced: "Global warming is real."

- **Various plant and animal species are migrating.** In response to the warming world, they are creeping northward and upward, with anticipated loss of biodiversity (Harley, 2011; Houghton, 2011).

- **The Arctic sea ice is melting.** The late-summer ice cover has shrunk from nearly 7.8 million sq. km (3 million sq. mi.) in the late 1970s to 4.33 million sq. km (1.67 million sq. mi.) in 2011. The West Antarctica and Greenland glacial ice sheets are also melting—faster than ever (Kerr, 2011).

- **The seas are rising.** Ocean water expands as it warms. Moreover, what happens in the Arctic doesn't stay in the Arctic. Projections of rising sea levels portend large problems for coastal and low-lying areas, including Pakistan, southern China, and Indian and Pacific Ocean islands (Houghton, 2011).

- **Extreme weather is increasing.** Any single weather event—even the record European heat of 2010, or the record 2011 Mississippi floods, Missouri tornadoes, and Texas heat and drought—cannot be attributed to climate change. Weird weather happens. Nevertheless, climate scientists predict that global warming will make extreme weather events—hurricanes, heat waves, droughts, and floods—more intense (Kerr, 2011). As precipitation in a warming and wetter world falls more as rain and less as snow, the likely result will be rainy-season floods and less dry-season snow and ice melt to sustain rivers.

PSYCHOLOGY AND CLIMATE CHANGE

Throughout its history, social psychology has responded to human events—to the civil rights era with studies of stereotyping and prejudice, to years of civil unrest and increasing crime with studies of aggression, to the women's movement with studies of gender development and gender-related attitudes. If global climate change is now "the greatest problem the world faces" (Houghton, 2011), surely we will see more and more studies of the likely effects of climate change on human behaviour, of public opinion about climate change, and of ways to modify the human sources of climate change. Already, such inquiry is underway.

Psychological effects of climate change

In 2010, 42 million people were forced by natural disasters to leave their homes—up from 17 million in 2009. More than 90 percent of these displacements were caused by weather-related hazards, making climate-related displacement "the defining challenge of our times," said Antonio Guerres, the U.N. high commissioner for refugees (Amland, 2011).

If temperatures increase by the expected 2 to 4 degrees Celsius this century, the resulting changes in water availability, agriculture, disaster risk, and sea level will necessitate massive resettlement (de Sherbinin et al., 2011). When drought or floods force people to leave their land, shelter, and work, as when sub-Saharan African farming and grazing lands become desert, the frequent result is increased poverty and hunger, earlier death, and loss of cultural identity. If an extreme weather event or climate change disrupted your ties to a place and its people, you could expect to feel grief, anxiety, and a sense of loss (Doherty & Clayton, 2011). For social and mental health, climate matters.

Got war? Blame the climate. Such is often the case, notes Jeffrey Sachs (2006). The recent deadly carnage in Darfur, Sudan, for example, had its roots in drought and the competition for water. And so it has happened across history. Many human maladies—from economic downturns to wars—have been traced to climate fluctuations (Zhang et al., 2011). When the climate changes, agriculture often suffers, leading to increased famine, epidemics, and overall misery. Poorer countries, with fewer resources, are especially vulnerable to climate-produced misery (Fischer & Van de Vliert, 2011). And when miserable, people become more prone to anger with their governments and with one another, leading to war. For social stability, climate matters.

As research on heat and aggression demonstrates in the laboratory and in everyday life, heat also amplifies short-term aggression. On hot days, neighbourhood violence and even batters hit by pitches in baseball games become more frequent. Violence is also more common in hotter seasons of the year, hotter summers, hotter years, hotter cities, and hotter regions (Anderson & Delisi, 2010). Craig Anderson and his colleagues project that if a 4°F (about 2°C) warming occurs, the United States will suffer at least 50 000 more serious assaults each year.

Public opinion about climate change

Is the Earth getting warmer? Are humans responsible? Will it matter to our grandchildren? Yes, yes, and yes, say published climate scientists—97 percent of whom agree that climate change is occurring and is human-caused (Anderegg et al., 2010). As one report in *Science* explained, "Almost all climate scientists are of one mind about the threat of global warming: It's real, it's dangerous, and the world needs to take action immediately" (Kerr, 2009).

In response, the European Community, Australia, and India have all passed either a carbon tax on coal or a carbon emissions trading system, and even China now has a limited plan that will make polluters pay for excess pollution. In China, India, and South Korea, a 2010 Pew survey found more than 70 percent of people willing to address climate change by paying more for energy (Rosenthal, 2011).

Yet such actions in Canada have been slow to gain acceptance. The current Conservative government in Canada has steadfastly refused to consider a carbon tax or an emission trading system. This is true even though 58 percent of Canadians believe "that global warming is a fact and is mostly caused by emissions from vehicles and industrial facilities" (Angus Reid, 2012). So in Canada, the population has largely accepted the truth of global warming, but does not elect politicians who promote the policies that actively combat global warming as seen in other countries.

In contrast, people in Britain and the United States are substantially less likely to believe that global warming is a fact and that it is caused by human activity, with only 42 percent of people from the U.S. and 43 percent of people from Britain endorsing these beliefs (Angus Reid, 2012). Why do so many people in Canada and the majority of people in the United States and Britain fail to accept the near-consensus scientific position? Why is global warming not a hotter topic? And what might be done to align scientific and public understandings?

By now, it's a familiar lesson: Vivid and recent experiences often overwhelm abstract statistics. Despite knowing the statistical rarity of shark attacks and plane crashes, vivid images of such—being readily available in memory—often hijack our emotions and distort our judgments. We make our intuitive judgments under the influence of the availability heuristic—and thus we often fear the wrong things. If an airline misplaces our bag, we likely will overweight our immediate experience; ignoring data on the airline's overall lost-bag rate, we belittle the airline. Our ancient brains come designed to attend to the immediate situation, not out-of-sight data and beyond-the-horizon dangers (Gifford, 2011). Likewise, people will often scorn global warming in the face of a winter freeze. One climate skeptic declared a record blizzard "a coup de grace" for global warming (Breckler, 2010).

As you may recall from Chapter 5, persuasive messages must first be understood. Thanks in part to the media's mixed messages—its framing of two opposing sides: those concerned about and those dismissive of climate change—only 39 percent of Americans in 2011 believed that "most scientists think global warming is happening." More perceived "a lot of disagreement among scientists" or didn't know enough to say (Leiserowitz et al., 2011). Perceiving uncertainty, and reassured by the natural human optimism bias, people discount the threat (Gifford, 2011).

People also exhibit a "system justification" tendency—a tendency to believe in and justify the way things are in their culture, and thus, especially when comfortable, to not want to change the familiar status quo (Feygina, Jost, & Goldsmith, 2010). We tend to like our habitual ways of living—of travelling, of eating, and of heating and cooling our spaces.

More encouraging news comes from an experiment that showed people global temperature trends. Regardless of their prior assumptions about global climate change, people were able to understand the trend and project it into the near future—and to adjust their beliefs. Education matters. We also benefit from framing energy savings in attention-getting ways. An information sheet or store sign might read, "If you do not install CFL light bulbs, you will lose $___." And use long time periods. Instead of saying, "This Energy Star refrigerator will save you $120 a year on your electric bills," say it "will save you $2400 in wasted energy bills over the next 20 years" (Hofmeister, 2010).

What shall we do? Eat, drink, and be merry, for tomorrow is doom? Behave as so many participants have in prisoners' dilemma games, by pursuing self-interest to our collective detriment? ("Heck, on a global scale, my consumption is infinitesimal; it makes my life comfortable and costs the world practically nothing.") Wring our hands, dreading that fertility plus prosperity equals calamity, and vow never to bring children into a doomed world?

Those more optimistic about the future see two routes to sustainable lifestyles: (a) increasing technological efficiency and agricultural productivity, and (b) moderating consumption and population.

NEW TECHNOLOGIES

One component in a sustainable future is improved eco-technologies. Today's new refrigerators consume half the energy of those sold a decade ago (Heap & Comim, 2005). We have replaced many incandescent bulbs with energy-saving fluorescent bulbs, replaced printed and delivered letters and catalogues with e-mail and e-commerce, and replaced many commuter kilometres driven with telecommuting.

There is also good news about cars. To begin with, today's middle-aged adults drive cars that get twice the mileage and produce a twentieth of the pollution of the ones they drove as teenagers. For the near future, we have hybrid cars, which conserve gasoline by using an electric power cell, and flex-fuel cars, which can run on ethanol produced from a variety of vegetable sources such as soybeans, or on a mixture of ethanol and gasoline.

Plausible future technologies include diodes that emit light for 20 years without bulbs; ultrasound washing machines that consume no water, heat, or soap; reusable and compostable plastics; cars running on fuel cells that combine hydrogen and oxygen and produce water exhaust; lightweight materials that are stronger than steel; and roofs and roads that double as solar energy collectors (N. Myers, 2000; Zhang et al., 2007).

Some energy solutions are low-tech. One Philippine non-profit is working with the government and volunteers to install zero-energy solar light bulbs in one million low-income homes. The "bulbs" are nothing more than discarded clear plastic soda bottles that, when filled with water and wedged in a hole in the roof—with half the bottle exposed to the sun and half jutting into the room—transmit 55 watts of light. The result? Daytime light is provided without electricity bills (Orendain, 2011).

Given the speed of innovation (who could have imagined today's world a century ago?), the future will surely bring solutions that we aren't yet imagining. Surely, say the optimists, the future will bring increased material well-being for more people requiring many fewer raw materials and much less polluting waste.

REDUCING CONSUMPTION

The second component of a sustainable future is the control of consumption. Instead of more people consuming and polluting more all the time, a stable population will need to consume and pollute less.

Thanks to family planning efforts, the world's population growth rate has decelerated, especially in developed nations. Even in less-developed countries, when food security has improved and women have become educated and empowered, birth rates have fallen. But even if birth rates everywhere instantly fell to a replacement level of 2.1 children per woman, the lingering momentum of population growth, fed by the bulge of younger humans, would continue for years to come.

Given that humans have already overshot the Earth's carrying capacity, individual consumption must moderate. With our material appetites continually swelling—as more people seek personal computers, air-conditioning, jet travel—what can be done to moderate consumption by those who can afford to over-consume?

One way is through public policies that harness the motivating power of incentives. As a general rule, we get less of what we tax, and more of what we reward. Many cities are using tax monies to build bike lanes and subsidize improved mass transportation, thus encouraging alternatives to cars. On jammed highways, many regions have created high-occupancy vehicle lanes that reward carpooling and penalize driving solo. Gregg Esterbrook (2004) noted that if the United States had raised its gasoline tax by 50 cents a decade ago, as was proposed, the country would now have smaller, more fuel-efficient cars (as do Europeans, with their higher petrol taxes) and would, therefore, import less oil. This, in turn, would have led to lower oil consumption, less global warming, lower gas prices, and a smaller trade deficit weighing down the economy. A higher gas tax would have similar effects in Canada.

Europe leads the way in incentivizing mass transit and bicycle use over personal vehicle use. In addition to the small vehicles incentivized by high fuel taxes, cities such as Vienna, Munich, Zurich, and Copenhagen have closed many city centre streets to car traffic. London and Stockholm drivers pay congestion fees when entering the heart of the city. Amsterdam is a bicycle haven. Dozens of German cities have "environmental zones" where only low CO_2 cars may enter (Rosenthal, 2011). The Netherlands has even experimented with a car meter that would tax drivers a fee for miles driven, rather like paying a phone fee for minutes talked (Rosenthal, 2011).

Some free-market proponents object to carbon taxes because they are taxes. Others respond that carbon taxes are simply payment for external damage to today's health and tomorrow's environment. If not today's CO_2 emitters, who should pay for the cost of tomorrow's more threatening floods, tornadoes, hurricanes, droughts, and sea rise? "Markets are truly free only when everyone pays the full price for his or her actions," contends Environmental Defense Fund economist Gernot Wagner (2011). "Anything else is socialism."

Another way to encourage greener homes and businesses is to harness the power of immediate feedback to the consumer by installing "smart meters" that provide a continuous readout of electricity use and its cost. Turn off a computer monitor or the lights in an empty room, and the meter displays the decreased wattage. Turn on the air-conditioning, and you immediately know the usage and cost. In Britain, where smart meters are being installed in businesses, Conservative Party leader David Cameron has supported a plan to have them installed in all homes. "Smart meters have the power to revolutionize people's relationship with the energy they use," he said to Parliament (Rosenthal, 2008).

In one survey, the top reason people gave for buying a Prius hybrid car was that it "makes a statement about me" (Clayton & Myers, 2009, p. 9). Indeed, argue Tom Crompton and Tim Kasser (2010), our sense of who we are—our identity—has profound implications for our climate-related behaviours. Does our social identity, the in-group that defines our circle of concern, include only those around us now? Or does it encompass vulnerable people in places unseen, our descendants and others in the future, and even the creatures in the planet's natural environment?

Support for new energy policies will require a shift in public consciousness not unlike that occurring during the 1960s civil rights movement and the 1970s women's movement. James Gustave Speth (2008) is calling for an enlarged identity—a "new consciousness"—in which people do the following:

- See humanity as part of nature.
- See nature as having intrinsic value that we must steward.
- Value the future and its inhabitants as well as the present.
- Appreciate our human interdependence, by thinking "we" and not just "me."
- Define quality of life in relational and spiritual rather than materialistic terms.
- Value equity, justice, and the human community.

Is there any hope that human priorities might shift from accumulating money to finding meaning, and from aggressive consumption to nurturing connections? The British government's plan for achieving sustainable development includes an emphasis on promoting personal well-being and social health. Perhaps social psychology can help point the way to greater well-being, by suggesting *ways to reduce consumption*—and also by documenting *materialism*, by informing people that *economic growth does not automatically improve human morale*, and by helping people understand *why materialism and money fail to satisfy* and encouraging *alternative, intrinsic values*.

● DOES MONEY BUY HAPPINESS?

What might social psychology contribute to our understanding of changing materialism? To what extent do money and consumption buy happiness? And why do materialism and economic growth not bring enduringly greater satisfaction?

Despite the recent economic recession, life for most people in Western countries is good. As we noted in the opening statement of this module, today's average North American enjoys luxuries unknown even to royalty in centuries past. Does money—and such associated luxuries—buy happiness? Few of us would answer yes. But ask a different question—"Would a *little* more money make you a *little* happier?"—and most of us will say yes. There is, we believe, a connection between wealth and well-being. That belief feeds what Juliet Schor (1998) has called the "cycle of work and spend"—working more to buy more.

INCREASED MATERIALISM

Although the Earth asks that we live more lightly upon it, materialism has surged. According to a 1990 Gallup poll, one in two women, two in three men, and four in five people earning more than $75 000 a year in the U.S. would like to be rich—although, to that half of the world's population who live on less than $2 a day, an income of $75 000 means they are already fabulously wealthy (Shah, 2005).

Materialism surged during the 1970s and 1980s. The most dramatic evidence came from a large-scale annual survey of nearly a quarter million students entering university. The proportion considering it "very important or essential" that they become "very well off financially" rose from 39 percent in 1970 to 74 percent in 2005. Those proportions virtually flipped with those who considered it very important to "develop a meaningful philosophy of life." Materialism is up; spirituality is down.

WEALTH AND WELL-BEING

Does consumption, indeed, enable "the good life"? Does being well-off produce—or at least correlate with—psychological well-being? Would people be happier if they could exchange a simple lifestyle for one with palatial surroundings, Alps ski vacations, and executive-class travel? Would they be happier if they won a publishers' sweepstakes and could choose from its suggested indulgences: a 13-metre yacht, deluxe motor home, designer wardrobe, luxury car, and private housekeeper? Social psychological theory and evidence offer some answers.

We can observe the traffic between wealth and well-being by asking, first, if rich nations are happier. There is, indeed, some correlation between national wealth and well-being (measured as self-reported happiness and life satisfaction). Scandinavians have been mostly prosperous and satisfied; Bulgarians are neither. But 1990s data revealed that once nations reached about $10 000 GNP per person, which was roughly the economic level of Ireland before 1990, higher levels of national wealth were not predictive of increased well-being. Better to be Irish than Bulgarian. But happiness was about the same for an average Irish person, or an average Belgian, Canadian, or Norwegian—with more than double the Irish purchasing power (Inglehart, 1990).

> *"Whoever said money can't buy happiness isn't spending it right."*
> LEXUS ADVERTISEMENT

We can ask, second, whether within any given nation, rich people are happier. In poor countries—where low income more often threatens basic human needs—being relatively well-off does predict greater well-being (Howell & Howell, 2008). In affluent countries, where most can afford life's necessities, affluence still matters—partly because people with more money perceive more control in their lives (Johnson & Krueger, 2006). But compared with poor countries, income matters little. Once a comfortable income level is reached, more and more money provides diminishing long-term returns. World values researcher Ronald Inglehart (1990, p. 242), therefore, found the income–happiness correlation to be "surprisingly weak."

Even the super-rich—for example, those on the *Forbes 100* list—have reported only slightly greater happiness than average (Diener, Horwitz, & Emmons, 1985). And winning a major lottery seems not to elevate well-being enduringly (Brickman, Coates, & Janoff-Bulman, 1978). Such jolts of joy have "a short half-life," noted Richard Ryan (1999).

We can ask, third, whether, over time, a culture's happiness rises with its affluence. Does our collective well-being float upward with a rising economic tide? Apparently not. Compared to their grandparents, today's young adults have grown up with much more affluence, but with slightly less happiness and at greater risk of depression and assorted social pathologies (Klerman & Weissman, 1989; Seligman, 1989).

> *"I always in the back of my mind figured a lot of money will buy you a little bit of happiness. But it's not really true."*
> GOOGLE BILLIONAIRE
> CO-FOUNDER SERGEY BRIN, 2006

It is hard to avoid a startling conclusion: Our becoming much better off over the last four decades has not been accompanied by one iota of increased subjective well-being. The same is true in the European countries, Japan, and the U.S., reported Richard Easterlin (1995). In Britain, for example, great increases in the percent of households with cars, central heating, and telephones were not accompanied by increased happiness. After a decade of extraordinary economic growth in China—from few owning a phone and 40 percent owning a colour television to most people now having such things—Gallup surveys revealed a decreasing proportion of people satisfied "with the way things are going in your life today" (Burkholder, 2005).

The findings are startling because they challenge modern materialism: *Economic growth has provided no apparent boost to humans.* More than ever, we have big houses and broken homes, high incomes and modest happiness. We excel at making a living but often fail at making a life. We celebrate our prosperity but yearn for purpose. We cherish our freedoms but long for connection.

MATERIALISM FAILS TO SATISFY

It is striking that economic growth in affluent countries has failed to satisfy. It is further striking that individuals who strive most for wealth tend to live with lower well-being, a finding that "comes through very strongly in every culture I've looked at," reported Richard Ryan (1999).

Seek extrinsic goals—wealth, beauty, popularity—and you may find anxiety, depression, and psychosomatic ills (Eckersley, 2005; Sheldon et al., 2004). Those who instead strive for intrinsic goals such as "intimacy, personal growth, and contribution to the community" experience a higher quality of life, concluded Tim Kasser (2000; Kasser & Ahuvia, 2002). Intrinsic values, Kasser (2011) adds, promote personal and social well-being and help immunize people against materialistic values. Those focused on close relationships, meaningful work, and concern for others enjoy inherent rewards that often prove elusive to those more focused on things or on their status and image.

"Why do you spend your money for that which is not bread, and your labour for that which does not satisfy?"
ISAIAH 55:2

Pause a moment and think: What is the single most personally satisfying event that you experienced in the last month? Ken Sheldon and his colleagues (2001) put that question (and similar questions about the last week and semester) to samples of university students. Then they asked them to rate the extent to which 10 different needs were met by the satisfying event. The students rated self esteem, relatedness (feeling connected with others), and autonomy (feeling in control) as the three emotional needs that most strongly accompanied the satisfying event. At the bottom of the list of factors predicting satisfaction was money and luxury.

People who identify themselves with expensive possessions experience fewer positive moods, reported Emily Solberg, Ed Diener, and Michael Robinson (2003). Such materialists tend to report a relatively large gap between what they want and what they have, and to enjoy fewer close, fulfilling relationships. Wealthier people also tend to savour life's simpler pleasures less (Quoidbach et al., 2010). Sipping tea with a friend, savouring a chocolate, finishing a project, and discovering a waterfall while hiking may pale alongside the luxuries enabled by wealth.

People focused on extrinsic and material goals also "focus less on caring for the Earth," reports Kasser (2011). "As materialistic values go up, concern for nature tends to go down . . .

Close, supportive relationships are a key element in well-being.

When people strongly endorse money, image, and status, they are less likely to engage in eco-logically beneficial activities like riding bikes, recycling, and re-using things in new ways."

But why do yesterday's luxuries, such as air-conditioning and television, so quickly become today's requirements? Two principles drive this psychology of consumption: our ability to adapt and our need to compare.

Our human capacity for adaptation

adaptation-level phenomenon
the tendency to adapt to a given level of stimulation and thus to notice and react to changes from that level

The **adaptation-level phenomenon** is our tendency to judge our experience (for example, of sounds, temperatures, or income) relative to a neutral level defined by our prior experience. We adjust our neutral levels—the points at which sounds seem neither loud nor soft, temperatures neither hot nor cold, events neither pleasant nor unpleasant—on the basis of our experience. We then notice and react to changes up or down from those levels.

Thus, as our achievements rise above past levels, we initially feel successful and satisfied. As our social prestige, income, or in-home technology improves, we feel pleasure. Before long, however, we adapt. What once felt good registers as neutral, and what formerly felt neutral now feels like deprivation.

Would it ever, then, be possible to create a social paradise? Donald Campbell (1975a) answered no: If you woke up tomorrow to your utopia—perhaps a world with no bills, no ills, someone who loves you unreservedly—you would feel euphoric, for a time. Yet before long, you would recalibrate your adaptation level and again sometimes feel gratified (when achieve-ments surpass expectations), sometimes feel deprived (when they fall below), and sometimes feel neutral.

To be sure, adaptation to some events, such as the death of a spouse, may be incomplete, as the sense of loss lingers (Diener, Lucas, & Scollon, 2006). Yet, as explained earlier, we generally underestimate our adaptive capacity. People have difficulty predicting the intensity and dura-tion of their future positive and negative emotions, a phenomenon called impact bias (Chapter 2) (Wilson & Gilbert, 2003). The elation from getting what we want—riches, top exam scores, the Toronto Blue Jays winning the World Series—evaporates more rapidly than we expect. We also sometimes "miswant." When first-year university students predicted their satisfaction with vari-ous housing possibilities shortly before entering their school's housing lottery, they focused on physical features. "I'll be happiest in a beautiful and well-located dorm," many students seemed to think. But they were wrong. When contacted a year later, it was the social features, such as a sense of community, that predicted happiness, reported Elizabeth Dunn of the University of British Columbia and her colleagues (2003). Likewise, Leaf Van Boven and Thomas Gilovich (2003) reported from surveys and experiments that positive experiences (often social experi-ences) leave people happier. The best things in life are not things.

Our wanting to compare

Much of life revolves around social comparison, a point made by the old joke about two hikers who meet a bear. One reaches into his backpack and pulls out a pair of sneakers. "Why bother putting those on?" asks the other. "You can't outrun a bear." "I don't have to outrun the bear," answers the first. "I just have to outrun you."

Similarly, happiness is relative to our comparisons with others, especially with others within our own groups (Lyubomirsky, 2001; Zagefka & Brown, 2005). Whether we feel good or bad depends on how we compare with others. We are slow-witted or clumsy only when others are smart or agile. Let one professional athlete sign a contract for $15 million a year and an $8-million-a-year teammate may now feel less satisfied. "Our poverty became a reality. Not because of our having less, but by our neighbours having more," recalled Will Campbell in *Brother to a Dragonfly.*

Further feeding our fever for luxury is the tendency to compare upward: As we climb the ladder of success or affluence, we mostly compare ourselves with peers who are at or above our current level, not with those who have less. People living in communities where a few residents are very wealthy tend to feel less satisfied as they compare upward (Fiske, 2011).

In developed and emerging economies worldwide, inequality has grown in recent years. In the 34 Organisation for Economic Co-operation and Development (OECD, 2011) countries, the richest 10 percent now average nine times the income of the poorest 10 percent. (The gap is less in the Scandinavian countries, and is substantially greater in Israel, Turkey, the United States, Mexico, and Chile.) Countries with greater inequality not only have greater health and social problems, but also higher rates of mental illness (Pickett & Wilkinson, 2011). And over time, years with more income inequality—and associated increases in perceived unfairness and lack of trust—correlate with less happiness among those with lower incomes (Oishi, Kesebir, & Diener, 2011).

The adaptation-level and social comparison phenomena give us pause. They imply that the quest for happiness through material achievement requires continually expanding affluence. But the good news is that adaptation to simpler lives can also happen. If we shrink our consumption by choice or by necessity, we will initially feel a pinch; but it will pass. "Weeping may tarry for the night, but joy comes with the morning," reflected the Psalmist. Indeed, thanks to our capacity to adapt and to adjust comparisons, the emotional impact of significant life events—losing a job or even a disabling accident—dissipates sooner than most people suppose (Gilbert et al., 1998).

TOWARD SUSTAINABILITY AND SURVIVAL

As individuals and as a global society, we face difficult social and political issues. How might a democratic society induce people to adopt values that emphasize happiness over materialism? How might a market economy mix incentives for prosperity with restraints that preserve a habitable planet? To what extent can we depend on technological innovations, such as alternative energy sources, to reduce our ecological footprint? And in the meantime, to what extent does the superordinate goal of preserving the Earth for our grandchildren call us each to limit our own liberties—our freedom to drive, burn, and dump whatever we wish?

> *"All our wants, beyond those which a very moderate income will supply, are purely imaginary."*
> HENRY ST. JOHN, *LETTER TO SWIFT,* 1719

A shift to postmaterialist values will gain momentum as people, governments, and corporations take these steps:

- Face the implications of population and consumption growth for pollution, climate change, and habitat and environmental destruction.

- Realize that materialist values make for less happy lives.

- Identify and promote the things in life that matter more than economic growth.

"If the world is to change for the better, it must have a change in human consciousness," said Czech poet-president Vaclav Havel (1990). We must discover "a deeper sense of responsibility

"However great the discrepancies between men's lots, there is always a certain balance of joy and sorrow which equalizes all."

LA ROCHEFOUCAULD, *MAXIMS*, 1665

toward the world, which means responsibility toward something higher than self." If people came to believe that stacks of unplayed CDs, closets full of seldom-worn clothes, and garages with luxury cars do not define the good life, then might a shift in consciousness become possible? Instead of being an indicator of social status, might conspicuous consumption become gauche?

Social psychology's contribution to a sustainable future will come partly through its consciousness-transforming insights into adaptation and social comparison. These insights also come from experiences that lower people's comparison standards and thereby cool luxury fever and renew contentment. In two such experiments, Marshall Dermer and his colleagues (1979) put university women through some imaginative exercises in deprivation. After viewing depictions of how grim life was in 1900, or after imagining and then writing about being burned and disfigured, the women expressed greater satisfaction with their own lives.

In another experiment, Jennifer Crocker and Lisa Gallo (1985) found that people who five times completed the sentence "I'm glad I'm not a . . ." afterwards felt less depressed and more satisfied with their lives than did those who had completed sentences beginning "I wish I were a . . .". Realizing that others have it worse helps us count our blessings. "I cried because I had no shoes," says a Persian proverb, "until I met a man who had no feet." Downward social comparison facilitates contentment.

Downward comparison to a hypothetical worse-off self also enhances contentment. In one experiment, Minkyung Koo and her colleagues (2008) invited people to write about how they might never have met their romantic partner. Compared to others who wrote about meeting their partner, those who imagined not having the relationship expressed more satisfaction with it. Can you likewise imagine how some good things in *your* life might never have happened? It's very easy for me to imagine not having chanced into an acquaintance that led to an invitation to author this book. Just thinking about that reminds me to count my blessings.

Social psychology also contributes to a sustainable and survivable future through its explorations of the good life. If materialism does not enhance quality of life, what does?

- **Close, supportive relationships.** As we saw in Chapter 10, our deep need to belong is satisfied by close, supportive relationships. Those supported by intimate friendships or a committed marriage are much likelier to declare themselves "very happy." Faith communities and other voluntary organizations are often a source of such connections, as well as of meaning and hope.

- **Positive thinking habits.** Optimism, self-esteem, perceived control, and extroversion also mark happy experiences and happy lives. One analysis of 638 studies of 420 000 people in 63 countries found that a sense of autonomy—feeling free and independent—consistently influences people's sense of well-being more than does wealth (Fischer & Boer, 2011).

- **Experiencing nature.** Carleton University students randomly assigned to a 17-minute nature walk near their campus ended up (to their and others' surprise) much happier than students who took a similar-length walk through campus walking tunnels (Nisbet & Zelenski, 2011). Japanese researchers report that "forest bathing"—walks in the woods—also helps lower stress hormones and blood pressure (Phillips, 2011).

- **Flow.** Work and leisure experiences that engage people's skills mark happy lives. Between the anxiety of being overwhelmed and stressed, and the apathy of being underwhelmed and bored, noted Mihaly Csikszentmihalyi (1990, 1999), lies a zone in which people experience *flow*, an optimal state in which, absorbed in an activity, they lose consciousness of self and time. When their experience is sampled using electronic pagers, people report greatest enjoyment not when mindlessly passive, but when unself-consciously absorbed in a mindful challenge. Ironically, in fact, the less expensive (and generally more involving) a leisure activity, the happier people are while doing it. Most people are happier gardening than power boating, and they are happier talking to friends than watching TV. Low consumption recreations prove most satisfying.

That is good news, indeed. Those things that make for the genuinely good life—close relationships, social networks based on belief, positive thinking, engaging activity—are enduringly sustainable. And that is an idea close to the heart of Jigme Singye Wangchuk, former king of Bhutan. "Gross national happiness is more important than gross national product," he believes. Writing from the Centre of Bhutan Studies in Bhutan, Sander Tideman (2003) explains: "Gross national happiness . . . aims to promote real progress and sustainability by measuring the quality of life, rather than the mere sum of production and consumption." Now other nations, too, are assessing national quality of life.

▶ SUMMING UP

HOW CAN HUMANITY CREATE A SUSTAINABLE FUTURE?

- There is overwhelming scientific evidence and consensus that global warming is a fact and caused by human activity. Global warming has psychological costs in that people must cope with the natural disasters, wars, and aggression that are promoted by global warming. Despite the scientific evidence, many people in Canada and the majority of people in the United States and Great Britain do not accept either its reality or that it is caused by human activity.

- Humanity can prepare for a sustainable future by increasing technological efficiency. We can also create incentives and change actions and attitudes to control population and moderate consumption.

- Attending to concepts in social psychology that address our attitudes and our behaviours may help accomplish those objectives. Rapid cultural change has happened in the last 40 years, and there is hope that in response to the global crisis it can happen again.

DOES MONEY BUY HAPPINESS?

- To judge from the expressed values of college and university students and the "luxury fever" that marked late-twentieth-century North America, today's Canadians and Americans—and to a lesser extent people in other Western countries—live in a highly materialistic age.

- People in rich nations report greater happiness and life satisfaction than those in poor nations, though with diminishing returns as one moves from moderately to very wealthy countries.

- Rich people within a country are somewhat happier than working-class people, though again more and more money provides diminishing returns (as evident in studies of the super rich and of lottery winners).

- Economic growth over time does not make people happier, as shown by the slight decline in self-reported happiness and the increasing rate of depression during the post-1960 years of increasing affluence.

- Two principles help explain why materialism fails to satisfy: the adaptation-level phenomenon and social comparison. When incomes and consumption rise, we soon adapt; when comparing with others, we may find our relative position unchanged.

- To build a sustainable and satisfying future, we can individually seek close relationships, and as a society promote them, through social networks based on belief, positive thinking habits, and engaging activity.

Glossary

A

acceptance conformity that involves both acting and believing in accord with social pressure

adaptation-level phenomenon the tendency to adapt to a given level of stimulation and thus to notice and react to changes from that level

aggression physical or verbal behaviour intended to hurt someone

altruism a motive to increase another's welfare without conscious regard for one's self-interests

arbitration resolution of a conflict by a neutral third party who studies both sides and imposes a settlement

attitude a favourable or unfavourable evaluative reaction toward something or someone, exhibited in one's beliefs, feelings, or intended behaviour

attitude inoculation exposing people to weak attacks on their attitudes so that when stronger attacks come, they will have refutations available

attractiveness having qualities that appeal to an audience. An appealing communicator (often someone similar to the audience) is most persuasive on matters of subjective preference.

attribution theory the theory of how people explain the behaviour of others—for example, by attributing it either to internal dispositions (enduring traits, motives, and attitudes) or to external situations

autokinetic phenomenon self (*auto*) motion (*kinetic*). The apparent movement of a stationary point of light in the dark. Perhaps you have experienced this when thinking you have spotted a moving satellite in the sky, only to realize later that it was merely an isolated star.

automatic processing implicit thinking that is effortless, habitual, and without awareness; roughly corresponds to intuition

availability heuristic a cognitive rule that judges the likelihood of things in terms of their availability in memory. If instances of something come readily to mind, we presume it to be commonplace.

avoidant attachment attachments are marked by discomfort over, or resistance to, being close to others

B

bargaining seeking an agreement through direct negotiation between parties to a conflict

behavioural confirmation a type of self-fulfilling prophecy whereby people's social expectations lead them to act in ways that cause others to confirm their expectations

behavioural medicine an interdisciplinary field that integrates and applies behavioural and medical knowledge about health and disease

belief perseverance persistence of your initial conceptions, as when the basis for your belief is discredited but an explanation of why the belief might be true survives

bystander effect the finding that a person is less likely to provide help when there are other bystanders

C

catharsis emotional release. The catharsis view of aggression is that aggressive drive is reduced when one "releases" aggressive energy, either by acting aggressively or by fantasizing aggression.

central route to persuasion occurs when interested people focus on the arguments and respond with favourable thoughts

channel of communication the way the message is delivered—whether face to face, in writing, on film, or in some other way

clinical psychology the study, assessment, and treatment of people with psychological difficulties

co-actors a group of people working simultaneously and individually on a non-competitive task

cognitive dissonance theory tension that arises when we are simultaneously aware of two inconsistent cognitions. For example, dissonance may occur when we realize that we have, with little justification, acted contrary to our attitudes or made a decision favouring one alternative despite reasons favouring another.

cohesiveness a "we feeling"—the extent to which members of a group are bonded together, such as by attraction for one another

collectivism giving priority to the goals of one's groups (often, one's extended family or work group) and defining one's identity accordingly

companionate love the affection we feel for those with whom our lives are deeply intertwined

complementarity the popularly supposed tendency, in a relationship between two people, for each to complete what is missing in the other

compliance conformity that involves publicly acting in accord with social pressure while privately disagreeing

confederate an accomplice of the experimenter

confirmation bias a tendency to search for information that confirms one's preconceptions

conflict a perceived incompatibility of actions or goals

conformity a change in behaviour or belief to accord with others

controlled processing explicit thinking that is deliberate, reflective, and conscious

correlational research the study of the naturally occurring relationships among variables

counterfactual thinking imagining alternative scenarios and outcomes that might have happened, but didn't

credibility believability. A credible communicator is perceived as both expert and trustworthy.

cults groups typically characterized by (1) the distinctive ritual of its devotion to a god or a person, (2) isolation from the surrounding "evil" culture, and (3) a charismatic leader; also called *new religious movements*. (A sect, by contrast, is a spinoff from a major religion.)

culture the enduring behaviours, ideas, attitudes, traditions, products, and institutions shared by a large group of people and transmitted from one generation to the next

D

deindividuation loss of self-awareness and evaluation apprehension; occurs in group situations that foster anonymity and draw attention away from the individual

demand characteristics cues in an experiment that tell the participant what behaviour is expected

dependent variable the variable being measured, so called because it may *depend* on manipulations of the independent variable

depressive realism the tendency of mildly depressed people to make accurate rather than self-serving judgments, attributions, and predictions

disclosure reciprocity the tendency for one person's intimacy of self-disclosure to match that of a conversational partner

discrimination unjustifiable negative behaviour toward a group or its members

displacement the redirection of aggression to a target other than the source of the frustration. Generally, the new target is a safer or more socially acceptable target.

dispositional attribution attributing behaviour to the person's disposition and traits

door-in-the-face technique a strategy for gaining a concession. After someone first turns down a large request (the door-in-the-face), the same requester counter-offers with a more reasonable request.

dual attitudes differing implicit (automatic) and explicit (consciously controlled) attitudes toward the same object. Verbalized explicit attitudes may change with education and persuasion; implicit attitudes change slowly, with practice that forms new habits.

E

egoism a motive (supposedly underlying all behaviour) to increase your own welfare; the opposite of *altruism*, which aims to increase someone else's welfare.

embodied cognition the mutual influence of bodily sensations on cognitive preferences and social judgments

empathy the vicarious experience of someone else's feelings; putting yourself in someone else's shoes

equality the equal distribution of rewards to all individuals

equity a condition in which the outcomes people receive from a relationship are proportional to what they contribute to it. *Note:* Equitable outcomes needn't always be equal outcomes.

ethnocentric believing in the superiority of your own ethnic and cultural group, and having a corresponding disdain for all other groups

evaluation apprehension concern for how others are evaluating us

experimental realism degree to which an experiment absorbs and involves its participants

experimental research studies that seek clues to cause–effect relationships by manipulating one or more factors (independent variables) while controlling others (holding them constant)

explanatory style a person's habitual way of explaining life events. A negative, pessimistic, and depressive explanatory style attributes failures to stable, global, and internal causes.

F

false consensus effect the tendency to overestimate the commonality of one's opinions and one's undesirable or unsuccessful behaviours

false uniqueness effect the tendency to underestimate the commonality of one's abilities and one's desirable or successful behaviours

field research research done in natural, real-life settings outside the laboratory

foot-in-the-door phenomenon the tendency for people who have first agreed to a small request to comply later with a larger request

free-ride benefiting from the group, but giving little in return

frustration the blocking of goal-directed behaviour

frustration-aggression theory the theory that frustration triggers a readiness to aggress

fundamental attribution error the tendency for observers to underestimate situational influences and overestimate dispositional influences on others' behaviour; also called *correspondence bias*, because we so often see behaviour as corresponding to a disposition

G

gender roles behaviour expectations (norms) for males and females

GRIT acronym for "graduated and reciprocated initiatives in tension reduction"—a strategy designed to de-escalate international tensions

group two or more people who, for longer than a few moments, interact with and influence one another and perceive one another as "us"

group polarization group-produced enhancement of members' pre-existing tendencies; a strengthening of the members' *average* tendency, not a split within the group

group-serving bias explaining away out-group members' positive behaviours; also attributing negative behaviours to their dispositions (while excusing such behaviour by one's own group)

groupthink "The mode of thinking that persons engage in when concurrence-seeking becomes so dominant in a cohesive in-group that it tends to override realistic appraisal of alternative courses of action."–Irving Janis (1971)

H

health psychology the study of the psychological roots of health and illness. It provides psychology's contribution to behavioural medicine.

heuristics a thinking strategy that enables quick, efficient judgments

hindsight bias the tendency to exaggerate, after learning an outcome, one's ability to have foreseen how something turned out; also known as the *I-knew-it-all-along phenomenon*

hostile aggression aggression driven by anger and performed as an end in itself

hypotheses testable propositions that describe relationships that may exist between events

I

illusion of control perception of uncontrollable events as subject to one's control or as more controllable than they are

illusory correlation perception of a relationship where none exists, or perception of a stronger relationship than actually exists

immune neglect the human tendency to underestimate the speed and the strength of the "psychological immune system," which enables emotional recovery and resilience after bad things happen

impact bias overestimating the enduring impact of emotion-causing events

Implicit Association Test (IAT) a computer-driven assessment of implicit attitudes that uses reaction times to measure people's automatic associations between attitude objects and evaluative words, where easier pairings (and faster responses) are taken to indicate stronger unconscious associations

independent self construing one's identity as a unique individual with particular abilities, traits, values, and dreams

independent variables experimental factors that a researcher manipulates

individualism the concept of giving priority to one's own goals over group goals and defining one's identity in terms of personal attributes rather than group identifications

informational influence conformity that results from accepting evidence about reality provided by other people

informed consent an ethical principle requiring that research participants be told enough to enable them to choose whether they wish to participate

ingratiation the use of strategies, such as flattery, by which people seek to gain another's favour

in-group bias the tendency to favour your own group

in-groups "us"—groups of people who share a sense of belonging, a feeling of common identity

insecure attachment attachments are marked by anxiety or ambivalence

instinctive behaviour an innate, unlearned behaviour pattern exhibited by all members of a species

instrumental aggression aggression that is a means to some other end

insufficient justification reduction of dissonance by internally justifying one's behaviour when external justification is "insufficient"

integrative agreements win–win agreements that reconcile both parties' interests to their mutual benefit

interdependent self construing one's identity in relation to others

J

just-world phenomenon the tendency of people to believe that the world is just, and that, therefore, people get what they deserve and deserve what they get

K

kin selection the idea that evolution has selected altruism toward one's close relatives to enhance the survival of mutually shared genes

L

leadership the process by which certain group members motivate and guide the group

learned helplessness the hopelessness and resignation learned when a human or animal perceives no control over repeated bad events

low-ball technique a tactic for getting people to agree to something. People who agree to an initial request will often still comply when the requester ups the ante. People who receive only the costly request are less likely to comply with it.

M

matching phenomenon the tendency for men and women to choose as partners those who are a "good match" in attractiveness and other traits

mediation an attempt by a neutral third party to resolve a conflict by facilitating communication and offering suggestions

mere-exposure effect the tendency for novel stimuli to be liked more or rated more positively after the rater has been repeatedly exposed to them

misattribution mistakenly attributing a behaviour to the wrong cause

misinformation effect incorporating "misinformation" into one's memory of the event, after witnessing an event and then receiving misleading information about it

moral exclusion the perception of certain individuals or groups as outside the boundary within which you apply moral values and rules of fairness

moral inclusion regarding others as within your circle of moral concern

mundane realism degree to which an experiment is superficially similar to everyday situations

N

naturalistic fallacy the error of defining what is good in terms of what is observable: for example, what's typical is normal; what's normal is good

need-based distribution the distribution of rewards based on need for those rewards

need for cognition the motivation to think and analyze; assessed by agreement with items such as "the notion of thinking abstractly is appealing to me" and disagreement with items such as "I only think as hard as I have to"

need to belong a motivation to bond with others in relationships that provide ongoing, positive interactions

non-zero-sum games games in which outcomes need not sum to zero. With cooperation, both can win; with competition, both can lose. (Also called *mixed-motive situations*.)

normative influence conformity based on a person's desire to fulfill others' expectations, often to gain acceptance

norms rules for accepted and expected behaviour, that prescribe "proper" behaviour

O

obedience acting in accord with a direct order

out-group homogeneity effect perception of out-group members as more similar to one another than are in-group members. Thus, "they are alike; we are diverse."

out-groups "them"—groups that people perceive as distinctively different from or apart from their in-group

overconfidence phenomenon the tendency to be more confident than correct—to overestimate the accuracy of one's beliefs

overjustification effect the result of bribing people to do what they already like doing; they may then see their action as externally controlled rather than intrinsically appealing

own-race bias the tendency for people to more accurately recognize faces of their own race

P

passionate love a state of intense longing for union with another. Passionate lovers are absorbed in one another; they feel ecstatic at attaining their partner's love, and they are disconsolate on losing it.

peripheral route to persuasion occurs when people are influenced by incidental cues, such as a speaker's attractiveness

persuasion the process by which a message induces change in beliefs, attitudes, or behaviours

physical-attractiveness stereotype the presumption that physically attractive people possess other socially desirable traits as well: What is beautiful is good.

planning fallacy the tendency to underestimate how long it will take to complete a task

pluralistic ignorance a false impression of how other people are thinking, feeling, or responding

possible selves images of what we dream of or dread becoming in the future

prejudice a negative prejudgment of a group and its individual members

primacy effect other things being equal, information presented first usually has the most influence

priming activating particular associations in memory

prosocial behaviour positive, constructive, helpful social behaviour; the opposite of antisocial behaviour

proximity geographical nearness. Proximity (more precisely, "functional distance") powerfully predicts liking.

R

racism (1) an individual's prejudicial attitudes and discriminatory behaviour toward people of a given race, or (2) institutional practices (even if not motivated by prejudice) that subordinate people of a given race

random assignment the process of assigning participants to the conditions of an experiment such that all persons have the same chance of being in a given condition

random sample survey procedure in which every person in the population being studied has an equal chance of inclusion

reactance a motive to protect or restore one's sense of freedom. Reactance arises when someone threatens our freedom of action.

realistic group conflict theory the theory that prejudice arises from competition between groups for scarce resources

recency effect information presented last sometimes has the most influence. Recency effects are less common than primacy effects.

reciprocity norm an expectation that people will help, not hurt, those who have helped them

regression toward the average the statistical tendency for extreme scores or extreme behaviour to return toward the person's average

relative deprivation the perception that one is less well off than others to whom one compares oneself

representativeness heuristic the tendency to presume, sometimes despite contrary odds, that someone or something belongs to a particular group if resembling (representing) a typical member

reward theory of attraction the theory that we like those whose behaviour is rewarding to us or whom we associate with rewarding events

role a set of norms that define how people in a given social position ought to behave

S

secure attachment attachments rooted in trust and marked by intimacy

self-affirmation theory a theory that people often experience self-image threat after engaging in an undesirable behaviour, and they compensate for this threat by affirming another aspect of the self. Threaten people's self-concept in one domain, and they will compensate either by refocusing or by doing good deeds in some other domain.

self-concept how a person answers the question, "Who am I?" provides a glimpse of his or her self-concept

self-disclosure revealing intimate aspects of oneself to others

self-esteem a person's overall self-evaluation or sense of self-worth

self-fulfilling prophecies beliefs that lead to their own fulfillment

self-handicapping protecting one's self-image with behaviours that create a handy excuse for later failure

self-monitoring being attuned to the way you present yourself in social situations and adjusting your performance to create the desired impression

self-perception theory the theory that when unsure of our attitudes, we infer them much as would someone observing us—by looking at our behaviour and the circumstances under which it occurs

self-presentation the act of expressing yourself and behaving in ways designed to create a favourable impression or an impression that corresponds to your ideals

self-schemas beliefs about self that organize and guide the processing of self-relevant information

self-serving attributions a form of self-serving bias; the tendency to attribute positive outcomes to yourself and negative outcomes to other factors

self-serving bias the tendency to perceive yourself favourably

sexism (1) an individual's prejudicial attitudes and discriminatory behaviour toward people of a given sex, or (2) institutional practices (even if not motivated by prejudice) that subordinate people of a given sex

situational attribution attributing behaviour to the environment

sleeper effect a delayed impact of a message; occurs when we remember the message but forget a reason for discounting it

social comparison evaluating your abilities and opinions by comparing yourself to others

social dominance orientation a motivation to have your own group be dominant over other social groups

social-exchange theory the theory that human interactions are transactions that aim to maximize one's rewards and minimize one's costs

social facilitation (1) original meaning: the tendency of people to perform simple or well-learned tasks better when others are present; (2) current meaning: the strengthening of dominant (prevalent, likely) responses owing to the presence of others

social identity the "we" aspect of our self-concept; the part of our answer to "Who am I?" that comes from our group memberships (examples: "I am Australian." "I am Catholic.")

social learning theory the theory that we learn social behaviour by observing and imitating and by being rewarded and punished

social loafing the tendency for people to exert less effort when they pool their efforts toward a common goal than when they are individually accountable

social neuroscience an integration of biological and social perspectives that explores the neural and psychological bases of social and emotional behaviours

social psychology the scientific study of how people think about, influence, and relate to one another

social representations socially shared beliefs; widely held ideas and values, including our assumptions and cultural ideologies. Our social representations help us make sense of our world.

social-responsibility norm an expectation that people will help those dependent upon them

social scripts culturally provided mental instructions for how to act in various situations

social trap a situation in which the conflicting parties, by rationally pursuing their own self-interest, become caught in mutually destructive behaviour

spontaneous trait inference an effortless, automatic inference of a trait after exposure to someone's behaviour

stereotypes beliefs about the personal attributes of a group of people. Stereotypes can be overgeneralized, inaccurate, and resistant to new information.

stereotype threat a disruptive concern, when facing a negative stereotype, that one will be evaluated based on a negative stereotype

subgrouping accommodating groups of individuals who deviate from one's stereotype by forming a new stereotype about this subset of the group

subtyping accommodating groups of individuals who deviate from one's stereotype by thinking of them as a special category of people with different properties

T

temporal comparisons comparisons between how the self is viewed now and how the self was viewed in the past or how the self is expected to be viewed in the future

theory an integrated set of principles that explain and predict observed events

two-factor theory of emotion arousal × its label = emotion

two-step flow of communication the process by which media influence often occurs through opinion leaders, who in turn influence others

References

Abbate, C. S., Isgro, A., Wicklund, R. A., & Boca, S. (2006). A field experiment on perspective-taking, helping, and self-awareness. *Basic and Applied Social Psychology, 28,* 283–287. (p. 302)

Abbey, A. (1987). Misperceptions of friendly behavior as sexual interest: A survey of naturally occurring incidents. *Psychology of Women Quarterly, 11,* 173–194. (p. 102)

Abbey, A. (1991). Misperception as an antecedent of acquaintance rape: A consequence of ambiguity in communication between women and men. In A. Parrot (Ed.), *Acquaintance rape.* New York: Wiley. (p. 102)

Abbey, A., & Andrews, F. M. (1985). Modeling the psychological determinants of life quality. *Social Indicators Research, 16,* 1–34. (p. 491)

ABC News. (2004, March 31). Bizarre hoax leads to strip searches (abcnews.go.com). (p. 208)

Abelson, R. (1972). Are attitudes necessary? In B. T. King & E. McGinnies (Eds.), *Attitudes, conflict and social change.* New York: Academic Press. (p. 122)

Abrams, D., Wetherell, M., Cochrane, S., Hogg, M. A., & Turner, J. C. (1990). Knowing what to think by knowing who you are: Self-categorization and the nature of norm formation, conformity and group polarization. *British Journal of Social Psychology, 29,* 97–119. (p. 253)

Abramson, L. Y., Metalsky, G. I., & Alloy, L. B. (1989). Hopelessness depression: A theory-based subtype. *Psychological Review, 96,* 358–372. (p. 476)

Ackerman, J. M., Griskevicius, V., & Li, N. P. (2011). Let's get serious: Communicating commitment in romantic relationships. *Journal of Personality and Social Psychology, 100,* 1079–1094. (p. 379)

Ackermann, R., & DeRubeis, R. J. (1991). Is depressive realism real? *Clinical Psychology Review, 11,* 565–584. (p. 476)

Adair, J. G., Dushenko, T. W., & Lindsay, R. C. L. (1985). Ethical regulations and their impact on research practice. *American Psychologist, 40,* 59–72. (p. 24)

Adams, D. (Ed.) (1991). The Seville statement on violence: Preparing the ground for the constructing of peace. UNESCO. (p. 316)

Adams, G., Garcia, D. M., Purdie-Vaughns, V., & Steele, C. M. (2006). The detrimental effects of a suggestion of sexism in an instruction situation. *Journal of Experimental Social Psychology, 42,* 602–615. (p. 113)

Adams, J. M., & Jones, W. H. (1997). The conceptualization of marital commitment: An integrative analysis. *Journal of Personality and Social Psychology, 72,* 1177–1196. (p. 392)

Addis, M. E., & Mahalik, J. R. (2003). Men, masculinity, and the contexts of help seeking. *American Psychologist, 58,* 5–14. (p. 282)

Aderman, D., & Berkowitz, L. (1983). Self-concern and the unwillingness to be helpful. *Social Psychology Quarterly, 46,* 293–301. (p. 277)

Adler, N. E., Boyce, T., Chesney, M. A., Cohen, S., Folkman, S., Kahn, R. L., & Syme, S. L. (1993). Socioeconomic inequalities in health: No easy solution. *Journal of the American Medical Association, 269,* 3140–3145. (p. 19)

Adler, N. E., Boyce, T., Chesney, M. A., Cohen, S., Folkman, S., Kahn, R. L., & Syme, S. L. (1994). Socioeconomic status and health: The challenge of the gradient. *American Psychologist, 49,* 15–24. (p. 19)

Adler, N. E., & Snibbe, A. C. (2003). The role of psychosocial processes in explaining the gradient between socioeconomic status and health. *Current Directions in Psychological Science, 12,* 119. (p. 489)

Adler, R. P., Lesser, G. S., Meringoff, L. K., Robertson, T. S., & Ward, S. (1980). The *effects of television advertising on children.* Lexington, MA: Lexington Books. (p. 190)

Adorno, T., Frenkel-Brunswik, E., Levinson, D., & Sanford, R. N. (1950). *The authoritarian personality.* New York: Harper. (p. 403)

Agerström, J., & Rooth, D-O. (2011). The role of automatic obesity stereotypes in real hiring discrimination. *Journal of Applied Psychology, 96,* 790–805. (p. 125)

Agnew, G. A., & Carron, A. V. (1994). Crowd effects and the home advantage. *International Journal of Sport Psychology, 25,* 53–62. (p. 236)

Agthe, M., Spörrle, M., & Maner, J. K. (2011). Does being attractive always help? Positive and negative effects of attractiveness on social decision making. *Personality and Social Psychology Bulletin, 37,* 1042–1054. (pp. 360, 363)

Aiello, J. R., & Douthitt, E. Z. (2001). Social facilitation from Triplett to electronic performance monitoring. *Group Dynamics: Theory, Research, and Practice, 5,* 163–180. (p. 237)

Aiello, J. R., Thompson, D. E., & Brodzinsky, D. M. (1983). How funny is crowding anyway? Effects of room size, group size, and the introduction of humor. *Basic and Applied Social Psychology, 4,* 193–207. (p. 236)

Ainsworth, M. D. S. (1973). The development of infant-mother attachment. In B. Caldwell & H. Ricciuti (Eds.), *Review of child development research* (Vol. 3). Chicago: University of Chicago Press. (p. 383)

Ainsworth, M. D. S. (1979). Infant-mother attachment. *American Psychologist, 34,* 932–937. (pp. 383, 384)

Ajzen, I. (1982). On behaving in accordance with one's attitudes. In M. P. Zanna, E. T. Higgins, & C. P. Herman (Eds.), *Consistency in social behavior: The Ontario Symposium,* vol. 2. Hillside, NJ: Erlbaum. (p. 126)

Ajzen, I., & Fishbein, M. (1977). Attitude-behavior relations: A theoretical analysis and review of empirical research. *Psychological Bulletin, 84,* 888–918. (p. 126)

Akhtar-Danesh, N., & Landeen, J. (2007). Relation between depression and sociodemographic factors. *International Journal of Mental Health Systems, 1,* 4. (p. 492)

Albarracin, D., Gillette, J. C., Earl, A. N., Glasman, L. R., Durantini, M. R., & Ho, M. (2005). A test of major assumptions about behavior change: A comprehensive look at the effects of passive and active HIV-prevention interventions since the beginning of the epidemic. *Psychological Bulletin, 131,* 856. (p. 176)

Albarracin, D., Johnson, B. T., Fishbein, M., & Muellerleile, P. A. (2001). Theories of reasoned action and planned behavior as models of condom use: A meta-analysis. *Psychological Bulletin, 127,* 142–161. (p. 127)

Allee, W. C., & Masure, R. M. (1936). A comparison of maze behavior in paired and isolated shell-parakeets (Melopsittacus undulatus Shaw) in a two-alley problem box. *Journal of Comparative Psychology, 22,* 131–155. (p. 234)

Allen, V. L., & Levine, J. M. (1969). Consensus and conformity. *Journal of Experimental Social Psychology, 5,* 389–399. (p. 215)

Allesøe, K., Hundrup, V. A., Thomsen, J. F., & Osler, M. (2010). Psychosocial work environment and risk of ischaemic heart disease in women: The Danish Nurse Cohort Study. *Occupational and Environmental Medicine, 67,* 318–322. (p. 485)

Allison, S. T., Mackie, D. M., & Messick, D. M. (1996). Outcome biases in social perception: Implications for dispositional inference, attitude change, stereotyping, and social behavior. *Advances in Experimental Social Psychology, 28,* 53–93. (p. 418)

Allison, S. T., Mackie, D. M., Muller, M. M., & Worth, L. T. (1993). Sequential correspondence biases and perceptions of change: The Castro studies revisited. *Personality and Social Psychology Bulletin, 19,* 151–157. (p. 105)

Allison, S. T., McQueen, L. R., & Schaerfl, L. M. (1992). Social decision making processes and the equal partitionment of shared resources. *Journal of Experimental Social Psychology, 28,* 23–42. (p. 458)

Allison, S. T., & Messick, D. M. (1985). The group attribution error. *Journal of Experimental Social Psychology, 21,* 563–579. (p. 418)

Alloy, L. B., & Abramson, L. Y. (1979). Judgment of contingency in depressed and nondepressed students: Sadder but wiser? *Journal of Experimental Psychology: General, 108,* 441–485. (p. 475)

Alloy, L. B., Abramson, L. Y., Whitehouse, W. G., Hogan, M. E., Tashman, N. A., Steinberg, D. L., Rose, D. T., & Donovan, P. (1999). Depressogenic cognitive styles: Predictive validity, information processing and personality characteristics, and developmental origins. *Behaviour Research and Therapy, 37,* 503–531. (p. 478)

Alloy, L. B., Albright, J. S., Abramson, L. Y., & Dykman, B. M. (1990). Depressive realism and nondepressive optimistic illusions: The role of the self. In R. E. Ingram (Ed.), *Contemporary psychological approaches to depression: Theory, research and treatment.* New York: Plenum. (p. 476)

Allport, F. H. (1920). The influence of the group upon association and thought. *Journal of Experimental Psychology, 3,* 159–182. (p. 234)

Allport, G. (1954). *The nature of prejudice.* Cambridge, MA: Addison-Wesley. (pp. 398, 436)

Allport, G. W. (1958). *The nature of prejudice* (abridged). Garden City, NY: Anchor Books. (pp. 402, 405, 407, 438, 440)

Allport, G. W., & Ross, J. M. (1967). Personal religious orientation and prejudice. *Journal of Personality and Social Psychology, 5,* 432–443. (p. 405)

Altemeyer, B. (1988). *Enemies of freedom: Understanding right-wing authoritarianism.* San Francisco: Jossey-Bass. (p. 404)

Altemeyer, B. (1992). *Six studies of right-wing authoritarianism among American state legislators.* Unpublished manuscript, University of Manitoba. (p. 404)

Altemeyer, B. (2004). Highly dominating, highly authoritarian personalities. *Journal of Social Psychology, 144,* 421. (p. 404)

Altemeyer, B., & Hunsberger, B. (1992). Authoritarianism, religious fundamentalism, quest, and prejudice. *International Journal for the Psychology of Religion, 2,* 113–133. (p. 404)

Alwin, D. F., Cohen, R. L., & Newcomb, T. M. (1991). *Political attitudes over the life span: The Bennington women after fifty years.* Madison, WI: University of Wisconsin Press. (p. 179)

Amato, P. R. (1986). Emotional arousal and helping behavior in a real-life emergency. *Journal of Applied Social Psychology, 16,* 633–641. (p. 288)

Ambady, N., Bernieri, F. J., & Richeson, J. A. (2000). Toward a histology of social behavior: Judgmental accuracy from thin slices of the behavioral stream. In M. P. Zanna (Ed.), *Advances in Experimental Social Psychology, 32,* 201–271. (p. 360)

Ambady, N., & Rosenthal, R. (1992). Thin slices of expressive behavior as predictors of interpersonal consequences: A meta-analysis. *Psychological Bulletin, 111,* 256–274. (p. 112)

Ambady, N., & Rosenthal, R. (1993). Half a minute: Predicting teacher evaluations from thin slices of nonverbal behavior and physical attractiveness. *Journal of Personality and Social Psychology, 64,* 431–441. (p. 112)

American College Health Association (ACHA). (2009). *American College Health Association-National College Health Assessment II: Reference group executive summary Fall 2008.* Baltimore: Author. (p. 471)

American Enterprise. (1992, January/February). "Women, men, marriages & ministers," 106. (p. 392)

American Psychological Association (1993). *Violence and youth: Psychology's response.* Vol I: Summary report of the American Psychological Association Commission on Violence and Youth. Washington DC: Public Interest Directorate, American Psychological Association. (pp. 314, 334)

Amland, B. H. (2011, June 6). Millions displaced by natural disasters last year. Associated Press. (p. 517)

Amodio, D. H., & Devine, P. G. (2010). Control in the regulation of intergroup bias. In R. R. Hassin, K. H. Ochsner, & Y. Trope (Eds.), *Self-control in society, mind, and brain.* New York: Oxford University Press. (p. 416)

Anastasi, J. S., & Rhodes, M. G. (2005). An own-age bias in face recognition for children and older adults. *Psychonomic Bulletin & Review, 12,* 1043–1047. (p. 420)

Anastasi, J. S., & Rhodes, M. G. (2006). Evidence for an own-age bias in face recognition. *North American Journal of Psychology, 8,* 237–252. (p. 420)

Anda, R., Williamson, D., Jones, D., Macera, C., Eaker, E., Glassman, A., & Marks, J. (1993). Depressed affect, hopelessness, and the risk of ischemic heart disease in a cohort of U.S. adults. *Epidemiology, 4,* 285–294. (p. 484)

Anderegg, W. R. L., Prall, J. W., Harold, J., & Schneider, S. H. (2010). Expert credibility in climate change. *PNAS, 107,* 12107–12109. (p. 517)

Andersen, S. M. (1998). *Service Learning: A National Strategy for Youth Development. A Position Paper issued by the Task Force on Education Policy.* Washington, DC: Institute for Communitarian Policy Studies, George Washington University. (pp. 275, 305)

Andersen, S. M., & Chen, S. (2002). The relational self: An interpersonal social-cognitive theory. *Psychological Review, 109,* 619–645. (p. 36)

Anderson, C. (2011, August 2). Norway: War games and toys pulled from shelves. *New York Times* (www.nytimes.com). (p. 338)

Anderson, C., Keltner, D., & John, O. P. (2003). Emotional convergence between people over time. *Journal of Personality and Social Psychology, 84,* 1054–1068. (p. 370)

Anderson, C., Srivastava, S., Beer, J. S., Spataro, S. E., & Chatman, J. A. (2006).

Knowing your place: Self-perceptions of status in face-to-face groups. *Journal of Personality and Social Psychology, 91,* 1094–1110. (p. 72)

Anderson, C. A. (1982). Inoculation and counter-explanation: Debiasing techniques in the perseverance of social theories. *Social Cognition, 1,* 126–139. (p. 84)

Anderson, C. A. (1999). Attributional style, depression, and loneliness: A cross-cultural comparison of American and Chinese students. *Personality and Social Psychology Bulletin, 25,* 482–499. (p. 74)

Anderson, C. A. (2003). Video games and aggressive behavior. In D. Ravitch and J. P. Viteritti (Eds.), *Kids stuff: Marking violence and vulgarity in the popular culture.* Baltimore, MD: Johns Hopkins University Press. (pp. 338, 342)

Anderson, C. A. (2004). An update on the effects of violent video games. *Journal of Adolescence, 27,* 113–122. (pp. 338, 342)

Anderson, C. A., & Anderson, D. C. (1984). Ambient temperature and violent crime: Tests of the linear and curvilinear hypotheses. *Journal of Personality and Social Psychology, 46,* 91–97. (p. 323)

Anderson, C. A., & Anderson, K. B. (1998). Temperature and aggression: Paradox, controversy, and a (fairly) clear picture. In R. G. Geen & E. Donnerstein (Eds.), *Human aggression: Theories, research, and implications for social policy.* San Diego: Academic Press. (p. 324)

Anderson, C. A., Anderson, K. B., Dorr, N., DeNeve, K. M., & Flanagan, M. (2000). Temperature and aggression. In M. P. Zanna (Ed.), *Advances in Experimental Social Psychology.* San Diego: Academic Press. (p. 324)

Anderson, C.A., Benjamin, A. J., Jr., & Bartholow, B.D. (1998). Does the gun pull the trigger? Automatic priming effects of weapon pictures and weapon names. *Psychological Science, 9,* 308–314. (p. 326)

Anderson, C. A., Berkowitz, L., Donnerstein, E., Huesmann, L. R., Johnson, J. D., Linz, D., Malamuth, N. M., & Wartella, E. (2003). The influence of media violence on youth. *Psychological Science in the Public Interest, 4*(3), 81–110. (pp. 334, 335)

Anderson, C. A., & Bushman, B. J. (1997). External validity of "trivial" experiments: The case of laboratory aggression. *Review of General Psychology, 1,* 19–41. (p. 343)

Anderson, C. A., & Bushman, B. J. (2001). Effects of violent video games on aggressive behavior, aggressive cognition, aggressive affect, physiological arousal, and prosocial behavior: A meta-analytic review of the scientific literature. *Psychological Science, 12,* 353–359. (p. 339)

Anderson, C. A., & Delisi, M. (2010). Implications of global climate change for violence in developed and developing countries. In J. Forgas, A. Kruglanski, & K. Williams (Eds.), *Social Conflict and Aggression.* New York: Psychology Press. (p. 517)

Anderson, C. A., Deuser, W. E., & DeNeve, K. M. (1995). Hot temperatures, hostile affect, hostile cognition, and arousal: Tests of a general model of affective aggression. *Personality and Social Psychology Bulletin, 21,* 434–448. (p. 325)

Anderson, C. A., Gentile, D. A., & Buckley, K. E. (2007). *Violent video game effects on children and adolescents: Theory, research, and public policy.* New York: Oxford University Press. (pp. 337, 344)

Anderson, C. A., & Harvey, R. J. (1988). Discriminating between problems in living: An examination of measures of depression, loneliness, shyness, and social anxiety. *Journal of Social and Clinical Psychology, 6,* 482–491. (p. 480)

Anderson, C. A., Horowitz, L. M., & French, R. D. (1983). Attributional style of lonely and depressed people. *Journal of Personality and Social Psychology, 45,* 127–136. (p. 69)

Anderson, C. A., Lepper, M. R., & Ross, L. (1980). Perseverance of social theories: The role of explanation in the persistence of discredited information. *Journal of Personality and Social Psychology, 39,* 1037–1049. (p. 83)

Anderson, C. A., Lindsay, J. J., & Bushman, B. J. (1999). Research in the psychological laboratory: Truth or triviality? *Current Directions in Psychological Science, 8,* 3–9. (pp. 29, 324)

Anderson, C. A., Sakamoto, A., Gentile, D. A., Ihori, N., Shibuya, A., Yukawa, S., Naito, M., & Kobayashi, K. (2008). Longitudinal effects of violent video games on aggression in Japan and the United States. *Pediatrics, 122,* e1067–e1072. (p. 339)

Anderson, C. A., & Sechler, E. S. (1986). Effects of explanation and counterexplanation on the development and use of social theories. *Journal of Personality and Social Psychology, 50,* 24–34. (p. 84)

Anderson, C. A., Shibuya, A., Ihori, N., Swing, E. L., Bushman, B. J., Sakamoto, A., Rothstein, C. R., & Saleen, M. (2010). Violent video game effects on aggression, empathy, and prosocial behavior in Eastern and Western countries: A meta-analytic review. *Psychological Bulletin, 136,* 151–173. (p. 339)

Anderson, R. (2004). A definition of peace. *Peace and Conflict: Journal of Peace Psychology. Special Issue: Assessing Cultures of Peace, 10,* 101–116. (p. 453)

Anderson, S. L., Adams, G., & Plaut, V. C. (2008). The cultural grounding of personal relationship: The importance of attractiveness in everyday life. *Journal of Personality and Social Psychology, 95,* 352–368. (p. 364)

Angus Reid. (2012, June). Global Warming Skepticism Higher in U.S. and Britain than Canada. Angus Reid (http://www.angusreidglobal.com/wp-content/uploads/2012/06/2012.06.27_Climate.pdf). (pp. 517, 518)

Angus Reid Public Opinion. (2011). Tories lead in Canada, NDP firmly in second place due to Quebec strength. Available at http://www.angus-reid.com/wpcontent/uploads/2011/04/2011.04.18_Politics_CAN.pdf (p. 178)

Anik, L., Aknin, L. B., Norton, M. I., & Dunn, E. W. (2010). Feeling good about giving: The benefits (and costs) of self-interested charitable behavior. In D. M. Oppenheimer & C. Y. Olivola (Eds.), *The science of giving: Experimental approaches to the study of charity.* New York: Psychology Press. (p. 275)

Anthony, D. B., Holmes, J. G., & Wood, J. V. (2007). Social acceptance and self-esteem: Tuning the sociometer to interpersonal value. *Journal of Personality and Social Psychology, 92,* 1024. (p. 41)

Archer, D., Iritani, B., Kimes, D. B., & Barrios, M. (1983). Face-ism: Five studies of sex differences in facial prominence. *Journal of Personality and Social Psychology, 45,* 725–735. (p. 406)

Archer, J. (1991). The influence of testosterone on human aggression. *British Journal of Psychology, 82,* 1–28. (p. 314)

Archer, J. (2006). Testosterone and human aggression: An evaluation of the challenge hypothesis. *Neuroscience and Biobehavioral Reviews, 30,* 319–345. (p. 312)

Archer, R. L., & Cook, C. E. (1986). Personalistic self-disclosure and attraction: Basis for relationship or scarce resource. *Social*

Psychology Quarterly, 49, 268–272. (p. 387)

Arendt, H. (1963). *Eichmann in Jerusalem: A report on the banality of evil.* New York: Viking Press. (p. 213)

Ariza, L. M. (2006, January). Virtual Jihad: The Internet as the ideal terrorism recruiting tool. *Scientific American,* pp. 18–21. (p. 251)

Arkes, H. R. (1990). *Some practical judgment/decision making research.* Paper presented at the American Psychological Association convention. (p. 175)

Arkes, H. R., & Tetlock, P. E. (2004). Attributions of implicit prejudice, or "would Jesse Jackson 'fail' the implicit association test?" *Psychological Inquiry, 15,* 257–278. (p. 126)

Arkin, R. M., Appleman, A., & Burger, J. M. (1980). Social anxiety, self-presentation, and the self-serving bias in causal attribution. *Journal of Personality and Social Psychology, 38,* 23–35. (p. 72)

Arkin, R. M., & Burger, J. M. (1980). Effects of unit relation tendencies on interpersonal attraction. *Social Psychology Quarterly, 43,* 380–391. (p. 356)

Arkin, R. M., Lake, E. A., & Baumgardner, A. H. (1986). Shyness and self-presentation. In W. H. Jones, J. M. Cheek, & S. R. Briggs (Eds.), *Shyness: Perspectives on research and treatment.* New York: Plenum. (p. 71)

Armitage, C. J., & Conner, M. (2001). Efficacy of the theory of planned behaviour: A meta-analytic review. *British Journal of Social Psychology, 40,* 471–499. (p. 127)

Armor, D. A., & Taylor, S. E. (1996). Situated optimism: Specific outcome expectancies and self-regulation. In M. P. Zanna (Ed.), *Advances in experimental social psychology,* vol. 30. San Diego, CA: Academic Press. (p. 65)

Arms, R. L., Russell, G. W., & Sandilands, M. L. (1979). Effects on the hostility of spectators of viewing aggressive sports. *Social Psychology Quarterly, 42,* 275–279. (p. 345)

Aron, A., & Aron, E. (1989). *The heart of social psychology,* 2nd ed. Lexington, MA: Lexington Books. (p. 201)

Aron, A., & Aron, E.N. (1994). Love. In A.L. Weber & J.H. Harvey (Eds.) *Perspective on close relationships.* Boston: Allyn & Bacon (p. 388)

Aron, A., Dutton, D. G., Aron, E. N., & Iverson, A. (1989). Experiences of falling in love. *Journal of Social and Personal Relationships, 6,* 243–257. (p. 372)

Aron, A., Fisher, H., Mashek, D. J., Strong, G., Li, H., & Brown, L. L. (2005). Reward, motivation, and emotion systems associated with early-stage intense romantic love. *Journal of Neurophysiology, 94*(1), 327. (pp. 378, 379, 380)

Aron, A., Melinat, E., Aron, E. N., Vallone, R. D., & Bator, R. J. (1997). The experimental generation of interpersonal closeness: A procedure and some preliminary findings. *Personality and Social Psychology Bulletin, 23,* 363–377. (p. 389)

Aron, A., Norman, C. C., Aron, E. N., McKenna, C., & Heyman, R. E. (2000). Couples' shared participation in novel and arousing activities and experienced relationship quality. *Journal of Personality and Social Psychology, 78,* 273–284. (p. 378)

Aronson, E. (1992). Stateways can change folkways. In R. M. Baird & S. E. Rosenbaum (Eds.), *Bigotry, prejudice, and hatred: Definitions, causes and solutions,* 185–201. (p. 136)

Aronson, E. (1988). *The social animal.* New York: Freeman. (p. 374)

Aronson, E., Brewer, M., & Carlsmith, J. M. (1985). Experimentation in social psychology. In G. Lindzey & E. Aronson (Eds.), *Handbook of social psychology,* vol. 1. Hillsdale, NJ: Erlbaum. (p. 27)

Aronson, E., & Linder, D. (1965). Gain and loss of esteem as determinants of interpersonal attractiveness. *Journal of Experimental Social Psychology, 1,* 156–171. (p. 374)

Aronson, E., & Mettee, D. R. (1974). *Affective reactions to appraisal from others. Foundations of interpersonal attraction.* New York: Academic Press. (p. 374)

Aronson, E., & Mills, J. (1959). The effect of severity of initiation on liking for a group. *Journal of Abnormal and Social Psychology, 59,* 177–181. (p. 183)

Aronson, E., Turner, J. A., & Carlsmith, J. M. (1963). Communicator credibility and communicator discrepancy as determinants of opinion change. *Journal of Abnormal and Social Psychology, 67,* 31–36. (pp. 170, 171)

Arriaga, X. B. (2001). The ups and downs of dating: Fluctuations in satisfaction in newly formed romantic relationships. *Journal of Personality and Social Psychology, 80,* 754. (p. 392)

Arriaga, X. B., & Agnew, C. R. (2001). Being committed: Affective, cognitive, and conative components of relationship commitment. *Personality and Social Psychology Bulletin, 27,* 1190. (p. 392)

Arrow, K. J., & 21 others. (2008). The promise of prediction markets. *Science, 320,* 877–878. (p. 264)

Asch, S. E. (1946). Forming impressions of personality. *Journal of Abnormal and Social Psychology, 41,* 258–290. (p. 173)

Asch, S. E. (1955, November). Opinions and social pressure. *Scientific American,* 31–35. (pp. 201, 215, 216)

Asendorpf, J. B. (1987). Videotape reconstruction of emotions and cognitions related to shyness. *Journal of Personality and Social Psychology, 53,* 541–549. (p. 480)

Ash, R. (1999). *The top 10 of everything 2000.* New York: DK Publishing. (p. 311)

Asher, J. (1987, April). Born to be shy? *Psychology Today,* 56–64. (p. 313)

Associated Press (AP). (1993, June 10). Walking past a dying man. *New York Times* (via Associated Press). (p. 293)

Associated Press (AP). (2007, January 15). Kids copying execution accidentally hang selves. *Grand Rapids Press,* p. A3. (p. 200)

Augoustinos, M., & Innes, J. M. (1990). Towards an integration of social representations and social schema theory. *British Journal of Social Psychology, 29,* 213–231. (p. 12)

Australian Attorney-General's Department. (2010, September). Literature review on the impact of playing violent video games on aggression. Commonwealth of Australia (www.ag.gov.au/cca). (p. 341)

Averill, J. R. (1983). Studies on anger and aggression: Implications for theories of emotion. *American Psychologist, 38,* 1145–1160. (p. 317)

Axelrod, R., & Dion, D. (1988). The further evolution of cooperation. *Science, 242,* 1385–1390. (p. 468)

Axsom, D., Yates, S., & Chaiken, S. (1987). Audience response as a heuristic cue in persuasion. *Journal of Personality and Social Psychology, 53,* 30–40. (p. 180)

Ayres, I. (1991). Fair driving: Gender and race discrimination in retail car negotiations. *Harvard Law Review, 104,* 817–872. (p. 433)

Azrin, N. H. (1967, May). Pain and aggression. *Psychology Today,* 27–33. (p. 322)

Baars, B. J., & McGovern, K. (1994). *How not to start a scientific revolution.* US: American Psychological Association. (p. 79)

Babad, E., Bernieri, F., & Rosenthal, R. (1991). Students as judges of teachers' verbal and nonverbal behavior. *American Educational Research Journal, 28,* 211–234. (p. 112)

Bachman, J. G., Johnston, L. D., O'Malley, P. M., & Humphrey, R. N. (1988). Explaining the recent decline in marijuana use: Differentiating the effects of perceived risks, disapproval, and general lifestyle factors. *Journal of Health and Social Behavior, 29,* 92–112. (p. 163)

Bachman, J. G., & O'Malley, P. M. (1977). Self-esteem in young men: A longitudinal analysis of the impact of educational and occupational attainment. *Journal of Personality and Social Psychology, 35,* 365–380. (p. 20)

Back, M. D., Schmukle, S. C., & Egloff, B. (2008). Becoming friends by chance. *Psychological Science, 19,* 439–440. (p. 355)

Bailenson, J. N., & Yee, N. (2005). Digital chameleons: Automatic assimilation of nonverbal gestures in immersive virtual environments. *Psychological Science, 16,* 814. (p. 165)

Baize, H. R., Jr., & Schroeder, J. E. (1995). Personality and mate selection in personal ads: Evolutionary preferences in a public mate selection process. *Journal of Social Behavior and Personality, 10,* 517–536. (p. 361)

Baker, L., & McNulty, J. K. (2010). Shyness and marriage: Does shyness shape even established relationships? *Personality and Social Psychology Bulletin, 36,* 665–676. (p. 388)

Baldwin, M. W., & Carrell, S. E., & Lopez, D. F. (1989). Priming relationship schemas: My advisor and the Pope are watching me from the back of my head. *Journal of Experimental Social Psychology, 26,* 435–454. (pp. 88, 89)

Baldwin, M. W., Keelan, J. P. R., Fehr, B., Enns, V., Koh-Rangarajoo, E. (1996). Social-cognitive conceptualization of attachment working models: Availability and accessibility effects. *Journal of Personality and Social Psychology, 71,* 94–109. (p. 383)

Banaji, M. R. (2004). The opposite of a great truth is also true: Homage of Koan #7. In J. T. Jost, M. R. Banaji, & D. A. Prentice (Eds.), *Perspectivism in social psychology: The yin and yang of scientific progress.* Washington, DC: American Psychological Association. (p. 401)

Bandura, A. (1979). The social learning perspective: Mechanisms of aggression. In H. Toch (Ed.), *Psychology of crime and criminal justice.* New York: Holt, Rinehart & Winston. (pp. 320, 321, 322)

Bandura, A. (1997). *Self-efficacy: The exercise of control.* New York: Freeman. (pp. 320, 322)

Bandura, A. (2004). Swimming against the mainstream: The early years from chilly tributary to transformative mainstream. *Behaviour Research and Therapy, 42,* 613–630. (p. 54)

Bandura, A., Ross, D., & Ross, S. A. (1961). Transmission of aggression through imitation of aggressive models. *Journal of Abnormal and Social Psychology, 63,* 575–582. (p. 320)

Bandura, A., & Walters, R. H. (1959). *Adolescent aggression.* New York: Ronald Press. (p. 320)

Bandura, A., & Walters, R. H. (1963). *Social learning and personality development.* New York: Holt, Rinehart and Winston. (p. 334)

Banks, S. M., Salovey, P., Greener, S., Rothman, A. J., Moyer, A., Beauvais, J., & Epel, E. (1995). The effects of message framing on mammography utilization. *Health Psychology, 14,* 178–184. (p. 168)

Barash, D. (1979). *The whisperings within.* New York: Harper & Row. (pp. 283, 284, 312)

Bargh, J. A. (1997). The automaticity of everyday life. In R. S. Wyer (Ed.) *The automaticity of everyday life: Advances in social cognition* (Vol. 10, pp. 1–61). Mahwah, NJ: Lawrence Erlbaum Associates. (p. 87)

Bargh, J. A., & Chartrand, T. L. (1999). The unbearable automaticity of being. *American Psychologist, 54,* 462–479. (pp. 87, 401)

Bargh, J. A., Chen, M., & Burrows, L. (1996). Automaticity and social behavior: Direct effects of trait construct and stereotype activation. *Journal of Personality and Social Psychology, 43,* 437–449. (p. 79)

Bargh, J. A., & McKenna, K. Y. A. (2004). The Internet and social life. *Annual Review of Psychology, 55,* 573–590. (p. 390)

Bargh, J. A., McKenna, K. Y. A., & Fitzsimons, G. M. (2002). Can you see the real me? Activation and expression of the "true self" on the Internet. *Journal of Social Issues, 58,* 33–48. (p. 390)

Bargh, J. A., & Raymond, P. (1995). The naive misuse of power: Nonconscious sources of sexual harassment. *Journal of Social Issues. Special Issue: Gender Stereotyping, Sexual Harassment, and the Law, 51*(1), 85–96. (p. 102)

Bar-Haim, Y., Ziv, T., Lamy, D., & Hodes, R. M. (2006). Nature and nurture in own-race face processing. *Psychological Science, 17,* 159–163. (p. 358)

Barlett, C. P., Harris, R. J., & Bruey, C. (2008). The effect of the amount of blood in a violence video game on aggression, hostility, and arousal. *Journal of Experimental Social Psychology, 44,* 539–546. (p. 341)

Barlett, C. P., & Rodeheffer, C. (2009). Effects of realism on extended violent and nonviolent video game play on aggressive thoughts, feelings, and physiological arousal. *Aggressive Behavior, 35,* 213–224. (p. 341)

Barnes, R. D., Ickes, W., & Kidd, R. F. (1979). Effects of the perceived intentionality and stability of another's dependency on helping behavior. *Personality and Social Psychology Bulletin, 5,* 367–372. (p. 282)

Barnett, M. A., King, L. M., Howard, J. A., & Melton, E. M. (1980). *Experiencing negative affect about self or other: Effects on helping behavior in children and adults.* Paper presented at the Midwestern Psychological Association convention. (p. 278)

Barnett, P. A., & Gotlib, I. H. (1988). Psychosocial functioning and depression: Distinguishing among antecedents, concomitants, and consequences. *Psychological Bulletin, 104,* 97–126. (p. 477)

Baron J., & Hershey, J. C. (1988). Outcome bias in decision evaluation. *Journal of Personality and Social Psychology, 54,* 569–579. (p. 416)

Baron, J., & Miller, J. G. (2000). Limiting the scope of moral obligations to help: A cross-cultural investigation. *Journal of Cross-Cultural Psychology, 31,* 703–725. (p. 281)

Baron, R. A. (1977). *Human aggression.* New York: Plenum Press. (p. 346)

Baron, R. A., Markman, G. D., & Bollinger, M. (2006). Exporting social psychology: Effects of attractiveness on perceptions of entrepreneurs, their ideas for new products, and their financial success. *Journal of Applied Social Psychology, 36,* 467–492. (p. 363)

Baron, R. S. (1986). Distraction-conflict theory: Progress and problems. In L. Berkowitz (Ed.), *Advances in experimental social psychology.* Orlando, FL: Academic Press. (p. 237)

Baron, R. S. (2000). Arousal, capacity, and intense indoctrination. *Personality and Social Psychology Review, 4,* 238–254. (p. 185)

Baron, R. S., Kerr, N. L., & Miller, N. (1992). *Group process, group decision, group action.* Pacific Grove, CA: Brooks/Cole. (p. 318)

Barongan, C., & Hall, G. C. N. (1995). The influence of misogynous rap music on sexual aggression against women. *Psychology of Women Quarterly, 19,* 195–207. (p. 335)

Barry, D. (1998). *Dave Barry Turns 50.* New York: Crown. (p. 63)

Bartholomew, K., & Horowitz, L. (1991). Attachment styles among young adults: A test of a four-category model. *Journal of Personality and Social Psychology, 61,* 226–244. (p. 383)

Bartholow, B. C., Anderson, C. A., Carnagey, N. L., & Benjamin, A. J., Jr. (2004). Interactive effects of life experience and situational cues on aggression: The weapons priming effect in hunters and nonhunters. *Journal of Experimental Social Psychology, 41,* 48–60. (p. 326)

Bartholow, B. D., Bushman, B. J., & Sestir, M. A. (2006). Chronic violent video game exposure and desensitization to violence: Behavioral and event-related brain potential data. *Journal of Experimental Social Psychology, 42,* 532. (p. 340)

Bartholow, B. D., & Heinz, A. (2006). Alcohol and aggression without consumption: Alcohol cues, aggressive thoughts, and hostile perception bias. *Psychological Science, 17,* 30. (p. 314)

Basile, K. C., Chen, J., Lynberg, M. C., & Saltzman, L. E. (2007). Prevalence and characteristics of sexual violence victimization. *Violence and Victims, 22,* 437–448. (p. 330)

Bassili, J. N. (1995). Response latency and the accessibility of voting intentions: What contributes to accessibility and how it affects vote choice. *Personality and Social Psychology Bulletin, 21,* 686–695. (p. 127)

Bassili, J. N. (2003). The minority slowness effect: Subtle inhibitions in the expression of views not shared by others. *Journal of Personality and Social Psychology, 84,* 261–276. (p. 267)

Bassili, J. N., & Roy, J. P. (1998). On the representation of strong and weak attitudes about policy in memory. *Political Psychology, 19,* 669–681. (p. 122)

Bastardi, A., Uhlmann, E. L., & Ross, L. (2011). Wishful thinking: Belief, desire, and the motivated evaluation of scientific evidence. *Psychological Science, 22,* 731–732. (p. 81)

Bastian, B., & Haslam, N. (2006). Psychological essentialism and stereotype endorsement. *Journal of Experimental Social Psychology, 42,* 228–235. (p. 103)

Batson, C. D. (1983). Sociobiology and the role of religion in promoting prosocial behavior: An alternative view. *Journal of Personality and Social Psychology, 45,* 1380–1385. (p. 303)

Batson, C. D. (1999a). Behind the scenes. In D. G. Myers, *Social psychology,* 6th edition. New York: McGraw-Hill. (p. 289)

Batson, C. D. (1999b). *Addressing the altruism question experimentally.* Paper presented at a Templeton Foundation/Fetzer Institute Symposium on Empathy, Altruism, and Agape, Cambridge, MA. (p. 289)

Batson, C. D. (2001). Addressing the altruism question experimentally. In S. G. Post, L. B. Underwood, J. P. Schloss, & W. B. Hurlbut (Eds.), *Altruism and altruistic love: Science, philosophy, and religion in dialogue.* New York: Oxford University Press. (p. 289)

Batson, C. D. (2006). "Not all self-interest after all": Economics of empathy-induced altruism. In D. De Cremer, M. Zeelenberg & J. K. Murnighan (Eds.), *Social psychology and economics,* 281–299. Mahwah, NJ: Lawrence Erlbaum Associates Publishers. (p. 68)

Batson, C. D. (2011). *Altruism in humans.* New York: Oxford University Press. (p. 286)

Batson, C. D., Chao, M. C., & Givens, J. M. (2009). Pursuing moral outrage: Anger at torture. *Journal of Experimental Social Psychology, 45,* 155–160. (p. 284)

Batson, C. D., Coke, J. S., Jasnoski, M. L., & Hanson, M. (1978). Buying kindness: Effect of an extrinsic incentive for helping on perceived altruism. *Personality and Social Psychology Bulletin, 4,* 86–91. (pp. 298, 306)

Batson, C. D., Duncan, B. D., Ackerman, P., Buckley, T., & Birch, K. (1981). Is empathic emotion a source of altruistic motivation? *Journal of Personality and Social Psychology, 40,* 290–302. (p. 288)

Batson, C. D., Eklund, J. H., Chermok, V. L., Hoyt, J. L., & Ortiz, B. G. (2007). An additional antecedent of empathic concern: Valuing the welfare of the person in need. *Journal of Personality and Social Psychology, 93,* 65–74. (p. 287)

Batson, C. D., Fultz, J., & Schoenrade, P. A. (1987). Distress and empathy: Two qualitatively distinct vicarious emotions with different motivational consequences. *Journal of Personality, 55,* 19–40. (p. 288)

Batson, C. D., Harris, A. C., McCaul, K. D., Davis, M., & Schmidt, T. (1979). Compassion or compliance: Alternative dispositional attributions for one's helping behavior. *Social Psychology Quarterly, 42,* 405–409. (p. 306)

Batson, C. D., Lishner, D. A., Carpenter, A., Dulin, L., Harjusola-Webb, S., Stocks, E. L., Gale, S., Hassan, O., & Sampat, B. (2003). "... As you would have them do unto you": Does imagining yourself in the other's place stimulate moral action? *Personality and Social Psychology Bulletin, 29,* 1190–1201. (p. 304)

Batson, C. D., Kobrynowicz, D., Dinnerstein, J. L., Kampf, H. C., & Wilson, A. D. (1997). In a very different voice: Unmasking moral hypocrisy. *Journal of Personality and Social Psychology, 72,* 1335–1348. (p. 123)

Batson, C. D., & Moran, T. (1999). Empathy-induced altruism in a prisoner's dilemma. *European Journal of Social Psychology, 29,* 909–924. (p. 465)

Batson, C. D., & Thompson, E. R. (2001). Why don't moral people act morally? Motivational considerations. *Current Directions in Psychological Science, 10,* 54–57. (p. 123)

Batson, C. D., Thompson, E. R., & Chen, H. (2002). Moral hypocrisy: Addressing some alternatives. *Journal of Personality and Social Psychology, 83*(2), 330–339. (p. 123)

Batson, C. D., Thompson, E. R., Seuferling, G., Whitney, H., & Strongman, J. A. (1999). Moral hypocrisy: Appearing moral to oneself without being so. *Journal of Personality and Social Psychology, 77,* 525–537. (p. 128)

Batson, C. D., & Ventis, W. L. (1982). *The religious experience: A social psychological perspective.* New York: Oxford University Press. (p. 405)

Bauman, C. W., & Skitka, L. J. (2010). Making attributions for behaviors: The prevalence of correspondence bias in the general population. *Basic and Applied Social Psychology, 32,* 269–277. (p. 106)

Baumann, L. J., & Leventhal, H. (1985). "I can tell when my blood pressure is up, can't I?" *Health Psychology, 4,* 203–218. (p. 482)

Baumeister, R. (2005). Rejected and alone. *The Psychologist, 18,* 732. (p. 355)

Baumeister, R. (2007). Is there anything good about men? Address to the American Psychological Association convention. (p. 435)

Baumeister, R. F. (1996). Self-regulation and ego threat: Motivated cognition, self deception, and destructive goal setting. In P. M. Gollwitzer, & J. A. Bargh (Eds.), *The psychology of action: Linking cognition and motivation to behavior.* (27–47). New York: Guilford Press. (p. 55)

Baumeister, R. F., & Bratslavsky, E. (1999). Passion, intimacy, and time: Passionate love as a function of change in intimacy. *Personality and Social Psychology Review, 3,* 49–67. (p. 387)

Baumeister, R. F., Bratslavsky, E., Finkenauer, C., & Vohs, D. K. (2001). Bad is stronger than good. *Review of General Psychology, 5,* 323–370. (p. 372)

Baumeister, R. F., Bratslavsky, E., Muraven, M., & Tice, D. M. (1998). Ego depletion: Is the active self a limited resource? *Journal of Personality and Social Psychology, 74,* 1252–1265. (p. 56)

Baumeister, R. F., Campbell, J. D., Krueger, J. I., & Vohs, K. D. (2003). Does high self-esteem cause better performance, interpersonal success, happiness, or healthier lifestyles? *Psychological Science in the Public Interest, 4*(1), 1–44. (pp. 54, 55, 59)

Baumeister, R. F., Chesner, S. P., Senders, P. S., & Tice, D. M. (1988). Who's in charge here? Group leaders do lend help in emergencies. *Personality and Social Psychology Bulletin, 14,* 17–22. (p. 105)

Baumeister, R. F., DeWall, C. N., & Vohs, K. D. (2009). Social rejection, control, numbness, and emotion: How not to be fooled by Gerber and Wheeler (2009). *Perspectives on Psychological Science, 4,* 489–493. (p. 353)

Baumeister, R. F., & Exline, J. J. (2000). Self-control, morality, and human strength. *Journal of Social and Clinical Psychology, 19,* 29–42. (p. 57)

Baumeister, R. F., & Leary, M. R. (1995). The need to belong: Desire for interpersonal attachment as a fundamental human motivation. *Psychological Bulletin, 117,* 495–527. (p. 352)

Baumeister, R. F., Muraven, M., & Tice, D. M. (2000). Ego depletion: A resource model of volition, self-regulation, and controlled processing. *Social Cognition, 18,* 130–150. (p. 56)

Baumeister, R. F., & Scher, S. J. (1988). Self-defeating behavior patterns among normal individuals: Review and analysis of common self-destructive tendencies. *Psychological Bulletin, 104,* 3–22. (p. 71)

Baumeister, R. F., & Wotman, S. R. (1992). *Breaking hearts: The two sides of unrequited love.* New York: Guilford. (p. 393)

Baumgardner, A. H., & Brownlee, E. A. (1987). Strategic failure in social interaction: Evidence for expectancy disconfirmation process. *Journal of Personality and Social Psychology, 52,* 525–535. (p. 71)

Baumhart, R. (1968). *An honest profit.* New York: Holt, Rinehart & Winston. (p. 63)

Baxter, T. L., & Goldberg, L. R. (1987). Perceived behavioral consistency underlying trait attributions to oneself and another: An extension of the actor-observer effect. *Personality and Social Psychology Bulletin, 13,* 437–447. (p. 108)

Bayer, E. (1929). Beitrage zur zeikomponenten theorie des hungers. *Zeitschrift fur Psychologie, 112,* 1–54. (p. 234)

Bazerman, M. H. (1986, June). Why negotiations go wrong. *Psychology Today,* 54–58. (p. 467)

Bazerman, M. H. (1990). *Judgment in managerial decision making,* 2nd ed. New York: Wiley. (p. 467)

Bazzini, D., Curtin, L., Joslin, S., Regan, S., & Martz, D. (2010). Do animated Disney characters portray and promote the beauty-goodness stereotype? *Journal of Applied Social Psychology, 40,* 2687–2709. (p. 362)

BBC (2008, November 21). Pirates "gained $150m this year" (news.bbc.co.uk). (p. 320)

Beals, K. P., Peplau, L. A., & Gable, S. L. (2009). Stigma management and well-being: The role of perceived social support, emotional processing, and suppression. *Personality and Social Psychology Bulletin, 35,* 867–879. (p. 388)

Beaman, A. L., Barnes, P. J., Klentz, B., & McQuirk, B. (1978). Increasing helping rates through information dissemination: Teaching pays. *Personality and Social Psychology Bulletin, 4,* 406–411. (p. 306)

Beaman, A. L., & Klentz, B. (1983). The supposed physical attractiveness bias against supporters of the women's movement: A meta-analysis. *Personality and Social Psychology Bulletin, 9,* 544–550. (p. 368)

Beaman, A. L., Klentz, B., Diener, E., & Svanum, S. (1979). Self-awareness and transgression in children: Two field studies. *Journal of Personality and Social Psychology, 37,* 1835–1846. (p. 247)

Bearak, B. (2010, July 9). South Africa braces for new attacks on immigrants. *New York Times* (www.nytimes.com). (p. 408)

Becker, D. V., Neel, R., Anderson, U. S. (2010). Illusory conjunctions of angry facial expressions follow intergroup biases. *Psychological Science, 21,* 938–940. (p. 423)

Becker, S. W., & Eagly, A. H. (2004). The heroism of women and men. *American Psychologist, 59,* 163–178. (p. 300)

Begue, L., Bushman, B., Giancola, P., Subra, B., & Rosset, E. (2010). "There is no such thing as an accident," especially when people are drunk. *Personality and Social Psychology Bulletin, 36,* 1301–1304. (p. 314)

Bell, B. E., & Loftus, E. F. (1988). Degree of detail of eyewitness testimony and mock juror judgments. *Journal of Applied Social Psychology, 18,* 1171–1192. (p. 498)

Bell, B. E., & Loftus, E. F. (1989). Trivial persuasion in the courtroom: The power of (a few) minor details. *Journal of Personality and Social Psychology, 56,* 669–679. (p. 498)

Bell, P. A. (1980). Effects of heat, noise, and provocation on retaliatory evaluative behavior. *Journal of Social Psychology, 110,* 97–100. (p. 323)

Bell, P. A. (2005). Reanalysis and perspective in the heat-aggression debate. *Journal of Personality and Social Psychology, 89,* 71–73. (p. 324)

Belson, W. A. (1978). *Television violence and the adolescent boy.* Westmead, UK: Saxon House, Teakfield Ltd. (pp. 332, 333)

Bem, D. J. (1972). *Self-perception theory.* In L. Berkowitz (Ed.), Advances in experimental social psychology. Vol. 6. New York: Academic Press. (pp. 145, 150)

Bem, D. J., & McConnell, H. K. (1970). Testing the self-perception explanation of dissonance phenomena: On the salience of premanipulation attitudes. *Journal of Personality and Social Psychology, 14,* 23–31. (p. 85)

Benjamin, Jr., L. T., & Simpson, J. A. (2009). The power of the situation: The impact of Milgram's obedience studies on personality and social psychology. *American Psychologist, 64,* 12–19. (p. 203)

Bennett, R. (1991, February). *Pornography and extrafamilial child sexual abuse: Examining the relationship.* Unpublished manuscript, Los Angeles Police Department Sexually Exploited Child Unit. (p. 329)

Bennis, W. (1984). Transformative power and leadership. In T. J. Sergiovani & J. E. Corbally (Eds.), *Leadership and organizational culture.* Urbana: University of Illinois Press. (p. 265)

Benton, S. L., Downey, R. G., Gilder, P. J., & Benton, S. A. (2008). College students' norm perception predicts reported use of protective behavioral strategies for alcohol consumption. *Journal of Studies on Alcohol and Drugs, 69,* 859–866. (p. 66)

Benzies, K., Keown, L., & Magill-Evans, J. (2009). Immediate and sustained effects of parenting on physical aggression in Canadian children aged 6 years and younger. *The Canadian Journal of Psychiatry, 54,* 55–64. (p. 321)

Berg, J. H. (1984). Development of friendship between roommates. *Journal of Personality and Social Psychology, 46,* 346–356. (pp. 376, 385)

Berg, J. H. (1987). Responsiveness and self-disclosure. In V. J. Derlega & J. H. Berg (Eds.), *Self-disclosure: Theory, research, and therapy.* New York: Plenum. (p. 387)

Berg, J. H., & McQuinn, R. D. (1986). Attraction and exchange in continuing and noncontinuing dating relationships. *Journal of Personality and Social Psychology, 50,* 942–952. (pp. 376, 388)

Berg, J. H., & Peplau, L. A. (1982). Loneliness: The relationship of self-disclosure and androgyny. *Personality and Social Psychology Bulletin, 8,* 624–630. (p. 387)

Berger, J., & Heath, C. (2008). Who drives divergence? Identity signaling, outgroup dissimilarity, and the abandonment of cultural tastes. *Journal of Personality and Social Psychology, 95,* 593–607. (p. 225)

Berglas, S., & Jones, E. E. (1978). Drug choice as a self-handicapping strategy in response to noncontingent success. *Journal of Personality and Social Psychology, 36,* 405–417. (p. 71)

Bergsieker, H. B., Shelton, J. N., & Richeson, J. A. (2010). To be liked versus respected: Divergent goals in interracial interactions. *Journal of Personality and Social Psychology, 99,* 248–264. (p. 442)

Berkman, L. F. (1995). The role of social relations in health promotion. *Psychosomatic Medicine, 57,* 245–254. (p. 487)

Berkowitz, L. (1954). Group standards, cohesiveness, and productivity. *Human Relations, 7,* 509–519. (p. 216)

Berkowitz, L. (1968, September). Impulse, aggression and the gun. *Psychology Today,* 18–22. (p. 325)

Berkowitz, L. (1975). Social norms, feelings, and other factors affecting helping and altruism. In L. Berkowitz (Ed.), *Advances in experimental social psychology* (Vol. 6). New York: Academic Press. (p. 281)

Berkowitz, L. (1978). Whatever happened to the frustration-aggression hypothesis? *American Behavioral Scientists, 21,* 691–708. (p. 317)

Berkowitz, L. (1981, June). How guns control us. *Psychology Today,* 11–12. (p. 325)

Berkowitz, L. (1983). Aversively stimulated aggression: Some parallels and differences in research with animals and humans. *American Psychologist, 38,* 1135–1144. (p. 323)

Berkowitz, L. (1984). Some effects of thoughts on anti- and prosocial influences of media events: A cognitive-neoassociation analysis. *Psychological Bulletin, 95,* 410–427. (p. 335)

Berkowitz, L. (1987). Mood, self-awareness, and willingness to help. *Journal of Personality and Social Psychology, 52,* 721–729. (p. 279)

Berkowitz, L. (1989). Frustration-aggression hypothesis: Examination and reformulation. *Psychological Bulletin, 106,* 59–73. (pp. 317, 323)

Berkowitz, L. (1995). A career on aggression. In G. G. Brannigan & M. R. Merrens (Eds.), *The social psychologists: Research adventures.* New York: McGraw-Hill. (p. 325)

Berkowitz, L., & Geen, R. G. (1966). Film violence and the cue properties of available targets. *Journal of Personality and Social Psychology, 3,* 525–530. (p. 334)

Berkowitz, L., & LePage, A. (1967). Weapons as aggression-eliciting stimuli. *Journal of Personality and Social Psychology, 7,* 202–207. (p. 326)

Berndsen, M., Spears, R., Pligt, J. V. D., & McGarty, C. (2002). Illusory correlation and stereotype formation: Making sense of group differences and cognitive biases. In C. McGarty, V. Y. Yzerbyt & R. Spears (Eds.), *Stereotypes as explanations: The formation of meaningful beliefs about social groups.* (pp. 90–110). New York: Cambridge University Press. (p. 422)

Bernhardt, P. C., Dabbs, J. M., Jr., Fielden, J. A., & Lutter, C. D. (1998). Testosterone changes during vicarious experiences of winning and losing among fans at sporting events. *Physiology & Behavior, 65,* 59. (p. 316)

Berns, G. S., Chappelow, J., Zink, C. F., Pagnoni, G., Martin-Skurski, M. E., & Richards, J. (2005). Neurobiological correlates of social conformity and independence during mental rotation. *Biological Psychiatry, 58,* 245. (p. 220)

Bernstein, M. J., Young, S. G., & Hugenberg, K. (2007). The cross-category effect. Mere social categorization is sufficient to elicit an own-group bias in face recognition. *Psychological Science, 18,* 706–712. (p. 420)

Berscheid, E. (1981). An overview of the psychological effects of physical attractiveness and some comments upon the psychological effects of knowledge of the effects of physical attractiveness. In W. Lucker, K. Ribbens, & J. A. McNamera (Eds.), *Logical aspects of facial form (craniofacial growth series).* Ann Arbor: University of Michigan Press. (p. 363)

Berscheid, E. (1985). Interpersonal attraction. In G. Lindzey & E. Aronson (Eds.), *The handbook of social psychology.* New York: Random House. (p. 491)

Berscheid, E., Boye, D., & Walster (Hatfield), E. (1968). Retaliation as a means of restoring equity. *Journal of Personality and Social Psychology, 10,* 370–376. (p. 135)

Berscheid, E., Dion, K., Walster (Hatfield), E., & Walster, G. W. (1971). Physical attractiveness and dating choice: A test of the matching hypothesis. *Journal of Experimental Social Psychology, 7,* 173–189. (pp. 358, 361)

Berscheid, E., Graziano, W., Monson, T., & Dermer, M. (1976). Outcome dependency: Attention, attribution, and attraction. *Journal of Personality and Social Psychology, 34,* 978–989. (p. 357)

Berscheid, E., & Peplau, L. A. (1983). The emerging science of relationships. In Kelley, H. H., Berscheid, E., Christensen, A., Harvey, J. H., Huston, T. L., Levinger, G., McClintock, E., Peplau, L. A. & Peterson, D. R. (Eds.), *Close relationships.* New York: Freeman. (p. 491)

Berscheid, E., Snyder, M., & Omoto, A. M. (1989). Issues in studying close relationships: Conceptualizing and measuring closeness. In C. Hendrick (Ed.), *Review of personality and social psychology*, Vol. 10. Newbury Park, CA: Sage. (p. 380)

Berscheid, E., & Walster (Hatfield), E. (1978). *Interpersonal attraction*. Reading, MA: Addison-Wesley. (p. 372)

Berscheid, E., Walster, G. W., & Hatfield (was Walster), E. (1969). *Effects of accuracy and positivity of evaluation on liking for the evaluator.* Unpublished manuscript. Summarized by E. Berscheid and E. Walster (Hatfield) (1978), *Interpersonal attraction*. Reading, MA: Addison-Wesley. (p. 372)

Bertrand, M., & Mullainathan, S. (2003). Are Emily and Greg more employable than Lakisha and Jamal? A field experiment on labor market discrimination. Massachusetts Institute of Technology, Department of Economics, Working Paper 03–22. (p. 429)

Besser, A., & Priel, B. (2005). The apple does not fall far from the tree: Attachment styles and personality vulnerabilities to depression in three generations of women. *Personality and Social Psychology Bulletin, 31,* 1052–1073. (p. 385)

Bettencourt, A., & Dorr, N. (1997). Collective self-esteem as a mediator of the relationship between allocentrism and subjective well-being. *Personality and Social Psychology Bulletin, 23,* 955–965. (p. 445)

Bettencourt, B. A., Dill, K. E., Greathouse, S. A., Charlton, K., & Mulholland, A. (1997). Evaluations of ingroup and outgroup members: The role of category-based expectancy violation. *Journal of Experimental Social Psychology, 33,* 244–275. (p. 420)

Bettencourt, B. A., Talley, A., Benjamin, A. J., & Valentine, J. (2006). Personality and aggressive behavior under provoking and neutral conditions: A meta-analytic review. *Psychological Bulletin, 132,* 751–777. (p. 313)

Beyer, L. (1990, Fall issue on women). Life behind the veil. *Time,* p. 37. (p. 436)

Bianchi, S. M., Milkie, M. A., Sayer, L. C., & Robinson, J. P. (2000). Is anyone doing the housework? Trends in the gender division of household labor. *Social Forces, 79,* 191–228. (p. 433)

Bickman, L. (1975). Bystander intervention in a crime: The effect of a mass-media campaign. *Journal of Applied Social Psychology, 5,* 296–302. (p. 301)

Bickman, L. (1979). Interpersonal influence and the reporting of a crime. *Personality and Social Psychology Bulletin, 5,* 32–35. (p. 301)

Bickman, L., & Green, S. K. (1977). Situational cues and crime reporting: Do signs make a difference? *Journal of Applied Social Psychology, 7,* 1–18. (p. 301)

Biernat, M. (1991). Gender stereotypes and the relationship between masculinity and femininity: A developmental analysis. *Journal of Personality and Social Psychology, 61,* 351–365. (p. 417)

Biernat, M. (2003). Toward a broader view of social stereotyping. *American Psychologist, 58,* 1019–1027. (p. 437)

Biernat, M., & Kobrynowicz, D. (1997). Gender- and race-based standards of competence: Lower minimum standards but higher ability standards for devalued groups. *Journal of Personality and Social Psychology, 72,* 544–557. (p. 420)

Biernat, M., Vescio, T. K., & Green, M. L. (1996). Selective self-stereotyping. *Journal of Personality and Social Psychology, 71,* 1194–1209. (pp. 70, 370)

Biernat, M., Vescio, T. K., & Theno, S. A. (1996). Violating American values: A "Value congruence" approach to understanding outgroup attitudes. *Journal of Experimental Social Psychology, 32,* 387–410. (p. 376)

Biernat, M., & Wortman, C. B. (1991). Sharing of home responsibilities between professionally employed women and their husbands. *Journal of Personality and Social Psychology, 60,* 844–860. (p. 433)

Billig, M., & Tajfel, H. (1973). Social categorization and similarity in intergroup behaviour. *European Journal of Social Psychology, 3,* 27–52. (p. 410)

Biner, P. M. (1991). Effects of lighting-induced arousal on the magnitude of goal valence. *Personality and Social Psychology Bulletin, 17,* 219–226. (p. 325)

Bingenheimer, J. B., Brennan, R. T., & Earls, F. J. (2005). Firearm violence exposure and serious violent behavior. *Science, 308,* 1323. (p. 321)

Binham, R. (1980, March–April). Trivers in Jamaica. *Science, 80,* pp. 57–67. (p. 284)

Bishop, G. D. (1984). Gender, role, and illness behavior in a military population. *Health Psychology, 3,* 519–534. (p. 483)

Bishop, G. D. (1987). Lay conceptions of physical symptoms. *Journal of Applied Social Psychology, 17,* 127–146. (p. 483)

Bishop, G. D. (1991). Understanding the understanding of illness: Lay disease representations. In J. A. Skelton & R. T. Croyle (Eds.), *Mental representation in health and illness.* New York: Springer-Verlag. (p. 483)

Blackburn, R. T., Pellino, G. R., Boberg, A., & O'Connell, C. (1980). Are instructional improvement programs off target? *Current Issues in Higher Education, 1,* 31–48. (p. 70)

Blackhart, G. C., Nelson, B. C., Knowles, M. L., & Baumeister, R. F. (2009). Rejection elicits emotional reactions but neither causes immediate distress nor lowers self-esteem: A meta-analytic review of 192 studies on social exclusion. *Personality and Social Psychology Review, 13,* 269–309. (p. 353)

Blair, C. A., Thompson, L. F., & Wuensch, K. L. (2005). Electronic helping behavior: The virtual presence of others makes a difference. *Basic and Applied Social Psychology, 27,* 171–178. (p. 291)

Blake, R. R., & Mouton, J. S. (1962). The intergroup dynamics of win-lose conflict and problem-solving collaboration in union-management relations. In M. Sherif (Ed.), *Intergroup relations and leadership.* New York: Wiley. (p. 466)

Blake, R. R., & Mouton, J. S. (1979). Intergroup problem solving in organizations: From theory to practice. In W. G. Austin and S. Worchel (Eds.), *The social psychology of intergroup relations.* Monterey, CA: Brooks/Cole. (p. 466)

Blanchard, F. A., & Cook, S. W. (1976). Effects of helping a less competent member of a cooperating interracial group on the development of interpersonal attraction. *Journal of Personality and Social Psychology, 34,* 1245–1255. (p. 137)

Blanton, H., Jaccard, J., Christie, C., & Gonzales, P. M. (2007). Plausible assumptions, questionable assumptions and post hoc rationalizations: Will the real IAT please stand up? *Journal of Experimental Social Psychology, 43,* 399–409. (p. 126)

Blanton, H., Jaccard, J., Gonzales, P. M., & Christie, C. (2006). Decoding the implicit association test: Implications for criterion prediction. *Journal of Experimental Social Psychology, 42,* 192–212. (p. 126)

Blanton, H., Pelham, B. W., DeHart, T., & Carvallo, M. (2001). Overconfidence as dissonance reduction. *Journal of Experimental Social Psychology, 37,* 373–385. (p. 143)

Blascovich, J., Wyer, N. A., Swart, L. A., & Kibler, J. L. (1997). Racism and racial categorization. *Journal of Personality and Social Psychology, 72,* 1364–1372. (p. 418)

Blass, T. (1990). *Psychological approaches to the Holocaust: Review and evaluation.* Paper presented to the American Psychological Association convention. (p. 223)

Blass, T. (1991). Understanding behavior in the Milgram obedience experiment: The role of personality, situations, and their interactions. *Journal of Personality and Social Psychology, 60,* 398–413. (p. 223)

Blass, T. (1996). Stanley Milgram: A life of inventiveness and controversy. In G. A. Kimble, C. A. Boneau, & M. Wertheimer (Eds.). *Portraits of pioneers in psychology,* Vol. II. Washington, DC: American Psychological Association. (p. 205)

Blass, T. (1999). The Milgram paradigm after 35 years: Some things we now know about obedience to authority. *Journal of Applied Social Psychology, 29,* 955–978. (p. 204)

Block J., & Funder, D. C. (1986). Social roles and social perception: Individual differences in attribution and error. *Journal of Personality and Social Psychology, 51,* 1200–1207. (p. 106)

Boden, J. M., Fergusson, D. M., & Horwood, L. J. (2007). Self-esteem and violence: Testing links between adolescent self-esteem and later hostility and violent behavior. *Social Psychiatry and Psychiatric Epidemiology, 42,* 881–891. (p. 55)

Boden, J. M., Fergusson, D. M., & Horwood, L. J. (2008). Does adolescent self esteem predict later life outcomes? A test of the causal role of self-esteem. *Development and Psychopathology, 20,* 319–339. (p. 53)

Bodenhausen, G. V. (1990). Stereotypes as judgmental heuristics: Evidence of circadian variations in discrimination. *Psychological Science, 1,* 319 322. (p. 417)

Bodenhausen, G. V. (1993). Emotions, arousal, and stereotypic judgments. A heuristic model of affect and stereotyping. In D. M. Mackie & D. L. Hamilton (Eds.), *Affect, cognition, and stereotyping: Interactive processes in group perception.* San Diego, CA: Academic Press. (p. 167)

Bodenhausen, G. V., & Macrae, C. N. (1998). Stereotype activation and inhibition. In R. S. Wyer, Jr., *Stereotype activation and inhibition: Advances in social cognition,* vol. 11. Mahwah, NJ: Erlbaum. (p. 416)

Bodenhausen, G. V., Sheppard, L. A., & Kramer, G. F. (1994). Negative affect and social judgment: The differential impact of anger and sadness. *European Journal of Social Psychology, 24,* 45–62. (p. 100)

Boehm, J. K., Peterson, C., Kivimaki, M., & Kubzansky, L. (2011). A prospective study of positive psychological well-being and coronary heart disease. *Health Psychology, 30,* 259–267. (p. 484)

Boer, D., Fischer, R., Strack, M., Bond, M. H., Lo, E., & Lam, J. (2011). How shared preferences in music create bonds between people: Values as the missing link. *Personality and Social Psychology Bulletin, 37,* 1159–1171. (p. 370)

Boggiano, A. K., Barrett, M., Weiher, A. W., McClelland, G. H., & Lusk, C. M. (1987). Use of the maximal-operant principle to motivate children's intrinsic interest. *Journal of Personality and Social Psychology, 53,* 866–879. (p. 148)

Boggiano, A. K., Harackiewicz, J. M., Bessette, J. M., & Main, D. S. (1985). Increasing children's interest through performance-contingent reward. *Social Cognition, 3,* 400–411. (p. 148)

Boggiano, A. K., & Ruble, D. N. (1985). Children's responses to evaluative feedback. In R. Schwarzer (Ed.), *Self-related cognitions in anxiety and motivation.* Hillsdale, NJ: Erlbaum. (p. 149)

Boldt, E. D. (1976). Acquiescence and conventionality in a communal society. *Journal of Cross Cultural Psychology, 7,* 21–36. (p. 216)

Bonanno, G. A., Rennicke, C., & Dekel, S. (2005). Self-enhancement among high-exposure survivors of the September 11th terrorist attack: Resilience or social maladjustment? *Journal of Personality and Social Psychology, 88,* 984–998. (p. 68)

Bond, C. F., Jr., DiCandia, C. G., & MacKinnon, J. R. (1988). Responses to violence in a psychiatric setting: The role of patient's race. *Personality and Social Psychology Bulletin, 14,* 448 458. (p. 444)

Bond, C. F., Jr., & Titus, L. J. (1983). Social facilitation: A meta-analysis of 241 studies. *Psychological Bulletin, 94,* 265–292. (p. 235)

Bond, M. H. (2004). Culture and aggression: From context to coercion. *Personality and Social Psychology Review, 8,* 62–78. (p. 321)

Bond, R., & Smith, P. B. (1996). Culture and conformity: A meta-analysis of studies using Asch's (1952b, 1956) line judgment task. *Psychological Bulletin, 119,* 111–137. (p. 223)

Bonnot, V., & Croizet, J-C. (2007). Stereotype internalization and women's math

performance: The role of interference in working memory. *Journal of Experimental Social Psychology, 43,* 857–866. (p. 442)

Bono, J. E., & Judge, T. A. (2004). Personality and transformational and transactional leadership: A meta-analysis. *Journal of Applied Psychology, 89,* 901. (p. 265)

Borgida, E., & Brekke, N. (1985). Psycholegal research on rape trials. In A. W. Burgess (Ed.), *Rape and sexual assault: A research handbook.* New York: Garland. (p. 415)

Borgida, E., Locksley, A., & Brekke, N. (1981). Social stereotypes and social judgment. In N. Cantor & J. Kihlstrom (Eds.), *Cognition, social interaction, and personality.* Hillsdale, NJ: Erlbaum. (p. 443)

Borkenau, P., & Liebler, A. (1993). Consensus and self-other agreement for trait inferences from minimal information. *Journal of Personality. Special Issue: Viewpoints on Personality: Consensus, Self-Other Agreement, and Accuracy in Personality Judgment, 61*(4), 477. (p. 91)

Bornstein, B. H., & Zicafoose, D. J. (1999). "I know I know it, I know I saw it": The stability of the confidence-accuracy relationship across domains. *Journal of Experimental Psychology: Applied, 5,* 76–88. (p. 499)

Bornstein, R. F. (1989). Exposure and affect: Overview and meta-analysis of research, 1968–1987. *Psychological Bulletin, 106,* 265–289. (p. 357)

Bornstein, R. F. (1999). Source amnesia, misattribution and the power of unconscious perceptions and memories. *Psychoanalytic Psychology, 16,* 155–178. (p. 357)

Bornstein, R. F., & D'Agostino, P. R. (1992). Stimulus recognition and the mere exposure effect. *Journal of Personality and Social Psychology, 63,* 545–552. (p. 357)

Bornstein, B. H., & Greene, E. (2011). Jury decision making: Implications for and from psychology. *Current Directions in Psychological Science, 20,* 63–67. (p. 511)

Bossard, J. H. S. (1932). Residential propinquity as a factor in marriage selection. *American Journal of Sociology, 38,* 219–224. (p. 356)

Bothwell, R. K., Brigham, J. C., & Malpass, R. S. (1989). Cross-racial identification. *Personality and Social Psychology Bulletin, 15,* 19–25. (p. 419)

Botvin, G. J., Epstein, J. A., & Griffin, K. W. (2008). A social influence model of alcohol use for inner-city adolescents: Family drinking, perceived drinking norms, and perceived social benefits of drinking. *Journal of Studies on Alcohol and Drugs, 69,* 397–405. (p. 189)

Botvin, G. J., Schinke, S., & Orlandi, M. A. (1995). School-based health promotion: Substance abuse and sexual behavior. *Applied & Preventive Psychology, 4,* 167–184. (p. 189)

Botwin, M. D., Buss, D. M., & Shackelford, T. K. (1997). Personality and mate preferences: Five factors in mate selection and marital satisfaction. *Journal of Personality, 65,* 107–136. (p. 371)

Bourgeois, M. J., Horowitz, I. A., & Lee, L. F. (1993). Effects of technicality and access to trial transcripts on verdicts and information processing in a civil trial. *Personality and Social Psychology Bulletin, 19,* 219–226. (p. 508)

Bourke, M. L., & Hernandez, A. E. (2009). The 'Butner Study' Redux: A report of the incidence of hands-on child victimization by child pornography offenders. *Journal of Family Violence, 24,* 183–191. (p. 329)

Bowen, E. (1988, April 4). Whatever became of Honest Abe? *Time.* (p. 5)

Bower, G. H. (1987). Commentary on mood and memory. *Behavioral Research and Therapy, 25,* 443–455. (pp. 100, 476)

Bowlby, J. (1980). Loss, sadness and depression. Vol. III of *Attachment and loss.* London: Basic Books. (p. 383)

Boyatzis, C. J., Matillo, G. M., & Nesbitt, K. M. (1995). Effects of the "Mighty Morphin Power Rangers" on children's aggression with peers. *Child Study Journal, 25,* 45–55. (p. 25)

Boyes, A. D., & Fletcher, G. J. O. (2007). Metaperceptions of bias in intimate relationships. *Journal of Personality and Social Psychology, 92,* 286–306. (p. 374)

Bradley, W., & Mannell, R. C. (1984). Sensitivity of intrinsic motivation to reward procedure instructions. *Personality and Social Psychology Bulletin, 10,* 426–431. (p. 149)

Brandon, R., & Davies, C. (1973). *Wrongful imprisonment: Mistaken convictions and their consequences.* Hamden, CT: Archon Books. (p. 498)

Branscombe, N. R., Schmitt, M. T., & Harvey, R. D. (1999). Perceiving pervasive discrimination among African Americans: Implications for group identification and well-being. *Journal of Personality and*

Social Psychology, 77, 135–149. (pp. 440, 447)

Brauer, M., Judd, C. M., & Gliner, M. D. (1995). The effects of repeated expressions on attitude polarization during group discussions. *Journal of Personality and Social Psychology, 68,* 1014–1029. (p. 252)

Brauer, M., Judd, C. M., & Jacquelin, V. (2001). The communication of social stereotypes: The effects of group discussion and information distribution on stereotypic appraisals. *Journal of Personality and Social Psychology, 81,* 463. (p. 249)

Bray, R. M., & Kerr, N. L. (1982). Methodological considerations in the study of the psychology of the courtroom. In N. L. Kerr & R. M. Bray (Eds.), *The psychology of the courtroom.* Orlando, FL: Academic Press. (p. 511)

Bray, R. M., & Noble, A. M. (1978). Authoritarianism and decisions of mock juries: Evidence of jury bias and group polarization. *Journal of Personality and Social Psychology, 36,* 1424–1430. (p. 509)

Breckler, S. J. (2010, April). In the heat of the moment. *Monitor on Psychology,* p. 39. (p. 518)

Breckler, S. J., & Wiggins, E. C. (1989). Affect versus evaluation in the structure of attitudes. *Journal of Experimental Social Psychology, 25,* 253–271. (p. 122)

Bregman, N. J., & McAllister, H. A. (1982). Eyewitness testimony: The role of commitment in increasing reliability. *Social Psychology Quarterly, 45,* 181–184. (p. 502)

Brehm, J. W. (1956). Post-decision changes in desirability of alternatives. *Journal of Abnormal Social Psychology, 52,* 384–389. (p. 143)

Brehm, S., & Brehm, J. W. (1981). *Psychological reactance: A theory of freedom and control.* New York: Academic Press. (p. 225)

Brenner, S. N., & Molander, E. A. (1977, January-February). Is the ethics of business changing? *Harvard Business Review,* 57–71. (p. 63)

Brewer, M. B. (1979). In-group bias in the minimal intergroup situation: A cognitive-motivational analysis. *Psychological Bulletin, 86,* 307–324. (p. 411)

Brewer, M. B. (1987). Collective decisions. *Social Science, 72,* 140–143. (p. 458)

Brewer, M. B. (1988). A dual process model of impression formation. In T. Srull & R.

Wyer (Eds.), *Advances in social cognition,* Vol. 1. Hillsdale, NJ: Erlbaum. (p. 437)

Brewer, M. B., & Silver, M. (1978). In-group bias as a function of task characteristics. *European Journal of Social Psychology, 8,* 393–400. (p. 410)

Brewer, N., & Wells, G. L. (2011). Eyewitness identification. *Current Directions in Psychological Science, 20,* 24–27. (p. 499)

Brickman, P. (1978). Is it real? In J. Harvey, W. Ickes, & R. Kidd (Eds.), *New directions in attribution research.* Vol. 2. Hillsdale, NJ: Erlbaum. (p. 224)

Brickman, P., Coates, D., & Janoff-Bulman, R. J. (1978). Lottery winners and accident victims: Is happiness relative? *Journal of Personality and Social Psychology, 36,* 917–927. (p. 522)

Brigham, J. C., Bennett, L. B., Meissner, C. A., & Mitchell, T. L. (2006). The influence of race on eyewitness testimony. In R. Lindsay, M. Toglia, D. Ross, & J. D. Read (Eds.), *Handbook of eyewitness psychology.* Mahwah, NJ: Erlbaum. (p. 500)

Brigham, J. C., & Williamson, N. L. (1979). Cross-racial recognition and age: When you're over 60, do they still all look alike? *Personality and Social Psychology Bulletin, 5,* 218–222. (p. 419)

Briñol, P., Petty, R. E., & Tormala, Z. L. (2004). Self-validation of cognitive responses to advertisements. *Journal of Consumer Research, 30,* 559–573. (p. 164)

Briñol, P., Petty, R. E., & Wagner, B. (2009). Body posture effects on self-evaluation: A self-validation approach. *European Journal of Social Psychology, 39,* 1053–1064. (p. 146)

Briñol, P., Tormala, Z. L., & Petty, R. E. (2002). *Source credibility as a determinant of self-validation effects in persuasion.* Poster presented at the European Association of Experimental Social Psychology, San Sebastian, Spain. (p. 164)

Britt, T. W., & Garrity, M. J. (2006). Attributions and personality as predictors of the road rage response. *British Journal of Social Psychology, 45,* 127–147. (p. 317)

Brock, T. C. (1965). Communicator-recipient similarity and decision change. *Journal of Personality and Social Psychology, 1,* 650–654. (p. 165)

Brockner, J., Rubin, J. Z., Fine, J., Hamilton, T. P., Thomas, B., & Turetsky, B. (1982). Factors affecting entrapment in escalating conflicts: The importance of timing. *Journal of Research in Personality, 16,* 247–266. (p. 457)

Broome, A., & Wegner, D. M. (1994). *Some positive effects of releasing socially anxious people from the need to please.* Paper presented to the American Psychological Society convention. (p. 480)

Brown, H. J., Jr. (1990). *P.S. I love you.* Nashville, TN: Rutledge Hill. (p. 63)

Brown, J. D., & Dutton, K. A. (1994). *From the top down: Self-esteem and self-evaluation.* Unpublished manuscript, University of Washington. (p. 51)

Brown, J. D., Novick, N. J., Lord, K. A., & Richards, J. M. (1992). When Gulliver travels: Social context, psychological closeness, and self-appraisals. *Journal of Personality and Social Psychology, 62,* 717–727. (p. 367)

Brown, J. D., & Taylor, S. E. (1986). Affect and the processing of personal information: Evidence for mood-activated self-schemata. *Journal of Experimental Social Psychology, 22,* 436–452. (pp. 100, 476)

Brown, R., Maras, P., Masser, B., Vivian, J., & Hewstone, M. (2001). Life on the ocean wave: Testing some intergroup hypotheses in a naturalistic setting. *Group Processes and Intergroup Relations, 4,* 81–97. (p. 316)

Brown, R., & Wootton-Millward, L. (1993). Perceptions of group homogeneity during group formation and change. *Social Cognition, 11,* 126–149. (p. 419)

Brown, R. P., Charnsangavej, T., Keough, K. A., Newman, M. L., & Rentfrom, P. J. (2000). Putting the "affirm" into affirmative action: Preferential selection and academic performance. *Journal of Personality and Social Psychology, 79,* 736–747. (p. 442)

Brown, R. P., Osterman, L. L., & Barnes, C. D. (2009). School violence and the culture of honor. *Psychological Science, 20,* 1400–1405. (p. 321)

Brown, S. L., Brown, R. M., House, J. S., & Smith, D. M. (2008). Coping with spousal loss: Potential buffering effects of self-reported helping behavior. *Personality and Social Psychology Bulletin, 34,* 849–861. (p. 275)

Brown, S. L., Nesse, R. M., Vinokur, A. D., & Smith, D. M. (2003). Providing social support may be more beneficial than receiving it. *Psychological Science, 14,* 320–327. (p. 488)

Brown, S. L., Smith, D. M., Schulz, R., Kabeto, M. U., Ubel, P. A., Poulin, M., Yi, J., Kim, C., & Langa, K. M. (2009). Caregiving behavior is associated with decreased mortality risk. *Psychological Science, 20,* 488–494. (p. 275)

Brown, V. R., & Paulus, P. B. (2002). Making group brainstorming more effective: Recommendations from an associative memory perspective. *Current Directions in Psychological Science, 11,* 208–212. (p. 263)

Brown, W. M., Price, M. E., Kang, J., Pound, N., Zhao, Y., & Yu, H. (2008). Fluctuating asymmetry and preferences for sex-typical bodily characteristics. *Proceedings of the National Academy of Sciences, 105,* 12938–12943 (pnas.org). (p. 365)

Browning, C. (1992). *Ordinary men: Reserve police battalion 101 and the final solution in Poland.* New York: HarperCollins. (p. 213)

Bruce, V. (1998). Fleeting images of shade: Identifying people caught on video. *The Psychologist, 11,* 331–337. (p. 499)

Bruck, M., & Ceci, S. (2004). Forensic developmental psychology: Unveiling four common misconceptions. *Current Directions in Psychological Science, 15,* 229–232. (p. 501)

Bruck, M., & Ceci, S. J. (1999). The suggestibility of children's memory. *Annual Review of Psychology, 50,* 419–439. (p. 501)

Bryan, J. H., & Test, M. A. (1967). Models and helping: Naturalistic studies in aiding behavior. *Journal of Personality and Social Psychology, 6,* 400–407. (p. 297)

Buckhout, R. (1974, December). Eyewitness testimony. *Scientific American,* 23–31. (p. 499)

Buehler, R., Griffin, D., & Ross, M. (1994). Exploring the "planning fallacy": When people underestimate their task completion times. *Journal of Personality and Social Psychology, 67,* 366–381. (p. 92)

Buehler, R., Griffin, D., & Ross, M. (2002). Inside the planning fallacy: The causes and consequences of optimistic time predictions. In T. Gilovich, D. Griffin & D. Kahneman (Eds.), *Heuristics and biases: The psychology of intuitive judgment,* 250–270. New York: Cambridge University Press. (pp. 48, 92)

Buehler, R., Peetz, J., & Griffin, D. (2010). Finishing on time: When do predictions influence completion times? *Organizational Behavior and Human Decision Processes, 111,* 23–32. (p. 92)

Buffardi, L. E., & Campbell, W. K. (2008). Narcissism and social networking websites. *Personality and Social Psychology Bulletin, 34,* 1303–1314. (p. 72)

Burchill, S. A. L., & Stiles, W. B. (1988). Interactions of depressed college students with their roommates: Not necessarily negative. *Journal of Personality and Social Psychology, 55,* 410–419. (p. 477)

Burger, J. M. (1987). Increased performance with increased personal control: A self-presentation interpretation. *Journal of Experimental Social Psychology, 23,* 350–360. (p. 264)

Burger, J. M. (1991). Changes in attributions over time: The ephemeral fundamental attribution error. *Social Cognition, 9,* 182–193. (p. 108)

Burger, J. M. (2009, January). Replicating Milgram: Would people still obey today? *American Psychologist, 64,* 1–11. (p. 204)

Burger, J. M., & Burns, L. (1988). The illusion of unique invulnerability and the use of effective contraception. *Personality and Social Psychology Bulletin, 14,* 264–270. (p. 64)

Burger, J. M., & Caldwell, D. F. (2003). The effects of monetary incentives and labeling on the foot-in-the-door effect: Evidence for a self-perception process. *Basic and Applied Social Psychology, 25,* 235–241. (p. 146)

Burger, J. M., & Guadagno, R. E. (2003). Self-concept clarity and the foot-in-the-door procedure. *Basic and Applied Social Psychology, 25,* 79–86. (p. 133)

Burger, J. M., Messian, N., Patel, S., del Prade, A., & Anderson, C. (2004). What a coincidence! The effects of incidental similarity on compliance. *Personality and Social Psychology Bulletin, 30,* 35–43. (pp. 216, 298)

Burger, J. M., & Pavelich, J. L. (1994). Attributions for presidential elections: The situational shift over time. *Basic and Applied Social Psychology, 15,* 359–371. (p. 108)

Burger, J. M., Soroka, S., Gonzago, K., Murphy, E., & Somervell, E. (2001). The effect of fleeting attraction on compliance to requests. *Personality and Social Psychology Bulletin, 27,* 1578–1586. (p. 164)

Burkholder, R. (2005, January 11). Chinese far wealthier than a decade ago, but are they happier? Gallup Poll (www.poll.gallup.com). (p. 522)

Burns, D. D. (1980). *Feeling good: The new mood therapy.* New York: Signet. (p. 475)

Burnstein, E. (2009). Robert B. Zajonc (1923–2008). *American Psychologist, 64,* 558–559. (p. 251)

Burnstein, E., Crandall, R., & Kitayama, S. (1994). Some neo-Darwinian decision rules for altruism: Weighing cues for inclusive fitness as a function of the biological importance of the decision. *Journal of Personality and Social Psychology, 67,* 773–789. (p. 284)

Burnstein, E., & Vinokur, A. (1977). Persuasive argumentation and social comparison as determinants of attitude polarization. *Journal of Experimental Social Psychology, 13,* 315–332. (p. 252)

Burnstein, E., & Worchel, P. (1962). Arbitrariness of frustration and its consequences for aggression in a social situation. *Journal of Personality, 30,* 528–540. (p. 317)

Burr, W. R. (1973). *Theory construction and the sociology of the family.* New York: Wiley. (p. 356)

Burson, K. A., Larrick, R. P., & Klayman, J. (2006). Skilled or unskilled, but still unaware of it: How perceptions of difficulty drive miscalibration in relative comparisons. *Journal of Personality and Social Psychology, 90*(1), 60. (p. 91)

Burt, R. S. (1986). *Strangers, friends and happiness.* GSS Technical Report No. 72. Chicago: National Opinion Research Center, University of Chicago. (p. 491)

Burton, C. M., & King, L. A. (2008). Effects of (very) brief writing on health: The two-minute miracle. *British Journal of Health Psychology, 13,* 9–14. (p. 489)

Bushman, B. J. (1993). Human aggression while under the influence of alcohol and other drugs: An integrative research review. *Current Directions in Psychological Science, 2,* 148–152. (p. 314)

Bushman, B. J. (1998). Priming effects of media violence on the accessibility of aggressive constructs in memory. *Personality and Social Psychology Bulletin, 24,* 537–545. (p. 337)

Bushman, B. J. (2002). Does venting anger feed or extinguish the flame? Catharsis, rumination, distraction, anger, and aggressive responding. *Personality and Social Psychology Bulletin, 28,* 724–731. (p. 345)

Bushman, B. J. (2005). Violence and sex in television programs do not sell products in advertisements. *Psychological Science, 16,* 702–708. (p. 180)

Bushman, B. J. (2007). That was a great commercial, but what were they selling? Effects of violence and sex on memory for products in television commercials. *Journal of Applied Social Psychology, 37,* 1784–1796. (p. 180)

Bushman, B. J., & Anderson, C. A. (1998). Methodology in the study of aggression: Integrating experimental and nonexperimental findings. In R. Geen & E. Donnerstein (Eds.), *Human aggression: Theories, research and implications for policy.* San Diego: Academic Press. (p. 343)

Bushman, B. J., & Anderson, C. A. (2001). Media violence and the American public: Scientific facts versus media misinformation. *American Psychologist, 56,* 477–489. (p. 335)

Bushman, B. J., & Anderson, C. A. (2002). Violent video games and hostile expectations: A test of the general aggression model. *Personality and Social Psychology Bulletin, 28,* 1679–1686. (p. 340)

Bushman, B. J., & Anderson, C. A. (2009). Comfortably numb: Desensitizing effects of violent media on helping others. *Psychological Science, 20,* 273–277. (pp. 336, 340)

Bushman, B. J., & Baumeister, R. (1998). Threatened egotism, narcissism, self-esteem, and direct and displaced aggression: Does self-love or self-hate lead to violence? *Journal of Personality and Social Psychology, 75,* 219–229. (p. 54)

Bushman, B. J., Baumeister, R. F., & Phillips, C. M. (2001). Do people aggress to improve their mood? Catharsis beliefs, affect regulation opportunity, and aggressive responding. *Journal of Personality and Social Psychology, 81,* 17–32. (p. 345)

Bushman, B. J., Baumeister, R. F., & Stack, A. D. (1999). Catharsis, aggression, and persuasive influence: Self-fulfilling or self-defeating prophecies? *Journal of Personality and Social Psychology, 76,* 367–376. (p. 345)

Bushman, B. J., Baumeister, R. F., Thomaes, S., Ryu, E., Begeer, S., & West, S. G. (2009). Looking again, and harder, for a link between low self-esteem and aggression. *Journal of Personality,* published online February 2, 2009. (p. 54)

Bushman, B. J., Bonacci, A. M., Pedersen, W. C., Vasquez, E. A., & Miller, N. (2005). Chewing on it can chew you up: Effects of rumination on triggered displaced aggression. *Journal of Personality and Social Psychology, 88,* 969. (p. 346)

Bushman, B. J., & Cooper, H. M. (1990). Effects of alcohol on human aggression: An integrative research review. *Psychological Bulletin, 107,* 341–354. (p. 314)

Bushman, B. J., & Geen, R. G. (1990). Role of cognitive-emotional mediators and individual differences in the effects of media violence on aggression. *Journal of Personality and Social Psychology, 58,* 156–163. (p. 335)

Bushman, B. J., Moeller, S. J., & Crocker, J. (2011). Sweets, sex, or self-esteem? Comparing the value of self-esteem boosts with other pleasant rewards. *Journal of Personality, 79,* 993–1012. (p. 52)

Bushman, B. J., Wang, M. C., & Anderson, C. A. (2005a). Is the curve relating temperature to aggression linear or curvilinear? Assaults and temperature in Minneapolis reexamined. *Journal of Personality and Social Psychology, 89,* 62–66. (p. 324)

Bushman, B. J., Wang, M. C., & Anderson, C. A. (2005b). Is the curve relating temperature to aggression linear or curvilinear? A response to Bell (2005) and to Cohn and Rotton (2005). *Journal of Personality and Social Psychology, 89,* 74–77. (p. 324)

Bushman, B. J., & Whitaker, J. L. (2010). Like a magnet: Catharsis beliefs attract angry people to violent video games. *Psychological Science, 21,* 790–792. (p. 341)

Buss, D. M. (1984). Toward a psychology of person-environment (PE) correlation: The role of spouse selection. *Journal of Personality and Social Psychology, 47,* 361–377. (p. 371)

Buss, D. M. (1985). Human mate selection. *American Scientist, 73,* 47–51. (p. 371)

Buss, D. M. (1989). Sex differences in human mate preferences: Evolutionary hypotheses tested in 37 cultures. *Behavioral and Brain Sciences, 12,* 1–49. (p. 365)

Butcher, S. H. (1951). *Aristotle's theory of poetry and fine art.* New York: Dover Publications. (p. 344)

Butler, A. C., Hokanson, J. E., & Flynn, H. A. (1994). A comparison of self-esteem lability and low trait self-esteem as vulnerability factors for depression. *Journal of Personality and Social Psychology, 66,* 166–177. (p. 478)

Butler, J. L., & Baumeister, R. F. (1998). The trouble with friendly faces: Skilled performance with a supportive audience. *Journal of Personality and Social Psychology, 75,* 1213–1230. (p. 236)

Butz, D. A., & Plant, E. A. (2006). Perceiving outgroup members as unresponsive: Implications for approach-related emotions, intentions, and behavior. *Journal of Personality and Social Psychology, 91,* 1066–1079. (p. 114)

Buunk, B. P., & van der Eijnden, R. J. J. M. (1997). Perceived prevalence, perceived superiority, and relationship satisfaction: Most relationships are good, but ours is the best. *Personality and Social Psychology Bulletin, 23,* 219–228. (p. 70)

Buunk, B. P., & Van Yperen, N. W. (1991). Referential comparisons, relational comparisons, and exchange orientation: Their relation to marital satisfaction. *Personality and Social Psychology Bulletin, 17,* 709–717. (p. 386)

Byers, S., & Wang, A. (2004). Understanding sexuality in close relationships from the social exchange perspective. In J. H. Harvey, A. Wenzel, & S. Sprecher (Eds.), *The handbook of sexuality in close relationships.* Mahwah, NJ: Erlbaum. (p. 375)

Bylsma, W. H., & Major, B. (1994). Social comparisons and contentment. *Psychology of Women Quarterly, 18,* 241–249. (p. 318)

Byrne, D. (1971). *The attraction paradigm.* New York: Academic Press. (p. 369)

Byrne, D., & Clore, G. L. (1970). A reinforcement model of evaluative responses. *Personality: An International Journal, 1,* 103–128. (p. 375)

Byrne, D., & Wong, T. J. (1962). Racial prejudice, interpersonal attraction, and assumed dissimilarity of attitudes. *Journal of Abnormal and Social Psychology, 65,* 246–253. (p. 418)

Bytwerk, R. L., & Brooks, R. D. (1980). *Julius Streicher and the rhetorical foundations of the holocaust.* Paper presented to the Central States Speech Association convention. (p. 169)

Cacioppo, J. T. (2007, October). The rise in collaborative science. *Association for Psychological Science Observer, 52* 53. (p. 262)

Cacioppo, J. T., & Patrick, W. (2008). *Loneliness: Human nature and the need for social connection.* New York: Norton. (p. 487)

Cacioppo, J. T., & Petty, R. E. (1981). Electromyograms as measures of extent and affectivity of information processing. *American Psychologist, 36,* 441–456. (p. 124)

Cacioppo, J. T., Berntson, G. G., & Decety, J. (2010). Social neuroscience and its relationship to social psychology. *Social Cognition, 28,* 675–685. (p. 9)

Cacioppo, J. T., Petty, R. E., Feinstein, J. A., & Jarvis, W. B. G. (1996). Dispositional differences in cognitive motivation: The life and times of individuals varying in need for cognition. *Psychological Bulletin, 119,* 197–253. (pp. 166, 180)

Cacioppo, J. T., Petty, R. E., & Morris, K. J. (1983). Effects of need for cognition on message evaluation, recall, and persuasion. *Journal of Personality and Social Psychology, 45,* 805–818. (p. 166)

Cacioppo, J. T., Uchino, B. N., Crites, S. L., Snydersmith, M. A., Smith, G., Berntson, G. G., & Lang, P. J. (1991). Relationship between facial expressiveness and sympathetic activation in emotion: A critical review, with emphasis on modeling underlying mechanisms and individual differences. *Journal of Personality and Social Psychology, 62,* 110–128. (p. 147)

Cafferty, J. (2011, March 15). Why is there no looting in Japan? www.caffertyfile.blogs.cnn.com. (p. 223)

Caldwell, H. K., Lee, H-J., MacBeth, A. H., & Young, W. S. (2008). Vasopressin: Behavioral roles of an "original" neuropeptide. *Progress in Neurobiology, 84,* 1–24. (p. 385)

Cameron, C. D., & Payne, B. K. (2011). Escaping affect: How motivated emotion regulation creates insensitivity to mass suffering. *Journal of Personality and Social Psychology, 100,* 1–15. (p. 287)

Cameron, J. J., Stinson, D. A., Gaetz, R., & Balchen, S. (2010). Acceptance is in the eye of the beholder: Self-esteem and motivated perceptions of acceptance from the opposite sex. *Journal of Personality and Social Psychology, 99,* 513–529. (p. 373)

Campbell, D. T. (1975a). On the conflicts between biological and social evolution and between psychology and oral tradition. *American Psychologist, 30,* 1103–1126. (pp. 11, 285, 524)

Campbell, D. T. (1975b). The conflict between social and biological evolution and the concept of original sin. *Zygon, 10,* 234–249. (pp. 283, 285)

Campbell, W. K. (2005). *When you love a man who loves himself.* Chicago: Sourcebooks. (p. 54)

Campbell, W. K., Bush, C. P., Brunell, A. B., & Shelton, J. (2005). Understanding the social costs of narcissism: The case of the Tragedy of the Commons. *Personality and Social Psychology Bulletin, 31,* 1358. (p. 457)

Campbell, W. K., & Foster, C. A. (2002). Narcissism and commitment in romantic relationships: An investment model analysis. *Personality and Social Psychology Bulletin, 28,* 484. (p. 392)

Campbell, W. K., Rudich, E., & Sedikides, C. (2002). Narcissism, self-esteem, and the positivity of self-views: Two portraits of self-love. *Personality and Social Psychology Bulletin, 28,* 358–368. (p. 54)

Campbell, W. K., & Sedikides, C. (1999). Self-threat magnifies the self-serving bias: A meta-analytic integration. *Review of General Psychology, 3,* 23–43. (p. 60)

Canadian Centre on Substance Abuse (1997). *Canadian profile: Alcohol, tobacco, & other drugs.* Ottawa: Canadian Centre on Substance Abuse. (p. 225)

Canter, D., Breaux, J., & Sime, J. (1980). Domestic, multiple occupancy, and hospital fires. In D. Canter (Ed.), *Fires and human behavior.* Hoboken, NJ: Wiley. (p. 292)

Cantril, H., & Bumstead, C. H. (1960). *Reflections on the human venture.* New York: New York University Press. (p. 267)

Caputo, D., & Dunning, D. (2005). What you don't know: The role played by errors of omission in imperfect self-assessments. *Journal of Experimental Social Psychology, 41*(5), 488. (p. 90)

Carducci, B. J., Cosby, P. C., & Ward, D. D. (1978). Sexual arousal and interpersonal evaluations. *Journal of Experimental Social Psychology, 14,* 449–457. (p. 378)

Carpenter, S. (2008, April/May). Buried prejudice. *Scientific American,* 32–39. (p. 401)

Carli, L. L. (1999). Cognitive reconstruction, hindsight, and reactions to victims and perpetrators. *Personality and Social Psychology Bulletin, 25,* 966–979. (p. 414)

Carli, L. L., & Leonard, J. B. (1989). The effect of hindsight on victim derogation. *Journal of Social and Clinical Psychology, 8,* 331–343. (p. 414)

Carlo, G., Eisenberg, N., Troyer, D., Switzer, G., & Speer, A. L. (1991). The altruistic personality: In what contexts is it apparent? *Journal of Personality and Social Psychology, 61,* 450–458. (p. 299)

Carlsmith, J. M., & Gross, A. E. (1969). Some effects of guilt on compliance. *Journal of Personality and Social Psychology, 11,* 232–239. (p. 277)

Carlson, J., & Hatfield, E. (1992). *The psychology of emotion.* Fort Worth, TX: Holt, Rinehart & Winston. (p. 381)

Carlson, J., & Miller, N. (1987). Explanation of the relation between negative mood and helping. *Psychological Bulletin, 102,* 91–108. (p. 277)

Carlson, M., Charlin, V., & Miller, N. (1988). Positive mood and helping behavior: A test of six hypotheses. *Journal of Personality and Social Psychology, 55,* 211–229. (p. 279)

Carlson, M., Marcus-Newhall, A., & Miller, N. (1990). Effects of situational aggression cues: A quantitative review. *Journal of Personality and Social Psychology, 58,* 622–633. (p. 317)

Carlston, D. E., & Shovar, N. (1983). Effects of performance attributions on others' perceptions of the attributor. *Journal of Personality and Social Psychology, 44,* 515–525. (p. 73)

Carlston, D. E., & Skowronski, J. J. (2005). Linking versus thinking: Evidence for the different associative and attributional bases of spontaneous trait transference and spontaneous trait inference. *Journal of Personality and Social Psychology, 89*(6), 884. (p. 82)

Carnagey, N. L., Anderson, C. A., & Bushman, B. J. (2007). The effect of video game violence on physiological desensitization to real-life violence. *Journal of Experimental Social Psychology, 43,* 489–496. (p. 340)

Carnevale, P. J., & Choi, D-W. (2000). Culture in the mediation of international disputes. *International Journal of Psychology, 35,* 105–110. (p. 465)

Carnevale, P. J., & Probst, T. M. (1998). Social values and social conflict in creative problem solving and categorization. *Journal of Personality and Social Psychology, 74,* 1300–1309. (p. 461)

Carney, D. R., Cuddy, A. J. C., & Yap, A. J. (2010). Power posing: Brief nonverbal displays affect neuroendocrine levels and risk tolerance. *Psychological Science, 21,* 1363–1368. (p. 146)

Carré, J. M., & McCormick, C. M. (2008). In your face: Facial metrics predict aggressiveness behaviour in the laboratory and in varsity and professional hockey players. *Proceedings of the Royal Society B, 275,* 2651–2656. (p. 315)

Carroll, D., Davey Smith, G., & Bennett, P. (1994, March). Health and socioeconomic status. *The Psychologist,* 122–125. (pp. 18, 489)

Carroll, J. S., Padilla-Walker, L. M., Nelson, L. J., Olson, C. D., Barry, C. M., & Madsen, S. D. (2008). Generation XXX: Pornography acceptance and use among emerging adults. *Journal of Adolescent Research, 23,* 6–30. (p. 327)

Carter, S. & Snow, C. (2004). *Helping singles enter better marriages using predictive models of marital success.* Paper presented at the annual meeting of the American Psychological Society, May 2004. (p. 369)

Carter, S. L. (1993). *Reflections of an affirmative action baby.* New York: Basic Books. (p. 420)

Cartwright, D. S. (1975). The nature of gangs. In D. S. Cartwright, B. Tomson, & H. Schwartz (Eds.), *Gang delinquency.* Monterey, CA: Brooks/Cole. (pp. 250, 321)

Carvallo, M., & Gabriel, S. (2006). No man is an island: The need to belong and dismissing avoidant attachment style. *Personality and Social Psychology Bulletin, 32,* 697–709. (p. 352)

Carver, C. S., Kus, L. A., & Scheier, M. F. (1994). Effect of good versus bad mood and optimistic versus pessimistic outlook on social acceptance versus rejection. *Journal of Social and Clinical Psychology, 13,* 138–151. (p. 477)

Carver, C. S., & Scheier, M. F. (1981). *Attention and self-regulation.* New York: Springer-Verlag. (p. 128)

Carver, C. S., & Scheier, M. F. (1986). Analyzing shyness: A specific application of broader self-regulatory principles. In W. H. Jones, J. M. Cheek, & S. R. Briggs (Eds.), *Shyness: Perspectives on research and treatment.* New York: Plenum. (p. 480)

Carver, C. S., Scheier, M. F., & Segerstrom, S. C. (2010). Optimism. *Clinical Psychology Review, 30,* 879–889. (p. 486)

Cash, T. F., & Janda, L. H. (1984, December). The eye of the beholder. *Psychology Today,* 46–52. (p. 363)

Caspi, A., & Herbener, E. S. (1990). Continuity and change: Assortative marriage and the consistency of personality in adulthood. *Journal of Personality and Social Psychology, 58,* 250–258. (p. 369)

Caspi, A., McClay, J., Moffitt, T., Mill, J., Martin, J., Craig, I. W., Taylor, A., & Poulton, R. (2002). Role of genotype in the cycle of violence in maltreated children. *Science, 297,* 851–854. (p. 313)

Cassidy, J. (2000). Adult romantic attachments: A developmental perspective on individual differences. *Review of General Psychology, 4,* 111–131. (p. 384)

Castelli, L., Carraro, L., Tomelleri, S., & Amari, A. (2007). White children's alignment to the perceived racial attitudes of the parents: Closer to the mother than father. *British Journal of Developmental Psychology, 25,* 353–357. (p. 403)

CBC (2002). Africville: Expropriating black Nova Scotians. Retrieved from http://archives.cbc.ca/society/racism/topics/96/ (p. 429)

CBC (2005). Racial profiling: Frequently asked questions. Retrieved from http://

www.cbc.ca/news/background/racial_profiling. (pp. 398, 430)

CBC 4 Kids. (1999, Nov. 15). A hero saves three children. Available at http://www.cs.cmu.edu/ dmg/MCALL/testing/1999-W47–1.qa.xml.qa_Q1.html. (p. 274)

Ceci, S. J., & Bruck, M. (1993a). Child witnesses: Translating research into policy. *Social Policy Report (Society for Research in Child Development), 7*(3), 1–30. (p. 501)

Ceci, S. J., & Bruck, M. (1993b). Suggestibility of the child witness: A historical review and synthesis. *Psychological Bulletin, 113,* 403–439. (p. 501)

Cemalcilar, Z., & Falbo, T. (2008). A longitudinal study of the adaptation of international students in the United States. *Journal of Cross-Cultural Psychology, 39,* 799–804. (p. 352)

Census Bureau (1993, May 4). Voting survey, reported by Associated Press. (p. 86)

Centers for Disease Control (CDC). (2008, Spring). Sexual violence: Facts at a glance. Centers for Disease Control and Prevention (www.cdc.gov/injury). (p. 330)

Centerwall, B. S. (1989). Exposure to television as a risk factor for violence. *American Journal of Epidemiology, 129,* 643–652. (p. 334)

Chaiken, S. (1979). Communicator physical attractiveness and persuasion. *Journal of Personality and Social Psychology, 37,* 1387–1397. (p. 165)

Chaiken, S. (1980). Heuristic versus systematic information processing and the use of source versus message cues in persuasion. *Journal of Personality and Social Psychology, 39,* 752–766. (p. 166)

Chaiken, S., & Eagly, A. H. (1976). Communication modality as a determinant of message persuasiveness and message comprehensibility. *Journal of Personality and Social Psychology, 34,* 605–614. (pp. 177, 179)

Chaiken, S., & Eagly, A. H. (1983). Communication modality as a determinant of persuasion: The role of communicator salience. *Journal of Personality and Social Psychology, 45,* 241–256. (p. 178)

Chaiken, S., & Maheswaran, D. (1994). Neuristic processing can bias systematic processing: Effects of source credibility, argument ambiguity, and task importance on attitude judgment. *Journal of Personality and Social Psychology, 66,* 460–473. (p. 162)

Chambers, J. R., & Windschitl, P. D. (2004). Biases in social comparative judgments: The role of nonmotivated factors in above-average and comparative-optimism effects. *Psychological Bulletin, 130,* 813. (p. 68)

Chan, M. K. H., Louis, W. R., & Jetten, J. (2010). When groups are wrong and deviants are right. *European Journal of Social Psychology, 40,* 1103–1109. (p. 267)

Chance, J. E., & Goldstein, A. G. (1981). Depth of processing in response to own and other-race faces. *Personality and Social Psychology Bulletin, 7,* 475–480. (p. 419)

Chandler, J., & Schwarz, N. (2009). How extending your middle finger affects your perception of others: Learned movements influence concept accessibility. *Journal of Experimental Social Psychology, 45,* 123–128. (p. 147)

Chapman, L. J., & Chapman, J. P. (1969). Genesis of popular but erroneous psychodiagnostic observations. *Journal of Abnormal Psychology, 74,* 272–280. (p. 472)

Chapman, L. J., & Chapman, J. P. (1971, November). Test results are what you think they are. *Psychology Today, 18–22,* 106–107. (p. 472)

Chartrand, T. L., & Bargh, J. A. (1999). The chameleon effect: The perception-behavior link and social interaction. *Journal of Personality and Social Psychology, 76,* 893–910. (p. 199)

Chatard, A., Guimond, S., & Selimbegovic, L. (2007). "How good are you in math?" The effect of gender stereotypes on students' recollection of their school marks. *Journal of Experimental Social Psychology, 43,* 1017–1024. (p. 436)

Check, J., & Malamuth, N. (1984). Can there be positive effects of participation in pornography experiments? *Journal of Sex Research, 20,* 14–31. (p. 329)

Chen, E. (2004). Why socioeconomic status affects the health of children: A psychosocial perspective. *Current Directions in Psychological Science, 13,* 112–115. (p. 489)

Chen, F. F., & Kenrick, D. T. (2002). Repulsion or attraction? Group membership and assumed attitude similarity. *Journal of Personality and Social Psychology, 83,* 111–125. (p. 370)

Chen, H., Luo, S., Yue, G., Xu, D., & Zhaoyang, R. (2009). Do birds of a feather flock together in China? *Personal Relationships, 16,* 167–186. (p. 369)

Chen, L.-H., Baker, S. P., Braver, E. R., & Li, G. (2000). Carrying passengers as a risk factor for crashes fatal to 16- and 17-year-old drivers. *Journal of the American Medical Association, 283,* 1578–1582. (p. 249)

Chen, S., Boucher, H. C., & Tapias, M. P. (2006). The relational self revealed: Integrative conceptualization and implications for interpersonal life. *Psychological Bulletin, 132,* 151–179. (p. 408)

Chen, S. C. (1937). Social modification of the activity of ants in nest-building. *Physiological Zoology, 10,* 420–436. (p. 234)

Chen, Z., Williams, K. D., Fitness, J., & Newton, N. C. (2008). When hurt will not heal: Exploring the capacity to relive social and physical pain. *Psychological Science, 19,* 789–795. (p. 355)

Chiao, J. Y., Bowman, N. E., & Gill, H. (2008) The political gender gap: Gender bias in facial inferences that predict voting behavior. *PLoS One 3*(10): e3666. (doi:10.1371/journal.pone.0003666). (p. 360)

Chida, Y., & Steptoe, A. (2009). The association of anger and hostility with future coronary heart disease: A meta-analytic review of prospective evidence. *Journal of the American College of Cardiology, 17,* 936–946. (p. 483)

Choi, I., & Choi, Y. (2002). Culture and self-concept flexibility. *Personality & Social Psychology Bulletin, 28,* 1508–1517. (p. 43)

Choi, I., Nisbett, R. E., & Norenzayan, A. (1999). Causal attribution across cultures: Variation and universality. *Psychological Bulletin, 125,* 47–63. (p. 109)

Christakis, N. A., & Fowler, J. H. (2009). *Connected: The surprising power of social networks and how they shape our lives.* New York: Little, Brown. (p. 199)

Chua, H. F., Boland, J. E., & Nisbett, R. E. (2005). Cultural variation in eye movements during scene perception. *Proceedings of the National Academy of Sciences, 102,* 12629–12633. (p. 42)

Chua-Eoan, H. (1997, April 7). Imprisoned by his own passions. *Time,* 40–42. (p. 182)

Church, G. J. (1986, January 6). China. *Time,* 6–19. (p. 241)

Cialdini, R. B. (1988). *Influence: Science and practice.* Glenview, IL: Scott, Foresman/Little, Brown. (pp. 134, 135, 139)

Cialdini, R. B. (1991). Altruism or egoism? That is (still) the question. *Psychological Inquiry, 2,* 124–126. (p. 289)

Cialdini, R. B. (1995). A full-cycle approach to social psychology. In G. G. Brannigan &

M. R. Merrens (Eds.), *The social psychologists: Research adventures.* New York: McGraw-Hill. (p. 302)

Cialdini, R. B. (2000). *Influence: Science and practice,* 4th edition. Boston: Allyn & Bacon. (p. 165)

Cialdini, R. B. (2003). Crafting normative messages to protect the environment. *Current Directions in Psychological Science, 12*(4), 105–109. (p. 304)

Cialdini, R. B. (2005). Basic social influence is underestimated. *Psychological Inquiry, 16,* 158–161. (p. 262)

Cialdini, R. B., Bickman, L., & Cacioppo, J. T. (1979). An example of consumeristic social psychology: Bargaining tough in the new car showroom. *Journal of Applied Social Psychology, 9,* 115–126. (p. 462)

Cialdini, R. B., Borden, R. J., Thorne, A., Walker, M. R., Freeman, S., & Sloan, L. R. (1976). Basking in reflected glory: Three (football) field studies. *Journal of Personality and Social Psychology, 39,* 406–415. (p. 409)

Cialdini, R. B., Cacioppo, J. T., Bassett, R., & Miller, J. A. (1978). Lowball procedure for producing compliance: Commitment then cost. *Journal of Personality and Social Psychology, 36,* 463–476. (p. 134)

Cialdini, R. B., Demaine, L. J., Barrett, D. W., Sagarin, B. J., & Rhoads, K. L. V. (2003). *The poison parasite defense: A strategy for sapping a stronger opponent's persuasive strength.* Unpublished manuscript, Arizona State University. (p. 188)

Cialdini, R. B., Kenrick, D. T., & Baumann, D. J. (1981). Effects of mood on prosocial behavior in children and adults. In N. Eisenberg-Berg (Ed.), *The development of prosocial behavior.* New York: Academic Press. (p. 277)

Cialdini, R. B., & Schroeder, D. A. (1976). Increasing compliance by legitimizing paltry contributions: When even a penny helps. *Journal of Personality and Social Psychology, 34,* 599–604. (p. 302)

Cialdini, R. B., Vincent, J. E., Lewis, S. K., Catalan, J., Wheeler, D., & Danby, B. L. (1975). Reciprocal concessions procedure for inducing compliance: The door-in-the-face technique. *Journal of Personality and Social Psychology, 31,* 206–215. (p. 302)

Cicerello, A., & Sheehan, E. P. (1995). Personal advertisements: A content analysis. *Journal of Social Behavior and Personality, 10,* 751–756. (p. 361)

Cikara, M., Bruneau, E. G., & Saxe, R. R. (2011). Us and them: Intergroup failures of empathy. *Current Directions in Psychological Science, 20,* 149–153. (p. 284)

Cioffi, D., & Garner, R. (1998). The effect of response options on decisions and subsequent behavior: Sometimes inaction is better. *Personality and Social Psychology Bulletin, 24,* 463–472. (p. 306)

Clark, M. S. (1984). Record keeping in two types of relationships. *Journal of Personality and Social Psychology, 47,* 549–557. (p. 386)

Clark, M. S. (1986). Evidence for the effectiveness of manipulations of desire for communal versus exchange relationships. *Personality and Social Psychology Bulletin, 12,* 414–425. (p. 386)

Clark, M. S., & Mills, J. (1979). Interpersonal attraction in exchange and communal relationships. *Journal of Personality and Social Psychology, 37,* 12–24. (p. 386)

Clark, M. S., & Mills, J. (1993). The difference between communal and exchange relationships: What it is and is not. *Personality and Social Psychology Bulletin, 19,* 684–691. (p. 386)

Clark, M. S., Mills, J., & Corcoran, D. (1989). Keeping track of needs and inputs of friends and strangers. *Personality and Social Psychology Bulletin, 15,* 533–542. (p. 386)

Clark, M. S., Mills, J., & Powell, M. C. (1986). Keeping track of needs in communal and exchange relationships. *Journal of Personality and Social Psychology, 51,* 333–338. (p. 386)

Clark, R. D., III (1995). A few parallels between group polarization and minority influence. In S. Moscovici, H. Mucchi-Faina, & A. Maass (Eds.), *Minority influence.* Chicago: Nelson-Hall. (p. 268)

Clark, R. D., III, & Maass, S. A. (1988). The role of social categorization and perceived source credibility in minority influence. *European Journal of Social Psychology, 18,* 381–394. (p. 216)

Clarke, A. C. (1952). An examination of the operation of residual propinquity as a factor in mate selection. *American Sociological Review, 27,* 17–22. (p. 356)

Clayton, S., & Myers, G. (2009). *Conservation psychology: Understanding and promoting human care for nature.* Hoboken, NJ: Wiley-Blackwell. (p. 520)

Cleghorn, J. (2000). *Beyond the bottom line: Redefining philanthropy in the 21st century.* Ketchum Leaders in Philanthropy Series. Toronto: Canadian Centre for Philanthropy. (p. 286)

Cleghorn, R. (1980, October 31). ABC News, meet the Literary Digest. *Detroit Free Press.* (p. 22)

Clevstrom, J., & Passariello, C. (2006, August 18). No kicks from "champagne." *Wall Street Journal,* A11. (p. 225)

Clifford, M. M., & Walster, E. H. (1973). The effect of physical attractiveness on teacher expectation. *Sociology of Education, 46,* 248–258. (p. 362)

Clore, G. L., Wiggins, N. H., & Itkin, G. (1975). Gain and loss in attraction: Attributions from nonverbal behavior. *Journal of Personality and Social Psychology, 31,* 706–712. (p. 374)

CNN. (2007, October 6). Jury awards $6.1 million in McDonald's strip search case (www.cnn.com). (p. 208)

Coan, J. A., Schaefer, H. S., & Davidson, R. J. (2006). Lending a hand: Social regulation of the neural response to threat. *Psychological Science, 17,* 1032–1039. (p. 487)

Coates, B., Pusser, H. E., & Goodman, I. (1976). The influence of "Sesame Street" and "Mister Rogers' Neighborhood" on children's social behavior in the preschool. *Child Development, 47,* 138–144. (p. 305)

Codol, J. P. (1976). On the so-called superior conformity of the self behavior: Twenty experimental investigations. *European Journal of Social Psychology, 5,* 457–501. (p. 70)

Cohen, B., Waugh, G., & Place, K. (1989). At the movies: An unobtrusive study of arousal attraction. *Journal of Social Psychology, 129,* 691–693. (p. 378)

Cohen, D. (1998). Culture, social organization, and patterns of violence. *Journal of Personality and Social Psychology, 75,* 408–419. (p. 321)

Cohen, D., & Nisbett, R. E. (1997). Field experiments examining the culture of honor: The role of institutions in perpetuating norms about violence. *Personality and Social Psychology Bulletin, 23,* 1188–1199. (p. 321)

Cohen, D., Nisbett, R. E., Bowdle, B. F., & Schwarz, N. (1996). Insult, aggression, and the southern culture of honor: An "Experimental Ethnography." *Journal of Personality and Social Psychology, 70,* 945–960. (p. 321)

Cohen, E. E. A., Ejsmond-Frey, R., Knight, N., & Dunbar, R. I. M. (2009, September 15). Rowers' high: Behavioural synchrony is correlated with elevated pain thresholds. *Biology Letters.* (doi: 10.1098/rsbl.2009.0670) (p. 238)

Cohen, G. L., Steele, C. M., & Ross, L. D. (1999). The mentor's dilemma: Providing critical feedback across the racial divide. *Personality and Social Psychology Bulletin, 25,* 1302–1318. (p. 442)

Cohen, M., & Davis, N. (1981). *Medication errors: Causes and prevention.* Philadelphia: G. F. Stickley Co. Cited by R. B. Cialdini (1989). *Agents of influence: Bunglers, smugglers, and sleuths.* Paper presented at the American Psychological Association convention. (p. 208)

Cohen, S. (1980). *Training to understand TV advertising: Effects and some policy implications.* Paper presented at the American Psychological Association convention. (p. 191)

Cohen, S. (2002). Psychosocial stress, social networks, and susceptibility to infection. In H. G. Koenig, & H. J. Cohen (Eds.), *The link between religion and health: Psychoneuroimmunology and the faith factor.* (101–123). New York: Oxford University Press. (p. 485)

Cohen, S. (2004). Social relationships and health. *American Psychologist. Special Issue: Awards Issue 2004, 59,* 676. (p. 485)

Cohen, S., Alper, C. M., Doyle, W. J., Treanor, J. J., & Turner, R. B. (2006). Positive emotional style predicts resistance to illness after experimental exposure to rhinovirus or influenza A virus. *Psychosomatic Medicine, 68,* 809–815. (p. 485)

Cohen, S., Doyle, W. J., Skoner, D. P., Rabin, B. S., & Gwaltney, J. M., Jr. (1997). Social ties and susceptibility to the common cold. *Journal of the American Medical Association, 277,* 1940–1944. (pp. 487, 489)

Cohen, S., Doyle, W. J., Turner, R., Alper, C. M., & Skoner, D. P. (2003). Sociability and susceptibility to the common cold. *Psychological Science, 14,* 389–395. (pp. 485, 487, 488)

Cohen, S., & Rodriguez, M. S. (1995). Pathways linking affective disturbances and physical disorders. *Health Psychology, 14,* 374–380. (p. 484)

Cohn, E. G. (1993). The prediction of police calls for service: The influence of weather and temporal variables on rape and domestic violence. *Environmental Psychology, 13,* 71–83. (p. 323)

Cohn, E. G., & Rotton, J. (2005). The curve is still out there: A reply to Bushman,

Wang, and Anderson (2005), Is the curve relating temperature to aggression linear or curvilinear? *Journal of Personality and Social Psychology, 89,* 67–70. (p. 324)

Cohrs, J. C., & Ibler, S. (2009). Authoritarianism, threat, and prejudice: An analysis of mediation and moderation. *Basic and Applied Social Psychology, 31,* 81–94. (p. 404)

Cohrs, J. C., Moschner, B., Maes, J., & Kielmann, S. (2005). The motivational bases of right-wing authoritarianism and social dominance orientation: Relations to values and attitudes in the aftermath of September 11, 2001. *Personality and Social Psychology Bulletin, 31,* 1425. (p. 404)

Cole, S. W., Arevalo, J. M. G., Takahashi, R., Sloan, E. K., Lutgendorf, S. K., Sood, A. K., Sheridan, J. F., & Seeman, T. E. (2010). Computational identification of gene-social environment interaction at the human IL6 locus. *PNAS, 107,* 5681–5686. (p. 485)

Coleman, L. M., Jussim, L., & Abraham, J. (1987). Students' reactions to teachers' evaluations: The unique impact of negative feedback. *Journal of Applied Social Psychology, 17,* 1051–1070. (p. 372)

Collins, N. L., & Miller, L. C. (1994). Self-disclosure and liking: A meta-analytic review. *Psychological Bulletin, 116,* 457–475. (p. 387)

Colman, A. M. (1991). Crowd psychology in South African murder trials. *American Psychologist, 46,* 1071–1079. See also, A. M. Colman (1991), Psychological evidence in South African murder trials. *The Psychologist, 14,* 482–486. (p. 252)

Comer, D. R. (1995). A model of social loafing in real work group. *Human Relations, 48,* 647–667. (p. 242)

Comstock, G. (2008). A sociological perspective on television violence and aggression. *American Behavioral Scientist, 51,* 1184–1211. (p. 335)

Conger, R. D., Cui, M., Bryant, C. M., & Elder, G. H. (2000). Competence in early adult romantic relationships: A developmental perspective on family influences. *Journal of Personality and Social Psychology, 79,* 224–237. (p. 385)

Conway, F., & Siegelman, J. (1979). *Snapping: America's epidemic of sudden personality change.* New York: Delta Books. (pp. 183, 184)

Conway, L. G., III, Suedfeld, P., & Tetlock, P. E. (2001). Integrative complexity and

political decisions that lead to war or peace. In D. J. Christie, R. V. Wagner, & D. Winter (Eds.), *Peace, conflict, and violence: Peace psychology for the 21st century.* Englewood Cliffs, NJ: Prentice-Hall. (p. 461)

Conway, M., & Ross, M. (1986). Remembering one's own past: The construction of personal histories. In R. Sorrentino & E. T. Higgins (Eds.), *Handbook of motivation and cognition.* New York: Guilford. (p. 86)

Cook, T. D., & Flay, B. R. (1978). The persistence of experimentally induced attitude change. In L. Berkowitz (Ed.), *Advances in experimental social psychology.* Vol. 11. New York: Academic Press. (p. 162)

Cooke, L., Chambers, L., Anez, E., Croker, H., Boniface, D., Yeomans, M., & Wardle, J. (2011). Eating for pleasure or profit: The effect of incentives on children's enjoyment of vegetables. *Psychological Science, 22,* 190–196. (p. 149)

Cooley, C. H. (1902). *Human nature and the social order.* New York: Schocken Books. (p. 40)

Coombs, R. H. (1991, January). Marital status and personal well-being: A literature review. *Family Relations, 40,* 97–102. (p. 493)

Cooper, H. (1983). Teacher expectation effects. In L. Bickman (Ed.), *Applied social psychology annual,* Vol. 4. Beverly Hills, CA: Sage. (p. 112)

Cooper, J. (1999). Unwanted consequences and the self: In search of the motivation for dissonance reduction. In (Eds.) E. Harmon-Jones & J. Mills. *Cognitive dissonance: Progress on a pivotal theory in social psychology.* Science conference series. (pp. 149–173). Washington, DC: American Psychological Association. (p. 140)

Cooper, M. (1999, Feb. 5). Officers in Bronx fire 41 shots, and an unarmed man is killed. *New York Times.* Available at www.nytimes.com. (p. 432)

Correll, J., Park, B., Judd, C. M., & Wittenbrink, B. (2002). The police officer's dilemma: Using ethnicity to disambiguate potentially threatening individuals. *Journal of Personality and Social Psychology, 83,* 1314–1329. (p. 430)

Correll, J., Park, B., Judd, C. M., & Wittenbrink, B. (2007). The influence of stereotypes on decisions to shoot. *European Journal of Social Psychology, 37,* 1102–1117. (p. 430)

Correll, J., Urland, G. R., & Ito, T. A. (2006). Event-related potentials and the decision

to shoot: The role of threat perception and cognitive control. *Journal of Experimental Social Psychology, 42,* 120–128. (pp. 430, 432)

Costanzo, M. (1998). *Just revenge.* New York: St. Martins. (pp. 311, 346)

Costello, C., Gaines, S. D., & Lynham, J. (2008). Can catch shares prevent fisheries' collapse? *Science, 321,* 1678–1682. (p. 458)

Cota, A. A., & Dion, K. L. (1986). Salience of gender and sex composition of ad hoc groups: An experimental test of distinctiveness theory. *Journal of Personality and Social Psychology, 50,* 770–776. (p. 226)

Cotton, J. L. (1981). *Ambient temperature and violent crime.* Paper presented at the Midwestern Psychological Association convention. (p. 323)

Cotton, J. L. (1986). Ambient temperature and violent crime. *Journal of Applied Social Psychology, 16,* 786–801. (p. 323)

Cottrell, N. B., Wack, D. L., Sekerak, G. J., & Rittle, R. M. (1968). Social facilitation of dominant responses by the presence of an audience and the mere presence of others. *Journal of Personality and Social Psychology, 9,* 245–250. (p. 237)

Courneya, K. S., & Carron, A. V. (1992). The home advantage in sport competitions: A literature review. *Journal of Sport and Exercise Psychology, 14,* 13–27. (p. 236)

Coyne, S. M., & Archer, J. (2005). The relationship between indirect and physical aggression on television and in real life. *Social Development, 14,* 324–338. (p. 332)

Cozzolino, P. J. (2011). Trust, cooperation, and equality: A psychological analysis of the formation of social capital. *British Journal of Social Psychology, 50,* 302–320. (p. 403)

Crabb, P. B., & Bielawski, D. (1994). The social representation of material culture and gender in children's books. *Sex Roles, 30,* 69–79. (pp. 132, 433)

Craig, W., & Harel, Y. (2004). Bullying, physical fighting, and victimization. In C. Currie (Ed.), *Young people's health in context: International report from the HSBC 2001/2 survey.* WHO Policy Series: Health policy for children and adolescents issue 4. Copenhagen: WHO Regional Office for Europe. (p. 310)

Crandall, C. S. (1988). Social contagion of binge eating. *Journal of Personality and Social Psychology, 55,* 588–598. (p. 216)

Crandall, C. S., Eshleman, A., & O'Brien, L. (2002). Social norms and the expression and suppression of prejudice: The struggle for internalization. *Journal of Personality and Social Psychology, 82*(3), 359–378. (p. 416)

Crano, W. D., & Mellon, P. M. (1978). Causal influence of teachers' expectations on children's academic performance: A cross-legged panel analysis. *Journal of Educational Psychology, 70,* 39–49. (p. 111)

Crawford, M., Stark, A. C., & Renner, C. H. (1998). The meaning of Ms.: Social assimilation of a gender concept. *Psychology of Women Quarterly, 22,* 197–208. (p. 399)

Crawford, T. J. (1974). Sermons on racial tolerance and the parish neighborhood context. *Journal of Applied Social Psychology, 4,* 1. (p. 174)

Crocker, J. (1981). Judgment of covariation by social perceivers. *Psychological Bulletin, 90,* 272–292. (p. 97)

Crocker, J., & Gallo, L. (1985). *The self-enhancing effect of downward comparison.* Paper presented at the American Psychological Association convention. (p. 526)

Crocker, J., Hannah, D. B., & Weber, R. (1983). Personal memory and causal attributions. *Journal of Personality and Social Psychology, 44,* 55–56. (p. 437)

Crocker, J., & Knight, K. M. (2005). Contingencies of self-worth. *Current Directions in Psychological Science, 14,* 200–203. (p. 56)

Crocker, J., Luhtanen, R. K., Cooper, M. L., & Bouvrette, S. (2003). Contingencies of self-worth in college students: Theory and measurement. *Journal of Personality and Social Psychology, 85,* 894–908. (p. 56)

Crocker, J., & Major, B. (1989). Social stigma and self-esteem: The self-protective properties of stigma. *Psychological Review, 96,* 608–630. (p. 447)

Crocker, J., & McGraw, K. M. (1984). What's good for the goose is not good for the gander: Solo status as an obstacle to occupational achievement for males and females. *American Behavioral Scientist, 27,* 357–370. (p. 420)

Crocker, J., & Park, L. E. (2004). The costly pursuit of self-esteem. *Psychological Bulletin, 130,* 392–414. (p. 56)

Crocker, J., Sommers, S., & Luhtanen, R. (2002). Hopes dashed and dreams fulfilled: Contingencies of self-worth in the graduate school admissions process. *Personality and Social Psychology Bulletin, 28,* 1275–1286. (p. 56)

Crocker, J., Thompson, L. L., McGraw, K. M., & Ingerman, C. (1987). Downward comparison, prejudice, and evaluations of others: Effects of self-esteem and threat. *Journal of Personality and Social Psychology, 52,* 907–916. (p. 412)

Crocker, J., Voelkl, K., Testa, M., & Major, B. (1991). Social stigma: The affective consequences of attributional ambiguity. *Journal of Personality and Social Psychology, 60,* 218–228. (p. 447)

Crocker, J., & Wolfe, C. (2001). Contingencies of self-worth. *Psychological Review, 108,* 593–623. (p. 51)

Crompton, T., & Kasser, T. (2010, July/August). Human identity: A missing link in environmental campaigning. *Environment Magazine,* pp. 23–33 (www.environmentmagazine.org). (p. 520)

Crosby, F., Bromley, S., & Saxe, L. (1980). Recent unobtrusive studies of black and white discrimination and prejudice: A literature review. *Psychological Bulletin, 87,* 546–563. (p. 429)

Crosby, F., Pufall, A., Snyder, R. C., O'Connell, M., & Whalen, P. (1989). The denial of personal disadvantage among you, me, and all the other ostriches. In M. Crawford & M. Gentry (Eds.), *Gender and thought.* New York: Springer-Verlag. (p. 447)

Crosby, F. J. (Ed.) (1987). *Spouse, parent, worker: On gender and multiple roles.* New Haven, CT: Yale University Press. (p. 493)

Crosby, J. R., & Monin, B. (2007). Failure to warn: How student race affects warnings of potential academic difficulty. *Journal of Experimental Social Psychology, 43,* 663–670. (p. 430)

Cross, P. (1977, Spring). Not can but will college teaching be improved? *New Directions for Higher Education, No. 17,* 1–15. (p. 70)

Cross, S. E., Liao, M-H., & Josephs, R. (1992). *A cross-cultural test of the self-evaluation maintenance model.* Paper presented at the American Psychological Association convention. (p. 43)

Cross-National Collaborative Group (1992). The changing rate of major depression. *Journal of the American Medical Association, 268,* 3098–3105. (p. 479)

Crowley, G. (1996, June 3). The biology of beauty. *Newsweek,* 61–69. (p. 360)

Croxton, J. S., Eddy, T., & Morrow, N. (1984). Memory biases in the reconstruction of interpersonal encounters. *Journal of Social & Clinical Psychology, 2*(4), 348. (p. 85)

Csikszentmihalyi, M. (1990). *Flow: The psychology of optimal experience.* New York: Harper & Row. (p. 526)

Csikszentmihalyi, M. (1999). If we are so rich, why aren't we happy? *American Psychologist, 54,* 821–827. (p. 526)

Cuddy, A. J. C., & 23 others. (2009). Stereotype content model across cultures: Towards universal similarities and some differences. *British Journal of Social Psychology, 48,* 1–33. (p. 402)

Cullum, J., & Harton, H. C. (2007). Cultural evolution: Interpersonal influence, issue importance, and the development of shared attitudes in college residence halls. *Personality and Social Psychology Bulletin, 33,* 1327–1339. (p. 217)

Cunningham, J. D. (1981). Self-disclosure intimacy: Sex, sex-of-target, cross-national, and generational differences. *Personality and Social Psychology Bulletin, 7,* 314–319. (p. 388)

Cunningham, M. R., Shaffer, D. R., Barbee, A. P., Wolff, P. L., & Kelley, D. J. (1990). Separate processes in the relation of elation and depression to helping: Social versus personal concerns. *Journal of Experimental Social Psychology, 26,* 13–33. (p. 279)

Cunningham, W. A., Raye, C. L., & Johnson, M. K. (2004). Implicit and explicit evaluation: FMRI correlates of valence, emotional intensity, and control in the processing of attitudes. *Journal of Cognitive Neuroscience. Special Issue: Social Cognitive Neuroscience, 16,* 1717. (p. 432)

Cutler, B. L., & Penrod, S. D. (1988). Improving the reliability of eyewitness identification: Lineup construction and presentation. *Journal of Applied Psychology, 73,* 281–290. (p. 503)

Cutler, B. L., Penrod, S. D., & Dexter, H. R. (1989). The eyewitness, the expert psychologist and the jury. *Law and Human Behavior, 13,* 311–332. (p. 505)

Cutler, B. L., Penrod, S. D., & Stuve, T. E. (1988). Juror decision making in eyewitness identification cases. *Law and Human Behavior, 12,* 41–55. (p. 505)

Cutrona, C. E. (1986). Behavioral manifestations of social support: A microanalytic investigation. *Journal of Personality and Social Psychology, 51,* 201–208. (p. 488)

Dabbs, J. M., & Janis, I. L. (1965). Why does eating while reading facilitate opinion change? An experimental inquiry. *Journal of Experimental Social Psychology, 1,* 133–144. (p. 167)

Dabbs, J. M., Jr. (1992). Testosterone measurements in social and clinical psychology. *Journal of Social and Clinical Psychology, 11,* 302–321. (p. 314)

Dabbs, J. M., Jr. (2000). *Heroes, rogues, and lovers : Testosterone and behavior.* New York: McGraw-Hill. (p. 315)

Dabbs, J. M., Jr., Carr, T. S., Frady, R. L., & Riad, J. K. (1995). Testosterone, crime, and misbehavior among 692 male prison inmates. *Personality and Individual Differences, 18,* 627–633. (p. 314)

Dabbs, J. M., Jr., & Morris, R. (1990). Testosterone, social class, and antisocial behavior in a sample of 4462 men. *Psychological Science, 1,* 209–211. (p. 314)

Dabbs, J. M., Jr., Riad, J. K., & Chance, S. E. (2001). Testosterone and ruthless homicide. *Personality and Individual Differences, 31,* 599. (p. 314)

Dabbs, J. M., Jr., Strong, R., & Milun, R. (1997). Exploring the mind of testosterone: A beeper study. *Journal of Research in Personality, 31,* 577–588. (p. 314)

Dalrymple, T. (2007). On evil. *New English Review* (www.newenglishreview.org). (p. 343)

Dando, C., Wilcock, R., & Milne, R. (2009). The cognitive interview: The efficacy of a modified mental reinstatement of context procedure for frontline police investigators. *Applied Cognitive Psychology, 23,* 138–147. (p. 503)

Dambrun, M., & Vatiné, E. (2010). Reopening the study of extreme social behaviors: Obedience to authority within an immersive video environment. *European Journal of Social Psychology, 40,* 760–773. (p. 206)

Damon, W. (1995). *Greater expectations: Overcoming the culture of indulgence in America's homes and schools.* New York: Free Press. (p. 20)

Danner, D. D., Snowdon, D. A., & Friesen, W. V. (2001). Positive emotions in early life and longevity: Findings from the Nun Study. *Journal of Personality and Social Psychology, 80,* 804–813. (p. 486)

Dardenne, B., Dumont, M., & Bollier, T. (2007). Insidious dangers of benevolent sexism: Consequences for women's performance. *Journal of Personality and Social Psychology, 93,* 764–779. (p. 402)

Darley, J., & Alter, A. (2009). Behavioral issues of punishment and deterrence. In E. Shafir (Ed.), *The behavioral foundations of policy.* Princeton, NJ: Princeton University Press. (p. 346)

Darley, J. M. (1995). Book review essay. *Political Psychology,* in press. (p. 299)

Darley, J. M., & Batson, C. D. (1973). From Jerusalem to Jericho: A study of situational and dispositional variables in helping behavior. *Journal of Personality and Social Psychology, 27,* 100–108. (pp. 297, 298)

Darley, J. M., & Berscheid, E. (1967). Increased liking as a result of the anticipation of personal contact. *Human Relations, 20,* 29–40. (p. 357)

Darley, J. M., & Gross, P. H. (1983). A hypothesis-confirming bias in labelling effects. *Journal of Personality and Social Psychology, 44,* 20–33. (p. 444)

Darley, J. M., & Latané, B. (1968). Bystander intervention in emergencies: Diffusion of responsibility. *Journal of Personality and Social Psychology, 8,* 377–383. (pp. 290, 291, 292, 294)

Darley, S., & Cooper, J. (1972). Cognitive consequences of forced noncompliance. *Journal of Personality and Social Psychology, 24,* 321–326. (p. 192)

Dasgupta, N., & Rivera, L. M. (2006). From automatic antigay prejudice to behavior: The moderating role of conscious beliefs about gender and behavioral control. *Journal of Personality and Social Psychology, 91,* 268–280. (p. 416)

Dashiell, J. F. (1930). An experimental analysis of some group effects. *Journal of Abnormal and Social Psychology, 25,* 190–199. (p. 234)

Dateline. (2000, June 20). *Dateline NBC.* New York: NBC. (p. 290)

Davidson, R. J., Putnam, K. M., & Larson, C. L. (2000). Dysfunction in the neural circuitry of emotion regulation-A possible prelude to violence. *Science, 289,* 591–594. (p. 313)

Davie, M. (1986). *The Titanic: The full story of a tragedy.* London: Collins. (p. 257)

Davies, M. F. (1997). Belief persistence after evidential discrediting: The impact of generated versus provided explanations on the likelihood of discredited outcomes. *Journal of Experimental Social Psychology, 33,* 561–578. (p. 83)

Davies, P. G., Spencer, S. J., Quinn, D. M., & Gerhardstein, R. (2002). Consuming images: How television commercials that elicit stereotype threat can restrain women academically and professionally. *Personality and Social Psychology Bulletin, 28,* 1615–1628. (p. 441)

Davila, J., Bradbury, T. N., Cohan, C. L., & Tochluk, S. (1997). Marital functioning and depressive symptoms: Evidence for a stress generation model. *Journal of Personality and Social Psychology, 73,* 849–861. (p. 493)

Davis, C. G., Lehman, D. R., Silver, R. C., Wortman, C. B., & Ellard, J. H. (1996). Self-blame following a traumatic event: The role of perceived avoidability. *Personality and Social Psychology Bulletin, 22,* 557–567. (p. 97)

Davis, C. G., Lehman, D. R., Wortman, C. B., Silver, R. C., & Thompson, S. C. (1995). The undoing of traumatic life events. *Personality and Social Psychology Bulletin, 21,* 109–124. (p. 97)

Davis, J. H., Kameda, T., Parks, C., Stasson, M., & Zimmerman, S. (1989). Some social mechanics of group decision making: The distribution of opinion, polling sequence, and implications for consensus. *Journal of Personality and Social Psychology, 57,* 1000–1012. (p. 509)

Davis, J. H., Kerr, N. L., Atkin, R. S., Holt, R., & Meek, D. (1975). The decision processes of 6- and 12-person mock juries assigned unanimous and two-thirds majority rules. *Journal of Personality and Social Psychology, 32,* 1–14. (p. 509)

Davis, J. H., Kerr, N. L., Strasser, G., Meek, D., & Holt, R. (1977). Victim consequences, sentence severity, and decision process in mock juries. *Organizational Behavior and Human Performance, 18,* 346–365. (p. 509)

Davis, J. H., Stasson, M. F., Parks, C. D., Hulbert, L., Kameda, T., Zimmerman, S. K., & Ono, K. (1993). Quantitative decisions by groups and individuals: Voting procedures and monetary awards by mock civil juries. *Journal of Experimental Social Psychology, 29,* 326–346. (p. 187)

Davis, J. L., & Rusbult, C. E. (2001). Attitude alignment in close relationships. *Journal of Personality and Social Psychology, 81,* 65–84. (p. 370)

Davis, K. E. (1985, February). Near and dear: Friendship and love compared. *Psychology Today,* 22–30. (p. 383)

Davis, K. E., & Jones, E. E. (1960). Changes in interpersonal perception as a means of reducing cognitive dissonance. *Journal of Abnormal and Social Psychology, 61,* 402–410. (p. 135)

Davis, L., & Greenlees, C. (1992). *Social loafing revisited: Factors that mitigate-and reverse-performance loss.* Paper presented at the Southwestern Psychological Association convention. (p. 242)

Davis, S. C., Diegel, S. W., & Boundy, R. G. (2011, June). *Transportation Energy Data Book: Edition 30* (Tables 3.1 and 3.2). Office of Energy Efficiency and Renewable Energy, U.S. Department of Energy. (p. 515)

Dawes, R. M. (1980a). Social dilemmas. *Annual Review of Psychology, 31,* 169–193. (p. 459)

Dawes, R. M. (1980b). You can't systematize human judgment: Dyslexia. In R. A. Shweder (Ed.), *New directions for methodology of social and behavioral science: Fallible judgment in behavioral research.* San Francisco: Jossey-Bass. (p. 117)

Dawes, R. M. (1990). The potential nonfalsity of the false consensus effect. In R. M. Hogarth (Ed.), *Insights in decision making: A tribute to Hillel J. Einhorn.* Chicago: University of Chicago Press. (p. 65)

Dawes, R. M. (1991). Social dilemmas, economic self-interest, and evolutionary theory. In D. R. Brown & J. E. Keith Smith (Eds.), *Frontiers of mathematical psychology: Essays in honor of Clyde Coombs.* New York: Springer-Verlag. (p. 455)

Dawes, R. M. (1994). *House of cards: Psychology and psychotherapy built on myth.* New York: Free Press. (pp. 20, 54)

Dawes, R. M. (1998). Behavioral decision making and judgment. In D. T. Gilbert, S. T. Fiske & G. Lindzey (Eds.), *The handbook of social psychology,* vols. 1 and 2 (4th ed.). (pp. 497–548). New York: McGraw-Hill. (p. 54)

Dawes, R. M., McTavish, J., & Shaklee, H. (1977). Behavior, communication, and assumptions about other people's behavior in a commons dilemma situation. *Journal of Personality and Social Psychology, 35,* 1–11. (p. 459)

Dawkins, R. (1976). *The selfish gene.* New York: Oxford University Press. (pp. 283, 285)

Dean, C. (2005, August 30). Scientific savvy? In U.S., not much. *New York Times* (www.nytimes.com). (p. 158)

Deary, I. J. (2005). Intelligence, health and death. *The Psychologist, 18,* 610. (p. 489)

DeBruine, L. M. (2002). Facial resemblance enhances trust. *Proceedings of the Royal Society of London, 269,* 1307–1312. (pp. 298, 299)

Decety, J., & Sommerville, J. A. (2003). Shared representations between self and other: A social cognitive neuroscience view. *Trends in Cognitive Sciences, 7,* 527–533. (p. 38)

Dechêne, A., Stahl, C., Hansen, J., & Wänke, M. (2010). The truth about the truth: A meta-analysis review of the truth effect. *Personality and Social Psychology Review, 14,* 238–257. (p. 175)

Deci, E. L., & Ryan, R. M. (1985). *Intrinsic motivation and self-determination in human behavior.* New York: Plenum. (p. 150)

Deci, E. L., & Ryan, R. M. (1987). The support of autonomy and the control of behavior. *Journal of Personality and Social Psychology, 53,* 1024–1037. (p. 58)

Deci, E. L., & Ryan, R. M. (1991). A motivational approach to self: Integration in personality. In R. Dienstbier (Ed.) Vol. 38. *Perspectives on motivation,* Lincoln, NE: University of Nebraska Press. Nebraska Symposium on Motivation, 237–288. (pp. 148, 150)

Deci, E. L., & Ryan, R. M. (1997). *Behaviorists in search of the null: Revisiting the undermining of intrinsic motivation by extrinsic rewards.* Unpublished manuscript, University of Rochester. (p. 148)

Deci, E. L., & Ryan, R. M. (Eds.). (2002). *Handbook of self-determination research.* Rochester, NY: University of Rochester Press. (p. 353)

Deci, E. L., & Ryan, R. M. (2008). Facilitating optimal motivation and psychological well-being across life's domains. *Canadian Psychology, 49,* 14–23. (p. 150)

De Hoog, N., Stroebe, W., & de Wit, J. B. F. (2007). The impact of vulnerability to and severity of a health risk on processing and acceptance of fear-arousing communications: A meta-analysis. *Review of General Psychology, 11,* 258–285. (p. 168)

de Hoogh, A. H. B., den Hartog, D. N., Koopman, P. L., Thierry, H., van den Berg, Peter T., van der Weide, Joost G., et al. (2004). Charismatic leadership, environmental dynamism, and performance. *European Journal of Work and Organizational Psychology, 13,* 447. (p. 265)

De Houwer, J., Thomas, S., & Baeyens, F. (2001). Associative learning of likes and dislikes: A review of 25 years of research on human evaluative conditioning. *Psychological Bulletin, 127,* 853–869. (p. 375)

Delgado, J. (1973). In M. Pines, *The brain changers.* New York: Harcourt Brace Jovanovich. (p. 129)

Dembroski, T. M., Lasater, T. M., & Ramirez, A. (1978). Communicator similarity, fear arousing communications, and compliance with health care recommendations. *Journal of Applied Social Psychology, 8,* 254–269. (p. 165)

Demoulin, S., Saroglou, V., & Van Pachterbeke, M. (2008). Infra-humanizing others, supra-humanizing gods: The emotional hierarchy. *Social Cognition, 26,* 235–247. (p. 411)

Denissen, J. J. A., Penke, L., Schmitt, D. P., & van Aken, M. A. G. (2008). Self-esteem reactions to social interactions: Evidence for sociometer mechanisms across days, people, and nations. *Journal of Personality and Social Psychology, 95,* 181–196. (p. 352)

Denrell, J. (2008). Indirect social influence. *Science, 321,* 47–48. (p. 220)

Denrell, J., & Le Mens, G. (2007). Interdependent sampling and social influence. *Psychological Review, 114,* 398–422. (p. 220)

Denson, T. F., Pedersen, W. C., & Miller, N. (2006). The displaced aggression questionnaire. *Journal of Personality and Social Psychology, 90,* 1032–1051. (p. 313)

DePaulo, B. (2006). *Singled out: How singles are stereotyped, stigmatized, and ignored, and still live happily ever after.* New York: St. Martin's. (p. 492)

DePaulo, B. M., Charlton, K., Cooper, H., Lindsay, J. J., & Muhlenbruck, L. (1997). The accuracy-confidence correlation in the detection of deception. *Personality and Social Psychology Review, 1,* 346–357. (p. 90)

Derks, B., Inzlicht, M., & Kang, S. (2008). The neuroscience of stigma and stereotype threat. *Group Processes and Intergroup Relations, 11,* 163–181. (p. 442)

Derlega, V., Metts, S., Petronio, S., & Margulis, S. T. (1993). *Self-disclosure.* Newbury Park, CA: Sage. (p. 387)

Dermer, M., Cohen, S. J., Jacobsen, E., & Anderson, E. A. (1979). Evaluative judgments of aspects of life as a function of vicarious exposure to hedonic extremes. *Journal of Personality and Social Psychology, 37,* 247–260. (p. 526)

Dermer, M., & Pyszczynski, T. A. (1978). Effects of erotica upon men's loving and liking responses for women they love. *Journal of Personality and Social Psychology, 36,* 1302–1309. (p. 378)

de Sherbinin, A., & 17 others. (2011). Preparing for resettlement associated with climate change. *Science, 334,* 456–457. (p. 517)

Desmarais, S. L., & Read, J. D. (2011). After 30 years, what do we know about what jurors know? A meta-analytic review of lay knowledge regarding eyewitness factors. *Law and Human Behavior, 35,* 200–210. (p. 505)

DeSteno, D., Petty, R. E., Wegener, D. T., & Rucker, D. D. (2000). Beyond valence in the perception of likelihood: The role of emotion specificity. *Journal of Personality and Social Psychology, 78,* 397–416. (p. 100)

Detweiler, J. B., Bedell, B. T., Salovey, P., Pronin, E., & Rothman, A. J. (1999). Message framing and sunscreen use: Gain-framed messages motivate beach-goers. *Health Psychology, 18,* 189–196. (p. 483)

Deutsch, M., & Gerard, H. B. (1955). A study of normative and informational social influence upon individual judgment. *Journal of Abnormal and Social Psychology, 51,* 629–636. (pp. 218, 219)

Devenport, J. L., Stinson, V., Cutler, B. L., & Kravitz, D. A. (2002). How effective are the cross-examination and expert testimony safeguards? Jurors' perceptions of the suggestiveness and fairness of biased lineup procedures. *Journal of Applied Psychology, 87,* 1042–1054. (p. 505)

Devine, P. A., Brodish, A. B., & Vance, S. L. (2005). Self-regulatory processes in interracial interactions: The role of internal and external motivation to respond without prejudice. In J. P. Forgas, K. D. Williams, & S. M. Laham (Eds.), *Social motivation. Conscious and unconscious processes.* New York: Cambridge University Press. (p. 416)

Devine, P. G. (1989). Stereotypes and prejudice: Their automatic and controlled components. *Journal of Personality and Social Psychology, 56,* 5–18. (p. 416)

Devine, P. G., Evett, S. R., & Vasquez-Suson, K. A. (1996). Exploring the interpersonal dynamics of intergroup contact. In R. Sorrentino & E. T. Higgins (Eds.), *Handbook of motivation and cognition: The interpersonal content,* vol. 3. New York: Guilford. (p. 440)

Devine, P. G., Forscher, P. S., Austin, A. J., & Cox, W. T. L. (2012). *Long-term reduction in implicit racial prejudice: A prejudice habit-breaking intervention.* Unpublished manuscript, University of Wisconsin. (p. 416)

Devine, P. G., & Malpass, R. S. (1985). Orienting strategies in differential face recognition. *Personality and Social Psychology Bulletin, 11*(1), 33–40. (p. 419)

Devine, P. G., & Sharp, L. B. (2008). Automatic and controlled processes in stereotyping and prejudice. In T. Nelson (Ed.), *Handbook of prejudice, stereotyping, and discrimination.* New York: Psychology Press. (p. 401)

DeVoe, S. E., House, J., & Zhong, C.-B. (2013). Fast food and financial impatience: A socio-ecological approach. *Journal of Personality and Social Psychology, 105,* 476–494. (p. 79)

De Vogli, R., Chandola, T., & Marmot, M. G. (2007). Negative aspects of close relationships and heart disease. *Archives of Internal Medicine, 167,* 1951–1957. (p. 487)

Devos-Comby, L., & Salovey, P. (2002). Applying persuasion strategies to alter HIV-relevant thoughts and behavior. *Review of General Psychology, 6,* 287–304. (p. 169)

de Waal, F. B. M. (2005–2006, Fall–Winter). The evolution of empathy. *Greater Good,* 6–9. (p. 288)

de Waal, F. B. M., Leimgruber, K., & Greenberg, A. R. (2008). Giving is self-rewarding for monkeys. *Proceedings of the National Academy of Sciences, 105,* 13685–13689. (p. 288)

DeWall, C. N., Baumeister, R. F., Stillman, T. F., & Gailliot, M. T. (2007). Violence restrained: Effects of self-regulation and its depletion on aggression. *Journal of Experimental Social Psychology, 43,* 62–76. (p. 57)

DeWall, C. N., & Bushman, B. J. (2011). Social acceptance and rejection: The sweet and the bitter. *Current Directions in Psychological Science, 20,* 256–260. (pp. 353, 354)

DeWall, C. N., Bushman, B. J., Giancola, P. R., & Webster, G. D. (2010a). The big, the bad, and the boozed-up: Weight moderates the effect of alcohol on aggression. *Journal of Experimental Social Psychology, 46,* 619–623. (p. 311)

DeWall, C. N., MacDonald, G., Webster, G. D., Masten, C. L., Baumeister, R. F., Powell, C., Combs, D., Schurtz, D. R., Stillman, T. F., Tice, D. M., & Eisenberger, N. I. (2010b). Acetaminophen reduces social pain: Behavioural and neural evidence. *Psychological Science, 21,* 931–937. (p. 354)

DeWall, C. N., Maner, J. K., & Rouby, D. A. (2009). Social exclusion and early-stage interpersonal perception: Selective attention to signs of acceptance. *Journal of Personality and Social Psychology, 96,* 729–741. (pp. 353, 355)

DeWall, C. N., Twenge, J. M., Gitter, S. A., Baumeister, R. F. (2009). It's the thought that counts: The role of hostile cognition in shaping aggressive responses to social exclusion. *Journal of Personality and Social Psychology, 96,* 45–59. (p. 353)

Diamond, J. (1996, December). The best ways to sell sex. *Discover,* 78–86. (p. 366)

Diamond, S. S. (1993). Instructing on death: Psychologists, juries, and judges. *American Psychologist, 48,* 423–434. (p. 508)

Dickerson, S. S., Gable, S. L., Irwin, M. R., Aziz, N., & Kemeny, M. E. (2009). Social-evaluative threat and proinflammatory cytokine regulation: An experimental laboratory investigation. *Psychological Science, 20,* 1237–1243. (p. 485)

Dicum, J. (2003, November 11). Letter to the editor. *New York Times,* p. A20. (p. 390)

DiDonato, T. E., Ullrich, J., & Krueger, J. I. (2011). Social perception as induction and inference: An intergrative model of intergroup differentiation, ingroup favoritism, and differential accuracy. *Journal of Personality and Social Psychology, 100,* 66–83. (p. 409)

Diekman, A. B., McDonald, M., & Gardner, W. L. (2000). Love means never having to be careful: The relationship between reading romance novels and safe sex behavior. *Psychology of Women Quarterly, 24,* 179–188. (p. 95)

Diekmann, K. A., Samuels, S. M., Ross, L., & Bazerman, M. H. (1997). Self-interest and fairness in problems of resource allocation: Allocators versus recipients. *Journal of Personality and Social Psychology, 72,* 1061–1074. (p. 61)

Diener, E. (1976). Effects of prior destructive behavior, anonymity, and group presence on deindividuation and aggression. *Journal of Personality and Social Psychology, 33,* 497–507. (pp. 245, 246)

Diener, E. (1979). Deindividuation, self-awareness, and disinhibition. *Journal of Personality and Social Psychology, 37,* 1160–1171. (p. 246)

Diener, E. (1980). Deindividuation: The absence of self-awareness and self-regulation in group members. In P. Paulus (Ed.), *The psychology of group influence.* Hillsdale, NJ: Erlbaum. (p. 247)

Diener, E., Horwitz, J., & Emmons, R. A. (1985). Happiness of the very wealthy. *Social Indicators, 16,* 263–274. (p. 522)

Diener, E., Lucas, R. E., & Scollon, C. N. (2006). Beyond the hedonic treadmill: Revising the adaptation theory of well-being. *American Psychologist, 61,* 305. (p. 524)

Diener, E., & Wallbom, M. (1976). Effects of self-awareness on antinormative behavior. *Journal of Research in Personality, 10,* 107–111. (pp. 128, 245, 247)

Dienstbier, R. A., Roesch, S. C., Mizumoto, A., Hemenover, S. H., Lott, R. C., & Carlo, G. (1998). Effects of weapons on guilt judgments and sentencing recommendations for criminals. *Basic and Applied Social Psychology, 20,* 93–102. (p. 326)

Dijksterhuis, A., Bos, M. W., Nordgren, L. F., & van Baaren, R. B. (2006a). Complex choices better made unconsciously? *Science, 313,* 760–761. (p. 88)

Dijksterhuis, A., & Nordgren, L. F. (2006b). A theory of unconscious thought. *Perspectives on Psychological Science, 1,* 95–109. (p. 88)

Dijksterhuis, A., Smith, P. K., van Baaren, R. B., & Wigboldus, D. H. J. (2005). The unconscious consumer: Effects of environment on consumer behavior. *Journal of Consumer Psychology, 15,* 193–202. (p. 160)

Dillehay, R. C., & Nietzel, M. T. (1980). Constructing a science of jury behavior. In L. Wheeler (Ed.), *Review of personality and social psychology* (Vol. 1). Beverly Hills, CA: Sage Publications. (p. 511)

Dion, K. K. (1972). Physical attractiveness and evaluations of children's transgressions. *Journal of Personality and Social Psychology, 24,* 207–213. (p. 362)

Dion, K. K. (1973). Young children's stereotyping of facial attractiveness. *Developmental Psychology, 9,* 183–188. (p. 362)

Dion, K. K. (1979). Physical attractiveness and interpersonal attraction. In M. Cook & G. Wilson (Eds.), *Love and attraction.* New York: Pergamon Press. (p. 362)

Dion, K. K., & Berscheid, E. (1974). Physical attractiveness and peer perception among children. *Sociometry, 37,* 1–12. (p. 362)

Dion, K. K., & Dion, K. L. (1985). Personality, gender, and the phenomenology of romantic love. In P. R. Shaver (Ed.), *Review of personality and social psychology,* vol. 6. Beverly Hills, CA: Sage. (p. 379)

Dion, K. K., & Dion, K. L. (1991). Psychological individualism and romantic love. *Journal of Social Behavior and Personality, 6,* 17–33. (p. 381)

Dion, K. K., & Dion, K. L. (1993). Individualistic and collectivistic perspectives on gender and the cultural context of love and intimacy. *Journal of Social Issues, 49,* 53–69. (p. 392)

Dion, K. K., & Dion, K. L. (1996). Cultural perspectives on romantic love. *Personal Relationships, 3,* 5–17. (p. 381)

Dion, K. K., & Stein, S. (1978). Physical attractiveness and interpersonal influence. *Journal of Experimental Social Psychology, 14,* 97–109. (p. 165)

Dion, K. L. (1975). Women's reactions to discrimination from members of the same or opposite sex. *Journal of Research in Personality, 9,* 294–306. (p. 447)

Dion, K. L. (1985). Responses to perceived discrimination and relative deprivation. In J. M. Olson, C. P. Herman, & M. P. Zanna (Eds.), *Relative deprivation and social comparison: The Ontario symposium,* vol. 4. Hillsdale, NJ: Erlbaum. (p. 318)

Dion, K. L. (1987). What's in a title? The Ms. stereotype and images of women's titles of address. *Psychology of Women Quarterly, 11,* 21–36. (p. 399)

Dion, K. L. (1998). *The social psychology of perceived prejudice and discrimination.* Colloquium presentation, Carleton University. (p. 440)

Dion, K. L., & Cota, A. A. (1991). The Ms. stereotype: Its domain and the role of explicitness in title preference. *Psychology of Women Quarterly, 15,* 403–410. (p. 399)

Dion, K. L., & Dion, K. K. (1988). Romantic love: Individual and cultural perspectives. In R. J. Sternberg & M. L. Barnes (Eds.), *The psychology of love.* New Haven, CT: Yale University Press. (p. 381)

Dion, K. L., Dion, K. K., & Keelan, J. P. (1990). Appearance anxiety as a dimension of social-evaluative anxiety: Exploring the ugly duckling syndrome. *Contemporary Social Psychology, 14*(4), 220–224. (p. 360)

Dion, K. L., & Earn, B. M. (1975). The phenomenology of being a target of prejudice. *Journal of Personality and Social Psychology, 32,* 944–950. (p. 447)

Dion, K. L., & Kawakami, K. (1996). *Canadian Journal of Behavioural Science, 28,* 203–213. (p. 448)

Dion, K. L., & Schuller, R. A. (1991). The Ms. stereotype: Its generality and its relation to managerial and marital status stereotypes. *Canadian Journal of Behavioural Science, 23,* 25–40. (p. 399)

DiPietro, L. (2000). Tackling race and sports: A review of *Taboo* by Jon Entine. *Scientific American.* May, pp. 112–118. (p. 399)

Dishion, T. J., McCord, J., & Poulin, F. (1999). When interventions harm: Peer groups and problem behavior. *American Psychologist, 54,* 755–764. (p. 251)

Dixon, J., Tropp, L. R., Durrheim, K., & Tredoux, C. (2010). "Let them eat harmony": Prejudice-reduction strategies and attitudes of historically disadvantaged groups. *Current Directions in Psychological Science, 19,* 76–80. (p. 453)

Doherty, T. J., & Clayton, S. (2011). The psychological impacts of global climate change. *American Psychologist, 66,* 265–276. (p. 517)

Dohrenwend, B., Pearlin, L., Clayton, P., Hamburg, B., Dohrenwend, B. P., Riley, M., & Rose, R. (1982). Report on stress and life events. In G. R. Elliott & C. Eisdorfer (Eds.), *Stress and human health: Analysis and implications of research* (A study by the Institute of Medicine/National Academy of Sciences). New York: Springer. (p. 488)

Dolinski, D. (2000). On inferring one's beliefs from one's attempt and consequences for subsequent compliance. *Journal of Personality and Social Psychology, 78,* 260–272. (p. 306)

Dolinski, D., & Nawrat, R. (1998). "Fear-then-relief" procedure for producing compliance: Beware when the danger is over. *Journal of Experimental Social Psychology, 34,* 27–50. (p. 278)

Dollard, J., Doob, L., Miller, N., Mowrer, O. H., & Sears, R. R. (1939). *Frustration and aggression.* New Haven, CT: Yale University Press. (p. 316)

Dolnik, L., Case, T. I., & Williams, K. D. (2003). Stealing thunder as a courtroom tactic revisited: Processes and boundaries. *Law and Human Behavior, 27,* 267. (p. 180)

Donaldson, Z. R., & Young, L. J. (2008). Oxytocin, vasopressin, and the neurogenetics of sociality. *Science, 322,* 900–904. (p. 382)

Donders, N. C., Correll, J., & Wittenbrink, B. (2008). Danger stereotypes predict racially biased attentional allocation. *Journal of Experimental Social Psychology, 44,* 1328–1333. (p. 432)

Donnellan, M. B., Larsen-Rife, D., & Conger, R. D. (2005). Personality, family history, and competence in early adult romantic relationships. *Journal of Personality and Social Psychology, 88,* 562–576. (pp. 55, 385)

Donnerstein, E. (1980). Aggressive erotica and violence against women. *Journal of Personality and Social Psychology, 39,* 269–277. (pp. 330)

Donnerstein, E. (1998). Why do we have those new ratings on television? Invited address to the National Institute on the Teaching of Psychology. (p. 331)

Donnerstein, E. (2011). The media and aggression: From TV to the Internet. In J. Forgas, A. Kruglanski, & K. Williams (Eds.). *The psychology of social conflict and aggression.* New York: Psychology Press. (p. 334)

Donnerstein, E., Linz, D., & Penrod, S. (1987). *The question of pornography.* London: Free Press. (pp. 328, 331)

Doob, A. N., & Kirshenbaum, H. M. (1973). Bias in police lineups-partial remembering. *Journal of Police Science and Administration, 1,* 287–293. (p. 504)

Doob, A. N., & McLaughlin, D. S. (1989). Ask and you shall be given: Request size and donations to a good cause. *Journal of Applied Social Psychology, 19,* 1049–1056. (p. 303)

Doob, A. N., & Roberts, J. (1988). Public attitudes toward sentencing in Canada. In N. Walker & M. Hough (Eds.), *Sentencing and the public.* London: Gower. (p. 96)

Doolittle, R. (2007). Bizarre assaults hit quiet town. *Toronto Star.* Available at www.thestar.com/News/GTA/article/260646. (p. 398)

D'Orlando, F. (2011). The demand for pornography. *Journal of Happiness Studies, 12,* 51–75. (p. 327)

Dotan-Eliaz, O., Sommer, K. L., & Rubin, S. (2009). Multilingual groups: Effects of linguistic ostracism on felt rejection and anger, coworker attraction, perceived team potency, and creative performance. *Basic and Applied Social Psychology, 31,* 363–375. (p. 353)

Dotsch, R., & Wigboldus, D. H. J. (2008). Virtual prejudice. *Journal of Experimental Social Psychology, 44,* 1194–1198. (p. 432)

Doty, R. M., Peterson, B. E., & Winter, D. G. (1991). Threat and authoritarianism in the United States, 1978–1987. *Journal of Personality and Social Psychology, 61,* 629–640. (p. 404)

Douglas, K. M., & McGarty, C. (2001). Identifiability and self-presentation: Computer-mediated communication and intergroup interaction. *British Journal of Social Psychology, 40,* 399–416. (p. 244)

Dovidio, J. F. (1991). The empathy-altruism hypothesis: Paradigm and promise. *Psychological Inquiry, 2,* 126–128. (p. 289)

Dovidio, J. F., Gaertner, S. L., Anastasio, P. A., & Sanitioso, R. (1992). Cognitive and motivational bases of bias: Implications of aversive racism for attitudes toward Hispanics. In S. Knouse, P. Rosenfeld, & A. Culbertson (Eds.), *Hispanics in the workplace.* Newbury Park, CA: Sage. (p. 401)

Dovidio, J. R., Brigham, J. C., Johnson, B. T., & Gaertner, S. L. (1996). Stereotyping, prejudice, and discrimination: Another look. In N. Macrae, M. Hewstone, & C. Stangor (Eds.), *Stereotypes and stereotyping.* New York: Guilford. (p. 400)

Downs, A. C., & Lyons, P. M. (1991). Natural observations of the links between attractiveness and initial legal judgments. *Personality and Social Psychology Bulletin, 17,* 541–547. (p. 506)

Draguns, J. G. (1990). Normal and abnormal behavior in cross-cultural perspective: Specifying the nature of their relationship. *Nebraska Symposium on Motivation 1989, 37,* 235–277. (p. 479)

Driskell, J. E., & Mullen, B. (1990). Status, expectations, and behavior: A meta-analytic review and test of the theory. *Personality and Social Psychology Bulletin, 16,* 541–553. (p. 217)

Dryer, D. C., & Horowitz, L. M. (1997). When do opposites attract? Interpersonal complementarity versus similarity. *Journal of Personality and Social Psychology, 72,* 592–603. (p. 371)

Duclos, S. E., Laird, J. D., Schneider, E., Sexter, M., Stern, L., & Van Lighten, O. (1989). Emotion-specific effects of facial expressions and postures on emotional experience. *Journal of Personality and Social Psychology, 57,* 100–108. (p. 146)

Dugger, C. W. (2001, April 22). Abortion in India spurred by sex text skew the ratio against girls. *New York Times.* Late edition, 12. (p. 436)

Dunbar, R. (1992). Neocortex size as a constraint on group size in primates. *Journal of Human Evolution, 22,* 469–493. (p. 458)

Dunbar, R. (2010, December 25). You've got to have (150) friends. *New York Times* (www.nytimes.com). (p. 458)

Duncan, B. L. (1976). Differential social perception and attribution of intergroup violence: Testing the lower limits of stereotyping of blacks. *Journal of Personality and Social Psychology, 34,* 590–598. (p. 423)

Dunfield, K. A., & Kuhlmeier, V. A. (2010). Intention-mediated selective helping in infancy. *Psychological Science, 21,* 523–527. (p. 280)

Dunn, E., & Ashton-James, C. (2008). On emotional innumeracy: Predicted and actual affective response to grand-scale tragedies. *Journal of Experimental Social Psychology, 44,* 692–698. (pp. 49, 303)

Dunn, E. W., Aknin, L. B., & Norton, M. I. (2008). Spending money on others promotes happiness. *Science, 319,* 1687–1688. (pp. 72, 275, 280)

Dunn, E. W., Wilson, T. D., & Gilbert, D. T. (2003). Location, location, location: The misprediction of satisfaction in housing lotteries. *Personality and Social Psychology Bulletin, 29,* 1421. (p. 524)

Dunning, D. (1995). Trait importance and modifiability as factors influencing self-assessment and self-enhancement motives. *Personality and Social Psychology Bulletin, 21,* 1297–1306. (p. 68)

Dunning, D. (2005). *Self-insight: Roadblocks and detours on the path to knowing thyself.* New York: Psychology Press. (p. 91)

Dunning, D. (2006). Strangers to ourselves? *The Psychologist, 19,* 600–603. (p. 48)

Dunning, D., Griffin, D. W., Milojkovic, J. D., & Ross, L. (1990). The overconfidence effect in social prediction. *Journal of Personality and Social Psychology, 58,* 568–581. (p. 90)

Dunning, D., Meyerowitz, J. A., & Holzberg, A. D. (1989). Ambiguity and self-evaluation. *Journal of Personality and Social Psychology, 57,* 1082–1090. (p. 62)

Dunning, D., Perie, M., & Story, A. L. (1991). Self-serving prototypes of social categories. *Journal of Personality and Social Psychology, 61,* 957–968. (p. 62)

Dunning, D., & Perretta, S. (2002). Automaticity and eyewitness accuracy: A 10- to 12-second rule for distinguishing accurate from inaccurate positive identifications. *Journal of Applied Psychology, 87,* 951–962. (p. 503)

Dunning, D., & Sherman, D. A. (1997). Stereotypes and tacit inference. *Journal of Personality and Social Psychology, 73,* 459–471. (p. 444)

Dutton, D. G., & Aron, A. (1989). Romantic attraction and generalized liking for others who are sources of conflict-based arousal. *Canadian Journal of Behavioural Science, 21,* 246–257. (p. 378)

Dutton, D. G., & Aron, A. P. (1974). Some evidence for heightened sexual attraction under conditions of high anxiety. *Journal of Personality and Social Psychology, 30,* 510–517. (p. 378)

Dutton, D. G., Boyanowsky, E. O., & Bond, M. H. (2005). Extreme mass homicide: From military massacre to genocide. *Aggression and Violent Behavior, 10,* 437–473. (p. 310)

Duval, S., Duval, V. H., & Neely, R. (1979). Self-focus, felt responsibility, and helping behavior. *Journal of Personality and Social Psychology, 37,* 1769–1778. (p. 301)

Dye, M. W. G., Green, C. S., & Bavelier, D. (2009). Increasing speed of processing with action video games. *Current Directions in Psychological Science, 18,* 321–326. (p. 341)

Eagly, A. (1994). *Are people prejudiced against women?* Donald Campbell Award invited address, American Psychological Association convention. (pp. 434, 435)

Eagly, A. H. (2009). The his and hers of prosocial behavior: An examination of the social psychology of gender. *American Psychologist, 64,* 644–658. (p. 300)

Eagly, A. H., Ashmore, R. D., Makhijani, M. G., & Longo, L. C. (1991). What is beautiful is good, but . . .: A meta-analytic review of research on the physical attractiveness stereotype. *Psychological Bulletin, 110,* 109–128. (pp. 362, 434)

Eagly, A. H., & Chaiken, S. (1993). *The psychology of attitudes.* San Diego: Harcourt Brace Jovanovich. (p. 160)

Eagly, A. H., & Chaiken, S. (1998). Attitude structure and function. In D. Gilbert, S. Fiske, and G. Lindzey (Eds.), *The handbook of social psychology,* 4th edition. New York: McGraw-Hill. (p. 160)

Eagly, A. H., & Crowley, M. (1986). Gender and helping behavior: A meta-analytic review of the social psychological literature. *Psychological Bulletin, 100,* 283–308. (pp. 282, 300)

Eagly, A. H., & Johnson, B. T. (1990). Gender and leadership style: A meta-analysis. *Psychological Bulletin, 108,* 233–256. (p. 265)

Eagly, A. H., Karau, S. J., & Makhijani, M. G. (1995). Gender and the effectiveness of leaders: A meta-analysis. *Psychological Bulletin, 117,* 125–145. (p. 399)

Eagly, A. H., Wood, W., & Chaiken, S. (1978). Causal inferences about communicators and their effect on opinion change. *Journal of Personality and Social Psychology, 36,* 424–435. (p. 164)

Easterbrook, G. (2004, May 25). The 50¢-a-gallon solution. *New York Times* (www.nytimes.com). (p. 519)

Easterlin, R. (1995). Will raising the incomes of all increase the happiness of all? *Journal of Economic Behavior and Organization, 27,* 35–47. (p. 522)

Eastwick, P. W., & Finkel, E. J. (2008). Sex differences in mate preferences revisited: Do people know what they initially desire in a romantic partner? *Journal of Personality and Social Psychology, 94,* 245. (p. 360)

Eastwick, P. W., Finkel, E. J., Krishnamurti, T., & Loewenstein, G. (2007a). Mispredicting distress following romantic breakup: Revealing the time course of the affective forecasting error. *Journal of Experimental Social Psychology, 44,* 800–807. (p. 49)

Eastwick, P. W., Finkel, E. J., Mochon, D., & Ariely, D. (2007b). Selective versus unselective romantic desire. *Psychological Science, 18,* 317–319. (p. 372)

Eaton, J., & Struthers, C. W. (2006). The reduction of psychological aggression across varied interpersonal contexts through repentance and forgiveness. *Aggressive Behavior, 32,* 195. (p. 317)

Ebbesen, E. B., Duncan, B., & Konecni, V. J. (1975). Effects of content of verbal aggression on future verbal aggression: A field experiment. *Journal of Experimental Social Psychology, 11,* 192–204. (p. 345)

Eberhardt, J. L. (2005). Imaging race. *American Psychologist, 60,* 181–190. (p. 432)

Eberhardt, J. L., Goff, P. A., Purdie, V. J., & Davies, P. G. (2004). Seeing black: Race, crime, and visual processing. *Journal of Personality and Social Psychology, 87,* 876. (p. 432)

Eckersley, R. (2005). Is modern Western culture a health hazard? *International Journal of Epidemiology,* published online November 22. (p. 523)

Edelson, M., Sharot, T., Dolan, R. J., & Dudai, Y. (2011). Following the crowd: brain substrates of long-term memory conformity. *Science, 333,* 108–111. (p. 197)

Edney, J. J. (1980). The commons problem: Alternative perspectives. *American Psychologist, 35,* 131–150. (p. 458)

Edwards, C. P. (1991). Behavioral sex differences in children of diverse cultures: The case of nurturance to infants. In M. Pereira & L. Fairbanks (Eds.), *Juveniles: Comparative socio-ecology.* Oxford: Oxford University Press. (p. 433)

Edwards, K. (1990). The interplay of affect and cognition in attitude formation and change. *Journal of Personality and Social Psychology, 59,* 202–216. (p. 167)

Edwards, K., & Bryan, T. S. (1997). Judgmental biases produced by instructions to disregard: The (paradoxical) case of emotional information. *Personality and Social Psychology Bulletin, 23,* 849–864. (p. 507)

Edwards, P. (2010). Anger over light sentence for racist attack. *Toronto Star.* Available at www.thestar.com/news/gta/article/764837. (p. 398)

Efran, M. G. (1974). The effect of physical appearance on the judgment of guilt, interpersonal attraction, and severity of recommended punishment in a simulated jury task. *Journal of Research in Personality, 8,* 45–54. (p. 506)

Egan, L. C., Santos, L. R., & Bloom, P. (2007). The origins of cognitive dissonance: Evidence from children and monkeys. *Psychological Science, 18,* 978–983. (p. 144)

Eibach, R. P., & Ehrlinger, J. (2006). "Keep your eyes on the prize": Reference points and racial differences in assessing progress toward equality. *Personality and Social Psychology Bulletin, 32,* 66–77. (p. 429)

Eisenberg, N., Fabes, R. A., Schaller, M., Miller, P., Carlo, G., Poulin, R., Shea, C., & Shell, R. (1991). Personality and socialization correlates of vicarious emotional responding. *Journal of Personality and Social Psychology, 61,* 459–470. (p. 299)

Eisenberger, N. I., Lieberman, M. D., & Williams, K. D. (2003). Does rejection hurt? An fMRI study of social exclusion. *Science, 302,* 290–292. (p. 354)

Eisenberger, R., & Armeli, S. (2001). Can salient reward increase creative performance without reducing intrinsic creative interest? *Journal of Personality and Social Psychology, 72,* 652–660. (p. 149)

Eisenberger, R., & Cameron, J. (1999). Detrimental effects of reward: Reality or myth? *American Psychologist, 51,* 1153–1166. (p. 149)

Eisenberger, R., & Rhoades, L. (2001). Incremental effects of reward on creativity. *Journal of Personality and Social Psychology, 81,* 728–741. (p. 149)

Eisenberger, R., Rhoades, L., & Cameron, J. (1999). Does pay for performance increase or decrease perceived self-determination and intrinsic motivation. *Journal of Personality and Social Psychology, 77,* 1026–1040. (p. 149)

Eisenberger, R. & Shanock, L. (2003). Rewards, intrinsic motivation, and creativity: A case study of conceptual and methodological isolation. *Creativity Research Journal, 15,* 121–130. (p. 149)

Eiser, J. R., Sutton, S. R., & Wober, M. (1979). Smoking, seat-belts, and beliefs about health. *Addictive Behaviors, 4,* 331–338. (p. 140)

Elder, G. H., Jr. (1969). Appearance and education in marriage mobility. *American Sociological Review, 34,* 519–533. (p. 361)

Eldersveld, S. J., & Dodge, R. W. (1954). Personal contact or mail propaganda? An experiment in voting turnout and attitude change. In D. Katz, D. Cartwright, S. Eldersveld, & A. M. Lee (Eds.), *Public opinion and propaganda.* New York: Dryden Press. (p. 176)

Ellemers, N., Van Rijswijk, W., Roefs, M., & Simons, C. (1997). Bias in intergroup perceptions: Balancing group identity with social reality. *Personality and Social Psychology Bulletin, 23,* 186–198. (p. 410)

Ellis, H. D. (1981). Theoretical aspects of face recognition. In G. H. Davies, H. D. Ellis, & J. Shepherd (Eds.), *Perceiving and remembering faces.* London: Academic Press. (p. 419)

Ellison, P. A., Govern, J. M., Petri, H. L., & Figler, M. H. (1995). Anonymity and aggressive driving behavior: A field study. *Journal of Social Behavior and Personality, 10,* 265–272. (p. 245)

Ellsworth, P. C., & Mauro, R. (1998). Psychology and law. In D. Gilbert, S. T. Fiske, & G. Lindzey (Eds.), *Handbook of social psychology,* 4th ed. New York: McGraw-Hill. (p. 508)

Elms, A. C. (1995). Obedience in retrospect. *Journal of Social Issues, 51,* 21–31. (p. 205)

Emmons, R. A., Larsen, R. J., Levine, S., & Diener, E. (1983). *Factors predicting satisfaction judgments: A comparative examination.* Paper presented at the Midwestern Psychological Association. (p. 491)

Emswiller, T., Deaux, K., & Willits, J. E. (1971). Similarity, sex, and requests for small favors. *Journal of Applied Social Psychology, 1,* 284–291. (p. 298)

Eng, P. M., Kawachi, I., Fitzmaurice, G., & Rimm, E. B. (2001). *Effects of marital transitions on changes in dietary and other health behaviors in men.* Paper presented to the American Psychosomatic Society meeting. (p. 488)

Engemann, K. M., & Owyang, M. T. (2003, April). So much for that merit raise: The link between wages and appearance. *The Regional Economist* (www.stlouisfed.org). (p. 363)

Ennis, B. J., & Verrilli, D. B., Jr. (1989). Motion for leave to file brief amicus curiae and brief of Society for the Scientific Study of Religion, American Sociological Association, and others. U.S. Supreme Court Case No. 88-1600, *Holy Spirit Association for the Unification of World Christianity, et al., v. David Molko and Tracy Leal.* On petition for write of certiorari to the Supreme Court of California. Washington, DC: Jenner & Block, 21 Dupont Circle NW. (p. 185)

Ennis, R., & Zanna, M. P. (1991). *Hockey assault: Constitutive versus normative violations.* Paper presented at the Canadian Psychological Association convention. (p. 320)

Epley, N., & Huff, C. (1998). Suspicion, affective response, and educational benefit of deception in psychological research. *Personality and Social Psychology Bulletin, 67,* 371–378. (p. 28)

Epley, N., Savitsky, K., & Kachelski, R. A. (1999, September/October). What every skeptic should know about subliminal persuasion. *Skeptical Inquirer,* 40–45. (p. 79)

Epstein, J. A., & Botvin, G. J. (2008). Media refusal skills and drug skill refusal techniques: What is their relationship with alcohol use among inner-city adolescents? *Addictive Behavior, 33,* 528–537. (p. 191)

Epstein, S. (1980). The stability of behavior: II. Implications for psychological research. *American Psychologist, 35,* 790–806. (p. 221)

Epstude, K., & Roese, N. J. (2008). The functional theory of counterfactual thinking. *Personality and Social Psychology Review, 12,* 168–192. (p. 96)

Erickson, B., Holmes, J. G., Frey, R., Walker, L., & Thibaut, J. (1974). Functions of a third party in the resolution of conflict: The role of a judge in pretrial conferences. *Journal of Personality and Social Psychology, 30,* 296–306. (p. 465)

Erickson, B., Lind, E. A. Johnson, B. C., & O'Barr, W. M. (1978). Speech style and impression formation in a court setting: The effects of powerful and powerless speech. *Journal of Experimental Social Psychology, 14,* 266–279. (p. 163)

Erikson, E. H. (1963). *Childhood and society.* New York: Norton. (p. 384)

Eron, L. D. (1987). The development of aggressive behavior from the perspective of a developing behaviorism. *American Psychologist, 42,* 425–442. (p. 332)

Eron, L. D., & Huesmann, L. R. (1980). Adolescent aggression and television. *Annals of the New York Academy of Sciences, 347,* 319–331. (p. 333)

Eron, L. D., & Huesmann, L. R. (1984). The control of aggressive behavior by changes in attitudes, values, and the conditions of learning. In R. J. Blanchard & C. Blanchard (Eds.), *Advances in the study of aggression,* vol. 1. Orlando, FL: Academic Press. (pp. 333, 347)

Eron, L. D., & Huesmann, L. R. (1985). The role of television in the development of prosocial and antisocial behavior. In D. Olweus, M. Radke-Yarrow, and J. Block (Eds.), *Development of antisocial and prosocial behavior.* Orlando, FL: Academic Press. (p. 333)

Escobar-Chaves, S. L., & Anderson, C. A. (2008). Media and risky behaviors. *The Future of Children, 18,* 147–180. (p. 336)

Escobar-Chaves, S. L., Tortolero, S. R., Markham, C. M., Low, B. J., Eitel, P., & Thickstun, P. (2005). Impact of the media on adolescent sexual attitudes and behaviors. *Pediatrics, 116,* 303–326. (p. 336)

Esser, J. K. (1998, February-March). Alive and well after 25 years. A review of groupthink research. *Organizational Behavior and Human Decision Processes, 73,* 116–141. (p. 259)

Esses, V. M. (1989). Mood as a moderator of acceptance of interpersonal feedback. *Journal of Personality and Social Psychology, 57,* 769–781. (p. 100)

Esses, V. M., Haddock, G., & Zanna, M. P. (1993a). Values, stereotypes, and emotions as determinants of intergroup attitudes. In D. Mackie & D. Hamilton (Eds.), *Affect, cognition and stereotyping: Interactive processes in intergroup perception.* San Diego, CA: Academic Press. (p. 401)

Esses, V. M., Haddock, G., & Zanna, M. P. (1993b). The role of mood in the expression of intergroup stereotypes. In M. P. Zanna & J. M. Olson (Eds.), *The psychology of prejudice: The Ontario symposium,* vol. 7. Hillsdale, NJ: Erlbaum. (p. 417)

Esses, V. M., Jackson, L. M., & Armstrong, T. L. (1998). Intergroup competition and attitudes toward immigrants and immigration: An instrumental model of group conflict. *Journal of Social Issues, 54,* 699–724. (p. 407)

Esses, V. M., & Webster, C. D. (1988). Physical attractiveness, dangerousness, and the Canadian criminal code. *Journal of Applied Social Psychology, 18,* 1017–1031. (p. 506)

Etaugh, C. E., Bridges, J. S., Cummings-Hill, M., & Cohen, J. (1999). "Names can never hurt me": The effects of surname use on perceptions of married women. *Psychology of Women Quarterly, 23,* 819–823. (p. 399)

Evans, G. W. (1979). Behavioral and physiological consequences of crowding in humans. *Journal of Applied Social Psychology, 9,* 27–46. (p. 237)

Evans, G. W., Lepore, S. J., & Schroeder, A. (1996). The role of interior design elements in human responses to crowding. *Journal of Personality and Social Psychology, 70,* 41–46. (p. 237)

Evans, R. I., Smith, C. K., & Raines, B. E. (1984). Deterring cigarette smoking in adolescents: A psycho-social-behavioral analysis of an intervention strategy. In A. Baum, J. Singer, & S. Taylor (Eds.), *Handbook of psychology and health: Social psychological aspects of health,* vol. 4, Hillsdale, NJ: Erlbaum. (p. 189)

Fabrigar, L. R., & Petty, R. E. (1999). The role of the affective and cognitive bases of attitudes in susceptibility to affectively and cognitively based persuasion. *Personality and Social Psychology Bulletin, 25,* 363–381. (p. 167)

Fabrigar, L. R., Priester, J. R., Petty, R. E., & Wegener, D. T. (1998). The impact of attitude accessibility on elaboration of persuasive messages. *Personality and Social Psychology Bulletin, 24,* 339–352. (pp. 180, 181)

Farquhar, J. W., Maccoby, N., Wood, P. D., Alexander, J. K., Breitrose, H., Brown, B. W., Jr., Haskell, W. L., McAlister, A. L., Meyer, A. J., Nash, J. D., & Stern, M. P. (1977, June 4). Community education for cardiovascular health. *Lancet,* 1192–1195. (p. 176)

Farrell, M. A. (2005). The effect of a market-oriented organisational culture on salesforce behaviour and attitudes. *Journal of Strategic Marketing, 13,* 261. (p. 190)

Farrelly, M. C., Davis, K. C., Duke, J., & Messeri, P. (2008, January 17). Sustaining "truth": Changes in youth tobacco attitudes and smoking intentions after three years of a national antismoking campaign. *Health Education Research* (doi:10.1093/her/cym087). (p. 168)

Farrelly, M. C., Healton, C. G., Davis, K. C., Messeri, P., Hersey, J. C., & Haviland, M. L. (2002). Getting to the truth: Evaluating national tobacco countermarketing campaigns. *American Journal of Public Health, 92,* 901–907. (p. 168)

Farris, C., Treat, T. A., Viken, R. J., & McFall, R. M. (2008). Perceptual mechanisms that characterize gender differences in decoding women's sexual intent. *Psychological Science, 19,* 348–354. (p. 102)

Farwell, L., & Weiner, B. (2000). Bleeding hearts and the heartless: Popular perceptions of liberal and conservative ideologies. *Personality and Social Psychology Bulletin, 26,* 845–852. (p. 109)

Faulkner, S. L., & Williams, K. D. (1996). *A study of social loafing in industry.* Paper presented to the Midwestern Psychological Association convention. (p. 241)

Fazio, R. (1987). Self-perception theory: A current perspective. In M. P. Zanna, J. M. Olson, & C. P. Herman (Eds.), *Social influence: The Ontario symposium,* vol. 5. Hillsdale, NJ: Erlbaum. (p. 152)

Fazio, R. H. (2007). Attitudes as object-evaluation associations of varying strength. *Social Cognition, 25,* 603–637. (p. 401)

Fazio, R. H., Effrein, E. A., & Falender, V. J. (1981). Self-perceptions following social interaction. *Journal of Personality and Social Psychology, 41,* 232–242. (p. 474)

Fazio, R. H., Jackson, J. R., Dunton, B. C., & Williams, C. J. (1995). Variability in automatic activation as an unobtrusive measure of racial attitudes: A bona fide pipeline? *Journal of Personality and Social Psychology, 69,* 1013–1027. (p. 401)

Fazio, R. H., & Zanna, M. P. (1981). Direct experience and attitude-behavior consistency. In L. Berkowitz (Ed.), *Advances in experimental social psychology,* Vol. 14. New York: Academic Press. (p. 128)

Fazio, R. H., Zanna, M. P., & Cooper, J. (1977). Dissonance versus self-perception: An integrative view of each theory's proper domain of application. *Journal of Experimental Social Psychology, 13,* 464–479. (p. 152)

Fazio, R. H., Zanna, M. P., & Cooper, J. (1979). On the relationship of data to theory: A reply to Ronis and Greenwald. *Journal of Experimental Social Psychology, 15,* 70–76. (p. 152)

Feather, N. T. (1983). Causal attributions for good and bad outcomes in achievement and affiliation situations. *Australian Journal of Psychology, 35,* 37–48. (p. 109)

Feather, N. T. (2005). Social psychology in Australia: Past and present. *International Journal of Psychology, 40,* 263–276. (p. 11)

Federal Bureau of Investigation (2008). Uniform crime report: Hate crimes 2008. Retrieved from: http://www.fbi.gov/about-us/cjis/ucr/hate-crime/2008 (p. 429)

Federal Trade Commission (FTC). (2003, June 12). Federal Trade Commission cigarette report for 2001 (www.ftc.gov/opa/2003/06/2001cigrpt.htm). (p. 190)

Feeney, J., Peterson, C., & Noller, P. (1994). Equity and marital satisfaction over the family life cycle. *Personality Relationships, 1,* 83–99. (p. 387)

Feeney, J. A. (1996). Attachment, caregiving, and marital satisfaction. *Personal Relationships, 3,* 401–416. (p. 383)

Feeney, J. A., & Noller, P. (1990). Attachment style as a predictor of adult romantic relationships. *Journal of Personality and Social Psychology, 58,* 281–291. (p. 383)

Fein, S., & Hilton, J. L. (1992). Attitudes toward groups and behavioral intentions toward individual group members: The impact of nondiagnostic information. *Journal of Experimental Social Psychology, 28,* 101–124. (p. 444)

Fein, S., & Spencer, S. J. (1997). Prejudice as self-image maintenance: Affirming the self through derogating others. *Journal of Personality and Social Psychology, 73,* 31–44. (p. 413)

Feinberg, M., & Willer, R. (2010). Apocalypse soon? Dire messages reduce belief in global warming by contradicting just-world beliefs. *Psychological Science, 22,* 34–38. (p. 169)

Feingold, A. (1988). Matching for attractiveness in romantic partners and same-sex friends: A meta-analysis and theoretical critique. *Psychological Bulletin, 104,* 226–235. (p. 361)

Feingold, A. (1990). Gender differences in effects of physical attractiveness on romantic attraction: A comparison across five research paradigms. *Journal of Personality and Social Psychology, 59,* 981–993. (p. 360)

Feingold, A. (1991). Sex differences in the effects of similarity and physical attractiveness on opposite-sex attraction.

Basic and Applied Social Psychology, 12, 357–367. (p. 360)

Feingold, A. (1992). Gender differences in mate selection preferences: A test of the parental investment model. *Psychological Bulletin, 112,* 125–139. (pp. 362, 363)

Feldman, R. S., & Prohaska, T. (1979). The student as Pygmalion: Effect of student expectation on the teacher. *Journal of Educational Psychology, 71,* 485–493. (p. 112)

Feldman, R. S., & Theiss, A. J. (1982). The teacher and student as Pygmalions: Joint effects of teacher and student expectations. *Journal of Educational Psychology, 74,* 217–223. (p. 112)

Felson, R. B. (1984). The effect of self-appraisals of ability on academic performance. *Journal of Personality and Social Psychology, 47,* 944–952. (p. 40)

Felson, R. B. (2000). A social psychological approach to interpersonal aggression. In V. B. Van Hasselt, & M. Hersen (Eds.), *Aggression and violence: An introductory text.* (pp. 9–22). Needham Heights, MA: Allyn & Bacon. (p. 311)

Ferguson, C. J., & Kilburn, J. (2010). Much ado about nothing: The misestimation and overinterpretation of violent video game effects in Eastern and Western nations: Comment on Anderson et al. (2010). *Psychological Bulletin, 136,* 174–178. (p. 341)

Fergusson, D. M., Horwood, L. J., & Shannon, F. T. (1984). A proportional hazards model of family breakdown. *Journal of Marriage and the Family, 46,* 539–549. (p. 392)

Fenigstein, A. (1984). Self-consciousness and the overperception of self as a target. *Journal of Personality and Social Psychology, 47,* 860–870. (p. 481)

Fenigstein, A., & Vanable, P. A. (1992). Paranoia and self-consciousness. *Journal of Personality and Social Psychology, 62,* 129–138. (p. 481)

Feshbach, N. D. (1980). *The child as "psychologist" and "economist": Two curricula.* Paper presented at the American Psychological Association convention. (pp. 190, 191)

Festinger, L. (1954). A theory of social comparison processes. *Human Relations, 7,* 117–140. (pp. 39, 252)

Festinger, L. (1957). *A theory of cognitive dissonance.* Stanford: Stanford University Press. (pp. 122, 140)

Festinger, L. (1987). *Reflections on cognitive dissonance theory: 30 years later.* Paper presented at the American Psychological Association convention. (p. 259)

Festinger, L., & Carlsmith, J. M. (1959). Cognitive consequences of forced compliance. *Journal of Abnormal and Social Psychology, 58,* 203–210. (pp. 140, 141, 142)

Festinger, L., & Maccoby, N. (1964). On resistance to persuasive communications. *Journal of Abnormal and Social Psychology, 68,* 359–366. (p. 180)

Festinger, L., Pepitone, A., & Newcomb, T. (1952). Some consequences of deindividuation in a group. *Journal of Abnormal and Social Psychology, 47,* 382–389. (p. 243)

Feygina, I., Jost, J. T., & Goldsmith, R. E. (2010). System justification, the denial of global warming, and the possibility of "system-sanctioned change." *Personality and Social Psychology Bulletin, 36,* 326–338. (p. 518)

Feynman, R. (1967). *The character of physical law.* Cambridge, MA: MIT Press. (p. 150)

Fichter, J. (1968). *America's forgotten priests: What are they saying?* New York: Harper. (p. 405)

Fiedler, F. E. (1987, September). When to lead, when to stand back. *Psychology Today,* 26–27. (p. 264)

Finkel, E. J., & Campbell, W. K. (2001). Self-control and accommodation in close relationships: An interdependence analysis. *Journal of Personality and Social Psychology, 81,* 263–277. (p. 57)

Finkel, E. J., Eastwick, P. W., Karney, B. R., Reis, H. T., & Sprecher, S. (2012). Online dating: A critical analysis from the perspective of psychological science. *Psychological Science in the Public Interest, 13,* 3–66. (p. 390)

Fischer, P., & Greitemeyer, T. (2006). Music and aggression: The impact of sexual-aggressive song lyrics on aggression-related thoughts, emotions, and behavior toward the same and the opposite sex. *Personality and Social Psychology Bulletin, 32,* 1165–1176. (p. 336)

Fischer, P., & Greitemeyer, T. (2010). A new look at selective-exposure effects: An integrative model. *Current Directions in Psychological Science, 19,* 384–389. (p. 140)

Fischer, P., Krueger, J., Greitemeyer, T., Kastenmüller, A., Vogrincic, C., Frey, D., Heene, M., Wicher, M., & Kainbacher, M. (2011). The bystander-effect: A

meta-analytic review on bystander intervention in dangerous and non-dangerous emergencies. *Psychological Bulletin, 137,* 517–537. (pp. 293, 503)

Fischer, R., & Boer, D. (2011). What is more important for national well-being: Money or autonomy? A meta-analysis of well-being, burnout, and anxiety across 63 societies. *Journal of Personality and Social Psychology, 101,* 164–184. (p. 526)

Fischer, R., & Chalmers, A. (2008). Is optimism universal? A meta-analytical investigation of optimism levels across 22 nations. *Personality and Individual Differences, 45,* 378–382. (p. 63)

Fischer, R., & Van de Vliert, E. (2011). Does climate undermine subjective well-being? A 58-nation study. *Personality and Social Psychology Bulletin, 37,* 1031–1041. (p. 517)

Fischhoff, B. (1982). Debiasing. In D. Kahneman, P. Slovic, & A. Tversky (Eds.), *Judgment under uncertainty: Heuristics and biases.* New York: Cambridge University Press. (p. 94)

Fischhoff, B., & Bar-Hillel, M. (1984). Diagnosticity and the base rate effect. *Memory and Cognition, 12,* 402–410. (p. 94)

Fishbein, D., & Thelen, M. H. (1981a). *Husband-wife similarity and marital satisfaction: A different approach.* Paper presented at the Midwestern Psychological Association convention. (p. 371)

Fishbein, D., & Thelen, M. H. (1981b). Psychological factors in mate selection and marital satisfaction: A review (Ms. 2374). *Catalog of Selected Documents in Psychology, 11,* 84. (p. 371)

Fishbein, M., & Ajzen, I. (1974). Attitudes toward objects as predictive of single and multiple behavioral criteria. *Psychological Review, 81,* 59–74. (p. 126)

Fisher, H. (1994, April). The nature of romantic love. *Journal of NIH Research,* 59–64. (p. 380)

Fisher, R. J. (1994). Generic principles for resolving intergroup conflict. *Journal of Social Issues, 50,* 47–66. (p. 466)

Fisher, R. P., & Geiselman, R. E. (1992). *Memory-enhancing techniques for investigative interviewing: The cognitive interview.* Springfield, IL: Charles C Thomas. (p. 503)

Fisher, R. P., Geiselman, R. E., & Amador, M. (1989). Field test of the cognitive interview: Enhancing the recollection of actual victims and witnesses of crime. *Journal of Applied Psychology, 74,* 722–727. (p. 503)

Fisher, R. P., Geiselman, R. E., & Raymond, D. S. (1987). Critical analysis of police interview techniques. *Journal of Police Science and Administration, 15,* 177–185. (p. 503)

Fisher, R. P., McCauley, M. R., & Geiselman, R. E. (1994). Improving eyewitness testimony with the Cognitive Interview. In D. F. Ross, J. D. Read, & M. P. Toglia (Eds.), *Adult eyewitness testimony: Current trends and developments.* Cambridge, England: Cambridge University Press. (p. 503)

Fiske, S. T. (1989). *Interdependence and stereotyping: From the laboratory to the Supreme Court (and back).* Invited address, American Psychological Association convention. (p. 430)

Fiske, S. T. (1992). Thinking is for doing: Portraits of social cognition from Daguerrotype to Laserphoto. *Journal of Personality and Social Psychology, 63,* 877–889. (p. 116)

Fiske, S. T. (1993). Controlling other people: The impact of power on stereotyping. *American Psychologist, 48,* 621–628. (p. 419)

Fiske, S. T. (2004). Mind the gap: In praise of informal sources of formal theory. *Personality and Social Psychology Review, 8,* 132–137. (p. 11)

Fiske, S. T. (2011). *Envy up, scorn down: How status divides us.* New York: Sage Foundation. (p. 525)

Fiske, S. T., Harris, L. T., & Cuddy, A. J. C. (2004). Why ordinary people torture enemy prisoners. *Science, 306,* 1482. (pp. 208, 212)

Fiske, S. T., Xu, J., Cuddy, A. C., & Glick, P. (1999). (Dis)respecting versus (Dis)liking: Status and interdependence predict ambivalent stereotypes of competence and warmth. *Journal of Social Issues, 55,* 473–489. (p. 402)

Fitzpatrick, A. R., & Eagly, A. H. (1981). Anticipatory belief polarization as a function of the expertise of a discussion partner. *Personality and Social Psychology Bulletin, 1,* 636–642. (p. 252)

Flay, B. R., Ryan, K. B., Best, J. A., Brown, K. S., Kersell, M. W., d'Avernas, J. R., & Zanna, M. P. (1985). Are social-psychological smoking prevention programs effective? The Waterloo study. *Journal of Behavioral Medicine, 8,* 37–59. (p. 189)

Fleming, M. A., Wegener, D. T., & Petty, R. E. (1999). Procedural and legal motivations to correct for perceived judicial biases. *Journal of Experimental Social Psychology, 35,* 186–203. (p. 507)

Fletcher, G. J. O., Fincham, F. D., Cramer, L., & Heron, N. (1987). The role of attributions in the development of dating relationships. *Journal of Personality and Social Psychology, 53,* 481–489. (p. 386)

Fletcher, G. J. O., Simpson, J. A., Thomas, G., & Giles, L. (1999). Ideals in intimate relationships. *Journal of Personality and Social Psychology, 76,* 72–89. (p. 376)

Fletcher, G. J. O., Tither, J. M., O'Loughlin, C., Friesen, M., & Overall, N. (2004). Warm and homely or cold and beautiful? Sex differences in trading off traits in mate selection. *Personality and Social Psychology Bulletin, 30,* 659. (p. 358)

Fletcher, G. J. O., & Ward, C. (1989). Attribution theory and processes: A cross-cultural perspective. In M. H. Bond (Ed.), *The cross-cultural challenge to social psychology.* Newbury Park, CA: Sage. (p. 423)

Flynn, F. J., & Wiltermuth, S. S. (2010). Who's with me? False consensus, brokerage, and ethical decision-making in organizations. *Academic of Management Journal, 53,* 1074–1089. (p. 65)

Foa, U. G., & Foa, E. B. (1975). *Resource theory of social exchange.* Morristown, NJ: General Learning Press. (p. 275)

Fogelman, E. (1994). *Conscience and courage: Rescuers of Jews during the Holocaust.* New York: Doubleday Anchor. (p. 303)

Follett, M. P. (1940). Constructive conflict. In H. C. Metcalf & L. Urwick (Eds.), *Dynamic administration: The collected papers of Mary Parker Follett.* New York: Harper. (p. 463)

Ford, R. (2008). Is racial prejudice declining in Britain? *British Journal of Sociology, 59,* 609–636. (p. 429)

Ford, T. E., Boxer, C. F., Armstrong, J., & Edel, J. R. (2008). More than "just a joke": The prejudice-releasing function of sexist humor. *Personality and Social Psychology Bulletin, 34,* 159–170. (p. 405)

Forgas, J. P. (1999). Behind the scenes. In D. G. Myers, *Social psychology,* 6th edition. New York: McGraw-Hill. (p. 100)

Forgas, J. P. (2007). When sad is better than happy: Negative affect can improve the quality and effectiveness of persuasive messages and social influence strategies. *Journal of Experimental Social Psychology, 43,* 513–528. (p. 167)

Forgas, J. P., Bower, G. H., & Krantz, S. E. (1984). The influence of mood on perceptions of social interactions. *Journal of Experimental Social Psychology, 20,* 497–513. (p. 100)

Forgas, J. P., Dunn, E., & Granland, S. (2008). Are you being served . . . ? An unobtrusive experiment of affective influences on helping in a department store. *European Journal of Social Psychology, 38,* 333–342. (p. 278)

Forgas, J. P., & Moylan, S. (1987). After the movies: Transient mood and social judgments. *Personality and Social Psychology Bulletin, 13,* 467–477. (p. 100)

Form, W. H., & Nosow, S. (1958). *Community in disaster.* New York: Harper. (p. 284)

Forster, E. M. (1976). *Aspects of the novel* (Ed. O. Stallybrass). Harmondsworth: Penguin. (Original work published 1927.) (p. 150)

Forsyth, D. R., Berger, R. E., & Mitchell, T. (1981). The effects of self-serving vs. other-serving claims of responsibility on attraction and attribution in groups. *Social Psychology Quarterly, 44,* 59–64. (p. 73)

Forsyth, D. R., Kerr, N. A., Burnette, J. L., & Baumeister, R. F. (2007). Attempting to improve the academic performance of struggling college students by bolstering their self-esteem: An intervention that backfired. *Journal of Social and Clinical Psychology, 26,* 447–459. (p. 52)

Foss, R. D. (1978). *The role of social influence in blood donation.* Paper presented at the American Psychological Association convention. (p. 301)

Fowler, J. H., & Christakis, N. A. (2008). Dynamic spread of happiness in a large social network: Longitudinal analysis over 20 years in the Framingham Heart Study. *British Medical Journal,* 337 (doi: 10.1136/bmj.a2338). (p. 477)

Frank, J. (1974). *Persuasion and healing: A comparative study of psychotherapy.* New York: Schocken. (p. 186)

Frank, J. D. (1982). Therapeutic components shared by all psychotherapies. In J. H. Harvey, & M. M. Parks (Eds.), *Psychotherapy research and behavior change,* Vol. 1 (pp. 9–37). Washington, DC: American Psychological Association. (p. 186)

Frank, R. (1999). *Luxury fever: Why money fails to satisfy in an era of excess.* New York: The Free Press. (p. 407)

Frasure-Smith, N., & Lespérance, F. (2005). Depression and coronary heart disease:

Complex synergism of mind, body, and environment. *Current Directions in Psychological Science, 14,* 39–43. (p. 484)

Frasure-Smith, N., Lespérance, F., Juneau, M., Talajic, M., & Bourassa, M. G. (1999). Gender, depression, and one-year prognosis after myocardial infarction. *Psychosomatic Medicine, 61,* 26–37. (p. 484)

Frasure-Smith, N., Lespérance, F., & Talajic, M. (1995). The impact of negative emotions on prognosis following myocardial infarction: Is it more than depression? *Health Psychology, 14,* 388–398. (p. 484)

Frederick, D. A., & Haselton, M. G. (2007). Why is muscularity sexy? Tests of the fitness indicator hypothesis. *Personality and Social Psychology Bulletin, 8,* 1167–1183. (p. 366)

Freedman, J. L., Birsky, J., & Cavoukian, A. (1980). Environmental determinants of behavioral contagion: Density and number. *Basic and Applied Social Psychology, 1,* 155–161. (p. 236)

Freedman, J. L., Cunningham, J. A., & Krismer, K. (1992). Inferred values and the reverse-incentive effect in induced compliance. *Journal of Personality and Social Psychology, 62,* 357–368. (p. 149)

Freedman, J. L., & Fraser, S. C. (1966). Compliance without pressure: The foot-in-the-door technique. *Journal of Personality and Social Psychology, 4,* 195–202. (p. 133)

Freedman, J. L., & Perlick, D. (1979). Crowding, contagion, and laughter. *Journal of Experimental Social Psychology, 15,* 295–303. (p. 236)

Freedman, J. L., & Sears, D. O. (1965). Warning, distraction, and resistance to influence. *Journal of Personality and Social Psychology, 1,* 262–266. (p. 180)

Freedman, J. S. (1965). Long-term behavioral effects of cognitive dissonance. *Journal of Experimental Social Psychology, 1,* 145–155. (p. 136)

Freeman, M. A. (1997). Demographic correlates of individualism and collectivism: A study of social values in Sri Lanka. *Journal of Cross-Cultural Psychology, 28,* 321–341. (p. 41)

French, J. R. P. (1968). The conceptualization and the measurement of mental health in terms of self-identity theory. In S. B. Sells (Ed.), *The definition and measurement of mental health.* Washington, DC: Department of Health, Education, and Welfare. (Cited by M. Rosenberg, 1979, Conceiving the self. New York: Basic Books.) (p. 63)

Freund, B., Colgrove, L. A., Burke, B. L., & McLeod, R. (2005). Self-rated driving performance among elderly drivers referred for driving evaluation. *Accident Analysis and Prevention, 37,* 613–618. (p. 64)

Frey, B. S., Savage, D. A., & Torgler, B. (2010). Interaction of natural survival instincts and internalized social norms exploring the Titanic and Lusitania disasters. *Proceedings of the National Academy of Sciences USA, 107,* 4862–4865. (p. 300)

Friedman, H. S., & DiMatteo, M. R. (1989). *Health psychology.* Englewood Cliffs, NJ: Prentice-Hall. (p. 483)

Friedman, H. S., Riggio, R. E., & Casella, D. F. (1988). Nonverbal skill, personal charisma, and initial attraction. *Personality and Social Psychology Bulletin, 14,* 203–211. (p. 371)

Friedman, R., & Elliot, A. J. (2008). The effect of arm crossing on persistence and performance. *European Journal of Social Psychology, 38,* 449–461. (p. 148)

Friedrich, J. (1996). On seeing oneself as less self-serving than others: The ultimate self-serving bias? *Teaching of Psychology, 23,* 107–109. (p. 70)

Friedrich, L. K., & Stein, A. H. (1973). Aggressive and prosocial television programs and the natural behavior of preschool children. *Monographs of the Society of Research in Child Development, 38* (4, Serial No. 151). (p. 305)

Friedrich, L. K., & Stein, A. H. (1975). Prosocial television and young children: The effects of verbal labeling and role playing on learning and behavior. *Child Development, 46,* 27–38. (p. 305)

Frieze, I. H., Olson, J. E., & Russell, J. (1991). Attractiveness and income for men and women in management. *Journal of Applied Social Psychology, 21,* 1039–1057. (p. 363)

Frisell, T., Lichtenstein, P., & Långström, N. (2011). Violent crime runs in families: A total population study of 12.5 million individuals. *Journal of Research in Psychiatry and the Allied Sciences, 41,* 97–105. (p. 313)

Froming, W. J., Walker, G. R., & Lopyan, K. J. (1982). Public and private self-awareness: When personal attitudes conflict with societal expectations. *Journal of Experimental Social Psychology, 18,* 476–487. (p. 128)

Fuller, S. R., & Aldag, R. J. (1998). Organizational Tonypandy: Lessons from a quarter century of the groupthink phenomenon. *Organizational Behavior and Human Decision Processes,* in press. (p. 259)

Funder, D. C. (1987). Errors and mistakes: Evaluating the accuracy of social judgment. *Psychological Bulletin, 101,* 75–90. (p. 116)

Funder, D. C., Levine, J. M., Mackie, D. M., Morf, C. C., Vazire, S. & West, S. G. (2014). Notice: PSPB articles by authors with retracted articles at PSPB or other journals: Stapel, Smeesters, and Sanna. *Personality and Social Psychology Bulletin, 40,* 132–135. (p. 28)

Furnham, A. (1982). Explanations for unemployment in Britain. *European Journal of Social Psychology, 12,* 335–352. (p. 109)

Furnham, A., & Gunter, B. (1984). Just world beliefs and attitudes towards the poor. *British Journal of Social Psychology, 23,* 265–269. (p. 415)

Gable, S. L., Gonzaga, G. C., & Strachman, A. (2006). Will you be there for me when things go right? Supportive responses to positive event disclosures. *Journal of Personality and Social Psychology, 91,* 904–917. (p. 387)

Gabrenya, W. K., Jr., Wang, Y.-E., & Latané, B. (1985). Social loafing on an optimizing task: Cross-cultural differences among Chinese and Americans. *Journal of Cross-Cultural Psychology, 16,* 223–242. (p. 242)

Gaebelein, J. W., & Mander, A. (1978). Consequences for targets of aggression as a function of aggressor and instigator roles: Three experiments. *Personality and Social Psychology Bulletin, 4,* 465–468. (p. 342)

Gaertner, L., Iuzzini, J., Witt, M. G., & Oriña, M. M. (2006). Us without them: Evidence for an intragroup origin of positive ingroup regard. *Journal of Personality and Social Psychology, 90,* 426–439. (p. 411)

Gaertner, L., Sedikides, C., & Chang, K. (2008). On pancultural self-enhancement: Well-adjusted Taiwanese self-enhance on personally valued traits. *Journal of Cross-Cultural Psychology, 39,* 463–477. (p. 61)

Gaertner, L., Sedikides, C., & Graetz, K. (1999). In search of self-definition: Motivational primacy of the individual self, motivational primacy of the collective self, or contextual primacy? *Journal of Personality and Social Psychology, 76,* 5–18. (p. 44)

Gailliot, M. T. (2008). Unlocking the energy dynamics of executive function: Linking executive functioning to brain glycogen.

Perspectives on Psychological Science, 3, 245–263. (p. 57)

Gailliot, M. T., & Baumeister, R. F. (2007). Self-regulation and sexual restraint. Dispositionally and temporarily poor self-regulatory abilities contribute to failures at restraining sexual behavior. *Personality and Social Psychology Bulletin, 33,* 173–186. (p. 57)

Galanter, M. (1989). *Cults: Faith, healing, and coercion.* New York: Oxford University Press. (p. 186)

Galanter, M. (1990). Cults and zealous self-help movements: A psychiatric perspective. *American Journal of Psychiatry, 147,* 543–551. (p. 186)

Galinsky, A. D., & Moskowitz, G. B. (2000). Perspective-taking: Decreasing stereotype expression, stereotype accessibility, and in-group favoritism. *Journal of Personality and Social Psychology, 78,* 708–724. (p. 465)

Galinsky, E., Aumann, K., & Bond, J. T. (2009). *Times are changing: Gender and generation at work and at home.* New York: Families and Work Institute. (p. 61)

Galizio, M., & Hendrick, C. (1972). Effect of musical accompaniment on attitude: The guitar as a prop for persuasion. *Journal of Applied Social Psychology, 2,* 350–359. (p. 167)

Gallo, L. C., & Matthews, K. A. (2003). Understanding the association between socioeconomic status and physical health: Do negative emotions play a role? *Psychological Bulletin, 129,* 10. (p. 489)

Gallup, G. G., Jr., & Frederick, D. A. (2010). The science of sex appeal: An evolutionary perspective. *Journal of General Psychology, 14,* 240–250. (p. 366)

Gallup, G. G., Jr., & Frederick, M. J., & Pipitone, R. N. (2008). Morphology and behavior: Phrenology revisited. *Review of General Psychology, 12,* 297–304. (p. 365)

Gallup, G. H., Jr., & Jones, T. (1992). *The saints among us.* Harrisburg, PA: Morehouse. (p. 405)

Gangestad, S. W., Simpson, J. A., Cousins, A. J., Garver-Apgar, C. E., & Christensen, P. N. (2004). Women's preferences for male behavioral displays change across the menstrual cycle. *Psychological Science, 15,* 203. (p. 366)

Gangestad, S. W., & Snyder, M. (2000). Self-monitoring: Appraisal and reappraisal. *Psychological Bulletin, 126,* 530–555. (p. 73)

Gangestad, S. W., & Thornhill, R. (1997). Human sexual selection and developmental stability. In J. A. Simpson & D. T. Kenrick (Eds.), *Evolutionary social psychology.* Mahway, NJ: Erlbaum. (p. 365)

Garb, H. N. (1994). Judgment research: Implications for clinical practice and testimony in court. *Applied and Preventive Psychology, 3,* 173–183. (p. 475)

Garb, H. N. (2005). Clinical judgment and decision making. *Annual Review of Clinical Psychology, 1,* 67. (p. 472)

Garcia-Marques, T., Mackie, D. M., Claypool, H. M., & Garcia-Marques, L. (2004). Positivity can cue familiarity. *Personality and Social Psychology Bulletin, 30,* 585. (p. 357)

Gardner, M. (1997, July/August). Heaven's Gate: The UFO cult of Bo and Peep. *Skeptical Inquirer,* 15–17. (p. 182)

Garrett, B. L. (2011, April 12). Getting it wrong: Convicting the innocent. *Slate* (www.slate.com). (pp. 499, 502)

Garry, M., Manning, C. G., Loftus, E. F., & Sherman, S. J. (1996). Imagination inflation: Imagining a childhood event inflates confidence that it occurred. *Psychonomic Bulletin & Review, 3,* 208–214. (p. 501)

Garver-Apgar, C. E., Gangestad, S. W., Thornhill, R., Miller, R. D., & Olp, J. J. (2006). Major histocompatibility complex alleles, sexual responsivity, and unfaithfulness in romantic couples. *Psychological Science, 17,* 830–834. (p. 371)

Gates, G. J. (2011, April). *How many people are lesbian, gay, bisexual, and transgender?* Los Angeles: The William Institute, UCLA School of Law. (p. 95)

Gates, M. F., & Allee, W. C. (1933). Conditioned behavior of isolated and grouped cockroaches on a simple maze. *Journal of Comparative Psychology, 15,* 331–358. (p. 234)

Gaucher, D., Friesen, J., & Kay, A. C. (2011). Evidence that gendered wording in job advertisements exists and sustains gender inequality. *Journal of Personality and Social Psychology, 101,* 109–128. (p. 400)

Gaunt, R. (2006). Couple similarity and marital satisfaction: Are similar spouses happier? *Journal of Personality, 74,* 1401–1420. (p. 369)

Gavanski, I., & Hoffman, C. (1987). Awareness of influences on one's own judgments: The roles of covariation detection and attention to the judgment process. *Journal of Personality and Social Psychology, 52,* 453–463. (p. 50)

Gawande, A. (2002). *Complications: A surgeon's notes on an imperfect science.* New York: Metropolitan Books, Holt and Company. (p. 63)

Gawronski, B., & Bodenhausen, G. V. (2006). Associative and propositional processes in evaluation: An integrative review of implicit and explicit attitude change. *Psychological Bulletin, 132,* 692–731. (p. 51)

Gazzaniga, M. (1985). *The social brain: Discovering the networks of the mind.* New York: Basic Books. (p. 129)

Gazzaniga, M. (1998). *The mind's past.* Berkeley, CA: University of California Press. (p. 89)

Gazzaniga, M. (2008). *Human: The science behind what makes us unique.* New York: Ecco. (p. 89)

Gazzaniga, M. S. (1992). *Nature's mind: The biological roots of thinking, emotions, sexuality, language, and intelligence.* New York: Basic Books. (p. 89)

Geen, R. G. (1998). Aggression and antisocial behavior. In D. Gilbert, S. Fiske, & G. Lindzey (Eds.), *Handbook of social psychology,* 4th ed. New York: McGraw-Hill. (p. 315)

Geen, R. G., & Gange, J. J. (1983). Social facilitation: Drive theory and beyond. In H. H. Blumberg, A. P. Hare, V. Kent, & M. Davies (Eds.), *Small groups and social interaction,* Vol. 1. London: Wiley. (p. 236)

Geen, R. G., & Thomas, S. L. (1986). The immediate effects of media violence on behavior. *Journal of Social Issues, 42*(3), 7–28. (p. 335)

Geers, A. L., Handley, I. M., & McLarney, A. R. (2003). Discerning the role of optimism in persuasion: The valence-enhancement hypothesis. *Journal of Personality and Social Psychology, 85,* 554–565. (p. 172)

Gentile, D. A. (2004, May 14). Quoted by K. Laurie in *Violent games* (ScienCentral. com). (p. 338)

Gentile, D. A., & Anderson, C. A. (2003). Violent video games: The newest media violence hazard. In D. A. Gentile (Ed.), *Media violence and children.* Westport, CT: Ablex. (p. 337)

Gentile, D. A., & Anderson, C. A. (2011, June 30). Don't read more into the Supreme Court's ruling on the California video game law. News release, Iowa State University. Newswise (www.newswise.com). (p. 341)

Gentile, D. A., Anderson, C. A., Yukawa, S., Ihori, N., Saleem, M., Ming, L. K., Shiuya,

A., Liau, A. K., Khoo, A., Bushman, B. J., Buesmann, L. R., & Sakamoto, A. (2009). The effects of prosocial video games on prosocial behaviors: International evidence from correlational, longitudinal, and experimental studies. *Personality and Social Psychology Bulletin, 35,* 752–763. (pp. 305, 341)

Gentile, D. A., Lynch, P. J., Linder, J. R., & Walsh, D. A. (2004). The effects of violent video game habits on adolescent hostility, aggressive behaviors, and school performance. *Journal of Adolescence, 27,* 5. (pp. 333, 339)

Gentile, D. A., Saleem, M., & Anderson, C. A. (2007). Public policy and the effects of media violence on children. *Social Issues and Policy Review, 1,* 15–61. (p. 335)

George, D., Carroll, P., Kersnick, R., & Calderon, K. (1998). Gender-related patterns of helping among friends. *Psychology of Women Quarterly, 22,* 685–704. (p. 300)

Gerard, H. B. (1999). A social psychologist examines his past and looks to the future. In A. Rodrigues, & R. V. Levine (Eds.), *Reflections on 100 years of experimental social psychology,* 47–81. New York: Basic Books. (p. 219)

Gerard, H. B., & Mathewson, G. C. (1966). The effects of severity of initiation on liking for a group: A replication. *Journal of Experimental Social Psychology, 2,* 278–287. (p. 183)

Gerard, H. B., Wilhelmy, R. A., & Conolley, E. S. (1968). Conformity and group size. *Journal of Personality and Social Psychology, 8,* 79–82. (p. 214)

Gerber, J., & Wheeler, L. (2009a). On being rejected: A meta-analysis of experimental research on rejection. *Perspectives on Psychological Science, 4,* 468–488. (p. 353)

Gerber, J., & Wheeler, L. (2009b). Rejoinder to Baumeister, DeWall, and Vohs (2009). *Perspectives on Psychological Science, 4,* 494–495. (p. 353)

Gerbner, G. (1994). The politics of media violence: Some reflections. In C. Hamelink & O. Linne (Eds.), *Mass communication research: On problems and policies.* Norwood, NJ: Ablex. (pp. 332, 336)

Gerbner, G., Gross, L., Signorielli, N., Morgan, M., & Jackson-Beeck, M. (1979). The demonstration of power: Violence profile No. 10. *Journal of Communication, 29,* 177–196. (p. 336)

Gergen, K. E. (1982). *Toward transformation in social knowledge.* New York: Springer-Verlag. (p. 306)

Gergen, K. J., Gergen, M. M., & Barton, W. H. (1973, October). Deviance in the dark. *Psychology Today,* 129–130. (p. 246)

Gerrig, R. J. & Prentice, D. A. (1991, September). The representation of fictional information. *Psychological Science, 2,* 336–340. (p. 95)

Gershoff, E. T. (2002). Corporal punishment by parents and associated child behaviors and experiences: A meta-analytic and theoretical review. *Psychological Bulletin, 128,* 539–579. (p. 321)

Gerstenfeld, P. B., Grant, D. R., & Chiang, C. (2003). Hate online: A content analysis of extremist Internet sites. *Analyses of Social Issues and Public Policy (ASAP), 3,* 29. (p. 251)

Gesch, C. B., Hammond, S. M., Hampson, S. E., Eves, A., & Crowder, M. J. (2002). Influence of supplementary vitamins, minerals and essential fatty acids on the antisocial behavior of young adult prisoners. Randomised, placebo-controlled trial. *British Journal of Psychiatry, 181,* 22–28. (p. 315)

Giancola, P. R., & Corman, M. D. (2007). Alcohol and aggression: A test of the attention-allocation model. *Psychological Science, 18,* 649–655. (p. 314)

Gibbons, F. X. (1978). Sexual standards and reactions to pornography: Enhancing behavioral consistency through self-focused attention. *Journal of Personality and Social Psychology, 36,* 976–987. (p. 128)

Gibbons, F. X., Eggleston, T. J., & Benthin, A. C. (1997). Cognitive reactions to smoking relapse: The reciprocal relation between dissonance and self-esteem. *Journal of Personality and Social Psychology, 72,* 184–195. (p. 140)

Gibbons, F. X., & Wicklund, R. A. (1982). Self-focused attention and helping behavior. *Journal of Personality and Social Psychology, 43,* 462–474. (p. 277)

Gibson, B., & Sanbonmatsu, D. M. (2004). Optimism, pessimism, and gambling: The downside of optimism. *Personality and Social Psychology Bulletin, 30,* 149–160. (p. 64)

Gifford, R. (2011). The dragons of inaction: Psychological barriers that limit climate change mitigation and adaptation. *American Psychologist, 66,* 290–302. (p. 518)

Gifford, R., & Hine, D. W. (1997). Toward cooperation in commons dilemmas. *Canadian Journal of Behavioural Science, 29,* 167–179. (p. 457)

Gigerenzer, G. (2007). *Gut feelings: The intelligence of the unconscious.* New York: Viking. (p. 89)

Gigerenzer, G., & Gaissmaier, W. (2011). Heuristic decision making. *Annual Review of Psychology, 62,* 451–482. (p. 116)

Gigone, D., & Hastie, R. (1993). The common knowledge effect: Information sharing and group judgment. *Journal of Personality and Social Psychology, 65,* 959–974. (p. 252)

Gilbert, D. (2007). *Stumbling on happiness.* New York: Knopf. (p. 47)

Gilbert, D. (2011, June 7). Introduction (to conversation with Timothy Wilson). *The Edge* (www.edge.org). (p. 47)

Gilbert, D. T., & Ebert, J. E. J. (2002). *Decisions and revisions: The affective forecasting of escapable outcomes.* Unpublished manuscript, Harvard University. (pp. 48, 59)

Gilbert, D. T., Giesler, R. B., & Morris, K. A. (1995). When comparisons arise. *Journal of Personality and Social Psychology, 69,* 227–236. (p. 40)

Gilbert, D. T., & Hixon, J. G. (1991). The trouble of thinking: Activation and application of stereotypic beliefs. *Journal of Personality and Social Psychology, 60,* 509–517. (p. 417)

Gilbert, D. T., & Jones, E. E. (1986). Perceiver-induced constraint: Interpretations of self-generated reality. *Journal of Personality and Social Psychology, 50,* 269–280. (p. 105)

Gilbert, D. T., Killingsworth, M. A., Eyre, R. N., & Wilson, T. D. (2009). The surprising power of neighborly advice. *Science, 323,* 1617–1619. (p. 49)

Gilbert, D. T., Krull, D. S., & Malone, P. S. (1990). Unbelieving the unbelievable: Some problems in the rejection of false information. *Journal of Personality and Social Psychology, 59,* 601–613. (p. 187)

Gilbert, D. T., Lieberman, M. D., Morewedge, C. K., & Wilson, T. D. (2004). The peculiar longevity of things not so bad. *Psychological Science, 15,* 14–19. (p. 50)

Gilbert, D. T., & Malone, P. S. (1995). The correspondence bias. *Psychological Bulletin, 117,* 21–38. (p. 102)

Gilbert, D. T., Pinel, E. C., Wilson, T. D., Blumberg, S. J., & Wheatley, T. P. (1998). Immune neglect: A source of durability bias in affective forecasting. *Journal of Personality and Social Psychology, 75,* 617–638. (pp. 49, 525)

Gilbert, D. T., Tafarodi, R. W., & Malone, P. S. (1993). You can't not believe everything you read. *Journal of Personality and Social Psychology, 65,* 221–233. (p. 187)

Gilbert, D. T., & Wilson, T. D. (2000). Miswanting: Some problems in the forecasting of future affective states. In J. Forgas (Ed.), *Feeling and thinking: The role of affect in social cognition.* Cambridge, UK: Cambridge University Press. (pp. 49, 50)

Gillath, O. M., Shaver, P. R., Baek, J-M., & Chun, D. S. (2008). Genetic correlates of adult attachment. *Personality and Social Psychology Bulletin, 34,* 1396–1405. (p. 385)

Gillis, J. (2011, December 16). As permafrost thaws, scientists study the risks. *New York Times* (www.nytimes.com). (p. 516)

Gilovich, T., & Douglas, C. (1986). Biased evaluations of randomly determined gambling outcomes. *Journal of Experimental Social Psychology, 22,* 228–241. (p. 98)

Gilovich, T., & Eibach, R. (2001). The fundamental attribution error where it really counts. *Psychological Inquiry, 12*(1), 23. (p. 110)

Gilovich, T., Kerr, M., & Medvec, V. H. (1993). Effect of temporal perspective on subjective confidence. *Journal of Personality and Social Psychology, 64,* 552–560. (p. 92)

Gilovich, T., & Medvec, V. H. (1994). The temporal pattern to the experience of regret. *Journal of Personality and Social Psychology, 67,* 357–365. (p. 97)

Gilovich, T., Savitsky, K., & Medvec, V. H. (1998). *The illusion of transparency: Biased assessments of others' ability to read our emotional states.* Unpublished manuscript, Cornell University. (p. 292)

Gilovich, T., Wang, R. F., Regan, D., & Nishina, S. (2003). Regrets of action and inaction across cultures. *Journal of Cross-Cultural Psychology, 34,* 61–71. (p. 97)

Giltay, E. J., Geleijnse, J. M., Zitman, F. G., Buijsse, B., & Kromhout, D. (2007). Lifestyle and dietary correlates of dispositional optimism in men: The Zutphen Elderly Study. *Journal of Psychosomatic Research, 63,* 483–490. (p. 486)

Giltay, E. J., Geleijnse, J. M., Zitman, F. G., Hoekstra, T., & Schouten, E. G. (2004). Dispositional optimism and all-cause and cardiovascular mortality in a prospective cohort of elderly Dutch men and women.

Archives of General Psychiatry, 61, 1126–1135. (p. 486)

Gino, F., Ayal, S., & Ariely, D. (2009). Contagion and differentiation in unethical behavior: The effect of one bad apple on the barrel. *Psychological Science, 20,* 393–398. (p. 217)

Ginsburg, B., & Allee, W. C. (1942). Some effects of conditioning on social dominance and subordination in inbred strains of mice. *Physiological Zoology, 15,* 485–506. (p. 319)

Glasman, L. R., & Albarracin, D. (2006). Forming attitudes that predict future behavior: A meta-analysis of the attitude-behavior relation. *Psychological Bulletin, 132,* 778–822. (p. 128)

Glass, D. C. (1964). Changes in liking as a means of reducing cognitive discrepancies between self-esteem and aggression. *Journal of Personality, 32,* 531–549. (p. 135)

Gleason, M. E. J., Masumi, I., Bolger, N., & Shrout, P. E. (2003). Daily supportive equity in close relationships. *Personality and Social Psychology Bulletin, 29,* 1036–1045. (p. 275)

Glenn, N. D. (1980). Aging and attitudinal stability. In O. G. Brim, Jr., & J. Kagan (Eds.), *Constancy and change in human development.* Cambridge, MA: Harvard University Press. (p. 179)

Glick, P., & Fiske, S. T. (1996). The ambivalent sexism inventory: Differentiating hostile and benevolent sexism. *Journal of Personality and Social Psychology, 70,* 491–512. (p. 434)

Glick, P., & Fiske, S. T. (2001). An ambivalent alliance: Hostile and benevolent sexism as complementary justifications for gender inequality. *American Psychologist, 56,* 109–118. (p. 402)

Glick, P., & Fiske, S. T. (2007). Sex discrimination: The psychological approach. In F. J. Crosby, M. S. Stockdale, & S. Ropp (Eds.), *Sex discrimination in the workplace: Multidisciplinary perspectives.* Malden, MA: Blackwell. (p. 434)

Glick, P., Lameiras, M., Fiske, S. T., Eckes, T., Masser, B., Volpato, C., et al. (2004). Bad but bold: Ambivalent attitudes toward men predict gender inequality in 16 nations. *Journal of Personality and Social Psychology, 86,* 713. (p. 434)

Gluszek, A., & Dovidio, J. F. (2010). The way *they* speak: A social psychological perspective on the stigma of nonnative accents in communication. *Personality*

and Social Psychology Review, 14, 214–237. (p. 408)

Gockel, C., Kerr, N. L., Seok, D-H., & Harris, D. W. (2008). Indispensability and group identification as sources of task motivation. *Journal of Experimental Social Psychology, 44,* 1316–1321. (p. 242)

Goel, S., Mason, W., & Watts, D. J. (2010). Real and perceived attitude agreement in social networks. *Journal of Personality and Social Psychology, 99,* 611–621. (p. 65)

Goethals, G. R., Messick, D. M., & Allison, S. T. (1991). The uniqueness bias: Studies of constructive social comparison. In J. Suls & T. A. Wills (Eds.), *Social comparison: Contemporary theory and research.* Hillsdale, NJ: Erlbaum. (p. 65)

Goethals, G. R., & Nelson, E. R. (1973). Similarity in the influence process: The belief-value distinction. *Journal of Personality and Social Psychology, 25,* 117–122. (p. 165)

Goethals, G. R., & Zanna, M. P. (1979). The role of social comparison in choice shifts. *Journal of Personality and Social Psychology, 37,* 1469–1476. (p. 254)

Goetz, J. L., Keltner, D., & Simon-Thomas, E. (2010). Compassion: An evolutionary analysis and empirical review. *Psychological Bulletin, 136,* 351–374. (p. 281)

Goggin, W. C., & Range, L. M. (1985). The disadvantages of hindsight in the perception of suicide. *Journal of Social and Clinical Psychology, 3,* 232–237. (p. 473)

Goh, J. O., Chee, M. W., Tan, J. C., Venkatraman, V., Hebrank, A., Leshikar, E. D., Jenkins, L., Sutton, B. P., Gutchess, A. H., & Park, D. C. (2007). Age and culture modulate object processing and object-science binding in the ventral visual area. *Cognitive, Affective & Behavioral Neuroscience, 7,* 44–52. (p. 42)

Goldberg, P. (1968). Are women prejudiced against women? *Transaction, 5,* 28–30. (p. 435)

Goldhagen, D. J. (1996). *Hitler's willing executioners.* New York: Knopf. (pp. 209, 213)

Goldman, W., & Lewis, P. (1977). Beautiful is good: Evidence that the physically attractive are more socially skillful. *Journal of Experimental Social Psychology, 13,* 125–130. (p. 363)

Goldstein, A. P. (1994). Delinquent gangs. In A. P. Goldstein, B. Harootunian, and J. C. Conoley (Eds.), *Student aggression: Prevention, control, and replacement.* New York: Guilford. (p. 342)

Goldstein, A. P., & Glick, B. (1994). Aggression replacement training: Curriculum and evaluation. *Simulation and Gaming, 25*, 9–26. (p. 347)

Goldstein, J. H., & Arms, R. L. (1971). Effects of observing athletic contests on hostility. *Sociometry, 34*, 83–90. (p. 345)

Golec de Zavala, A., Cichocka, A., Eidelson, R., & Jayawickreme, N. (2009). Collective narcissism and its social consequences. *Journal of Personality and Social Psychology, 97*, 1074–1096. (p. 55)

Goleman, D. (1993, June 22). Scientist at work: Ervin Staub; studying the pivotal role of bystanders. *New York Times.* (p. 293)

Gómez, Á., Brooks, M. L., Buhrmeister, M. D., Váquez, A., Jetten, J., & Swann, Jr., W. B. (2011). On the nature of identity fusion: Insights into the construct and a new measure. *Journal of Personality and Social Psychology, 100*, 918–933. (p. 408)

Gonsalkorale, K., & Williams, K. D. (2006). The KKK would not let me play: Ostracism even by a despised outgroup hurts. *European Journal of Social Psychology, 36*, 1–11. (p. 354)

Gonsalves, B., Reber, P. J., Gitelman, D. R., Parrish, T. B., Mesulam, M., & Paller, K. A. (2004). Neural evidence that vivid imagining can lead to false remembering. *Psychological Science, 15*, 655. (p. 502)

Gonzaga, G. C., Campos, B., & Bradbury, T. (2007). Similarity, convergence, and relationship satisfaction in dating and married couples. *Journal of Personality and Social Psychology, 93*, 34–48. (p. 369)

Gonzaga, G. C., Keltner, D., Londahl, E. A., & Smith, M. D. (2001). Love and the commitment problem in romantic relations and friendship. *Journal of Personality and Social Psychology, 81*, 247–262. (p. 377)

González-Vallejo, C., Lassiter, G. D., Bellezza, F. S., & Lindberg, M. J. (2008). "Save angels perhaps": A critical examination of unconscious thought theory and the deliberation-without-attention effect. *Review of General Psychology, 12*, 282–296. (p. 88)

Goodhart, D. E. (1986). The effects of positive and negative thinking on performance in an achievement situation. *Journal of Personality and Social Psychology, 51*, 117–124. (p. 65)

Goodsell, C. A., Gronlund, S. D., & Carlson, C. A. (2010). Exploring the sequential lineup advantage using WITNESS. *Law and Human Behavior, 34*, 445–459. (p. 504)

Gordijn, E. H., De Vries, N. K., & De Dreu, C. K. W. (2002). Minority influence on focal

and related attitudes: Change in size, attributions and information processing. *Personality and Social Psychology Bulletin, 28*, 1315. (p. 509)

Gordon, R., & Mentzel, R. K. (1990). Sympathy and altruism in response to disasters. *Journal of Social Psychology, 130*, 309–316. (p. 288)

Gordon, R. A. (1996). Impact of ingratiation on judgments and evaluations: A meta-analytic investigation. *Journal of Personality and Social Psychology, 71*, 54–70. (p. 372)

Gortmaker, S. L., Must, A., Perrin, J. M., Sobol, A. M., & Dietz, W. H. (1993). Social and economic consequences of overweight in adolescence and young adulthood. *New England Journal of Medicine, 329*, 1008–1012. (p. 24)

Gotlib, I. H., & Colby, C. A. (1988). How to have a good quarrel. In P. Marsh (Ed.), *Eye to eye: How people interact.* Topsfield, MA: Salem House. (p. 464)

Gottlieb, J., & Carver, C. S. (1980). Anticipation of future interaction and the bystander effect. *Journal of Experimental Social Psychology, 16*, 253–260. (p. 301)

Gottman, J. (with N. Silver) (1994). *Why marriages succeed or fail.* New York: Simon & Schuster. (p. 393)

Gould, M. S., & Shaffer, D. (1986). The impact of suicide in television movies: Evidence of imitation. *New England Journal of Medicine, 315*, 690–694. (p. 200)

Gould, S. J. (1988, July). Kropotkin was no crackpot. *Natural History*, 12–21. (p. 458)

Gouldner, A. W. (1960). The norm of reciprocity: A preliminary statement. *American Sociological Review, 25*, 161–178. (p. 280)

Gove, W. R., Style, C. B., & Hughes, M. (1990). The effect of marriage on the well-being of adults: A theoretical analysis. *Journal of Family Issues, 11*, 4–35. (p. 492)

Granstrom, K., & Stiwne, D. (1998). A bipolar model of groupthink: An expansion of Janis's concept. *Small Group Research, 29*, 32–56. (p. 259)

Gray, C., Russell, P., & Blockley, S. (1991). The effects upon helping behaviour of wearing pro-gay identification. *British Journal of Social Psychology, 30*, 171–178. (p. 298)

Gray, J. D., & Silver, R. C. (1990). Opposite sides of the same coin: Former spouses' divergent perspectives in coping with their divorce. *Journal of Personality and Social Psychology, 59*, 1180–1191. (p. 61)

Graziano, W. G., Jensen-Campbell, L. A., & Finch, J. F. (1997). The self as a mediator between personality and adjustment. *Journal of Personality and Social Psychology, 73*, 392–404. (p. 57)

Green, A. R., Carney, D. R., Pallin, D. J., Ngo, L. H., Raymond, K. L., Iezzoni, L. I., & Banaji, M. R. (2007). Implicit bias among physicians and its prediction of thrombolysis decisions for Black and White patients. *Journal of General Internal Medicine, 22*, 1231–1238. (p. 430)

Green, M. C., Strange, J. J., & Brock, T. C. (Eds.) (2002). *Narrative impact: Social and cognitive foundations.* Mahwah, NJ: Erlbaum. (p. 95)

Greenberg, J. (1986). Differential intolerance for inequity from organizational and individual agents. *Journal of Applied Social Psychology, 16*, 191–196. (p. 460)

Greenberg, J. (2008). Understanding the vital human quest for self-esteem. *Perspectives on Psychological Science, 3*, 48–55. (p. 53)

Greenberg, J., Landau, M. J., Kosloff, S., & Solomon, S. (2008). How our dreams of death transcendence breed prejudice, stereotyping, and conflict. In T. Nelson (Ed.), *Handbook of prejudice, stereotyping, and discrimination.* New York: Psychology Press. (p. 413)

Greenberg, J., Pyszczynski, T., Solomon, S., Rosenblatt, A., Veeder, M., Kirkland, S., & Lyon, D. (1990). Evidence for terror management theory II: The effects of mortality salience on reactions to those who threaten or bolster the cultural worldview. *Journal of Personality and Social Psychology, 58*, 308–318. (p. 412)

Greenberg, J., Pyszczynski, T., Solomon, S., Simon, L., & Breus, M. (1994). Role of consciousness and accessibility of death-related thoughts in mortality salience effects. *Journal of Personality and Social Psychology, 67*, 627–637. (p. 412)

Greenberg, J., Solomon, S., & Pyszczynski, T. (1997). Terror management theory of self-esteem and cultural worldviews: Empirical assessments and conceptual refinements. *Advances in Experimental Social Psychology, 29*, in press. (p. 69)

Greenwald, A. G. (1975). On the inconclusiveness of crucial cognitive tests of dissonance versus self-perception theories. *Journal of Experimental Social Psychology, 11*, 490–499. (p. 150)

Greenwald, A. G. (1980). The totalitarian ego: Fabrication and revision of personal history. *American Psychologist, 35*, 603–618. (p. 86)

Greenwald, A. G. (1992). New look 3: Unconscious cognition reclaimed. *American Psychologist, 47,* 766–779. (p. 89)

Greenwald, A. G., & Banaji, M. R. (1995). Implicit social cognition: Attitudes, self-esteem, and stereotypes. *Psychological Review, 102,* 4–27. (p. 87)

Greenwald, A. G., Banaji, M. R., Rudman, L. A., Farnham, S. D., Nosek, B. A., & Mellott, D. S. (2002). A unified theory of implicit attitudes, stereotypes, self-esteem, and self-concept. *Psychological Bulletin, 109,* 3–25. (p. 124)

Greenwald, A. G., Banaji, M. R., Rudman, L. A., Farnham, S. D., Nosek, B. A., & Rosier, M. (2000). Prologue to a unified theory of attitudes, stereotypes, and self-concept. In J. P. Forgas (Ed.), *Feeling and thinking: The role of affect in social cognition and behavior.* New York: Cambridge University Press. (p. 401)

Greenwald, A. G., McGhee, D. E., Schwartz, J. L. K. (1998). Measuring individual differences in implicit cognition: The implicit association test. *Journal of Personality and Social Psychology, 74,* 1464–1480. (p. 401)

Greenwald, A. G., Nosek, B. A., & Banaji, M. R. (2003). Understanding and using the implicit association test: I. An improved scoring algorithm. *Journal of Personality and Social Psychology, 85,* 197–216. (p. 124)

Greenwald, A. G., Poehlman, T. A., Uhlmann, E. L., & Banaji, M. R. (2008). Understanding and using the Implicit Association Test: III. Meta-analysis of predictive validity. *Journal of Personality and Social Psychology, 97*(1), 17–41. (pp. 124, 401)

Greenwald, A. G., Oakes, M. A., & Hoffman, H. G. (2003). Targets of discrimination: Effects of race on responses to weapons holders. *Journal of Experimental Social Psychology, 39,* 399–405. (p. 430)

Greenwald, A. G., & Schuh, E. S. (1994). An ethnic bias in scientific citations. *European Journal of Social Psychology, 24,* 623–639. (p. 432)

Greitemeyer, T. (2009). Effects of songs with prosocial lyrics on prosocial thoughts, affect, and behavior. *Journal of Experimental Social Psychology, 45,* 186–190. (p. 305)

Greitemeyer, T. (2011). Exposure to music with prosocial lyrics reduces aggression: First evidence and test of the underlying mechanism. *Journal of Experimental Social Psychology, 47,* 28–36. (pp. 305, 347)

Greitemeyer, T., & McLatchie, N. (2011). Denying humanness to others: A newly discovered mechanism by which violent video games increase aggressive behavior. *Psychological Science, 22,* 659–665. (p. 340)

Greitemeyer, T., & Osswald, S. (2010). Effects of prosocial video games on prosocial behavior. *Journal of Personality and Social Psychology, 98,* 211–221. (p. 305)

Greitemeyer, T., Osswald, S., & Brauer, M. (2010). Playing prosocial video games increases empathy and decreases Schadenfreude. *Emotion, 10,* 796–802. (p. 305)

Griffin, D., & Buehler, R. (1993). Role of construal processes in conformity and dissent. *Journal of Personality and Social Psychology, 65,* 657. (pp. 220, 221)

Griffitt, W. (1970). Environmental effects on interpersonal affective behavior. Ambient effective temperature and attraction. *Journal of Personality and Social Psychology, 15,* 240–244. (p. 323)

Griffitt, W., & Veitch, R. (1971). Hot and crowded: Influences of population density and temperature on interpersonal affective behavior. *Journal of Personality and Social Psychology, 17,* 92–98. (p. 323)

Griskevicius, V., Tybur, J. M., Gangestad, S. W., Perea, E. F., Shapiro, J. R., & Kenrick, D. T. (2009). Aggress to impress: Hostility as an evolved context-dependent strategy. *Journal of Personality and Social Psychology, 96,* 980–994. (p. 312)

Griskevicius, V., Tybur, J. M., Sundie, J. M., Cialdini, R. B., Miller, G. F., & Kenrick, D. T. (2007). Blatant benevolence and conspicuous consumption: When romantic motives elicit strategic costly signals. *Journal of Personality and Social Psychology, 93,* 85–102. (p. 282)

Groenenboom, A., Wilke, H. A. M., & Wit, A. P. (2001). Will we be working together again? The impact of future interdependence on group members' task motivation. *European Journal of Social Psychology, 31,* 369. (p. 242)

Gronlund, S. D. (2004a). Sequential lineups: Shift in criterion or decision strategy? *Journal of Applied Psychology, 89,* 362–368. (p. 504)

Gronlund, S. D. (2004b). Sequential lineup advantage: Contributions of distinctiveness and recollection. *Applied Cognitive Psychology, 19,* 23–37. (p. 504)

Gross, A. E., & Crofton, C. (1977). What is good is beautiful. *Sociometry, 40,* 85–90. (p. 367)

Gross, J. T. (2001). *Neighbors: The destruction of the Jewish community in Jedwabne, Poland.* Princeton: Princeton University Press. (p. 310)

Grote, N. K., & Clark, M. S. (2001). Perceiving unfairness in the family: Cause or consequence of marital distress? *Journal of Personality and Social Psychology, 80,* 281. (p. 387)

Grove, J. R., Hanrahan, S. J., & McInman, A. (1991). Success/failure bias in attributions across involvement categories in sport. *Personality and Social Psychology Bulletin, 17,* 93–97. (p. 60)

Grube, J. W., Kleinhesselink, R. R., & Kearney, K. A. (1982). Male self-acceptance and attraction toward women. *Personality and Social Psychology Bulletin, 8,* 107–112. (p. 413)

Gruder, C. L. (1977). Choice of comparison persons in evaluating oneself. In J. M. Suls & R. L. Miller (Eds.), *Social comparison processes.* Washington, DC: Hemisphere. (p. 40)

Gruder, C. L., Cook, T. D., Hennigan, K. M., Flay, B., Alessis, C., & Kalamaj, J. (1978). Empirical tests of the absolute sleeper effect predicted from the discounting cue hypothesis. *Journal of Personality and Social Psychology, 36,* 1061–1074. (p. 162)

Gruendl, M. (2005, accessed December 14). Beautycheck (www.beautycheck.de). (p. 365)

Gruman, J. C., & Sloan, R. P. (1983). Disease as justice: Perceptions of the victims of physical illness. *Basic and Applied Social Psychology, 4,* 39–46. (p. 415)

Grunberger, R. (1971). *The 12-year-Reich: A social history of Nazi Germany 1933–1945.* New York: Holt, Rinehart & Winston. (p. 138)

Grush, J. E. (1980). Impact of candidate expenditures, regionality, and prior outcomes on the 1976 Democratic presidential primaries. *Journal of Personality and Social Psychology, 38,* 337–347. (p. 175)

Grush, J. E., & Glidden, M. V. (1987). *Power and satisfaction among distressed and non-distressed couples.* Paper presented at the Midwestern Psychological Association convention. (p. 464)

Guadagno, R. E., Rhoads, K. V. L., & Sagarin, B. J. (2011). Figural vividness and persuasion: Capturing the "elusive" vividness effect. *Personality and Social Psychology Bulletin, 37*, 626–638. (p. 169)

Guay, F., Mageau, G. A., & Vallerand, R. J. (2003). On the hierarchical structure of self-determined motivation: A test of top-down, bottom-up, reciprocal, and horizontal effects. *Personality & Social Psychology Bulletin, 29*(8), 992–1004. (p. 58)

Gueguen, N. & Jacob, C. (2001). Fundraising on the Web: The effect of an electronic foot-in-the-door on donation. *CyberPsychology and Behavior, 4*, 705–709. (p. 133)

Guerin, B. (1993). *Social facilitation.* Paris: Cambridge University Press. (p. 235)

Guerin, B. (1994). What do people think about the risks of driving? Implications for traffic safety interventions. *Journal of Applied Social Psychology, 24*, 994–1021. (p. 63)

Guerin, B. (1999). Social behaviors as determined by different arrangements of social consequences: Social loafing, social facilitation, deindividuation, and a modified social loafing. *The Psychological Record, 49*, 565–578. (p. 235)

Guimond, S., Dambrun, N., Michinov, N., & Duarte, S. (2003). Does social dominance generate prejudice? Integrating individual and contextual determinants of intergroup cognitions. *Journal of Personality and Social Psychology, 84*, 697–721. (p. 403)

Guiness, O. (1993). *The American hour: A time of reckoning and the once and future role of faith.* New York: Free Press. (p. 391)

Gupta, U., & Singh, P. (1982). Exploratory study of love and liking and type of marriages. *Indian Journal of Applied Psychology, 19*, 92–97. (pp. 381, 382)

Gutierres, S. E., Kenrick, D. T., & Partch, J. J. (1999). Beauty, dominance, and the mating game: Contrast effects in self-assessment reflect gender differences in mate selection. *Journal of Personality and Social Psychology, 25*, 1126–1134. (p. 367)

Hacker, H. M. (1951). Women as a minority group. *Social Forces, 30*, 60–69. (p. 402)

Hackman, J. R. (1986). The design of work teams. In J. Lorsch (Ed.), *Handbook of organizational behavior.* Englewood Cliffs, NJ: Prentice-Hall. (p. 242)

Hadden, J. K. (1969). *The gathering storm in the churches.* Garden City, NY: Doubleday. (p. 405)

Haddock, G., Maio, G. R., Arnold, K., & Huskinson, T. (2008). Should persuasion be affective or cognitive? The moderating effects of need for affect and need for cognition. *Personality and Social Psychology Bulletin, 34*, 769–778. (p. 180)

Haddock, G, & Zanna, M.P. (1994). Preferring "housewives" to "feminists." *Psychology of Women Quarterly, 18*, 25–52. (p. 434)

Hafer, C. L. (2000). Do innocent victims threaten the belief in a just world? Evidence from a modified Stroop task. *Journal of Personality and Social Psychology, 79*(2), 165–173. (p. 414)

Hafer, C. L., & Bègue, L. (2005). Experimental research on just-world theory: Problems, developments, and future challenges. *Psychological Bulletin, 131*, 128. (p. 414)

Hafer, C. L., & Olson, J. M. (2003). An analysis of empirical research on the scope of justice. *Personality and Social Psychology Review, 7* (4), 311–323. (p. 414)

Hagerty, M. R. (2000). Social comparisons of income in one's community: Evidence from national surveys of income and happiness. *Journal of Personality and Social Psychology, 78*, 764–771. (p. 318)

Haidt, J. (2003). The moral emotions. In R. J. Davidson (Ed.), *Handbook of affective sciences.* Oxford: Oxford University Press. (p. 297)

Haidt, J. (2006). *The happiness hypothesis: Finding modern truth in ancient wisdom.* New York: Basic Books. (p. 37)

Halberstadt, J. (2006). The generality and ultimate origins of the attractiveness of prototypes. *Personality and Social Psychology Review, 10*, 166–183. (p. 365)

Hall, D. L., Matz, D. C., & Wood, W. (2010). Why don't we practice what we preach? A meta-analytic review of religious racism. *Personality and Social Psychology Review, 14*, 126–139. (p. 404)

Hall, T. (1985, June 25). The unconverted: Smoking of cigarettes seems to be becoming a lower-class habit. *Wall Street Journal, 1*, 25. (p. 86)

Halverson, A. M., Hallahan, M., Hart, A. J., & Rosenthal, R. (1997). Reducing the biasing effects of judges' nonverbal behavior with simplified jury instruction. *Journal of Applied Psychology, 82*, 590–598. (p. 508)

Hamblin, R. L., Buckholdt, D., Bushell, D., Ellis, D., & Feritor, D. (1969, January). Changing the game from get the teacher to learn. *Transaction, 20–25*, 28–31. (p. 346)

Hamermesh, D. S. (2011). *Beauty pays: Why attractive people are more successful.* Princeton, NJ: Princeton University Press. (p. 363)

Hamilton, D. L., & Gifford, R. K. (1976). Illusory correlation in interpersonal perception: A cognitive basis of stereotypic judgments. *Journal of Experimental Social Psychology, 12*, 392–407. (p. 422)

Hamilton, D. L., & Rose, T. L. (1980). Illusory correlation and the maintenance of stereotypic beliefs. *Journal of Personality and Social Psychology, 39*, 832–845. (p. 422)

Hampson, R. B. (1984). Adolescent prosocial behavior: Peer-group and situational factors associated with helping. *Journal of Personality and Social Psychology, 46*, 153–162. (p. 299)

Hancock, K. J., & Rhodes, G. (2008). Contact, configural coding and the other-race effect in face recognition. *British Journal of Psychology, 99*, 45–56. (p. 419)

Harbaugh, W. T., Mayr, U., & Burghart, D. R. (2007). Neural responses to taxation and voluntary giving reveal motives for charitable donations. *Science, 316*, 1622–1625. (p. 275)

Harber, K. D. (1998). Feedback to minorities: Evidence of a positive bias. *Journal of Personality and Social Psychology, 74*, 622–628. (p. 430)

Harber, K. D., Stafford, R., & Kennedy, K. A. (2010). The positive feedback bias as a response to a self-image threat. *Journal of Social Psychology, 49*, 207–218. (p. 430)

Hardin, G. (1968). The tragedy of the commons. *Science, 162*, 1243–1248. (p. 455)

Hardy, C., & Latané, B. (1986). Social loafing on a cheering task. *Social Science, 71*, 165–172. (p. 239)

Hardy, C. L., & Van Vugt, M. (2006). Nice guys finish first: The competitive altruism hypothesis. *Personality and Social Psychology Bulletin, 32*, 1402–1413. (p. 275)

Haritos-Fatouros, M. (1988). The official torturer: A learning model for obedience to the authority of violence. *Journal of Applied Social Psychology, 18*, 1107–1120. (p. 211)

Harkins, S. G. (1981). *Effects of task difficulty and task responsibility on social loafing.* Presentation to the First International Conference on Social Processes in Small Groups, Kill Devil Hills, NC. (p. 239)

Harkins, S. G., & Jackson, J. M. (1985). The role of evaluation in eliminating social loafing. *Personality and Social Psychology Bulletin, 11*, 457–465. (p. 240)

Harkins, S. G., Latané, B., & Williams, K. (1980). Social loafing: Allocating effort or taking it easy? *Journal of Experimental Social Psychology, 16*, 457–465. (p. 239)

Harkins, S. G., & Petty, R. E. (1981). Effects of source magnification of cognitive effort on attitudes: An information-processing view. *Journal of Personality and Social Psychology, 40*, 401–413. (p. 180)

Harkins, S. G., & Petty, R. E. (1982). Effects of task difficulty and task uniqueness on social loafing. *Journal of Personality and Social Psychology, 43*, 1214–1229. (p. 242)

Harkins, S. G., & Petty, R. E. (1987). Information utility and the multiple source effect. *Journal of Personality and Social Psychology, 52*, 260–268. (p. 180)

Harkins, S. G., & Szymanski, K. (1989). Social loafing and group evaluation. *Journal of Personality and Social Psychology, 56*, 934–941. (p. 242)

Harkness, K. L., Sabbagh, M. A., Jacobson, J. A., Chowdrey, N. K., & Chen, T. (2005). Enhanced accuracy of mental state decoding in dysphoric college students. *Cognition & Emotion, 19*, 999. (p. 476)

Harmon-Jones, E., & Allen, J. J. B. (2001). The role of affect in the mere exposure effect: Evidence from psychophysiological and individual differences approaches. *Personality and Social Psychology Bulletin, 27*, 889–898. (p. 357)

Harmon-Jones, E., Brehm, J. W., Greenberg, J., Simon, L., & Nelson, D. E. (1996). Evidence that the production of aversive consequences is not necessary to create cognitive dissonance. *Journal of Personality and Social Psychology, 70*, 5–16. (pp. 152, 412)

Harmon-Jones, E., Gerdjikov, T., & Harmon-Jones, C. (2008). The effect of induced compliance on relative left frontal cortical activity: A test of the action-based model of dissonance. *European Journal of Social Psychology, 38*, 35–45. (p. 151)

Harrel, W. A. (1994). Effects of blind pedestrians on motorists. *Journal of Social Psychology, 134*, 529–539. (p. 281)

Harries, K. D., & Stadler, S. J. (1988). Heat and violence: New findings from Dallas field data, 1980–1981. *Journal of Applied Social Psychology, 18*, 129–138. (p. 323)

Harris, J. R. (1998). *The nurture assumption.* New York: Free Press. (p. 385)

Harris, L. T., & Fiske, S. T. (2006). Dehumanizing the lowest of the low: Neuroimaging responses to extreme out-groups. *Psychological Science, 17*, 847. (p. 432)

Harris, M. J., & Rosenthal, R. (1985). Mediation of interpersonal expectancy effects: 31 meta-analyses. *Psychological Bulletin, 97*, 363–386. (p. 112)

Harris, M. J., & Rosenthal, R. (1986). Four factors in the mediation of teacher expectancy effects. In R. S. Feldman (Ed.), *The social psychology of education.* New York: Cambridge University Press. (p. 112)

Harrison, A. A. (1977). Mere exposure. In L. Berkowitz (Ed.), *Advances in experimental social psychology* (Vol. 10). New York: Academic Press, 39–83. (p. 357)

Hart, A. J., & Morry, M. M. (1997). Trait inferences based on racial and behavioral cues. *Basic and Applied Social Psychology, 19*, 33–48. (p. 430)

Hart, A. J., Whalen, P. J., Shin, L. M., & others. (2000, August). Differential response in the human amygdala to racial outgroup vs. ingroup face stimuli. *Neuroreport: For Rapid Communication of Neuroscience Research, 11*, 2351–2355. (p. 416)

Hart, W., Albarracin, D., Eagly, A. H., Brechan, I., Lindberg, M. J., & Merrill, L. (2009). Feeling validated versus being correct: A meta-analysis of selective exposure to information. *Psychological Bulletin, 135*, 555–588. (p. 140)

Hartup, W. W., & Stevens, N. (1997). Friendships and adaptation in the life course. *Psychological Bulletin, 121*, 355–370. (p. 491)

Haselton, M. G., & Nettle, D. (2006). The paranoid optimist: An integrative evolutionary model of cognitive biases. *Personality and Social Psychology Review, 10*, 47. (p. 65)

Haslam, S. A., & Oakes, P. J. (1995). How context-independent is the group homogeneity effect? A response to Bartsch and Judd. *European Journal of Social Psychology, 25*, 469–475. (p. 419)

Hass, R. G., Katz, I., Rizzo, N., Bailey, J., & Eisenstadt, D. (1991). Cross-racial appraisal as related to attitude ambivalence and cognitive complexity. *Personality and Social Psychology Bulletin, 17*, 83–92. (p. 430)

Hastie, R., Penrod, S. D., & Pennington, N. (1983). *Inside the jury.* Cambridge, MA: Harvard University Press. (pp. 509, 510)

Hatfield, E. (1988). Passionate and compassionate love. In R. J. Sternberg & M. L. Barnes (Eds.), *The psychology of love.* New Haven, CT: Yale University Press. (p. 377)

Hatfield (Walster), E., Aronson, V., Abrahams, D., & Rottman, L. (1966). Importance of physical attractiveness in dating behavior. *Journal of Personality and Social Psychology, 4*, 508–516. (p. 360)

Hatfield, E., Cacioppo, J. T., & Rapson, R. (1992). The logic of emotion: Emotional contagion. In M. S. Clark (Ed.), *Review of personality and social psychology.* Newbury Park, CA: Sage. (p. 147)

Hatfield, E., & Rapson, R. L. (1987). Passionate love/sexual desire: Can the same paradigm explain both? *Archives of Sexual Behavior, 16*, 259–278. (p. 378)

Hatfield, E., & Sprecher, S. (1986). *Mirror, mirror: The importance of looks in everyday life.* Albany, NY: SUNY Press. (p. 381)

Hatfield, E., Traupmann, J., Sprecher, S., Utne, M., & Hay, J. (1985). Equity and intimate relations: Recent research. In W. Ickes (Ed.), *Compatible and incompatible relationships.* New York: Springer-Verlag. (p. 386)

Hatfield, E., & Walster, G. W. (1978). *A new look at love.* Reading, MA: Addison-Wesley. (Note: originally published as Walster, E., & Walster, G. W.) (p. 376)

Hatfield (was Walster), E., Walster, G. W., & Berscheid, E. (1978). *Equity: Theory and research.* Boston: Allyn and Bacon. (p. 385)

Hatzfeld, J. (2007). *Machete season: The killers in Rwanda speak.* New York: Farrar, Straus and Giroux. (p. 343)

Haugtvedt, C. P., & Wegener, D. T. (1994). Message order effects in persuasion: An attitude strength perspective. *Journal of Consumer Research, 21*, 205–218. (p. 174)

Havas, D. A., Glenberg, A. M., Gutowski, K. A., Lucarelli, M. J., & Davidson, R. J. (2010). Cosmetic use of Botulinum Toxin-A affects processing of emotional language. *Psychological Science, 21*, 895–900. (p. 146)

Havel, V. (1990). *Disturbing the peace.* New York: Knopf. (p. 525)

Hazan, C. (2004). Intimate attachment/capacity to love and be loved. In C. Peterson & M. E. P. Seligman (Eds.), *The values in action classification of strengths and virtues.* Washington, DC: American Psychological Association. (p. 384)

Hazan, C., & Shaver, P. R. (1994). Attachment as an organizational framework for research on close relationships. *Psychological Inquiry, 5*, 1–22. (p. 393)

He, Y., Ebner, N. C., & Johnson, M. K. (2011). What predicts the own-age bias in face recognition memory? *Social Cognition, 29*, 97–109. (p. 420)

Headey, B., & Wearing, A. (1987). The sense of relative superiority-central to well-being. *Social Indicators Research, 20,* 497–516. (p. 63)

Heap, B., & Comim, F. (2005). Consumption and happiness: Christian values and an approach towards sustainability. Capability and Sustainability Centre, St. Edmund's College, University of Cambridge. Address to Christians in Science annual meeting. (p. 518)

Hearold, S. (1986). A synthesis of 1043 effects of television on social behavior. In G. Comstock (Ed.), *Public communication and behavior,* Vol. 1. Orlando, FL: Academic Press. (p. 304)

Health Canada. (2012). Canadian tobacco use monitoring survey (CTUMS). Available at http://www.hc-sc.gc.ca/hc-ps/tobac-tabac/research-recherche/stat/ctums-esutc_2012-eng.php. (p. 331)

Hedge, A., & Yousif, Y. H. (1992). Effects of urban size, urgency, and cost on helpfulness: A cross-cultural comparison between the United Kingdom and the Sudan. *Journal of Cross-Cultural Psychology, 23,* 107–115. (p. 284)

Heider, F. (1958). *The psychology of interpersonal relations.* New York: Wiley. (p. 102)

Heine, S. J., & Hamamura, T. (2007). In search of East Asian self-enhancement. *Personality and Social Psychology Review, 11,* 4–27. (p. 61)

Heine, S. J., Kitayama, S., Lehman, D. R., Takata, T., Ide, E., Leung, C., & Matsumoto, H. (2001). Divergent consequences of success and failure in Japan and North America: An investigation of self-improving motivations and malleable selves. *Journal of Personality and Social Psychology, 81,* 599–615. (p. 44)

Heine, S. J., & Lehman, D. R. (1995). Cultural variation in unrealistic optimism: Does the West feel more invulnerable than the East? *Journal of Personality and Social Psychology, 68,* 595–607. (p. 74)

Heine, S. J., & Lehman, D. R. (1997). The cultural construction of self-enhancement: An examination of group-serving biases. *Journal of Personality and Social Psychology, 72,* 1268–1283. (pp. 74, 423)

Heine, S. J., & Lehman, D. R. (1997a). Culture, dissonance, and self-affirmation. *Personality and Social Psychology Bulletin, 23,* 389–400. (p. 144)

Heine, S. J., Lehman, D. R., Markus, H. R., & Kitayama, S. (1999). Is there a universal need for positive self-regard? *Psychological Review, 106,* 766–794. (pp. 41, 45)

Heine, S. J., Takemoto, T., Moskalenko, S., Lasaleta, J., & Heinrich, J. (2008). Mirrors in the head: Cultural variation in objective self-awareness. *Personality and Social Psychology Bulletin, 34,* 879–887. (p. 247)

Hellman, P. (1980). *Avenue of the righteous of nations.* New York: Atheneum. (p. 274)

Helmrich, R. L. (1997, May). Managing human error in aviation. *Scientific American,* 62–67. (p. 260)

Helweg-Larsen, M., & LoMonaco, B. L. (2008). Queuing among U2 fans: Reactions to social norm violations. *Journal of Applied Social Psychology, 38,* 2378–2393. (p. 196)

Hemsley, G. D., & Doob, A. N. (1978). The effect of looking behavior on perceptions of a communicator's credibility. *Journal of Applied Social Psychology, 8,* 136–144. (p. 163)

Hendersen-King, E. I., & Nisbett, R. E. (1996). Anti-black prejudice as a function of exposure to the negative behavior of a single black person. *Journal of Personality and Social Psychology, 71,* 654–664. (p. 421)

Hendrick, S. S., & Hendrick, C. (1995). Gender differences and similarities in sex and love. *Personal Relationships, 2,* 55–65. (p. 379)

Hendrick, S. S., Hendrick, C., & Adler, N. L. (1988). Romantic relationships: Love, satisfaction, and staying together. *Journal of Personality and Social Psychology, 54,* 980–988. (p. 388)

Hennenlotter, A., Dresel, C., Castrop, F., Ceballos Baumann, A., Wohschlager, A., & Haslinger, B. (2008). The link between facial feedback and neural activity within central circuitries of emotion: New insights from Botulinum Toxin-induced denervation of frown muscles. *Cerebral Cortex, 19,* 537–542. (p. 146)

Hennigan, K. M., Del Rosario, M. L., Health, L., Cook, T. D., Wharton, J. D., & Calder, B. J. (1982) Impact of the introduction of television on crime in the United States: Empirical findings and theoretical implications. *Journal of Personality and Social Psychology, 42,* 461–477. (p. 319)

Henrich, J., McElreath, R., Barr, A., Ensminger, J., Barrett, C., Bolyanatz, A., Cardenas, J. C., Gurven, M., Gwako, E., Henrich, N., Lerorogol, C., Marlowe, F., Tracer, D., & Ziker, J. (2006). Costly punishment across human societies. *Science, 312,* 1767–1770. (p. 275)

Henslin, M. (1967). Craps and magic. *American Journal of Sociology, 73,* 316–330. (p. 98)

Hepworth, J. T., & West, S. G. (1988). Lynchings and the economy: A time-series reanalysis of Hovland and Sears (1940). *Journal of Personality and Social Psychology, 55,* 239–247. (p. 407)

Herlocker, C. E., Allison, S. T., Foubert, J. D., & Beggan, J. K. (1997). Intended and unintended overconsumption of physical, spatial, and temporal resources. *Journal of Personality and Social Psychology, 73,* 992–1004. (p. 457)

Herzog, S. M., & Hertwig, R. (2009). The wisdom of many in one mind: Improving individual judgments with dialectical bootstrapping. *Psychological Science, 20,* 231–237. (p. 263)

Heslin, P. A. (2009). Better than brainstorming? Potential contextual boundary conditions to brainwriting for idea generation in organizations. *Journal of Occupational and Organizational Psychology, 82,* 129–145. (p. 263)

Hewstone, M. (1990). The 'ultimate attribution error?' A review of the literature on intergroup causal attribution. *European Journal of Social Psychology, 20,* 311–335. (p. 424)

Hewstone, M. (1994). Revision and change of stereotypic beliefs: In search of the elusive subtyping model. In S. Stroebe & M. Hewstone (Eds.), *European review of social psychology,* vol. 5. Chichester, England: Wiley. (p. 437)

Hewstone, M., & Fincham, F. (1996). Attribution theory and research: Basic issues and applications. In M. Hewstone, W. Stroebe, and G. M. Stephenson (Eds.), *Introduction to social psychology: A European perspective.* Oxford, UK: Blackwell (p. 102)

Hewstone, M., Hantzi, A., & Johnston, L. (1991). Social categorisation and person memory: The pervasiveness of race as an organizing principle. *European Journal of Social Psychology, 21,* 517–528. (p. 417)

Hewstone, M., Hopkins, N., & Routh, D. A. (1992). Cognitive models of stereotype change: Generalization and subtyping in young people's views of the police. *European Journal of Social Psychology, 22,* 219–234. (p. 437)

Higbee, K. L., Millard, R. J., & Folkman, J. R. (1982). Social psychology research during the 1970s: Predominance of experimentation and college students. *Personality and Social Psychology Bulletin, 8,* 180–183. (p. 24)

Higgins, E. T., & McCann, C. D. (1984). Social encoding and subsequent attitudes, impressions and memory: "Context-driven" and motivational aspects of processing. *Journal of Personality and Social Psychology, 47,* 26–39. (p. 132)

Higgins, E. T., & Rholes, W. S. (1978). Saying is believing: Effects of message modification on memory and liking for the person described. *Journal of Experimental Social Psychology, 14,* 363–378. (p. 132)

Hilgard, E. R., & Loftus, E. F. (1979). Effective interrogation of the eyewitness. *International Journal of Clinical and Experimental Hypnosis, 17,* 342–359. (p. 503)

Hilmert, C. J., Kulik, J. A., & Christenfeld, N. J. S. (2006). Positive and negative opinion modeling: The influence of another's similarity and dissimilarity. *Journal of Personality and Social Psychology, 90,* 440. (p. 217)

Hilton, J. L., & von Hippel, W. (1990). The role of consistency in the judgment of stereotype-relevant behaviors. *Personality and Social Psychology Bulletin, 16,* 430–448. (p. 80)

Hine, D. W., & Gifford, R. (1996). Attributions about self and others in commons dilemmas. *European Journal of Social Psychology, 26,* 429–445. (p. 457)

Hinsz, V. B. (1990). Cognitive and consensus processes in group recognition memory performance. *Journal of Personality and Social Psychology, 59,* 705–718. (p. 261)

Hinsz, V. B., Tindale, R. S., & Vollrath, D. A. (1997). The emerging conceptualization of groups as information processors. *Psychological Bulletin, 121,* 43–64. (p. 252)

Hirschman, R. S., & Leventhal, H. (1989). Preventing smoking behavior in school children: An initial test of a cognitive-development program. *Journal of Applied Social Psychology, 19,* 559–583. (p. 189)

Hirt, E. R. (1990). Do I see only what I expect? Evidence for an expectancy-guided retrieval model. *Journal of Personality and Social Psychology, 58,* 937–951. (p. 84)

Hirt, E. R., & Markman, K. D. (1995). Multiple explanation: A consider-an-alternative strategy for debiasing judgments. *Journal of Personality and Social Psychology, 69,* 1069–1088. (p. 84)

Hirt, E. R., Zillmann, D., Erickson, G. A., & Kennedy, C. (1992). Costs and benefits of allegiance: Changes in fans' self-ascribed competencies after team victory versus defeat. *Journal of Personality and Social Psychology, 63,* 724–738. (p. 477)

Hitsch, G. J., Hortacsu, A., & Ariely, D. (2006, February). What makes you click? Mate preferences and matching outcomes in online dating. MIT Sloan Research Paper No. 4603–06 (ssrn.com/abstract = 895442). (p. 361)

Hobden, K. L., & Olson, J. M. (1994). From jest to antipathy: Disparagement humor as a source of dissonance-motivated attitude change. *Basic and Applied Social Psychology, 15,* 239–249. (p. 141)

Hodges, B. H., & Geyer, A. L. (2006). A nonconformist account of the Asch experiments: Values, pragmatics, and moral dilemmas. *Personality and Social Psychology Review, 10,* 2. (p. 201)

Hoffman, L. W. (1977). Changes in family roles, socialization, and sex differences. *American Psychologist, 32,* 644–657. (p. 406)

Hoffman, M. L. (1981). Is altruism part of human nature? *Journal of Personality and Social Psychology, 40,* 121–137. (p. 288)

Hofmeister, B. (2010). Bridging the gap: Using social psychology to design market interventions to overcome the energy efficiency gap in residential energy markets. *Southeastern Environmental Law Journal, 19,* pp. 1ff. Available at SSRN: http://ssrn.com/abstract51892906. (p. 518)

Hogan, R., Curphy, G. J., & Hogan, J. (1994). What we know about leadership: Effectiveness and personality. *American Psychologist, 49,* 493–504. (p. 265)

Hogg, M. A. (1992). *The social psychology of group cohesiveness: From attraction to social identity.* London: Harvester Wheatsheaf. (p. 408)

Hogg, M. A. (2006). Social identity theory. In P. J. Burke (Ed.), *Contemporary social psychological theories.* Stanford, CA: Stanford University Press. (p. 408)

Hogg, M. A. (2008). Social identity processes and the empowerment of followers. In R. E. Riggio, I. Chaleff, & J. Lipman-Blumen (Eds.), *The art of followership: How great followers create great leaders and organizations.* San Francisco: Jossey-Bass. (p. 408)

Hogg, M. A. (2010). Human groups, social categories, and collective self: Social identity and the management

of self-uncertainty. In R. M. Arkin, K. C. Oleson, & P. J. Carroll (Eds.), *Handbook of the uncertain self.* New York: Psychology Press, 2010. (p. 408)

Hogg, M. A., & Hains, S. C. (1998). Friendship and group identification: A new look at the role of cohesiveness in groupthink. *European Journal of Social Psychology, 28,* 323. (p. 259)

Hogg, M. A., Turner, J. C., & Davidson, B. (1990). Polarized norms and social frames of reference: A test of the self-categorization theory of group polarization. *Basic and Applied Social Psychology, 11,* 77–100. (p. 253)

Holland, R. W., Hendriks, M., & Aarts, H. (2005). Smells like clean spirit: Nonconscious effects of scent on cognition and behavior. *Psychological Science, 16*(9), 689. (p. 79)

Holland, R. W., Meertens, R. M., & Van Vugt, M. (2002). Dissonance on the road: Self-esteem as a moderator of internal and external self-justification strategies. *Personality and Social Psychology Bulletin, 28,* 1712–1724. (p. 152)

Hollander, E. P. (1958). Conformity, status, and idiosyncrasy credit. *Psychological Review, 65,* 117–127. (p. 265)

Holmberg, D., & Holmes, J. G. (1994). Reconstruction of relationship memories: A mental models approach. In N. Schwarz & S. Sudman (Eds.), *Autobiographical memory and the validity of retrospective reports.* New York: Springer-Verlag. (p. 86)

Holmes, J. G., & Rempel, J. K. (1989). Trust in close relationships. In C. Hendrick (Ed.), *Review of personality and social psychology,* Vol. 10. Newbury Park, CA: Sage. (p. 387)

Holtgraves, T. (1997). Styles of language use: Individual and cultural variability in conversational indirectness. *Journal of Personality and Social Psychology, 73,* 624–637. (p. 43)

Holtgraves, T., & Srull, T. K. (1989). The effects of positive self-descriptions on impressions: General principles and individual differences. *Personality and Social Psychology Bulletin, 15,* 452–462. (p. 73)

Holtzworth, A., & Jacobson, N. S. (1988). An attributional approach to marital dysfunction and therapy. In J. E. Maddux, C. D. Stoltenberg, & R. Rosenwein (Eds.), *Social processes in clinical and counseling psychology.* New York: Springer-Verlag. (p. 102)

Holtzworth-Munroe, A., & Jacobson, N. S. (1985). Causal attributions of married couples: When do they search for causes? What do they conclude when they do? *Journal of Personality and Social Psychology, 48*(6), 1398–1412. (p. 102)

Honigman, R. J., Phillips, K. A., & Castle, D. J. (2004). A review of psychosocial outcomes for patients seeking cosmetic surgery. *Plastic and Reconstructive Surgery, 113*, 1229–1237. (p. 362)

Hoorens, V. (1993). Self-enhancement and superiority biases in social comparison. In W. Stroebe & M. Hewstone (Eds.), *European review of social psychology*, vol. 4. Chichester, UK: Wiley. (pp. 63, 357)

Hoorens, V. (1995). Self-favoring biases, self-presentation and the self-other asymmetry in social comparison. *Journal of Personality, 63*, 793–819. (p. 63)

Hoorens, V., Nuttin, J. M., Herman, I. E., & Pavakanun, U. (1990). Mastery pleasure versus mere ownership: A quasi-experimental cross-cultural and cross-alphabetical test of the name letter effect. *European Journal of Social Psychology, 20*, 181–205. (p. 357)

Hoorens, V., Smits, T., & Shepperd, J. A. (2008). Comparative optimism in the spontaneous generation of future life-events. *British Journal of Social Psychology, 47*, 441–451. (p. 63)

Hoover, C. W., Wood, E. E., & Knowles, E. S. (1983). Forms of social awareness and helping. *Journal of Experimental Social Psychology, 19*, 577–590. (p. 302)

Hormuth, S. E. (1986). Lack of effort as a result of self-focused attention: An attributional ambiguity analysis. *European Journal of Social Psychology, 16*, 181–192. (p. 71)

Horner, V., Proctor, D., Bonnie, K. E., Whiten, A., & de Waal, F. B. M. (2010). Prestige affects cultural learning in chimpanzees. *PLoS One, 5*, e10625 (www .plosone.org). (pp. 217, 288)

Hornstein, H. (1976). *Cruelty and kindness.* Englewood Cliffs, NJ: Prentice-Hall. (p. 312)

Horowitz, S. V., & Boardman, S. K. (1994). Managing conflict: Policy and research implications. *Journal of Social Issues, 50*, 197–211. (p. 464)

Horwitz, A. V., White, H. R., & Howell-White, S. (1997). Becoming married and mental health: A longitudinal study of a cohort of young adults. *Journal of Marriage and the Family, 58*, 895–907. (p. 493)

Hoshino-Browne, E., Zanna, A. S., Spencer, S. J., Zanna, M. P., Kitayama, S., &

Lackenbauer, S. (2005). On the cultural guises of cognitive dissonance: The easterners and westerners. *Journal of Personality and Social Psychology, 89*, 294–310. (p. 144)

Houghton, J. (2011). Global warming, climate change and sustainability: A challenge to scientists, policymakers and religious believers. Cambridge, England: The International Society for Science and Religion (www.issr.org .uk/latest-news/ global-warming). (pp. 515, 516)

House, R. J., & Singh, J. V. (1987). Organizational behavior: Some new directions for I/O psychology. *Annual Review of Psychology, 38*, 669–718. (p. 265)

Houston, V., & Bull, R. (1994). Do people avoid sitting next to someone who is facially disfigured? *European Journal of Social Psychology, 24*, 279–284. (p. 362)

Hovland, C. I., Lumsdaine, A. A., & Sheffield, F. D. (1949). *Experiments on mass communication. Studies in social psychology in World War II* (Vol. III). Princeton, NJ: Princeton University Press. (pp. 159, 166, 172)

Hovland, C. I., & Sears, R. (1940). Minor studies of aggression: Correlation of lynchings with economic indices. *Journal of Psychology, 9*, 301–310. (p. 407)

Howard, D. J. (1997). Familiar phrases as peripheral persuasion cues. *Journal of Experimental Social Psychology, 33*, 231–243. (p. 160)

Howell, R. T., & Howell, C. J. (2008). The relation of economic status to subjective well-being in developing countries: A meta-analysis. *Psychological Bulletin, 134*, 536–560. (p. 522)

Hoyle, R. H. (1993). Interpersonal attraction in the absence of explicit attitudinal information. *Social Cognition, 11*, 309–320. (p. 370)

Hsee, C. K., & Hastie, R. (2006). Decision and experience: Why don't we choose what makes us happy? *Trends in Cognitive Sciences, 10*, 31–37. (p. 59)

Huart, J., Corneille, O., & Becquart, E. (2005). Face-based categorization, context-based categorization, and distortions in the recollection of gender ambiguous faces. *Journal of Experimental Social Psychology, 41*, 598. (p. 436)

Huberman, B., & Lukose, R. (1997). Social dilemmas and internet congestion. *Science, 277*, 535–537. (p. 456)

Huddy, L., & Virtanen, S. (1995). Subgroup differentiation and subgroup bias among

Latinos as a function of familiarity and positive distinctiveness. *Journal of Personality and Social Psychology, 68*, 97–108. (p. 419)

Huesmann, L. R., Lagerspetz, K., & Eron, L. D. (1984). Intervening variables in the TV violence-aggression relation: Evidence from two countries. *Developmental Psychology, 20*, 746–775. (p. 333)

Huesmann, L. R., Moise-Titus, J., Podolski, C-L., & Eron, L. D. (2003). Longitudinal relations between children's exposure to TV violence and their aggressive and violent behavior in young adulthood: 1977–1992. *Developmental Psychology, 39*, 201–222. (pp. 313, 333)

Hugenberg, K. & Bodenhausen, G. V. (2003). Facing prejudice: Implicit prejudice and the perception of facial threat. *Psychological Science, 14*, 640–643. (pp. 430, 431)

Hugenberg, K., Young, S. G., Bernstein, M. J., & Sacco, D. F. (2010). The categorization-individuation model: An integrative account of the other-race recognition deficit. *Psychological Review, 117*, 1168–1187. (p. 420)

Hui, C. H., Triandis, H. C., & Yee, C. (1991). Cultural differences in reward allocation: Is collectivism the explanation? *British Journal of Social Psychology, 30*, 145–157. (p. 460)

Hull, J. G., & Young, R. D. (1983). The self-awareness-reducing effects of alcohol consumption: Evidence and implications. In J. Suls & A. G. Greenwald (Eds.), *Psychological perspectives on the self*, Vol. 2. Hillsdale, NJ: Erlbaum. (pp. 247, 481)

Hunt, P. J., & Hillery, J. M. (1973). Social facilitation in a location setting: An examination of the effects over learning trials. *Journal of Experimental Social Psychology, 9*, 563–571. (p. 235)

Huston, A. C., Donnerstein, E., Fairchild, H., Feshbach, N. D., Katz, P. A., & Murray, J. P. (1992). *Big world, small screen: The role of television in American society.* Lincoln, NE: University of Nebraska Press. (p. 332)

Huston, T. L. (1973). Ambiguity of acceptance, social desirability, and dating choice. *Journal of Experimental Social Psychology, 9*, 32–42. (p. 361)

Huston, T. L., & Chorost, A. F. (1994). Behavioral buffers on the effect of negativity on marital satisfaction: A longitudinal study. *Personal Relationships, 1*, 223–239. (p. 380)

Hyde, J. S., Fennema, E. H., & Lamon, S. J. (1990). Gender differences in mathematics performance: A meta-analysis. *Psychological Bulletin, 107.* (p. 399)

Hyde, J. S., Mezulis, A. H., & Abramson, L. Y. (2008). The ABCs of depression: Integrating affective, biological, and cognitive models to explain the emergence of the gender difference in depression. *Psychological Review, 115,* 291–313. (p. 478)

Hyman, H. H., & Sheatsley, P. B. (1956 & 1964). Attitudes toward desegregation. *Scientific American, 195*(6), 35–39, and *211*(1), 16–23. (p. 428)

Ickes, B. (1980). *On disconfirming our perceptions of others.* Paper presented at the American Psychological Association convention. (p. 109)

Ickes, W., Layden, M. A., & Barnes, R. D. (1978). Objective self-awareness and individuation: An empirical link. *Journal of Personality, 46,* 146–161. (p. 247)

Ickes, W., Patterson, M. L., Rajecki, D. W., & Tanford, S. (1982). Behavioral and cognitive consequences of reciprocal versus compensatory responses to preinteraction expectancies. *Social Cognition, 1,* 160–190. (pp. 223, 437)

Ijzerman, H., & Semin, G. R. (2009). The thermometer of social relations: Mapping social proximity on temperature. *Psychological Science, 20,* 1214–1220. (p. 80)

Imai, Y. (1994). Effects of influencing attempts on the perceptions of powerholders and the powerless. *Journal of Social Behavior and Personality, 9,* 455–468. (p. 61)

Imhoff, R., & Banse, R. (2009). Ongoing victim suffering increases prejudice: The case of secondary anti-Semitism. *Psychological Science, 20,* 1443–1447. (p. 414)

Imhoff, R., Dotsch, R., Bianchi, M., Banse, R., & Wigboldus, D. (2011). Facing Europe: Visualizing spontaneous ingroup projection. *Psychological Science, 22,* 1583–1590. (p. 65)

Imhoff, R., & Erb, H-P. (2009). What motivates nonconformity? Uniqueness seeking blocks majority influence. *Personality and Social Psychology Bulletin, 35,* 309–320. (p. 226)

Ingham, A. G., Levinger, G., Graves, J., & Peckham, V. (1974). The Ringelmann effect: Studies of group size and group performance. *Journal of Experimental Social Psychology, 10,* 371–384. (p. 239)

Inglehart, M. R., Markus, H., & Brown, D. R. (1989). The effects of possible selves on academic achievement-a panel study. In J. P.

Forgas & J. M. Innes (Eds.), *Recent advances in social psychology: An international perspective.* Amsterdam: North-Holland – Elsevier Science Publishers. (p. 38)

Inglehart, R. (1990). *Culture shift in advanced industrial society.* Princeton, NJ: Princeton University Press. (pp. 492, 522)

Inglehart, R. F., & Welzel, C. (2005). Liberalism, postmaterialism and the growth of freedom." *International Review of Sociology, 15,* 81–108. (p. 58)

Insko, C. A., Nacoste, R. W., & Moe, J. L. (1983). Belief congruence and racial discrimination: Review of the evidence and critical evaluation. *European Journal of Social Psychology, 13,* 153–174. (p. 370)

International Telecommunication Union (ITU). (2010). *The world in 2010: ICT facts and figures.* ITU (www.itu.int/ict). (p. 352)

Inzlicht, M., McKay, L., & Aronson, J. (2006). Stigma as ego depletion: How being the target of prejudice affects self-control. *Psychological Science, 17,* 262–269. (p. 440)

Inzlicht, M., & Schmeichel, B. J. (2012). What is ego depletion? Toward a mechanistic revision of the resource model of self-control. *Perspectives on Psychological Science, 7,* 450–463. (p. 57)

Ireland, M. E., & Pennebaker, J. W. (2010). Language style matching in writing: Synchrony in essays, correspondence, and poetry. *Journal of Personality and Social Psychology, 99,* 549–571. (p. 148, 199)

Ireland, M. E., Slatcher, R. B., Eastwick, P. W., Scissors, L. E., Finkel, E. J., & Pennebaker, J. W. (2011). Language style matching predicts relationship initiation and stability. *Psychological Science, 22,* 39–44. (p. 369)

Isen, A. M., Clark, M., & Schwartz, M. F. (1976). Duration of the effect of good mood on helping: Footprints on the sands of time. *Journal of Personality and Social Psychology, 34,* 385–393. (p. 279)

Isen, A. M., & Means, B. (1983). The influence of positive affect on decision-making strategy. *Social Cognition, 2,* 28–31. (p. 100)

Isen, A. M., Shalker, T. E., Clark, M., & Karp, L. (1978). Affect, accessibility of material in memory, and behavior: A cognitive loop. *Journal of Personality and Social Psychology, 36,* 1–12. (p. 279)

Isozaki, M. (1984). The effect of discussion on polarization of judgments. *Japanese Psychological Research, 26,* 187–193. (p. 249)

Ito, T. A., Miller, N., & Pollock, V. E. (1996). Alcohol and aggression: A meta-analysis on the moderating effects of inhibitory cues, triggering events, and self-focused attention. *Psychological Bulletin, 120,* 60–82. (p. 314)

Iyengar, S. S., & Lepper, M. R. (2000). When choice is demotivating: Can one desire too much of a good thing? *Journal of Personality and Social Psychology, 79,* 995–1006. (p. 58)

Jackman, M. R., & Senter, M. S. (1981). Beliefs about race, gender, and social class different, therefore unequal: Beliefs about trait differences between groups of unequal status. In D. J. Treiman & R. V. Robinson (Eds.), *Research in stratification and mobility* (Vol. 2). Greenwich, CT: JAI Press. (p. 434)

Jackson, J. M., & Latané, B. (1981). All alone in front of all those people: Stage fright as a function of number and type of co-performers and audience. *Journal of Personality and Social Psychology, 40,* 73–85. (p. 236)

Jackson, L. A., Hunter, J. E., & Hodge, C. N. (1995). Physical attractiveness and intellectual competence: A meta-analytic review. *Social Psychology Quarterly, 58,* 108–122. (p. 362)

Jackson, L. A., Sullivan, L. A., & Hodge, C. N. (1993). Stereotype effects on attributions, predictions, and evaluations: No two social judgments are quite alike. *Journal of Personality and Social Psychology, 65,* 69–84. (p. 423)

Jacobs, R. C., & Campbell, D. T. (1961). The perpetuation of an arbitrary tradition through several generations of a laboratory microculture. *Journal of Abnormal and Social Psychology, 62,* 649–658. (p. 198)

Jacoby, S. (1986, December). When opposites attract. *Reader's Digest,* 95–98. (p. 371)

Jacques-Tiura, A. J., Abbey, A., Parkhill, M. R., & Zawacki, T. (1997). Why do some men misperceive women's sexual intentions more frequently than others do? An application of the confluence model. *Personality and Social Psychology Bulletin, 33,* 1467–1480. (p. 331)

Jaffe, Y., Shapir, N., & Yinon, Y. (1981). Aggression and its escalation. *Journal of Cross-Cultural Psychology, 12,* 21–36. (pp. 343, 344)

Jaffe, Y., & Yinon, Y. (1983). Collective aggression: The group-individual paradigm in the study of collective anti-social behavior. In H. H. Blumberg, A. P. Hare, V. Kent, & M. Davies (Eds.), *Small groups and social interaction* (Vol. 1). Cambridge: Wiley. (p. 343)

James, W. (1890, reprinted 1950). *The principles of psychology*, vol. 2. New York: Dover Publications. (p. 147)

James, W. (1902, reprinted 1958). *The varieties of religious experience.* New York: Mentor Books. (p. 404)

Jamieson, D. W., Lydon, J. E., Stewart, G., & Zanna, M. P. (1987). Pygmalion revisited: New evidence for student expectancy effects in the classroom. *Journal of Educational Psychology, 79,* 461–466. (p. 113)

Janis, I. (1989). *Crucial decisions: Leadership in policymaking and crisis management.* New York: Free Press. (p. 461)

Janis, I. L. (1971, November). Groupthink. *Psychology Today,* 43–46. (pp. 255, 256)

Janis, I. L. (1982). Counteracting the adverse effects of concurrence-seeking in policy-planning groups: Theory and research perspectives. In H. Brandstatter, J. H. Davis, & G. Stocker-Kreichgauer (Eds.), *Group decision making.* New York: Academic Press. (pp. 255, 260)

Janis, I. L., Kaye, D., & Kirschner, P. (1965). Facilitating effects of eating while reading on responsiveness to persuasive communications. *Journal of Personality and Social Psychology, 1,* 181–186. (p. 167)

Jankowiak, W. R., & Fischer, E. F. (1992). A cross-cultural perspective on romantic love. *Ethnology, 31,* 149–155. (p. 378)

Jaremka, L. M., Gabriel, S., & Carvallo, M. (2011). What makes us feel the best also makes us feel the worst: The emotional impact of independent and interdependent experiences. *Self and Identity, 10,* 44–63. (p. 393)

Jason, L. A., Rose, T., Ferrari, J. R., & Barone, R. (1984). Personal versus impersonal methods for recruiting blood donations. *Journal of Social Psychology, 123,* 139–140. (p. 301)

Jelalian, E., & Miller, A. G. (1984). The perseverance of beliefs: Conceptual perspectives and research developments. *Journal of Social and Clinical Psychology, 2,* 25–56. (p. 83)

Jellison, J. M., & Green, J. (1981). A self-presentation approach to the fundamental attribution error: The norm of internality. *Journal of Personality and Social Psychology, 40,* 643–649. (p. 109)

Jemmott, J. B., III., & Locke, S. E. (1984). Psychosocial factors, immunologic mediation, and human susceptibility to infectious diseases: How much do we know? *Psychological Bulletin, 95,* 78–108. (p. 485)

Jenkins, A. C., Macrae, C. N., & Mitchell, J. P. (2008). Repetition suppression of ventromedial prefrontal activity during judgments of self and others. *Proceedings of the National Academy of Sciences, 105,* 4507–4512 (www.pnas.org). (p. 432)

Jennings, D. L., Amabile, T. M., & Ross, L. (1982). Informal covariation assessment: Data-based vs theory-based judgments. In D. Kahneman, P. Slovic, & A. Tversky (Eds.), *Judgment under uncertainty: Heuristics and biases.* New York: Cambridge University Press. (p. 97)

Jetten, J., Hornsey, M. J., & Adarves-Yorno, I. (2006). When group members admit to being conformist: The role of relative intragroup status in conformity self-reports. *Personality and Social Psychology Bulletin, 32,* 162. (p. 217)

Ji, L., Guo, T., Zhang, Z., & Messervey, D. (2009). Looking into the past: Cultural differences in perception and representation of past information. *Journal of Personality and Social Psychology, 96,* 761–769. (p. 109)

Job, V., Dweck, C., & Walton, G. (2010). Ego depletion: Is it all in your head? Implicit theories about willpower affect self-regulation. *Psychological Science, 21,* 1686–1693. (p. 57)

John, L. K., Loewenstein, G., & Prelec, D. (2012). Measuring the prevalence of questionable research practices with incentives for truth telling. *Psychological Science, 23,* 524–532. (p. 28)

Johnson, A. L., Crawford, M. T., Sherman, S. J., Rutchick, A. M., Hamilton, D. L., Ferreira, M. B., & Petrocelli, J. V. (2006). A functional perspective on group memberships: Differential need fulfilment in group typology. *Journal of Experimental Social Psychology, 42,* 707–719. (p. 233)

Johnson, B. T., & Eagly, A. H. (1990). Involvement and persuasion: Types, traditions, and the evidence. *Psychological Bulletin, 107,* 375–384. (p. 180)

Johnson, D. J., & Rusbult, C. E. (1989). Resisting temptation: Devaluation of alternative partners as a means of maintaining commitment in close relationships. *Journal of Personality and Social Psychology, 57,* 967–980. (p. 368)

Johnson, D. W., & Johnson, R. T. (1995). Teaching students to be peacemakers: Results of five years of research. *Peace and Conflict: Journal of Peace Psychology, 1,* 417–438. (p. 464)

Johnson, D. W., & Johnson, R. T. (2000). The three Cs of reducing prejudice and discrimination. In S. Oskamp (Ed.), *Reducing prejudice and discrimination.* Mahwah, NJ: Erlbaum. (p. 464)

Johnson, D. W., & Johnson, R. T. (2003). Field testing integrative negotiations. *Peace and Conflict, 9,* 39–68. (p. 464)

Johnson, J. D., Bushman, B. J., & Dovidio, J. F. (2008). Support for harmful treatment and reduction of empathy toward blacks: "Remnants" of stereotype activation involving Hurricane Katrina and "Lil' Kim." *Journal of Experimental Social Psychology, 44,* 1506–1513. (p. 437)

Johnson, J. D., Jackson, L. A., & Gatto, L. (1995). Violent attitudes and deferred academic aspirations: Deleterious effects of exposure to rap music. *Basic and Applied Social Psychology, 16,* 27–41. (p. 335)

Johnson, J. G., Cohen, P., Smailes, E. M., Kasen, S. & Brook, J. S. (2002). Television viewing and aggressive behavior during adolescence and adulthood. *Science, 295,* 2468–2471. (p. 333)

Johnson, M. H., & Magaro, P. A. (1987). Effects of mood and severity on memory processes in depression and mania. *Psychological Bulletin, 101,* 28–40. (pp. 100, 476)

Johnson, M. K., Rowatt, W. C., Barnard-Brak, L. M., Patock-Peckham, J. A., LaBouff, J. P., & Carlisle, R. D. (2011). A mediational analysis of the role of right-wing authoritarianism and religious fundamentalism in the religiosity-prejudice link. *Personality and Individual Differences, 50,* 851–856. (p. 404)

Johnson, R. D., & Downing, L. J. (1979). Deindividuation and valence of cues: Effects of prosocial and antisocial behavior. *Journal of Personality and Social Psychology, 37,* 1532–1538. (p. 246)

Johnson, R. W., Kelly, R. J., & LeBlanc, B. A. (1995). Motivational basis of dissonance: Aversive consequences or inconsistency. *Personality and Social Psychology Bulletin, 21,* 850–855. (p. 152)

Johnson, W., & Krueger, R. F. (2006). How money buys happiness: Genetic and environmental processes linking finances and life satisfaction. *Journal of*

Personality and Social Psychology, 90, 680. (p. 522)

Joiner, T. E., Jr. (1994). Contagious depression: Existence, specificity to depressed symptoms, and the role of reassurance seeking. *Journal of Personality and Social Psychology, 67,* 287–296. (p. 477)

Joiner, T. E., Jr. (1999). The clustering and contagion of suicide. *Current Directions in Psychological Science, 8,* 89–92. (p. 200)

Joinson, A. N. (2001). Self-disclosure in computer-mediated communication: The role of self-awareness and visual anonymity. *European Journal of Social Psychology, 31,* 177–192. (p. 390)

Jonas, K. (1992). Modelling and suicide: A test of the Werther effect. *British Journal of Social Psychology, 31,* 295–306. (p. 200)

Jones, C. R., Fazio, R. H., & Olson, M. A. (2009). Implicit misattribution as a mechanism underlying evaluative conditioning. *Journal of Personality and Social Psychology, 96,* 933–948. (p. 161)

Jones, E. E. (1964). *Ingratiation.* New York: Appleton-Century-Crofts. (p. 372)

Jones, E. E. (1976). How do people perceive the causes of behavior? *American Scientist, 64,* 300–305. (p. 107)

Jones, E. E., & Davis, K. E. (1965). From acts to dispositions: The attribution process in person perception. In L. Berkowitz (Ed.), *Advances in experimental social psychology* (Vol. 2). New York: Academic Press. (p. 103)

Jones, E. E., & Harris, V. A. (1967). The attribution of attitudes. *Journal of Experimental Social Psychology, 3,* 2–24. (p. 105)

Jones, E. E., & Nisbett, R. E. (1971). *The actor and the observer: Divergent perceptions of the cases of behavior.* Morristown, NJ: General Learning Press. (p. 107)

Jones, E. E., Rock, L., Shaver, K. G., Goethals, G. R., & Ward, L. M. (1968). Pattern of performance and ability attribution: An unexpected primacy effect. *Journal of Personality and Social Psychology, 10,* 317–340. (p. 173)

Jones, J. M. (1983). The concept of race in social psychology: From color to culture. In L. Wheeler & P. Shaver (Eds.), *Review of personality and social psychology,* Vol. 4. Beverly Hills, CA: Sage. (p. 439)

Jones, J. M. (1988). *Piercing the veil: Bicultural strategies for coping with prejudice and racism.* Invited address at the national conference, "Opening Doors: An Appraisal of Race Relations in America," University of Alabama, June 11. (p. 370)

Jones, J. M. (2003). TRIOS: A psychological theory of the African legacy in American culture. *Journal of Social Issues, 59,* 217–242. (p. 370)

Jones, J. M. (2004). TRIOS: A model for coping with the universal context of racism? In G. Philogène (Ed.), *Racial identity in context: The legacy of Kenneth B. Clark.* Washington, DC: American Psychological Association. (p. 370)

Jones, J. T., & Cunningham, J. D. (1996). Attachment styles and other predictors of relationship satisfaction in dating couples. *Personal Relationships, 3,* 387–399. (p. 383)

Jones, R. A., & Brehm, J. W. (1970). Persuasiveness of one- and two-sided communications as a function of awareness there are two sides. *Journal of Experimental Social Psychology, 6,* 47–56. (p. 172)

Jordan, C. H., Spencer, S. J., & Zanna, M. P. (2005). Types of high self-esteem and prejudice: How implicit self-esteem relates to ethnic discrimination among high explicit self-esteem individuals. *Personality & Social Psychology Bulletin, 31*(5), 693–702. (p. 56)

Jordan, C. H., Spencer, S. J., Zanna, M. P., Hoshino-Browne, E., & Correll, J. (2003). Secure and defensive high self-esteem. *Journal of Personality and Social Psychology, 85,* 969–978. (pp. 56, 152)

Josephson, W. L. (1987). Television violence and children's aggression: Testing the priming, social script, and disinhibition predictions. *Journal of Personality and Social Psychology, 53,* 882–890. (p. 335)

Jost, J. T., & Kay, A. C. (2005). Exposure to benevolent sexism and complementary gender stereotypes: Consequences for specific and diffuse forms of system justification. *Journal of Personality and Social Psychology, 88,* 498. (pp. 402, 434)

Jourard, S. M. (1964). *The transparent self.* Princeton, NJ: Van Nostrand. (p. 388)

Jourden, F. J., & Heath, C. (1996). The evaluation gap in performance perceptions: Illusory perceptions of groups and individuals. *Journal of Applied Psychology, 81,* 369–379. (p. 70)

Judd, C. M., Blair, I. V., & Chapleau, K. M. (2004). Automatic stereotypes vs. automatic prejudice: Sorting out the possibilities in the Payne (2001) weapon paradigm. *Journal of Experimental Social Psychology, 40,* 75–81. (p. 432)

Judd, C. M., Park, B., Ryan, C. S., Brauer, M., & Kraus, S. (1995). Stereotypes and ethnocentrism: Diverging interethnic perceptions of African American and White American youth. *Journal of Personality and Social Psychology, 69,* 460–481. (p. 439)

Judd, C. M., Ryan, C. S., & Park, B. (1991). Accuracy in the judgment of in-group and out-group variability. *Journal of Personality and Social Psychology, 61,* 366–379. (p. 419)

Judge, T. A., LePine, J. A., & Rich, B. L. (2006). Loving yourself abundantly: Relationship of the narcissistic personality to self and other perceptions of workplace deviance, leadership, and task and contextual performance. *Journal of Applied Psychology, 91,* 762–776. (p. 55)

Jussim, L. (1986). Self-fulfilling prophecies: A theoretical and integrative review. *Psychological Review, 93,* 429–445. (p. 112)

Jussim, L. (2005). Accuracy in social perception: Criticisms, controversies, criteria, components, and cognitive processes. In M. P. Zanna (Ed.), *Advances in experimental social psychology, vol. 37* (pp. 1–93). San Diego, CA: Elsevier Academic Press. (pp. 12, 80, 112, 116)

Jussim, L. (2012). *Social perception and social reality: Why accuracy dominates bias and self-fulfilling prophecy.* New York: Oxford University Press. (pp. 113, 443)

Jussim, L., McCauley, C. R., & Lee, Y-T. (1995). Introduction: Why study stereotype accuracy and inaccuracy? In Y. T. Lee, L. Jussim, & C. R. McCauley (Eds.), *Stereotypes accuracy: Toward appreciating group differences.* Washington, DC: American Psychological Association. (p. 399)

Jussim, L., Robustelli, S. L., & Cain, T. R. (2009). Teacher expectations and self-fulfilling prophecies. In K. R. Wenzel & A. Wigfield (Eds.), *Handbook of motivation at school.* New York: Routledge/Taylor & Francis. (pp. 111, 112)

Kagan, J. (1989). Temperamental contributions to social behavior. *American Psychologist, 44,* 668–674. (p. 313)

Kagan, J. (2009). Historical selection. *Review of General Psychology, 13,* 77–88. (p. 11)

Kagehiro, D. K. (1990). Defining the standard of proof in jury instructions. *Psychological Science, 1,* 194–200. (pp. 508)

Kahan, D. M., Jenkins-Smith, H., & Braman, D. (2010). Cultural cognition of scientific consensus. *Journal of Risk Research, 14,* 147–174. (p. 163)

Kahle, L. R., & Berman, J. (1979). Attitudes cause behaviors: A cross-lagged panel analysis. *Journal of Personality and Social Psychology, 37,* 315–321. (p. 126)

Kahlor, L., & Morrison, D. (2007). Television viewing and rape myth acceptance among college women. *Sex Roles, 56,* 729 739. (p. 328)

Kahn, M. W. (1951). The effect of severe defeat at various age levels on the aggressive behavior of mice. *Journal of Genetic Psychology, 79,* 117–130. (p. 319)

Kahneman, D., & Miller, D. T. (1986). Norm theory: Comparing reality to its alternatives. *Psychological Review, 93,* 75–88. (p. 97)

Kahneman, D., & Snell, J. (1992). Predicting a changing taste: Do people know what they will like? *Journal of Behavioral Decision Making, 5,* 187–200. (p. 357)

Kahneman, D., & Tversky, A. (1979). Intuitive prediction: Biases and corrective procedures. *Management Science, 12,* 313–327. (p. 90)

Kahneman, D., & Tversky, A. (1995). Conflict resolution: A cognitive perspective. In K. Arrow, R. Mnookin, L. Ross, A. Tversky, & R. Wilson (Eds.), *Barriers to the negotiated resolution of conflict.* New York: Norton. (p. 467)

Kaiser, C. R., & Pratt-Hyatt, J. S. (2009). Distributing prejudice unequally: Do Whites direct their prejudice toward strongly identified minorities? *Journal of Personality and Social Psychology, 96,* 432–445. (p. 403)

Kaiser Family Foundation. (2005, November 9). Sex on TV 4 (www.kff.org). (p. 336)

Kalick, S. M. (1977). Plastic surgery, physical appearance, and person perception. Unpublished doctoral dissertation, Harvard University. Cited by E. Berscheid in, An overview of the psychological effects of physical attractiveness and some comments upon the psychological effects of knowledge of the effects of physical attractiveness. In W. Lucker, K. Ribbens, & J. A. McNamera (Eds.), *Logical aspects of facial form* (craniofacial growth series). Ann Arbor: University of Michigan Press, 1981. (p. 362)

Kalin, R., & Berry, J. W. (1995). Ethnic and civic self-identity in Canada: Analyses of 1974 and 1991 national surveys. *Canadian Ethnic Studies, 27,* 1–15. (pp. 39, 400)

Kalven, H., Jr., & Zeisel, H. (1966). *The American jury.* Chicago: University of Chicago Press. (pp. 508, 510)

Kameda, T., & Sugimori, S. (1993). Psychological entrapment in group decision making: An assigned decision rule and a groupthink phenomenon. *Journal of Personality and Social Psychology, 65,* 282–292. (p. 267)

Kammer, D. (1982). Differences in trait ascriptions to self and friend: Unconfounding intensity from variability. *Psychological Reports, 51,* 99–102. (p. 108)

Kanagawa, C., Cross, S. E., & Markus, H. R. (2001). "Who am I?" The cultural psychology of the conceptual self. *Personality and Social Psychology Bulletin, 27,* 90–103. (p. 41)

Kandel, D. B. (1978). Similarity in real-life adolescent friendship pairs. *Journal of Personality and Social Psychology, 36,* 306–312. (p. 371)

Kanekar, S., & Nazareth, A. (1988). Attributed rape victim's fault as a function of her attractiveness, physical hurt, and emotional disturbance. *Social Behaviour, 3,* 37–40. (p. 102)

Kanten, A. B., & Teigen, K. H. (2008). Better than average and better with time: Relative evaluations of self and others in the past, present, and future. *European Journal of Social Psychology, 38,* 343–353. (p. 61)

Kaplan, M. F. (1989). Task, situational, and personal determinants of influence processes in group decision making. In E. J. Lawler (Ed.), *Advances in group processes* (vol. 6). Greenwich, CT: JAI Press. (p. 254)

Kaplan, M. F., Wanshula, L. T., & Zanna, M. P. (1993). Time pressure and information integration in social judgment: The effect of need for structure. In O. Svenson & J. Maule (Eds.), *Time pressure and stress in human judgment and decision making.* Cambridge: Cambridge University Press. (p. 417)

Kaprio, J., Koskenvuo, M., & Rita, H. (1987). Mortality after bereavement: A propsective study of 95,647 widowed persons. *American Journal of Public Health, 77,* 283–287. (p. 488)

Karau, S. J., & Williams, K. D. (1993). Social loafing: A meta-analytic review and theoretical integration. *Journal of Personality and Social Psychology, 65,* 681–706. (pp. 240, 242)

Karau, S. J., & Williams, K. D. (1997). The effects of group cohesiveness on social loafing and social compensation. *Group Dynamics: Theory, Research, and Practice, 1,* 156–168. (p. 242)

Karberg, J. C., & James, D. J. (2005). Substance dependence, abuse, and treatment of jail inmates, 2002. Bureau of Justice Statistics Special Report. Washington, DC: U.S. Department of Justice. (p. 314)

Karna, A., Voeten, M., Little, T. D., Poskiparta, E., Kalijonen, A., & Salmivalli, C. (2011). A large-scale evaluation of the KiVa antibullying program. *Child Development, 82,* 311–330. (p. 343)

Karney, B. R., & Bradbury, T. N. (1995). The longitudinal course of marital quality and stability: A review of theory, method, and research. *Psychological Bulletin, 118,* 3–34. (p. 393)

Kashima, E. S., & Kashima, Y. (1998). Culture and language: the case of cultural dimensions and personal pronoun use. *Journal of Cross-Cultural Psychology, 29,* 461–486. (p. 42)

Kashima, Y., & Kashima, E. S. (2003). Individualism, GNP, climate, and pronoun drop: Is individualism determined by affluence and climate, or does language use play a role? *Journal of Cross-Cultural Psychology, 34,* 125–134. (p. 42)

Kasser, T. (2000). Two versions of the American dream: Which goals and values make for a high quality of life? In E. Diener and D. Rahtz (Eds.), *Advances in quality of life: Theory and research.* Dordrecht, Netherlands: Kluwer. (p. 523)

Kasser, T. (2011). High price of materialism. Animated video. Center for the New American Dream (www.newdream.org). (p. 523)

Kasser, T., & Ahuvia, A. (2002). Materialistic values and well-being in business students. *European Journal of Social Psychology, 32,* 137. (p. 523)

Kassin, S. M., Drizin, S. A., Grisso, T., Gudjonsson, G. H., Leo, R. A., & Redlich, A. D. (2010). Police-induced confessions: Risk factors and recommendations. *Law and Human Behavior, 34,* 3–38. (p. 502)

Kassin, S. M., Goldstein, C. C., & Savitsky, K. (2003). Behavioral confirmation in the interrogation room: On the dangers of presuming guilt. *Law and Human Behavior, 27*(2), 187. (p. 113)

Kassin, S. M., Tubb, V. A., Hosch, H. M., & Memon, A. (2001). On the 'general acceptance' of eyewitness testimony research: A new survey of the experts. *American Psychologist, 56,* 405–416. (p. 505)

Katz, A. M., & Hill, R. (1958). Residential propinquity and marital selection: A review of theory, method, and fact. *Marriage and Family Living, 20,* 237–335. (p. 356)

Katz, E. (1957). The two-step flow of communication: An up-to-date report on a hypothesis. *Public Opinion Quarterly, 21,* 61–78. (p. 176)

Katz, J., Beach, S. R. H., & Joiner, T. E., Jr. (1999). Contagious depression in dating couples. *Journal of Social and Clinical Psychology, 18,* 1–13. (p. 477)

Katzev, R., Edelsack, L., Steinmetz, G., & Walker, T. (1978). The effect of reprimanding transgressions on subsequent helping behavior: Two field experiments. *Personality and Social Psychology Bulletin, 4,* 126–129. (p. 302)

Katzev, R., & Wang, T. (1994). Can commitment change behavior? A case study of environmental actions. *Journal of Social Behavior and Personality, 9,* 13–26. (p. 219)

Kaufman, J., & Zigler, E. (1987). Do abused children become abusive parents? *American Journal of Orthopsychiatry, 57,* 186–192. (p. 321)

Kawachi, I., Kennedy, B. P., & Wilkinson, R. G. (1999). Crime: Social disorganization and relative deprivation. *Social Science and Medicine, 48,* 719–731. (pp. 318, 490)

Kawakami, K., & Dion, K. L. (1993). The impact of salient self-identities on relative deprivation and action intentions. *European Journal of Social Psychology, 23,* 525–540. (p. 318)

Kawakami, K., & Dion, K. L. (1995). Social identity and affect as determinants of collective action: Toward an integration of relative deprivation and social identity theories. *Theory & Psychology, 5,* 551–577. (p. 318)

Kawakami, K., Dovidio, J. F., Moll, J., Hermsen, S., & Russin, A. (2000). Just say no (to stereotyping): Effects of training in the negation of stereotypic associations on stereotype activation. *Journal of Personality and Social Psychology, 78,* 871–888. (p. 401)

Kawakami, K., Dunn, E., Kiarmali, F., & Dovidio, J. F. (2009). Mispredicting affective and behavioral responses to racism. *Science, 323,* 276–278. (pp. 123, 212)

Kay, A. C., Jost, J. T., Mandisodza, A. N., Sherman, S. J., Petrocelli, J. V., & Johnson, A. L. (2007). Panglossian ideology in the service of system justification: How complementary stereotypes help us to rationalize inequality. In M. P. Zanna (Ed.), *2005 Society of Experimental Social Psychology Conference, 2005,* San Diego,

CA (pp. 305–358). San Diego: Elsevier Academic Press. (p. 402)

Kay, A. C., Jost, J. T., & Young, S. (2005). Victim derogation and victim enhancement as alternate routes to system justification. *Psychological Science, 16,* 240. (p. 402)

Keating, J. P., & Brock, T. C. (1974). Acceptance of persuasion and the inhibition of counterargumentation under various distraction tasks. *Journal of Experimental Social Psychology, 10,* 301–309. (p. 180)

Keelan, J. P., Dion, K. K., & Dion, K. L. (1998). Attachment style and relationship satisfaction: Test of a self-disclosure explanation. *Canadian Journal of Behavioural Science, 30,* 24–35. (p. 383)

Keller, E., & Berry, J. L. (2003). *The influentials.* New York: Simon & Schuster. (p. 176)

Keller, J., & Dauenheimer, D. (2003). Stereotype threat in the classroom: Dejection mediates the disrupting threat effect on women's math performance. *Personality and Social Psychology Bulletin, 29,* 371–381. (p. 442)

Kellerman, J., Lewis, J., & Laird, J. D. (1989). Looking and loving: The effects of mutual gaze on feelings of romantic love. *Journal of Research in Personality, 23,* 145–161. (p. 394)

Kellermann, A. L. (1997). Comment: Gunsmoke-changing public attitudes toward smoking and firearms. *American Journal of Public Health, 87,* 910–912. (p. 327)

Kellermann, A. L. & 9 others (1993). Gun ownership as a risk factor for homicide in the home. *New England Journal of Medicine, 329,* 1984–1991. (p. 327)

Kelley, H. H. (1973). The process of causal attribution. *American Psychologist, 28,* 107–128. (pp. 103, 104)

Kelley, H. H., & Stahelski, A. J. (1970). The social interaction basis of cooperators' and competitors' beliefs about others. *Journal of Personality and Social Psychology, 16,* 66–91. (p. 113)

Kelley, K., Dawson, L., & Musialowski, D. M. (1989). Three faces of sexual explicitness: The good, the bad, and the useful. In D. Zillmann & J. Bryant (Eds.), *Pornography: Research advances and policy considerations.* Hillsdale, NJ: Erlbaum. (p. 345)

Kelly, D. J., Liu, S., Ge, L., Quinn, P. C., Slater, A. M., Lee, K., Liu, Q., & Pascalis, O. (2007). Cross-race preferences for same-race faces extended beyond the African versus Caucasian contrast in 3-month-old infants. *Infancy, 11,* 87–95. (pp. 358, 419)

Kelly, D. J., Quinn, P. C., Slater, A. M., Lee, K., Gibson, A., Smith, M., Ge, L., & Y Pascalis, O. (2005). Three-month-olds, but not newborns prefer own-race faces. *Developmental Science, 8,* F31–F36. (pp. 358, 419)

Kelman, H. C. (1997). Group processes in the resolution of international conflicts: Experiences from the Israeli-Palestinian case. *American Psychologist, 52,* 212–220. (p. 466)

Kelman, H. C. (1998). *Building a sustainable peace: The limits of pragmatism in the Israeli-Palestinian negotiations.* Address to the American Psychological Association convention. (p. 465)

Kenny, D. A., & Acitelli, L. K. (2001). Accuracy and bias in the perception of the partner in a close relationship. *Journal of Personality and Social Psychology, 80,* 439–448. (p. 370)

Kenny, D. A., & Nasby, W. (1980). Splitting the reciprocity correlation. *Journal of Personality and Social Psychology, 38,* 249–256. (p. 372)

Kenrick, D. T., & Gutierres, S. E. (1980). Contrast effects and judgments of physical attractiveness: When beauty becomes a social problem. *Journal of Personality and Social Psychology, 38,* 131–140. (p. 366)

Kenrick, D. T., Gutierres, S. E., & Goldberg, L. L. (1989). Influence of popular erotica on judgments of strangers and mates. *Journal of Experimental Social Psychology, 25,* 159–167. (p. 366)

Kenrick, D. T., & MacFarlane, S. W. (1986). Ambient temperature and horn-honking: A field study of the heat/aggression relationship. *Environment and Behavior, 18,* 179–191. (p. 323)

Kenrick, D. T., & Trost, M. R. (1987). A biosocial theory of heterosexual relationships. In K. Kelly (Ed.), *Females, males, and sexuality.* Albany: State University of New York Press. (p. 381)

Kenworthy, J. B., Hewstone, M., Levine, J. M., Martin, R., & Willis, H. (2008). The phenomenology of minority-majority status: Effects of innovation in argument generation. *European Journal of Social Psychology, 38,* 624–636. (p. 267)

Kernis, M. H. (2003). High self-esteem: A differentiated perspective. In E. C. Chang & L. J. Sanna (Eds.), *Virtue, vice, and personality: The complexity of behavior.* Washington, DC: APA Books. (p. 56)

Kerr, N. L. (1981). Social transition schemes: Charting the group's road to agreement. *Journal of Personality and Social Psychology, 41,* 684–702. (p. 509)

Kerr, N. L. (1983). Motivation losses in small groups: A social dilemma analysis. *Journal of Personality and Social Psychology, 45,* 819–828. (p. 242)

Kerr, N. L. (1989). Illusions of efficacy: The effects of group size on perceived efficacy in social dilemmas. *Journal of Experimental Social Psychology, 25,* 287–313. (p. 458)

Kerr, N. L. (1992). Norms in social dilemmas. In D. Schroeder (Ed.), *Social dilemmas: Psychological perspectives.* New York: Praeger. (p. 459)

Kerr, N. L., Atkin, R. S., Stasser, G., Meek, D., Holt, R. W., & Davis, J. H. (1976). Guilt beyond a reasonable doubt: Effects of concept definition and assigned decision rule on the judgments of mock jurors. *Journal of Personality and Social Psychology, 34,* 282–294. (p. 509)

Kerr, N. L., & Bruun, S. E. (1981). Ringelmann revisted: Alternative explanations for the social loafing effect. *Personality and Social Psychology Bulletin, 7,* 224–231. (p. 240)

Kerr, N. L., & Bruun, S. E. (1983). Dispensibility of member effort and group motivation losses: Free-rider effects. *Journal of Personality and Social Psychology, 44,* 78–94. (p. 242)

Kerr, N. L., & Kaufman-Gilliland, C. M. (1997). ". . and besides, I probably couldn't have made a difference anyway": Justification of social dilemma defection via perceived self-inefficacy. *Journal of Experimental Social Psychology, 33,* 211–230. (p. 458)

Kerr, N. L., & MacCoun, R. J. (1985). The effects of jury size and polling method on the process and product of jury deliberation. *Journal of Personality and Social Psychology, 48,* 349–363. (p. 219)

Kerr, R. A. (2009). Amid worrisome signs of warming, 'climate fatigue' sets in. *Science, 326,* 926–928. (p. 517)

Kerr, R. A. (2011). Humans are driving extreme weather; time to prepare. *Science, 334,* 1040. (p. 516)

Kidd, J. B., & Morgan, J. R. (1969). A predictive information system for management. *Operational Research Quarterly, 20,* 149–170. (p. 70)

Kiecolt-Glaser, J. K., Loving, T. J., Stowell, J. R., Malarkey, W. B., Lemeshow, S., Dickinson, S. L., & Glaser, R. (2005). Hostile marital interactions, proinflammatory cytokine production, and wound healing. *Archives of General Psychiatry, 62,* 1377–1384. (p. 485)

Kiecolt-Glaser, J. K., Malarkey, W. B., Chee, M., Newton, T., Cacioppo, J. T., Mao, H-Y., & Glaser, R. (1993). Negative behavior during marital conflict is associated with immunological down-regulation. *Psychosomatic Medicine, 55,* 395–409. (p. 485)

Kiesler, C. A. (1971). *The psychology of commitment: Experiments linking behavior to belief.* New York: Academic Press. (p. 187)

Kihlstrom, J. F., & Cantor, N. (1984). Mental representations of the self. In L. Berkowitz (Ed.), *Advances in experimental social psychology,* vol. 17. New York: Academic Press. (p. 38)

Kim, H., & Markus, H. R. (1999). Deviance or uniqueness, harmony or conformity? A cultural analysis. *Journal of Personality and Social Psychology, 77,* 785–800. (p. 43)

Kim, H. S., & Sherman, D. K. (2007). "Express yourself": Culture and the effect of self-expression on choice. *Journal of Personality and Social Psychology, 92,* 1–11. (p. 43)

Kimball, M. M. (1989). A new perspective on women's math achievement. *Psychological Bulletin, 105,* 198–214. (p. 399)

Kimmel, A. J. (1998). In defense of deception. *American Psychologist, 53,* 803–804. (p. 28)

Kimmel, M. J., Pruitt, D. G., Magenau, J. M., Konar-Goldband, E., & Carnevale, P. J. D. (1980). Effects of trust, aspiration, and gender on negotiation tactics. *Journal of Personality and Social Psychology, 38,* 9–22. (p. 463)

Kinder, D. R., & Sears, D. O. (1985). Public opinion and political action. In G. Lindzey & E. Aronson (Eds.), *The handbook of social psychology,* 3rd ed. New York: Random House. (p. 82)

King, L. A. (2001). The health benefits of writing about life goals. *Personality and Social Psychology Bulletin, 27,* 798–807. (p. 489)

Kingdon, J. W. (1967). Politicans' beliefs about voters. *The American Political Science Review, 61,* 137–145. (p. 60)

Kingston, D. A., Malamuth, N. M., Federoff, P., & Marshall, W. L. (2009). The importance of individual differences in pornography use: Theoretical perspectives and implications for treating sexual offenders. *Journal of Sex Research, 46,* 216–232. (p. 328)

Kinnier, R. T., & Metha, A. T. (1989). Regrets and priorities at three stages of life. *Counseling and Values, 33,* 182–193. (p. 97)

Kinzler, K. D., Shutts, K., Dejesus, J., & Spelke, E. S. (2009). Accent trumps race in guiding children's social preferences. *Social Cognition, 27,* 623–634. (p. 408)

Kirsh, S. J. (2006). Cartoon violence and aggression in youth. *Aggression and Violent Behavior, 11,* 547–557. (p. 332)

Kitayama, S. (1996). *The mutual constitution of culture and the self: Implications for emotion.* Paper presented to the American Psychological Society convention. (p. 40)

Kitayama, S. (1999). Behind the scenes. In D. G. Myers, *Social psychology,* 6th edition. New York: McGraw-Hill. (p. 45)

Kitayama, S., & Karasawa, M. (1997). Implicit self-esteem in Japan: Name letters and birthday numbers. *Personality and Social Psychology Bulletin, 23,* 736–742. (p. 357)

Kitayama, S., & Markus, H. R. (1995). Culture and self: Implications for internationalizing psychology. In N. R. Godlberger & J. B. Veroff (Eds.), *The culture and psychology reader.* New York: New York University Press. (p. 41)

Kitayama, S., & Markus, H. R. (2000). The pursuit of happiness and the realization of sympathy: Cultural patterns of self, social relations, and well-being. In E. Diener & E. M. Suh (Eds.), *Subjective well-being across cultures.* Cambridge, MA: MIT Press. (p. 45)

Kite, M. E. (2001). Changing times, changing gender roles: Who do we want women and men to be? In R. K. Unger (Ed.), *Handbook of the psychology of women and gender.* New York: Wiley. (p. 433)

Klaas, E. T. (1978). Psychological effects of immoral actions: The experimental evidence. *Psychological Bulletin, 85,* 756–771. (p. 132)

Klauer, K. C., & Voss, A. (2008). Effects of race on responses and response latencies in the weapon identification task: A test of six models. *Personality and Social Psychology Bulletin, 34,* 1124–1140. (p. 432)

Kleck, R. E., & Strenta, A. (1980). Perceptions of the impact of negatively valued physical characteristics on social interaction. *Journal of Personality and Social Psychology, 39,* 861–873. (p. 439)

Klein, J. G. (1991). Negative effects in impression formation: A test in the political arena. *Personality and Social Psychology Bulletin, 17,* 412–418. (p. 372)

Klein, O., Snyder, M., & Livingston, R. W. (2004). Prejudice on the stage: Self-monitoring and the public expression of group attitudes. *British Journal of Social Psychology, 43,* 299–314. (p. 73)

Klein, S. B., Lax, M. L., & Gangi, C. E. (2010). A call for an inclusive approach to the social cognitive neurosciences. *Social Cognition, 28,* 748–756. (p. 9)

Klein, W. M., & Kunda, Z. (1992). Motivated person perception: Constructing justifications for desired beliefs. *Journal of Experimental Social Psychology, 28,* 145–168. (p. 357)

Kleinke, C. L. (1977). Compliance to requests made by gazing and touching experimenters in field settings. *Journal of Experimental Social Psychology, 13,* 218–223. (p. 207)

Kleinsmith, J., Kasser, T., & McAndrew, F. T. (2006). Guns, testosterone, and aggression: An experimental test of a mediational hypothesis. *Psychological Science, 17,* 568. (p. 315)

Klentz, B., Beaman, A. L., Mapelli, S. D., & Ullrich, J. R. (1987). Perceived physical attractiveness of supporters and nonsupporters of the women's movement: An attitude-similarity-mediated error (ASME). *Personality and Social Psychology Bulletin, 13,* 513–523. (p. 368)

Klerman, G. L., & Weissman, M. M. (1989). Increasing rates of depression. *Journal of the American Medical Association, 261,* 2229–2235. (p. 522)

Klopfer, P. H. (1958). Influence of social interaction on learning rates in birds. *Science, 128,* 903. (p. 234)

Klucharev, V., Hytönen, K., Rijpkema, M., Smidts, A., & Fernández, G. (2009). Reinforcement learning signal predicts conformity. *Neuron, 61,* 140–151. (p. 219)

Knight, J. A., & Vallacher, R. R. (1981). Interpersonal engagement in social perception: The consequences of getting into the action. *Journal of Personality and Social Psychology, 40,* 990–999. (p. 357)

Knight, P. A., & Weiss, H. M. (1980). *Benefits of suffering: Communicator suffering, benefiting, and influence.* Paper presented at the American Psychological Association convention. (p. 164)

Knowles, E. D., & Peng, K. (2005). White selves: Conceptualizing and measuring a dominant-group identity. *Journal of Personality and Social Psychology, 89,* 223–241. (p. 227)

Knowles, E. S. (1983). Social physics and the effects of others: Tests of the effects of audience size and distance on social judgment and behavior. *Journal of Personality and Social Psychology, 45,* 1263–1279. (p. 236)

Knox, R. E., & Inkster, J. A. (1968). Postdecision dissonance at post-time. *Journal of Personality and Social Psychology, 8,* 319–323. (p. 143)

Knudson, R. M., Sommers, A. A., & Golding, S. L. (1980). Interpersonal perception and mode of resolution in marital conflict. *Journal of Personality and Social Psychology, 38,* 751–763. (p. 464)

Koehler, D. J. (1991). Explanation, imagination, and confidence in judgment. *Psychological Bulletin, 110,* 499–519. (p. 94)

Koehler, D. J., & Poon, C. S. K. (2006). Self-predictions overweight strength of current intentions. *Journal of Experimental Social Psychology, 42*(4), 517. (p. 91)

Koehler, D. J., White, R. J., & John, L. K. (2011). Good intentions, optimistic self-predictions, and missed opportunities. *Social Psychological and Personality Science, 2,* 90–96. (p. 91)

Koenig, L. B., McGue, M., & Iacono, W. G. (2008). Stability and change in religiousness during emerging adulthood. *Developmental Psychology, 44,* 531–543. (p. 178)

Koestner, R., & Wheeler, L. (1988). Self-presentation in personal advertisements: The influence of implicit notions of attraction and role expectations. *Journal of Social and Personal Relationships, 5,* 149–160. (p. 361)

Kohn, N. W., Paulus, P. B., & Choi, Y. (2011). Building on the ideas of others. An examination of the idea combination process. *Journal of Experimental Social Psychology, 47,* 554–561. (p. 263)

Kolivas, E. D., & Gross, A. M. (2007). Assessing sexual aggression: Addressing the gap between rape victimization and perpetration prevalence rates. *Aggression and Violent Behavior, 12,* 315–328. (p. 102)

Konrath, S. H., O'Brien, E. H., & Hsing, C. (2011). Changes in dispositional empathy in American college students over time: A meta-analysis. *Personality & Social Psychology Review, 15,* 180–198. (p. 55)

Koo, M., Algoe, S. B., Wilson, T. D., & Gilbert, D. T. (2008). It's a wonderful life: Mentally subtracting positive events improves people's affective states, contrary to their affective forecasts. *Journal of Personality and Social Psychology, 95,* 1217–1224. (pp. 51, 526)

Koomen, W., & Bahler, M. (1996). National stereotypes: Common representations and ingroup favouritism. *European Journal of Social Psychology, 26,* 325–331. (p. 399)

Koop, C. E. (1987). Report of the Surgeon General's workshop on pornography and public health. *American Psychologist, 42,* 944–945. (pp. 328, 329)

Koriat, A., Lichtenstein, S., & Fischhoff, B. (1980). Reasons for confidence. *Journal of Experimental Social Psychology: Human Learning and Memory, 6,* 107–118. (p. 94)

Korn, J. H., & Nicks, S. D. (1993). *The rise and decline of deception in social psychology.* Poster presented at the American Psychological Society convention. (p. 27)

Koss, M. P., Heise, L., & Russo, N. F. (1994). The global health burden of rape. *Psychology of Women Quarterly, 18,* 509–537. (p. 330)

Krackow, A., & Blass, T. (1995). When nurses obey or defy inappropriate physician orders: Attributional differences. *Journal of Social Behavior and Personality, 10,* 585–594. (p. 208)

Krahe, B. (1998). Sexual aggression among adolescents: Prevalence and predictors in a German sample. *Psychology of Women Quarterly, 22,* 537–554. (p. 330)

Krahe, B., Moller, I., Huesmann, L. R., Kirwil, L., Felber, J., & Berger, A. (2010). Desensitization to media violence: Links with habitual media violence exposure, aggressive cognitions, and aggressive behavior. *Journal of Personality and Social Psychology, 100,* 630–646. (p. 335)

Kramer, A. E. (2008, August 32). Russia's collective farms: Hot capitalist property. *New York Times* (www.nytimes.com). (p. 241)

Kraus, M. W., Piff, P. K., & Keltner, D. (2011). Social class as culture: the convergence of resources and rank in the social realm. *Current Directions in Psychological Science, 20,* 246–250. (p. 402)

Kraus, S. J. (1995). Attitudes and the prediction of behavior: A meta-analysis of the empirical literature. *Personality and Social Psychology Bulletin, 21,* 58–75. (p. 124)

Kraut, R. E. (1973). Effects of social labeling on giving to charity. *Journal of Experimental Social Psychology, 9,* 551–562. (p. 303)

Kravitz, D. A., & Martin, B. (1986). Ringelmann rediscovered: The original article. *Journal of Personality and Social Psychology, 50,* 936–941. (p. 238)

Krebs, D. (1970). Altruism-An examination of the concept and a review of the literature. *Psychological Bulletin, 73,* 258–302. (p. 275)

Krebs, D. (1975). Empathy and altruism. *Journal of Personality and Social Psychology, 32,* 1134-1146. (p. 276)

Krebs, D., & Adinolfi, A. A. (1975). Physical attractiveness, social relations, and personality style. *Journal of Personality and Social Psychology, 31,* 245-253. (p. 358)

Krebs, D. L. (1998). The evolution of moral behaviors. In C. Crawford & D. L. Krebs (Eds.), *Handbook of evolutionary psychology: Ideas, issues, and applications.* Mahwah, NJ: Erlbaum. (p. 285)

Krendl, A. C., Richeson, J. A., Kelley, W. M., & Heatherton, T. F. (2008). The negative consequences of threat: A functional magnetic resonance imaging investigation of the neural mechanisms underlying women's underperformance in math. *Psychological Science, 19,* 168-175. (p. 442)

Krisberg, K. (2004). Successful 'truth' anti-smoking campaign in funding jeopardy: New commission works to save campaign. *Nation's Health, 34*(4). (p. 165)

Krizan, Z., & Suls, J. (2008). Losing sight of oneself in the above-average effect: When egocentrism, focalism, and group diffuseness collide. *Journal of Experimental Social Psychology, 44,* 929-942. (p. 62)

Krosnick, J. A. (2010, June 8). The climate majority. *New York Times* (www.nytimes.com). (p. 158)

Krosnick, J. A., & Alwin, D. F. (1989). Aging and susceptibility to attitude change. *Journal of Personality and Social Psychology, 57,* 416-425. (p. 178)

Krosnick, J. A., & Schuman, H. (1988). Attitude intensity, importance, and certainty and susceptibility to response effects. *Journal of Personality and Social Psychology, 54,* 940-952. (p. 23)

Krueger, A. B., & Malečková, J. (2009). Attitudes and action: Public opinion and the occurrence of international terrorism. *Science, 325,* 1534-1536. (p. 122)

Krueger, J., & Clement, R. W. (1994). Memory-based judgments about multiple categories: A revision and extension of Tajfel's accentuation theory. *Journal of Personality and Social Psychology, 67,* 35-47. (pp. 65, 418)

Krueger, J., & Rothbart, M. (1988). Use of categorical and individuating information in making inferences about personality. *Journal of Personality and Social Psychology, 55,* 187-195. (p. 444)

Krueger, J. I., & Funder, D. C. (2003a). Towards a balanced social psychology: Causes, consequences and cures for the problem-seeking approach to social behavior and cognition. *Behavior and Brain Sciences, 27,* 313-349. (p. 116)

Krueger, J. I., & Funder, D. C. (2003b). Social psychology: A field in search of a center—Response. *Behavior and Brain Sciences, 27,* 361-376. (p. 116)

Krueger, R. F., Hicks, B. M., & McGue, M. (2001). Altruism and antisocial behavior: Independent tendencies, unique personality correlates, distinct etiologies. *Psychological Science, 12,* 397-402. (p. 299)

Kruger, J., & Dunning, D. (1999). Unskilled and unaware of it: How difficulties in recognizing one's own incompetence lead to inflated self-assessments. *Journal of Personality and Social Psychology, 77,* 1121-1134. (p. 90)

Kruger, J., Epley, N., Parker, J., & Ng, Z. (2005). Egocentrism over e-mail: Can we communicate as well as we think? *Journal of Personality and Social Psychology, 89*(6), 925. (p. 97)

Kruger, J., & Evans, M. (2004). If you don't want to be late, enumerate: Unpacking reduces the planning fallacy. *Journal of Experimental Social Psychology, 40*(5), 586. (p. 94)

Kruger, J., & Gilovich, T. (1999). "Naïve cynicism" in everyday theories of responsibility assessment: On biased assumptions of bias. *Journal of Personality and Social Psychology, 76,* 743-753. (p. 60)

Kruger, J., Gordon, C. L., & Kuban, J. (2006). Intentions in teasing: When "just kidding" just isn't good enough. *Journal of Personality and Social Psychology, 90,* 412-425. (p. 389)

Kruglanski, A. W., & Ajzen, I. (1983). Bias and error in human judgment. *European Journal of Social Psychology, 13,* 1-44. (p. 116)

Kruglanski, A. W., & Fishman, S. (2006). Terrorism between "syndrome" and "tool." *Current Directions in Psychological Science, 15,* 45. (p. 311)

Kruglanski, A. W., Gelfand, M., & Gunaratna, R. (2010, January). Detainee deradicalization: A challenge for psychological science. *APS Observer, 23,* 20-22. (p. 171)

Kruglanski, A. W., & Golec de Zavala, A. (2005). Individual motivations, the group process and organizational strategies in suicide terrorism. *Psychology and Sociology (Psycologie et sociologie).* (p. 185)

Kruglanski, A. W., & Webster, D. M. (1991). Group members' reactions to opinion deviates and conformists at varying degrees of proximity to decision deadline and of environmental noise. *Journal of Personality and Social Psychology, 61,* 212-225. (p. 267)

Krull, D. S., Loy, M. H-M., Lin, J., Wang, C-F., Chen, S., & Zhao, X. (1999). The fundamental fundamental attribution error: Correspondence bias in individualist and collectivist cultures. *Personality and Social Psychology Bulletin, 25,* 1208-1219. (p. 109)

Kubany, E. S., Bauer, G. B., Pangilinan, M. E., Muroka, M. Y., & Enriquez, V. G. (1995). Impact of labeled anger and blame in intimate relationships. *Journal of Cross-Cultural Psychology, 26,* 65-83. (p. 346)

Kubey, R., & Csikszentmihalyi, M. (2002, February). Television addiction is no mere metaphor. *Scientific American, 286,* 74-82. (p. 337)

Kugihara, N. (1999). Gender and social loafing in Japan. *Journal of Social Psychology, 139,* 516-526. (p. 242)

Kuiper, N. A., & Higgins, E. T. (1985). Social cognition and depression: A general integrative perspective. *Social Cognition, 3,* 1-15. (p. 477)

Kunda, Z., Fong, G. T., Sanitioso, R., & Reber, E. (1993). Directional questions direct self-conceptions. *Journal of Experimental Social Psychology, 29,* 63-86. (p. 474)

Kunda, Z., & Oleson, K. C. (1995). Maintaining stereotypes in the face of disconfirmation: Constructing grounds for subtyping deviants. *Journal of Personality and Social Psychology, 68,* 565-579. (p. 437)

Kunda, Z., & Oleson, K. C. (1997). When exceptions prove the rule: How extremity of deviance determines the impact of deviant examples on stereotypes. *Journal of Personality and Social Psychology, 72,* 965-979. (p. 437)

Kunda, Z., & Sherman-Williams, B. (1993). Stereotypes and the construal of individuating information. *Personality and Social Psychology Bulletin, 19,* 90-99. (p. 437)

Kunda, Z., & Sinclair, L. (1999). Motivated reasoning with stereotypes: Activation, application, and inhibition. *Psychological Inquiry, 10,* 12-22. (p. 445)

Kunda, Z. & Spencer, S. J. (2003). When do stereotypes come to mind and when do they color judgment? A goal-based theoretical framework for stereotype activation and application. *Psychological Bulletin, 129,* 522–544. (p. 416)

Kunkel, D. (2001, February 4). Sex on TV. Menlo Park, CA: Henry J. Kaiser Family Foundation (www.kff.org). (p. 336)

Kunst-Wilson, W. R., & Zajonc, R. B. (1980). Affective discrimination of stimuli that cannot be recognized. *Science, 207,* 557–558. (p. 357)

Kuntsche, E. K., Picket, W., Overpeck, M. Craig, W., Boyce, W., & de Matos, M. G. (2006). Television viewing and forms of bullying among adolescents from eight countries. *Journal of Adolescent Health, 39,* 908–915. (p. 332)

Kupper, N., & Denollet, J. (2007). Type D personality as a prognostic factor in heart disease: Assessment and mediating mechanisms. *Journal of Personality Assessment, 89,* 265–276. (p. 483)

Kutner, L., & Olson, C. K. (2008). *Grand theft childhood: The surprising truth about violent video games and what parents can do* (pp. 111–137). New York: Simon & Schuster. (p. 341)

Lagerspetz, K. (1979). Modification of aggressiveness in mice. In S. Feshbach & A. Fraczek (Eds.), *Aggression and behavior change.* New York: Praeger. (p. 313)

Lagerspetz, K. M. J., Bjorkqvist, K., Berts, M., & King, E. (1982). Group aggression among school children in three schools. *Scandinavian Journal of Psychology, 23,* 45–52. (p. 342)

Laird, J. D. (1974). Self-attribution of emotion: The effects of expressive behavior on the quality of emotional experience. *Journal of Personality and Social Psychology, 29,* 475–486. (p. 146)

Laird, J. D. (1984). The real role of facial response in the experience of emotion: A reply to Tourangeau and Ellsworth, and others. *Journal of Personality and Social Psychology, 47,* 909–917. (p. 146)

Lakin, J. L., & Chartrand, T. L. (2003). Using nonconscious behavioral mimicry to create affiliation and rapport. *Psychological Science, 14,* 334–339. (p. 369)

Lakin, J. L., Chartrand, T. L., & Arkin, R. M. (2008). I am too just like you: Nonconscious mimicry as an automatic behavioral responses to social exclusion. *Psychological Science, 19,* 816–821. (p. 355)

Lalancette, M-F., & Standing, L. (1990). Asch fails again. *Social Behavior and Personality, 18,* 7–12. (p. 224)

Lalonde, R. N. (1992). The dynamics of group differentiation in the face of defeat. *Personality and Social Psychology Bulletin, 18,* 336–342. (p. 60)

Lalwani, A. K., Shavitt, S., & Johnson, T. (2006). What is the relation between cultural orientation and socially desirable responding? *Journal of Personality and Social Psychology, 90,* 165–178. (p. 43)

Lamal, P. A. (1979). College student common beliefs about psychology. *Teaching of Psychology, 6,* 155–158. (p. 84)

Lambert, N. M., Negash, S., Stillman, T. F., Olmstead, S. B., & Fincham, F. D. (2012). A love that doesn't last: Pornography consumption and weakened commitment to a romantic partner. *Journal of Social and Clinical Psychology, 31,* 410–438. (pp. 328, 330)

Landers, A. (1969, April 8). Syndicated newspaper column. April 8, 1969. Cited by L. Berkowitz in The case for bottling up rage. *Psychology Today,* September, 1973, 24–31. (p. 344)

Landers, A. (1985, August). Is affection more important than sex? *Reader's Digest,* pp. 44–46. (p. 22)

Lane, D. J., Gibbons, F. X., O'Hara, R. E., & Gerrard, M. (2011). Standing out from the crowd: How comparison to prototypes can decrease health-risk behavior in young adults. *Basic and Applied Social Psychology, 33,* 228–238. (p. 217)

Langer, E. J. (1977). The psychology of chance. *Journal for the Theory of Social Behavior, 7,* 185–208. (p. 98)

Langer, E. J., & Imber, L. (1980). The role of mindlessness in the perception of deviance. *Journal of Personality and Social Psychology, 39,* 360–367. (p. 420)

Langer, E. J., & Rodin, J. (1976). The effects of choice and enhanced personal responsibility for the aged: A field experiment in an institutional setting. *Journal of Personality and Social Psychology, 334,* 191–198. (p. 57)

Langer, E. J., & Roth, J. (1975). Heads I win, tails it's chance: The illusion of control as a function of the sequence of outcomes in a purely chance task. *Journal of Personality and Social Psychology, 32,* 951–955. (p. 173)

Langford, D. J., Crager, S. E., Shehzad, Z., Smith, S. B., Sotocinal, S. G., Levenstadt, J. S., Chanda, M. L., Levitin, D. J., & Mogil, J. S. (2006). Social modulation of pain as evidence for empathy in mice. *Science, 312,* 1967–1970. (p. 288)

Langlois, J., Kalakanis, L., Rubenstein, A., Larson, A., Hallam, M., & Smoot, M. (1996). *Maxims and myths of beauty: A meta-analytic and theoretical review.* Paper presented to the American Psychological Society convention. (p. 363)

Langlois, J. H., Kalakanis, L., Rubenstein, A. J., Larson, A., Hallam, M., & Smoot, M. (2000). Maxims or myths of beauty? A meta-analytic and theoretical review. *Psychological Bulletin, 126,* 390–423. (pp. 362, 363, 364)

Langlois, J. H., & Roggman, L. A. (1990). Attractive faces are only average. *Psychological Science, 1,* 115–121. (p. 364)

Langlois, J. H., Roggman, L. A., Casey, R. J., Ritter, J. M., Rieser-Danner, L. A., & Jenkins, V. Y. (1987). Infant preferences for attractive faces: Rudiments of a stereotype? *Developmental Psychology, 23,* 363–369. (p. 362)

Langlois, J. H., Roggman, L. A., & Musselman, L. (1994). What is average and what is not average about attractive faces? *Psychological Science, 5,* 214–220. (p. 364)

Larrick, R. P., Timmerman, T. A., Carton, A. M., and Abrevaya, J. (2011). Temper, temperature, and temptation: Heat-related retaliation in baseball. *Psychological Science, 23*(6), 1–6. (p. 323)

Larsen, K. (1974). Conformity in the Asch experiment. *Journal of Social Psychology, 94,* 303–304. (p. 224)

Larsen, K. S. (1990). The Asch conformity experiment: Replication and transhistorical comparisons. *Journal of Social Behavior and Personality, 5*(4), 163–168. (p. 224)

Larsen, R. J., & Diener, E. (1987). Affect intensity as an individual difference characteristic: A review. *Journal of Research in Personality, 21,* 1–39. (p. 313)

Larson, J. R., Jr., Foster-Fishman, P. G., & Keys, C. B. (1994). Discussion of shared and unshared information in decision-making groups. *Journal of Personality and Social Psychology, 67,* 446–461. (p. 252)

Larsson, K. (1956). *Conditioning and sexual behavior in the male albino rat.* Stockholm: Almqvist & Wiksell. (p. 234)

Larwood, L. (1978). Swine flu: A field study of self-serving biases. *Journal of Applied Social Psychology, 18,* 283–289. (p. 63)

Larwood, L., & Whittaker, W. (1977). Managerial myopia: Self-serving biases in organizational planning. *Journal of Applied Psychology, 62,* 194–198. (p. 70)

Lassiter, G. D. (2010). Psychological science and sound public policy: Video recording of custodial interrogations. *American Psychologist, 65,* 768–779. (p. 502)

Lassiter, G. D., Diamond, S. S., Schmidt, H. C., & Elek, J. K. (2007). Evaluating videotaped confessions. *Psychological Science, 18,* 224–226. (p. 108)

Lassiter, G. D., & Dudley, K. A. (1991). The a priori value of basic research: The case of videotaped confessions. *Journal of Social Behavior and Personality, 6,* 7–16. (p. 108)

Lassiter, G. D., Geers, A. L., Handley, I. M., Weiland, P. E., & Munhall, P. J. (2002). Videotaped interrogations and confessions: A simple change in camera perspective alters verdicts in simulated trials. *Journal of Applied Psychology, 87,* 867–874. (p. 108)

Lassiter, G. D., & Irvine, A. A. (1986). Videotaped confessions: The impact of camera point of view on judgments of coercion. *Journal of Applied Social Psychology, 16,* 268–276. (p. 108)

Lassiter, G. D., & Munhall, P. J. (2001). The genius effect: Evidence for a nonmotivational interpretation. *Journal of Experimental Social Psychology, 37,* 349–355. (p. 63)

Lassiter, G. D., Munhall, P. J., Berger, I. P., Weiland, P. E., Handley, I. M., & Geers, A. L. (2005). Attributional complexity and the camera perspective bias in videotaped confessions. *Basic and Applied Social Psychology, 27,* 27–35. (p. 108)

Latané, B., & Dabbs, J. M., Jr. (1975). Sex, group size and helping in three cities. *Sociometry, 38,* 180–194. (p. 291)

Latané, B., & Darley, J. M. (1968). Group inhibition of bystander intervention in emergencies. *Journal of Personality and Social Psychology, 10,* 215–221. (p. 291)

Latané, B., & Darley, J. M. (1970). *The unresponsive bystander: Why doesn't he help?* New York: Appleton-Century-Crofts. (pp. 290, 299)

Latané, B., & Nida, S. (1981). Ten years of research on group size and helping. *Psychological Bulletin, 89,* 308–324. (p. 291)

Latané, B., & Rodin, J. (1969). A lady in distress: Inhibiting effects of friends and strangers on bystander intervention. *Journal of Experimental Social Psychology, 5,* 189–202. (p. 293)

Latané, B., Williams, K., & Harkins, S. (1979). Many hands make light the work: The causes and consequences of social loafing. *Journal of Personality and Social Psychology, 37,* 822–832. (p. 239)

Lau, G. P., Kay, A. C., & Spencer, S. J. (2008). Loving those who justify inequality: The effects of system threat on attraction to women who embody benevolent sexist ideals. *Psychological Science, 19,* 20. (p. 434)

Laughlin, P. R. (1996). Group decision making and collective induction. In E. H. Witte & J. H. Davis (Eds.), *Understanding group behavior: Consensual action by small groups.* Mahwah, NJ: Erlbaum. (p. 261)

Laughlin, P. R., & Adamopoulos, J. (1980). Social combination processes and individual learning for six-person cooperative groups on an intellective task. *Journal of Personality and Social Psychology, 38,* 941–947. (p. 261)

Laughlin, P. R., Hatch, E. C., Silver, J. S., & Boh, L. (2006). Groups perform better than the best individuals on letters-to-numbers problems: Effects of group size. *Journal of Personality and Social Psychology, 90,* 644–651. (p. 261)

Laughlin, P. R., Zander, M. L., Knievel, E. M., & Tan, T. K. (2003). Groups perform better than the best individuals on letters-to-numbers problems: Informative equations and effective strategies. *Journal of Personality and Social Psychology, 85,* 684–694. (p. 261)

Laumann, E. O., Gagnon, J. H., Michael, R. T., & Michaels, S. (1994). *The social organization of sexuality: Sexual practices in the United States.* Chicago: University of Chicago Press. (p. 102)

Lazarsfeld, P. F. (1949). The American soldier—an expository review. *Public Opinion Quarterly, 13,* 377–404. (p. 14)

Lazer, D., & others. (2009). Computational social science. *Science, 323,* 721–723. (p. 251)

Leary, M. (1994). *Self-presentation: Impression management and interpersonal behavior.* Pacific Grove, CA: Brooks/Cole. (p. 139)

Leary, M. R. (1998). The social and psychological importance of self-esteem. In R. M. Kowalski & M. R. Leary (Eds.), *The social psychology of emotional and behavioral problems.* Washington, DC: American Psychological Association. (pp. 20, 41, 52)

Leary, M. R. (2001). Social anxiety as an early warning system: A refinement and extension of the self-presentation theory of social anxiety. In S. G. Hofmann & P. M. DiBartolo (Eds.), *From social anxiety to social phobia: Multiple perspectives.* Needham Heights, MA: Allyn & Bacon. (p. 139)

Leary, M. R. (2004a). *The curse of the self: Self-awareness, egotism, and the quality of human life.* New York: Oxford University Press. (p. 37)

Leary, M. R. (2004b). The self we know and the self we show: Self-esteem, self-presentation, and the maintenance of interpersonal relationships. In M. Brewer & M. Hewstone (Eds.), *Emotion and motivation.* Malden, MA: Usishers. (pp. 41, 52, 73, 139)

Leary, M. R. (2007). Motivational and emotional aspects of the self. *Annual Review of Psychology, 58,* 317–344. (pp. 52, 139)

Leary, M. R. (2010). Affiliation, acceptance, and belonging: The pursuit of interpersonal connection. In S. T. Fiske, D. T. Gilbert, & G. Lindzey (Eds.), *Handbook of social psychology,* 5th edition. Hoboken, NJ: Wiley. (p. 139)

Leary, M. R., & Baumeister, R. F. (2000). The nature and function of self-esteem: Sociometer theory. In M. P. Zanna (Ed.) *Advances in Experimental Social Psychology, 32* (1–62). San Diego, CA: Academic Press. (p. 10)

Leary, M. R., & Kowalski, R. M. (1995). *Social anxiety.* New York: Guilford. (p. 480)

Leary, M. R., Kowalski, R. M., Smith, L., & Phillips, S. (2003). Teasing, rejection, and violence: Case studies of the school shootings. *Aggressive Behavior, 29,* 202–214. (p. 353)

Leary, M. R., Nezlek, J. B., Radford-Davenport, D., Martin, J., & McMullen, A. (1994). Self-presentation in everyday interactions: Effects of target familiarity and gender composition. *Journal of Personality and Social Psychology, 67,* 664–673. (p. 72)

Leary, M. R., Twenge, J. M., & Quinlivan, E. (2006). Interpersonal rejection as a determinant of anger and aggression. *Personality and Social Psychology Review, 10,* 111–132. (p. 353)

LeDoux, J. (1994, June). Emotion, memory and the brain. *Scientific American,* 50–57. (p. 88)

LeDoux, J. (1996). *The emotional brain: The mysterious underpinnings of emotional life.* New York: Simon & Schuster. (p. 88)

Lee, F., Hallahan, M., & Herzog, T. (1996). Explaining real-life events: How culture and domain shape attributions. *Personality and Social Psychology Bulletin, 22,* 732–741. (p. 109)

Lee, S., Rogge, R. D., & Reis, H. T. (2010). Assessing the seeds of relationship decay: Using implicit evaluations to detect the early stages of disillusionment. *Psychological Science, 21,* 857–864. (p. 125)

Lee, Y.-P., & Bond, M. H. (1996). *How friendship develops out of personality and values: A study of interpersonal attraction in Chinese culture.* Unpublished manuscript, Chinese University of Hong Kong. (p. 369)

Lee, Y.-T., & Seligman, M. E. P. (1997). Are Americans more optimistic than the Chinese? *Personality and Social Psychology Bulletin, 23,* 32–40. (p. 74)

Lehavot, K., & Lambert, A. J. (2007). Toward a greater understanding of antigay prejudice: On the role of sexual orientation and gender role violation. *Basic and Applied Social Psychology, 29,* 279–292. (p. 370)

Lehman, D. R., Krosnick, J. A., West, R. L., & Fan, L. (1992). The focus of judgment effect: A question wording effect due to hypothesis confirmation bias. *Personality and Social Psychology Bulletin, 18,* 690–699. (p. 23)

Lehman, D. R., Lempert, R. O., & Nisbett, R. E. (1988). The effects of graduate training on reasoning: Formal discipline and thinking about everyday-life events. *American Psychologist, 43,* 431–442. (p. 117)

Leippe, M. R. (1985). The influence of eyewitness nonidentification on mock-jurors. *Journal of Applied Social Psychology, 15,* 656–672. (p. 498)

Leippe, M. R. (1994). The appraisal of eyewitness testimony. In D. F. Ross, J. D. Read, & M. P. Toglia (Eds.), *Adult eyewitness testimony: Current trends and developments.* New York: Cambridge. (p. 499)

Leippe, M. R., & Eisenstadt, D. (1994). Generalization of dissonance reduction: Decreasing prejudice through induced compliance. *Journal of Personality and Social Psychology, 67,* 395–413. (p. 142)

Leippe, M. R., & Elkin, R. A. (1987). *Dissonance reduction strategies and accountability to self and others: Ruminations and some initial research.* Presentation to the Fifth International Conference on Affect, Motivation, and Cognition, Nags Head Conference Center. (p. 142)

Leiserowitz, A., Maibach, E., Roser-Renouf, C., & Smith, N. (2011). *Climate change in the American mind: Americans' global warming beliefs and attitudes in May 2011.* Yale University and George Mason University. New Haven, CT: Yale Project on Climate Change Communication. (p. 518)

Lemay, E. P., Jr., Clark, M. S., & Greenberg, A. (2010). What is beautiful is good because what is beautiful is desired: Physical attractiveness stereotyping as projection of interpersonal goals. *Personality and Social Psychology Bulletin, 36,* 339–353. (p. 362)

Lemyre, L., & Smith, P. M. (1985). Intergroup discrimination and self-esteem in the minimal group paradigm. *Journal of Personality and Social Psychology, 49,* 660–670. (p. 412)

Lench, H. C., Quas, J. A., & Edelstein, R. S. (2006). My child is better than average: The extension and restriction of unrealistic optimism. *Journal of Applied Social Psychology, 36,* 2963–2979. (p. 64)

Lenhart, A. (2010, April 20). *Teens, cell phones and texting.* Pew Internet and American Life Project. Pew Research Center (www.pewresearch.org). (p. 352)

Lenton, A. P., & Francesconi, M. (2010). How humans cognitively manage an abundance of mate options. *Psychological Science, 21,* 528–533. (p. 363)

Leodoro, G., & Lynn, M. (2007). The effect of server posture on the tips of Whites and Blacks. *Journal of Applied Social Psychology, 37,* 201–209. (p. 301)

Leone, C. & Hawkins, L. B. (2006). Self-monitoring and close relationships. *Journal of Personality, 74,* 739–778. (p. 73)

Lepore, S. J., Ragan, J. D., & Jones, S. (2000). Talking facilitates cognitive-emotional processes of adaptation to an acute stressor. *Journal of Personality and Social Psychology, 78,* 499–508. (p. 489)

Lepper, M. R., & Greene, D. (Eds.) (1979). *The hidden costs of reward.* Hillsdale, NJ: Erlbaum. (p. 148)

Lerner, M. J. (1980). *The belief in a just world: A fundamental delusion.* New York: Plenum. (p. 414)

Lerner, M. J., & Miller, D. T. (1978). Just world research and the attribution process: Looking back and ahead. *Psychological Bulletin, 85,* 1030–1051. (p. 414)

Lerner, M. J., & Simmons, C. H. (1966). Observer's reaction to the "innocent victim": Compassion or rejection? *Journal of Personality and Social Psychology, 4,* 203–210. (p. 414)

Lerner, M. J., Somers, D. G., Reid, D., Chiriboga, D., & Tierney, M. (1991). Adult children as caregivers: Egocentric biases in judgments of sibling contributions. *The Gerontologist, 31,* 746–755. (p. 63)

Leshner, A. I. (2005, October). Science and religion should not be adversaries. *APS Observer* (www.psychologicalscience.org). (p. 17)

Leung, K., & Bond, M. H. (1984). The impact of cultural collectivism on reward allocation. *Journal of Personality and Social Psychology, 47,* 793–804. (p. 460)

Levav, J., & Fitzsimons, G. J. (2006). When questions change behavior: The role of ease of representation. *Psychological Science, 17,* 207–213. (p. 127)

Leventhal, H. (1970). Findings and theory in the study of fear communications. In L. Berkowitz (Ed.), *Advances in experimental social psychology* (Vol. 5). New York: Academic Press. (p. 168)

Levesque, M. J., Nave, C. S., & Lowe, C. A. (2006). Toward an understanding of gender differences in inferring sexual interest. *Psychology of Women Quarterly, 30,* 150–158. (p. 102)

Levin, S., Matthews, M., Guimond, S., Sidanius, J., Pratto, F., Kteily, N., Pitpitan, E. V., & Dover, T. (2011). Assimilation, multiculturalism, and colorblindness: Mediated and moderated relationships between social dominance orientation and prejudice. *Journal of Experimental Social Psychology, 47,* 208–214. (p. 403)

Levine, J. M. (1989). Reaction to opinion deviance in small groups. In P. Paulus (Ed.), *Psychology of group influence: New perspectives.* Hillsdale, NJ: Erlbaum. (pp. 267, 268)

Levine, J. M., & Moreland, R. L. (1985). Innovation and socialization in small groups. In S. Moscovici, G. Mugny, & E. Van Avermaet (Eds.), *Perspectives on minority influence.* Cambridge: Cambridge University Press. (p. 268)

Levine, M., & Crowther, S. (2008). The responsive bystander: How social group membership and group size can encourage as well as inhibit bystander intervention. *Journal of Personality and Social Psychology, 95,* 1429–1439. (p. 295)

Levine, R. (2003). *The power of persuasion: How we're bought and sold.* New York: Wiley. (pp. 63, 190)

Levine, R. V. (2001). Cross-cultural differences in helping strangers. *Journal of Cross-Cultural Psychology, 32,* 543–560. (p. 295)

Levine, R. V. (2003). The kindness of strangers. *American Scientist, 91,* 226–233. (pp. 295, 296)

Levine, R. V., Martinez, T. S., Brase, G., & Sorenson, K. (1994). Helping in 36 U.S. cities. *Journal of Personality and Social Psychology, 67,* 69–82. (p. 295)

Levine, R. V., Norenzayan, A., & Philbrick, K. (2001). Cross-cultural differences in helping strangers. *Journal of Cross-Cultural Psychology, 32*(5), 543–560. (p. 295)

Levinson, H. (1950). *The science of chance: From probability to statistics.* New York: Rinehart. (p. 459)

Levitan, L. C., & Visser, P. S. (2008). The impact of the social context on resistance to persuasion: Effortful versus effortless responses to counter-attitudinal information. *Journal of Experimental Social Psychology, 44,* 640–649. (p. 192)

Levy, S. R., Stroessner, S. J., & Dweck, C. S. (1998). Stereotype formation and endorsement: The role of implicit theories. *Journal of Personality and Social Psychology, 74,* 1421–1436. (p. 423)

Levy-Leboyer, C. (1988). Success and failure in applying psychology. *American Psychologist, 43,* 779–785. (p. 168)

Lewandowski, G. W., & Bizzoco, N. M. (2007). Addition through subtraction: Growth following the dissolution of a low-quality relationship. *Journal of Positive Psychology, 2,* 40–54. (p. 393)

Lewicki, P. (1985). Nonconscious biasing effects of single instances on subsequent judgments. *Journal of Personality and Social Psychology, 48,* 563–574. (p. 375)

Lewin, K. (1936). *A dynamic theory of personality.* New York: McGraw-Hill. (p. 223)

Lewin, K. (1952). *Field theory in social science. Selected theoretical papers by Kurt Lewin.* London: Tavistock. (p. 6)

Lewinsohn, P. M., Hoberman, H., Teri, L., & Hautziner, M. (1985). An integrative theory of depression. In S. Reiss & R. Bootzin (Eds.), *Theoretical issues in behavior therapy.* New York: Academic Press. (p. 478)

Lewinsohn, P. M., & Rosenbaum, M. (1987). Recall of parental behavior by acute depressives, remitted depressives, and nondepressives. *Journal of Personality and Social Psychology, 52,* 611–619. (p. 477)

Lewis, C. S. (1974). *The horse and his boy.* New York: Collier Books. (p. 142)

Lewis, D. O. (1998). *Guilty by reason of insanity.* London: Arrow. (p. 313)

Lewis, R. S., Goto, S. G., & Kong, L. L. (2008). Culture and context: East Asian American and European American differences in P3 event-related potentials and self-construal. *Personality and Social Psychology Bulletin, 34,* 623–634. (p. 42)

Leyens, J.-P., Camino, L., Parke, R. D., & Berkowitz, L. (1975). Effects of movie violence on aggression in a field setting as a function of group dominance and cohesion. *Journal of Personality and Social Psychology, 32,* 346–360. (p. 334)

Leyens, J.-P., Cortes, B., Demoulin, S., Dovidio, J. F., Fiske, S. T., Gaunt, R., Paladino, M-P., Rodriquez-Perez, A., Rodriquez-Torrez, R., & Vaes, J. (2003). Emotional prejudice, essentialism, and nationalism. *European Journal of Social Psychology, 33,* 703–717. (p. 411)

Leyens, J-P., Demoulin, S., Vaes, J., Gaunt, R., & Paladino, M. P. (2007). Infra-humanization: The wall of group differences. *Social Issues and Policy Review, 1,* 139–172. (p. 411)

Li, N. P., Bailey, J. M., Kenrick, D. T., & Linsenmeier, J. A. W. (2002). The necessities and luxuries of mate preferences: Testing the tradeoffs. *Journal of Personality and Social Psychology, 82,* 947–955. (p. 365)

Li, Y., Johnson, E. J., & Zaval, L. (2011). Local warming: Daily temperature influences belief in global warming. *Psychological Science, 22,* 454–459. (p. 96)

Liberman, A., & Chaiken, S. (1992). Defensive processing of personally relevant health messages. *Personality and Social Psychology Bulletin, 18,* 669–679. (p. 170)

Lichtblau, E. (2003, March 18). U.S. seeks $289 billion in cigarette makers' profits. *New York Times* (www.nytimes.com). (p. 190)

Lichtblau, E. (2005, August 24). Profiling report leads to a demotion. *New York Times* (www.nytimes.com). (p. 429)

Lichtenstein, S., & Fischhoff, B. (1980). Training for calibration. *Organizational Behavior and Human Performance, 26,* 149–171. (p. 94)

Lieberman, M. D., Ochsner, K. N., Gilbert, D. T., & Schacter, D. L. (2001). Do amnesics exhibit cognitive dissonance reduction? The role of explicit memory and attention in attitude change. *Psychological Science, 12,* 135–140. (p. 152)

Lilienfeld, S. O., Fowler, K. A., Lohr, J. M., & Lynn, S. J. (2005). Pseudoscience, nonscience, and nonsense in clinical psychology: Dangers and remedies. In R. H. Wright, & N. A. Cummings (Eds.), *Destructive trends in mental health: The well-intentioned path to harm.* (187–218). New York: Routledge. (p. 472)

Lilienfeld, S. O., Wood, J. M., & Garb, H. N. (2000). The scientific status of projective techniques. *Psychological Science in the Public Interest, 1,* 27–66. (p. 472)

Lindsay, R. C. L., Semmler, C., Weber, N., Brewer, N., & Lindsay, M. R. (2008). How variations in distance affect eyewitness reports and identification accuracy. *Law and Human Behavior, 32,* 526–535. (p. 499)

Lindsay, R. C. L., & Wells, G. L. (1985). Improving eyewitness identifications from lineups: Simultaneous versus sequential lineup presentation. *Journal of Applied Psychology, 70,* 556–564. (p. 504)

Lindsay, R. C. L., Wells, G. L., & Rumpel, C. H. (1981). Can people detect eyewitness-identification accuracy within and across situations? *Journal of Applied Psychology, 66,* 79–89. (p. 498)

Lindskold, S. (1978). Trust development, the GRIT proposal, and the effects of conciliatory acts on conflict and cooperation. *Psychological Bulletin, 85,* 772–793. (p. 468)

Lindskold, S., & Collins, M. G. (1978). Inducing cooperation by groups and individuals. *Journal of Conflict Resolution, 22,* 679–690. (p. 468)

Lindskold, S., & Finch, M. L. (1981). Styles of announcing conciliation. *Journal of Conflict Resolution, 25,* 145–155. (p. 468)

Lindskold, S., Bennett, R., & Wayner, M. (1976). Retaliation level as a foundation for subsequent conciliation. *Behavioral Science, 21,* 13–18. (p. 468)

Lindskold, S., Betz, B., & Walters, P. S. (1986). Transforming competitive or cooperative climate. *Journal of Conflict Resolution, 30,* 99–114. (p. 468)

Lindskold, S., & Han, G. (1988). GRIT as a foundation for integrative bargaining. *Personality and Social Psychology Bulletin, 14,* 335–345. (p. 468)

Lindskold, S., Han, G., & Betz, B. (1986a). Repeated persuasion in interpersonal conflict. *Journal of Personality and Social Psychology, 51,* 1183–1188. (p. 468)

Lindskold, S., Han, G., & Betz, B. (1986b). The essential elements of communication in the GRIT strategy. *Personality and Social Psychology Bulletin, 12,* 179–186. (p. 468)

Lindskold, S., Walters, P. S., Koutsourais, H., & Shayo, R. (1981). *Cooperators, competitors, and response to GRIT.* Unpublished manuscript, Ohio University. (p. 468)

Linssen, H., & Hagendoorn, L. (1994). Social and geographical factors in the explanation of the content of European nationality stereotypes. *British Journal of Social Psychology, 33,* 165–182. (p. 399)

Linville, P. W., Gischer, W. G., & Salovey, P. (1989). Perceived distributions of the characteristics of in-group and out-group members: Empirical evidence and a computer simulation. *Journal of Personality and Social Psychology, 57,* 165–188. (p. 419)

Lippa, R. A. (2007). The preferred traits of mates in a cross-national study of heterosexual and homosexual men and women: An examination of biological and cultural influences. *Archives of Sexual Behavior, 36,* 193–208. (p. 358)

Lipsitz, A., Kallmeyer, K., Ferguson, M., & Abas, A. (1989). Counting on blood donors: Increasing the impact of reminder calls. *Journal of Applied Social Psychology, 19,* 1057–1067. (p. 133)

LISPOP (Laurier Institute for the Study of Public Opinion and Policy. (2011). http://www.lispop.ca/fedblog2011. (p. 21)

Little, A., & Perrett, D. (2002). Putting beauty back in the eye of the beholder. *The Psychologist, 15,* 28–32. (p. 364)

Livingston, R. W. (2001). What you see is what you get: Systematic variability in perceptual-based social judgment. *Personality and Social Psychology Bulletin, 27,* 1086. (p. 363)

Livingstone, S., & Haddon, L. (2009). *EU Kids Online: Final report.* LSE, London: EU Kids Online. (p. 334)

Locke, E. A., & Latham, G. P. (1990). Work motivation and satisfaction: Light at the end of the tunnel. *Psychological Science, 1,* 240–246. (p. 264)

Locke, K. D., & Horowitz, L. M. (1990). Satisfaction in interpersonal interactions as a function of similarity in level of dysphoria. *Journal of Personality and Social Psychology, 58,* 823–831. (p. 371)

Locksley, A., Borgida, E., Brekke, N., & Hepburn, C. (1980). Sex stereotypes and social judgment. *Journal of Personality and Social Psychology, 39,* 821–831. (pp. 410, 443)

Locksley, A., Hepburn, C., & Ortiz, V. (1982). Social stereotypes and judgments of individuals: An instance of the base-rate fallacy. *Journal of Experimental Social Psychology, 18,* 23–42. (p. 443)

Lockwood, P. (2002). Could it happen to you? Predicting the impact of downward comparisons on the self. *Journal of Personality and Social Psychology, 87,* 343–358. (p. 40)

Lockwood, P., Dolderman, D., Sadler, P., & Gerchak, E. (2004). Feeling better about doing worse: Social comparisons within romantic relationships. *Journal of Personality and Social Psychology, 87,* 80. (p. 52)

Lockwood, P., & Kunda, Z. (1997). Superstars and me: Predicting the impact of role models on the self. *Journal of Personality and Social Psychology, 73,* 91–103. (p. 39)

Loewenstein, G., & Schkade, D. (1999). Wouldn't it be nice? Predicting future feelings. In D. Kahneman, E. Diener, & N. Schwarz (Eds.), *Understanding well-being: Scientific perspectives on enjoyment and suffering.* New York: Russell Sage Foundation, 85–105. (p. 48)

Lofland, J., & Stark, R. (1965). Becoming a worldsaver: A theory of conversion to a deviant perspective. *American Sociological Review, 30,* 862–864. (p. 184)

Loftin, C., McDowall, D., Wiersema, B., & Cottey, T. J. (1991). Effects of restrictive licensing of handguns on homicide and suicide in the District of Columbia. *New England Journal of Medicine, 325,* 1615–1620. (p. 327)

Loftus, E. F. (1974, December). Reconstructing memory: The incredible eyewitness. *Psychology Today,* 117–119. (p. 498)

Loftus, E. F. (1979a). *Eyewitness testimony.* Cambridge, MA: Harvard University Press. (pp. 498, 500)

Loftus, E. F. (1979b). The malleability of human memory. *American Scientist, 67,* 312–320. (pp. 498, 500)

Loftus, E. F. (2001, November). Imagining the past. *The Psychologist, 14,* 584–587. (p. 500)

Loftus, E. F. (2003). Make-believe memories. *American Psychologist, 58*(11), 867. (p. 85)

Loftus, E. F. (2007). Memory distortions: Problems solved and unresolved. In M. Garry & H. Hayne (Eds.), *Do justice and let the sky fall: Elizabeth Loftus and her contributions to science, law, and academic freedom.* Mahway, NJ: Erlbaum. (p. 85)

Loftus, E. F. (2011, September). Intelligence gathering post-9/11. *American Psychologist, 66,* 532–541. (pp. 498, 502)

Loftus, E. F., & Bernstein, D. M. (2005). Rich false memories: The royal road to success. In A. F. Healy (Ed.), *Experimental cognitive psychology and its applications.* Washington, DC: American Psychological Association. (p. 84)

Loftus, E. F., & Klinger, M. R. (1992). Is the unconscious smart or dumb? *American Psychologist, 47,* 761–765. (p. 89)

Loftus, E. F., Miller, D. G., & Burns, H. J. (1978). Semantic integration of verbal information into a visual memory. *Journal of Experimental Social Psychology: Human Learning and Memory, 4,* 19–31. (p. 500)

Logel, C., Walton, G. M., Spencer, S. J., Iserman, E. C., von Hippel, W., & Bell, A. E. (2009a). Interacting with sexist men triggers social identity threat among female engineers. *Journal of Personality and Social Psychology, 96,* 1089–1103. (p. 441)

Logel, C. E. R., Iserman, E. C., Spencer, S. J., Davies, P. G., & Quinn, D. M. (2009b). The perils of avoiding negative thoughts: Thought suppression as a mediator of stereotype threat. *Journal of Experimental Social Psychology, 45,* 299–312. (p. 442)

Lombardo, J. P., Weiss, R. F., & Buchanan, W. (1972). Reinforcing and attracting functions of yielding. *Journal of Personality and Social Psychology, 21,* 359–368. (p. 376)

London, P. (1970). The rescuers: Motivational hypotheses about Christians who saved Jews from the Nazis. In J. Macaulay & L. Berkowitz (Eds.), *Altruism and helping behavior.* New York: Academic Press. (p. 304)

Lord, C.G., Desforges, D.M., Ramsey, S.L., Trezza, G.R., & Lepper, M.R. (1991). Typicality effects in attitude-behavior consistency: Efffects of category discrimination and category knowledge. *Journal of Experimental Social Psychology, 27,* 550–575. (p. 444)

Lord, C. G., Lepper, M. R., & Preston, E. (1984). Considering the opposite: A corrective strategy for social judgment. *Journal of Personality and Social Psychology, 47,* 1231–1243. (p. 84)

Lord, C. G., Ross, L., & Lepper, M. (1979). Biased assimilation and attitude polarization: The effects of prior theories on subsequently considered evidence. *Journal of Personality and Social Psychology, 37,* 2098–2109. (p. 81)

Lord, W. (1955). *A night to remember.* New York: Holt. (p. 256)

Lortie-Lussier, M., Lemieux, S., & Godbout, L. (1989). Reports of a public manifestation: Their impact according to minority influence theory. *Journal of Social Psychology, 129,* 285–295. (p. 264)

Lott, A. J., & Lott, B. E. (1961). Group cohesiveness, communication level, and conformity. *Journal of Abnormal and Social Psychology, 62,* 408–412. (p. 216)

Lott, A. J., & Lott, B. E. (1974). The role of reward in the formation of positive interpersonal attitudes. In T. Huston (Ed.), *Foundations of interpersonal attraction*. New York: Academic Press. (p. 375)

Loughman, S., & Haslam, N. (2007). Animals and androids: Implicit associations between social categories and nonhumans. *Psychological Science, 18,* 116–121. (p. 411)

Lovett, F. (1997). Thinking about values (report of December 13, 1996 Wall Street Journal national survey). *The Responsive Community, 7*(2), 87. (p. 63)

Lowenstein, D. (2000 May 20). Interview. *The World*. www.cnn.com/TRANSCRIPTS/0005/20/stc.00.html. (p. 338)

Lücken, M., & Simon, B. (2005). Cognitive and affective experiences of minority and majority members: The role of group size, status, and power. *Journal of Experimental Social Psychology, 41,* 396–413. (p. 267)

Lueptow, L. B., Garovich, L., & Lueptow, M. B. (1995). The persistence of gender stereotypes in the face of changing sex roles: Evidence contrary to the sociocultural model. *Ethology and Sociobiology, 16,* 509–530. (p. 434)

Lumsdaine, A. A., & Janis, I. L. (1953). Resistance to "counter-propaganda" produced by one-sided and two-sided "propaganda" presentations. *Public Opinion Quarterly, 17,* 311–318. (p. 172)

Lumsden, A., Zanna, M. P., & Darley, J. M. (1980). *When a newscaster presents counter-additional information: Education or propaganda?* Paper presented to the Canadian Psychological Association annual convention. (p. 159)

Lutsky, L. A., Risucci, D. A., & Tortolani, A. J. (1993). Reliability and accuracy of surgical resident peer ratings. *Evaluation Review, 17,* 444–456. (p. 47)

Lydon, J., & Dunkel-Schetter, C. (1994). Seeing is committing: A longitudinal study of bolstering commitment in amniocenesis patients. *Personality and Social Psychology Bulletin, 20,* 218–227. (p. 207)

Lydon, J. E., Meana, M., Sepinwall, D., Richards, N., & Mayman, S. (1999). The commitment calibration hypothesis: When do people devalue attractive alternatives? *Personality and Social Psychology Bulletin, 25,* 152–161. (p. 368)

Lykken, D. T. (1997). The American crime factory. *Psychological Inquiry, 8,* 261–270. (p. 250)

Lykken, D. T., & Tellegen, A. (1993). Is human mating adventitious or the result of lawful choice? A twin study of mate selection. *Journal of Personality and Social Psychology, 65,* 56–68. (p. 356)

Lynch, J. W., Kaplan, G. A., Pamuk, E. R., Cohen, R. D., Heck, K. E., Balfour, J. L., & Yen, I. H. (1998). Income inequality and mortality in metropolitan areas of the United States. *American Journal of Public Health, 88,* 1074–1080. (p. 490)

Lynch, J. W., Smith, G. D., Kaplan, G. A., & House, J. S. (2000). Income inequality and health: A neo-material interpretation. *British Medical Journal, 320,* 1200–1204. (p. 490)

Lynn, M., & Oldenquist, A. (1986). Egoistic and nonegoistic motives in social dilemmas. *American Psychologist, 41,* 529–534. (p. 459)

Lyons, L. (2003, September 23). Oh, boy: Americans still prefer sons. *Gallup Poll Tuesday Briefing* (www.gallup.com). (p. 436)

Lyubomirsky, S. (2001). Why are some people happier than others? The role of cognitive and motivational processes in well-being. *American Psychologist, 56,* 239–249. (p. 524)

Lyubomirsky, S., Sousa, L., & Dickerhoof, R. (2006). The costs and benefits of writing, talking, and thinking about life's triumphs and defeats. *Journal of Personality and Social Psychology, 90,* 692–708. (p. 489)

Ma, V., & Schoeneman, T. J. (1997). Individualism versus collectivism: A comparison of Kenyan and American self-concepts. *Basic and Applied Social Psychology, 19,* 261–273. (p. 41)

Maass, A. (1998). Personal communication from Universita degli Studi di Padova. (p. 268)

Maass, A. (1999). Linguistic intergroup bias: Stereotype perpetuation through language. In M. P. Zanna (Ed.), *Advances in Experimental Social Psychology, 31,* 79–121. (p. 423)

Maass, A., & Clark, R. D., III (1984). Hidden impact of minorities: Fifteen years of minority influence research. *Psychological Bulletin, 95,* 428–450. (p. 268)

Maass, A., & Clark, R. D., III (1986). Conversion theory and simultaneous majority/minority influence: Can reactance offer an alternative explanation? *European Journal of Social Psychology, 16,* 305–309. (p. 268)

Maass, A., Milesi, A., Zabbini, S., & Stahlberg, D. (1995). Linguistic intergroup bias: Differential expectancies or in-group protection? *Journal of Personality and Social Psychology, 68,* 116–126. (p. 423)

Maass, A., Volparo, C., & Mucchi-Faina, A. (1996). Social influence and the verifiability of the issue under discussion: Attitudinal versus objective items. *British Journal of Social Psychology, 35,* 15–26. (p. 268)

Maccoby, N. (1980). Promoting positive health behaviors in adults. In L. A. Bond & J. C. Rosen (Eds.), *Competence and coping during adulthood*. Hanover, NH: University Press of New England. (pp. 176, 177)

Maccoby, N., & Alexander, J. (1980). Use of media in lifestyle programs. In P. O. Davidson & S. M. Davidson (Eds.), *Behavioral medicine: Changing health lifestyles*. New York: Brunner/Mazel. (p. 176)

MacCoun, R. J., & Kerr, N. L. (1988). Asymmetric influence in mock jury deliberation: Jurors' bias for leniency. *Journal of Personality and Social Psychology, 54,* 21–33. (p. 510)

MacDonald, G., & Leary, M. R. (2005). Why does social exclusion hurt? The relationship between social and physical pain. *Psychological Bulletin, 131,* 202. (p. 354)

MacDonald, G., Zanna, M. P., & Holmes, J. G. (2000). An experimental test of the role of alcohol in relationship conflict. *Journal of Experimental Social Psychology, 36,* 182–193. (pp. 314, 482)

MacDonald, T. K., & Ross, M. (1997). *Assessing the accuracy of predictions about dating relationships: How and why do lovers' predictions differ from those made by observers?* Unpublished manuscript, University of Lethbridge. (p. 47)

MacDonald, T. K., Zanna, M. P., & Fong, G. T. (1995). Decision making in altered states: Effects of alcohol on attitudes toward drinking and driving. *Journal of Personality and Social Psychology, 68,* 973–985. (p. 481)

Mack, D., & Rainey, D. (1990). Female applicants' grooming and personnel selection. *Journal of Social Behavior and Personality, 5,* 399–407. (p. 363)

Mackinnon, S. P., Jordan, C. H., & Wilson, A. E. (2011). Birds of a feather sit together: Physical similarity predicts seating choice. *Personality and Social Psychology Bulletin, 37,* 879–892. (p. 369)

MacLin, O. H., Zimmerman, L. A., & Malpass, R. S. (2005). PC Eyewitness and the sequential superiority effect:

Computer-based lineup administration. *Law and Human Behavior, 29,* 303. (p. 504)

Macrae, C. N., Alnwick, M. A., Milne, A. B., & Schloerscheidt, A. M. (2002). Person perception across the menstrual cycle: Hormonal influences on social-cognitive functioning. *Psychological Science, 13,* 532–536. (p. 366)

Macrae, C. N., & Bodenhausen, G. V. (2000). Social cognition: Thinking categorically about others. *Annual Review of Psychology, 51,* 93–120. (p. 417)

Macrae, C. N., & Bodenhausen, G. V. (2001). Social cognition: Categorical person perception. *British Journal of Psychology, 92,* 239–255. (p. 417)

Macrae, C. N., Bodenhausen, G. V., Milne, A. B., & Jetten, J. (1994). Out of mind but back in sight: Stereotypes on the rebound. *Journal of Personality and Social Psychology, 67,* 808–817. (p. 416)

Macrae, C. N., & Johnston, L. (1998). Help, I need somebody: Automatic action and inaction. *Social Cognition, 16,* 400–417. (p. 87)

Macrae, C. N., Stangor, C., & Milne, A. B. (1994). Activating social stereotypes: A functional analysis. *Journal of Experimental Social Psychology, 30,* 370–389. (p. 417)

Maddux, J. E. (1993). The mythology of psychopathology: A social cognitive view of deviance, difference, and disorder. *The General Psychologist, 29*(2), 34–45. (pp. 472, 475)

Maddux, J. E. (2008). Positive psychology and the illness ideology: Toward a positive clinical psychology. *Applied Psychology: An International Review, 57,* 54–70. (p. 471)

Maddux, J. E., & Rogers, R. W. (1983). Protection motivation and self-efficacy: A revised theory of fear appeals and attitude change. *Journal of Experimental Social Psychology, 19,* 469–479. (p. 169)

Maddux, W. W., Galinsky, A. D., Cuddy, A. J. C., & Polifroni, M. (2008). When being a model minority is good . . . and bad: Realistic threat explains negativity towards Asian Americans. *Personality and Social Psychology Bulletin, 34,* 74–89. (p. 465)

Maddux, W. W., Mullen, E., & Galinsky, A. D. (2008). Chameleons bake bigger pies and take bigger pieces: Strategic behavioral mimicry facilitates negotiation outcomes. *Journal of Experimental Social Psychology, 44,* 461–468. (p. 407)

Madon, S., Jussim, L., & Eccles, J. (1997). In search of the powerful self-fulfilling prophecy. *Journal of Personality and Social Psychology, 72,* 791–809. (p. 112)

Mae, L., Carlston, D. E., & Skowronski, J. (1999). Spontaneous trait transference to familiar communicators: Is a little knowledge a dangerous thing? *Journal of Personality and Social Psychology, 77,* 233–246. (p. 82)

Maio, G. R., Bell, D., & Esses, V. M. (1996). Ambivalence in persuasion: The processing of messages about immigrant groups. *Journal of Experimental Social Psychology, 32,* 513–536. (p. 171)

Maio, G. R., & Olson, J. M. (1990). Involvement and persuasion: Evidence for different types of involvement. *Canadian Journal of Behavioural Science, 27,* 64–78. (p. 180)

Major, B., Quinton, W. J., & McCoy, S. K. (2002). Antecedents and consequences of attributions to discrimination: Theoretical and empirical advances. In M. P. Zanna (Ed.). *Advances in experimental social psychology* (Vol. 34) (pp. 251–330). San Diego: Academic Press. (p. 447)

Malamuth, N. M. (1996). The confluence model of sexual aggression. In D. M. Buss & N. M. Malamuth (Eds.), *Sex, power, conflict: Evolutionary and feminist perspectives.* New York: Oxford University Press. (p. 331)

Malamuth, N. M. (2003). Criminal and noncriminal sexual aggressors: Integrating psychopathy in a hierarchical-mediational confluence model. In R. A. Prentky, E. Janus, & M. Seto (Eds.), *Sexually coercive behavior: Understanding and management.* New York: Annals of the New York Academy of Sciences. (p. 331)

Malamuth, N. M., & Check, J. V. P. (1981). The effects of media exposure on acceptance of violence against women: A field experiment. *Journal of Research in Personality, 15,* 436–446. (pp. 328)

Malamuth, N. M., Haber, S., Feshbach, S., & others. (1980, March). *Journal of Research in Personality, 14,* 121–137. (p. 328)

Malkiel, B. G. (1985). *A random walk down Wall Street,* 4th ed. New York: W. W. Norton. (p. 92)

Malkiel, B. G. (1995, June). Returns from investing in equity mutual funds 1971 to 1991. *Journal of Finance,* 549–572. (p. 92)

Malle, B. F. (2006). The actor-observer asymmetry in attribution: A (surprising) meta-analysis. *Psychological Bulletin, 132,* 895–919. (p. 107)

Mallet, R. K., & Swim, J. K. (2003). Collective guilt in the United States: Predicting support for social policies that alleviate social injustice. In N. Branscombe & B. Doosje (Eds.), *Collective guilt: International perspectives.* New York: Cambridge University Press. (p. 460)

Maner, J. K., Gailliot, M. T., & Miller, S. L. (2009). The implicit cognition of relationship maintenance: Inattention to attractive alternatives. *Journal of Experimental Social Psychology, 45,* 174–179. (p. 392)

Maner, J. K., Miller, S. L., Schmidt, N. B., & Eckel, L. A. (2008). Submitting to defeat: Social anxiety, dominance threat, and decrements in testosterone. *Psychological Science, 19,* 764–768. (p. 316)

Manis, M., Cornell, S. D., & Moore, J. C. (1974). Transmission of attitude-relevant information through a communication chain. *Journal of Personality and Social Psychology, 30,* 81–94. (p. 132)

Manis, M., Nelson, T. E., & Shedler, J. (1988). Stereotypes and social judgment: Extremity, assimilation, and contrast. *Journal of Personality and Social Psychology, 55,* 28–36. (p. 445)

Mann, L. (1981). The baiting crowd in episodes of threatened suicide. *Journal of Personality and Social Psychology, 41,* 703–709. (p. 244)

Manning, R., Levine, M., & Collins, A. (2007). The Kitty Genovese murder and the social psychology of helping: The parable of the 38 witnesses. *American Psychologist, 62,* 555–562. (p. 290)

Marcus, S. (1974, January 13). Review of *Obedience to authority. New York Times Book Review,* 1–2. (p. 205)

Marcus-Newhall, A., Pedersen, W. C., Carlson, M., & Miller, N. (2000). Displaced aggression is alive and well: A meta-analytic review. *Journal of Personality and Social Psychology, 78,* 670–689. (p. 317)

Marigold, D. C., Holmes, J. G., & Ross, M. (2007). More than words: Reframing compliments from romantic partners fosters security in low self-esteem individuals. *Journal of Personality and Social Psychology, 92,* 232. (p. 373)

Markey, P. M., Wells, S. M., & Markey, C. N. (2002). In S. P. Shohov (Ed.), *Advances in Psychology Research, 9,* 94–113. Huntington, NY: Nova Science. (p. 133)

Markman, H. J., Floyd, F. J., Stanley, S. M., & Storaasli, R. D. (1988). Prevention of marital distress: A longitudinal investigation.

Journal of Consulting and Clinical Psychology, 56, 210–217. (p. 394)

Markman, K. D., & McMullen, M. N. (2003). A reflection and evaluation model of comparative thinking. *Personality and Social Psychology Review, 7,* 244–267. (p. 97)

Marks, G., & Miller, N. (1987). Ten years of research on the false-consensus effect: An empirical and theoretical review. *Psychological Bulletin, 102,* 72–90. (p. 65)

Markus, H. (2001, October 7). Culture and the good life. Address to the Positive Psychology Summit conference, Washington, DC. (p. 43)

Markus, H., & Kitayama, S. (1991). Culture and the self: Implications for cognition, emotion, and motivation. *Psychological Review, 98,* 224–253. (pp. 44, 74)

Markus, H., & Nurius, P. (1986). Possible selves. *American Psychologist, 41,* 954–969. (p. 38)

Markus, H., & Wurf, E. (1987). The dynamic self-concept: A social psychological perspective. *Annual Review of Psychology, 38,* 299–337. (p. 38)

Markus, H. R. (2005). On telling less than we can know: The too tacit wisdom of social psychology. *Psychological Inquiry, 16,* 180–184. (p. 8)

Markus, H. R., & Kitayama, S. (1994). A collective fear of the collective: Implications for selves and theories of selves. *Personality and Social Psychology Bulletin, 20,* 568–579. (p. 196)

Marsden, P., & Attia, S. (2005). A deadly contagion? *The Psychologist, 18,* 152–155. (p. 320)

Marsh, H. W., Kong, C-K., & Hau, K-T. (2000). Longitudinal multilevel models of the big-fish-little-pond effect on academic self-concept: Counterbalancing contrast and reflected-glory effects in Hong Kong schools. *Journal of Personality and Social Psychology, 78,* 337–349. (p. 39)

Marsh, H. W., & O'Mara, A. (2008). Reciprocal effects between academic self-concept, self-esteem, achievement, and attainment over seven adolescent years: Unidimensional and multidimensional perspectives of self-concept. *Personality and Social Psychology Bulletin, 34,* 542–552. (p. 52)

Marsh, H. W., & Young, A. S. (1997). Causal effects of academic self-concept on academic achievement: Structural equation models of longitudinal data. *Journal of Educational Psychology, 89,* 41–54. (p. 40)

Marshall, L. (Ed.) (1912). *Sinking of the Titanic and great sea disasters.* Philadelphia, PA: Universal Book and Bible House. (p. 256)

Marshall, R. (1997). Variances in levels of individualism across two cultures and three social classes. *Journal of Cross-Cultural Psychology, 28,* 490–495. (p. 41)

Martens, A., Kosloff, S., Greenberg, J., Landau, M. J., & Schmader, R. (2007). Killing begets killing: Evidence from a bug-killing paradigm that initial killing fuels subsequent killing. *Personality and Social Psychology Bulletin, 33,* 1251–1264. (p. 136)

Martin, L. L., & Erber, R. (2005). Can social psychology impart any wisdom to the world? *Psychological Inquiry, 16*(4), 151. (p. 116)

Martin, R. (1996). Minority influence and argument generation. *British Journal of Social Psychology, 35,* 91–103. (p. 267)

Martin, R., Hewstone, M., & Martin, P. Y. (2007). Majority versus minority influence: The role of message processing in determining resistance to counterpersuasion. *European Journal of Social Psychology, 38,* 16–34. (p. 267)

Martin, R., Martin, P. Y., Smith, J. R., & Hewstone, M. (2008). Majority versus minority influence and prediction of behavioural intentions and behaviour. *Journal of Experimental Social Psychology, 43,* 763–771.

Martino, S. C., Collins, R. L., Kanouse, D. E., Elliott, M., & Berry, S. H. (2005). Social cognitive processes mediating the relationship between exposure to television's sexual content and adolescents' sexual behavior. *Journal of Personality and Social Psychology, 89,* 914–924. (p. 336)

Maruyama, G., Rubin, R. A., & Kingbury, G. (1981). Self-esteem and educational achievement: Independent constructs with a common cause? *Journal of Personality and Social Psychology, 40,* 962–975. (p. 20)

Marvelle, K., & Green, S. (1980). Physical attractiveness and sex bias in hiring decisions for two types of jobs. *Journal of the National Association of Women Deans, Administrators, and Counselors, 44*(1), 3–6. (p. 363)

Masserman, J. H., Wechkin, S., & Terris, W. (1964). "Altruistic" behavior in rhesus monkeys. *American Journal of Psychiatry, 121,* 584–585. (p. 288)

Massey, C., Simmons, J. P., & Armor, D. A. (2011). Hope over experience: Desirability and the persistence of optimism. *Psychological Science, 22,* 274–281. (p. 64)

Mast, M. S., & Hall, J. A. (2006). Women's advantage at remembering others' appearance: A systematic look at the why and when of a gender difference. *Personality and Social Psychology Bulletin, 32,* 353–364. (p. 360)

Mastekaasa, A. (1995). Age variations in the suicide rates and self-reported subjective well-being of married and never married persons. *Journal of Community & Applied Social Psychology, 5,* 21–39. (p. 493)

Masuda, T., Gonzalez, R., Kwan, L., & Nisbett, R. E. (2008). Culture and aesthetic preference: Comparing the attention to context of East Asians and Americans. *Personality and Social Psychology Bulletin, 34,* 1260–1275. (p. 42)

Masuda, T., & Kitayama, S. (2004). Perceiver-induced constraint and attitude attribution in Japan and the US: A case for the cultural dependence of the correspondence bias. *Journal of Experimental Social Psychology, 40,* 409. (p. 109)

Matthews, K. A. (2005). Psychological perspectives on the development of coronary heart disease. *American Psychologist, 60,* 783–796. (p. 484)

Maxwell, G. M. (1985). Behaviour of lovers: Measuring the closeness of relationships. *Journal of Personality and Social Psychology, 2,* 215–238. (p. 383)

Mayer, J. D., & Salovey, P. (1987). Personality moderates the interaction of mood and cognition. In K. Fiedler & J. Forgas (Eds.), *Affect, cognition, and social behavior.* Toronto: Hogrefe. (pp. 100, 476)

Mazur, A., & Booth, A. (1998). Testosterone and dominance in men. *Behavioral and Brain Sciences, 21,* 353–363. (p. 316)

Mazzella, R., & Feingold, A. (1994). The effects of physical attractiveness, race, socioeconomic status, and gender of defendants and victims on judgments of mock jurors: A meta-analysis. *Journal of Applied Social Psychology, 24,* 1315–1344. (p. 506)

Mazzoni, G., & Memon, A. (2003). Imagination can create false autobiographical memories. *Psychological Science, 14,* 186. (p. 501)

Mazzuca, J. (2002, August 20). Teens shrug off movie sex and violence. Gallup Tuesday Briefing (www.gallup.com). (p. 336)

McAlister, A., Perry, C., Killen, J., Slinkard, L. A., & Maccoby, N. (1980). Pilot study of smoking, alcohol and drug abuse prevention. *American Journal of Public Health, 70,* 719–721. (p. 189)

McAndrew, F. T. (1981). Pattern of performance and attributions of ability and gender. *Journal of Personality and Social Psychology, 7,* 583–587. (p. 173)

McAndrew, F. T. (2009). The interacting roles of testosterone and challenges to status in human male aggression. *Aggression and Violent Behavior, 14,* 330–335. (p. 312)

McCann, C. D., & Hancock, R. D. (1983). Self-monitoring in communicative interactions: Social cognitive consequences of goal-directed message modification. *Journal of Experimental Social Psychology, 19,* 109–121. (p. 73)

McCarthy, J. F., & Kelly, B. R. (1978a). Aggression, performance variables, and anger self-report in ice hockey players. *Journal of Psychology, 99,* 97–101. (p. 320)

McCarthy, J. F., & Kelly, B. R. (1978b). Aggressive behavior and its effect on performance over time in ice hockey athletes: An archival study. *International Journal of Sport Psychology, 9,* 90–96. (p. 320)

McCauley, C. (1989). The nature of social influence in groupthink: Compliance and internalization. *Journal of Personality and Social Psychology, 57,* 250–260. (p. 258)

McCauley, C. (1998). Group dynamics in Janis's theory of groupthink: Backward and forward. *Organizational Behavior and Human Decision Processes, 73,* 142–163. (p. 259)

McCauley, C. R. (2002). Psychological issues in understanding terrorism and the response to terrorism. In C. E. Stout (Ed.), *The psychology of terrorism* (Vol. 3). Westport, CT: Praeger/Greenwood. (p. 251)

McCauley, C. R., & Segal, M. E. (1987). Social psychology of terrorist groups. In C. Hendrick (Ed.), *Group processes and intergroup relations: Review of personality and social psychology* (Vol. 9). Newbury Park, CA: Sage. (p. 251)

McClure, J. (1998). Discounting causes of behavior: Are two reasons better than one? *Journal of Personality and Social Psychology, 74,* 7–20. (p. 104)

McConahay, J. B. (1986). Modern racism, ambivalence, and the Modern Racism Scale. In J. F. Dovidio & S. L. Gaertner (Eds.). *Prejudice, discrimination, and racism* (91–125). San Diego, CA: Academic Press. (p. 400)

McCullough, J. L., & Ostrom, T. M. (1974). Repetition of highly similar messages and attitude change. *Journal of Applied Psychology, 59,* 395–397. (p. 358)

McDonald, M. M., Asher, B. D., Kerr, N. L., & Navarrete, C. D. (2011). Fertility and intergroup bias in racial and minimal-group contexts: Evidence for shared architecture. *Psychological Science, 22,* 860–865. (p. 366)

McFarland, C., & Ross, M. (1985). *The relation between current impressions and memories of self and dating partners.* Unpublished manuscript, University of Waterloo. (p. 86)

McFarland, C., & White, K., & Newth, S. (2003). Mood acknowledgement and correction for the mood-congruency bias in social judgment. *Journal of Experimental Social Psychology, 39,* 483–491. (p. 101)

McGillicuddy, N. B., Welton, G. L., & Pruitt, D. G. (1987). Third-party intervention: A field experiment comparing three different models. *Journal of Personality and Social Psychology, 53,* 104–112. (p. 467)

McGlone, M. S., & Tofighbakhsh, J. (2000). Birds of a feather flock conjointly (?): Rhyme as reason in aphorisms. *Psychological Science, 11,* 424–428. (p. 175)

McGlynn, R. P., Tubbs, D. D., & Holzhausen, K. G. (1995). Hypothesis generation in groups constrained by evidence. *Journal of Experimental Social Psychology, 31,* 64–81. (p. 261)

McGrath, J. E. (1984). *Groups: Interaction and performance.* Englewood Cliffs, NJ: Prentice-Hall. (p. 233)

McGraw, A. P., Mellers, B. A., & Tetlock, P. E. (2005). Expectations and emotions of Olympic athletes. *Journal of Experimental Social Psychology, 41,* 438–446. (p. 96)

McGregor, I., & Marigold, D. C. (2003). Defensive zeal and the uncertain self: What makes you so sure? *Journal of Personality & Social Psychology, 85*(5), 838–852. (p. 56)

McGregor, I., Nail, P. R., Marigold, D. C., & Kang, S. (2005). Defensive pride and consensus: Strength in imaginary numbers. *Journal of Personality and Social Psychology, 89,* 978. (p. 56)

McGregor, I., Newby-Clark, I. R., & Zanna, M. P. (1998). Epistemic discomfort is moderated by simultaneous accessibility of inconsistent elements. In E. Harmon-Jones and J. Mills (Eds.), *Cognitive dissonance theory 40 years later: A revival with revisions and controversies.* Washington, DC: American Psychological Association. (p. 152)

McGregor, I., Zanna, M. P., Holmes, J. G., & Spencer, S. J. (2001). Conviction in the face of uncertainty: Going to extremes and being oneself. *Journal of Personality and Social Psychology, 80,* 472–478. (p. 413)

McGuire, A. (2002, August 19). Charity calls for debate on adverts aimed at children. *The Herald* (Scotland), 4. (p. 190)

McGuire, W. J. (1964). Inducing resistance to persuasion: Some contemporary approaches. In L. Berkowitz (Ed.), *Advances in experimental social psychology* (Vol. 1). New York: Academic Press. (p. 188)

McGuire, W. J. (1978). An information-processing model of advertising effectiveness. In Davis, H.L., & Silk, A. J., (Eds.) *Behavioral and management sciences in marketing.* New York: John Wiley & Sons, Inc. (p. 160)

McGuire, W. J., McGuire, C. V., & Winton, W. (1979). Effects of household sex composition on the salience of one's gender in the spontaneous self-concept. *Journal of Experimental Social Psychology, 15,* 77–90. (p. 226)

McGuire, W. J., McGuire, C. V., Child, P., & Fujioka, T. (1978). Salience of ethnicity in the spontaneous self-concept as a function of one's ethnic distinctiveness in the social environment. *Journal of Personality and Social Psychology, 36,* 511–520. (p. 227)

McGuire, W. J., & Padawer-Singer, A. (1978). Trait salience in the spontaneous self-concept. *Journal of Personality and Social Psychology, 33,* 743–754. (p. 226)

McKelvie, S. J. (1995). Bias in the estimated frequency of names. *Perceptual and Motor Skills, 81,* 1331–1338. (p. 95)

McKelvie, S. J. (1997). The availability heuristic: Effects of fame and gender on the estimated frequency of male and female names. *Journal of Social Psychology, 137,* 63–78. (p. 95)

McKenna, F. P., & Myers, L. B. (1997). Illusory self-assessments—Can they be reduced? *British Journal of Psychology, 88,* 39–51. (p. 63)

McKenna, K. Y. A., & Bargh, J. A. (1998). Coming out in the age of the Internet:

Identity demarginalization through virtual group participation. *Journal of Personality and Social Psychology, 75,* 681–694. (pp. 251, 390)

McKenna, K. Y. A., & Bargh, J. A. (2000). Plan 9 from cyberspace: The implications of the Internet for personality and social psychology. *Personality and Social Psychology Review, 4,* 57–75. (pp. 251, 390)

McKenna, K. Y. A., Green, A. S., & Gleason, M. E. J. (2002). What's the big attraction? Relationship formation on the Internet. *Journal of Social Issues, 58,* 9–31. (p. 390)

McKenzie-Mohr, D., & Zanna, M. P. (1990). Treating women as sexual objects: Look to the (gender schematic) male who has viewed pornography. *Personality and Social Psychology Bulletin, 16,* 296–308. (p. 345)

McMillen, D. L., & Austin, J. B. (1971). Effect of positive feedback on compliance following transgression. *Psychonomic Science, 24,* 59–61. (p. 276)

McMillen, D. L., Sanders, D. Y., & Solomon, G. S. (1977). Self-esteem, attentiveness, and helping behavior. *Journal of Personality and Social Psychology, 3,* 257–261. (p. 278)

McNulty, J. K. (2010). When positive processes hurt relationships. *Current Directions in Psychological Science, 19,* 167–171. (p. 394)

McNulty, J. K., O'Mara, E. M., & Karney, B. R. (2008). Benevolent cognitions as a strategy of relationship maintenance: "Don't sweat the small stuff" . . . But it is not all small stuff. *Journal of Personality and Social Psychology, 94,* 631–646. (p. 102)

Mead, G. H. (1934). *Mind, self, and society.* Chicago: University of Chicago Press. (p. 40)

Medalia, N. Z., & Larsen, O. N. (1958). Diffusion and belief in collective delusion: The Seattle windshield pitting epidemic. *American Sociological Review, 23,* 180–186. (p. 199)

Medvec, V. H., Madey, S. F., & Gilovich, T. (1995). When less is more: Counterfactual thinking and satisfaction among Olympic medalists. *Journal of Personality and Social Psychology, 69,* 603–610. (p. 96)

Medvec, V. H., & Savitsky, K. (1997). When doing better means feeling worse: The effects of categorical cutoff points on counterfactual thinking and satisfaction. *Journal of Personality and Social Psychology, 72,* 1284–1296. (p. 97)

Meehl, G. A., Tebaldi, C., Walton, G., Easterling, D., & McDaniel, L. (2009). Relative increase of record high maximum temperatures compared to record low minimum temperatures in the U.S. *Geophysical Research Letters, 36,* L23701. (p. 516)

Mehl, M. R., & Pennebaker, J. W. (2003). The sounds of social life: A psychometric analysis of students' daily social environments and natural conversations. *Journal of Personality and Social Psychology, 84,* 857–870. (pp. 8, 352)

Mehl, M. R., Vazire, S., Holleran, S. E., & Clark, C. S. (2010). Eavesdropping on happiness: Well-being is related to having less small talk and more substantive conversations. *Psychological Science, 21,* 539–541. (p. 388)

Meindl, J. R., & Lerner, M. J. (1984). Exacerbation of extreme responses to an out-group. *Journal of Personality and Social Psychology, 47,* 71–84. (p. 413)

Meissner, C. A., & Brigham, J. C. (2001). Thirty years of investigating the own-race bias in memory for faces: A meta-analytic review. *Psychology, Public Policy, & Law, 7,* 3–35. (p. 419)

Meissner, C. A., Brigham, J. C., & Butz, D. A. (2005). Memory for own- and other-race faces: A dual-process approach. *Applied Cognitive Psychology, 19,* 545–567. (p. 500)

Meissner, C. A., Tredoux, C. G., Parker, J. F., & MacLin, O. H. (2005). Eyewitness decisions in simultaneous and sequential lineups: A dual-process signal detection theory analysis. *Memory & Cognition, 33,* 783. (p. 504)

Meleshko, K. G. A., & Alden, L. E. (1993). Anxiety and self-disclosure: Toward a motivational model. *Journal of Personality and Social Psychology, 64,* 1000–1009. (p. 480)

Memon, A., Meissner, C. A., & Fraser, J. (2011). The cognitive interview: A meta-analytic review and study space analysis of the past 25 years. *Psychology, Public Policy, and Law, 16,* 340–372. (p. 503)

Merikle, P. M., Smilek, D., & Eastwood, J. D. (2001). Perception without awareness: Perspectives from cognitive psychology. *Cognition. Special Issue: The Cognitive Neuroscience of Consciousness, 79*(1–2), 115. (p. 80)

Merton, R. K. (1948). The self-fulfilling prophecy. *Antioch Review, 8,* 193–210. (p. 111)

Merton, R. K., & Kitt, A. S. (1950). Contributions to the theory of reference group behavior. In R. K. Merton & P. F. Lazarsfeld (Eds.), *Continuities in social research: Studies in the scope and method of the American soldier.* Glencoe, IL: Free Press. (p. 318)

Messick, D. M., & Sentis, K. P. (1979). Fairness and preference. *Journal of Experimental Social Psychology, 15,* 418–434. (p. 460)

Meyers, S. A., & Berscheid, E. (1997). The language of love: The difference a preposition makes. *Personality and Social Psychology Bulletin, 23,* 347–362. (p. 377)

Michaels, J. W., Blommel, J. M., Brocato, R. M., Linkous, R. A., & Rowe, J. S. (1982). Social facilitation and inhibition in a natural setting. *Replications in Social Psychology, 2,* 21–24. (p. 235)

Mickelson, K. D., Kessler, R. C., & Shaver, P. R. (1997). Adult attachment in a nationally representative sample. *Journal of Personality and Social Psychology, 73,* 1092–1106. (p. 383)

Mikula, G. (1984). Justice and fairness in interpersonal relations: Thoughts and suggestions. In H. Taijfel (Ed.), *The social dimension: European developments in social psychology,* Vol. 1, Cambridge: Cambridge University Press. (p. 460)

Mikulincer, M., Florian, V., & Hirschberger, G. (2003). The existential function of close relationships: Introducing death into the science of love. *Personality and Social Psychology Review, 7,* 20–40. (p. 352)

Mikulincer, M., & Shaver, P. R. (2001). Attachment theory and intergroup bias: Evidence that priming the secure base schema attenuates negative reactions to out-groups. *Journal of Personality and Social Psychology, 81,* 97–115. (p. 413)

Mikulincer, M., Shaver, P. R., Gillath, O., & Nitzberg, R. A. (2005). Attachment, caregiving, and altruism: Boosting attachment security increases compassion and helping. *Journal of Personality and Social Psychology, 89,* 817–839. (p. 287)

Milgram, A. (2000). My personal view of Stanley Milgram. In T. Blass (Ed.), *Obedience to authority: Current perspectives on the Milgram paradigm.* Mahwah, NJ: Erlbaum. (p. 204)

Milgram, S. (1961, December). Nationality and conformity. *Scientific American,* December, 45–51. (p. 223)

Milgram, S. (1965). Some conditions of obedience and disobedience to authority. *Human Relations, 18,* 57–76. (pp. 203, 205)

Milgram, S. (1974). *Obedience to authority.* New York: Harper and Row. (pp. 5, 203, 210, 213, 214, 217, 222)

Milgram, S., Bickman, L., & Berkowitz, L. (1969). Note on the drawing power of crowds of different size. *Journal of Personality and Social Psychology, 13,* 79–82. (p. 215)

Millar, M. G. (2011). Predicting dental flossing behavior: The role of implicit and explicit responses and beliefs. *Basic and Applied Social Psychology, 33,* 7–15. (p. 125)

Miller, A. G. (1986). *The obedience experiments: A case study of controversy in social science.* New York: Praeger. (p. 204)

Miller, A. G. (2006). *Exonerating harm-doers: Some problematic implications of social-psychological explanations.* Paper presented to the Society of Personality and Social Psychology convention. (p. 213)

Miller, A. G., Ashton, W., & Mishal, M. (1990). Beliefs concerning the features of constrained behavior: A basis for the fundamental attribution error. *Journal of Personality and Social Psychology, 59,* 635–650. (p. 105)

Miller, C. E., & Anderson, P. D. (1979). Group decision rules and the rejection of deviates. *Social Psychology Quarterly, 42,* 354–363. (p. 219)

Miller, C. T., & Felicio, D. M. (1990). Person-positivity bias: Are individuals liked better than groups? *Journal of Experimental Social Psychology, 26,* 408–420. (p. 443)

Miller, D. T., Downs, J. S., & Prentice, D. A. (1998). Minimal conditions for the creation of a unit relationship: The social bond between birthdaymates. *European Journal of Social Psychology, 28,* 475–481.. (p. 409)

Miller, D. T., & McFarland, C. (1987). Pluralistic ignorance: When similarity is interpreted as dissimilarity. *Journal of Personality and Social Psychology, 53,* 298–305. (p. 253)

Miller, G., Tybur, J. M., & Jordan, B. D. (2007). Ovulatory cycle effects on tip earnings by lap dancers: Economic evidence for human estrus? *Evolution and Human Behavior, 28,* 375–381. (p. 366)

Miller, G. E., & Blackwell, E. (2006). Turning up the heat: Inflammation as a mechanism linking chronic stress, depression, and heart disease. *Current Directions in Psychological Science, 15,* 269–272. (p. 484)

Miller, G. E., Chen, E., & Parker, K. J. (2011). Psychological stress in childhood and susceptibility to the chronic diseases of aging: Moving toward a model of behavioral and biological mechanisms. *Psychological Bulletin, 137,* 959–997. (p. 485)

Miller, J. G. (1984). Culture and the development of everyday social explanation. *Journal of Personality and Social Psychology, 46,* 961–978. (p. 109)

Miller, K. I., & Monge, P. R. (1986). Participation, satisfaction, and productivity: A meta-analytic review. *Academy of Management Journal, 29,* 727–753. (p. 58)

Miller, L. (2004). Psychotherapeutic interventions for survivors of terrorism. *American Journal of Psychotherapy, 58,* 1. (p. 209)

Miller, L. C. (1990). Intimacy and liking: Mutual influence and the role of unique relationships. *Journal of Personality and Social Psychology, 59,* 50–60. (p. 387)

Miller, L. C., Berg, J. H., & Archer, R. L. (1983). Openers: Individuals who elicit intimate self-disclosure. *Journal of Personality and Social Psychology, 44,* 1234–1244. (p. 387)

Miller, L. E., & Grush, J. E. (1986). Individual differences in attitudinal versus normative determination of behavior. *Journal of Experimental Social Psychology, 22,* 190–202. (p. 128)

Miller, N., & Campbell, D. T. (1959). Recency and primacy in persuasion as a function of the timing of speeches and measurements. *Journal of Abnormal and Social Psychology, 59,* 1–9. (p. 173)

Miller, N., & Marks, G. (1982). Assumed similarity between self and other: Effect of expectation of future interaction with that other. *Social Psychology Quarterly, 45,* 100–105. (p. 357)

Miller, N., Maruyama, G., Beaber, R. J., & Valone, K. (1976). Speed of speech and persuasion. *Journal of Personality and Social Psychology, 34,* 615–624. (p. 164)

Miller, P. A., & Eisenberg, N. (1988). The relation of empathy to aggressive and externalizing/antisocial behavior. *Psychological Bulletin, 103,* 324–344. (p. 287)

Miller, P. A., Kozu, J., & Davis, A. C. (2001). Social influence, empathy, and prosocial behavior in cross-cultural perspective. In W. Wosinska, R. B. Cialdini, D. W. Barrett, & J. Reykowski (Eds.), *The practice of social influence in multiple cultures.* Mahwah, NJ: Erlbaum. (p. 298)

Miller, P. J. E., Niehuis, S., & Huston, T. L. (2006). Positive illusions in marital relationships: A 13-year longitudinal study. *Personality and Social Psychology Bulletin, 32,* 1579–1594. (p. 374)

Miller, P. J. E., & Rempel, J. K. (2004). Trust and partner-enhancing attributions in close relationships. *Personality and Social Psychology Bulletin, 30,* 695. (p. 383)

Miller, R. L., Brickman, P., & Bolen, D. (1975). Attribution versus persuasion as a means for modifying behavior. *Journal of Personality and Social Psychology, 31,* 430–441. (p. 115)

Miller, R. S. (1997). Inattentive and contented: Relationship commitment and attention to alternatives. *Journal of Personality and Social Psychology, 73,* 758–766. (p. 392)

Miller, R. S., & Schlenker, B. R. (1985). Egotism in group members: Public and private attributions of responsibility for group performance. *Social Psychology Quarterly, 48,* 85–89. (p. 73)

Millett, K. (1975). The shame is over. *Ms.,* January, 26–29. (p. 388)

Milyavskaya, M., Gingras, I., Mageau, G. A., Koestner, R., Gagnon, H., Fang, J., & Boiché, J. (2009). Balance across contexts: Importance of balanced need satisfaction across various life domains. *Personality and Social Psychology Bulletin, 35,* 1031–1045. (p. 353)

Mims, P. R., Hartnett, J. J., & Nay, W. R. (1975). Interpersonal attraction and help volunteering as a function of physical attractiveness. *Journal of Psychology, 89,* 125–131. (p. 282)

Mio, J. S., Thompson, S. C., & Givens, G. H. (1993). The commons dilemma as a metaphor: Memory, influence, and implications for environmental conservation. *Metaphor and Symbolic Activity, 8,* 23–42. (p. 459)

Mirsky, S. (2009, January). What's good for the group. *Scientific American,* p. 51. (p. 285)

Mischel, W. (1968). *Personality and assessment.* New York: Wiley. (p. 222)

Mishna, F., Cook, C., Gadallo, T., Daciuk, J., & Solomon, S. (2010). Cyberbullying behaviors among middle and high school students. *American Journal of Orthopsychiatry, 80,* 362–374. (p. 310)

Mita, T. H., Dermer, M., & Knight, J. (1977). Reversed facial images and the mere-exposure hypothesis. *Journal of*

Personality and Social Psychology, 35, 597–601. (p. 358)

Mitchell, G., Tetlock, P. E., Mellers, B. A., & Ordonez, L. D. (1993). Judgments of social justice: Compromises between equality and efficiency. *Journal of Personality and Social Psychology, 65,* 629–639. (p. 460)

Mitchell, J., McCrae, C. N, & Banaji, M. R. (2006). Dissociable medial prefrontal contributions to judgments of similar and dissimilar others. *Neuron, 18,* 655–663. (p. 432)

Mitchell, T. R., & Thompson, L. (1994). A theory of temporal adjustments of the evaluation of events: Rosy prospection and rosy retrospection. In C. Stubbart, J. Porac, & J. Meindl (Eds.), *Advances in managerial cognition and organizational information processing.* Greenwich, CT: JAI Press. (p. 85)

Mitchell, T. R., Thompson, L., Peterson, E., & Cronk, R. (1997). Temporal adjustments in the evaluation of events: The "rosy view." *Journal of Experimental Social Psychology, 33,* 421–448. (p. 85)

Moffitt, T., & 12 others. (2011). A gradient of childhood self-control predicts health, wealth, and public safety. *PNAS, 108*(7): 2693–2698. (p. 313)

Moffitt, T., Caspi, A., Sugden, K., Taylor, A., Craig, I. W., Harrington, H., McClay, J., Mill, J., Martin, J., Braithwaite, A., & Poulton, R. (2003). Influence of life stress on depression: Moderation by a polymorphism in the 5-HTT gene. *Science, 301,* 386–389. (p. 313)

Moghaddam, F. M., & Studer, C. (1997). The sky is falling, but not on me: A cautionary tale of illusions of control, in four acts. *Cross-Cultural Research: The Journal of Comparative Social Science, 31,* 155–167. (p. 448)

Mojzisch, A., & Schulz-Hardt, S. (2010). Knowing others' preferences degrades the quality of group decisions. *Journal of Personality and Social Psychology, 98,* 784–808. (p. 260)

Moller, I., & Krahe, B. (2008). Exposure to violent video games and aggression in German adolescents: A longitudinal analysis. *Aggressive Behavior, 34,* 1–14. (p. 339)

Monson, T. C., Hesley, J. W., & Chernick, L. (1982). Specifying when personality traits can and cannot predict behavior: An alternative to abandoning the attempt to predict single-act criteria. *Journal of Personality and Social Psychology, 43,* 385–399. (p. 223)

Monteith, M. J. (1993). Self-regulation of prejudiced responses: Implications for progress in prejudice-reduction efforts. *Journal of Personality and Social Psychology, 65,* 469–485. (p. 416)

Montoya, R. M. (2008). I'm hot, so I'd say you're not: The influence of objective physical attractiveness on mate selection. *Personality and Social Psychology Bulletin, 34,* 1315–1331. (p. 361)

Montoya, R. M., & Insko, C. A. (2008). Toward a more complete understanding of the reciprocity of liking effect. *European Journal of Social Psychology, 38,* 477–498. (p. 372)

Moody, K. (1980). *Growing up on television: The TV effect.* New York: Times Books. (p. 190)

Moons, W. G., & Mackie, D. M. (2007). Thinking straight while seeing red: The influence of anger on information processing. *Personality and Social Psychology Bulletin, 33,* 706–720. (p. 167)

Moons, W. G., Mackie, D. M., & Garcia-Marques, T. (2009). The impact of repetition-induced familiarity on agreement with weak and strong arguments. *Journal of Personality and Social Psychology, 96,* 32–44. (p. 175)

Moor, B. G., Crone, E. A., & van der Molen, M. W. (2010). The heartbrake of social rejection: Heart rate deceleration in response to unexpected peer rejection. *Psychological Science, 21,* 1326–1333. (p. 354)

Moore, D. A., & Swift, S. A. (2011). The three faces of overconfidence in organizations. In D. De Cremer, R. van Dick, & J. K. Murnighan (Eds.), *Social psychology and organizations.* New York: Routledge/Taylor & Francis. (p. 163)

Moore, D. A., Swift, S. A., Sharek, Z. S., & Gino, F. (2010). Correspondence bias in performance evaluation: Why grade inflation works. *Personality and Social Psychology Bulletin, 36,* 843–852. (p. 104)

Moore, D. L., & Baron, R. S. (1983). Social facilitation: A physiological analysis. In J. T. Cacioppo & R. Petty (Eds.), *Social psychophysiology.* New York: Guilford Press. (p. 236)

Moore, D. W. (2004, April 20). Ballot order: Who benefits? *Gallup Poll Tuesday Briefing* (www.gallup.com). (p. 173)

Mor, N., & Winquist, J. (2002). Self-focused attention and negative affect: A meta-analysis. *Psychological Bulletin, 128,* 638. (p. 478)

Morales, L. (2011, May 27). U.S. adults estimate that 25% of Americans are gay or lesbian [news release]. Retrieved from www.gallup.com/poll/147824/adults-estimate-americans-gay-lesbian.aspx. (p. 95)

Moreland, R. L., & Zajonc, R. B. (1977). Is stimulus recognition a necessary condition for the occurrence of exposure effects? *Journal of Personality and Social Psychology, 35,* 191–199. (p. 357)

Morgan, C. A., III, Hazlett, G., Doran, A., Garrett, S., Hoyt, G., Thomas, P., et al. (2004). Accuracy of eyewitness memory for persons encountered during exposure to highly intense stress. *International Journal of Law and Psychiatry, 27,* 265. (p. 499)

Mori, K., & Mori, H. (2009). Another test of the passive facial feedback hypothesis: When your face smiles, you feel happy. *Perceptual and Motor Skills, 109,* 1–3. (p. 146)

Morier, D., & Seroy, C. (1994). The effect of interpersonal expectancies on men's self-presentation of gender role attitudes to women. *Sex Roles, 31,* 493–504. (p. 132)

Morling, B., & Lamoreaux, M. (2008). Measuring culture outside the head: A meta-analysis of individualism collectivism in cultural products. *Personality and Social Psychology Bulletin, 12,* 199–221. (p. 43)

Morris, W. N., & Miller, R. S. (1975). The effects of consensus-breaking and consensus-preempting partners on reduction of conformity. *Journal of Experimental Social Psychology, 11,* 215–223. (p. 215)

Morrow, L. (1983, August 1). All the hazards and threats of success. *Time,* 20–25. (p. 106)

Moscovici, S. (1985). Social influence and conformity. In G. Lindzey & E. Aronson (Eds.), *The handbook of social psychology,* 3rd ed. Hillsdale, NJ: Erlbaum. (p. 267)

Moscovici, S. (1988). Notes towards a description of social representations. *European Journal of Social Psychology, 18,* 211–250. (p. 12)

Moscovici, S. (2001). Why a theory of social representation? In K. Deaux & G. Philogène (Eds.), *Representations of the social: Bridging theoretical traditions.* Malden, MA: Blackwell. (p. 12)

Moscovici, S., Lage, S., & Naffrechoux, M. (1969). Influence of a consistent minority on the responses of a majority in a color perception task. *Sociometry, 32,* 365–380. (p. 267)

Moscovici, S., & Zavalloni, M. (1969). The group as a polarizer of attitudes. *Journal of Personality and Social Psychology, 12,* 124–135. (p. 249)

Motherhood Project. (2001, May 2). Watch out for children: A mothers' statement to advertisers. Institute for American Values (http://www.americanvalues.org/pdfs/watchout.pdf). (p. 191)

Moyer, K. E. (1976). *The psychobiology of aggression.* New York: Harper & Row. (p. 313)

Moyer, K. E. (1983). The physiology of motivation: Aggression as a model. In C. J. Scheier & A. M. Rogers (Eds.), *G. Stanley Hall Lecture Series* (Vol. 3). Washington, DC: American Psychological Association. (p. 313)

Moynihan, D. P. (1979). Social science and the courts. *Public Interest, 54,* 12–31. (p. 11)

Mucchi-Faina, A., Maass, A., & Volpato, C. (1991). Social influence: The role of originality. *European Journal of Social Psychology, 21,* 183–197. (p. 267)

Muehlenhard, C. L. (1988). Misinterpreted dating behaviors and the risk of date rape. *Journal of Social and Clinical Psychology, 6,* 20–37. (p. 102)

Mueller, C. W., Donnerstein, E., & Hallam, J. (1983). Violent films and prosocial behavior. *Personality and Social Psychology Bulletin, 9,* 83–89. (p. 335)

Mullen, B. (1986a). Atrocity as a function of lynch mob composition: A self-attention perspective. *Personality and Social Psychology Bulletin, 12,* 187–197. (p. 342)

Mullen, B. (1986b). Stuttering, audience size, and the other-total ratio: A self-attention perspective. *Journal of Applied Social Psychology, 16,* 139–149. (p. 236)

Mullen, B., Anthony, T., Salas, E., & Driskell, J. E. (1994). Group cohesiveness and quality of decision making: An integration of tests of the groupthink hypothesis. *Small Group Research, 25,* 189–204. (p. 259)

Mullen, B., & Baumeister, R. F. (1987). Group effects on self-attention and performance: Social loafing, social facilitation, and social impairment. In C. Hendrick (Ed.), *Group processes and intergroup relations: Review of personality and social psychology,* Vol. 9. Newbury Park, CA: Sage. (pp. 237, 240)

Mullen, B., Brown, R., & Smith, C. (1992). Ingroup bias as a function of salience, relevance, and status: An integration. *European Journal of Social Psychology, 22,* 103–122. (p. 410)

Mullen, B., Bryant, B., & Driskell, J. E. (1997). Presence of others and arousal: An integration. *Group Dynamics: Theory, Research, and Practice, 1,* 52–64. (p. 234)

Mullen, B., & Copper, C. (1994). The relation between group cohesiveness and performance: An integration. *Psychological Bulletin, 115,* 210–227. (p. 256)

Mullen, B., Copper, C., & Driskell, J. E. (1990). Jaywalking as a function of model behavior. *Personality and Social Psychology Bulletin, 16,* 320–330. (p. 217)

Mullen, B., & Goethals, G. R. (1990). Social projection, actual consensus and valence. *British Journal of Social Psychology, 29,* 279–282. (p. 65)

Mullen, B., & Hu, L. (1989). Perceptions of ingroup and outgroup variability: A meta-analytic integration. *Basic and Applied Social Psychology, 10,* 233–252. (p. 419)

Mullen, B., & Riordan, C. A. (1988). Self-serving attributions for performance in naturalistic settings: A meta-analytic review. *Journal of Applied Social Psychology, 18,* 3–22. (p. 60)

Mullen, B., Salas, E., & Driskell, J. E. (1989). Salience, motivation, and artifact as contributions to the relation between participation rate and leadership. *Journal of Experimental Social Psychology, 25,* 545–559. (p. 267)

Muller, R. A. (2011, October 21). The case against global-warming skepticism. *Wall Street Journal* (online.wsj.com). (p. 516)

Muller, S., & Johnson, B. T. (1990). *Fear and persuasion: A linear relationship?* Paper presented at the Eastern Psychological Association convention. (p. 168)

Mullin, C. R., & Linz, D. (1995). Desensitization and resensitization to violence against women: Effects of exposure to sexually violent films on judgments of domestic violence victims. *Journal of Personality and Social Psychology, 69,* 449–459. (p. 328)

Munro, G. D., Ditto, P. H., Lockhart, L. K., Fagerlin, A., Gready, M., & Peterson, E. (1997). *Biased assimilation of sociopolitcal arguments: Evaluating the 1996 U.S. Presidential debate.* Unpublished manuscript, Hope College. (p. 82)

Muraven, M., & Slessareva, E. (2003). Mechanisism of self-control failure: Motivation and limited resources. *Personality and Social Psychology Bulletin, 29,* 894–906. (p. 57)

Muraven, M., Tice, D. M., & Baumeister, R. F. (1998). Self-control as a limited resource: Regulatory depletion patterns. *Journal of Personality and Social Psychology, 74,* 774–790. (p. 56)

Murphy, C. (1990, June). New findings: Hold on to your hat. *The Atlantic,* 22–23. (p. 14)

Murphy-Berman, V., Berman, J. J., Singh, P., Pachauri, A., & Kumar, P. (1984). Factors affecting allocation to needy and meritorious recipients: A cross-cultural comparison. *Journal of Personality and Social Psychology, 46,* 1267–1272. (p. 460)

Murray, D. R., Trudeau, R., & Schaller, M. (2011). On the origins of cultural differences in conformity: Four tests of the pathogen prevalence hypothesis. *Personality and Social Psychology Bulletin, 37,* 318–329. (p. 223)

Murray, S. L., Gellavia, G. M., Rose, P., & Griffin, D. W. (2003). Once hurt, twice hurtful: How perceived regard regulates daily marital interactions. *Journal of Personality and Social Psychology, 84,* 126–147. (p. 114)

Murray, S. L., & Holmes, J. G. (1997). A leap of faith? Positive illusions in romantic relationships. *Personality and Social Psychology Bulletin, 23,* 586–604. (p. 374)

Murray, S. L., Holmes, J. G., Gellavia, G., Griffin, D. W., & Dolderman, D. (2002b). Kindred spirits? The benefits of egocentrism in close relationships. *Journal of Personality and Social Psychology, 82,* 563–581. (p. 370)

Murray, S. L., Holmes, J. G., & Griffin, D. W. (1996a). The self-fulfilling nature of positive illusions in romantic relationships: Love is not blind, but prescient. *Journal of Personality and Social Psychology, 71,* 1155–1180. (pp. 114, 374)

Murray, S. L., Holmes, J. G., & Griffin, D. W. (1996b). The benefits of positive illusions: Idealization and the construction of satisfaction in close relationships. *Journal of Personality and Social Psychology, 70,* 79–98. (p. 374)

Murray, S. L., Holmes, J. G., & Griffin, D. W. (2000). Self-esteem and the quest for felt security: How perceived regard regulates attachment processes. *Journal of Personality and Social Psychology, 78,* 478–498. (pp. 114, 373)

Murray, S. L., Holmes, J. G., MacDonald, G., & Ellsworth, P. C. (1998). Through the looking glass darkly? When self-doubts turn into relationship insecurities. *Journal of Personality and Social Psychology, 75,* 1459–1480. (p. 56)

Murray, S. L., Rose, P., Bellavia, G. M., Holmes, J. G., & Kusche, A. G. (2002a). When rejection stings: How self-esteem constrains relationship-enhancement processes. *Journal of Personality and Social Psychology, 83,* 556–573. (pp. 56, 376)

Murray, S. L., Rose, P., Holmes, J. G., Derrick, J., Podchaski, E. J., Bellavia, G., et al. (2005). Putting the partner within reach: A dyadic perspective on felt security in close relationships. *Journal of Personality and Social Psychology, 88,* 327. (p. 373)

Murstein, B. L. (1986). *Paths to marriage.* Newbury Park, CA: Sage. (p. 361)

Muson, G. (1978, March). Teenage violence and the telly. *Psychology Today,* 50–54. (p. 332)

Mussweiler, T. (2006). Doing is for thinking! Stereotype activation by stereotypic movements. *Psychological Science, 17,* 17–21. (p. 148)

Myers, D. G. (1978). Polarizing effects of social comparison. *Journal of Experimental Social Psychology, 14,* 554–563. (p. 254)

Myers, D. G. (1993). *The pursuit of happiness.* New York: Avon. (pp. 99, 493)

Myers, D. G. (2000). *The American paradox: Spiritual hunger in an age of plenty.* New Haven, CT: Yale University Press. (pp. 59, 99, 392, 514)

Myers, D. G. (2010). *Psychology,* 9th edition. New York: Worth Publishers. (p. 86)

Myers, D. G., & Bishop, G. D. (1970). Discussion effects on racial attitudes. *Science, 169,* 778–789. (p. 250)

Myers, J. N. (1997, December). Quoted by S. A. Boot, Where the weather reigns. *World Traveler, 86,* 88, 91, 124. (p. 263)

Myers, N. (2000). Sustainable consumption: The meta-problem. In B. Heap & J. Kent (Eds.), *Towards sustainable consumption: A European perspective.* London: The Royal Society. (pp. 327, 519)

Nadler, A. (1991). Help-seeking behavior: Psychological costs and instrumental benefits. In M. S. Clark (Ed.), *Prosocial behavior.* Newbury Park, CA: Sage. (p. 282)

Nadler, A., & Fisher, J. D. (1986). The role of threat to self-esteem and perceived control in recipient reaction to help: Theory development and empirical validation. In L. Berkowitz (Ed.), *Advances in experimental social psychology,* vol. 19. Orlando, FL: Academic Press. (p. 281)

Nadler, A., Goldberg, M., & Jaffe, Y. (1982). Effect of self-differentiation and anonymity in group on deindividuation. *Journal of Personality and Social Psychology, 42,* 1127–1136. (p. 247)

Nagar, D., & Pandey, J. (1987). Affect and performance on cognitive task as a function of crowding and noise. *Journal of Applied Social Psychology, 17,* 147–157. (p. 237)

Nail, P. R., MacDonald, G., & Levy, D. A. (2000). Proposal of a four-dimensional model of social response. *Psychological Bulletin, 126,* 454–470. (pp. 197, 225)

Nair, H., Manchanda, P., & Bhatia, T. (2008, May). Asymmetric social interactions in physician prescription behavior: The role of opinion leaders. Stanford University Graduate School of Business Research Paper No. 1970 (ssrn.com/abstract = 937021). (p. 177)

National Center for Health Statistics (NCHS). (1991). Family structure and children's health: United States, 1988 (by Deborah A. Dawson). *Vital and Health Statistics,* Series 10, No. 178, CHHS Publication No. PHS 91–1506. (p. 421)

National Center for Health Statistics (NCHS). (2008, August 6). National ambulatory medical care survey: 2006 summary. *National Health Statistics Report,* No. 3 (by D. K. Cherry, E. Hing, D. A. Woodwell, & E. A. Rechtsteiner). Centers for Disease Control and Prevention: National Center for Health Statistics. Available at www.cdc.gov/nchs/data/nhsr/nhsr003.pdf. (p. 487)

National Safety Council. (2008). Transportation mode comparisons, from *Injury Facts* (via correspondence with Kevin T. Fearn, Research & Statistical Services Department). (p. 96)

National Television Violence Study. (1997). Thousand Oaks, CA: Sage. (p. 331)

Navarrete, C. D., McDonald, M. M., Molina, L. E., & Sidanius, J. (2010). Prejudice at the nexus of race and gender: An outgroup male target hypothesis. *Journal of Personality and Social Psychology, 98,* 933–945. (p. 517)

Naylor, T. H. (1990). Redefining corporate motivation, Swedish style. *Christian Century, 107,* 566–570. (p. 265)

Neal, D. T., & Chartrand, T. L. (2011). Embodied emotion perception: Amplifying and dampening facial feedback modulates emotion perception accuracy. *Social Psychological and Personality Science, 2,* 673–678. (p. 146)

Neff, K. D. (2011). Self-compassion, self-esteem, and well-being. *Social and Personality Psychology Compass, 5,* 1–12. (p. 56)

Neff, L. A., & Karney, B. R. (2005). To know you is to love you: The implications of global adoration and specific accuracy for marital relationships. *Journal of Personality and Social Psychology, 88,* 480. (p. 388)

Nelson, L., & LeBoeuf, R. (2002). *Why do men overperceive women's sexual intent? False consensus vs. evolutionary explanations.* Paper presented to the annual meeting of the Society for Personality and Social Psychology. (p. 102)

Nelson, L. D., & Morrison, E. L. (2005). The symptoms of resource scarcity: Judgments of food and finances influence preferences for potential partners. *Psychological Science, 16,* 167. (p. 364)

Nelson, L. J., & Miller, D. T. (1995). The distinctiveness effect in social categorization: You are what makes you unusual. *Psychological Science, 6,* 246. (p. 420)

Nelson, T. E., Acker, M., & Manis, M. (1996). Irrepressible stereotypes. *Journal of Experimental Social Psychology, 32,* 13–38. (p. 444)

Nelson, T. E., Biernat, M. R., & Manis, M. (1990). Everyday base rates (sex stereotypes): Potent and resilient. *Journal of Personality and Social Psychology, 59,* 664–675. (p. 444)

Nemeth, C. (1979). The role of an active minority in intergroup relations. In W. G. Austin and S. Worchel (Eds.), *The social psychology of intergroup relations.* Monterey, CA: Brooks/Cole. (p. 267)

Nemeth, C. J. (1999). Behind the scenes. In D. G. Myers, *Social psychology,* 6th edition. New York: McGraw-Hill. (p. 268)

Nemeth, C. J. (2011). Minority influence theory. In P. Van Lange, A. Kruglanski, & E. T. Higgins (Eds.), *Handbook of theories in social psychology.* New York: Sage. (p. 267)

Nemeth, C. J., Brown, K., & Rogers, J. (2001a). Devil's advocate versus authentic dissent: Stimulating quantity and quality. *European Journal of Social Psychology, 31,* 1–13. (p. 260)

Nemeth, C. J., Connell, J. B., Rogers, J. D., & Brown, K. S. (2001b). Improving decision making by means of dissent. *Journal of Applied Social Psychology, 31,* 48. (p. 260)

Nemeth, C., & Chiles, C. (1988). Modelling courage: The role of dissent in fostering independence. *European Journal of Social Psychology, 18,* 275–280. (p. 216)

Nemeth, C. J., & Ormiston, M. (2007). Creative idea generation: Harmony versus stimulation. *European Journal of Social Psychology, 37,* 524–535. (p. 259)

Nemeth, C. J., Personnaz, B., Personnaz, M., & Goncalo, J. A. (2004). The liberating role of conflict in group creativity: A study in two countries. *European Journal of Social Psychology, 34,* 365–374. (p. 262)

Nemeth, C., & Wachtler, J. (1974). Creating the perceptions of consistency and confidence: A necessary condition for minority influence. *Sociometry, 37,* 529–540. (p. 268)

Neumann, R., & Strack, F. (2000). Approach and avoidance: The influence of proprioceptive and exteroceptive cues on encoding of affective information. *Journal of Personality and Social Psychology, 79,* 39–48. (p. 199)

Newby-Clark, I. R. (2005). Plans and predictions for exercise frequency change. *Basic and Applied Social Psychology, 27,* 97–106. (p. 90)

Newcomb, T. M. (1961). *The acquaintance process.* New York: Holt, Rinehart and Winston. (pp. 356, 369)

Newell, B. R., Wong, K. Y., Cheung, J. C. H., & Rakow, T. (2008, August 23). Think, blink, or sleep on it? The impact of modes of thought on complex decision making. *Quarterly Journal of Experimental Psychology* (DOI: 10.1080/17470210802215202). (p. 88)

Newman, H. M., & Langer, E. J. (1981). Postdivorce adaptation and the attribution of responsibility. *Sex Roles, 7,* 223–231. (p. 69)

Newman, L. S. (1993). How individualists interpret behavior: Idiocentrism and spontaneous trait inference. *Social Cognition, 11,* 243–269. (p. 109)

Nias, D. K. B. (1979). Marital choice: Matching or complementation? In M. Cook and G. Wilson (Eds.), *Love and attraction.* Oxford: Pergamon. (p. 371)

Nichols, J. (2003, February 9). Man overdoses online as chatters watch him die. *Grand Rapids Press,* A20. (p. 293)

Nicholson, C. (2007, January). Framing science: Advances in theory and technology are fueling a new era in the science of persuasion. *APS Observer* (www.psychologicalscience.org). (p. 168)

Nicholson, N., Cole, S. G., & Rocklin, T. (1985). Conformity in the Asch situation: A comparison between contemporary British and U. S. university students. *British Journal of Social Psychology, 24,* 59–63. (p. 224)

Nie, N. H., & Erbring, L. (2000, February 17). *Internet and society: A preliminary report.* Stanford, CA: Stanford Institute for the Quantitative Study of Society. (p. 389)

Nielsen. (2008a, May). *Nielsen's three screen report.* The Nielsen Company (www.nielsen.com). (p. 331)

Nielsen. (2008b, February 14). Nielsen reports DVR playback is adding to TV viewing levels. The Nielsen Company (www.nielsen.com). (p. 331)

Niemi, R. G., Mueller, J., & Smith, T. W. (1989). *Trends in public opinion: A compendium of survey data.* New York: Greenwood Press. (p. 345)

Nigro, G. N., Hill, D. E., Gelbein, M. E., & Clark, C. L. (1988). Changes in the facial prominence of women and men over the last decade. *Psychology of Women Quarterly, 12,* 225–235. (p. 407)

Nijstad, B. A., & Stroebe, W. (2006). How the group affects the mind: A cognitive model of idea generation in groups. *Personality and Social Psychology Review, 10,* 186–213. (p. 262)

Nijstad, B. A., Stroebe, W., & Lodewijkx, H. F. M. (2006). The illusion of group productivity. A reduction of failures explanation. *European Journal of Social Psychology, 36,* 31–48. (p. 262)

Nisbet, E. K., & Zelenski, J. M. (2011). Underestimating nearby nature: Affective forecasting errors obscure the happy path to sustainability. *Psychological Science, 22,* 1101–1106. (p. 526)

Nisbett, R. (2003). *The geography of thought: How Asians and Westerners think differently . . . and why.* New York: Free Press. (p. 42)

Nisbett, R. E., Fong, G. T., Lehman, D. R., & Cheng, P. W. (1987). Teaching reasoning. *Science, 238,* 625–631. (p. 117)

Nisbett, R. E., & Masuda, T. (2003). Culture and point of view. *Proceedings of the National Academy of Sciences, 100,* 11163–11170. (p. 42)

Nisbett, R. E., & Ross, L. (1980). *Human inference: Strategies and shortcomings of social judgment.* Englewood Cliffs, NJ: Prentice-Hall. (pp. 115, 117)

Nisbett, R. E., & Ross, L. (1991). *The person and the situation.* New York: McGraw-Hill. (p. 265)

Nix, G., Watson, C., Pyszczynski, T., & Greenberg, J. (1995). Reducing depressive affect through external focus of attention. *Journal of Social and Clinical Psychology, 14,* 36–52. (p. 479)

Nock, M. K., Park, J. M., Finn, C. T., Deliberto, T. L., Dour, H. J., & Banaji, M. R. (2010). Measuring the suicidal mind: Implicit cognition predicts suicidal behavior. *Psychological Science, 21,* 511–517. (p. 125)

Nolan, S. A., Flynn, C., & Garber, J. (2003). Prospective relations between rejection and depression in young adolescents. *Journal of Personality and Social Psychology, 85,* 745–755. (p. 352)

Nolen-Hoeksema, S. (2003). *Women who think too much: How to break free of overthinking and reclaim your life.* New York: Holt. (p. 478)

Noller, P., & Fitzpatrick, M. A. (1990). Marital communication in the eighties. *Journal of Marriage and the Family, 52,* 832–843. (p. 393)

Noon, E., & Hollin, C. R. (1987). Lay knowledge of eyewitness behaviour: A British survey. *Applied Cognitive Psychology, 1,* 143–153. (p. 505)

Noor, M., Brown, R., Gonzalez, R., Manzi, J., & Lewis, C. A. (2008). On positive psychological outcomes: What helps groups with a history of conflict to forgive and reconcile with each other? *Personality and Social Psychology Bulletin, 34,* 819–832. (p. 465)

Nordgren, L. F., Banas, K., & MacDonald, G. (2011). Empathy gaps for social pain: Why people underestimate the pain of social suffering. *Journal of Personality and Social Psychology, 100,* 120–128. (pp. 288, 353)

Norem, J. K., & Cantor, N. (1986). Defensive pessimism: Harnessing anxiety as motivation. *Journal of Personality and Social Psychology, 51,* 1208–1217. (p. 65)

Norton, M. I., Frost, J. H., & Ariely, D. (2007). Less is more: The lure of ambiguity, or why familiarity breeds contempt. *Journal of Personality and Social Psychology, 92,* 97–105. (p. 370)

Nosek, B. A. (2007). Implicit-explicit relations. *Current Directions in Psychological Science, 16,* 65–69. (p. 51)

Nosek, B. A., Hawkins, C. B., & Frazier, R. S. (2011). Implicit social cognition: From measures to mechanisms. *Trends in Cognitive Sciences, 15,* 152–159. (p. 124)

Nosek, B. A., Smyth, F. L., Hansen, J. J., Devos, T., Lindner, N. M., Ranganath, K.

A., Smith, C. T., Olson, K. R., Chugh, D., Greenwald, A. G., & Banaji, M. R. (2007). Pervasiveness and correlates of implicit attitudes and stereotypes. *European Review of Social Psychology, 18,* 36–88. (p. 401)

Notarius, C., & Markman, H. J. (1993). *We can work it out.* New York: Putnam. (p. 394)

Nowak, M. A., & Highfield, R. (2011). *Super-Cooperators: Altruism, evolution, and why we need each other to succeed.* New York: Free Press. (p. 283)

Nuttin, J. M., Jr. (1987). Affective consequences of mere ownership: The name letter effect in twelve European languages. *European Journal of Social Psychology, 17,* 318–402. (p. 357)

Oaten, M., & Cheng, K. (2006a). Improved self-control: The benefits of a regular program of academic study. *Basic and Applied Social Psychology, 28,* 1. (p. 57)

Oaten, M., & Cheng, K. (2006b). Longitudinal gains in self-regulation from regular physical exercise. *British Journal of Health Psychology, 11,* 717–733. (p. 57)

Oddone-Paolucci, E., Genuis, M., & Violato, C. (2000). A meta analysis of the published research on the effects of pornography. In C. Violata (Ed.), *The changing family and child development.* Aldershot, UK: Ashgate Publishing. (p. 328)

O'Dea, T. F. (1968). Sects and cults. In D. L. Sills (Ed.), *International encyclopedia of the social sciences* (Vol. 14). New York: Macmillan. (p. 185)

Ohbuchi, K., & Kambara, T. (1985). Attacker's intent and awareness of outcome, impression management, and retaliation. *Journal of Experimental Social Psychology, 21,* 321–330. (p. 324)

O'Hegarty, M., , L. L., Yonokyan, G., Nelson, D., & Wortley, P. (2007). Young adults' perceptions of cigarette warning labels in the United States and Canada. *Preventing Chronic Disease: Public Health Research, Practice, and Policy, 30,* 467–473. (p. 168)

Oishi, S., Kesebir, S., & Diener, E. (2011). Income inequality and happiness. *Psychological Science, 22,* 1095–1100. (p. 525)

Oishi, S., Lun, J., & Sherman, G. D. (2007). Residential mobility, self-concept, and positive affect in social interactions. *Journal of Personality and Social Psychology, 93,* 131–141. (p. 43)

O'Keefe, D. J., & Jensen, J. D. (2011). The relative effectiveness of gain-framed and loss-framed persuasive appeals concerning obesity-related behaviors: Meta-analytic evidence and implications. In R. Batra, P. A. Keller, & V. J. Strecher (Eds.), *Leveraging consumer psychology for effective health communications: The obesity challenge* (pp. 171–185). Armonk, NY: Sharpe. (p. 169)

O'Leary, K. D., Christian, J. L., & Mendell, N. R. (1994). A closer look at the link between marital discord and depressive symptomatology. *Journal of Social and Clinical Psychology, 13,* 33–41. (p. 393)

Olfson, M., & Pincus, H. A. (1994). Outpatient therapy in the United States: II. Patterns of utilization. *American Journal of Psychiatry, 151,* 1289–1294. (p. 483)

Oliner, S. P., & Oliner, P. M. (1988). *The altruistic personality: Rescuers of Jews in Nazi Europe.* New York: The Free Press. (p. 304)

Olson, I. R., & Marchuetz, C. (2005). Facial attractiveness is appraised in a glance. *Emotion, 5,* 498. (p. 363)

Olson, J. M., & Cal, A. V. (1984). Source credibility, attitudes, and the recall of past behaviours. *European Journal of Social Psychology, 14,* 203–210. (p. 163)

Olson, J. M., Roese, N. J., & Zanna, M. P. (1996). Expectancies. In E. T. Higgins & A. W. Kruglanski (Eds.), *Social psychology: Handbook of basic principles.* New York: Guilford Press. (p. 113)

Olson, J. M., & Zanna, M. P. (1993). Attitudes and attitude change. *Annual Review of Psychology, 44,* 117–154. (p. 122)

Olweus, D. (1979). Stability of aggressive reaction patterns in males: A review. *Psychological Bulletin, 86,* 852–875. (p. 313)

Olweus, D., Mattsson, A., Schalling, D., & Low, H. (1988). Circulating testosterone levels and aggression in adolescent males: A causal analysis. *Psychosomatic Medicine, 50,* 261–272. (p. 314)

Omoto, A. M., & Snyder, M. (2002). Considerations of community: The context and process of volunteerism. *American Behavioral Scientist, 45,* 846–867. (p. 301)

Open Secrets. (2005). 2004 election overview: Winning vs. spending (www.opensecrets.org). (p. 175)

Opotow, S. (1990). Moral exclusion and injustice: An introduction. *Journal of Social Issues, 46,* 1–20. (p. 303)

Orbell, J. M., van de Kragt, A. J. C., & Dawes, R. M. (1988). Explaining discussion-induced cooperation. *Journal of Personality and Social Psychology, 54,* 811–819. (p. 458)

Orendain, S. (2011, December 29). In Philippine slums, capturing light in a bottle. National Public Radio (www.npr.org). (p. 519)

Organisation for Economic Co-operation and Development (OECD). (2011). *An overview of growing income inequalities in OECD countries: Main findings.* Paris: Author (www.oecd.org/dataoecd/40/12/49170449.pdf) (p. 525)

Orive, R. (1984). Group similarity, public self-awareness, and opinion extremity: A social projection explanation of deindividuation effects. *Journal of Personality and Social Psychology, 47,* 727–737. (p. 246)

Ornstein, R. (1991). *The evolution of consciousness: Of Darwin, Freud, and cranial fire: The origins of the way we think.* New York: Prentice-Hall. (p. 133)

Osbeck, L. M., Moghaddam, F. M., & Perreault, S. (1996). Similarity and attraction among majority and minority groups in a multicultural context. *International Journal of Intercultural Relations, 20,* 1–10. (p. 370)

Osborne, J. W. (1995). Academics, self-esteem, and race: A look at the underlying assumptions of the disidentification hypothesis. *Personality and Social Psychology Bulletin, 21,* 449–455. (p. 441)

Osgood, C. E. (1962). *An alternative to war or surrender.* Urbana, IL: University of Illinois Press. (p. 467)

Osgood, C. E. (1980). *GRIT: A strategy for survival in mankind's nuclear age?* Paper presented at the Pugwash Conference on New Directions in Disarmament, Racine, WI. (p. 467)

Oskamp, S. (1991). *Curbside recycling: Knowledge, attitudes, and behavior.* Paper presented at the Society for Experimental Social Psychology meeting, Columbus, Ohio. (p. 127)

Osofsky, M. J., Bandura, A., & Zimbardo, P. G. (2005). The role of moral disengagement in the execution process. *Law and Human Behavior, 29,* 371–393. (p. 136)

Osterhouse, R. A., & Brock, T. C. (1970). Distraction increases yielding to propaganda by inhibiting counterarguing. *Journal of Personality and Social Psychology, 15,* 344–358. (p. 180)

Ostrom, T. M., & Sedikides, C. (1992). Outgroup homogeneity effects in natural and minimal groups. *Psychological Bulletin, 112,* 536–552. (p. 418)

Ouellette, J. A., & Wood, W. (1998). Habit and intention in everyday life: The multiple processes by which past behavior predicts future behavior. *Psychological Bulletin, 124,* 54–74. (p. 128)

Oyserman, D., Coon, H. M., & Kemmelmeier, M. (2002a). Rethinking individualism and collectivism: Evaluation of theoretical assumptions and meta-analyses. *Psychological Bulletin, 128,* 3–72. (p. 42)

Oyserman, D., Kemmelmeier, M., & Coon, H. M. (2002b). Cultural psychology, a new look: Reply to Bond (2002), Fiske (2002), Kitayama (2002), and Miller (2002). *Psychological Bulletin, 128,* 110–117. (p. 42)

Packer, D. J. (2008). Identifying systematic disobedience in Milgram's obedience experiments: A meta-analytic review. *Perspectives on Psychological Science, 3*(4), 301–304. (p. 204)

Packer, D. J. (2009). Avoiding groupthink: Whereas weakly identified members remain silent, strongly identified members dissent about collective problems. *Psychological Science, 20,* 546–548. (p. 259)

Padgett, V. R. (1989). *Predicting organizational violence: An application of 11 powerful principles of obedience.* Paper presented at the American Psychological Association convention. (p. 207)

Page, S. E. (2007). *The difference: How the power of diversity creates better groups, firms, schools, and societies.* Princeton, NJ: Princeton University Press. (pp. 259, 267)

Pallak, M. S., Mueller, M., Dollar, K., & Pallak, J. (1972). Effect of commitment on responsiveness to an extreme consonant communication. *Journal of Personality and Social Psychology, 23,* 429–436. (p. 171)

Pallak, S. R., Murroni, E., & Koch, J. (1983). Communicator attractiveness and expertise, emotional versus rational appeals, and persuasion: A heuristic versus systematic processing interpretation. *Social Cognition, 2,* 122–141. (p. 165)

Palmer, D. L. (1996). Determinants of Canadian attitudes toward immigration: More than just racism? *Canadian Journal of Behavioural Science, 28,* 180–192. (p. 407)

Palmer, E. L., & Dorr, A. (Eds.) (1980). *Children and the faces of television: Teaching, violence, selling.* New York: Academic Press. (p. 190)

Paloutzian, R. (1979). *Pro-ecology behavior: Three field experiments on litter pickup.* Paper presented at the Western Psychological Association convention. (p. 175)

Paluck, E. L. (2009). Reducing intergroup prejudice and conflict using the media: A field experiment in Rwanda. *Journal*

of *Personality and Social Psychology, 96,* 574–587. (p. 169)

Pandey, J., Sinha, Y., Prakash, A., & Tripathi, R. C. (1982). Right-left political ideologies and attribution of the causes of poverty. *European Journal of Social Psychology, 12,* 327–331. (p. 109)

Papastamou, S., & Mugny, G. (1990). Synchronic consistency and psychologization in minority influence. *European Journal of Social Psychology, 20,* 85–98. (p. 267)

Pape, R. A. (2003, September 22). Dying to kill us. *New York Times* (www.nytimes.com). (p. 311)

Parashar, U. D., Gibson, C. J., Bresse, J. S., & Glass, R. I. (2006). Rotavirus and severe childhood diarrhea. *Emerging Infectious Diseases, 12,* 304–306. (p. 96)

Parents Television Council (PTC). (2007, January 10). *Dying to entertain: Violence on prime time broadcast TV, 1998 to 2006.* (www.parentstv.org). (p. 332)

Park, B., & Rothbart, M. (1982). Perception of out-group homogeneity and levels of social categorization: Memory for the subordinate attributes of in-group and out-group members. *Journal of Personality and Social Psychology, 42,* 1051–1068. (p. 419)

Parke, R. D., Berkowitz, L., Leyens, J. P., West, S. G., & Sebastian, J. (1977). Some effects of violent and nonviolent movies on the behavior of juvenile delinquents. In L. Berkowitz (Ed.), *Advances in experimental social psychology* (Vol. 10). New York: Academic Press. (p. 334)

Parker, K. D., Ortega, S. T., & VanLaningham, J. (1995). Life satisfaction, self-esteem, and personal happiness among Mexican and African Americans. *Sociological Spectrum, 15,* 131–145. (p. 492)

Parks, C. D., & Rumble, A. C. (2001). Elements of reciprocity and social value orientation. *Personality and Social Psychology Bulletin, 27,* 1301–1309. (p. 468)

Pascarella, E. T., & Terenzini, P. T. (1991). *How college affects students: Findings and insights from twenty years of research.* San Francisco: Jossey-Bass. (p. 250)

Patterson, G. R., Chamberlain, P., & Reid, J. B. (1982). A comparative evaluation of parent training procedures. *Behavior Therapy, 13,* 638–650. (p. 320)

Patterson, G. R., Littman, R. A., & Bricker, W. (1967). Assertive behavior in children: A step toward a theory of aggression.

Monographs of the Society of Research in Child Development (Serial No. 113), *32,* 5. (p. 319)

Patterson, T. E. (1980). The role of the mass media in presidential campaigns: The lessons of the 1976 election. *Items, 34,* 25–30. Social Science Research Council, 605 Third Avenue, New York, NY 10016. (p. 358)

Paulhus, D. (1982). Individual differences, self-presentation, and cognitive dissonance: Their concurrent operation in forced compliance. *Journal of Personality and Social Psychology, 43,* 838–852. (p. 139)

Paulhus, D. L. (1998). Interpersonal and intrapsychic adaptiveness of trait self-enhancment: A mixed blessing? *Journal of Personality and Social Psychology, 75,* 1197–1208. (p. 480)

Paulhus, D. L., & Lim, D. T. K. (1994). Arousal and evaluative extremity in social judgments: A dynamic complexity model. *European Journal of Social Psychology, 24,* 89–99. (p. 101)

Paulhus, D. L., & Morgan, K. L. (1997). Perceptions of intelligence in leaderless groups: The dynamic effects of shyness and acquaintance. *Journal of Personality and Social Psychology, 72,* 581–591. (p. 480)

Paulhus, D. L., & Williams, K. M. (2002). The Dark Triad of personality: Narcissism, Machiavellianism and psychopathy. *Journal of Research in Personality, 36,* 556–563. (p. 54)

Paulus, P. B. (1998). Developing consensus about groupthink after all these years. *Organizational Behavior and Human Decision Processes,* in press. (p. 259)

Paulus, P. B., & Coskun, H. (2012). Group creativity: Understanding collaborative creativity processes. In J. M. Levine (Ed.), *Group processes.* Boca Raton, FL: Psychology Press. (p. 263)

Paulus, P. B., Dzindolet, M., & Kohn, N. W. (2011). Collaborative creativity—Group creativity and team innovation. In M. D. Mumford (Ed.), *Handbook of organizational creativity.* New York: Elsevier. (pp. 262, 263)

Paulus, P. B., Larey, T. S., & Ortega, A. H. (1995). Performance and perceptions of brainstormers in an organizational setting. *Basic and Applied Social Psychology, 17,* 249–265. (p. 262)

Paulus, P. B., & Yang, H. (2000). Idea generation in groups: A basis for creativity in organizations. *Organizational Behavior and Human Decision Processes, 82,* 76–87. (p. 262)

Payne, B. K. (2001). Prejudice and perception: The role of automatic and controlled processes in misperceiving a weapon. *Journal of Personality and Social Psychology, 81,* 181–192. (p. 432)

Payne, B. K. (2006). Weapon bias: Split-second decisions and unintended stereotyping. *Current Directions in Psychological Science, 15,* 287–291. (p. 432)

Pedersen, A., & Walker, I. (1997). Prejudice against Australian Aborigines: Old-fashioned and modern forms. *European Journal of Social Psychology, 27,* 561–587. (p. 401)

Pedersen, A., Zachariae, R., & Bovbjerg, D. H. (2010). Influence of psychological stress on upper respiratory infection—A meta-analysis of prospective studies. *Psychosomatic Medicine, 72,* 823–832. (p. 485)

Pedersen, W. C., Gonzales, C., & Miller, N. (2000). The moderating effect of trivial triggering provocation on displaced aggression. *Journal of Personality and Social Psychology, 78,* 913–927. (p. 317)

Peetz, J. & Buehler, R. (2009). Is there a budget fallacy? The role of savings goals in the prediction of personal spending. *Personality and Social Psychology Bulletin, 35,* 1579–1591. (pp. 48, 92)

Peetz, J., Buehler, R., & Britten, K. (2011). Only minutes a day: Reframing exercise duration affects exercise intentions and behavior. *Basic and Applied Social Psychology, 33,* 118–127. (p. 483)

Peetz, J., Gunn, G. R., & Wilson, A. E. (2010). Crimes of the past: Defensive temporal distancing in the face of past in-group wrongdoing. *Personality and Social Psychology Bulletin, 36,* 598–611. (p. 67)

Pegalis, L. J., Shaffer, D. R., Bazzini, D. G., & Greenier, K. (1994). On the ability to elicit self-disclosure: Are there gender-based and contextual limitations on the opener effect? *Personality and Social Psychology Bulletin, 20,* 412–420. (p. 387)

Pelham, B. W. (2009, October 22). About one in six Americans report history of depression. www.gallup.com. (p. 471)

Pennebaker, J. (1990). *Opening up: The healing power of confiding in others.* New York: William Morrow. (p. 489)

Pennebaker, J. W. (1982). *The psychology of physical symptoms.* New York: Springer-Verlag. (p. 482)

Pennebaker, J. W., & O'Heeron, R. C. (1984). Confiding in others and illness rate among spouses of suicide and accidental death victims. *Journal of Abnormal Psychology, 93,* 473–476. (p. 488)

Pennebaker, J. W., Rime, B., & Sproul, G. (1996). Stereotypes of emotional expressiveness of northerners and southerners: A cross-cultural test of Montesquieu's hypotheses. *Journal of Personality and Social Psychology, 70,* 372–380. (p. 399)

Penner, L. A., Dertke, M. C., & Achenbach, C. J. (1973). The "flash" system: A field study of altruism. *Journal of Applied Social Psychology, 3,* 362–370. (p. 282)

Pennington, N., & Hastie, R. (1993). The story model for juror decision making. In R. Hastie (Ed.), *Inside the juror: The psychology of juror decision making.* New York: Cambridge University Press. (p. 507)

Pentland, A. (2010). To signal is human. *American Scientist, 98,* 204–211. (p. 163)

Penton-Voak, I. S., Perrett, D. I., & Peirce, J. W. (2001). *Computer graphic studies of the role of facial similarity in judgements of attractiveness.* New Brunswick, NJ: Transaction Publishers. (p. 365)

Peplau, L. A., & Fingerhut, A. W. (2007). The close relationships of lesbians and gay men. *Annual Review of Psychology, 58,* 405–424. (p. 492)

Peplau, L. A., & Gordon, S. L. (1985). Women and men in love: Gender differences in close heterosexual relationships. In V. E. O'Leary, R. K. Unger, & B. S. Wallston (Eds.), *Women, gender, and social psychology.* Hillsdale, NJ: Erlbaum. (p. 379)

Pereira, C., Vala, J., & Costa-Lopes, R. (2010). From prejudice to discrimination: The legitimizing role of perceived threat in discrimination against immigrants. *European Journal of Social Psychology, 40,* 1231–1250. (p. 407)

Pereira, J. (2003, January 10). Just how far does First Amendment protection go? *Wall Street Journal,* B1, B3. (p. 338)

Perkins, H. W. (1991). Religious commitment, Yuppie values, and well-being in post-collegiate life. *Review of Religious Research, 32,* 244–251. (p. 491)

Perlman, D., & Rook, K. S. (1987). Social support, social deficits, and the family: Toward the enhancement of well-being. In S. Oskamp (Ed.), *Family processes and problems: Social psychological aspects.* Newbury Park, CA: Sage. (p. 491)

Perls, F. S. (1973). Ego, hunger and aggression: The beginning of Gestalt therapy. Random House, 1969. Cited by Berkowitz in The case for bottling up rage. *Psychology Today,* July, 24–30. (p. 344)

Perrin, S., & Spencer, C. (1981). Independence or conformity in the Asch experiment as a reflection of cultural or situational factors. *British Journal of Social Psychology, 20,* 205–209. (p. 224)

Persico, N., Postelwaite, A., & Silverman, D. (2004). The effect of adolescent experience on labor market outcomes: The case of height. *Journal of Political Economy, 112,* 1019–1053. (p. 363)

Pessin, J. (1933). The comparative effects of social and mechanical stimulation on memorizing. *American Journal of Psychology, 45,* 263–270. (p. 234)

Pessin, J., & Husband, R. W. (1933). Effects of social stimulation on human maze learning. *Journal of Abnormal and Social Psychology, 28,* 148–154. (p. 234)

Peters, E., Romer, D., Slovic, P., Jamieson, K. H., Whasfield, L., Mertz, C. K., & Carpenter, S. M. (2007). The impact and acceptability of Canadian-style cigarette warning labels among U.S. smokers and nonsmokers. *Nicotine and Tobacco Research, 9,* 473–481. (p. 168)

Peterson, C., & Bossio, L. M. (2000). Optimism and physical well-being. In E. C. Chang (Ed.), *Optimism and pessimism.* Washington, DC: APA Books. (p. 486)

Peterson, C., & Seligman, M. E. P. (1987). Explanatory style and illness. *Journal of Personality, 55,* 237–265. (p. 486)

Peterson, C., Schwartz, S. M., & Seligman, M. E. P. (1981). Self-blame and depression symptoms. *Journal of Personality and Social Psychology, 41,* 253–259. (p. 69)

Peterson, C., Seligman, M. E. P., & Vaillant, G. E. (1988). Pessimistic explanatory style is a risk factor for physical illness: A thirty-five-year longitudinal study. *Journal of Personality and Social Psychology, 55,* 23–27. (p. 486)

Peterson, C., & Steen, T. A. (2002). Optimistic explanatory style. In C. R. Snyder & S. J. Lopez (Ed.), *Handbook of positive psychology.* London: Oxford University Press. (p. 476)

Peterson, J. L., & Zill, N. (1981). Television viewing in the United States and children's intellectual, social, and emotional development. *Television and Children, 2*(2), 21–28. (p. 336)

Peterson, R. S., & Nemeth, C. J. (1996). Focus versus flexibility: Majority and minority influence can both improve performance. *Personality and Social Psychology Bulletin, 22,* 14–23. (p. 267)

Petrocelli, J. V., Percy, E. J., Sherman, S. J., & Tormala, Z. L. (2011). Counterfactual potency. *Journal of Personality and Social Psychology, 100,* 30–46. (p. 97)

Pettigrew, T. F. (1958). Personality and socio-cultural factors in intergroup attitudes: A cross-national comparison. *Journal of Conflict Resolution, 2,* 29–42. (p. 405)

Pettigrew, T. F. (1979). The ultimate attribution error: Extending Allport's cognitive analysis of prejudice. *Personality and Social Psychology Bulletin, 55,* 461–476. (p. 423)

Pettigrew, T. F. (1980). Prejudice. In S. Thernstrom et al. (Eds.), *Harvard encyclopedia of American ethnic groups.* Cambridge, MA: Harvard University Press. (p. 423)

Pettigrew, T. F. (1997, May 12). *New York Times,* 20. (p. 401)

Pettigrew, T. F. (1998). Intergroup contact theory. *Annual Review of Psychology,* in press. (p. 401)

Pettigrew, T. F., Christ, O., Wagner, U., Meertens, R. W., van Dick, R., & Zick, A. (2008a). Relative deprivation and intergroup prejudice. *Journal of Social Issues, 64,* 385–401. (p. 408)

Pettigrew, T. F., & Meertens, R. W. (1995). Subtle and blatant prejudice in western Europe. *European Journal of Social Psychology, 25,* 57–76. (p. 408)

Pettigrew, T. F., Jackson, J. S., Brika, J. B., Lemaine, G., Meertens, R. W., Wagner, U., & Zick, A. (1998). Outgroup prejudice in western Europe. *European Review of Social Psychology, 8,* 241–273. (p. 412)

Pettigrew, T. F., Wagner, U., & Christ, O. (2008b). Who opposes immigration? Comparing German with North American findings. *DuBois Review, 4,* 19–40. (p. 412)

Petty, R. E., & Briñol, P. (2008). Persuasion: From single to multiple to metacognitive processes. *Perspectives on Psychological Science, 3,* 137–147. (p. 161)

Petty, R. E., & Cacioppo, J. T. (1979). Effects of forewarning of persuasive intent and involvement on cognitive response and persuasion. *Personality and Social Psychology Bulletin, 5,* 173–176. (p. 171)

Petty, R. E., & Cacioppo, J. T. (1986). *Communication and persuasion: Central and peripheral routes to attitude change.* New York: Springer-Verlag. (p. 160)

Petty, R. E., Cacioppo, J. T., & Goldman, R. (1981). Personal involvement as a determinant of argument-based persuasion. *Journal of Personality and Social Psychology, 41,* 847–855. (p. 166)

Petty, R. E., Haugtvedt, C. P., & Smith, S. M. (1995). Elaboration as a determinant of attitude strength: Creating attitudes that are persistent, resistant, and predictive of behavior. In R. E. Petty & J. A. Krosnick (Eds.), *Attitude strength: Antecedents and consequences.* Hillsdale, NJ: Erlbaum. (pp. 161, 162)

Petty, R. E., Schumann, D. W., Richman, S. A., & Strathman, A. J. (1993). Positive mood and persuasion: Different roles for affect under high and low elaboration conditions. *Journal of Personality and Social Psychology, 64,* 5–20. (p. 167)

Petty, R. E., & Wegener, D. T. (1998). Attitude change: Multiple roles for persuasion variables. In D. Gilbert, S. Fiske, & G. Lindzey (Eds), *Handbook of Social Psychology,* 4th edition. New York: McGraw-Hill. (pp. 161, 172)

Petty, R. E., & Wegener, D. T. (1999). The elaboration likelihood model: Current status and controversies. In S. & Y. Trope (Eds.). *Dual-process theories in social psychology* (41–72). New York: Guilford. (p. 160)

Petty, R. E., Wegener, D. T., & Fabrigar, L. R. (1997). Attitudes and attitude change. *Annual Review of Psychology, 48,* 609–647. (p. 152)

Pew Research Center. (2000, May 10). *Tracking online life: How women use the Internet to cultivate relationships with family and friends.* Washington, DC: Pew Internet and American Life Project. (p. 390)

Pew Research Center. (2006, February 13). Not looking for love: Romance in America. Pew Internet and American Life Project (pewresearch.org). (p. 356)

Pew Research Center. (2007, July 18). Modern marriage: "I like hugs. I like kisses. But what I really love is help with the dishes." Pew Research Center (pewresearch.org). (p. 386)

Pew Research Center. (2008). Video Gamers Galore. Retrieved from pewresearch.org/databank/dailynumber/?NumberID5787, June 5, 2009. (p. 338)

Phelan, J. E., & Rudman, L. A. (2010). Reactions to ethnic deviance: The role of backlash in racial stereotype maintenance. *Journal of Personality and Social Psychology, 99,* 265–281. (p. 436)

Phillips, A. L. (2011). A walk in the woods. *American Scientist, 69,* 301–302. (p. 526)

Phillips, D. P. (1985). Natural experiments on the effects of mass media violence on fatal aggression: Strengths and weaknesses of a new approach. In L. Berkowitz (Ed.), *Advances in experimental social psychology,* Vol. 19. Orlando, FL: Academic Press. (p. 200)

Phillips, D. P., Carstensen, L. L., & Paight, D. J. (1989). Effects of mass media news stories on suicide, with new evidence on the role of story content. In D. R. Pfeffer (Ed.), *Suicide among youth: Perspectives on risk and prevention.* Washington, DC: American Psychiatric Press. (p. 200)

Pickett, K., & Wilkinson, R. (2011). *The spirit level: Why greater equality makes societies stronger.* New York: Bloomsbury. (pp. 403, 525)

Piliavin, I. M., Rodin, J., & Piliavin, J. A. (1969). Good Samaritanism: An underground phenomenon. *Journal of Personality and Social Psychology, 13,* 289–299. (p. 294)

Piliavin, J. A. (2003). Doing well by doing good: Benefits for the benefactor. In C. L. M. Keyes, & J. Haidt (Eds.), *Flourishing: Positive psychology and the life well-lived.* 227–247. (p. 275)

Piliavin, J. A., Evans, D. E., & Callero, P. (1982). Learning to "Give to unnamed strangers": The process of commitment to regular blood donation. In E. Staub, D. Bar-Tal, J. Karylowski, & J. Reykawski (Eds.), *The development and maintenance of prosocial behavior: International perspectives.* New York: Plenum. (pp. 275, 306)

Piliavin, J. A., & Piliavin, I. M. (1973). *The Good Samaritan: Why does he help?* Unpublished manuscript, University of Wisconsin. (p. 276)

Pincus, J. H. (2001). *Base instincts: What makes killers kill?* New York: W. W. Norton & Co., Inc. (p. 313)

Pinel, E. C. (1999). Stigma consciousness: The psychological legacy of social stereotypes. *Journal of Personality and Social Psychology, 76,* 114–128. (p. 440)

Pinel, E. C. (2002). Stigma consciousness in intergroup contexts: The power of conviction. *Journal of Experimental Social Psychology, 38,* 178–185. (p. 114)

Pinker, S. (2008). *The sexual paradox: Men, women, and the real gender gap.* New York: Scribner. (p. 435)

Pinker, S. (2011, September 27). A history of violence. The Edge (www.edge.org). (p. 348)

Pinkus, R. T., Lockwood, P., Schimmack, U., & Fournier, M. A. (2008). For better and for worse: Everyday social comparisons between romantic partners. *Journal of Personality and Social Psychology, 95,* 1180–1201. (p. 52)

Place, S. S., Todd, P. M., Penke, L., & Asendorpf, J. B. (2009). The ability to judge the romantic interest of others. *Psychological Science, 20,* 22–26. (p. 377)

Plaks, J. E., & Higgins, E. T. (2000). Pragmatic use of stereotyping in teamwork: Social loafing and compensation as a function of inferred partner-situation fit. *Journal of Personality and Social Psychology, 79,* 962–974. (p. 242)

Plant, E. A., Devine, P. G., & Peruche, B. M. (2010). Regulatory concerns for interracial interactions: Approaching egalitarianism versus avoiding prejudice. *Personality and Social Psychology Bulletin, 36,* 1135–1147. (p. 416)

Plant, E. A., Goplen, J., & Kunstman, J. W. (2011). Selective responses to threat: The roles of race and gender in decisions to shoot. *Personality and Social Psychology, 37,* 1274–1281. (p. 431)

Platow, M. J., Haslam, S. A., Both, A., Chew, I., Cuddon, M., Goharpey, N., et al. (2005). "It's not funny if they're laughing": Self-categorization, social influence, and responses to canned laughter. *Journal of Experimental Social Psychology, 41,* 542–550. (p. 199)

Plaut, V. C., Adams, G., & Anderson, S. L. (2009). Does attractiveness buy happiness? "It depends on where you're from." *Personal Relationships, 16,* 619–630. (p. 363)

Pliner, P., Hart, H., Kohl, J., & Saari, D. (1974). Compliance without pressure: Some further data on the foot-in-the-door technique. *Journal of Experimental Social Psychology, 10,* 17–22. (p. 133)

Poincaré, J. H. (1905). *Science and Hypothesis.* (W. J. Greenstreet, Trans.). London: Walter Scott Publishing Co. (Original work published 1901). (p. 17)

Pomazal, R. J., & Clore, G. L. (1973). Helping on the highway: The effects of dependency and sex. *Journal of Applied Social Psychology, 3,* 150–164. (p. 282)

Poniewozik, J. (2003, November 24). All the news that fits your reality. *Time,* p. 90. (p. 80)

Popenoe, D. (2002). *Seven Secrets to a Happy Marriage.* New York: Ladies Home Journal. (p. 392)

Pornpitakpan, C. (2004). The persuasiveness of source credibility: A critical review of

five decades' evidence, *Journal of Applied Social Psychology, 34,* 243–281. (p. 164)

Post, J. M. (2005). The new face of terrorism: Socio-cultural foundations of contemporary terrorism. *Behavioral Sciences and the Law, 23,* 451–465. (p. 251)

Postmes, T., & Spears, R. (1998). Deindividuation and antinormative behavior: A meta-analysis. *Psychological Bulletin, 123,* 238–259. (p. 246)

Postmes, T., Spears, R., & Cihangir, S. (2001). Quality of decision making and group norms. *Journal of Personality and Social Psychology, 80,* 918–930. (p. 259)

Pratkanis, A. R., Greenwald, A. G., Leippe, M. R., & Baumgardner, M. H. (1988). In search of reliable persuasion effects: III. The sleeper effect is dead. Long live the sleeper effect. *Journal of Personality and Social Psychology, 54,* 203–218. (p. 162)

Pratkanis, A. R., & Turner, M. E. (1996). The procative removal of discriminatory barriers: Affirmative action as effective help. *Journal of Social Issues, 52,* 111–132. (p. 281)

Pratto, F., Sidanius, J., Stallworth, L. M., & Malle, B. F. (1994). Social dominance orientation: A personality variable predicting social and political attitudes. *Journal of Personality and Social Psychology, 67,* 741–763. (p. 403)

Prentice-Dunn, S., & Rogers, R. W. (1980). Effects of deindividuating situational cues and aggressive models on subjective deindividuation and aggression. *Journal of Personality and Social Psychology, 39,* 104–113. (p. 247)

Prentice-Dunn, S., & Rogers, R. W. (1989). Deindividuation and the self-regulation of behavior. In P. B. Paulus (Ed.), *Psychology of group influence,* 2nd ed. Hillsdale, NJ: Erlbaum. (p. 247)

Presson, P. K., & Benassi, V. A. (1996). Illusion of control: A meta-analytic review. *Journal of Social Behavior and Personality, 11,* 493–510. (p. 98)

Price, G. H., Dabbs, J. M., Jr., Clower, B. J., & Resin, R. P. (1974). *At first glance-Or, is physical attractiveness more than skin deep?* Paper presented at the Eastern Psychological Association convention. Cited by K. L. Dion & K. K. Dion (1979). Personality and behavioral correlates of romantic love. In M. Cook & G. Wilson (Eds.), *Love and attraction.* Oxford: Pergamon. (p. 368)

Prislin, R., & Pool, G. J. (1996). Behavior, consequences, and the self: Is all well

that ends well? *Personality and Social Psychology Bulletin, 22,* 933–948. (p. 152)

Pritchard, I. L. (1998). *The effects of rap music: On aggressive attitudes toward women.* Master's thesis, Humboldt State University. (p. 335)

Prohaska, V. (1994). "I know I'll get an A": Confident overestimation of final course grades. *Teaching of Psychology, 21,* 141–143. (p. 64)

Pronin, E., Berger, J., & Molouki, S. (2007). Alone in a crowd of sheep: Asymmetric perceptions of conformity and their roots in an introspection illusion. *Journal of Personality and Social Psychology, 92,* 585–595. (p. 223)

Pronin, E., Gilovich, T., & Ross, L. (2004). Objectivity in the eye of the beholder: Divergent perceptions of bias in self versus others. *Psychological Review, 111*(3), 781. (p. 110)

Pronin, E., Kruger, J., Savitsky, K., & Ross, L. (2001). You don't know me, but I know you: The illusion of asymmetric insight. *Journal of Personality and Social Psychology, 81,* 639–656. (p. 63)

Pronin, E., Lin, D. Y., & Ross, L. (2002). The bias blind spot: Perceptions of bias in self versus others. *Personality and Social Psychology Bulletin, 28,* 369–381. (p. 61)

Pronin, E., & Ross, L. (2006). Temporal differences in trait self-ascription: When the self is seen as an other. *Journal of Personality and Social Psychology, 90*(2), 197. (pp. 61, 108)

Prothrow-Stith, D. (with M. Wiessman) (1991). *Deadly consequences.* New York: HarperCollins. (p. 464)

Pruitt, D. G. (1986, July). Trends in the scientific study of negotiation. *Negotiation Journal,* 237–244. (pp. 463, 467)

Pruitt, D. G. (1998). Social conflict. In D. Gilbert, S. T. Fiske, & G. Lindzey (Eds.), *Handbook of social psychology,* 4th ed. New York: McGraw-Hill. (p. 463)

Pruitt, D. G., & Lewis, S. A. (1975). Development of integrative solutions in bilateral negotiation. *Journal of Personality and Social Psychology, 31,* 621–633. (p. 463)

Pruitt, D. G., & Lewis, S. A. (1977). The psychology of integrative bargaining. In D. Druckman (Ed.), *Negotiations: A social-psychological analysis.* New York: Halsted. (p. 463)

Pryke, S., Lindsay, R. C. L., Dysart, J. E., & Dupuis, P. (2004). Multiple independent identification decisions: A method of calibrating eyewitness identifications. *Journal of Applied Psychology, 89*(1), 73. doi:10.1037/0021-9010.89.1.73. (p. 504)

Pryor, J. B., DeSouza, E. R., Fitness, J., Hutz, C., Kumpf, M., Lubbert, K., et al. (1997). Gender differences in the interpretation of social-sexual behavior: A cross-cultural perspective on sexual harassment. *Journal of Cross-Cultural Psychology, 28*(5), 509. (p. 102)

Pryor, J. H., Hurtado, S., DeAngelo, L., Blake, L. P., & Tran, S. (2010). *The American freshman: National norms fall 2010.* Los Angeles: Higher Education Research Institute, UCLA. (p. 62)

Pryor, J. H., Hurtado, S., Sharkness, J., & Korn, W. S. (2007). *The American freshman: National norms for Fall 2007.* Los Angeles: Higher Education Research Institute, UCLA. (p. 300)

Przybylski, A. K., Rigby, C. S., & Ryan, R. M. (2010). A motivational model of video game engagement. *Review of General Psychology, 14,* 154-166. (p. 341)

Public Opinion (1984, August/September). *Vanity Fair, 22.* (p. 63)

Purvis, J. A., Dabbs, J. M., Jr., & Hopper, C. H. (1984). The "opener": Skilled user of facial expression and speech pattern. *Personality and Social Psychology Bulletin, 10,* 61-66. (p. 388)

Putnam, R. (2000). *Bowling alone.* New York: Simon & Schuster. (pp. 305, 336, 337, 389, 390)

Pyszczynski, T., & Greenberg, J. (1987). Self-regulatory perseveration and the depressive self-focusing style: A self-awareness theory of reactive depression. *Psychological Bulletin, 102,* 122-138. (p. 71)

Pyszczynski, T., Hamilton, J. C., Greenberg, J., & Becker, S. E. (1991). Self-awareness and psychological dysfunction. In C. R. Snyder & D. O. Forsyth (Eds.), *Handbook of social and clinical psychology: The health perspective.* New York: Pergamon. (p. 478)

Quoidbach, J., & Dunn, E. W. (2010). Personality neglect: The unforeseen impact of personal dispositions on emotional life. *Psychological Science, 21,* 1783-1786. (p. 108)

Quoidbach, J., Dunn, E. W., Petrides, K. V., & Mikolajczak, M. (2010). Money giveth, money taketh away: The dual effect of wealth on happiness. *Psychological Science, 21*(6), 759-763. (p. 523)

Raine, A. (1993). *The psychopathology of crime: Criminal behavior as a clinical disorder.* San Diego, CA: Academic Press. (p. 313)

Raine, A. (2005). The interaction of biological and social measures in the explanation of antisocial and violent behavior. In D. M. Stoff & E. J. Susman (Eds.), *Developmental psychobiology of aggression.* New York: Cambridge University Press. (p. 313)

Raine, A. (2008). From genes to brain to antisocial behavior. *Current Directions in Psychological Science, 17,* 323-328. (p. 313)

Raine, A., Lencz, T., Bihrle, S., LaCasse, L., & Colletti, P. (2000). Reduced prefrontal gray matter volume and reduced autonomic activity in antisocial personality disorder. *Archives of General Psychiatry, 57,* 119-127. (p. 313)

Raine, A., Stoddard, J., Bihrle, S., & Buchsbaum, M. (1998). Prefrontal glucose deficits in murderers lacking psychosocial deprivation. *Neuropsychiatry, NeuroPsychology, & Behavioral Neurology, 11,* 1-7. (p. 313)

Rajecki, D. W., Bledsoe, S. B., & Rasmussen, J. L. (1991). Successful personal ads: Gender differences and similarities in offers, stipulations, and outcomes. *Basic and Applied Social Psychology, 12,* 457-469. (p. 361)

Ramirez, J. M., Bonniot-Cabanac, M-C., & Cabanac, M. (2005). Can aggression provide pleasure? *European Psychologist, 10,* 136-145. (p. 345)

Randler, C., & Kretz, S. (2011). Assortative mating in morningness-eveningness. *International Journal of Psychology, 46,* 91-96. (p. 369)

Rank, S. G., & Jacobson, C. K. (1977). Hospital nurses' compliance with medication overdose orders: A failure to replicate. *Journal of Health and Social Behavior, 18,* 188-193. (p. 208)

Rapoport, A. (1960). *Fights, games, and debates.* Ann Arbor: University of Michigan Press. (p. 454)

Rawls, J. (1971). *A theory of justice.* Cambridge, MA: Belknap Press of Harvard University Press. (p. 460)

Rawn, C. D., & Vohs, K. D. (2011). People use self-control to risk personal harm: An intra-interpersonal dilemma. *Personality and Social Psychology Review, 15,* 267-289. (p. 72)

Read, J. D., & Desmarais, S. L. (2009). Lay knowledge of eyewitness issues: A Canadian evaluation. *Applied Cognitive Psychology, 23,* 301-326. (p. 505)

Reed, D. (1989, November 25). Video collection documents Christian resistance to Hitler. Associated Press release in *Grand Rapids Press,* B4, B5. (p. 405)

Regan, D. T., & Cheng, J. B. (1973). Distraction and attitude change: A resolution. *Journal of Experimental Social Psychology, 9,* 138-147. (p. 180)

Regan, D. T., & Fazio, R. (1977). On the consistency between attitudes and behavior: Look to the method of attitude formation. *Journal of Experimental Social Psychology, 13,* 28-45. (p. 128)

Regan, P. C. (1998). What if you can't get what you want? Willingness to compromise ideal mate selection standards as a function of sex, mate value, and relationship context. *Personality and Social Psychology Bulletin, 24,* 1294-1303. (p. 376)

Reicher, S., Spears, R., & Postmes, T. (1995). A social identity model of deindividuation phenomena. In W. Storebe & M. Hewstone (Eds.), *European review of social psychology* (Vol. 6). Chichester, England: Wiley. (p. 246)

Reid, P., & Finchilescu, G. (1995). The disempowering effects of media violence against women on college women. *Psychology of Women Quarterly, 19,* 397-411. (p. 336)

Reis, H. T., Maniaci, M. R., Caprariello, P. A., Eastwick, P. W., & Finkel, E. J. (2011). Familiarity does indeed promote attraction in live interaction. *Journal of Personality and Social Psychology, 101,* 557-570. (p. 357)

Reis, H. T., Nezlek, J., & Wheeler, L. (1980). Physical attractiveness in social interaction. *Journal of Personality and Social Psychology, 38,* 604-617. (p. 358)

Reis, H. T., & Shaver, P. (1988). Intimacy as an interpersonal process. In S. Duck (Ed.), *Handbook of personal relationships: Theory, relationships and interventions.* Chichester, UK: Wiley. (p. 387)

Reis, H. T., Smith, S. M., Carmichael, C. L., Caprariello, P. A., Tsa, F.-F., Rodrigues, A., & Maniaci, M. R. (2010). Are you happy for me? How sharing positive events with others provides personal and interpersonal benefits. *Journal of Personality and Social Psychology, 99,* 311-329. (p. 387)

Reis, H. T., Wheeler, L., Spiegel, N., Kernis, M. H., Nezlek, J., & Perri, M. (1982). Physical attractiveness in social interaction: II. Why does appearance affect social experience? *Journal of Personality and Social Psychology, 43,* 979-996. (p. 358)

Reisenzein, R. (1983). The Schachter theory of emotion: Two decades later. *Psychological Bulletin, 94*, 239–264. (p. 325)

Renaud, H., & Estess, F. (1961). Life history interviews with one hundred normal American males: "Pathogenecity" of childhood. *American Journal of Orthopsychiatry, 31*, 786–802. (p. 474)

Ressler, R. K., Burgess, A. W., & Douglas, J. E. (1988). *Sexual homicide patterns*. Boston: Lexington Books. (p. 329)

Reynolds, J., Stewart, M., MacDonald, R., & Sischo, L. (2006). Have adolescents become too ambitious? High school seniors' educational and occupational plans, 1976 to 2000. *Social Problems, 53*, 186–206. (p. 64)

Rhine, R. J., & Severance, L. J. (1970). Ego-involvement, discrepancy, source credibility, and attitude change. *Journal of Personality and Social Psychology, 16*, 175–190. (p. 171)

Rhodes, G. (2006). The evolutionary psychology of facial beauty. *Annual Review of Psychology, 57*, 199. (pp. 364, 365)

Rhodes, G., Sumich, A., & Byatt, G. (1999). Are average facial configurations attractive only because of their symmetry? *Psychological Science, 10*, 52–58. (p. 365)

Rhodewalt, F. (1987). *Is self-handicapping an effective self-protective attributional strategy?* Paper presented at the American Psychological Association convention. (p. 71)

Rhodewalt, F., Saltzman, A. T., & Wittmer J. (1984). Self-handicapping among competitive athletes: The role of practice in self-esteem protection. *Basic and Applied Social Psychology, 5*, 197–209. (p. 71)

Rholes, W. S., Newman, L. S., & Ruble, D. N. (1990). Understanding self and other. Developmental and motivational aspects of perceiving persons in terms of invariant dispositions. In E. T. Higgins & R. M. Sorrentino (Eds.), *Handbook of motivation and cognition: Foundations of social behavior,* Vol. 2. New York: Guilford. (p. 109)

Rice, B. (1985, September). Performance review: The job nobody likes. *Psychology Today*, 30–36. (p. 61)

Rice, M. E., & Grusec, J. E. (1975). Saying and doing: Effects on observer performance. *Journal of Personality and Social Psychology, 32*, 584–593. (p. 297)

Richards, Z., & Hewstone, M. (2001). Subtyping and subgrouping: Processes for the prevention and promotion of stereotype change. *Personality and Social Psychology Review, 5*, 52–73. (p. 438)

Richardson, L. F. (1960). Generalized foreign policy. *British Journal of Psychology Monographs Supplements, 23*. Cited by A. Rapoport in *Fights, games, and debates.* Ann Arbor: University of Michigan Press, 1960, p. 15. (p. 452)

Richeson, J. A., & Trawalter, S. (2008). The threat of appearing prejudiced, and race-based attentional biases. *Psychological Science, 19*, 98–102. (p. 416)

Richtel, M. (2007, June 2). For pornographers, Internet's virtues turn to vices. *New York Times* (www.nytimes.com). (p. 327)

Ridge, R. D., & Reber, J. S. (2002). "I think she's attracted to me": The effect of men's beliefs on women's behavior in a job interview scenario. *Basic and Applied Social Psychology, 24*, 1–14. (p. 114)

Riess, M., Rosenfeld, P., Melburg, V., & Tedeschi, J. T. (1981). Self-serving attributions: Biased private perceptions and distorted public descriptions. *Journal of Personality and Social Psychology, 41*, 224–231. (p. 72)

Rietzschel, E. F., Nijstad, B. A., & Stroebe, W. (2006). Productivity is not enough: A comparison of interactive and nominal brainstorming groups on idea generation and selection. *Journal of Experimental Social Psychology, 42*, 244–251. (p. 262)

Riggs, J. M. (1992). Self-handicapping and achievement. In A. K. Boggiano & T. S. Pittman (Eds.), *Achievement and motivation: A social-developmental perspective.* New York: Cambridge University Press. (p. 71)

Riordan, C. A. (1980). *Effects of admission of influence on attributions and attraction.* Paper presented at the American Psychological Association convention. (p. 376)

Risen, J. L., & Critcher, C. R. (2011). Visceral fit: While in a visceral state, associated states of the world seem more likely. *Journal of Personality and Social Psychology, 100*, 777–793. (p. 96)

Risen, J. L., Gilovich, T., & Dunning, D. (2007). One-shot illusory correlations and stereotype formation. *Personality and Social Psychology Bulletin, 33*, 1492–1502. (p. 422)

Riva, P., Wirth, J. H., & Williams, K. D. (2011). The consequences of pain: The social and physical overlap on psychological responses. *European Journal of Social Psychology, 41*, 681–687. (p. 354)

Robberson, M. R., & Rogers, R. W. (1988). Beyond fear appeals: Negative and positive persuasive appeals to health and self-esteem. *Journal of Applied Social Psychology, 18*, 277–287. (p. 168)

Robins, R. W., & Beer, J. S. (2001). Positive illusions about the self: Short-term benefits and long-term costs. *Journal of Personality and Social Psychology, 80*, 340–352. (pp. 55, 64)

Robins, R. W., Mendelsohn, G. A., Connell, J. B., & Kwan, V. S. Y. (2004). Do people agree about the causes of behavior? A social relations analysis of behavior ratings and causal attributions. *Journal of Personality and Social Psychology, 86*, 334–344. (p. 103)

Robinson, J. (2002, October 8). What percentage of the population is gay? *Gallup Tuesday Briefing* (www.gallup.com). (p. 421)

Robinson, M. S., & Alloy, L. B. (2003). Negative cognitive styles and stress-reactive rumination interact to predict depression: A prospective study. *Cognitive Therapy and Research, 27*, 275. (p. 478)

Robinson, T. N., Wilde, M. L., Navracruz, L. C., Haydel, F., & Varady, A. (2001). Effects of reducing children's television and video game use on aggressive behavior. *Archives of Pediatric and Adolescent Medicine, 155*, 17–23. (p. 347)

Rochat, F. (1993). *How did they resist authority? Protecting refugees in Le Chambon during World War II.* Paper presented at the American Psychological Association convention. (p. 211)

Rochat, F., & Modigliani, A. (1995). The ordinary quality of resistance: From Milgram's laboratory to the village of Le Chambon. *Journal of Social Issues, 51*, 195–210. (p. 211)

Roese, N. J., & Jamieson, D. W. (1993). Twenty years of bogus pipeline research: A critical review and meta-analysis. *Psychological Bulletin, 114*, 363–375. (p. 400)

Roese, N. L., & Olson, J. M. (1994). Attitude importance as a function of repeated attitude expression. *Journal of Experimental Social Psychology, 66*, 805–818. (p. 152)

Rogers, C. R. (1980). *A way of being.* Boston: Houghton Mifflin. (p. 388)

Rogers, R. W., & Prentice-Dunn, S. (1981). Deindividuation and anger-mediated interracial aggression: Unmasking regressive racism. *Journal of Personality and Social Psychology, 41*, 63–73. (p. 429)

Rohrer, J. H., Baron, S. H., Hoffman, E. L., & Swander, D. V. (1954). The stability of autokinetic judgments. *Journal of Abnormal and Social Psychology, 49*, 595–597. (p. 198)

Rokeach, M. (1968). *Beliefs, attitudes, and values.* San Francisco: Jossey-Bass. (p. 370)

Rokeach, M., & Mezei, L. (1966). Race and shared beliefs as factors in social choice. *Science, 151*, 167–172. (p. 418)

Romer, D., Gruder, D. L., & Lizzadro, T. (1986). A person-situation approach to altruistic behavior. *Journal of Personality and Social Psychology, 51*, 1001–1012. (p. 299)

Rook, K. S. (1987). Social support versus companionship: Effects on life stress, loneliness, and evaluations by others. *Journal of Personality and Social Psychology, 52*, 1132–1147. (p. 488)

Rooth, D-O. (2007). Implicit discrimination in hiring: Real-world evidence. IZA Discussion Paper No. 2764, University of Kalmar, Institute for the Study of Labor (IZA). (p. 430)

Rosenbaum, M. E. (1986). The repulsion hypothesis: On the nondevelopment of relationships. *Journal of Personality and Social Psychology, 51*, 1156–1166. (p. 370)

Rosenbaum, M. E., & Holtz, R. (1985). *The minimal intergroup discrimination effect: Out-group derogation, not in-group favorability.* Paper presented at the American Psychological Association convention. (p. 411)

Rosenberg, L. A. (1961). Group size, prior experience and conformity. *Journal of Abnormal and Social Psychology, 63*, 436–437. (p. 215)

Rosenblatt, A., & Greenberg, J. (1988). Depression and interpersonal attraction: The role of perceived similarity. *Journal of Personality and Social Psychology, 55*, 112–119. (p. 371)

Rosenblatt, A., & Greenberg, J. (1991). Examining the world of the depressed: Do depressed people prefer others who are depressed? *Journal of Personality and Social Psychology, 60*, 620–629. (p. 371)

Rosenbloom, S. (2008, January 3). Putting your best cyberface forward. *New York Times,* Style section. (p. 72)

Rosenbloom, T., Shahar, A., Perlman, A., Estreich, D., & Kirzner, E. (2007). Success on a practical driver's license test with and without the presence of another testee. *Accident Analysis and Prevention, 39*, 1296–1301. (p. 235)

Rosenfeld, D., Folger, R., & Adelman, H. F. (1980). When rewards reflect competence: A qualification of the overjustification effect. *Journal of Personality and Social Psychology, 39*, 368–376. (p. 149)

Rosenhan, D. L. (1970). The natural socialization of altruistic autonomy. In J. Macaulay & L. Berkowitz (Eds.) *Altruism and helping behavior.* New York: Academic Press. (p. 304)

Rosenhan, D. L. (1973). On being sane in insane places. *Science, 179*, 250–258. (p. 473)

Rosenthal, E. (2008, July 15). Britons shine a light on energy use at home. *New York Times* (www.nytimes.com). (p. 520)

Rosenthal, E. (2010, May 24). Climate fears turn to doubts among Britons. *New York Times* (www.nytimes.com). (p. 158)

Rosenthal, E. (2011, October 15). Where did global warming go? *New York Times* (www.nytimes.com). (pp. 517, 520)

Rosenthal, R. (1985). From unconscious experimenter bias to teacher expectancy effects. In J. B. Dusek, V. C. Hall, & W. J. Meyer (Eds.), *Teacher expectancies.* Hillsdale, NJ: Erlbaum. (p. 111)

Rosenthal, R. (1991). Teacher expectancy effects: A brief update 25 years after the Pygmalion experiment. *Journal of Research in Education, 1*, 3–12. (p. 112)

Rosenthal, R. (2002). Covert communication in classrooms, clinics, courtrooms, and cubicles. *American Psychologist, 57*(11), 839. (p. 112)

Rosenthal, R. (2003). Covert communication in laboratories, classrooms, and the truly real world. *Current Directions in Psychological Science, 12*(5), 151. (p. 113)

Rosenthal, R. (2006). Applying psychological research on interpersonal expectations and covert communication in classrooms, clinics, corporations, and courtrooms. In S. I. Donaldson, D. E. Berger, & K. Pezdek (Eds.), *Applied psychology: New frontiers and rewarding careers.* Mahwah, NJ: Erlbaum. (p. 111)

Rosenthal, R., & Jacobson, L. (1968). *Pygmalion in the classroom: Teacher expectation and pupils' intellectual development.* New York: Holt, Rinehart & Winston. (p. 111)

Ross, L. (1977). The intuitive psychologist and his shortcomings: Distortions in the attribution process. In L. Berkowitz (Ed.), *Advances in experimental social psychology* (Vol. 10). New York: Academic Press. (p. 105)

Ross, L. (1981). The "intuitive scientist" formulation and its developmental implications. In J. H. Havell & L. Ross (Eds.), *Social cognitive development: Frontiers and possible futures.* Cambridge, UK: Cambridge University Press. (p. 36)

Ross, L. (1988). Situationist perspectives on the obedience experiments. Review of A. G. Miller's *The obedience experiments. Contemporary Psychology, 33*, 101–104. (p. 203)

Ross, L., Amabile, T. M., & Steinmetz, J. L. (1977). Social roles, social control, and biases in social-perception processes. *Journal of Personality and Social Psychology, 35*, 485–494. (pp. 106, 107)

Ross, L., & Anderson, C. A. (1982). Shortcomings in the attribution process: On the origins and maintenance of erroneous social assessments. In D. Kahneman, P. Slovic, & A. Tversky (Eds.), *Judgment under uncertainty: Heuristics and biases.* New York: Cambridge University Press. (p. 83)

Ross, L., & Lepper, M. R. (1980). The perseverance of beliefs: Empirical and normative considerations. In R. A. Shweder (Ed.), *New directions for methodology of behavioral science: Fallible judgment in behavioral research.* San Francisco: Jossey-Bass. (p. 84)

Ross, L., & Ward, A. (1995). Psychological barriers to dispute resolution. In M. P. Zanna (Ed.), *Advances in experimental social psychology,* vol. 27. San Diego: Academic Press. (p. 465)

Ross, L., & Ward, A. (1996). Naive realism in everyday life: Implications for social conflict and misunderstanding. In T. Brown, E. Reed, & E. Turiel (Eds.), *Values and knowledge.* Hillsdale, NJ: Erlbaum. (p. 459)

Ross, M., & Buehler, R. (1994). Creative remembering. In U. Neisser & R. Fivush (Eds.), *The remembering self.* New York: Cambridge University Press. (p. 84)

Ross, M., & Fletcher, G. J. O. (1985). Attribution and social perception. In G. Lindzey & E. Aronson (Eds.), *The handbook of social psychology,* 3rd ed. New York: Random House. (p. 100)

Ross, M., McFarland, C., & Fletcher, G. J. O. (1981). The effect of attitude on the recall of personal histories. *Journal of Personality and Social Psychology, 40*, 627–634. (p. 86)

Ross, M., & Newby-Clark, I. R. (1998). Construing the past and future. *Social Cognition, 16*, 133–150. (p. 90)

Ross, M., & Sicoly, F. (1979). Egocentric biases in availability and attribution. *Journal of Personality and Social Psychology, 37,* 322 336. (pp. 61, 68)

Ross, M. & Wilson, A. E. (2002). It feels like yesterday: Self-esteem, valence of personal past experiences, and judgments of subjective distance. *Journal of Personality and Social Psychology, 82,* 792–803. (p. 66)

Roszell, P., Kennedy, D., & Grabb, E. (1990). Physical attractiveness and income attainment among Canadians. *Journal of Psychology, 123,* 547–559. (p. 363)

Rotenberg, K. J., Gruman, J. A., & Ariganello, M. (2002). Behavioral confirmation of the loneliness stereotype. *Basic and Applied Social Psychology, 24,* 81–89. (p. 114)

Rothbart, M., & Birrell, P. (1977). Attitude and perception of faces. *Journal of Research Personality, 11,* 209 215. (p. 82)

Rothbart, M., Fulero, S., Jensen, C., Howard, J., & Birrell, P. (1978). From individual to group impressions: Availability heuristics in stereotype formation. *Journal of Experimental Social Psychology, 14,* 237 255. (p. 421)

Rothbart, M., & Taylor, M. (1992). Social categories and social reality. In G. R. Semin & K. Fielder (Eds.), *Language, interaction and social cognition.* London: Sage. (p. 227)

Rothman, A. J., & Salovey, P. (1997). Shaping perceptions to motivate healthy behavior: The role of message framing. *Psychological Bulletin, 121,* 3–19. (p. 483)

Rotton, J., & Frey, J. (1985). Air pollution, weather, and violent crimes: Concomitant time-series analysis of archival data. *Journal of Personality and Social psychology, 49,* 1207–1220. (p. 323)

Rotundo, M., Nguyen, D-H., & Sackett, P. R. (2001). A meta-analytic review of gender differences in perceptions of sexual harrassment. *Journal of Applied Psychology, 86,* 914–922. (p. 102)

Rowe, D. C., Almeida, D. M., & Jacobson, K. C. (1999). School context and genetic influences on aggression in adolescence. *Psychological Science, 10,* 277–280. (p. 313)

Royal Society (2010, September). *Climate change: A summary of the science.* London: The Royal Society. (pp. 515, 516)

Ruback, R. B., Carr, T. S., & Hoper, C. H. (1986). Perceived control in prison: Its relation to reported crowding, stress, and symptoms. *Journal of Applied Social Psychology, 16,* 375–386. (p. 58)

Rubin, J. Z. (1986). *Can we negotiate with terrorists: Some answers from psychology.*

Paper presented at the American Psychological Association convention. (p. 320)

Rubin, Z. (1973). *Liking and loving: An invitation to social psychology.* New York: Holt, Rinehart and Winston. (pp. 377, 394)

Rudolph, U., Roesch, S. C., Greitemeyer, T., & Weiner, B. (2004). A meta-analytic review of help giving and aggression from an attributional perspective: Contributions to a general theory of motivation. *Cognition & Emotion, 18,* 815. (p. 282)

Rule, B. G., Taylor, B. R., & Dobbs, A. R. (1987). Priming effects of heat on aggressive thoughts. *Social Cognition, 5,* 131–143. (p. 323)

Rule, N. O., Rosen, K. S., Slepian, M. L., & Ambady, N. (2011). Mating interest improves women's accuracy in judging male sexual orientation. *Psychological Science, 22,* 881–886. (p. 366)

Rusbult, C. E. (1980). Commitment and satisfaction in romantic associations: A test of the investment model. *Journal of Experimental Social Psychology, 16,* 172 186. (p. 375)

Rusbult, C. E., Johnson, D. J., & Morrow, G. D. (1986). Impact of couple patterns of problem solving on distress and non-distress in dating relationships. *Journal of Personality and Social Psychology, 50,* 744–753. (p. 393)

Rusbult, C. E., Morrow, G. D., & Johnson, D. J. (1987). Self-esteem and problem-solving behaviour in close relationships. *British Journal of Social Psychology, 26,* 293–303. (p. 393)

Rushton, J. P. (1975). Generosity in children: Immediate and long-term effects of modeling, preaching, and moral judgment. *Journal of Personality and Social Psychology, 31,* 459–466. (p. 297)

Rushton, J. P. (1991). Is altruism innate? *Psychological Inquiry, 2,* 141–143. (p. 284)

Rushton, J. P., Brainerd, C. J., & Pressley, M. (1983). Behavioral development and construct validity: The principle of aggregation. *Psychological Bulletin, 94,* 18–38. (p. 222)

Rushton, J. P., & Campbell, A. C. (1977). Modeling, vicarious reinforcement and extraversion on blood donating in adults: Immediate and long-term effects. *European Journal of Social Psychology, 7,* 297–306. (p. 297)

Rushton, J. P., Chrisjohn, R. D., & Fekken, G. C. (1981). The altruistic personality and the self-report altruism scale. *Personality*

and Individual Differences, 2, 293–302. (p. 299)

Rushton, J. P., Fulker, D. W., Neale, M. C., Nias, D. K. B., & Eysenck, H. J. (1986). Altruism and aggression: The heritability of individual differences. *Journal of Personality and Social Psychology, 50,* 1192–1198. (p. 313)

Russell, G. W. (1983). Psychological issues in sports aggression. In J. H. Goldstein (Ed.), *Sports violence.* New York: Springer-Verlag. (p. 345)

Russell, N. J. C., & Gregory, R. J. (2005). Making the undoable doable: Milgram, the Holocaust, and modern government. *American Review of Public Administration, 35,* 327–349. (p. 207)

Ruvolo, A., & Markus, H. (1992). Possible selves and performance: The power of self-relevant imagery. *Social Cognition, 9,* 95–124. (p. 57)

Ryan, C. S. (1996). Accuracy of Black and White college students' in-group and out-group stereotypes. *Personality and Social psychology Bulletin, 22,* 1114–1127. (p. 419)

Ryan, R. (1999, February 2). Quoted by A. Kohn, In pursuit of affluence, at a high price. *New York Times* (via www.nytimes.com). (p. 522)

Ryckman, R. M., Robbins, M. A., Kaczor, L. M., & Gold, J. A. (1989). Male and female raters' stereotyping of male and female physiques. *Personality and Social Psychology Bulletin, 15,* 244–251. (p. 24)

Rydell, R. J., McConnell, A. R., & Beilock, S. L. (2009). Multiple social identities and stereotype threat: Imbalance, accessibility, and working memory. *Journal of Personality and Social Psychology, 96,* 949–966. (p. 442)

Rydell, R. J., Rydell, M. T., & Boucher, K. L. (2010). The effect of negative performance stereotypes on learning. *Journal of Personality and Social Psychology, 99,* 883–896. (p. 441)

Ryff, C. D., & Singer, B. (2000). Interpersonal flourishing: A positive health agenda for the new millennium. *Personality and Social Psychology Review, 4,* 30–44. (p. 487)

Saad, L. (2002, November 21). Most smokers wish they could quit. Gallup News Service (www.gallup.com/poll/releases/pr021121.asp). (p. 140)

Sabini, J., & Silver, M. (1982). *Moralities of everyday life.* New York: Oxford University Press. (p. 213)

Sachs, J. D. (2006, July). Ecology and political upheaval. *Scientific American, 291,* 37. (p. 517)

Sack, K., & Elder, J. (2000, July 11). Poll finds optimistic outlook but enduring racial division. *New York Times* (www.nytimes.com). (p. 409)

Sacks, C. H., & Bugental, D. P. (1987). Attributions as moderators of affective and behavioral responses to social failure. *Journal of Personality and Social Psychology, 53,* 939–947. (p. 478)

Sagarin, B. J., Cialdini, R. B., Rice, W. E., & Serna, S. B. (2002). Dispelling the illusion of invulnerability: The motivations and mechanisms of resistance to persuasion. *Journal of Personality and Social Psychology, 83,* 526–541. (p. 187)

Sagarin, B. J., Rhoads, K. v L., & Cialdini, R. B. (1998). Deceiver's distrust: Denigration as a consequence of undiscovered deception. *Personality and Social Psychology Bulletin, 24,* 1167–1176. (p. 65)

Sageman, M. (2004). *Understanding terror networks.* Philadelphia: University of Pennsylvania Press. (p. 251)

Saks, M. J., & Hastie, R. (1978). *Social psychology in court.* New York: Van Nostrand Reinhold. (p. 497)

Sakurai, M. M. (1975). Small group cohesiveness and detrimental conformity. *Sociometry, 38,* 340–357. (p. 216)

Sales, S. M. (1972). Economic threat as a determinant of conversion rates in authoritarian and nonauthoritarian churches. *Journal of Personality and Social Psychology, 23,* 420–428. (p. 185)

Sales, S. M. (1973). Threat as a factor in authoritarianism: An analysis of archival data. *Journal of Personality & Social Psychology, 28,* 44–57. (p. 404)

Salganik, M. J., Dodds, P. S., & Watts, D. J. (2006). Experimental study of inequality and unpredictability in an artificial cultural market. *Science, 311,* 854–856. (p. 254)

Salmela-Aro, K., & Nurmi, J-E. (2007). Self-esteem during university studies predicts career characteristics 10 years later. *Journal of Vocational Behavior, 70,* 463–477. (p. 53)

Salmivalli, C. (2009). Bullying and the peer group: A review. *Aggression and Violent Behavior, 15,* 112–120. (p. 311)

Salmivalli, C., Kaukiainen, A., Kaistaniemi, L., & Lagerspetz, K. M. J. (1999). Self-evaluated self-esteem, peer-evaluated self-esteem, and defensive egotism as predictors of adolescents' participation in bullying situations. *Personality and Social Psychology Bulletin, 25,* 1268–1278. (p. 343)

Salovey, P., Mayer, J. D., & Rosenhan, D. L. (1991). Mood and healing: Mood as a motivator of helping and helping as a regulator of mood. In M. S. Clark (Ed.), *Prosocial behavior.* Newbury Park, CA: Sage. (p. 278)

Salovey, P., Schneider, T. R., & Apanovitch, A. M. (2002). Message framing in the prevention and early detection of illness. In J. P. Dillard & M. Pfau (Eds.), *The persuasion handbook: Theory and practice.* Thousand Oaks, CA: Sage. (p. 483)

Saltzstein, H. D., & Sandberg, L. (1979). Indirect social influence: Change in judgmental processor anticipatory conformity. *Journal of Experimental Social Psychology, 15,* 209–216. (p. 218)

Sampson, E. E. (1975). On justice as equality. *Journal of Social Issues, 31*(3), 45–64. (p. 460)

Sanbonmatsu, D. M., Akimoto, S. A., & Gibson, B. D. (1994). Stereotype-based blocking in social explanation. *Personality and Social Psychology Bulletin, 20,* 71–81. (p. 437)

Sanbonmatsu, D. M., & Fazio, R. H. (1990). The role of attitudes in memory-based decision making. *Journal of Personality and Social Psychology, 59,* 614–622. (p. 122)

Sande, G. N., Goethals, G. R., & Radloff, C. E. (1988). Perceiving one's own traits and others': The multifaceted self. *Journal of Personality and Social Psychology, 54,* 13–20. (p. 108)

Sanders, G. S. (1981a). Driven by distraction: An integrative review of social facilitation and theory and research. *Journal of Experimental Social Psychology, 17,* 227–251. (p. 237)

Sanders, G. S. (1981b). Toward a comprehensive account of social facilitation: Distraction/conflict does not mean theoretical conflict. *Journal of Experimental Social Psychology, 17,* 262–265. (p. 237)

Sanders, G. S., & Baron, R. S. (1977). Is social comparison irrelevant for producing choice shifts? *Journal of Experimental Social Psychology, 13,* 303–314. (p. 254)

Sanders, G. S., Baron, R. S., & Moore, D. L. (1978). Distraction and social comparison as mediators of social facilitation effects. *Journal of Experimental Social Psychology, 14,* 291–303. (p. 237)

Sanderson, C. A., & Cantor, N. (2001). The association of intimacy goals and marital satisfaction: A test of four mediational hypotheses. *Personality and Social Psychology Bulletin, 27,* 1567. (p. 388)

Sani, F., Herrera, M., & Bowe, M. (2009). Perceived collective continuity and ingroup identification as defence against death awareness. *Journal of Experimental Social Psychology, 45,* 242–245. (p. 413)

Sanislow, C. A., III, Perkins, D. V., & Balogh, D. W. (1989). Mood induction, interpersonal perceptions, and rejection in the roommates of depressed, nondepressed-disturbed, and normal college students. *Journal of Social and Clinical Psychology, 8,* 345–358. (p. 477)

Sanitioso, R., Kunda, Z., & Fong, G. T. (1990). Motivated recruitment of autobiographical memories. *Journal of Personality and Social Psychology, 59,* 229–241. (p. 68)

Sansone, C. (1986). A question of competence: The effects of competence and task feedback on intrinsic interest. *Journal of Personality and Social Psychology, 51,* 918–931. (p. 149)

Sapolsky, R. M. (2005). The influence of social hierarchy on primate health. *Science, 308,* 648. (pp. 489, 491)

Sartre, J-P. (1946/1948). *Anti-Semite and Jew.* New York: Shocken Books. (p. 4)

Sasaki, J. Y., & Kim, H. S. (2011). At the intersection of culture and religion: A cultural analysis of religion's implications for secondary control and social affiliation. *Journal of Personality and Social Psychology, 101,* 401–414. (p. 42)

Saslow, L. R., Muise, A., Impett, E. A., & Dubin, M. (2013). Can you see how happy we are? Facebook images and relationship satisfaction. *Social Psychological and Personality Science, 4,* 411-418. (p. 388)

Sassenberg, K., Moskowitz, G. B., Jacoby, J., & Hansen, N. (2007). The carry-over effect of competition: The impact of competition on prejudice towards uninvolved outgroups. *Journal of Experimental Social Psychology, 43,* 529–538. (p. 407)

Sato, K. (1987). Distribution of the cost of maintaining common resources. *Journal of Experimental Social Psychology, 23,* 19–31. (p. 456)

Saucier, D. A., & Miller, C. T. (2003). The persuasiveness of racial arguments as a subtle measure of racism. *Personality and Social Psychology Bulletin, 29,* 1303–1315. (p. 81)

Saucier, G., Akers, L. G., Shen-Miller, S., Kneževič, G., & Stankov, L. (2009). Patterns of thinking in militant extremism. *Perspectives on Psychological Science, 4,* 256–271. (p. 404)

Sauer, J., Brewer, N., Zweck, T., & Weber, N. (2010). The effect of retention interval on the confidence–accuracy relationship for eyewitness identification. *Law and Human Behavior, 34,* 337–347. (pp. 499, 503)

Sauerland, M., & Sporer, S. L. (2009). Fast and confident: Postdicting eyewitness identification accuracy in a field study. *Journal of Experimental Psychology: Applied, 15,* 46–62. (p. 499)

Savani, K., Stephens, N. M., & Markus, H. R. (2011). The unanticipated interpersonal and societal consequences of choice: Victim blaming and reduced support for the public good. *Psychological Science, 22,* 795–802. (p. 415)

Savitsky, K., Medvec, V. H., & Gilovich, T. (1997). Remembering and regretting: The Zeigarnik effect and the cognitive availability of regrettable actions and inactions. *Personality and Social Psychology Bulletin, 23,* 248–257. (p. 97)

Savitsky, K., Van Voven, L., Epley, N., & Wright, W. M. (2005). The unpacking effect in allocations of responsibility for group tasks. *Journal of Experimental Social Psychology, 41,* 447–457. (p. 61)

Sbarra, D. A., Law, R. W., & Portley, R. M. (2011). Divorce and death: A meta-analysis and research agenda for clinical, social, and health psychology. *Perspectives on Psychological Science, 6,* 454–474. (p. 485)

Scalia, A. (2011). Opinion of the Supreme Court of the United States, *Brown v. Entertainment Merchants Association.* June 27, 2011. (p. 341)

Schachter, S. (1951). Deviation, rejection and communication. *Journal of Abnormal and Social Psychology, 46,* 190–207. (pp. 219, 267)

Schachter, S., & Singer, J. E. (1962). Cognitive, social and physiological determinants of emotional state. *Psychological Review, 69,* 379–399. (pp. 324, 378)

Schafer, R. B., & Keith, P. M. (1980). Equity and depression among married couples. *Social Psychology Quarterly, 43,* 430–435. (p. 386)

Schaffner, P. E. (1985). Specious learning about reward and punishment. *Journal of Personality and Social Psychology, 48,* 1377–1386. (p. 99)

Schaffner, P. E., Wandersman, A., & Stang, D. (1981). Candidate name exposure and voting: Two field studies. *Basic and Applied Social Psychology, 2,* 195–203. (p. 358)

Schaller, M., & Cialdini, R. B. (1988). The economics of empathic helping: Support for a mood management motive. *Journal of Experimental Social Psychology, 24,* 163–181. (p. 289)

Schaller, M., & Cialdini, R. B. (1990). Happiness, sadness, and helping: A motivational integration. In E. T. Higgins, & R. M. Sorrentino (Eds.). *Handbook of motivation and cognition: Foundations of social behavior.* Vol. 2. (pp. 265–296). New York: Guilford Press. (p. 279)

Schein, E. H. (1956). The Chinese indoctrination program for prisoners of war: A study of attempted brainwashing. *Psychiatry, 19,* 149–172. (p. 138)

Schiffenbauer, A., & Schiavo, R. S. (1976). Physical distance and attraction: An intensification effect. *Journal of Experimental Social Psychology, 12,* 274–282. (p. 236)

Schimel, J., Arndt, J., Pyszczynski, T., & Greenberg, J. (2001). Being accepted for who we are: Evidence that social validation of the intrinsic self reduces general defensiveness. *Journal of Personality and Social Psychology, 80,* 35–52. (p. 56)

Schimel, J., Pyszczynski, T., Greenberg, J., O'Mahen, H., & Arndt, J. (2000). Running from the shadow: Psychological distancing from others to deny characteristics people fear in themselves. *Journal of Personality and Social Psychology, 78,* 446. (p. 371)

Schimel, J., Simon, L., Greenberg, J., Pyszczynski, T., Solomon, S., & Waxmonsky, J. (1999). Stereotypes and terror management: Evidence that mortality salience enhances stereotypic thinking and preferences. *Journal of Personality and Social Psychology, 77,* 905–926. (p. 412)

Schimmack, U., Oishi, S., & Diener, E. (2005). Individualism: A valid and important dimension of cultural differences between nations. *Personality and Social Psychology Review, 9,* 17. (p. 42)

Schirmer, A., Teh, K., Wang, S., Vijayakumar, R., Ching, A., Nithianantham, D.,

Escoffier, N., & Cheok, A. (2011). Squeeze me, but don't tease me: Human and mechanical touch enhance visual attention and emotion discrimination. *Social Neuroscience, 6*(3), 219–230. (p. 301)

Schkade, D. A., & Kahneman, D. (1998). Does living in California make people happy? A focusing illusion in judgments of life satisfaction. *Psychological Science, 9,* 340–346. (p. 50)

Schlenker, B. R. (1976). *Egocentric perceptions in cooperative groups: A conceptualization and research review.* Final Report, Office of Naval Research Grant NR 170–797. (p. 69)

Schlenker, B. R., & Leary, M. R. (1982). Social anxiety and self-presentation: A conceptualization and model. *Psychological Bulletin, 92,* 641–669. (pp. 73, 480)

Schlenker, B. R., & Leary, M. R. (1985). Social anxiety and communication about the self. *Journal of Language and Social Psychology, 4,* 171–192. (p. 480)

Schlenker, B. R., & Miller, R. S. (1977a). Egocentrism in groups: Self-serving biases or logical information processing? *Journal of Personality and Social Psychology, 35,* 755–764. (p. 69)

Schlenker, B. R., & Miller, R. S. (1977b). Group cohesiveness as a determinant of egocentric perceptions in cooperative groups. *Human Relations, 30,* 1039–1055. (p. 69)

Schlenker, B. R., Phillips, S. T., Boniecki, K. A., & Schlenker, D. R. (1995). Championship pressures: Choking or triumphing in one's own territory? *Journal of Personality and Social Psychology, 68*(4), 632–643. (p. 236)

Schlenker, B. R., & Weigold, M. F. (1992). Interpersonal processes involving impression regulation and management. *Annual Review of Psychology, 43,* 133–168. (p. 72)

Schlesinger, A., Jr. (1949). The statistical soldier. *Partisan Review, 16,* 852–856. (p. 14)

Schmader, T., Johns, M., & Forbes, C. (2008). An integrated process model of stereotype threat effects on performance. *Psychological Review, 115,* 336. (p. 442)

Schmiege, S. J., Klein, W. M. P., & Bryan, A. D. (2010). The effect of peer comparison information in the context of expert recommendations on risk perceptions and subsequent behavior. *European Journal of Social Psychology, 40,* 746–759. (p. 202)

Schmitt, D. P., Alcalay, L., Allensworth, M., Allik, J., Ault, L., Austers, I., et al. (2004).

Patterns and universals of adult romantic attachment across 62 cultural regions: Are models of self and of other pancultural constructs? *Journal of Cross-Cultural Psychology, 35*, 367. (p. 384)

Schmitt, D. P., & Allik, J. (2005). Simultaneous administration of the Rosenberg Self-Esteem Scale in 53 nations: Exploring the universal and culture-specific features of global self-esteem. *Journal of Personality and Social Psychology, 89*, 623–642. (p. 60)

Schnall, S., & Laird, J. D. (2003). Keep smiling: Enduring effects of facial expressions and postures on emotional experience and memory. *Cognition and Emotion, 17*, 787–797. (p. 146)

Schneider, M. E., Major, B., Luhtanen, R., & Crocker, J. (1996). Social stigma and the potential costs of assumptive help. *Personality and Social Psychology Bulletin, 22*, 201–209. (p. 281)

Schneider, T. R., Salovey, P., Pallonen, U., Mundorf, N., Smith, N. F., & Steward, W. T. (2000). Visual and auditory message framing effects on tobacco smoking. *Journal of Applied Social Psychology, 31*(4), 667–682. (p. 483)

Schoeneman, T. J. (1994). Individualism. In V. S. Ramachandran (Ed.), *Encyclopedia of Human Behavior.* San Diego, CA: Academic Press. (p. 41)

Schor, J. B. (1998). *The overworked American.* New York: Basic Books. (p. 521)

Schulz, J. W., & Pruitt, D. G. (1978). The effects of mutual concern on joint welfare. *Journal of Experimental Social Psychology, 14*, 480–492. (p. 465)

Schulz-Hardt, S., Frey, D., Luthgens, C., & Moscovici, S. (2000). Biased information search in group decision making. *Journal of Personality and Social Psychology, 78*, 655–669. (p. 259)

Schuman, H., & Kalton, G. (1985). Survey methods. In G. Lindzey & E. Aronson (Eds.), *Handbook of social psychology,* Vol. 1. Hillsdale, NJ: Erlbaum. (p. 23)

Schuman, H., & Ludwig, J. (1983). The norm of even-handedness in surveys as in life. *American Sociological Review, 48*, 112–120. (p. 22)

Schuman, H., & Scott, J. (1989). Generations and collective memories. *American Sociological Review, 54*, 359–381. (p. 179)

Schutte, J. W., & Hosch, H. M. (1997). Gender differences in sexual assault verdicts. *Journal of Social Behavior and Personality, 12*, 759–772. (p. 102)

Schwartz, B. (2000). Self-determination: The tyranny of freedom. *American Psychologist, 55*, 79–88. (p. 58)

Schwartz, B. (2004). *The tyranny of choice.* New York: Ecco/HarperCollins. (p. 58)

Schwartz, S. H. (1975). The justice of need and the activation of humanitarian norms. *Journal of Social Issues, 31*(3), 111–136. (p. 281)

Schwartz, S. H., & Gottlieb, A. (1981). Participants' post-experimental reactions and the ethics of bystander research. *Journal of Experimental Social Psychology, 17*, 396–407. (p. 295)

Schwarz, N., Bless, H., Strack, F., Klumpp, G., Rittenauer-Schatka, H., & Simons, A. (1991). Ease of retrieval of information: Another look at the availability heuristic. *Journal of Personality and Social Psychology, 61*, 195–202. (p. 95)

Schwarz, N., & Clore, G. L. (1983). Mood, misattribution, and judgments of well-being: Informative and directive functions of affective states. *Journal of Personality and Social Psychology, 45*, 513–523. (p. 47)

Schwarz, N., & Kurz, E. (1989). What's in a picture? The impact of face-ism on trait attribution. *European Journal of Social Psychology, 19*, 311–316. (p. 407)

Schwarz, N., Strack, F., Kommer, D., & Wagner, D. (1987). Soccer, rooms, and the quality of your life: Mood effects on judgments of satisfaction with life in general and with specific domains. *Journal of Applied Social Psychology, 17*, 69–79. (p. 100)

Schweitzer, K., Zillmann, D., Weaver, J. B., & Luttrell, E. S. (1992, Spring). Perception of threatening events in the emotional aftermath of a televised college football game. *Journal of Broadcasting and Electronic Media,* 75–82. (p. 100)

Scott, J. P., & Marston, M. V. (1953). Non-adaptive behavior resulting from a series of defeats in fighting mice. *Journal of Abnormal and Social Psychology, 48*, 417–428. (p. 319)

Sears, D. O. (1979). *Life stage effects upon attitude change, especially among the elderly.* Manuscript prepared for Workshop on the Elderly of the Future, Committee on Aging, National Research Council, Annapolis, MD, May 3–5. (p. 178)

Sears, D. O. (1986). College sophomores in the laboratory: Influences of a narrow data base on social psychology's view of human nature. *Journal of Personality and Social Psychology, 51*, 515–530. (p. 178)

Sedikides, C. (1993). Assessment, enhancement, and verification determinants of the self-evaluation process. *Journal of Personality and Social Psychology, 65*, 317–338. (p. 68)

Sedikides, C., Gaertner, L., & Toguchi, Y. (2003). Pancultural self-enhancement. *Journal of Personality and Social Psychology, 84*, 60–79. (p. 61)

Segal, H. A. (1954). Initial psychiatric findings of recently repatriated prisoners of war. *American Journal of Psychiatry, 61*, 358–363. (p. 138)

Segal, N. L. (1984). Cooperation, competition, and altruism within twin sets: A reappraisal. *Ethology and Sociobiology, 5*, 163–177. (p. 283)

Segal, N. L., & Hershberger, S. L. (1999). Cooperation and competition between twins: Findings from a Prisoner's Dilemma game. *Evolution and Human Behavior, 20*, 29–51. (p. 283)

Segerstrom, S. C., McCarthy, W. J., Caskey, N. H., Gross, T. M., & Jarvik, M. E. (1993). Optimistic bias among cigarette smokers. *Journal of Applied Social Psychology, 23*, 1606–1618. (p. 487)

Segerstrom, S. C., & Miller, G. E. (2004). Psychological stress and the human immune system: A meta-analytic study of 30 years of inquiry. *Psychological Bulletin, 130*, 601. (p. 485)

Seibt, B., & Forster, J. (2004). Stereotype threat and performance: How self-stereotypes influence processing by inducing regulatory foci. *Journal of Personality and Social Psychology, 87*(1), 38–56. (p. 442)

Seidel, E., Eickhoff, S. B., Kellermann, T., Schneider, F., Gur, R. C., Habel, U., & Birgit, D. (2010). Who is to blame? Neural correlates of causal attribution in social situations. *Social Neuroscience, 5*, 335–350. (p. 60)

Seligman, M. (1994). *What you can change and what you can't.* New York: Knopf. (p. 20)

Seligman, M. E. P. (1975). *Helplessness: On depression, development and death.* San Francisco: W. H. Freeman. (p. 57)

Seligman, M. E. P. (1989). Explanatory style: Predicting depression, achievement, and health. In M. D. Yapko (Ed.), *Brief therapy approaches to treating anxiety and depression.* New York: Brunner/Mazel. (p. 522)

Seligman, M. E. P. (1991). *Learned optimism.* New York: Knopf. (pp. 57, 478, 479)

Seligman, M. E. P. (1998). The prediction and prevention of depression. In D. K. Routh & R. J. DeRubeis (Eds.), *The science of clinical psychology: Accomplishments and future directions.* Washington, DC: American Psychological Association. (p. 479)

Seligman, M. E. P. (2002). *Authentic happiness: Using the new positive psychology to realize your potential for lasting fulfillment.* New York: Free Press. (p. 479)

Sentyrz, S. M., & Bushman, B. J. (1997). *Mirror, mirror on the wall, who's the thinnest one of all? Effects of self-awareness on consumption of fatty, reduced-fat, and fat-free products.* Unpublished manuscript, Iowa State University. (p. 247)

Shaffer, D. R., Pegalis, L. J., & Bazzini, D. G. (1996). When boy meets girls (revisited): Gender, gender-role orientation, and prospect of future interaction as determinants of self-disclosure among same- and opposite-sex acquaintances. *Personality and Social Psychology Bulletin, 22,* 495–506. (p. 387)

Shah, J. Y. (2005). The automatic pursuit and management of goals. *Current Directions in Psychological Science, 14,* 10. (p. 521)

Sharot, T., Velasquez, C. M., & Dolan, R. J. (2010). Do decisions shape preference? Evidence from blind chance. *Psychological Science, 21,* 1231–1235. (p. 143)

Sharpe, D., & Faye, C. (2009). A second look at debriefing practices: Madness in our methods? *Ethics and Behavior, 19,* 432–447. (p. 28)

Shaver, P. R., & Hazan, C. (1993). Adult romantic attachment: Theory and evidence. In D. Perlman & W. Jones (Eds.), *Advances in personal relationships,* vol. 4. Greenwich, CT: JAI. (p. 383)

Shaver, P. R., & Hazan, C. (1994). Attachment. In A. L. Weber & J. H. Harvey (Eds.), Perspectives on close relationships. Boston: Allyn & Bacon. (p. 383)

Shaver, P. R., & Mikulincer, M. (2011). An attachment-theory framework for conceptualizing interpersonal behavior. In L. M. Horowitz & S. Strack (Eds.), *Handbook of interpersonal psychology: Theory, research, assessment, and therapeutic interventions.* Hoboken, NJ: Wiley. (p. 383)

Shaw, M. E. (1981). *Group dynamics: The psychology of small group behavior.* New York: McGraw-Hill. (p. 233)

Sheese, B. E., & Graziano, W. G. (2005). Deciding to defect: The effects of video-game violence on cooperative behavior. *Psychological Science, 16,* 354. (p. 340)

Sheldon, K. M., Elliot, A. J., Youngmee, K., & Kasser, T. (2001). What is satisfying about satisfying events? Testing 10 candidate psychological needs. *Journal of Personality and Social Psychology, 80,* 325–339. (p. 523)

Sheldon, K. M., & Niemiec, C. P. (2006). It's not just the amount that counts: Balanced need satisfaction also affects well-being. *Journal of Personality and Social Psychology, 91,* 331–341. (p. 353)

Sheldon, K. M., Ryan, R. M., Deci, E. L., & Kasser, T. (2004). The independent effects of goal contents and motives on well-being: It's both what you pursue and why you pursue it. *Personality and Social Psychology Bulletin, 30,* 475. (p. 523)

Shell, R. M., & Eisenberg, N. (1992). A developmental model of recipients' reactions to aid. *Psychological Bulletin, 111,* 413–433. (p. 281)

Shelton, J. N., & Richeson, J. A. (2006). Ethnic minorities' racial attitudes and contact experiences with white people. *Cultural Diversity and Ethnic Minority Psychology, 12,* 149–164. (p. 448)

Shelton, J. N., Richeson, J. A., & Vorauer, J. D. (2006). Threatened identities and interethnic interactions. *European Review of Social Psychology, 17,* 321–358. (p. 448)

Shen, H., Wan, F., & Wyer, R. S., Jr. (2011). Cross-cultural differences in the refusal to accept a small gift: The differential influence of reciprocity norms on Asians and North Americans. *Journal of Personality and Social Psychology, 100,* 271–281. (p. 281)

Sheppard, B. H., & Vidmar, N. (1980). Adversary pretrial procedures and testimonial evidence: Effects of lawyer's role and machiavelianism. *Journal of Personality and Social Psychology, 39,* 320–322. (p. 502)

Shepperd, J. A. (2003). *Interpreting comparative risk judgments: Are people personally optimistic or interpersonally pessimistic?* Unpublished manuscript, University of Florida. (p. 63)

Shepperd, J. A., & Arkin, R. M. (1991). Behavioral other-enhancement: Strategically obscuring the link between performance and evaluation. *Journal of Personality and Social Psychology, 60,* 79–88. (p. 71)

Shepperd, J. A., & Taylor, K. M. (1999). Ascribing advantages to social comparison targets. *Basic and Applied Social Psychology, 21,* 103–117. (pp. 40, 242)

Shepperd, J. A., & Wright, R. A. (1989). Individual contributions to a collective effort: An incentive analysis. *Personality and Social Psychology Bulletin, 15,* 141–149. (p. 242)

Sherif, M. (1935). A study of some social factors in perception. *Archives of Psychology,* No. 187. (p. 197)

Sherif, M. (1937). An experimental approach to the study of attitudes. *Sociometry, 1,* 90–98. (p. 197)

Sherif, M., & Sherif, C. (1969). *Social Psychology.* New York: Harper & Row. (p. 198)

Sherman, J. W. (1996). Development and mental representation of stereotypes. *Journal of Personality and Social Psychology, 70,* 1126–1141. (p. 421)

Sherman, J. W., Kruschke, J. K., Sherman, S. J., Percy, E. J., Petrocelli, J. V., & Conrey, F. R. (2009). Attentional processes in stereotype formation: A common model for category accentuation and illusory correlation. *Journal of Personality and Social Psychology, 96,* 305–323. (p. 422)

Sherman, J. W., Lee, A. Y., Bessenoff, G. R., & Frost, L. A. (1998). Stereotype efficiency reconsidered: Encoding flexibility under cognitive load. *Journal of Personality and Social Psychology, 75,* 589–606. (p. 417)

Shih, M., Pittinsky, T. L., & Ambady, N. (1999). Stereotype susceptibility: Identity salience and shifts in quantitative performance. *Psychological Science, 10,* 80–83. (p. 442)

Short, J. F., Jr. (Ed.) (1969). *Gang delinquency and delinquent subcultures.* New York: Harper & Row. (p. 321)

Shostak, M. (1981). *Nisa: The life and words of a !Kung woman.* Cambridge, MA: Harvard University Press. (p. 380)

Shotland, R. L. (1989). A model of the causes of date rape in developing and close relationships. In C. Hendrick (Ed.), *Review of personality and social psychology,* Vol. 10. Beverly Hills, CA: Sage. (p. 102)

Shotland, R. L., & Stebbins, C. A. (1983). Emergency and cost as determinants of helping behavior and the slow accumulation of social psychological knowledge. *Social Psychology Quarterly, 46,* 36–46. (p. 281)

Shotland, R. L., & Straw, M. K. (1976). Bystander response to an assault: When a man attacks a woman. *Journal of Personality and Social Psychology, 34,* 990–999. (p. 293)

Showers, C., & Ruben, C. (1987). *Distinguishing pessimism from depression: Negative expectations and positive coping mechanisms.* Paper presented at the American Psychological Association convention. (p. 65)

Shrauger, J. S. (1975). Responses to evaluation as a function of initial self-perceptions. *Psychological Bulletin, 82,* 581–596. (p. 372)

Shrauger, J. S., & Schoeneman, T. J. (1979, May). Symbolic interactionist view of self-concept: Through the looking glass darkly. *Psychological Bulletin, 86,* 549–573. (p. 40)

Shriver, E. R., Young, S. G., Hugenberg, K., Bernstein, M. J., & Lanter, J. R. (2008, February). Class, race, and the face: Social context modulates the cross-race effect in face recognition. *Personality and Social Psychology Bulletin, 34,* 260–274. (p. 420)

Sidanius, J., Van Laar, C., Levin, S., & Sinclair, S. (2004). Ethnic enclaves and the dynamics of social identity on the college campus: The good, the bad, and the ugly. *Journal of Personality and Social Psychology, 87,* 96–110. (p. 403)

Sieverding, M., Decker, S., & Zimmerman, F. (2010). Information about low participation in cancer screening demotivates other people. *Psychological Science, 21,* 941–943. (p. 202)

Sigall, H. (1970). Effects of competence and consensual validation on a communicator's liking for the audience. *Journal of Personality and Social Psychology, 16,* 252–258. (p. 376)

Silk, J. B., Alberts, S. C., & Altmann, J. (2003). Social bonds of female baboons enhance infant survival. *Science, 302,* 1231–1234. (p. 284)

Silver, M., & Geller, D. (1978). On the irrelevance of evil: The organization and individual action. *Journal of Social Issues, 34,* 125–136. (p. 213)

Silver, N. (2009, May 9). Bush may haunt Republicans for generations (www.fivethirtyeight.com). (p. 178)

Silvia, P. J. (2005). Deflecting reactance: The role of similarity in increasing compliance and reducing resistance. *Basic and Applied Social Psychology, 27,* 277–284. (p. 216)

Simmons, W. W. (2000, December). When it comes to having children, Americans

still prefer boys. *The Gallup Poll Monthly,* 63–64. (p. 436)

Simon, H. A. (1957). *Models of man: Social and rational.* New York: Wiley. (p. 116)

Simon, P. (1996, April 17). American provincials. *Christian Century,* 421–422. (p. 23)

Simon, R. (2011). SCOTUS: Violence OK. Sex? Maybe. Politico.com column, June 28, 2011. (p. 338)

Simonton, D. K. (1994). *Greatness: Who makes history and why.* New York: Guilford. (p. 266)

Simpson, J. A. (1987). The dissolution of romantic relationships: Factors involved in relationship stability and emotional distress. *Journal of Personality and Social Psychology, 53,* 683–692. (p. 393)

Simpson, J. A., Gangestad, S. W., & Lerma, M. (1990). Perception of physical attractiveness: Mechanisms involved in the maintenance of romantic relationships. *Journal of Personality and Social Psychology, 59,* 1192–1201. (p. 368)

Simpson, J. A., Rholes, W. S., & Nelligan, J. S. (1992). Support seeking and support giving within couples in an anxiety-provoking situation: The role of attachment styles. *Journal of Personality and Social Psychology, 62,* 434–446. (p. 383)

Simpson, J. A., Rholes, W. S., & Phillips, D. (1996). Conflict in close relationships: An attachment perspective. *Journal of Personality and Social Psychology, 71,* 899–914. (p. 384)

Sinclair, L., & Kunda, Z. (1999). Reactions to a Black professional: Motivated inhibition and activation of conflicting stereotypes. *Journal of Personality and Social Psychology, 77,* 885–904. (pp. 445, 446)

Sinclair, L., & Kunda, Z. (2000). Motivated stereotyping of women: She's fine if she praised me but incompetent if she criticized me. *Personality and Social Psychology Bulletin, 26,* 1329–1342. (p. 445)

Sinclair, S., Dunn, E., & Lowery, B. S. (2004). The relationship between parental racial attitudes and children's implicit prejudice. *Journal of Experimental Social Psychology, 41,* 283–289. (p. 403)

Singer, M. (1979). *Cults and cult members.* Address to the American Psychological Association convention. (p. 184)

Singh, D. (1993). Adaptive significance of female physical attractiveness: Role of waist-to-hip ratio. *Journal of Personality and Social Psychology, 65,* 293–307. (p. 366)

Singh, D. (1995). Female judgment of male attractiveness and desirability for relationships: Role of waist-to-hip ratio and financial status. *Journal of Personality and Social Psychology, 69,* 1089–1101. (p. 366)

Singh, D., & Randall, P. K. (2007). Beauty is in the eye of the plastic surgeon: Waist-hip ratio (WHR) and women's attractiveness. *Personality and Individual Differences, 43,* 329–340. (p. 366)

Singh, R., & Ho, S. J. (2000). Attitudes and attraction: A new test of the attraction, repulsion and similarity-dissimilarity asymmetry hypotheses. *British Journal of Social Psychology, 39,* 197–211. (p. 370)

Singh, R., & Teoh, J. B. P. (1999). Attitudes and attraction: A test of two hypotheses for the similarity-dissimilarity asymmetry. *British Journal of Social Psychology, 38,* 427–443. (p. 370)

SIPRI. (2011). Appendix 4A. Military expenditure data, 2001–10. Stockholm International Peace Research Institute (www.sipri.org/yearbook/2011/04/04A). (p. 453)

Sittser, G. L. (1994, April). Long night's journey into light. *Second Opinion,* 10–15. (p. 97)

Sivarajasingam, V., Moore, S., & Shepherd, J. P. (2005). Winning, losing, and violence. *Injury Prevention, 11,* 69–70. (p. 316)

Sivard, R. L. (1996). *World military and social expenditures 1996,* 16th edition. Washington, DC: World Priorities. (p. 310)

Six, B., & Eckes, T. (1996). Metaanalysen in der Einstellungs-Verhaltens-Forschung. *Zeitschrift für Sozialpsychologie,* 7–17. (p. 127)

Skaalvik, E. M., & Hagtvet, K. A. (1990). Academic achievement and self-concept: An analysis of causal predominance in a developmental perspective. *Journal of Personality and Social Psychology, 58,* 292–307. (p. 20)

Skinner, B. F. (1971). *Beyond freedom and dignity.* New York: Knopf. (p. 276)

Skitka, L. R., Bauman, C. E., & Mullen, E. (2004). Political tolerance and coming to psychological closure following the September 11, 2001 terrorist attacks: An integrative approach. *Personality and Social Psychology Bulletin, 30,* 743–756. (p. 370)

Skitka, L. J., & Tetlock, P. E. (1993). Providing public assistance: Cognitive and motivational processes underlying liberal and conservative policy preferences. *Journal of Personality and Social Psychology, 65,* 1205–1223. (p. 281)

Skurnik, I., Yoon, C., Park, D. C., & Schwarz, N. (2005). How warnings about false claims become recommendations. *Journal of Consumer Research, 31,* 713. (p. 175)

Slatcher, R. B., & Pennebaker, J. W. (2006). How do I love thee? Let me count the words: The social effects of expressive writing. *Psychological Science, 17,* 660–664. (p. 391)

Sloan, J. H., Kellerman, A. L., Reay, D. T., Ferris, J. A., Koepsell, T., Rivara, F. P., Rice, C., Gray, L., & LoGerfo, J. (1988). Handgun regulations, crime, assaults, and homicide: A tale of two cities. *New England Journal of Medicine, 319,* 1256–1261. (p. 326)

Slopen, N., Glynn, R. J., Buring, J., & Albert, M. A. (2010, November 23). Job strain, job insecurity, and incident cardiovascular disease in the Women's Health Study (Abstract 18520). *Circulation, A18520* (circ.ahajournals org). (p. 485)

Slotow, R., Van Dyke, G., Poole, J., Page, B., & Klocke, A. (2000). Older bull elephants control young males. *Nature, 408,* 425–426. (p. 342)

Slotter, E. B., & Gardner, W. L. (2009). Where do you end and I begin? Evidence for anticipatory, motivated self-other integration between relationship partners. *Journal of Personality and Social Psychology, 96,* 1137–1151. (p. 388)

Slotter, E. B., Gardner, W. L., & Finkel, E. (2010). Who am I without you? The influence of romantic breakup on the self-concept. *Personality and Social Psychology Bulletin, 36,* 147–160. (pp. 36, 392)

Slovic, P. (1972). From Shakespeare to Simon: Speculations–and some evidence–about man's ability to process information. *Oregon Research Institute Research Bulletin, 12*(2). (p. 115)

Slovic, P. (2007). "If I look at the mass I will never act": Psychic numbing and genocide. *Judgment and Decision Making, 2,* 79–95. (p. 303)

Slovic, P., & Fischhoff, B. (1977). On the psychology of experimental surprises. *Journal of Experimental Psychology: Human Perception and Performance, 3,* 455–551. (p. 14)

Slovic, P., & Västfjäll, D. (2010). Affect, moral intuition, and risk. *Psychological Inquiry, 21,* 387–398. (p. 303)

Smith, A. (1976). *The wealth of nations.* Book 1. Chicago: University of Chicago Press. (Originally published, 1776.) (p. 457)

Smith, A. E., & Haney, C. (2011). Getting to the point: Attempting to improve juror comprehension of capital penalty phase instructions. *Law and Human Behavior, 35,* 339–350. (p. 508)

Smith, D. E., Gier, J. A., & Willis, F. N. (1982). Interpersonal touch and compliance with a marketing request. *Basic and Applied Social Psychology, 3,* 35–38. (p. 207)

Smith, H. (1976). *The Russians.* New York: Balantine Books. Cited by B. Latané, K. Williams, and S. Harkins in, Many hands make light the work. *Journal of Personality and Social Psychology,* 1979, *37,* 822–832. (p. 241)

Smith, H. J., & Tyler, T. R. (1997). Choosing the right pond: The impact of group membership on self-esteem and group-oriented behavior. *Journal of Experimental Social Psychology, 33,* 146–170. (p. 408)

Smith, P. B. (2005). Is there an indigenous European social psychology? *International Journal of Psychology, 40,* 254–262. (p. 5)

Smith, P. B., & Tayeb, M. (1989). Organizational structure and processes. In M. Bond (Ed.), *The cross-cultural challenge to social psychology.* Newbury Park, CA: Sage. (p. 265)

Smith, R. H., Turner, T. J., Garonzik, R., Leach, C. W., Urch-Druskat, V., & Weston, C. M. (1996). Envy and Schadenfreude. *Personality and Social Psychology Bulletin, 22,* 158–168. (p. 40)

Smith, T. W. (1998, December). *American sexual behavior: Trends, socio-demographic differences, and risk behavior.* National Opinion Research Center GSS Topical Report No. 25. (p. 421)

Smith, V. L., & Ellsworth, P. C. (1987). The social psychology of eyewitness accuracy: Misleading questions and communicator expertise. *Journal of Applied Psychology, 72,* 294–300. (p. 501)

Snopes. (2008, accessed July 30). The naked truth (www.snopes.com/humor/iftrue/pollster.asp). (p. 208)

Snyder, C. R. (1978). The "illusion" of uniqueness. *Journal of Humanistic Psychology, 18,* 33–41. (p. 63)

Snyder, C. R. (1980). The uniqueness mystique. *Psychology Today,* March, 86–90. (p. 226)

Snyder, C. R., & Higgins, R. L. (1988). Excuses: Their effective role in the negotiation of reality. *Psychological Bulletin, 104,* 23–35. (p. 68)

Snyder, M. (1981). Seek, and ye shall find: Testing hypotheses about other people. In E. T. Higgins, C. P. Herman, & M. P. Zanna (Eds.), *Social cognition: The Ontario symposium on personality and social psychology.* Hillsdale, NJ: Erlbaum. (p. 474)

Snyder, M. (1984). When belief creates reality. In L. Berkowitz (Ed.), *Advances in experimental social psychology,* Vol. 18. New York: Academic Press. (pp. 114, 474)

Snyder, M. (1987). *Public appearances/private realities: The psychology of self-monitoring.* New York: Freeman. (p. 73)

Snyder, M., Campbell, B., & Preston, E. (1982). Testing hypotheses about human nature: Assessing the accuracy of social stereotypes. *Social Cognition, 1,* 256–272. (p. 474)

Snyder, M., Grether, J., & Keller, K. (1974). Staring and compliance: A field experiment on hitch-hiking. *Journal of Applied Social Psychology, 4,* 165–170. (pp. 282, 301)

Snyder, M., & Haugen, J. A. (1994). Why does behavioral confirmation occur? A functional perspective on the role of the perceiver. *Journal of Experimental Social Psychology, 30,* 218–246. (p. 25)

Snyder, M., & Haugen, J. A. (1995). Why does behavioral confirmation occur? A functional perspective on the role of the target. *Personality and Social Psychology Bulletin, 21,* 963–974. (p. 25)

Snyder, M., & Swann, W. B., Jr. (1976). When actions reflect attitudes: The politics of impression management. *Journal of Personality and Social Psychology, 34,* 1034–1042. (p. 128)

Snyder, M., Tanke, E. D., & Berscheid, E. (1977). Social perception and interpersonal behavior: On the self-fulfilling nature of social stereotypes. *Journal of Personality and Social Psychology, 35,* 656–666. (p. 114)

Sober, E., & Wilson, D. S. (1998). *Unto others: The evolution and psychology of unselfish behavior.* Cambridge, MA: Harvard University Press. (p. 285)

Solano, C. H., Batten, P. G., & Parish, E. A. (1982). Loneliness and patterns of self-disclosure. *Journal of Personality and Social Psychology, 43,* 524–531. (p. 387)

Solberg, E. C., Diener, E., & Robinson, M. D. (2003). Why are materialists less satisfied? In T. Kasser & A. D. Kanner (Eds.), *Psychology and consumer culture: The struggle for a good life in a materialistic world.* Washington, DC: APA Books. (p. 523)

Solberg, E. C. , Diener, E., Wirtz, D., Lucas, R. E., & Oishi, S. (2002). Wanting, having, and satisfaction: Examining the role of desire discrepancies in satisfaction with income. *Journal of Personality and Social Psychology, 83,* 725. (p. 318)

Solomon, H., & Solomon, L. Z. (1978). *Effects of anonymity on helping in emergency situations.* Paper presented at the Eastern Psychological Association convention. (p. 301)

Solomon, H., Solomon, L. Z., Arnone, M. M., Maur, B. J., Reda, R. M., & Rother, E. O. (1981). Anonymity and helping. *Journal of Social Psychology, 113,* 37–43. (p. 301)

Solomon, L. Z., Solomon, H., & Stone, R. (1978). Helping as a function of number of bystanders and ambiguity of emergency. *Personality and Social Psychology Bulletin, 4,* 318–321. (p. 294)

Solomon, S., Greenberg, J., & Pyszczynski, T. (2000). Pride and prejudice: Fear of death and social behavior. *Current Directions in Psychological Science, 9,* 200–203. (p. 412)

Son Hing, L. S., Bobocel, D. R., Zanna, M. P., & McBride, M. V. (2007). Authoritarian dynamics and unethical decision making: High social dominance orientation leaders and high right-wing authoritarianism followers. *Journal of Personality and Social Psychology, 92,* 67. (p. 404)

Sorokowski, P., & others. (2011). Attractiveness of leg length: Report from 27 nations. *Journal of Cross-Cultural Psychology, 42,* 131–139. (p. 364)

Sparrell, J. A., & Shrauger, J. S. (1984). *Self-confidence and optimism in self-prediction.* Paper presented at the American Psychological Association convention. (p. 65)

Spears, R., Ellemers, N., & Doosje, B. (2009). Strength in numbers or less is more? A matter of opinion and a question of taste. *Personality and Social Psychology Bulletin, 35,* 1099–1111. (p. 66)

Spector, P. E. (1986). Perceived control by employees: A meta-analysis of studies concerning autonomy and participation at work. *Human Relations, 39,* 1005–1016. (p. 264)

Speer, A. (1971). *Inside the Third Reich: Memoirs.* (R. Winston & C. Winston. trans.). New York: Avon Books. (p. 258)

Spence, A., & Townsend, E. (2007). Predicting behaviour towards genetically modified food using implicit and explicit attitudes. *British Journal of Social Psychology, 46,* 437–457. (p. 124)

Spencer, S. J., Fein, S., Wolfe, C. T., Fong, C., & Dunn, M. A. (1998). Automatic activation of stereotypes: The role of self-image threat. *Personality and Social Psychology Bulletin, 24,* 1139–1152. (p. 413)

Spencer, S. J., Steele, C. M., & Quinn, D. M. (1999). Stereotype threat and women's math performance. *Journal of Experimental Social Psychology, 35,* 4–28. (pp. 440, 441)

Speth, J. G. (2008). Foreword. In A. A. Leiserowitz & L. O. Fernandez, *Toward a new consciousness: Values to sustain human and natural communities.* New Haven: Yale School of Forestry & Environmental Studies. (p. 520)

Spiegel, H. W. (1971). *The growth of economic thought.* Durham, NC: Duke University Press. (p. 64)

Spielmann, S. S., Joel, S., MacDonald. G., & Kogan, A. (2013b). Ex appeal: Current relationship quality and emotional attachment to ex-partners. *Social Psychological and Personality Science, 4,* 175–180. (p. 393)

Spielmann, S. S., MacDonald, G., Maxwell, J. A., & Joel, S. (2013a). Settling for less out of fear of being single. *Journal of Personality and Social Psychology, 105,* 961–977. (p. 392)

Spielman, S. S., MacDonald, G., & Wilson, A. E. (2009). On the rebound: Focusing on someone new helps anxiously attached individuals let go of ex-partners. *Personality and Social Psychology Bulletin, 35,* 1382–1394. (pp. 373, 393)

Spitz, H. H. (1999). Beleaguered Pygmalion: A history of the controversy over claims that teacher expectancy raises intelligence. *Intelligence, 27,* 199–234. (p. 112)

Spivak, J. (1979, June 6). *Wall Street Journal.* (p. 241)

Sporer, S. L. (2008). Lessons from the origins of eyewitness testimony research in Europe. *Applied Cognitive Psychology, 22,* 737–757. (p. 499)

Sporer, S. L., & Horry, R. (2011). Recognizing faces from ethnic in-groups and out-groups: Importance of outer face features and effects of retention interval. *Applied Cognitive Psychology, 25,* 424–431. (p. 419)

Sporer, S. L., Trinkl, B., & Guberova, E. (2007). Matching faces. Differences in processing speed of out-group faces by different ethnic groups. *Journal of Cross-Cultural Psychology, 38,* 398–412. (p. 419)

Sprecher, S. (1987). The effects of self-disclosure given and received on affection for an intimate partner and stability of the relationship. *Journal of Personality and Social Psychology, 4,* 115–127. (p. 388)

Sprecher, S., Aron, A., Hatfield, E., Cortese, A., Potapova, E., & Levitskaya, A. (1994). Love: American style, Russian style, and Japanese style. *Personal Relationships, 1,* 349–369. (pp. 360, 381)

Srivastava, S., McGonigal, K. M., Richards, J. M., Butler, E. A., & Gross, J. J. (2006). Optimism in close relationships: How seeing things in a positive light makes them so. *Journal of Personality and Social Psychology, 91,* 143–153. (p. 114)

Stalder, D. R. (2008). Revisiting the issue of safety in numbers: The likelihood of receiving help from a group. *Social Influence, 3,* 24–33. (p. 291)

Stam, H., Lubeck, I., & Radtke, H. L. (1998). Repopulating social psychology texts: Disembodied "subjects" and embodied subjectivety. In Bayer, B. M., & Shotter, J., (Eds.) *Reconstructing the psychological subject: Bodies, practices and technologies. Inquiries in social construction.* (153–186). London: Sage Publications, Inc. (p. 204)

Stangor, C., & McMillan, D. (1992). Memory for expectancy-congruent and expectancy-incongruent information: A review of the social and social developmental literatures. *Psychological Bulletin, 111,* 42–61. (p. 437)

Stanley, D., Phelps, E., & Banaji, M. (2008). The neural basis of implicit attitudes. *Current Directions in Psychological Science, 17,* 164–170. (p. 126)

Stanovich, K. E., & West, R. F. (2008). On the relative independence of thinking biases and cognitive ability. *Journal of Personality and Social Psychology, 94,* 672–695. (p. 115)

Staples, B. (2000, June 26). Playing "catch and grope" in the schoolyard. *New York Times* (www.nytimes.com). (p. 314)

Stark, E., Kim, A., Miller, C., & Borgida, E. (2008). Effects of including a graphic warning label in advertisements for reduced-exposure products: Implications for persuasion and policy. *Journal of Applied Social Psychology, 38,* 281–293. (p. 168)

Stark, R., & Bainbridge, W. S. (1980). Networks of faith: Interpersonal bonds and recruitment of cults and sects. *American Journal of Sociology, 85,* 1376–1395. (pp. 184, 185)

Stasser, G. (1991). Pooling of unshared information during group discussion. In

S. Worchel, W. Wood, & J. Simpson (Eds.), *Group process and productivity.* Beverly Hills, CA: Sage. (p. 252)

Stasser, G., Kerr, N. L., & Bray, R. M. (1981). The social psychology of jury deliberations: Structure, process, and product. In N. L. Kerr & R. M. Bray (Eds.), *The psychology of the courtroom.* New York: Academic Press. (p. 510)

Statistics Canada. (1997). The Justice Data Factfinder. *Juristat: Canadian Centre for Justice Statistics, 17,* number 13. (pp. 433, 497)

Statistics Canada. (1998). General social survey: Overview of the time use of Canadians in 1998. Ottawa: Statistics Canada. (p. 433)

Statistics Canada. (2009). Police reported hate crimes in Canada, 2009. Retrieved from: http://www.statcan.gc.ca/pub/85-002-x/2011001/article/11469-eng.htm. (p. 429)

Staub, E. (1978). *Positive social behavior and morality: Social and personal influences,* vol. 1. Hillsdale, NJ: Erlbaum. (p. 276)

Staub, E. (1989). *The roots of evil: The origins of genocide and other group violence.* Cambridge: Cambridge University Press. (pp. 211, 304)

Staub, E. (1990). Moral exclusion: Personal goal theory, and extreme destructiveness. *Journal of Social Issues, 46,* 47–64. (p. 303)

Staub, E. (1991). Altruistic and moral motivations for helping and their translation into action. *Psychological Inquiry, 2,* 150–153. (pp. 289, 304)

Staub, E. (1992). The origins of caring, helping, and nonaggression: Parental socialization, the family system, schools, and cultural influence. In Oliner, P. M., Oliner, S. P., Baron, L., Blum, L. A., Krebs, D. L., & Smolenska, M. Z. (Eds.), *The origins of caring, helping, and nonaggression: Parental socialization, the family system, schools, and cultural influence.* New York: New York University Press. (p. 304)

Staub, E. (1996). Altruism and aggression in children and youth: Origins and cures. In R. Feldman (Ed.), *The psychology of adversity.* Amherst, MA: University of Massachusetts Press. (p. 342)

Staub, E. (1997a). *Halting and preventing collective violence: The role of bystanders.* Background paper for symposium organized by the Friends of Raoul Wallenberg, Stockholm, June 13–16. (p. 295)

Staub, E. (1997b). Blind versus constructive patriotism: Moving from embeddedness in the group to critical loyalty and action. In D. Bar-Tal and E. Staub (Eds.), *Patriotism in the lives of individuals and nations.* Chicago: Nelson-Hall. (p. 408)

Staub, E. (2003). *The psychology of good and evil: Why children, adults, and groups help and harm others.* New York: Cambridge University Press. (p. 211)

Staub, E. (2005). The roots of goodness: The fulfillment of basic human needs and the development of caring, helping and nonaggression, inclusive caring, moral courage, active bystandership, and altruism born of suffering. In G. Carlo & C. P. Edwards (Eds.), *Moral motivation through the life span: Theory, research, applications. Nebraska Symposium on Motivation* (Vol. 51). Lincoln, NE: University of Nebraska Press. (pp. 305, 408)

Staub, E., & Bar-Tal, D. (2003). Genocide, mass killings, and intractable conflict. In D. Sears, L. Huddy, & R. Jervis (Eds.). *Handbook of political psychology.* New York: Oxford University Press. (p. 461)

Staub, E., & Pearlman, L. A. (2005a). Advancing healing and reconciliation. In L. Barbanel & R. Sternberg (Eds.), *Psychological interventions in times of crisis* (213–243). New York: Springer. (p. 466)

Staub, E., & Pearlman, L. A. (2005b). Psychological recovery and reconciliation after the genocide in Rwanda and in other post-conflict settings. In R. Sternberg & L. Barbanel (Eds.), *Psychological interventions in times of crisis.* New York: Springer. (p. 466)

Steblay, N., Dysart, J. E., Fulero, S., & Lindsay, R. C. L. (2001). Eyewitness accuracy rates in sequential and simultaneous lineup presentations: A meta-analytic comparison. *Law and Human Behavior, 25,* 459–473. (p. 504)

Steblay, N. M. (1987). Helping behavior in rural and urban environments: A meta-analysis. *Psychological Bulletin, 102,* 346–356. (p. 284)

Steele, C. M. (1988). The psychology of self-affirmation: Sustaining the integrity of the self. In L. Berkowitz (Ed.), *Advances in experimental social psychology,* Vol. 21. Orlando, FL: Academic Press. (p. 151)

Steele, C. M. (1997). A threat in the air: How stereotypes shape intellectual identity and performance. *American Psychologist, 52,* 613–629. (pp. 40, 441)

Steele, C. M. (2010). *Whistling Vivaldi: And other clues to how stereotypes affect us.* New York: Norton. (p. 440)

Steele, C. M., & Aronson, J. (1995). Stereotype threat and the intellectual test performance of African Americans. *Journal of Personality and Social Psychology, 69,* 797–811. (p. 441)

Steele, C. M., & Josephs, R. A. (1990). Alcohol myopia: Its prized and dangerous effects. *American Psychologist, 45,* 921–933. (p. 481)

Steele, C. M., Southwick, L. L., & Critchlow, B. (1981). Dissonance and alcohol: Drinking your troubles away. *Journal of Personality and Social Psychology, 41,* 831–846. (p. 152)

Steele, C. M., Spencer, S. J., & Lynch, M. (1993). Self-image resilience and dissonance: The role of affirmational resources. *Journal of Personality and Social Psychology, 64,* 885–896. (p. 151)

Steele, C. M., Spencer, S. J., Aronson, J. (2002). Contending with group image: The psychology of stereotype and social identity threat. In Zanna, M. P. (Ed.), *Advances in experimental social psychology,* 34, 379–440. San Diego, CA: Academic Press, Inc. (p. 440)

Stein, A. H., & Friedrich, L. K. (1972). Television content and young children's behavior. In J. P. Murray, E. A. Rubinstein, & G. A. Comstock (Eds.), *Television and social learning.* Washington, DC: Government Printing Office. (p. 305)

Stein, D. D., Hardyck, J. A., & Smith, M. B. (1965). Race and belief: An open and shut case. *Journal of Personality and Social Psychology, 1,* 281–289. (p. 418)

Stelter, B. (2008, November 25). Web suicide viewed live and reaction spur a debate. *New York Times* (www.nytimes.com). (p. 244)

Stelzl, M., Janes, L., & Seligman, C. (2008). Champ or chump: Strategic utilization of dual social identities of others. *European Journal of Social Psychology, 38,* 128–138. (p. 411)

Stephan, W. G., Berscheid, E., & Walster, E. (1971). Sexual arousal and heterosexual perception. *Journal of Personality and Social Psychology, 20,* 93–101. (p. 378)

Stephens, N. M., Markus, H. R., & Townsend, S. S. M. (2007). Choice as an act of meaning: The case of social class. *Journal of Personality and Social Psychology, 93,* 814–830. (p. 223)

Sternberg, R. J. (1988). Triangulating love. In R. J. Sternberg & M. L. Barnes (Eds.), *The psychology of love.* New Haven, CT: Yale University Press. (p. 394)

Sternberg, R. J. (1998). *Cupid's arrow: The course of love through time.* New York: Cambridge University Press. (p. 377)

Sternberg, R. J. (2003). A duplex theory of hate and its development and its application to terrorism, massacres, and genocide. *Review of General Psychology, 7,* 299–328. (p. 310)

Sternberg, R. J., & Grajek, S. (1984). The nature of love. *Journal of Personality and Social Psychology, 47,* 312–329. (p. 383)

Stewart, K. D., & Bernhardt, P. C. (2010). Comparing Millennials to pre-1987 students and with one another. *North American Journal of Psychology, 12,* 579–602. (p. 55)

Stewart-Williams, S. (2007). Altruism among kin vs. nonkin: Effects of cost of help and reciprocal exchange. *Evolution and Human Behavior, 28,* 193–198. (p. 283)

Stinson, D. A., Cameron, J. J., Wood, J. V., Gaucher, D. G., & Holmes, J. G. (2009). Deconstructing the "reign of error": Interpersonal warmth explains the self-fulfilling prophecy of anticipated acceptance. *Personality and Social Psychology Bulletin, 35,* 1165–1178. (p. 373)

Stinson, V., Devenport, J. L., Cutler, B. L., & Kravitz, D. A. (1996). How effective is the presence-of-counsel safeguard? Attorney perceptions of suggestiveness, fairness, and correctability of biased lineup procedures. *Journal of Applied Psychology, 81,* 64–75. (p. 505)

Stinson, V., Devenport, J. L., Cutler, B. L., & Kravitz, D. A. (1997). How effective is the motion-to-suppress safeguard? Judges' perceptions of the suggestiveness and fairness of biased lineup procedures. *Journal of Personality and Social Psychology, 82,* 211–220. (p. 505)

Stirrat, M., & Perrett, D. I. (2010). Valid facial cues to cooperation and trust: Male facial width and trustworthiness. *Psychological Science, 21,* 349–354. (p. 315)

Stix, G. (2008, March). When markets beat the polls. *Scientific American Mind,* 38–45. (p. 264)

Stone, A. A., Hedges, S. M., Neale, J. M., & Satin, M. S. (1985). Prospective and cross-sectional mood reports offer no evidence of a "blue Monday" phenomenon. *Journal of Personality and Social Psychology, 49,* 129–134. (p. 47)

Stone, A. L., & Glass, C. R. (1986). Cognitive distortion of social feedback in depression. *Journal of Social and Clinical Psychology, 4,* 179–188. (p. 100)

Stone, J. (2000, November 6). Quoted by Sharon Begley, The stereotype trap. *Newsweek.* (p. 441)

Stone, J., Lynch, C. I., Sjomeling, M., & Darley, J. M. (1999). Stereotype threat effects on Black and White athletic performance. *Journal of Personality and Social Psychology, 77,* 1213–1227. (pp. 152, 441)

Stone, L. (1977). *The family, sex and marriage in England, 1500–1800.* New York: Harper & Row. (p. 392)

Stoner, J. A. F. (1961). *A comparison of individual and group decisions involving risk.* Unpublished master's thesis, Massachusetts Institute of Technology, 1961. Cited by D. G. Marquis in, Individual responsibility and group decisions involving risk. *Industrial Management Review, 3,* 8–23. (p. 248)

Storms, M. D., & Thomas, G. C. (1977). Reactions to physical closeness. *Journal of Personality and Social Psychology, 35,* 412–418. (p. 236)

Stouffer, S. A., Suchman, E. A., DeVinney, L. C., Star, S. A., & Williams, R. M., Jr. (1949). *The American soldier: Adjustment during army life* (Vol. 1.). Princeton, NJ: Princeton University Press. (p. 318)

Stowell, J. R., Oldham, T., & Bennett, D. (2010). Using student response systems ("clickers") to combat conformity and shyness. *Teaching of Psychology, 37,* 135–140. (p. 217)

Strachman, A., & Schimel, J. (2006). Terror management and close relationships: Evidence that mortality salience reduces commitment among partners with different worldviews. *Journal of Social and Personal Relationships, 23,* 965. (p. 352)

Strack, F., & Deutsch, R. (2004). Reflective and impulsive determinants of social behavior. *Personality and Social Psychology Review, 8*(3), 220–247. (p. 87)

Strack, F., Martin, L. & Stepper, S. (1988). Inhibiting and facilitating conditions of the human smile: A nonobtrusive test of the facial feedback hypothesis. *Journal of Personality and Social Psychology, 54,* 768–777. (p. 146)

Strack, S., & Coyne, J. C. (1983). Social confirmation of dysphoria: Shared and private reactions to depression. *Journal of Personality and Social Psychology, 44,* 798–806. (p. 477)

Straus, M. A., & Gelles, R. J. (1980). *Behind closed doors: Violence in the American family.* New York: Anchor/Doubleday. (p. 320)

Streeter, S. A., & McBurney, D. H. (2003). Waist–hip ratio and attractiveness: New evidence and a critique of "a critical test." *Evolution and Human Behavior, 24,* 88–98. (p. 366)

Strick, M., van Baaren, R. B., Holland, R. W., & van Knippenberg, A. (2009). Humor in advertisements enhances product liking by mere association. *Journal of Experimental Psychology: Applied, 15,* 35–45. (p. 167)

Stroebe, W. (2012). The truth about Triplett (1898), but nobody seems to care. *Perspectives on Psychological Science, 7,* 54–57. (p. 234)

Stroebe, W., & Diehl, M. (1994). Productivity loss in idea-generating groups. In W. Stroebe & M. Hewstone (Eds.), *European review of social psychology,* vol. 5. Chichester: Wiley. (p. 262)

Stroessner, S. J., Hamilton, D. L., & Lepore, L. (1990). *Intergroup categorization and intragroup differentiation: Ingroup-outgroup differences.* Paper presented at the American Psychological Association convention. (p. 417)

Stroessner, S. J., & Mackie, D. M. (1993). Affect and perceived group variability: Implications for stereotyping and prejudice. In D. M. Mackie & D. L. Hamilton (Eds.), *Affect, cognition, and stereotyping: Interactive processes in group perception.* San Diego, CA: Academic Press. (p. 417)

Strong, S. R. (1978). Social psychological approach to psychotherapy research. In S. L. Garfield & A. E. Bergin (Eds.), *Handbook of psychotherapy and behavior change,* 2nd ed. New York: Wiley. (p. 186)

Stroufe, B., Chaikin, A., Cook, R., & Freeman, V. (1977). The effects of physical attractiveness on honesty: A socially desirable response. *Personality and Social Psychology, 3,* 59–62. (p. 282)

Strube, M. J. (2005). What did Triplett really find? A contemporary analysis of the first experiment in social psychology. *American Journal of Psychology, 118,* 271–286. (p. 234)

Stukas, A. A., Snyder, M., & Clary, E. G. (1999). The effects of "mandatory volunteerism" on intentions to volunteer. *Psychological Science, 10,* 59–64. (p. 142)

Sue, S., Smith, R. E., & Caldwell, C. (1973). Effects of inadmissible evidence on the decisions of simulated jurors: A moral dilemma. *Journal of Applied Social Psychology, 3,* 345–353. (p. 507)

Suedfeld, P. (2000). Reverberations of the Holocaust fifty years later: Psychology's contributions to understanding persecution and genocide. *Canadian Psychology, 41,* 1–9. (p. 295)

Suls, J., & Tesch, F. (1978). Students' preferences for information about their test performance: A social comparison study. *Journal of Applied Social Psychology, 8,* 189–197. (p. 40)

Summers, G., & Feldman, N. S. (1984). Blaming the victim versus blaming the perpetrator: An attributional analysis of spouse abuse. *Journal of Social and Clinical Psychology, 2,* 339–347. (p. 415)

Sun, C., Bridges, A., Wosnitzer, R., Scharrer, E., & Liberman, R. (2008). A comparison of male and female directors in popular pornography: What happens when women are at the helm? *Psychology of Women Quarterly, 32,* 312–325. (p. 327)

Sundstrom, E., De Meuse, K. P., & Futrell, D. (1990). Work teams: Applications and effectiveness. *American Psychologist, 45,* 120–133. (p. 265)

Sunstein, C. R. (2001). *Republic.com.* Princeton, NJ: Princeton University Press. (p. 251)

Sunstein, C. R. (2007). On the divergent American reactions to terrorism and climate change. *Columbia Law Review, 107,* 503–557. (p. 96)

Sunstein, C. R. (2009). *Going to extremes: How like minds unite and divide.* New York: Oxford University Press. (pp. 249, 251)

Sunstein, C. R., & Hastie, R. (2008). *Four failures of deliberating groups.* Economics Working Paper Series, University of Chicago Law School (www.law.uchicago.edu). (p. 259)

Surowiecki, J. (2004). *The wisdom of crowds.* New York: Doubleday. (p. 263)

Sussman, N. M. (2000). The dynamic nature of cultural identity throughout cultural transitions: Why home is not so sweet. *Personality and Social Psychology Review, 4,* 355–373. (p. 224)

Svenson, O. (1981). Are we all less risky and more skillful than our fellow drivers? *Acta Psychologica, 47,* 143–148. (p. 63)

Swann, W. B., Jr. (1984). Quest for accuracy in person perception: A matter of pragmatics. *Psychological Review, 91,* 457–475. (p. 116)

Swann, W. B., Jr. (1996). *Self-traps: The elusive quest for higher self-esteem.* New York: Freeman. (p. 68)

Swann, W. B., Jr. (1997). The trouble with change: Self-verification and allegiance to the self. *Psychological Science, 8,* 177–180. (p. 68)

Swann, W. B., Jr., Chang-Schneider, C., & Angulo, S. (2007). Self-verification in relationships as an adaptive process. In J. Wood, A. Tesser, & J. Holmes (Eds.) *Self and relationships.* New York: Psychology Press. (pp. 52, 93)

Swann, W. B., Jr., & Gill, M. J. (1997). Confidence and accuracy in person perception: Do we know what we think we know about our relationship partners? *Journal of Personality and Social Psychology, 73,* 747–757. (p. 90)

Swann, W. B., Jr., Gómez, Á., Seyle, D. C., Morales, J. F., & Huici, C. (2009). Identity fusion: The interplay of personal and social identities in extreme group behavior. *Journal of Personality and Social Psychology, 96,* 995–1011. (p. 408)

Swann, W. B., Jr., & Predmore, S. C. (1985). Intimates as agents of social support: Sources of consolation or despair? *Journal of Personality and Social Psychology, 49,* 1609–1617. (p. 388)

Swann, W. B., Jr., & Read, S. J. (1981). Acquiring self-knowledge: The search for feedback that fits. *Journal of Personality and Social Psychology, 41,* 1119–1128. (p. 93)

Swann, W. B., Jr., Rentfrow, P. J., & Gosling, S. D. (2003). The precarious couple effect: Verbally inhibited men 1 critical, disinhibited women = bad chemistry. *Journal of Personality and Social Psychology, 85,* 1095–1106. (p. 93)

Swann, W. B., Jr., Stein-Seroussi, A., & Giesler, R. B. (1992a). Why people self-verify. *Journal of Personality and Social Psychology, 62,* 392–401. (p. 93)

Swann, W. B., Jr., Stein-Seroussi, A., & McNulty, S. E. (1992b). Outcasts in a white lie society. The enigmatic worlds of people with negative self-conceptions. *Journal of Personality and Social Psychology, 62,* 618–624. (p. 93)

Swann, W. B., Jr., Wenzlaff, R. M., Krull, D. S., & Pelham, B. W. (1991). Seeking truth, reaping despair: Depression, self-verification and selection of relationship partners. *Journal of Abnormal Psychology, 101,* 293–306. (pp. 93, 374)

Swap, W. C. (1977). Interpersonal attraction and repeated exposure to rewarders and punishers. *Personality and Social Psychology Bulletin, 3,* 248–251. (p. 357)

Sweeney, J. (1973). An experimental investigation of the free rider problem. *Social Science Research, 2,* 277–292. (p. 240)

Sweeney, P. D., Anderson, K., & Bailey, S. (1986). Attributional style in depression: A meta-analytic review. *Journal of Personality and Social Psychology, 50,* 947–991. (p. 476)

Sweeny, K., Melnyk, D., Miller, W., & Shepperd, J. A. (2010). Information avoidance: Who, what, when, and why. *Review of General Psychology, 14,* 340–353. (p. 140)

Swim, J., Borgida, E., Maruyama, G., & Myers, D. G. (1989). Joan McKay vs. John McKay: Do gender stereotypes bias evaluations? *Psychological Bulletin, 105,* 409–429. (p. 435)

Swim, J. K. (1994). Perceived versus meta-analytic effect sizes: An assessment of the accuracy of gender stereotypes. *Journal of Personality and Social Psychology, 66,* 21–36. (p. 434)

Swim, J. K., Aikin, J. K., Hall, W. S., & Hunter, B. A. (1995). Sexism and racism: Old-fashioned and modern prejudices. *Journal of Personality and Social Psychology, 68,* 199–214. (pp. 400, 433)

Swim, J. K., & Cohen, L. L. (1997). Overt, covert, and subtle sexism. *Psychology of Women Quarterly, 21,* 103–118. (p. 433)

Swim, J. K., Cohen, L. L., & Hyers, L. L. (1998). Experiencing everyday prejudice and discrimination. In J. K. Swim & C. Stangor (Eds.), *Prejudice: The target's perspective.* San Diego: Academic Press. (p. 439)

Swim, J. K., & Hyers, L. L. (1998). Excuse me—What did you just say?!: Women's public and private reactions to sexist remarks. *Journal of Experimental Social Psychology,* in press. (p. 212)

Swindle, R., Jr., Heller, K., Bescosolido, B., & Kikuzawa, S. (2000). Responses to nervous breakdowns in America over a 40-year period: Mental health policy implications. *American Psychologist, 55,* 740–749. (p. 479)

Tafarodi, R. W., Lo, C., Yamaguchi, S., Lee, W. W.-S., & Katsura, H. (2004). The inner self in three countries. *Journal of Cross-Cultural Psychology, 35,* 97–117. (p. 44)

Tajfel, H. (1970, November). Experiments in intergroup discrimination. *Scientific American,* 96–102. (p. 410)

Tajfel, H. (1981). *Human groups and social categories: Studies in social psychology.* London: Cambridge University Press. (pp. 11, 410)

Tajfel, H. (1982). Social psychology of intergroup relations. *Annual Review of Psychology, 33,* 1–39. (p. 410)

Tajfel, H., & Billig, M. (1974). Familiarity and categorization in intergroup behavior. *Journal of Experimental Social Psychology, 10,* 159–170. (p. 410)

Takooshian, H., & Bodinger, H. (1982). Bystander indifference to street crime. In L. Savitz & N. Johnston (Eds.), *Contemporary criminology.* New York: Wiley. (p. 293)

Tang, S-H., & Hall, V. C. (1995). The overjustification effect: A meta-analysis. *Applied Cognitive Psychology, 9,* 365–404. (p. 149)

Tanner, R. J., Ferraro, R., Chartrand, T. L., Bettman, J. R., & van Baaren, R. (2008). Of chameleons and consumption: The impact of mimicry on choice and preferences. *Journal of Consumer Research, 34,* 754–766. (p. 199)

Tapp, J. L. (1980). Psychological and policy perspectives on the law: Reflections on a decade. *Journal of Social Issues, 36*(2), 165–192. (p. 510)

Tarmann, A. (2002, May/June). Out of the closet and onto the Census long form. *Population Today, 30,* 1, 6. (p. 421)

Tarrant, M., Dazeley, S., & Cottom, T. (2009). Social categorization and empathy for outgroup members. *British Journal of Social Psychology, 48,* 427–446. (p. 284)

Taubes, G. (1992). Violence epidemiologists tests of hazards of gun ownership. *Science, 258,* 213–215. (p. 327)

Taylor, D. A., Gould, R. J., & Brounstein, P. J. (1981). Effects of personalistic self-disclosure. *Personality and Social Psychology Bulletin, 7,* 487–492. (p. 387)

Taylor, D. G., Sheatsley, P. B., & Greeley, A. M. (1978). Attitudes toward racial integration. *Scientific American, 238*(6), 42–49. (p. 418)

Taylor, D. M., & Doria, J. R. (1981). Self-serving and group-serving bias in attribution. *Journal of Social Psychology, 113,* 201–211. (p. 70)

Taylor, D. M., Wright, S. C., Moghaddam, F. M., & Lalonde, R. N. (1990). The personal/group discrimination discrepancy: Perceiving my group, but not myself, to be a target for discrimination. *Personality and Social Psychology Bulletin, 16,* 254–262. (p. 448)

Taylor, L. S., Fiore, A. T., Mendelsohn, G. A., & Cheshire, C. (2011). "Out of my league": A real-world test of the matching hypothesis. *Personality and Social Psychology Bulletin, 37,* 942–954. (p. 361)

Taylor, S. E. (1981). A categorization approach to stereotyping. In D. L. Hamilton (Ed.), *Cognitive processes in stereotyping and intergroup behavior.* Hillsdale, NJ: Erlbaum. (p. 418)

Taylor, S. E. (1989). *Positive illusions: Creative self-deception and the healthy mind.* New York: Basic Books. (p. 476)

Taylor, S. E., Crocker, J., Fiske, S. T., Sprinzen, M., & Winkler, J. D. (1979). The generalizability of salience effects. *Journal of Personality and Social Psychology, 37,* 357–368. (p. 420)

Taylor, S. E., & Fiske, S. T. (1978). Salience, attention, and attribution: Top of the head phenomena. In L. Berkowitz (Ed.), *Advances in experimental social Psychology* (Vol. 11). New York: Academic Press. (p. 420)

Taylor, S. E., Lerner, J. S., Sherman, D. K., Sage, R. M., & McDowell, N. K. (2003). Are self-enhancing cognitions associated with healthy or unhealthy biological profiles? *Journal of Personality and Social Psychology, 85,* 605. (p. 68)

Taylor, S. E., Repetti, R. L., & Seeman, T. (1997). Health psychology: What is an unhealthy environment and how does it get under the skin? *Annual Review of Psychology, 48,* 411–447. (p. 488)

Taylor, S. E., Saphire-Bernstein, S., & Seeman, T. E. (2010). Are plasma oxytocin in women and plasma vasopressin in men biomarkers of distressed pair-bond relationships? *Psychological Science, 21,* 3–7. (p. 380)

Taylor, S. P., & Chermack, S. T. (1993). Alcohol, drugs and human physical aggression. *Journal of Studies on Alcohol,* Supplement No. 11, 78–88. (p. 314)

Tedeschi, J. T., Nesler, M., & Taylor, E. (1987). *Misattribution and the bogus pipeline: A test of dissonance and impression management theories.* Paper presented at the American Psychological Association convention. (p. 139)

Teger, A. I. (1980). *Too much invested to quit.* New York: Pergamon Press. (p. 457)

Teigen, K. H. (1986). Old truths or fresh insights? A study of students' evaluations of proverbs. *British Journal of Social Psychology, 25,* 43–50. (p. 15)

Teigen, K. H., Evensen, P. C., Samoilow, D. K., & Vatne, K. B. (1999). Good luck and bad luck: How to tell the difference. *European Journal of Social Psychology, 29,* 981–1010. (p. 97)

Telch, M. J., Killen, J. D., McAlister, A. L., Perry, C. L., & Maccoby, N. (1981). *Long-term follow-up of a pilot project on smoking prevention with adolescents.* Paper presented at the American Psychological Association convention. (p. 189)

Tennen, H., & Affleck, G. (1987). The costs and benefits of optimistic explanations and dispositional optimism. *Journal of Personality, 55,* 377–393. (p. 486)

Tenney, E. R., MacCoun, R. J., Spellman, B. A., & Hastie, R. (2007). Calibration trumps confidence as a basis for witness credibility. *Psychological Science, 18,* 46–50. (p. 499)

Tennov, D. (1979). *Love and limerence: The experience of being in love.* New York: Stein and Day, 22. (p. 278)

Tepperman, L., & Curtis, J. (1995). A life satisfaction scale for use with national adult samples from the USA, Canada and Mexico. *Social Indicators Research, 35,* 255–270. (p. 492)

Tesser, A. (1988). Toward a self-evaluation maintenance model of social behavior. In L. Berkowitz (Ed.), *Advances in experimental social psychology,* Vol. 21. San Diego, CA: Academic Press. (p. 52)

Tesser, A., Martin, L., & Mendolia, M. (1995). The impact of thought on attitude extremity and attitude-behavior consistency. In R. E. Petty and J. A Krosnick (Eds.), *Attitude strength: Antecedents and consequences.* Hillsdale, NJ: Erlbaum. (p. 252)

Tesser, A., Millar, M., & Moore, J. (1988). Some affective consequences of social comparison and reflection processes: The pain and pleasure of being close. *Journal of Personality and Social Psychology, 54,* 49–61. (p. 410)

Tesser, A., Rosen, S., & Conlee, M. C. (1972). News valence and available recipient as determinants of news transmission. *Sociometry, 35,* 619–628. (p. 132)

Tetlock, P. E. (1983). Accountability and complexity of thought. *Journal of Personality and Social Psychology, 45,* 74–83. (p. 132)

Tetlock, P. E. (1985). Integrative complexity of American and Soviet foreign policy rhetoric: A time-series analysis. *Journal of Personality and Social Psychology, 49,* 1565–1585. (p. 465)

Tetlock, P. E. (1998). Close-call counterfactuals and belief-system defenses: I was not almost wrong but I was almost right. *Journal of Personality and Social Psychology, 75,* 639–652. (p. 93)

Tetlock, P. E. (1999). Theory-driven reasoning about plausible pasts and probable futures in world politics: Are we prisoners of our preconceptions? *American Journal of Political Science, 43,* 335–366. (p. 93)

Tetlock, P. E. (2005). *Expert political judgment: How good is it? How can we know?* Princeton, NJ: Princeton University Press. (p. 93)

Tetlock, P. E., Peterson, R. S., McGuire, C., Chang, S., & Feld, P. (1992). Assessing political group dynamics: A test of the groupthink model. *Journal of Personality and Social Psychology, 63,* 403–425. (p. 259)

t'Hart, P. (1998). Preventing groupthink revisited: Evaluating and reforming groups in government. *Organizational Behavior and Human Decision Processes, 73,* 306–326. (p. 259)

Thomas, G. C., & Batson, C. D. (1981). Effect of helping under normative pressure on self-perceived altruism. *Social Psychology Quarterly, 44,* 127–131. (p. 306)

Thomas, G. C., Batson, C. D., & Coke, J. S. (1981). Do Good Samaritans discourage helpfulness? Self-perceived altruism after exposure to highly helpful others. *Journal of Personality and Social Psychology, 40,* 194–200. (p. 306)

Thompson, L. (1990). An examination of naive and experienced negotiators. *Journal of Personality and Social Psychology, 59,* 82–90. (p. 463)

Thompson, L. (1998). *The mind and heart of the negotiator.* Upper Saddle River, NJ: Prentice-Hall. (p. 463)

Thompson, L., Valley, K. L., & Kramer, R. M. (1995). The bittersweet feeling of success: An examination of social perception in negotiation. *Journal of Experimental Social Psychology, 31,* 467–492. (p. 463)

Thompson, L. L., & Crocker, J. (1985). *Prejudice following threat to the self-concept. Effects of performance expectations and attributions.* Unpublished manuscript, Northwestern University. (p. 412)

Thompson, W. C., Cowan, C. L., & Rosenhan, D. L. (1980). Focus of attention mediates the impact of negative affect on altruism. *Journal of Personality and Social Psychology, 38,* 291–300. (p. 277)

Thompson, W. C., Fong, G. T., & Rosenhan, D. L. (1981). Inadmissible evidence and juror verdicts. *Journal of Personality and Social Psychology, 40,* 453–463. (p. 511)

Thornton, B., & Maurice, J. (1997). Physique contrast effect: Adverse impact of idealized body images for women. *Sex Roles, 37,* 433–439. (p. 367)

Tice, D. M., Butler, J. L., Muraven, M. B., & Stillwell, A. M. (1995). When modesty prevails: Differential favorability of self-presentation to friends and strangers. *Journal of Personality and Social Psychology, 69,* 1120–1138. (p. 72)

Tideman, S. (2003). Announcement of Operationalizing Gross National Happiness conference, February 18–20, 2004. Distributed via the Internet. (p. 527)

Time. (1992, March 30). The not so merry wife of Windsor, 38–39. (p. 391)

Timmerman, T. A. (2007). "It was a thought pitch": Personal, situational, and target influences on hit-by-pitch events across time. *Journal of Applied Psychology, 92,* 876–884. (p. 317)

Tindale, R. S., Davis, J. H., Vollrath, D. A., Nagao, D. H., & Hinsz, V. B. (1990). Asymmetrical social influence in freely interacting groups: A test of three models. *Journal of Personality and Social Psychology, 58,* 438–449. (p. 510)

Todorov, A., Mandisodza, A. N., Goren, A., & Hall, C. C. (2005). Inferences of competence from faces predict election outcomes. *Science, 308,* 1623–1626. (p. 360)

Tomasello, M. (2009). *Why we cooperate.* Boston: MIT Press. (p. 288)

Tormala, Z. L., Briñol, P., & Petty, R. E. (2006). When credibility attacks: The reverse impact of source credibility on persuasion. *Journal of Experimental Social Psychology, 42,* 684–691. (p. 164)

Toronto News (1977, July 26). (p. 60)

Totterdell, P., Kellett, S., Briner, R. B., & Teuchmann, K. (1998). Evidence of mood linkage in work groups. *Journal of Personality and Social Psychology, 74,* 1504–1515. (p. 199)

Towles-Schwen, T., & Fazio, R. H. (2006). Automatically activated racial attitudes as predictors of the success of interracial roommate relationships. *Journal of Experimental Social Psychology, 42,* 698–705. (p. 126)

Trautwein, U, & Lüdtke, O. (2006). Self-esteem, academic self-concept, and achievement: How the learning environment moderates the dynamics of self-concept. *Journal of Personality and Social Psychology, 90,* 334–349. (p. 20)

Travis, L. E. (1925). The effect of a small audience upon eye-hand coordination. *Journal of Abnormal and Social Psychology, 20,* 142–146. (p. 234)

Trawalter, S., & Richeson, J. A. (2006). Regulatory focus and executive function after interracial interactions. *Journal of Experimental Social Psychology, 42,* 406–412. (p. 448)

Trawalter, S., Todd, A. R., Baird, A. A., & Richeson, J. A. (2008). Attending to threat: Race-based patterns of selective attention. *Journal of Experimental Social Psychology, 44,* 1322–1327. (p. 432)

Trewin, D. (2001). *Australian social trends 2001.* Canberra: Australian Bureau of Statistics. (p. 331)

Triandis, H. C. (1982). *Incongruence between intentions and behavior: A review.* Paper presented at the American Psychological Association convention. (p. 124)

Triandis, H. C. (1994). *Culture and social behavior.* New York: McGraw-Hill. (pp. 41, 391)

Triandis, H. C. (2000). Culture and conflict. *International Journal of Psychology, 55,* 145–152. (p. 45)

Triandis, H. C., Bontempo, R., Villareal, M. J., Asai, M., & Lucca, N. (1988). Individualism and collectivism: Cross-cultural perspectives on self-ingroup relationships. *Journal of Personality and Social Psychology, 54,* 323–338. (p. 381)

Triplett, N. (1898). The dynamogenic factors in pacemaking and competition. *American Journal of Psychology, 9,* 507–533. (p. 233)

Trolier, T. K., & Hamilton, D. L. (1986). Variables influencing judgments of correlational relations. *Journal of Personality and Social Psychology, 50,* 879–888. (p. 97)

Trost, M. R., Maass, A., & Kenrick, D. T. (1992). Minority influence: Personal relevance biases cognitive processes and reverses private acceptance. *Journal of Experimental Social Psychology, 28,* 234–254. (p. 267)

Trzesniewski, K. H., Donnellan, M. B., Moffitt, T. E., Robins, R. W., Poulton, R., & Caspi, A. (2006). Low self-esteem during adolescence predicts poor health, criminal behavior, and limited economic prospects during adulthood. *Developmental Psychology, 42,* 381–390. (pp. 53, 55)

Tsang, J-A. (2002). Moral rationalization and the integration of situational factors and psychological processes in immoral behavior. *Review of General Psychology, 6,* 25–50. (p. 213)

Turner, C. W., Hesse, B. W., & Peterson-Lewis, S. (1986). Naturalistic studies of the long-term effects of television violence. *Journal of Social Issues, 42*(3), 51–74. (p. 332)

Turner, J. C. (1981). The experimental social psychology of intergroup behaviour. In J. Turner & H. Giles (Eds.), *Intergroup behaviour.* Oxford, England: Blackwell. (p. 408)

Turner, J. C. (1984). Social identification and psychological group formation. In H. Tajfel (Ed.), *The social dimensions: European developments in social psychology* (Vol. 2). London: Cambridge University Press. (pp. 11, 410)

Turner, J. C. (1987). *Rediscovering the social group: A self-categorization theory.* New York: Basil Blackwell. (p. 233)

Turner, J. C. (2000). Social identity. In A. E. Kazdin (Ed.), *Encyclopedia of Psychology, 7.* Washington, DC: American Psychological Association. (p. 408)

Turner, M. E., & Pratkanis, A. R. (1993). Effects of preferential and meritorious selection on performance: An examination of intuitive and self-handicapping perspectives. *Personality and Social Psychology Bulletin, 19,* 47–58. (p. 71)

Turner, M. E., & Pratkanis, A. R. (1994). Social identity maintenance prescriptions for preventing groupthink: Reducing identity protection and enhancing intellectual conflict. *International Journal of Conflict Management, 5,* 254–270. (p. 256)

Turner, M. E., & Pratkanis, A. R. (1997). Mitigating groupthink by stimulating constructive conflict. In C. K. W. De Dreu & E. Van de Vliert (Eds.), *Using conflict in organizations.* London: Sage. (p. 259)

Turner, M. E., Pratkanis, A. R., Probasco, P., & Leve, C. (1992). Threat cohesion, and group effectiveness: Testing a social identity maintenance perspective on groupthink. *Journal of Personality and Social Psychology, 63,* 781–796. (p. 256)

Turner, N., Barling, J., Epitropaki, O., Butcher, V., & Milner, C. (2002). Transformational leadership and moral reasoning. *Journal of Applied Psychology, 87,* 304. (p. 265)

TV Guide (1977, January 26), 5–10. (p. 332)

Tversky, A., & Kahneman, D. (1973). Availability: A neuristic for judging frequency and probability. *Cognitive Psychology, 5,* 207–302. (p. 95)

Tversky, A., & Kahneman, D. (1974). Judgment under uncertainty: Heuristics and biases. *Science, 185,* 1123–1131. (p. 98)

Tversky, A., & Kahneman, D. (1983). Extensional versus intuitive reasoning: The conjunction fallacy in probability judgment. *Psychological Review, 90,* 293–315. (p. 95)

Twenge, J. M. (2006). *Generation Me.* New York: Free Press. (p. 55)

Twenge, J. M., Baumeister, R. F., Tice, D. M., & Stucke, T. S. (2001). If you can't join them, beat them: Effects of social exclusion on aggressive behavior. *Journal of Personality and Social Psychology, 81,* 1058–1069. (p. 353)

Twenge, J. M., & Campbell, W. K. (2008). Increases in positive self-views among high school students: Birth cohort changes in anticipated performance, self-satisfaction, self-liking, and self-competence. *Psychological Science, 19,* 1082–1086. (p. 64)

Twenge, J. M., Catanese, K. R., & Baumeister, R. F. (2002). Social exclusion causes self-defeating behavior. *Journal of Personality and Social Psychology, 83,* 606–615. (p. 353)

Twenge, J. M., Catanese, K. R., & Baumeister, R. F. (2003). Social exclusion and the deconstructed state: Time perception, meaninglessness, lethargy, lack of emotion, and self-awareness. *Journal of Personality and Social Psychology, 85,* 409–423. (p. 352)

Twenge, J. M., & Foster, J. D. (2008). Mapping the scale of the narcissism epidemic: Increases in narcissism 2002–2007 within ethnic groups. *Journal of Research in Personality, 42,* 1619–1622. (p. 55)

Twenge, J. M., & Foster, J. D. (2010). Birth cohort increases in narcissistic personality traits among American college students, 1982–2009. *Social Psychological and Personality Science, 1,* 99–106. (p. 55)

Twenge, J. M., Konrath, S., Foster, J. D., Campbell, W. K., & Bushman, B. J. (2008). Egos inflating over time: A cross-temporal meta-analysis of the Narcissistic Personality Inventory. *Journal of Personality, 76,* 875–902. (p. 55)

Twenge, J. M., Zhang, L., Catanese, K. R., Dolan-Pascoe, B., Lyche, L. F., &

Baumeister, R. F. (2007). Replenishing connectedness: Reminders of social activity reduce aggression after social exclusion. *British Journal of Social Psychology, 46,* 205–224. (p. 353)

Tyler, T. R., & Lind, E. A. (1990). Intrinsic versus community-based justice models: When does group membership matter? *Journal of Social Issues, 46,* 83–94. (p. 303)

Tyler, T. R., Rasinski, K. A., & Spodick, N. (1985). Influence of voice on satisfaction with leaders: Exploring the meaning of process control. *Journal of Personality and Social Psychology, 48,* 72–81. (p. 265)

Tzeng, M. (1992). The effects of socioeconomic heterogamy and changes on marital dissolution for first marriages. *Journal of Marriage and the Family, 54,* 609–619. (p. 392)

Uchino, B. N., Cacioppo, J. T., & Kiecolt-Glaser, J. K. (1996). The relationship between social support and physiological processes: A review with emphasis on underlying mechanisms and implications for health. *Psychological Bulletin, 119,* 488–531. (p. 488)

Uleman, J. S. (1989). A framework for thinking intentionally about unintended thoughts. In J. S. Uleman & J. A. Bargh (Eds.), *Unintended thought: The limits of awareness, intention, and control.* New York: Guilford. (p. 103)

Unger, R. K. (1979). *Whom does helping help?* Paper presented at the Eastern Psychological Association convention, April. (p. 275)

Unger, R. K. (1985). Epistomological consistency and its scientific implications. *American Psychologist, 40,* 1413–1414. (p. 12)

United Nations (UN). (1991). *The world's women 1970–1990: Trends and statistics.* New York: United Nations. (pp. 132, 433, 436)

United Nations (UN). (2006). *Ending violence against women: From words to action.* Study of the Secretary-General. New York: United Nations (www.un.org). (p. 436)

Unkelbach, C., Forgas, J. P., & Denson, T. F. (2008). The turban effect: The influence of Muslim headgear and induced affect on aggressive responses in the shooter bias paradigm. *Journal of Experimental Social Psychology, 44,* 1409–1413. (p. 432)

Unkelbach, C., & Memmert, D. (2010). Crowd noise as a cue in referee decisions contributes to the home advantage.

Journal of Sport & Exercise Psychology, 32, 483–498. (p. 202)

Väänänen, A., Buunk, B. P., Kivimäki, M., Pentti, J., & Vahtera, J. (2005). When it is better to give than to receive: Long-term health effects of perceived reciprocity in support exchange. *Journal of Personality and Social Psychology, 89,* 176. (p. 488)

Vaillant, G. E. (1977). *Adaptation to life.* Boston: Little, Brown. (p. 85)

Vaillant, G. E. (1997). *Report on distress and longevity.* Paper presented to the American Psychiatric Association convention. (p. 484)

Valcour, M. (2007). Work-based resources as moderators of the relationship between work hours and satisfaction with work-family balance. *Journal of Applied Psychology, 92,* 1512–1523. (p. 58)

Valdesolo, P., & DeSteno, D. (2007). Moral hypocrisy: Social groups and the flexibility of virtue. *Psychological Science, 18,* 689–690. (p. 123)

Valdesolo, P., & DeSteno, D. (2008). The duality of virtue: Deconstructing the moral hypocrite. *Journal of Experimental Social Psychology, 44,* 1334–1338. (p. 123)

Valentine, T., & Mesout, J. (2009). Eyewitness identification under stress in the London Dungeon. *Applied Cognitive Psychology, 23,* 151–161. (p. 499)

Valentine, T., Pickering, A., & Darling, S. (2003). Characteristics of eyewitness identification that predict the outcome of real lineups. *Applied Cognitive Psychology, 17,* 969. (p. 503)

Vallone, R. P., Griffin, D. W., Lin, S., & Ross, L. (1990). Overconfident prediction of future actions and outcomes by self and others. *Journal of Personality and Social Psychology, 58,* 582–592. (p. 91)

Vallone, R. P., Ross, L., & Lepper, M. R. (1985). The hostile media phenomenon: Biased perception and perceptions of media bias in coverage of the "Beirut Massacre." *Journal of Personality and Social Psychology, 49,* 577–585. (pp. 80, 81)

van Baaren, R. B., Holland, R. W., Karremans, R. W., & van Knippenberg, A. (2003b). *Mimicry and interpersonal closeness.* Unpublished manuscript, University of Nijmegen. (p. 369)

van Baaren, R. B., Holland, R. W., Kawakami, K., & van Knippenberg, A. (2004). Mimicry and prosocial behavior. *Psychological Science, 15,* 71. (p. 199)

van Baaren, R. B., Holland, R. W., Steenaert, B., & van Knippenberg, A. (2003a). Mimicry for money: Behavioral consequences of imitation. *Journal of Experimental Social Psychology, 39,* 393–398. (p. 369)

Van Boven, L., & Gilovich, T. (2003). To do or to have? That is the question. *Journal of Personality and Social Psychology, 85,* 1193. (p. 524)

Vandello, J. A., Cohen, D., & Ransom, S. (2008). U.S. southern and northern differences in perceptions of norms about aggression: Mechanisms for the perpetuation of a culture of honor. *Journal of Cross-Cultural Psychology, 39,* 162–177. (p. 321)

van der Plight, J., Eise, J. R., & Spears, R. (1987). Comparative judgments and preferences: The influence of the number of response alternatives. *British Journal of Social Psychology, 26,* 269–280. (p. 22)

Vanderslice, V. J., Rice, R. W., & Julian, J. W. (1987). The effects of participation in decision-making on worker satisfaction and productivity: An organizational simulation. *Journal of Applied Social Psychology, 17,* 158–170. (p. 264)

van Dijk, W. W., Finkenauer, C., & Pollmann, M. (2008). The misprediction of emotions in track athletics: Is experience the teacher of all things? *Basic and Applied Social Psychology, 30,* 369–376. (p. 49)

Van Knippenberg, D., & Wilke, H. (1992). Prototypicality of arguments and conformity to ingroup norms. *European Journal of Social Psychology, 22,* 141–155. (p. 165)

Van Lange, P. A. M., & Visser, K. (1999). Locomotion in social dilemmas: How people adapt to cooperative, tit-for-tat, and noncooperative partners. *Journal of Personality and Social Psychology, 77,* 762–773. (p. 468)

Vanman, E. J., Paul, B. Y., Kaplan, D. L., & Miller, N. (1990). Facial electromyography differentiates racial bias in imagined cooperative settings. *Psychophysiology, 27,* 563. (p. 416)

van Straaten, I., Engels, R. C. M. E., Finkenauer, C., & Holland, R. W. (2009). Meeting your match: How attractiveness similarity affects approach behavior in mixed-sex dyads. *Personality and Social Psychology Bulletin, 35,* 685–697. (p. 361)

Van Vugt, M., Van Lange, P. A. M., & Meertens, R. M. (1996). Commuting by car or public transportation? A social dilemma analysis of travel mode judgements. *European Journal of Social Psychology, 26,* 373–395. (p. 459)

Van Yperen, N. W., & Buunk, B. P. (1990). A longitudinal study of equity and satisfaction in intimate relationships. *European Journal of Social Psychology, 20,* 287–309. (p. 386)

Vargas, R. A. (2009, July 6). "City of Heroes" character "Twixt" becomes game's most hated outcast courtesy of Loyola professor. *The Times-Picayune* (www.nola.com). (p. 219)

Vasquez, E. A., Denson, T. F., Pedersen, W. C., Stenstrom, D. M., & Miller, N. (2005). The moderating effect of trigger intensity on triggered displaced aggression. *Journal of Experimental Social Psychology, 41,* 61. (p. 317)

Vaughan, K. B., & Lanzetta, J. T. (1981). The effect of modification of expressive displays on vicarious emotional arousal. *Journal of Experimental Social Psychology, 17,* 16–30. (p. 147)

Vazire, S., & Mehl, M. R. (2008). Knowing me, knowing you: The accuracy and unique predictive validity of self-ratings and other-ratings of daily behavior. *Journal of Personality and Social Psychology, 95,* 1202–1216. (p. 48)

Vega, V., & Malamuth, N. M. (2007). Predicting sexual aggression: The role of pornography in the context of general and specific risk factors. *Aggressive Behavior, 33,* 104–117. (p. 329)

Verkuyten, M., & Yildiz, A. A. (2007). National (dis)identification and ethnic and religious identity: A study among Turkish-Dutch Muslims. *Personality and Social Psychology, 33,* 1448–1462. (p. 409)

Verplanken, B. (1991). Persuasive communication of risk information: A test of cue versus message processing effects in a field experiment. *Personality and Social Psychology Bulletin, 17,* 188–193. (p. 162)

Vescio, T. K., Gervais, S. J., Snyder, M., & Hoover, A. (2005). Power and the creation of patronizing environments: The stereotype-based behaviors of the powerful and their effects on female performance in masculine domains. *Journal of Personality and Social Psychology, 88,* 658–672. (p. 402)

Veysey, B. M., & Messner, S. F. (1999). Further testing of social disorganization theory: An elaboration of Sampson and Groves's "Community structure and crime." *Journal of Research in Crime and Delinquency, 36,* 156–174. (p. 250)

Vidmar, N. (1979). The other issues in jury simulation research. *Law and Human Behavior, 3,* 95–106. (p. 510)

Vidmar, N., & Laird, N. M. (1983). Adversary social roles: Their effects on witnesses' communication of evidence and the assessments of adjudicators. *Journal of Personality and Social Psychology, 44,* 888–898. (p. 502)

Visher, C. A. (1987). Juror decision making: The importance of evidence. *Law and Human Behavior, 11,* 1–17. (p. 498)

Visintainer, M. A., & Seligman, M. E. (1983, July/August). The hope factor. *American Health,* 59–61. (p. 484)

Visintainer, M. A., & Seligman, M. E. P. (1985). *Tumor rejection and early experience of uncontrollable shock in the rat.* Unpublished manuscript, University of Pennsylvania. See also, M. A. Visintainer et al. (1982). Tumor rejection in rats after inescapable versus escapable shock. *Science, 216,* 437–439. (p. 485)

Visser, P. S., & Krosnick, J. A. (1998). Development of attitude strength over the life cycle: Surge and decline. *Journal of Personality and Social Psychology, 75,* 1389. (p. 179)

Visser, P. S., & Mirabile, R. R. (2004). Attitudes in the social context: The impact of social network composition on individual-level attitude strength. *Journal of Personality and Social Psychology, 87,* 779–795. (p. 192)

Vitelli, R. (1988). The crisis issue assessed: An empirical analysis. *Basic and Applied Social Psychology, 9,* 301–309. (p. 27)

Vogel, T., Kutzner, F., Fiedler, K., & Freytag, P. (2010). Exploiting attractiveness in persuasion: Senders' implicit theories about receivers' processing motivation. *Personality and Social Psychology Bulletin, 36,* 830–842. (p. 165)

Vohs, K. D., Baumeister, R. F., & Ciarocco, N. J. (2005). Self-regulation and self-presentation: Regulatory resource depletion impairs impression management and effortful self-presentation depletes regulatory resources. *Journal of Personality and Social Psychology, 88,* 632. (p. 72)

Vohs, K. D., Baumeister, R. F., Schmeichel, B. J., Twenge, J. M., Nelson, N. M., & Tice, D. M. (2008). Making choices impairs subsequent self-control: A limited-resource account of decision making,

self-regulation, and active initiative. *Journal of Personality and Social Psychology, 94,* 883–898. (p. 59)

von Hippel, F. N. (2011, March 22). It could happen here. *New York Times* (www.nytimes.com). (p. 96)

von Hippel, W., Brener, L., & von Hippel, C. (2008). Implicit prejudice toward injecting drug users predicts intentions to change jobs among drug and alcohol nurses. *Psychological Science, 19,* 7–12. (p. 430)

von Hippel, W., Silver, L. A., & Lynch, M. B. (2000). Stereotyping against your will: The role of inhibitory ability in stereotyping and prejudice among the elderly. *Personality and Social Psychology Bulletin, 26,* 523–532. (p. 416)

Vorauer, J. D., Hunter, A. J., Main, K. J., & Roy, S. A. (2000). Meta-stereotype activation: Evidence from indirect measures for specific evaluative concerns experienced by members of dominant groups in intergroup interaction. *Journal of Personality and Social Psychology, 78,* 690–707. (p. 448)

Vorauer, J. D., Main, K. J., & O'Connell, G. B. (1998). How do individuals expect to be viewed by members of lower status groups? Content and implications of meta-stereotypes. *Journal of Personality and Social Psychology, 75,* 917–937. (pp. 440, 448)

Vorauer, J. D., & Miller, D. T. (1997). Failure to recognize the effect of implicit social influence on the presentation of self. *Journal of Personality and Social Psychology, 73,* 281–295. (p. 36)

Vorauer, J. D., & Ratner, R. K. (1996). Who's going to make the first move? Pluralistic ignorance as an impediment to relationship formation. *Journal of Social and Personal Relationships, 13,* 483–506. (p. 253)

Vul, E., & Pashler, H. (2008). Measuring the crowd within: Probabilistic representations within individuals. *Psychological Science, 19,* 646–647. (p. 263)

Wagner, G. (2011, September 7). Going green but getting nowhere. *New York Times* (www.nytimes.com). (p. 520)

Wagner, U., Christ, O., & Pettigrew, T. F. (2008). Prejudice and group-related behavior in Germany. *Journal of Social Issues, 64,* 403–416. (p. 400)

Wagstaff, G. F. (1983). Attitudes to poverty, the Protestant ethic, and political affiliation: A preliminary investigation. *Social*

Behavior and Personality, 11, 45–47. (p. 109)

Walfish, D. (2001). China's census: National count reveals major societal changes. *Science, 292* (5523), 1823. (p. 436)

Walker, L. J., & Frimer, J. A. (2007). Moral personality of brave and caring exemplars. *Journal of Personality and Social Psychology, 93,* 845–860. (p. 299)

Walker, P. M., & Hewstone, M. (2008). The influence of social factors and implicit racial bias on a generalized own-race effect. *Applied Cognitive Psychology, 22,* 441–453. (p. 419)

Walker, R. (2004, December 5). The hidden (in plain sight) persuaders. *New York Times Magazine.* (p. 176)

Wallace, D. S., Paulson, R. M., Lord, C. G., & Bond, C. F., Jr. (2005). Which behaviors do attitudes predict? Meta-analyzing the effects of social pressure and perceived difficulty. *Review of General Psychology, 9,* 214–227. (p. 127)

Wallace, M. (1969, November 25). *New York Times.* (p. 209)

Waller, J. (2002). *Becoming evil: How ordinary people commit genocide and mass killing.* Oxford: Oxford University Press. (pp. 135, 213)

Walster (Hatfield), E. (1965). The effect of self-esteem on romantic liking. *Journal of Experimental Social Psychology, 1,* 184–197. (p. 373)

Walster (Hatfield), E., Aronson, V., Abrahams, D., & Rottman, L. (1966). Importance of physical attractiveness in dating behavior. *Journal of Personality and Social Psychology, 4,* 508–516. (p. 358)

Walster (Hatfield), E., & Festinger, L. (1962). The effectiveness of "overheard" persuasive communications. *Journal of Abnormal and Social Psychology, 65,* 395–402. (p. 164)

Walster (Hatfield), E., Walster, G. W., & Berscheid, E. (1978). *Equity: Theory and research.* Boston: Allyn and Bacon. (p. 460)

Walther, E., Weil, R., & Düsing, J. (2011). The role of evaluative conditioning in attitude formation. *Current Directions in Psychological Science, 20,* 190–196. (p. 161)

Walther, J. B., Van Der Heide, B., Kim, S-Y., Westerman, D., & Tong, S. T. (2008). The role of friends' appearance and behavior on evaluations of individuals on Facebook: Are we known by the company we keep? *Human Communication Research, 34,* 28–49. (p. 72)

Walton, G. M., & Spencer, S. J. (2009). Latent ability: Grades and test scores systematically underestimate the intellectual ability of negatively stereotyped students. *Psychological Science, 20*(9), 1132–1139. (p. 399)

Walum, H., Westberg, L., Heinningsson, S., Neiderhiser, J. M., Reiss, D., Igl, W., Ganiban, J. M., Spotts, E. L., Pedersen, N. L., Eriksson, E., & Lichtenstein, P. (2008). Genetic variation in the vasopressin receptor 1a gene (*AVPR1A*) associates with pair-bonding behavior in humans. *Proceedings of the National Academy of Sciences, 105*, 14153–14156. (pp. 382, 385)

Ward, W. C., & Jenkins, H. M. (1965). The display of information and the judgment of contingency. *Canadian Journal of Psychology, 19*, 231–241. (p. 97)

Warnick, D. H., & Sanders, G. S. (1980). The effects of group discussion on eyewitness accuracy. *Journal of Applied Social Psychology, 10*, 249–259. (p. 261)

Warr, P., & Payne, R. (1982). Experiences of strain and pleasure among British adults. *Social Science and Medicine, 16*, 1691–1697. (p. 487)

Warren, N. C. (2005, March 4). Personal correspondence from founder of eHarmony. com. (p. 369)

Wason, P. C. (1960). On the failure to eliminate hypotheses in a conceptual task. *Quarterly Journal of Experimental Psychology, 12*, 129–140. (p. 93)

Waters, E. A., Klein, W. M. P., Moser, R. P., Yu, M., Waldron, W. R., McNeel, T. S., & Freedman, A. N. (2011). Correlates of unrealistic risk beliefs in a nationally representative sample. *Journal of Behavioral Medicine, 34*, 225–235. (p. 64)

Watkins, E. R. (2008). Constructive and unconstructive repetitive thought. *Psychological Bulletin, 134*, 163–206. (p. 477)

Watson, D. (1982, November). The actor and the observer: How are their perceptions of causality divergent? *Psychological Bulletin, 92*, 682–700. (p. 109)

Watson, R. I., Jr. (1973). Investigation into deindividuation using a cross-cultural survey technique. *Journal of Personality and Social Psychology, 25*, 342–345. (p. 245)

Watt, S. E., & Badger, A. J. (2009). Effects of social belonging on homesickness: An application of the belongingness hypothesis. *Personality and Social Psychology Bulletin, 35*, 516–530. (p. 352)

Watt, S. E., & Larkin, C. (2010). Prejudiced people perceive more community

support for their views: The role of own, media, and peer attitudes in perceived consensus. *Journal of Applied Social Psychology, 40*, 710–731. (p. 65)

Weary, G., & Edwards, J. A. (1994). Social cognition and clinical psychology: Anxiety, depression, and the processing of social information. In R. Wyer & T. Srull (Eds.), *Handbook of social cognition*, vol. 2. Hillsdale, NJ: Erlbaum. (p. 99)

Weary, G., Harvey, J. H., Schwieger, P., Olson, C. T., Perloff, R., & Pritchard, S. (1982). Self-presentation and the moderation of self-serving biases. *Social Cognition, 1*, 140–159. (p. 72)

Webb, T. L., & Sheeran, P. (2006). Does changing behavioral intentions engender behavior change? A meta-analysis of the experimental evidence. *Psychological Bulletin, 132*, 249–268. (p. 127)

Weber, A. L., & Harvey, J. H. (1994). *Perspective on close relationships*. Boston, MA: Allyn & Bacon, Pearson Education. (p. 388)

Weber, B., & Hertel, G. (2007). Motivation gains of inferior group members: A meta-analytical review. *Journal of Personality and Social Psychology, 93*, 973–993. (p. 242)

Weber, N., Brewer, N., Wells, G. L., Semmler, C., & Keast, A. (2004). Eyewitness identification accuracy and response latency: The unruly 10–12-second rule. *Journal of Experimental Psychology: Applied, 10*, 139. (p. 503)

Wegner, D. M., & Erber, R. (1992). The hyperaccessibility of suppressed thoughts. *Journal of Personality and Social Psychology, 63*, 903–912. (p. 416)

Wehr, P. (1979). *Conflict regulation*. Boulder, CO: Westview Press. (p. 466)

Weiner, B. (1980). A cognitive (attribution)-emotion-action model of motivated behavior: An analysis of judgments of help-giving. *Journal of Personality and Social Psychology, 39*, 186–200. (p. 282)

Weiner, B. (1981). *The emotional consequences of causal ascriptions*. Unpublished manuscript, UCLA. (p. 317)

Weiner, B. (1985). "Spontaneous" causal thinking. *Psychological Bulletin, 97*, 74–84. (p. 101)

Weiner, B. (1995). *Judgments of responsibility: A foundation for a theory of social conduct*. New York: Guilford. (p. 102)

Weiner, B. (2008). Reflections on the history of attribution theory and research: People, personalities, publications, problems. *Social Psychology, 39*, 151–156. (p. 101)

Weiner, B. (2010). The development of an attribution-based theory of motivation: A history of ideas. *Educational Psychologist, 45*, 28–36. (p. 101)

Weiner, B., Osborne, D., & Rudoph, U. (2011). An attributional analysis of reactions to poverty: The political ideology of the giver and the perceived morality of the receiver. *Personality and Social Psychology Review, 15*, 199–213. (p. 109)

Weinstein, N., & Ryan, R. M. (2010). When helping helps: Autonomous motivation for prosocial behavior and its influence on well-being for the helper and recipient. *Journal of Personality and Social Psychology, 98*, 222–244. (p. 275)

Weinstein, N. D. (1980). Unrealistic optimism about future life events. *Journal of Personality and Social Psychology, 39*, 806–820. (p. 63)

Weinstein, N. D. (1982). Unrealistic optimism about susceptibility to health problems. *Journal of Behavioral Medicine, 5*, 441–460. (p. 63)

Weis, R., & Cerankosky, B. C. (2010). Effects of video-game ownership on young boys' academic and behavioral functioning: A randomized, controlled study. *Psychological Science, 21*, 463–470. (p. 341)

Weiss, J., & Brown, P. (1976). *Self-insight error in the explanation of mood*. Unpublished manuscript, Harvard University. (p. 47)

Wells, G. L. (1984). The psychology of lineup identifications. *Journal of Applied Social Psychology, 14*, 89–103. (p. 504)

Wells, G. L. (1986). Expert psychological testimony: Empirical and conceptual analyses of effects. *Law and Human Behavior, 10*, 83–95. (p. 505)

Wells, G. L. (1992). Naked statistical evidence of liability: Is subjective probability enough? *Journal of Personality and Social Psychology, 62*, 739–752. (p. 508)

Wells, G. L. (1993). What do we know about eyewitness identification? *American Psychologist, 48*, 553–571. (p. 504)

Wells, G. L. (2005). Helping experimental psychology affect legal policy. In N. Brewer, & K. D. Williams (Eds.), *Psychology and law: An empirical perspective*. New York: Guilford Press. 483–500. (p. 504)

Wells, G. L. (2008). Field experiments on eyewitness identification: Towards a better understanding of pitfalls and prospects. *Law and Human Behavior, 32*, 6–10. (p. 504)

Wells, G. L., Ferguson, T. J., & Lindsay, R. C. L. (1981). The tractability of eyewitness confidence and its implications for triers of fact. *Journal of Applied Psychology, 66,* 688–696. (p. 502)

Wells, G. L., & Leippe, M. R. (1981). How do triers of fact enter the accuracy of eyewitness identification? Memory for peripheral detail can be misleading. *Journal of Applied Psychology, 66,* 682–687. (p. 498)

Wells, G. L., Lindsay, R. C. L., & Ferguson, T. (1979). Accuracy, confidence, and juror perceptions in eyewitness identification. *Journal of Applied Psychology, 64,* 440–448. (p. 498)

Wells, G. L., Lindsay, R. C. L., & Tousignant, J. P. (1980). Effects of expert psychological advice on human performance in judging the validity of eyewitness testimony. *Law and Human Behavior, 4,* 275–285. (p. 498)

Wells, G. L., Memon, A., & Penrod, S. D. (2006). Eyewitness evidence: Improving its probative value. *Psychological Science in the Public Interest, 7,* 45–75. (p. 499)

Wells, G. L., & Murray, D. M. (1983). What can psychology say about the Neil v. Biggers criteria for judging eyewitness accuracy? *Journal of Applied Psychology, 68,* 347–362. (p. 499)

Wells, G. L., Olson, E. A., & Charman, S. D. (2002). The confidence of eyewitnesses in their identifications from lineups. *Current Directions in Psychological Science, 11,* 151–154. (p. 499)

Wells, G. L., & Olson, E. A. (2003). Eyewitness testimony. *Annual Review of Psychology, 54,* 277–295. (p. 504)

Wells, G. L., & Petty, R. E. (1980). The effects of overt head movements on persuasion: Compatibility and incompatibility of responses. *Basic and Applied Social Psychology, 1,* 219–230. (p. 148)

Wells, G. L., Steblay, N. K., & Sysart, J. E. (2011). *A test of the simultaneous vs. sequential lineup methods: An initial report of the AJS eyewitness identification field studies.* Des Moines, IA: American Judicature Society. (p. 504)

Wells, G. L., & Turtle, J. W. (1987). Eyewitness testimony research: Current knowledge and emergent controversies. *Canadian Journal of Behavioral Science, 19,* 363–388. (p. 505)

Wener, R., Frazier, W., & Farbstein, J. (1987, June). Building better jails. *Psychology Today,* 40–49. (p. 58)

Wenzlaff, R. M., & Prohaska, M. L. (1989). When misery prefers company: Depression, attributions, and responses to others' moods. *Journal of Experimental Social Psychology, 25,* 220–233. (p. 371)

Werner, C. M., Stoll, R., Birch, P., & White, P. H. (2002). Clinical validation and cognitive elaboration: Signs that encourage sustained recycling. *Basic and Applied Social Psychology, 24,* 185–203. (p. 171)

West, S. G., & Brown, T. J. (1975). Physical attractiveness, the severity of the emergency and helping: A field experiment and interpersonal simulation. *Journal of Experimental Social Psychology, 11,* 531–538. (p. 282)

West, S. G., Whitney, G., & Schnedler, R. (1975). Helping a motorist in distress: The effects of sex, race, and neighborhood. *Journal of Personality and Social Psychology, 31,* 691–698. (p. 282)

Weyant, J. M. (1984). Applying social psychology to induce charitable donations. *Journal of Applied Social Psychology, 14,* 441–447. (p. 303)

Weyant, J. M., & Smith, S. L. (1987). Getting more by asking for less: The effects of request size on donations of charity. *Journal of Applied Social Psychology, 17,* 392–400. (p. 303)

Whatley, M. A., Webster, J. M., Smith, R. H., & others. (1999). The effect of a favor on public and private compliance: How internalized is the norm of reciprocity? *Basic and Applied Social Psychology, 21,* 251–261. (p. 281)

Wheeler, L., Koestner, R., & Driver, R. E. (1982). Related attributes in the choice of comparison others: It's there, but it isn't all there is. *Journal of Experimental Social Psychology, 18,* 489–500. (p. 40)

White, G. L. (1980). Physical attractiveness and courtship progress. *Journal of Personality and Social Psychology, 39,* 660–668. (p. 361)

White, G. L., & Kight, T. D. (1984). Misattribution of arousal and attraction: Effects of salience of explanations for arousal. *Journal of Experimental Social Psychology, 20,* 55–64. (p. 378)

White, K., & Lehman, D. R. (2005). Culture and social comparison seeking: The role of self-motives. *Personality and Social Psychology Bulletin, 31,* 232. (p. 45)

White, M. J., & Gerstein, L. H. (1987). Helping: The influence of anticipated social sanctions and self-monitoring. *Journal of Personality, 55,* 41–54. (p. 300)

Whitechurch, E. R., Wilson, T. D., & Gilbert, D. T. (2011). "He loves me, he loves me not . . ."; Uncertainty can increase romantic attraction. *Psychological Science, 22,* 172–175. (p. 372)

Whitley, B. E., Jr. (1987). The effects of discredited eyewitness testimony: A meta-analysis. *Journal of Social Psychology, 127,* 209–214. (p. 498)

Whitman, R. M., Kramer, M., & Baldridge, B. (1963). Which dream does the patient tell? *Archives of General Psychology, 8,* 277–282. (p. 474)

Whittaker, J. O., & Meade, R. D. (1967). Social pressure in the modification and distortion of judgment: A cross-cultural study. *International Journal of Psychology, 2,* 109–113. (p. 223)

Whooley, M. A., de Jonge, P., Vittinghoff, E., Otte, C., Moos, R., Carney, R. M., Ali, S., Dowray, S., Na, B., Feldman, M. C., Schiller, N. B., & Browner, W. S. (2008). Depressive symptoms, health behaviors, and risk of cardiovascular events in patients with coronary heart disease. *Journal of the American Medical Association, 300,* 2379–2388. (p. 486)

Whyte, G. (1993). Escalating commitment in individual and group decision making: A prospect theory approach. *Organizational Behavior and Human Decision Processes, 54,* 430–455. (p. 250)

Wicker, A. W. (1969). Attitudes versus actions: The relationship of verbal and overt behavioral responses to attitude objects. *Journal of Social Issues, 25*(4), 41–78. (p. 123)

Widom, C. S. (1989). Does violence beget violence? A critical examination of the literature. *Psychological Bulletin, 106,* 3–28. (p. 321)

Wiebe, D. J. (2003). Homicide and suicide risks associated with firearms in the home: A national case-control study. *Annals of Emergency Medicine, 41,* 771–782. (p. 327)

Wiegman, O. (1985). Two politicians in a realistic experiment: Attraction, discrepancy, intensity of delivery, and attitude change. *Journal of Applied Social Psychology, 15,* 673–686. (p. 162)

Wiesel, E. (1985, April 6). The brave Christians who saved Jews from the Nazis. *TV Guide,* 4–6. (p. 274)

Wieselquist, J., Rusbult, C. E., Foster, C. A., & Agnew, C. R. (1999). Commitment, prorelationship behavior, and trust in close relationships. *Journal of Personality and Social Psychology, 77,* 942–966. (p. 386)

Wikipedia. (2008, accessed July 30). Strip search prank call scam (en.wikipedia.org). (p. 208)

Wilder, D. A. (1977). Perception of groups, size of opposition, and social influence. *Journal of Experimental Social Psychology, 13,* 253–268. (p. 215)

Wilder, D. A. (1978). Perceiving persons as a group: Effect on attributions of causality and beliefs. *Social Psychology, 41,* 13–23. (p. 418)

Wilder, D. A. (1981). Perceiving persons as a group: Categorization and intergroup relations. In. D. L. Hamilton (Ed.). *Cognitive processes in stereotyping and intergroup behavior.* Hillsdale, NJ: Lawrence Erlbaum. (p. 410)

Wilder, D. A. (1990). Some determinants of the persuasive power of in-groups and out-groups: Organization of information and attribution of independence. *Journal of Personality and Social Psychology, 59,* 1202–1213. (p. 165)

Wilder, D. A. (1996). Challenging stereotypes about stereotypes. *PsycCRITIQUES, 41,* 429–430. (p. 438)

Wilder, D. A., & Shapiro, P. (1991). Facilitation of outgroup stereotypes by enhanced ingroup identity. *Journal of Experimental Social Psychology, 27,* 431–452. (p. 411)

Wilder, D. A., & Shapiro, P. N. (1989). Role of competition-induced anxiety in limiting the beneficial impact of positive behavior by out-group members. *Journal of Personality and Social Psychology, 56,* 60–69. (p. 437)

Wilkes, J. (1987, June). Murder in mind. *Psychology Today,* 27–32. (p. 311)

Wilkinson, G. S. (1990, February). Food sharing in vampire bats. *Scientific American, 262,* 76–82. (p. 284)

Wilkinson, R., & Pickett K. (2009). *The spirit level: Why greater equality makes societies stronger.* New York: Penguin. (p. 490)

Wilkowski, B. M., & Robinson, M. D. (2008). The cognitive basis of trait anger and reactive aggression: An integrative analysis. *Personality and Social Psychology Bulletin, 12,* 3–21. (p. 313)

Willard, G., & Gramzow, R. H. (2009). Beyond oversights, lies, and pies in the sky: Exaggeration as goal projection. *Personality and Social Psychology Bulletin, 35,* 477–492. (p. 69)

Williams, D. K., Bourgeois, M. J., & Croyle, R. T. (1993). The effects of stealing thunder in criminal and civil trials. *Law and Human Behavior, 17,* 597–609. (p. 172)

Williams, E. F., & Gilovich, T. (2008). Do people really believe they are above average? *Journal of Experimental Social Psychology, 44,* 1121–1128. (p. 62)

Williams, J. E., Satterwhite, R. C., & Best, D. L. (1999). Pancultural gender stereotypes revisited: The Five Factor model. *Sex Roles, 40,* 513–525. (p. 434)

Williams, J. E., Satterwhite, R. C., & Best, D. L. (2000). *Five-factor gender stereotypes in 27 countries.* Paper presented at the XV Congress of the International Association for Cross-Cultural Psychology, Pultusk, Poland. (p. 434)

Williams, K. D. (2002). *Ostracism: The power of silence.* New York: Guilford. (pp. 9, 353)

Williams, K. D. (2007). Ostracism. *Annual Review of Psychology, 58,* 425–452. (p. 353)

Williams, K. D., Cheung, C. K. T., & Choi, W. (2000). Cyberostracism: Effects of being ignored over the Internet. *Journal of Personality and Social Psychology, 79,* 748–762. (pp. 9, 354)

Williams, K. D., Harkins, S., & Latané, B. (1981). Identifiability as a deterrent to social loafing: Two cheering experiments. *Journal of Personality and Social Psychology, 40,* 303–311. (p. 241)

Williams, K. D., Jackson, J. M., & Karau, S.J. (1992). Collective hedonism: A social loafing analysis of social dilemmas. In D. A. Schroeder (Ed.) *Social Dilemmas: Social Psychological Perspectives.* New York: Praeger. (p. 240)

Williams, K. D., & Karau, S. J. (1991). Social loafing and social compensation: The effects of expectations of coworker performance. *Journal of Personality and Social Psychology, 61,* 570–581. (p. 242)

Williams, K. D., & Nida, S. A. (2011). Ostracism: Consequences and coping. *Current Directions in Psychological Science, 20,* 71–75. (p. 354)

Williams, K. D., Nida, S. A., Baca, L. D., & Latané, B. (1989). Social loafing and swimming: Effects of identifiability on individual and relay performance of intercollegiate swimmers. *Basic and Applied Social Psychology, 10,* 73–81. (p. 240)

Williams, K. D., & Zadro, L. (2001). Ostracism: On being ignored, excluded and rejected. In M. Leary (Ed.), *Interpersonal rejection.* New York: Oxford. (p. 9)

Williams, L. E., & Bargh, J. A. (2008). Experiencing physical warmth promotes interpersonal warmth. *Science, 322,* 606–607. (p. 80)

Williams, M. J., & Eberhardt, J. L. (2008). Biological conceptions of race and the motivation to cross racial boundaries. *Journal of Personality and Social Psychology, 94,* 1033–1047. (p. 423)

Williams, T. M. (Ed.) (1986). *The impact of television: A natural experiment in three communities.* Orlando, FL: Academic Press. (p. 334)

Williamson, G. M., & Clark, M. S. (1989). Providing help and desired relationship type as determinants of changes in moods and self-evaluations. *Journal of Personality and Social Psychology, 56,* 722–734. (p. 277)

Willis, F. N., & Hamm, H. K. (1980). The use of interpersonal touch in securing compliance. *Journal of Nonverbal Behavior, 5,* 49–55. (p. 207)

Willis, J., & Todorov, A. (2006). First impressions: Making up your mind after a 100-ms exposure to a face. *Psychological Science, 17,* 592–598. (p. 103)

Wilson, A. E., & Ross, M. (2001). From chump to champ: People's appraisals of their earlier and present selves. *Journal of Personality and Social Psychology, 80,* 572–584. (pp. 66, 67)

Wilson, D. K., Kaplan, R. M., & Schneiderman, L. J. (1987). Framing of decisions and selections of alternatives in health care. *Social Behaviour, 2,* 51–59. (p. 483)

Wilson, D. S., & Wilson, E. O. (2008). Evolution for "the good of the group." *American Scientist, 96,* 380–389. (p. 285)

Wilson, E. O. (1978). *On human nature.* Cambridge, MA: Harvard University Press. (pp. 283, 284)

Wilson, J. P., & Petruska, R. (1984). Motivation, model attributes, and prosocial behavior. *Journal of Personality and Social Psychology, 46,* 458–468. (p. 299)

Wilson, L. C., & Scarpa, A. (2011). The link between sensation seeking and aggression: A meta-analytic review. *Aggressive Behavior, 37,* 81–90. (p. 325)

Wilson, R. S., & Matheny, A. P., Jr. (1986). Behavior-genetics research in infant temperament: The Louisville twin study. In R. Plomin & J. Dunn (Eds.), *The study of temperament: Changes, continuities, and challenges.* Hillsdale, NJ: Erlbaum. (p. 313)

Wilson, S. J., & Lipsey, M. W. (2005). The effectiveness of school-based violence prevention programs for reducing disruptive and aggressive behavior. Revised Report for the National Institute of Justice

School Violence Prevention Research Planning Meeting, May 2005. (p. 347)

Wilson, T. D. (1985). Strangers to ourselves: The origins and accuracy of beliefs about one's own mental states. In J. H. Harvey & G. Weary (Eds.), *Attribution in contemporary psychology*. New York: Academic Press. (p. 50)

Wilson, T. D. (2002). *Strangers to ourselves: Discovering the adaptive unconscious*. Cambridge, MA: Harvard University Press. (p. 50)

Wilson, T. D., Dunn, D. S., Kraft, D., & Lisle, D. J. (1989). Introspection, attitude change, and attitude-behavior consistency: The disruptive effects of explaining why we feel the way we do. In L. Berkowitz (Eds.), *Advances in experimental social psychology*, Vol. 22. San Diego, CA: Academic Press. (p. 50)

Wilson, T. D., & Gilbert, D. T. (2003). Affective forecasting. *Advances in Experimental Social Psychology, 35*, 346–413. (pp. 48, 50, 524)

Wilson, T. D., & Gilbert, D. T. (2005). Affective forecasting: Knowing what to want. *Current Directions in Psychological Science, 14*, 131–134. (p. 49)

Wilson, T. D., Laser, P. S., & Stone, J. I. (1982). Judging the predictors of one's mood: Accuracy and the use of shared theories. *Journal of Experimental Social Psychology, 18*, 537–556. (p. 47)

Wilson, T. D., Lindsey, S., & Schooler, T. Y. (2000). A model of dual attitudes. *Psychological Review, 107*, 101–126. (p. 51)

Wilson, W. R. (1979). Feeling more than we can know: Exposure effects without learning. *Journal of Personality and Social Psychology, 37*, 811–821. (p. 357)

Winch, R. F. (1958). *Mate selection: A study of complementary needs*. New York: Harper & Row. (p. 371)

Winter, F. W. (1973). A laboratory experiment of individual attitude response to advertising exposure. *Journal of Marketing Research, 10*, 130–140. (p. 358)

Wirth, J. H., Sacco, D. F., Hugenberg, K., & Williams, K. D. (2010). Eye gaze as relational evaluation: Averted eye gaze leads to feelings of ostracism and relational devaluation. *Personality and Social Psychology Bulletin, 36*, 869–882. (p. 377)

Wiseman, R. (1998, Fall). Participatory science and the mass media. *Free Inquiry*, pp. 56–57. (p. 506)

Wisman, A., & Koole, S. L. (2003). Hiding in the crowd: Can mortality salience promote affiliation with others who oppose one's worldviews? *Journal of Personality and Social Psychology, 84*, 511–526. (p. 352)

Wittenbrink, B. (2007). Measuring attitudes through priming. In B. Wittenbrink & N. Schwarz (Eds.), *Implicit measures of attitudes*. New York: Guilford. (p. 401)

Wittenbrink, B., Judd, C. M., & Park, B. (1997). Evidence for racial prejudice at the implicit level and its relationship with questionnaire measures. *Journal of Personality and Social Psychology, 72*, 262–274. (p. 401)

Wixon, D. R., & Laird, J. D. (1976). Awareness and attitude change in the forced-compliance paradigm: The importance of when. *Journal of Personality and Social Psychology, 34*, 376–384. (p. 85)

Wohl, M. J. A., & Enzle, M. E. (2002). The deployment of personal luck: Sympathetic magic and illusory control in games of pure chance. *Personality and Social Psychology Bulletin, 28*, 1388–1397. (p. 98)

Wojciszke, B., Bazinska, R., & Jaworski, M. (1998). On the dominance of moral categories in impression formation. *Personality and Social Psychology Bulletin, 24*, 1251–1263. (p. 376)

Wolf, S. (1987). Majority and minority influence: A social impact analysis. In M. P. Zanna, J. M. Olson, & C. P. Herman (Eds.), *Social influence: The Ontario symposium on personality and social psychology*, Vol. 5. Hillsdale, NJ: Erlbaum. (p. 268)

Wolf, S., & Latané, B. (1985). Conformity, innovation and the psycho-social law. In S. Moscovici, G. Mugny, & E. Van Avermaet (Eds.), *Perspectives on minority influence*. Cambridge: Cambridge University Press. (p. 268)

Wolf, S., & Montgomery, D. A. (1977). Effects of inadmissible evidence and level of judicial admonishment to disregard on the judgments of mock jurors. *Journal of Applied Social Psychology, 7*, 205–219. (p. 507)

Women on Words and Images (1972). *Dick and Jane as victims: Sex stereotyping in children's readers*. Princeton: Women on Words and Images. Cited by C. Tavris & C. Offir (1977) in *The longest war: Sex differences in perspective*. New York: Harcourt Brace Jovanovich, p. 177. (p. 406)

Wood, J. V., Heimpel, S. A., & Michela, J. L. (2003). Savoring versus dampening: Self-esteem differences in regulating positive affect. *Journal of Personality and Social Psychology, 85*, 566. (p. 68)

Wood, J. V., Perunovic, W. Q. E., & Lee, J. W. (2009). Positive self-statements: Power for some, peril for others. *Psychological Science, 20*, 860–866. (p. 40)

Wood, J. V., Saltzberg, J. A., & Goldsamt, L. A. (1990a). Does affect induce self-focused attention? *Journal of Personality and Social Psychology, 58*, 899–908. (pp. 277, 478)

Wood, W., Conway, M., Pushkar, D., & Dugas, M. J. (2005). People's perceptions of women's and men's worry about life issues: Worrying about love, accomplishment, or money? *Sex Roles, 53*, 545. (p. 434)

Wood, W., Rhodes, N., & Whelan, M. (1989). Sex differences in positive well-being: A consideration of emotional style and marital status. *Psychological Bulletin, 106*, 249–264. (p. 492)

Woodzicka, J. A., & LaFrance, M. (2001). Real versus imagined gender harassment. *Journal of Social Issues, 57*(1), 15–30. (p. 48)

Woolhandler, S., Campbell, T., & Himmelstein, D. U. (1991). Costs of health care administration in the United States and Canada. *New England Journal of Medicine, 349*, 768–775. (p. 491)

Woolley, A. W., Chabris, C. F., Pentland, A., Hasmi, N., & Malone, T. W. (2010). Evidence for a collective intelligence factor in the performance of human groups. *Science, 330*, 686–688. (p. 259)

Worchel, S., & Brown, E. H. (1984). The role of plausibility in influencing environmental attributions. *Journal of Experimental Social Psychology, 20*, 86–96. (p. 236)

Worchel, S., Jenner, S. M., & Hebl, M. R. (1998). Changing the guard: How origin of new leader and disposition of ex-leader affect group performance and perceptions. *Small Group Research, 29*, 436. (p. 242)

Word, C. O., Zanna, M. P., & Cooper, J. (1974). The nonverbal mediation of self-fulfilling prophecies in interracial interaction. *Journal of Experimental Social Psychology, 10*, 109–120. (p. 439)

Workman, E. A., & Williams, R. L. (1980). Effects of extrinsic rewards on intrinsic motivation in the classroom. *Journal of School Psychology, 18*, 141–147. (p. 149)

World Meteorological Organization. (2011, November). *WMO greenhouse gas bulletin: The state of greenhouse gases in the atmosphere based on global observations through*

2010. Geneva: World Meteorological Organization. (p. 516)

Worringham, C. J., & Messick, D. M. (1983). Social facilitation of running: An unobtrusive study. *Journal of Social Psychology, 121,* 23–29. (p. 237)

Wraga, M., Helt, M., Jacobs, E., & Sullivan, K. (2007). Neural basis of stereotype-induced shifts in women's mental rotation performance. *Social Cognitive and Affective Neuroscience, 2,* 12–19. (p. 442)

Wright, D. B., Boyd, C. E., & Tredoux, C. G. (2001). A field study of own-race bias in South Africa and England. *Psychology, Public Policy, & Law, 7,* 119–133. (p. 420)

Wright, D. B., & Stroud, J. N. (2002). Age differences in lineup identification accuracy: People are better with their own age. *Law and Human Behavior, 26,* 641–654. (p. 420)

Wright, E. F., Lüüs, C. A., & Christie, S. D. (1990). Does group discussion facilitate the use of consensus information in making causal attributions? *Journal of Personality and Social Psychology, 59,* 261–269. (p. 261)

Wright, R. (2003, June 29). Quoted by Thomas L. Friedman, "Is Google God?" *New York Times* (www.nytimes.com). (p. 251)

Wrosch, C., & Miller, G. E. (2009). *Depressive symptoms can be useful: Self-regulatory and emotional benefits of dysphoric mood in adolescence.* Unpublished manuscript. (p. 65)

Wu, D. Y. H., & Tseng, W. S. (1985). Introduction: the characteristics of chinese culture. In D. Y. H. Wu and W. S. Tseng (Eds.), *Chinese culture and mental health.* San Diego, CA: Academic Press. (p. 74)

Wylie, R. C. (1979). *The self-concept (Vol. 2): Theory and research on selected topics.* Lincoln, NE: University of Nebraska Press. (p. 63)

Wynne, C. D. L., & de Waal, F. B. M. (2006). Chimps are from Mars, bonobos from Venus. *Ethology, 112*(3), 310–311. (p. 288)

Yamaguchi, S., Greenwald, A. G., Banaji, M. R., Murakami, F., Chen, D., Shiomura, K., Kobayashi, C., Cai, H., & Krendl, A. (2007). Apparent universality of positive implicit self-esteem. *Psychological Science, 18,* 498–500. (p. 61)

Yarmey, A. D. (2003a). Eyewitness identification: Guidelines and recommendations for identification procedures in the United States and in Canada. *Canadian Psychology, 44,* 181–189. (p. 505)

Yarmey, A. D. (2003b). Eyewitnesses. In D. Carson and R. Bull (Eds.), *Handbook of Psychology in legal contexts,* 2nd ed. Chichester, England: Wiley. (p. 505)

Ybarra, M. L., Mitchell, K. J., Hamburger, M., Diener-West, M., & Leaf, P. J. (2011). X-rated material and perpetration of sexually aggressive behavior among children and adolescents: Is there a link? *Aggressive Behavior, 37,* 1–18. (p. 329)

Ybarra, M. L., West, M. D., Markow, D., Leaf, P. J., Hamburger, M. & Boxer, P. (2008). Linkages between Internet and other media violence with seriously violent behavior by youth. *Pediatrics, 122,* 929–937. (p. 334)

Ybarra, O. (1999). Misanthropic person memory when the need to self-enhance is absent. *Personality and Social Psychology Bulletin, 25,* 261–269. (p. 56)

Young, L. (2009). Love: Neuroscience reveals all. *Nature, 457,* 148. (p. 382)

Young, S. G., Bernstein, M. J., & Hugenberg, K. (2010). When do own-group biases in face recognition occur? Encoding versus post-encoding. *Social Cognition, 28,* 240–250. (p. 420)

Younger, J., Aron, A., Parke, S., Chatterjee, N., & Mackey, S. (2010). Viewing pictures of a romantic partner reduces experimental pain: Involvement of neural reward systems. *PLoS One, 5*(10), e13309. (p. 354)

Younger, J. C., Walker, L., & Arrowood, J. A. (1977). Postdecision dissonance at the fair. *Personality and Social Psychology Bulletin, 3,* 284–287. (p. 143)

Yousif, Y., & Korte, C. (1995). Urbanization, culture, and helpfulness. *Journal of Cross Cultural Psychology, 26,* 474–489. (p. 295)

Yovetich, N. A., & Rusbult, C. E. (1994). Accommodative behavior in close relationships: Exploring transformation of motivation. *Journal of Experimental Social Psychology, 30,* 138–164. (p. 394)

Yuchtman (Yaar), E. (1976). Effects of social-psychological factors on subjective economic welfare. In B. Strumpel (Ed.), *Economic means for human needs.* Ann Arbor: Institute for Social Research, University of Michigan. (p. 318)

Yuille, J. C., & Cutshall, J. L. (1986). A case study of eyewitness memory of a crime. *Journal of Applied Psychology, 71,* 291–301. (p. 498)

Yukl, G. (1974). Effects of the opponent's initial offer, concession magnitude, and concession frequency on bargaining

behavior. *Journal of Personality and Social Psychology, 30,* 323–335. (p. 462)

Yzerbyt, V. Y., & Leyens, J-P. (1991). Requesting information to form an impression: The influence of valence and confirmatory status. *Journal of Experimental Social Psychology, 27,* 337–356. (p. 372)

Zadro, L., Boland, C., & Richardson, R. (2006). How long does it last? The persistence of the effects of ostracism in the socially anxious. *Journal of Experimental Social Psychology, 42,* 692–697. (p. 354)

Zagefka, H., & Brown, R. (2005). Comparisons and perceived deprivation in ethnic minority settings. *Personality and Social Psychology Bulletin, 31,* 467. (p. 524)

Zagefka, H., Noor, M., Brown, R., De Moura, G. R., & Hopthrow, T. (2011). Donating to disaster victims: Responses to natural and humanly caused events. *European Journal of Social Psychology, 41,* 353–363. (p. 281)

Zajonc, R. B. (1965). Social facilitation. *Science, 149,* 269–274. (p. 234)

Zajonc, R. B. (1968). Attitudinal effects of mere exposure. *Journal of Personality and Social Psychology, 9,* Monograph Suppl. No. 2, part 2. (p. 357)

Zajonc, R. B. (1970, February). Brainwash: Familiarity breeds comfort. *Psychology Today,* 32–35, 60–62. (p. 357)

Zajonc, R. B. (1980). Feeling and thinking: Preferences need no inferences. *American Psychologist, 35,* 151–175. (p. 357)

Zajonc, R. B. (1998). Emotions. In D. Gilbert, S. T. Fiske, & G. Lindzey (Eds.), *Handbook of social psychology,* 4th ed. New York: McGraw-Hill. (p. 357)

Zajonc, R. B. (2000). *Massacres: Mass murders in the name of moral imperatives.* Unpublished manuscript, Stanford University. (pp. 251, 343)

Zaki, J., Schirmer, J., & Mitchell, J. P. (2011). Social influence modulates the neural computation of value. *Psychological Science, 22,* 894–900. (pp. 197, 220)

Zanna, M. P. (1993). Message receptivity: A new look at the old problem of open- vs. closed-mindedness. In A. Mitchell (Ed.), *Advertising: Exposure, memory and choice.* Hillsdale, NJ: Erlbaum. (p. 170)

Zanna, M. P., & Cooper, J. (1974). Dissonance and the pill: An attributional approach to studying the arousal properties of dissonance. *Journal of Personality and Social Psychology, 29,* 703–709. (pp. 150, 151)

Zanna, M. P., Crosby, F., & Loewenstein, G. (1987). Male reference groups and discontent among female professionals. In B. A. Gutek & L. Larwood (Eds.), *Women's career development.* Newbury Park, CA: Sage. (p. 318)

Zanna, M. P., & Olson, J. M. (1982). Individual differences in attitudinal relations. In M. P. Zanna, E. T. Higgins, & C. P. Herman, (Eds.) *Consistency in social behavior: The Ontario symposium,* Vol. 2. Hillsdale, NJ: Erlbaum. (p. 73)

Zanna, M. P., Olson, J. M., & Fazio, R. H. (1981). Self-perception and attitude-behavior consistency. *Personality and Social Psychology Bulletin, 7,* 252–256. (p. 128)

Zanna, M. P., & Pack, S. J. (1975). On the self-fulfilling nature of apparent sex differences in behavior. *Journal of Experimental Social Psychology, 11,* 583–591. (p. 132)

Zaragoza, M. S., & Mitchell, K. J. (1996). Repeated exposure to suggestion and the creation of false memories. *Psychological Science, 7,* 294–300. (p. 501)

Zarkadi, T., Wade, K. A., & Stewart, N. (2009). Creating fair lineups for suspects with distinctive features. *Psychological Science, 20,* 1448–1453. (p. 504)

Zebrowitz-McArthur, L. (1988). Person perception in cross-cultural perspective. In M. H. Bond (Ed.), *The cross-cultural challenge to social psychology.* Newbury Park, CA: Sage. (p. 506)

Zebrowitz, L. A., Collins, M. A., & Dutta, R. (1998). The relationship between appearance and personality across the life span. *Personality and Social Psychology Bulletin, 24,* 736–749. (p. 367)

Zebrowitz, L. A., Olson, K., & Hoffman, K. (1993). Stability of babyfaceness and attractiveness across the life span. *Journal of Personality and Social Psychology, 64,* 453–466. (p. 367)

Zebrowitz-McArthur, L. (1988). Person perception in cross-cultural perspective. In M. H. Bond (Ed.), *The cross-cultural challenge to social psychology.* Newbury Park, CA: Sage. (p. 109)

Zhang, D. D., Lee, H. F., Wong, C., Li, B., Pei, Q., Zhang, J., & An, Y. (2011). The causality analysis of climate change and large-scale human crisis. *PNAS, 108,* 17296–17301. (p. 517)

Zhang, Y. F., Wyon, D. P., Fang, L., & Melikov, A. K. (2007). The influence of heated or cooled seats on the acceptable ambient temperature range. *Ergonomics, 50,* 586–600. (p. 519)

Zhong, C.-B., & DeVoe, S. E. (2010). You are how you eat: Fast food and impatience. *Psychological Science, 21,* 619–622. (p. 79)

Zhong, C-B, & Leonardelli, G. F. (2008). Cold and lonely: Does social exclusion literally feel cold? *Psychological Science, 19,* 838–842. (pp. 80, 355)

Zhu, Y., Zhang, L., Fan, L., & Han, S. (2007). Neural basis of cultural influence on self-representation. *NeuroImage, 34,* 1310–1316. (p. 43)

Zick, A., Pettigrew, T. F., & Wagner, U. (2008). Ethnic prejudice and discrimination in Europe. *Journal of Social Issues, 64,* 233–251. (p. 404)

Zillmann, D. (1988). Cognition-excitation interdependencies in aggressive behavior. *Aggressive Behavior, 14,* 51–64. (p. 325)

Zillmann, D. (1989a). Aggression and sex: Independent and joint operations. In H. L. Wagner & A. S. R. Manstead (Eds.), *Handbook of psychophysiology: Emotion and social behavior.* Chichester, UK: Wiley. (pp. 325, 335)

Zillmann, D. (1989b). Effects of prolonged consumption of pornography. In D. Zillmann & J. Bryant (Eds.), *Pornography: Research advances and policy considerations.* Hillsdale, NJ: Erlbaum. (pp. 325, 366)

Zillmann, D., & Paulus, P. B. (1993). Spectators: Reactions to sports events and effects on athletic performance. In R. N. Singer, N. Murphey, & L. K. Tennant (Eds.), *Handbook of research on sport psychology.* New York: Macmillan. (p. 235)

Zillmann, D., & Weaver, J. B., III. (1999). Effects of prolonged exposure to gratuitous media violence on provoked and unprovoked hostile behavior. *Journal of Applied Social Psychology, 29,* 145–165. (p. 334)

Zillmann, D., & Weaver, J. B. (2007). Aggressive personality traits in the effects of violence imagery on unprovoked impulsive aggression. *Journal of Research in Personality, 41,* 753–771. (p. 335)

Zimbardo, P. G. (1970). The human choice: Individuation, reason, and order versus deindividuation, impulse, and chaos. In W. J. Arnold & D. Levine (Eds.), *Nebraska symposium on motivation, 1969.* Lincoln: University of Nebraska Press. (p. 244)

Zimbardo, P. G. (1971). *The psychological power and pathology of imprisonment.* A statement prepared for the U.S. House of Representatives Committee on the Judiciary, Subcommittee No. 3: Hearings on Prison Reform, San Francisco, CA, October 25. (p. 130)

Zimbardo, P. G. (1972). *The Stanford prison experiment.* A slide/tape presentation produced by Philip G. Zimbardo, Inc., P. O. Box 4395, Stanford, CA 94305. (p. 130)

Zimbardo, P. G. (2002, April). Nurturing psychological synergies. *APA Monitor, 5,* 38. (p. 244)

Zimbardo, P. G. (2004a). A situationist perspective on the psychology of evil: Understanding how good people are transformed into perpetrators. In A. G. Miller (Ed.), *The social psychology of good and evil.* New York: Guilford. (p. 130)

Zimbardo, P. G. (2004b, May 3). Awful parallels: Abuse of Iraqi inmates and SPE. Comments to Social Psychology of Personality and Social Psychology listserv. (p. 130)

Zimmer, C. (2005, November). The neurobiology of the self. *Scientific American,* 93–101. (p. 38)

Zitek, E. M., & Hebl, M. R. (2007). The role of social norm clarity in the influenced expression of prejudice over time. *Journal of Experimental Social Psychology, 43,* 867–876. (p. 405)

Zuckerman, E. W., & Jost, J. T. (2001). What makes you think you're so popular? Self-evaluation maintenance and the subjective side of the "friendship paradox." *Social Psychology Quarterly, 64,* 207–223. (p. 52)

Zuwerink, J. R., Monteith, M. J., Devine, P. G., & Cook, D. A. (1996). Prejudice toward blacks: With and without compunction? *Basic and Applied Social Psychology, 18,* 131–150. (p. 416)

Acknowledgements

Chapter 2

Figure 2-2, p. 39, Adapted from P. Lockwood and Z. Kunda, "Superstars and me: Predicting the impact of role models on the self," *Journal of Personality and Social Psychology, 73*(1), 91–103. Copyright © 1997 by the American Psychological Association. Adapted with permission.

Figure 2-4, p. 43, Kim & Markus, 1999.

Figure 2-5, p. 44, Markus & Kitayama, 1991.

Figure 2-6, p. 54, Adapted with permission from Figure 2, p. 435, in Bushman et al., "Looking Again, and Harder, for a Link Between Low Self-Esteem and Aggression," *Journal of Personality 77*:2, April 2009. © 2009, Copyright the Authors. Journal compilation © 2009, Wiley Periodicals, Inc.

Figure 2-8, p. 67, Adapted from A. Wilson and M. Ross, "From chump to champ: People's appraisals of their earlier and present selves," *Journal of Personality and Social Psychology, 80*(4), 572–584. Copyright © 2001 by the American Psychological Association. Adapted with permission.

Chapter 3

Figure 3-3, p. 89, Adapted from Baldwin, M. W., Carrell, S. E., & Lopez, D. F. (1990). "Priming relationship-schemas: My advisor and the Pope are watching me from the back of my mind," *Journal of Experimental Social Psychology, 26*, 435–454.

Figure 3-4, p. 100, Reprinted from *Journal of Experimental Social Psychology, 20*. J. P. Forgas, G. H. Bower and S. E. Kranz, "The Influence of Mood on Perceptions of Social Interactions." Copyright 1984, with permission from Elsevier.

Chapter 4

Figure 4-5, p. 151, Adapted from M. P. Zanna and J. Cooper, "Dissonance and the pill: An attributional approach to studying the arousal properties of dissonance," *Journal of Personality and Social Psychology, 29*(5), 703–709. Copyright © 1974 by the American Psychological Association. Adapted with permission.

Chapter 5

Figure 5-1, p. 160, Adapted from W. J. McGuire. "An Information-Processing Model of Advertising Effectiveness," in *Behavioral and Management Science in Marketing*, H. L. Davis and A. J. Silk, eds. Copyright © 1978. Reprinted by permission of John Wiley & Sons.

Figure 5-10, p. 181, Based on L. R. Fabrigar, J. R. Priester, R. E. Petty, and D. T. Wegener, "The impact of attitude accessibility on elaboration of persuasive messages," *Personality and Social Psychology Bulletin, 24*(4), 1998, 339–352.

Chapter 6

Figure 6-3, p. 203, Figure 13: "Learner demands to be shocked" p. 91. From *Obedience to Authority: An Experimental View*, by Stanley Milgram. Copyright © 1974 by Stanley Milgram. Reprinted by permission of HarperCollins Publishers and by Pinter & Martin, Ltd.

Figure 6-4, p. 205, From S. Milgram, 1965, "Some Conditions of Obedience and Disobedience to Authority," *Human Relations, 18*, pp. 57–76. Copyright © 1965, The Tavistock Institute.

Text excerpt, p. 211, Abridged from the original for this book and from Milgram, 1977, with permission of Alexandra Milgram.

Figure 6-5, p. 215, Data from Milgram, Bickman, & Berkowitz, 1969

Figure 6-6, p. 216, Adapted from Asch, "Opinions and Social Pressure," *Scientific American*, November 1955.

Figure 6-7, p. 221, Adapted from D. Griffin and R. Buehler, "Role of construal process in conformity and dissent," *Journal of Personality and Social Psychology, 65*(4), 657–669. Copyright © 1993 by the American Psychological Association. Adapted with permission.

Chapter 7

Figure 7-3, p. 240, From K. D. Williams, J. M. Jackson, & S. J. Karau, in *Social Dilemmas: Perspectives on Individuals and Groups*, edited by D. A. Schroeder.

Copyright © 1992 by Praeger Publishers. Reprinted with permission of Greenwood Publishing Group, Inc., Westport, CT.

Chapter 8

Text excerpt, p. 274, Canadian Broadcasting Corporation

Figure 8-2, p. 281, From M.A. Whatley, J. M. Webster, R. H. Smith, & A. Rhodes, 1999, "The Effect of a Favor on Public and Private Compliance: How Internalized is the Norm of Reciprocity?" *Basic and Applied Social Psychology, 21*, pp. 251–259. Copyright © 1999 Psychology Press. Reprinted by permission of the publisher. (Taylor & Francis Ltd, http://www.tandf.co.uk/journals).

Figure 8-6, p. 296, Adapted from R.V. Levine (2003). "The kindness of strangers." *American Scientist, 91*, 226–233.

Chapter 9

Figure 9-4, p. 326, Adapted from Statistics Canada, Canadian Crime Statistics, 1996, Catalogue no. 85-002 XPE, Vol. 17, no. 8; and U.S. Federal Bureau of Investigation Uniform Crime Report. This does not constitute an endorsement by Statistics Canada of this product.

Figure 9-8, p. 339, Adapted from Craig A. Anderson and Brad J. Bushman, "Effects of violent video games on aggressive behavior, aggressive cognition, aggressive effect, psychological arousal and prosocial behavior: A meta-analytic review of the scientific literature," *Psychological Science, 12*, No. 5, pp. 353–359. Reprinted by permission of Blackwell Publishing.

Chapter 10

Figure 10-3, p. 368, Based on J. E. Lydon, M. Meana, D. Sepinwell, N. Richards, and S. Mayman, "The commitment calibration hypothesis: When do people devalue attractive alternatives?" *Personality and Social Psychology Bulletin, 25*, 1999, pp. 152–161.

Figure 10-9, p. 388, From Weber/Harvey, *Perspective on Close Relationships*, Figure "Love: An Overlapping of Selves—you become part of me, I part of you," © 1994 Allyn & Bacon. Reproduced by permission of Pearson Education, Inc.

Chapter 11

Figure 11-3, p. 419, From P. G. Devine & R. S. Malpass, "Orienting Strategies in Differential Face Recognition," *Personality and Social Psychology Bulletin, 11*, pp. 33–40. Copyright © 1985. Reprinted by permission of Sage Publications, Inc.

Chapter 12

Figure 12-2, p. 435, Data from Gallup Polls (brain.gallup.com).

Figure 12-3, p. 438, Adapted from D. A. Wilder, A. F. Simon, and M. Faith, "Enhancing the impact of counterstereotypic information, dispositional attributions for deviance," *Journal of Personality and Social Psychology, 71*(2), 276–287. Copyright © 1996 by the American Psychological Association. Adapted with permission.

Figure 12-6, p. 446, Based on Z. Kunda & L. Sinclair, "Motivated reasoning with stereotypes: Activation, application, and inhibition," *Psychological Inquiry, 10*(1), 1999, 12–22.

Figure 12-7, p. 448, Based on D. M. Taylor, S. C. Wright, F. M. Moghaddam, & R. N. Lalonde, "The personal/group discrimination discrepancy: Perceiving my group, but not myself, to be a target for discrimination," *Personality and Social Psychology Bulletin, 16*(2), 1990, 254–262.

Module B

Figure B–3, p. 481, Adapted from T. K. MacDonald, M. P. Zanna, and G. T. Fong, "Decision making in altered states: Effects of alcohol on attitudes toward drinking and driving," *Journal of Personality and Social Psychology, 68*(6), 973–985. Copyright © 1995 by the American Psychological Association. Adapted with permission.

Figure B–6, p. 490, From Richard Wilkinson and Kate Pickett, *The Spirit Level: Why Greater Equality Makes Societies Stronger* (Penguin, 2009). http://www.equalitytrust.org.uk/resources/slides. Reprinted by permission of Penguin Group, Ltd.

Figure B–7, p. 492, Adapted from Akhtar-Danesh, N., & Landeen, J. (2007). Relation between depression and sociodemographic factors. *International Journal of Mental Health Systems, 1*, 4.

Module D

Figure D–1, p. 515, Data from Global Footprint Network, 2006, www.footprintnetwork.org.

Photo Credits

Chapter 1

Pages 2, 3, © denis_pc/iStock/360/Getty Images; page 5, © Jonathan Hayward/The Canadian Press; page 13, Alison Derry/McGraw-Hill Ryerson; page 19, © Jon Bower/Age Fotostock; page 25, © Byron Peter/Photo Researchers/Getty Images; page 27, © Ryan Remiorz/The Canadian Press.

Chapter 2

Pages 34, 35, © Alexandra Dean; page 45, © AP Photo/Julie Jacobson; page 46, Pixtal/SuperStock; page 50, © AP Images/Gene Blythe; page 53, Forsterforest / Dreamstime.com / GetStock.com; page 62, Mast3r / Dreamstime.com / GetStock.com; page 66, © Larry Dale Gordon/Getty Images; page 70, © PhotoDisc/Getty Images; page 73, © Tibor Bognar/Corbis.

Chapter 3

Pages 76, 77, Arindambanerjee / Dreamstime.com / GetStock.com; page 81, © Ian Barrett/The Canadian Press; page 82, © Bettman/CORBIS; page 83, © PhotoDisc/Getty Images; page 86, © PhotoDisc/Getty Images; page 92, Steve Cole/Getty Images; page 99, © Rob Melnychuk/Getty Images RF; page 101, © Digital Vision/Photodisc/Getty Images; page 103, © Moodboard/Corbis RF; page 106, © Everett Collection; page 109, John Lehmann/The Globe and Mail; page 110, © Esbin-Anderson/The Image Works; page 113, Mike Kemp/Getty Images.

Chapter 4

Pages 120, 121, © Steven J. Spencer; page 122, © Jonathan Hayward/The Canadian Press; page 125, Jstudio/Dreamstime.com/GetStock.com; page 127, © Kevin P. Casey / Corbis; page 130, © Phillip Zimbardo; page 131 (top), © AP Images; page 131 (bottom left), © Ralph Bower/Vancouver Sun; page 131 (bottom right), © Victoria Times Colonist/The Canadian Press; page 134, © XiXinXing/iStock/360/Getty Images; page 135, © Canadian Blood Services; page 137, © Kevin Frayer/The Canadian Press; page 138, Ginaellen/Dreamstime.com/GetStock.com; page 141, © EPA/DENNIS M. SABANGAN/Landov; page 143, © Anton Vengo/Purestock; page 145 (left, middle, right), © Colin Young-Wolff/PhotoEdit; page 146 (left and right), Courtesy Fritz Strack; page 147, © PEOPLE AND TECHNOLOGY by VISION /Alamy.

Chapter 5

Pages 156, 157, © REUTERS/CHRIS WATTIE/Landov; page 158, Ad developed by ChangeMakers for the Winnipeg Regional Health Authority; page 166, © AP Photo/Press Association; page 169 (left), © Sun Media Corporation. Reprinted by permission; page 169 (right), From Strick, M., Van Baaren, R. B., Holland, R. W., & Van Knippenberg, A. (2009). Humor in advertisements enhances product liking by mere association. *Journal of Experimental Psychology: Applied, 15*, 35–45, Experiment 3. p. 238; page 170 (top left), Licensed under Health Canada copyright; page 170 (top right), Copyright © Province of British Columbia. All rights reserved. Reproduced with permission of the Province of British Columbia. Licensed under Health Canada copyright; page 170 (middle left), Licensed under Health Canada copyright; page 170 (middle right), Licensed under Health Canada copyright; page 170 (bottom left), Licensed under Health Canada copyright; page 170 (bottom right), Courtesy © Health Sciences Centre Winnipeg. Licensed under Health Canada copyright; page 178, © Time Life Pictures/Getty Images; page 186, © AP Photo/Richard Vogel; page 188, © Rachel Epstein/The Image Works; page 190, Igorr / Dreamstime.com / GetStock.com; page 191, © Michelle D. Bridwell/PhotoEdit.

Chapter 6

Pages 194, 195, © MedioImages/Corbis RF; page 202, From Opinions and Social Pressure, Asch, Solomon E. November 1955. Reprinted with permission. Copyright © 1955 by *Scientific American*, a division of

Nature America, Inc. All rights reserved; page 206, Stanley Milgram, 1965, from the film *Obedience,* distributed by the Pennsylvania State University, PCR; page 209, © AP Photo; page 210, © Benny Gool/Capetown Independent Newspaper; page 211, Courtesy Alexandra Milgram; page 215, © James A. Sugar/Corbis; page 218 (top), © AP Photo; page 221, © Ryan Remiorz/The Canadian Press; page 222, © Zia Soleil/Getty Images; page 226, © AP Photo/Joe Hermosa; page 227, Image Source/Getty Images.

Chapter 7
Pages 230, 231, Sergeibach/Dreamstime.com/GetStock.com; page 234, © Ryan McVay/Thinkstock; page 236, © Mike Okoniewski; page 239, Courtesy Alan G. Ingham; page 241 (top), © Royalty-Free/Corbis; page 241 (bottom), Thinkstock Images/Getty Images; page 242, Dave Chidley/The Canadian Press; page 243, Lucas Oleniuk/GetStock.com; page 244, © Phillip Zimbardo; page 246, © Rich Lam/Getty Images; page 253, © Creatas/PunchStock RF; page 255, © The Kobal Collection at Art Resource, NY; page 258, © Frank Gunn/The Canadian Press; page 261, © Bruce Meyer/Sygma/Corbis; page 262, Skypixel/Dreamstime.com/GetStock.com; page 266, © Mark Richards/PhotoEdit.

Chapter 8
Pages 272, 273, © Darryl Brooks/Dreamstime.com; page 286, McGraw-Hill Companies Inc./Ken Karp, photographer; page 289, © Joe Gibbons/St. John's Telegram/The Canadian Press; page 293, © Peter Dazeley/Getty Images RF; page 294, © Charles Platiau/Reuters/Corbis; page 295, © Tatianatatiana/Dreamstime.com/GetStock.com; page 299, Courtesy Lisa DeBruine; page 305, © ARNE DEDERT/dpa/Landov.

Chapter 9
Pages 308, 309, © AP Photo/Thibault Camus; page 313, © Jeff Share/Black Star; page 314, © Jose Mercado; page 315, © AP Photo/Matt Dunham; page 317, © Intst/Dreamstime.com/GetStock.com; page 319, © SolStock/

istock/360/Getty Images; page 321 (left, right), © Albert Bandura; page 323, © AP Photo/Jack Smith; page 326, © Chuck Stoody/The Canadian Press; page 327, Ingram Publishing; page 329, © Jim Rankin/The Toronto Star/The Canadian Press; page 340, © Andrew Lichtenstein/The Image Works; page 342, © Gus van Dyk, Pilanesberg, South Africa.

Chapter 10
Pages 350, 351, Purestock/SuperStock; page 353, © Getty Images; page 354, Eisenberger, N. I., Lieberman, M. D., & Williams, K. D. (2003). Does rejection hurt? An fMRI study of social exclusion. *Science, 302,* 290–292. © 2003 American Association for the Advancement of Science; page 357, © PhotoDisc/Getty Images RF; page 360, © Peter Scholey/Getty Images RF; page 361, © AP Photo; page 364, Jose Luis Pelaez, Inc/Blend Images/Getty Images; page 365 (left), © Oliver Bodmer/Zuma Press; page 365 (right), From Braun, C., Gruendl, M., Marberger, C., & Scherber, C. (2001). Beautycheck - Causes and Consequences of Human Facial Attractiveness as presented at the German Students Award 2000/2001; page 367 (left), © Rick Smolan/Stock Boston; page 367 (middle left), © John Lund/Getty Images; page 367 (middle right), © Catherine Karnow/Woodfin Camp; page 367 (right), © Royalty-Free/Corbis; page 369, © The Granger Collection, NYC; page 375 (left, middle, right), Courtesy Dr. Pawel Lewicki, University of Tulsa, Oklahoma; page 376, © Joe Polillio; page 379, From Aron, A. Fisher, H., Mashek, D. J., Strong, G., Li, H., & Brown, L. L. (2005). Reward, movitation, and emotion systems associated with early-stage intense romantic love. *Journal of Neurophysiology, 94,* 327–337. Image courtesy of Lucy L. Brown; page 380, © Tetra Images / Alamy; page 381, © Blend Images/iStockphoto; page 384, Ximagination / Dreamstime.com/GetStock.com; page 385, © Elizabeth Crews/The Image Works.

Chapter 11
Pages 396, 397, Adrian Wyld/The Canadian Press; page 399, © Digital Vision/Getty Images; page 400, The McGraw-Hill

Companies, Inc./Christopher Kerrigan, photographer; page 402, © National Archives of Canada/The Canadian Press; page 409 (top), © Brand X Photos/PhotoDisc RF; page 409 (bottom), © Digital Vision/PhotoDisc RF; page 410, © Rex Features/APA Images/The Canadian Press; page 411 (top), © AP Photo; page 412, David R. Frazier Photolibrary, Inc./GetStock.com; page 413, © 1999 Allan Tannenbaum; page 418, James Blascovich; page 421, © AP Photo/Eugene Hoshik;

Chapter 12
Pages 426, 427, © Ryan McVay/Getty Images RF; page 428, © Nova Scotia Archives, Bob Brooks fonds, 1989-468 vol. 16; page 431, © Kurt Hugenberg and Galen Bodenhausen (2003); page 432 (left and right), Correll, J., Park, B., Judd, C.M., & Wittenbrink, B. (2002). The police officer's dilemma: Using ethnicity to disambiguate potentially threatening individuals. *Journal of Personality and Social Psychology, 83,* 1316. Fig. 1. Images courtesy Josh Correll; page 437, Pierre Obendrauf, *The Gazette;* page 443, © Image Source/Alamy; page 445, Andresr / Dreamstime.com / GetStock.com; page 449, Creatista / Dreamstime.com/ GetStock.com.

Module A
Page 452, Courtesy Steven J. Spencer; page 454, © Andrew Vaughan/The Canadian Press; page 459, © Joseph Sohm, ChromoSohm/Corbis; page 466, © Mark Antman/The Image Works.

Module B
Page 470, David Buffington/Getty Images; page 486, © Jacques Chenet.

Module C
Page 496, © Tektite/Dreamstime.com/GetStock.com; page 500, Courtesy Elizabeth Loftus; page 501, Courtesy Elizabeth Loftus.

Module D
Page 514, Getty Images/Photodisc; page 523, © Kayte M. Deioma/PhotoEdit.

Name Index

A

Abbate, C. S., 302
Abbey, A., 102, 491
ABC News, 208
Abelson, R., 122
Abraham, J., 372
Abrams, D., 253
Abramson, L., 475, 476, 478
Achenbach, C. J., 282
Acitelli, L. K., 370
Acker, M., 444
Ackerman, J. M., 379
Ackermann, R., 476
Adair, J. G., 24
Adamopoulos, J., 261
Adams, D., 316
Adams, G., 113, 363, 364
Adams, J. M., 392
Adarves-Yorno, I., 217
Addams, C., 185
Addis, M. E., 282
Adelman, H. F., 149
Aderman, D., 277
Adinolfi, A. A., 359
Adler, N. E., 19, 489
Adler, N. L., 388
Adler, R. P., 190
Adorno, T., 403
Aesop, 359
Affleck, H., 486
Agerström, J., 125
Agnew, C. R., 392
Agnew, G. A., 236
Agthe, M., 360, 363
Ahuvia, A., 523
Aiello, J. R., 236, 237
Ainsworth, M., 383, 384
Ajzen, I., 116, 126, 127, 127f
Akhart-Danesh, N., 492f
Akimoto, S. A., 437
Aknin, L. B., 280
Al-Sadat, A., 465
Albarracin, D., 127, 128, 176
Alberts, S. C., 284
Aldag, R. J., 259
Alden, L. E., 480
Alexander, J., 176
Allee, W. C., 234, 319
Allen, J., 358

Allen, V. L., 215
Allesøe, K., 485
Allik, J., 60
Allison, S., 418
Allison, S. T., 65, 105, 458
Alloy, L., 475, 476, 478
Almeida, D. M., 313
Allport, F. W., 234
Allport, G. W., 398, 402, 405, 407, 436, 438, 440
Altemeyer, B., 404
Alter, A., 346
Altmann, J., 284
Alwin, D. E., 178, 179
Amabile, T. M., 97, 106, 107f
Amador, M., 503
Amato, P., 288
Ambady, N., 112, 360, 442
American College Health Association (ACHA), 471
American Enterprise, 392
American Psychological Association, 314, 334, 505t
Amland, B. H., 517
Amodio, D. M., 416
Amos, 368
Amundsen, R., 264
Anastasi, J. S., 420
Anda, R., 484
Anderegg, W. R. L., 517
Andersen, S., 275
Andersen, S. M., 36, 305
Anderson, C. A., 29, 69, 72, 74, 83, 84, 323, 324, 325f, 326, 334–339, 339f, 340–343, 370, 480, 517
Anderson, D. C., 323, 324
Anderson, K., 476
Anderson, P., 66
Anderson, P. D., 219
Anderson, R., 453
Anderson, S. L., 363, 364
Andrews, F. M., 491
Angier, N., 348
Angulo, S., 52
Angus Reid, 178, 517, 518
Anik, L., 275
Anthony, D. B., 41
Antoninus, M. A., 16, 159
Apanovitch, A. M., 483

Appleman, A. J., 72
Applewhite, M. H., 181, 182, 185
Archer, D., 406, 407
Archer, J., 312, 314, 332
Archer, R. L., 387
Arendt, H., 213
Ariely, D., 217, 361, 370
Ariganello, M., 114
Aristotle, 8, 344, 351, 359, 370, 458
Ariza, L. M., 251
Arkes, H. R., 126, 175
Arkin, R. M., 71, 72, 355, 356
Armeli, S., 149
Armitage, C. J., 127
Armor, D. A., 64, 65
Arms, R. L., 345
Armstrong, T. L., 407
Arneli, S., 148
Aron, A., 201, 372, 378, 379f, 380, 388, 389
Aron, E., 201, 388, 389
Arone, S., 212, 243, 245
Aronson, E., 27, 136, 170, 171f, 183, 374
Aronson, J., 440, 441, 443
Arriaga, X. B., 392
Arrow, J., 264
Arrowood, A. J., 143
Asch, S. E., 173, 200–202, 209–211, 214, 214t, 215, 216f, 217, 218, 220, 223, 224
Asendorpf, J. B., 480
Ash, E., 311
Asher, S. R., 313
Ashton, W. A., 105
Ashton-James, C. E., 49, 303
Associated Press, 200, 293
Attia, S., 320
Augoustinos, M., 12
Aumann, K., 61
Austin, J. B., 276
Averill, J., 317
Axelrod, R., 468
Axent-Gyorgyi, A., 235
Axsom, D., 180
Ayal, S., 217
Ayres, I., 433
Azrin, N. H., 322

B

Baars, B. J., 79
Babad, E., 112
Bach, R., 59
Bachman, J. G., 20, 163
Back, M., 355
Bacon, F., 491
Badger, A. J., 352
Baeyens, F., 375
Bähler, M., 399
Bailenson, J. N., 165
Bailey, S., 476
Bainbridge, W. S., 184, 185
Baize, H. R., 361
Baker, L. R., 388
Baldridge, B. J., 474
Baldwin, M. W., 88, 89f, 383
Balogh, D. W., 477
Banaji, M. R., 87, 124, 125, 126, 401, 432
Banas, K., 288, 353
Bandura, A., 42, 59, 136, 320, 321, 322f, 334, 335
Banks, S. M., 168
Banse, R., 414
Banting, F., 36
Bar-Haim, Y., 359
Bar-Hillel, M., 94
Bar-Tal, D., 461
Barash, D. P., 283, 284, 312
Bargh, J. A., 79, 80, 87, 102, 199, 251, 390, 401
Barkley, C., 312
Barlett, C. P., 341
Barnes, R. D., 247, 282
Barnett, M. A., 278
Barnett, P. A., 477
Baron, J., 281, 416
Baron, R. A., 346, 363
Baron, R. S., 185, 236, 237, 254, 318
Barongan, C., 335
Barry, B., 400
Barry, D., 63
Barsotti, C., 152, 163
Bartholomew, K., 383, 384
Bartholow, B. D., 314, 326, 340
Barton, W. H., 246
Basile, K. C., 330

Bassili, J. N., 122, 127, 267
Bastardi, A., 81
Bastian, B., 103
Batson, C. D., 68, 123, 128, 284, 286, 287, 288f, 288, 289, 297, 298, 303, 304, 306, 405, 465
Batten, P. G., 387
Bauman, C. W., 106, 370
Baumann, L. J., 277, 482
Baumgardner, A. H., 71
Baumeister, R. F., 10, 54, 55, 56, 57, 59, 71, 72, 105, 236, 237, 240, 345, 352, 353, 355, 372, 387, 392, 393, 435
Baumhart, R., 63
Baxter, T. L., 108
Bayer, E., 234
Bazerman, M. H., 467
Bazinska, R., 376
Bazzini, D., 362, 387
BBC, 320
Beach, S. R. H., 477
Beals, K. P., 388
Beaman, A. L., 247, 306, 368
Bearak, B., 408
Becker, S., 300
Becker, V., 423
Beer, J. S., 55, 64
Bègue, L., 314, 414
Bell, B. E., 498
Bell, D. W., 171
Bell, P. A., 323, 324
Bellock, S. L., 442
Belson, W. A., 332
Bem, D., 85, 145, 150
Benassi, V. A., 98
Benjamin, A. J. Jr., 326
Benjamin, L. T. Jr., 203
Bennett, D., 217
Bennett, P., 18
Bennett, T., 329
Bennis, W. G., 265
Benthin, A. C., 140
Benton, S. L., 66
Benzien, J., 210
Benzies, K., 321
Berg, J. H., 376, 385, 387, 388
Berger, J., 223, 225
Berger, R., 73
Berglas, S., 71
Bergsieker, H., 442
Berkman, L. F., 487
Berkowitz, L., 215f, 216, 277, 279, 281, 317, 317f, 323, 325, 326, 334, 335
Berman, J. J., 126

Bernardo, P., 329
Berndsen, M., 422
Bernhardt, P. C., 55, 316
Bernieri, F., 112, 360
Berns, G. S., 220
Bernstein, D. M., 84
Bernstein, M. J., 420
Berry, D., 506
Berry, J. L., 176
Berry, J. W., 39
Berscheid, E., 114, 135, 357, 359, 361, 362, 363, 364, 372, 377, 378, 380, 385, 460, 491
Bertrand, M., 429
Bertuzzi, T., 326
Berwick, S., 397–398
Besser, A., 385
Best, D. L., 434
Bettencourt, B. A., 313, 420, 445
Beyer, L., 436
Bhatia, T., 177
Bianchi, S. M., 433
Bickman, L., 215f, 301, 462
Bielawski, D. M., 132, 433
Biernat, M. R., 70, 370, 417, 420, 433, 437, 444
Billig, M. G., 410
bin Laden, O., 212
Biner, P., 325
Bingenheimer, J. B., 321
Bingham, J., 419
Bingham, P. M., 284
Birrell, P., 82
Bishop, G. D., 250, 250f, 483
Bizzoco, N., 393
Blackburn, R. T., 70
Blackhart, G. C., 353
Blackstone, W., 510
Blackwell, E., 484
Blair, J., 291
Blake, R. R., 466
Blanchard, F. A., 137
Blanton, H., 126, 143
Blascovich, J., 418
Blass, T., 204, 206, 208, 223
Bledsoe, S. B., 361
Block, J., 106
Blockley, S., 298
Boardman, S. K., 464
Boden, J. M., 53, 55
Bodenhausen, G. V., 51, 100, 167, 416, 417, 430, 431f
Bodinger, H., 293
Boehm, S. H., 484
Boer, D., 370, 526
Boggiano, A. K., 148, 149

Boland, C., 354
Boland, J. E., 42
Boldt, E. D., 216
Bollier, T., 402
Bollinger, M., 363
Bombeck, E., 190
Bonanno, G., 68
Bond, A. J., 321
Bond, C. F. Jr., 235, 444
Bond, J. T., 61
Bond, M. H., 310, 369, 460
Bond, R., 223
Bonniot-Cabanac, M-C., 345
Bonnot, V., 442
Bono, J. E., 265
Booth, A., 316
Borgida, E., 415, 435, 443, 510
Borkenau, P., 91
Bornstein, B. H., 499, 511
Bornstein, R. F., 357, 358
Bossard, J. H. S., 356
Bossio, L. M., 486
Boswell, J., 413
Bothwell, R. K., 419
Botvin, G. J., 189, 191
Botwin, M. D., 371
Bouchard, L., 463
Boucher, H. C., 408
Boucher, K. L., 441
Boundy, R. G., 515
Bourgeois, M. J., 172, 508
Bourke, M. L., 329
Bovbjerg, D. H., 485
Bowe, M., 413
Bowen, E., 5
Bower, G. H., 100, 101f, 476
Bowlby, J., 383
Bowman, S., 264
Boyanowsky, E. O., 310
Boyatzis, C. J., 25
Boye, D., 135
Boyes, A. D., 374
Bradbury, T., 369
Bradbury, T. N., 393
Bradley, E., 290, 291
Bradley, W., 149
Brainerd, C. J., 222
Braman, D., 163
Brandon, R., 498
Branscombe, N. R., 440, 447
Bratslavsky, E., 387
Brauer, M., 249, 252, 305
Braun, C., 365f
Bray, R. M., 509, 510, 511
Breaux, J., 292
Breckler, S. J., 122, 518
Bregman, N. J., 502

Brehm, J. W., 143, 172, 225
Brehm, S. S., 225
Brekke, N., 415, 443
Brener, L., 430
Brennan, R. T., 321
Brenner, S. N., 63
Brewer, M. B., 27, 410, 411, 437, 458
Brewer, N., 499
Bricker, W., 320
Brickman, P., 224, 522
Brigham, J. C., 419, 500
Brin, S., 522
Briñol, P., 146, 161, 164
Britt, T. W., 317
Britten, K., 483
Brock, T. C., 95, 165, 180
Brockner, J., 457
Brodzinsky, D. M., 236
Bromley, S., 429
Brookins, S., 293
Brooks, R. D., 169
Broome, A., 480
Brounstein, P., 387
Brown, D. R., 38
Brown, E. H., 236
Brown, H. J. Jr., 63
Brown, J., 47, 51
Brown, J. D., 100, 367, 476
Brown, R., 316, 321, 410, 419, 442, 524
Brown, R. M., 135
Brown, S. L., 275, 488
Brown, T. J., 282
Brown, V. R., 263
Brown, W. M., 365
Browning, C., 213
Browning, E. B., 377
Browning, R., 381, 474
Brownlee, E. A., 71
Bruce, V., 499
Bruck, M., 501
Bruey, C., 341
Bruneau, E., 284
Bruun, S. E., 240, 242
Bryan, J., 297
Bryan, T. S., 507
Bryant, B., 234
Bryant, J., 325
Buchanan, W., 376
Buckhout, R., 499
Buckley, K. E., 337
Buehler, R., 48, 84, 92, 220, 221f, 483
Buffardi, L. E., 72
Buffett, W., 305
Bugental, D. P., 478

Bull, R., 362
Bundy, T., 329
Burchill, S. A. L., 477
Burger, J. M., 64, 72, 108, 133, 146, 164, 204, 216, 264, 298, 356
Burgess, A. W., 329
Burghart, D., 275
Burkholder, J. P., 522
Burns, D. D., 475
Burns, L., 64
Burnstein, E., 251, 252, 284, 317
Burr, W. R., 356
Burson, A. K., 91
Burt, R. S., 491
Burton, C. M., 489
Burton, R., 200
Bushman, B. J., 52, 54, 54f, 180, 247, 314, 324, 335, 336, 337, 339f, 340, 341, 343, 345, 346, 354, 437
Bushnell, N., 338
Buss, D. M., 317, 365, 371
Butcher, S. H., 344
Butler, A. C., 478
Butler, J. L., 236
Butz, D. A., 114, 500
Buunk, A. P., 386
Buunk, B. P., 70
Byatt, G., 365
Byers, E. S., 375
Bylsma, W. H., 318
Byrne, D., 369, 375, 418
Bytwerk, R. L., 169

C

Cabanac, M., 345
Cacioppo, J. T., 9, 124, 147, 160, 166, 171, 180, 262, 462, 487, 488
Cafferty, J., 223
Cain, T. R., 111
Cal, A. V., 163
Caldwell, C., 507
Caldwell, D., 146
Caldwell, H. K., 385
Callero, P. L., 275
Calley, W., 209
Cameron, C. D., 287
Cameron, D., 520
Cameron, J., 149, 255, 373
Campbell, A. C., 297
Campbell, D. T., 11, 173, 198, 283, 285, 524
Campbell, L., 392
Campbell, T., 491

Campbell, W. K., 54, 56, 60, 64, 72, 457, 525
Campos, B., 369
Canadian Centre on Substance Abuse, 225
Canadian Community Health Survey, 492f
Canadian Tobacco Use Monitoring Survey, 158
Canter, D., 292
Cantor, N., 38, 65, 388
Cantril, H., 267
Caputo, D., 90
Carducci, B. J., 378
Carli, L. L., 414
Carlo, G., 299
Carlsmith, J. M., 27, 140, 141, 141t, 142f, 170, 171f, 277
Carlson, C. A., 504
Carlson, J. G., 381
Carlson, M., 277, 279, 317
Carlston, D. E., 73, 82
Carnagey, N. L., 340
Carnegie, A., 347
Carnegie, D., 372, 374
Carnevale, P. J., 461, 465
Carney, D. R., 146
Carpenter, S. J., 401
Carr, R. B., 58
Carré, J. M., 315
Carrell, S. E., 89f
Carroll, D., 18
Carroll, J. S., 327
Carroll, M. D., 489
Carron, A. V., 236, 236t
Carter, J., 259
Carter, S., 369, 420
Cartwright, D. S., 250, 321
Carvallo, M., 352, 393
Carver, C. S., 128, 301, 477, 480, 486
Case, T. I., 180
Casella, D., 371
Cash, T. F., 363
Caspi, A., 313, 369
Cassidy, J., 384
Castelli, L., 403
Castle, D. J., 362
Castro, F., 105
Catanese, K. R., 352
CBC, 274, 398, 429, 430
Ceci, S. J., 501
Cemalcilar, Z., 352
Census Bureau, 86
Centers for Disease Control and Prevention (CDC), 330
Centerwall, B. S., 334

Cerankosky, B. C., 341
Chaiken, S., 160, 164, 165, 166, 170, 177, 178, 179f, 180
Chalmers, A., 63
Chamberlain, P., 320
Chambers, J. R., 68
Chan, M. K. H., 267
Chance, J. E., 419
Chance, S. E., 314
Chandler, J., 147
Chandola, T., 487
Chang, K., 61
Chang-Schneider, C., 52
Chao, M., 284
Chapman, J. P., 472
Chapman, L. J., 472
Chapman, M., 422
Charles I, King, 40
Charlin, V., 279
Chartrand, T. L., 87, 146, 199, 355, 369, 401
Chatard, A., 436
Check, J., 328, 329
Chen, E., 485
Chen, F. F., 369, 370
Chen, L., 249
Chen, S., 36, 408
Chen, S. C., 234
Chen, W., 489
Chen, Z., 355
Cheng, J. B., 180
Cheng, K., 57
Chermack, S. M., 314
Chernick, L., 223
Cherry, D., 162
Chesterfield, Lord, 166
Chesterfield, P. S., 297, 419
Cheung, C. K. T., 9, 354
Chiang, C. P., 251
Chiao, J., 360
Chida, Y., 483
Chiles, C., 216
Choi, D-W., 465
Choi, I., 43, 109
Choi, J., 43
Choi, W., 9, 354
Choi, Y., 263
Chorost, A. F., 380
Christ, O., 400
Chrisjohn, R. D., 299
Christenfeld, N., 217
Christiakis, N. A., 199, 477
Christian, J. L., 393
Christie, S. D., 261
Chua, H. F., 42
Chua-Eoan, H., 182
Church, A. H., 241

Churchill, W., 159, 459
Cialdini, R. B., 65, 133, 134, 135, 139, 165t, 188, 262, 277, 279, 286, 289, 302, 303, 304, 409, 462
Ciano, G., 69
Ciarocco, N. J., 72
Ciccone, M., 65
Cicerello, A., 361
Cicero, 280, 359, 506
Cihangir, S., 259
Cikara, M., 284
Cioffi, D., 306
Clark, M. S., 277, 279, 362, 386, 387, 387f
Clark, R. D. III, 216, 268
Clarke, A. C., 356
Clarkson, T., 405
Clary, E. G., 142
Clayton, S., 517, 520
Cleghorn, J., 286
Cleghorn, R., 22
Clement, R. W., 65, 418
Clevstrom, J., 225
Clifford, M. M., 362
Clore, G. L., 47, 282, 374, 375
CNN, 208
Coan, J. A., 487
Coates, B., 305
Coates, D., 522
Codol, J. P., 70
Cohen, B., 378
Cohen, D., 321
Cohen, E. E. A., 238
Cohen, G. L., 442
Cohen, L. L., 439
Cohen, M., 208
Cohen, R. L., 179
Cohen, S., 485, 487, 488f, 489
Cohn, E., 323, 324
Cohrs, J. C., 404
Coke, J. S., 306
Colby, C. A., 464
Cole, S. G., 224
Cole, S. W., 485
Coleman, L., 372
Collins, A., 290
Collins, M. A., 367
Collins, N. L., 387
Colman, A. M., 252
Comer, D. R., 242
Comim, F., 518
Comstock, G., 335
Confucius, 93
Conger, R. D., 55, 385
Conlee, M. C., 132
Conner, M., 127

Conolley, E. S., 215
Conrad, J., 86
Conway, F., 183, 184
Conway, L. G. III, 461
Conway, M., 86
Cook, C. E., 387
Cook, S. W., 137
Cook, T. D., 162
Cooke, L. J., 149
Cooley, C. H., 40
Coombs, R., 493
Coon, H. M., 42
Cooper, H., 314
Cooper, H. M., 112
Cooper, J., 140, 150, 151, 151f, 152, 192, 439
Cooper, M., 432
Copper, C., 217, 256
Corcoran, D. M., 386
Corman, M. D., 314
Cornell, S. D., 132
Correl, J., 430, 432
Cosby, P. C., 378
Coskun, H., 263
Costa-Lopes, R., 407
Costanzo, M., 311, 346
Costello, C., 458
Cota, A. A., 226, 399
Cothan, F., 168
Cottom, T., 284
Cotton, J. L., 323
Cottrell, N. B., 237
Courneya, K. S., 236t
Cowan, C. L., 277
Coyne, J. C., 477
Coyne, S. M., 332
Cozzolino, P. J., 403
Crabb, P. B., 132, 433
Craig, W. M., 310
Crandall, C. S., 216, 284, 416
Crane, F., 388
Crano, W., 111
Crawford, M., 399
Crawford, T. J., 174
Crick, F., 262, 263
Critcher, C. R., 96
Crocker, J., 51, 52, 56, 97, 412, 420, 437, 447, 526
Crofton, C., 367
Croizet, J.-C., 442
Crompton, T., 520
Crone, E. A., 354
Crosby, F. J., 318, 429, 447, 493
Crosby, J. R., 430
Cross, P., 70
Cross, S. E., 41, 43

Cross-National Collaborative Group, 479
Crowley, M., 282, 300, 360
Crowther, S., 295
Croxton, J., 85
Croyle, R. T., 172
Csikszentmihaly, M., 337, 527
Cuddy, A. J. C., 146, 402
Cullum, J. G., 217
Cullum, L., 414
Cunningham, J. A., 149
Cunningham, J. D., 383, 388
Cunningham, M. R., 279
Cunningham, W. A., 432
Curphy, G. J., 265
Curtis, J., 492
Cutler, B. L., 503, 505
Cutrona, C. E., 488
Cutshall, J., 498

D

Dabbs, J., 388
Dabbs, J. M., 167, 291, 314, 315
D'Agostino, P. R., 358
Dalrymple, T., 343
Dambrun, M., 206
Damon, W., 20
Dando, C. J., 503
Danner, D., 486
Dardenne, B., 402
Darley, J. M., 159, 290, 291, 291f, 292f, 294, 297, 298, 299, 300, 346, 357, 444
Darley, S., 192
Darwin, C., 17, 147, 235, 284, 345
Dasgupta, N., 416
Dashiell, J. F., 234
Dateline, 290
Dauenheimer, D., 442
Davidson, B., 253
Davidson, R., 313
Davidson, R. J., 487
Davie, M., 257
Davies, C., 498
Davies, P. G., 441
Davies, W. H., 83
Davila, J., 493
Davis, A. C., 298
Davis, C. G., 97
Davis, H. L., 160f
Davis, J. H., 187, 509, 510
Davis, J. L., 370
Davis, K. E., 103, 135, 383
Davis, L., 242
Davis, N., 208
Davis, S. C., 515

Dawes, R., 20, 54, 65, 117
Dawes, R. M., 455, 458, 459
Dawkins, R., 283, 285
Dawson, L., 345
Dazeley, S., 284
De Dreu, C. K. W., 509
de Hoog, N., 168
de Hoogh, A. H. B., 265
De Houwer, J., 375
de Meuse, K. P., 265
de Sherbinin, A., 517
De Tocqueville, A., 318
De Vogli, R., 487
de Vries, N. K., 509
de Waal, F. B. M., 288
de Wit, J. B. F., 168
Dean, C., 158
Deary, I., 489, 490
DeBruine, L. M., 298, 299f
Decety, J., 38
Dechêne, A., 175
Deci, E. L., 58, 148, 150, 353
Delgado, J., 129
Delisi, M., 517
Dembroski, T. M., 165
Demoulin, S., 411
DeNeve, K. M., 325f
Denissen, J. J. A., 352
Denollet, J., 483
Denrell, J., 220
Denson, T. F., 313, 432
DePaulo, B. M., 90, 492
DeReubeis, R. J., 476
Derks, B., 442
Derlega, V. J., 387
Dermer, M., 359, 378, 526
Dertke, M. C., 282
Desmarais, S. L., 505
DeSteno, D., 100, 123
Detweiler, J. B., 483
Deuser, W. E., 325f
Deutsch, M., 218, 219, 457
Deutsch, R., 87
Devenport, J. L., 505
Devine, P. G., 401, 416, 419f, 440
DeVoe, S. E., 79
DeVos-Comby, L., 169
DeWall, C. N., 57, 314, 353, 354, 355
Dexter, H. R., 505
Diallo, A., 432
Diamond, J., 366
Diamond, S. S., 508
Dickerhoof, R., 489
Dickerson, S. S., 485
Dicum, J., 390
DiDonato, T. E., 409

Diegel, S. W., 515
Diehl, M., 262
Diekman, A. B., 95
Diekmann, K. A., 61
Diener, E., 42, 128, 245, 245f, 246, 247, 313, 522, 523, 524, 525
Dienstbier, R. A., 326
Dietrich, M., 372
Dijksterhuis, A., 88, 160
Dill, K., 340
Dillehay, R. D., 511
DiMatteo, M. R., 483
Dion, D., 468
Dion, K. K., 165, 360, 362, 364, 379, 380, 381, 383, 392, 447
Dion, K. L., 226, 318, 319, 360, 379, 381, 383, 392, 399, 440, 447, 448
DiPietro, G., 399
Dishion, T. J., 251
Disraeli, B., 129
Dixon, J., 453
Dobbs, A. R., 323
Dodge, R. W., 176
Doherty, T. J., 517
Dohrenwend, B. P., 488
Dolan, R. J., 143
Dolinski, D., 278, 306
Dollard, J., 316
Dolnik, L., 180
Donaldson, Z. R., 382
Donders, N. C., 432
Donnellan, B., 385
Donnellan, M. B., 55
Donnerstein, E., 328, 330f, 331, 334, 335
Doob, A. N., 96, 163, 303, 504
Doolittle, R., 398
Doosje, B., 66
Doria, J. R., 70
D'Orlando, F., 327
Dorr, A., 190
Dorr, N., 445
Dotan-Eliaz, O., 353
Dotsch, R., 432
Doty, R. G., 404
Douglas, C., 98
Douglas, J. E., 329
Douglas, K. M., 244
Douthitt, E. A., 237
Dovidio, J. F., 289, 400, 401, 408, 437
Downing, L., 246
Downs, C., 506
Downs, J. S., 409
Doyle, A. C., 10, 16, 255

Draguns, J. G., 479
Drapeau, J., 48, 92
Driskell, J. E., 217, 234, 267
Driver, R., 40
Dryer, D. C., 371
Duck, J. M., 175
Duclos, S. E., 146
Dudley, K. A., 108
Dugger, C. W., 436
Dukes, H., 475
Dumont, M., 402
Dunbar, R., 458
Duncan, B. L., 423
Dunfield, K. A., 280
Dunkel-Schetter, C., 207
Dunn, E. W., 48, 73, 277, 283, 524
Dunn, L., 403
Dunning, D., 48, 61, 62, 68, 90,
    91, 422, 444, 503
Dushenko, T. W., 24
Düsing, J., 161
Dutta, R., 367
Dutton, D., 310, 378, 384
Dutton, K. A., 51
Duval, S., 109, 301
Duval, V. H., 301
Dweck, C. S., 57, 423
Dye, M. W. G., 341
Dziekanski, R., 5
Dzindolet, M. T., 262

E

Eagly, A. H., 160, 164, 177, 178,
    179f, 180, 252, 265, 282,
    300, 362, 399, 434, 435
Earls, F. J., 321
Earn, B. M., 447
Easterlin, R., 522
Eastwick, P. W., 49, 360, 372
Eastwood, J. D., 80
Eaton, J., 317
Ebbesen, E. B., 345
Eberhardt, J. L., 432
Ebert, J. E. J., 48, 59
Ebner, N. C., 420
Eccles, J., 112
Ecclesiastes, 491
Eckersley, R., 523
Eckes, T., 127
Edelson, M. G., 197
Edelstein, R., 64
Eden, A., 468
Edney, J. J., 458
Edwards, C. P., 398
Edwards, J. A., 99, 167
Edwards, J. J., 433

Edwards, K., 507
Effrein, E. A., 474
Efran, M., 506
Egan, L., 144
Eggleston, T. J., 140
Ehrlinger, J., 429
Eibach, R. P., 110, 429
Eichmann, A., 205, 209, 213
Einstein, A., 310, 475
Eisenberg, N., 281, 287, 299
Eisenberger, N. I., 354f
Eisenberger, R., 149
Eisenhower, D. D., 310
Eisenstadt, D., 142
Eiser, J. R., 140
Elder, G. H. Jr., 361
Elder, J., 409
Eldersveld, S., 176
Eliot, G., 369
Eliot, T. S., 115, 170
Elkin, R. A., 142
Ellemers, N., 66, 410
Elliot, A., 148
Ellis, H., 419
Ellison, P., 245
Ellsworth, P. C., 501, 508
Elms, A. C., 205
Emerson, R. W., 80, 123, 140,
    211, 244, 267, 372, 414
Emmons, R. A., 491, 522
Emswiller, T., 298
Eng, P. M., 488
Engemann, K. M., 363
Ennis, B. J., 185, 320
Enzle, M., 98
Epley, N., 28, 79
Epstein, J. A., 189, 191
Epstein, S., 222
Epstude, K., 96
Erb, H.-P., 226
Erber, R., 116, 416
Erbring, L., 389
Erickson, B., 163
Erickson, S. K., 465
Erikson, E. H., 384
Eron, L. D., 332, 333, 333f, 347
Escobar-Chaves, L. S., 336
Eshleman, A., 416
Esser, J. K., 259
Esses, V. M., 100, 171, 401, 407,
    412, 417, 506
Esterbrook, G., 519
Estes, F., 474
Etaugh, C. E., 399
Etzioni, A., 196
Evans, D. E., 275
Evans, G. W., 237

Evans, M., 94
Evans, M. A., 369
Evans, R. I., 189
Evett, S. R., 440
Exline, J. J., 57

F

Fabrigar, L. R., 152, 167, 180, 181f
Falbo, T., 352
Falender, V. J., 474
Farbstein, F., 58
Farquhar, J. W., 176
Farrell, C., 190
Farrelly, M. C., 168
Farris, K. B., 102
Farwell, L., 109
Faulkner, S. L., 241
Faye, C., 28
Fazio, R. H., 122, 126, 128, 152,
    161, 401, 474
Feather, N. T., 11, 109
Federal Bureau of Investigation,
    326f, 429
Federal Trade Commission,
    190, 338
Feeney, J., 387
Feeney, J. A., 383
Fein, S., 413, 444
Feinberg, M., 169
Feingold, A., 360, 361, 362,
    363, 506
Fekken, G. C., 299
Feldman, N. S., 415
Feldman, R. S., 112, 113
Felicio, D. M., 443
Felson, R. B., 40, 311
Fenigstein, A., 481
Fennema, E., 399
Ferguson, C. J., 341
Ferguson, S., 391
Ferguson, T. J., 502
Fergusson, D. M., 53, 55, 392
Feshbach, N. D., 190, 191
Festinger, L., 39, 122, 140, 141,
    141t, 142f, 152, 164, 180,
    243, 252, 259
Feygina, J. T., 518
Feynman, R., 150
Fichter, J. H., 405
Fiedler, F. E., 264
Fielder, L., 226
Finch, J. F., 57
Fincham, F. D., 102
Finchilescu, G., 336
Fingerhut, A. W., 492
Finkel, E., 360, 390

Finkel, E. J., 36, 57, 392
Finkenauer, C., 49
Fischer, E. F., 378
Fischer, G. W., 419
Fischer, P., 140, 293, 336, 503
Fischer, R., 63, 526
Fischhoff, B., 14, 94
Fishbein, D., 371
Fishbein, M., 126, 127, 127f
Fisher, E., 411
Fisher, H., 380
Fisher, J. D., 281
Fisher, L., 497, 507, 508
Fisher, R. J., 466, 503, 517
Fishman, S., 311
Fiske, S. T., 11, 117, 208,
    402, 419, 420, 430, 432,
    434, 525
Fitzpatrick, A. R., 252
Fitzpatrick, M. A., 393
Fitzsimons, G. J., 127
Fitzsimons, G. M., 390
Flay, B. R., 162, 189
Fleet, F., 257
Fleming, M., 507
Fletcher, G. J. O., 86, 100, 359,
    374, 376, 386, 423
Florian, V., 352
Flynn, C., 352
Flynn, F., 65
Flynn, H. A., 478
Foa, E. B., 275
Foa, U. G., 275
Fogelman, E., 303
Folger, R., 149
Folkman, J. R., 24
Follett, M. P., 463
Fonda, H., 232, 509
Fong, G. T., 68, 474, 481, 481f
Footprint Network, 515f
Forbes, C., 442
Forbes, M., 227
Ford, J. D., 405
Ford, R., 429
Forgas, J. P., 100, 100f, 101, 167,
    278, 432
Form, W. H., 284
Forster, E. M., 150
Förster, J., 442
Forsyth, D. R., 52, 73
Foss, R. D., 301
Foster, C. A., 392
Foster, J. D., 55
Foster-Fishman, P. G., 252
Fowler, J. H., 199, 477
Fradon, D., 69
Francesconi, M., 363

Frank, A., 147
Frank, B., 407
Frank, J. D., 186
Franklin, B., 36
Fraser, J., 503
Fraser, S. C., 133
Frasure-Smith, N., 484
Frazier, R. S., 124
Frazier, W., 58
Frederick, D. A., 366
Freedman, J. L., 133, 136, 149, 180, 236
Freeman, M. A., 41
French, R., 69
French, S., 63
Freud, S., 7, 61, 147, 310, 311, 439
Freund, B., 64
Frey, B., 300
Frey, J., 323
Friedman, H. S., 371, 483
Friedman, R., 148
Friedrich, J., 70
Friedrich, L. K., 305
Friesen, J., 400
Frisen, W. V., 486
Frieze, I. H., 363
Frimer, J. A., 299
Frisell, T., 313
Froming, W. J., 128
Fromkin, H., 226
Fromm, E., 362
Frost, J. H., 370
Fuller, S. R., 259
Fuller, T., 221
Fulton, R., 267
Fultz, J., 288f, 289
Funder, D. C., 28, 106, 116
Furnham, A., 109, 415
Futrell, D., 265

G

Gable, S. L., 387, 388
Gabrenya, W. K. Jr., 242
Gabriel, S., 352, 393
Gaebelein, J. W., 342
Gaeddert, W., 461
Gaertner, S. L., 44, 61, 411
Gailliot, M. T., 57
Gaines, S. D., 458
Gaissmaier, W., 116
Galanter, M., 186
Galinsky, A. D., 407, 465
Galinsky, E., 61
Galizio, M., 167
Gallo, L. C., 489, 526

Gallup, G. H. Jr., 178, 365, 366, 405, 435f
Gange, J. J., 236
Gangestad, S. W., 73, 365, 366, 368
Garb, H. N., 472, 475
Garber, J., 352
Garcia-Marques, T., 175, 358
Gardner, N., 182
Gardner, W. L., 36, 95, 388, 392
Garner, R., 306
Garovich, L., 434
Garrett, B. L., 499, 502
Garrity, M. J., 317
Garry, M., 501
Garver-Apgar, C. E., 371
Gates, G. J., 95
Gates, M. F., 234
Gatto, K., 335
Gaucher, D., 400
Gaunt, R., 369
Gavanski, I., 50
Gawande, A., 63
Gawronski, B., 51
Gazzaniga, M., 89, 129
Geen, R. G., 236, 315, 334, 335
Geers, A. L., 172
Geiselman, R. E., 503
Gelfand, M., 171
Geller, D., 213
Gelles, R., 320
Genovese, K., 290, 293
Gentile, D. A., 305, 333, 335, 337, 338, 339, 341
Genuis, M., 328
George, D., 300
George, H., 201
Gerard, H. B., 183, 214, 218, 219
Gerber, J. P., 353
Gerbner, G., 332, 336
Gerdjikov, T., 151
Gergen, K. J., 246, 306
Gergen, M. M., 246
Gerrig, R. J., 95
Gershoff, E., 321
Gerstein, L. H., 300
Gerstenfeld, P. B., 251
Gesch, B., 315
Geyer, A. L., 201
Giancola, P. R., 314
Gibbons, F. X., 128, 140, 277
Gibson, B., 64
Gibson, B. D., 437
Gier, J., 207
Giesler, R. B., 40
Gifford, R., 422, 457, 518
Gigerenzer, G., 89, 116

Gigone, D., 252
Gilbert, D. T., 40, 47, 48, 49, 50, 59, 102, 105, 187, 372, 417, 524, 525
Gill, M. J., 90
Gillath, O., 385
Gillis, J., 516
Gilman, C. P., 158
Gilovich, T., 60, 62, 92, 96, 97, 98, 110, 292, 422, 524
Giltay, E. J., 486
Gino, F., 217
Ginsburg, B. E., 319
Givens, J., 284
Glasman, L. R., 128
Glass, C., 100, 135
Gleason, M. E. J., 275, 390
Glenn, N. D., 179
Glick, B., 347
Glick, P., 402, 434
Glidden, M. V., 464
Gliner, M. D., 252
Global Footprint Network, 515f
Gluszek, A., 408
Gockel, C., 242
Godbout, L., 264
Goel, S., 65
Goethals, G. R., 65, 108, 165, 254
Goethe, J. W., 146, 172
Goetz, J. L., 281
Goggin, W. C., 473
Goh, J., 42
Goldberg, L. L., 367
Goldberg, L. R., 108
Goldberg, M., 247
Goldberg, P., 435
Goldhagen, D. J., 209, 213
Golding, W., 244
Goldman, R., 166
Goldman, W., 363
Goldsamt, L. A., 277
Goldsmith, R. E., 518
Goldstein, A. G., 419
Goldstein, A. P., 342, 347
Goldstein, C. C., 113
Goldstein, J. H., 345
Golec de Davala, A., 55, 185
Goleman, D., 293
Gómez, A., 408
Gonsalkorale, K., 354
Gonsalves, B., 502
Gonzaga, G. C., 369, 377, 387
Gonzales, C., 317
Gonzalez-Vallejo, C., 88
Goodhart, D. E., 65
Goodman, I., 305
Goodsell, C. A., 504

Goplen, J., 431
Gordjin, E., 509
Gordon, S. L., 372, 379
Gortmaker, S. L., 24
Gotlib, I. H., 464, 477
Goto, S. G., 42
Gottlieb, J., 301
Gottlieb, M. C., 295
Gottman, J., 393
Gould, M. S., 200
Gould, R., 387
Gould, S. J., 458
Gouldner, A. W., 280
Gove, W. R., 492
Govern, J., 245
Graetz, K., 44
Grajek, S., 383
Gramzow, R. H., 69
Granstrom, K., 259
Grant, D. R., 251
Graves, J., 239f
Gray, C., 298
Gray, J. D., 61
Graziano, W. G., 57, 340
Greeley, A., 418
Green, A. R., 430
Green, A. S., 390
Green, J., 109
Green, M. C., 95
Green, M. L., 70
Green, S., 363
Green, S. K., 301
Greenberg, A., 362
Greenberg, A. R., 288
Greenberg, J., 53, 69, 71, 371, 412, 413, 460
Greene, D., 148
Greene, E., 511
Greenlees, C., 242
Greenwald, A. G., 86, 87, 89, 124, 125, 150, 401, 430, 432
Gregory, A., 197
Gregory, R., 207
Greitemeyer, T., 140, 305, 336, 340, 347
Grether, J., 282
Griffin, D., 48
Griffin, D. W., 92, 220, 221f, 374
Griffin, K. W., 189
Griffitt, W., 323
Griskevicius, V., 282, 312, 379
Groenenboom, A., 242
Gronlund, C. A., 504
Gross, A. E., 277, 367
Gross, A. M., 102
Gross, J. T., 310
Gross, P. H., 444

Grote, M., 387, 387f
Grove, J. R., 60
Grube, J. W., 413
Gruder, C. L., 40, 162, 299
Gruendl, M., 365f
Gruman, J. A., 114
Gruman, J. C., 415
Grunberger, R., 138
Grusec, J. E., 297
Grush, J. E., 128, 175
Grush, R., 464
Guadagno, R. E., 133, 169
Guardian, 315
Guay, F., 58
Guberova, E., 419
Gueguen, N., 133
Guerin, B., 63, 235
Guerres, A., 517
Guimond, S., 403, 436
Guiness, O., 391
Gunaratna, R., 171
Gunn, G., 67
Gunter, B., 415
Gupta, U., 381, 382f
Guthrie, W., 223
Gutierres, S. E., 366, 367

H

Hacker, H. M., 402
Hackman, J. R., 242
Hadden, J. K., 405
Haddock, G., 180, 401, 417, 434
Haddon, L., 334
Haefeli, W., 68
Hafer, C. L., 414
Hagendoorn, L., 399
Hagerty, M., 530
Hagerty, M. R., 318
Hagtvet, K. A., 20
Haidt, J., 37, 297
Hains, S. C., 259
Halberstadt, J., 365
Haldane, J. B. S., 283
Hall, D. L., 404
Hall, G. C. N., 335
Hall, J. A., 360
Hall, T., 86
Hall, V. C., 149
Hallahan, M., 109
Hallam, J., 335
Halverson, A. M., 508
Hamamura, T., 61
Hamblin, R. L., 346
Hamermesh, D., 363
Hamilton, D. L., 97, 417, 422

Hamm, H. K., 207
Hammerstein, O., 147
Hampson, R. B., 299
Hancock, K., 419
Hancock, R. D., 73
Handelsman, J. B., 132f
Handley, I. M., 172
Haney, C., 508
Hannah, D. B., 437
Hanrahan, S. J., 60
Hansen, P., 361
Hantzi, A., 417
Harbaugh, W. T., 275
Harber, J., 430
Harber, K. D., 112f
Harburg, E. Y., 356
Hardin, G., 455
Hardy, C. H., 239
Hardy, C. L., 275
Hardyck, J. A., 418
Harel, Y., 310
Hargrove, B., 418
Haritos-Fatouros, M., 211
Harkins, S. G., 180, 239, 240, 241, 242
Harkness, K. L., 476
Harley, C. D. G., 516
Harmon-Jones, C., 151
Harmon-Jones, E., 151, 152, 358, 412
Harper, E., 267
Harper, S., 80
Harrel, W. A., 281
Harries, K. D., 323
Harris, E., 353
Harris, J. R., 385
Harris, L. T., 432
Harris, M. J., 112
Harris, R., 341
Harris, V. A., 105, 105f
Harrison, A. A., 358
Hart, A. J., 430
Hart, J., 416
Hart, P. T., 259
Hart, W., 140
Hartnett, J. J., 282
Harton, H. C., 217
Hartup, W. W., 491
Harvey, J. H., 388f
Harvey, R. D., 440
Harvey, R. J., 480
Haselton, M. G., 65, 366
Haslam, N., 103, 411
Haslam, S. A., 419
Hass, R. G., 430
Hastie, R., 59, 252, 259, 497, 507, 509, 510, 510f

Hatfield, E. C., 147, 164, 360, 362, 373, 376, 377, 378, 380, 381, 385, 386
Hatzfeld, J., 343
Hau, K. T., 39
Haugen, J., 25
Haugtvedt, C. P., 161, 174
Havas, D. A., 146
Havel, V., 525
Hawkins, C. B., 124
Hawkins, L. B., 73
Hawthorne, N., 130
Hazan, C., 383, 384, 393
Hazlitt, W., 402, 475
He, Y., 420
Headey, B., 63
Health Canada, 331
Heap, B., 518
Hearold, S., 304
Heath, C., 70, 225
Hebl, M. R., 242, 405
Hecato, 372
Hedge, A., 284
Heider, F., 102
Heimpel, S. A., 68
Heine, S. J., 41, 44, 45, 61, 74, 144, 247, 423
Heinz, A., 314
Heise, L., 330t
Heisenberg, W., 12
Hellman, P., 274
Helmreich, R. L., 260
Helwig-Larsen, M., 196
Hemsley, G., 163
Henderson-King, E. I., 421
Hendrick, C., 167, 379, 388
Hendrick, S. S., 379, 388
Henley, M., 366
Hennenlotter, A., 146
Hennigan, K., 319
Henrich, J., 275
Henslin, M., 98
Hepburn, C., 443
Hepworth, J. T., 407
Herbener, E. S., 369
Herlocker, C. E., 457
Hernandez, A., 329
Herrera, M., 413
Hershberger, S. L., 283
Hershey, J. C., 416
Hertel, G., 242
Hertwig, R., 263
Herzog, S. M., 263
Herzog, T., 109
Heschel, A., 158
Hesley, J. W., 223
Heslin, P. A., 263

Hesse, B., 332
Hewstone, M., 102, 267, 417, 419, 424, 437, 437, 438
Hicks, B. M., 299
Higbee, K. L., 24
Higgins, E. T., 132, 242, 477
Higgins, R. L., 68
Highfield, R., 283
Hilgard, E., 503
Hill, R., 356
Hillery, J. M., 235
Hilmert, C. J., 217
Hilton, J. L., 80, 444
Himmelstein, D. U., 491
Himmler, H., 207
Hinckley, J. Jr., 422
Hine, D. W., 457
Hinsz, V. B., 252, 261
Hippocrates, 323
Hirschberger, G., 352
Hirschman, R. S., 189
Hirt, E. R., 84, 477
Hitchcock, A., 332
Hitler, A., 55, 92, 161, 212, 258
Hitsch, G. J., 361
Hixon, J. G., 417
Ho, S. Y., 370
Hobbes, T., 311
Hobden, K. L., 141
Hodge, C. N., 362, 423
Hodges, B., 201
Hoffman, B., 475
Hoffman, C., 50, 406
Hoffman, K., 367
Hoffman, M. L., 288
Hofling, C. K., 207
Hofmeister, J., 518
Hogan, J., 265
Hogan, R., 265
Hogg, M. A., 175, 253, 259, 408
Hokanson, J. E., 478
Holland, R. W., 79, 152
Hollander, E. P., 265
Hollin, C. R., 505
Holmberg, D., 86
Holmes, J. G., 41, 86, 314, 373, 374, 387
Holmes, O. W., 499
Holmes, S., 10, 16
Holt, R., 509
Holtgraves, T. M., 43, 73
Holtz, R., 411
Holtzworth-Munroe, A., 102
Holyfield, E., 323
Holzberg, A. D., 62

Holzhausen, K. G., 261
Honigman, R., 362
Hoorens, V., 63, 358
Hoover, C. W., 302
Hopkins, N., 437
Hopper, C., 388
Hopper, T. S., 58
Hormuth, S. E., 71
Horner, V., 217, 288
Hornsey, M. J., 217
Hornstein, H. A., 312
Horowitz, I. A., 508
Horowitz, L. M., 69, 371, 383
Horowitz, S. V., 464
Horry, R., 419
Hortacsu, A., 361
Horwitz, A. V., 493, 522
Horwood, L. J., 53, 55
Hosch, H. M., 102, 505t
Hoshino-Browne, E., 144
Houghton, J., 515
Houghton, R. A., 516
House, J., 79
House, R. J., 265
Houston, V., 362
Howard, D. J., 160
Howell, C. J., 522
Howell, R. T., 522
Howell-White, S., 493
Hovland, C. I., 159, 166, 172,
     172f, 407
Hoyle, R. H., 370
Hsee, C. K., 59
Hsing, C., 55419
Huart, J., 436
Huberman, B. A., 456
Huddy, L., 419
Huesmann, L. R., 313, 333,
     333f, 347
Huff, C., 28
Hugenberg, K., 420, 430, 431f
Hughes, M., 492
Hui, C. H., 460
Hull, J. G., 247, 481
Hume, D., 13
Hunsberger, B., 404
Hunt, P., 235
Hunter, J. E., 362
Husband, R. W., 234
Hussein, S., 200
Huston, A. C., 332, 361
Huston, T. L., 374, 380
Huxley, T. H., 235
Hyde, J. S., 399, 478
Hyers, L., 212
Hyers, L. L., 439
Hyman, H. H., 428

I

Iacono, W. G., 178
Ibler, S., 404
Ickes, W., 109, 223, 247, 282, 437
Ijzerman, H., 80
Imai, Y., 61
Imber, L., 420
Imhoff, R., 65, 226, 414
Ingham, A. G., 239, 239f
Inglehart, M. R., 38, 58, 492, 522
Inkster, J. A., 143
Innes, J. M., 12
Insko, C. A., 370, 372
Intergovernmental Panel on
     Climate Change (IPCC), 515
International
     Telecommunication
     Union, 352
Inzlicht, M., 57, 440, 442
Ireland, M. E., 148, 199, 369
Isaiah, 523
Isen, A. M., 100, 279, 279f
Isozaki, M., 249
Itkin, S., 374
Ito, T., 314
Iyengar, S. S., 58

J

Jackman, M. R., 434
Jackson, E. F., 423
Jackson, J. M., 109, 236, 240,
     240f
Jackson, L. A., 335, 362
Jackson, L. M., 407
Jacob, C., 133
Jacobs, R. C., 198
Jacobson, C. K., 208
Jacobson, K. C., 313
Jacobson, L., 111
Jacobson, N. S., 102
Jacoby, S., 371
Jacques-Tiura, A. J., 331f
Jaffe, Y., 247, 343, 344f
James, H., 369
James, J., 314
James, W., 71, 145, 147, 404
Jamieson, D. W., 113, 400
Janda, L. H., 363
Janes, L. M., 411
Janis, I. L., 167, 167f, 172, 255,
     256, 259, 260, 461
Jankowiak, W. R., 378
Janoff-Bullman, R., 522
Jaremka, L. M., 393
Jason, L., 301

Jaworski, M., 376
Jelalian, E., 83
Jellison, J. M., 109
Jemmott, J. B. III, 485
Jenkins, A. C., 432
Jenkins, H. M., 97
Jenkins-Smith, H., 163
Jenner, S., 242
Jennings, D., 97
Jensen, J. D., 169
Jensen-Campbell, L. A., 57
Jervis, R., 80
Jetten, J., 217, 267
Ji, L., 109
Job, V., 57
John, L. J., 28
John, L. K., 91
John, O. P., 370
Johns, M., 442
Johnson, A. L., 233
Johnson, B., 411
Johnson, B. T., 168, 180, 265, 336
Johnson, C., 356
Johnson, D. J., 368
Johnson, D. W., 464
Johnson, H., 386
Johnson, J. D., 152, 335, 437
Johnson, J. G., 333
Johnson, M. H., 100, 476
Johnson, M. K., 404, 420, 432
Johnson, N., 336
Johnson, N. S., 441
Johnson, R. D., 246
Johnson, R. T., 464
Johnson, S., 413
Johnson, T. P., 43
Johnson, W., 522
Johnston, L., 87
Johnston, L. C., 417
Joiner, T. E., 200, 477
Joinson, A. N., 390
Jonas, K., 200
Jones, C. R., 161
Jones, E. E., 71, 103, 105, 105f,
     107, 135
Jones, J. M., 182, 183, 184, 185,
     187, 370, 439
Jones, J. T., 372, 383
Jones, R. A., 172, 173
Jones, T. K., 405
Jones, W. H., 392
Jordan, B. D., 366
Jordan, C. H., 56, 152, 369
Josephs, R., 43
Josephs, R. A., 481
Josephson, W. L., 335
Jost, J. T., 52, 402, 434, 518

Joubert, 218
Jourard, S., 387, 388
Jourden, F. J., 70
Judd, C., 432, 439
Judd, C. M., 252, 401
Judd, J. W., 419
Judge, T. A., 55, 265
Julian, J. W., 264
Jussim, L., 12, 80, 111, 112, 112f,
     113, 116, 372, 399, 443

K

Kachelski, R. A., 79
Kagan, J., 11, 313
Kagehiro, D. K., 508
Kahan, D. M., 163
Kahle, L. R., 126
Kahlor, L. A., 328
Kahn, A., 461
Kahn, M. W., 319
Kahneman, D., 50, 90, 95, 97,
     98, 99, 262, 263, 358, 467
Kaiser, C. R., 403
Kaiser Family Foundation, 336
Kalick, M., 362
Kalin, R., 39, 400
Kalton, G., 23
Kalven, H. Jr., 508, 509, 510
Kambara, T., 324
Kameda, T., 267
Kammer, D., 108
Kanagawa, C., 41
Kandel, D. B., 371
Kandinsky, W., 410
Kanekar, S., 102
Kang, S., 442
Kanten, A. B., 61
Kaplan, M. F., 254, 417, 510
Kaplan, R. M., 483
Kaprio, J., 488
Karasawa, M., 358
Karau, S. J., 240, 240f, 242, 399
Karberg, J., 314
Karna, A., 343
Karney, B. R., 102, 388, 393
Kashima, E. S., 42
Kashima, Y., 42
Kasser, T., 315, 520, 523
Kassin, S. M., 113, 502, 505t
Katz, A. M., 356
Katz, E., 176
Katz, J., 477
Katzev, R., 302
Katzev, T., 219
Kaufman, J., 321
Kaufman-Gilliland, C. M., 458

Kawachi, I., 318, 490
Kawakami, K., 123, 212, 318, 401, 448
Kay, A. C., 400, 402, 434
Kaye, D., 167f
Kearney, K., 413
Keating, J. P., 180
Keelan, J., 360
Keelan, J. P. R., 383
Keillor, G., 61
Keith, P., 386
Keller, E. B., 176
Keller, J., 442
Keller, K., 282
Kellerman, A., 327
Kellerman, J., 394
Kelley, H. H., 104, 104f, 113
Kelley, K., 345
Kelly, B. R., 320
Kelly, D. J., 359, 419
Kelly, R. J., 152
Kelman, H. C., 465, 466
Keltner, D., 281, 370, 402
Kemmelmeir, M., 42
Kennedy, B. P., 318
Kenny, D. A., 370, 372
Kenrick, D. T., 267, 277, 323, 366, 370, 381
Kenworthy, L., 267
Keown, L. A., 321
Kernis, M. H., 56
Kerr, M., 92
Kerr, N. L., 219, 240, 242, 318, 458, 459, 509, 510, 511, 516, 517
Kesebir, S., 525
Kessler, R. C., 383
Key, E., 345
Keys, C. B., 252
Kibler, J. L., 418
Kidd, J. B., 70
Kidd, R. F., 282
Kiecolt-Glaser, J. K., 485, 488
Kierkegaard, S., 14
Kiesler, C. A., 187
Kight, T. D., 378
Kihlstrom, J. F., 38, 84
Kilburn, J., 341
Kim, H. S., 42, 43, 43f
Kimball, M. M., 399
Kimmel, A. J., 28
Kimmel, M. J., 463
Kinder, D. R., 82
King, L. A., 489
King, L. L., 372
Kingdon, J. W., 60
Kingsbury, G. G., 20

Kingston, D. A., 328
Kinnier, R. T., 97
Kinzler, K. D., 408
Kipling, R., 412
Kirschner, P., 167f
Kirsh, S. J., 332
Kirshenbaum, H. M., 504
Kitaigorodskii, A. I., 14
Kitayama, S., 40, 41, 44f, 45, 74, 109, 196, 284, 358
Kite, M. E., 433
Kitt, A. S., 318
Klaas, E. T., 132
Klauer, K. C., 432
Klebold, D., 353
Kleck, R. E., 439
Klee, P., 410
Klein, D. J., 9
Klein, R., 372
Klein, S. B., 73
Klein, W. M., 357
Kleinhesselink, R., 413
Kleinke, C. L., 207
Kleinsmith, J., 315
Klentz, B., 368
Klerman, G. L., 522
Klinger, M., 89
Klopfer, P. H., 234
Klucharev, V., 219
Knight, J. A., 357, 359
Knight, P. A., 164
Knowles, E., 227, 236
Knowles, E. S., 302
Knox, R., 143
Knudson, R. M., 464
Kobrynowicz, M., 420
Koch, J., 165
Koebel, F., 258
Koebel, S., 258
Koehler, D. J., 91, 94
Koenig, A. M., 178
Koestner, R., 40
Koestner, R. F., 361
Kohn, N. W., 262, 263
Kolivas, E. D., 102
Kong, C. K., 39
Kong, L. L., 42
Konrath, S. H., 55
Koo, M., 526
Koole, S. L., 352
Koomen, W., 399
Koop, C. E., 328, 329
Koresh, D., 182, 185
Koriat, A., 94
Korn, J. H., 27
Korte, C., 295
Koskenvuo, M., 488

Koss, M. P., 330t
Kowalski, R. M., 480
Kozu, J., 298
Krackow, A., 208
Krahe, B., 330t, 335, 339
Kramer, A. E., 241
Kramer, G. P., 100
Kramer, M., 474
Kramer, R. M., 463
Krantz, S., 100f
Kraus, M. W., 402
Kraus, S. J., 124
Kraut, R. E., 303
Kravitz, D. A., 238
Krebs, D., 275, 276, 285, 359
Krendl, A. C., 442
Kressel, K., 467
Kretz, S., 369
Krisberg, K., 165
Krismer, K., 149
Krizan, Z., 62
Kropotkin, P., 458
Krosnick, J. A., 23, 158, 178, 179
Krueger, A., 122
Krueger, J., 65, 116, 418
Krueger, J. I., 409
Krueger, R. F., 522
Krueger, W. K., 299
Kruger, J., 60, 90, 94, 97, 389
Kruglanski, A. W., 116, 171, 185, 267, 311
Krull, D. S., 109, 187
Kubany, E. S., 346
Kubey, R., 337
Kugihara, N., 242
Kuhlmeier, V. A., 280
Kuiper, N. A., 477
Kulechov, L. V., 82
Kulik, J. A., 217
Kunda, Z., 39, 39f, 68, 357, 416, 437, 437, 445, 446f, 474
Kunkel, S., 336
Kunst-Wilson, W., 358
Kuntsche, E. N., 332
Kuntsman, J. W., 431
Kupper, N., 483
Kurz, E., 407
Kus, L. A., 477
Kutner, L. A., 341

L

La Rochefoucauld, 128, 135, 376, 526
LaFrance, M., 48
Lage, S., 267
Lagerspetz, K., 313, 342

Laird, J. D., 85, 146, 394
Laird, N., 502
Lake, E. A., 71
Lakin, J. L., 355, 369
Lalancette, M-F., 224
Lalonde, R. N., 60
Lalwani, A. K., 43
Lam, R., 397–398
Lamal, P. A., 84
Lambert, A. J., 370
Lambert, N., 328, 330
Lamon, S. J., 399
Lamoreaux, M., 43
Landeen, J., 492f
Landers, A., 22, 344
Landon, A., 22
Lane, T., 217
Langer, E. J., 57, 58, 69, 98, 173, 420
Langford, D. J., 288
Langlois, J. H., 362, 363, 364
Långström, N., 313
Lanzetta, J. T., 147
Lao-tzu, 48, 61
Larey, T. S., 262
Larkin, C., 65
Larrick, R. P., 323
Larsen, K. S., 224
Larsen, O. N., 199
Larsen, R. J., 313
Larsen-Rife, D., 55
Larson, C. L., 313
Larson, J. R. Jr., 252
Larsson, K., 234
Larwood, L., 63, 70
Lasater, T. M., 165
Laser, T. D., 47
Lassiter, G. D., 63, 108, 502
Latané, B., 236, 239, 241, 242, 268, 290, 291, 291f, 292f, 293, 294, 299, 300
Latham, G. P., 264
Lau, G. P., 434
Laughlin, P. R., 261
Laumann, E. O., 102
Laurier Institute for the Study of Public Opinion and Policy (LISPOP), 20
Law, R. W., 485
Layden, M. A., 247
Lazarsfeld, P. F., 14
Lazer, D., 251
Le Mens, G., 220
Leary, M. R., 10, 20, 37, 41, 52, 72, 73, 139, 352, 353, 354, 480
LeBlanc, B. A., 152

LeBoeuf, R., 102
LeDoux, J. E., 88
Lee, C., 460
Lee, J. W., 40
Lee, L. F., 508
Lee, R. Y. P., 369
Lee, S., 125
Lee, Y. T., 74, 109, 399
Lefebvre, L. M., 74
Lehavot, K., 370
Lehman, D. R., 23, 45, 74, 117, 144, 423
Leimgruber, K., 288
Leippe, M. R., 142, 498, 499
Leiserowitz, A., 518
Lemay, E. P. Jr., 362
Lemieux, S., 264
Lempert, R. O., 117
Lemyre, L., 412
Lench, H. C., 64
L'Engle, M., 115, 116
Lenhart, A., 352
Lennon, J., 422
Lenton, A. P., 363
Leodoro, G., 301
Leonard, J. B., 414
Leonardelli, G. J., 80, 355
Leone, C., 73
LePage, A., 326
LePine, J. A., 55
Lepine, M., 318
Lepore, L., 417
Lepore, S., 489
Lepore, S. J., 237
Lepper, M., 80, 81, 81f, 83, 84, 148
Lepper, M. R., 58
Lerma, M., 368
Lerner, M. J., 63, 413, 414
Leshner, A., 17
Leung, K., 460
Levav, J., 127
Leventhal, H., 168, 189, 482
Levesque, M. J., 102
Levin, S., 403
Levine, J. M., 215, 267, 268
Levine, M., 290, 295
Levine, R., 190
Levine, R. V., 63, 295, 296f
Levinger, G., 239f, 455
Levinson, M., 459
Levitan, L. C., 192
Levy, D. A., 197
Levy, S. R., 423
Levy-Leboyer, C., 168
Lewandowski, G., 393
Lewicki, P., 375, 375f
Lewin, K., 6, 223, 265

Lewinsohn, P. M., 477, 478
Lewis, C. S., 142, 143, 180, 491
Lewis, D. O., 313
Lewis, E. D., 42
Lewis, J., 394
Lewis, P., 363
Lewis, R., 380
Lewis, R. S., 42
Lewis, S. A., 463
Leyens, J. P., 334, 372, 411
Li, N., 365
Li, N. P., 379
Li, Y., 96
Liao, M., 43
Liberman, A., 170
Lichtblau, E., 190, 429
Lichtenberg, 225
Lichtenstein, P., 313
Lichtenstein, S., 94
Lieberman, M. D., 152, 354f
Liebler, A., 91
Lilienfeld, S. O., 472
Lim, D. T. K., 101
Lin, D. Y., 61
Lind, E. A., 303
Linder, D., 374
Lindsay, R. C. L., 24, 498, 499, 502, 504
Lindsey, S., 50
Lindskold, S., 468
Linssen, H. M., 399
Linville, P., 419
Linz, D., 328, 331
Lippa, R. A., 359
Lipsey, M., 347
Lipsitz, A., 133
Little, A., 364
Littman, R. A., 319
Livingston, R. W., 73, 363
Livingstone, S., 334
Lizzadro, T., 299
Locke, E. A., 264
Locke, J., 216
Locke, K. D., 371
Locke, S. B., 485
Locksley, A., 410, 443
Lockwood, P., 39, 39f, 40, 52
Lodewijkx, H. F. M., 262
Loewenstein, G., 28, 48, 318
Lofland, J., 184
Loftin, C., 327
Loftus, E. F., 84, 85, 89, 125, 498, 500, 502, 503
Logel, C. E. R., 441, 442
Lombardo, J. P., 376
LoMonaco, B., 196
London, P., 304

Lopez, D. F., 89f
Lopyan, K. J., 128
Lord, C. G., 81, 84, 444
Lord, W., 256
Lorenz, K., 311, 312
Lortie-Lussier, M., 264
Lott, A. J., 216, 375
Lott, B. E., 216, 375
Loughman, S., 411
Louis, W. R., 267
Lovett, F., 63
Lowe, C. A., 102
Lowenstein, D., 338
Lowery, B. S., 403
Lubek, H. J., 204
Lucas, R. E., 524
Lücken, M., 267
Lüdtke, O., 20
Ludwig, J., 22
Lueptow, L. B., 434
Lueptow, M. B., 434
Lukose, R. M., 456
Lumsdaine, A. A., 159, 172, 172f
Lumsden, A., 159
Lun, J., 43
Lutsky, N., 47
Lüüs, C. A. E., 261
Lydon, J., 207, 368, 368f
Lykken, D. T., 250, 356
Lynch, J. W., 490
Lynch, M., 151
Lynch, M. E., 416
Lynham, J., 458
Lynn, M., 301, 459
Lyons, D., 436
Lyons, P., 506
Lyubomirsky, S., 489, 524

M

Ma, V., 41
Maas, J., 236
Maass, A., 216, 267, 268, 423, 424
Macchiavelli, N., 72
Maccoby, N., 176, 177f, 180
MacCoun, R. J., 219, 510
MacDonald, G., 48, 197, 288, 314, 353, 354, 373, 393
MacDonald, S., 314
MacDonald, T. K., 47, 481, 481f, 482
MacFarlane, S. W., 323
Mack, D., 363
Mackie, D. M., 167, 175, 417, 418
Mackinnon, S. P., 369
Macleod, J., 36
MacLin, O. H., 504

Macrae, C. N., 366, 416, 417, 432
Macrae, N., 87
Madey, S. F., 96
Maddux, J. E., 169, 471, 472, 475
Maddux, W. M., 407, 465
Madison, J., 92
Madon, S., 112
Mae, L., 82
Maeder, G., 184
Magaro, P. A., 100, 476
Mageau, G. A., 58
Magill-Evans, J., 321
Mahalik, J. R., 282
Maheswaran, D., 162
Main, K. J., 440
Maio, G. R., 171, 180
Major, B., 318, 447
Makhijani, M., 399
Malamuth, N., 328, 329, 331f
Maleckóvá, J., 122
Malkiel, B., 92
Malle, B., 107
Mallet, R. K., 460
Malone, D. T., 187
Malone, P. S., 102
Malpass, R. G., 419, 419f, 504
Manchanda, P., 177
Mandela, N., 9
Mander, A., 342
Maner, J. K., 316, 353, 355, 360, 392
Manis, M., 132, 444, 445
Mankoff, R., 218, 372, 415
Mann, L., 244
Mannell, R. C., 149
Manning, R., 290
Marchuetz, C., 363
Marcus, S., 205
Marcus-Newhall, A., 317
Marigold, D. C., 56, 373
Markey, P., 133
Markman, G. D., 363
Markman, H. J., 394
Markman, K. D., 84, 97
Marks, G., 65, 357
Markus, H. R., 8, 38, 41, 43, 43f, 44f, 45, 57, 74, 196, 415
Marmot, M. G., 487
Marsden, P., 320
Marsh, H. W., 39, 40, 52
Marshall, R., 41, 256
Marston, M-V., 319
Martens, A., 136
Martin, B., 238
Martin, H., 257
Martin, L., 252
Martin, L. L., 116

Martin, P. Y., 267
Martin, R., 267
Martino, S. C., 336
Maruyama, G. M., 20, 435
Marvelle, K., 363
Marx, K., 235, 318, 460
Mason, W., 65
Masserman, J. H., 288
Massey, C., 64
Mast, M. S., 360
Mastekaasa, A., 493
Masuda, T., 42, 109
Masure, R. H., 234
Matheny, A., 313
Mathewson, G. C., 183
Matthews, K. A., 489
Matthews, S. C., 484
Matz, D. C., 404
Maugham, W. S., 367
Maurice, J. K., 367
Mauro, R., 508
Maxwell, G. M., 383
Mayer, J. D., 100, 278, 476
Mayr, U., 275
Mazur, A., 316
Mazzella, R., 506
Mazzoni, G., 501
Mazzuca, J., 336
McAlister, A., 189, 189f
McAllister, H. A., 502
McAndrew, F. T., 173, 312, 315
McBurney, D. H., 366
McCann, C. D., 73, 132
McCarthy, J. F., 320
McCauley, C., 251, 258, 259, 399
McCauley, M., 503
McClure, J., 104
McConahay, J. B., 400
McConnell, A. R., 442
McConnell, H. K., 85
McCord, J., 251
McCormick, C. M., 315
McCoy, S., 447
McCullough, J. L., 359
McDonald, M., 95
McDonald, M. M., 366
McFarland, C., 86, 101, 253
McGarty, C., 244
McGillicuddy, N., 467
McGlone, M. S., 175
McGlynn, F. D., 261
McGovern, K., 79
McGrath, J. E., 233
McGraw, A. P., 96
McGraw, K. M., 420
McGregor, I., 56, 152, 413
McGue, M., 178, 299

McGuire, C. V., 226
McGuire, W. J., 160f, 188, 190,
    226, 227
McInman, A. D., 60
McKay, L., 440
McKelvie, S. J., 95
McKenna, F. P., 63
McKenna, K. Y. A., 251, 390
McKenzie-Mohr, D., 345
McLarney, A., 172
McLatchie, N., 340
McLaughlin, D. S., 303
McLuhan, M., 174
McMillan, D., 437
McMillen, D., 276, 278
McMullen, M. N., 97
McNulty, J. K., 388, 394
McNulty, S. E., 102
McQueen, L. R., 458
McQuinn, R. D., 376, 388
McTavish, J., 459
Mead, G. H., 40
Meade, R. D., 223
Means, B., 100
Medalia, N., 199
Medvec, V. H., 92, 96, 97, 292
Meehl, G. A., 516
Meertens, R. W., 152, 408, 459
Mehl, M. R., 8, 48, 352, 388
Meindl, J. R., 413
Meissner, A., 419
Meissner, C. A., 500, 503, 504
Meleshko, K. A., 480
Mellers, B. A., 96
Mellon, P., 111
Memmert, D., 202
Memon, A., 501, 503, 505t
Mendell, N. R., 393
Mendolia, M., 252
Mentzel, R. K., 288
Merikle, P., 80
Merton, R., 111
Merton, R. K., 318
Mesout, J., 499
Messick, D. M., 65, 237, 418, 460
Messner, S. F., 250–251
Metha, A. T., 97
Mettee, D. R., 374
Meyerowitz, J. A., 62
Meyers, S., 377
Mezei, L., 418
Mezulis, A. H., 478
Michaels, J., 235
Michela, J. L., 68
Mickelson, K. D., 383
Middleton, T., 398
Mikula, G., 460

Mikulincer, M., 287, 352, 383, 413
Milgaard, D., 497, 498, 507, 508
Milgram, A., 204, 211
Milgram, S., 5, 202–214, 203f,
    205f, 214t, 215, 215f, 217,
    222, 223, 327, 345
Mill, J. S., 197, 258
Millar, M., 410
Millar, M. G., 125
Millard, R. J., 24
Miller, A. G., 105, 204, 213
Miller, C. E., 219
Miller, C. T., 81, 109, 443
Miller, D. L., 83
Miller, D. T., 36, 97, 253, 409,
    414, 420
Miller, F. A., 58
Miller, G., 366, 496–497, 507, 508
Miller, G. E., 65, 484, 485
Miller, J. G., 281, 298
Miller, L., 209
Miller, L. C., 387
Miller, L. E., 128
Miller, N., 65, 164, 173, 277, 279,
    313, 314, 317, 318, 357
Miller, P. A., 287, 298
Miller, P. J. E., 374, 383
Miller, R. L., 115
Miller, R. S., 69, 73, 215, 392
Miller, W., 225, 370
Millett, K., 388
Mills, J., 183, 386
Milne, A. B., 417
Milun, R., 314
Milyavskaya, M., 353
Mims, P. R., 282
Ming, Y., 421
Mio, J. S., 459
Mirabile, R. R., 192
Mirsky, S., 285
Mischel, W., 222
Mishal, M., 105
Mishna, F., 310
Mita, T., 359
Mitchell, G., 460
Mitchell, J., 380
Mitchell, J. P., 197, 432
Mitchell, K. J., 501
Mitchell, T., 73
Mitchell, T. R., 85
Modigliani, A., 211
Moe, J. L., 370
Moeller, S. J., 52
Moffitt, T. E., 313
Moghaddam, F. M., 370, 448
Mojzisch, A., 260
Molander, E. A., 63

Moller, I., 339
Molouki, S., 223
Monge, P. R., 58
Monin, B., 430
Monroe, M., 200
Monson, T. C., 223
Montaigne, 97, 128
Monteith, M. J., 416
Montgomery, D. A., 507
Montoya, R. M., 361, 372
Moody, K., 190
Moon, S. M., 182
Moons, W. G., 167, 175
Moor, B. G., 354
Moore, D., 184
Moore, D. A., 104, 163
Moore, D. L., 236, 237
Moore, D. W., 173
Moore, J., 410
Moore, J. C., 132
Moore, S., 316, 326
Mor, N., 478
Morales, L., 95
Moran, T., 465
Moreland, R. L., 268, 358
Morgan, C. A., 499
Morgan, K., 480
Morgan, J. R., 70
Mori, H., 146
Mori, K., 146
Morier, D., 132
Morling, B., 43
Mormille, A., 290
Morris, K., 166
Morris, K. A., 40
Morris, R., 314
Morris, W. N., 215
Morrison, D., 328
Morrison, E. L., 364
Morrow, L., 196
Morry, M. M., 430
Moscovici, S., 12, 249, 267, 268
Moskowitz, G. B., 465
Motherhood Project, 191
Mouton, J. S., 466
Moyer, K. E., 313
Moylan, S., 100
Moynihan, D. P., 11
Mucchi-Faina, A., 267
Muehlenhard, C. L., 102
Mueller, J., 345
Mueller, U., 335
Mugny, G., 267
Mullainathan, S., 429
Mullen, B., 60, 65, 217, 234,
    236, 237, 240, 256, 259,
    267, 342, 410, 419

Mullen, E., 370, 407
Muller, R., 516
Muller, S., 168
Mullin, C. R., 328
Munhall, P. J., 63
Munro, G. D., 82
Muraven, M., 56, 57
Murphy, C. M., 14
Murphy-Berman, V., 460
Murray, D., 56, 223
Murray, D. M., 499
Murray, S. L., 114, 370, 373, 374
Murroni, E., 165
Murstein, B., 361
Musgrave, S., 130, 131
Musialowski, D., 345
Musil, R., 138
Muson, G., 332
Musselman, L., 364
Mussweiler, T., 148
Myers, D., 199, 250, 250f,
    254f, 435
Myers, D. G., 59, 392, 493, 514n
Myers, J., 263
Myers, K. M., 86, 99
Myers, L. B., 63
Myers, N., 327, 519, 520

N

Nacoste, R. W., 370
Nadler, A., 247, 281, 282
Naffrechoux, M., 267
Nagar, D., 237
Nail, P. R., 197, 225
Nair, H., 177
Nasby, W., 372
Nasser, G. A., 468
National Academy of Sciences,
    515
National Center for Health
    Statistics (NCHS), 421, 487
National Safety Council, 96
National Television Violence
    Study, 331
Navarette, C. D., 417
Nawrat, R., 278
Nay, W. R., 282
Naylor, J. C., 265
Nazareth, A. M., 102
Neal, T. L., 146
Neely, R., 301
Neff, K., 56
Neff, L. A., 388
Neiburger, C. S., 406
Nelligan, J. S., 383
Nelson, E., 165

Nelson, L., 102, 420
Nelson, L. D., 364
Nelson, T. E., 444, 445
Nemeth, C. J., 216, 259, 260,
    262, 267, 268
Nesler, M. S., 139
Nettle, D., 65
Nettles, B. L., 182, 185
Neumann, R., 199
Newby-Clark, I. R., 90, 152
Newcomb, T. M., 178, 179, 243,
    356, 369
Newell, B. R., 88
Newman, L. S., 109
Newman, R. I., 69
Newth, S., 101
Nezlek, J. B., 359
Nguyen, D-H., 102
Nias, D. K. B., 371
Nichols, J., 293
Nicholson, C., 168
Nicholson, N., 224
Nicks, S. D., 27
Nida, S., 291, 354
Nie, N. H., 389
Niebuhr, R., 64
Niehuis, S., 374
Nielsen, 331
Niemi, G. J., 345
Niemiec, C. P., 353
Nietzel, M. T., 511
Nietzsche, F., 408
Night, D., 427–428
Nigro, G. N., 407
Nijstad, B. A., 262
Nisa, 380
Nisbett, E. K., 526
Nisbett, R. E., 42, 42f, 107, 109,
    115, 117, 265, 321, 421
Nix, B. D., 479
Nock, S. L., 125
Noble, A. M., 509
Nolan, S. A., 352
Nolen-Hoeksema, S., 478
Noller, P., 74, 383, 387, 393
Noon, E., 505
Noor, M., 465
Nordgren, L. F., 288, 353
Norem, J. K., 65
Norenzayan, A., 109, 295
North, O., 209
Norton, M. I., 280, 370
Nosek, B. A., 51, 124, 125, 401
Nosow, S., 284
Notarius, C. I., 394
Novalis, 216
Nowak, M., 283

Nurius, P., 38
Nurmi, J.-E., 53
Nuttin, J. M. Jr., 358

O

Oakes, P. J., 419
Oaten, M., 57
O'Brien, E. H., 55
O'Brien, L. T., 416
O'Connell, G. B., 440
Oddone-Paolucci, E., 328
O'Dea, T. F., 185
Ohbuchi, K., 324
O'Heeron, R. C., 488
O'Hegarty, M., 168
Oishi, S., 42, 43, 525
O'Keefe, D. J., 169
Oldenquist, A., 459
Oldham, T., 217
O'Leary, K. D., 393
Oleson, K. C., 437
Olfson, M., 483
Oliner, P. M., 304
Oliner, S. P., 304
Olson, C. K., 341
Olson, E. A., 504
Olson, I. R., 363
Olson, J. M., 73, 113, 122, 128,
    141, 152, 163, 180, 414
Olson, K., 367
Olson, M. A., 161
Olweus, D., 313, 314
O'Malley, P. M., 20
O'Mara, A., 52
O'Mara, E. M., 102
Omoto, A. M., 301, 380
Open Secrets, 175
Opotow, S., 303
Orbell, J. M., 458
Orendain, S., 519
Organisation for Economic
    Co-operation and
    Development (OECD), 525
Orive, R., 246
Orlandi, M. A., 189
Ormiston, M., 259
Ornstein, R., 133
Ortega, A. H., 262
Ortega, S. T., 492
Ortiz, V., 443
Orwell, G., 86
Osbeck, L. M., 370
Osborne, D., 109
Osborne, J. W., 441
Osgood, C. E., 467, 468
Oskamp, S., 127

Osofsky, M. J., 136
Osswald, S., 305
Osterhouse, R. A., 180
Ostrom, T. M., 359, 418
Ouellette, J. A., 128
Ovid, 275, 361
Owyang, M. T., 363
Oyserman, D., 42

P

Pack, S. J., 132, 134
Packer, D. J., 204, 259
Padawer-Singer, A., 226
Padgett, V. R., 207
Page, S. E., 259, 267
Pallak, M. S., 165, 171
Palmer, D. L., 407
Palmer, E. L., 190
Paloutzian, R., 175
Paluck, E. L., 169
Pandey, J., 109, 237
Papastamou, S., 267
Pape, R., 311
Parashar, U. D., 96
Parents Television Council, 332
Parish, E. A., 387
Park, B. M., 419
Park, C. M., 401
Park, L. E., 56
Parke, R. D., 334
Parker, K. D., 492
Parker, K. J., 485
Parks, C. D., 468
Parliament of the World
    Religions, 304
Pascal, B., 87
Pascarella, E. T., 250
Pashler, H., 263
Passariello, C., 225
Patrick, B., 487
Patterson, G. R., 319, 320, 359
Paulhus, D. L., 54, 101, 139,
    479, 480
Pauling, L., 460
Paulus, P. B., 235, 259, 262, 263
Pavelich, J. L., 108
Payne, B. K., 287, 432
Payne, R., 487
Pearson, L. B., 468
Peckham, V., 239f
Pedersen, A., 401
Pedersen, A. F., 485
Pedersen, W. C., 313, 317
Peetz, J., 48, 67, 92, 483
Pegalis, L. J., 387
Pelham, B. W., 471

Peng, K., 227
Pennebaker, J. W., 8, 148, 199, 352, 391, 399, 482, 488, 489
Penner, L., 282
Pennington, N., 507, 509
Penrod, S. D., 328, 331, 503, 505, 509
Pentland, S., 163
Penton-Voak, I. S., 364, 365
Pepitone, A., 243
Peplau, L. A., 379, 387, 388, 491, 492
Pereira, C., 407
Pereira, J., 338
Perie, M., 62
Perkins, D. V., 477
Perkins, H. W., 491
Perlman, L. A., 466, 491
Perls, F. S., 344
Perrault, S., 370
Perrett, D. I., 315, 364, 365
Perretta, S., 503
Perrin, S., 224
Persico, N., 363
Perunovic, W. Q. E., 40
Pessin, J., 234
Peters, E., 168
Peterson, B. E., 404
Peterson, C., 69, 387, 476, 486
Peterson, J. L., 336
Peterson, R. S., 267
Peterson-Lewis, S., 332
Peto, R., 121
Petrocelli, J. V., 97
Petruska, R., 299
Pettigrew, J. D., 401, 412
Pettigrew, T. F., 401, 404, 405, 408, 423
Petty, R. E., 124, 146, 148, 152, 160, 161, 162, 164, 166, 167, 171, 172, 180, 242, 507
Pew Research Center, 338, 356, 386, 390
Phelan, J. E., 436
Phelps, E., 126
Philbrick, K., 295
Phillips, A. C., 526
Phillips, C. M., 345
Phillips, D., 384
Phillips, D. P., 200
Phillips, K. A., 362
Pickett, K., 403, 490f, 525
Pierce, J., 365
Piff, P. K., 402
Piliavin, I. M., 276, 294
Piliavin, J. A., 275, 276, 306
Pincus, H. A., 483

Pincus, J. H, 313
Pinel, E. C., 114, 440
Pinker, S., 348, 435
Pinkus, R. T., 52
Pittinsky, T., 442
Place, K., 378
Place, S. S., 377
Plaks, J. E., 242
Plant, E. A., 114, 416, 431
Plato, 334, 434
Platow, M., 199
Plaut, V. C., 363, 364
Pliner, P., 133
Poincaré, J. H., 17
Pollmann, M. M. H., 49
Pollock, V. E., 314
Pomazal, J. R., 282
Pompitakpan, C., 164
Poniewozik, J., 80
Pool, G. J., 152
Poon, C. S. K., 91
Popenoe, D., 392
Pornpitakpan, C., 164
Portley, R. M., 485
Postlewaite, A., 363
Postmes, T., 246, 259
Poulin, F., 251
Powell, M. C., 386
Pratkanis, A. R., 71, 162, 259, 281
Pratt-Hyatt, J. S., 403
Pratto, F., 403
Predmore, S. C., 388
Prelec, D., 28
Prentice, D. A., 95, 409
Prentice-Dunn, S., 247, 429
Pressley, M., 222
Presson, B. K., 98
Preston, E., 84
Price, G. H., 368
Priel, B., 385
Prislin, R., 152
Pritchard, C., 335
Probst, T., 461
Prohaska, M. L., 371
Prohaska, T., 65, 112, 113
Pronin, E., 61, 63, 108, 110, 223
Prost, J., 251
Prothrow-Stith, D., 464
Pruitt, D. G., 463, 465, 467
Pryke, S., 504
Pryor, J. B., 102
Pryor, J. H., 62, 300
Przybylski, A. K., 341
Psalms, 472
Public Opinion, 63
Purvis, J. A., 388
Pusser, H. E., 305

Putnam, K. M., 313
Putnam, R., 305, 336, 337, 390
Putnam, R. D., 389
Pyszczynski, T., 69, 71, 378, 412, 478

Q
Quas, J. A., 64
Quinlivan, E., 353
Quinn, D. M., 440, 441f
Quinton, W. J., 447
Quoidbach, J., 108, 523

R
Radloff, C., 108
Radtke, H. L., 204
Raine, A., 313
Raines, B. E., 189
Rainey, D., 363
Rajecki, D. W., 361
Ramirez, A., 165
Ramirez, J. M., 345
Randall, P. K., 366
Randler, C., 369
Range, L. M., 473
Rank, S. G., 208
Ransom, S., 321
Rapoport, A., 454
Rapson, R., 148, 378
Rasinski, K. A., 265
Rasmussen, J. L., 361
Ratner, R. K., 253
Rawls, J., 460
Rawn, C. D., 72
Raye, C. L., 432
Raymond, P., 102
Read, J. D., 505
Read, S. J., 93
Reagan, R., 422
Reber, J., 114
Reed, D., 405
Regan, D. T., 128, 180, 376
Reicher, S., 246
Reid, J. B., 320
Reid, P., 336
Reid, S., 130, 131
Reis, H. T., 125, 358, 359, 387
Reisenzein, R., 325
Rempel, J. K., 383, 387
Renaud, H., 474
Renner, C. H., 399
Repetti, R. L., 488
Ressler, R. K., 329
Reynolds, J., 64
Rhine, R. J., 171

Rhoades, L., 149
Rhoads, K., 65
Rhoads, K. V. L., 169
Rhodes, G., 364, 365, 419
Rhodes, M. G., 420
Rhodes, N., 492
Rhodewalt, F., 71
Rholes, W. S., 109, 132, 383, 384
Riad, J. K., 314
Rice, B., 61
Rice, M. E., 297
Rice, R. W., 264
Rich, B. L., 55
Richards, K., 361
Richards, Z., 438
Richardson, L. F., 452
Richardson, R., 354
Richeson, J. A., 360, 416, 442, 448
Richtel, M., 327
Ridge, R. D., 114
Riess, M., 72
Rietzschel, E. F., 262
Rigby, C. S., 341
Riggio, R. E., 371
Riggs, J. M., 71
Ringelmann, M., 238
Riordan, C. A., 60, 376
Risen, J. L., 96, 422
Risucci, D. A., 47
Rita, H., 488
Riva, P., 354
Rivera, L. M., 416
Robberson, M. R., 168
Roberts, J. V., 96
Robins, G., 103
Robins, R. W., 55, 64
Robinson, B. A., 421
Robinson, M. D., 313, 523
Robinson, M. S., 478
Robinson, T. N., 347
Robustelli, S. L., 111
Rochat, F., 211
Rocklin, T., 224
Rodeheffer, C., 341
Rodgers, R., 147
Rodin, J., 57, 58, 293
Rodriguez, M. S., 484
Roese, N. L., 96, 152, 400
Roese, N. J., 113
Roethke, T., 51
Rogers, C., 283
Rogers, C. R., 388
Rogers, R. W., 168, 169, 247, 429
Rogge, R. D., 125
Roggman, L., 364
Rohrer, J. H., 198
Rokeach, M., 370, 418

Romer, D., 299
Rook, K. S., 488, 491
Rooney, A., 375
Roosevelt, F. D., 22
Rooth, D. O., 125, 430
Rose, P., 109
Rose, T. L., 422
Rosen, S., 132
Rosenbaum, M. E., 370, 411, 477
Rosenberg, L. A., 215
Rosenblatt, A., 371
Rosenbloom, S., 72
Rosenbloom, T., 235
Rosenfeld, D., 149
Rosenhan, D. L., 277, 278, 304, 473
Rosenthal, E., 158, 517, 520
Rosenthal, R., 111, 112, 113
Rosenzweig, D., 137
Ross, D., 320
Ross, L., 36, 61, 80, 81, 81f, 83, 84, 97, 105, 106, 107f, 108, 110, 115, 117, 203, 265, 459, 465
Ross, L. D., 442
Ross, M., 47, 48, 61, 62, 66, 67f, 68, 86, 90, 92, 100, 373
Ross, M. J., 405
Ross, S. A., 320
Roszell, P., 363
Rotenberg, K. J., 114
Roth, J., 173
Rothbart, M., 82, 227, 419, 421
Rothman, A. J., 483
Rotton, J., 323, 324
Rotundo, M., 102
Rouby, D. A., 353, 355
Rousseau, J-J., 311
Routh, D. A., 437
Rowe, D. C., 31, 313
Roy, J-P., 122
Royal Society, 515, 516
Ruback, R. B., 58
Ruben, C., 65
Rubin, J. Z., 320
Rubin, R. A., 20
Rubin, Y., 353
Rubin, Z., 377, 394
Ruble, D. N., 109, 149
Rudich, E. A., 54
Rudman, L. A., 436
Rudolph, U., 109, 282
Ruge, J., 316
Rule, B. G., 323
Rule, N., 366
Rumble, A. C., 468
Rumpel, C., 498

Rusbult, C. E., 368, 370, 375, 393, 394
Rushton, J. P., 222, 284, 299, 313
Rushton, P., 297
Russell, B., 72, 245, 359
Russell, G. W., 288, 345
Russell, N., 207
Russell, P., 298
Russo, N. F., 330t
Ruvolo, A., 57
Ryan, C. S., 419
Ryan, R. M., 58, 148, 150, 275, 341, 353, 522
Ryckman, R. M., 24
Rydell, M. T., 441
Rydell, R. J., 441, 442
Ryff, C. D., 487

S

Saad, L., 140
Sabini, J., 213
Sachs, J., 517
Sack, K., 409
Sackett, P. R., 102
Sacks, C. H., 478
Sagarain, B. J., 65, 169, 187
Sageman, M., 251
Saks, M. J., 497
Sakurai, M. M., 216
Salas, E., 267
Saleem, M., 335
Sales, S. M., 185, 404
Salganik, M., 254
Salmela Aro, K., 53
Salmivalli, C., 311, 343
Salovey, P., 100, 168, 278, 419, 476, 483
Saltzberg, J. A., 277
Saltzman, A. T., 71
Saltzstein, H. D., 218
Sampson, E. E., 460
Sanbonmatsu, D. M., 64, 122, 437
Sancton, T., 294
Sandberg, L., 218
Sande, G. N., 108
Sanders, D. Y., 278
Sanders, G. S., 237, 254, 261
Sanderson, C. A., 388
Sanderson, E., 276
Sandilands, M. L., 345
Sani, F., 413
Sanislow, C. A. III, 477
Sanitioso, R., 68
Sansone, C., 149
Saphire-Bernstein, S., 380
Sapolsky, R. M., 489, 491

Saroglou, V., 411
Sartre, J. P., 4, 487
Sasaki, J. Y., 42
Saslow, L. R., 388
Sassenberg, K., 407
Sato, K., 456
Satterwhite, R. C., 434
Saucier, D. A., 81, 404
Sauer, J. D., 499, 503
Sauerland, M., 499
Savani, K., 415
Savitsky, K., 61, 79, 97, 113, 292
Saxe, L., 429
Saxe, R., 284
Sbarra, D. A., 485
Scalia, A., 341
Scarpa, A., 325
Schachter, S., 219, 267, 324, 325, 378
Schaefer, H. S., 487
Schaerfi, L., 458
Schafer, R., 386
Schaffner, P. E., 99, 359
Schaller, M., 279, 286, 289
Scheier, M. F., 128, 477, 480, 486
Schein, E., 138
Scher, S. J., 71
Schiavo, R. S., 236
Schiffenbauer, A., 236
Schimel, J., 56, 352, 412
Schimel, J. P., 371
Schimmack, U., 42
Schinke, S., 189
Schirmer, J., 197, 301
Schkade, D., 48, 50
Schlenker, B. R., 69, 72, 73, 480
Schlenker, D. R., 236t
Schlesinger, A. Jr., 14
Schmader, T., 442
Schmeichel, B. J., 57
Schmiege, S., 202
Schmitt, D. P., 60, 384
Schmitt, M. T., 440
Schnall, S., 146
Schnedler, R., 282
Schneider, C., 281
Schneider, T. R., 483
Schneiderman, L. J., 483
Schoeneman, T. J., 40, 41
Schoenrade, P. A., 288f
Schooler, S., 51
Schopenhauer, A., 472
Schor, J. B., 521
Schroeder, A., 237
Schroeder, D. A., 240f, 302, 303
Schroeder, J. E., 361
Schuh, E., 432, 433

Schuller, R. A., 399
Schulz, R. W., 465
Schulz-Hardt, S., 259, 260
Schuman, H., 22, 23, 179
Schutte, J. W., 102
Schwartz, B., 58
Schwartz, D. A., 295
Schwartz, M., 279, 281
Schwartz, S. M., 69
Schwarz, N., 47, 95, 100, 147, 407
Schweitzer, K., 100
Scollon, C. N., 524
Scott, J., 179
Scott, J. P., 319
Scott, R. F., 264
Sears, D. O., 82, 178, 180
Sears, R., 407
Sechler, E. S., 84
Sedikides, C., 44, 54, 60, 61, 68, 418
Seeman, T. E., 380, 488
Segal, H. A., 138
Segal, M., 251
Segal, N. L., 283
Segerstrom, S. C., 485, 486, 487
Seibt, B., 442
Seidel, E. M., 60
Seligman, C., 411
Seligman, M. E. P., 20, 57, 69, 74, 478, 479, 484, 485, 486, 522
Selimbegovic, L., 436
Semin, G. R., 80
Seneca, 203, 388
Senter, M., 434
Sentis, K. P., 460
Sentyrz, S. M., 247
Sestir, M. A., 340
Seroy, C., 132
Severance, L. J., 171
Shackelford, T. K., 371
Shaffer, D., 200
Shaffer, D. R., 387
Shah, A., 521
Shakespeare, W., 82, 115, 128, 166, 219, 224, 324
Shaklee, H., 459
Shanock, L., 149
Shapir, N., 343
Shapiro, P. N., 411, 437
Sharot, T., 143
Sharp, L. B., 401
Sharpe, D., 28
Shatford, R., 504
Shaver, P., 383, 387, 393, 413
Shavitt, S., 43
Shaw, G. B., 255, 406

Shaw, M., 233
Sheatsley, P. B., 418, 428
Shedler, J., 445
Sheehan, E. P., 361
Sheeran, P., 127
Sheese, B. E., 340
Sheffield, F. D., 159, 172f
Sheldon, K. M., 353, 523
Shell, R. M., 281
Shelton, J. N., 442
Shelton, N., 448
Shen, H., 281
Shepherd, J., 316
Sheppard, B. H., 502
Sheppard, L., 100
Shepperd, J. A., 40, 63, 71, 242
Sherif, C. W., 198f
Sherif, M., 197, 198, 198f, 200, 201, 214t
Sherman, D. K., 43, 444
Sherman, J. W., 417, 421, 422
Sherman-Williams, B., 437
Shih, M., 442
Short, J. F. Jr., 321
Shostak, M., 380
Shotland, R. L., 102, 281, 293
Shovar, N., 73
Showers, C., 65
Shrauger, J. S., 40, 65, 372
Shriver, E. R., 420
Sicoly, F., 61, 62, 68
Sidanius, J., 403
Siegelman, J., 183, 184
Sieverding, M., 202
Sigall, H., 376
Silk, A. J., 160f
Silk, J. B., 284
Silver, L. A., 416
Silver, M., 178, 213, 410
Silver, R. C., 61
Silverman, D., 363
Silvia, P. J., 216
Sime, J., 292
Simmons, C. H., 414
Simmons, J., 64
Simmons, R., 436
Simon, B., 267
Simon, H., 116
Simon, P., 23
Simon, R., 338
Simon-Thomas, E., 281
Simonton, D. K., 266
Simpson, J. A., 203, 368, 383, 384, 393
Sinclair, L., 445, 446f
Sinclair, S., 403
Singer, B., 487

Singer, J. E., 324, 378
Singer, M., 184
Singh, D., 366
Singh, J. V., 265
Singh, P., 381, 382f
Singh, R., 370
Sittser, G. L., 97
Sivarajasingham, V., 316
Sivard, R. L., 310
Six, B., 127
Skaalvik, E. M., 20
Skinner, B. F., 276
Skitka, L. J., 106, 281, 470
Skowronski, J. J., 82
Skurnik, I., 175
Slatcher, R., 391
Slessareva, E., 57
Sloan, J. H., 326
Sloan, R. P., 415
Slopen, N., 485
Slotter, E. B., 36, 388, 392
Slovic, P., 14, 115, 303
Smilek, D., 80
Smith, A., 64, 289, 457
Smith, A. K., 508
Smith, C., 410
Smith, C. A., 501
Smith, C. K., 189
Smith, D. E., 207
Smith, E. J., 255–258
Smith, G. D., 18
Smith, H., 241
Smith, H. J., 408
Smith, M. B., 418
Smith, P. B., 5, 223, 265
Smith, P. M., 412
Smith, R., 507
Smith, R. H., 40
Smith, S. L., 303
Smith, S. M., 161
Smith, T. W., 345, 421
Smits, T., 63
Snell, J., 358
Snibbe, A. C., 489
Snopes, 208
Snow, C., 369
Snowdon, D. A., 486
Snyder, C. R., 63, 68, 226
Snyder, M., 25, 73, 114, 128, 142, 282, 301, 380, 474
Sober, E., 285
Solano, C. H., 387
Solberg, E. C., 523
Solberg, N. L., 318
Solomon, G. S., 278
Solomon, H., 294, 301
Solomon, L. Z., 294, 301

Solomon, S., 69, 412
Sommer, K. L., 353
Sommerville, J. A., 38
Son Hing, L. S., 404
Sophocles, 167
Sorokowski, P., 364
Sousa, L., 489
Sparrell, J. A., 65
Spears, R., 66, 246, 259
Spector, P. E., 264
Speer, A., 258
Spence, A., 124
Spencer, C. P., 224
Spencer, H., 167
Spencer, S. J., 151, 399, 413, 416, 434, 440, 441f, 443
Speth, J. G., 520
Spiegel, H. W., 64
Spielman, S., 373
Spielmann, S. S., 392, 393
Spinoza, B., 374
Spitz, H. H., 112
Spivak, G., 241
Spodick, N., 265
Sporer, S., 499
Sporer, S. L., 419
Spörrle, M., 360
Sprecher, S., 360, 381, 388
Srivastava, S., 114
Srull, T. K., 73
St. Augustine, 429
St. John, H., 525
Stack, A. D., 345
Stadler, D., 291
Stadler, S. J., 323
Stahelski, A. J., 113
Stam, H. J., 204
Standing, L. G., 224
Stang, D. J., 359
Stangor, C., 417, 437
Stanley, D., 126
Stanovich, K. E., 115
Stanton, E. C., 318
Staples, B., 314
Stark, A., 399
Stark, R., 168, 184, 185
Stasser, G., 252, 509, 510
Statistics Canada, 326f, 429, 433, 492f, 497
Staub, E., 211, 276, 289, 295, 303, 304, 305, 342, 408, 461, 466
Stebbins, C. A., 281
Steblay, N. M., 284, 504
Steele, C. M., 40, 125, 151, 152, 440, 441, 441f, 442, 443, 481
Steen, T. A., 476

Stein, A., 305
Stein, D. D., 418
Stein, S., 165
Steinem, G., 329
Steinmetz, J. L., 106, 107f
Stelter, B., 244
Stelzl, M., 411
Stephan, W. G., 378
Stephens, N., 223
Stephens, N. M., 415
Steptoe, A., 483
Sternberg, R. J., 310, 377, 377f, 383, 394
Stevens, M., 199
Stevens, N., 491
Stewart, K. D., 55
Stewart-Williams, S., 283
Stiles, W. B., 477
Stinson, D., 373
Stinson, V., 505
Stirrat, M., 315
Stiwne, D., 259
Stix, G., 264
Stockholm International Peace Research Institute, 453
Stoen, G., 183
Stone, J., 441
Stone, J. I., 47, 100, 152
Stone, L., 392
Stone, R., 294
Stoner, J. A. F., 248
Storms, M. D., 236
Story, A. L., 62
Stouffer, S. A., 318
Stowell, J. R., 217
Strachman, A., 352, 387
Strack, F., 87, 146, 199
Strack, S., 477
Strange, J. J., 95
Strauss, M., 320
Straw, M. K., 293
Streeter, S. A., 366
Strenta, A., 439
Strick, M., 167
Stroebe, W., 168, 234, 262
Stroessner, S. J., 417, 423
Strong, R. A., 314
Strong, S., 186
Stroud, J. N., 420
Stroufe, R., 282
Strube, M. J., 234
Struthers, C. W., 317
Studer, C., 448
Stukas, A. A., 142
Stuve, T. E., 505
Style, B. C., 492
Sue, S., 507

Suedfeld, P., 295, 461
Sugimori, S., 267
Sullivan, L. A., 423
Suls, J. M., 40, 62
Sumich, A., 365
Summers, G., 415
Sun, C., 327
Sundstrom, E., 265
Sunstein, C., 96, 249, 251, 259
Surowiecki, J., 263
Sussman, N. M., 224
Sutton, S. R., 140
Svenson, O., 63
Swann, W. B. Jr., 52, 68, 90, 93, 116, 128, 374, 388, 408, 474
Swap, W. C., 358
Swart, L. A., 418
Sweeney, J., 240
Sweeney, P. D., 476
Sweeny, K., 140
Swift, J., 47, 85, 227, 405
Swift, S. A., 163, 460
Swindle, R., 479
Syrus, P., 133
Szymanski, K., 242

T

Tacitus, 402
Tafarodi, R. W., 44, 187
Tajfel, H., 11, 268, 408, 410
Takooshian, H., 293
Tang, S. H., 149
Tanke, E. D., 114
Tanner, R. J., 199
Tapias, M. P., 408
Tapp, J. L., 510
Tarmann, A., 421
Tarrant, M., 284
Taubes, G., 327
Tayeh, M., 265
Taylor, B. R., 323
Taylor, D. G., 387
Taylor, D. M., 70, 448, 448f, 449
Taylor, K., 40
Taylor, K. M., 242
Taylor, L. S., 361
Taylor, M., 227
Taylor, R. D., 139
Taylor, S. E., 63, 65, 68, 100, 380, 418, 420, 476, 478, 488
Taylor, S. P., 314
Tedeschi, J. T., 139
Teger, A. I., 457
Teigen, K. H., 15, 61, 97
Telch, M. J., 189f
Tellegen, A., 356

Temple, W., 182
Tennen, H., 486
Tenney, E. R., 499
Tennov, D., 278
Teoh, J. B. P., 370
Tepperman, L., 492
Terenzini, P. T., 250
Terris, W., 288
Terry, D. J., 175
Tesch, F. E., 40
Tesser, A., 52, 132, 252, 410
Test, M. A., 297
Tetlock, P. E., 93, 96, 126, 132, 259, 281, 461, 465
t'Hart, P., 259
Thatcher, M., 320
Theiss, A. J., 112
Thelen, M. H., 371
Theno, S. A., 370
Theroux, P., 85
Thomas, G. C., 236, 306
Thomas, L., 311
Thomas, S., 375
Thomas, S. L., 335
Thompson, D. E., 236
Thompson, L., 85, 463
Thompson, L. F., 291
Thompson, L. L., 412
Thompson, W., 277
Thompson, W. C., 511
Thoreau, H. D., 83
Thornhill, R., 365
Thorton, B., 367
Tice, D. M., 56, 72
Tideman, S., 527
Time, 391
Timmerman, T. A., 317
Tindale, R. S., 252, 510
Titus, L. J., 235
Tobey, B., 287
Todorov, A., 103, 360
Tofighbakhsh, J., 175
Toguchi, Y., 61
Tolstoy, L., 137, 363, 368
Tomasello, M., 288
Tomorrow, T., 337
Tormala, Z. L., 164
Toronto News, 60
Toronto Sun, 428
Tortolani, A. J., 47
Totterdell, P., 199
Towles-Schwen, T., 126
Townsend, E., 124
Trautwein, U., 20
Travis, L. E., 234
Trawalter, S., 416, 432, 448
Trewin, D., 331

Triandis, H. C., 41, 45, 124, 381, 391, 460
Trinkl, B., 419
Triplett, N., 233, 234
Trivers, R., 284
Trolier, T. K., 97
Trost, M. R., 267, 381
Trudeau, G. B., 23f, 91f
Trudeau, P. E., 67
Trzesniewski, K. H., 53, 55
Tsang, J-A., 213
Tseng, W. S., 74
Tuan, Y-F., 247
Tubb, V. A., 505t
Tubbs, D. D., 261
Turner, C., 332
Turner, J. A., 170, 171f
Turner, J. C., 11, 233, 253, 408, 410
Turner, M. E., 71, 256, 259, 281
Turner, N., 265
Turtle, J. W., 505
TV Guide, 332
Tversky, A., 90, 95, 99, 262, 263, 467
Twain, M., 16, 374, 382
Twenge, J. M., 55, 64, 352, 353
Twohy, M., 393
Tybur, J. M., 366
Tyler, T. R., 265, 303, 408
Tyson, M., 323
Tzeng, O., 392

U

Uchino, B. N., 488
Uleman, J., 103
Ullrich, J., 409
Unger, R. K., 12, 275
United Nations, 433, 436
Unkelbach, C., 202, 432
Ustinov, P., 356

V

Väänänen, A., 488
Vaillant, G. E., 85, 486
Vala, J., 407
Valcour, P. M., 58
Valdesolo, P., 123
Valentine, T., 499, 503
Vallacher, R. R., 357
Vallerand, R. J., 58
Valley, K. L., 463
Valliant, G., 484
Vallone, R. P., 80, 81f, 91
van Baaren, R., 199, 369
Van Boven, L., 524

van de Kragt, A., 458
Van de Vliert, E., 517
van der Eijnden, R. J. J. M., 70
van der Molen, M. W., 354
van der Plight, J., 22
Van Dijk, J., 49
Van Doren, C., 196
van Knippenberg, A., 165
Van Lange, P. A. M., 459, 468
Van Pachterbeke, M., 411
Van Straaten, I., 361
Van Vugt, M., 152, 275, 459
Van Yperen, N. W., 386
Vanable, P., 481
Vandello, J. A., 321
Vanderslice, R. R., 264
VanLinganham, J., 492
Vanman, E. J., 416
Vargas, R. A., 219
Vasquez, E., 317
Vasquez-Suson, K. A., 440
Västfjäll, D., 303
Vatiné, E., 206
Vaughan, K. B., 147
Vazire, S., 48
Vedas, B., 293
Vega, V., 329
Veitch, R., 323
Velasquez, C. M., 143
Ventis, W. L., 405
Verkuyten, M. J. A. M., 409
Verplanken, B., 162
Verrilli, D. B. Jr., 185
Vescio, T., 402
Vescio, T. K., 70, 370
Veysey, B., 250
Vidmar, N., 502, 510
Vinokur, A., 252
Violato, C., 328
Virgil, 163, 362
Virtanen, S. V., 419
Visher, C., 498
Visintainer, M. A., 484, 485
Visser, K., 468
Visser, P. S., 179, 192
Vitelli, S., 27
Vogel, T., 165
Vohs, K. D., 59, 72, 353
Vollrath, D. A., 252
Volpato, C., 267
von Goethe, J. W., 128, 200
von Hippel, C., 430
von Hippel, W., 80, 96, 416, 430
Vonnegut, K., 410
Vorauer, J. D., 36, 253, 440, 448
Voss, A., 432
Vul, E., 263

W

Wachtler, J., 268
Wagner, B., 146
Wagner, G., 520
Wagner, R. V., 400
Wagner, U., 404
Wagstaff, J. F., 109
Walfish, S., 436
Walker, G. R., 128
Walker, I., 401
Walker, L., 143
Walker, L. J., 299
Walker, P. M., 419
Walker, R., 176
Wallace, D. S., 127
Wallace, M., 209
Wallbom, M., 128, 247
Waller, J., 135, 213
Walster (Hatfield), E., 135, 164,
     359, 362, 372, 373, 376,
     378, 385, 460
Walster, G. W., 460
Walters, R. H., 320, 334
Walther, E., 161
Walther, J., 72
Walton, G. M., 57, 399
Walum, H., 382, 385
Wan, F., 281
Wandersman, A., 359
Wang, A., 375
Wang, M. C., 324
Wang, T., 219
Wangchuk, J. S., 527
Wanshula, L. T., 417
Ward, A., 459, 465, 465
Ward, C., 423
Ward, C. D., 378
Ward, W. C., 97
Warnick, D., 261
Warr, P., 487
Warren, N., 369
Wason, P. C., 93
Waters, E. A., 64
Watkins, E. R., 477
Watson, D., 109
Watson, J., 262, 263
Watson, R. I. Jr., 245
Watt, S. E., 65, 352
Watts, D. J., 65
Waugh, G., 378
Wearing, A., 63
Weaver, J. B. III, 334, 335
Weary, G., 72, 99
Webb, T. L., 127
Weber, A. L., 388f
Weber, B., 242

Weber, N. S., 503
Weber, R., 437
Webster, C. D., 506
Webster, D. M., 267
Wechkin, S., 288
Wegener, D. T., 152, 160, 161,
     172, 174, 507
Wegner, D. M., 416, 480
Wehr, P., 466
Weigold, M. F., 72
Weil, R., 161
Weiner, B., 101, 102, 109,
     282, 317
Weinstein, N., 63, 275
Weis, R., 341
Weiss, H. M., 164
Weiss, R. D., 47
Weiss, R. F., 376
Weissman, M. M., 522
Wells, G. L., 148, 498, 499, 502,
     504, 505, 508
Welzel, C., 58
Wener, R., 58
Wenzlaff, R. M., 371
Werner, C. M., 171
West, R. F., 115
West, S. G., 282, 407
Weyant, J. M., 303
Whatley, M., 281, 281f
Wheeler, L., 40, 353,
     359, 361
Whelan, M., 492
Whitaker, J. L., 341
Whitchurch, E. R., 372
White, G., 361
White, G. L., 378
White, H. R., 493
White, K., 45, 101
White, M. J., 300
White, R. J., 91
Whitehead, A. N., 128
Whitley, B. E. Jr., 498
Whitman, R. M., 474
Whitman, W., 126, 355
Whitney, G., 282
Whittaker, J. O., 223
Whittaker, W., 70
Whooley, M. A., 486
Whyte, G., 250
Wicker, A., 123
Wicklund, R. A., 277
Widom, C., 321
Wiebe, D. J., 327
Wiegman, O., 162
Wiesel, E., 274
Wieselquist, J., 386
Wigboldus, D. H. J., 432

Wiggins, E. C., 122
Wiggins, N. H., 374
Wikipedia, 208
Wilberforce, W., 405
Wilde, O., 267
Wilder, D. A., 165, 215, 410,
     411, 418, 437, 438f
Wilhelmy, R. A., 214
Wilke, H., 165
Wilke, H. A. M., 242
Wilkes, D. E. Jr., 311
Wilkinson, G. S., 284
Wilkinson, R. A., 403, 490f, 525
Wilkinson, R. G., 318
Wilkowski, B. M., 313
Willard, G., 69
Willer, R., 169
Williams, D. K., 172
Williams, E., 62
Williams, J. E., 434
Williams, K., 239
Williams, K. D., 9, 180, 240,
     240f, 241, 242, 353,
     354, 354f
Williams, K. M., 54
Williams, L. E., 80
Williams, M. J., 423
Williams, R. L., 149
Williams, T. M., 334
Williamson, G. M., 277
Williamson, N. L., 419
Willis, F. N., 207
Willis, J., 103
Wilson, A., 325
Wilson, A. E., 66, 67, 67f, 369,
     373, 393
Wilson, D. K., 483
Wilson, D. S., 285
Wilson, E. O., 283, 284, 285
Wilson, J. P., 299
Wilson, J. Q., 284
Wilson, R., 274, 283, 286,
     313, 483
Wilson, S. J., 347
Wilson, T. D., 47, 48, 49, 50, 51,
     372, 524
Wilson, W. R., 358
Wiltermuth, S., 65
Winch, R., 371
Windschitl, P. D., 68
Winquist, J., 478
Winter, D. G., 404
Winter, F. W., 359
Winton, W., 226
Wirth, J. H., 354, 377
Wiseman, R., 506
Wisman, A., 352

Wit, A. P., 242
Wittenbrink, B., 401, 432
Wittmer, J., 71
Wixon, D. R., 85
Wober, M., 140
Wodehouse, P. G., 279
Wohl, M., 98
Wojciszke, B., 376
Wolf, S., 268, 507
Wolfe, C., 51
Wolfenshohn, J., 317
*Women on Words and
     Images,* 406
Wong, T. J., 418
Wood, D., 54
Wood, E. E., 302
Wood, J. V., 40, 41, 68, 478
Wood, V. R., 277
Wood, W., 128, 164, 404, 492
Wood, W-J., 434
Woods, T., 164
Woodzicka, J., 48
Woolhandler, S., 491
Woolley, J., 259
Wootton-Millward, L., 419
Worchel, S., 236, 242, 317
Word, C., 439
Workman, E. A., 149
World Meteorological
     Organization, 516
Worringham, C., 237
Wortman, C., 433
Wotman, S., 393
Wraga, M., 442
Wright, D. B., 420
Wright, K. D., 261
Wright, R. A., 242, 251
Wrosch, C., 65
Wu, D. Y. H., 74
Wuensch, K. L., 201
Wurf, E., 38
Wyer, N., 418
Wyer, R. S., 281
Wylie, R. C., 63
Wynne, C. D. L., 288

Y

Yamaguchi, S., 61
Yang, H-C., 262
Yap, A. J., 146
Yarmey, A. D., 505
Yates, S., 180
Ybarra, O., 56, 329, 334
Yee, L., 341
Yee, N., 165
Yildiz, A. A., 409

Yinon, Y., 343
Young, A. S., 40
Young, L. J., 382
Young, R. D., 247, 481
Young, S., 402
Young, S. G., 420
Younger, J. C., 143, 354
Yousif, Y., 284, 295
Yovetich, N. A., 394
Yuchtman, E., 318
Yuille, J., 498
Yukl, G., 462
Yzerbyt, V. Y., 372

Z

Zachariae, R., 485
Zadro, L., 9, 354
Zagefka, H., 281, 524
Zajonc, R. B., 234, 235, 235f,
    237, 251, 343, 357, 358
Zaki, J., 197, 220
Zanna, M. P., 73, 113, 122, 128,
    132, 134, 150, 151, 151f,
    152, 159, 170, 254, 314,
    318, 320, 345, 401, 417,
    434, 439, 481, 481f

Zaragoza, S., 501
Zarkardi, T., 504
Zavalloni, M., 249
Zebrowitz, L. A., 367
Zebrowitz-McArthur, L.,
    109, 506
Zeisel, H., 508, 509, 510
Zelenski, J. M., 526
Zhang, D. D., 517, 519
Zhong, C. B., 79, 80, 355
Zhu, Y., 43
Zick, A., 404
Zickafoose, D., 499

Ziegler, J., 43f, 59f
Zigler, E., 321
Zill, N., 336
Zillman, D., 235, 325, 334,
    335, 367
Zimbardo, P. G., 130, 131, 136,
    244, 246
Zimmer, C., 38
Zimmerman, L. A., 504
Zitek, E. M., 405
Zuckerman, E. W., 52
Zuwerink, J. R., 416

Subject Index

A

Abu Ghraib, 212
academic achievement, and self-esteem, 19–20, 52
accentuation phenomenon, 250
acceptance
  see also conformity and compliance, 183
  defined, 197
accuracy *vs.* confidence, 505t
achievement, and self-concept, 19–20
active experience, 174–176
active participation, 252
actor-observer difference, 107–108
adaptation-level phenomenon, 524
additive tasks, 238
advertising, and children, 190–191
advice, 13
aeronautical engineering, 24
affective forecasting, 48–49
Africville, 428, 429
age
  and attitudes, 178–179
  of audience, 178–179
  generational explanation, 178
  life cycle explanation, 178
aggression
  adaptive nature of, 312
  aggression cues, 325–327
  alcohol and, 314
  altered perceptions, 336
  arousal, 324–325
  attacks, 324
  aversive incidents, 322–324
  biochemical influences, 314–316
  as biological phenomenon, 311–316
  biology and behaviour, 315–316
  catharsis, 341, 344–346
  cognitive priming, 337
  correlational studies, 332
  and culture, 245, 321–322

culture change and world violence, 348
defined, 310
described, 310–311
desensitization, 335–336
displaced aggression, 316–317, 407–408
distorted perceptions of sexual reality, 328
evolutionary psychology, 312
experimental studies, 329–330, 334–335
and the family, 320–321
frustration-aggression theory, 316–319, 317f, 407–408
genetic influences, 313
group influences, 342–344, 344f
guns, 325–326, 326f, 346
heat, 323–324
hostile aggression, 311, 323, 325f
influences on, 322–344
instinct theory, 312
instinctive behaviour, 312
instrumental aggression, 311
as learned social behaviour, 319–322
media awareness education, 330–331
media influences, 327–342
murders, 311, 326f
and narcissism, 54f
neural influences, 312–313
observational learning, 320–322
pain, 322–323
poor diet, 315
and pornography, 327–331, 330f
primates *vs.* humans, 312–313
reducing aggression, 344–348
relative deprivation, 318–319
retaliation, 316, 345–346
rewards of, 319–320
scapegoat theory, 407–408
and self-esteem, 54f
sexual violence, 327–331

sexually aggressive men, 331f
silent aggression, 311
social aggression, 311
social learning theory, 320–322, 322f, 346–347
social scripts, 336
television, influences of, 25, 331–337
terrorism, 311, 320
and testosterone, 314–315
theories of aggression, 311–322
time drain, 337
types of aggression, 311
video games, 337–342, 339f
wars, 311
weapons, 326f
against women, 328–330
aggression cues, 325–327
aggressive behaviours, 25, 339
alcohol
  and aggression, 314
  myopia, 481–482, 481f
  and social situations, 481
altered perceptions, 336
altruism
  altruistic norms, 458–459
  ambiguity, reducing, 300–302
  anonymity, 294, 301
  attributing helpful behaviour to, 305–306
  comparison and evaluation of theories, 285–288, 285t
  and culture, 296f
  defined, 274
  egoistic distress reduction, 288, 288f
  empathy and distress, 288–289
  encouraging altruistic behaviour, 300–307, 304f
  evolutionary psychology, 282–285
  examples of, 274
  and foot-in-the-door phenomenon, 133–135
  and gender, 282, 300

genuine altruism, 286–289, 288f
Good Samaritan parable, 274
group selection, 284–285
guilt, 276–277, 302–302
how to increase helping, 300–307, 304f
kin selection, 283–284
learning about, 306–307
modelling altruism, 304–305
money and happiness, 280
moral inclusion, 303–304
and number of bystanders, 290–297
overjustification effect, 305–306
personality traits, 299–300
and prejudice, 413
and prosocial models, 297
reciprocity norm, 280–281, 284
responsibility, increase in, 300–302
rewards, 275–279
self-image, concern for, 302–303
similarity to victim, 298
social-exchange theory, 274–279
and social norms, 280–282
social-responsibility norm, 281–282
socialization and, 303–307
teaching altruism, 303–304
theories of altruism, 285–289, 285t
time pressures, 297–298
when we help, 289–298
who helps, 298–300
why we help, 274–289
altruistic norms, 458–459
ambiguity, and altruism, 300–302
ambiguous events, 291–293
ambiguous information, 81
ambiguous reality, 200
The American Paradox: Spiritual Hunger in an Age of Plenty (Myers), 514n
amygdala, 126

analytical reasoning, 50–51
ancestors' fate, 41
anecdotes, power of, 96
anger-prone personality, 483
anonymity, 244–246, 245f, 301
anticipation of interaction, 357
anticipatory liking, 357
anticonformity
   motivation for, 225–227
   reactance, 225
   uniqueness, assertion of,
      226–227
anti-smoking programs, 168
antisocial behaviour, and self-
   esteem, 55
antisocial tendencies, 342
anxiety, 480–482
anxious-ambivalent attachment,
   384
approval, 373–374
arbitration, 466–467
arguments, 252
arousal
   and aggression, 324–325
   and deindividuation, 247
   dissonance as arousal,
      150–152
   dominant responses,
      facilitation of, 234
   effects of, 235f
   mere presence of others,
      233–235, 235f, 237–238
   and passionate love, 377–379
   and romantic responses, 378
   and self-affirmation theory,
      151
   sexual arousal, 325
   television, 335
   video games, 341
arousing and distracting
   activities, 246–247
Asch's studies of group
   pressure, 200–202,
   201f, 214t
assumption of responsibility,
   293–295
assumptions, power of, 81
attachment
   anxious-ambivalent
      attachment, 384
   avoidant attachment, 383
   and close relationships,
      382–385
   dismissive attachment,
      383–384
   fearful attachment, 383–384
   insecure attachment, 384

internal working models, 384
   preoccupied attachment, 384
   secure attachment, 383
   styles, 383–385
attacks, 324
attitude alignment, 370
attitude inoculation, 188,
   192–193
attitudes
   accessibility of, and
      persuasion, 181f
   and active participation, 252
   and age, 178–179
   behaviour, effect on, 8–9,
      51, 145f
   benevolent attitudes, 434
   and conformity and
      obedience, 210–212
   defined, 122
   and disease, 486–487
   dissimilar attitudes, 370–371
   drunk driving, 481f
   dual attitude system, 51, 401
   and expectations, 505t
   experience and, 128
   explicit attitudes, 51, 124
   and expressions, 146–148
   facial expressions, 146–148
   hostile attitudes, 434
   and hypocrisy, 123–124
   implicit attitudes, 51, 124
   minimal social influences,
      124–126
   in novel, 130
   and persuasive messages, 159
   power of, 127–128
   and prediction of behaviour,
      124–128
   predictive accuracy of,
      126–127
   reconstruction of past
      attitudes, 85–86
   and self-conscious people, 128
   self-perception theory, and
      attitude formation, 150
attitudes-follow-behaviour
   principle
   cognitive dissonance theory,
      140–145
   comparison of theories,
      150–152
   culture, 144–145
   cults, 183
   evil acts, 135–137
   explanations of, 129
   foot-in-the-door phenomenon,
      133–135, 183

gender roles, 131–132
impression management,
   139–140
moral acts, 135–137
role-playing, 129–132
self-justification, 140–145
self-perception theory, 139,
   145–150, 152
self-presentation theory,
   139–140
social movements, 138–139
when saying becomes
   believing, 132–133
attraction
   attribution, 372–373
   beautiful is good stereotype,
      363–364
   complementarity, 371
   and dating, 359–360
   dissimilarity breeds dislike,
      370–371
   and evolution, 365–366
   first impressions, 363
   gaining another's esteem,
      373–374
   ingratiation, 372
   interaction and, 356–357
   likeness leads-to-liking effect,
      369–370
   liking by association, 375
   liking those who like us,
      371–374
   love and, 367–368
   matching phenomenon, 361
   mere-exposure effect,
      357–359
   mutual liking, 371–374
   open, honest relationship,
      374
   opposites, 371
   physical attractiveness, 165,
      359–368
   proximity and, 355–359
   reward theory of attraction,
      375–376
   and self-esteem, 373
   similarity, 165, 368–371
   social comparison, 366–367
attractiveness, 164–166,
   359–368. See physical
   attractiveness
attribution theory, 102
attributions
   attraction, 372–373
   causality, 101–104
   cognitive source of prejudice,
      423–424

common-sense attributions,
   104
and culture, 109
dispositional attribution,
   102–103, 109
fundamental attribution error,
   104–107, 105f, 107–108,
   107f, 110
group-serving bias, 423–424
helpful behaviour to altruistic
   motives, 305–306
inferring traits, 103
Kelley's theory of
   attributions, 104, 104f
language, and external
   attributions, 109
misattribution, 102
prejudice, 423–424
and reactions, 110f
self-serving attributions,
   60–61
situational attribution,
   103, 109
and social-responsibility
   norm, 281–282
and stereotype change, 438f
audience
   age of audience, 178–179
   counterarguing, 179–180
   cults, 184–185
   distraction, 180
   peripheral cues, 180–181
   and persuasion, 178–181
   thoughts of, 179–181
   uninvolved audiences,
      180–181
authoritarian personality,
   403–404
authority
   closeness and legitimacy,
      and obedience, 207–208
   institutional authority, 208
   persuasion, 165t
autokinetic phenomenon, 198
automatic prejudice, 401,
   430, 432
automatic processing, 51, 88
automatic stereotyping, 432
autonomy, 353
availability heuristics, 95–96
aversive incidents
   and aggression, 322–324
   attacks, 324
   heat, 323–324
   pain, 322–323
avoidance, 383
avoidant attachment, 383

B

bad luck, 97
bargaining, 462–463
beautiful is good stereotype, 363–364
behaviour
  affect on attitudes, 129–139
  aggressive behaviours, 339
  attitudes, and prediction of behaviour, 122–128
  attitudes, effect of, 8–9, 51, 145f
  biological roots of, 9
  and biology, interaction between, 315–316
  and conformity and obedience, 210–212
  and culture, 101–110
  depressed mood and, 476–477
  discrimination, 399–400
  and evolution, 282–285
  examining attitudes specific to, 126–127
  and expectations, 114–115
  expected behaviour. See norms
  helping behaviour. See altruism
  instinctive behaviour, 312
  looking good, as motivator, 71–74
  mental after-effects of, 129
  minimal social influences, 124–126
  objective behavioural dimensions, 61–62
  past behaviour, reconstruction of, 86
  personality, effect of, 9
  planned behaviour, 127f
  predicting our behaviour, 47–48, 91
  prosocial behaviour, 303–307, 335, 341–342
  self-defeating behaviour, 71
  social influences, effect of, 8
  subjective behaviour dimensions, 61–62
  television, effects of, 332–335
behaviour problems
  anxiety, 480–482
  depression, 475–480
  shyness, 480–482
behaviour tendency, 398

behavioural confirmation, 114–115
behavioural medicine, 482
Beirut massacre, 80, 81f
Belet Huen, 243
belief perseverance, 83–84
beliefs
  challenging, 187
  changing after conforming, 221f
belonging, and social identity, 412–414
benevolent sexism, 434
bias
  blind spot, 60
  camera perspective bias, 108
  competitive, individualist biases, 12
  confirmation bias, 93, 474
  correspondence bias, 104–107
  cross-race bias, 505t
  detection of, in behaviour, 429–430
  experimenter bias, 111
  false consensus bias, 370
  fundamental attribution error, 104–107
  gender bias, 433–436
  group-serving bias, 70, 423–424
  hindsight bias, 15
  impact bias, 49
  implicit bias, 124
  in-group bias, 303, 409–412
  in interpretations, 444–446
  knowledge of issues, 23–24
  linguistic intergroup bias, 424
  media bias, 80, 81f
  in memories, 444–446
  mug-shot-induced bias, 505t
  own-age bias, 420
  own-race bias, 419, 419f
  perception of, 81f
  response bias, 22–23
  self-serving bias. See self-serving bias
  study of, 110
  subtle biases in social psychology, 12
  survey, 21–24
big egos, 54, 54f
bio-psycho-social organisms, 9
biochemical influences on aggression, 314–316

biology
  and aggression, 311–316
  and behaviour, interaction between, 9, 315–316
  and culture, 312
  natural selection, 285
  passionate love and, 378
black bloc tactics, 78
blame-the-victim process, 211
blind optimism, 64
blindsight, 88
blood chemistry, 314
body dysmorphic disorder, 471
boomerang effect, 225
boredom, 358
the brain
  and aggression, 311, 312–313
  and conformity, 220
  and love, 379f
  and stereotyping, 432
brainstorming, 262–263
brainwashing, 13, 138
brainwriting, 263
bullying, 343
bystander effect, 293
bystander passivity
  assumption of responsibility, 293–295
  decision tree, 291f
  interpretation, 291–293
  nations as bystanders, 295
  noticing, 291
  number of bystanders, effect of, 290–297
  research ethics, 295–297
  similarity to victim, 298
  smoke-filled room experiment, 292f
  time pressures, 297–298

C

camera perspective bias, 108
Canada
  alcohol and tobacco use, 158, 331
  aggression in, 320, 325–326, 333–334
  immigration, 407–408
  married people in, 492
  multiculturalism, 398, 399, 400
  murders in, 326, 326f, 333–334
  prejudice and discrimination in, 400, 413, 429, 448
  rape experiences in, 330t
  self-concept, 144

  social identity, 39
  Tri-Council, 28
  weapon use, 326f
cancer screening, 202
carbon taxes, 520
cases, distinctive, 421–422
castration, 315
categorization, 417–420
catharsis, 341, 344–346
causality, attributing, 101–104
causation, 19–21, 20f, 25
central executive, 57
central route to persuasion, 160, 161f
chameleon effect, 199
channel of communication
  active experience vs. passive reception, 174–176
  defined, 174
  personal vs. media influence, 176–178
charismatic leaders, 182
cheating, 247
children
  advertising, influence of, 190–191
  and aggression, 320–321
  altruism, teaching, 303–304
  attitude inoculation, 188
  conflict management, 464
  and depression, 478–479
  and dissonance, 144
  expectations, and behaviour, 115
  games they play, 337–338
  and Halloween anonymity, 245, 245f
  peer pressure to smoke, 189, 189f
  and physical-attractiveness stereotype, 362–364
  sexual scripts, 336
  television viewing, 332–333, 333f
  video games, 337–343
choices-influence-preferences effect, 143
Cinderella effect, 25
classification, 417–420
climate change
  evidence of, 515–516
  psychological effects of, 516–517
  psychology and, 516–518
  public opinion about, 517–518
  skepticism, 158

clinical psychology
  accuracy of clinical
      judgments, 471–473
  behaviour problems,
      475–482
  better clinical practice, 475
  defined, 471
  hindsight, 473
  illusory correlation,
      97–98, 472
  overconfidence, 473
  self-confirming diagnoses,
      473–475
close relationships
  see also love
  arranged marriages *vs.* love
      marriages, 382f
  attachment, 382–385
  collectivism and, 242
  and culture, 241–242
  detachment process,
      392–394
  divorce, 391–392
  ending relationships,
      391–394
  equity, 385–387
  and expectations, 113–115
  and happiness, 491–493
  happily *vs.* unhappily
      married, 5
  and health, 487–491
  individualism and, 41
  long-term equity, 386
  love, 367–368, 376–382
  marital attachment, and
      happiness, 492–493
  open, honest relationship,
      374
  perceived equity and
      satisfaction, 386–387
  physical attractiveness of
      loved ones, 367–368,
      368f
  positive illusions, 374
  predictions of, 47–48
  self-disclosure, 387–391
  successful couples, 393–394
  supportive relationships, 526
co-actors, 233
cognition, 42–44, 180,
      398, 401
cognitive dissonance theory
  application of, 140
  and culture, 42–44, 144–145
  defined, 140
  dissonance after decisions,
      143–144

dissonance as arousal,
      150–152
  insufficient justification
      effect, 140–142, 142f
cognitive priming, 337
cognitive processes
  anxiety, 480–482
  depression, 475–480
  prejudice, 417–424
  shyness, 480–482
cognitive response approach,
      159
cohesiveness, 216–217
colds, and sociability, 488f
collapse of compassion, 287
collective narcissism, 54–55
collectivism
  cognitive dissonance, 144
  consensus information, 65
  defined, 41
  intimate relationships,
      formation of, 387
  language, 43
  and the self, 41–45
  and self-esteem, 44–45
  and social loafing, 242
  variations in, 42
commitment
  effect of, on social loafing,
      242
  prior commitments, 187–188
  relationship commitment,
      and related
      attractiveness, 368f
common-sense attributions,
      13–16, 104
common-sense psychology, 102
communal qualities, 41
communication
  channel of communication,
      174–178
  controlled communication,
      463–466
  fear-rousing communications,
      168–169
  persuasion. *See* persuasion
  two-step flow of
      communication,
      176–177
the communicator
  attractiveness and liking,
      164–166
  credibility, 162–164, 171f
  cults, 183–184
communities, and group
      polarization, 250–251
community spirit, 284

companionate love, 380–382
comparison
  downward, 526
  media comparison, 177–178
  self-serving bias, and, 61–62
  social comparison. *See* social
      comparison
  temporal comparison, 66–67
  upward, 40
compassion fatigue, 295
competence, 353
complementarity, 371
compliance
  see also conformity
  and acceptance, 183
  defined, 197
  with legitimate authority,
      207–208
compliant confessions, 502
compliments, 372–373
companionate love, 380–382
competition, and prejudice,
      407
compromise, 463
concepts, formation of, 12
conciliation, 467–468
confederate, 10, 198–199
confidence, and eyewitness
      testimony, 502
confidence *vs.* accuracy, 505t
confidence malleability, 505t
confident speaking, 162
confiding, and health, 488–489
confirmation bias, 93, 474
confirming evidence, 81
conflict
  constructive fighting, 464t
  creation of conflict, 453–462
  defined, 453
  misperception, 460–462
  non-zero-sum games, 457
  perceived injustice, 460
  Prisoners' Dilemma, 454–455,
      455f, 456f, 457, 459
  resolution of, 462–468
  social dilemmas, 453–459
  Tragedy of the Commons,
      455–457
conformity
  acceptance, 197
  anti-conformity, motivation
      for, 225–227
  behaviour and attitudes,
      210–212
  and the brain, 219–220
  changing beliefs after
      conforming, 221f

classic conformity and
      obedience studies,
      197–214, 213t
  cohesiveness, 216–217
  compliance, 197
  conformists, 221–224
  and culture, 223–224
  defined, 196–197
  gender prejudice, 406
  group influence, liberating
      effects of, 208–209
  group size, 214–215, 215f
  groupthink, and conformity
      pressure, 257
  informational influence, 219,
      220–221
  negative value judgment, 196
  no prior commitment,
      217–219
  normative influence,
      219–220, 221
  obedience, 197, 206–209
  and personality, 222–223
  predicting conformity,
      214–219
  prejudice, 405–406
  public response, 217
  reactance, 225
  reasons for conformity,
      219–221
  situation, power of, 212–214
  and social movements,
      104–107
  social roles, 224
  status, 217
  suggestibility, 198–200
  unanimity, 215–216, 216f
  and uniqueness, 226–227
  varieties of, 197
conformity and obedience
      studies
  Asch's studies of group
      pressure, 200–202, 201f,
      214t
  Milgram's obedience studies,
      203–206, 203f, 205f,
      214t
  reflections on, 209–214
  Sherif's studies of norm
      formation, 197–200,
      198f, 214t
  summary, 214t
confounded variables, 21
conscious self-presentation,
      72–73
consensus, 104
consensus information, 65

Conservative Party, 178
consistency, 104, 165t, 267
construal processes, 82
construction of memories, 84–86
constructive fighting, 464t
consumption, reduction of, 519–521
contact, 176–177, 284
contrast effect, 366–367
control
    in experimental research, 24–25
    illusion of control, 98–99
    personal control, 57–58
    self-control, 56–59, 247
    social control, 186–187
controlled communications, 463–466
controlled consciousness, 89
controlled processing, 87–88
conventional wisdom, 16
cooling-off period, 135
cooperation, 238, 299f, 382, 409, 457–459
cooperative intent, 468
correlation
    vs. causation, 19–21, 20f
    illusory correlation, 97–98, 472, 475
    obesity, marital status and income, 24–25
    quantifying, 20–21
    recognition of, 26t
    status-longevity correlation, 18–19, 20f
    television viewing and behaviour, 332–334
    temperature and aggression, 323–324
    time-lagged correlation, 21
    violence on television, 25
correlational research
    advantages and disadvantages of, 18
    aggression against women, 328
    and causation, 19–21
    cause-effect relations, 21
    defined, 18
    detecting natural associations, 18–24
    and experiments, 24–25, 26t, 29f
    longitudinal research, 21
    prejudice against obese, 24–25

recognizing, 26t
status and longevity, 18–19
television violence viewing, 25
correspondence bias, 104–107
cosmetic surgery, 362, 367
counterarguing, 188
counterarguments, 179–180, 188
counterfactual thinking, 96–97
courtroom
    eyewitness testimony, 497–506
    individual jurors, influences on, 506–508
    jury as group, influences on, 508–510
    simulated juries, 510–511
credibility, 162–164, 165, 171f
credible source, 170–171
cross-race bias, 505t
crowd within, 263–264
crowding, 236–237
cruelty, 5
cults
    attitudes-follow-behaviour principle, 183
    audience, 184–185
    the communicator, 183–184
    compliance, effect of, 183
    defined, 182
    extreme persuasion, 181–187
    foot-in-the-door phenomenon, 183
    group effects, 185–187
    the message, 184
    persuasive elements of, 183–185
cultural diversity, 109
cultural psychology, 46
cultural racism, 370–371
culture
    and aggression, 321–322
    and altruism, 296f
    and attributions, 109
    and behaviour, 101–110
    and biology, 312
    and cognitive dissonance, 42–44, 144–145
    and conformity, 223–224
    conformity, and negative value judgment, 196
    consensus information, 65
    cultural diversity, 109
    cultural racism, 370–371
    cultural similarity, 111–115
    defined, 11

Eastern cultural assumptions, 109, 144, 479
and emotional expression, 146–148
facial expressions, 146–148
false beliefs, perpetuation of, 198
and friendships, 284
and fundamental attribution error, 109
and gender stereotypes, 433
and group behaviour, 241–242
individualism. See individualism
language, influence of, 109
love, variations in, 378–379
multiculturalism, 398, 399, 400
and norms, 283
perceptions, 43f
and persuasion, 158
and physical attractiveness, 364–365
pigeonholing, 42
self and, 41–45
and self-esteem, 44–45
social influence, impact on, 8, 238–242
and social loafing, 241–242
and social relations, 321–322
social roles, 224
thinking, effect on, 41–44
and uniqueness, 226–227
values, differences in, 11
Western cultural assumptions, 41–42, 479
world violence, and change, 348
cyberbalkanization, 390
cyberostracism, 354

D

dating, and attractiveness, 359–360
death instinct, 312
deciding-becomes-believing effect, 143
decision tree, 291f
decisions, and dissonance, 143–144
defections from the majority, 268
defendant's attractiveness, 506
deflation, 353

deindividuation
    arousing and distracting activities, 246–247
    defined, 243
    diminished self-awareness, 247
    group size, 243–244
    physical anonymity, 244–246, 244f
    unrestrained behaviours, 243
demand characteristics, 27
democratic leadership, 265
dental flossing, 202
dependent variable, 25
depersonalization, 206–207
depression
    depressive realism, 476
    described, 475
    distortion, 475–476
    explanatory style, 476, 477f
    health risks of, 484
    and marital status, 492f
    negative thinking and, 476–480
    and stress, 477–478
    vicious cycle of, 479f
depressive realism, 476
deprivation, 318–319
desensitization, 335–336
detachment process, 392–394
diet, and aggression, 315
differences, perceived, 420–423
diffusion of responsibility, 342
diminished self-awareness, 247
disagreement, 170
disclosure reciprocity, 387
discomfort, 170
discrepancy, 170–171, 171f
discrimination
    see also prejudice
    defined, 400
    effect of, 438–440
    gender discrimination, 434–436
    influence of prejudice on, 430–433
    obesity and, 26
    perceived discrimination, 439, 447–448
    personal/group discrimination, 448, 448f
    discrepancy, 170–171, 171f
    vs. prejudice, 400
    and self-esteem, 447
    self-fulfilling prophecy, 438–440
    without awareness, 430–433

disinhibition, 335, 342
dismissive attachment, 383
displaced aggression, 316–317, 407
displacement, 316
disposition and behaviour, 9
dispositional attribution, 102–103, 109
dissimilarity, 370–371
dissonance
    as arousal, 150–152
    and decisions, 143–144
    minimizing, 140
    and the pill, 151f
distinctiveness
    and attributions, 104
    cases, 421–422
    events, 422–423
    extreme cases, 423
    illusory correlation, 97–98
    people, 420–421
    and prejudice, 420–423
    and self-consciousness, 439–440
    shortcut to judging groups, 421
    stereotypes, 421
    stigma consciousness, 440
distracting activities, 246 247
distraction, 180, 237
distress, 288
divorce, 391–392
door-in-the-face technique, 302
Draw-a-Person test, 472
driven by distraction, 237
drivers, and self-serving bias, 63
drunk-driving attitudes, 481f
drug education programs, 189
dual attitude system, 51, 401
dual processing, 7, 126
due process, 507

E

ecological footprint, 515f
eco-technologies, 518–519
education
    health, 177f
    of jurors, 505–506
    media awareness education, 330–331
    persuasion as, 159
egoism, 276
egoistic distress reduction, 288, 288f
electronic brainstorming, 263
elevation, 297

embodied cognition, 80
emotional expression, 146–148
emotional reactions, 88
emotions
    expressions, influence of, 146–148
    and eyewitness testimony, 499
    fear-arousing communications, 168–169
    good feelings, effect of, 167–168
    and illness, 483–487
    perception of, 166–169
    predicting our future feelings, 48–50
    vs. reason, 166–169
    and self-perception theory, 145
    stereotype threat and, 442
    two-factor theory of emotion, 378
    video games, and aggressive feelings, 339–340
empathy, 55, 287
ending relationships, 391–394
environmental influences, 323–324
environmental zones, 520
equality, 460
equity, 385–387, 460
erotic photographs, 49
errors, reducing, 503–506
ethics
    of experimentation, 27–28
    explanation of experiment, 201
    informed consent, 295
    Milgram's studies, 204–206
    and self-serving bias, 63
    twofold obligation, 295, 297
    university ethics committees, 28
ethnicity, 417
ethnocentric, 403
evaluation apprehension, 237, 240, 244
events
    distinctive, 422–423
    perceiving and interpreting, 80–82
everyday life
    group brainstorming, 263–264
    group polarization, 250–251
    social loafing, 240–242

social psychology in, 10
evil acts, 135–137, 211–212
evolution
    and aggression, 312
    and altruism, 283–284
    and attraction, 365–366
    and behaviour, 282–285
    genetic self-interest, 284
    instinct theory, 312
    kin selection, 283–284
    physical attractiveness, 365–366
    reciprocity, 284
evolutionary psychology, 9, 282–285, 312, 365–366
excess choice, 58 59
exchanging benefits, and equity, 385–386
expectations
    and attitudes, 505t
    and children's behaviour, 115
    influence of, 113–115
    of our social world, 111–115
    self-fulfilling prophecy, 111, 112f
    teacher expectations and student performance, 111–113, 112f
experimental realism, 27, 201
experimental research
    aggression against women, 328–330
    confederate, 10, 198–199
    control, 24–25
    and correlations, 24–25, 26t, 29f
    defined, 18
    demand characteristics, 27
    dependent variables, 25
    described, 24
    ethics of experimentation, 27–28
    experimental realism, 27
    generalizations from laboratory to life, 29
    independent variables, 24
    informed consent, 28
    manipulating variables, 24–25
    and mundane realism, 27
    prejudice against obese, 24–25
    random assignment, 25–26, 25f
    recognizing, 26t

television violence viewing, 25, 334–335
experimenter bias, 111
expertise, perceived, 88, 163
explanatory style, 476, 477f, 486–487
explicit attitudes, 51, 124
explicit memory, 88
explicit prejudice, 428
explicit self-esteem, 56
express yourself, 43
expressions
    and attitudes, 146–148
    emotional expression, and culture, 146–148
    of prejudice, 400
external causes, 105
external rewards, 275
extreme persuasion, 181–187
extrinsic motivation, 149f
eyewitness testimony
    confidence of witness, 502
    double-blind testing, 504
    false lineup identifications, minimization of, 504
    inaccuracy of, 498–500
    influences on, 505t
    jurors, education of, 505–506
    misinformation effect, 500 502, 500f, 501f
    persuasiveness, 498
    reduction of error, 503–506
    reliability of, 497–506
    retelling, 502–503
    training for police interviewers, 503

F

faces
    see also physical attractiveness
    computer averaged faces, and attractiveness, 365
    facial expressions, 42, 82, 146–148, 389
    recall and high-stress situations, 500
facial expressions, 42, 82, 146–148, 389
facts, 17
failure, 40, 71
fallacies
    naturalistic fallacy, 13
    planning fallacy, 48
false confessions, 502
false consensus bias, 370

false consensus effect, 65
false lineup identifications, 504
false memories, 501–502
false modesty, 73
false uniqueness effect, 65–66
family, and aggression, 320–321
favour, reciprocation of, 281f
favourable stereotype, 434
fear of failure, 71
fear-rousing communications,
    168–169
fearful attachment, 383
federalists, 14, 23
feel bad-do good scenario,
    277–278
feel good-do good scenario,
    278–279
feelings
    see also emotions
    expressions, influence of,
        146–148
    good feelings, effect of,
        167–168
    predicting our future feelings,
        48–50
    video games, and aggressive
        feelings, 339–340
feminist critics, 12
field research, 18
fighting constructively, 464t
final-offer arbitration, 467
first impressions, 363
fitting in
    and self-definition, 37–38
    social comparison, 39–40
flow, 527
folie à deux, 185
folk tale, 4
foot-in-the-door phenomenon,
    133–135, 183
Forbes 100 list, 522
forest bathing, 526
fragile self-esteem, 55–56
fraud, 28
free-ride, 240
friendship
    complementarity, 371
    and culture, 284
    and groupthink, 259
    and happiness, 491
    long-term equity, 386
    mere-exposure effect, 357–359
    mutual liking, 371–374
    norms, 280
    physical attractiveness,
        359–368
    proximity and, 355–359

relationship rewards,
    375–376
similarity, 368–361
frustration
    aggression as response to,
        316–319, 407–408
    defined, 316
    vs. deprivation, 318
    objective reality, 318
    scapegoat theory, 407–408
frustration-aggression theory
    classic theory, 317f
    defined, 316
    displacement, 316–317
    relative deprivation, 318–319
    revision of theory, 317
full house, 236
functional distance, 356
fundamental attribution error
    actor-observer difference,
        107–108
    attributions, 423–424
    camera perspective bias, 108
    changes in perspective,
        107–108
    and culture, 109
    defined, 105
    described, 104–107
    fundamental nature of, 109
    illustration of, 105f
    misperception and, 107f, 461
    perspective and situational
        awareness, 107–108
    prejudice, 423–424
    reasons for, 107–108
    self-awareness, 108–109
    social dilemmas, 457
    study of, 110
future technologies, 518–519

G

G-20 summit, 77–78, 245–246
gain-framed messages, 169
gambling, 98
game shows, 263
gangs, 342–343
gender
    and altruism, 300
    awareness of, 226
    bias, 435–436
    changing attitudes, 435f
    discrimination, 434–436
    gender roles, 131–132,
        433–434
    gender socialization, 433–434
    love, variations in, 378–379

marital attachment, and
    happiness, 492–493
medical treatment, seeking,
    483
passionate love, 378–379
prejudice, and conformity,
    406
prejudice based on, 433–436
and receiving help, 282
and self-disclosure, 387–388
stereotypes, 399, 433–434
gender-based prejudice,
    433–436
gender-inclusive language, 138
gender socialization, 433–434
generalization of positive
    attitudes, 398
Generation Me, 55
generational explanation, 178
genes and genetics
    and aggression, 313
    altruism, 282–285
    attachment, 385
    genetic selfishness, and
        altruistic behaviour, 286
    kin selection, 283–284
genetic self-interest, 284
genocide, 310, 343
Genovese, Kitty, 290, 293
genuine altruism, 286–289, 288f
The Geography of Thought
    (Nisbett), 42
global warming, 517–518
"going along with the crowd,"
    219
good feelings, 167–168
good life, 12
good luck, 97
Good Samaritan parable, 274
good subjects, 27
Google, 263
gravity, 17
"great person" theory of
    leadership, 265
greed, 5–6
GRIT, 467–468
group identities, 295
group immersion, and
    anonymity, 245f
group polarization
    in communities, 250–251
    defined, 249
    discussion, 250f
    in everyday life, 250–251
    experiments, 249–250
    explanations for, 252–254
    illustration of, 249f

informational influence, 252
intensification of opinions,
    247–254
on the Internet, 251
jury as a group, 509, 510f
misperception and, 461
normative influence,
    252–254
pluralistic ignorance, 253
research on, 253
risky shift phenomenon,
    248–249
schools, 250
social comparison, 253–254
terrorist organizations, 251
group selection, 284–285
group-serving bias, 70, 423–424
group size
    and conformity, 214–215,
        215f
    and deindividuation,
        243–244
    and social dilemmas, 458
    and social loafing, 240f
groups
    aggression, influences on,
        342–344, 344f
    Asch's studies of group
        pressure, 200–202, 201f,
        214t
    and brainstorming, 262–263
    categorization, 417–420
    co-actors, 233
    cohesiveness, 216–217
    cults, and group effects,
        185–187
    and culture, 241–242
    defined, 233
    deindividuation, 243–247
    group polarization, 247–254
    groupthink, 255–264
    and humans, 408
    in-group, 408
    in-group bias, 409–412
    jury as group, influences on,
        508–510
    leadership, 264–266
    liberating effects of group
        influence, 208–209
    minority influence, 266–268,
        509
    out-group, 408, 410–412,
        413–414
    problem solving, 261–264
    reference groups, 252–253
    social facilitation, 233–238
    social loafing, 238–242

unanimity, 215–216, 216f
unquestioned belief in
   morality of, 257
groupthink
   and brainstorming, 263–264
   closed-mindedness,
      257–258
   conformity pressure, 257
   critique of, 259
   defined, 256
   everyday examples, 263–264
   group problem solving,
      261–264
   illusion of invulnerability,
      256
   illusion of unanimity,
      257–258
   mindguards, 258
   misperception and, 461
   overestimate of might and
      right, 256–257
   prevention of, 260–261
   rationalization, 257
   self-censorship, 257
   stereotyped view of
      opponent, 257
   symptoms of, 256–258
   the *Titanic*, 255–256
   uniformity, 257–258
   unquestioned belief in
      group's morality, 257
   Walkerton water crisis, 258
growth-promoting listeners, 388
guilt, 276–277, 302–303
guns, 326–327, 326f, 346

H

handguns, 326–327, 326f, 346
happiness, 280, 491–493,
   521–527
health
   and close relationships,
      487–491
   and confiding, 488–489
   and illness, 482–487
   and income inequality, 490f
   and inequality, 489–491
   and optimism, 484–487
   and persuasion, 158
   and poverty, 489–491
   and self-efficacy, 59
   and self-serving bias, 63
   and social relationships,
      487–493
health education, 177f
health psychology

defined, 482
emotions and illness,
   483–487
optimism and health,
   484–487
reactions to illness,
   482–483
social relationships, 487–493
socially constructed
   disorders, 472
stress and illness, 484f
symptoms, 482–483
treatment, 483
healthier living, 158
healthy self-concept, 20
heart disease, 483–484, 487
heat, 323–324
heroism, 211
heuristics
   availability heuristics, 95–96
   defined, 94
   representativeness heuristics,
      94–95
   rule-of-thumb heuristics,
      94–95
hidden-camera method, 164
hidden third factor, 332
hidden values, 12–13
high self-esteem, 40, 52, 54, 54f,
   55–56, 68
hindsight, 473
hindsight bias, 15
the Holocaust, 8, 158, 207, 209,
   211, 213
   see also Nazi Germany
home advantage in team sports,
   235, 236t
hopelessness, 485, 486
hormones
   aggression, 314
   stress hormones, 9
   testosterone, 314–315
hostile aggression, 311, 323,
   325f
hostile sexism, 434
hostility, 113–114
hubris, 70
humility, 70
Hurricane Katrina, 49
hypoactive sexual desire
   disorder, 471
hypocrisy, 123–124
hypotheses
   defined, 17
   forming and testing, 16–18
   purposes of, 17

I

I-knew-it-all-along
   phenomenon, 15
illness
   emotions and, 483–487
   explanatory style and,
      486–487
   health and, 482–487
   reactions to, 482–483
   and stress, 484f, 485
illusion, capacity for, 89
illusion of control, 98–99
illusion of invulnerability, 256
illusion of transparency, 292
illusion of unanimity, 257–258,
   268
illusory correlation, 97–98,
   472, 475
illusory optimism, 64
illusory thinking
   illusion of control, 98–99
   illusory correlation, 97–98,
      472
   limits of intuition, 89–90
imagination inflation, 501–502
imitation, 335
immoral acts, 135–127
immune neglect, 50
impact bias, 49
Implicit Association Test (IAT),
   124–125, 401
implicit attitudes, 51, 124
implicit bias, 124
implicit cognition, 401
implicit measures, 23
implicit memory, 88
implicit self-esteem, 56
impression management,
   71–74, 139–140
impulse buying, 49
incest taboo, 280
income and marital status, and
   obesity correlation, 24–25
income inequality, and health
   problems, 490f
incompatibility *vs.*
   misconceptions, 461f
incompetence, and
   overconfidence, 90–91
independent self, 41, 44f, 44t
independent variables, 24
individualism
   cognitive dissonance, 144
   defined, 41
   and the self, 41–42
   and self-esteem, 44–45

and Tragedy of the
   Commons, 456
variations in, 42
ineffective appeals, 192
inequality, and health, 489–491
inequity
   marital distress, and, 387f
   perceived, 386–387
informational influence, 219,
   220–221, 252, 510
informed consent, 28, 295
infrahumanization, 411
ingratiation, 372
in-group, 408
in-group bias, 303, 409–412
injustice, perceived, 460
inoculation programs, 188–192
insecure attachment, 384
insight, 63
instinct theory, 312
instinctive behaviour, 312
institutional authority, 208
institutional supports, 406–407
instrumental aggression, 311
insufficient justification,
   140–142, 142f
   definition, 141
integrative agreements, 463
intellectual conceit, 90
intelligence
   and self-serving bias, 63
   and social status, 20
interaction, 274–275, 300, 301,
   356–357
interdependent self, 41, 43,
   44f, 44t
intergroup relations
   cooperation, 409
   generalization of positive
      attitudes, 399
   group identities, 295
   superordinate goals, 525
internal causes, 102
internal rewards, 275, 276–279
internal working models, 384
internalized confessions, 502
Internet
   and anonymity, 244
   cyberostracism, 354
   and group polarization, 251
   intimacy or isolation, 389–390
   and violence, 334
interpretation, bias in, 444–446
interpretation of events, 80–82,
   291–293
intrinsic motivation, 148–150,
   149f

intuition
about the self, 46–51
limits of, 89–90
powers of, 6–7, 87–89
predicting our feelings, 48–50
predicting our own
behaviour, 46–48
social intuitions, 6–7
and self-concept, 37–51
intuitive judgments, 87–90
Iraq, 8

J

Japan, 8, 41
Japanese-style management,
265
judgments. *See* social judgment
jurors and juries
defendant's physical
attractiveness and, 506
education of, 505–506
group polarization, 509, 510f
individual jurors, influences
on, 506–508
influences, 506–511
informational influence, 510
judicial instructions and,
506–507
jury as group, influences on,
508–510
leniency, effect of, 510
minority influence, 509
normative influence, 510
simulated juries, 510–511
social influences, 508–509
statistical information,
comprehension of,
507–508
story of trial and, 507
understanding, increasing, 508
just-world phenomenon, 414–416

K

kin selection, 283–284
knowledge of issues, and bias,
23–24
Kulechov effect, 82

L

labelling, 12–13
language
collectivist language, 41–42
culture, influence of, 109

external attributions, 109
gender-inclusive language,
138
group-serving bias, 423–424
jury instruction and, 506–507
preferences, 357–358
purpose of, 43
value judgments within,
12–13
law and social science. *See*
courtroom; jurors and
juries
leadership
defined, 264
democratic leadership, 265
"great person" theory of
leadership, 265
social leadership, 264–265
task leadership, 264–265
transactional leadership, 265
transformational leadership,
265–266
learned helplessness, 57,
58f, 485
learning
about altruism, 306–307
aggression, 319–322, 322f
by doing, 305
observational learning,
320–322
social learning theory,
320–322, 322f, 346–347
Lemmings, 305
leniency, 510
Liberal Party, 21
life cycle explanation, 178
likeness-leads-to-liking effect,
369–370
liking, 164–166, 165t, 350–395
see also attraction
liking by association, 357–358,
375, 375f
liking those who like us,
371–374
lineup instructions, 505t
linguistic intergroup bias, 424
Literary Digest, 22
long-term equity, 386
longevity, and status, 18–19, 19f
longitudinal research, 21
looking-glass self, 40
love
see also close relationships
arranged marriages *vs.* love
marriages, 382f
and attractiveness, 367–368,
377–379

brain and, 379f
companionate love, 380–382
and culture, 378–379
described, 377, 378
and gender, 378–379
overlapping of selves, 388f
passionate love, 377–379
two-factor theory of emotion,
378
types, 377f
love bombing, 186
low-ball techniques, 134
low self-esteem, 20, 40, 41,
53–54, 54f, 55–56, 68, 373
luck, 97

M

major themes in social
psychology, 6–10, 7f
mammalian pair bonding, 383
mammograms, and fear-
arousing communications,
168
marital attachment, and
happiness, 492–493
marital distress, and inequity,
387f
marital status and depression,
492f
marital status and income, and
obesity correlation, 24–25
marriage. *See* close
relationships
mastery experiences, 59
Marxist critics, 12
matching phenomenon, 361
materialism
adaptation-level
phenomenon, 524
failure to satisfy, 522–525
increased materialism, 521
social comparisons, 524–525
wealth and well-being,
521–522
media
aggression, influences on,
327–342
comparison of, 177–178
influence, 176–178
media awareness education,
330–331
pornography, 327–331
sexual violence, 327–331
stereotype threat, 440–443,
441f, 442f
television, 331–337

two-step flow of
communication,
176–177
video games, 337–342, 339f
media bias, 80–81, 81f
medial prefrontal cortex, 38
mediation, 462, 463–466
medical treatment, 483
memory
bias in, 444–446
construction of memories,
84–86
explicit memory, 88
false memories, 500–502
implicit memory, 88
misinformation effect, 85,
500–502, 500f, 501f
moods, effect of, 476–477
past attitudes, reconstruction
of, 85–86
past behaviour,
reconstruction of, 86
positive memories, 85–86
priming, 79
rosy retrospection, 85
stereotypes, influence of,
440–442
men
see also gender
falling in love, 361
looks, and attraction, 360
sexually aggressive men,
331f
stereotypes about, 402
mere-exposure effect, 357–359
mere presence of others,
233–235, 237–238
mere repetition, 175
message
audience, 178–181
content of, and persuasion,
166–174
cults, 184
difficult messages, 179f
discrepancy, 170–171, 171f
easy messages, 179f
fear-rousing communications,
168–169
good feelings, effect of,
167–168
one-sided appeals, 171–173,
172f
personal *vs.* media influence,
176–178
primacy *vs.* recency,
173–174, 174f
reason *vs.* emotion, 166–169

two-sided appeals, 171–173, 172f
written message, 177–178, 179f
meta-stereotypes, 440
Milgram's obedience studies, 203–206, 203f, 205f, 214t
mimic and mirror, 165
mimicry, 199, 369
mindguards, 258
minimal group situations, 233
minority influence
consistency, 267
defections from the majority, 268
jury as a group, 509
minority slowness effect, 267
self-confidence, 268
minority slowness effect, 267
misattribution, 102
misconceptions *vs.* incompatibility, 461f
misidentifications, 504
misinformation effect, 85, 500–502, 500f, 501f
misperception, 107f, 460–462, 461f, 463–466
mistrust, 465
miswant, 49
modelling altruism, 304–305
moment of truth, 92
money
and happiness, 275, 280, 521–527
predictions, 48
mood
depressed moods, and negative thinking, 476–480
and helpfulness, 279f
and judgment, 99–101
memory, effect on, 476–477
and perception, 100f
self-knowledge, 47
and self-presentation, 72
and social judgment, 99–101
and thinking, 100–101
mood infusion, 100
mood linkage, 199
moral acts, 135–137
moral disengagement, 135–136
moral exclusion, 303
moral hypocrisy, 123–124, 128
moral imperative, 343
moral inclusion, 303
morality
legislation of, 137
unquestioned belief in, 257

motivation
for anti-conformity, 225–227
avoidance of prejudice, 416–417
extrinsic motivation, 149f
frustration and aggression, 407–408
internal rewards, 275, 276–279
intrinsic motivation, 148–150, 149f
just-world phenomenon, 414–416
need for cognition, 180
need to belong, 352
and prejudice, 407–417
rewards, 275–279
self-esteem, 52–56
social identity theory, 408–414
motives *vs.* perceptions, 68
mug-shot-induced bias, 505t
multiculturalism, 398–399, 400
multiple-choice tests, 15
mundane realism, 27, 201
murders, 311, 326–327, 326f, 333–334

N

name letter effect, 358
narcissism, 54–55, 54f
nation of the dead, 309–310
natural associations, 18–29, 19f, 26t, 29f
natural disasters, 49
natural mimicry, 369
natural selection, 285
naturalistic fallacy, 13
Nazi Germany, 5, 8, 82, 138, 169, 207, 209, 211, 212, 213
see also the Holocaust
need-based distribution, 460
need for cognition, 180
need to belong, 352
negative events
explanations for, 60–61
and impact bias, 49
negative persuasion, 172
negative thinking, 476–480
neurobiology, 9
neuroscience
and aggression, 312–313
social neuroscience, 9
new consciousness, 520

New Democratic Party (NDP), 21, 23–24, 178
new technologies, 518–519
no prior commitment, 217–219
Nobel Prize, 36, 262
non-zero-sum games, 457
normative influence, 219–220, 221, 252–254, 510
norms
and altruism, 280–282
altruistic norms, 458–459
and culture, 281
defined, 129
reciprocity norm, 280–281, 285
Sherif's studies of norm formation, 197–200, 198f, 214t
social-responsibility norm, 281–282
universal norms, 280
noticing, 291

O

obedience
see also conformity
Asch's studies of group pressure, 200–202, 201f, 214t
behaviour and attitudes, 210–212
classic conformity and obedience studies, 197–214, 214t
closeness and legitimacy of the authority, 207–208
conditions that breed obedience, 206–209
defined, 197
factors, 206–209
group influence, liberating effects of, 208–209
institutional authority, 208
Milgram's obedience studies, 203–206, 203f, 205f, 214t
Sherif's studies of norm formation, 197–200, 198f, 214t
situation, power of, 212–214
soldiers, 207, 209
victims' distance, 206–207
obesity, prejudice against, 24–25
objective behavioural dimensions, 61–62

objective reality, 164
observable traits, 41
observational learning, 320–322
Occam's razor, 173
one-sided appeals, 171–173, 172f
Ontario Human Rights Commission, 430
open, honest relationship, 374
openers, 387–388
operationalization, 17–18
opposites, 371
oppositional defiance disorder, 471
optimism, 63–65, 172, 484–487
orgasmic disorder, 471–472
ostracism, 353–354, 354f
out-group, 408, 410–412, 413–414
out-group homogeneity effect, 418
overconfidence
in clinical judgments, 473
and incompetence, 90–91
overconfidence phenomenon, 90–94
planning fallacy, 94
remedies for, 93–94
overconfidence phenomenon, 90–94
overjustification effect, 148–150, 305–306
overpersonalization, 481–482
own-age bias, 420
own-race bias, 419, 419f
oxygen of publicity, 320

P

pain, 322–323
parental support, 63
Parti Quebecois, 23
passionate love, 377–379
passive reception, 174–176, 252
peace
achievement of, 462–468
applications in the real world, 468
arbitration, 462, 466–467
bargaining, 462–463
conciliation, 467–468
GRIT, 467–468
mediation, 462, 463–466
people, distinctive, 420–421
people-watching, 16

perception
  altered perceptions, 336
  of bias, 81f
  culture, 43f
  of differences, 418–420
  distinctiveness, 420–423
  discrimination, 439–440,
    447–448
  of emotion, 166–169
  of equity, and satisfaction,
    386–387
  of events, 80–82
  of expertise, 88, 163
  of facial expressions, 146
  of inequity and marital
    distress, 386–387, 387f
  of injustice, 460
  and mood, 100f
  vs. motives, 68
  misperception, 460–462,
    463–466
  of prejudice, 417–424
  of sexual reality, 328
  shifting perceptions, and
    conflict, 461–462
  of similarities, 418–420
  of social worlds, 78–86
  trustworthiness, 163–164
peripheral cues, 160–161,
  180–181
peripheral route to persuasion,
  160–161, 161f
persistence, 267, 268
person, power of the, 225–227
personal appeal, 301–302
personal commitment, 187–188
personal control, 57
personal/group discrimination
  discrepancy, 448, 448f
personal history, 43–44
personal identity, 44, 408, 409f
personal influence,
  176–178, 301
personal judgment, and
  stereotypes, 442–446
personality
  and altruism, 299–300
  anger-prone personality, 483
  authoritarian personality,
    403–404
  behaviour, effect on, 9
  and conformity, 222–223
  social dominance
    orientation, 403, 404
  Type A personality, 483
personality disposition, 9
personality psychology, 4–5

perspective
  actor-observer difference,
    107–108
  camera perspective bias, 108
  change in, over time, 108
  and situational awareness,
    107–108
persuasion
  active experience vs. passive
    reception, 174–176
  age, 178–179
  attitude accessibility, 181f
  attitude inoculation, 188,
    191–192
  attitudes follow behaviour,
    183
  and attractiveness, 164–166
  audience, 178–181, 184–185
  central route to persuasion,
    160, 161f
  challenging beliefs, 187
  channel of communication,
    174–178
  the communicator, 162–166,
    183–184
  comprehension, 177–178
  constructive uses of, 186–187
  counterarguments, 180, 188
  credibility, 162–164
  cults, 181–187
  and culture, 158
  defined, 158
  different routes and purposes,
    161–162
  difficult messages, 179f
  discrepancy, 170–171, 171f
  easy messages, 179f
  as education, 159
  extreme persuasion, 181–187
  eyewitness testimony, 498
  fear-rousing communications,
    168–169
  good feelings, effect of,
    167–168
  group effects, 185–187
  and health, 158
  ineffective appeals, 192
  influencing variables, 184f
  inoculation programs,
    188–192
  and liking, 164–166
  message content, 166–174, 184
  negative persuasion, 172
  one-sided appeals, 171–173,
    172f
  paths to persuasion,
    159–162, 161f

perceived expertise, 163
perceived trustworthiness,
  164–164
peripheral cues, 180–181
peripheral route to
  persuasion, 160–161,
  161f
personal commitment,
  strengthening, 187–188
personal vs. media influence,
  176–178
persuasive elements,
  183–185
positive persuasion, 172
power of, 157–159
primacy vs. recency,
  173–174, 174f
and prior commitments,
  187–188
propaganda, 159, 169
reason vs. emotion, 166–169
resistance to, 187–192
six persuasion principles,
  165t
thought, 179–181
two-sided appeals, 171–173,
  172f
pessimism, 63–65, 172,
  475–476, 477–478, 486
physical anonymity, 244–246,
  244f
physical appeal, 165
physical attractiveness
  across cultures, 364–365
  and attraction, 359–368
  beautiful is good stereotype,
    363–364
  of the communicator,
    164–166
  computer averaged faces, 365
  and dating, 359–360
  of defendants, 506
  and evolution, 365–366
  first impressions, 363
  and liking, 164–166
  of loved ones, 367–368
  matching phenomenon, 361
physical-attractiveness
  stereotype, 362–364
  and relationship
    commitment, 368f
  social comparison, 366–367
  subjective nature of, 364–368
physical-attractiveness
  stereotype, 362–364
physical punishment, 347
planned behaviour, 127f

planning fallacy, 48, 94
pluralistic ignorance, 253, 292
poison parasite defence, 188
police interviewers, 503
political correctness, 12
political debate, 81–82
polls, 21
pop psychology, 109
pornography, and aggression,
  327–331, 330f
positive events, explanations
  for, 60–61
positive illusions, 374
positive memories, 85–86
positive persuasion, 172
possible selves, 38
post-decision dissonance,
  143–144
post-event information, 505t
postmaterialist values, 525
posture and performance, 148
poverty, and health, 489–491
power of the person, 225–227
The Power of Persuasion: How
  We're Bought and Sold
  (Levine), 190
Power Rangers, 25
preconceptions, 78–80, 82
prediction markets, 264
predictions
  about our behaviour, 47–48
  about our future feelings,
    48–50
  affective forecasting, 48–49
  attitudes, and behaviour,
    126–127
  of conformity, 214–219
  money and, 48
  relationship, fate of, 64
  in research, 16–17, 18
  theoretical predictions, 17
prejudgments, 398, 436–438
prejudice
  attitude of, 398, 400
  attributions, 423–424
  authoritarian personality,
    403–404
  automatic prejudice, 401,
    430, 432
  avoidance of prejudice, and
    motivation, 416–417
  categorization, 417–420
  cognitive sources of, 417–424
  conformity, 405–406
  consequences of, 428–436
  defined, 398
  vs. discrimination, 400

distinctiveness, 420–423, 439–440
ethnocentric, 403
explicit prejudice, 428
facing, 431f
frustration and aggression, 407–408
fundamental attribution error, 423
gender prejudice, 433–436
gender roles, 402
group-serving bias, 423–424
implicit prejudice, 430
in-group bias, 409–413
institutional supports, 406–407
just-world phenomenon, 414–416
measuring, 400–401
motivational sources of, 407–417
nature and power of, 398–401
need for status, self-regard and belonging, 412–414
against obesity, 24–25
out-group homogeneity effect, 418
own-race bias, 419, 419f
perceived similarities and differences, 418–420
perceptions of, 447–448
personal judgment, 442–446
prejudgments, 398, 436–438
racial prejudice, 428–433
vs. racism, 400
reactions to, 446–449
realistic group conflict theory, 407
and religion, 404–405
scapegoat theory, 407–408
self-consciousness, 439–440
self-fulfilling prophecy, 399, 438–440
self-perpetuating stereotypes, 436–438
vs. sexism, 400
social desirability and, 22–23
social dominance orientation, 403
social identity theory, 408–414
social inequalities, 401–403
social sources of, 401–407
socialization, 403–406
vs. stereotype, 398–399, 402

stereotype threat, 440–442, 441f, 442f
stigma consciousness, 440
subtle forms of, 400–401, 429–430
values and, 11
preoccupied attachment, 384
pride, 70
primacy effect, 173–174, 174f
primal attractions, 366
priming, 79–80, 89f
principle of aggregation, 126
prior commitments, 217–219
Prisoners' Dilemma, 454–455, 455f, 456f, 457, 458
probability neglect, 96
problem-solving, group, 261–264
process of thoughts, 27
professional advice, 13
professional competence, 63
professional opinion, 223
propaganda, 159, 169
prosocial behaviour, 297, 303–307, 335, 342
prosocial models, 297, 304–305
prosocial value orientation, 304
proverbs, 15
proximity
    anticipation of interaction, 357
    defined, 355
    interaction, 356–357
    mere-exposure effect, 357–359
psychological concepts, hidden values in, 12–13
psychological immune system, 50
psychological pain, 322–323
psychotherapy, 186
PsycINFO, 37
public commitment, 218–219
public image, 302
public opinion, 21, 517–518
public response, 217
punishment, 346–347
punitive behaviour, 330f

Q
quantifying correlations, 20
Quebec sovereignty, 14, 23
questions
    order of, 22
    wording of, 23–24, 505t

R
race, categorization by, 417–418, 418f
racial attitudes. See prejudice
racism
    see also prejudice
    cultural, 370–371
    defined, 400
    vs. prejudice, 400
random assignment, 26–27, 26f
random events, 97
random sample, 21, 27
rape experiences, 330t
rape myth, 328
rationalization, 257
reactance, 225
reactions, and attributions, 110f
reactions to illness, 482–483
reactive devaluation, 466
realism, 65
realistic group conflict theory, 407
reason vs. emotion, 166–169
recency effect, 173–174, 174f
reciprocity, 165t, 284
reciprocity norm, 280–281, 285
recollections, 85–86
reduction of error, 503–506
reference groups, 252–253
regression toward the average, 98–99
regulation of social dilemmas, 458
rejection, pain of, 354f
relating to others, 9–10
relationships
    close relationships. See close relationships
    ending relationships, 391–394
    and health, 487–493
    love, 367–368, 376–382
    related attractiveness, and commitment, 368f
    and self-esteem, 10
    social relationships, 36, 526
relative deprivation, 318–319
religion, and prejudice, 404–405
repetition, 175
representativeness, 22
representativeness heuristics, 94–95
research methods
    correlational research, 18–23, 20f, 26t, 39f

experimental research, 18, 24–28, 26t, 29f
experimenter bias, 111
field research, 18
generalizations from laboratory to life, 29
hypotheses, forming and testing, 16–18
longitudinal research, 21
manipulating variables, 24–25
random assignment, 26–27, 26f
survey research, 21–24
theory, 16–17
time-lagged correlations, 21
resisting persuasion, 187–192
response bias, 22–23
responsibility
    and altruism, 300–302
    assumption of, 293–295
responsibility diffusion, 342
retaliation, 316, 321, 345–346
retelling events, 502–503
reward theory of attraction, 375–376
rewards, 275–276, 319–320, 375–376
rich-poor gap, 525
rioters, 243
risky shift phenomenon, 248–249
risk vs. caution, 254f
role
    defined, 129
    effects of, 224
    gender roles, 131–132
    social roles, 224
role-playing, 129–132
romantic love. See love
rope-pulling, 239f
rosy retrospection, 85
rule-of-thumb heuristics, 94–95

S
sadder-but-wiser effect, 476
satisfaction
    and materialism, 522–525
    and perceived equity, 386–387
    and social comparison, 40
saying, and believing, 132–133
scapegoat theory, 407–408
scarcity, 165t
Schaudenfreude, 284
schemas, 38, 88

school
    group polarization in, 250
    success in, 65
science, subjective aspects of,
    11–12
secure attachment, 383
secure self-esteem, 55–56
the self
    in action, 56–59
    and culture, 41–45
    defining, 36, 37f
    evaluation of, 60–70
    independent self, 41, 44f, 44t
    interdependent self, 41, 43,
        44f, 44t
    intuitions about, 47–51
    looking-glass self, 40
    possible selves, 38
    sense of self, 37–38
    social comparison, 39–40, 39f
    social self, 38
self-affirmation theory, 151
self-analysis, 50–51
self-awareness, 36, 110, 247,
    301–302
self-blame, 476, 478–479
self-censorship, 257, 374
self-concept
    daily experiences, 40
    defined, 37
    healthy self-concept, and
        achievement, 20
    importance of, 37–38
    independent vs.
        interdependent, 44f, 44t
    intuition, 37–51
    malleability of, 44
    self and culture, 41–44
    self-determination, 57–59
    self-knowledge, 47–51
    sense of self, 37–38
    social identity, 38–41, 408,
        410–411
    spontaneous self-concepts,
        226
self-concern, 36
self-confidence, 268
self-confirming diagnoses,
    473–475
self-consciousness, 98, 128,
    439–440
self-construal, 44f
self-contradictory acts, 152
self-control, 56–59, 247
self-defeating behaviour, 71
self-determination, 57–59
self-disclosure, 387–391

self-doubt, 65
self-efficacy
    and health and happiness, 58
    and optimism, 65
self-esteem
    and achievement, 19–20, 52
    and aggression, 54f
    and antisocial behaviour, 55
    and attraction, 373
    and communal qualities, 41
    and culture, 44–45
    dark side, 53–56
    defined, 51
    explicit self-esteem, 56
    fragile self-esteem, 55–56
    gaining another's esteem,
        373–374
    high self-esteem, 40, 52, 54,
        54f, 55–56, 68
    implicit self-esteem, 56
    low self-esteem, 20, 40, 41,
        53–54, 54f, 55–56, 68,
        373
    maintenance motive, 52
    motivation, 52–53
    narcissism and, 54–56, 54f
    observable traits, 41
    and perceptions of prejudice,
        447
    and personal identity, 409f
    positive messages and, 40
    and relationships, 10
    secure self-esteem, 55–56
    and self-organization, 37
    and self-serving bias, 68–70
    and social identity, 408, 409f
    success and, 40
    threats, 52–53
    and violence, 54
self-evaluation, 39, 39f, 60–70,
    89f
self-focus, 479
self-fulfilling prophecy
    defined, 111
    and discrimination, 438–438
    influence of, 113–115
    teacher expectations and
        student performance,
        111–113, 112f
self-handicapping, 71
self-image, 302–303
self-inflation, 40–41
self-interest, and judgment, 36
self-justification, 140–144
self-knowledge
    dual attitude system, 51, 401
    immune neglect, 50

impact bias, 49
planning fallacy, 48
predicting behaviour, 47–48
predicting feelings, 48–50
self-analysis, 50–51
self-monitoring, 73, 442
self-perception theory
    defined, 145
    described, 145–146
    expressions and attitude,
        146–148
    intrinsic motivations,
        148–150
    overjustification effect,
        148–150
    physical attractivness, 367
    when not self-contradicting,
        152
self-perpetuating stereotypes,
    436–438
self-persuasion, 129, 152
self-presentation
    conscious self-presentation,
        72–73
    defined, 72
    false modesty, 73–74
    impression management,
        71–74, 139–140
    self-handicapping, 71
    self-monitoring, 73
    social influence on, 36
    and social networking, 72
self-presentation theory, 139
self-presented modesty, 74
self-regard, and social identity,
    412–414
self-reports, 51
self-sacrifice, 283
self-schema, 38
self-serving attributions, 60–61
self-serving bias
    as adaptive, 68–69
    comparisons with others,
        61–62
    defined, 60
    and driving, 63
    and ethics, 63
    evaluating self, 60–67
    explanations for, 67f, 68
    false consensus effect, 65
    false uniqueness effect, 65–66
    group self-serving bias, 70
    and health, 63
    and humility, 70
    and insight, 63
    and intelligence, 63
    as maladaptive, 69–70

and marriage, 61
misperception and, 461
negative events, explanations
    for, 60–61
objective behavioural
    dimensions, 61–62
parental support, 63
perceptions vs. motives, 68
positive events, explanations
    for, 60–61
and pride, 70
and professional
    competence, 63
reflections on, 68–70
and self-esteem, 68–70
and stress, 68–69
subjective behaviour
    dimensions, 61–62
temporal comparison, 66–67,
    67f
types of, 63
unrealistic optimism, 63–65
and virtues, 63
self-verification, 93
self-worth, 275
sensitivity to diversity, 399
sensory overload, 295
sex, 443
sexism, 400, 402, 434
sexual arousal, 49, 325
sexual assault, 328
sexual scripts, 336
sexual violence
    aggression against women,
        328–329
    correlational studies, 328
    depictions of, in
        pornography, 327–328
    distorted perceptions of
        sexual reality, 328
    experimental studies,
        328–329
    increase in incidents of,
        328–330
    media awareness education,
        330–331
    rape myth, acceptance of,
        328
    violent pornography,
        exposure to, 329
Sherif's studies of norm
    formation, 197–200, 198f,
    214t
shifting perceptions, 461–462
shyness, 480–482
silent aggression, 311
silent treatment, 353

similarity
  and attraction, 165, 368–371
  bystander passivity, 290
  and cooperation, 299f
  cultural similarity, 223–224
  and liking, 369–370
  perceived similarities,
      371–372, 418–420
  to victim, 298
simplistic thinking, 461
simulated juries, 510–511
situational anxiety, 481–482
situational attribution, 103, 109
situational awareness, and
      perspective, 107–108
situational influences
  conformity, predicting,
      214–219
  the person, influence of,
      173–174, 301
  power of, 8, 212–214, 299
sleeper effect, 162
smart meters, 520
smoke-filled room experiment,
      292f
smoking, and children,
      189, 189f
snap judgments, 7, 88
soccer referee decisions, 202
social acceptance, 41
social aggression, 311
social animal, 353
social anxiety, 480–482
social arousal, 235f
social attachment, 352
social behaviour, 5, 8, 36,
      50–51, 319–322
social beliefs
  behavioural confirmation,
      115–117
  belief perseverance, 83–84
  challenging beliefs, 187
  changing, after conforming,
      221f
  constructing, 78–79
  importance of, 6
  and mental construction of
      events, 83–84
  saying, and believing,
      132–133
  self-fulfilling, 5
social capital, 281
social cocoon, 186
social comparison
  defined, 39
  and group polarization,
      250–251

and materialism, 524–525
  physical attractiveness,
      366–367
  and self-evaluation,
      39–40, 39f
social competence, 353
social contagion
  and aggressive tendencies,
      342
  chameleon effect, 199
  suggestibility, 198–199
social control, 186
Social Credit Party, 23–24
social desirability, 22–23
social dilemmas
  altruistic norms, appeal to,
      458–459
  described, 453–454
  Prisoners' Dilemma, 454–455,
      455f, 456f, 457, 458
  regulation, 458
  resolution of, 457–459
  small groups, 458
  social trap, 454
  Tragedy of the Commons,
      455–457
social dominance orientation,
      403, 404
social-exchange theory
  defined, 275
  described, 274–275
  egoism, 276
  feel bad-do good scenario,
      exceptions to, 277–278
  feel good-do good scenario,
      278–279
  guilt, 276–277
  internal rewards, 276–279
  rewards, 275–276
  weakness in, 276
social exclusion, 41
social facilitation
  crowding, 236–237
  defined, 234
  driven by distraction, 237
  evaluation apprehension,
      237
  mere presence of others,
      233–235, 237–238
  reasons for arousal, 235f,
      237–238
  vs. social loafing, 241f
social history, 11
social identity
  and belonging, 412–414
  categorization and, 418
  defined, 38

Europe and, 11
  in-group, 408
  in-group bias, 409–412
  motivational source of
      prejudice, 408–414
  other people's judgments,
      40–41
  out-group, 408, 410–412,
      413–414
  perceived prejudice and
      discrimination, 403–406
  self-enhancing, 424t
  self-esteem, 408, 409f
  self-regard, need for, 412–414
  social comparisons, 39–40
  status, need for, 412–414
  success and failure, 40
social image, 220–221
social implosion, 185
social indoctrination, 138
social inequalities, and
      prejudice, 401–403
social influence
  and behaviour, 8, 124–126
  culture, impact of, 8, 223–224
  jurors and juries, 508–510
  and personality, 222–223
social intuitions, 6–7
social judgment
  clinical judgment, 471
  confirmation bias, 93
  counterfactual thinking,
      96–97
  heuristics, 94–96
  illusory thinking, 97–99
  intuitive judgment, 87–90
  mood and, 99–101
  overconfidence
      phenomenon, 90–94
  other people's judgments,
      40–41
  self-interest and, 36
social leadership, 264–265
social learning theory, 320–322,
      322f, 346–347
social loafing
  challenging tasks, effect of,
      242
  collective effort of teams,
      238–240
  commitment, effect of, 242
  and culture, 241–242
  defined, 239
  in everyday life, 240–242
  free riders, 240
  group size, effect of, 240f
  vs. social facilitation, 241f

social movements,
      138–139, 267
social networking, 72
social neuroscience, 9
social norms. See norms
social perception, 78
social proof, 165t
social psychology
  behaviour, and effect of
      social influences, 8
  behaviour, and effect of
      personal attitudes and
      dispositions, 8–9
  biological roots of social
      behaviour, 9
  and climate change, 516–518
  and common sense, 13–16
  defined, 4, 4f
  everyday life and, 10
  hidden values and, 11–13
  and human values, 10–13
  major themes in, 6–10, 7f
  materialism, 521–525
  new technologies, 518–519
  obvious values and, 11
  parameters of, 4–6
  vs. personality psychology,
      4–5
  purposes of, 4–6
  questions, 5–6
  reducing consumption,
      519–521
  relating to others, 9–10
  research methods, 16–29
  social intuitions, power of,
      6–7
  social reality, construction
      of, 6
  sustainability and survival,
      525–527
  unexamined assumptions, 12
  wealth and well-being,
      521–522
social reality, construction of, 6
social rejection, 219, 354
social relations
  see also aggression; altruism;
      attraction; relationships
  culture and, 321–322
  reward theory of attraction,
      375–376
social relationships, and self, 36
social representations, 12
social-responsibility norm,
      281–282
social roles, 224
social scripts, 336

social self, 38
social situations, 480
social status, and intelligence, 20
social support
    confiding, 488–389
    and happiness, 491
    and health, 488–489
social surroundings, 36
social trap, 454
social world
    behavioural confirmation,
        114–115
    expectations of, 111–115
    explaining, 101–110
    judging, 87–101
    perception of, 78–86
socialization
    altruism, 303–307
    gender socialization, 433
    and prejudice, 403–406
socially constructed disorders,
    483
sociology, 4
soldiers, 14, 209
Somalia, 212, 243
source credibility, 162–164
sovereignty, 14, 23
speed dating, 49, 360, 363
spoken appeals, 174–175
spontaneous categorization,
    417–418
spontaneous self-concepts, 226
spontaneous trait inference,
    103
spontaneous trait transference,
    82
start-small-and-build
    technique, 139
statistical information,
    507–508
status
    and conformity, 217
    and longevity, 18–19, 19f
    marital, 24–25
    need for, and social identity,
        412–414
    unequal status, 401–403
stereotype threat, 440–442,
    441f, 442f
stereotypes
    actions and thinking, 148
    automatic stereotyping, 432
    beautiful is good stereotype,
        363–364
    change in, and attributions,
        438f
    defined, 398

and distinctiveness, 421
favourable stereotypes, 434
gender stereotypes, 401,
    433–434
harsher evaluation of target,
    446f
influence on judgment,
    442–446
interpretations, influence on,
    444–446
memories, influence on,
    444–446
overgeneralization, 399
and personal judgment,
    442–446
physical-attractiveness
    stereotype, 362–364
vs. prejudice, 398–399, 402
reactions to, 446–449
self-enhancing social
    identities, supporting,
    424t
self-perpetuating stereotypes,
    436–438
stereotyped view of
    opponent, 257
strong stereotypes, 444
subgrouping, 438
subtyping, 437
and unequal status, 401–402
stigma consciousness, 440
Stop Watch Gang, 130–131
strangers, helping, 296f
stress
    and depression, 477–478
    health effects of, 484f
    and illness, 484f, 485
    and self-serving bias, 68–69
    and stereotype threat, 442
student expectations, and
    teacher performance,
        111–113, 112f
subgrouping, 438
subjective aspects of science,
    11–12
subjective behaviour
    dimensions, 61–62
subjective preference, 165
subliminal priming, 89f
subliminal stimuli, 79–80,
    88–89
subtyping, 437
success
    and failure, 40
    in school, 65

and self-control, 57
and self-esteem, 40
and subjective qualities,
    61–62
suggestibility, 198–200
suicide, 200
superordinate goals, 525
suppressing thoughts and
    emotions, 442
survey research
    biases, sensitivity to, 23
    described, 21
    order of questions, 22
    random sample, 21
    response bias, 22–23
    social desirability, 22–23
    unrepresentative sample, 22
    wording of question, 24
survivable future, 525–527
sustainability
    consumption, reduction of,
        519–521
    eco-technologies, 518–519
    enabling sustainable living,
        515–521
    psychology and climate
        change, 516–518
    and survival, 525–527
    sustainable future, 515–521
Swiss Air flight 111, 260–261
symptoms
    explaining, 482–483
    noticing, 482
system justification
    tendency, 518

T

task leadership, 264–265
teacher expectations, and
    student performance,
        111–113, 112f
television
    and aggression, 331–337
    altered perceptions, 336
    arousal, 335
    behaviour, effects on,
        332–335
    catharsis, 341
    children, and latent criminal
        activity, 333f
    cognitive priming, 337
    correlating viewing and
        behaviour, 332–334
    desensitization, 335–336
    disinhibition, 335
    hidden third factor, 332–333

imitation, 335
prosocial behaviour, 335
prosocial models, 304–305
social scripts, 336
thinking, effects on, 335–337
time drain, 337
viewing, and violence,
    25, 335
viewing experiments,
    334–335
temperament, 313, 385
temporal comparison, 66–67
temporary climate, 323
terror management theory, 53,
    69, 413
terrorism, 311, 320
terrorist organizations, group
    polarization in, 251
totalitarian egos, 86
terrorism, 311
testosterone, and aggression,
    314–315
theoretical explanation, 17
theoretical predictions, 17
theory, 16–18
thinking
    Asian and Western thinking,
        42–43, 42f
    automatic processing, 51, 88
    controlled processing, 88
    counterfactual thinking,
        96–97
    culture, effect of, 41–45
    heuristics, 95–96
    illusory thinking, 97–99, 472
    intuition and, 7
    and mood, 100–102
    negative thinking, 476–480
    persuasion and, 179–181
    positive thinking, 526
    simplistic thinking, 461
    stereotype threat and, 442
    television, effects of, 335–337
    unconscious thinking, 88
    video games, and aggressive
        thinking, 340
third variable, 21
threatened punishment, 346
time delay, 463
time drain, 337
time-lagged correlations, 21
time pressures, 297–298
time-shifting, 331
Titanic, 255–256
totalitarian egos, 86
Tragedy of the Commons,
    455–457

traits, inference of, 103
transactional leadership, 265
transformational leadership, 265–266
treatment, 483
trial story, 507
Tri-Council, 28
truisms, 188
trustworthiness, 163–164
two-factor theory of emotion, 378
two-sided appeals, 171–173, 172f
two-step flow of communication, 176–177
Type A personality, 483
tyranny of freedom, 58

U

unanimity, 215–216, 216f, 257–258
unanticipated reward, 149
unattended stimuli, 79
unconscious mind, 7
unconscious thinking, 88
unequal status, 401–403
unhappy people, 99
uniforms, 245–246

uninvolved audiences, 180–181
uniqueness, 65–66, 226–227
universal norms, 280
university ethics committees, 28
unrealistic optimism, 63–65
unrepresentative samples, 22
unrestrained behaviours, 243

V

value judgments, 12–13
values
    concept formation, 12
    differences across time and culture, 11
    hidden values, 12–13
    labelling, 12–13
    naturalistic fallacy, 13
    obvious values, 11
    postmaterialist values, 525
    psychological concepts, 12–13
    and social psychology, 10–13
    and subjective aspects of science, 11–12
variables
    dependent variable, 25
    independent variables, 24

victimization, 438–439
victims
    blame-the-victim process, 211
    discrimination and, 438–439
    distance of, 206–207
    similarity to, 298
video games, 337–342, 339f
violence
    operationalizing, 17
    and self-esteem, 54
    sexual violence, 327–331
    and television viewing, 25, 334–335
    world, and culture change, 348
virtues, 63
vivid stories, 169
voting, and looks, 360

W

Walkerton, Ontario water crisis, 258
wars, 8, 311, 311
wealth, and well-being, 521–522
weather forecasting, 263
weird beliefs, 158

well-being
    and good or bad events, 49
    and social relationships, 487–493
    and wealth, 521–522
Werther effect, 200
win-win situations, 163
women
    see also gender
    aggression against, 328–330
    looks, and attraction, 360
    math performance, and stereotype threat, 441f
    as "openers," 387–388
    prejudice against, 433–436
    self-disclosure, 388
    stereotypes of, 433–434
women-are-wonderful effect, 434
world population growth, 515f
world violence, 348
written vs. taped messages, 177–178, 179f

Z

Zimbardo's prison study, 130–131